THE CONTEXT OF SCRIPTURE

VOLUME II

Monumental Inscriptions from the Biblical World

THE CONTEXT OF SCRIPTURE

Canonical Compositions, Monumental Inscriptions, and Archival Documents from the Biblical World

General Editor William W. Hallo
Associate Editor K. Lawson Younger, Jr.

The Context of Scripture

VOLUME II

Monumental Inscriptions from the Biblical World

Editor

WILLIAM W. HALLO

Associate Editor

K. LAWSON YOUNGER, JR.

Consultants

HARRY A. HOFFNER, JR.
ROBERT K. RITNER

TUTA SUB AEGIDE PALLAS · 1683 ·

BRILL
LEIDEN · BOSTON · KÖLN
2000

This book is printed on acid-free paper.

Cover: The Israel Stela of Merneptah (Text 2.6). Courtesy of the Cairo Museum. For a photograph of the entire stela, with highlighting of "Israel" see H. Shanks, ed. *Ancient Israel* (2nd ed.; Washington, Biblical Archaeology Society, 1999), p. 78.

Library of Congress Cataloging-in-Publication Data

The context of Scripture / editor, William W. Hallo ; associate editor, K. Lawson Younger.
p. cm.
Includes bibliographical references and index.
Contents: v. I. Canonical compositions from the biblical world.
ISBN 9004106189 (alk. paper)
1. Bible. O.T.—Extra-canonical parallels. 2. Middle Eastern literature—Relation to the Old Testament. 3. Bible. O.T.—History of contempory events—Sources. 4. Middle Eastern literature – –Translations into English. I. Hallo, William W. II. Younger. K. Lawson.
BS1180.C66 1996
220.9'5—dc21 96-48987
CIP

Die Deutsche Bibliothek – CIP-Einheitsaufnahme

The context of scripture : canonical compositions, monumental inscriptions, and archival documents from the biblical world / ed. William W. Hallo. – Leiden ; New York ; Köln : Brill
NE: Hallo, William W. [Hrsg.]
Vol. I Canonical compositions from the biblical world. – 1997
ISBN 90-04-10618-9

ISBN 90 04 10619 7 (Vol. II)
ISBN 90 04 09629 9 (Set)

PRINTED IN THE NETHERLANDS

CONTENTS

WEST SEMITIC MONUMENTAL INSCRIPTIONS

AKKADIAN MONUMENTAL INSCRIPTIONS

SUMERIAN MONUMENTAL INSCRIPTIONS

PREFACE

The second volume of *The Context of Scripture* appears at the beginning of the new millennium rather than the end of the old one as planned but it has benefitted from the interval by incorporating some of the desiderata voiced by the reviewers of the first volume. They have, on the whole, been generous in their praise, both of the goals of the project and of the extent to which these goals have been met. Some of them have questioned the title and subtitles as to their meaning[1] — a matter addressed to a certain extent in the Introduction to the present volume — or their validity,[2] or both.[3]

In particular, it has been asked why comparison or contrast with biblical passages should dictate the choice of ancient Near Eastern texts here presented. To rephrase the question: what is the relevance, not of the ancient Near Eastern texts for the Hebrew Bible — a matter addressed in the Introduction to Volume I — but of the Bible for the study of (other) ancient Near Eastern texts.

Methodologically, this question could be answered by stressing the value of avoiding the approach of *obscurum per obscurius* or, to put it more positively, of approaching the less familiar via the more familiar — and the Bible remains by far the most familiar ancient Near Eastern text in wide circles of the English-speaking or English-reading world. A fuller answer to the question must be reserved for the Introduction to Volume III. In the meantime, it may be pointed out that, in fact, the scope of the project extends to many texts which display no obvious parallels to the Bible. A glance at the column of biblical comparisons (positive and negative) will reveal many such texts.[4] They were chosen for other reasons, some of them listed in the Preface to Volume I.

While the procedural outlines of the first volume have continued to characterize the second, there is a noticeable disparity in size between the two. This disparity was planned from the beginning, though both volumes have grown beyond initial estimates. Within the present volume, there is a further disparity between the Akkadian and the Sumerian sections, though it is (slightly) more apparent than real. Given the resort to both languages in the monumental inscriptions of some dynasties, especially in the Old Babylonian period, sometimes involving bilingual versions of one and the same inscription, it was decided to accommodate *all* the building and display inscriptions of the dynasties of Isin I, Larsa, Uruk and Babylon I in the Akkadian section regardless of their language(s).

Other bilingual inscriptions have been dealt with variously: the bilingual edict of Hattushili I (2.15) in the Hittite section without special reference to the Akkadian version; the treaties between Hatti and Amurru (2.17A-C) in the Hittite section with significant variants from the Akkadian versions in the footnotes; the Hadad-yith^{c}i stele (2.34) on the basis of its Aramaic version, with variants from the Akkadian noted in the footnotes; and the Azatiwada inscriptions separately in the (hieroglyphic) Hittite and Phoenician sections respectively (2.21 and 2.31).

The third and concluding volume will include full indices that will illustrate further connections, not only between the biblical text and the various other corpora, but among the different corpora themselves. The reader's patience is asked as we move to consummate these efforts.

It remains to thank the many people who have helped to keep this project on track: the contributors, the consultants, David Orton who first conceived the project and Marijke Wiersma who took it over when Dr. Orton left Brill to begin his own publishing enterprise, Mattie Kuiper who coordinated Brill's efforts, and, above all, K. Lawson Younger, Jr., without whose tireless labors at every stage this project could not have been realized.

William W. Hallo
February 9, 2000

---

[1] See e.g. D. I. Block, *Review and Expositor* 94 (1997) 607f.
[2] See e.g. O. Loretz, *UF* 28 (1996) 791-793.
[3] See e.g. N. Wyatt, *JSOT* 79 (1998) 168f.
[4] So noted e.g. by R. S. Hendel, *BR* 14/4 (1998) 14f.

ACKNOWLEDGEMENTS

The following publishers permitted the reprinting of portions of books:

Texts 2.7 (pp. 42-51): Miriam Lichtheim, *Ancient Egyptian Literature*. 3 Volumes. The University of California Press,© 1973-1980. Regents of The University of California.

Texts 2.4A-G and 2.5A-B (pp. 23-39): K. A. Kitchen, *Ramesside Inscriptions Translated & Annotated, Translations*. I. Oxford: Blackwell Reference, 1993; and *Ramesside Inscriptions Translated & Annotated, Notes & Comments,* II. Oxford: Blackwell Reference, 1996.

Texts 2.130; 2.131; 2.132; 2.133; 2.153; 2.154; (pp. 332-361, 408-414): Martha T. Roth, *Law Collections from Mesopotamia and Asia Minor*. SBLWAW 6. Atlanta, GA: Scholars Press, 1995.

ADDITIONAL ABBREVIATIONS AND SYMBOLS

(* For abbreviations not listed here, please consult volume 1)

AaG — S. Segert. *Altaramäische Grammatik. Mit Bibliographie, Glossar.* Leipzig: Verlag Enzyklopädie, 1975.

ABAW — Abhandlungen der Bayerischen Akademie der Wissenschaften.

AbB 13 — W. H. van Soldt. *Letters in the British Museum.* Part 2. Altbabylonische Briefe in Umschrift und Übersetzung 13. Leiden: E. J. Brill, 1994.

AC — J. J. Koopmans, Editor. *Aramäische Chrestomathie. Ausgewählte Texte (Inschriften, Ostraka und Papyri) bis zum 3. Jahrhundert v. Chr.* Leiden: Nederlands Instituut voor het Nabije Oosten, 1962.

AHI — G. I. Davies. *Ancient Hebrew Inscriptions. Corpus and Concordance.* Cambridge: Cambridge University Press, 1991.

AJBI — *The Annual of the Japanese Biblical Institute.*

AKM — Abhandlungen für die Kunde des Morgenlandes.

AMI — *Archäologische Mitteilungen aus Iran.*

ANE — Ancient Near East(ern).

ANEP^2 — J. B. Pritchard. *The Ancient Near East in Pictures Relating to the Old Testament.* 2nd Edition. Princeton: Princeton University Press, 1969.

ARINH — F. M. Fales, Editor. *Assyrian Royal Inscriptions: New Horizons in Literary, Ideological and Historical Analysis.* Orientis Antiqvi Collectio 17. Rome: Istituto per l'Oriente.

ARRIM — *Annual Review of the Royal Inscriptions of Mesopotamia Project.* Toronto, 1983-1991.

Assyria 1995 — S. Parpola and R. M. Whiting. Editors. *Assyria 1995. Proceedings of the 10th Anniversary Symposium of the Neo-Assyrian Text Corpus Project, Helsinki, September 7-11, 1995.* Helsinki: The Neo-Assyrian Text Corpus Project, 1997.

AT — D. J. Wiseman. *The Alalakh Texts.* Occasional Publications of the British Institute of Archaeology at Ankara 2. London: British Institute of Archaeology, 1953.

BAT 1990 — A. Biran, et al., Editors. *Biblical Archaeology Today 1990.* Jerusalem: Israel Exploration Society, 1993.

Bib — *Biblica.*

BiMes 6 — M. Gibson and R. D. Biggs, Editors. *Seals and Sealing in the Ancient Near East.* BiMes 6.

BIN — Babylonian Inscriptions in the Collection of J. B. Nies.

BMB — *Bulletin du Musée de Beyrouth.*

BN — *Biblische Notizien.*

BSMS — *Bulletin of the Society for Mesopotamian Studies.* Toronto.

CAI — W. E. Auffrecht. *A Corpus of Ammonite Inscriptions.* Ancient Near Eastern Texts and Studies 4. Lewiston/Queenston/Lampster: The Edwin Mellen Press, 1989.

CHLI 1 — *Corpus of Hieroglyphic Luwian Inscriptions.* Volume 1: J. D. Hawkins. *The Hieroglyphic Luwian Inscriptions of the Iron Age.* UISK 8.1. Berlin and New York: Walter de Gruyter, 2000.

CHLI 2 — *Corpus of Hieroglyphic Luwian Inscriptions.* Volume 2: H. Çambel. With a contribution by W. Röllig and tables by J. D. Hawkins. *Karatepe-Aslantaş. The Inscriptions: Facsimile Edition.* UISK 8.2. Berlin and New York: Walter de Gruyter, 1999.

DAE — P. Grelot. *Documents araméens d'Égypte.* LAPO 5. Paris: Éditions du Cerf, 1972.

DCPP — E. Lipiński, Editor. *Dictionnaire de la civilisation phénicienne et punique.* Leuven: Peeters, 1992.

DISO — C. F. Jean and J. Hoftijzer. *Dictionaire des inscriptions sémitiques de l'ouest.* Leiden: Brill, 1965.

DLE — L. Lesko. *A Dictionary of Late Egyptian.* 5 vols. Providence: BC Scribe, 1982-1990.

DMOA — Documenta et Monumenta Orientis Antiqui. Leiden: E. J. Brill.

DP — F.-M. Allotte de la Fuÿe, Editor. *Documents présargoniques.* Paris, E. Leroux, 1908-1920.

EAEHL — M. Avi-Yonah, Editor. *Encyclopedia of Archaeological Excavations in the Holy Land.* Englewood Cliffs, NJ: Prentice-Hall, 1975.

EMRT — W. W. Hallo. *Early Mesopotamia Royal Titles: a Philologic and Historical Analysis.* AOS 43. New Haven: American Oriental Society, 1957.

ENES — B. Buchanan. *Early Near Eastern Seals in the Yale Babylonian Collection.* Introduction and Seal Inscriptions by W. W. Hallo. New Haven and London: Yale University Press, 1981.

EPE — B. Porten. *Elephantine Papyri in English: Three Millennia of Cross-Cultural Continuity and Change.* Leiden: E. J. Brill, 1996.

ESE — M. Lidzbarki. *Ephemeris für semitische Epigraphik.* Giessen: Alfred Töpelmann, 1902, 1915.

EVO — *Egitto e Vicino Oriente.*

Glossar — W. Erichsen. *Demotisches Glossar.* Copenhagen: E. Munksgaard, 1954.

GPP — S. Segert. *A Grammar of Phoenician and Punic.* München: Beck, 1976.

HAL — W. Baumgartner, et al. *Hebräisches und Aramäisches Lexikon zum alten Testament.* Leiden: E. J. Brill, 1967-.

HAR — *Hebrew Annual Review.*

HdO — Handbuch der Orientalistik.

HML 1 — Paul Åström, Editor. *High, Middle or Low? Acts of an International Colloquium on Absolute Chronology Held at the University of Gothenburg 20th - 22nd August 1987.* Part 1. Gothenburg: Paul Åströms Förlag, 1987.

HML 3 — Paul Åström, Editor. *High, Middle or Low? Acts of an International Colloquium on Absolute Chronology Held at the University of Gothenburg 20th - 22nd August 1987.* Part 3. Gothenburg: Paul Åströms Förlag, 1989.

HNE — M. Lidzbarski. *Handbuch der Nordsemitischen Epigraphik.* Weimar: E. Felber, 1898.

IAK — E. Ebeling, B. Meissner, and E. F. Weidner. *Die Inschriften der altassyrischen Könige.* Leipzig: Quelle and Meyer, 1924.

Ist. Mit. — *Istanbuler Mitteilungen.*

ITP — H. Tadmor. *The Inscriptions of Tiglath-Pileser III King of Assyria.* Jerusalem: The Israel Academy of Sciences and Humanities, 1994.

JA — *Journal Asiatique.*

Mariette, *Mon. div.* — A. Mariette. *Monuments divers recueillis en Égypte et en Nubie.* Paris: F. Viewig, E. Bouillon, 1872-1889.

MDAIA — *Mitteilungen des deutschen archäologischen Instituts, Athenische Abteilung.*

MDP — Mémoires (de la) Délegation en Perse. Paris: E. Leroux.

MFA — Boston Museum of Fine Arts.

Moscati — S. Moscati, Editor. *The Phoenicians.* New York: Abbeville Press, 1988.

MPAIBL — *Mémoires presentées par divers savants à l'Académie des Inscriptions et Belles-Lettres.*

NAG — M. Liverani, Editor. *Neo-Assyrian Geography.* Quaderni di Geografia Storica 5. Rome: Università di Roma "La Sapienza," 1995.

NBK — P.-R. Berger. *Die neubabylonischen Königsinschriften.* AOAT 4/1. Kevelaer: Butzon & Bercker; Neukirchen-Vluyn: Neukirchener Verlag, 1973.

NDB — J. D. Douglas, Editor. *New Bible Dictionary.* Wheaton, IL: Tyndale House Publishers, 1982.

NEAEHL E. Stern, Editor. *The New Encyclopedia of Archaeological Excavations in the Holy Land*. Jerusalem: The Israel Exploration Society & Carta, 1993.

NEASB *Near Eastern Archaeology Society Bulletin.*

NSI G. A. Cooke. *A Textbook of North-Semitic Inscriptions*. Oxford: The Clarendon Press, 1903.

OEANE E. M. Meyers, Editor. *The Oxford Encyclopedia of Arachaeology in the Near East*. 5 volumes. New York and Oxford: Oxford University Press, 1997.

Origins W. W. Hallo. *Origins: the Ancient Near Eastern Background of Some Modern Western Institutions*. SHCANE 6. Leiden: E. J. Brill, 1996.

PNA K. Radner, Editor. *The Prosopography of the Neo-Assyrian Empire*. Helsinki: The Neo-Assyrian Text Corpus Project, 1998-.

POANE K. Watanabe, Editor. *Priests and Officials in the Ancient Near East. Papers of the Second Colloquium on the Ancient Near East — The City and its Life held at the Middle Eastern Culture Center in Japan (Mitaka, Tokyo)*. Heidelberg: C. Winter, 1999.

PPG J. Friedrich and W. Röllig. *Phönizisch-punische Grammatik*. AnOr 46. Rome: Pontificium Institutum Biblicum, 1970.

RAI 33 J.-M. Durand, Editor. *La Femme dans le Proche-Orient Antique*. Paris: Editions Recherche sur les Civilizations, 1987.

RAI 39 H. Waezoldt and H. Hauptmann, Editors. *Assyrien im Wandel der Zeiten*. Heidelberger Studien zum Alten Orient 6. Heidelberg: Heidelberger Orientverlag, 1997.

RIMA 3 *The Royal Inscriptions of Mesopotamia. Assyrian Periods*. Volume 3. A. K. Grayson. *Assyrian Rulers of the Early First Millennium BC II (858-745 BC)*. Toronto: University of Toronto, 1996.

RIMB 2 *The Royal Inscriptions of Mesopotamia. Babylonian Periods*. Volume 2. G. Frame. *Rulers of Babylonia from the Second Dynasty of Isin to the End of Assyrian Domination (1157-612 BC)*. Toronto: University of Toronto, 1995.

RIME 2 *Royal Inscriptions of Mesopotamia: Early Periods*. Volume 2. D. Frayne. *Sargonic and Gutian Periods*. Toronto: University of Toronto, 1993.

RIME 3/1 *The Royal Inscriptions of Mesopotamia: Early Periods*. Volume 3/1. D. O. Edzard. *Gudea and His Dynasty*. Toronto: University of Toronto Press, 1997.

RIME 3/2 *Royal Inscriptions of Mesopotamia: Early Periods*. Volume 3/2. D. Frayne. *Ur III Period (2112-2004 BC)*. Toronto: University of Toronto, 1997.

RIME 4 *Royal Inscriptions of Mesopotamia: Early Periods*. Volume 4. D. Frayne. *Old Babylonian Period (2003-1595 BC)*. Toronto: University of Toronto, 1990.

RTC F. Thureau-Dangin. *Recueil de tablettes chaldéennes*. Paris: E. Leroux, 1903.

RTAT W. Beyerlin, et al. *Religionsgechichtliches Textbuch zum Alten Testament*. Göttingen: Vandenhoeck & Ruprecht, 1975.

SBLMS SBL Monograph Series.

SD Studia et Documenta ad Iura Orientis Antiqui Pertinentia.

SHCANE Studies in the History and Culture of the Ancient Near East. Leiden: Brill.

SJOT *Scandinavian Journal of the Old Testament.*

SO Samaria Ostraca. G. A. Reisner. et al., *Harvard Excavations at Samaria*. 2 Vols. Cambridge, MA: Harvard University Press, 1924, and idem, *Israelite Ostraca from Samaria*. Harvard University, Palastinian (sic) Expedition. Boston, n.d.

Studies Albright H. Goedicke, Editor. *Near Eastern Studies in Honor of W. F. Albright*. Baltimore: Johns Hopkins University Press, 1971.

Studies Altheim R. Stiehl and H. E. Stier, Editors. *Beiträge zur alten Geschichte und deren Nachleben: Festschrift für Franz Altheim zum 6.10.1968*. 2 vols. Berlin: De Gruyter, 1969.

Studies Anderson J. T. Butler, E. W. Conrad, and B. C. Ollenburger, Editors. *Understanding the Word: Essays in Honour of Bernhard W. Anderson*. JSOTSup 37. Sheffield: JSOT Press, 1985.

Studies Artzi P. Artzi, J. Klein and A. J. Skaist, Editors. *Bar-Ilan Studies in Assyriology dedicated to Pinhas Artzi*. Bar-Ilan Studies in Near Eastern Languages and Culture. Ramat Gan: Bar-Ilan University Press, 1990.

Studies Astour G. D. Young, M. W. Chavalas, and R. E. Averbeck. Editors. *Crossing Boundaries and Linking Horizons: Studies in Honor of Michael C. Astour on His 80th Birthday*. Bethesda, Maryland: CDL, 1997.

Studies Böhl M. A. Beek, et al., Editors. *Symbolae Biblicae et Mesopotamicae Francisco Mario Theodoro De Liagre Böhl Dedicatae*. Leiden: E. J. Brill, 1973.

Studies Borger S. M. Maul. Editor. *Festschrift für Rykle Borger zu seinem 65. Geburtstag am 24. Mai 1994: tikip santakki mala basmu*. Groningen: Sytx, 1998.

Studies Carratelli Ed. by F. Imparati, Editor. *Studi di storia e di filologia anatolica dedicati a Giovanni Pugliese Carratelli*. Firenze: Elite, 1988.

Studies Cross P. D. Miller, P. D. Hanson, and S. D. McBride, Editors. *Ancient Israelite Religion: Essays in Honor of Frank Moore Cross*. Philadelphia: Fortress Press, 1987.

Studies Daumas *Hommages à François Daumas*. Institut d'Égyptologie, Université Paul Valéry. Montpellier: Université de Montpellier, 1986.

Studies David *Symbolae iuridicae et historicae Martino David dedicatae* 2 Vols. Leiden: E. J. Brill, 1968.

Studies Driver D. Winton Thomas, Editor. *Hebrew and Semitic Studies Presented to G. R. Driver*. Oxford: Clarendon, 1963.

Studies Dupont-Sommer *Hommages à André Dupont-Sommer*. Paris: Maisonneuve, 1971.

Studies Edel M. Görg and E. B. Pusch, Editors. *Festschrift Elmar Edel, 12. März 1979*. AAT 1. Bamberg: M. Görg, 1979.

Studies Ehrman Y. L. Arbeitman, Editor. *Fucus. A Semitic/Afrasian Gathering in Remembrance of Albert Ehrman*. Current Issues in Linguistic Theory 58. Amsterdam/Philadelphia: John Benjamins, 1988.

Studies Frerichs J. Magness and S. Gitin, Editors. *Hesed ve-Emet: Studies in Honor of Ernest S. Frerichs*. Brown Judaic Studies 320. Atlanta: Scholars Press, 1998.

Studies Galling A. Kuschke and E. Kutsch. Editors. *Archäologie und Altes Testament. Festschrift für Kurt Galling, zum 8. Januar 1970*. Tübingen: J. C. B. Mohr (Paul Siebeck), 1970.

Studies Garelli D. Charpin and F. Joannès, Editors. *Marchands, Diplomates et empereurs: Études sur la civilisation mésopotamienne offertes à P. Garelli*. Paris: Éditions Recherche sur les Civilisations, 1991.

Studies Glueck J. A. Sanders, Editor. *Near Eastern Archaeology in the Twentieth Century. Essays in Honor of Nelson Glueck*. Garden City, NY: Doubleday, 1970.

Studies Greenfield Z. Zevit, S. Gitin, and M. Sokoloff, Editors. *Solving Riddles and Untying Knots: Biblical, Epigraphic and Semitic Studies in Honor of Jonas C. Greenfield*. Winona Lake, IN: Eisenbrauns, 1995.

Studies Grelot *La Vie de la parole: de l'ancien au nouveau testament: études d'exégèse et d'herméneutique bibliques offertes à Pierre Grelot*. Paris: Desclée, 1987.

Studies Horn L. T. Geraty and L. G. Herr, Editors. *The Archaeology of Jordan and Other Studies Presented to Siegfried H. Horn*. Berrien Springs: Andrews University Press,

1986.

Studies Kantor A. Leonard, Jr. and B. Beyer Williams. Editors. *Essays in Ancient Civilization Presented to Helene 1. Kantor*. Chicago: The Oriental Institute, 1989.

Studies Karageorghis G. C. Ioannidès, Editor. *Studies in Honour of Vassos Karageorghis*. Nicosia: The Society of Cypriot Studies, 1992.

Studies King M. D. Coogan, J. C. Exum, and L. E. Stager. Editors. *Scripture and Other Artifacts: Essays on the Bible and Archaeology in Honor of Philip J. King*. Louisville: Westminster/John Knox, 1994.

Studies Kutscher G. B. Sarfati, P. Artzi, J. C. Greenfield and M. Kaddari. Editors. *Studies in Hebrew and Semitic Languages Dedicated to the Memory of Yechezkel Kutscher*. Ramat-Gan: Bar-Ilan University Press, 1980.

Studies Landsberger H. G. Güterbock and T. Jacobsen, Editors. *Studies in Honor of Benno Landsberger on his Seventy-fifth Birthday April 21, 1965*. AS 16. Chicago: University of Chicago Press, 1965.

Studies Levine R. Chazan, W.W. Hallo, and L.H. Schiffman, Editors. *Ki Baruch Hu: Ancient Near Eastern, Biblical, and Judaic Studies in Honor of Baruch A. Levine*. Winona Lake, IN: Eisenbrauns, 1999.

Studies McNamara K. J. Cathcart and M. Maher, Editors. *Targumic and Cognate Studies. Essays in Honour of Martin McNamara*. JSOTSup 230. Sheffield: Sheffield Academic Press, 1996.

Studies Macuch M. Macuch, C. Müller-Kessler, B. G. Fragner, Editors. *Studia Semitica necnon Iranica: Rudolpho Macuch septuagenario ab amicis et disciplulis dedicata*. Wiesbaden: Harrassowitz, 1989.

Studies Maspero J. Sainte Fare Garnot, Editor. *Mélanges Maspero*. Volume 1: *Orient ancien*. Mémoires publiés par les membres de l'Institut français d'archéologie orientale du Caire 66/4. Cairo: Institut français d'archéologie orientale, 1961.

Studies Mellink J. V. Canby, et al. editors. *Ancient Anatolia, Aspects of Change and Cultural Development. Essays in Honor of Machteld J. Mellink*. Madison: University of Wisconsin, 1986.

Studies Meriggi O. Carruba, editor. *Studia mediterranea Piero Meriggi dicata*. Studia mediterranea 1. Pavia: Aurora Edizione, 1979.

Studies Milik Z. J. Kapera, Editor. *Intertestamental Essays in Honour of Józef Tadeusz Milik*. Kraków: Enigma Press, 1992.

Studies Myers H. N. Bream, Editor. *A Light unto My Path: Old Testament Studies in Honor of Jacob M. Myers*. Philadelphia: Temple University Press, 1974.

Studies Otten E. Neu and C. Rüster, editors. *Documentum Asiae Minoris Antiquae. Festschrift für Heinrich Otten zum 75. Geburtstag*. Wiesbaden: Harrassowitz, 1988.

Studies Özgüç K. Emre, et al., editors. *Anatolia and the Ancient Near East. Studies in Honor of Tahsin Özgüç*. Ankara: Türk Tarih Kurumu Basimevi, 1989.

Studies van der Ploeg W. C. Delsman, et al. Editors. *Von Canaan bis Kerala: Festschrift für Professor Mag. Dr. Dr. J. P. M. van der Ploeg O.P.* AOAT 211. Kevelaer: Verlag Butzon & Bercker and Neukirchen-Vluyn: Neukirchener Verlag, 1982.

Studies Puhvel D. Disterheft, M. Huld and J. Greppin, editors. *Studies in Honor of Jaan Puhvel: Part One. Ancient Languages and Philology*. Washington, DC: Institute for the Study of Man, 1997.

Studies Sarna M. Brettler and M. Fishbane, Editors. *Minḥah le-Naḥum: Biblical and Other Studies Presented to Nahum N. Sarna in Honour of his 70th Birthday*. JSOTSup 154. Sheffield: Sheffield Academic Press, 1993.

Studies Smith E. Robbins and S. Sandahl, Editors. *Corolla Torontonensis. Studies in Honour of Ronald Morton Smith*. Toronto: TSAR, 1994.

Studies von Soden M. Dietrich and O. Loretz, Editors. *Vom Alten Orient zum Alten Testament. Festschrift für Wolfram Freiherrn von Soden zum 85. Geburtstag am 19. Juni 1993*. AOAT. Kevelaer: Butzon & Bercker; Neukirchen-Vluyn: Neukirchener Verlag, 1995.

Studies Soggin D. Garrone and F. Israel, Editors. *Storia e tradizioni di Israele. Scritti in onore di J. Alberto Soggin*. Brescia: Paideia, 1991.

Studies Spycket *Collectanea Orientalia. Histoire, arts de l'espace et industrie de la terre. Études offertes en hommage à Agnes Spycket*. Civilisations du proche-orient. Serie 1. Archéologie et environment 3. Neuchatel-Paris: Recherches et publications, 1996.

Studies Tufnell J. N. Tubb, Editor. *Palestine in the Bronze and Iron Ages. Papers in Honour of Olga Tufnell*. London: Institute of Archaeology, 1985.

Studies Young J. Coleson and V. Matthews, Editors. *"Go to the land I will show you": Studies in Honor of Dwight W. Young*. Winona Lake, IN: Eisenbrauns, 1996.

Symposia F. M. Cross, Editor. *Symposia Celebrating the Seventy-Fifth Anniversary of the Founding of the American Schools of Oriental Research (1900-1975)*. Cambridge, MA: ASOR, 1979.

TAD B. Porten and A. Yardeni. *Textbook of Aramaic Documents from Ancient Egypt*. 4 Volumes. Jerusalem: The Hebrew University, 1986-1999.

TAPhS Transactions of the American Philosophical Society. Philadelphia.

TRE *Theologische Realenzyklopädie*. Berlin/New York: Walter de Gruyter, 1971-.

TGI^2 K. Galling, editor. *Textbuch zur Geschichte Israels*. 2nd Edition. Tübingen, 1968.

UISK Untersuchungen zur indogermanischen Sprach- und Kulturwissenschaft, N.F.

Urk. III H. Schäfer, Editor. *Urkunden des ägyptischen Altertums*. Abteilung III: *Urkunden der älteren Äthiopenkönige*. Leipzig: J. C. Hinrichs, 1905, 1908.

VAB 4 S. Langdon. *Die neubabylonischen Königsinschriften*. Vorderasiatische Bibliothek 4. Leipzig: J. C. Hinrichs, 1912.

VS 1 Vorderasiatische Schriftdenkmäler der Königlichen Museen zu Berlin 1. Leipzig: J. C. Hinrichs, 1907.

VS 14 W. Förtsch. *Altbabylonische Wirtschaftstexte aus der Zeit Lugalanda's und Urukagina's*. Vorderasiatische Schriftdenkmäler der Königlichen Museen zu Berlin 14/1. Leipzig: J. C. Hinrichs, 1916.

WAI K. A. D. Smelik. *Writings from Ancient Israel: A Handbook of Historical and Religious Documents*. Edinburgh: T. & T. Clark, 1991.

YNER Yale Near Eastern Researches.

1 R H. C. Rawlinson and E. Norris. *The Cuneiform Inscriptions of Western Asia*. Volume 1: *A Selection from the Historical Inscriptions of Chaldea, Assyria, & Babylonia*. London, 1861.

3 R H. C. Rawlinson and G. Smith. *The Cuneiform Inscriptions of Western Asia*. Volume 3: *A Selection from the Miscellaneous Inscriptions of Assyria*. London, 1870.

5 R H. C. Rawlinson and Th. G. Pinches. *The Cuneiform Inscriptions of Western Asia*. Volume 5: *A Selection from the Miscellaneous Inscriptions of Assyria*. London, 1880.

OTHER ABBREVIATIONS

(* For abbreviations not listed here, please consult volume 1)

BH	Biblical Hebrew
MT	Masoretic Text
NH	New Hittite

LIST OF CONTRIBUTORS

WALTER E. AUFRECHT
University of Lethbridge

RICHARD E. AVERBECK
Trinity International University — Divinity School

RICHARD H. BEAL
University of Chicago

PAUL-ALAIN BEAULIEU
Harvard University

GARY BECKMAN
University of Michigan

MORDECHAI COGAN
The Hebrew University, Jerusalem

JOSEPH A. FITZMYER, S.J.
Georgetown University

DOUGLAS FRAYNE
University of Toronto

WILLIAM W. HALLO
Yale University

GORDON HAMILTON
Huron College

J. D. HAWKINS
University of London

J. F. HEALEY
University of Manchester

MICHAEL HELTZER
University of Haifa

RICHARD S. HESS
Denver Seminary

JAMES K. HOFFMEIER
Trinity International University — Divinity School

HARRY A. HOFFNER, JR.
University of Chicago

VICTOR HUROWITZ
Ben Gurion University of the Negev

BURKHART KIENAST
Albert-Ludwigs-Universität, Freiburg im Breisgau

K. A. KITCHEN
University of Liverpool, *emeritus*

BARUCH A. LEVINE
New York University

MIRIAM LICHTHEIM
University of California, Berkley, *emerita*

P. KYLE MCCARTER
Johns Hopkins University

ALAN MILLARD
University of Liverpool

WAYNE T. PITARD
University of Illinois

BEZALEL PORTEN
The Hebrew University, Jerusalem

MARVIN A. POWELL
Northern Illinois University

ROBERT K. RITNER
University of Chicago

MARTHA ROTH
University of Chicago

STANISLAV SEGERT
University of California, Los Angeles, *emeritus*

ITAMAR SINGER
Tel Aviv University

K. A. D. SMELIK
Universitaire Faculteit voor Protestantse Godgeleerdheid te Brussel

JEFFREY H. TIGAY
University of Pennsylvania

K. LAWSON YOUNGER, JR.
Trinity International University — Divinity School

INTRODUCTION

THE BIBLE AND THE MONUMENTS

William W. Hallo[1]

More than a century ago, a book appeared under the title of *The Bible and the Monuments*. It was subtitled *The Primitive Hebrew Records in the Light of Modern Research*, and its author bore the impressive name of William Saint Chad Boscawen.[2] His was only one in a long line of books that capitalized on the fruits of archaeological exploration of the Near East to bring new life to biblical history and literature. But in common with other works of its time and type, it used the term "monuments" loosely to describe whatever in the way of written or artistic evidence had been turned up by the spade of the excavator. Thus he dealt in one chapter with creation legends, in another with the Deluge, and in a third with the Egyptian Book of the Dead and other evidence of beliefs in an afterlife. When students of the ancient Near East speak of monuments today, they tend to have a more restricted category of evidence in mind. In my case, I have developed a particular taxonomy of documentation based on the cuneiform writings of Mesopotamia, which the projected three volumes of *The Context of Scripture* proposes to extend to the Egyptian, Hittite and West Semitic evidence as well. It has been defended in print in several places,[3] but needs to be presented here afresh.

In ancient Mesopotamia, clay was abundantly available and was thus the writing medium of choice. If a document was intended to be preserved for a limited length of time, it was typically inscribed on a clay tablet in one or at most two copies and deposited in an archive for subsequent retrieval. Such documents as letters, accounts, contracts, and court-cases answer these descriptions and may be called archival. If, on the other hand, a composition was intended for long-time preservation, it might still be inscribed in clay, either on a tablet shaped much like an archival text, or on a variety of other shapes such as cylinders, prisms, round or square "school-tablets" or extract tablets which were wider than they were long; but regardless of their shape, such compositions typically appear in multiple copies. They were ultimately the product of the scribal schools, and constituted their curriculum or canon. They may therefore be labelled canonical, though not in the sense in which that term is usually employed in biblical scholarship, that is to say with the implications of divine inspiration or binding authority attached to the biblical canon. Rather, the term is here used in its more general, literary sense, as when literary critics speak of the Chaucer canon to identify all the works that can safely be attributed to that author, or of the Western canon to identify the different authors whose works constitute by general consent the shared literary heritage of the Western tradition.

When using the term in this sense, one can detect several successive canons in the millennial literary tradition of ancient Mesopotamia. The individual compositions that make up those successive canons exhibit certain common distinctive traits, a dozen of which I have summarized elsewhere.[4] They include the standardization of such external features as the length of each composition, its division into lines and chapters, the ordering of separate compositions in a fixed sequence, their study in that sequence in the schools, whether in whole or in part, the creation of commentaries and other scholastic explanatory texts, their augmentation with other compositions copied from archival or monumental sources, and above all their replication in numerous exemplars as a result of their use in the school curriculum or, occasionally, for private libraries.

Multiple copies in clay also served to preserve another sort of text, namely bricks and cones, typically employed in temples, palaces and other public buildings. Clay was, however, not the only medium for writing, even in Mesopotamia. Thus other building inscriptions, such as foundation deposits and door-sockets, resorted to imported stone or even metal to achieve durability. So did additional genres such as votive inscriptions, weights, and seals. From the largest to the smallest, these genres all alike constitute monuments — structures or objects intended to last for all time as memorials to those kings and other mortals who built or dedicated them, or to those deities to whom they were

[1] The essence of this paper was first presented to Kenrick Theological Seminary, St. Louis, November 11, 1999, Anne Marie Kitz presiding. It was revised for presentation to the Midwest meeting of the Society of Biblical Literature/American Oriental Society, Chicago, February 13, 2000.

[2] 2nd ed. (London/New York, Eyre and Spottiswoode, 1895). For some of Boscawen's other publications, see F. H. Weissbach, *RlA* 2 (1938) 60; R. Borger, *Handbuch der Keilschriftliteratur* 1 (1967) 32, 2 (1975) 22; D. B. Weisberg, YOS 17 (1980) xix and n. 18.

[3] Notably W. W. Hallo, *The Ancient Near East: a History* (New York, Harcourt Brace, 1971) 154-158; 2nd. ed. (1998) 154-157.

[4] W. W. Hallo, "The Concept of Canonicity in Cuneiform and Biblical Literature: A Comparative Appraisal," in *SIC* 4 (1991) 1-19.

dedicated. All became parts of the structures or objects which they commemorate. They may therefore be called monumental inscriptions. In special cases, uninscribed monuments may also be added to this category if their iconography bore mute witness to a comparable commemoration.

While thus carefully delineating the three principal categories of documentation from each other by the combined criteria of form and function, the proposed taxonomy allows for some intermediate genres. Thus for example the ancient records of land sales which are sometimes designated in modern terminology as "boundary-stones" (*kudurru*) are formally monumental in that they are inscribed on stone but functionally archival in that they deal with real estate transactions.[5] The taxonomy also leaves room for transitions from one category to another. More specifically, the curriculum included instruction in the writing of archival texts, and for this purpose drew on the archives to create textbooks of contracts, court cases, letters, including royal correspondence, etc. And the curriculum specifically included the copying of monuments, as attested in descriptions of the life of the Old Babylonian scribal schools.[6] Such monuments thus often found their way into the canon as can be demonstrated for royal inscriptions, "law codes," cadastres, treaties and other genres preserved either as models of good style or for their intrinsic value. Often enough, archival or monumental texts are preserved for us *only* in their canonical guise. They may nevertheless be legitimately included among the archives and monuments to which they presumably go back rather than among the canonical texts with which they have been found.

To what extent do these classifications apply beyond the borders of Mesopotamia? On the face of it, it should not be difficult to do so in the case of the Hittites, who essentially adopted the cuneiform writing conventions of Mesopotamia. It must, however, be added at once that the discoveries in Hattusha have been overwhelmingly of canonical compositions. Only the more recent excavations at Hittite sites outside the capital city have begun to turn up archival documents in significant numbers; this has notably been the case at Maṣat.[7] As for monumental texts, these are nearly all clay tablet copies of what must have been originally inscriptions on stone or metal. This is presumably true of the Hittite Laws, and is certainly true of some or all of the Hittite treaties, as most dramatically shown by the bronze version of the treaty between Tudhaliyash IV and his cousin Kurunta, the ruler of the petty kingdom of Tarhuntashsha.[8] According to the end of this text, it was prepared in seven copies, one for Kurunta and the others deposited before various deities, i.e., presumably, their statues. None of the other copies, whether on metal or clay, has survived.

The Egyptian situation is different but also capable of being correlated with the Mesopotamian taxonomy. Whether Mesopotamia inspired the first attempts at writing in Egypt or not, certain it is that Egypt used clay tablets as a writing surface only much later when, in the Amarna period, Akkadian became the *lingua franca* of the Near East. Rather, Egypt discovered papyrus as an ideal medium for its archival documents and canonical compositions, with clay potsherds or ostraca as a distinctly less popular alternative. As for monuments, there was no lack of stone or metal to preserve these for all time. Much the same situation prevailed in most of the West Semitic speaking area — with one notable exception, namely Israel.

What then of the Israelites? As far as the biblical text itself is concerned, it is of course quintessentially canonical in its entirety — and that in both senses of the term. But a closer look suggests at least the hypothetical possibility that its present canonical shape may have developed out of other categories, as demonstrably happened often in Mesopotamia. In other words, it may harbor what in some cases may be regarded as originally archival and monumental texts. Long ago, James A. Montgomery wrote an article on what he called "Archival data in the Book of Kings."[9] He was referring to passages in the Books of Kings which seemed to emanate from royal archives, such as the lists of Solomon's officers and provincial lieutenants (1 Kgs 4), or of the cities he built (1 Kgs 9:15, 17), or of his building activities in Jerusalem (1 Kgs 7:2-8). More recently, Baruch A. Levine identified what he called "The descriptive ritual texts of the Pentateuch,"[10] using a term which he and I had previously applied to certain Ugaritic and Mesopotamian account texts.[11] His parade example was Numbers 7, a chapter often consigned to oblivion because of its seemingly endless and pointless repetition of identical entries in the long list of offerings brought by the leaders of the twelve tribes at the dedication of the desert tabernacle.[12] Levine showed graphically that the material could be represented in two-dimensional format and then resembled comparable account texts from Babylonia. If it was not a genuine copy of an archival document, it certainly suggested the existence of such texts as a model for the biblical author.

---

[5] I. J. Gelb, P. Steinkeller and R. M. Whiting, Jr., *Earliest Land Tenure Systems in the Near East: Ancient Kudurrus* (OIP 104) (1991).

[6] Hallo, *SIC* 3 (1990) 9-11; *SIC* 4 (1991) 8 and 17, nn. 79f.

[7] J. Klinger, "Das Corpus der Maṣat-Briefe," *ZA* 85 (1995) 74-108.

[8] Below, *COS* 2.18. Cf. the review article of Otten's edition by Dietrich Sürenhagen, *OLZ* 87 (1992) 341-371.

[9] *JBL* 53 (1934) 46-52.

[10] *JAOS* 85 (1965) 307-318.

[11] Hallo, *SIC* 3 (1990) 9f.

[12] Cf. also J. Milgrom, "The Chieftain's Gifts: Numbers, Chapter 7," *HAR* 9 (1985) 221-225.

What is true of archival origins is equally valid, mutatis mutandis, for monumental origins. I am not suggesting the Decalogue in this connection. But analogies have been drawn, again some time ago, between certain biblical psalm genres, notably the psalms of thanksgiving, and West Semitic inscriptions on steles such as the Aramaic stele of King Zakkur of Hamath; Zobel, Ginsberg and Greenfield all commented on this analogy.[13] More recently I entered the lists with a proposal to add the prayer of Hezekiah in Isaiah 38 to the list.[14] It is called a "writing" (*mktb*) in the Hebrew text, and a *proseuché* in the Septuagint, but it may be related to the Psalm genre (16, 56-60) called a *mktm* in Hebrew, and consistently rendered by "writing on a stele" (*stélographía*) in the Greek versions. If so, these six historical or rather biographical psalms of the Psalter may be added to the roster. It may be noted that most modern translations leave the word *mktm* untranslated, but the New Jerusalem Bible ventures "In a quiet voice," while Buber and Rosenzweig proposed "Sühngedicht," a prayer about sin. Perhaps these translations were influenced by the root meaning of *ktm* in Akkadian and Arabic, i.e. to cover, conceal.

The appeal to the Zakkur Stele reminds us that the finite corpus of the biblical canon has been supplemented and illuminated by a ceaseless accretion of other West Semitic writings in the form of monuments from all over the soil of Israel and its immediate neighbors. Since the very beginnings of modern exploration of the Levant, these have furnished evidence in Ugaritic, Phoenician, Aramaic and every other kind of West Semitic language and dialect. The majority of them have involved royal inscriptions.

We may cite by way of illustration the famous Mesha Stele found at Dhiban in Jordan in 1868 and recording the triumph of that Moabite king over his Israelite oppressor, presumably Ahab (874-853) and/or his son Joram (Jehoram) (852-841).[15] More recently the record has been enriched by a find from the same period (i.e. the late ninth century BCE) but from the northern frontier of Israel. There the ongoing excavations at Tell Dan have unearthed two fragments of an Aramaic stele celebrating the triumph of a Syrian king, probably Hazael of Damascus, over the combined forces of the kings of Israel and Judah, the latter referred to there, interestingly enough, as "[the kin]g of the house of David."[16] (This phrase has now also been tentatively identified in the Mesha Stele by the simple restoration of a single lost letter.)[17] And it is only a couple of years since the excavation at Eqron, once one of the five principal Philistine cities, turned up an inscription of Achish son of Padi king of Eqron that fits into the history of the seventh century as recorded both in the Bible[18] and the Assyrian monuments, where both Padi and Achish appear, the latter as Ikausu.[19] The Assyrian inscriptions have mostly been found in Assyria itself, of course, but it is worth recalling that some were erected in Palestine and have turned up there; for example fragments of standard victory steles of Sargon II from Samaria and Ashdod.[20] Similarly, Egyptian royal inscriptions were erected in Palestine to commemorate Egyptian triumphs there. One may mention in this connection two steles of Seti I (1289-1278 BCE) found at Beth Shan.[21] The second of these even mentions Apiru in conflict with Asiatics (*amu*) of *rhm*, sometimes interpreted as the basis for an assumed tribe of *banu rahāmi* with an eponymous ancestor called *Abu-Rahāmi* = Abraham![22]

What then of the comparable harvest, from the biblical period, of Hebrew monuments in general, and of royal inscriptions in particular? Here we come up against the curious fact that it has been meager to the point of non-existence! Let us look at the evidence. Probably the single most familiar Hebrew monument is the so-called Siloam Inscription.[23] It was found in 1880 when Palestine was still under Ottoman rule, and to this day the original remains housed in the Archaeological Museum in Istanbul despite all attempts to reclaim it for Israel.[24] It records the completion of the tunnel whereby water was to be brought securely from the Pool of Siloam into the walled city of Jerusalem, presumably in the event of a siege.[25]

Because of its unique character as virtually the only monumental inscription of its kind from Israel or Judah in the

---

[13] See the references in Hallo, *Studies Kramer* (1976) 209f, and below, 2.35.

[14] W. W. Hallo, "The Royal Correspondence of Larsa: I. A Sumerian Prototype for the Prayer of Hezekiah?" in *Studies Kramer* (1976) 209-224.

[15] Below, 2.23.

[16] Below, 2.39.

[17] A. Lémaire, "'House of David' restored in Moabite inscription," *BAR* 20/3 (1994) 30-37; idem, "La dynastique Davidique (*Byt Dwd*) dans deux inscriptions ouest-sémitiques du IXe S. Av. J.-C." *SEL* 11 (1994) 17-19.

[18] Achish is familiar as king of Gath in the time of Saul (1 Sam 21:27-29) and Solomon (1 Kgs 2:30f.)

[19] Below, 2.42. S. Gitin, T. Dothan and J. Naveh, "A Royal Dedicatory Inscription from Eqron," *IEJ* 47 (1997) 1-16. Cf. A. Demsky, *BAR* 24/5 (1998) 56; V. Sasson, "The Inscription of Achish, Governor of Ekron, and Philistine Dialect, Cult and Culture," *UF* 29 (1997b) 627-639.

[20] See the illustrations in Mordechai Cogan and Hayim Tadmor, *II Kings. A New Translation with Introduction and Commentary* (Garden City, NY: Doubleday & Company, 1988) pl. 11.

[21] Below, 2.4B and 2.4D.

[22] Mario Liverani, "Un'ipotesi sul nome di Abramo," *Henoch* 1 (1979) 9-18; ref. courtesy Oded Tammuz.

[23] Below, 2.28.

[24] H. Shanks, "Returning Cultural Artifacts — Turkey Is All Take, No Give," *BAR* 17/3 (1991) 12; "Please Return the Siloam Inscription to Jerusalem," *BAR* 17/3 (1991) 58-60.

[25] Cf. J. A. Hackett, *BAR* 23/2 (Mar/Apr 1997) 42f.

biblical period, there have been recent attempts to reassign it to the early post-biblical period, when such inscriptions become more common. But these attempts have been decisively refuted by the palaeographic evidence. In fact, there is general consensus that the inscription belongs to the reign of Hezekiah who, as the Book of Chronicles informs us (II Chr 32:30; cf. 2 Kgs 20:20), "stopped the upper outlet of the waters of Gihon and directed them straight down on the West side of the City of David. He said in effect: why should the king of Assyria come and find much water?" (cf. 2 Chr 32:4). The siege envisaged was that of Sennacherib and the Assyrian army in 701 BCE. Granted all this, it becomes all the more curious that the king is mentioned neither by name nor by title in the entire inscription! It seems to be the exception that proves the rule!

Another exception is provided by the mortuary inscription of King Uzziah (= Azariah) of Judah (792-740).[26] Mortuary inscriptions are fairly standard in the biblical world. Both kings and commoners have left us examples; those in cuneiform have been conveniently catalogued and described by Bottero,[27] those in West Semitic by Müller.[28] It has even been suggested that the Bible preserves an allusion to an epitaph in Job 19:23-27.[29] But the funerary inscription of Uzziah turns out to be something else: the record of a reburial. Dating to the first century BCE and inscribed in Aramaic, it says in effect: "Here were brought the bones of Uzziah, king of Judah. Do not open!"[30] Whether this had something to do with his leprosy as implied by the Chronicler (2 Chr 26:23) I leave for others to ponder.

There is, it is true, a class of inscriptions that mentions the king by title, and another that mentions him by name. In the former category are the stone stamp seals inscribed "Belonging to the king" (*lmlk*) which are presumed to have existed (though none have ever been found) on the basis of the impressions they have left on the handles of numerous clay jars which were used to hold and transport wine or olive oil during the period of the Divided Monarchy, more specifically during the reign of — again — Hezekiah.[31] More than 1700 such impressions have been found from some 65 different sites, nearly all adding one of four place-names.[32]

In the latter category are all those stamp seals and seal impressions inscribed by servants of such Judahite kings as Azariah, Ahaz and Hezekiah, and such Israelite kings as Jeroboam.[33] Such inscriptions are typically of the form "belonging to Ushna servant of Ahaz";[34] we can recognize the royal name but it is never accompanied by the royal title. This is in conformity with long-standing Near Eastern usage, but it also seems to fit neatly into a recognizable Israelite pattern. It is almost as if to the Decalogue had been added an eleventh commandment: thou shalt not commemorate the royal name and title in a monumental inscription! There is not even a word for royal inscription in biblical Hebrew, as there is in Sumerian (MU-SAR) and Akkadian (*musarû, šumu šaṭru*).

Of course there was one form of monument identified by name and specifically condemned and that was the commemorative stele or *maṣṣeba*.[35] It was originally regarded as a legitimate sign of the divine presence, as in the case of Jacob's *maṣṣeba* at Bethel (Gen 28:18 etc.)[36] and as the designation of a Jewish gravestone to this day. But it was proscribed elewhere in the Pentateuch and was seen under the monarchy as a symbol of Canaanite idol worship, on a par with the image (*pesel*) of the decalogue with which it was often paired.[37]

The peculiarities of the Israelite situation can be adduced to account for the absence of certain other elements familiar from the Mesopotamian repertoire of royal monuments.[38] The Israelites did not normally build in clay, the favorite medium for bricks and cones; they did not use pivot stones for the doors of monumental buildings, nor construct

---

[26] Cogan and Tadmor, *II Kings*, 167 and pl. 11.

[27] "Les inscriptions funéraires cunéiformes," in *La Mort, les morts dans les sociétés anciennes* (Actes du Colloque sur l'Idéologie Funéraire, Ischia, 1977) (Cambridge: Cambridge University Press, 1981).

[28] Hans-Peter Müller, "Die phönizische Grabinschrift aus dem Zypern-Museum KAI 30 und die Formgeschichte des nordwestsemitischen Epitaphs," *ZA* 65 (1975) 104-132.

[29] Kurt Galling, "Die Grabinschrift Hiobs," *WO* 2 (1954) 3-6.

[30] Cogan and Tadmor, *II Kings* 167 and fig. 5.

[31] This date is suggested, i.a., by "the fact that most of these jars were found in destruction levels caused by the retaliatory Assyrian invasion of 701 BCE" according to J. H. Tigay, below, 2.77.

[32] Hebron and Ziph in Judah, Socho in the Shephelah, and an otherwise unknown place *mmšt*; cf. Tigay, below, p. 202 and n. 67.

[33] A. R. Millard below, 2.70R.

[34] N. Avigad and B. Sass, *Corpus of West Semitic Stamp Seals* (Revised and completed by B. Sass. Jerusalem: Israel Academy of Sciences and Humanities, Israel Exploration Society, and Institute of Archaeology, Hebrew University of Jerusalem, 1997) No. 5 and frontispiece.

[35] My thanks to John Ahn for reminding me of this fact.

[36] R. Kutscher, "The Mesopotamian god Zaqar and Jacob's Maṣṣebāh," *Beer Sheva* 3 (1988) 125-130 (in Hebrew).

[37] See Roland de Vaux, *Ancient Israel: Its Life and Institutions*, tr. John McHugh (New York etc., McGraw-Hill, 1961) 285f.; Tryggve N.D. Mettinger, *No Graven Image? Israelite Aniconism in its Ancient Near Eastern Context* (Coniectanea Biblica, Old Testament Series 42; Stockholm: Almqvist & Wiksell International, 1995) esp. p. 24.

[38] Hallo, "The Royal Inscriptions of Ur: A Typology," *HUCA* 33 (1962) 1-43; E. Sollberger and J.-R. Kupper, *Inscriptions Royales Sumeriennes et Akkadiennes* (Paris: Cerf, 1971) 25-36: "L'inscription royale comme genre littéraire."

elaborate foundation boxes filled with inscribed stone foundation tablets (in the guise of model bricks) and other foundation deposits. But that still leaves room for other royal monuments: building inscriptions in stone; votive dedications; seals inscribed to or by the king; weights royally authorized and guranteed, mortuary inscriptions and others. Their total absence remains to be explained.

If there has been little attention paid to the fact of this absence, there is even less discussion of its possible cause or causes. Perhaps the question has been ignored on the grounds of the old truism that absence of evidence is not evidence of absence. Most scholars feel safer explaining the presence of phenomena than their absence. Perhaps that would be my safest course too. But I have long preached the contextual approach, in which contrast is as important as comparison, and here is a contrast worthy of the name. Scholars have periodically assembled great compendia of monuments from Egypt, Syria, Assyria and Babylonia, culminating in such stately series of volumes as *The Royal Inscriptions of Mesopotamia* from the University of Toronto. But there is never going to be even a single volume of "The Royal Inscriptions of Judah and Israel." Even the most recent and comprehensive *Handbook of Ancient Hebrew Inscriptions* is mostly devoted to seals and ostraca, the latter more properly at home among archival texts.[39] Why are there no royal inscriptions among them?

We can rule out the accidents of discovery. The soil of the Holy Land is the most carefully and thoroughly excavated real estate on the face of the earth, and has been such for over a century. (This is assuming we date the beginnings of scientific excavation no earlier than Sir Flinders Petrie in 1890.)[40] The chance that future discoveries will turn up a whole genre of Hebrew (or Aramaic) inscriptions overlooked so far is remote at best, especially given the many discoveries of non-Israelite monuments already made. Nor need we be long detained by a second possibility, namely that all traces of such inscriptions have been destroyed by the many wars the land of Israel has experienced and the many enemies it has faced. Other peoples of the biblical world faced just as much conflict and hostility yet their monuments have survived or reemerged.

A third possible explanation is equally unconvincing, namely that the period of the monarchy was so short on literacy that monumental inscriptions would have lacked a readership. But this is, to begin with, the wrong way to phrase matters. Monumental inscriptions are not addressed to a literate readership but rather to a largely illiterate *audience*, who would be read to by the minority of trained scribes and other literate alumni of the scribal schools. This is well known from Babylonia where literacy was limited to the elite classes even in periods such as that of Hammurapi's when such schooling was more widely available than at other periods. In the famous stele(s) inscribed with his laws, Hammurapi specifically says:

> Let any wronged man who has a lawsuit come before the statue of me (*ṣalmia*), the king of justice, and let him have my inscribed stela (*narī šaṭram*) read aloud to him, thus may he hear my precious pronouncements and let my stela reveal his lawsuit for him.[41]

Moreover literacy was vastly easier to achieve in areas of West Semitic speech using "alphabetic" writing than it had ever been in the areas of cuneiform (and hieroglyphic) writing. Investigations by Aaron Demsky and others have shown that Israel, in particular, did not lag behind in the spread of literacy, and even the biblical text preserves traces of a spelling lesson, albeit in sarcastic form, when the prophet is mocked as a would-be school teacher, with "*ṣaw* for *ṣaw*, *qaw* for *qaw*, a little one here a little one there" (Isa 28:9-13).[42]

The real reason for the absence of royal monuments from Israel must be sought elsewhere. Again the contextual approach can guide us. One of the most salient contrasts between Israel and its Near Eastern context is seen in the role of the king in the respective spheres. In the high civilizations of Mesopotamia and Egypt and in the Syrian, Anatolian and other areas in contact with them, kingship had arrived on the scene together with the other chief ingredients of civilization — urbanism, capital formation, writing, and metallurgy. In Egypt, the early kings were put on a virtual par with the gods themselves; in Mesopotamia, there was only a reluctant and temporary flirtation with the notion of divine kingship; among the Hittites, royalty had to die before being accorded divine honors.[43] But everywhere kingship was held in high honor; the king was the warrant for his country's weal or woe; his cultic leadership was a prerequisite; his death meant disaster,[44] especially if premature, as for instance in the case of Sargon II of Assyria.[45]

---

[39] Shmuel Aḥituv, *Handbook of Ancient Hebrew Inscriptions* (The Biblical Encyclopaedia Library 7; Jerusalem: Mosad Bialik, 1992) (in Hebrew).

[40] W. F. Albright, *The Archaeology of Palestine* (Harmondsworth: Penguin Books, 1949) 29.

[41] M. T. Roth, *Law Collections from Mesopotamia and Asia Minor* (SBLWAW 6; Atlanta: Scholars Press, 1995) 134; below p. 352.

[42] A. Demsky, "Abecedaries," *COS* 1 (1997) 362-365; Hallo, "Isaiah 28:9-13 and the Ugaritic Abecedaries," *JBL* 77 (1958) 324-338; *Origins: the Ancient Near Eastern Background of Some Modern Western Institutions* (SHCANE 6; Leiden: Brill, 1996) 37f.

[43] Hallo, *Origins* 207.

[44] W. W. Hallo, "The Death of Kings: Traditional Historiography in Contextual Perspective," *Studies Tadmor* (1991) 148-165.

[45] Cf. ibid., 162; Hallo, "Disturbing the Dead," *Studies Sarna* (1993) 185-192, esp. pp. 190f.

Not so in Israel. There the norm was theocracy: God was the only legitimate king ever since the exaltation of God celebrated in the archaic Song of the Sea (Exod 15; esp. v. 18). He assumed most of the roles played by the king, and especially the divine king, in the surrounding cultures; the other royal roles were shared in Israel by priesthood and laity. Only the military role was not so easily assigned elsewhere. When Samuel reluctantly agreed to institute a mortal kingship — more reluctantly, according to the biblical record, than God himself — it was in response to the popular demand: "Give us a king to judge us, like the other nations" (1 Sam 8:5). So far from being an institution coeval with the beginnings of (its) history, kingship was regarded as a late aberration, an accommodation to foreign norms forced on the people by external circumstances such as the threat of annihilation at the hands of enemies under more permanent dynastic leadership and more united than the disparate tribes of Israel. Samuel's warnings of the excesses of kingship were so nearly fulfilled already in the United Monarchy, specifically under Solomon, that critics tend to regard them as inspired by that experience. And when the monarchical experiment had run its course after the failure of the divided monarchy, first in the North then in the South, it was not long before theocracy was reestablished. There were attempts to restore the Davidic monarchy as well but they ended in abject failure, and the hopes for a future restoration were relegated to a distant Messianic time which in Jewish belief is yet to come, despite or perhaps because of periodic attempts to hasten its arrival or even to declare it arrived.

In such an essentially anti-monarchic setting, there was little or no room for the type of royal propaganda that emanated from the royal chanceries elsewhere in the ancient Near East. In Israel, kings were well advised to ruffle as few feathers as possible. Other Near Eastern kings celebrated their achievements and the "sacraments" of their own lifetimes not only in monumental inscriptions but also in royal hymns, date formulas, and statuary. The bombastic tones in which they glorified their roles is unmistakable even when they assigned due credit to their deities. Israel may have tolerated an occasional hymn thought to be in honor of an unnamed king such as Psalm 45. But the lion's share of its hymns were composed in honor of God, including the Psalms which began "The Lord reigneth" (*yhwh mlk*) as if in defiant assertion of the theocratic ideal.

In fact, Israel kept a critical eye on its monarchs: the northern kingdom which favored a kind of charismatic kingship was ever ready to throw over an unsatisfactory monarch in favor of a whole new dynasty; the southern kingdom, while it adhered to the dynastic principle of succession, passed severe judgement on its kings and, if the Deuteronomic point of view is taken as a guide, found the great majority of them wanting. Bombastic royal inscriptions, or other monuments to royal pride, might only have jeopardized the whole idea of monarchy, fanning the flames of distrust of and dissent from it that simmered just below the surface.

Was there, finally, room for some uninscribed or non-royal monuments? The recent discovery of a prototype of the priestly blessing, familiar from Numbers 6:24-26, inscribed on two small silver amulets in the form of scrolls from the cemetery at Ketef Hinnom, and dating to the mid-seventh or early sixth century alerts us to this possibility.[46] One may also cite the occasional weight inscribed with its size though never with the authority of a king or other official who had established that weight as in the ancient Near Eastern pattern.[47] References to ᵓ*šyw* and ᵓ*šyhw* the king in newly published votive inscriptions have been tentatively linked to Joash of Israel and Joash of Judah respectively.[48] But we virtually lack the votive inscriptions or even the mortuary inscriptions which are the most common examples of private monuments in the Near Eastern context.[49]

So to return to our starting point: when we speak today of "the Bible and the monuments," we are no longer referring indiscriminately, like Saint Chad Boscawen a century ago, to all the evidence that archaeology has unearthed from the ancient Near East. Nor, certainly, do we refer to monuments of biblical Israel itself turned up by the spade on Israel's own soil - seeing that these are virtually non-existent. Rather we mean those inscriptions from the surrounding cultures which were intended by their authors for all time, whether royal or private, building or votive or mortuary, weights or seals, rediscovered on their original stone and metal surfaces or preserved in copies on clay and papyrus. These monuments often throw welcome new light on the biblical record; they form a significant part of "the context of scripture."

[46] G. Barkay, "The Divine Name Found in Jerusalem," *BAR* 9/2 (1983) 14-19. Below, 2.83.

[47] Below, 2.81.

[48] Below, 2.47 and 2.50.

[49] For some examples, see below, 2.47B-D, 48, 52-54.

EGYPTIAN MONUMENTAL INSCRIPTIONS

A. ROYAL INSCRIPTIONS

1. EIGHTEENTH DYNASTY INSCRIPTIONS

THE TOMB BIOGRAPHY OF AHMOSE OF NEKHEB (2.1)

James K. Hoffmeier

Ahmose, the son of Baba and Abena, was a highly decorated naval officer from ancient Nekheb. In his tomb biography, he offers one of the most important historical witnesses to the rise of the 18th Dynasty. His distinguished career lasted from the reign of King Ahmose (1550-1525 BCE) into that of Thutmose I (1504-1492 BCE). Most significantly, his references to the battles against Avaris remain the only surviving records of the so-called "expulsion of the Hyksos." Following the fall of Avaris, Ahmose speaks of besieging the city of Sharuhen in southern Canaan, thought to be the place to which the Hyksos elite fled. The three-year campaign in Canaan appears to have laid the foundation for Egypt's empire in the Levant upon which Thutmose I and III built.

The text of this biography has a number of grammatical complexities because the standard rules of Middle Egyptian grammar are not always followed, while Late Egyptian is not as yet in full bloom.

Introduction (lines 1-4a)
The naval commander, Ahmose son of Abena, the justified (i.e. deceased), says, "let me speak to you, everyone and let me inform you of the honors that happened to me. I was rewarded with gold seven times in the presence of the entire land, and (given) male and female servants likewise. I was endowed with many great fields. The name of the brave is in that which he has done.[1] It will not perish from this land forever."

Service under Ahmose (lines 4b-8)
He spoke the following: "I was reared in the city of Nekheb.[2] My father was a soldier of the King of Upper and Lower Egypt, Seqenenre,[3] the justified, whose name is Baba, son of Rainet. Then I was made a soldier in order to replace him on the boat, 'Wild Bull,' during the lifetime of the Lord of the Two Lands, Nebpehtyre,[4] the justified. While I was a lad, before I had taken a wife, I slept in a net hammock.[5]

After this, I established a home. Subsequently I was taken to the northern fleet because of my bravery. Then I accompanied the Sovereign, life, prosperity, and health,[6] on foot,[7] following his travels on chariot."[8]

War against the Hyksos (lines 8-14)
"When the city of Avaris[9] was besieged, I was brave on foot in his majesty's presence. Subsequently I was assigned to the boat 'Coronation in Memphis.'[10] Then there was fighting on the water of Pajdku[11] of Avaris. Subsequently I made a capture, I having carried off a hand which was reported[12] to the Royal Herald. Then the gold of valor

[1] Rather than being a relative form (*irt.n.f*), this could be perfective pass. part., i.e. "what is done for him." Goedicke (1974:33) has argued for this understanding.

[2] Ancient Nekheb is located near modern el-Kab, south of Luxor.

[3] Seqenenre Tao is the 17th Dynasty Theban ruler who apparently initiated the conflict with the Hyksos, and may have died in the process. His two sons, Kamose and Ahmose followed him to the throne, the latter being the one credited with ousting the Hyksos and founding the 18th Dynasty.

[4] The pre-nomen of Ahmose, the first king of the Dynasty 18th according to Manetho's reconstruction.

[5] The translation of *smt šnw* is problematic. "Hammock" is the translation first proffered by Gardiner (Gardiner and Gunn 1918:49) and has been followed by several subsequent translators (*ANET* 233; *CDME* 225). This rendering has been questioned by Goedicke (1974:34-35) who argues that Gardiner read into the Egyptian terms "a quaint projection of traditions of H. M. Navy onto ancient Egypt." He suggests this sentence might be translated: "I spent the night in clothing the ropes," acknowledging he is not certain what it means.

[6] "life, prosperity, and health." This is the standard blessing after allusions to the living Pharaoh [Ed.]

[7] Lit., "on my feet." Ahmose might be considered a "marine." Once he sailed to the point of conflict, he fought on land.

[8] This is the first occurrence of the word *wrrt*, "chariot," in an Egyptian text (Hoffmeier 1999:193).

[9] The Greek vocalization of Egyptian *Ḥwt wᶜrt*, Avaris, the capital of the Hyksos, is identified with the site of Tell el-Dabᶜa (Bietak 1996).

[10] Goedicke (1974:38) may be correct in proposing that *ḫᶜm Mn-nfr* refers to a secondary coronation ceremony for King Ahmose at Memphis. However, his idea that the boat determinative after this expression refers to the journey to Memphis for this event rather than the name of the boat to which Ahmose was assigned is not particularly convincing. Alternatively, perhaps, the name of the boat simply commemorates the coronation ceremony in Memphis.

[11] Recent investigations at Tell el-Dabᶜa have revealed that in ancient times, the Pelusiac branch of the Nile, a number of tributaries, canals and pools were in proximity to the city. "The water of Pajdku" is likely one of these phenomena.

[12] The grammatical form of "report," *smiṯ*, is problematic. Below in line 13 of this text, the same construction occurs, but *smiw* is written. In the case of the first example, the *ṯ* ending is peculiar, and may be an archaic writing for *t*. In which case, an inf. (Gardiner 1969 §281) or

was given to me. Subsequently there was more fighting in this (same) place and I again made a capture there and carried off a hand. Then the gold of valor was given to me again. Then there was fighting in the south of Egypt[13] in this city. Subsequently I carried off a prisoner of war after I went down to the water. Look, he was carried off as a prisoner on that course[14] of the city, after I carried him across the water. It was reported to the Royal Herald. Subsequently[15] I was rewarded with gold again. Then Avaris was plundered and I carried off plunder from there: a man, three maidservants, for a total of four, and his majesty gave them to me as servants."

Campaign to Canaan (lines 15-16a)
"Then Sharuhen[16] [a] was besieged for three years.[17] Then his majesty plundered it. Subsequently I carried off plunder from there: two maid servants and a hand. Then the gold of valor was given to me. Look, the plunder of the men servants was given to me."

Nubian Campaigns (lines 16b-24a)
"After his majesty slew Asian Bedouin,[18] he then sailed south to Khenet-hen-nefer[19] in order to destroy Nubian tribesmen.[20] Then his majesty made a great heap of corpses from them. Subsequently I carried off plunder from there: two live men and three hands. Then I was rewarded with gold again. Look, two maid-servants were given to me. His majesty sailed north,[21] he being joyful at the bravery and victory, because he had seized southerners and northerners.

Then Aata came to the South, his fate bringing about his doom, the gods of Upper Egypt taking hold of him. He was found by his majesty in Tenet-taa.[22] His majesty carried him off as the prisoner-of-war, and all his people being easy prey. Subsequently, I carried off two Nubian fighters[23] as captives from the boat of Aata. Then one gave to me five persons as shares and a field of five *stt*[24] in my city. The same was done for all the sailors.

Subsequently that enemy, whose name is Tetian, came, after he had gathered to himself trouble makers.[25] Then his majesty slaughtered him and his crew was annihilated.[26] Subsequently three people and a field of five *stt* in my city were given to me."

Service under Amenhotep I (lines 24b-29a)
Then I transported the king of Upper and Lower Egypt, Djeserkare,[27] the justified. He sailed to Kush[28] [b] in order to expand the border of Egypt. His majesty struck down that Nubian tribesman in the midst of his army. They were carried off in neck constraints, without losing one of them.[29] The one who fled was laid low like those who did not exist.[30] [c]

a Josh 19:6

b Gen 10:6-7; 2 Kgs 19:9; Esth 1:1; 1 Chr 1:8; Isa 18:1; 20:3; Ezek 29:10, 30:4

c Josh 10:20

perfective pass. part. (Gardiner 1969 §361) are possibilities. For this translation, the latter option is followed. The *w* ending in the second occurrence might indicate the pass. *sḏm.f* form, with the subject, "it" being understood. While the sense of both sentences is fairly evident, the precise grammatical understanding is uncertain.

[13] *Kmt.*

[14] *Wꜣt* usually means path, but could mean a water course (*Wb* 1:246-247). Ahmose's bravery is particularly noteworthy because he crossed over this canal (or tributary) to capture the prisoner who would have been closer to the city of Avaris.

[15] This line (13) reads, *ꜥḥꜥ.n tw mk*. The placement of the particle *mk* after the initial element in the sentence is a problem, since it should stand at the beginning of a sentence (Gardiner 1969 §234). In lines 16 and 18, the formula *wn.in tw* begins the sentences followed by one beginning with *mk*. Perhaps a scribal error occurred in line 13 in which two lines, like those in 16 and 18, were conflated.

[16] Sharuhen is located in southern Canaan to judge from Josh 19:6 which locates it within Simeon, the southernmost Israelite tribal territory. Albright (1929:7) proposed that Tell el-Farah (S) was Sharuhen. This identification has been challenged by a number of archaeologists in recent years who prefer Tell el-ꜥAjjul. Those arguing for this position include Kempinski (1974:145-152), Stewart (1974) and Weinstein (1981:241; 1991:106). Despite the compelling case that has been made for Tell el-ꜥAjjul, the case remains to be settled, as the archaeological evidence is too ambiguous (Hoffmeier 1989:182-184; 1991:117-120). It will likely take an inscription from one of these sites to confirm the identification of Sharuhen. [Rainey (1993) suggests the possibility of locating Sharuhen at Tell Abū Hureira (Tel Haror).] [KLY]

[17] Goedicke (1974:40-41) argues that *m rnpwt ḫmt* should be read as "in three years." For him this does not represent a three year long siege, but three consecutive years of campaigning. His reason for doing so is that the preposition *m* is not typically used to indicate duration of time. Gardiner (1969 §162.2), however, points to this very text to illustrate that *m* can be used to express time duration.

[18] I.e. *Mntyw stt.*

[19] A region within Nubia (Gardiner *AEO* 1:48).

[20] I.e. *Iwnw-sttyw.*

[21] Lit., "Sailing north by his majesty."

[22] The determinative used with this toponym is the water sign, suggestive of a body of water, but its location is uncertain.

[23] These are *Mgꜣ*, apparently a tribal name that subsequently came to refer to a specific para-military fighting force (Schulman 1964:25).

[24] Approximately 3.3 acres.

[25] I.e. *ẖꜣkw ibw*, "disaffected ones" (*CDME* 200).

[26] Lit., "into that which does not exist."

[27] The pre-nomen of Amenhotep I, the second king of the 18th Dynasty.

[28] During the New Kingdom, Kush is situated south of the Third Cataract (Trigger, Kemp, O'Connor and Lloyd 1983:256).

[29] Lit., "without a loss of them."

[30] Line 25 ends by saying that none were lost, followed immediately by "the one who fled." While to a western audience, such statements appear to be contradictory, clearly it was not to the Egyptians. A similar juxtaposition regarding enemies is present in Josh 10:20 where reference is made to the total annihilation of the populace of Makkedah, followed immediately by the mention of survivors. For further discussion of this phenomenon, see Hoffmeier 1997:41.

Now I was at the head of our army. I fought truly well, his majesty having seen my bravery. I carried off two hands which were presented to his majesty. Then his people and his cattle were sought out. Subsequently I carried off a prisoner of war who was presented to his majesty. From the 'Upper Well' I brought him back to Egypt in two days. Subsequently I was rewarded with gold. I carried off two maid servants as plunder, besides these which I had presented to him. Then I was appointed as a 'Warrior of the Ruler'."

Thutmose I's Nubian Campaign (lines 29b-35)
"Then I transported the king of Upper and Lower Egypt, Aakheperkare,[31] the justified. He sailed south to Khenet-hen-nefer in order to destroy insurrection throughout foreign lands and to subdue those who enter from the dessert region.

I was brave in his presence in the rough water while pushing boats over the rapids.[32] Then I was appointed as crew commander. Then his majesty, life, prosperity, and health, [...] Then his majesty raged like a panther concerning it. His majesty fired his first arrow, sticking in the neck of that enemy. Then these [enemies (?) [...] fl]ed, weakened by his Uraeus[33] which in a moment turned them into carnage. Their subjects were carried off as prisoners-of-war. His majesty sailed north with foreign lands in his grip. That feeble Nubian tribesman was hung upside down at the bow of his majesty's boat. They docked at Karnak."

Thutmose I's Euphrates Campaign (lines 36-39)
"After these things, there was an expedition to Retenu[34] in order to take vengeance throughout foreign lands. His majesty arrived at Naharin.[35] [d] His majesty, life, prosperity, and health, discovered that enemy rallying troops. His majesty made a great heap of them. Countless were the prisoners-of-war which his majesty carried off from his victories.

Now I was at the head of our army. His majesty saw how brave I was when I carried off a chariot, its horse, and the rider[36] as a prisoner-of-war who was presented to his majesty. Then I was rewarded with gold again."

Conclusion (line 40)
"I am (now) elderly, having reached old age. My honors are before (me) a second time. [Bel]oved by my [lord?]. I [rest] in the tomb that I myself made."

d Gen 24:10; Deut 23:4; Judg 3:8; Ps 60:2; 1 Chr 19:6

[31] The prenomen of Thutmose I, successor to Amenhotep I.

[32] Sailing through the hazardous waters of the 1st and 2nd cataracts was notoriously dangerous. There was always the potential for loss of ships and human life. Hence, Ahmose's courage at this point of the journey was noteworthy.

[33] This is the cobra that is perched on the brow of king or attached to his crown.

[34] Retenu is a general term that include the area of Lebanon and Syria. Egyptian scribes could distinguish between upper and lower Retenu, but the dividing line between the two regions is unclear (Gardiner *AEO* 2:142*-149*).

[35] Aram Naharaim is attested in the Bible (see ***d*** above), referring to the land between the Euphrates and Balih or Habur. Nahar is a Semitic word for river, attested in Heb., Ug. and Akk. (*KB*[3] 599).

[36] Lit., "the one who was on it."

REFERENCES

Text: Loret 1910; Sethe *Urk.* IV:1-11. Translations and studies: Albright 1929; *ANET* 233-234; Bietak 1996. Gardiner and Gunn 1918; Goedicke 1974; Hoffmeier 1989; 1991; 1997; 1999; Kempinski 1974; Lichtheim *AEL* 2:12-15; Schulman 1964; Stewart 1974; Trigger, Kemp, O'Connor and Lloyd 1983.

THUTMOSE III (2.2)

THE ANNALS OF THUTMOSE III (2.2A)

James K. Hoffmeier

These annals are among the most celebrated of ancient Egyptian historical texts. The annals are carved in raised relief on walls that surrounded the bark shrine of Amun which likewise was erected by Thutmose III. K. Sethe's collation of the annals (*Urk.* IV:625-756), despite its predisposition to offer speculative restorations, has served as the standard transcription. The historical and geographical aspects of the annals have been widely studied, and so have the forms and sources used in the composition of the annals. Earlier studies by M. Noth (1943) and H. Grapow (1947) laid the foundation for the more recent investigations of A. J. Spalinger (1974; 1977; 1982) and Redford (1986). Grapow believed that the principal source behind the annals was the daybook. Surviving daybooks date back to the Middle Kingdom and continue to be found through the New Kingdom. Redford (1986:103-121) was able to identify 16 examples of daybooks for study. The *Tagebuchstil* or "daybook style" is rather mundane with log-like records, characterized by the use of bare infinitives. A good example of this form is found in the 6th campaign, a translation of which is offered below.

Spalinger argued for the existence of a second source along with the daybook, viz. "the scribal war diary." Lines 93-94 of the annals refers to daily recording of the events of the campaign on a leather scroll. Unfortunately for Spalinger's ingenious suggestion, the scroll is not given a name. The fact that no Egyptian text mentions a "scribal war diary" leads Redford (1986:122) to reject Spalinger's hypothesis. Instead, Redford suggests that behind the detailed record of the first campaign stands a special document that complemented the daybook, "the Daybook (*hrwyt*) of the King's Palace" (1986:124-125). There is little doubt that military scribes recorded the acts of the king and other significant events while on the campaign, even "daily" as suggested by the statement in line 93. Additionally, the military scribe (*sš mšʿw*) Tjaneny reports that he followed Thutmose III on his campaigns, and states: "I saw the victories of the king which he made over every foreign land ... It was I who recorded the victories which he achieved over all foreign lands, it being put into writing according to what was done" (*Urk.* IV, 4, 9-10). Thus it is evident that whatever the name of the source or sources behind the annals may be, they were based upon eye-witnesses who immediately recorded salient details for future editing, expansions and recording on stelae and temple walls.

The same combination of long, detailed reports, like the Megiddo expedition, and short terse accounts, like most of the succeeding campaigns (cf. the 5th and 6th campaigns), is a feature also attested in Israel's military narratives in the book of Joshua (see Hoffmeier 1994). Joshua 1-8 contain lengthy, detailed reports about the initial Israelite campaigns in Canaan, whereas Joshua 10:28-11:14 is recorded in very stylized, repetitive expressions that look intriguingly like the *Tagbuchstil*. In a comprehensive, comparative study of ancient Near Eastern military writings of the 2nd Millennium BCE, Younger (1990) has shown that features they exhibit are very similar to those found in Hebrew military reports found in the Bible. This work, along with a study comparing the Joshua narratives with the Annals of Thutmose III (Hoffmeier 1994), demonstrates that the style and structuring of Hebrew military writings was influenced by ancient Near Eastern scribal tradition rather than an Israelite innovation by the Deuteronomic Historian as some biblical scholars have opined (e.g. Weinfeld 1972; Van Seters 1990).

The First Asiatic Campaign
Introduction (lines 1-6a)
Horus, Strong Bull arising in Thebes; [Two Ladies, Enduring of Kingship like Re in the Sky; Horus of Gold, Mighty in Strength and of Holy Diadem]; the King of Upper and Lower Egypt, Lord of the Two Lands, Menkheperre; Bodily [Son of Re, Thutmose (III), of Beautiful Form, given life forever].

His majesty commanded that the [victories which his father Amun gave him be recorded as][1] an inscription in the temple which his majesty had made for [his father Amun in order to record] each campaign along with the booty [which his majesty] brought [from it and the tribute of] every [foreign land] which his father Re gave to him.[2]

The Initiation of the First Campaign (lines 6b-13a)
Regnal year 22, fourth month of winter, day 25: [His majesty passed by the fortress of] Tjaru[3] on the first victorious campaign, [in order to drive off the attackers] of Egypt's borders in bravery, [in victory, in strength and justice].[4] Now for a [great] period of years [...][5] anarchy, every one [showing hostility towards][6] his [neighbor] [...].[7] Now it happened in other times that the troops which were there are (now) in the city of Sharuhen,[a] while

a Josh 19:6

[1] Throughout the Annals, the names of Amun and Amun-Re have been deliberately expunged by the iconoclasts of the Amarna period.

[2] The name of the sun-god Re is not obliterated here as with the case of Amun throughout this text. Clearly, Re's name was not offensive to the Aten iconoclasts.

[3] Traditionally, Tjaru has been identified with Tell Abu-Sefêh, a few km east of Qantara East. Recent excavations at the site have revealed an impressive fort. However, only remains of the Greco-Roman periods have surfaced thus far. Around five kilometers north of Tell Abu Sefêh, excavations at Tell Hebua have unearthed a major New Kingdom site, including a massive fort. Hebua now appears to be the more likely site for Tjaru, Egypt's frontier town. For a recent discussion of these sites and the identity of Tjaru, see Hoffmeier 1997:83-188 and Abd El-Maksoud 1999.

[4] This line can be restored with some certainty because of its appearance in lines 15-16.

[5] The reading of this critical lacuna is disputed. Its importance lies in the description of the condition of the empire in Syria-Palestine that prompted Thutmose's immediate attention after his gaining full control of the throne upon the death of Hatshepsut. Redford (1979:338) made a careful study of this text and rejected Sethe's restoration (*ḥḳ*ꜣ*.n.sn t*ꜣ *pn wn m* — "they ruled this land which was in"). Instead he proposes the reading to be *iw rṯnw ḥryt* — "Retenu was terrified." More recently still, Murnane (1989) has questioned the restoration of Retenu because the *ṯ* sign is not clear, but still thinks the provenance for the unrest is Asia. He restores *Sṯt* later in the line.

[6] This is Redford's restoration (1979:339).

[7] This lacuna, like the one in the previous line, is very critical because it gives details about the conditions in Canaan that prompted Thutmose's military action. A number of different readings have been offered for the partially legible text. Sethe (*Urk.* IV, 648.4) restored it as *wr.sn nty m ḥwt wʿrt*, "their chieftains who had been in Avaris." This reading lays the blame for the current rebellion on descendants of Hyksos chieftains who had lived in Egypt until ca. 1540 BCE. While it is true that Hatshepsut in the Speos Artemidos inscription at a slightly earlier date blamed the Hyksos for the conditions of temples in Egypt, it seems unlikely that a century later, and several generations removed from the expulsion of the Hyksos, the current crisis in Canaan could be connected with the "chieftains who had been in Avaris." Because of the speculative nature of Sethe's restoration, it is now largely rejected, although for many decades, his understanding influenced some Egyptologist and Syro-Palestinian archaeologists into thinking that the destruction of MB II sites in Canaan resulted from systematic, vengeful attacks on cities associated with the Hyksos (for a recent defense of this views, see Weinstein 1981; 1991; for a critique of this position, see Hoffmeier 1989).

beginning at Yursa[8] to the farthest northlands are in rebellion against his majesty.[9]

Celebration of the anniversary of the king's coronation at Gaza (lines 13b-18a)

Regnal year 23, the first month of summer, day four, the day of the Festival of the King's Coronation at the city "That which the Ruler Captured," [whose Syrian name] is Gaza.[b] [Regnal year 23], first month of summer, day five, departing from this place in bravery, [in victory], in strength and justice, in order to overthrow that feeble enemy and in order to expand the borders of Egypt[10] according to what his [brave] and victorious father [Amun-Re] ordained that he conquer.

War Counsel at Yehem (lines 18b-56a)

Regnal year 23, first month of summer, day 16 at the city of Yehem.[11] [His majesty] ordered a consultation with his victorious army in order to say the following: "That feeble enemy of Kadesh[12] [c] has entered Megiddo,[d] and he is [there] at this moment, having rallied to himself the chieftains of [every] foreign land [who had been] allies of Egypt,[13] as well as (those) from as far away as Naharin in (or being) [...], Kharu[14] and Kedy,[15] their horses, their armies and [their people].[16]

And he says, so it is rumored, "I will take a stand to [fight against his majesty here] at Megiddo. (Now) tell me [what is your opinion?]"[17] They said to his majesty, "What is it like, traveling on this road which becomes narrow, since it is reported, the enemies are there, standing [outside],[18] [and they are] becoming more numerous? Will not the horses have to go in single file[19] and [the army] and people likewise? Will our lead troops[20] be fighting (there) while those at the rear are standing around here in Aruna,[21] not able to fight. Now there are two (other) [roa]ds here. One of the roads, it [is favorable to (?)][22] our [lord] and it comes [out] at Taanach?[23] [e] The other is at the road north of Djefti,[24] so that we would come out north of Megiddo. Now then, let our victorious lord proceed on whichever of [them] is bes[t in] his opinion,[25] but do not make us go on th[at di]fficult[26] road."

Then intelligence reports [were brought] concer[ning that feeble enemy],[27] [...] concerning [that] plan which they had discussed previously.[28] What was said in the majesty of the palace,[29] "I [swear][30] [f] as Re loves me and my father [Amun] praises me, as my nose is refreshed by life and

b Gen 10:19; Deut 2:23; Josh 11:22; 13:3; 15:47; Judg 1:8; 1 Sam 6:17

c 2 Sam 24:6

d Josh 12:21, etc.

e Josh 12:21; 17:11; 21:25; Judg 1:27; 5:19; 1 Kgs 4:12; 1 Chr 7:29

f Num 14:21; 14:28; Deut 32:4; Pss 63:4; 104:33; 116:2; Isa 49:18; Jer 22:24; 46:18; Ezek 5:11; 14:16

[8] Identified with Tell Jemmeh, located around 13 km. south of Gaza (Aḥituv 1984:202-203).

[9] This statement is somewhat obscure, but it appears to be reporting that the garrison which had been stationed at a point further north had been forced to retreat to the south, viz. Sharuhen. It might be that when the Prince of Kadesh, the ringleader of the rebellion, occupied Megiddo (cf. line 20), he ousted the Egyptian troops.

[10] *Kmt*.

[11] Yehem's name is preserved in the Arabic toponym Khirbet Yamma, situated 3 km. north of Sochoh, Tell er-Ras (Aḥituv 1984:198). The distance traveled by Thutmose III and his army since the departure from Gaza is 72 km. in eleven days. Subsequently, Amenhotep II camped at this site.

[12] Not to be confused with Kadesh-Barnea in northeastern Sinai, but northern Kadesh, on the Orontes River, in Syria. The site is identified with Tell Nebi Mend (Gardiner *AEO* 1:137).

[13] Lit. "who had been on the water of Egypt."

[14] A general term for Syria, perhaps equivalent to Retenu (Gardiner *AEO* 1:180-183).

[15] The land north of Alalakh and Aleppo, and west of Carchemish, running to the Mediterranean (Gardiner *AEO* 1:132-136).

[16] The expression "army and people (*rmṯ*)" occurs several times in the Annals. "People" apparently refers to non-combat, support personnel essential to the mission.

[17] This line was restored by Sethe as *ntt m ib.tn*, lit. "what is in your heart."

[18] It is unclear whether this means the rebel forces are waiting at the other end of the Kina Valley, or in a general sense, outside of Megiddo. Regarding the former, Faulkner (1942:14) argued "'standing ready at its mouth'" (his translation) should not be taken too literally," because Thutmose was able to lead this troops through the valley "virtually unopposed."

[19] Lit. "horse after [horse]."

[20] *Ḥ*ᶜ*t* lit. means in front, and here "those in front," and hence has been translated "vanguard" (*CDME* 162; Lichtheim *AEL* 2:31).

[21] The king's strategy session occurs at Yehem. Aruna, where the narrow pass begins, was still approximately 20 km ahead. Thus "here" (ᶜᵓ) does not mean "here in Yehem," but at Aruna. Aruna is identified with Khirbet ᶜArah, situated near the modern village by the same name (Aḥituv 1984:67).

[22] Sethe restored this break as "[beneficial to] our lord," a reading rejected as "certainly wrong" by Faulkner (1942:5), but he offers no alternative. Lichtheim (*AEL* 2:31) speculates a reading "[to our east]."

[23] Taanach is identified with Tell Taᶜinnik, located about 8 km southeast of Megiddo (Aḥituv 1984:184-185), guarding one of the entrances to the Jezreel Valley. The close relationship between Megiddo and Taanach is well reflected in the Bible. Of the seven references to Taanach cited in note ***e***, only Josh 21:25 does not also mention Megiddo.

[24] For Hebrew *sphath*, a town located at Khirbet Sitt Leila which looks out upon the northern road proposed by Thutmose's general (Aḥituv 1984:204-205).

[25] Lit. "on the best for his heart of them."

[26] The word used here is *štᵓ*, most commonly meaning secret or mysterious, but also difficult or hard, "schwierig" (*Wb* 4:551).

[27] Faulkner (1942:5 n. g) believes that Sethe's restoration is quite plausible.

[28] Apparently Thutmose's spies returned with a report on the placement of the rebel forces, which apparently influenced the king's decision on the route to take.

[29] *Stp sᵓ* is an expression meaning protection (*Wb* 4:339), with the addition of the house determinative for the royal court or palace (*Wb* 4:340-341). Faulkner (1942:3) renders *stp sᵓ* as "royal tent," since on a military campaign, the king's tent was his traveling palace,

[30] Lit. "As I live." This oath formula is the same one used in Israel (cf references in note *f*).

dominion. My majesty will proceed on this Aruna road. Let whoever desires among you to go on those roads of which you speak, and let whoever desires among you to come in the following of my majesty. Do not let them say,[31] those enemies who are an abomination to Re, 'Has his majesty proceeded on another road because he is afraid of us,' so they will say."

They said to him, "May your father Amun, lord of the thrones of the Two Lands who is foremost at Karnak, do [what is in your heart]. See here, we are followers of your majesty: anywhere that [your majesty] goes, there a servant will be, behind [his] lord."

[His majesty gave the] (following) command to his whole army: ["Your victorious lord will] protect[32] [your march on th]at road which becomes nar-[row]." [His majesty had made] an oath, saying, "I will not let [my victorious army] go out in front of my majesty in [this place." Now his majesty had determined][33] that he would go out leading his army in person. [Everyone] was briefed[34] on the marching orders, horses in single file, [his majesty] being at the head of his army.

The Stop-over at Aruna (lines 56b-82)
Regnal year 23, first month of summer, day 19,[35] awaking in [life] in the tent of life,[36] prosperity, and health at the city of Aruna. Journeying northwards by my majesty under <my> father [Amun-Re Lord of the thrones of the two lands] that he may [blaze the trail][37] in front of me, Re-horakhty encourag[ing[38] my victorious army], <my> father [Amun s]trengthened the powerful ar[m of my majesty]. [... Horus(?) as protection][39] over my majesty.

Exiting (the narrow pass) by [his maj]esty [at the front of] his [army], organized in many divisions, [without encountering] a single [enemy].[40] [Their] southern flanks were in Taanach, [while their] northern flank was in the sout[hern] bend [of ...].[41] [Then] his majesty cried out concerning [this] r[oad] ...] "They are defeated," while that [feeble] enemy [...][42] [text is virtually unreadable through the end of line 69] [Give] praise to him, [extol the power] of his majesty on account of the greatness of his powerful arm more than [any king].[43] [... of][44] the army of his majesty in Aruna. Now the rear of the victorious army of his majesty was (still) at the [city] of Aruna, while the front was coming out into the Valley of Kina, they having filled the mouth of this valley.

Then they said to his majesty (life, prosperity, and health), "Look here, his majesty and his victorious army have come out and have filled the valley. Let our victorious lord listen to us this time. Let our lord guard for us the rear of his army and his people. When the rear of our army comes outside (the valley) to us, then we will fight against these foreigners and we will not be concerned for the rear of our army." His majesty secured the outside. [He] sat [...] there, guarding the rear of his victorious army. Now when the [le]ad troops had

[31] Here this line is understood as *m di kꜣ.sn*, the negative *m* + negatival complement, *di*, "do not let" (cf. Gardiner 1969 §341). Lichtheim (*AEL* 2:31) and Faulkner (1942:3) understand the first two signs to read as *ink*, "behold."

[32] This word is partially preserved, the first sign, *n*, is preserved, while the smaller sign beneath it is obliterated. Sethe (*Urk. IV* 652 n. a) indicates that a number of signs could fit, including *ḫ*, but he opts for *ḥ* reading the word as *nḥm*, meaning, "guard and protect" (*Wb* 2:296). Alternatively, if *ḫ* is the missing sign, the word would be *nḫ*, also meaning "protect" (*Wb* 2:304). Either reading makes good sense in view of the fear of Thutmose's officers to go through the Aruna pass.

[33] If Sethe's restoration is correct, the line lit. reads, "his majesty placed in his heart," hence the meaning "determined" (*CDME* 155).

[34] Lit. "caused to know."

[35] Three days had passed since the consultation had taken place in Yehem. This distance from Yehem to Aruna should only have taken a day to travel. Since this date marks the beginning of day 19, Thutmose and his army might have arrived the night before.

[36] It has been suggested that this formula, which occurs elsewhere in the annals, as well as in the military documents of Amenhotep II and Ramesses II (see Hoffmeier 1977:16-17 for references and discussion), signaled the beginning of a new day in the daybook which served as the source for the Annals (Spalinger 1975:222). See also *COS* 2.1, note 6.

[37] The idiom, *wpi wꜣwt* (lit. "open the ways") occurs in the Armant Stela (line 12), but it is the king who blazes the trail whereas here in the Annals, it is Amun-Re who "blazes the trail."

[38] Lit. "making firm the heart."

[39] The falcon on the standard, a determinative that often accompanies the writing of Horus, is visible. The appearance of Horus here makes sense since the falcon usually flies over the head of the king in the iconography.

[40] Sethe's restoration is possible, but, in the absence of evidence, was rejected by Faulkner (1942:7). Lichtheim (*AEL* 2:31), however, follows it.

[41] Understanding this critical line is problematic because of two lacunae. Sethe posits "of the Kina Valley" for the second break. It is hard to believe, however, that Thutmose could lead his troops right by the coalition's forces in the narrow pass without a skirmish. Lichtheim (*AEL* 2:35 n. 6) thinks that restoring Kina Valley may be erroneous.

[42] The break at this critical juncture prevents one from knowing with certainty why the king was so elated. Thutmose's excitement may stem from either seeing no defenders as he exits the ravine, hence, "they are as good as defeated," or, there was such a small force posted that they were quickly overwhelmed. This latter point is preferred by Faulkner (1942:9 n. v) because he finds it unlikely that the Prince of Kadesh would not have placed some troops at this possible point of egress.

[43] Sethe restores this as [*nṯrw nbw*] "all the gods." This reading is unlikely because the king is never described in terms superior to deity.

[44] Sethe's restoration reads: "[he guarded the rear of] the army of his majesty ..." Faulkner (1942:9 n. y) left this space blank, while acknowledging that the reading is possible. Lichtheim (*AEL* 2:31) adopts the reading.

finished coming out on this road, it was noon.[45]

Setting up camp at Megiddo (lines 83-84a)
His majesty arrived south of Megiddo, on the banks of the Kina Brook, at seven in the evening. Then the camp was set up there for his majesty. Then he made the following command to the entire army, [saying]: "Make your preparations, get your weapons ready because one will engage in fighting with that feeble enemy in the morning,[46] because one [...]

Resting in the enclosure[47] of life, prosperity, and health.[48] Making provisions for the officers and distributing rations to the attendants. Sentries were posted for the army, saying to them: "Be courageous, be courageous, keep awake, keep awake!"

Awaking in life in the tent of life, prosperity, and health. One came to brief his majesty,[49] "the coast is clear[50] and the troops north and south are also (safe)."

The Battle at Megiddo (lines 84b-89)
Year 23, first month of summer, day 21.[51] The exact day of the festival of the new moon.[52] The appearance of the king at dawn. Now orders were given to the entire army to deploy[53] [...]. His majesty set off on his electrum chariot, equipped with an impressive array of weapons, like a strong-armed Horus, Lord of Action, like Montu of Thebes, his father [Amun] making his arms victorious. The southern flank of his majesty's army was at the southern mountain [by?] the Kina [brook], and the northern flank was northwest of Megiddo, while his majesty was in the middle of them, [Amun] protecting his body in the melee and the strength of [Seth fills] his limbs. Then his majesty overpowered them while leading his army. They saw his majesty overpower them. They fled, falling headlong [toward] Megiddo with fearful faces, they having abandoned their horses and chariots of gold and silver in order that they be dragged and hoisted by their clothes into this city.

Now because the people had sealed this city against th[em,[54] they let down] garments in order to hoist them up into this city. Now if only the army of his majesty had not set their minds to looting the possessions of those enemies,[55] th[ey] would have [taken] Megiddo at that time. Now (even) the feeble enemy of Kadesh and the feeble enemy of this city were being dragged, scrambling, to get them into their city. The fear of his majesty had penetrated [their limbs], their arms were exhausted, [for (?)] his Uraeus overpowered them.

Meanwhile, their horses and chariots of gold and silver were taken easily as [booty].[56] Their troo[ps] were lying around on (their) backs[57] like fish in the bight of a net as his majesty's victorious army tallied their possessions.

Now the tent belonging to [that] feeble [enemy] which was dec[orated with gold][58] was plundered.[59] [...] The whole army was shouting, giving praise to [Amun for the victor]ies which he gave to his son [today, and they gave thanks] to his majesty, extolling his victory. They presented the plunder which they had carried off, hands, prisoners of war, horses, gold and silver chariots and pla[in

[45] Lit. "the shadow turned."

[46] Lit. "seven hours from the turning of the day," i.e. seven hours after noon, since the king and the lead battalion reached the exiting point of the valley at noon. In his commentary on this passage, Faulkner (1942:10 n. bb) proposes that Thutmose and the lead battalion departed Aruna around 7:30 A.M., arriving at noon, and the last battalion would have departed around 2:30 P.M. in order to cover the ca. 15-16 km by 7:00 P.M.

[47] The word here is *ʿʿny*. Three different words are used to described the royal camp and tent. *Ihy* (line 83), *ʿʿny* (line 84) and *im* (lines 57 and 84) which apparently reflects a tripartite structure. When this terminology is viewed in the light of Ramesses II's camp at Kadesh, depicted at Luxor and Abu Simbel Temples (Wrezinski 1938-41:82, 170), the three-fold structure is evident. An outer wall marks the perimeter of the camp. *Ihy* appears to be the general term for this enclosure. The *ʿʿny* is possibly a smaller enclosure within the camp in which the king's tent (*im*) is located (Hoffmeier 1977:16, 18).

[48] This formula is the opposite of "awaking the tent" which pointed to the beginning of the day in the daybook (cf. note 36 above). The "resting" formula, which also occurs in the Memphis Stela of Amenhotep II (see *COS* 2.3 below), could be denoting the end of the daybook entry (Hoffmeier 1977:17).

[49] Lit. "one came to say." The formula "one came" (*iw.tw*) is a standard formula for introducing a report (Spalinger 1982:1-33).

[50] Lit. "the desert or waste-land is safe." Faulkner's translation, "the cost is clear," beautifully captures the meaning of this expression (1942:11 n. gg).

[51] The reading "day 21" has been questioned by Faulkner (1942:11 n. hh) and others (e.g. Parker 1957) because if Thutmose's army had passed through the Aruna Valley on the 19th, they could not possibly have stayed undetected for another day before the battle began on the morning of the 21st. There is no doubt that this missing day poses a problem.

[52] This lunar date is a pivotal datum in establishing Thutmose III's accession date, with 1504 BCE and 1490 BCE being favored by some (cf. Parker, 1957; Lello 1978; Casperson 1986), while others prefer 1479 BCE (Kitchen 1987; 1989; Hornung 1987).

[53] The verb *ss*, or *sni*, assuming the walking legs sign is lost in the lacuna, means "pass" or "spread out" (*CDME* 246; *Wb* 3:454). In the "Tale of Sinuhe" (B 128), in a military setting, this word appears to mean "draw" weapons. Hence, "deploy" here makes good sense.

[54] *Ḥr.s* is visible, but there appears to be room for the *n* over the plural strokes. The reading would be *sn*, the third pl. suffix-pronoun.

[55] I.e. from the camp outside the city and the chariotry that was abandoned.

[56] Lit. "taken, made as easy prey." Faulkner (*CDME* 29) considered the expression *is ḥʾḳ* to mean "easy prey."

[57] Lit. "lying down in prostration." The determinative for both words shows a figure lying on its back.

[58] This restoration is likely correct, based upon the booty list. Line 97 mentions the seven tent poles that were decorated in silver.

[59] The seizure of the enemy's tent may have special military significance in Near Eastern context (cf. Hoffmeier 1991:18-19).

ones].[60]

The Siege of Megiddo (lines 90-94a)
[...] [His majesty gave] orders to his army, saying, "Capture w[ell], capture w[ell, Oh my vi]ctorious [army!] Look, [all foreign lands are] are placed [in this city according to the decree] of Re today, because every chieftain of all [northe]rn lands is bottled up within it, and because the capture of Megiddo is the capture of 1000 cities, so capture firmly, capture firmly. Lo[ok ...] [...] troop [commanders to equi[p their army in order to inform] every [man] of his position, they having measured [this] city, encircling (it) with a ditch, enclosing (it) with fresh branches of all their fruit trees.[61] [g] His majesty himself was at a fort east of th[is] city, [keeping wa]tch [over it, night and day]. [...] its enclo]sure being a thick wall [...] was its thickness. It was named "Menkheperre-Trapper-of-Asiatics." People were put on guard at his majesty's enclosure.[62] They were told, "Be courageous, be courageous, keep awake, keep awake!" [Now] his majesty [... Not o]ne of them [was allowed to go] out beyond this wall, except to come in order to knock on the door of their fortress.[63]

As a matter of fact, everything which his majesty did to this city, to that feeble enemy and his feeble army, was recorded daily by its name, by the name of the expedition, and [by the] name[s] of the tr[oop] commanders. [... in order to put it into writing according to this command]. They are recorded on a leather scroll that is in the temple of [Amun] today.

The Surrender of Megiddo (lines 94b-95)
Now the chieftains of this foreign land came on their bellies in order to kiss the ground because of the awe of his majesty, in order to beg for the breath of their nostril because of the greatness of his powerful arm and the vastness of the awe [of Amu]n over every foreign land [...] foreign land. Now [all] the chieftains, [ca]rried off by the awe of his majesty, bore their tribute of silver, gold, lapis lazuli and copper, bearing grain, wine, cattle and flocks for the army of his majesty; one company of them carried tribute on the journey south. Now his majesty reappointed the chieftains of [every city ...].

g Deut 20:19-20

h 1 Kgs 22:34; 2 Chr 18:33

The Booty List (lines 96-102a)
[The list of booty which his majesty carried off from the city of] Megiddo:
3400 prisoners-of-war
83 hands
2041 horses
191 foals
6 stallions
... colts
The gold decorated chariot and golden (chariot) pole of that enemy.
The fine, gold decorated chariot of the chieftain of [Megiddo].
[...]
892 chariots of his feeble army, totalling 924.
The fine, bronze mail coat[64] [h] of that enemy.
The fine bronze mail coat of the chieftain of Meg[iddo].
20 mail [...] coats of his feeble army.
502 bows
7 fine silver decorated tent poles of the tent of that enemy.
Now [his majesty's] army captured [the livestock of this city]
[...]
387 [...]
1929 cows
2000 goats
20,500 sheep

The list of that which was carried away afterwards by the king of the possessions of the palace of that enemy from Yenoam,[65] from Inuges, from Herenkaru,[66] and the property of those cities which had been loyal to him which were carried away because of [the awe of his majesty].
[...]
[the wives of that enemy along with those who were with him ...]
and 38 [Marayanu][67] belonging to them.
87 children of that enemy and the chieftains who were with him and 5 Marayanu belonging to them.
1796 male, female servants and their children.
103 who surrendered and defected from that enemy because of hunger.
A total of 2503.

[60] The reading n^{cc} seems certain (Faulkner 1942:14 n. rr), and means "smooth" or "undecorated" (*CDME* 126; *Wb* 2:208), and seems to refer to undecorated or plain chariots over against decorated types used by the kings or highest ranking officers.

[61] The mention of "fruit trees" is especially interesting in that the Egyptians felt no obligation to preserve fruit bearing trees as a humanitarian gesture to the local population whereas the Hebrews are specifically instructed to discriminate between fruit and non-fruit bearing trees for siege equipment (Deut 20:19-20). They were not to cut down the former. Cf. also *COS* 2.2B, note 19a. and *COS* 2.113C, note 3.

[62] Cf. note 47.

[63] This expression apparently means to surrender (cf. Lichtheim *AEL* 2:35, n. 8).

[64] Lit. "bronze tunic for fighting." The word "tunic" (*mss*) is written with a leather hide determinative, suggesting that the leather coat had small bronze plates attached to it. This type of armor is depicted on a Canaanite charioteer in the scene on Thutmose IV's chariot body.

[65] Located in southern Bashan (Aḥituv 1984:199), possibly el-ʾAbadiyeh (Aharoni 1979:443). See *COS* 2.6, note 4.

[66] A city-state in Upper Retenu, Syria (Gardiner *AEO* 1:169).

[67] An Indo-European word for an elite chariot warrior (Gardiner 1961:203).

Additionally, precious stones, gold, bowls, and a variety of vessels. [...], a large jar of Syrian workmanship, vases, bowls, plates, a variety of drinking cups, large vessels, [x+]27 knives, adding up to 1784 *deben*.[68] Golden disks which were hand crafted and many silver disks, adding up to 966 *deben* and one *kite*.[69] A silver statue being formed [... statue of that enemy who] was there (?). A (statue) head of gold. 3 human-headed staves. 6 carrying chairs of that enemy (made) of ivory, ebony, *ssnḏm*-wood and decorated in gold. 6 footstools[70] of theirs. 6 large offering tables (made) of ebony and *ssnḏm*-wood. A bed of *ssnḏm*-wood decorated with gold and gems, (made) in the form of a bed[71] belonging to that enemy, and decorated with gold entirely. An ebony statue of that enemy which was decorated with gold, the head of which is (made) of la[pis lazuli]. [...] bronze vessels, and many clothes of that enemy.

Harvesting the Fields of Megiddo (lines 102b-103a)
Now the fields were divided into plots and assigned to royal agents[72] in order to reap their harvest. A list of the harvest which was taken away for his majesty from the fields of Megiddo: 207,300 [+ x] sacks of wheat, apart from gleanings taken[73] by the army of his majesty. [...]

The Fifth Asiatic Campaign (lines 3-5)[74]
Regnal year 29. Now [his] majesty[was in Dja]hy[75] destroying foreign nations which had been rebellious towards him on his fifth victorious campaign. Now his majesty plundered the city of War[t]et. [...] Giving praise to his majesty by his army. Giving adoration to [Amun] for the victories [which he] had given to his son. They were happy and pleased with his majesty more than anything. Thereafter, his majesty proceeded to the offering storehouse. Giving offerings to [Amun]-Re-Harakhty consisting of oxen, fowl, short-horned cattle [...] [on behalf of, life, prosperity, and health, the king of Upper and Lower Egypt], Menkheper[re], given life forever.

The list of the plunder which was brought from this city and from the troops of that enemy of Tunip:[76] 1 chieftain of this city; 329 Syrian warriors, 100 *deben* of fine gold, lapis lazuli, turquoise, and vessels of bronze and copper ...

The Sixth Asiatic Campaign (lines 9-10)[77]
Regnal year 30. Now his majesty was in the foreign land of Retenu[78] on this 6th victorious campaign of his majesty. Arriving at the city of Kadesh, destroying it, cutting down its trees and plucking its barley. Proceeding from Shesryt,[79] arriving at the City of Djamer,[80] arriving at the city of Irtjet (*Irṯwt*).[81] Doing likewise against it.

The list of the gifts[82] which were brought by the chieftain of Retenu because of the awe of his majesty ...

[68] One *deben* weighs 91 grams.
[69] This measurement is a tenth of a *deben*.
[70] The Egyptian word is *hdm*, a Semitic loan word (*KB*³ 225).
[71] Apparently this word refers to a type of couch or bed (*DLE* 4:44). This word survives into Coptic where it means "bed, bier" (Černý 1976:330).
[72] Lit. "agents of the palace, life, prosperity, and health."
[73] Lit. "cuttings which were taken."
[74] Text in *Urk. IV*, 685-687.
[75] This term seems to generally apply to the area of Palestine/Canaan, as compared with Syria, *Ḫ*ꜣ*rw* (Gardiner *AEO* 1:182*), but it is admittedly vague (Redford 1992:255).
[76] Located in Naharin (Gardiner *AEO* 1:179*).
[77] Text in *Urk IV*, 689-690.
[78] See *COS* 2.1, note 34.
[79] A north Syrian city in the region of Kadesh.
[80] A coastal city in North Syria (Gardiner *AEO* 1:136*).
[81] A north Syrian city in the region of Kadesh.
[82] The word used here is *inw*, lit. "that which is brought." Bleiberg (1996) has argued that the traditional translations, tribute and booty, do not take into account ancient economic considerations, and thus he opts for the meaning "official gift."

REFERENCES

Text: *Urk*. IV, 647-667, 685-687, 689-690. Translations and studies: *ANET* 234-238; Lichtheim *AEL* 2:12-15.

THE GEBEL BARKAL STELA OF THUTMOSE III (2.2B)

James K. Hoffmeier

Found in the temple built by Thutmose III at Gebel Barkal in the Fourth Cataract region, this stela offers an overview of Pharaoh's military accomplishments and hunting heroics. While much of what is reported on the stela is recorded in the Annals, it does, nevertheless, provide important supplemental information. For instance, the duration of the siege of Megiddo, not mentioned in the Annals, is given as seven months (line 20). The text moves back and forth between sober historical statements and grandiose claims, a common historiographic practice in Egyptian royal inscriptions (Hoffmeier 1992).

Of special interest is the mention of a miraculous star (a shooting star?) which appeared while on a foreign campaign. This "miracle" *(bi(ꜣ)yt)* overwhelmed the enemy, and spooked the horses, resulting in an impressive victory for Thutmose III. This miracle is clearly attributed to Amun-Re who was acting on the king's behalf (lines 36-37). On the use of divine intervention in ancient Near Eastern historiography, as well as the use of hyperbolic statements about military prowess and success, see Hoffmeier 1994; 1997:38-43; Weinfeld 1983:121-147; Younger 1990:165-266.

Royal titles (line 1a)
Regnal year 47, third month of the inundation season, day 10 under the majesty of Horus, Strong Bull arising in Thebes; Two Ladies, Enduring of Kingship like Re in the Sky; Horus of Gold, of Holy Diadem, Mighty in Strength; the King of Upper and Lower Egypt, Menkheperre; the Beloved, Bodily Son of Re, Lord of Every Foreign Land, Thutmose (III), of Beautiful Form.

The king's bravery and might reviewed (lines 1b-8a)
He made it as his monument for his father [Amun-Re],[1] Lord of the Thrones of the Two Lands in the fortress (called) "Destroying Foreigners," making for him an eternal dwelling since he magnifies the victories of my majesty more than any king who ever existed, I having seized Southerners through the order of his *Ka*[2] and Northerners in accordance with his governance.

He created the Son of Re, Thutmose, Ruler of Thebes, may he be granted life like Re forever, the good god who captures with his powerful arm, smiting southerners and beheading northerners, who shatters the heads of evil characters, slaughtering Asian Bedouin[3] and overthrowing defiant desert dwellers, who subdues the marshlands and strikes down the tribesmen of Ta-Seti,[4] and vanquishes the foreign lands who attacked him.

He is one who faces aggressively the battlefield in a state of rage, all foreign lands being united, standing as one prepared to fight; there is no coward[5] (among them) because of trust in (their) numerous squadrons, and no end of people and horses. With fearless hearts they came, their hearts being charged. The mighty powerful one overthrew them, the strong-armed one[6] who tramples his enemies.

He is a king who fights alone, without a multitude to back him up. He is more effective than a myriad of numerous armies. An equal to him has not been, (he is) a warrior who extends his arm[7] on the battlefield, no one can touch him.[8] He is one who immediately overwhelms all foreign lands while at the head of his army, as he shoots between the two divisions of troops, like a star he crosses the sky, entering into the throng, [while a bl]ast[9] of his flame is against them[10] with fire, turning into nothing[11] those who lie prostrate in their blood. It

[1] Throughout this stela, the name and epithets of Amun-Re were erased during the period of Akhenaten's iconoclasm.

[2] The *kꜣ* or *ku* is one of the attributes of humans and deities. The traditional translation "spirit" is inadequate for it assumes Greek or Judaeo-Christian anthropology. Some prefer rendering it as alter ego.

[3] *Šꜥt mntyw stt.*

[4] This is the name of the first southern nome of Egypt that included the area of present day Aswan (Montet 1961:13-14). This area served as the dividing line between Egypt and Nubia, and in earlier periods, Ta-Seti may have been considered to be within Nubia, and hence, during the New Kingdom, the name appears to include Nubia. Thutmose was hunting in the *ḫꜣst* of Ta-seti, either the desert or highlands region, the area away from the Nile Valley.

[5] The word *bhw* means "fugitive," i.e. one who flees (*Wb* 1:467). In this military context, the word "coward" seems appropriate.

[6] *Ṯmꜣ-ꜥ*.

[7] *Pr-ꜥ*, lit. "extending the arm." This idiom may have its counterpart in the Bible; viz. Heb. *zᵉrôaᶜ nᵉṭûyâ*, "outstretched arm" in the Exodus narratives (Hoffmeier 1986:378-387; Görg 1986:323-330). The use of this expression, and its counterpart, *yād ḥᵃzāqāh*, "strong hand, to describe the struggle between Yahweh and Pharaoh, may deliberately have been chosen because of the Egyptian symbolic significance.

[8] Lit. "there is not standing in his vicinity."

[9] There is a small break in the text, which almost certainly reads *wn thy*.

[10] The pronoun is feminine singular, referring back to *wmt* which we have rendered as "throng."

[11] *Ir st m tm wn*, lit. "making them into that which does not exist."

is his uraeus[12] that overthrows them for him, his flaming serpent that subdues his enemies, with the result that numerous armies of Mitanni were overthrown in the space of an hour, annihilated completely like those who had not existed, in the manner of those who are burned, because of that which the arms of the good god performed, great of might in the mêlée, who slaughters everyone, by himself alone, the king of Upper and Lower Egypt, Menkheperre, may he live forever.

He is Horus, the strong-armed one, an excellent fortress for his armies, a refuge for the people,[a] one who subdues all lands when they invade,[13] one who rescues[b] Egypt on the field of battle, a defender who is not afraid of ravenous ones. He is a stout-hearted bull. His southern border is to the Horns of the Earth,[14] to the southernmost part of this land, and the northern to the far reaches of Asia,[15] towards the supports of heaven.[c] With heads bowed they come to him in quest of his breath of life.[16]

a Deut33:27; Pss 9:10[9]; 46:2[1]; 62:8

b Pss 18:17; 22:8; 143:9

c 2 Sam 2:8; Job 26:11

d Jer 1:18; Ezek 4:3

Campaign to Mesopotamia (lines 8b-16a)
He is a king who is valorous like Montu,[17] who captures but no one captures from his hand, who tramples all rebellious foreign lands, there was no one to protect them in that land of Naharin[18] because its lord had fled out of fear. I hacked up his cities and villages[19] and set fire to them, my majesty having reduced them to mounds. They will not be repopulated, my majesty having carried off all their people as prisoners of war and their cattle without limit and their property as well. From it I took grain and plucked their barley. I cut down all their orchards and all their fruit trees.[19a] Their territory has been cut off, my majesty demolished it, it having turned into [...] on which there are no trees. Now my majesty traveled to the far reaches of Asia. I had many boats built of Ash-wood[20] on the mountains of the god's land[21] in the vicinity of the Lady of Byblos[22] which were placed on wagons[23] and oxen carted (them). They traveled in fro[nt ...] of my majesty in order to cross that great river which flows in between this foreign land and Naharin. But he is a king to be hailed because of his arms in the mêlée, who crossed the Euphrates after the one who had attacked him, at the head of his armies seeking that feeble enemy [from] the land of Mitanni. Now he is the one who flees in fear before his majesty to another distant land.

Then, my majesty set up my stela on that mountain of Naharin being hewn from the mountain on the western side of the Euphrates. There is no opponent of mine in the southern lands, northerners come bowing because of my awe. It was Re who ordained it concerning me, I having surrounded that which his eye has encircled. He gave to me the length and breadth of the land, I having bound together the Nine Bows,[24] the islands in the midst of the sea, the Aegean and rebellious foreign lands. I turned back in a southerly direction to Egypt,[25] having strong-armed Naharin, great was the terror in the mouths of the desert dwellers, their gates being sealing because of it, and they do not come outside in fear of the bull. He is a king who is a champion,[26] an excellent fortress for his armies, a rampart of iron[d] [...], he attacks every land with his powerful arm, without a myriad of men to back him up, who shoots to hit each time he takes aim, his arrows do not miss, a strong arm, its like has not existed, a Montu who is brave on the battlefield.

Hunting Elephants in Syria (lines 16b-18a)
Here is another act of victory which Re ordained for me. He repeated for me great acts of bravery by the Lake of Ny.[27] He allowed me to corral a (herd) of elephants. My majesty fought them, a herd

[12] The cobra that regularly appears on the king's crown.

[13] Lit. "when smiting the land before his face" (*m ḥwi tꜣ r ḥr.f*).

[14] Also in line 28. The location and identity of this designation is uncertain, but it clearly represents the southern counterpart to the "supports of heaven" in the north. These expressions likely mean the northern and southern extremities of the earth.

[15] The term used here is *Stt*.

[16] Williams (1969:93-94) suggested that the Heb. expression "breath of life" (e.g. Gen 2:7; Lam 4:20; 2 Chr 35:25) was an Egyptianism.

[17] War-god of Thebes whose cult gained prominence beginning with the 11th Dynasty.

[18] See *COS* 2.1, note 35 above.

[19] *Wḥyt* when written with the people determinative usually means "family" or "tribe" as is the case here. However, when the city-sign is used, the meaning is "village." We have rendered *wḥyt* as villages, despite the fact that the "peoples" sign is used, because of the parallelism with "cities" which immediately precedes it.

[19a] See *COS* 2.2A, note 61.

[20] Traditionally, *ꜥš* was thought to be "cedar" (*Wb* 1:228; *CDME* 49), although juniper has also been suggested (Gardiner *AEO* 1:8 n. 1).

[21] This expression is often used for the land of Punt (*Wb* 5:225; *CDME* 293). Here, however, a Phoenician context is obvious. "God's land" seems to signify a place where exotic goods are obtained.

[22] The local deity associated with the Egyptian goddess Hathor (Bleeker 1973:72).

[23] *Wrryt* is the common word for chariot. Given the light frame and thin wheels of Egyptian chariots, their value for transporting heavy materials would have been limited. Clearly a cart is the vehicle in question.

[24] A popular expression for the enemies of Egypt.

[25] *Tꜣ mri*.

[26] *Pr-ꜥ*, lit. "one who extends his arm," i.e. is active, athletic.

[27] This land is located in Syria, somewhere south of Alalakh and north of Kadesh (Gardiner *AEO* 2:167*).

of 120! Never had the like been done by any king since the time of god, those who had worn the white crown. It is without exaggeration and without falsehood that I have said this. <I> did it in accordance with that which [Amun-Re, lord of the thrones of the Two Lands] ordained for me, who leads my majesty on the right path according to his excellent plans. For me he has united the Black Land and Red Land,[28] and that which the sun-disc[29] encircles is in my grasp.

The First Asian Campaign (lines 18b-27a)
Now let me report to you, pay attention folks! On the first campaign, he ordained for me the lands of Retenu[30] when they came in order to engage (in battle) with my majesty with a myriad of men, hundreds of thousands with the headmen of all foreign lands, standing on their chariots, comprising 330 chieftains, each one with their armies.

Now they were in the Kina Valley,[31] ready, indeed, in a narrow pass. A fortunate thing occurred by my hand against them. My majesty attacked them. Whereupon they immediately fled, falling headlong. They entered Megiddo[e] and my majesty shut them up for a period of seven months before they came out, imploring my majesty, saying "Give us your breath O our Lord. The people[32] of Retenu will never again rebel against you."

Then that feeble enemy and his chieftains who were with him, had all their children sent out[f] to my majesty with gifts and bearing much tribute of gold and silver, all their horses which were with them, their magnificent chariots of gold and silver, and those which were undecorated, all their mail armor,[33] their bows, their arrows and all their weapons of combat. It is these with which they came bearing (arms) in order to fight from afar against his majesty. Instead they brought them as tribute to my majesty. Now they were standing on their walls, giving praise to my majesty, seeking that the breath of life be given to them. Then my majesty had an oath of allegiance administered,[34] saying, "Never again will we do evil against Menkheperre, may he live for ever, our lord in our lifetime, since we have seen his awe. It was because of his love that he gave us breath. It was his father [Amun-Re, lord of the thrones of the two lands?] who performed it, it was indeed not a human hand." Then my majesty permitted them to set out on the roads to their cities. Since I had taken their chariotry, they all set out on donkeys. I carried off their citizens to Egypt and their property also. It was my father who gave them to me, [Amun-Re] the magnificent god, the one who accomplishes successfully, whose plans do not fail, who sent my majesty in order to seize lands. All foreigners who were united, I overthrew them in accordance with his decree in the way he is accustomed to doing. He caused me to smite all foreigners without there being one to challenge him. It was my mace which overthrew the Asiatics,[35] my club which smote the Nine Bows. My majesty subdued all lands, Retenu being under my sandals, and Nubians being the vassals of my majesty.

Nubian and Levantine Tribute (lines 27b-32)
They pay me taxes as a unity, a levy of millions of taxes of numerous products of the Horns of the Earth, abundant gold of Wawat,[36] there being no limit to its amount. (Boats) were built there for the palace (life prosperity and health), each and every year, viz. Khementyw-ships and boats, more than (the available) crews of sailors, besides the tribute of the Nubians which consisted of ivory and ebony.[37] An abundance of timber comes to me from Kush,[38] [g] including beams of dome-palm, limitless furniture made of acacia from the Southland. My armies in Kush which are there in great number, hewed them [...] the multitude of dome-palm boats which my majesty brought in victory. [Timber] is also hewed for me in Djahy[39] each and every year, including real ʿAsh-wood of Lebanon which was brought to the palace (life prosperity and health). An abundance of timber comes to me in Egypt[40]

e Josh 12:21; 17:11; Judg 1:27; 5:19; etc.

f Gen 33:4-9

g Gen 10:6-7; 2 Kgs 19:9; Esth 1:1; 1 Chr 1:8; Isa 18:1; 20:3; Ezek 29:10; 30:4

[28] I.e. Egypt.

[29] I.e. *itn*, the Aten.

[30] See *COS* 2.1, note 34.

[31] This valley is identified with Wadi es-Sitt which leads into the Jezreel Valley (Aḥituv 1984:159).

[32] Lit. "foreigners."

[33] Lit. "all their tunics for fighting."

[34] Morschauser (1988:93-103) has made a compelling case for the expression *sḏf tryt* meaning "to pardon"; however, the traditional interpretation remains a viable option.

[35] *ʿꜣmw*.

[36] During the New Kingdom, Wawat is located south of the First Cataract, and probably included the Second Cataract region (Trigger, Kemp, O'Connor and Lloyd 1983:256).

[37] The Egyptian word is *hbny*, the source of the English word, ebony.

[38] During the New Kingdom, Kush is situated south of the Third Cataract (Trigger, Kemp, O'Connor and Lloyd 1983:256).

[39] This term seems to generally apply to the area of Palestine/Canaan, as compared with Syria, *Ḫꜣrw* (Gardiner *AEO* 1:182*), but it is admittedly vague (Redford 1992:255).

[40] *Kmt*, lit., "the Black Land," a reference to Egypt's Nile Valley.

which is shipped south, real [...] of Negu[41] with the choicest of the God's Land,[42] sturdy [... timber] reaching the palace without its season passing each and every year. My troops which are from the garrisons in Ullaza[43] come [...] which consist of 'Ash-wood from victories of my majesty according to the plan of my father [Amun-re] who ordained for me all foreigners. I let none (remain) of it for the Asiatics;[44] it is wood that he loves. He subdues in order that they testify to my lordship, they being troubled so that [...] might be pacified.[45]

The Miraculous Star (lines 33-37a)
[...] my [majesty]. Pay attention, oh people of the south land, who are in the pure mountain, which is called "Thrones of the Two Lands"[46] among people, (yet) it is unknown; then you will know the miracle of [Amun-Re] in the presence of the Two Lands.[47] [...] not [... sentr]ies were in the very act of being posted at night in order to do their regular watch. There were two astronomers (present). A star approached, coming to the south of them. The like had not happened before. It shot straight toward them (the enemy), not one of them could stand [...] falling headlong. Now then [...] was behind them with fire in their faces. Not one of them retaliated;[48] no one looked back. Their chariotry is gone, they (the horses?) having bolted[49] in [...] in order that all foreigners might see the awe of my majesty.

With joyful heart I turned back in a southerly direction, having celebrated for my lord [Amun-Re] who had ordained the victories and who put the dread [of me?] [...] in my life time. Among the foreigners he placed the fear of me so that they might flee far from me. Everyone on whom the sun shines is bound under my sandals.

The king addresses his courtiers (lines 37b-42a)[50]
My majesty myself says: [...] victory, that I was greatly skilled because of the valor and victory which my august father, Amun[-Re], Lord of the Thrones of the Two Lands, gave to me, he having made me lord of the five divisions, the ruler of that which the sun-disc encircles. Victory [...] the northerners, dread of my majesty to the southern territories. There is no road against me, he having sealed up for me the entire land. There was no limit to what accrued to me because of victory, he having placed my awe in Upper Retenu. [...] they [brought (?)] their gifts every season to me at the place where my majesty is. The mountainous areas mine for me what is in them comprising every fine product. What it concealed from other kings has revealed itself [for me (?) ...] every valuable precious stone, all kinds of sweet smelling plants which flourish in Punt, every fine product of the southland. Everything arriving as trade for my majesty belongs to him that I might fill his house and that I might compensate him (for) his protection. [...] on the battlefield. Moreover, I will put wonderful gifts of all lands from [...][51] which his valorous arm had taken, he having ordained it for me from every foreigner.

The courtiers respond (lines 42b-44a)
These courtiers [replied? ... Amun-Re, Lord] of the thrones of the Two Lands, the Great God of the beginning of time,[52] the Primeval One who created your beauty and gave to you every land. Govern it for him, knowing that you have come from him. It is he, moreover, who led your majesty on the [right][53] path [...]

The king speaks (lines 44b-48a)
[I have placed] dread of me in the farthest reaches of Asia, without my messenger being hindered. It was my army who cut down the flag poles of the terraced-foothills of 'Ash-wood [...]. [...] for the monuments of my fathers, all the gods of Upper and Lower Egypt. My majesty hewed rowing boats of 'Ash-wood [...] on the shore of Lebanon in the fort [...][54] All of the chieftains of Lebanon [made ?]

[41] The geographical area in which the city of Byblos (*kpn*) was situated (Redford 1992:43).

[42] This expression is elsewhere used for Punt and the Byblos area, and thus seems to refer to a distant land from which exotic and precious materials and objects were obtained.

[43] A Levantine coastal city (Redford 1992:91).

[44] *Sttyw*.

[45] The lacuna at the beginning of line 33 makes the translation of this sentence uncertain. An alternative to the translation offered here is "[their crime (?)] is pardoned." Faulkner also offers the meaning "pardon" for *ḥtp* (*CDME* 179), a meaning that could fit this context.

[46] This is the Egyptian name of the mountain called in Arabic "Gebel Barkal."

[47] *Tmw* is an imperfective pass. part. of the negative verb *tm*. Helck suggested a likely restoration for the lacuna — "the like of which had never been seen before" (1955:7).

[48] *N gm* ꜥ *ḏrt.f* lit. means "could not find his hand," i.e. could not respond, and thus, retaliate.

[49] The word *ḫꜣrw* is extremely rare. It is not listed in *Wb*. Faulkner (*CDME* 184) includes it as a hapax, rendering it "bolt?"

[50] The following is an address by Thutmose, apparently to his courtiers, judging by the fact that the *smrw* appear to respond beginning at the end of line 43. Unfortunately, the verb associated with *smrw inp*, "these courtiers," is also missing.

[51] The reading of this lacuna is uncertain. Helck offered the meaning "the finest," but offered no explanation for the reading (Cummings 1982:5).

[52] Lit. "the first occasion," *sp tpy*, a synonym for creation.

[53] In line 18 it is stated that "(Amun-Re) leads my majesty on the right path according to his excellent plans" — *šsm ḥm.i ḥr mṯn nfr m sḫrw.f mnḫ*. In some form this line is apparently being repeated by the courtiers.

[54] Believing that Egyptian naval operations were based at Byblos, Helck thought that this city might have been named in the lacuna (1961:11,

the royal boats in order that their workers[55] sail south in order to bring all the wonderful things [...] belonging to the [...][56] land to the Palace (life, prosperity, and health). The chieftains of [...]. [It is] the chieftains of Retenu who drag the flagpoles with oxen to the shore; it is they who come with tribute to the place where his majesty is, the Royal Residence in [...] bearing all the fine products which are brought as wonderful things of [the south], being taxed from the required, annual tribute just like all the underlings of my majesty.

The people extol the king (lines 48b-50)
What the people said [...] [...]. Foreigners [...] your awe. Your battle-cry reaches to the Horns of the Earth, respect of you makes their hearts quiver, reaching (?) [...] the people [...] [...] all [Nub(?)]ians who would transgress your plans. It is your father [...]. His majesty was in [...].

n. 3).
[55] Lit. "those with them," *im(y).sn*. "Them" must refer back to the chieftains of Lebanon, a reference to their servants or workers who transported the tribute back to Egypt.
[56] The sign is unclear.

REFERENCES

Text: MFA 23.733; Reisner 1933:24-29, pls. iii-v; Helck 1955:§§1227-1243 and de Buck 1970:56-63; Translations: *ANET* 238; Cummings 1982:1-7.

THE ARMANT STELA OF THUTMOSE III (2.2C)

James K. Hoffmeier

The Armant Stela of Thutmose III was discovered in the temple of Montu at Armant, near ancient Thebes. The inscription can be classified as a summary or collection (*sḫwy*) of the king's athletic prowess, and it recalls the heroic events of the first campaign. "Summaries" are well attested as a scribal reporting device.[1] As with the Annals and the Gebel Barkal Stela, reference is specifically made to the narrow Kina Valley through which Thutmose led his troops to attack the rebel alliance at Megiddo. Mention is also made to the Euphrates campaign, the king's eighth which occurred in year 33. While there are two year 22 dates in the text, towards the end of the stela, year 29 also appears. The span of time covered by the collection of reports, then, is at least eleven years. The Armant Stela does not provide historical information beyond what is known from the Annals and Gebel Barkal Stela, but its reports on the king's hunting exploits are the most thorough, and references to shooting arrows through a copper target set the standard for Amenhotep II to emulate.

Introduction (lines 1-3)
Long live the Horus: Strong Bull arising in Thebes; Two Ladies, Enduring of Kingship like Re in the Sky; Horus of Gold, of Holy Diadem, Mighty in Strength; the King of Upper and Lower Egypt, Lord of Action, Menkheperre; the Bodily Son of Re, Thutmose (III) Ruler of Truth, who is loved by Montu of Thebes who resides in Armant,[2] may he live eternally. Regnal year twenty-two, second month of winter, day 10. A summary of the acts of bravery and victory of that which this good god performed comprising every act of athleticism[3] beginning with the first generation of that which the Lord of the gods and the Lord of Armant, who exulted in his victories, did for him in order to have his bravery recounted for millions of years to come, besides the acts of athleticism which his majesty performed through time. If they were reported specifically by occurrence,[4] they would be too many to record.

Body (lines 4-17)
When he fired (arrows) at a metal ingot, every shaft was split like marsh papyrus. Subsequently he placed an example of it in the temple of Amun, (it) being a target of hammered copper three fingers thick,[5] his arrow in it, it having passed through it, he causing three palms[6] to come out the back in order to cause his followers to pray for the strength of his arms in valor and victory. It is without

[1] See Younger 1990:249-253.
[2] Egyptian *Iwn mnt*, the temple site where this stela was discovered. The present day town of Armant is located 13.5 km south of Luxor (Gardiner *AEO* 2:22*).
[3] See The Gebel Barkal Stela" (*COS* 2.4), note 7 above.
[4] Lit. "according to its name."
[5] Approximately 56 mm.
[6] Approximately 225 mm.

deception and fabrication, and without exaggerated claims that I state the truth regarding that which he performs among and in front of his whole army. Should he take time for recreation in (the form of) hunting in any foreign land, more numerous is the amount which he bags than the take of his entire army! He slew seven lions by shooting arrows in an instant and carried off a herd of twelve wild bulls in one hour after breakfast time occurred, their tails being (displayed) behind him.[7] As he was returning from Naharin,[8] [a] he finished off 120 elephants in the highlands of Ny.[9] He ferried across the Euphrates River[10] and trampled the cities on both sides, they being destroyed forever with fire. On the [east] side he erected a victory stela. He felled a rhino by shooting (arrows) on the southern highland of Ta-Seti,[11] after he proceeded to Miu[12] in order to search for the one who had rebelled against him in that land. He set up a stela there, just as he had down in the farthest reaches of [Asia]. His majesty didn't delay in going to the land of Djahy[13] in order to slay the rebels who were there and to give gifts to those who are loyal to him. Indeed, the names attest [...] every [...] at its season. His majesty returns each occasion, his attack happens in bravery and victory, he causing that Egypt be in its (original) state, just as it was when Re was in it as king.[14] [Regnal year 22, fourth month of winter, day 20(?)] from Memphis[15] in order to slay the lands of feeble Retenu[16] on the first occasion of victory. It was his majesty who blazed the trail and broke open all its roads for his army after [...] made [... Meg]iddo.[b] At the head of his whole army, his majesty entered on that road which narrows greatly, while all foreign lands gathered and were standing ready at its opening [...] falling exhausted, fleeing headlong toward their cities along with the chieftain who was in [...] for them, begging [...], bearing their gifts on their back. With a joyful heart, his majesty returned, this entire land having become [his] vassal [... Asiatic]s at one time bearing tribute [...] Regnal year 29, 4th month of winter, day [...]

[the rest of the text is completely lost]

a Gen 24:10; Deut 23:5; Judg 3:8; Ps 60:2[1]; 1 Chr 19:6

b Josh 12:21, 17:11; Judg 1:27, 5:19

[7] From the earliest portrayals of Egyptian kings, e.g., the Scorpion and Narmer mace heads, they are shown wearing a bulls tail behind them. Even earlier, on the "Hunters Palette," each hunter is shown with a tail attached to the back of their kilts. Apparently, this very early practice was continued in the New Kingdom too.

[8] See *COS* 2.1, note 35 above.

[9] Thutmose I had also hunted elephants in the land of Ny. This land is located in Syria, somewhere south of Alalakh and north of Kadesh (Gardiner *AEO* 2:167*).

[10] Eg. *itrw pẖ r wr*.

[11] See *COS* 2.2B, note 4.

[12] An unidentified Nubian site in the Third Cataract region (Trigger, Kemp, O'Connor and Lloyd 1983:257).

[13] This term seems to generally apply to the area of Palestine/Canaan, as compared with Syria, *ḫ*ʾ*rw* (Gardiner *AEO* 1:182*), but it is admittedly vague (Redford 1992:255).

[14] In column I of the Turin Canon (*COS* 1:37D) the pre-dynastic rulers are listed, and they are the gods, including Osiris, Seth, Horus and Thoth. Re may well have been the first god listed, but the top of column I is completely lost. It appears that the statement used here alludes to this glorious age when the gods ruled on earth.

[15] Lit. "White Walls," another name for Memphis (Montet 1957:27-29).

[16] See *COS* 2.1, note 34.

REFERENCES

Text: Mond and Myers 1940:182, pls. ciii, lxxxviii; Helck 1955 §§1244-1247; de Buck 1970:64-65. Translations and studies: *ANET* 234; Cummings 1982:7-9.

THE MEMPHIS AND KARNAK STELAE OF AMENHOTEP II (2.3)

James K. Hoffmeier

Amenhotep II (1427-1400 BCE) succeeded his father, Thutmose III, and continued his father's military policy in Syria-Palestine. In so doing, Amenhotep assured that the empire he received would be successfully maintained by his successors. He conducted at least two military campaigns into the Levant which are reported on two nearly identical stelae, the one discovered at Karnak, and the other at Memphis. The translation offered here is based upon the Memphis text. The campaigns are dated to regnal years 7 and 9, and are especially of interest to students of historical geography of Syria-Palestine. The content of the stela combines the more sober reports of the annalistic style, mingled with some of the exaggerated claims of accomplishment, like those of Thutmose III in his Gebel Barkal stela. For a discussion of the differences in style and implications for Biblical studies, see the introductory comments on the Annals of Thutmose III.

Date and introduction (lines 1-3a)
Regnal year 7, 1st month of summer, day 25 under the majesty of Horus, Strong Bull with Sharp Horns; Two Ladies, of Mighty Splendor who was coronated in Thebes; Golden Horus, Who Conquers with His Might in all lands; The King of Upper and Lower Egypt, Lord of the Two Lands, Aakherperu-re; Son of Re, Lord of Diadems, Possessor of a Powerful Arm,[1] Amenhotep, Divine Ruler of Heliopolis,[2] may he be given life forever.

The Good God, the likeness of Re, the Son of Amun upon his throne. He formed him with strength and might more than that which exists. His mace struck Naharin,[3] while his bow trampled Nubia,[4] [a] who conquered with strength and might like Montu,[5] being armed with his weapons. His heart is satisfied when he sees them after he decapitated the trouble makers.

Campaign to Shamashu-Adom (lines 3b-4a)
His majesty went to Retenu[6] on his first victorious campaign in order to widen his border and to give gifts to those who were loyal to him. His face was powerful like Bastet,[7] [b] like Seth[8] in his moment of rage. His majesty arrived at Shamashu-Adom.[9] He hacked it up in a brief moment like a lion roaming the hills, his majesty being in his chariot which is called, "Amun is Valiant ..."[10]

A record of that which [his majesty] captured [on that day]: 35 live Asiatics and 22 bulls.

Campaign in Syria (lines 4b-15a)
His majesty crossed the Orontes (River) on water, wading like Resheph.[11] [c] Subsequently he turned himself around to view the rear guard of his army. He noticed a few Asiatics[12] coming, creeping forward, equipped with weapons for fighting in order to attack the army of the king. His majesty charged after them like the swoop of the divine falcon. They halt, their hearts becoming weak, as one after the other fell on his companion, including their commander. There was no one with his majesty except himself with his valiant, powerful arm.[13] His majesty slew them with arrows.

It was in a state of elation that he returned, like valiant Montu he celebrated. A record of that which his majesty captured on that day: 2 chieftains, 6 Maryanu,[14] including their chariots, horses and all their weapons of war.

Journeying south, his majesty arrived at Ny.[15] Its chieftain and all his people, male and female alike surrendered to his majesty, their eyes fixed on staring.

His majesty arrived at Ugarit.[16] He surrounded all those who defied him. He slew them like those who did not exist, being placed beside those who lay prostrate. Resting in the tent[17] of his majesty in the area of Tjarkha[18] on the east of Shasherem. Mendjat was plundered.

His majesty arrived at Hatjera.[19] Its chieftain surrendered[20] to his majesty, with his children and his possessions. Peace offerings were presented to his majesty by (the land) of Inka.

a Exod 6:25, etc.

b Ezek 30:17

c Deut 32:24, etc.

[1] *Nb ḫpš*. The use of this expression may have a counterpart in the Bible, viz. *yad h^azaqah*, "strong hand." It is used to describe the struggle between Yahweh and Pharaoh in the Exodus narrative, and may deliberately have been chosen because of the Egyptian symbolic significance (Hoffmeier 1986:378-387; Görg 1986:323-330).

[2] Eg. *iwnw*, the cult center of the sun-god Atum-Re, located north of Memphis. The biblical writers were aware of this important city (Gen 41:45, 50; 46:20), calling it *ᵓôn*, and symbolically "house of the sun" (Jer 19:8).

[3] See *COS* 2.1, note 35 above.

[4] *tᵓ nḥsy*, "land of Nehesy." The name Phinehas, Aaron's grandson, is derived from this word (Exod 6:25; Num 31:6; Judg 20:28; etc.) (Kitchen 1982a).

[5] Cf. above, *COS* 2.2B, note 17.

[6] *COS* 2.1, note 34.

[7] Cat goddess whose name is reflected in her cult center, Bubastis, a northeast Delta city. This name is attested as Pi-Beseth (Ezek 30:17).

[8] The deity who was associated with storm (and hence identified with Canaanite Baal) and the desert regions.

[9] While attested with some frequency in Egyptian texts, the identity of this site remains uncertain. It has been identified with Beth-Shemesh of Josh 19:22 in northeastern Issachar which might be Tell el Abeidiyeh (Aḥituv 1984:174-176).

[10] The remainder of the name appears to be corrupt. While several different readings have been proposed, there is no consensus about the reading (see Helck's note on *Urk.* IV, 1302.3 in Cummings 1982:32).

[11] A Levantine storm-god who is also associated with warfare.

[12] *Sttyw*.

[13] Cf. note 1.

[14] See *COS* 2.2A, note 67.

[15] See *COS* 2.2B, note 27.

[16] Read *ikᵓṯy*, but is thought by some to be the famous coastal city of northern Syria (Cummings 1982:30; Gardiner *AEO* 1:164*), while recognizing that the '*r*' is omitted. Ugarit is located at modern Ras Shamra on the coast of Syria, north of Byblos.

[17] This formula is the opposite of "awaking the tent" which pointed to the beginning of the day in the daybook (cf. *COS* 2.2A, note 36). The "resting" formula, which also occurs in the Annals, line 49, could be noting the end of the day book entry (Hoffmeier 1977:17).

[18] The identity of the toponyms in line 9 are not known, but they appear to be in the vicinity of Ugarit.

[19] The location of Hatjera and Inka is uncertain; however, Amenhotep appears to be moving from Ugarit and the coastal area of Syria-Lebanon in a southwesterly direction towards Kadesh (cf. n. 21).

[20] Lit., "came out in peace."

His majesty arrived at Kadesh.[21] [a] Its chieftain surrendered. They were made to swear an oath of allegiance,[22] and all their children [likewise]. Then his majesty shot (arrows) at a target of hammered copper in their presence on the south side of this town. Then one (i.e. the king) went hunting in woods of Lebiu.[23] Gazelles, *mꜣswt*,[24] hares, an endless number of wild assess were bagged.

His majesty went by chariot[25] to Khasbu, alone, without a companion. In just a short time he returned from there. He carried off 16 live Maryanu at the rear of his chariot, 20 hands at the foreheads of his horses, and 60 bulls being led in front of him. Gifts were given[26] to his majesty by this city.

Now at that time, his majesty traveled south within the Valley of Sharon.[b] He a discovered a messenger of the chieftain of Naharin carrying a document around his neck. He carried him off as a prisoner-of-war at the rear of the chariot. His majesty went from Sibyn[27] on chariot[28] to Egypt,[29] a Marya(n)u being a prisoner-of-war on his horse alone with him.[30]

The Arrival at Memphis and the Record of the Booty (lines 15b-17a)

His majesty arrived at Memphis, he being elated [as] a strong bull.[31] A record of this booty: 550 Maryanu, 240 of their wives; 640 Canaanites; 232 sons of chieftains; 323 daughters of chieftains; 270 concubines of the chieftains of every foreign land, including 2214 of their festive, silver and gold arm jewelry; 820 horses, 730 chariots including all their weapons of war. Now at that time the divine wife, the queen and princ[ess] [...] were watching the victories of his majesty.

Second Asiatic Campaign (lines 17b-20a)

Regnal year 9, 3rd month of winter, day 25. His majesty went to Retenu on his second victorious campaign to the city of Aphek.[32] [c] It (i.e. the people of the city) came out with gifts because of the great victories of pharaoh,[33] life, prosperity, and health. His majesty [we]nt on his chariot, equipped with weapons of combat to the city of Yehem.[34] At this time his majesty plundered the villages of Mapesin[35] and the villages of Khatjen and the two cities on the west of Socho.[36]

Now at that time the ruler raged like a divine falcon, his chariots were shooting like a star in the sky. His majesty entered (the fray). Its chieftains, children and wives were carried off as prisoners-of-war, and all its inhabitants likewise, and all its property without end: its cattle, its chariots, and all the herds in front of him.

The King's Dream (lines 20b-22a)

A Pleasant thing which happened to his majesty: The majesty of this august god, Amun-Re, Lord of the Throne of the Two Lands came before his

a 2 Sam 24:6

b Isa 33:9; 35:2; 1 Chr 5:16; 27:29

c Josh 12:18; 13:4; 19:30; 1 Sam 4:1; 29:1; 1 Kgs 20:26, 30; 2 Kgs 13:17

[21] *COS* 2.2A, note 12.

[22] Morschauser (1988:93-103) has made a compelling case for the expression *stf tryt* meaning "to pardon"; however, the traditional interpretation remains a viable option.

[23] Situated near one of the sources of the Orontes river in Syria. The name is preserved in the Arab village of Labwe (Aḥituv 1984:131).

[24] An unidentifiable wild animal.

[25] Only the horse sign is written, leading Helck to translate this line as "His majesty set out on horseback" (Cummings 1982:31). The fact that he returns from this solo mission with captives behind his chariot (*wrrt*) suggests that rather than reading *ssm*, for horse, it is an abbreviation for *ḥtry*, chariot. Edel (1953:116) also reads the horse sign as *ḥtr*. This interpretation makes sense in view of the fact that horseback riding during the New Kingdom was rather limited (Schulman 1957).

[26] Read *rdi.t(w) ḥtpw*. This could mean "peace was offered," i.e. they surrendered, or, as we have rendered it "gifts were given." *Ḥtpw* can mean both gifts or offerings, and peace (*CDME* 179-180). There are numerous examples in the Bible of kings presenting gifts, usually gold and silver, to an advancing king as a sign of capitulation. Toi of Hamath sent his son, Joram, to David after the Israelites had defeated Hadadezer of Damascus. 2 Sam 8:10 mentions that utensils of silver, gold and bronze were offered. Similarly, Ahaz of Judah sent "silver and gold" as a present to Tiglath-pileser III (2 Kgs 16:8), thus becoming his vassal so that the Assyrian would fight against Israel and Damascus who had been attacking Jerusalem. Likewise, Hezekiah of Judah gave gold and silver to Sennacherib to prevent him from further destruction of his kingdom (2 Kgs 18:14-15). Based on this practice, the ruler of Khashbu may have been doing the same to Amenhotep II.

[27] It is unclear whether this is the name of a settlement, which is otherwise unattested, or a geographical feature of some sort.

[28] Cf. n. 25.

[29] *Tꜣ mri*.

[30] In this case the horse sign could actually be read *ssm*. On a stela showing the triumphant Amenhotep III returning from a Nubian campaign in his chariot (Petrie 1897 pl. x), four Nubian captives are depicted on backs of the two horses, and another prisoner is riding on the chariot pole between the chariot body and the rear ends of the horses. Based upon this scene, Amenhotep II may have been displaying his captives similarly.

[31] The epithet "strong bull" plays on the king's Horus name (cf. line 1).

[32] Located in the Valley of Acco, south of the city of Acco, and north of the Carmel range (Aḥituv 1984:62).

[33] The title, Pharaoh, *pr ꜥꜣ*, lit. "great house," is an epithet that initially applied to the palace as early as the Old Kingdom (*WB* 1:516) and only becomes attached to the king sometime in middle of the 18th Dynasty. From Genesis onwards in the Bible, the title "Pharaoh" is the Heb. vocalization of this Eg. expression.

[34] Yehem's name is preserved in the Arabic toponym Khirbet Yamma, situated 3 km. north of Sochoh which is found at Tell er-Ras (Aḥituv 1984:198). Thutmose III mentions stopping over at this site on his way to Megiddo. Cf. *COS* 2.2A, note 11.

[35] Villages were scattered throughout the land of Canaan; most of their names have not survived. In Amenhotep's records he mentions several. Villages were linked to urban centers, a point not missed in the Bible (Num 21:25, 32; Deut 2:23; 3:5; Josh 13:28; 15:32-62; Judg 1:27).

[36] Socho is an important site on the Via Maris. It is identified with Tell er-Ras/Khirbet Shuweikat (Aḥituv 1984:178).

majesty during sleep, in order to encourage[37] his son, Aakheperure. His father Amun-Re was the guardian of his body, while protecting the ruler.

Military Campaign in the Levant (lines 22b-29a)
His majesty went out on his chariot at dawn to the city of Ituryn and Migdalen.[38] Subsequently, his majesty, life, prosperity, and health, was powerful like the power of Sakhmet[39] and Theban Montu. He carried off 34 of their chieftains, 57 Maryanu, 231 living Asiatics, 372 hands, 54 horses, 54 chariots, including all their weapons of war, all their champions of Retenu, their children, their wives and all their property. After his majesty reviewed the very great amount of booty, they were turned into prisoners-of-war. Two trenches were made all around them and, look, they were filled with fire. His majesty watched over them until the break of day, his battle axe being in his right hand, he being alone with no one with him. At that time, the army was far from him, except for the personal servants of pharaoh.

Now after daybreak of the second day, his majesty set out on his chariot at dawn, equipped with the power and panoply of Montu on the anniversary of his majesty's coronation.

Then Anakharat[40] [d] was plundered. A record of that which his majesty alone captured on that day: 17 living Maryanu, 6 children of the chieftains, 68 living Asiatics, 123 hands, 7 teams of horses, 7 chariots of silver and gold including their weapons of war, 443 bulls, 370 cows, and all sorts of cattle beyond counting. His entire army was bringing away very much booty beyond counting.

His majesty arrived <at> Hukti. The chieftain of Giboa-Shemen,[41] whose name is Kaka, his wife, his children and all his subjects likewise were carried off. Another[42] chieftain was appointed in his place.

Return to Memphis (lines 29b-33)
His majesty arrived at the city of Memphis, he being satisfied because every foreign country and every land is under his sandals.[e] A record of the plunder which his majesty carried off: 127 chieftain<s> of Retenu, 179 brother<s> of the chieftains, 3600 Apiru,[43] 15,200 live Shasu,[44] 36,000 Syrians,[45] 15,070 live Nagasuites,[46] 30,652 of their family members, totaling 89,600[47] and their endless property likewise. All their herds and all their endless cattle, 60 gold and silver chariots, 1032 painted chariots, including all their weapons of war being 13,500, through the might of Amun-Re, his august father who loves him and who is your protection, and who decreed valor for him.

Now at that time the chieftain of Naharin, the chieftain of Hatti,[48] and the chieftain of Sangar[49] [f] heard of the great victories which <his majesty> had accomplished. Each one tried to outdo his counterpart with gifts of every foreign land. They thought on account of their grandfathers to implore his majesty, to go that the breath of life[50] be given to them. "We shall carry our taxes to your palace, Son of Re, Amenhotep, divine ruler of Heliopolis, ruler of rulers, a panther who rages in every foreign land and in this land forever."

d Josh 19:19
e Josh 1:3; Ps 110:1
f Gen 10:10; 11:2; Josh 7:21; Isa 11:11; Dan 1:2; etc.

[37] Lit., "in order to give valor or bravery to his son." Dreams were seen as a vehicle of divine communication throughout the Near East (e.g. see the Gudea cylinders below, *COS* 2.155) as well as among the Hebrews.

[38] Identified with Khirbet el-Majdal, which preserves the ancient name, in the northern end of the Sharon Plain. However, there is no corresponding archaeological evidence from this site. Nearby Tell edh-Dhrur does have evidence for the Late Bronze Age, and evidence of multiple destructions during this period (Aḥituv 1984:142).

[39] Sakhmet is the leonine goddess who is known for her violent outbursts and sending plagues, as well as being a protectress against plague.

[40] This site is identified with Anaharat of Josh 19:19, within the tribal territory of Issachar. Tell el-Ajjul (N) and Tell Mukharkhash have been suggested as the location of this site, with the latter being more likely (Ahituv 1982:59).

[41] Could mean "Hill of Eight," (Rainey 1973:74-75) or "Hill of Oil" which is thought to be identified with Tell es-Samn, by the Kishon Brook, just south of the Carmel Range (Aḥituv 1984:100).

[42] The text reads *dhnw.k*, which makes no sense. Edel (1953:123) rightly emends *k* (2nd person suffix) to *ky* (demonstrative adjective).

[43] This is the Eg. writing for the Akk. *ḫabiru*/*ḫapiru* of the Amarna letters. Earlier generations of biblical scholars believed that this word was to be equated with ᶜ*brî*, Hebrew. This equation has been largely rejected on the grounds that *ḫabiru* appears to have a sociological rather than ethnic application. Moreover, the Habiru are found at different locations and times around the Near East, proving that the term could not be limited to the Hebrews of the Bible ("Habiru" *ABD* 3:6-10). Scholars have not completely abandoned the idea that the term *ḫabiru* could be applied to the Israelites (Lemche 1985:421-429). It could be that *ḫabiru* originally designated groups of outlaws or was a derogatory expression, and yet it is clear from the occurrence in the stela of Amenhotep II that they were identified as a specific group like the other ethnic groups taken prisoners by the king. If the large numbers are to be believed, Apiru/Habiru were not just small bands of marauders in Amenhotep's day.

[44] A generic term used by the Egyptians of desert dwellers, bedouin (*Wb* 4:412).

[45] I.e. *ḫꜣrw*.

[46] Nahasse of the Amarna letters, located within Upper Retenu, not far from Aleppo (Gardiner *AEO* 1:146*).

[47] The total given, 89,600, is actually wrong, the correct total being 101,128! The use of large numbers in this section has given rise to a number of explanations: 1. The figures are exaggerated and thus not reliable, 2. They represent a grand total for all the king's expeditions, 3. The large figures represent a change in strategy by Amenhotep from selective to mass deportations like the Neo-Assyrians. For a review of the different views see, Hoffmeier 1997:113.

[48] Hatti is the term from which the English term "Hittites" is derived. Hatti is located in central Turkey, the capital being Hattuša. The people of Hatti may be one and the same as the *bᵉnê ḥet* of the Bible (Gen 10:14; 15:20; 23:3; Josh 1:4; Judg 3:5).

[49] Sangar is equated with *šanḫar*, i.e. Babylonia, Shinᶜar of the Bible (Gardiner *AEO* 1:209*).

[50] See *COS* 2.2B, note 16 above.

REFERENCES

Text: *Urk.* IV., 1300-1309; Edel 1953:97-175. Translations: Edel 1953:97-175; Helck 1961:1300-1309; *ANET* 245-247; Cummings 1982:29-33.

2. NINETEENTH DYNASTY INSCRIPTIONS

SETHOS I (2.4)

KARNAK, CAMPAIGN FROM SILE TO PA-CANAAN, YEAR 1 (2.4A)
(East Side, Lower Register)

K. A. Kitchen

To celebrate his northern wars, about 1294/85 BCE, Sethos I placed three registers of scenes on either side of the north doorway into the Great Hypostyle Hall at Karnak temple in Thebes. On the east side, the registers read from bottom to top (normal in the New Kingdom), but the top register is lost. On the west side opinions differ as to whether one should read also from bottom to top or the reverse. Here, in the east side's bottom register, the scenes divide from the middle. Very appropriately, the first three scenes move left/eastward, along the north-Sinai coast road (clearing off the wandering Shasu folk on the way), then to tribute at a town [name lost], and finally action near "the city of Canaan," probably Gaza. Then, from the mid-point to the right/westward, the king returns to Egypt in triumph, then offers to the gods in gratitude. In each scene, rhetorical praise of the king accompanies his figure. As appropriate, topographical data are given (settlements, wells, etc.).

Defeat of the Shasu tribesmen (KRI I 6.15-7.9)
(i. Rhetorical text over king)
The Good god, Sun[a] of Egypt, Moon[b] of all lands,
Montu in the foreign lands, who is not repulsed,
Bold-hearted like Baal,
there is none who can retreat from him,
on the day of marshalling for the battle.
He has extended the boundaries of Egypt to the limits of heaven on every side.
(As for) the hil[ls of the] rebels, — none could [get pas]t them, because of the fallen ones of Shasu[1] who had attacked [him?]. His Majesty cap[tured th]em totally, so that none escaped.
(ii. Minor epigraphs: a. cartouches)
Menmare, Sethos I Merenamun.
(b. Vulture)
Nekhbet, White One of Nekhen.
(c) Over the horses [... lost ...].
(iii. Forts and wells at bottom of scene)
(Fort I) The Stronghold of Menmare, "The ... is his Protection."
(Below I at J) The Fort of Sethos I [Merenptah].
(Fort K) Settlement [which] His Majesty [built] a[new].
(Water L) The Well Ibseqeb (*ᵓIbsqb*)[2]
(Below fort M) The Well of Sethos I Merenptah.
(At right edge of scene) [...]mat.

Receipt of tribute at town [X] (KRI 7.10-8.4)
(i. Rhetorical text over the king)
The Good god, achieving with his arms, archer[c] like Montu who resides in Thebes, [strong bull, sharp-horned, bold-heart]ed, who tramples Asia, setting his boundaries according as his heart dictates; his arm is not repulsed in all lands.

Victorious King who protects Egypt, who breaches the wall(s) in rebellious foreign lands. He causes the chiefs of Khurru (i.e. Syria-Palestine) to cease from all boasting by their mouths; his strong arm[3] is mighty in valor and victory, and his power like (that of) the Son of Nut.

(ii. Minor epigraphs: a. cartouches) Lord of Both Lands, Menmare, Lord of Crowns, Sethos I [Mer]en-a[mun].
(b. Over the horses) First Great (Chariot-)Span of His Majesty, "Amun decrees him Valor," which is (also) named "Anath is Content."

a Ps 84:12 [11]
b Ps 89:37-38[36-37]; Cant 6:10
c Gen 49:24

[1] The Shasu were encountered by the Egyptians all the way from the margins of the East Delta along the North Sinai coastal zone through the eastern fringes of Palestine and Syria. For the main documentation on them, see Giveon 1971; but their name is not Semitic (or the *s* would have appeared as *ṯ* — it is most easily taken as deriving from Egyptian *š(ᵓ)s*, "to wander," hence "wanderers." It is not an ethnic term, but was applied to semi-nomadic groups (such as the Edomites of Papyrus Anastasi VI:54-56), but not provenly to early Israel.
[2] The name of this well may be NW Semitic, e.g. *ᵓeb segub*, "exalted greenery," perhaps referring to its surrounding vegetation.
[3] The "strong arm" of Pharaoh seems to be reflected in biblical usage, esp. the phrase "outstretched arm" found mostly in Exod-Deut, with later echoes in Pss and the prophets. See Hoffmeier 1986; 1997:151; and Görg 1986 for discussions.

(iii. Forts and wells)
(Below fort N) The Well, "Menmare Great of Victories."
(Water O) The Well, "Sweet (Water)."[d]

d Exod 15:25

(Upper fort P) Settlement which His Majesty built anew, with/at the Well Hu[.]ututi (*ḫ-[.]wtwti*)
(Below P fort at Q) The Fort of Menmare, Heir of Re.
(Circular feature R) "Wide Pool" ([y]*m rbt*).[4] [e]

e Num 20:11; 24:7

(Lower left fort S) The Well (of) Menmare.
(Water T) *Nḫs* of the Chief.[5]
(Upper left fort U) Settlement of [Raphia??]

Victory near the city of Pa-Canaan, Year 1 (KRI I 8.5-8.15)

(i. Dated rhetorical text over fallen foes)
Year 1 (of) the King of Southern and Northern Egypt, Menmare. The destruction which the sturdy arm of Pharaoh, LPH,[6] made <among> the fallen foes of Shasu, beginning from the fortress of Sile as far as Pa-Canaan.

His Majesty seized upon them like a terrifying lion,[f] turning them into corpses throughout their valleys, wallowing in their blood as if (they) had never existed. Any who slip through his fingers tell of his power to (far-)distant foreign countries — "it is the might of Father Amun who has decreed for you valor and victory over every foreign country."

f Gen 49:9; Num 24:9; Deut 33:20, 22; Jer 49:19

(ii. Minor epigraphs: a. cartouches) King of Southern and Northern Egypt, Menmare, Son of Re, Sethos I Merenptah, given life like Re, and beloved of Montu (and) Astarte.
(b. Horus-Falcon) The Behdetite, Lord of heaven — may he give life, stability, dominion and health like Re. (c. Vulture) Nekhbet, White One of Nekhen — may she give life.
(d. Over the horses) First Great (Chariot-)Span of His Majesty, "Victory in Thebes."
(iii. Fort, upper left) Settlement of Pa-Canaan.

Triumphal return to Egypt (KRI I 9.1-10.9)

(i. Rhetorical text over king)
Year 1, "Renaissance," (of) the King of Southern and Northern Egypt, Lord of Both Lands, Menmare, given life.

Now, one came to tell His Majesty: "The fallen (foemen) of Shasu are plotting rebellion. Their tribal chiefs are united in one place, stationed on the mountain ridges of Khurru. They have lapsed into confusion and quarrelling; each slays his fellow. They disregard the edicts of the Palace."

The heart of His Majesty, LPH, was pleased at it. Now, as for the Good god, he rejoices at beginning a fight, he is glad about his attacker, his heart is satified at seeing blood — he cuts off the heads of the dissidents. More than a day of jubilation loves he a moment of trampling (such) down. His Majesty slays them all at once, he leaves no heirs among them. Who(ever) escapes his hand is (but) a prisoner brought to Nile-land.

(ii. Minor epigraphs: a. cartouches) King of Southern and Northern Egypt, Lord of Both Lands, Menmare, Son of Re, Lord of Crowns, Sethos I Merenamun, given life like Re.
(b. Vulture) Nekhbet, the White One of Nekhen; may she give life, stability and dominion like Re.
(c. Over horses) First Great (Chariot-)Span of His Majesty, LPH, "Amun, he gives strength."
(iii. Prince behind the king) Following the King at his forays in the foreign countries of Syria (Retenu), by the Hereditary Noble and Count, grandee of who[se nam]e one boasts, true King's Scribe, beloved of him, [General??], bodily King's Son, beloved of him, [Ramesse]s,[7] [justified?].
(iv. Canal, forts and wells [from right to left, i.e., west to east])
(Canal A) The (boundary) Canal.
(Building before canal B) The Fortress of Sile.
(Fort D) The Dwelling of the Lion.
(Middle fort E) The Keep (*migdol*)[8] of Menmare.
(Well F) The Well of Hapan/Hatjan (*Ḫpn/Ḫṯn*).[9]
(Fort G) Udjo of Sethos I Merenptah.
(Well H) The Well of the District of Imy-ᶜa(?).
(v. Dignitaries welcoming the king) The prophet<s>, grandees, leaders of the South and North are come to acclaim the Good god on his return from the land of Retenu (Syria) bringing great and abundant plunder, the like of which has never been seen since the time of the god.

⌜They⌝ say in adoring His Majesty, in magnifying his might: "Welcome you are, from the foreign countries, your attack has succeeded! You are triumphant, your enemies are beneath you.[g] Your duration as King is like Re in heaven, in slaking your heart <against> the Nine Bows. Re has set your boundaries, his arms are (magical) protection around you. Your mace was upon the head(s) of every foreign land, the<ir> chiefs are fallen to your sword!"

g Josh 10:24

Presentation of prisoners and spoil to Amun (KRI I 10.10-11.9)

(i. Text over the spoils)
[Presentation] of tribute by His Majesty [to his father] Amun, when he returned from the foreign land of despised Retenu (Syria): "The chiefs of the

[4] Cp. Heb. and Ug. *ym*, "sea/lake," and Common Semitic *rb(b)*, "great/wide"; or render as "many waters," and cf. Num 20:11, 24:7.
[5] The word *nḫs* may be related to Akk. *nuḫšu*, "abundance" (here, of water), for the "chief."
[6] LPH is the abbreviation for the blessing formula, "life, prosperity, health."
[7] Replacing an earlier (non-royal) name and epithets: "[X, who traverses] foreign [count]ries [for] his lord?"
[8] Using a term for "tower/keep," familiar also in BH, used as, and as part of, place-names, including in the East Delta.
[9] The name "Hatjan" may be related to Heb. *ḥsn*, "wealth/abundance," again of water and/or surrounding vegetation at the well so named.

foreign lands are prisoners, with their tribute on their backs — of every sort of precious vessel from their lands, of silver, gold, real lapis-lazuli, through the valor that you gave me over every foreign land." [h]

(ii. Cartouches) Lord of Both Lands, Menmare, Lord of Crowns, Sethos I Merenamun.

(Vulture) [Udjo].

(iii. Text over upper row of prisoners)

The chiefs of the foreign countries who knew not Egypt, whom His Majesty brought (back) by his victory from the land of despised Retenu. They said, in magnifying His Majesty, in praising his victories: "Hail to you! How great is your name, how powerful your strength! The (foreign) land that is loyal to you has joy; who(ever) infringes your boundaries is fettered(?). As your Spirit endures! We knew not Egypt, and our fathers did not tread it. Grant us the breath of your giving!"

(iv. Text over lower row of prisoners)

The spoils which His Majesty brought (back) from the Shasu, whom His Majesty himself vanquished in Year 1, "Renaissance."

(v. Speech of Amun)

[Words spoken by Am]un-Re, Lord of the Thrones of the Two Lands: "My bodily S[on], (my) beloved, Lord of Both Lands, Menmare! I put the fear of you into every foreign land, your mace is upon the head(s) of their chiefs. They come to you, united as one, with a (tribute) load on their backs because of your war-cry."

h Josh 6:19, 24

REFERENCES

Text-editions: definitive, Epigraphic Survey 1986 pls. 2-8; handbook ed., *KRI* 1:6-11; 7:422-423. Translations: Epigraphic Survey 1986:3-26; Kitchen 1993a:6-9. Older references plus notes, Kitchen 1993b:12-17.

FIRST BETH-SHAN STELA, YEAR 1 (2.4B)
(Palestine Archaeological Museum, Jerusalem, S.884)

K. A. Kitchen

On his campaign in Year 1 (1294 or 1290 BCE), Sethos I probably penetrated as far as Phoenicia. Then on his return southward, he found disturbances in the Beth-Shan district, just south of the Sea of Galilee. The local chiefs of Hammath and Pella (W and E of the Jordan) had blockaded nearby Rehob and seized the important center of Beth-Shan. So the pharaoh sent out three strike-forces: against rebel Hammath, the captured Beth-Shan, and neighboring Yenoam. Beth-Shan is Tell Husn (at modern Beisan), where this stela was found.

Scene (KRI I 11.10-14)

(Winged disc at top) The Behdetite, great god, with dappled plumage, Lord of heaven.

(King offers incense and libation to Re-Harakhti)

(Over king) The Good god, Lord of Both Lands, Menmare, given life like Re.

(Behind king) All protection and life attend him!

(Between king and deity) Performing incense[a] and libation.

(Over deity) Re-Harakhti, great god, Lord of heaven; may he give all life.

Main text (KRI I 11.15-12.14)

Year 1, 3rd month of Shomu, Day 10. (Long) live:
Horus-Falcon, Strong Bull, Appearing in Thebes, Bringing life to Both Lands;
Nebty-Ruler, Renewing birth, Powerful of arm, Subduing the Nine Bows;
Golden Horus, Repeating epiphanies, Rich in forces in all lands;
King of Southern and Northern Egypt, Lord of Both Lands, Menmare Made by Re,
Son of Re, Lord of Crowns, Sethos I Merenptah, beloved of Re-Harakhti, the great god.
The Good god, sturdy in wielding his sword, hero valiant like Montu;
abounding in captures(?), knowing his ability, skilled wherever he is;
who speaks with his mouth and acts with his arms.
Valiant leader of his army, valiant warrior amid the battle,
a Bast who grasps as a warrior, who enters into the mass of Asiatics,
who makes them prostrate, who tramples down the chiefs of Retenu (Syria),
who vanquishes who(ever) transgresses his path.
He causes the chiefs of Khurru to go back on all the boasting of their mouth(s);[b]
every foreign land of the far north, their chiefs (say): "Where can we (go)?"
They spend nights, made witness(?) in his name, frantic(?) in their minds.
It is the power of his father Amun which decrees for him valor and victory.

On this day, one came to inform His Majesty thus:
"The despicable chief who is in the town of

a Deut 33:10

b Isa 52:15

Hammath[1] has gathered to himself many people, seizing the town of Beth-Shan, and is joined up with those from Pahil (Pella)[2]; he is preventing the chief of Rehob[3] from coming out."

Then His Majesty sent out the First Division of Amun, "Rich in Bows," against the town of Hammath; the First Division of Re, "Abounding in Valor," against the town of Beth-Shan; and the First Division of Sutekh, "Strong of Bows," against the town of Yenoam.[4] And so, when the span of a day had elapsed, they were (all) fallen to the might of His Majesty, the King of Southern and Northern Egypt, Menmare, Son of Re, Sethos I Merenptah, given life.

[1] Ancient Hammath is the present large Tell el-Hammeh (not excavated), some 15 miles south of Beth-Shan.

[2] Pahil (classical Pella) is to be located at Khirbet Fahil, some 7 miles south-east of Beth-Shan, across the Jordan; for excavations there, cf. *NEAEHL* 3:1174-1180.

[3] Rehob is at modern Tell es-Sarem, some 4 miles due south of Beth-Shan; for excavations there, see Mazar 1999.

[4] Yenoam's location is much discussed. The likeliest site is still Tell el-Abeidiyeh (or Ubeidiyeh), about 15 miles north of Beth-Shan, at a fitting distance, in a loop of the Jordan with trees, rather like the setting by water with trees in the Sethos relief-scene (references, Kitchen 1993b:18). The proposal by Na᾿aman (1977) to place it nearly 30 miles away across the Jordan at Tell esh-Shihab is theoretically possible, but the supposed evidence is not watertight.

REFERENCES

Text: Rowe 1930:26-29, pls. 41, 47:3; *KRI* 1:11-12. Translation: Kitchen 1993a:9-10, and notes and older references, Kitchen 1993b:17-19.

KARNAK, CAMPAIGN TO YENOAM AND LEBANON (YEAR 1 OR LATER) (2.4C)
(East Side, Middle Register)

K. A. Kitchen

In this register, two successive war-scenes have Sethos I conquering Yenoam and [X-1], then *Qdr* in a land *Hnm* and [X-2] in [Leban]on. Lebanese chiefs fell timber for him. The mention of Yenoam may link the scenes with Year 1 (cf. Yenoam on the Year 1 stela, just above), but there is no guarantee that Yenoam did not feature in a later campaign. *Qdr* and *Hnm* are geographically obscure; *Qdr* might possibly be Gadara on the Yarmuk river (east of the Jordan), on the way to Tell esh-Shihab, where a stela of Sethos I was found.

Victory at Yenoam (KRI I 13.1-4)
(i. City of Yenoam) Town of Yenoam.
(ii. Over the horses) (1st Version): First Great (Chariot-)Span of His Majesty, "Amun [subdu]es the Nine Bows [for] him."
(2nd Version): First Great (Chariot-)Span of His Majesty, "Amun [silenc]es(?) the Nine Bows."
(All other texts in this scene are lost).

Submission by the chiefs of Lebanon (KRI I 13.5-14.9)
(i. Main texts above king and chariot)
(a. Before the king) [The chiefs of] Lebanon, they cut [timbers [a] for] the great river-barge U[serha]t, and likewise for the great flagstaves of Amun.
(b. Cartouches) [King of Southern and Northern Egypt, M]en[mare, Son of Re, Sethos I Merenptah], given life. (c.i. [Vulture]). [Nekhbet ...], may she endow him [with ...], with life and dominion, [... like] Re every day.
(c.ii. Over the horses and chariot) [(Long) live:]
[*Falcon-King*, Strong Bull, Appearing in Thebes, Bringing life to Both Lands;]
Nebty-Ruler, Renewing birth, [Powerful of arm, Subduing the Nine Bows;]
[*Golden Horus*], Repeating [epiphanies], Rich in forces [in all lands;]
[King of Southern and Northern Egypt, Menmare, S]on of [Re], Sethos I Merenptah, given life.

[The Good god ..., Sovereign] satisfied with victory; mighty [in power, like the Son of Nut? ...;] [strong-]armed, who achieves [with his arms, ..., who protects?] his army.

[Hero? ... (etc.) ...]; one [breath]es [the breath of his giving; ...]. More than a day [of jubilation, he loves tramp]ling (them) down. [... a Montu?] when he sees the battle-line, [...] his heart is satisfied at making [slaughter? (in) extending] the boundaries of Egypt. [He takes Asiatics as servant]s(?), to fill the workshops, [...] conifers [...].

(ii. Speech of fanbearer) Said by the Fanbearer on the King's Right Hand, (in) his reply to the Good god: "It is done according to all that you say, O Horus who brings life to Both Lands! You are like Montu against every foreign country. The chiefs of Retenu behold you, and your renown (pervades) their (very) bodies."

[a] 2 Sam 5:11; 1 Kgs 5:6, 10

(iii. Speech of the Lebanese chiefs)
The great chiefs of Lebanon, they say in adoring the Lord of Both Lands, in magnifying his power: "You are seen like your father Re, and one lives by beholding you."

(iv. Forts: a. Over the chiefs' speech) [Town of X, in the land of ?Lebano]n.
(b. Below the horses) Town of Qader, in the land of Hinuma.

King binds captives (KRI I 14.10-12)
(i. Before the king)
[Captures] which His Majesty has [brought] off, on his own two feet. Every foreign country, he has brought them off as prisoners — Menmare, Sethos I Merenamun.
(ii. Behind the king)
Horus, strong in arm, Lord who performs the rituals, and who overthrows his enemies.

King returns, carrying and leading captives (KRI I 14.13-16)
(i. Rhetorical text) [... val]or and [victory? ...] Nine Bows.
[...] he has/to him [...] seized? [... Mont]u [...].
(ii. Over the horses) First Great (Chariot-)Span of His Majesty, "Great of Victories."
(iii. Over lower group of prisoners)
Great chiefs of Retenu, whom His Majesty brought off as prisoners.
Presentation of Prisoners and Spoils to the Theban Triad (KRI I 15.1-14)
(i. Speech of Amun) Words spoken by Amun-Re, Lord of the Thrones of Both Lands:
"Welcome in peace, O Good god, Lord of Both Lands, Menmare! I set your victories over every foreign country, and the fear of you in the hearts of the Nine Bows. Their chiefs come to you as one, with a (tribute) load on their backs. I grant you the lands in fear of you, and the Nine Bows bowing down at your war-cry."
(ii. Mut and Khons) Mut the Mighty, Lady of Asheru, Lady of heaven, Mistress of all the Gods, — may she give all life like Re.
Khons-in-Thebes, Neferhotep, the great god, Lord of heaven.
(iii. Vulture and king) Nekhbet. King of Southern and Northern Egypt, Menmare, Son of Re, Sethos I Merenamun, given life like Re forever.
(iv. Presentation of gifts) Presentation of tribute by His Majesty to his father Amun, when he returned from the land of despicable Retenu, (consisting) of silver, gold, lapis-lazuli, turquoise, red jasper, and every (kind of) precious stone.[b] The chiefs of the foreign lands are enclosed in his grasp, to fill the workshops of his father Amun — "by the valor that you granted me!"
(v. Upper file of prisoners) His Majesty returned from Upper Retenu, after extending the boundaries of Egypt, [and after?] destroying [the land of the Men]tiu(?), [their chiefs] being [prisoners], with [their] tribute [on their backs ...] [... rest lost ...]
(vi. Lower file of prisoners) Chiefs of foreign countries that knew not Egypt, whom His Majesty brought off as prisoners, [their] tribute [on their backs? ...].

b Josh 6:19, 24

REFERENCES

Text: definitive, Epigraphic Survey 1986: pls. 9-14; handbook ed., *KRI* 1:13-15; 7:423-424. Translations: Epigraphic Survey 1986:27-43, and Kitchen 1993a:10-12, with notes and older references in Kitchen 1993b:19-20.

SECOND BETH-SHAN STELA, [YEAR LOST] (2.4D)
(Palestine Archaeological Museum, Jerusalem, S.885A/B)

K. A. Kitchen

Regrettably, the year-date is broken away on this monument, but is likely to have been [Year 2 or later]. Again, on his way back south, the king was obliged to quell dissidents, seemingly in Lower Galilee, as his troops "turned back" to deal with the matter. The ᶜApiru are here given the determinative of an armed man; so they were regarded in this case as armed bands by the Egyptians.

Scenes (KRI I 15.15)
(lost - king worships deity, either side)

Main text (KRI I 16.1-15)
[Year x, month/season y, Day z. (Long) live:]
Horus-Falcon, Strong Bull, Appearing in Thebes, [Bringing life to Both Lands;]
[*Nebty-Ruler*, Renewing birth, Powerful of] arm, [Subduing the Nine Bows;]
[*Golden Horus*], Repeating epiphanies, Rich in forces in all lands;
King of Southern and Northern Egypt, Lord of Both Lands, Menmare Heir of Re, [Bodily Son of Re, his beloved], Lord of Crowns, [Sethos I Merenptah], beloved of Amun-Re, Lord of the Thrones of Both Lands, and given life like Re [forever].

[The Good god who achieves with] his arms, an iron rampart [a] on the field on the day of battle, [who calms(?) the heart] of the people, who knows his ability, resolute on behalf of his army on the day of battle like a young bull;[b] powerful lion,[c] falcon of Khepri in the Mansion of the Prince, Son of Sekhmet, beloved of Bast.

Sphinxlike image[1] amid the foreign countries that infringe his boundary, he has curbed all lands by reason of the dread [of him in the]ir [hearts]. He causes the Asiatics to retreat, who had drawn their bows — a king to [be boasted of] to the height of heaven, a master to be bragged about forever.

On this day, now, [one came to inform His Ma]jesty, LPH, thus:

"The ᶜApiru of the mountain of Yarmutu,[2] along with the Tayaru[3] [folk, they] are arisen, attacking the Asiatics of Ruhma."

Then said [His Majesty]: "Who [do they] think they are, these despicable Asiatics, in [taking up] their [arms] for yet more trouble? They shall find out about him whom they did not know — [the Ruler val]iant like a falcon *and* a strong bull wide-striding and sharp-horned, [spreading his wings (firm)] as flint, and every limb as iron,[d] to hack up the [entire] land of Dja[hy]!" [4]

Then His Majesty, LPH, commanded a detachment of men from his ample [infantry and ch]ariotry to turn back against the land of Djahy. When a period of two days had elapsed, [they returned in peace] from the land(?)/mountain(?) of Yarmutu, bringing the impost [?from these Asiatics?, and] prisoner(s) as plunder [wrought by His Majesty?] — it was/by the power of his father Amun-Re that decreed for him valor and vic[tory [forever?] — (even) the King of Southern and Northern Egypt, Lord of Both Lands, Menmare Heir of Re, Son of Re, Lord of [Crowns], Sethos I Merenptah, like Re.

a Jer 1:18; Ezek 4:3

b Deut 33:17

c Gen 49:9; Deut 33:20, 22

d Job 40:18; Isa 48:4

[1] Cp. the pharaoh shown as a sphinx with kingly head, vanquishing foes, as of Tuthmosis IV (ca. 1390 BCE; *ANEP* no. 393) and Tutankhamun (ca. 1330 BCE; Desroches-Noblecourt 1963:61, pl. xix), with derived motif on gold bowl at Syrian Ugarit (14th/13th centuries BCE; Smith 1965: fig. 48), as well as in earlier and later periods.

[2] Yarmutu may be related to the northern Yarmuth, Josh 21:29 (with its possible name-variants, Remeth, Ramoth, in Josh 19:21, and 1 Chr 6:65), near the later "Belvoir" of the crusaders.

[3] Tayaru and Ruhma are (so far) unknown entities; Albright (1952:30-31) did compare Tayaru with the Tiria of 1 Chr 4:16, in name but not location (much further south).

[4] Djahy is a rather elastic term in Egyptian, covering a fair-sized area including Canaan and up into Lebanon (cf. Gardiner *AEO* 1:145′-146′).

REFERENCES

Text: Rowe 1930: pls. 42-44, 45:1; Grdseloff 1949; Albright 1952; handbook edition, *KRI* 1:15-16. Translation, notes, other references: Kitchen 1993a:12-13, and 1993b:20-21.

KARNAK, CAMPAIGN AGAINST THE HITTITES (UNDATED) (2.4E)
(West Side, Lower Register)

K. A. Kitchen

Originally, two whole registers on the west half of this wall dealt with northern wars of Sethos I: the bottom one, a clash with the Hittites, and the top one the king's attack on Qadesh and Amurru. It is significant that the two are separated by a middle register that focuses on a wholly different locale — a war in the west with the Libyans. This suggests that the top and bottom registers may commemorate two separate campaigns, before and after a Libyan war. Which came first is uncertain. Artistic convention would favor bottom-to-top (Hatti, then Qadesh/Amurru), but allusions in the texts, and geographical progression may rather favor a clash in Amurru and Qadesh first, then with Hatti from the north.

(Scene hidden behind 22nd-Dynasty Wall — not accessible.)

Sethos I in battle with the Hittites (KRI I 17.10-18.4)

(i. Over the Hittites) The despicable land of Hatti, amongst whom His Majesty, LPH, has wrought great slaughter.

(ii. Rhetorical text)

Horus-Falcon, Strong Bull, Appearing in Thebes, Bringing life to Both Lands,
King of Southern and Northern Egypt, Lord of Both Lands, Menmare, Son of Re, Sethos I Merenamun.
The Good god, strong in power, a hero valiant like Montu;
Powerful one, powerful like him who begot him,
illuminating Both Lands like Him of the Horizon.
Mighty in strength like the Son of Nut,
the strength of the Two Lords is in his actions;
Who stalks the battlefield like Him of Ombos,

great of terror like Baal against the foreign lands.
Uniter of Both Lands, (even) while he was in the nest,
his power has protected Egypt.
Re has made his boundary for him to the limits of what the Sun-Disc illumines;
Divine Falcon of dappled plumage,
traversing the heaven(s) like thc majesty of Re.

Southern jackal, fast, circling this land in an hour;
Fearsome Lion who travels the difficult paths of every foreign land.
Strong Bull,[a] sharp-horned, stout-hearted,
who treads down the Asiatics, who tramples the Hittites,
who slays their chiefs, (left) wallowing in their blood,
who enters among them like a fiery flame,
reducing them to non-existence.

(iii. Minor epigraphs: a. Falcon) The Behdetite, great god — may he give [all] valor [and victory ...]; may he give [all] life, stability and dominion, [... rest lost ...].
(b. King) The Good god, powerful and res[olute?], Lord of Both Lands, [Menmare], Lord of Crowns, Sethos I Merenamun, Image of Re at the head of Both Lands.
(c. Winged disc) The Behdetite. (d. Vulture) Nekhebet, the White One of Nekhen; — may she give life and dominion. (e. Behind king) (Magical) protection, life, stability and dominion. [(f. Over horses) lost].

Triumphal return with prisoners (KRI I 18.5-19.6)
(i. Rhetorical text over prisoners and king's chariot)
The Good god, in strength manifest,
mighty in power like Montu residing in Thebes;
Young Bull,[a] the sharp-horned,
resolute, trampling down hundreds of thousands;
Strong Lion,[b]
roaming the difficult paths of every foreign land;
Southern jackal, speeding and roaming,
circling this land in an hour,
seeking out his foes in every foreign land.
Valiant warrior without equal, archer[c] who knows his ability;
who projects his might like a mountain of copper;
(when) he is pacified, they can breathe his breath (of life).
There comes Retenu to him in obeisance,
(and) the land of Lib<ya>[1] on their feet.
He lets go(?) seed as he wishes, in this despicable land of Hatti,
their chiefs are fallen to his sword, reduced to non-existence.
How mighty is his power against them,
(just) like fire when he destroys their towns.

(ii. Further text behind the king)
Victorious King, mighty in power, whose battle-cry is like the Son of Nut's; he has returned triumphant, he has hacked up the foreign lands, he has trampled down the Hatti-land. He puts an end to the rebels, and every foreign land languishes, becoming peaceable as dread of His Majesty has entered into them. His scourge(?) has broken their will ("heart"), and the foreign lands are bound before him; he cares nothing for even hundreds of thousands gathered (together).
(iii. Cartouches) Lord of Both Lands, Menmare, Lord of Crowns, Sethos I Merenamun.
(iv. Over the horses) First Great (Chariot-)Span of His Majesty, "Amun grants him the strong arm."
(v. Over lower row of prisoners) Chiefs of foreign lands who knew not Egypt, whom His Majesty has brought as prisoners (with) their tribute on their backs, (it) being all the choicest of their countries.

Presentation of prisoners and spoils to Amun and the Gods (KRI I 19.7-20.11)
(i. Presentation by the king) [Presentation] of tribute by the Good god to his father Amun-Re, Lord of [the Throne]s of Both Lands, [when] he returned from the land of Hatti — hacking up the rebels and trampling down the Asiatics in their places — with silver and gold, lapis-lazuli and turquoise, [with every kind of] noble [gemstone],[d] according as he decreed for him valor and victory over all foreign lands.
(ii. Vulture and cartouches) Udjo; may she give life and dominion. King of Southern and Northern Egypt, Menmare, Son of Re, Sethos I Merenamun, chosen by Re in the Bark of <millions>.
(iii. Over upper file of prisoners) The great chiefs of despicable Retenu, whom His Majesty has brought off by his victories from the land of Hatti, so to fill the storehouse(s)[e] of [his] noble [father] Amun-Re, Lord of the Thrones of Both Lands, according as he has granted (him) valor against the South and victory over the North.

The chiefs of the foreign countries, they say in extolling His Majesty, LPH, and in magnifying his strength: "Hail to you, King of Egypt, Sun of the Nine Bows! Mighty is your power, Lord of the Gods! You have brought (captive) the (far) limit(s) of the foreign lands, and you have bound them under the feet[f] of your son, the Horus-falcon who brings life to the Two Lands."

(iv. Over lower row of prisoners) Mighty is your power, O Victorious King! How great is your power! You are like Montu over every foreign land, your force

a Deut 33:17
b Gen 49:9; Deut 33:20, 22
c Gen 49:24
d Josh 6:19, 24
e Josh 6:19, 24
f Josh 10:24

[1] The mentions here of Syria ("Retenu") and of Libya might be held to indicate that campaigns in Syria and Libya carved above this register had occurred earlier than the Hittite conflict shown here; however, there is always the possibility that we simply have a flight of rhetorical language normal in these label-texts to war-scenes.

is (just) like his.
(v. Speech of Amun) Words spoken: "I grant you all valor and all victory. I grant you all flat lands and all foreign countries under your sandals. I grant you the lifespan of Re and the years of Atum. I grant you an eternity in jubilees like Re. I grant you all food and provision. I grant you all life, stability and dominion, and all health." — (So), Amun-Re, Lord of the Thrones of Both Lands, presiding over Karnak.

(vi. The other gods: a. Mut-Bastet) Mut the Mighty, [Lady] of Asheru, Bast Mistress of Karnak, Lady of charm, sweet of love: — "I grant you the [thro]ne of Geb, and the lifespan of Re in heaven." (b. Khons) Khons in Thebes, Neferhotep, Falcon (or Horus), Lord of joy.
(c. Maat) Words spoken by Maat Daughter of Re: "My bodily son, (my) beloved, Lord of Both Lands, Lord of the strong arm, Menmare — I grant you an eternity in jubilees like Re."

REFERENCES

Text-editions: definitive, Epigraphic Survey 1986: pls. 33-36; handbook ed., *KRI* 1:17-20; 7:424-425. Translations and notes: Epigraphic Survey 1986:103-114; and Kitchen 1993a:14-17; 1993b:22-23.

KARNAK, CAMPAIGN AGAINST THE LIBYANS (UNDATED) (2.4F)
(West Side, Middle Register)

K. A. Kitchen

As with all three registers on this western side, an initial scene is now hidden away around the corner, under later (22nd Dynasty) stonework that was part of the masonry for the great forecourt built by Shoshenq I, ca. 925 BCE. The visible scenes are limited to a victorious battle, the king killing a Libyan leader, and the triumphal return to Egypt.

(Scene hidden behind 22nd-Dynasty Wall - not accessible.)

Sethos I in Battle with the Libyans (KRI I 20.15-21.4)
(i. Minor epigraphs: a. cartouches) Lord of Both Lands, Menmare, Lord of Crowns, Sethos I Merenamun. (b. Over the horses) First Great (Chariot-)Span of His Majesty, "Trampling down the Foreign Lands." (c. Behind the king) Horus strong in arm, Lord who performs the rituals — may all protection, life, stability and dominion attend him!

(ii. Rhetorical text) [The Good god ...], [the strong arm]ed,[a] Lo[rd of po]wer, val[iant li]ke Montu, who fights and captures in every foreign land; a hero without equal, who achieves with his strong arm, so that the Two Lands know, and so that the entire land shall see (it).

He is like Baal[1] (as) he treads the mountains. Dread of him has crushed the foreign lands, his name is victorious, and his power is strong; there is none who can withstand him.

Sethos I spears a Libyan Chief (KRI I 21.6-17)
(i. Rhetorical text) [The Good god ...], who overthrows those who rebel against him, who smites the tribesfolk and tramples down the Mentiu/Beduin and the distant foreign lands of Libya (*Tehenu*), [?making a great slaughter] amongst them, [... fall]en, their chiefs, [... under] the feet of the Falcon.

(ii. Before the king) Striking down the chiefs of Libya. (iii. Minor epigraphs: a. cartouches) [...], Men[mare], [...], Sethos I [Merenamun], given dominion like Re. (b. Falcon) May he give life and dominion.
(c. Fan) May all protection, life, stability and dominion attend him like Re!
(d. Above and behind the king) Horus strong in arm, Lord of Both Lands, Lord who performs the rituals, smiting every foreign land, Lord of the strong arm, trampling down the Nine Bows.
(e. Terminal text) Shall endure the King, Lord of Both Lands, Lord of the strong arm,[b] Menmare, trampling down the chiefs of the foreign lands of Lib[ya] (*Temehu*) like Re.
(iv. Prince Ramesses added behind king at left) Hereditary Prince, Senior King's Son, of his (own) body, beloved of him, Ramesses.
(v. Prince [formerly, an official] behind Libyan chief at right) (Original text [KRI VII 425:6]): Troop-Commander and Fanbearer, Mehy.]
(Added text of prince): Hereditary Prince, Eldest King's Son, of his (own) body, [...].

Triumphal Return with Prisoners (KRI I 22.1-13)
(i. Rhetorical text, before and above the prisoners)
[The Good god who returns, having triumphed over the chiefs of every land; he has trampled down the rebellious foreign countries] who had transgressed his boundaries. He is like Montu, [he has taken up

[a] Exod 3:19-20; 6:1
[b] Exod 3:19-20; 6:1

[1] Comparisons of the pharaoh with Baal are quite frequent in the Ramesside period, as here and above *COS* 2.4A, (i). Likewise with the goddess ᶜAstarte, as in *COS* 2.4A.

the mace, like Horus in his panoply], his bow is with [him like Bast], his arrow is like (that of) the Son of Nut. No foreign land can stand be[fore him, the dread of him is in their hearts, all foreign lands ..., have become at pe]ace — he causes them to cease standing on the battlefield, (as) they forget (even how) to draw the bow, spending the day in the caves,[c] hidden away like foxes. Dread of His Majesty [is in all lands, per]vading their hearts, [?inasmuch as his father Amun has given him] valor and victory.

(ii. Text above lower file of prisoners) [Chiefs of the foreign lands that knew not Egypt, whom His Majesty brought off as] prisoner(s) from the ⌜foreign land⌝ of Lib<ya>, by the power of his father Amun.

(iii. Minor epigraphs. a. Over the horses) First Great (Chariot-)Span <of> His Majesty, "Valiant is Amun."

(b. Cartouches) Lord of Both Lands, Menmare, Lord of Crowns, Sethos I Merenamun, given life.

(c. Vultures at right): Nekhbet, White One of Nekhen. (At left): [... lost ...].

Presentation of prisoners and spoil to the Theban triad (KRI I 23.1-24.4)

(i. Text above the spoils) Presentation of tribute by His Majesty to his father Amun-Re, (consisting) of silver and gold, lapis-lazuli and turquoise, and of every noble gemstone [d] — "by the valor which you give me over every foreign land."

(ii. Text before the king) Presentation of tribute by the Good god to his father Amun, from the rebellious chiefs of the foreign lands ignorant of Egypt, (with) their tribute on their backs, to fill every workshop with slaves male and female — "by the victories which you gave me over every land."

(iii. Text above upper file of prisoners) His Majesty has returned from the foreign lands, his at[tack] having succeeded. He has plundered Retenu (Syria), he has slain their chiefs. He has caused the Asiatics to say: "Who is this? He is like a flame in its shooting forth, unchecked by water!" He causes all rebels to desist from all boasting with their mouths — he has taken away the (very) breath of their nostrils.

(iv. Text above lower file of prisoners) Chiefs of the foreign lands of Libya (*Tehenu*) [...].

(v. Minor epigraphs: a. cartouches) King of Southern and Northern Egypt, Lord who performs the rituals, Menmare, Son of Re, Lord of Crowns, Sethos I Merenamun, given life like Re.

(b. Vultures, at left) May she give life, stability and dominion like Re. (At right]: Nekhbet, White One of Nekhen; may she give all valor.

(vi. Speech of Amun)

Words spoken by Amun-Re, Lord of the Thrones of Both Lands: "(My) bodily son whom I love, Lord of Both Lands, Menmare! My heart is glad through love for you, and I rejoice at the sight of your beauty. I set the war-cry of Your Majesty upon every foreign land. [Your mace] is upon the head(s) of their chiefs — [they] come to you in unison, to Nile-land, carrying all their goods loaded on their backs."

(vii. Mut) Mut, Lady of Asheru, Lady of heaven, Mistress of all the Gods: "[I grant to you] eternity as King of the Two Lands, you having appeared like Re."

(viii. Khons-Thoth) Khons in Thebes, Neferhotep, Horus, Lord of joy, Thoth Lord of Karnak: "I give to you valor against the South and victory over the North" — may all protection, life, stability and dominion attend him like Re.

c Josh 10:16

d Josh 6:19, 24

REFERENCES

Texts: definitive, Epigraphic Survey 1986: pls. 27-32; handbook ed., *KRI* 1:20-24. Translations with notes and older references: Epigraphic Survey 1986:87-101; Kitchen 1993a:17-19, 1993b:23-25.

KARNAK, CAMPAIGN AGAINST QADESH AND AMURRU (UNDATED) (2.4G)

(West Side, Top Register)

K. A. Kitchen

Here, except for an inaccessible scene round the corner (walled-over in the 22nd Dynasty), only one scene remains, of the king in battle, the scenes of his return to Egypt and presentation to the gods being now lost. But the remaining scene has him vanquishing Amurru, a kingdom in the Lebanon mountains that bears the name of the Amorites, and Qadesh, focus of an epic battle in his son's reign (*COS* 2.5 below).

(Scene hidden behind 22nd-Dynasty wall — not accessible)

Sethos I attacks Qadesh and Amurru (*KRI* I 24)

(i. Rhetorical text) [The Good god who slays] te[ns of thousands],[a] raging [like the Son of] Nut, (with Montu at [his right and Seth] at his left, a hero [without his equal], a warrior worth ("of") millions, [who protects] his army, a rampart [b] for myriads; [stout-hearted?] (when) he sees multitudes,

a 1 Sam 18:7; 21:12; 29:5

b Jer 1:18; Ezek 4:3

[he cares] nothing for myriads en masse; one who enters [into the mass of Asiatics, and who makes them [prostra]te, who tramples down [their] settlements, [and devas]tates [their] villages [upon] his paths, [a strong bull, sharp-horned?] who crushs [myriads ...].

(ii. Text on the fort) The ascent which Pharaoh, LPH, made to destroy the land of Qadesh (and) the land of Amurru.[1]

(iii. Text at right of fort) Town of Qadesh.

(iv. Over the horses) <First> Great Chariot-Span [of] His majesty, ["..."].

(v. Terminal line at right; KRI VII 426) [Shall endure the King, Lord of Both Lands, Menmare, arisen upon the] Horus-throne, and destroying the rebellious foreign lands [...].

Text of obliterated official (KRI VII 426)
The Troop-commander and Fanbearer, Me[hy, justified].[2]

Triumphal return (KRI VII 425)
[...] according as he gives him valor against every foreign land.

Prisoners to the gods (KRI VII 425)
(i. Amun): [...] to see me.
(ii. Mut): [... I give you ...] everlasting as joyful ruler.
(iii. Behind Mut): [... all ...] attend her like Re.

[1] Qadesh and Amurru are here close neighbors, as is geographically true; Qadesh-on-Orontes closely adjoined the north-east border of the mountain-state of Amurru. The text here speaks of "the land of the Amurru"; or probably better, of "him of Amurru," meaning the Amurrite ruler, which foreshadows well-attested usage in the Qadesh-texts of Ramesses II. Originally, "Amurru" had been a Mesopotamian term for the area of Syria west of the River Euphrates and Gebel Bishri, and for people in that area ("Amorites"); but already in texts from Mari and Alalakh (early 2nd millennium BCE) it had begun to have a more restricted use, culminating in the specific 14th/13th-century kingdom of Amurru in Lebanon envisaged in the Amarna letters, in Hittite and Ugaritic records and in these texts of Sethos I and Ramesses II. See Klengel 1969:178-183; 1992:39-43, 160-161, with references.

[2] The high official Mehy was originally present in three scenes on these walls — in the Year 1 (bottom) register, west side; in the Libyan war series and in this series (east side), in each case replaced by a figure of Ramesses II as Prince (not king). Mehy must have played an important role at court and probably in these wars, to be honored with a place in these great temple-scenes; on his emergence into a political role next to his father (as prince-regent), young Ramesses evidently considered that he (not a mere commoner) should feature here, especially if he went on his father's later campaigns.

REFERENCES

Texts: definitive, Epigraphic Survey 1986: pls. 22-26; handbook ed., *KRI* 1:24; 7:425. Translations, notes and older references: Epigraphic Survey 1986:79-85; Kitchen 1993a:19-20; 1993b:25-26.

RAMESSES II (2.5)

THE BATTLE OF QADESH — THE POEM, OR LITERARY RECORD (2.5A)

K. A. Kitchen

In this epic clash of arms between Muwatallis II of Hatti and Ramesses II of Egypt in the latter's Year 5 (1275 BC), it is now clear that Ramesses won the battle on the day, but Egypt lost politically by its results: Qadesh was not taken, Amurru returned to Hatti, and the Egyptian province of Upe (around Damascus) fell into Hittite control temporarily. However, as his personal valor had in some measure saved the day (but aided by the timely arrival of reinforcements), the pharaoh felt justified in presenting his narrow personal triumph to Egypt and its gods in a suitably grandiose composition in both image and word. Thus, two great tableaux were carved upon the temple walls, one of the Egyptian camp as attacked by the Hittites as the Egyptian relief-force arrived, and one of the king triumphantly pushing back the Hittite forces into and over the River Orontes. Alongside these scenes was engraved a 'literary record', the so-called Poem (most of it actually poetical, but with prose segments as needed), and in the first tableau a supplementary text, now known as the Bulletin, mainly prose but with a touch of poetry as needed. The entire work was inscribed on major temples in Egypt and Nubia: so, at Thebes (Karnak, Luxor, Ramesseum), at Abydos, at Abu Simbel in Nubia; northern temples are too destroyed to preserve copies. The Poem also was copied as a purely literary piece (without the scenes) on papyrus.

(1-6)[1] Beginning of the Triumph of the King of Southern and Northern Egypt, Usimare Setepenre,
Son of Re, {beloved of the Gods},
Ramesses II Meriamun,[2] given life forever,
which he achieved: against the Hatti-land,
Naharina, and against the land of Arzawa;
against Pidassa, (and) against the Dardanaya (land);
against the land of Masa, against the land of Qarqisha, and Lukka;
against Carchemish, Qode, (and the) land of Qadesh;
against the land of Ugarit, (and) Mushnatu.[3]

(7-24) Now, His Majesty was a youthful lord, a hero without peer;
arms were powerful, his heart bold,
his strength (was) like Montu's in his hour:
Fine in appearance like Atum,
at seeing his beauty, one rejoices.
Mighty in victories over all foreign countries,
one never knows when he may begin to fight.
Strong rampart [a] around his army,
their shield on the day of fighting.
An archer unequalled,[b]
more valiant than hundred-thousands rolled into one.
Going straight ahead, entering the throng,
his heart confident in his strength.
Ruthless in the hour of combat,
like fire in the instant that it devours.
Determined like a bull poised in the arena,
he thinks nothing (even) of every land combined.
Even a thousand men [c] cannot withstand him,
hundred-thousands despair just at the sight of him.
Master (through) fear, great of war-cry,
in the hearts of all lands.
Mighty in renown, rich in splendour,
like Sutekh on the mountain-tops.
[Dreaded] in the hearts of foreigners,
like a fierce lion in a valley of wild game.
Going forth bravely,
returning after triumphing personally,
without speaking boastfully.
Effective in counsel,
good at planning,
one finds (the needful) in his first reply.

a Jer 1:18; Ezek 4:3

b Gen 49:24

c 1 Sam 18:7; 21:12; 29:5

Rescuer of his infantry on the day of battle,
great protector of his chariotry.
Bringing his followers (safe home), saving his troops,
his heart (steady) as a mountain of copper.
(Such is) the King of Southern and Northern Egypt,
Usimare Setepenre,
the Son of Re,[4] Ramesses II, given life.[5]

(25-40) So now, His Majesty issued supplies to his infantry and chariotry, (and the) Sherden-warriors that His Majesty had captured, when he brought them in by the triumph of his strong arm; they being kitted-out with all their weapons, and the plan of campaign given to them.

Thus, His Majesty travelled north, his infantry and chariotry accompanying him. He made a good start to the march in Year 5, 2nd month of Shomu, Day 9, {to the despised land of Syria, on his 2nd campaign of victory}.

His Majesty passed the fortress of Sile, he being strong as Montu at his forays. All foreign lands trembled before him, their chiefs presenting their tribute; and every (would-be) rebel submitting through fear of the wrath of His Majesty. His army went through the (narrow) passes just like someone on the (open) roads of Egypt.

Some time after this, see, His Majesty was in Ramesses II the Town, which is in the Valley of the Conifers. His Majesty travelled on northwards. Now when His Majesty had reached the ridge of Qadesh, then His Majesty went straight on, like his father Montu, Lord of Thebes; and he crossed the ford of (the river) Orontes, with the 1st Army-Division of Amun who gives victory to Usimare Setepenre.[6] (Thus) His Majesty arrived at the town of Qadesh.

(41-55) Now, the despicable Fallen (chief) of Hatti had come; he had gathered round himself all foreign countries to the (furthest) limits of the sea:
The entire land of Hatti had come; that of Naharina likewise, and that of Arzawa;
Dardanaya, that of Gasgas, that *(var.:* those) of Masa;
those of Pidassa, that of Arwanna, that of Qarqisha, (and) Lukku;

[1] The "line-numbers" given in the text are the modem P(oem) paragraph-numbers applied to the text since Kuentz's edition; for typographical neatness, the cipher "P" is omitted.

[2] Hereinafter abbreviated to "Ramesses II."

[3] The home locations of most of the Hittite allies can be defined, even if sometimes only broadly. Naharina is the Eg. term for Mitanni/Hanigalbat in the great west bend of the Euprates. Arzawa is in the south part of Anatolia, and Pidassa to the north of Arzawa. Dardanaya, Masa, Qarqisha and Lukka (cf. Lycia) were all in the western parts of Anatolia. Qode is an Eg. term that loosely embraces north Syria and perhaps Cilicia (Kizzuwatna). North-Syrian Carchemish on the Euprates was the Hittite administrative capital for their Syrian vassals; Ugarit was the seaport city-state near modern Latakia; Mushnatu (for Mushanipa?) was also probably in north Syria.

[4] P. Ch. Beatty adds: {Beloved of the Gods} here.

[5] P. Ch. Beatty adds: {forever and eternally, like his father Re}.

[6] P. Ch. Beatty here adds {L.P.H., [Son of Re, Ramesses II, L.P.H.}

Kizzuwatna, Carchemish, Ugarit, Qode;
the entire land of Nuhasse; Mushnatu; (and) Qadesh;[7]
he left not (even one) country which was not brought, of every distant land.
Their rulers were there with him, each man with his forces;
their chariotry was vast in extent, unequalled;
they covered hill and valley, they were like the locust-swarm in their multitude;[d]
he left no money ("silver") in his land, he had stripped himself of all his property;
he gave it to all the(se) countries, to bring them with him, to fight.[e]
Now, the despicable Fallen (chief) of Hatti, along with the many lands that were with him, stood hidden and ready, on the North-East of the (town) of Qadesh.

(56-74) Now, His Majesty was all alone, with (just) his followers,
the division of Amun marching behind him;
the division of Pre crossing the ford, in the area South[8] of the town of Shabtuna, at a distance of 1 *iter* from where His Majesty was;
the division of Ptah being to the South of the town of Arnam;
(and) the division of Seth (still) marching along the road.
His Majesty had drawn the first battle-line from all the leaders of his army.
Now, they were on the shore *(or* bank) in the land of Amurru.
Now, the despicable Ruler of Hatti stood amidst the army which was with him,
he could not come out to fight, for fear of His Majesty.
So, he sent out men and chariotry, abundant, exceedingly numerous like the sand,
they being three men to a chariot-span,[f]
{they formed their units of three, every runner of the land of of the fallen ones of Hatti},
they being armed with every (kind of) weapon of war.

See, they had been made to stand hidden behind the town of Qadesh. Then they emerged on the South side of Qadesh, and attacked the division of Pre at its middle, as they were marching, unaware, and not prepared for fighting. Then His Majesty's troops and chariotry collapsed before them.

(75-91) Now His Majesty was established on the North of the town of Qadesh, on the West side of the Orontes. Then one came to report it to His Majesty. Then His Majesty appeared (gloriously) like his father Montu, he took his panoply of war, and girded himself in his coat of mail; he was like Baal in his hour. The great (chariot)-span which bore His Majesty was (named) *Victory in Thebes*, of the Great Stable of Usimare Setepenre, *Beloved of Amun*, of the Residence.

Then His Majesty set forth at a gallop, he plunged into the midst of the forces of the Hittite foe, he being entirely on his own, no-one else with him.

So, His Majesty went on to look around him; he found 2,500 chariot-spans hemming him in, all around him, even all the champions ("runners") of the Hittite foe, along with the numerous foreign countries who were with them:

from Arzawa, Masa and Pidassa; {from Gasgas, Arwanna and Qizzuwatna; from Aleppo, Ugarit, Qadesh and Lukka;} they were three men to a chariot-span, acting as a unit. But there was no high officer with me, no charioteer, no army-soldier, no shield-bearer. But my army and my chariotry melted away before them, none could withstand them, to fight with them.

(92-120) Then said His Majesty:
"Indeed, what's up with you, my father Amun?
Has a father ever ignored his son?
Now, have I done anything without you?
Do I not go and stop at your word?
I have not disobeyed a(ny) plan that you commanded![9]
How (much) great(er) is he, the great Lord of Egypt,
(than) to allow foreigners to approach his path!
What are they to you, O Amun,
these Asiatics, despicable and ignorant of God!
Have I not made for you monuments in great multitude?
I have filled your temple with my captures!
I built for you my Memorial Temple,[10] [g]
and I assigned you all my property by testament.
I presented to you every land in (its) entirety,
to supply your sacred offerings.
I caused to be offered to you myriads of cattle,
with all sweet-smelling herbs.[h]
I neglected no good deed,
to fail to do them in your courts.
I built for you great {stone} pylon-towers,
and erected their flagstaves myself.
I brought for you obelisks from Elephantine,

d Judg 6:5; Joel 1:4-7
e 1 Kgs 15:18-19; 2 Kgs 16:7-9
f Exod 14:7; Josh 11:4
g 1 Kgs 8:20
h 1 Kgs 8:62-64

[7] The Gasgas or Gasgaeans were unruly tribesfolk who lived north of the Hittite central homeland, and Arwanna adjoined the Gasgaean zone. Kizzuwatna was a former kingdom centered on Cilicia (around Tarsus), while Nuhasse comprised lesser Syrian states neighboring on the northern course of the Orontes.

[8] Raifé: "West."

[9] In his devotion to the god Amun, Ramesses II was the perfect "Deuteronomist"! He repeatedly emphasizes his obedience to the divine will and commands (here; and Poem, 108-110, 120ff.), cf. Deut, passim. Cf. Kitchen 1970:16-19.

[10] Lit., "my Temple of Millions of Years."

it being I who acted as stone-carrier.
I directed for you ships on the sea,
to ferry for you the products of foreign countries.
What will people think, if (even) a minor mishap befalls him that depended on your counsel? Do good to him who counts on you — then people will serve you with a will.
I have called on you, O Amun,
while I am amidst multitudes whom I know not.
All the foreign countries have united against me,
I being (left) entirely alone, no one else with me.
My regular troops have abandoned me,
not one of them has looked for me, from my chariotry.
When I kept on shouting out to them,
none of them heeded me, as I called out.
Amun I found more help to me than millions of troops,
than hundred-thousands of chariotry,
than ten-thousands of men, whether brothers or offspring,
(even) if united in one will.
There is no achievement of (however) many men,
but Amun is more help than them!
I have attained this (much), O Amun, by the counsels of your mouth;
I have never ("not") overstepped your counsel.

(121-127) See, I made petition from the back of beyond,[11]
my voice echoing in Thebes.[i]
The moment I called to him, I found Amun came,
he gave me his hand, being with me, and I was happy.
As (close as) face to face, he spoke out (from) behind me:
"Forward! I am with you, I am your father, my hand is with you!
I am more useful to you than hundred-thousands of men,
I am the Lord of Victory, who loves bravery."

(128-142) My heart I found strong, my mind joyful,
All I did came off (well), I was just like Montu.
I shot to my right, and captured to my left,
I was like Seth in his moment,[12] in their sight.
I found that the 2,500 chariots, in whose midst I was, fell prostrate before my horses.
None of them was able to fight,
their hearts quailed in their bodies through fear of me.
All their arms were weak, they could not shoot,
they could not steady their minds, to seize their javelins.

i 1 Kgs 8:29-30, 42, 44

I made them plunge into the water, as crocodiles plunge,
so, they fell on their faces, one on (top of) another.
I slaughtered them just as I wished,
none looked behind him, no other turned around,
whoever of them fell, he did not rise again.

(143-165) Now, the despicable Ruler of Hatti was standing amidst his infantry and chariotry,
watching the attack by His Majesty, alone, on his own,
having with him neither his infantry nor his chariotry;
so he [=the Hittite] just stood, — turning back, cringing, fearful.
Then he sent forth many chiefs, each of them with his chariot-spans,
equipped with their weapons of war:
the Ruler of Arzawa and the one of Masa;
the Ruler of Arwanna, the one of Lukku, the one of Dardanaya;[13]
the Ruler of Carchemish, the Ruler of Qarqisha, and the one of Aleppo;
the brothers of Him of Hatti, all assembled as one.
They united as one thousand chariot-spans,
and came straight on forward into the fire!
I launched myself against them, being like Montu;
I gave them a taste of my fist ("hand") in the space of a moment.
I wrought mayhem among them, slain on the spot,
One cried out to another amongst them, (saying):
"He is no mere man, he that is among us!
(it's) Seth great of power, (very) Baal in person!
Not the acts of a mere man are the things that he does,
they belong to one utterly unique!
One who defeats myriads, no troops with him, no chariotry.
Let's come away quickly, let's flee before him,
let's seek life for ourselves, that we may breathe air!
See, he who would venture out to approach him,
at once, his hand and all his limbs go weak.
None can draw a bow or even (wield) a spear,
when they see him coming, striding in from a distance."

(166-204) Now, His Majesty was after them like a griffon,
I slaughtered among them, without letting up.
I raised my voice to call out to my troops, saying:
"Stand firm, be bold-hearted, my troops,[14]
see my triumph, (all) on my own,
with only Amun to be my protector, his hand

[11] Lit., "from the furthest end of the foreign lands."
[12] In some versions, Montu (at Abydos) and Baal (P. Sallier) are substituted for Seth.
[13] P. Sallier adds: "the one of Gasgas."
[14] P. Sallier adds (wrongly): "and my chariotry" (who are addressed in P173).

with me.
And how cowardly are your hearts, my chariotry, it's no use trusting in you either!
Was there not one of you, for whom I did good in my land?
Did I not arise as Lord, when you were poor?
I caused you to become great men by my beneficence daily,
I set a son over his father's property, I expelled all evil that had been in this land.
I left your servants for you(r use), I gave you (back) others who had been taken from you.
(As for) anyone who requested petitions, "I'll do (it, — here) I am," I said to him daily.
No master has done for his army, the things that I have done at your wish.
I allowed you to dwell in your towns, without doing military service.
My chariotry equally, I sent home on the road to their towns, saying:
'I shall find them just as (easily as) today, in the hour of meeting for battle.'
Now see — you did a rotten trick, all together as one:
Not a man of you stood firm to give me a hand as I fought.
As the spirit of my father Amun endures, O that I were in Egypt!
Like the Forefather of my forefathers, they who saw no Syrians,
(who never fought Him, even remotely!)
And not one of you having come to boast of your ('his') service, in the land of Egypt."
How much better, (just) to raise many monuments for Thebes, city of Amun!
The wrong that my troops and chariotry did is greater than can be told.
See, Amun has given me his victory,
no troops being with me, and no chariotry.
He has caused every distant land to see my victory by my strong arm,[j]
I being alone, no high officer with me,
no charioteer, no soldier of the infantry, no groom.
The foreign lands that beheld me shall tell of my fame ("name")
as far as distant lands yet unknown.
As for any of them that escaped my hand,
they stood, turning back, looking at what I had done.
If I penetrated amid millions of them, their legs could not stay firm, and they fled.
All those who shot in my direction, their arrows then scattered when they reached me.

(205-213) Now when Menna my shield-bearer saw that a huge number of chariots hemmed me in,
then he was dismayed, his heart sank, and stark fear possessed his body.
Then he said to His Majesty:
"My good Lord, O mighty Ruler,
great Protector of Egypt on the day of battle,
we stand alone in the midst of the foe!
See, the troops and chariotry have abandoned us,
why do you stay to save them?
Let's get clear, save us, O Usimare Setepenre!"

(214-223) Then said His Majesty to his shieldbearer:
"Be firm, be bold-hearted, my shield-bearer!
I shall go into them like the pounce of a falcon,
killing, slaughtering, felling to the ground.
What are these effeminate weaklings to you,
for millions of whom I care nothing?"
Then His Majesty set off quickly, and he went off at a gallop,
into the midst of the foe, for the 6th time of attacking them.
I was like Baal in the moment of his power,
I killed among them, I did not let up.[15]

(224-250) Then, when my troops and my chariotry saw me,
that I was like Montu, my arm strong,
Amun my father being with me instantly,
turning all the foreign lands into straw before me,
then they presented themselves one by one,
to approach the camp at evening time.
They found all the foreign lands, amongst which I had gone,
lying overthrown in their blood,
namely all the fine(st) warriors of the Hatti-(land),
the children and brethren of their ruler.
I had made white the countryside of the land of Qadesh,
None could find space to tread, by reason of their sheer number.
Then my army came to praise me,[16]
their faces [amazed/averted], at seeing what I had done.
My officers came to extol my strong arm,[j]
And likewise my chariotry, boasting of my name, thus:
"What a fine warrior, who stiffens morale,
that you should rescue your troops and chariotry!
You are the son of Amun, achieving with his arms,
you devastate the land of Hatti by your valiant arm.
You are the fine(st) warrior, without your peer,
the king who fights on his army's behalf, on the day of conflict.
You are great-hearted, foremost in the battle-line,

j Exod 3:20; 6:1

[15] P. Sallier adds (wrongly, P. 223 *bis & ter*): "Then His Majesty called to his troops and chariorty, likewise (to) his chiefs who could not fight; and His Majesty said to them:"
[16] Or possibly, "to thank me" (praise me because of them).

you did not bother about any of the lands, (even) united as one.
You are great in victory in front of your army,
in the presence of the entire land, without boastful claims.
O Protector of Egypt, who curbs the foreign lands,
You have broken the back of Hatti forever!"

(251-276) Then said His Majesty to his troops and his officers,
and likewise (to) his chariotry:
"What's wrong with you, my officers, my troops and my chariotry,
who do not know (how to) fight?
Does a man not make himself honored in his city,
at his return, when he has played the hero before his lord?
Fair indeed is fame ("name") won in battle, over and over,
from of old, a man is respected because of his strong arm.
Have I done no good to (even) one of you,
(for) your abandoning me, alone amidst the strife?
How lucky, indeed, is he among who is alive,
(for) your sniffing the air, while I was (left) on my own!
Don't you know in your minds, that I am your rampart of iron? [k]
What will be said in gossip, when it is heard of,
your abandoning me, I being (left) alone, without companion?
And neither high officer, chariot-warrior nor soldier came,
to give me a hand, as I fought!
I repulsed a million foreign lands, on my own,
with (only) *Victory in Thebes* and *Mut is Content*,
my great chariot-steeds.
It was they whom I found to help me,
when all alone I fought with multitudinous foreign lands!
I shall stoop to feeding them myself, personally,
every day that I am in the Palace!
It was they whom I found amidst the strife,
with the charioteer Menna, my shield-bearer,
and with my household butlers who were at my side,
those who are my witnesses regarding the fighting.
See, I found them!"
My Majesty desisted from (further) valor and triumph,
(for) I had overthrown myriads by my strong arm.

(277-320) When dawn came, I marshalled the battle-line in the fight,
I was prepared to fight like an eager bull.
I appeared against them like Montu,
arrayed in the accoutrements of valor and victory.
I entered into the battle-lines, fighting like the pounce of a falcon,
my Uraeus-serpent overthrowing my enemies for me,
she spat her fiery flame in the face(s) of my foes.
I was like Re, in his appearing at the dawn,
my rays, they burned up the bodies of the rebels.
One of them called out to his fellows:
"Look out, beware, don't approach him!
See, Sekhmet the Mighty is she who is with him,
she's along with him, on his horse, her hand with him!
As for anyone who goes to approach him,
then a fiery flame comes to burn up his body!"
Then they took (their) stand at a distance,
doing homage with their hands before me.
Thereupon My Majesty seized them,
killing among them, without letting up,
(as) they sprawled before my horses,
lying overthrown together in their blood.
Thereupon the despicable, defeated Ruler of Hatti sent (a message),
honoring my name like (that of) Re, saying:
"You are (very) Sutekh, Baal in person,
dread of you is like a torch-brand [l] in the land of Hatti."
Then he despatched his envoy, bearing a letter in his hand, in the mighty name of My Majesty, sending greetings to the majesty of the palace of:
Horus-Falcon, Strong Bull, Beloved of Maat,
Sovereign who protects his army, valiant through his strong arm;
Rampart for his troops on the day of battle;
King of Southern and Northern Egypt, Usimare Setepenre,
Son of Re, Lion, possessor of the strong arm,
Ramesses II, given life forever.
This (humble) servant speaks, he makes it known that:[17]
You are the (very) Son of Re, who came forth from his body;
he assigned to you all lands together, united as one.
As for the land of Egypt and the land of Hatti, they are yours,
your servants — they are under your feet,[m]
Pre your august father has granted them to you.
Do not overwhelm us!
See, your power is great.
your might lies heavy upon the land of Hatti.
Is it good that you kill your servants,

k Jer 1:18; Ezek 4:3
l Gen 15:17
m Jos 10:24

[17] P. Sallier here needlessly adds: "O Pharaoh, my good Lord, fine son of Pre-Harakhti."

your face fierce against them, without your pity (on them)?
See, you spent yesterday, slaughtering myriads.[n]
You came today, and you left no heirs!
Do not be (so) harsh in your words, O Victorious king!
Peace is better than war; grant us breath!"

(321-330) So, My Majesty desisted in life and dominion,
I being like Montu his moment (of triumph), when his attack has succeeded.

Then My Majesty had brought in to me all the leaders of my infantry and my chariotry, and all my high officers, assembled all together, in order to let them hear the matter about which he [= Hittite king] had sent word. Then I caused them to hear the words that the despicable Ruler of Hatti had sent to me.

Then they spoke out in unison: "Excellent, indeed, is peace, O Sovereign our Lord! There is no dishonor ('blame') in peace, when you make it. Who shall resist you on the day of your wrath?"

(331-343) Then His [*var*.: My] Majesty decreed that his word be heeded.
I [*var*.: he] turned peacefully southwards.
His Majesty set off back to Egypt peacefully, with his troops and chariotry,
all life, stability and dominion being with him,
the gods and goddesses being the talismanic protection for his body,
and subduing for him all lands, through fear of him.
It was the might of His Majesty that protected his army,
all foreign lands praising his fair countenance.
Arrival peacefully in Egypt, at Pi-Ramesse Great-in-Victories,[o]
and resting in his Palace of life and dominion, like Re who is in his horizon.
The gods of the land <come> to him in greeting, saying:
"Welcome, our beloved Son, King of Southern and Northern Egypt, Usimare Setepenre, Son of Re, Ramesses II, given life! — according as they have granted him a million jubilees and eternity upon the throne of Re, all lands and all foreign lands being overthrown and slain beneath his sandals, eternally and forever.

(P. Sallier, Colophon)
This text [was written] in Year 9, 2nd month of Shomu, Day <1>, of the King of Southern and Northern Egypt, Usima[re] Setepenre, LPH, Son of Re, Ramesses II, LPH, given life eternally and forever like his father Re.

It has come to completion successfully ... For the spirit of the Chief Archivist [of the Treasury of Pharaoh, LPH, Amenemone,] the Scribe of the Treasury of Pharaoh, [LPH], A[men]emwia, and [the Scribe of] the Treasury of Pharaoh, [LPH ...]. Made by the Scribe Pentaweret [...].

n 1 Sam 18:7; 21:12; 29:5

o Exod 1:11

REFERENCES

Texts: Kuentz 1928-34; *KRI* 1:2-147. Translations: Gardiner 1960; Kitchen 1996:2-26; Davies 1997:55-96. Latest commentary: Kitchen 1999:3-55 with extensive bibliography.

THE BATTLE OF QADESH — THE "BULLETIN" TEXT (2.5B)

K. A. Kitchen

The so-called "Bulletin" is a compact text that gives details supplementary to the main account in the "Poem." By its position in the first great tableau-scene, it functions as a label-text to that part of the scene (the king interrogating two Hittite spies). But its length and cohesion also ranks it as almost an independent text within the overall composition.

(1-2)[1] Year 5, 3rd month of Shomu, Day 9, under the Majesty of:
Horus-Falcon, Strong Bull, Beloved of Maat;
King of Southern and Northern Egypt, Usimare Setepenre, Son of Re, Ramesses II, given life forever.

(3-6) Now, His Majesty was in Syria (*Djahy*) on his 2nd victorious campaign. A happy awakening in life, prosperity and health, in His Majesty's tent, on the ridge South of Qadesh. After this, in the early morning, His Majesty appeared as when Re shines, and he assumed the accoutrements of his father Montu.

(7-28) The Lord [=the King] proceeded North, and (His Majesty) reached the area South of the town of Shabtuna. There came two Shasu, from the Shasu

[1] The "line-numbers" given in the text are the modern B(ulletin) paragraph-numbers used since Kuentz's edition; for typographical neatness,

tribesfolk, to say to His Majesty:

"It is our brothers, who are tribal chiefs with the Fallen One of Hatti, who have sent us to His Majesty, saying: 'We shall become servants of Pharaoh, LPH, and we shall separate ourselves from the Ruler of Hatti.'"

Then said His Majesty to them: "Where are they, your brothers who [se]nt you to speak of this matter to His Majesty?"

Then said they to His Majesty: "They are where the despicable Chief of Hatti is, for the Fallen One of Hatti is in the land of Aleppo, to the North of Tunip. He feared Pharaoh, LPH, too much to come southward, when he heard that Pharaoh, LPH, was coming northward."

Now, these (two) Shasu said these things, and lied [a] to His Majesty. (For) it was the Fallen One of Hatti who had sent them, to find out ("see") where His Majesty was, so as to prevent His Majesty's army from being prepared to fight with the Fallen One of Hatti.

Now, the Fallen One of Hatti had sent the Shasu to say these things to His Majesty, having come with his troops and chariotry, along with the rulers of every land that was in the territory of the land of Hatti, and their troops and chariotry, which he had brought with him as allies, to fight with His Majesty's army, he standing ready and prepared behind Old Qadesh — but His Majesty did not know that they were there, The two Shasu who were in the (royal) presence were interrogated(?).

(29-32) So, His Majesty travelled on northward, arriving at the North-West of Qadesh. The camp of His Majesty's army was pitched there, and His Majesty sat on the throne of electrum, to the North of Qadesh, on the West side of the (river) Orontes.

(33-51) Then came a scout [b] who was in His Majesty's service, bringing in two scouts of the Fallen One of Hatti; they were ushered into the (royal) presence.

Then said His Majesty to them: "What are you?" What they said: "We belong <to> the Ruler of Hatti — he it is who sent us, to see where His Majesty is."

His Majesty said to them: "Where is he himself, the Ruler of Hatti? See, I have heard that he is in the land of Aleppo, to the North of Tunip."

They said [to] His Majesty: "See, the despicable Ruler of Hatti has (already) come, along with the many foreign lands that accompany him, whom he has brought with him as allies, [from all the foreign lands who belong to the area of Hatti]:[2]

[the land of Dardanaya],[3] the land of Naharina;
that of Gasgas, those of Masa, those of Pidassa;
the land of Qarqisa, and Lukku, (and) the land of Carchemish;
the land of Arzawa, the land of Ugarit, that of Arwanna;
the land of Alshe, Mushnatu, and Qadesh;
Aleppo, and the entire land of Qode.

They are furnished with their infantry and chariotry, [bearing their combat-weapons];[4] they are more numerous than the sands of the seashore.[c] See, they stand equipped, ready to fight, behind Old Qadesh!"

(52-80) Then His Majesty had the high officers summoned into the (royal) presence, to let them hear all the words that the Fallen One of Hatti's two spies had spoken.

Then said His Majesty to them: "You see the situation (in) which are the garrison-commanders and governors of foreign territories, together with the chiefs of the lands of Pharaoh, LPH, (that) they stand (there) saying daily to Pharaoh, LPH: 'The despicable Ruler of Hatti is in the land of Aleppo, north of Tunip, having fled before His Majesty, when he heard (the report): "See, Pharaoh has come!" — so they say, speaking to His Majesty daily!' But see, I have heard this very hour, from these two spies from the Fallen One of Hatti, that the despicable Fallen One of Hatti has (already) come, with the numerous foreign countries accompanying him, with men and chariotry, as many as the sand (of the shore).[c] See, they stand hidden behind Old Qadesh — [so, it is said][5] — and my governors of foreign territories and my chiefs, in whose charge are the lands of Pharaoh, LPH, could not tell us that they [= Hatti] had arrived!"

The high officers who were in the (royal) presence spoke and replied to the Good [god] thus: "(This is) a great crime that the governors of foreign territories and chiefs (of Pharaoh, LPH) have committed, (in) not causing (the location) of the Fallen One of Hatti, wherever he is, to be reported to them, that they might report it to Pharaoh, LPH, daily."

Then the Vizier was ordered to hurry up His Majesty's army that was (still) marching (from) South of the town of Shabtuna, in order to fetch them to where His Majesty was.

a Josh 9
b Num 13; 1 Kgs 20:17
c Josh 11:4

the cipher "B" is here omitted.

[2] Bracketed wording in Luxor texts, omitted at Ramesseum and Abu Simbel.

[3] Bracketed wording at Ramesseum and Abu Simbel, omitted at Luxor.

[4] Bracketed wording at Ramesseum and Abu Simbel (omitted at Luxor), which omit Aleppo (included at Luxor).

[5] Bracketed words in Ramesseum and Abu Simbel texts; omitted at Luxor.

But (even) as His Majesty sat talking with the high officers, the despicable Fallen One of Hatti came with his troops and his chariotry, and also the numerous foreign lands that were accompanying him. They crossed the ford (just) South of Qadesh, then they entered in amongst His Majesty's troops as they marched unawares.

(81-83) Then His Majesty's troops and chariotry quailed before them, on their way North, to where His Majesty was. Then the foes from the Fallen One of Hatti surrounded His Majesty's subordinates who were by his side.

(84-105) Then His Majesty caught sight of them, so he arose quickly.
(Then) he raged against them, like his father Montu (Lord of Thebes).
He took up his panoply of war, he girded himself with his coat of mail,
— he was like Sutekh [*var.*: Baal] in his moment of power.
Then he mounted ("Victory-in-Thebes"),[6] his chariot-span [*var.*: horses],
he setting off quickly, being all alone.
His Majesty was strong, and his heart firm,
none could stand before him.
All his patch blazed with fire,
he burnt up every foreign land with his hot breath.
His eyes became savage when he saw them,
his might flared like fire against them.
He paid no heed to (even) a million aliens,
he looked upon them as on chaff.
Then His Majesty entered into the hostile ranks of the fallen ones of Hatti,
along with the many foreign lands who were with them,
His Majesty being like Sutekh great in strength,
like Sekhmet in the moment of her fury.
His Majesty slew all the hostile ranks of the despicable Fallen One of Hatti,
along with all of his great chiefs and his brothers,
likewise all the rulers of all the foreign lands that came with him,
and their troops and chariotry, fallen on their faces, one upon another.
His Majesty slaughtered and slew them, fallen on the spot,
as they (lay) sprawling before his horses,
His Majesty being alone, none other with him.
So His Majesty forced the hostile ranks of the fallen ones of Hatti to plunge on their faces,
sprawling, one upon another, plunging like crocodiles, into the waters of Orontes.

(106-110) "I was after them like a griffon, I defeated all the foreign lands, being alone,
my troops and chariotry abandoned me, none of them stood looking back.
As Re lives for me and loves me, and as my father Atum favours me,
regarding everything of which My Majesty has spoken,
— I truly did them, in the presence of my troops and my chariotry."

(Luxor palimpsest continues — fragmentary):
[...] I was like Montu, his strength [being with me? ...] all [... *much lost* ...]
[...] like serpents [... *very large loss* ...] [...] them, alighting [...]

[remainder very fragmentary]

[6] Name of chariot-span, in Luxor text, omitted in Ramesseum and Abu Simbel texts; the latter have "Baal" for "Sutekh," and Abu Simbel "horses" for "span."

REFERENCES

Text: Kuentz 1928-34; *KRI* 2:102-124. Translations: Gardiner 1960; Kitchen 1996:14-18; Davies 1997:86-96; and latest commentary, Kitchen 1999:3-55 passim, with extensive earlier references.

THE (ISRAEL) STELA OF MERNEPTAH (2.6)

James K. Hoffmeier

Discovered in 1896 by Sir Flinders Petrie in western Thebes, the Merneptah Stela instantly became one of the most important documents from the ancient Near East, thanks to the appearance on it of the name "Israel" (Petrie 1897, pl. 13-14). Now over a century later, this reference remains the earliest occurrence of Israel outside of the Bible. In recent years, as more minimalist readings of the Hebrew scriptures have increased, this stela's reference to Israel has considerable interest for biblical historians as they attempt to explain Israel's origins in Canaan apart from the Bible.

Merneptah, the thirteenth son of Ramesses II, reigned a decade, beginning in 1213 BCE. According to Kenneth Kitchen (1982b:215), a major military campaign against Libyan tribes occurred in summer of year 5. Thus the stela, which is dated to regnal year 5, was set up to celebrate this triumph. Hence the Libyan campaign occupies the majority of the stela. This means that the king's sortie to the Levant, in which the Israelites were encountered, must have occurred no earlier than year 2 and before the Libyan campaign (1211-1208 BCE). Consequently the earlier campaign to Canaan did not receive as much notice on this stela as the recently concluded victory over the Libyans. In all, the stela has 28 lines, 23 of which deal with the battle with the Libyans, while the closing paean in which Israel occurs, begins towards the end of line 26 and runs to the very end of line 27. Since this short hymn mentions Tehenu (the main Libyan tribe) first among the eight toponyms, the hymn must be regarded as celebrating all the king's victories, from his first campaign into the Levant up to the most recent victory against the Libyans. These factors must be kept in view because it was not the writer's intent to give a full report on the events in Asia. It could well be that earlier annals or victory stelae, which have not survived or await discovery, documented this campaign.

The stela as a whole is generally recognized to be hymnic in nature. John Wilson called it a "Hymn of Victory" (*ANET* 376), while Ronald J. Williams saw it as "a series of hymns" (*DOTT* 137), and Miriam Lichtheim refers to it as "The Poetical Stela of Merneptah" (*AEL* 2:73). Both the literary structure of the stela as well as that of the final paean, have attracted considerable scholarly study in recent years. While there is general agreement that the Israel pericope is chiastic in structure, and may reflect on Israel's geo-political status in the Levant, there is no consensus regarding how to relate the toponyms to each other. A number of scholars, however, believe that Israel and Hurru (a general term for Syria-Canaan) are used in parallelism. This association suggests that the Israelites are a significant enough presence to be compared with Hurru. It has long been noted that the writing of Israel uses the determinative (semantic indicator) for an ethnic group, and not for a geographic region or city. This scenario is in complete agreement with the picture portrayed in the books of Joshua and Judges, viz. the Israelites had no clearly defined political capital city, but were distributed over a region.

A concluding historiographic note needs to be made. In the "origins of Israel" debate of the 1980's and 1990's, many critical scholars rejected the historical value of the Joshua narratives on the grounds that they are tendentious, as well as theological and ideological in nature. These same tendencies permeate the Merneptah Stela. Nevertheless, these same scholars readily accept the historical value of this important text.

The (foreign) chieftains lie prostrate, saying "Peace."[1] Not one lifts his head among the Nine Bows.[2]
Libya is captured,[3] while Hatti[a] is pacified.
Canaan is plundered, Ashkelon[b] is carried off, and Gezer[c] is captured.
Yenoam[4] is made into non-existence; Israel is wasted, its seed[5] is not; and Hurru[6] is become a widow because of Egypt.
All lands united themselves in peace. Those who went about are subdued by the king of Upper and Lower Egypt ... Merneptah.

a Gen 15:20; 23:3; 25:9; Exod 3:8; 13:5; Josh 1:4; 3:10
b Josh 13:3; Judg 1:18; 14:19; 1 Sam 6:17
c Josh 10:33; 12:12; Judg 1:29; 2 Sam 5:25; 1 Kgs 9:15, 16, 17

[1] The Semitic word, *shalom* is written.
[2] A longstanding Eg. expression for its enemies.
[3] The line reads, *ḥfʿ n tḥnw*. The problem with this text is the function of the preposition, *n*, which makes no sense grammatically, esp. given that all the verbs in this paean are either passive *sḏm.f* forms or old perfectives, neither of which are written with *n* after the verb. This appears to be a scribal error (cf. Hoffmeier 1997:45, n. 27).
[4] Identified with Tell el-Ubeidiya, south of the Sea of Galilee (Aḥituv 1984:206-208). See also *COS* 2.2A, note 65; 2.4B, note 4.
[5] The Eg. word *prt* can apply equally to seeds, i.e. grain, as to human offspring. The latter interpretation has been generally accepted. The former position has recently been advocated by Hasel (1994:48-50), but the traditional understanding seems to fit the context better (Stager 1985:61*; Hoffmeier 1997:28, 45 n. 26).
[6] A generic, Egyptian term for Syria.

REFERENCES

Text: Petrie, 1887; *KRI* 4:12-19. Translations: *ANET* 376-378; Williams in *DOTT* 137-141; Lichtheim *AEL* 2:73-77. Studies: Fecht 1983; Ahlström and Edelman 1985; Stager 1985; Bimson 1991; Hasel 1994; Kitchen 1994-97; Hoffmeier 1997:27-31; Niccacci 1997.

3. LATE INSCRIPTIONS

THE VICTORY STELA OF KING PIYE (PIANKHY) (2.7)

Miriam Lichtheim

The great "Victory Stela of King Piye,"[1] on which the king narrates his conquest of all of Egypt, is the foremost historical inscription of the Late Period. It equals the New Kingdom Annals of Thutmosis III in factualness and surpasses them in vividness. It also paints the portrait of a Nubian king who was forceful, shrewd, and generous. He meant to rule Egypt but he preferred treaties to warfare, and when he fought he did not glory in the slaughter of his adversaries in the manner of an Assyrian king. Like all members of his egyptianized dynasty, he was extremely pious and especially devoted to Amun, whom he worshiped in his Nubian residence, Napata, and of course in the god's own hallowed city, Thebes.

The large round-topped stela of gray granite was discovered in 1862 in the ruins of the temple of Amun at Napata, the Nubian capital at the foot of Gebel Barkal. The temple of Amun, erected in the New Kingdom, had been much enlarged by Piye. The stela measures 1.80 by 1.84 m and the sides are 0.43 m thick. It is inscribed on all four sides with a total of one hundred and fifty-nine lines.

The relief in the lunette shows on the left Amun enthroned, with Mut standing behind him and King Piye before him. Behind Piye, King Namart of Hermopolis leads up a horse. With him is his wife whose right arm is raised in a gesture of prayer. In the register below are the prostrate figures of Kings Osorkon IV, Iuput II, and Peftuaubast. Behind them, also kissing the ground, are five rulers: the prince Pediese and four chiefs of the Libyan Ma (or, Meshwesh): Patjenfi, Pemai, Akanosh, and Djedamenefankh. The words inscribed before these subjected rulers are mostly destroyed.

Piye, King of Nubia, was in control of Upper Egypt, with an army of his stationed there. While at Napata, the news reached him that Tefnakht of Sais, the Great Chief of the Ma, who ruled the entire western Delta, was extending his conquests southward. He had formed an alliance with a number of chiefs, including King Namart of Hermopolis, and had turned south to besiege Heracleopolis whose ruler, Peftuaubast, was allied with Piye. Piye first decided to send reinforcements to his army in Egypt, and when this army failed to win decisive victories, he himself led another army into Egypt.

In the twentieth year of his reign, ca. 734 BCE, Piye[1a] sailed to Egypt. After halting at Thebes to celebrate the Opet festival of Amun, he tightened the siege of Hermopolis until King Namart surrendered. He then rescued the besieged Peftuaubast at Heracleopolis and received his homage. Thereafter he proceeded to capture the strongholds that stood between him and Memphis. The great walled city of Memphis, which refused to surrender, was stormed in heavy fighting. Then the rulers of the Delta hastened to surrender; only Tefnakht of Sais still held out. Eventually Tefnakht admitted defeat and, treating through an envoy, made his submission. Loaded with booty, a triumphant Piye sailed home to Napata.

The direct factual style of the inscription makes it a historical document of the first order. It is also the most important in a series of royal inscriptions of the Nubian Twenty-fifth Dynasty.

Introduction

(1) Year 21, first month of the first season, under the majesty of the King of Upper and Lower Egypt, Piye (Piankhy) [beloved-of-Amun], ever living. Command spoken by my majesty:

"Hear what I did, exceeding the ancestors,
I the King, image of god,
Living likeness of Atum!
Who left the womb marked as ruler,
Feared by those greater than he!
His father knew, his mother perceived:
He would be ruler from the egg,[2]

[1] In recent years several scholars reached the conclusion that the name of the king, hitherto read Piankhy, was really Pi or Piye. In the latest discussion of the name Vittmann proposed that, whereas the Nubian form was Pi or Piye, the Egyptians understood it as Piankhy. Thus some scholars now write Pi(ankhy). I have after some hesitation chosen Piye. The reading of the king's name: von Beckerath 1969; Janssen 1968:172; Leclant 1966:152; Parker 1966:111-114; Priese 1968:166-175; Vittmann 1974:12-16.

[1a] [It is within this general historical context that the enigmatic "So" king of Egypt is mentioned in 2 Kgs 17:4. The identification of So is still debated. The following are the possibilities:

1) *Śôʾ* = Osorkon IV. The name "So" is a hypocoristicon of Osorkon. See Kitchen 1986:372-374; Yoyotte 1961.
2) *Śôʾ* = Sais. *Śôʾ* is a rendering of "Sais" or perhaps a *nisbe* derived from the toponym. Hence the king would be Tefnakhte I of Sais. See most recently Redford 1992:346; Christensen 1989; Day 1992.
3) *Śôʾ* = a title. A) = *tʾ* "vizier." See Yeivin 1952; B) *nśw* — "king." See Krauss 1978; Donner 1977:433.
4) *Śôʾ* = Pi(hanky). King *Śôʾ* is to be identified with Pi(hanky), the father of Shabako, the founder of the 25th Nubian Dynasty. See Green 1993; Naʾaman (1990:216) uses the argument of option 3B above and identifies the king as Pi(hanky).] [KLY]

[2] I.e., born to be a ruler. [Gilula 1967 sees in these lines a close parallel to Jer 1:4, 5.] [WWH]

The good god, beloved of gods,
The Son of Re, who acts with his arms,
Piye beloved-of-Amun."

Tefnakht's advance

One came to say to his majesty: "The Chief of the West, the count and grandee in Netjer,[3] Tefnakht, is in the nome of ...,[4] (3) in the nome of Xois,[5] in Hapy,[6] in ...,[7] in Ayn,[8] in Pernub,[9] and in the nome of Memphis. He has conquered the entire West from the coastal marshes to Itj-tawy,[10] sailing south with a numerous army, with the Two Lands united behind him, and the counts and rulers of domains are as dogs at his feet.

"No stronghold has closed [its gates in] the nomes of Upper Egypt. Mer-Atum,[11] Per-Sekhem-kheperre,[12] Hut-Sobk,[13] Permedjed,[14] Tjeknesh,[15] all towns of the West[16] have opened the gates for fear of him. When he turned around to the nomes of the East they opened to him also: Hut-benu,[17] Teudjoi,[18] Hut-nesut,[19] Per-nebtepih.[20]

Now [he is] (5) besieging Hnes.[21] He has encircled it completely,[22] not letting goers go, not letting entrants enter,[a] and fighting every day. He has measured it in its whole circuit. Every count knows his wall.[23] He has made every man besiege his portion, to wit the counts and rulers of domains." His majesty heard [it] with delight, laughing joyously.

Then those chiefs, the counts and generals who were in their towns,[24] sent to his majesty daily, saying: "Have you been silent in order to forget the Southland, the nomes of Upper Egypt, while Tefnakht conquers (all) before him and finds no resistance? Narmart,[25] [ruler of Hermopolis], (7) count of Hutweret,[26] has demolished the wall of Nefrusi.[27] He has thrown down his own town[28] out of fear of him who would seize it for himself in order to besiege another town. Now he has gone to be at his (Tefnakht's) feet; he has rejected the water of his majesty.[29] He stays with him like one of [his men in] the nome of Oxyrhynchos. He (Tefnakht) gives him gifts to his heart's content of everything he has found."

[a] Josh 6:1

Piye orders his troops in Egypt to attack and sends reinforcements

His majesty wrote to the counts and generals who were in Egypt, the commander Purem, and the commander Lemersekny, and every commander of his majesty who was in Egypt: "Enter combat, engage in battle; surround ..., (9) capture its people, its cattle, its ships on the river! Let not the farmers go to the field, let not the plowmen plow. Beset the Hare nome; fight against it daily!" Then they did so.

Then his majesty sent an army to Egypt and charged them strictly:[30] "Do not attack by night in the manner of draughts-playing; fight when one can see.[31] Challenge him to battle from afar. If he proposes to await the infantry and chariotry of

[3] Netjer, not identified with certainty, may be the region of Buto; see Yoyotte 1961:154-155.
[4] The scribe did not fill in the nome sign. Probably the Harpoon nome, the 7th nome of Lower Egypt, in the northwest corner of the Delta, was meant; see Yoyotte 1961:154.
[5] The 6th nome of Lower Egypt.
[6] A name for the double nome of Sais; see Yoyotte 1961:155.
[7] The sign is destroyed; a territory adjacent to Hapy must be meant.
[8] A name for the marshy regions of Imau (or: Iamu), the metropolis of the 3rd nome of Lower Egypt.
[9] This town has not been identified.
[10] The old residence of the Middle Kingdom, south of Memphis. It marked the southern boundary of Tefnakht's domains at the beginning of his new campaign.
[11] Meidum in the Fayyum.
[12] "House of Osorkon I," near El-Lahun and Gurob; see Yoyotte 1961:135, n. 1.
[13] Crocodilopolis, the capital of the Fayyum.
[14] Oxyrhynchos, the metropolis of the 19th nome of Upper Egypt.
[15] A town in the 19th nome of Upper Egypt.
[16] I.e., on the west bank of the Nile. The towns are listed from north to south.
[17] A town in the 18th nome of Upper Egypt.
[18] Town in the 18th nome of Upper Egypt, modern El-Hiba.
[19] Another town in the 18th nome.
[20] Aphroditopolis (modern Atfih), the metropolis of the 22nd nome of Upper Egypt. These four towns on the east bank are listed from south to north, thus showing that Tefnakht had made a circular sweep.
[21] Heracleopolis Magna, the metropolis of the 20th nome of Upper Egypt.
[22] Lit., "He made himself into a tail-in-the-mouth," i.e., he encircled the town like a coiled snake.
[23] I.e., each chief allied with him was encamped before a section of the wall.
[24] I.e., the Eg. petty rulers of Upper Egypt who were loyal to Piye.
[25] Namart of Hermopolis was one of four Eg. rulers who claimed the title "king" at this time. His domain was the Hare nome, the 15th nome of Upper Egypt.
[26] Hutweret is Herwer, an important town in the Hare nome.
[27] Another town in the Hare nome.
[28] The fortress of Nefrusi.
[29] I.e., Namart has joined Tefnakht and repudiated his allegiance to Piye.
[30] Piye's charge to his army was explained by Gardiner 1935.
[31] I.e., they should not attack by stealth as in a game where one party tries to outwit the other.

another town, then sit still until his troops come. Fight when he proposes. Also if he has allies in another town, let (11) them be awaited. The counts whom he brings to help him, and any trusted Libyan troops, let them be challenged to battle in advance, saying: 'You whose name we do not know, who musters the troops! Harness the best steeds of your stable, form your battle line, and know that Amun is the god who sent us!'"[32]

"When you have reached Thebes at Ipet-sut, go into the water. Cleanse yourselves in the river; wear the best linen.[33] Rest the bow; loosen the arrow. Boast not (13) to the lord of might, for the brave has no might without him.[34] He makes the weak-armed strong-armed, so that the many flee before the few, and a single one conquers a thousand men! Sprinkle yourselves with water of his altars; kiss the earth before his face. Say to him:

'Give us the way,
May we fight in the shade of your arm!
The troop you sent, when it charges,
May the many tremble before it!'"

Then they placed themselves on their bellies before his majesty:

"It is your name that makes our strength,
Your counsel brings your army into port;
Your bread is in our bellies on every way,
Your beer (15) quenches our thirst.
It is your valor that gives us strength,
There is dread when your name is recalled;
No army wins with a cowardly leader,
Who is your equal there?

You are the mighty King who acts with his arms,
The chief of the work of war!"

They sailed north and arrived at Thebes; they did as his majesty had said.

Sailing north on the river they met many ships going south with soldiers and sailors, all kinds of fighting troops from Lower Egypt, equipped with weapons of warfare, (17) to fight against his majesty's army. Then a great slaughter was made of them, whose number is unknown. Their troops

b 1 Kgs 11:40, etc.

c Josh 6:1

and ships were captured, and taken as prisoners to where his majesty was.[35]

Battle at Heracleopolis

They proceeded toward Hnes and challenged to battle. List of the counts and kings of Lower Egypt: **check spelling of Hnes**

King Namart and King Iuput.
Chief of the Ma, Sheshonq[b] of Per-Usirnebdjedu[36]
And Great Chief of the Ma, Djedamenefankh of Per-Banebdjedet[37]
And his eldest son, the commander of Per-Thoth-weprehwy.[38]
The troops of Prince Bakennefi and his eldest son, the Count and Chief of the Ma, (19) Nesnaisu of Hesbu.[39]
Every plume-wearing chief of Lower Egypt.
And King Osorkon of Perbast[40] and the district of Ranofer.[41]
All the counts, all the rulers of domains in the west, in the east, and in the isles of the midst were united in their allegiance at the feet of the great Chief of the West, the Ruler of the domains of Lower Egypt, the prophet of Neith, mistress of Sais, the *setem*-priest of Ptah, Tefnakht.

They went forth against them; they made a great slaughter of them, exceedingly great. Their ships on the river were captured. The remnant made a crossing and landed on the west side in the vicinity of Perpeg. At dawn of the next day the troops of his majesty crossed over (21) against them and troops mingled with troops. They slew many of their men and countless horses. Terror befell the remnant and they fled to Lower Egypt from the blow that was great and exceedingly painful.

List of the slaughter made of them. Men: [...][42]

King Namart fled upstream southward when he was told, "Khmun is faced with war from the troops of his majesty; its people and its cattle are being captured." He entered into Un,[43] while his majesty's army was on the river and on the riverbanks (23) of the Hare nome. They heard it and surrounded the Hare nome on its four sides, not letting goers go, not letting entrants enter.[c]

[32] The aim of Piye's charge was that his troops should fight a few large decisive battles rather than many small skirmishes. And he was confident that Amun was on his side.

[33] I take this to be the word *tpy* of *Wb.* 5:292.15-16, rather than *Wb.* 5:291.17.

[34] Gardiner rendered, "Boast not of being lords of might." But *nb*, "lord," is in the sing., and the "lord of might" is Amun, who is referred to in the next sentence.

[35] I.e., to Napata.

[36] Busiris, the metropolis of the 9th nome of Lower Egypt.

[37] Mendes, the metropolis of the 16th nome of Lower Egypt.

[38] Hermopolis Parva, the metropolis of the 15th nome of Lower Egypt.

[39] The 11th nome of Lower Egypt.

[40] King Osorkon IV of Bubastis.

[41] Ranofer has not been definitely localized; see Gomaà 1974:132-134.

[42] A blank space.

[43] Khmun and Un together formed Hermopolis Magna.

Piye resolves to go to Egypt
They wrote to report to the majesty of the King of Upper and Lower Egypt, Piye beloved of Amun, given life, on every attack they had made, on every victory of his majesty. His majesty raged about it like a panther: "Have they left a remnant of the army of Lower Egypt, so as to let some of them escape to report the campaign, instead of killing and destroying the last of them? I swear, as Re loves me, as my father Amun favors me, I shall go north myself! I shall tear down (25) his works. I shall make him abandon fighting forever!"

"When the rites of New Year are performed, and I offer to my father Amun at his beautiful feast, when he makes his beautiful appearance of the New Year, he shall send me in peace to view Amun at his beautiful feast of Ipet.[44] I shall convey him in his processional bark to Southern Ipet at his beautiful feast of 'Night of Ipet,' and the feast of 'Abiding in Thebes,' which Re made for him in the beginning. I shall convey him to his house, to rest on his throne, on the day of 'Bringing in the God,' in the third month of the inundation, second day. And I shall let Lower Egypt taste the taste of my fingers!"

Then the army that was here in (27) Egypt heard of the anger his majesty held against them. They fought against Permedjed of the Oxyrhynchite nome; they captured it like a cloudburst. They wrote to his majesty — his heart was not appeased by it.

Then they fought against "the Crag Great-of-Victories."[45] They found it filled with troops, all kinds of fighters of Lower Egypt. A siege tower was made against it; its wall was overthrown. A great slaughter was made of them, countless numbers, including a son of the Chief of the Ma, Tefnakht. They wrote of it to his majesty — his heart was not appeased by it.

(20) Then they fought against Hut-benu; its interior was opened; his majesty's troops entered it. They wrote to his majesty — his heart was not appeased by it.

d Judg 9:15

Piye goes to Egypt and besieges Hermopolis
First month of the first season, day 9, his majesty went north to Thebes. He performed the feast of Amun at the feast of Ipet. His majesty sailed north to the harbor of the Hare nome. His majesty came out of the cabin of the ship. The horses were yoked, the chariot was mounted, while the grandeur of his majesty attained the Asiatics and every heart trembled before him.

His majesty burst out to (31) revile his troops, raging at them like a panther: "Are you continuing to fight while delaying my orders? It is the year for making an end, for putting fear of me in Lower Egypt, and inflicting on them a great and severe beating!"

He set up camp on the southwest of Khmun. He pressed against it every day. An embankment was made to enclose the wall. A siege tower was set up to elevate the archers as they shot, and the slingers as they hurled stones and killed people there each day.

Days passed, and Un was a stench to the nose, for lack of air to (33) breathe.[46] Then Un threw itself on its belly, to plead before the king. Messengers came and went with all kinds of things beautiful to behold: gold, precious stones, clothes in a chest, the diadem from his head, the uraeus that cast his power,[47] without ceasing for many days to implore his crown.

Then they sent his wife, the royal wife and royal daughter, Nestent, to implore the royal wives, the royal concubines, the royal daughters, and the royal sisters. She threw herself on her belly in the women's house before the royal women: "Come to me, royal wives, royal daughters, royal sisters, that you may appease Horus, lord of the palace, great of power, great of triumph! Grant (35) ....[48]

(51) "Lo, who guides you, who guides you?[49] Who then guides you, who guides you? [You have abandoned] the way of life! Was it the case that heaven rained arrows?[50] I was [content] that Southerners bowed down and Northerners (said), 'Place us in your shade!'[d] Was it bad that ... with

[44] I.e., after celebrating the New Year's feast at Napata, Piye would proceed to Thebes in time for the feast of Ipet (Opet), one of the principal feasts of Amun at Thebes.

[45] A fortress in the 18th nome; cf. Gardiner *AEO* 2:93*.

[46] Priese 1972:124, discussed the various translations of this sentence and proposed to render: "When the third day had begun — Hermopolis having become rotten to the nose in that it lacked the free breath of its nose — Hermopolis placed itself on its belly." I do not find this convincing. Neither the reading "three days" is probable, nor the reading *m sp n nḏm fnd.s*, which is too wordy to suit the terseness and economy of this narrative style. I read *m ḫnm fnd.s*. Furthermore, it is not likely that the decisive result of the siege, i.e., the town's turning too foul to be habitable, would be told in a parenthesis; and *iw* probably introduces the main clause, since this is classical Eg.

[47] I.e., King Namart's crown.

[48] A long lacuna: lines 35-50 are almost entirely destroyed. This missing portion contained the intercession of Piye's women, Piye's acceptance of the surrender of Hermopolis, and King Namart's appearance before him.

[49] Piye is speaking.

[50] Piye makes the point that his rule of Egypt had been benign. He had not oppressed the people and had contented himself with the loyalty of their rulers.

his gifts?[51] The heart is the rudder. It capsizes its owner through that which comes from the wrath of god. It sees fires as coolness .... (55) He is not grown old who is seen with his father. Your nomes are full of children."

He[52] threw himself on his belly before his majesty, [saying: "Be appeased], Horus, lord of the palace! It is your power that has done it to me. I am one of the King's servants who pays taxes into the treasury. ... (57) their taxes. I have done for you more than they." Then he presented silver, gold, lapis lazuli, turquoise, copper, and all kinds of precious stones. The treasury was filled with this tribute. He brought a horse with his right hand, and in his left hand a sistrum of gold and lapis lazuli.[53]

His majesty arose in splendor (59) from his palace and proceeded to the temple of Thoth, lord of Khmun. He sacrificed oxen, shorthorns, and fowl to his father Thoth, lord of Khmun, and the Ogdoad in the temple of the Ogdoad.[54] And the troops of the Hare nome shouted and sang, saying:

"How good is Horus at peace in (61) his town,
The Son of Re, Piye!
You make for us a jubilee,
As you protect the Hare nome!"

His majesty proceeded to the house of King Namart. He went through all the rooms of the palace, his treasury and his storehouse. He (Namart) presented (63) the royal wives and royal daughters to him. They saluted his majesty in the manner of women, while his majesty did not direct his gaze at them.

His majesty proceeded to the stable of the horses and the quarters of the foals. When he saw they had been [left] (65) to hunger he said: "I swear, as Re loves me, as my nose is refreshed by life: that my horses were made to hunger pains me more than any other crime you committed in your recklessness![55] I would teach you to respect your neighbors. (67) Do you not know god's shade is above me and does not let my action fail? Would that another, whoever he might be, had done it for me! I would not have to reprimand him for it.[56] I was fashioned in the womb, created in the egg of the god! (69) The seed of the god is in me! By his *ka*, I act not without him; it is he who commands me to act!"

e 2 Sam 22:6; Ps 18:6

f Judg 9:15

Then his goods were assigned to the treasury, and his granary to the endowment of Amun in Ipet-sut.[57]

Heracleopolis reaffirms its loyalty, other towns surrender

There came the ruler of Hnes Peftuaubast,[58] bearing tribute (71) to Pharaoh: gold, silver, all kinds of precious stones, and the best horses of the stable. He threw himself on his belly before his majesty and said: **check spelling of Hnes above and below**

"Hail to you, Horus, mighty King,
Bull attacking bulls!
The netherworld seized me,[e]
I foundered in darkness,
O you who give me (73) the rays of his face!
I could find no friend on the day of distress,
Who would stand up on battle day,
Except you, O mighty King,
You drove the darkness from me!
I shall serve with my property,
Hnes (75) owes to your dwelling;
You are Harakhti above the immortal stars!
As he is king so are you,
As he is immortal you are immortal;
King of Upper and Lower Egypt, Piye ever living!"

His majesty sailed north to the entrance of the canal beside Re-hone,[59] and found Per-Sekhem-kheperre with its wall raised, its gate closed, and filled with all kinds of fighters of Lower Egypt. Then his majesty sent to them, saying: "O you who live in death, you who live in death; you poor wretches, you who live in death! If the moment passes without your opening to me, you will be counted slain according to the King's judgment. Do not bar the gates of your life, so as to be brought to the block this day! Do not desire death and reject life! (79) ... before the whole land."

Then they sent to his majesty, saying:

"Lo, god's shade[f] is above you,
Nut's Son gave you his arms!
Your heart's plan happens instantly,
Like the word of mouth of god.
Truly, you are born of god,
For we see (it) by the work of your arms!
Lo, your town and its gates
[...];

[51] Perhaps restore: "Was it bad that the King of the Hare nome came with gifts?"
[52] King Namart.
[53] This is how Namart is depicted on the scene at the top of the stela, only the hands are reversed.
[54] The eight primeval gods whose cult center was Hermopolis.
[55] Hornung (1962:115-116) discussed the meaning of *kf³-ib* and proposed "profligacy, recklessness" for this instance. This is suitable here but not in some other cases. I have suggested that two different roots of *kf³* may be involved. See Lichtheim *AEL* 1:77-78, n. 27.
[56] If this is the correct translation, the meaning is obscure.
[57] In all conquered towns Piye allocated part of the booty to Amun of Thebes.
[58] The ruler of Heracleopolis was one of the four rulers who claimed the title "king" and the only one who had remained loyal to Piye.
[59] Modern El-Lahun; cf. Gardiner *AEO* 2:116*.

May entrants enter, goers go,
May his majesty do as he wishes!"

They came out with a son of the Chief of the Ma, Tefnakht. The troops of his majesty entered it, and he did not slay one of all the people he found. (81) [...] and treasurers, in order to seal its possessions. Its treasuries were allocated to the treasury, its granaries as endowment to his father Amun-Re, lord of Thrones-of-the-Two-Lands.

His majesty sailed north. He found Mer-Atum, the house of Sokar, lord of Sehedj, closed and unapproachable. It had resolved to fight. [...]; fear of (his) grandeur sealed their mouth. His majesty sent to them, saying: "Look, two ways are before you; choose as you wish. Open, you live; close, you die.[g] My majesty will not pass by a closed town!" Then they opened immediately. His majesty entered the town. (85) He sacrificed [...], [to] Menhy, foremost of Sehedj. Its treasury was allocated to the treasury, its granary as endowment to Amun in Ipet-sut.

g Deut 30:15

His majesty sailed north to Itj-tawy. He found the rampart closed, the walls filled with valiant troops of Lower Egypt. Then they opened the gates and threw themselves on their bellies before [his majesty, saying to] his majesty:

"Your father gave you his heritage,
Yours are the Two Lands, yours those in it,
Yours is all that is on earth!"

His majesty went to offer a great sacrifice to the gods of this town: oxen, shorthorns, fowl, and everything good and pure. Its storehouse was allocated to the treasury, its granary as endowment to (85) his father Amun-Re.

Capture of Memphis
[His majesty proceeded to] Memphis. He sent to them, saying: "Do not close, do not fight, O home of Shu since the beginning! Let the entrant enter, the goer go; those who would leave shall not be hindered! I shall offer an oblation to Ptah and the gods of Memphis. I shall sacrifice to Sokar in Shetit. I shall see South-of-his-Wall.[60] And I shall sail north in peace! [...]. [The people of] Memphis will be safe and sound; one will not weep over children. Look to the nomes of the South! No one was slain there, except the rebels who had blasphemed god; the traitors were executed."

They closed their fort. They sent out troops against some of his majesty's troops, consisting of artisans, builders, and sailors (87) [who had entered] the harbor of Memphis. And the Chief of Sais[61] arrived in Memphis by night to charge his soldiers, his sailors, all the best of his army, consisting of 8,000 men, charging them firmly:

"Look, Memphis is filled with troops of all the best of Lower Egypt, with barley, emmer, and all kinds of grain, the granaries overflowing; with weapons [of war] of all kinds. A rampart [surrounds it]. A great battlement has been built, a work of skilled craftsmanship. The river surrounds its east side; one cannot fight there. The stables here are filled with oxen; the storehouse is furnished with everything: silver, gold, copper, clothing, incense, honey, resin. I shall go to give gifts to the chiefs of Lower Egypt. I shall open their nomes to them.[62] I shall be (89) [...], [in a few] days I shall return." He mounted a horse (for) he did not trust his chariot,[63] and he went north in fear of his majesty.

At dawn of the next day his majesty arrived at Memphis. When he had moored on its north, he found the water risen to the walls and ships moored at [the houses of] Memphis. His majesty saw that it was strong, the walls were high with new construction, and the battlements manned in strength. No way of attacking it was found. Every man of his majesty's army had his say about some plan of attack. Some said: "Let us blockade (91) [...], for its troops are numerous." Others said: "Make a causeway to it, so that we raise the ground to its wall. Let us construct a siege tower, setting up masts and using sails as walls for it. You should divide it thus on each of its sides with ramparts and [a causeway] on its north, so as to raise the ground to its wall, so that we find a way for our feet."

Then his majesty raged against them like a panther, saying: "I swear, as Re loves me, as my father Amun favors me, ... according to the command of Amun! This is what people say: (93) '... and the nomes of the South opened to him from afar, though Amun had not put (it) in their hearts, and they did not know what he had commanded. He (Amun) made him in order to show his might, to let his grandeur be seen.' I shall seize it like a cloudburst, for [Amun-Re] has commanded me!"

Then he sent his fleet and his troops to attack the harbor of Memphis. They brought him every ship, every ferry, every *shry*-boat, all the many ships that were moored in the harbor of Memphis, with the bow rope fastened to its houses. (95) [There was not] a common soldier who wept among all the troops of his majesty. His majesty himself came to

[60] Ptah.
[61] Tefnakht.
[62] This probably means that Tefnakht would restore to the northern chiefs the towns he had captured from them, in order to gain their help for the defense of Memphis and the Delta.
[63] Gilula (1977:296) points out that *nḥty* is the root *nḥt* "believe, trust," and not *nḥi*, "wish, ask for."

line up the many ships.

His majesty commanded his troops: "Forward against it! Mount the walls! Enter the houses over the river! When one of you enters the wall, no one shall stand in his vicinity, no troops shall repulse you! To pause is vile. We have sealed Upper Egypt; we shall bring Lower Egypt to port. We shall sit down in Balance-of-the Two-Lands!"[64]

Then Memphis was seized as by a cloudburst. Many people were slain in it, or brought as captives to where his majesty was.

Now (97) [when] it dawned on the next day his majesty sent people into it to protect the temples of god for him. The arm was raised over the holy of holies of the gods.[h] Offerings were made to the Council (of the gods) of Memphis. Memphis was cleansed with natron and incense. The priests were set in their places.

His majesty proceeded to the house of [Ptah]. His purification was performed in the robing room. There was performed for him every rite that is performed for a king when he enters the temple. A great offering was made to his father Ptah South-of-his-Wall of oxen, shorthorns, fowl, and all good things. Then his majesty went to his house.

Then all the districts in the region of Memphis heard (it). Hery-pedemy, (99) Peninewe, Tower-of-Byt, Village-of-Byt, they opened the gates and fled in flight, and it was not known where they had gone.

Three rulers surrender

Then came King Iuput,[65] and the Chief of the Ma, Akanosh,[66] and Prince Pediese,[67] and all counts of Lower Egypt, bearing their tribute, to see the beauty of his majesty.

Then the treasuries and granaries of Memphis were allocated as endowment to Amun, to Ptah, and to the Ennead in Memphis.

Piye visits the sanctuaries of Heliopolis

At dawn of the next day his majesty proceeded to the East. (101) An offering was made to Atum in Kheraha,[68] the Ennead in Per-Pesdjet,[69] and the cavern of the gods in it,[70] consisting of oxen, shorthorns, and fowl, that they might give life-prosperity-health to the King of Upper and Lower Egypt, Piye ever living.

His majesty proceeded to On[i] over that mountain of Kheraha on the road of Sep[71] to Kheraha. His majesty went to the camp on the west of Iti.[72] His purification was done: he was cleansed in the pool of Kebeh; his face was bathed in the river of Nun, in which Re bathes his face. He proceeded to the High Sand[73] in On. A great oblation was made on the High Sand in On before the face of Re at his rising, consisting of white oxen, milk, myrrh, incense, and all kinds of (103) sweet-smelling plants.

Going in procession to the temple of Re.[74] Entering the temple with adorations. The chief lector-priest's praising god and repulsing the rebels from the king.[75] Performing the ritual of the robing room; putting on the *sdb*-garment; cleansing him with incense and cold water; presenting him the garlands of the Pyramidion House; bringing him the amulets.

Mounting the stairs to the great window to view Re in the Pyramidion House. The king stood by himself alone. Breaking the seals of the bolts, opening the doors; viewing his father Re in the holy Pyramidion House; adorning[76] the morning-bark of Re and the evening-bark of Atum. Closing the doors, applying the clay, (105) sealing with the king's own seal, and instructing the priests: "I have inspected the seal. No other king who may arise shall enter here." They placed themselves on their bellies before his majesty, saying: "Abide forever without end, Horus beloved of On!"

Entering the temple of Atum. Worshiping the image of his father Atum-Khepri, Great one of On.

Then came King Osorkon[77] to see the beauty of his majesty.

h Exod 30:10, etc.

i Gen 41:45, 50; 46:20

[64] Memphis.

[65] Iuput II, ruler of Leontopolis (*Tꜣ-rmw, Tnt-tmw*), one of the four "kings."

[66] This important Libyan chief ruled in Sebennytos (*Ṯb-nṯr*), the metropolis of the 12th nome of Lower Egypt, and controlled a large territory around it, including the towns of Iseopolis (Per-hebyt) and Diospolis Inferior (Sema-behdet). See Yoyotte 1961:159-161, and Gomaà 1974:69-71. He had not joined Tefnakht's alliance, and along with Iuput and Pediese, he now came to make his submission.

[67] The ruler of Athribis. He too appears to have remained neutral; see Yoyotte 1961:162-163.

[68] A town south of Heliopolis called "Babylon" by the Greeks. See Gardiner *AEO* 2:131*-144*.

[69] Ibid., pp. 141*-142*. Gardiner examined the question whether Per-Pesdjet, the "House of the Ennead," was a place distinct from Kheraha or merely another name for it, and he leaned to the latter view.

[70] The "cavern" means a source of the inundation. In addition to the "twin sources" of the Nile at Elephantine, Kheraha claimed possession of a source.

[71] A god of the region, spelled Sepa in earlier texts.

[72] Name of the canal of Heliopolis.

[73] An often-mentioned sacred place in Heliopolis.

[74] The principal temple of Heliopolis.

[75] A symbolic act.

[76] It is not clear whether the word is *ḏsr* and just what ritual act the king is performing.

[77] Osorkon IV of Bubastis, the last of the four kings to surrender.

Piye holds court at Athribis
At dawn of the next day his majesty proceeded to the harbor at the head of his ships. He crossed over to the harbor of Kemwer.[78] The camp of his majesty was set up on the south of Keheny, in the east (107) of Kemwer.

Then came those kings and counts of Lower Egypt, all the plume-wearing chiefs, all viziers, chiefs, king's friends from the west, the east, and the isles in their midst, to see the beauty of his majesty. Prince Pediese threw himself on his belly before his majesty, saying: "Come to Athribis, that you may see Khentikhety,[79] that Khuyet[80] may protect you, that you may offer an oblation to Horus in his house, of oxen, shorthorns, and fowl. When you enter my house, my treasury will be open to you. I shall present you with my father's possessions. I shall give you gold as much as you wish, (109) turquoise heaped before you, and many horses of the best of the stable, the choicest of the stall."

His majesty proceeded to the house of Horus Khentykhety. An offering of oxen, shorthorns, and fowl was made to his father Horus Khentykhety, lord of Athribis. His majesty went to the house of Prince Pediese. He (Pediese) presented him with silver, gold, lapis lazuli, and turquoise, a great quantity of everything, and clothing of royal linen of every number,[81] couches laid with fine linen, myrrh and ointment in jars, and stallions and mares, all the best of his stable.

He purified himself by a divine oath before these kings and great chiefs of (111) Lower Egypt: "Anyone who hides his horses and conceals his wealth[82] shall die the death of his father! I have said this in order that you bear out your servant with all that you know of me. Tell if I have concealed from his majesty anything of my father's house: gold bars, precious stone, vessels of all kinds, armlets, bracelets of gold, necklaces, collars wrought with precious stones, amulets for every limb, headbands, earrings, all royal adornments, all vessels for the king's purification of gold and precious stones. All these I have presented (113) to the King, and garments of royal linen by the thousands of the very best of my house. I know you will be satisfied with it. Proceed to the stable, choose what you wish, all the horses you desire!" Then his majesty did so.

Then said these kings and counts to his majesty: "Let us go to our towns to open our treasuries, that we may choose according to what your heart may desire, and bring to you the best of our stables, the finest of our horses." Then his majesty did so.

List of the northern rulers
List of their names:[83]

King Osorkon in Perbast and the district of Ranofer,[84]
King Iuput in Tentremu and Taan,[85]
Count Djedamenefankh (115) in Per-Banebdjedet[86] and Granary-of-Re,[87]
His eldest son, the general in Per-Thoth-weprehwy,[88] Ankh-hor,
Count Akanosh in Tjeb-neter, Per-hebyt, and Sema-behdet,[89]
Count and Chief of the Ma, Patjenfi in Per-Sopd and Granary-of-Memphis,[90]
Count and Chief of the Ma, Pemai in Per-Usirnebdjedu,[91]
Count and Chief of the Ma, Nesnaisu in Hesbu,[92]
Count and Chief of the Ma, Nekhthor-neshnu in Per-gerer,[93]
Chief of the Ma, Pentweret,
Chief of the Ma, Pentbekhent,[94]
Prophet of Horus, lord of Khem,[95] (117) Pedihorsomtus,
Count Herbes in Per-Sakhmet-nebetsat and in

[78] The 10th nome of Lower Egypt, the metropolis of which was Athribis.
[79] The principal god of Athribis who was identified with Horus.
[80] A local goddess.
[81] Perhaps a reference to the number of threads in a fabric by which its fineness was determined.
[82] Assuming that *š*ꜣ*w* "worth, value, weight," could be used in the sense of a person's material worth, i.e., his wealth.
[83] The list is arranged according to rank.
[84] See nn. 40-41 and 77.
[85] See n. 65. Taan has not been identified.
[86] See n. 37.
[87] Location uncertain. See Gomaà 1974:88.
[88] Hermopolis Parva, see n. 37. On the two rulers see Gomaà 1974:86-89.
[89] See n. 66.
[90] Patjenfi's residence, Per-Sopd (modern Saft el-Henna) was the metropolis of the 22nd nome of Lower Egypt. His other town, "Granary-of-Memphis," has not been localized. This chief had not participated in Tefnakht's alliance. On the rulers of Per-Sopd, see Gomaà 1974:101-104.
[91] Pemai was the ruler of Busiris. His predecessor, Sheshonq, had been a member of Tefnakht's coalition. On these dynasts of Busiris, see Yoyotte 1961:165-172, and Gomaà 1974:60-67.
[92] See n. 39. Nesnaisu had been an important member of Tefnakht's coalition.
[93] This chief has not been mentioned previously. His town in the eastern Delta has not been localized with certainty; see Gomaà 1974:105-106.
[94] Two minor chiefs not previously mentioned.
[95] Khem = Letopolis was the metropolis of the 2nd nome of Lower Egypt.

Per-Sakhmet-nebetrehsa,[96]
Count Djedkhiu in Khentnefer,[97]
Count Pebes in Kheraha and Per-Hapy,[98]

with all their good tribute [of] gold, silver, [precious stones], couches laid with fine linen, myrrh in (119) jars, [...] of good value, horses [...]

[...] [after] this one came to tell (121) his majesty: "[... the wall ...]. He has set fire to [his] treasury [and to the ships] on the river. He has garrisoned Mesed (123) with soldiers ...."[99] Then his majesty sent soldiers of his to see what was happening there, he being the protector of Prince Pediese. They returned to report (125) to his majesty, saying: "We have slain every man we found there." Then his majesty gave it (the town) to Prince Pediese as a gift.

Tefnakht announces his submission

The Chief of the Ma, Tefnakht, heard it[100] (127), and a messenger was sent to where his majesty was with cajoling words, saying: "Be gracious! I cannot see your face in the days of shame; I cannot stand before your flame; I dread your grandeur! For you are Nubti, foremost of the Southland,[101] and Mont, (129) the mighty bull! Whatever town you turn your face to, you will not be able to find your servant there, until I have reached the islands of the sea! For I fear your wrath on account of those fiery words which are hostile to me!"

"Is your majesty's heart (131) not cooled by the things you did to me? While I am under a just reproach, you did not smite me in accordance with (my) crime. Weigh in the balance, count by weight, and multiply it against me threefold! (But) leave the seed, that you may gather it in time. Do not cut down (133) the grove to its roots! Have mercy! Dread of you is in my body; fear of you is in my bones!"

"I sit not at the beer feast; the harp is not brought for me. I eat the bread of the hungry; I drink the water of (135) the thirsty, since the day you heard my name! Illness is in my bones, my head is bald, my clothes are rags, till Neith is appeased toward me! Long is the course you led against me, and your face is against me yet! It is a year (137) that has purged my *ka* and cleansed your servant of his fault! Let my goods be received into the treasury: gold and all precious stones, the best of the horses, and payment of every kind.[102] Send me (139) a messenger quickly, to drive the fear from my heart! Let me go to the temple in his presence, to cleanse myself by a divine oath!"

His majesty sent the chief lector-priest Pediamennest-tawy and the commander Purem. He (Tefnakht) presented (141) him with silver and gold, clothing and all precious stones. He went to the temple; he praised god; he cleansed himself by a divine oath, saying: "I will not disobey the King's command. I will not thrust aside (143) his majesty's words. I will not do wrong to a count without your knowledge. I will only do what the King said. I will not disobey what he has commanded." Then his majesty's heart was satisfied with it.

Final surrenders, Piye returns to Nubia

One came to say (145) to his majesty: "Hut-Sobk[103] has opened its gate; Meten[104] has thrown itself on its belly. No nome is shut against his majesty, of the nomes of the south and the north. The west, the east, and the islands in the midst are on their bellies in fear of him, (147) and are sending their goods to where his majesty is, like the subjects of the palace."

At dawn of the next day there came the two rulers of Upper Egypt and the two rulers of Lower Egypt, the uraeus wearers,[105] to kiss the ground to the might of (149) his majesty. Now the kings and counts of Lower Egypt who came to see his majesty's beauty, their legs were the legs of women. They could not enter the palace because they were uncircumcised[j] (151) and were eaters of fish, which is an abomination to the palace. But King Namart entered the palace because he was clean and did not eat fish. The three stood (153) there while the one entered the palace.

Then the ships were loaded with silver, gold, copper, and clothing; everything of Lower Egypt, every product of Syria, and all plants of god's land.[106] His majesty (155) sailed south, his heart joyful, and all those near him shouting. West and East took up the announcement, shouting around his majesty. This was their song of jubilation:

"O mighty ruler, O mighty ruler,
(157) Piye, mighty ruler!

j Gen 17:14; Exod 12:48; 1 Sam 17:26; Isa 52:1

[96] Two fortresses in the 2nd nome.
[97] A town in the nome of Memphis; see Gardiner *AEO* 2:120*-122*, and Gomaà 1974:51.
[98] Twin towns south of Heliopolis; see Gardiner *AEO* 2:131*-144.
[99] I.e., Tefnakht had occupied the town of Mesed (Mosdai) north of Athribis, on the border of Pediese's realm.
[100] When Tefnakht heard that the resistance of Mesed had been crushed he surrendered but without appearing in person.
[101] The god Seth.
[102] Or, "equipped with everything," referring to the horses.
[103] See n. 13.
[104] The nome of Aphroditopolis, the 22nd nome of Upper Egypt.
[105] The four kings: Namart, Peftuaubast, Iuput II, and Osorkon IV.
[106] This term for foreign regions south and east of Egypt seems to refer specifically to wooded areas. It could also be employed for woodlands within Egypt, as in the "Victory Stela of Psamtik II" (see Lichtheim *AEL* 2:86, n. 2).

You return having taken Lower Egypt,
You made bulls into women!
Joyful is the mother who bore you,
The man who begot you!
The valley dwellers[107] worship her,
The cow (159) that bore the bull!
You are eternal,
Your might abides,
O ruler loved of Thebes!"

[107] The inhabitants of Upper Egypt.

REFERENCES

Text: Mariette 1872-89 pls. 1-6. *Urk. III*, 1-56. Additional fragments: Loukianoff 1926:86-89 and 2 pls.; Dunham 1970:12, 48, 77-81. Translations: Breasted 1906-07 4:§§796-883; Bresciani 1969:470-484; Lichtheim *AEL* 3:66-84 (reproduced here). Studies: Baer 1973:4-25; Gardiner 1935:219-223; Gomaà 1974; Kitchen 1986:362-398; Logan and Westenholz 1971-72:111-119; Priese 1972:16-32, 99-124; Yoyotte 1961:121-181.

B. MORTUARY INSCRIPTIONS

1. PYRAMID TEXTS

PYRAMID TEXTS 213 AND 219 (2.8)
("The Conquest of Death")

Robert K. Ritner

First carved in the Fifth Dynasty tomb of Unas (ca. 2350 BCE), the collection of 759 spells known as the "Pyramid Texts" was originally restricted to royal use, appearing in varying numbers in the pyramids of nine kings and queens of the Sixth to Eighth Dynasties. The texts stress the divinity and immortality of the monarch, and provide the earliest extensive commentary on the role of Osiris, the god of the dead. In spell 213, the individual body parts of the deceased are identified with divine counterparts, a technique that was to become a standard feature of Egyptian "magico-religious" practice.[1] The resultant image of the king is as an anthropomorphic Anubis, with the limbs of the primordial creator, Atum. In spell 219, the fate of the king is paired directly with that of the revived Osiris, initiating another fundamental technique of ritual pronouncements. Implicit here, though quite explicit elsewhere, is the threat that injury to the king would result in injury to the gods.[2]

Pyramid Text 213 (§§134-135)
Hail, King Unas! Not dead have you gone forth! Living have you gone forth! Be seated upon the throne of Osiris with your sceptre in your hand, so that you might issue commands to the living, and with your lotus-bud sceptre in your hand, so that commands might be issued to those whose places are secret ("the dead"). Your arm(s) are as (those of) Atum; your shoulders are as (those of) Atum; you belly is as (that of) Atum; your back is as (that of) Atum; your posterior is (that of) Atum; your legs are as (those of) Atum; your face is as (that of) Anubis. May you encircle the Mounds of Horus; may your encircle the Mounds of Seth.[3]

Pyramid Text 219 (§§167-193)
Recitation:
O Atum, this one is that (great-grand)son of yours, Osiris, whom you have caused that he be healthy and that he live. As he lives, so this king Unas lives. He doesn't die — this king Unas doesn't die. He doesn't perish — this king Unas doesn't perish. He doesn't mourn — this king Unas doesn't mourn.[4] He mourns — this king Unas mourns.

O Shu, this one is that (grand)son of yours, Osiris, whom you have caused that he be healthy and that he live. As he lives, so this king Unas lives. He doesn't die — this king Unas doesn't die. He doesn't perish — this king Unas doesn't perish. He doesn't mourn — this king Unas doesn't mourn. He mourns — this king Unas mourns.

O Tefnut, this one is that (grand)son of yours, Osiris, whom you have caused that he be healthy and that he live. As he lives, so this king Unas lives. He doesn't die — this king Unas doesn't die. He doesn't perish — this king Unas doesn't perish. He doesn't mourn — this king Unas doesn't mourn. He mourns — this king Unas mourns.

O Geb, this one is that son of yours, Osiris, whom you have caused that he be healthy and that he live. As he lives, so this king Unas lives. He doesn't die — this king Unas doesn't die. He doesn't perish — this king Unas doesn't perish. He doesn't mourn — this king Unas doesn't mourn. He mourns — this king Unas mourns.

O Nut, this one is that son of yours, Osiris, whom you have caused that he be healthy and that he live. As he lives, so this king Unas lives. He doesn't die — this king Unas doesn't die. He doesn't perish — this king Unas doesn't perish. He doesn't mourn — this king Unas doesn't mourn. He mourns — this king Unas mourns.

O Isis, this one is that brother of yours, Osiris,

[1] See Massart 1959 and Ritner 1993:40.

[2] For such "threats," see Grapow 1911; Sauneron 1951; Ritner 1993:22 and the references indexed on 311.

[3] The "tells" or "settlements" of Horus and Seth denote the fertile and desert regions allotted respectively to these deities. For the notion of "encircling" as "controlling" mounds and other territory, see Ritner 1993:57-67. Following Sethe, earlier translators have preferred: "The Mounds of Horus go about for (= 'serve') you. The Mounds of Seth go about for (='serve') you."

[4] Or "As he doesn't die — this king Unas doesn't die." The negative statements in this passage are taken as future forms in Allen 1984: 130.

whom you have caused that he be healthy and that he live. As he lives, so this king Unas lives. He doesn't die — this king Unas doesn't die. He doesn't perish — this king Unas doesn't perish. He doesn't mourn — this king Unas doesn't mourn. He mourns — this king Unas mourns.

O Seth, this one is that brother of yours, Osiris, who has been caused that he be healthy and that he live and that he punish you.[5] As he lives, so this king Unas lives. He doesn't die — this king Unas doesn't die. He doesn't perish — this king Unas doesn't perish. He doesn't mourn — this king Unas doesn't mourn. He mourns — this king Unas mourns.

O Nephthys, this one is that brother of yours, Osiris, whom you have caused that he be healthy and that he live. As he lives, so this king Unas lives. He doesn't die — this king Unas doesn't die. He doesn't perish — this king Unas doesn't perish. He doesn't mourn — this king Unas doesn't mourn. He mourns — this king Unas mourns.

O Thoth, this one is that brother of yours, Osiris, who has been caused that he be healthy and that he live and that he punish you. As he lives, so this king Unas lives. He doesn't die — this king Unas doesn't die. He doesn't perish — this king Unas doesn't perish. He doesn't mourn — this king Unas doesn't mourn. He mourns — this king Unas mourns.

O Horus, this one is that father of yours, Osiris, whom you have caused that he be healthy and that he live. As he lives, so this king Unas lives. He doesn't die — this king Unas doesn't die. He doesn't perish — this king Unas doesn't perish. He doesn't mourn — this king Unas doesn't mourn. He mourns — this king Unas mourns.

O Great Ennead, this one is that Osiris, whom you have caused that he be healthy and that he live. As he lives, so this king Unas lives. He doesn't die — this king Unas doesn't die. He doesn't perish — this king Unas doesn't perish. He doesn't mourn — this king Unas doesn't mourn. He mourns — this king Unas mourns.

O Little Ennead, this one is that Osiris, whom you have caused that he be healthy and that he live. As he lives, so this king Unas lives. He doesn't die — this king Unas doesn't die. He doesn't perish — this king Unas doesn't perish. He doesn't mourn — this king Unas doesn't mourn. He mourns — this king Unas mourns.

O Nut(?),[6] this one is that son of yours, Osiris, regarding whom you have said: "One has been (re)born to your[7] father," for whom you have wiped his mouth when his mouth was opened by his son Horus, whom he loves, when his limbs were numbered by the gods. As he lives, so this king Unas lives. He doesn't die — this king Unas doesn't die. He doesn't perish — this king Unas doesn't perish. He doesn't mourn — this king Unas doesn't mourn. He mourns — this king Unas mourns.

[Address to Osiris in his various forms]

In your name of "He who is in Heliopolis," who endures enduringly in his enduring necropolis. As he lives, so this king Unas lives. He doesn't die — this king Unas doesn't die. He doesn't perish — this king Unas doesn't perish. He doesn't mourn — this king Unas doesn't mourn. He mourns — this king Unas mourns.

In your name of "He who is in the Busirite nome," chief of his nomes. As he lives, so this king Unas lives. He doesn't die — this king Unas doesn't die. He doesn't perish — this king Unas doesn't perish. He doesn't mourn — this king Unas doesn't mourn. He mourns — this king Unas mourns.

In your name of "He who is in The Mansion of Selqet," the pacified spirit. As he lives, so this king Unas lives. He doesn't die — this king Unas doesn't die. He doesn't perish — this king Unas doesn't perish. He doesn't mourn — this king Unas doesn't mourn. He mourns — this king Unas mourns.

In your name of "He who is in the God's Booth,"[8] who is within the fumigation, he of the coffer, he of the chest, he of the sack. As he lives, so this king Unas lives. He doesn't die — this king Unas doesn't die. He doesn't perish — this king Unas doesn't perish. He doesn't mourn — this king Unas doesn't mourn. He mourns — this king Unas mourns.

In your name of "He who is in the Mansion of the *pꜣꜥr*-wood mace." As he lives, so this king Unas lives. He doesn't die — this king Unas doesn't die. He doesn't perish — this king Unas doesn't perish. He doesn't mourn — this king Unas doesn't mourn. He mourns — this king

[5] Seth, in company with Thoth, is punished for the murder of Osiris.

[6] The signs are unclear, and may indicate the tomb addressed as "City" (so Faulkner 1969:41) or the goddess of the lower heaven, Naunet (so Sethe and, with hesitation, Wilson *ANET* 33). A slight correction in carving would yield Nut, noted in § 171 as the proper mother of Osiris.

[7] Pl.

[8] The embalming booth.

Unas mourns.

In your name of "He who is in Orion," with your season in heaven and your season on earth. O Osiris, turn your face that you might look at this king Unas, your effective seed that came forth from you. As he lives, so this king Unas lives. He doesn't die — this king Unas doesn't die. He doesn't perish — this king Unas doesn't perish. He doesn't mourn — this king Unas doesn't mourn. He mourns — this king Unas mourns.

In your name of "He who is in Dep." Your hand is around the offering, your daughter. Provide yourself with it. As he lives, so this king Unas lives. He doesn't die — this king Unas doesn't die. He doesn't perish — this king Unas doesn't perish. He doesn't mourn — this king Unas doesn't mourn. He mourns — this king Unas mourns.

In your name of "He who is in the Mansion of the Great Cow." Your hands are around the offering, your daughter. Provide yourself with it. As he lives, so this king Unas lives. He doesn't die — this king Unas doesn't die. He doesn't perish — this king Unas doesn't perish. He doesn't mourn — this king Unas doesn't mourn. He mourns — this king Unas mourns.

In your name of "He who is in Hermopolis Magna." Your hands are around the offering, your daughter. Provide yourself with it. As he lives, so this king Unas lives. He doesn't die — this king Unas doesn't die. He doesn't perish — this king Unas doesn't perish. He doesn't mourn — this king Unas doesn't mourn. He mourns — this king Unas mourns.

In your name of "He who is in Hermopolis Parva." Your hands are around the offering, your daughter. Provide yourself with it. As he lives, so this king Unas lives. He doesn't die — this king Unas doesn't die. He doesn't perish — this king Unas doesn't perish. He doesn't mourn — this king Unas doesn't mourn. He mourns — this king Unas mourns.

In your name of "He who is in the City of Lakes." What you have eaten is the Eye (of Horus); your belly is encircled[9] under it. Your son Horus has released it for you so that you might live by means of it. As he lives, so this king Unas lives. He doesn't die — this king Unas doesn't die. He doesn't perish — this king Unas doesn't perish. He doesn't mourn — this king Unas doesn't mourn. He mourns — this king Unas mourns.

The body of this king Unas is your body. The flesh of this king Unas is your flesh. The bones of this king Unas are your bones. As you go, so goes this king Unas. As this king Unas goes, so go you.

[9] Signifying "protected." Following Sethe, translators have suggested "rounded out," meaning "to be full."

REFERENCES

Texts and Translations: Sethe 1908:80-81, 93-111; 1935:1-4, 72-99; Faulkner 1969:40-41, 46-48; Wilson 1969:32-33.

2. COFFIN TEXTS

COFFIN TEXT 261 (2.9)
("The Deceased as Divine Magician")

Robert K. Ritner

This spell provides the longest Egyptian theological discussion of Heka, eldest son of the creator and embodiment of the deity's ineluctable generative and destructive power (*heka*), conventionally termed "magic." By direct identification with Heka, the deceased controls the underlying force of the universe and gains command over the gods themselves.

TO BECOME THE GOD HEKA.

O noble ones who are before the Lord of the universe, behold, I have come before you. Respect me in accordance with what you know. I am he whom the Unique Lord made before two things ("duality") had yet come into being in this land by his sending forth his unique Eye when he was alone, by the going forth from his mouth, when his myriads of *ka*-spirits were the protection of his companions,[1] when he spoke with Khepri and himself that he might be more powerful than he, when he took authoritative Logos (Hu) upon his mouth.

I am indeed the son of Him who gave birth to the universe.[2] I am the protection of that which the Unique Lord ordained. I am he who caused the Ennead to live. I am one who does what he wishes, the father of the gods, whose standard is exalted, who endows a god in accordance with that which He who gave birth to the universe[3] has ordained, the noble god who eats, who speaks with his mouth. Be silent for me; Bow down to me! Shod have I come, O bulls of heaven. In this my great dignity of "Lord of *ka*-Spirits," heir of Re-Atum, have I seated myself, O bulls of heaven.

I have come specifically that I might take my seat and that I might receive my dignity; for to me belonged the universe before you gods had yet come into being. Descend, you who have come in the end! I am Heka.

[1] A var. adds: "who shone in his Eye."
[2] Or "who gave birth to Atum." A var. adds: "who was born before his mother yet existed."
[3] Or "who gave birth to Atum."

REFERENCES

Text: de Buck 1947:382-389. Translations and Discussions: Ritner 1993:17; Faulkner 1973: 199-201; Barguet 1986:489-490.

COFFIN TEXT 159 (2.10)
("Spell for Knowing the Souls of the Easterners")

Robert K. Ritner

Depicting the wonders of the region from which the sun rises, this spell (with its parallel Coffin Text 161 and descendants Book of the Dead 109 and 149b) details the otherworldly paradise known as "The Field of Reeds" where both the grain and the blessed inhabitants are giants in size.

ENTERING AND EXITING FROM THE EASTERN GATES OF HEAVEN AMONG THE FOLLOWERS OF RE. KNOWING THE SOULS OF THE EASTERNERS.[1]

I know that central gate[2] from which Re exits in the east - with its south as the Lake of Water-fowl, in the place where Re sails by the wind, with its north as the Pools of Geese, in the place where Re sails by rowing.[3] I am the guardian of the halyard in the boat of the god. I am one who rows without wearying in the bark of Re.[4]

I know those two sycamore trees that are of turquoise, between which Re exits, which go casting shade at every eastern gate from which Re shines. I know that Field of Reeds of Re. The wall that is around it is of iron. The height of its barley is four cubits.[5] Its ear is one cubit. Its stalk is three cubits.[6] Its emmer wheat is seven cubits. Its ear is two cubits. Its stalk is five cubits. It is the horizon dwellers, nine cubits in their height,[7] who reap it beside the Souls of the Easterners.

I KNOW THE SOULS OF THE EASTERNERS. THEY ARE HARAKHTY, THE *KHURER*-CALF, AND THE MORNING STAR.[8]

[1] Common var.: "I know the souls of the Easterners."
[2] Var. adds: "of heaven."
[3] As on the earthly Nile, one travels south by wind and sail and north by current and rowing.
[4] The deceased claims a pivotal role in the solar bark, using either method of navigation.
[5] Common var.: "five cubits."
[6] Common var.: "four cubits."
[7] Common var.: "horizon dwellers of nine cubits."
[8] Common var.: "ONE (lit., "IT") IS HARAKHTY. ONE IS THE *KHURER*-CALF. ONE IS THE MORNING STAR."

REFERENCES

Text: de Buck 1938:363-372. Translations and Discussions: Wilson *ANET* 33; Faulkner 1973: 137-138; Barguet 1986:576.

3. THE BOOK OF THE DEAD

BOOK OF THE DEAD 109 (2.11)
(Variant of Coffin Text 159)

Robert K. Ritner

The New Kingdom vignette depicts the deceased standing behind the spotted *Khurer*-calf, with his arms raised in daily adoration of a seated Re-Harakhty. The spell is a counterpart to Coffin Text 160 (*COS* 1.21) and Book of the Dead 108 for "Knowing the Souls of the Westerners." For discussion, see Sethe 1924:1-20; and the bibliography in Hornung 1979:482.

As in the earlier Coffin Texts, the remarkable size of the underworld grain varies between sources, though the total height should equal the measure of the ear added to that of the stalk. Barley of five cubits (at 20.6 in. or 523 mm per cubit) would be over eight feet (2.615 m), while emmer of seven cubits would be just under twelve feet tall (3.661 m). Comparison of the Coffin Text and Book of the Dead versions shows that the latter follow many of the "variant" readings in the earlier source.

SPELL FOR KNOWING THE SOULS OF THE EASTERNERS.

It is NN who will say: "I know that eastern gate of heaven whose south is the Lake of Waterfowl, with its north as the Pool of Geese, in the place where Re sails by wind and by rowing. I am the guardian[1] of the halyards in the boat of the god. I am one who rows without wearying in the bark of Re.

I know those two sycamore trees of turquoise, between which Re exits, which go casting shadows at every eastern gate from which Re exits. I know the Field of Reeds. Its wall is of iron. Its barley is five cubits. Its ear is two cubits. Its stalk is three cubits.[2] Its emmer wheat is seven cubits.[3] Its ear is four cubits.[4] Its stalk is three cubits. It is the blessed spirits, each one of nine cubits in height, who reap it beside the Souls of the Easterners.

I know the souls of the Easterners. One is Harakhty. One is the *Khurer*-calf. One is the Morning Star.

Adoring Re every day. NN has built the city of the god. I know it. I know its name. Its name is Field of Reeds.

[1] Var.: "one who tends the halyards."
[2] Var.: list barley of seven cubits, with a stalk of three or five cubits.
[3] Variants include: "four" or "eight cubits."
[4] Var.: "three cubits."

REFERENCES

Text: Naville 1886:247-248. Translations and Discussions: Barguet 1967:143; Allen 1974:86; Hornung 1979:209-210; and Faulker 1985:102.

BOOK OF THE DEAD 125 (2.12)
("The Negative Confession")

Robert K. Ritner

The most famous of all Book of the Dead chapters, Spell 125 contains the celebrated protestation of innocence by the deceased before an underworld tribunal of forty-two gods, corresponding to the like-numbered nomes, or provinces, of Egypt. The duality of the "Two Truths" also reflects geographical, not ethical, considerations, as the goddesses correspond to the dual nature of the Egyptian kingdom, with two regions (Upper and Lower Egypt), royal titles, tutelary deities, insignia, etc. Although Spell 125 does not specifically mention the weighing of the heart before this tribunal and its overseer Osiris, god of the dead,[1] the accompanying vignette regularly depicts this *psychostasis*. The address by the deceased serves as a preamble to this pivotal event, purifying him from all misdeeds (literally, "things protected against/excluded") that he may in fact have done. Since the list of

[1] Though surely indicated by "that day of the reckoning of characters in the presence of Wennefer" and by the placing of "the scale in its proper position in the Land of Silence."

infractions includes seemingly unavoidable actions such as winking, impatience, aggressiveness and wading in flowing water, as well as all forms of sexual activity, this "ethical code" is not absolute, but reflects restrictions and abstinence preparatory for entrance into a sacred space and state.

Following two declarations of innocence, the reciter defends his knowledge of religious mysteries in response to hostile questions posed by the constituent elements of the judgment hall itself. While cryptic, these responses detail ritual enactments of the mysteries of Osiris, slain by the severed leg of Seth, discovered in Phoenician Byblos, interred, shattered and scattered. The concluding rubric provides instructions for utilizing Spell 125 in ritual mysticism by the living. Attested from the Eighteenth Dynasty onward, Spell 125 survives well into the Hellenistic period, when it appears in a Demotic funerary papyrus written in the reign of Nero and in Greek translation as an initiatory recitation for priestly induction.

WHAT IS SAID WHEN ARRIVING AT THIS HALL OF TWO TRUTHS, PURGING NN OF ALL MISDEEDS THAT HE HAS DONE AND SEEING THE FACES OF THE GODS.[2]

RECITATION BY NN: "Hail to you, great god, Lord of the Two Truths! I have come before you, my lord, just so that you might bring me so that I might see your beauty. I know you and I know your name and the names of the forty-two gods who are with you in this Hall of the Two Truths, who live on those who preserve evil, who swallow their blood on that day of the reckoning of characters in the presence of Wennefer.[3] Behold, The Two Daughters, His Two Eyes, {Lord} of Truth is your name. Behold, I have come before you bringing to you Truth, having repelled for you falsehood.

I have not committed wrongdoing against anyone.[a]
I have not mistreated cattle.[4]
I have not done injustice in the place of Truth.
I do not know that which should not be.
I have not done evil.
I have not daily made labors in excess of what should be done for me.
My name has not reached the bark of the Governor (i.e., Re).[5]
I have not debased a god.[6]
I have not deprived an orphan.
I have not done that which the gods abominate.
I have not slandered a servant to his superior.
I have not caused pain.[7]
I have not caused weeping.
I have not killed.
I have not commanded to kill.
I have not made suffering for anyone.
I have not diminished the offering loaves in the temples.
I have not damaged the offering cakes of the gods.
I have not stolen the cakes of the blessed dead.
I have not copulated.[8]
I have not been lascivious.[9]
I have not added to nor have I subtracted from the offering measure.
I have not subtracted from the aroura measure.[10 b]
I have not encroached upon fields.[11]
I have not added to the weight of the balance.
I have not tampered with the plummet of the scales.[b]
I have not taken milk from the mouths of children.
I have not deprived the flocks of their pasturage.
I have not snared birds of the branches of the gods.
I have not trapped fish in their marshes.
I have not diverted water in its season.
I have not erected a dam against flowing water.
I have not extinguished a fire at its critical moment.
I have not neglected the days concerning their meat offerings.
I have not driven away the cattle of the god's property.
I have not stopped a god in his procession.
I am pure, I am pure, I am pure, I am pure!

My purity is the purity of that great phoenix that is in Heracleopolis, because I am indeed that nose of the Lord of breath, who vivifies all the subjects on that day of filling the Eye of Horus in Heliopolis in the second month of winter, last day, in the presence of the Lord of this land. I am one who has seen the filling of the Eye of Horus in Heliopolis. Evil shall not happen against me in this land or in this Hall of the Two Truths

a Job 31

b-b Lev 19:35; Deut 25:13-16; Amos 8:5; Micah 6:10; Prov 11:1; 20:10

[2] Variants: "Spell for descending to the Hall of the Two Truths {and learning what is in it} by NN."
[3] "The Perfect Being," an epithet of Osiris, now surviving as the surname Onofrio.
[4] Common var.: "I have not mistreated associates."
[5] Var.: "Governor of slaves."
[6] Var.: "I have not debased a deed of the king in my time."
[7] Common var.: "I have not caused hunger."
[8] Var.: "I have not copulated with a boy."
[9] Var.: "I have not been lascivious in the sanctuary of my local god."
[10] Var.: I have not subtracted from the palm-measure (1/7 of a cubit)."
[11] Var.: "I have not falsified the half-aroura of field."

because I know the names of the gods who are in it, the followers of the great god.[12]

O Wide-of-Stride, who has come forth from Heliopolis, I have not committed wrongdoing.

O Embracer-of-Fire, who has come forth from Egyptian Babylon, I have not robbed.

O Beaky,[13] who has come forth from Hermopolis, I have not been envious.

O Swallower-of-Shadows, who has come forth from the cavern, I have not stolen.

O Rough of Face, who has come forth from the Memphite necropolis, I have not killed people.

O Twin-Lions, who has come forth from heaven, I have not damaged the offering measure.

O He-Whose-Eyes-Are-Flint, who has come forth from Letopolis, I have not committed crookedness.

O Firey-One, who has come forth backwards, I have not stolen a god's property.

O Smasher-of-Bones, who has come forth from Heracleopolis, I have not told lies.

O Sender-of-Flames, who has come forth from Memphis, I have not seized food.

O Cavern-dweller, who has come forth from the West, I have not been sullen.

O White-Toothed-One, who has come forth from the Faiyum, I have not transgressed.[14]

O Eater-of-Blood,[15] who has come forth from the slaughtering-block, I have not slain sacred cattle.

O Eater-of-Entrails, who has come forth from the Court of Thirty, I have not committed usury.[16]

O Lord of Truth, who has come forth from The-Place-of-the-Two-Truths, I have not robbed bread-rations.

O Wanderer, who has come forth from Bubastis, I have not eavesdropped.[17]

O Pale-One, who has come forth from Heliopolis, I have not blabbered.[18]

O Doubly-Evil-Viper, who has come forth from Busiris, I have not disputed except concerning my own property.

O *Wamemti*-Viper, who has come forth from the place of execution, I have not copulated with a man's wife.[19]

O He-Who-Sees-That-Which-He-Has-Brought-Away, who has come forth from the House of Min, I have not been lascivious.

O Chief of the Nobles, who has come forth from Kom el-Hîsn, I have not caused terror.

O Wrecker, who has come forth from Xois, I have not transgressed.

O Disturber, who has come forth from the sanctuary, I have not been hot-tempered.[20]

O Child, who has come forth from the Heliopolitan Nome, I have not turned a deaf ear to words of truth.

O Proclaimer of Speech, who has come forth from Wensi, I have not made disturbance.

O Bastet, who has come forth from the shrine, I have not winked.[21]

O He-Whose-Face-Is-Behind-Him, who has come forth from the pit, I have not masturbated; I have not copulated with a catamite.[22]

O Hot-Footed-One, who has come forth from the dusk, I have not dissembled.[23]

O Dark-One, who has come forth from the darkness, I have not reviled.

O He-Who-Brings-Away-His-Offering, who has come forth from Sais, I have not been aggressive.[24]

O Lord of Faces, who has come forth from the Heroonopolite Nome, I have not been impatient.[25]

O Accuser, who has come forth from Wetenet, I have not transgressed my nature; I have not washed out a god.[26]

O Lord of Horns, who has come forth from Siut, I have not been verbose in matters.

O Nefertum, who has come forth from Memphis, I have not sinned; I have not done wrong.

O He-Who-Is-Not-Abandoned, who has come forth from Busiris, I have not reviled the king.

O He-Who-Has-Acted-According-to-His-Heart, who has come forth from Antaeopolis, I have

---

12 Var.: "Then you (Osiris) will protect NN from these gods who are with you in the Hall of the Two Truths."

13 An epithet of Thoth, the long-beaked ibis.

14 Address to the crocodile Sobek. Variants conclude: "regarding the property of Osiris" or "against another."

15 Used to signify "cannibal" in Coptic.

16 Translated variously "extorted," "profiteered," or "practiced usury," the infraction (*ḥnwy.t*) is perhaps related to "greed" (*ḥnt*). Faulkner's "perjury" derives from the Demotic substitution: "I did not commit falsehood [...]."

17 Var. concludes: "on another in his house."

18 Lit., "The speech/mouth of NN has not run on."

19 For this passage, see Heerma van Voss 1973.

20 Var.: "My speech has not been heated."

21 Var. adds: "at another."

22 For this passage, see Heerma van Voss 1973.

23 Lit., "I have not swallowed my heart." In medical texts, "swallowing the heart" is a physiological designation for "fainting."

24 Elsewhere always a positive designation of a warrior: "champion."

25 Lit., "my heart has not been hasty."

26 Faulkner (1985:32) understands: "I have not washed out (the picture of) a god."

not waded in water.[27]

O Surging-One, who has come forth from the Abyss, I have not raised my voice.

O Commander of the subjects, who has come forth from his shrine, I have not reviled a god.

O Provider of goodness, who has come forth from the Harpoon Nome, I have not been puffed up.

O Nehebkau, who has come forth from Thebes, I have not made distinctions on my behalf.

O Serpent-Whose-Head-Is-Erect, who has come forth from the cavern, my possessions have not increased except by my own property.

O Serpent-Who-Has-Brought-Away-His-Portion, who has come forth from the Land of Silence, I have not debased the god in my town."

RECITATION BY NN:

"Hail to you, you gods.[28] I know you; I know your names. I shall not fall to your slaughter. You will not report my misdeed to this god in whose following you are. No fault of mine will come forth concerning you. You will speak Truth concerning me in the presence of the Lord of All, because I have done Truth in Egypt. I have not cursed a god. No fault of mine has come forth concerning a king who was in his reign.

Hail to you gods who are in this Hall of the Two Truths, who have no lies in their bodies, who live on Truth in Heliopolis, who swallow their putrifaction[29] in the presence of Horus who is in his Aten-disk. May you save me from Babai, who lives on the entrails of the great ones on that day of the great reckoning. Behold me; I have come before you without falsehood of mine, without guilt of mine, without evil of mine, without a witness against me, without anyone against whom I have done anything.[30] As I live on Truth, so I consume Truth. I have done what people say and that on account of which the gods are pleased. I have contented the god with that which he loves.[31] I have given bread to the hungry, water to the thirsty, clothing to the naked, and a boat to the boatless. I have made divine offerings for the gods, invocation-offerings for the blessed dead. Save me, then. Protect me, then. You will not report against me in the presence of the great god. I am pure of mouth, pure of hands, one to whom "Welcome!" is said at seeing him, because I have heard that speech[32] said by the Donkey and the Cat in the house of the One of the Gaping Mouth,[33] I being a witness before him[34] when he gave a shriek. I have seen the splitting of the persea tree within the Memphite necropolis.[35] I am one who provides assistance in the presence of the gods, who knows the requirements of their bodies. I have come here specifically to testify to Truth, to place the scale in its proper position in the Land of Silence. O he who is high upon his standard, Lord of the *atef*-crown, who has made his name as Lord of Breath,[36] may you save me from your messengers, who inflict bloody injury,[37] who create punishment, who are without compassion, because I have done Truth for the Lord of Truth, since I am pure, my front clean, my back cleansed, my middle as a pool of Truth. There is no limb of mine lacking in purity. As I have washed in the pool of the South, so I have rested in the city of the North, in the field of grasshoppers in which the crew of Re bathes in that second hour of night and third of day, which soothes the hearts of the gods when they pass by it by night or day."

"Let him come," so they say regarding me.

"Who are you?" so they say regarding me.

"What is your name?" so they say regarding me.

"I am the stalk of the papyrus plant, He-Who-is-in-the-Moringa-tree is my name."[38]

"By what have you passed?" so they say regarding me.

"By the city north of the moringa tree I passed."[39]

"What did you see there?"

"It was the calf and the thigh."

"What did you say to them?"

"I have seen rejoicing in the lands of the Phoenicians."

"What did they give to you?"

"It was a firebrand and a column of faience."

[27] Var.: "in flowing water."

[28] Var. adds: "who are in this Hall of the Two Truths."

[29] Var.: "who swallow/consume Truth."

[30] Var.: "for I have not done anything against him."

[31] Var.: "the gods with that which they love."

[32] Var.: "great word/speech."

[33] A reference to the punishment of Seth in donkey form by the cat goddess Mafdet; see Borghouts 1978:38, no. 59.

[34] Var.: "He-Whose-Face-Is-Behind-Him being my witness."

[35] A reference to Re's victory against Apep described in Book of the Dead 17 (*COS* 1.10).

[36] Epithets of Osiris.

[37] See Ritner 1993:170.

[38] Epithet of Osiris.

[39] For the following Osirian mysteries, see Ritner 1993:150, n. 678.

"What did you do with them?"
"I buried them on the bank of the lake of Two Truths in the evening meal rite."
"What did you find there on the bank of the Two Truths?"
"It was a scepter of flint, whose name is Breath-Giver."
"What did you do with the firebrand and column of faience after you had buried them?"
"I lamented over them. I dug them up. I extinguished the fire. I broke the column and threw it in the lake."
"Come, then, enter by this portal of the Hall of the Two Truths, since you know us."

"I shall not let you enter by me," so say the door-posts of this portal, "unless you have said my name."
"'Plummet of Truthfulness' is your name."
"I shall not let you enter by me," so says the right door-leaf of this portal, "unless you have said my name."
"'Scale-pan which bears Truth' is your name."
"I shall not let you enter by me," so says the left door-leaf of this portal, "unless you have said my name."
"'Scale-pan of wine' is your name."
"I shall not let you enter by me," so says the threshold of this portal, "unless you have said my name."
"'Ox of Geb' is your name."
"I shall not open for you," so says the bolt of this portal, "unless you have said my name."
"'Toe of his mother' is you name."
"I shall not open for you," so says the hasp of this portal, "unless you have said my name."
"'Living Eye of Sobek, Lord of Bakhu' is your name."
"I shall not open for you, I shall not let you enter by me," so says the door-keeper of this portal, "unless you have said my name."
"'Breast of Shu which he placed as protection for Osiris' is your name."
"We shall not let you pass by us," so say the cross-timbers of this portal, "unless you have said our name."
"'Children of Renenutet' is your name."
"You know us. Pass, then, by us."

"You shall not tread upon me," so says the floor of this Hall of the Two Truths."
"Why, then, since I am pure?"
"Because we do not know the names of your feet with which you would tread upon us. Say it to me then."
"'He who is inducted into the presence of Min' is the name of my right foot. "'Flower of Nephthys'[40] is the name of my left foot."
"Tread, then, upon us. You know us."
"I shall not announce you," so says the door-keeper of this hall, "unless you have said my name."
"'He who perceives hearts, who examines bodies' is your name."
"To which god on duty shall I announce you, then?"
"Tell it to the Interpreter of the Two Lands."
"Who is the Interpreter of the Two Lands?"
"It is Thoth."

"Come," so says Thoth, "Why have you come?"
"I have come here expressly to report."
"What is your condition?"
"I am pure from all misdeeds. I excluded myself from the strife of those who are in their days. I am not among them."
"To whom, then, shall I announce you?"
"To him whose roof is of fire, with its walls of living uraei, and the floor of whose house is in flood."
"Who is he?"
"He is Osiris."
"Proceed, then. Behold, you are announced. Your bread is the Eye of Horus; your beer is the Eye of Horus; your invocation offerings on earth are the Eye of Horus," so says he regarding me.

What should be done when being present in the Hall of Two Truths. A man should say this spell when pure and clean, dressed in clothing, shod in white sandals, painted with black eye-paint, anointed with the finest myrrh-oil, and having offered fresh meat, fowl, incense, bread, beer, and vegetables. Now make for yourself this image[41] in drawing upon pure ground with Nubian ochre, overlaid with soil on which neither pig nor goats have trod. As for the one for whom this book is done, he will flourish and his children will flourish. He will be a confidant of the king and his entourage. There shall be given to him a cake, a jug of beer, a loaf and a large portion of meat from upon the altar of the great god. He cannot be turned back from any portal of the West. He will be ushered in with the kings of Upper and Lower Egypt. He will be a follower of Osiris.[42] Truly effective, millions of times.

[40] Var.: "He who opens heaven for Hathor."
[41] Presumably the corresponding vignette of the weighing of the heart.
[42] Var. adds: "He goes forth in any transformation that he desires, being a living *ba*-spirit forever and ever."

REFERENCES

Text: Maystre 1937; and Naville 1886:275-335 and plates cxxxiii-cxxxix. Translations and discussions: Wilson *ANET* 34-36; Barguet 1967:157-164; Allen 1974:97-101; Lichtheim 1976 3:124-132; Hornung 1979:233-245 and 491-493; Faulkner 1985:29-34; and Rosati 1991:88-96. For the Demotic version, see Lexa 1977. For the Greek translation, see Merkelbach 1968:7-30; 1987.

4. HARPER SONGS

CONTRASTING HARPER SONGS FROM THE TOMB OF NEFERHOTEP (2.13)
("The Good Fortune of the Dead")

Robert K. Ritner

Offering a traditional and a skeptical response to the fate of the dead, these banquet songs are part of a trio carved on the walls of Theban Tomb 50, dating to the reign of Horemheb (ca. 1319-1292 BCE). The first song to be read by the tomb visitor (conventionally termed the *second* Neferhotep song) forms a reaction to these contrasting approaches (see *COS* 1.31). Adjacent to this is the song extolling the rewards of piety and ritual (Neferhotep "III"), while the skeptical song (Neferhotep "I") is placed in the rear corridor. This last text continues the *carpe diem* philosophy of the Intef Harper Song (see *COS* 1.30), and is paralleled by a song in the Theban tomb of Paser.

Neferhotep Song "III"
Beginning of the Song:
Remember, O heart, that day of mooring (death),
Let it be placed in the heart of him who possesses a burial, who reckons(?) ... [...] him,
For indeed, there exists none who evades it,
The strong and weak in the same manner.
He who sails north or south within a lifetime,
Moors at the bank thereafter.

O God's Father,[1] what a salvation is yours,
Since you united with the lords of eternity.
How enduring is your name forever,
Glorified in the necropolis.
Every god whom you have served since your existence,
You have entered before them eye to eye,
They are prepared to receive your soul
And to protect your dignity.
They have doubled the work of your hands,
They shall purify your beauty.
They have established the altar of your mummy,
Every god bearing his food offerings.
They say to you: "Come in peace, O servant beneficent for our spirits,"
Namely the God's Father of Amon, Neferhotep, begotten by the judge Amenemone the justified.

O God's Father, I have heard your praises beside the lords of eternity.
It is said regarding you:
"He has dragged the bark of Sokar."
You have placed the Sokar bark on its sledge;
You have encircled the walls in his following,
When his breast acquires brilliance.
"He has erected the *djed*-pillar as a *setem*-priest in his duty,
Who takes the hoe on the day of hacking the earth."[2]
"He has recited the festival liturgy of Busiris."
Your existence is good before the gods.
You are remembered for your goodness,
Inasmuch as it is you who enters into Heliopolis,
Who knows the mystery within it,
Namely the lector priest, who satisfied the heart of Amun, Neferhotep the justified.

O God's Father, your soul has advanced,
Your burial has passed.
Anubis has placed his hands upon you,
The Two Sisters[3] have embraced you.
Purification is made for you anew,
You being assigned with crafts of eternity:
A stone deity in its true form,[4]
Ointment from upon the hands of Shesmu,[5]
Clothing from the work of Taiyt,[6]
The Children of Horus as your protection.
The Two Kites[7] have seated themselves outside for you;
They have mourned for your name,

[1] The priestly title of the tomb owner, Neferhotep.
[2] For these ceremonial activities associated with the festival of Sokar, inert deity of death, see Schott 1934.
[3] Isis and Nephthys.
[4] A possible designation of the *shawabty* (var. *ushebti*) figure, detailed in Chapter 6 of the Book of the Dead and intended to perform eternal tasks for the deceased in the underworld.
[5] God of the wine press.
[6] Goddess of weaving.
[7] Isis and Nephthys.

Inasmuch as it is you whose existence was beneficent on earth for your lord Amun,
God's Father of Amun, Neferhotep the justified.

O God's Father, you are remembered in Heliopolis,
You are imaged[8] in Thebes.
There need be no searching for you for eternity;
Your name shall not be forgotten,
Inasmuch as you are one who is justified in the Estate of Ptah,
Who enters eye to eye in the Great Place.
Who is skilled in dignity in His great processions,
Who ascertains the extent of eternity by his measuring rods.
You are more exalted and happier than you have ever been.

O praised Neferhotep the justifed,
Your soul is justified,
And your enemies are overthrown forever.

Neferhotep Song "I"
Statement of the singer with the harp who is in the tomb of the Osiris Neferhotep the justified, who says:
"How still is this righteous lord!
The good fate has occurred.
Bodies pass away since the time of the god;
Generations come into their places.
Re presents himself in the mornings;
Atum sets in Manu (the western mountain).
Men beget;
Women conceive.
Every nose breathes the air;
Dawn comes, and all their children have come to their tombs.

Make holiday, O God's Father!
Place incense together with fine oil to your nose;
Garlands of lotus and mandragora flowers at your breast,
Your sister,[9] who is in your heart, seated beside you.
Place song and music before you,
Let all evil be cast behind.
Recall to yourself only joy,
Until the coming of that day of mooring
At the Land that Loves Silence,
Where the Son-whom-He-Loves[10] is not weary.

Make holiday, Neferhotep the justified,
O excellent God's Father,
Whose hands are pure!
They[11] have heard all that has happened to those:
Their houses are crumbled,
Their places do not exist,
They are like that which had never occurred since the time of the god.
The [... trees] on the bank of your lake,
May your spirit be seated beneath them,
May it drink their waters.

Follow your heart thoroughly!
[...]
Give bread to the one who has no field,
That you may acquire a good name throughout eternity.
You have looked at the *setem*-priests, [clad in] panther [skins],
As they libate to the ground, with bread as offering loaves,
[What is it for?][12]
The chantresses crying [...]
Their mummies are set up before Re;
Their people are in mourning.
[...] does not [...] coming at its time,
Fate reckoning his days.[13]
Awake [...],
Sitting powerlessly in what was made for his shade.[14]

Make holiday, O you whose hands are pure,
God's Father Neferhotep [the justified]! [...]
There is no work for the granaries of Egypt;
Its court is rich in [...],
Return me(?) to learn what remains concerning him.
A brief moment has not been added to [...] desert.
Those who used to have granaries with bread for offerings,
[And those who had none (?)] likewise,
They will spend their happy hour in [...],
[...] the time gone forth, the day of breaking hearts,
The one that places the house in [...]
Recall to yourself the day of your being dragged,
To the land that mingles [people ...].

[Follow your heart (?)] thoroughly!
There is no coming back.
Beneficial to [you is ...]
You are a righteous and true one,
Whose abomination is falsehood.
There is love of rightness [...]
[... protect(?)] the weak from the powerful,

---

[8] Earlier translations adopt an unsubstantiated meaning "protected."
[9] A figurative term for "beloved" or "wife."
[10] Epithet of Horus, who performs mortuary duties for his father Osiris.
[11] Translators have tacitly emended: "I have heard ..."
[12] Restored from the parallel in the tomb of Paser, see Schott 1950:135.
[13] Even the pious priest is subject to death.
[14] A description of the helpless corpse in the tomb.

The one who is in [...] doesn't hasten(?),
[...] who has no protector, who binds the one who is constricted(?) [...]
Give abundance to your happiness to perfection!
[...] Maat, Min and Isis,

The nourishment that gives [...]
[...] you.
In old age she dispatches you to the place of truth,
Without [...]

REFERENCES

Text: Hari 1985:11-15 and 36-40 and pls. iv and xxvi; and Lichtheim 1945. Translations and discussions: Breasted 1912:185-188; 1933:166-168; Schott 1950:131-135; Müller 1899:31-33.

5. GRAVE INSCRIPTIONS

HYMN FROM THE TOMB OF AY (2.14)

Robert K. Ritner

This hymn of the God's Father, and later Pharaoh, Ay derives from the east wall thickness of his private tomb at Amarna. Reflecting the official theology of the contemporary Atenist cult, the prayer stresses the universality of Aten, the visible solar disk, and the prophetic role of his son, Akhenaten. The hymnist's figurative expressions of abundance in terms of human measures of the sand, the sea and the mountains are paralleled in the later text of Isaiah.[1]

Adoration of the living Re-Harackhty, rejoicing in the horizon in his name as the Light (Shu) which is in the Aten (the sun disk), given life forever and ever, and of the King of Upper and Lower Egypt Neferkheperure-Waenre,[2] son of the Sun, Akhenaten, long in his lifetime, and the great royal wife Neferneferuaten[3] Nefertiti, living forever and ever.

Praises be to you when you rise in the horizon, O living Aten, lord of eternity!
Kissing the ground be at your rising in the heaven to illuminate every land with your beauty, with your rays on your son whom you love, your hands bearing millions of jubilees for the King of Upper and Lower Egypt Neferkheperure-Waenre, your child who came forth from your rays. May you confer on him your lifetime and your years. May you hearken for him to that which is in his heart. May you love him and cause him to be like Aten. May you rise to give him eternity; may you set to give him everlastingness. May you form him in the morning like your manifestations. May you fashion him in your image like Aten, the ruler of Maat, who came forth from eternity, the son of Re, who uplifts his beauty and who administers for him the production of his rays: the King of Upper and Lower Egypt who lives on Maat, Lord of the Two Lands, Neferkheperure-Waenre and the great royal wife Neferneferuaten Nefertiti, living forever and ever.

The God's Father, favorite of the Good god,[4] fanbearer at the right hand of the king, overseer of all the horses of his Majesty, true royal scribe whom he loves, Ay, who says:
"Hail to you, O living Aten, who rises in heaven inundating hearts, at whose appearance all lands are in festival, their hearts glad in jubilation since their lord, who made himself, is risen over them. Your son presents Maat to your beautiful countenance as joyfully you behold him. From you he has come forth, an eternal son come forth from the Aten, an effective one for him who is effective for him, who gratifies the heart of the Aten when he rises in heaven. He rejoices for his son, as he embraces him with his rays and gives to him an eternity as king like the Aten: Neferkheperure-Waenre, my god who made me, who transformed my *ka*-spirit. May you cause that I be fulfilled by beholding you unceasingly. Your character is like the Aten's: abounding in property, an inundation surging daily, giving life to Egypt, with silver and gold like the sands of the banks, while the land awakens to acclaim the one powerful by means of his *ka*-spirit. O he whom the Aten has born, you will be eternal, Neferkheperure-Waenre, alive and healthy inasmuch as he

[1] For a comparison of the hymn with Isa 40:12, see Couroyer 1966.
[2] Throne name of Akhenaten: "Beautiful are the Manifestations of Re; The Unique One of Re."
[3] Throne name of Queen Nefertiti: "Beautiful is the beauty of Aten."
[4] The "good god" is an epithet of the king.

has born you."

The God's Father, fanbearer at the right hand of the king, overseer of all the horses of his Majesty, true royal scribe whom he {loves}, Ay, who says: "I was one true to the king, one whom he transformed, one scrupulous for the Lord of the Two Lands, efficacious for his lord. I followed the *ka*-spirit of His Majesty as his favorite who sees his beauty when he appears in his palace, while I was at the head of the great ones and the royal companions, the first of all the followers of his Majesty. He has placed Maat in my body. Falsehood is my abomination, for I know that Warenre, my lord who is knowledgeable like Aten and truly perceptive, has rejoiced at such. He has doubled for me my rewards in silver and gold, while I am the first of the great ones at the head of the subjects. My character, my good nature, has made my position there. My lord instructed me just so that I might enact his teachings. I have lived by adoring his *ka*-spirit; I have been fulfilled by following him - my breath by which I live, my north wind, my millions of inundations surging daily, Neferkheperure-Waenre. May you give to me a long lifetime in your favor. How prosperous is your favorite, O son of the Aten! All that he does is stable and thriving; the *ka*-spirit of the Lord of the Two Lands is with him forever. Thus he is fulfilled in life when he has reached old age.

O my lord, who fashions people, who transforms a lifetime, who makes a good fate for his favorite, who is satisfied by truth, whose abomination is falsehood, how prosperous is he who hears your teaching of life! May he be fulfilled by beholding you unceasingly, his eyes seeing the Aten daily. May you grant to me a goodly old age as your favorite. May you grant to me a goodly burial by the decree of your *ka*-spirit in my tomb which you decreed for me that I rest therein in this mountain of Akhet-Aten, the place of the elect. May I hear your pleasant voice in the Mansion of the Benben, when you do that which your father the living Aten praises. May he cause you to be eternal! May he reward you with jubilees like the number of the sandbanks, measured in *oipe*-units, like the reckoning of the sea, measured by remainder-units. The itemization and counting of the mountains, weighed with the balance,[a] or the feathers of birds or leaves of trees are like the jubilees of king Waenre, forever and ever, as an enduring king for the great royal wife whom he loves, who is united with her beauty, and who pacifies the Aten with a pleasant voice and with her beautiful hands bearing the sistra, the Lady of the Two Lands, Neferneferuaten Nefertiti, living forever and ever, while she is beside Waenre forever and ever just as heaven endures bearing what is in it.

Your father the Aten has risen in the heaven to protect you every day inasmuch as he has born you. May you give to me the pure offering bread that has gone forth from your presence from the surplus of your father Aten as the gift of your *ka*-spirit. May you grant that my *ka*-spirit exist for me stable and thriving as when I was on earth following your *ka*-spirit, after it has mounted up by name to the place of the elect in which you have caused that I rest. My mouth holds Maat; let my name be uttered because of it as you have decreed, for I am like all of your elect who follow your *ka*-spirit. May I go bearing your rewards after old age. For the *ka*-spirit of the fanbearer at the right hand of the king, the true royal scribe whom he loves, the God's Father Ay, who lives again.

a Isa 40:12

REFERENCES

Text: Sandman 1938:90-93; de Garis Davies 1908:17-18 and pl. xxv. Translations and discussions: Murnane 1995:110-112; Davies 1908:28-29; Couroyer 1966.

EGYPTIAN BIBLIOGRAPHY

ABD EL-MAKSOUD, M.
1998 *Tell Heboua (1981-1991)*. Enquête archéologique sur la deuxième période intermédiaire et le nouvel empire à l'extrémité orientale du delta. Paris: Éditions Recherche sur les Civilisations.
AHARONI, Y.
1979 *The Land of the Bible: A Historical Geography*. Rev. ed. by A. F. Rainey. Philadelphia. Westminster Press.
AHLSTRÖM, G., and D. EDELMAN.
1985 "Merneptah's Israel." *JNES* 44:59-61.
AḤITUV, S.
1984 *Canaanite Toponyms in Ancient Egyptian Documents*. Jerusalem/Leiden: Magnes/Brill.
ALBRIGHT, W. F.
1929 "Progress in Palestinian Archaeology during the Year 1928." *BASOR* 33:1-10.
1952 "The Smaller Beth-shan Stele of Sethos I (1309-1290 B.C.)." *BASOR* 125:24-32.
ALLEN, T. G.
1974 *The Book of the Dead or Going Forth by Day*. SAOC 37. Chicago: The University of Chicago Press.
BAER, K.
1973 "The Libyan and Nubian Kings of Egypt: Notes on the Chronology of Dynasties XXII to XXVI." *JNES* 32:4-25.
BARGUET, P.
1967 *Le Livre des Morts des anciens Égyptiens*. LAPO 1. Paris: Les Éditions du Cerf.
1986 *Textes des sarcophages égyptiens du Moyen Empire*. LAPO 12. Paris: Les Éditions du Cerf.
VON BECKERATH, J.
1969 "Zu den Namen des kuschitischen Königs Pi'anchy." *MDAIK* 24:58-62.
BIETAK, M.
1996 *Avaris: Capital of the Hyksos*. London: The British Museum.
BIMSON, J.
1991 "Merneptah's Israel and Recent theories of Israelite Origins." *JSOT* 49:20-23.
BLEEKER, C. J.
1973 *Hathor and Thoth*. Leiden: Brill.
BLEIBERG, E. L.
1996 *The Official Gift in Ancient Egypt*. Norman/London: University of Oklahoma Press.
BORGHOUTS, J. F.
1978 *Ancient Egyptian Magical Texts*. Nisaba 9. Leiden: E. J. Brill.
BREASTED, J. H.
1906-07 *Ancient Records of Egypt*. 5 volumes. Chicago: University of Chicago Press. Reprint, 1962.
1912 *Development of Religion and Thought in Ancient Egypt*. New York: Charles Scribner's Sons.
1933 *The Dawn of Conscience*. New York: Charles Scribner's Sons.
BRESCIANI, E.
1969 *Letteratura e poesia dell' antico egitto*. Turin.
DE BUCK, A.
1947 *The Egyptian Coffin Texts*. Vol. 3: *Texts of Spells 164-267*. OIP 64. Chicago: The University of Chicago.
1970 *Egyptian Reading Book*. Leiden: Nederlands Institut voor het Nabije Oosten.
CASPERSON, L.
1986 "The Lunar Dates of Thutmose III." *JNES* 45:139-150.
ČERNÝ, J.
1976 *Coptic Etymological Dictionary*. Cambridge: Cambridge University Press.
CHRISTENSEN, D. L.
1989 "The Identity of 'King So' in Egypt (2 Kings XVII 4)." *VT* 39:140-153.
COUROYER, B.
1966 "Isaïe XL, 12." *RB* 73:186-196.
CUMMINGS, B.
1982 *Egyptian Historical Records of the Later Eighteenth Dynasty*. Warminster: Aris & Phillips.
DAVIES, B. G.
1997 *Egyptian Historical Inscriptions of the Nineteenth Dynasty*. Documenta Mundi, Aegyptiaca 2. Jonsered [Gothenburg]: Paul Aströms förlag.
DAVIES, N. de G.
1908 *The Rock Tombs of El Amarna*. Part 6: *Tombs of Parennefer, Tutu, and Aÿ*. London: Egypt Exploration Society.
DAY, J.
1992 "The Problem of 'So, King of Egypt' in 2 Kings xvii 4." *VT* 42:289-301.
DESROCHES-NOBLECOURT, C.
1963 *Tutankhamen, Life and Death of a Pharaoh*. London: Connoisseur/Michael Joseph.
DONNER, H.
1977 "The Separate States of Israel and Judah." Pp. 381-434 in *Israelite and Judaean History*. Ed. by J. H. Hayes and J. M. Miller. London/Philadelphia: Westminster.
DUNHAM, D.
1970 *The Barkal Temples*. Boston: Musuem of Fine Arts.
EDEL, E.
1953 "Die Stelen Amenophis' II aus Karnak und Memphis." *ZDPV* 69:98-175.

EPIGRAPHIC SURVEY
1986 *The Battle Reliefs of King Sety I.* RIK 4. Chicago: The Oriental Institute.
FAULKNER, R. O.
1942 "The Battle of Megiddo." *JEA* 28:2-15.
1969 *The Ancient Egyptian Pyramid Texts.* Oxford: Clarendon Press.
1973 *The Ancient Egyptian Coffin Texts.* Vol. 1: *Spells 1-354.* Warminster: Aris & Phillips.
1985 *The Book of the Dead.* Rev. edition. London: The British Museum.
FECHT, G.
1983 "Die Israelstele, Gestalt und Aussage." Pp. 106-138 in *Studies Brunner.*
GARDINER, A. H.
1935 "Piankhi's Instructions to his Army." *JEA* 21:219-223.
1960 *The Kadesh Inscriptions of Ramesses II.* Oxford: Griffith Institute/OUP.
1961 *Egypt of the Pharaohs.* New York/London: Oxford University Press.
1969 *Egyptian Grammar.* Oxford: The Griffith Institute.
GARDINER, A. H., and B. GUNN.
1918 "New Renderings of Egyptian Texts." *JEA* 5:36-56.
GILULA, M.
1967 "An Egyptian Parallel to Jeremiah I 4-5." *VT* 17:114.
1977 "Egyptian *nḥt* = Coptic *naḥte* 'To Believe.'" *JNES* 36:295-296.
GIVEON, R.
1971 *Les bédouins Shosou des documents égyptiens.* Leiden: Brill.
GOEDICKE, H.
1974 "Some Remarks Concerning the Inscription of Ahmose, Son of Ebana." *JARCE* 11:31-41.
1980 "The Background to Thutmosis III's Foreign Policy." *JSSEA* 10:201-213.
GOMAÀ, F.
1974 *Die libyschen Fürstentümer des Deltas vom Tod Osorkons II bis zur Wiedervereinigung Ägyptens durch Psametik I.* BTAVO, Reihe B 6. Wiesbaden: L. Reichert.
GÖRG, M.
1986 "'Der Starke Arm Pharaos' — Beobachtungen zum Belegspektrum einer Metaphor in Palästina und Ägypten." Pp. 323-330 in *Studies Daumas.*
GRAPOW, H.
1911 "Bedrohungen der Götter durch den Verstorbenen." *ZÄS* 49:48-54.
1947 *Studien zu den Annalen Thutmosis des Dritten und zu ihnen verwandten historischen Berichten des Neuen Reiches.* Abhandlungen der Deutschen Akademie der Wissenschaften zu Berlin. Jarg. 1947. Phil.-hist. Kl. 2. Berlin: Akademie-Verlag.
GRDSELOFF, B.
1949 *Une stèle scythopolitaine du roi Séthos Ier.* Cairo: Imprimerie Le Scribe Égyptien.
GREEN, A. R. W.
1993 "The Identity of King So of Egypt — An Alternative Interpretation," *JNES* 52:99-108.
HARI, R.
1985 *La tombe thébaine du père divin Neferhotep.* Geneva: Éditions de Belles-Lettres.
HASEL, M.
1994 "Israel in the Merneptah Stela." *BASOR* 296:45-61.
HEERMA VAN VOSS, M.
1973 "Drie Egyptische Geboden." Pp. 185-187 in *Studies Böhl.*
HELCK, W.
1955 *Urkunden der 18. Dynastie: historische Inscriften Thutmosis' III. und Amenophis' III.* Urkunden des ägyptischen Altertums 17. Berlin: Akademie Verlag.
1961 *Urkunden der 18. Dynastie: Übersetzung zu den Heften 17-22.* Berlin: Akademie Verlag.
HOFFMEIER, J. K.
1977 "Tents in Egypt and the Ancient Near East." *JSSEA* 7:13-28.
1986 "The Arm of God Versus the Arm of Pharaoh in the Exodus Narratives." *Bib* 67:378-387.
1989 "Reconsidering Egypt's Part in the Termination of the Middle Bronze Age in Palestine." *Levant* 21:181-193.
1991 "The Aftermath of David's Triumph Over Goliath: 1 Samuel 17:54 in Light of Near Eastern Parallels." *Archaeology in the Biblical World* 1:18-23.
1991 "James Weinstein's 'Egypt and the Middle Bronze IIC/Late Bronze IA Transition': A Rejoinder." *Levant* 23:117-124.
1992 "The Problem of 'History' in Egyptian Royal Inscriptions." Pp. 291-299 in *VI Congresso Internazionale di Egittologia Atti* I. Turin.
1994 "The Structure of Joshua 1-11 and the Annals of Thutmose III." Pp. 165-179 in *FTH.*
1997 *Egypt in Israel: The Evidence for the Authenticity of the Exodus Tradition.* New York/Oxford: Oxford University Press.
1999 "Chariots." Pp. 193-195 in *Encyclopedia of the Archaeology of Ancient Egypt.* Ed. By Kathryn A. Bard. London: Routledge.
HORNUNG, E.
1962 *ZÄS* 87:115-116.
1979 *Das Totenbuch der Ägypter.* Zürich: Artemis Verlag.
1987 "Lang order kurz? — das Mittlere und Neue Reich Ägyptens als Prüfstein." Pp. 27-36 in *HML.*
JANSSEN, J. J.
1968 "The Smaller Dâkhla Stela." *JEA* 54:165-172.
KEMPINSKI, A.
1974 "Tell el-ᶜAjjul — Beth-Aglayim or Sharuhen?" *IEJ* 24:145-152.

KITCHEN, K. A.
1970 "Ancient Orient, 'Deuteronism' and the Old Testament." Pp. 1-24 in *New Perspectives on the Old Testament.* edited by J. B. Payne. Waco, TX: Word Books.
1982a "Phinehas." P. 934 in *NBD.*
1982b *Pharaoh Triumphant: The Life and Times of Ramesses II.* Warminster: Aris and Phillips.
1986 *The Third Intermediate Period in Egypt (1100-650 BC)*[2]. Warminster: Aris and Phillips. 1st edition 1973; 3rd edition 1996.
1987 "The Basics of Egyptian Chronology in Relation to the Bronze Age" pp. 37-53 in *HML 1.*
1989 "Supplementary Notes on 'The Basics of Egyptian Chronology.'" Pp. 151-159 in *HML 3.*
1993a *Ramesside Inscriptions Translated & Annotated, Translations.* I. Oxford: Blackwell Reference.
1993b *Ramesside Inscriptions Translated & Annotated, Notes & Comments,* I. Oxford: Blackwell Reference.
1994-97 "The Physical Text of Merenptah's Victory Hymn (The 'Israel Stela')." *JSSEA* 24:71-76.
1996 *Ramesside Inscriptions Translated & Annotated, Translations.* II. Oxford: Blackwell Reference.
1999 *Ramesside Inscriptions Translated & Annotated, Notes & Comments,* II. Oxford: Blackwell Reference.

KLENGEL, H.
1969 *Geschichte Syriens im 2. Jahrtausend v. u. Z.,* 2. Berlin: Akademie-Verlag.
1992 *Syria 3000 to 300 B.C.* Berlin: Akademie-Verlag.

KRAUSS, R.
1978 "Sōᵓ, König von ägypten — ein Deutungsvorschlag." *MDOG* 110:49-54.

KUENTZ, C.
1928-34 *La bataille de Qadech.* Cairo: IFAO.

LECLANT, J.
1966 *OLZ* 61:152.

LELLO, G.
1978 "Thutmose III's First Lunar Date." *JNES* 37:327-330.

LEMCHE, N. P.
1985 *Early Israel: Anthropological and Historical Studies on the Israelite Society before the Monarchy.* Leiden: Brill.

LEXA, F.
1977 *Das demotische Totenbuch der Pariser Nationalbibliothek.* Milan: Cisalpino-Golliardica. Reprint of Leipzig: J. C. Hinrich'sche Buchhandlung, 1910.

LICHTHEIM, M.
1945 "The Songs of the Harpers." *JNES* 4:178-212 and pls. i-vii.
1976 *AEL.*

LOGAN, T. J., and J. G. WESTENHOLZ.
1971-72 "*Sḏm.f* and *Sḏm.n.f* Forms in the Pey (Piankhy) Inscription." *JARCE* 9:111-119.

LORET, V.
1910 *L'inscription d'Ahmes fils d'Abana.* Cairo: Bibliothèque d'étude.

LOUKIANOFF, G.
1926 *Ancient Egypt,* n.v.

MARIETTE, A.
1872-89 *Monuments divers recueillis en Égypte et en Nubie.* Paris: F. Vieweg.

MASSART, A.
1959 "A propos des «listes» dans les textes funéraires et magiques." *Analecta Biblica* 12:227-246.

MAYSTRE, C.
1937 *Les déclarations d'innocence (Livre des Morts, chapitre 125).* Recherches d'archéologie, de philologie et d'histoire 8. Cairo: IFAO.

MAZAR, A.
1999 "The 1997-1998 Excavations at Tel Rehov: Preliminary Report." *IEJ* 49:1-42.

MERKELBACH, R.
1968 "Ein ägyptischer Priestereid," *Zeitschrift für Papyrologie und Epigraphik* 2:7-30.
1987 *Die Unschuldserklärungen und Berichten im ägyptischen Totenbuch, in der römischen Elegie und im antiken Rome.* Giessen: Universitätsbibliothek Giessen.

MOND, R., and O. H. MYERS.
1940 *Temples of Armant.* 2 Vols. London: Egypt Exploration Society.

MONTET, P.
1957-61 *Géographie de l'Égypte Ancienne* I & II. Paris: Imprimerie Nationale.

MORSCHAUSER, S.
1988 "The End of the *Sḏf(3)-Tr(yt)* 'Oath'." *JARCE* 25:93-103.

MÜLLER, W. M.
1899 *Die Liebespoesie der alten Ägypter.* Leipzig: J. G. Hinrichs.

MURNANE, W. J.
1989 "Rhetorical History? The Beginning of the Thutmose III's First Campaign in Western Asia." *JARCE* 26:183-189.
1995 *Texts from the Amarna Period in Egypt.* WAW 5. Atlanta: Scholars Press.

NAᵓAMAN, N.
1977 "Yeno'am." *Tel Aviv* 4:168-177.
1990 "The Historical Background to the Conquest of Samaria (720 BC)." *Biblica* 71:211-216.

NAVILLE, É.
1886 *Das aegyptische Todtenbuch der XVIII. bis XX. Dynastie aus verschiedenen Urkunden zusammengestellt und herausgegeben.* 2 vols. Berlin: A. Asher & Co.

NICCACCI, A.
1997 "La Stèle d'Israël: Grammaire et stratégie de communication." *Études égyptologiques et bibliques à la mémoire du Père B. Couroyer. Cahier de la Revue Biblique* 36:43-107.
NOTH, M.
1943 "Die Annalen Thutmose III. als Geschichtsquelle." *ZDPV* 66:156-174.
PARKER, R. A.
1957 "The Lunar Dates of Thtumose III and Ramesses II." *JNES* 16:39-43.
1966 "King Py, a Historical Problem." *ZÄS* 93:111-114.
PETRIE, W. M. F.
1897 *Six Temples at Thebes: 1896*. London: Bernard Quaritch.
PRIESE, K.-H.
1968 "Der Name des Königs 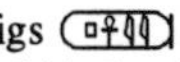." *MIO* 14:166-175.
1972a "Der Beginn der kuschitischen Herrschaft in Ägypten." *ZÄS* 98:16-32.
1972b "Zu Sprache der ägyptischen Inschriften der Könige von Kusch." *ZÄS* 98:99-124.
RAINEY, A.
1973 "Amenhotep II's Campaign to Takshi." *JARCE* 10:71-75.
1993 "Sharuḥân/Sharuhen — The Problem of Identification." *EI* 24:178*-187*.
REDFORD, D. B.
1979 "The Historical Retrospective at the Beginning of Thutmose III's Annals." Pp. 338-342 in *Studies Edel*.
1986 *Pharaonic King-Lists, Annals and Day-Books: A Contribution to the Study of the Egyptian Sense of History*. Mississauga: Benben Publications.
1992 *Egypt, Canaan, and Israel in Ancient Times*. Princeton: Princeton University Press.
REISNER, G. A., and M. B. REISNER.
1933 "Inscribed Monuments from Gebel Barkal." Pt. 2 *ZÄS* 69:24-29, pls iii-v.
RITNER, R. K.
1993 *The Mechanics of Ancient Egyptian Magical Practice*. SAOC 54. Chicago: The Oriental Institute.
ROSATI, G.
1991 *Libro dei Morti*. Testi del Vicino Oriente antico 1.2. Brescia: Paideia Editrice.
ROWE, A.
1930 *The Topography and History of Beth-Shan*. Philadephia: Pennsylvania: University Press.
SANDMAN, M.
1938 *Texts from the Time of Akhenaten*. Bibliotheca Aegyptiaca 8. Brussels: Fondation Égyptologique Reine Élisabeth.
SAUNERON, S.
1951 "Aspects et sort d'un thème magique égyptien: les menaces incluant les dieux." *BSFE* 8:11-21.
SCHOTT, S.
1934 "The Feasts of Thebes." Pp. 78-88 in *Work in Western Thebes 1931-33*. Ed. by H. Nelson and U. Hölscher. OIC 18. Chicago: The University of Chicago.
1950 *Ägyptische Liebeslieder*. Zurich: Artemis Verlag.
SCHULMAN, A. R.
1957 "Egyptian Representation of Horsemen and Riding in the New Kingdom." *JNES* 16:263-271 and pls. xxxvii-xli.
1964 *Military Rank, Title and Organization in the Egyptian New Kingdom*. MÄS 6. Berlin: Verlag Bruno Hessling.
SETHE, K.
1908 *Die altägyptischen Pyramidentexte*. Vol. 1. Leipzig: J. C. Hinrichs'sche Buchhandlung.
1924 "Die Sprüche für das Kennen der Seelen der heiligen Orte." *ZÄS* 59:1-20.
1935 *Übersetzung und Kommentar zu den altägyptischen Pyramidentexten*. Vol. 1. Hamburg: J. J. Augustin.
SMITH, W. S.
1965 *Interconnections in the Ancient Near East*. New Haven: Yale University Press.
SPALINGER, A. J.
1974 "Some Notes on the Battle of Megiddo and Reflections on Egyptian Military Writing." *MDAIK* 30:221-229.
1977 "A Critical Analysis of the 'Annals' of Thutmose III (Stücke V-VI)." *JARCE* 14:41-54.
1982 *Aspects of the Military Documents of the Ancient Egyptians*. YNER 9. New Haven and London: Yale University Press.
STAGER, L. E.
1985 "Merneptah, Israel and the Sea Peoples: New Light on an Old Relief." *EI* 18:56-64.
STEWART, J. R. et. al.
1974 *Tell el-^{c}Ajjul: The MB Age Remains*. Götenborg: Studies in Mediterranean Archaeology 38.
TRIGGER, B., B. KEMP, D. O'CONNOR, and A. LLOYD.
1983 *Ancient Egypt: A Social History*. Cambridge: Cambridge University Press.
VAN SETERS, J.
1990 "Joshua's Campaign and Near Eastern Historiography." *SJOT* 2:1-12.
VITTMANN, G.
1974 "Zur Lesung des Königsnamens 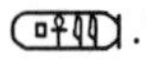." *Or* 43:12-16.
WEINFELD, M.
1972 *Deuteronomy and the Deuteronomic School*. Oxford: Clarendon.
WEINSTEIN, J.
1981 "The Egyptian Empire in Palestine: A Reassessment." *BASOR* 241:1-28.
1991 "Egypt and the Middle Bronze IIC/Late Bronze IA Transition in Palestine." *Levant* 23:105-115.
WILLIAMS, R. J.
1958 *DOTT* 137-141.
1969 "Some Egyptianisms in the Old Testament." Pp. 93-98 in *Studies Wilson*.

WILSON, J. A.
1969 *ANET*³.
WREZINSKI, W.
1938-41 *Atlas zur Altaegyptischen Kulturgeschichte*. Leipzig: J. C. Hinrichs'sche Buchhandlung.
YEIVIN, S.
1952 "Who Was 'Śő' the King of Egypt?" *VT* 2:164-168.
YOUNGER, K. L., Jr.
1990 *Ancient Conquest Accounts: A Study of Ancient Near Eastern and Biblical History Writing*. JSOTSup 98. Sheffield: Sheffield Academic Press.
YOYOTTE, J.
1961 "Les Principautés du Delta au temps de l'anarchie libyenne." Pp. 121-181 in *Studies Maspero*.

HITTITE MONUMENTAL INSCRIPTIONS

A. ROYAL INSCRIPTIONS

1. EDICTS AND PROCLAMATIONS

BILINGUAL EDICT OF ḪATTUŠILI I (2.15)

Gary Beckman

The reign of one of the earliest Hittite Great Kings, Ḫattušili I, was plagued by dissension within his own family, culminating in several plots against his rule by members of the younger generation. In this document, which is presented in both Hittite and Akkadian in parallel columns,[1] Ḫattušili justifies his disinheritance of one adopted son, Labarna, and the nomination of another, Muršili, as successor to the throne. This edict was directed to various influential groups in Hittite society, whose active cooperation was necessary because the newly-designated heir was still a child. In places the discourse here is somewhat confusing, for it contains numerous quotations, which are not always introduced by verbs of speech. In §§11, 19, and 21b-22 the king addresses his new son Muršili, and in §23 his wife(?) Ḫaštayar. Although this proclamation is said to have been made by the king from his sickbed in the Anatolian town of Kuššar, and the tenor of the text indeed suggests that he lay near death, it is possible that Ḫattušili recovered from this crisis, since another tradition relates that he perished in battle in northern Syria. In any event, we know that Muršili I duly succeeded his adoptive father.

§1 (i/ii.1-7) [The Great King] Tabarna[2] spoke to the ranks of the army and to the dignitaries: I am now ill. I designated the young Labarna to you: "He shall sit securely (upon the throne)!" I, the king, had named him as my son. I continually instructed him[3] and looked after him constantly. But he showed himself a youth not fit to be seen. He didn't shed tears. He didn't show mercy. He was cold. He was heartless.

§2 (i/ii.8-13) I, the king, apprehended him and had him brought to my couch: "What (is this)? No one will ever again raise his sister's child (as his own foster son)!" But he didn't accept the word of the king. He always took the advice of his mother, that snake. His brothers and sisters continually sent cool words to him, and he consistently listened to their words. I, the king, heard (of this), and I indeed quarrelled with him.

§3 (i/ii.14-19) "But enough!" (I said). "He is no longer my son!" Whereupon his mother bellowed like an ox: "They have torn my bull-calf[4] [from] my living womb, (as if I were) a cow, and they have deposed him. (And now) you will kill [him]!" But have I, the king, done him any evil? [Haven't I elevated him] to the priesthood? I have always singled him out for goodness and kindness. [Yet] he showed no sympathy when commanded by the king. How can he then show sympathy on his [own] toward Ḫattuša?

§4 (i/ii.20-25) His mother is a snake. Henceforth he will always heed (first) the words of his mother, and of his brothers and sisters. And when he draws near, it will be to take vengeance that he approaches! [And concerning my troops], my dignitaries, [and] my subjects who surround(?) the king, [he will vow]: "They will be massacred on account of the king!" So he will proceed [to destroy] them. He will begin to shed blood and will have [no] fear!

§5 (i/ii.26-29) It will come about that in regard to those who are citizens of Ḫattuša he will thus draw near to [take away] the cattle and sheep of whoever (owns any). [I ...ed my] external enemies [... and] I held [my land(?)] in peace(?). It shall not come about that he hereafter establishes [...]

§6 (i/ii.30-36) [He] shall now in no way go down freely (in exile from Ḫattuša). I have now given my son Labarna a house. I have given him [arable land] in plenty. I have given him cattle in plenty. I have given [him sheep in plenty]. He shall continue to eat and drink (his fill). [As long as he is on his best behavior], he shall come up from time to time (to Ḫattuša to visit). But if he begins [to cause trouble(?)], or (if he spreads) any

[1] Columns i and iv are Akk., ii and iii Hittite.

[2] This title of the Hittite king, which has an alternate form Labarna, was also adopted as a personal name by certain members of the Hittite royal house. Some scholars believe that the development was in the opposite direction, and that like Latin Caesar, T/Labarna was originally the personal name of an important ruler and only later borrowed as a title by his successors. On this problem see Tischler 1988.

[3] Read contra Sommer and Falkenstein 1938. Hoffner follows Forrer in reading the Akk. of i 4: *ar-ṭú-up ú-u'-ú-ri-šu*. See also the colophon.

[4] Read i.15: GUD *bi-ri*.

slander, [or] and [...], he will not be permitted to come up (again), but [shall remain on his own estate].

§7 (i/ii.37-41) Muršili is now my son. [You must acknowledge] him. You must enthrone him. [...] In place of the lion, [the god will set up only] (another) lion. [And in the hour] when a call to arms goes forth, [or] when perhaps [a rebellion becomes serious], you, my subjects and high noblemen, must be [of assistance to my son].

§8 (ii.42-47) [(Only) when] three years (have passed) shall he go on a campaign. [For the present] I will make [a valiant king of him]. If for the moment (this) is not yet (so), [honor him nonetheless(?)]. He is the progeny of your monarch. Raise him to be a valiant [king. If] you take him (with you) on campaign [while he is still a child], bring [him] back [safely]. Your clan shall be [united] like that of the *wetna*,[5] and it shall be [...] His subjects are born [of one mother].

§9 (ii.48-52) A single liver, a single set of lungs, and a single [ear] have been allotted [to you (all)].[6] Don't] vie with one another for preeminence. None of you shall be the opponent (of another). None of you shall transgress (this) command. You musn't commit this [deed] of the cities of Šinaḫḫuwa and Ubariya. Slander shall not be established (among you). (If it is), my son will carry out my (wishes) [against you].

§10 (ii.53-57) [No] one shall think: "In secret the king [does] what he pleases (saying): 'I can justify it, whether it (really) is, or whether it is not.'" [Such] slander shall *never* be established as true. Rather, you [who yourselves] now acknowledge my advice and my wisdom, instruct my son in wisdom.

§11 (ii.58-62) [Not] one (of you) shall hinder the other [in his own interests], nor shall one [promote] the other in his own interests. The elders shall not keep on speaking (to you courtiers). [My son] shall [not] be called [...] The elders of Ḫattuša shall not keep on speaking to you, (my son). No one shall speak to you at all — [not a man of Kuššar(?)], nor a man of Ḫemuwa, nor a man of Tamalikya, nor [a man of Zalpa(?)], nor (anyone of) the (general) population.[7]

§12 (ii.63-67) [Consider (the case of)] my [son] Ḫuzziya: I, the king, [made] him [lord] over the city of Tappaššanda. But those (people there) got his attention, speaking abusively to him. They [acted] in a hostile fashion [against me] (saying): "Rebel against your father. The great estates [of Tappaššanda] — they [haven't been exempted (from taxes and corvée)], but you will grant an exemption."

§13 (ii.68-74) So I, [the king], deposed [Ḫuzziya]. Then [even in Ḫattuša itself] the citizens of Ḫattuša [become hostile (to me)]. They got the attention of a daughter (of mine). And [since she had male] offspring, they acted in a hostile manner [against me] (in regard to her, saying): "[There is no heir for] your father's [throne]. A subject will sit (upon it). A subject [will become king]." And furthermore [she made] the city of Ḫattuša and the great [households disloyal], so that [the high noblemen] and courtiers became hostile [to me. Thus] she incited [the entire land].

§14 (i/ii.75-iii.5) Out of enmity she killed the citizens [of Ḫattuša ...], but these persons [... she killed]. (As for) the citizens of Ḫattuša: from him whose [ox was taken], from him whose ram was taken, from him whose [vine-yard] and fields were taken — (his) [threshing-floor(?)] and [servants(?) were also taken].[a] The ox which he harnessed — his ox [and his sheep(?) were killed(?)]. [Now ...] both these [...] subjects of the king [...] them the men of [...] and the craftsmen [...] and their fields she took. ... Do I, the king, know nothing (of it) [...]?

§16 (iii.6-12a) When [I] heard [that] she had put [the citizens] of Ḫattuša to death, I sought tears (i.e., remorse) for them [from her]. Had [I] not sought (them from her),[8] you would have slandered me with (your) tongue (saying): "[He has] expelled [his daughter]." I, the king, did [not do] anything (to her). [Whereupon she said: "Why] have you given me so little?" (So, I, the king, replied): "[If I hadn't given] you only a little, if I had given you more cattle, if I had given [you more] sheep, I would have been drinking the blood (of the land)."[9]

§17 (iii.13-22) [This daughter had debased my person(?)] and my name, [so] I, [the king], took [(my) daughter and brought her down] here[10] from Ḫattuša. And I replaced land for

[a] 1 Sam 12:3

[5] An unidentified wild animal.

[6] This metaphor indicates that the nobility should behave as if it shared emotions (liver), life (lungs), intelligence and knowledge (ears).

[7] Ḫattušili here cautions both his nobles and his heir Muršili against becoming involved in intrigues engaged in by prominent residents of the most important towns in Ḫatti.

[8] Read iii.7-8: *ták-ku-ma-na-*<*aš*>*ta* / *Ú-UL-ma ša-an-*[*ḫu-un* ...].

[9] The king fears that if his daughter were given abundant resources, she would only use them to stir up trouble in Ḫatti.

[10] To Kuššar.

land; [cattle for cattle] I replaced.[11] She has rejected (her) father's word and has drunk [the life's blood of the citizens of Ḫattuša]. Now she [has been banished from the city]. If she were to come to my household, [she would surely disrupt] my household. [If] she were to come to Ḫattuša, she would cause [it] to revolt [once more. A house has been allotted(?)] to her in the country — now (she shall stay there, and) she shall eat [and drink].

§18 (iii.23-25) [You] shall not do [her any harm]. She did (me) harm, but I shall not do (her) [harm in return]. She [would not call] me father, so I shall not call her daughter.

§19 (iii.26-32) Up until now no one [in my family] has heeded my command. [But you, my son], Muršili, you must heed it. Keep [(your) father's words]. If you keep your father's word, you [must eat (only) bread] and drink (only) water. When the prime of young adulthood is [within] you, then eat two or three times a day, and treat yourself. [But when] old age is within you, drink your fill, setting aside [(your) father's] word.

§20 (iii.33-45) You are my foremost subjects. You [must keep] my words, those of the king. You may (only) eat bread and drink (only) water. Then [Ḫattuša] will stand tall, and my land will be [at peace]. But if you don't keep the king's word, you won't live [much longer(?)], but will perish. [Whoever] confounds the king's words, right now he [...] my [...] Such a person should not be a high-ranking servant. [His throat(?)] shall be slit. Didn't his sons set aside these words of my grandfather [...]? In Šanaḫuitta my grandfather had proclaimed his son Labarna (as heir to the throne). [But afterwards] his subjects and high noblemen had confounded his words [and] set Papaḫdilmaḫ (on the throne). How many years have now passed, and [how many (of them)] have escaped (their fate)? The households of the high noblemen — where are they? Haven't they perished?

§21a (iii.46-51) You (my subjects) must keep my words, those of Labarna, the Great King. [As long as] you keep [them], Ḫattuša will stand tall, and you will set your land [at peace]. You shall eat (only) bread and drink (only) water. But if you don't keep them, your land will fall under foreign control. Be very careful about the business [of the gods]. Their sacrificial loaves, their libations, their [stews(?)], and their meal must (always) be kept available for them. §21b (iii-iv.51-54) You (Muršili) must [not] postpone (them), nor fall behind (in your deliveries). If you were to [postpone (them)], it would be evil, (as indeed was) the former (condition). So be [it]!

§22 (iii-iv.55-63) [The Great King], Labarna, spoke to his son Muršili: "I have given you my words. They shall read this [tablet] aloud in your presence every month. Thus you will be able to impress my [words] and my wisdom into (your) heart, [and] to rule successfully over my [subjects] and the high noblemen. If you [observe] an offense in anyone — whether someone offends before a deity, or someone speaks some (irresponsible) word — consult the assembly. Slander must be referred to the same assembly.[12] My son, always do what is in your heart."

§23 (iii-iv.64-72) The Great King, Labarna, says repeatedly to Ḫaštayar: "Don't forsake me!" (In order that) the king not speak thus to her, the courtiers say as follows to him: "She now still keeps on consulting the Old Women." The king says as follows [to them]: "Is she now still consulting the Old Women? I don't know."[13] (And the king says to Ḫaštayar:) "Furthermore, don't forsake me! [No!] Always consult me [alone]. I will reveal my words to you. Wash me as is fitting, hold me to your breast, and at your breast protect me from the earth!"[14]

Colophon: The tablet of Tabarna, the Great King: When the Great King, Tabarna, took ill in the city of Kuššar and instructed the young Muršili for kingship.

[11] The king here assigns to his daughter property in lieu of that near Ḫattuša which he has confiscated.

[12] On this institution see Beckman 1982 and Marazzi 1984.

[13] The "Old Women" were diviners and practioners of magic whose services were often to be utilized by members of the Hittite court in the centuries which followed.

[14] These concluding lines seem to be a request for proper burial rites.

REFERENCES

Text: *CTH* 6. KUB 1.16 + KUB 40.65. Edition: Sommer and Falkenstein 1938 (without KUB 40.65 join). Translations: T. Bryce 1982:99-130; Klock-Fontanille 1996. Studies: Bryce 1998:89-110; Beckman 1982; Carratelli 1994; Giorgieri 1991; Hoffner 1980:300-302; Marazzi 1984, 1986:1-23; de Martino 1989; Melchert 1991; Pecchioli Daddi 1992; Steiner 1996; Bryce 1998:89-100.

2. ANNALS

THE TEN YEAR ANNALS OF GREAT KING MURŠILI II OF ḪATTI (2.16)

Richard H. Beal

This composition is known from five copies. The best preserved is KBo 3.4 + KUB 23.125. This appears to be a copy from approximately the reign of Muršili's grandson Tudḫaliya IV (Grélois 1988:38-44). The other copies, KBo 16.1, KUB 19.38 (+) KUB 14.21, KBo 16.4, and KBo 16.2 (+) 113/e, appear to be slightly earlier (Grélois 1988:38-44). All of the copies were found at Boğazköy. The main copy, KBo 3.4 + KUB 23.125, as well as KUB 19.38 (+) KUB 14.21 were found by Winckler's excavations before World War I, which means they were found either in Building E, a building facing the innermost courtyard of the citadel's palace or in the archive rooms of the Great Temple in the lower city. More specific information was lost in the course of unpacking the tablets in Berlin. But see H. Klengel 1993 on Winckler's diaries. Of the copies found more recently, KBo 16.1 and KBo 16.2 are from the archive Building A on the citadel, while KBo 16.4 is from the Great Temple archive.

The main text was transliterated by Forrer 1926, no. 48. The primary edition of this text is Goetze 1933. Additional duplicates were published by Otten 1955. A newer edition was published by Grélois 1988, and a translation by del Monte 1993:32-33, 57-72.

There is also a more detailed version of the Annals of Muršili, known as the "Comprehensive" or "Detailed" Annals. This was also edited by Goetze 1933. Additional fragments or joins were published by Otten 1955, Houwink ten Cate 1966, 1967, 1979 and 1979a, Kammenhuber 1970:547-550, del Monte 1985a, Beal 1992:380f. n. 1439 and a new translation published by del Monte 1993:33-40, 73-131.

The ancient title of the "Comprehensive Annals" was "The Manly Deeds of Muršili." Although no copy preserves a title, this was likely to have been the title of the "Ten Year Annals" as well. As one might guess from its modern name, the "Ten Year Annals" describes events, largely military in nature, during the first ten years of Muršili's reign. In the so called "Comprehensive Annals" the record of events continues at least until the twenty-first year of the king. It also gives more detail and includes more campaigns not directly led by the king. For as Muršili states in the conclusion of the "Ten Year Annals," "the enemy lands which the royal princes and lords overcame are not included here." The latter statement is only partially correct: note the campaign of Nuwanza described in the 9th year of the Ten Year Annals.

It is useful to note that while the battles with the great or medium-sized powers such as Arzawa and Azzi and places that we can place on the map such as Nuḫašše and Qidš(a) (Kinza) interest us the most, and also appear to figure more prominently in Muršili's presentation, it is wars with the barbarian Kaška peoples which require most of Muršili's time. Their very lack of central organization made the Kaška easy to defeat but impossible to subdue, rather like trying to dig away the edge of a hill of sand. After spending his accession year in the all-important effort of winning the god's favor, Muršili had to go against the Kaška in his first three years. Only partway through his third year could he finally turn his attention to the powerful but relatively distant Arzawa. After spending a year and a half on campaign here, for all or parts of the next three years (5, 6, 7) he returned to fight the Kaška, who had presumably taken advantage of the army's absence. In the ninth year, the Kaška in both Pala and Yaḫrešša/Piggainarešša required Muršili's attention along with bigger and more distant Kinza, Assyria, and Azzi-Ḫayaša. Finally, almost all of the additional years described only in the "Full/Comprehensive Annals" (11-21+) detail nothing but campaigns against the Kaška.

The Ten Year Annals are interesting as a particularly complete example of Hittite historical composition. They begin with a prologue (as do many Hittite historical compositions) and end with an echoing epilogue, "clearly already in view, as the prologue was being written. Each presupposes the other" (Hoffner 1980:312). The theme of the composition is that when the youngster Muršili came to the throne after the unexpected deaths of his heroic father Šuppiluliuma I and equally heroic elder brother Arnuwanda II, the neighboring lands insulted him for his youth and inexperience and, adding injury to insult, revolted. Then, with the considerable help of the gods, he, Muršili, subdued with his own hands in ten years all those who had insulted him.

This need of Muršili to demonstrate to history that he was indeed manly and that the gods did indeed support him can perhaps be further explained by several things not mentioned in either set of annals. First and foremost, his father and brother had died of plague, brought back from a punitive expedition against Egypt (*COS* 1:160 A i 47ff.). This plague was to ravage the Hittite lands for at least twenty years thereafter,[1] that is through the entire period covered

---

[1] There is a mention of the plague having ravaged the Hittite lands for twenty years during the course of the 18th year of the Comprehensive Annals.

by the Ten Year Annals. It is the subject of four prayers by Muršili (*COS* 1:156-160). In what seems likely to have been the earliest plague prayer (now known as the "fourth"), Muršili says that repeated inquiries of the gods[2] by himself and his father have failed to find the divine cause of the plague and that he is concerning himself with temple building in a bid for the gods' mercy.[3] This must have been weighing on Muršili as he was composing the Ten Year annals. His mention that he prioritized festivals may be a reflection of this problem.

In addition, with Muršili's mother dead, Muršili was saddled with a strong-willed Babylonian princess as stepmother and queen. Making matters far worse was the fact that Muršili's beloved wife, Gaššulawiya, was on very bad terms with her step-mother-in-law, the queen. The situation was to climax with Gaššulawiya dead and deeply mourned by Muršili ("Throughout the days of life [my soul] goes down to the dark netherworld [on her account]") and the queen accused of witchcraft and demoted.[4] This may all have happened during the composition of the Ten Year Annals, for while Muršili was in Azzi on campaign, a solar eclipse was seen over Ḫattuša, which the queen repeatedly said "did not signify the death of the king, but did signify [the death of the king's wife]."[5] If the restoration is correct, such talk may have indeed caused poor Gaššulawiya to die at this time. Regardless, the domestic discontent and the eclipse portending death or another's lordship[6] must have been of concern to Muršili as he was writing the Ten Year Annals.

Finally, del Monte (1993:14) suggests that the death in Muršili's ninth year of Šarri-Kušuḫ, his elder brother and right arm, left Muršili fully on his own for the first time, and that this played a role in Muršili's issuing these annals. Probably all these events played a part in making the theme of the Ten Year Annals proof of the king's ability and the gods' trust in him. In contrast, the Full Annals, written over a decade later, appear to have another theme: "loyalty versus treason" (del Monte 1993:15-17).

In Muršili's view, it is the gods running before his army that give him the margin of victory. In the Ten Year Annals the repeated phrase is "the Sungoddess of Arinna, my lady, the victorious Stormgod, my lord, Mezzulla and all the gods ran before me." In the Comprehensive Annals, on the other hand, the phrase is somewhat different: "The victorious Stormgod, my lord, the Sungoddess of Arinna, my lady, the Stormgod of Ḫattuša, the Protective Deity (dLAMMA) of Ḫattuša, the Stormgod of the Army, *IŠTAR* of the countryside, and all the gods ran before me." The gods were also seen to intervene directly in human affairs by throwing a thunderbolt at the enemy. However, human will was also certainly seen as a causal factor. For example, because the enemy thought Muršili was an inexperienced child, they revolted. Letters from Muršili to the enemy and his replies are quoted, as are challenges to battle over intractable points. The text often gives the casus belli as seen by Muršili (usually refusal to return fugitives in the case of foreign powers or refusal to continue to supply troops, i.e. revolt for parts of the empire). Sometimes Muršili gives his reasoning for choosing a particular course of action and sometimes even the enemy's reasoning is surmised (both often given in first person). While the purpose of the text is to demonstrate the king's manhood, actions performed by armies and detachments not under Muršili's direct command are nevertheless mentioned. The text also manages successfully to discuss several campaigns going on simultaneously on different fronts. Sometimes Muršili even describes the terrain. All in all, the historical writings of Muršili II show considerable historical sophistication. (On Muršili's historiography, see Cancik 1976:102-151, Hoffner 1980:311-315, and del Monte 1993:13-17).

Muršili II is also responsible another major Hittite historical text, "The Manly Deeds of Šuppiluliuma" (*COS* 1:185-192).

Introduction

[Thus speaks] My Majesty[7] Muršili, the Great King, King of the land of Ḫatti, the hero, son of Šuppiluliuma, Great King, the hero.

Before I sat down on my father's throne, all the enemy foreign lands began hostilities. When my father became a god,[8] Arnuwanda, my brother, sat on his father's throne. But, afterwards he, too,

[2] For one of the primary methods, the oracular inquiry, see later examples in *COS* 1:204-211.

[3] The other three prayers mention that 20 years of plague have now passed. The badly broken "third" prayer's preserved sections mention no "causes," so it may actually be the second. By the time of the so called "first" prayer oracular inquiry had turned up a cause: his father's treachery toward Tudḫaliya the younger. The "second" prayer is probably the last in line since further causes have now been found, and since for the first time Muršili accepts his guilt in all of these misdeeds by the principle of the "sins of the father are visited on the son." Cf. Exod 20:5; etc. These prayers are transliterated and translated by Goetze (1930); cf. *COS* 1.60.

[4] KUB 14.4 = CTH 70, ed. poorly by de Martino (1998), KBo 4.8 + Izmir "1277" w. dupl. 1206/u + 245/w, ed. Hoffner 1983.

[5] ([*ŠA* DAM LUGAL-*wa* ÚŠ *išiy*]*aḫta* *UL*-*wa* *ŠA* LUGAL ÚŠ *išiyaḫta*) KUB 14.4 iv.25-26, with restoration courtesy of H. A. Hoffner (orally). Since this is the text detailing the queen's crimes, the restoration is likely to be correct.

[6] Ibid., iv.27.

[7] Lit., "My Sungod." The Hittite king was not worshipped as a god until he died and even then only became a minor god in his own right (not a sungod). The title is probably borrowed from Egypt, but makes sense to the Hittites due to the Mesopotamian-influenced concept of the Sungod as god of justice, and hence of kingship.

[8] Cf. note 7.

became sick.[9] When the enemy lands heard that my brother Arnuwanda was sick, the enemy lands began hostilities.

And when my brother Arnuwanda became a god, those enemy lands which had not yet begun hostilities, they too began hostilities. The enemy foreign lands said as follows: "His father, who was king of Ḫatti, was a heroic king. He kept the enemy lands defeated and he has become a god. His son who sat on his father's throne was also in the prime of life, and he got sick and he also became a god.

Now, the one who has sat down on his father's throne is a child.[10] He will not (be able to) save the borders of Ḫatti and Ḫatti itself."

Because my father was establishing garrisons in the land of Mitanni,[11] he tarried in a garrison, and the festivals of the Sungoddess of Arinna, my lady, lapsed.

When I, My Majesty, sat on my father's throne, while I had not yet gone against any of the enemy foreign lands who were in a state of hostilities with me, I concerned myself with and performed the regular festivals of the Sungoddess of Arinna, my lady. I held up my hand to the Sungoddess of Arinna, my lady, and said as follows: "O Sungoddess of Arinna, my lady! The enemy foreign lands who have called me a child and belittled me, have begun seeking to take away the borders of the Sungoddess of Arinna, my lady. Stand by me, O Sungoddess of Arinna, my lady. Destroy those enemy foreign lands before me." The Sungoddess of Arinna heard my words and stood by me. After I sat down on my father's throne, in ten years I vanquished these enemy foreign lands and destroyed them.

Year 1

The Kaška[12] of the land of Durmitta began hostilities with me and [came] for battle against me. Subsequently the (other) Kaška also came. They began to attack the land of Durmitta. I, My Majesty, went against them. I attacked the leading districts of the Kaška-Land — Ḫalila and Dudduška. I looted them including their transplantees,[13] cattle and sheep and brought them away to Ḫattuša. The towns of Ḫalila and Dudduška I burned down.

When the Kaška heard about the destruction of Ḫalila and Dudduška, the whole land of the Kaška came to help and came for battle against me. I, My Majesty, fought them. The Sungoddess of Arinna, my lady, the victorious[14] Stormgod, my lord, Mezzulla and all the gods ran before me. I defeated the levies[15] of the Kaška and killed them. The Kaška of the land of Durmitta resubmitted and they began to give [me troops].

[Then] I, [My Majesty,] returned. Because the Kaška of the land of Išḫupitta had become hostile and ceased giving me troops, I, My Majesty, went to the land of Išḫupitta. I attacked the town of [...]ḫumiššena. I looted it including its transplantees, cattle and sheep and brought them away to Ḫattuša, while the town I burned down. I resubjugated the Kaška of the land of Išḫupitta. They began to give me troops. All this I did in one year.

Year 2

In the following year I went [to the Upper Land,] because the district of Tipiya had become hostile and ceased giving me troops. I, My Majesty, attacked Katḫaiduwa. I brought its transplantees, cattle, and sheep back to Ḫattuša, [while the town I burned down.]

Then I [retur]ned [from Tipiya to Ḫattuša]. Because the land of Išḫupitta had [again] become hostile, [I sent ...] and he defeated it again a second time. Those who [had been the head of the rebellion] escaped there. Nunnata [and Pazzanna, my servants ...-d] and [I chased(?)] them [to Kammama] in the land of the Kaška. [No one(?) esc]aped. [When I demanded those] people [who had been] the head of the rebellion, [they seized and killed] them. I, My Majesty, [made] Kammama [my servants again]. The [Sungoddess of Arinna,] my lady, [the victorious Stormgod, my lord,]

[9] The plague which carried off two Hittite kings in rapid succession is probably the same which caused Muršili to compose at least four progressively more desperate plague prayers (see note 3 above). The plague was perhaps brought back by prisoners taken during Arnuwanda's punitive attack on Egyptian territory in Syria-Palestine.

[10] Two elder brothers, Telipinu, "priest" of Kizzuwatna and later king of Aleppo and Piyaššili/Šarri-Kušuḫ, king of Karkamiš were passed over in the succession. Perhaps these younger brothers of crown prince Arnuwanda had given up their at-the-time-theoretical rights to the throne in return for their appanage states or perhaps they were not children of the queen and so were disqualified from the Great Kingship.

[11] A Hurrian imperial state, ruled by an Indo-European family, stretching across upper Mesopotamia from the Mediterranean sea to the Zagros and centered on the land of Ḫanigalbat, with its capital at Waššukanni, so far unlocated, in upper Mesopotamia. After several generations of hostilities, Šuppiluliuma I in a campaign of strategic genius attacked them through the Ergani Maden pass from the north and penetrated quickly to Waššukkani, destroying their power, installing a puppet king, and annexing the Syrian third of their empire. See Güterbock 1956:84-96, 110-114; Beckman 1996:30-54; and Moran 1992.

[12] On the Kaškaeans, see my introduction to this text. See also von Schuler 1965.

[13] NAM.RA = Hitt. *arnuwala-*, these are civilian captives, largely intended to be resettled in Ḫatti. See Alp 1950-51; Beal 1988:277, n. 42; Klinger 1992. The usual translation "deportee" is to be avoided since they are not being expelled from the empire but rather moved within it.

[14] Underlying the Sumerogram NIR.GÁL is Luwian *muwatalli-*, which *CLL* 151 renders "overpowering, mighty." The adj. is ultimately based upon the Luwian *muwa-* "to overpower." My translation "victorious" is based on an oral suggestion of J. D. Hawkins.

[15] ERÍN.MEŠ *NĀRĀRU* = *warriš* ERÍN.MEŠ-*za*, lit., "help-troops," see Beal 1992:56-71.

Mezzulla, [and all] the gods [ran before me, and I defeated Palḫuišša(?).[16] I looted it including its transplantees,] cattle and sheep [and brought them] away [to Ḫattuša.] All this [I did in one year].

Year 3

In the following year [I did ... When Arnuwanda(?)],[17] my brother, in [...], [the troops of the town of Attārimma], the troops of the town of Ḫuwaršanašša and the troops of the town of [Šuruda fled before him and went] to [Arzawa.[18] I sent a messenger] to Uḫḫa-ziti. [I] wrote to him as follows: "People [who belong to me — the troops of Attārimma,] the troops of Ḫuwaršanašša [and the troops of Šuruda] — came [to you. Give them back to me.]" But Uḫḫa-ziti [wrote back] to me [as follows]: "[I will] not [give] any[one back] to you. [...] by force [...]" [He mustered] his troops [...]

[He stood] for battle behind the town of Tikkukkuwa. I, [My Majesty] fought [him]. The Sungoddess of [Arinna, my lady, the] victorious [Stormgod], my lord, Mezzula [and all the god]s ran before me and [I defeated] the enemy and destroyed them. I burned down Tikkukkuwa [...]. I also burned the district of Dašma[ḫa ...]

[I went to ..].-ittakattaša, [and it ...] I attacked. [...], and I [...]-d [...] for the second time(?) [...]

Then I went forth to Išḫupitta. I attacked Palḫuišša. The Pišḫuruan enemy stood behind Palḫuišša for battle against me. I fought them. The Sungoddess of Arinna, my lady, the victorious[19] Stormgod, my lord, Mezzulla and all the gods ran before me. I destroyed the Pišḫuruan enemy behind Palḫuišša, then I burned down the town.

From Palḫuišša I came back to Ḫattuša. I set my infantry and horse-troops in motion and in that same year I went against Arzawa. I sent a messenger to Uḫḫaziti.[a] I wrote to him as follows: "Because I asked you to return my subjects who came to you and you did not give them back and you kept calling me a child and you kept belittling me. Now, come, we will fight. Let the Stormgod, my lord, decide our lawsuit." [b]

[a] Num 20:14; 21:21; Josh 11:1; Judg 11; 1 Kgs 20:3

[b] Judg 11:27

When I had gone and when I had arrived in Lawaša, the victorious Stormgod, my lord, showed his divine power. He shot a lightning bolt. My troops saw the lightning bolt and the land of Arzawa saw it. The lightning bolt went and struck Arzawa.[20] [c] It struck Apāša (Ephesus?), the city of Uḫḫaziti. Uḫḫaziti fell on his knees and became ill. When Uḫḫaziti became ill, he did not subsequently come against me for battle. (Instead) he sent his son Piyama-dLAMMA with infantry and horse-troops against me. He stood for battle against me at the Āštarpa River in Walma. I My Majesty fought him. The Sungoddess of Arinna, my lady, the victorious Stormgod, my lord, Mezzulla and all the gods ran before me. I defeated Piyama-^{d}LAMMA, son of Uḫḫaziti, with his infantry and his horse-troops, and I destroyed them. Then I pursued him and I went across to Arzawa. I went to Apāša into the city of Uḫḫaziti. Uḫḫaziti did not resist me and fled before me. He went across into the sea by ship(??)/to the islands(??).[21] There he remained.

[c] Josh 10:11-15

All the land of Arzawa fled. Some (potential) transplantees fled to Mt. Arinnanda and they held Mt. Arinnanda. Other (potential) transplantees fled to the town of Puranda and they held Puranda. Yet other (potential) tranplantees fled across into the sea with Uḫḫaziti. I, My Majesty, pursued the transplantees on Mt. Arinnanda. I battled Mt. Arinnanda. The Sungoddess of Arinna, my lady, the victorious Stormgod, my lord, Mezzulla and all the gods ran before me. I vanquished Mt. Arinnanda. The transplantees whom I, My Majesty, brought back for the royal estate numbered 15,500. Those whom the Hittite lords, infantry and horse-troops brought back were innumerable. Then I sent the tranplantees to Ḫattuša and they were led away.

When I vanquished Mt. Arinnanda, I returned to the Āštarpa river and at the Āštarpa river I built a walled military camp. There I celebrated the Festi-

---

[16] Previous editors have restored "Kammama" here. Indeed the transition from discussion of Kammama to Palḫuiša would seem in the above translation to be rather abrupt. However, according to the Full Annals (KUB 14.15 i 1-21), Kammama turned over the fugitives and submitted voluntarily, whereas Palḫuiša was attacked and plundered. Since Muršili again attacked and this time burned Palḫiša in his third year, it is possible that a third town, whose name was lost in both texts is to be restored here and in KUB 14.15 i 1.

[17] Since this past event happened in Northwestern Anatolia, it seems likely that a campaign led by Šuppiluliuma I's crown prince Arnuwanda is meant. del Monte 1993:62 and n. 14 prefers to restore a different brother, Šarri-kušuḫ, King of Karkamiš, here.

[18] On this state see Heinhold-Krahmer 1977.

[19] Cf. note 14 above.

[20] For discussion of divine intervention in Hittite military records, see Hoffner 1980:327-328, and in ancient warfare narrations, see Younger 1990:145-146, 208-211; and Weinfeld 1983:139.

[21] :*guršawanza*. The word is quite rare. Goetze 1933:50f., 216. translated "by ship." Starke 1981 has since suggested a translation "to the islands" (followed by Melchert, *CLL* 113 and del Monte 1993:64). His arguments include the following. A genitival adjective *guršawanašši-* formed from our word and describing a type of terrain occurs in field texts, KUB 8.75 i 12, where it is found in similar position to *ŠA* ÍD "of the river" (Starke, 1981:144). "Island land" makes better sense than "ship land." An ergative/personified form occurs in a Luwian language offering text, KUB 35.107 ii.7, transliterated by Starke 1985:236-240. Starke's case would be quite convincing except for another example of the word, RS 25.421:48 (Laroche 1968:774f.), which he missed. Translating this passage "sweet Dilmun (i.e. Bahrain) dates arrive 'from the island'" surely makes sense, but why should "from the island" have a GIŠ "wood" determinative? Dates arriving from Dilmun "by ship" makes equal if not better sense and "ships" not "islands" could be expected to have a "wood" determinative. Unless the same word is used for both "ship" and "island"

val of the Year. All this I did in one year.

Year 4

When it became Spring — as long as Uḫḫaziti was sick and was in the midst of sea (i.e. on an island) his sons were with him. Uḫḫaziti died in the midst of sea, but his sons split up. One son was still in the midst of the sea, but one, Tapalazunauli, returned from the sea. Since all (remaining) of Arzawa had gone [...] up to Puranda, Tapalazunauli (also) went up to Puranda. When I had taken care of the Festival of the Year, I went to Puranda for battle. Tapalazunauli came down from Puranda with infantry and horse-troops for battle against me. He stood for battle against me in his own territory.[22] I, My Majesty, fought him. The Sungoddess of Arinna, my lady, the victorious Stormgod, my lord, Mezzulla and all the gods ran before me. I defeated Tapalazunauli, [son of Uḫḫaziti,] and his infantry and horse-troops and destroyed him. Then I pursued him. I went and surrounded Puranda and shut it up; I took away its water.

[When] I had shut up Puranda, Tapalazunauli, son of Uḫḫaziti, who was up in Puranda, became afraid. He fled down from Puranda at night. He took charge of [his wife,] his children, and the (potential) transplantees together with (their) provisions[23]; he led them down from Puranda. However, when I, My Majesty, heard: 'Tapalazunauli fled down [at night] and he took charge of his wife, his children and the (potential) transplantees together with (their) provisions and led them down,' I, My Majesty, sent my infantry and horse-troops after him. They harried Tapalazunauli on the road. They captured his wife, his children, and the transplantees and brought them back. Tapalazunauli escaped alone, a single person. The aforementioned infantry and horse-troops kept for themselves the transplantees whom they had ha[rried] on the road.

When it had come about that I had shut up Puranda for [x] days, I [attack]ed [Puranda. The Sungoddess of Arinna, my lady, the victorious Stormgod,] my [lord,] Mezzulla [and all the gods ran before me.] I vanquished Puranda. [The transplantees whom I, My Majesty, brought back for the royal estate] numbered 16,[X]00. Those [transplantees,] cattle and sheep [which the Hittite lords, infantry and horse-troops brought back] were [innumerable. Then I sent them to Ḫattuša and they] were led away.

[...] was in [the midst of the sea ...Piyama]-ᵈLA[MMA,] son of Uḫḫaziti, [... departed] from the sea [and took refuge(?)] with the king of Aḫḫiyawa[24] [...] I, [My Majesty] sent [...] by ship. [...-ed ...] and they brought him away. [The transplantees with him] they also brought away. [The transplantees from ...] and the transplantees from Lipa consisted of [ ] transplantees. I sent [them to Ḫattuša] and they were led away.

[When] I came back [to the Še]ḫa-[River Land,][25] I would have fought [Manapa-Tarḫunta who] was [lord] in Šeḫa-River Land. However, when [Manapa-Tarḫunta] heard about me: "The Hittite king is coming," [he became] afraid and so [he did not] then [come] against me. He sent [to] me his mother and old men and old women. They came and [fell down] at my feet. Because the women fell down at my feet, I had mercy on the women and so[26] I did [not] enter the Šeḫa-River Land. They handed over to me the Hittite transplantees who were in Šeḫa-River Land. There were 4,000 transplantees whom they handed over. I sent them back to Ḫattuša and they led them away. Manapa-Tarḫunta and Šeḫa-River Land I made into my subjects.[27] [d]

d Josh 9

Then I went to Mirā. I gave Mirā to Mašḫuiluwa; I gave Šeḫa-River Land to Manapa-Tarḫunta; and I gave Ḫapalla to Targašnalli. I made these lands into my subjects where they were. I imposed military obligations on them and they began to give me troops. Because I wintered within Arzawa, in two years the Sungoddess of Arinna, my lady, the victorious Stormgod, my lord, Mezzulla and all the gods ran before me and I overcame Arzawa. Some (of Arzawa) I brought away to Ḫattuša and some I made into my subjects where they were. I imposed military obligations on them and they began to give me troops. The transplantees whom I, My Majesty, brought back for the royal estates, because I overcame all of Arzawa, numbered all together[28] 66,000. Those whom the Hittite lords, infantry and horse-troops brought back were innumerable. When I had overcome all of Arzawa, then I came away to Ḫattuša. All this I did in the one year since I had wintered in Arzawa.

(wooden island = ship), the meaning of *guršawanza* is still not settled.

[22] Lit. "his fields and meadows."

[23] *šaramnaz*. The translation follows a suggestion of H. A. Hoffner (personal communication). It was previously translated "from (their) place of refuge" (Goetze 1933:220), "down from above" (Friedrich 1952:184), "from the acropolis" (Alp 1954:456-58) and "from the palace" (Alp 1979:18-25).

[24] = Achaea, that is some Mycenaean Greek state. Although still a contentious issue, this equation is now accepted my most Hittitologists. See Güterbock 1983b; 1984; Bryce 1988; 1989; 1998:59f., 321f., 342f.; Marazzi 1992.

[25] Restoration with Goetze 1933:66 and Grélois 1988:65, rather than with Forrer 1926:82 "When I came back aw[ay from the sea]."

[26] See *CHD* s.v. *namma* 6c.

[27] See Younger 1990:202-203.

[28] Hitt. 1-*etta*, lit. "in one (sum)."

Year 5
The next year I went to Mt. Ašḫarpaya. Since the Kaška had possession of Mt. Ašḫarpaya, they had cut the Pala-roads. I fought these Kaška of Mt. Ašḫarpaya. The Sungoddess of Arinna, my lady, the victorious Stormgod, my lord, Mezzulla and all the gods ran before me and I overcame Mt. Ašḫarpaya which the Kaška had held. I destroyed it. I emptied Mt. Ašḫarpaya and then departed. When I arrived in Šammaḫa, I entered Ziulila.

While my father was in Mitanni, the Arawannan enemy by continually attacking Kiššiya kept it greatly oppressed. I, My Majesty, went to Arawanna and attacked Arawanna. The Sungoddess of Arinna, my lady, the victorious Stormgod, my lord, Mezzulla and all the gods ran before me and I overcame all Arawanna. The transplantees whom I brought back from Arawanna for the royal estates numbered 3,500. The transplantees, cattle and sheep that the Hittite lords, infantry and horse-troops brought back were innumerable. When I had overcome Arawanna, then I came back to Ḫattuša. All this I did in one year.

Year 6
The next year I went to Zimurriya.[29] The Kaška who had occupied Mt. Tarikarimu by force in the time of my grandfather, subsequently became a danger for Hittite territory.[30] They came and attacked Hittite territory[31] and they oppressed it greatly. I, My Majesty went and attacked Mt. Tarikarimu, which the Kaška had occupied. The Sungoddess of Arinna, my lady, the victorious Stormgod, my lord, Mezzulla and all the gods ran before me and I overcame the Kaška of Mt. Tarikarimu and destroyed them. I emptied Mt. Tarikarimu and burned the whole land of Zimurriya. Then I returned to Ḫattuša. All this I did in one year.

Year 7
The next year I went to Tipiya.[32] While my father was in Mitanni, Piḫḫuniya, man of Tipiya, marched and repeatedly attacked the Upper Land. He advanced as far as Zazziša and he looted the Upper Land and carried it (i.e. the loot) down into the land of the Kaška. He took all the land of Ištitina and turned it into his pasture.

Thereafter, Piḫḫuniya did not rule like a Kaškan. When in Kaška there had never been a single ruler, suddenly this Piḫḫuniya ruled like a king. I, My Majesty, went toward him and sent him a messenger. I wrote to him: "Send out to me my subjects whom you took and led down into Kaška." Piḫḫuniya wrote back to me as follows: "I will not give anything back to you. And if you come to fight me, I will not take a stand to fight you anywhere in my own territory,[33] I will come to your land and I will take a stand to fight you in the midst of your land." When Piḫḫuniya had written this back to me and did not give my subjects back to me, I went to fight him. I attacked his land. The Sungoddess of Arinna, my lady, the victorious Stormgod, my lord, Mezzulla and all the gods ran before me. I overcame the whole land of Tipiya and burned it. I captured Piḫḫuniya and brought him back to Ḫattuša. Then I returned from Tipiya. Since Piḫḫuniya had taken Ištitina, I rebuilt it and made it a Hittite land again.

When I had overcome Tipiya, I sent a messenger [e] to Anniya, king of Azzi.[34] I wrote to him: "[Return to me] my subjects who came to you while my father was in Mitanni."

e Num 20:14; 21:21; Josh 11:1; Judg 11; 1 Kgs 20:3

[Remainder of Year 7 is broken away in the Ten Year Annals; Continuation of the 7th year according to the Full Annals (KUB 14.17 iii 2ff.)]

[...] He (Anniya) came [and marched to Dankuwa. He at[tacked it, and plundered] it of [transplantees, cattle and sheep.] He [carr]ied [them] down into Ḫayaša.[35]

[When I, My Majesty, heard about it], I wrote to him, "[...] they [...]-ed there nothing to/for me. None of the men of Ištitina(?) [...] me/for me. [But you] came, [marched] to Dankuwa, [attac]ked [it, plundered it] of [transplantees, cattle and sheep, and carried them] down into Ḫayaša." [Anniya, the lord] of Azzi, [wrote] back to me as follows:

[29] The reading ^{URU}*Zi-mur-ri-ya* follows Hoffner 1976:336, based on ^{URU}*Zi-mu-ri-ya* in the historical fragment KBo 22:54 rev. 4, 5, on the obv. of which the Kaška are mentioned, in preference to the *Zi-ḫar-ri-ya* of Goetze 1933:80 and del Monte and Tischler 1978:498.

[30] Lit. "Ḫattuša."

[31] Lit. "Ḫattuša."

[32] The Comprehensive Annals, which are badly broken in this section, first describe a revolt in Nuḫašše. When an Egyptian army is reported to be approaching Hittite territory, Muršili quickly sent general Kantuzzili to aid his brother Šarri-Kušuḫ, king of Karkamiš, in suppressing the revolt and presumably holding off the Egyptians until Muršili could personally bring the rest of the army. Fortunately the Egyptians were defeated. Since the text does not use the regular formula "My gods ran before them and they defeated PN/GN" (for some examples, see Goetze 1933:38f. i.28, 106f. i.22) or give credit to the victorious generals, but simply says "the Egyptians were defeated and did not come" the Egyptians, may have been defeated by some third party before reaching the Hittite border. See Bryce 1988 for more details and a suggested scenario for Muršili's relations with Nuḫašše. Muršili on hearing the news was able to turn around and instead head for Tipiya.

[33] Lit. "field and meadow."

[34] Anniya's kingdom of Azzi-Ḫayaša was located to the northeast of the Hittites, perhaps in the valley of the Kelkit İrmak. For references and discussion see del Monte and Tischler 1978:59f., 63f.

[35] Part of the combined kingdom of Azzi-Ḫayaša, see note 34.

"[Why] do you keep writing to me? If some [deportees] came and (if) there are some who are (still) coming in to me, [we do not give them up.] But if you are continually seeking [...]." I wrote back to him as follows: "I came and encamped at the border of your land. I did not attack your land and I did not plunder it of transplantees, cattle and sheep. You started hostilities [with My Majesty] and came and [attacked] Dankuwa [and empti]ed [it.] Let the gods take a stand on my side and judge the [legal case] on my side." [f]

f Judg 11:27

[Because] he began to speak ev[il] words [to me], I became ho[stile to him.] I went (against) him. The town of Ura, which was the first outpost of the land of Azzi, is situated in a hard to reach place. Whoever hears these tablets (read), let him send and let him [behold how] this town of Ura was built.[36] [When] Anniya, lord of Azzi [...]

[Aside from a mention of a campaign by Muršili's brother Šarri-Kušuḫ, king of Karkamiš, while Muršili was in Ištitina, the remainder of the 7th year is entirely broken away in the Full Annals.]

Year 8

[Entirely broken away in the Ten Year Annals. Some of the missing information can be gleaned from the badly broken section in the Full Annals]

[...] Man[apa-Tarḫunta ...] a woman [...] the man of the town of [...] it/them [...] / to me [...] thus [...]

[long gap in the text]

[I sent ... with orders] "seize [...]" [Then, I sent my brother [Šarri-Kušuḫ to ...]. I, [however], returned [to ...]. I encamped in [...]. I myself, in Ḫattuša [...]. [I] would [have ...-ed] troops and horse-troops [against] them. But when the [men] of Ḫayaša [heard] "His Majesty is coming," they sent [a messenger] to [me] saying "O lord, because they heard [...] they were afraid [...] ... We will bring [...] and hand over [...] to the lor]d(?). [...] comes, then let the lords come forth [...] We will b[ring] back the Hittite transplantees who are coming in to us, and hand them over."

When the men of Ḫayaša replied to me in this way, at that time the goddess Ḫebat of Kummanni troubled me with regard to the festival of invocation.

Year 9

[The beginning of Year 9 is broken away in the Ten Year Annals; some of the missing information may be gleaned from the Full Annals.]

[I] sai[d], "Hand over [the Hittite transplantees who are coming to you ... and I will not then go] against the men [of Ḫayaša.]" [However,] the men of Ḫayaša [...] and [did not hand over] the Hittite transplantees. So [I wrote] again [to] Anniya as follows. "[You have not] yet [begun] to give anything back to me. Some [you brought(?)] to the city of Ḫayaša and the land of Ḫayaša [kept(?)] and some you even took for yourself." He brought [word] to Ḫattuša:[37] "The Hittite transplantees have not been compensated for [by(?)] Azziyan [transplantees] either. If some Hittite transplantees are coming over to us, we will not give them over." When the men of Ḫayaša did not hand back the Hittite transplantees to My Majesty, [...(my general)] built a [fortress ...] and he departed.

While I was in Tiliur[a], (the people of) Wāšulana revolted against Ḫūdupianza, the royal prince who ruled Palā. I sent Nuwanza, Chief of the Wine[38] [with infantry] and horse-troops and they departed for the sake of Ḫūdupianza. They went to Wāšulana and they attacked Wāšulana. My gods ran before them and they defeated Wāšulana and burned it down. They looted [it including its transplantees], cattle, and sheep and carried [them] off [to Ḫattuša.]

[When I needed to celebrate] the festival of invocation of Ḫebat of Kummanni,[39] I went to Kizzuwatna.[40] When I arrived in Kizzuwatna, my brother Šarri-Kušuḫ, [the king of] Karkamiš[41] drove to Kizzuwatna to meet me and we got together. [Then] they [brought] [me] a terrible message. Šarri-Kušuḫ, my [brother, the king of] Karkamiš, got sick and died. They [ca]rried him to Ḫattuša and in Ḫattuša they performed the rites of the dead. The thr[eshold(?)] of the god which I [...]-d, the [...] of the gods [...]. I came away and in K[izzuwatna] I lamented.

The men of Nu[ḫašše[42] began hostilities] and [they] besieged [...] ... [They wrote(?)] to the king of [... and] to other enemies [of My Majesty]. [...] When [the men of] Ḫayaša [heard that] enemies were arising [against My Majesty,] they did not [...]. They mustered [their troops and attacked] the land of Išt[itina. [They] surrounded [the city of Kannu-

[36] Verification of written annals is invited. See Hoffner 1980:315.

[37] The preceding broken passage can be differently understood following del Monte 1993:91: "Aniya [wrote] back [to me:] '[You are not beginning] to hand anything back to me. [You have come] against Ḫayaša, you have [devastated] the land of Ḫayaša; some you took for yourself and you have carried [them away] to Ḫattuša.'"

[38] The title of a senior general in the Hittite army. This officer ranked below only the king, the crown prince (at this time too young to be in the field), the king of Karkamiš, and the Chief of the Royal Body Guards (GAL *MEŠEDI*). See Beal 1992:342-56.

[39] Classical Comana Cataoniae, near modern Şar, east south-east of Kayseri on the Seyhan River, which was the major cult center of Kizzuwatna, is still unexcavated.

[40] The Cilician Plain and the valleys leading north from it. On the history of Kizzuwatna, see Kümmel 1980; Beal 1986.

[41] See Güterbock 1956:120-121.

[42] A land of many small states in Syria south of Aleppo, west of Meskene, east of Amurru and north of Qids (Qadeš); see Klengel 1969:18-57

wara. ...] Before PN [...] [While they came against Ištit]ina with infantry and horse-troops and destroyed] the land of [Ištitina] and surrounded the city [of Kannuwa]ra, I had gone [to Kummanni to celebrate] the invocation festival. [...] and I did not want in any way to [...] [I] did not want to [... aw]ay from before [...] I became [...] [...] me not. If while I was far away things [would] improve.

This is what I went and did. I gave infantry and horse-troops to [Kurunta] and I sent him to Nuḫašše. I gave him the following orders: "Since the men of Nuḫašše are hostile, go and destroy their harvest and besiege them." Kurunta went leading troops and horse-troops. He destroyed the harvest of the land of Nuḫašše and besieged them. Because the kings of Nuḫašše had transgressed the oaths of me and my father, the oath gods showed their divine power. [...] ... They summoned his own flesh and blood[43] against them. When Niqmadda,[44] eldest son of Aitakkama,[45] who was king of Kinza,[46] saw how they were besieged and further how their grain was running out, he killed Aitakkama his father. They (sc. the oath gods) turned [Niqmadd]a and the land of Kinza back to my side. (The Kinzans) submitted themselves to me. I did not take Niqmadda as my servant on the spot. Now, because they had transgressed oaths, I said [to them] "let the oath gods make them [...]. Let the son kill his father and let brother kill brother. Let his own [flesh and blood] finish them off.

[Kurunta ...] and [went] up to the city of Kinza and he seized the city of Kinza.

[Then], because the infantry and horse-troops of Ḫayaša [came] in the direction of the Upper Land and destroyed the land of Ištitina and surrounded the city of Kannuwara and because I had left Nuwanza, the Chief of the Wine [in the Upp]er [Land] with all the generals, infantry and horse-troops, I wrote to Nuwanza [as follows]: "The enemy from Ḫayaša has just come [in the direction of the Upper Land] and has destroyed Ištitina and has surrounded the city of Kannuwara. [Go] with infantry and horse-troops to the aid of Kannuwara and chase [the enemy] away from Kannuwara."

[Nuwanza, the Chief of the Wine], with infantry and horse-troops was marching to Kannuwara to help. When [Nuwanza ...], the ranking officers are saying the following words to him: "(Success) has not been ascertained [for you by augury] and extispicy."[47] [So Nuwanza, the Chief of the] Wine, sent a messenger [to me with a letter saying]: "[I do not have (?)] an augur and diviner and (success) has not been ascertained [for me by augury] and extispicy. [If] you [would only] write [to me the oracular answer]."

[When Nuwanza, the Chief of the Wine], had written that [to me], [I was celebrating the festival of invocation] in [Kizzuwat]na. [...] I summoned [...] I completed [the festival(?)]. [If] I had gone to help [Ištitina] and had chased the [Ḫayašan enemy away from Kannuwara], the [king of Assyria(?) would have] conquered Karkamiš and [...] it. If I had [gone] against those enemies [and had] defeated them, when the [Assyrians] would have heard, would [they] not have [said] as follows: "His father conquered Karkamiš[48] and it stands [...]. His (Muršili's) brother whom he (Šuppiluliuma) made king in Karkamiš has died and he (Muršili) has not gone to Karkamiš and put Karkamiš in order; he has gone to some other land." When I had thought this over, I took oracles by augury and extispicy in advance[49] for Nuwanza, the Chief of the Wine. (Success) was ascertained for him by augury and by extispicy. I sent Nanaziti, the Royal Prince, after Nuwanza with a letter saying: "Just now I have taken oracles by augury and extispicy in advance for you and (success) was ascertained for you by augury and extispicy. Go now! The Storm-god, My Lord, has already given that Ḫayašan enemy to you. You will kill him."

When I had sent Nanaziti, the royal prince, after Nuwanza the Chief of the Wine, I went to the land of Karkamiš. When I arrived in the city of Aštata,[50] I went up into the city of Aštata and built a fortress up there. Then I garrisoned it. The troops whom Kurunta had led for destroying the harvest of Nuḫašše brought Niqmadda before me because he had killed his father Aitakkama, king of Kinza. I

and most recently Beckman 1996:50.

[43] Lit. "fat."

[44] The reading of this prince's name as the common North West Semitic name Niqmad (= *Níg-ma-*ᵈU) rather than NÍG.BA-ᵈU, as Goetze 1933:112f. read, is the suggestion of Albright *BASOR* 95 (1944) 31f.

[45] The double dealing of Aitakkama, or Etakkama, and his switch of sides from the Egyptians/Mitannians to the Hittites during Šuppiluliuma I's conquest of Syria is documented in several letters from Tell el-Amarna; see Moran 1992:380 (index).

[46] This city's name, probably actually pronounced something like Qidš(a), as the Hittite "Kinza" and Aitakkama's own rendering, "Qidši" (EA 189 obv. 11, genitive) clearly show, is usually misvocalized by modern scholars as "Kadesh" or "Qadeš" by modern scholars. Its site is Tell Nebi Mend. See Klengel 1969:139-177.

[47] Lit. "by birds and by flesh."

[48] This conquest is described by Muršili in his "Deeds of Šuppiluliuma" (see Güterbock 1956:92-96). Karkamiš is modern Jereblus, where the Turkish-Syrian border crosses the Euphrates. It was briefly excavated before this border line was drawn. For discussion and bibliography, see Hawkins 1980a. On Hittite administration there see most recently Beckman 1992.

[49] *CHD* s.v. *peran* 3 a 2′.

[50] Modern Meskene, downstream from Karkamiš. French excavations and subsequent clandestine digging before the site was covered by Lake

took him into my service.

When I went from Aštata into Karkamiš, ... I reorganized the land of Karkamiš. Then I made [...]-šarruma, son of Šarri-Kušuḫ king in the land of Karkamiš and I made the land of Karkamiš swear allegiance to him. Then I made Talmi-Šarruma, son of Telipinu, king in Aleppo and I made the land of Aleppo swear allegiance to him.

[The Ten Year Annals resume here]

[...] in fear [...] I turned [...] did not [stand] for battle against me. [Since] I had left [the infantry and horse-troops in the Upper Land, Nuwanza, the Chief of the Wine], came [with infantry and horse-troops] to help. He went [to Kannuwara to figh]t [against Azzi]. The infantry and horse-troops of Azzi stood [for battle against Nuwanza, the Chief of the Wine. Nuwanza overcame them.] Concerning prisoners and killed, [they were innumerable.]

[When] I, [My Majesty], came up from Kizzuwatna, [little of] the year [remain]ed to me. So I didn't then go to Azzi. [Since Yaḫrešša] had begun hostilities against [me] and did not give me troops and kept attacking [...], I, My Majesty, [went] to Yaḫrešša. I attacked Yaḫrešša. The Sun-goddess of Arinna, my lady, the victorious Storm-god, my lord, Mezzulla and all [the gods] ran before me. I overcame Yaḫrešša[-city] and then I burned it down. Then I continued to the land of Piggainarešša. I attacked the Kaška of Piggainarešša, and I overcame them. I burned down Piggainarešša. I plundered it of transplantees, cattle and sheep. and brought them away to Ḫattuša. When I had overcome Yaḫrešša and Piggainarešša, I then came back to Ḫattuša. All this I did in one year.

Year 10

The next year I went to Azzi. The infantry and horse-troops of Azzi did not stand for battle against me. The whole land took to fortified cities. Two of these fortified cities, Aripšā and Dukkamma, I fought. The Sungoddess of Arinna, my lady, the victorious Stormgod, my lord, Mezzulla and all the gods ran before me. Aripšā and Dukkamma I captured in battle. The transplantees whom I, My Majesty, brought back for the royal estates numbered 3,000. Those whom the Hittite lords, infantry and horse-troops brought back were not included.

Conclusion

Since I sat down on my father's throne, I have ruled ten years as king. These enemy lands I overcame with my own hands. The enemy lands which the royal princes and lords overcame are not included here. Whatever more the Sungoddess of Arinna, my lady, repeatedly gives to me (to do), I will carry it out and put it down (on clay).[51]

[The remainder of the column is uninscribed. There is no colophon]

Assad have produced numerous tablets. See Huehnergard 1993 and Margueron 1993. On Hittite administration there see Beckman 1992.

[51] Or: place it down before (the goddess).

REFERENCES

Editions: Forrer 1926, no. 48; Goetze 1933; Grélois 1988. Translations: Friedrich 1925:9-12; Kümmel 1985; del Monte 1993:32-33, 57-72. Studies: Houwink ten Cate 1966; 1967; 1979; Hoffner 1980:311-315.

B. "FUNCTIONAL" INSCRIPTIONS

1. TREATIES

THE TREATIES BETWEEN ḪATTI AND AMURRU (2.17)

Itamar Singer

The Amurru treaties represent the largest series of Hittite vassal treaties with a Syrian state: four separate treaties extending from the mid-14th to the late 13th centuries BCE. In comparison, Carchemish and Ugarit are represented with two treaties each (plus royal decrees), whereas only one each is attested from Aleppo, Mitanni, Tunip, Nuḫḫašše, Alašia, and Mukiš(?). This state of preservation is in itself indicative of the relative importance of the strategic kingdom of Amurru flanking the southern border of the Hittite Empire. The treaties, especially their historical introductions, contain invaluable information on the troubled history of this Levantine state during the century and a half of its existence (Singer 1991a; Klengel 1992:160-174; Bryce 1998:181-189, 249-251, 262-263, 344-347). Although they in fact dealt with the same historical background of Hittite-Amorite relations, the resourceful legal draftsmen of the Hittite chancery did not mechanically repeat the same narrative time and again but, rather, skillfully adapted their discourse to the changing needs of the imperial political propaganda.

The decisive political act which shaped the development of Hittite-Amorite relations was Aziru's voluntary submission to Šuppiluliuma at an early stage of the Hittite penetration into Syria (Singer 1990:155-159). As an acknowledged Egyptian dependency for many generations, Amurru's defection to the Hittite camp remained an open wound in the pride of the Pharaohs, and sixty-five years later Ramesses II attempted unsuccessfully to reverse the course of events at the Battle of Qadesh. With the advent of peace, the former frontierland turned into one of the main hubs of amicable contact between the Hittite and the Egyptian empires. New problems agitated the Hittite court in its last decades — the growing Assyrian danger from without and dynastic rivalries from within. All these dramatic developments are vividly echoed in the Amurru treaties: the emphasis on Amurru's voluntary joining of the Hittite camp and its treacherous *volte-face* to Egypt before Qadesh, the deposition and restoration of Bentešina on the throne of Amurru, the military and trade embargo on Assyria, and the concern to ensure Amurru's ongoing support for the ruling line of Hittite kings.

Another aspect which may be followed in these treaties is the growing "Hittitization" of Amurru through reciprocal royal marriages and their resulting cultural impact (Singer 1992). A typical Canaanite state under Egyptian influence in the Amarna Age, Amurru gradually opened up to northern influences brought in by two Hittite princesses and the ensuing close ties between the two royal courts. The last document in the series was already composed for a king whose mother and wife were both Hittite princesses, and his father Bentešina absorbed "Hittite values" in his re-educational sojourn in Hatti. An Akkadian translation may have become superfluous, which may explain why the Šaušgamuwa treaty only came down to us in two Hittite copies (Beckman 1996:99).

TREATY BETWEEN ŠUPPILULIUMA AND AZIRU (2.17A)

Itamar Singer

There are six duplicates of the Akkadian version of the treaty but only one in Hittite. The following is a composite translation based primarily on the better-preserved Hittite text. Significant variants in the Akkadian version are indicated in the footnotes. Additional restorations are afforded by parallel Syrian treaties, notably those between Šuppiluliuma I and Tette of Nuḫḫašše (*CTH* 53), and between Muršili II and Niqmepa of Ugarit (*CTH* 66), and also by the later treaties with Amurru (Duppi-Tešub, Bentešina and Šaušgamuwa). The paragraphs correspond to the original division lines of the text.

Preamble and main stipulations of the treaty

(i.1-13): [Thus says My Majesty, Šuppiluliuma, Great King, king of Hatti, hero, beloved [of the Storm-god:] I, My Majesty, have taken you in vassalage and [I have seated] you upon [the throne of your father]. If you, [Azira,[1] from this day on] until the end of days do not protect the king of Hatti, your lord, and the land of Hatti; and as your soul, your head, [your wives, your sons] and *your land*[2] [are dear] to you, in the same way may the king's soul, the king's head, the king's body and the land of Hatti be likewise dear to you [forever]! Until the end of days you should keep [the treaty and the peace] of the king of Hatti, [of his sons and grandsons], and of the land of Hatti. 300 shekels [of refined gold] of firstclass quality shall be your [annual] tribute [to the king] of Hatti; it shall be weighed out [with the weights] of the merchants [of

[1] Both the Hittite and the Akk. versions use the form Azira throughout the text.

[2] The Hittite text actually has the curious form "his(!) land (and ?) city".

Hatti]. [You] Azira [must appear] yearly before My Majesty, [your lord], in the land of Hatti.

Historical background

(i.14-26)[3] Previously, suddenly [all the kings, (namely)] — the king of Egypt, the king of Hurri,[4] the king of [Qatna(?) / Aštata(?)], the king of Nuḫḫašše, the king of Niya, the king of [Kinza(?)],[5] the king of Mukiš, the king of Ḫalab, the king of Karkamiš — all of these kings suddenly became hostile [towards My Majest]y. But Azira, king of [Amurru], rose up from the gate of Egypt and submitted himself to My Majesty, king of Hatti. And I, My Majesty, Great King, [accordingly(?) rejoiced] very much. *Should* I, My Majesty, the Great King, not have accordingly rejoiced very much, as I [...] to Azira? When Azira [knelt down] at the feet [of My Majesty] — (indeed) he came from the gate of Egypt and knelt down [at the feet of My Majesty] — I, My Majesty, Great King, [took up] Azira and ranked him among his brothers.[6]

Military clauses

(ii.9′-24′) Whoever is My Majesty's friend should also be your friend; whoever is My Majesty's enemy should also be your enemy.[a] If the king of Hatti (goes) to the land of [Hurri], or to the land of Egypt, or to the land of Kara(n)duniya (Babylon), or to the land of Aštata, or to the land of Alši, [or to whatever enemy lands that are] close to your border and are hostile [towards My Majesty], or to whatever friendly lands that are friends to My Majesty and are close to your border — (namely) the land of [Niya(?),[7] the land of Kinza] and the land of Nuḫḫašše — (who) turn and become hostile [towards the king of Hatti, and if the king of Hatti goes to war] against that enemy, and if you, Azira, do not mobilize wholeheartedly with troops and chariots and do not fight him wholeheartedly —

(ii.25′-39′) Or if I, My Majesty, send to you, Azira, to your aid either a prince or a high-ranking lord with (his) troops and his chariots, or if I send to attack another land, and you, Azira, do not mobilize wholeheartedly with troops and chariots and you do not attack that enemy, and you commit some [evil by saying as follows]: "Although I am under oath, I do not know at all whether he will defeat the enemy or whether the enemy will defeat him"; and if you write to [that] enemy (saying): "[Behold! The troops and the chariots] of Hatti are coming to attack. Be on guard!" — thereby you will break the oath.

(ii.40′-46′) [...] troops and chariots of Hatti, [... of] Hatti, they should [no]t seize a single person [...]. [If] you [do not seize(?) him and do not] deliver him to the king of Hatti — thereby you will break the oath.

(ii.47′-56′) [If some] other [enemy] rises up against the king of Hatti and [attacks] the land of [Hatti], (or if) someone starts a revolt [against the king of] Hatti, [and you], Azira, hear about it but do not come wholeheartedly to the aid of [My Majest]y with troops and chariots; if it is not [possible] for you (to come), Azira, send to the aid of the king of Hatti either [your son] or your brother with troops and chariots.

(ii.56′-iii.3′ [8]) Or if someone oppresses Azira, either [...] or anyone else, and you send to the king of Hatti (saying): "[Come] to my rescue!" then I, My Majesty, will [come to your] aid, or I will] send either a prince or a high-ranking [lord] with troops and chariots and they will defeat that enemy [for you].

(iii.4′-16′) [Now(?)], because Azira has turned of his ow[n will to] My Majesty's servitude, I, My Majesty, will s[end him] lords of Hatti, troops [and chariots from the land of] Hatti to the land of Amurru. [And since] they will go up to your cities, you (must) protect them and provision them.[9] [b] They should walk like brothers before you. You must protect [the king of] Hatti, but if some man of Hatti seeks evil against you, Azira, and he seeks to get h[old of either] a city or your(!)[10] land — thereby he will break the oath.

Extradition of deportees, conspirators and fugitives

(iii.17′-28′) Whatever deportees of that land [My Majesty] has carried off — deportees of the land of Hurri, deportees of the land of Kinza, deportees of the land of Niya and deportees of the land of Nuḫḫašše — if some man or woman flees from Ḫattuša

a Exod 23:22

b Judg 8:4-17

[3] For the restoration of the list of kings and the rest of this passage, see Singer 1990:145.

[4] Instead of Hurri the Akk. version has *A-mur-[ri]*. This could be a scribal error, or perhaps a confusion between two parallel geopolitical terms, for which see Singer 1991b.

[5] Kinza is the cuneiform writing for Qadesh on the Orontes.

[6] In the Hittite version there follow one or two very fragmentary paragraphs in the remainder of the first column and in the first eight lines of the second.

[7] Beckman 1996:34 suggests restoring Mukiš(?), but this land is quite distant from Amurru's border. Cf. also §8 for the same group of lands (Kinza, Niya, Nuḫḫašše) in a similar context.

[8] Most of this paragraph is lost in the Hittite version; the translation follows here the Akk. version A obv 27′-30′.

[9] The sense of the rare Hittite verb *išḫaššarwaḫḫ-* is provided by the parallel section in the Duppi-Tešub treaty (A ii.32′-33′): "... give them regularly to eat and to drink." Cf. Beckman 1996:57; Friedrich 1926:18f.

[10] The text actually has "his land" (followed by an erasure).

and enters your land, you should not say as follows: "Although I am sworn to the treaty, I (don't want to) know anything. [Are they(?)] in my land?" [You], Azira, should rather capture them and send them to the king of Hatti.

(iii.29′-34′) [If] someone speaks [evil words about] My Majesty to you,[c] Azira — whether [a man of Hatt]i or your own subject — but you, Azira, do not seize him and send him to the king of Hatti — thereby you will break the oath.

(iii.35′-44′) Whatever men of Amurru reside in the land of Hatti - whether a nobleman or a slave of Azira's land - if you request him from the king of Hatti and the king of Hatti [gives] him back to you, then take him. But if the king of Hatti does not give him back to you and he flees and comes to you, and you Azira take him — thereby you will break the oath.

(iv.1′-5′; F I′-3′) [If] some [people(?) rise and come to the land of Azira, and you, Azira, speak unfavorable things before them and you direct them] towards the moun[tains or towards another land, and if] you, [Azira, do not seize and extradite hi]m to the king of Hatti — thereby [you will break the oath.]

(iv.6′-11′) If a man of H[atti] comes as a fugitive [from the land of Hatti] and he turns to [you, Azira, seize him and extradite] him to the king [of Hatti]. But [if you do not extradite him — thereby you will break the oath.]

(iv.12″-14″ = F 8′-9′) [If a fugitive flees] from the land of Amurru [and comes to the land of Hatti, the king of Hatti does not (have to) seize and extradite him. It is not right for the king of Hatti to return] a fugitive.[d] [But if a fugitive flees from the land of Hatti and comes to the land of Amurru, you, Azira, [should not detain him], but should release him to the land of Hatti. [If you detain him] — thereby you will [break the oath.]

(iv.15″-18″) If you, [Azira, want something(?) you should request it] from the king of Hatti. [If the king of Hatti gives it to you], take it, but you should not take what [the king of Hatti does not give to you].

c Exod 22:28; Lev 24

d Exod 21:12-14; Num 35

e Deut 3:9; Ps 29:6

f Deut 4:26; 30:19; 31:28

Treason

(iv.19″-26″): You, Azira, [I have taken to vassalage (?) and I have placed] you on [the throne of your father (?)]. If you, [Azira, do not seek] the well-being [of Hatti and] the hand of Šuppiluliuma, [Great King, king of Hatti], but (rather) you seek the well-being of another [land — either the land of Hurri(?)] or the land of Eg[ypt] — and [you seek] another's [hand] — thereby you will break the oath.[11]

Summoning the divine witnesses

(iv.30″-32″) Behold, I have summoned [the Thousand Gods to assembly for this oath and I have called them to witness. Let] them be witnesses![12]

(A rev. 1′-11′) ... Ḫuwaššana of] Ḫupišna, [Tapišuwa of Išḫupita, the Lady of Landa], Kuniyawani [of Landa, NIN.PÌSAN.PÌSAN of] Kinza, Mount Lablana,[13] [Mount Šariyana,[14][e] Mount Pišaiša,] the *lulaḫḫi* gods, the *ḫabiru* gods, Er[eškigal, all the male] deities [and all the female deities of the land of Hatti], all the male deities and all the female deities [of the land of Kizzuwatna], all the male deities and all the female deities of Amurru, [all the primeval gods]: Nara, Namšara, Minki, [Tuḫuši, Ammunki, Ammizzadu], Alalu, Antu, [Anu, Apantu, Enlil, Ninlil], mountains, rivers, springs, great [sea, heaven and earth,[f] winds and clouds]. Let them be witnesses to this treaty [and to the oath]!

Curses and blessings

(A rev. 12′-16′) [All the words of the treaty and of the oath which are inscribed] on this tablet, [if Azira does not keep these words of] the treaty and of the oath [and he breaks the oath], let these oath gods destroy Azira [together with his head, his wives, his sons, his grandsons, his house], his town, his land, and all [his possesions]!

(A rev. 17′-20′) [But if Azira keeps these words of the treaty] and of the oath which are [inscribed on this tablet], let these oath gods protect [Azira together with his head, his wives, his sons, his grandsons], his house, his town, his land, [and his possessions]!

[11] There follows a very fragmentary short paragraph (iv.27″-29″).

[12] The rest of the Hittite tablet is uninscribed, but copy A of the Akk. version adds three more paragraphs: a list of witness deities (partly restored from similar lists in other Syrian treaties), a curse and a blessing.

[13] Mt. Lebanon.

[14] Mt. Sirion (the Anti-Lebanon).

REFERENCES

Text: *CTH* 49: Akkadian: A. KUB 3.7 + KUB 3.122 + KUB 4.94. B. KUB 3.19 (+) KUB 48.71. C. KBo 28-140. D. Bo 9200. E. KBo 28.118. F. Bo 9201. Hittite: KBo 10.12 (+) 13 (+) 12a. Editions: Weidner 1923:70-75, 146-149 (Akkadian); Freydank 1959 (Hittite); del Monte 1986:116-141 (both). Translations and Studies: Goetze 1955:529-530; Klengel 1964; 1977; Singer 1990:144-50; 1991a:154-58; Beckman 1996:32-37; 1997:96-97.

TREATY BETWEEN MURŠILI AND DUPPI-TEŠUB (2.17B)

Itamar Singer

The Akkadian version is preserved in one text, the Hittite in four duplicates. The composite translation is based primarily on the Hittite version, with restorations afforded by the Akkadian version and other Amurru treaties. Significant variants in the Akkadian version are indicated in the footnotes. The paragraphs correspond to the original division lines in the text.

Preamble

(B i.1-2) [Thus says] My Majesty, Muršili, Great King, king [of Hatti, hero], beloved of the Storm-god, [son of] Šuppiluliuma, [Great King, king of Hatti, hero].

Historical background

(B i.3-12) Duppi-Tešub! Your grandfather Azira[1] submitted to my father.[2] When it came about that the kings of Nuḫḫašše and the king of Kinza[3] became hostile, Azira did not become hostile.[4] When my father fought his enemies, Azira likewise fought them. Just as Azira protected my father, my father protected Azira together with his land. He did not seek to harm him in any way, and Azira did not anger my father in any way. He kept delivering to him[5] the 300 shekels of refined gold of first-class quality that had been decreed.[6] My father died[7] and I sat on the throne of my father. And just as Azira had been in [the time of my father], so he was in my time.

(B i.13-21) When it came about that the kings of Nuḫḫašše and the king of Kinza became again hostile in my time, Azira, your grandfather, and DU-Tešub, your father, [did not join] them. They supported only me in (my) overlordship.[8] [And when Azira became old] and was no longer able to go on military campaign,[a] [just as Azira] went to battle with troops and chariots, DU-Tešub likewise went to battle [with the troops and the chariots of the land of Amurru]. And I, My Majesty, destroyed those [enemies. ...] Azira, your father, to my father [...] came [...] I gave to DU-Tešub [...[9]]

(A i.11′-18′) When your father died, according [to the request of your father] I did not reject you. Since your father during (his) *lifetime*(?)[10] had often mentioned yo[ur na]me before me, therefore I took care of you. You fell ill and became sick, but even though you were sick, I, My Majesty, still installed you in the position of your father and for you I made [...], your brothers, and the land of Amurru swore allegiance to you.

Main stipulations of the treaty and relations with Egypt

(A i.19′-34′, B obv. 9′-10′) When I, My Majesty, took care of you according to the word of your father, and installed you in the place of your father, behold, I have made you swear an oath to the king of Hatti, to the land of Hatti, and to my sons and my grandsons.[b] Keep the oath of the king and the hand of the king, and I, My Majesty, will protect you, Duppi-Tešub. When you shall take your wife and if you produce a son, he shall later be king in the land of Amurru. And as I, My Majesty, protect you, I will likewise protect your son. You, Duppi-Tešub, protect in the future the king of Hatti, the land of Hatti, my sons, and my grandsons. The tribute which was imposed upon your grandfather and upon your father — they delivered 300 shekels of refined gold of first-class quality by the weights of the land of Hatti — you shall deliver likewise. Do not turn your eyes towards another (land)! Your ancestors paid tribute to Egypt, [but] you [should not pay tribute to Egypt because E]gypt has become an enemy [...[11]]

(D ii.1′-3′) If [the king of Egypt(?) will become My Majesty's friend, you too] should be his friend, [and] you may keep sending your messenger [to Egypt(?)].

(D ii.4′-9′) But [if] you commit [trea]chery, and while the king of Egypt [is hos]tile to My Majesty you secretly [send] your messenger to him [and you become hosti]le to the king of Hatti, and [you cast] off the hand of the king of Hatti becoming (a subject) of the king of Egypt, [thereby] you, Duppi-Tešub, will break the oath.[c]

a 2 Sam 18:1-4
b 2 Chr 36:13
c Exod 34:12, 15

[1] Both the Hittite and Akk. versions use the form Azira throughout the text.

[2] Akk. version has: "He c[ame] to my father, [and] my father made him his subject." For this restoration of the first verb (instead of the traditional "he was hostile"), see Singer 1990:150f.

[3] The cuneiform writing for Qadesh on the Orontes. Cf. *COS* 2.16, note 46.

[4] Akk. version adds: "As he was friendly (before), he remained friendly."

[5] Akk. version adds: "year by year".

[6] Akk. version adds: "... by my father for your grandfather. He never withheld (his tribute) and he never angered him."

[7] Lit., "became god" in Hittite; "went to his fate" in Akk.

[8] Akk.: "As they (Aziru and DU-Tešub) held to the hand of my [father], likewise they held to my hand."

[9] The Akk. version breaks off. The Hittite version resumes after a large gap.

[10] See Starke 1990:543f.

[11] About four lines are entirely lost.

Military clauses
(D ii.10′-17′, A ii.1′-12′) [Whoever is My Majesty's] enemy shall be your enemy, [and whoever is My Majesty's friend] shall be your friend.[d] [And if any of(?)] the *protectorate*[12] lands [becomes hostile] to the king of Hatti, and if I, My Majesty, go [to fight] that [land], and you do not mobilize whole[heartedly with troops and chariots, or do] not fight [the enemy] without hesitation [or ..., or you say] as follows: "[Although I am a sworn] man, let them defeat [the enemy or let] the enemy [defeat] them," [or if] you send a man to that [land] to warn [him as follows]: "Behold, the troops and the chariots of the land of Hatti are coming. Defend yourselves!" — (thereby) you will break the oath.

(A ii.13′-24′) As I, My Majesty, protect you, Duppi-Tešub, be an auxiliary force to My Majesty and the land of [Hatti]. And if some [evil] matter arises in the land of Hatti, and [someone] revolts against My Majesty, and you hear (of it), lend assistance with your [troops] and chariots. Take a stand immediately to help [the land of Hat]ti. But if it is not possible for you to lend assistance, send either your son or your brother with your troops and chariots to help the king of Hatti. If you do not send your [son] or your brother with your troops and chariots to help the king of Hatti — (thereby) you will break the oath.

(A ii.25′-29′) If someone oppresses you, Duppi-Tešub, in some matter, or someone revolts against you, and you write to the king of Hatti, and the king of Hatti sends troops and chariots to help you, <...>[13] — (thereby) you will break the oath.

(A ii.30′-37′) If sons of Hatti bring you, Duppi-Tešub, troops and chariots, and since they will go up to (your) cities, you, Duppi-Tešub, must regularly give them to eat and to drink. But if (any Hittite) undertakes an evil matter against Duppi-Tešub, (such as) the plunder of his land or of his cities, or if he seeks to depose Duppi-Tešub from the kingship in the land of Amurru — (thereby) he will break the oath.

Extradition of deportees, conspirators and fugitives
(A ii.38′-45′) Whatever deportees of the land of Nuḫḫašše and deportees of the land of Kinza my father carried off, or I carried off — if one of these deportees flees from me and comes to you, and you do not seize him and extradite him to the king of Hatti, but instead you tell him thus: "[Carry on(?)], go where (you want to) go; I do not know you" — (thereby) you will break the oath of the gods.

d Exod 23:22; 2 Chr 19:2

(A ii.46′-iii.11) If someone should bring up before you, Duppi-Tešub, evil words about the king or about the land of Hatti, you shall not conceal it from the king. If My Majesty should somehow confidently give orders to you: "Do this or that thing,"[14] that one among those things which is not possible to perform make an appeal about it right on the spot: "I cannot do this thing and I won't do it"; it (will happen) according to what the king decides. But if you won't do a thing which is possible to perform and you repulse the king, or if you do not observe the matter that the king tells you confidently — (thereby) you will break the oath.

(A iii.12-22) If (the population of) some land or a fugitive rebels and goes to the land of Hatti, and passes through your land, you must set them on the right track and show (them) the road to the land of Hatti, and tell them favorable words. Do not direct them elsewhere. If you do not set them on their way, and you do not conduct them to the road (leading) to Hatti, but rather you turn their eyes towards the mountain, or if you speak evil words before them — (thereby) you will break the oath.

(A iii.23-29) Or if the king of Hatti beleaguers some land and he causes them (i.e. its inhabitants) to flee, and they enter your land, if you want to take anything, ask the king of Hatti for it. Do not take [it as you wi]sh. If you take [anything] as you wish and you conceal it — <(thereby) you will break the oath>.[15]

(A iii.30-33) Furthermore, if a fugitive en[ters your land in flight], seize him and extradite him. [But if a fugitive flees from the land of Amurru and comes in fli]ght [to the land of Hatti, the king of Hatti does not (have to) seize and extradite him.][16]

Summoning the divine witnesses
(D iii.5′-6′) [Behold, let the thousand gods sta]nd by for this oath! Let them observe and listen!

(D iii.7′-17′) [Sun-god of Heaven, Sun-goddess] of Arinna, Storm-god of Heaven, Storm-god of Hatti, [Šeri (and) Ḫu]ri, Mount Nanni and Mount Ḫazzi,[17] [Storm-god of the Gate-house, Storm-god of] the Army, Storm-god of Ḫalab, Storm-god of Zippalanda, Storm-god of Nerikka, Storm-god of Liḫ-

[12] For the meaning of *kuriwana-*, see, e.g., Otten 1969:28f.

[13] The scribe left out the rest of this entry, which is in fact continued in the next paragraph. Cf. the parallel entry in the Aziru treaty, ii.56–iii.16′ (see *COS* 2.17A).

[14] Lit., "Do these things or this thing."

[15] The recurring closing formula is omitted.

[16] Restored from the parallel clause in the Aziru treaty (iv.12″-14″) (see *COS* 2.17A). There follows a break of uncertain length concluded by the very fragmentary first four lines of D iii.

[17] The Casius (*Ṣaphōn*) and Anti-Casius Mountains.

zina, Storm-god of the Ruin Mound, [Storm-god of Ḫišš]ašpa(!), Storm-god of Šahpina, Storm-god of Šapinuwa, [Storm-god of Pittiyar]igga, Storm-god of Šamuha, Storm-god of Ḫurma, [Storm-god of Šari]šša, Storm-god of Rescue, Storm-god of Uda, [Storm-god of Kizz]uwatna, Storm-god of Išḫupitta, [Storm-god of Amurru(?)[18]], Storm-god of Argata, Storm-god of Dunippa, [Storm-god of Ḫal]ab of Dunip, Milku [of the land of Amur]ru.

e Deut 3:9; Ps 29:6

(D iii.18′-23′) [Tutelary-god, Tutelary-god] of Hatti, Zitḫariya, Karzi, [Ḫapantal]iya, Tutelary-god of Garaḫna, Tutelary-god of the Field, [Tutelary-god of the *kurša*[19]], Aya (Ea), Alladu, [Telipinu] of Turmitta, [Telipinu] of Tawiniya, Telipinu [of Ḫanḫana], Bunene, Ašgašipa.

(D iii.24′-A iv.3) [Moon-god Lord of the Oath, Išḫara] Queen of the Oath, [Ḫebat Queen of Heaven, Ištar Lady of the Field, Ištar of Ninuwa, Ištar of Ḫattarina, Ninatta], Kulitta, War-god of Hatti, War-god of Ellaya, War-god of Arziya, Iyarriš, Zampana.

(A iv.4-20) Ḫantidašu of Ḫurma, Apara of Šamuha, Kataḫḫa of Ankuwa, [the Queen] of Gatapa, Ammamma of Taḫurpa, Ḫallara of Dunna, Ḫuwaššana of Ḫupišna, Tapišuwa of Išḫ[upitta], Lady of Landa, Kunniyawanni of Landa, NIN.PÌSAN-PÌSAN of Kinza, Mount Lablana,[20] Mount Šariyana,[21] Mount Pišaiša, *lulaḫḫi* gods, *ḫabiru* gods, [Ereškigal], the male deities (and) the female deities of the land of Hatti, the male (and) the female deities of the land of Amurru, [all] the primeval gods — Nara, Napšara, [Minki], Tuḫuši, Ammunki, Amizzadu, Alalu, Anu, Antu, Apantu, Enlil, Ninlil, mountains, rivers, springs, great sea, heaven and earth, winds, clouds. Let them be witnesses to this treaty and to the oath!

Curses and blessings[22]

(A iv.21-26) All the words of the treaty and the oath which are written on this tablet — if Duppi-Tešub [does not keep these] words of the treaty and of the oath, then let these oath gods destroy Duppi-Tešub together with his head, his wife, his son, his grandson, his house, his city, his land and together with his possessions.

(A iv.27-32) But if Duppi-Tešub observes these words of the treaty and of the oath which are written on this tablet, let these oath gods protect Duppi-Tešub together with his head, his wife, his son, his grandson, his city, his land, your(!) house, your(!) subjects [and together with his possessions!]

Colophon

(C rev. 11′) [First tablet of Duppi-Tešub's treat]y. Complete.

[18] For the restoration of the list of the gods of Amurru, see Singer 1991a:180f.
[19] Either "fleece" or "hunting bag," for which see Güterbock 1989.
[20] Mt. Lebanon.
[21] Mt. Sirion (the Anti-Lebanon).
[22] These paragraphs are written entirely in Akk. in the Hittite version.

REFERENCES

Text: *CTH* 62: Akkadian: KUB 3.14; Hittite: A. KBo 5.9. B. KUB 3.119 (+) KUB 14.5 (+) KUB 19.48 + KUB 23.6 (+) KBo 22.39. C. KUB 21.49. Editions: Weidner 1923:76-79 (Akkadian); Friedrich 1926:1-48, 179-181 (Hittite); del Monte 1986:156-177 (both). Studies: Goetze 1955:203-05; Cornil and Lebrun 1975-76:96-100; del Monte 1985b; Singer 1990:150-151; Lebrun 1992:17-26; Beckman 1996:32-37.

TREATY BETWEEN TUDḪALIYA AND ŠAUŠGAMUWA (2.17C)
(excerpts)

Itamar Singer

This treaty has come down to us only in two Hittite duplicates. The main text (A) has numerous erasures and insertions, some of them quite telling. The excerpts presented below include the historical introduction and other fragments dealing with Amurru's foreign relations, past and future. The remaining text includes the regular repertory of stipulations as also found in the Aziru and the Duppi-Tešub treaties. The paragraphs correspond to the original division lines in the text.

Preamble

(A i.1-7) [Thus says *tabarna* Tutḫaliy]a, Great King, [king of] Hatti, hero, beloved of the Sun-goddess of Arinna, [son of Ḫattušili, Great King, king of] Hatti, hero, [grandson of] Muršili, Great King, king of Hatti, hero, [descendant] of Tutḫaliya, [Great King, king of] Hatti, hero.

Historical background

(A i.8-12) I, My Majesty, [have taken you], Šaušgamuwa, [by the hand and] have made [you (my)] brother-in-law. You [shall not alter the words] of the treaty tablet which [I have made] for you!

(A i.13-27) [In the past] the land of Amurru had not been defeated by the force of arms of the land of Hatti. At the time when [Aziru] came to the (great)grandfather[1] of My Majesty, [Šuppilul]iuma, in the land of Hatti, the lands of Amurru[2] were still [hostile]; they [were] subjects of the king of Hurri. Even so, Aziru was loyal to him, although he did [not def]eat him by force of arms. Aziru, your (great-great-)grandfather,[1] protected Šuppiluliuma as overlord, and he also protected the land of Hatti. Thereafter, he protected Muršili as overlord, and he also protected the land of Hatti. In no way did he commit an offense against Hatti.

(A i.28-39) But when Muwatalli, the brother of My Majesty's father, reigned, the men of the land of Amurru committed an offense against him and announced to him as follows: "We were voluntary[3] subjects, but now we are no longer your subjects." And they went after the king of the land of Egypt. The brother of My Majesty's father, Muwatalli, and the king of the land of Egypt fought over the men of the land of Amurru, and Muwatalli defeated him. He conquered the land of Amurru by the force of arms and subjugated it. And he made Šabili king in the land of Amurru.

(A i.40-48) When Muwatalli, the brother of My Majesty's father, died, the father of My Majesty, Ḫattušili, became king. He deposed Šabili and made Bentešina, your father, king in the land of Amurru. He protected the father of My Majesty and he also protected the land of Hatti. In no way did he commit an offense against Hatti.

Loyalty to the Hittite dynasty

(A ii.1-7) I, My Majesty, Great King, have taken you, Šaušgamuwa, by the hand, and have made you (my) brother-in-law. I gave you my sister in marriage and have made you king in the land of Amurru. Protect My Majesty as overlord, and thereafter protect the sons, grandsons, and offspring of My Majesty as overlords. You shall not desire another overlord[4] for yourself. This matter should be placed under oath for you.

(A ii.8-19) Because I have made you, Šaušgamuwa, (my) brother-in-law, protect My Majesty as overlord. Thereafter protect the sons, the grandsons, and the offspring of My Majesty as overlords. But you shall not desire anyone (else) as overlord from among those who are brothers of My Majesty, (or) those who are legitimate sons of secondary wives of My Majesty's father, (or) any other royal offspring who are bastards for you. You shall not behave like Mašturi: Muwatalli took Mašturi, who was king of the Šeḫa River Land, and made him (his) brother-in-law; he gave him his sister Massanauzzi[5] in marriage, and he made him king of the Šeḫa River Land.

(A ii.20-38) But when Muwatalli died, Urḫi-Tešub, son of Muwatalli, became king. [My father] took away the kingship from Urḫi-Tešub.[6] Mašturi committed treachery. Although it was Muwatalli who had taken him up and who had made him (his) brother-in-law, Mašturi did not protect his son Urḫi-Tešub,[7] but went over to my father (thinking): "Should I protect a bastard? Should I *act on behalf of* a bastard's son?"[8] Will you perhaps behave like Mašturi? If someone brings difficulties upon My Majesty, or upon the sons, the grandsons, or the offspring of My Majesty, and you, Šaušgamuwa, together with your wives, your sons, your troops and your chariots, do not help wholeheartedly, and are not ready to die for him, together with your wives and your sons — this shall be placed under oath for you.

Foreign relations and embargo on Assyria

(A iv.1-18) The kings who are equal to me (are) the king of Egypt, the king of Karanduniya (Babylon), the king of Assyria <and the king of Aḫḫiyawa.>[9] If the king of Egypt is My Majesty's friend, he shall also be your friend; but if he is My Majesty's enemy, he shall also be your enemy. And if the king of Karanduniya is My Majesty's friend, he shall also be your friend; but if he is My Majesty's enemy, he shall also be your enemy. Since the king of Assyria is My Majesty's enemy, he shall also be your enemy.[10] Your merchant shall not enter into Assyria and you shall not allow his merchant into your land. He shall not pass through your land. But if he enters into your land, you should seize him and send him off to My Majesty.[11] This matter should be placed under oath for you.

[1] Lit. "grandfather" (written, over erasure).

[2] The "lands of Amurru" (in plural) refers to the Syrian states ruled by Mitanni before the Hittite takeover. See Singer 1991b and cf. Zaccagnini 1988.

[3] Lit. "out of love."

[4] Written over the erased "another offspring".

[5] For the reading of the logographically written name DINGER.MEŠ-IR, see Edel 1976:32f.

[6] This sentence was added over an erasure.

[7] The sentence "He committed a treachery" was erased, but can still be read on the tablet.

[8] This sentence, the sense of which is not quite clear, was added above the line.

[9] The last name has been erased, but is still clearly readable on the tablet.

[10] The sentence on Assyria is written over erasure.

[11] This sentence and the remaining paragraph was squeezed in the column-divider.

(A iv.19-22)[12] Because I, My Majesty, have begun war with the king of Assyria, just as My Majesty, you should (also) go and mobilize (your) troops (and your) chariots. Just as it is a matter of urgency and *diligence* for My Majesty, it shall likewise be a matter of urgency and *diligence* for you. You should mobilize wholeheartedly (your) troops (and) chariots. This matter should be placed under oath for you.

(A iv.23ff.) [Do not let] a ship of [*Aḫḫ*]*iyawa*[13] go to him." [...] but when he dispatches them [...] the deity of your land [...].[14]

[12] This entire paragraph is written in minuscule script; the last line has been erased.

[13] For a failed attempt to restore "[bat]tle ship" instead of "ship of [Aḫḫ]iyawa", see Steiner 1989 and cf. Singer 1991a:171, n. 56.

[14] The rest of the column is lost.

REFERENCES

Text: *CTH* 105 (only Hittite versions): A. 93 / w (+) KUB 23.1 + KUB 31.43 (+) KUB 23.37 (+) 720 / v (+) 670 / v. B. 1198 / u + 1436 / u + 69 / 821 + KUB 8.82. Editions: Kühne and Otten 1971. Studies: Sommer 1932:320-327; Ranoszek 1950; Zaccagnini 1988; Steiner 1989; Singer 1991a; 1991b; Beal 1992; Klengel 1992:173; Beckman 1996:98-102; Cohen 1997; Bryce 1998; Klengel 1999.

THE TREATY OF TUDḪALIYA IV WITH KURUNTA OF TARḪUNTAŠŠA ON THE BRONZE TABLET FOUND IN ḪATTUŠA (2.18)

Harry A. Hoffner, Jr.

§1 (i.1-5) The words of the Tabarna, Tudḫaliya, Great King, King of the Land of Ḫatti, Hero, son of Ḫattušili (III), Great King, King of the Land of Ḫatti, Hero, grandson of Muršili (II), Great King, King of the Land of Ḫatti, Hero, great-grandson of Šuppiluliuma (I), Great King, King of the Land of Ḫatti, Hero, descendant (and namesake) of Tudḫaliya, Great King, King of the Land of Ḫatti, Hero.

Ḫattušili III and Kurunta

§2 (i.6-13) When my father, Ḫattušili (III), made war on Urḫi-Tešub (= Muršili III),[1] son of Muwatalli (II), he deposed him from kingship, but no treason was proven against Kurunta.[2] Kurunta was in no way involved in whatever treasonous acts the men of Ḫatti committed. Even before this, King Muwatalli had entrusted him to my father Ḫattušili to raise, and even before this, my father was raising him.

§3 (i.14-21) But when my father (Ḫattušili III) had deposed (Kurunta's older brother) Urḫi-Tešub from kingship, my father took Kurunta and installed him in kingship in the land of Tarḫuntašša. And my father made treaty tablets for him (concerning) what obligations my father made for him and how he set boundaries for him, and Kurunta has them.[3]

Kurunta's Borders

His[4] boundaries are set as follows: In the direction of the land of Pitašša (to the W?), Mt. Ḫawa and the *kantanna* of Zarniya and the city Šanantarwa are your boundary. But the *kantanna* of the town of Zarniya remains in the land of the Ḫulaya River, while the town of Šanantarwa remains in the land of Pitašša.

§4 (i.22-28) Previously in the direction of the land of Pitašša (to the WNW?) his[5] boundary was the town of Nahhanta.[6] But then my father reduced his territory,[7] so that on the treaty tablet of my father the grotto springs[8] of the town of Arimmatta were made his boundary. Now I, My Majesty, have reestablished for him the former boundary. So from the land of Pitašša: from the boundary of Arimmatta:

[1] This was the conflict that led to the overthrow of Urḫi-Tešub and the accession of Ḫattušili III. For the sequence of events in this conflict see Bryce 1998:284-288.

[2] A brother of Urḫi-Tešub. For general discussions of this man Kurunta see Otten 1988:3-5; van den Hout 1995:82-95; Bryce 1998:296ff., 335f., 354f., and Mora 1998. Kurunta depicted himself as "Great King" on a rock relief published by Dinçol 1998.

[3] The tablets of the treaty with Ḫattušili III which Kurunta had in his possession at the time this new treaty was being made by Tudḫaliya IV would have been invalidated thereby.

[4] Ulmi-Tešub Treaty variant (hereafter UTT): "your."

[5] UTT also: "his."

[6] The boundary descriptions in §4 differ from UTT obv. 19', which reads: "In the direction of the boundary of the land of Pitašša the grotto springs (^{d}KASKAL.KUR.MEŠ) of (the city) Arimmatta are his boundary."

[7] Lit., "drew in his boundary."

[8] Or "underground river." The word is the Sumerogram ^{d}KASKAL.KUR, lit., "(divine) road (of) the netherworld." See Gordon 1967.

Naḫḫanta and Hauttašša form the boundary. Naḫḫanta and Hauttašša themselves belong to the land of the Ḫulaya River.

§5 (i.29-42) In the direction of Mt. Huwatnuwanta (to the NNW?), the *ḫallapuwanza* is its/his border, but the *ḫallapuwanza* belongs to the Ḫulaya River Land. In the direction of Kuwarsawanta up behind, the *ḫuwaši* stone of the Dog is the boundary. In the direction of Ušša (to the N?), Zarata is its/his boundary, but the city Zarata (belongs) to the Ḫulaya River Land. In the direction of Wanzataruwa the town Harazzuwa is his boundary, but Harazzuwa (itself) belongs to the Land of Ušša. In my father's first written treaty the town Šuttasna was his boundary in the direction of Mt. Kuwakuwaliya. But later my father himself made the town Šantimma the boundary. Šantimma (itself), however, belongs to the Land of the Ḫulaya River. In the direction of the towns Wanzatarwa and Kunzinasa his boundary is Mt. Arlanta and the town Alana. Alana belongs to the Land of the Ḫulaya River, but the water which is on Mt. Arlanta belongs jointly to the Land of the Ḫulaya River and Ḫatti.

§6 (i.43-47) In the direction of the town Šinwanta, Mount Lula and the Damnaššara-Mountains form its boundary. But the city Ninainta belongs to the Ḫulaya River Land. The TUKUL of the Gold Charioteer which is behind, belongs to His Majesty. In the direction of Zarnušašša, the city Harmima used to be its boundary. But I, My Majesty, made Uppaššana its boundary. Uppaššana itself belongs to the Ḫulaya River Land.

§7 (i.48-52) In the direction of Zarwiša Mt. Šarlaimmi, the grotto springs, and the water(s) of *ḫinnaru* are his boundary. In the direction of the high mountain (the city) Šaliya is his boundary. But (the city) Šaliya itself belongs to the land of Ḫatti. In the direction of Ušaula (the cities) Ḫaššuwanta, Mila, Palmata, Ḫašḫaša, Šura and Šimmuwanta form his boundary. But these cities belong to the Ḫulaya River Land.

§8 (i.53-67) In the direction of the territory of Ḫawaliya (to the NNE?), the cities Walwara, Ḫarḫašuwanta, Tarapa,[9] Šarnanta, Tupiša, Parayašša and the *upati* of Nata form the boundary. But these cities and the *upati* of Nata belong to the Ḫulaya River Land. In the direction of the "place" (on) the sea (to the E?), the cities Mata, Šanhata, Šurimma, Šaranduwa, Ištapanna, the *upati* of Šalluša, Tatta, (and) Daša form his boundary. But these cities belong to the Ḫulaya River Land. In the direction of the border-territory of Šaranduwa (to the S?), the sea is his boundary. In the direction of the border-territory of Parha (to the W),[10] the Kaštaraya River[11] forms his boundary. And if the king of Ḫatti should undertake a campaign up against it (Parha?), and should take possession of the Land of Parha also by force of arms, then that (city) too would belong to the king of Tarḫuntašša. In the direction of the border-territory of Walma (to the WNW?), the cities Huwahhuwarwa, Alluprata, Kaparuwa, Ḫaššuwanta, Walippa (and) Wala form his boundary, but these cities belong to the Ḫulaya River Land.

Hittite Enclaves in Tarḫuntašša

§9 (i.68-90) These are cities of the king of Ḫatti which were inside the land of Tarḫuntašša: Anta, the ruined cities of Anta, Lahhuiyašši, Waštišša, Hudduwašša, Handawa, Daganza, Šimmuwa, Šahita, the men of Kammama (as) Men of the Long Weapon, Walištašša (and its) Golden Charioteers, Inurta, Wattanna, Malhuwaliyata, Kašuriya, Šawiya, Pariyašša, Annauliliya, Puhanta, Gurtanašša, the pomegranate-men, Aralla, the men of Araunna, Uppaššana, the augurs — (insofar as) one resides within the borders of the land, they too are given (to Kurunta). From Mattarwanta (and) Parašša the tent men, from Dagannunta and Munanta the scribes of the *tuppaš* chest, from Ayara the custodians/keepers of *nawilaš*, from Tarapa[12] the spear men, from Wattašša (and) Talwišuwanta two TUKULs. The potters (remain) behind, and also the cupbearers remain behind: they are given to the gods of Tarḫuntašša. The *duddušḫialla*-men from Iyasanta, the city Azzuwašši, the *ḫuwantala*-men from Wašḫaniya remain (or: are present). The *warpatala*-men from Adara as well as the cupbearers remain (or: are present). Respecting whatever *šarikuwaš* troops, craftsmen or Men of the Long Weapon remain in the land of Tarḫuntašša and the Ḫulaya River Land, my father gave to him (i.e., to Kurunta) these cities with their mud (i.e., without additional population); he did not give them to him with population. Therefore I, Tudḫaliya, Great King, made a representation before my father

[9] Perhaps the Derbe known in the Greco-Roman period.

[10] Classical Perge in the Plain of Pamphylia.

[11] Classical Cestrus (modern Aksu) just to the East of Perge.

[12] Perhaps the Derbe known in the Greco-Roman period.

father, and he gave them (i.e., the cities) to him with population. But it is not written (so) on the treaty tablet of my father.

Kurunta's Access to the Eternal Rock Mausoleum[13]

§10 (i.91-101, ii.1-3) With respect to the matter of the eternal rock mausoleum, my father took it from the mouth of Maraššanta, (who had said:) "Kurunta should not approach the eternal rock mausoleum." My father (once) made a tablet for Maraššanta, which Maraššanta (still) has. But my father did not yet know how the wording of the eternal rock mausoleum inside (*andan*) the *kuntarra* of Tešub was (lit. "is") inscribed: how from now on the eternal rock mausoleum will never be taken away from Kurunta. Now when he came to hear the wording, my father reversed his ruling. And when I, Tudḫaliya, Great King, succeeded to the throne, I sent a man who saw how the word of the eternal rock mausoleum inside the *kuntarra* of Tešub was inscribed: "from now on the eternal rock mausoleum will never be taken away from Kurunta." Therefore if Maraššanta ever brings the tablet which he has (which prohibited Kurunta from going up to the eternal rock mausoleum), let it not be accepted.

Changes in Boundaries

§11 (ii.4-20) No goatherd may go into the Ḫulaya River Land, which is the boundary (area) of the land of Tarḫuntašša. And if they drive up from the Ḫulaya River Land to the Great Saltlick Rock,[14] let them not take from him (i.e., Kurunta) the saltlick right(s). It is given to the king of Tarḫuntašša, and he may regularly take the salt. My father Ḫattušili gave to Kurunta, king of Tarḫuntašša, the town of Šarmana, Pantarwanta, and Mahrimma, together with their fields, grounds, meadows, sheep pastures, the whole saltlick, and the whole *liki*-.[15] Also I, My Majesty, Tudḫaliya the Great King, have given them to him. Therefore let no other person encroach upon the salt of the town of Šarmana. And in Dunna one *kuwappala* has been given to the storm-god of lightning, and (yet) it remains (i.e., still belongs) to [the king] of Tarḫuntašša. If Kurunta, the king of Tarḫuntašša, subsequently "makes"[16] one *kuwappala*, my father Ḫattušili, Great King, allowed it to him, and I Tudḫaliya, Great King, allowed it to him also. So let it be allowed to him.

§12 (ii.21-30)[17] Because all the Hittites supported(?) the gods of Tarḫuntašša,[18] they shall not appropriate those tribute payments and ritual provisions for the gods of Tarḫuntašša from what my father gave to Kurunta, king of Tarḫuntašša, and what I gave to him. But if now I, My Majesty, should choose some place for the (delivery of) cattle and sheep, who will appropriate it (as) the ritual provisions for the gods? They will begin to give to the gods of Tarḫuntašša annually two hundred cattle and one thousand sheep. But if I do not give him any place, let them give annually to the gods of Tarḫuntašša from the *ariyatt(a)*- of Ḫattuša two hundred cattle and one thousand sheep.

Tudḫaliya and Kurunta as Childhood Friends

§13 (ii.31-42) I, Tudḫaliya the Great King, before I became king, the god already previously had brought Kurunta and me together in friendship. Already previously we were dear and good to each other. We even were parties to an oath: "Each shall be loyal to the other."[19] But at that time my father had placed an older brother[20] in the rank of *tuḫukanti*-.[21] At that time he had not yet decided that I should become king. But even at that time Kurunta was loyal to me and swore allegiance to me personally as follows: "Even if your father does not install you in kingship, in whatever place your father puts you I will be loyal to you only. I am your servant." I too swore my allegiance to Ku-

[13] On this section see Beal 1993.

[14] On *lapana*- "saltlick" and its derivatives in Luwian and Hittite see Watkins 1997.

[15] This word *liki*- does not occur in the corresponding passage in the UTT KBo 4.10 obv. 35, but of course MUN does. Melchert 1994:255 (cited with approval by Watkins) must be a native Hittite synonym of Luwian *lapana*-.

[16] *HW*[2] 1:220 "(d.h., dem Gott gibt)." But perhaps rather it means "makes the one *k.* (previously given to the god his own)."

[17] ii.21-80 has no antecedent in the preserved parts of UTT.

[18] Cf. Gordon 1965 §7, obv. 41.

[19] Cf. the friendship, mutual loyalty, and even oath between David and Jonathan (1 Sam 18-23, esp. 23:18).

[20] Bryce 1998:299f., who follows the view that Ulmi-Tešub is the same person as Kurunta and that the UTT belongs to Ḫattušili III and therefore precedes the Bronze Tablet, proposes that this "older brother" of Tudḫaliya IV was Ḫattušili III's son Nerikkaili who as *tuḫukanti*-heads the list of human witnesses in UTT. On this man see van den Hout 1995:95-105. The Nerikkaili of the Bronze Tablet witness list, who is called simply "prince" (DUMU LUGAL), might be another man, a son of Tudḫaliya IV, although Otten and van den Hout think it more likely that he is the same person mentioned in UTT.

[21] The Hittite (or Luwian) word *tuḫukanti*- is generally thought to mean "crown prince", and although Houwink ten Cate 1992:262-63 argues it merely means "heir presumptive" or "second in line," a view that appears to be followed by van den Hout 1995, this would simply be the

Kurunta: "I too will be loyal to you."

The Designation of Tudḫaliya

§14 (ii.43-52) But when my father deposed my brother, whom he had placed in the rank of *tuḫukanti*-, he installed me in kingship. And when my father saw the high regard and love which existed between Kurunta and me, my father brought us together and made us swear: "May each (of us) be loyal to the other." And so it was my father too who made us swear (to each other), and we became separately (i.e., independently) parties to a (mutual) oath. Kurunta was loyal to me: he never broke the oaths which he swore before me. And I, My Majesty, on my part promised him: "If the gods recognize me, so that I become king, nothing but good will come to you from me." [a]

[a] 1 Sam 18-23

The Death of Ḫattušili III

§15 (ii.53-56) But when my father at that time became a god (i.e., died), although (some) lands adopted a wait-and-see policy,[22] even at that time Kurunta put his life on the line for me. He was loyal to me and broke none of the oaths which he had sworn.

§16 (ii.57-66) And when the deity took me, and I became king, I made the following treaty with Kurunta. I gave even cities which do not lie on the treaty tablet of my father together with field, fallow and NAM.RA, with everything, to be subjects of Kurunta, king of the land of Tarḫuntašša. (Respecting) whoever dwells in the Ḫulaya River Land, the entire (land)[23] remains subject to Kurunta, king of the Land of Tarḫuntašša. I redrew the boundaries in a manner favorable to him. I gave the eternal rock mausoleum back to him. In the future let no one take the eternal rock mausoleum away from the descendant of Kurunta.

Future Validity of Treaty

§17 (ii.67-78) In the future let this treaty be valid for Kurunta, king of the land of Tarḫuntašša, for as long as Tudḫaliya, (king) of the land of Ḫatti, keeps these. And let the descendant of Tudḫaliya thereafter keep the descendant of Kurunta in the land of Tarḫuntašša in kingship in the same way. Let him not allow them to be killed or demoted(?).[24] As I, Tudḫaliya, Great King, am loyal to Kurunta, afterwards let my son and my grandson be loyal to the descendant of Kurunta in the same way. And as I am loyal to Kurunta— if he lacks something, I will compensate him. And if some difficulty (i.e., crisis)[25] befalls the descendant of Kurunta, let my son or my grandson compensate him in the same way; let him not allow him to be either destroyed or diminished.

The Carchemish Treaty

§18 (ii.79-83) Let the protocol of the king of the land of Carchemish be allowed to him with respect to the Great Throne. Let only the crown prince (of Ḫatti) be greater than the king of the land of Tarḫuntašša; let no one else be greater than he. What royal insignia/protocol[26] is allowed to the king of the land of Carchemish, let it be allowed also to the king of the land of Tarḫuntašša.

Kurunta's Wife, Heir, Successor

§19 (ii.84-94) Concerning what stands written on the treaty tablet of my father (Ḫattušili III): "Put in kingship in the land of Tarḫuntašša the son of the woman whom the (Hittite) queen[27] gives you as a wife," — when they made the treaty tablet during my father's reign, you, Kurunta, had not taken that woman. Whether now Kurunta takes that woman or doesn't take her, that ruling (of my father) will not be enforced. Whatever son Kurunta prefers, whether the son of his wife or the son of some other woman, whatever son is the choice of Kurunta, whatever son Kurunta prefers, let him place him in kingship in the land of Tarḫuntašša. Let no one overrule Kurunta in this matter.

Security of Kurunta's line even in the event of treason

§20 (ii.95-102, iii.1-20) Let this treaty be valid for Kurunta, his son and his grandson. I, My Majesty, will not throw out your son.[28] I will not accept (in your son's place) your brother or anyone else. Your descendant alone[29] will possess the land of Tarḫuntašša which I have

meaning of "crown prince" in English, "heir apparent to the throne."

[22] Hittite: *arša tiyat*, translation after Otten 1988:19.

[23] Or perhaps: "everything."

[24] Luwian: *zantalanuna=ya*. Tentative translation based upon the apparent alternation with *tepnummanzi=ya* in line 77.

[25] The same Hittite verb *nakkišzi* occurs below in §21 iii.22, 28. Whereas here in §17 (ii 76) it is parallel to *wakšiyazi* "is lacking" in ii.74, later in §21 it is parallel to GÙB-*lišzi* "something unfortunate happens."

[26] Hittite *šaklaiš*.

[27] That is, Puduḫepa.

[28] Lines ii.96–iii.20 recapitulate §2' (KBo 4.10 + KUB 40.69 + 1548/u obv. 7'-14') of Ḫattušili III's earlier treaty with the king of Tarḫuntašša. For a parallel aligned transliteration see van den Hout 1995:22-25.

[29] UTT: "your son and grandson."

given to you. They will not take it away from him. And even if some son or grandson of yours commits treason[30] (against Ḫatti), the king of the land of Ḫatti will examine him, and if treason is proved against him, they[31] shall do to him whatever the king of the land of Ḫatti decides.[32] [b] (iii.1) But they may not take from him his 'house' (i.e., his dynasty) and land, nor may he (i.e., the emperor)[33] give it to another descendant (i.e., to a brother or cousin, some other descendant of Muwatalli II). Or if — since the matter of the land of Tarḫuntašša was subsequently formulated as follows: "In the future let no one take the kingship of the land of Tarḫuntašša away from the (primary) line of Muwatalli's descendants" — someone does this thing: he gives it (i.e., the land) to another line of Muwatalli's descendants, thus taking it away from the descendant of Kurunta, let the storm-god of Ḫatti and the sun-goddess of Arinna destroy whoever does that thing. In the future let only the descendant of Kurunta hold kingship over the land of Tarḫuntašša.[34] But let only a descendant on the male side hold[35] it; let them not accept the descendant of a daughter.[36] And[37] if some son or grandson of Kurunta exercises kingship over the land of Tarḫuntašša, and some misfortune[38] befalls him (lit. "someone") because of a god's decision (lit. word of a god), so that he must relinquish the kingship of Tarḫuntašša, let them take only a descendant of Kurunta and install him in kingship in the land of Tarḫuntašša. Let them not give it to any other descendant. If he has no descendant in the male line,[39] let them search for a descendant of the daughter of Kurunta. Even if it (scil. the descendant) is in a foreign country, let them bring it back even from there, and let them install him/her in kingship[40] in the land of Tarḫuntašša.

b 1 Sam 20; 22:16; 2 Sam 19:23; 1 Kgs 2:42

c 1 Kgs 22

Kurunta's line must ensure the succession and permanence of Tudḫaliya's descendants

§21 (iii.21-31)[41] If some descendant (lit. seed) of Tudḫaliya exercises kingship in the land of Ḫatti, and some difficulty[42] befalls him, whatever descendant of Kurunta exercises kingship in the land of Tarḫuntašša should be ready to die for him.[43] [c] And just as Kurunta was loyal to Tudḫaliya, so afterwards the descendant of Kurunta should also be loyal to the descendant of Tudḫaliya. The descendant of Kurunta should also be loyal to the descendant of Tudḫaliya and should not allow him to die or be demoted. If some difficulty befalls the descendant of Tudḫaliya, and he must step down from the kingship of the land of Ḫatti, what descendant of Kurunta stands in kingship in the land of Tarḫuntašša must make war on the (new) king of Ḫatti; he must not serve (him).

Tarḫuntašša's obligation to provide troops

§22 (iii.32-42)[44] My father, Ḫattušili, abolished for him (Kurunta) the (providing of) chariotry and infantry of the Ḫulaya River Land which the administration holds for you (Kurunta) in Ḫatti, and I too, My Majesty, Great King, have abolished it for him. In the future a contingent of 100 foot soldiers supplied by him shall march on a campaign of the land of Ḫatti. The administration may not demand further troops from him. Whenever a troop contingent is demanded of him, they shall require no more than 100 foot soldiers and no chariotry at all. But if a king of equal status arises against the Hittite king, or if My Majesty initiates a campaign from the Lower Land,[45] a contingent of 200 foot soldiers may be recruited from him. But they may not serve as garrison troops.

30 Lit. "sins" (*waštai*).
31 UTT: "he."
32 Lit. "whatever is the wish of the king of the land of Ḫatti." UTT then adds: "If he deserves to die, he shall die."
33 UTT: "nor may they give ...."
34 UTT lacks "Or if ... destroy whoever does that thing" and instead of "let only the descendant of Kurunta hold ..." reads "let only the descendant of Ulmi-Tešub take ...."
35 UTT: "take."
36 UTT: "let them not accept a daughter."
37 The next two sentences in my English translation are lacking in UTT.
38 GÙB-*lišzi*; see notes on §§17 and 21.
39 UTT adds: "then let it be retracted, and."
40 UTT: "in lordship."
41 §21 had no antecedent in UTT.
42 Hittite: *nakkišzi*. See above note on §17.
43 Cp. the willingness of Jehoshaphat of Judah to risk death in battle to assist his ally, Ahab of Israel (1 Kgs 22).
44 iii.32-36 are paralleled in UTT obv. 42'-44'.
45 An area adjacent to Tarḫuntašša.

Tarḫuntašša's exemption from taxes and corvée

§23 (iii.43-56) Concerning the fact that the entire land belongs to him and that as a whole it forms his front line of border posts — if now a call for help arises from somewhere, no one may require help from the Ḫulaya River Land. And against the cities in the midst of the land of Ḫatti, in the midst of the territory of Mt. Huwatnuwanta, in the midst of Kizzuwatna, Ḫurniya, Ikkuwaniya, and Pitašša — which belong in whatever land to the storm-god of lightning, the god of Parša, Šauška of Inuita, the cities that belong to the house of the king of Tarḫuntašša — against them no obligation to taxes and corvée shall stand. No call for military assistance is binding upon them. No one shall pester them to require taxes and corvée. For the sake of the gods of Tarḫuntašša I have exempted them.

§24 (iii.57-77) Concerning this which my father (Ḫattušili III) gave to Kurunta, and what I, My majesty, gave to him, the treaty which we made for him, in the future let no one change it. When I, My Majesty, carefully reviewed the taxes and corvée of the gods of (Kurunta), the king of Tarḫuntašša, (I saw that) it was too burdensome and that he could not manage it. What cult procedure the king of Tarḫuntašša supports in the land of Tarḫuntašša, corresponds to the procedure of Ḫattuša, Arinna and Zippalanda. Because the support of ceremonies and provisions for the gods was too burdensome for him, I remitted what my father and I, My Majesty, gave to Kurunta, for the sake of the Tešub of Lightning, Šarruma son of Tešub, and all the gods of Tarḫuntašša, and I exempted him. Let no one[46] take anything away from him. Let no one subject him to taxes and corvée. Whoever should take away the kingship of the land of Tarḫuntašša from a descendant of Kurunta or reduce it or command that it be abolished or should take away from him whatever my father and I have given him, or should alter a single word of this tablet,[d] may the sun-goddess of Arinna and the storm-god of Ḫatti take away the kingship of the land of Ḫatti from that person.

The divine witnesses to the treaty

§25 (iii.78-98, iv.1-4) The Thousand Gods[47] have now been called to assembly for (attesting the contents of) this treaty tablet that I have just executed for you. Let them see, hear, and be witnesses thereto — the sun-god of heaven, the sun-goddess of Arinna, the storm-god of heaven, the storm-god of Ḫatti, the storm-god of the army, the storm-god of Ḫiššašḫapa, the storm-god of Zippalanda, the storm-god of Nerik, the storm-god of Aleppo, the storm-god of Uda, the storm-god of Kizzuwatna, the storm-god of Šamuḫa, the storm-god of Šapinuwa, the mighty storm-god, the storm-god of lightning, the (god) of *lulut*, the patron god, the patron god of Ḫatti, Āla, Karzi, Ḫapantaliya, the patron god of the countryside, the patron god of the hunting bag,[48] Zitḫariya, Šarruma, Ḫebat the queen of heaven, Ḫebat of Uda, Ḫebat of Kizzuwatna, Šawuška of Šamuḫa, Šawuška of the coun-tryside, Šawuška of Lawazantiya, Šawuška of Nineveh, Šawuška of Ḫattarina, Ninatta, Kulitta, the moon-god king of the oath, NIN.GAL queen of the oath, Išḫara goddess of Arušna, the warrior-god, the warrior-god of Ḫatti, the warrior-god of Ellaya, the warrior-god of Arziya, Yarri, Zappana, Ḫantitaššu of Ḫurma, Abara of Šamuḫa, Ḫataḫḫa of Ankuwa, Ammama of Taḫurpa, GAZ.BA.A.A of Ḫubišna, Ḫallara of Dunna, Lelwani, the *lulaḫḫi*- and *ḫabiri*-gods, (all) the male and female deities, heaven and earth,[e] the great sea, the mountains,[f] rivers and springs of the land of Ḫatti and of the land of Tarḫuntašša.

(iv.5-15) If you, Kurunta, fail to comply with these treaty clauses, and do not remain loyal to My Majesty and subsequently the descendants of My Majesty as your rulers, or if you should desire for yourself the kingship of the land of Ḫatti, or if you side with someone who causes trouble for My Majesty or for the descendants of My Majesty instead of making war against him, then may these oath-deities destroy you together with your posterity. But if you, Kurunta, take to heart the words of this tablet, and you desire My Majesty and subsequently the descendants of My Majesty as your rulers, and you remain loyal to them, then may these same deities take good care of you, and may you grow old under the protection of My Majesty.

§26 (iv.16-29) But whoever causes trouble for Kurunta in this land and takes it away from him, or subsequently takes it away from the descendant of Kurunta, or reduces his territory, or takes anything away that I have given to him, or alters even a single word of this tablet,[g] may these oath-deities destroy

d Deut 4:2; 13:1 [12:32]

e Deut 4:26; 30:19; 31:28

f Ezek 6:3; 36:1, 4; Micah 6:1-2

g Deut 4:2; 13:1 [12:32]

[46] That is, no future king of Ḫatti.

[47] The official term for the Hittite pantheon.

[48] Cf. above *COS* 2.2.17B, note 19.

him. What I, My Majety, have given to Kurunta, king of the land of Tarḫuntašša, and what borders I have set for him, no one must ever take away from the descendants of Kurunta. Not even the king (of Ḫatti) should ever take them and give them to his son. He must not give them to any other descendant. Let no one contest his right to it. Let only the direct line of Kurunta's descendants possess the kingship of the land of Tarḫuntašša forever. Whoever causes trouble for him and takes something away from him may these oath-deities destroy together with that man's posterity.

§27 (iv.30-43) Ḫalwa-ziti, the scribe, the son of Lupakki of Ukkiya, inscribed this tablet in the city of Tawa in the presence of the following witnesses: Prince Nerikkaili, Ḫuzziya the chief of the palace guards, Prince Kurakura, Ini-Tešub king of Carchemish, Mašturi king of the Šeḫa River Land,[49] Šauška-muwa the king's son-in-law, Uppara-muwa the *anduwašalli*, Tattamaru the chief of the guard of the left side, Prince Eḫli-Šarruma, Aba-muwa chief of the chariot drivers, Prince Ḫešmi-Šarruma, Prince Taki-Šarruma, Prince En-Šarruma, Alalimi chief of the military tribunes, Alantalli king of the land of Mera,[50] Bentešina king of the land of Amurru, Šaḫurunuwa chief of the wood scribes, Ḫattuša-LAMMA the field marshal, GAL-^{d}U chief of the chariot drivers, Ḫuršaniya the field marshal, Zuzuḫḫa chief of the chariot warriors, Šalikka chief of the guards of the right side, Tapa-ziti the decurio, Tuttu commander of the storehouses, Walwa-ziti chief of the scribes, Kammaliya chief scribe of the kitchen staff, Nana-zi chief of the scribes and overseer of the food-servers — and all sorts of military commanders, magistrates and all the royal family.

h Deut 10:2

Colophon[51]

(iv.44-51) This (treaty) was made into seven tablets and sealed with the seals of the sun-goddess of Arinna and the storm-god of Ḫatti. One tablet was placed before the sun-goddess of Arinna,[52] *h* one before the storm-god of Ḫatti, one before Lelwani, one before Ḫebat of Kizzuwatna, one before the storm-god of lightning, and one in the king's house before Zitḫariya. And Kurunta, king of Tarḫuntašša, keeps one in his house.

[49] Located on the western end of Asia Minor.
[50] Located on the western end of Asia Minor.
[51] On this colophon see Börker-Klähn 1993.
[52] Cp. the keeping of the two tablets of the Sinai covenant in the ark of the testimony (Deut 10:2).

REFERENCES

Edition: Otten 1988. Other Tarḫuntašša treaties and protocols: *CTH* 96 (544/f, treated in SBo II [1942] 10f., 82); *CTH* 97 (StBoT 57); *CTH* 106 (KBo 4.10++, edited van den Hout 1995). Studies: Beal 1993; Beckman 1989-1990; Börker-Klähn 1993; Börker-Klähn 1994; Bryce 1998; Dinçol 1998; Heinhold-Krahmer 1991-92; Hoffner 1992; Houwink ten Cate 1992; Imparati 1992a; Imparati 1992b; 1992c; Laroche 1948; Melchert 1990; Mora 1998; Otten 1989; Singer 1996; Stefanini 1992; Sürenhagen 1992; van den Hout 1984.

2. LAWS

HITTITE LAWS (2.19)

Harry A. Hoffner, Jr.

The Hittite laws were first written down in the Old Kingdom (ca. 1650-1500 BCE). They are therefore later than the Sumerian law collections of Ur-Nammu and Lipit-Ishtar and the Akkadian laws of Eshnunna and Hammurabi, but earlier than the Middle Assyrian laws and the laws of the Hebrew Bible. A New Kingdom revision (KBo 6.4), called the Late Parallel Version and abbreviated PT for "Parallel Text," contains 41 sections numbered with roman numerals. I have interleaved the Late Parallel Version with the Main Version of Series One in the manner of Goetze 1969. In order to distinguish it more clearly from the copies of the Old Hittite recension I have indented the translation of paragraphs from the Late Parallel Version. Two paragraphs from the Old Hittite Telipinu Edict, edited by Hoffmann 1984, have been appended in order to supply the Hittite law on murder.

§1 [If] anyone kills[a] [a man] or a woman in a [quarr]el,[b] he shall [bring him] (for burial) and shall give 4 persons (lit. heads), male or female respectively. He shall look [to his house for it.][1]

§2 [If] anyone kills[c] [a male] or female slave in a quarrel, he shall bring him (for burial) [and] shall give [2] persons (lit. heads), male or female respectively. He shall look to his house for it.

§3 [If] anyone strikes a free [man] or woman so that he dies, but it is an accident,[2] [d] he shall bring him (for burial) and shall give 2 persons (lit. heads). He shall look to his house for it.

§4 If anyone strikes a male or female slave so that he dies, but it is an accident, he shall bring him (for burial) and shall give one person (lit. head). He shall look to his house for it.

§II (= late version of §§3-4) [If anyone] strikes [a (free) man,] so that he dies, but it is an accident, [he shall pay ... shekels of silver.] If it is a (free) woman (or) a female slave (or: if the woman is a slave), he shall pay 80 shekels of silver.[3]

§5 If anyone kills a merchant (variant: a Hittite merchant)[4] (in a foreign land), he shall pay 4,000 shekels (lit. 100 minas) of silver. He shall look to his house for it. If it is in the lands of Luwiya (= Arzawa) or Pala, he shall pay the 4,000 shekels of silver and also replace his goods. If it is in the land of Hatti, he shall (also) bring the merchant himself (for burial).

§III (= late version of §5) [If] anyone kills a Hittite [merchant] in the midst of his goods, he shall pay [... s minas hekels of silver], and he shall make threefold compensation for his goods. But [if] (the merchant) is not in possession of goods, and someone kills him in a quarrel, he shall pay 240 shekels of silver. If it is only an accident, he shall pay 80 shekels of silver.

§6 If a person, man or woman, is killed in another city, (the victim's heir) shall deduct 12,000 square meters (= 3 acres)[5] from the land of the person on whose property the person was killed and shall take it for himself.

a Exod 21:12

b Exod 21:18

c Exod 21:20

d Deut 19:5-6; Num 35

e Deut 21:1-2

f Exod 21:24; Lev 24:20; Deut 19:21

g Exod 21:26-27

h Exod 21:18-19

§IV (= late version of §6) If a man is found killed on another person's property, if he is a free man, he shall give his property, house, and 6040 shekels of silver. If it is a woman, he shall give (no property, but) 120 shekels of silver. But if (the place where the dead person was found) is not private property, but uncultivated open country, they shall measure 3 miles in all directions,[e] and whatever village is determined to lie within that radius, he shall take those (same payments from the villagers).[6] If there is no village, he shall forfeit (his claim).

§7 If anyone blinds a free person or knocks out his tooth,[7] [f] they used to pay 40 shekels of silver. But now he shall pay 20 shekels of silver. He shall look to his house for it.

§V (= late version of §7) If anyone blinds a free man in a quarrel, he shall pay 40 shekels of silver. If it is an accident, he shall pay 20 shekels of silver.

§8 If anyone blinds a male or female slave or knocks out his tooth,[g] he shall pay 10 shekels of silver. He shall look to his house for it.

§VI (= late version of §8) If anyone blinds a male slave in a quarrel, he shall pay 20 shekels of silver. If it is an accident, he shall pay 10 shekels of silver.

§VII (= late version of §§7-8) If anyone knocks out a free man's tooth — if he knocks out 2 or 3 teeth — he shall pay 12 shekels of silver. If it is a slave, he shall pay 6 shekels of silver.

§9 If anyone injures a person's head, they used to pay 6 shekels of silver: the injured party took 3 shekels of silver, and they used to take 3 shekels of silver for the palace. But now the king has waived the palace share, so that only the injured party takes 3 shekels of silver.

§VIII (= late version of §9) If anyone injures a (free) man's head, the injured man shall take 3 shekels of silver.

§10 If anyone injures a person and temporarily incapacitates him, he shall provide medical care for him. In his place he shall provide a person to work on his estate until he recovers. When he recovers, (his assailant) shall pay him 6 shekels of silver and shall pay the physician's fee as well.[h]

[1] The significance of this phrase has been much debated (Güterbock and Hamp 1956; Haase 1956; 1962; Souček 1961; Güterbock 1983b). I favor Güterbock's view that the claimant person entitled to make a claim in the case is entitled to recover damages from the estate of the perpetrator.

[2] Lit., "(only) his hand is at fault."

[3] Given the price of a slave, this fine of 2 minas (= 80 shekels) seems inordinately high.

[4] So OH manuscript. NH reads "a Hittite merchant."

[5] Hittite: 100 *gipeššar* = 3.3 IKU = 3 acres = 1 hectar, worth about 8.25 shekels silver according to §183. The fine in the late version (all his land plus 40 shekels) is much higher.

[6] Or perhaps: "he shall take those very (people who inhabit the village)."

[7] Cf. §§18-22.

§IX (= late version of §10) If anyone injures a free man's head, he shall provide medical care for him. In his place he shall provide a person to work on his estate until he recovers. When he recovers, (his assailant) shall pay him 10 shekels of silver and shall pay the 3 shekel physician's fee as well. If it is a slave, he shall pay 2 shekels of silver.

§11 If anyone breaks a free person's arm or leg, he shall pay him 20 shekels of silver. He shall look to his house for it.

§X (= late version of §11) If anyone breaks a free man's arm or leg, if (the injured man) is permanently handicapped(?), he shall pay him 20 shekels of silver. If he is not permanently handicapped(?), he shall pay him 10 shekels of silver.

§12 If anyone breaks a male or female slave's arm or leg, he shall pay 10 shekels[8] of silver. He shall look to his house for it.

§XI (= late version of §12) If anyone breaks a slave's arm or leg, if he is permanently handicapped(?), he shall pay him 10 shekels of silver. If he is not permanently handicapped(?), he shall pay him 5 shekels of silver.

§13 If anyone bites off the nose of a free person, he shall pay 40 shekels of silver. He shall look to his house for it.

§XII (= late version of §13) If anyone bites off the nose of a free man, he shall pay 30 minas (i.e., 1,200 shekels)[9] of silver. He shall look to his house for it.

§14 If anyone bites off the nose of a male or female slave, he shall pay 3 shekels of silver. He shall look to his house for it.

§XIII (= late version of §14) If anyone bites off the nose of a male or female slave, he shall pay 15 minas (i.e., 600 shekels)[10] of silver.

§15 If anyone tears off the ear of a free person, he shall pay 12 shekels of silver. He shall look to his house for it.

§XIV (= late version of §15) If anyone tears off the ear of a free man, he shall pay 12 shekels of silver.

§16 If anyone tears off the ear of a male or female slave, he shall pay him 3 shekels of silver.

§XV (= late version of §16) If anyone tears off the ear of a male or female slave, he shall pay 6 shekels of silver.

§17 If anyone causes a free woman to miscarry, [if] it is her tenth month,[11] he shall pay 10 shekels of silver, if it is her fifth month, he shall pay 5 shekels of silver. He shall look to his house for it.

§XVI (= late version of §17) If anyone causes a free woman to miscarry,[i] he shall pay 20 shekels of silver.

§18 If anyone causes a female slave to miscarry,[12] if it is her tenth month, he shall pay 5 shekels of silver.

§XVII (= late version of §18) If anyone causes a female slave to miscarry, he shall pay 10 shekels of silver. [...]

§19a If a Luwian abducts[j] a free person, man or woman, from the land of Hatti, and leads him away to the land of Luwiya/Arzawa, and subsequently the abducted person's "owner"[13] recognizes him, (the abductor) shall forfeit (lit. bring) his entire house.[14]

§19b If a Hittite abducts a Luwian man in the land of Hatti itself, and leads him away to the land of Luwiya, formerly they gave 12 persons (lit. heads), but now he shall give 6 persons. He shall look to his house for it.

§20 If a Hittite man abducts a Hittite male slave[k] from the land of Luwiya, and leads him here to the land of Hatti, and subsequently the abducted person's owner recognizes him, (the abductor) shall pay him 12 shekels of silver. He shall look to his house for it.

§21 If anyone abducts the male slave of a Luwian man from the land of Luwiya and brings him to the land of Hatti, and his owner (later) recognizes him, (the owner) shall only take (back) his own slave: there shall be no compensation.

§22a If a male slave runs away, and someone brings him back, if he seizes him nearby, he shall give him (i.e., the finder) shoes.

§22b If (he seizes him) on the near side of the (Maraššanta) River, he shall pay 2 shekels of silver. If on the far side of the river, he shall pay him 3 shekels of silver.

§23a If a male slave runs away and goes to the land of Luwiya, (his owner) shall pay 6 shekels of silver to whomever brings him back.

§23b If a male slave runs away and goes into an enemy country, whoever brings him back shall keep him for himself.

§24 If a male or female slave runs away, he/she at whose hearth his/her owner finds him/her

i Exod 21:22

j Exod 21:16; Deut 24:7; Amos 1:6

k Exod 20:17; Deut 5:21

[8] Later variant: "6 shekels."

[9] Perhaps a scribal error for "30 shekels." See also in §XIII.

[10] Perhaps a scribal error for "15 shekels."

[11] Remainder of the paragraph in manuscript C reads: "he shall pay 20 shekels of silver."

[12] Remainder of the paragraph in manuscript C reads: "he shall pay 10 shekels of silver."

[13] Since the victim is a free person, "owner" probably indicates only the head of his household.

[14] Or: "(The claimant) shall confiscate(?) his (i.e., the abductor's) entire house." See Hoffner 1997b 30 note 46.

shall pay one month's wages: 12 shekels of silver for a man, 6 shekels of silver for a woman.[15]

§25a [If] a person is impure in a vessel or a vat,[16] they used to pay 6 shekels of silver: s/he who is impure/guilty pays 3 shekels of silver,[17] and they used to take 3 shekels for the [king]'s house.[18]

§25b But now the king has [waived] the palace's share. S/he who is impure/guilty only pays 3 shekels of silver.[19] S/he shall look to his/her house for it.

§26a If a woman re[fuses][20] a man, [the man] shall give [her ...], and [the woman shall take] a wage for her seed.[21] But the man [shall take the land] and the children. [...]

§26b But if a man divor[ces][l] a woman, [and she ...s, he shall] s[ell her.] Whoever buys her [shall] pa[y him] 12 shekels of silver.

§27 If a man takes his wife and leads [her] away to his house, he shall carry her dowry[m] in (to his house). If the woman [dies] th[ere] (in his house), they shall burn her personal possessions, and the man shall take her dowry. If she dies in her father's house, and there [are] children,[22] the son(s) is/are his, but the man shall not [take] her dowry.

§28a If a daughter (or: young woman) has been promised to a man, but another man runs off with her, he who runs off with her shall give to the first man whatever he paid and shall compensate him.[23] The father and mother (of the woman) shall not make compensation.

§28b If her father and mother give her to another man,[n] the father and mother shall make compensation (to the first man).

§28c If the father and mother refuse (to do so),[24] they shall separate her from him.[25]

§XX (= late version of §28) [*Too broken for connected translation.*]

§XXI [*Too broken for connected translation*]

§29 If a daughter has been betrothed (lit. bound) to a man, and he pays a brideprice[o] for her, but afterwards the father and mother abrogate reject[26] it (sc. the agreement), they shall separate her from the man, but they[27] shall restore the brideprice double.

§XXII (= late version of §29) [*Too broken for connected translation.*]

§30 But if before a man has taken the daughter (sexually) he refuses her, he shall forfeit the brideprice which he has paid.

§XXIII (= late version of §30) If a man [...s] a young woman, the brideprice which [he paid, ...].

§31 If a free man and a female slave are lovers and come together (i.e., live together), and he takes her as his wife, and they make a house and children, but (if) afterwards either they become estranged or they each find a new marriage partner, they shall divide the house equally, and the man shall take the children, with the woman taking one child.

§XXIV (= late version of §31) [*Too broken for connected translation.*]

§32 If a male slave [takes] a [free] woman (in marriage), [and they make a home and children, when they divide their house], (if they separate,) they shall divide their possessions [equally, and the free woman shall take] most of [the children,] with [the male slave taking] one child.

§33 (Translation of A) If a male slave takes a female slave (in marriage), [and they have children,] when they divide their house, they shall divide their possessions equally, [the slave woman shall take] mos[t of the children], with the male slave [taking] one child.

§34 If a male slave pays a brideprice for a woman and takes her as his wife, no one shall free her from slavery.[p]

§XXVI (= late version of §32 or 34) If a male slave [..., and takes] her [in] ma[rriage...]

§35 If a herdsman[28] [takes]elopes with a free woman [in marriage] and does not pay a brideprice for her, she will become a slave for[29] (only) 3 years.[30]

l Deut 24:1-4; Jer 3:1; Mal 2:16

m Gen 30:20; 1 Kgs 9:16

n Deut 28:30; Judg 15:1-3

o Exod 22:15-16; Deut 22:28-29; 2 Sam 3:14

p Exod 21:2-11

---

[15] So the OH manuscript. The NH manuscript substitutes: "shall pay one year's wages: 100 shekels of silver for a man, 50 shekels of silver for a woman."

[16] Although the Hittite wording cannot support the translation "brings impurity into a vessel or vat," yet the act referred to must be urinating or in some other manner defiling the vessel and its contents.

[17] Another manuscript reads "[the victim] ta[kes] 3 shekels of silver."

[18] So the OH manuscript. The NH manuscript has: "for the palace."

[19] Another manuscript reads: "The victim [takes three shekels of silver]."

[20] Another manuscript reads: "divorces."

[21] I.e., she shall be paid for the number of children she has borne?

[22] Variant: "and he/she has a son."

[23] Another manuscript reads: "As soon as (*kuššan*) he runs off ... they (i.e., the parents) shall compensate ..."

[24] Another manuscript reads: "But if it is not the wish of the father and mother."

[25] Another manuscript adds: "who runs off with her."

[26] Same verb (*ḫulle-*) as in §173a.

[27] Another manuscript has a singular verb.

[28] So the OH manuscript. The NH manuscript substitutes: "If a steward or a herdsman."

[29] Or, less likely: "after." See §175.

[30] So the OH manuscript. NH reads: "If a steward or a herdsman elopes with a free woman and does not pay a brideprice for her, she will

§36 If a slave pays a brideprice for a free young man and acquires him as a son-in-law, no one shall free him from slavery.

§37 If anyone elopes with a woman, and a group of supporters goes after them, if 3 or 2 men are killed, there shall be no compensation: "You (singular) have become a wolf."

§38 If persons are engaged in a lawsuit, and some supporter goes to them, if a litigant becomes furious and strikes the supporter, so that he dies, there shall be no compensation.

§XXXII (= late version of §38) If a person [...], and if/when [a supporter(?) ...] and he/she becomes angry [...], and he/she dies, [if(?) ...], and he/she dies, [...].

§39 But if he holds another person's land, he shall perform the *šaḫḫan*-services entailed by it. [But if] he refuses(?)[31] [the *šaḫḫan*-obligation,] he shall relinquish the land: he shall not sell it.

§XXXIII (= late version of §39) If [anyone holds] vacated [land], he shall work [it,] and not [...]

§40 If a man who has a TUKUL-obligation defaults, and a man owing *šaḫḫan*-services has stepped (in his place), the man owing *šaḫḫan*-services shall say: "This is my TUKUL-obligation, and this other is my obligation for *šaḫḫan*-services." He shall secure for himself a sealed deed concerning the land of the man having the TUKUL-obligation, he shall hold the TUKUL-obligation and perform the *šaḫḫan*-services. But if he refuses the TUKUL-obligation, they will declare the land to be that of a man having a TUKUL-obligation who has defaulted,[32] and the men of the village will work it.[33] If the king gives an *arnuwalaš*-man, they will give him land, and he will become a TUKUL-(man).

§XXX (= late version of §40) If a free man [defaults], and a man owing *šaḫḫan*-services [has stepped in his place, the man owing *šaḫḫan*-services shall declare: "This is my ...], and this other is [my] obligation for *šaḫḫan*-services." He shall secure for himself a sealed deed concerning [the land of the man having the ...-obligation, he shall ... the ...-obligation] and perform [the *šaḫḫan*-services. But if he refuses the ...-obligation, they will declare the land] vacated, [and the men of the village will work it]. If the king [gives an *arnuwala*-man], they will give [him land, and he will become a ...-(man)].

§41 If a man owing *šaḫḫan*-services defaults, and a man having a TUKUL-obligation has stepped in his place, the man having the TUKUL-obligation shall say: "This is my TUKUL-obligation, and this other is obligation for *šaḫḫan*-services." He shall secure for himself a sealed deed concerning the land of the man owing *šaḫḫan*-services. He shall hold the TUKUL-obligation and perform the *šaḫḫan*-services. But if he refuses (to do) the *šaḫḫan*-services, they will take for the palace the land of the man owing *šaḫḫan*-services. And the obligation for *šaḫḫan*-services shall cease.

§XXXI (= late version of §41) [*See §41 for probable translation.*]

§42 If anyone hires a person, and that person goes on a military campaign[34] and he is killed, if the hire has been paid, there shall be no compensation. But if the hire has not been paid, the hirer shall give one slave.[35]

§43 If a man is crossing a river with his ox, and another man pushes him off (the ox's tail), seizes the tail of the ox, and crosses the river, but the river carries off the owner of the ox, (the dead man's heirs) shall take that man (who pushes him off).

§44a If anyone shoves a man into a fire, so that he dies, (the guilty party) shall give one person (lit. head) a son in return.

§44b If anyone performs a purification ritual on a person, he shall dispose of the remnants (of the ritual) in the incineration dumps. But if he disposes of them in someone's house,[36] it is sorcery (and) a case for the king.

§XXXIV (= late version of §44b?) ... and he shall make it ritually pure again. If in the house anything goes wrong, he shall make it pure again. And he shall make compensation for whatever is lost.

§45 If anyone finds implements, [he shall bring] them back to their owner. He (the owner) will reward him. But if (the finder) does not give them (back), he shall be considered a thief.

§XXXV (= late version of §§45 and 71) If anyone finds implements or an ox, a sheep, a horse, (or) an ass, he shall drive it back to its owner, and (the owner) will lead it away. But if he cannot find its owner, he shall secure witnesses (that he is only maintaining custody).

become a slave for (only) 3 years."

[31] One NH manuscript has "releases," while another has "casts off," "rejects."

[32] A later manuscript reads "they declare the land of the TUKUL-man vacant."

[33] A later manuscript reads "men will work it for the village."

[34] Or: "on a (business) trip."

[35] A later manuscript adds: "And as hire he shall pay 12 shekels of silver. As the hire of a woman he shall pay 6 shekels of silver."

[36] Another manuscript reads: "on someone's land or house."

Afterwards (when) its owner finds it, he shall produce it according to the law — carry off in full what was lost. But if he does not secure witnesses, and afterwards its owner finds it (in his possession), he shall be considered a thief,[q] and he shall make threefold compensation.

§46 If in a village someone holds land (lit. fields) as an inheritance share, if the [larger part of] the land has been given to him/her, (s)he shall render the *luzzi*-services. But if the sm[aller part] (of) the land [has been given] to him/her, (s)he shall not render the *luzzi*-services: they shall render them from the house of his/her father.[37] If an heir cuts out for himself new(?) idle land, or the men of the village give land to him/her (in addition to his inherited land), (s)he shall render the *luzzi*-services (on the new land).

§XXXVIII (= late version of §46) If anyone holds land and obligation to perform *šaḫḫan*-services as an inheritance share in a village, if the land was given him in its entirety, he shall render the *luzzi*-services. If the land was not given him in its entirety, but only a small portion was given to him, he shall not render the *luzzi*-services. They shall render them from his father's estate. If the land of the heir is vacated, and the men of the village give him (other public) land, he shall render the *luzzi*-services.

§47a If anyone holds land by a royal grant, [he shall] not [have to render] *šaḫḫan*- and *luzzi*-services. Furthermore, the king shall provide him with food at royal expense.[38]

§47b If anyone buys all the land of a man having a TUKUL-obligation, he shall render the *luzzi*-services. But if he buys only the largest portion of the land, he shall not render the *luzzi*-services. But if he carves out for himself new idle land, or the men of the village give (him land), he shall render the *luzzi*-services.

§XXXVI (= late version of §47a) If anyone holds land by a royal grant, he shall perform the *luzzi*-services. But if the king exempts him, he shall not perform the *luzzi*-services.

§XXXVII (= late version of §47b) If anyone buys all the land of a TUKUL-man, and the (former) owner of the land dies, (the new owner) shall perform whatever (*šaḫḫan*-services) the king determines. But if the (former) owner is still living, or (there is) an estate of the (former) owner of the land, whether in that country or another country, he shall not perform the *šaḫḫan*-services.

[q] Exod 20:17; Deut 5:21

§XXXIXa (= late version of §47) If anyone holds land by a royal grant, he shall perform the *luzzi*-services devolving on the land. If they exempt him from the palace, he shall not render the *luzzi*-services.

§XXXIXb If anyone buys all the land of a TUKUL-man, they shall ask the king, and he shall render whatever *luzzi*-services the king says. If he buys in addition someone (else)'s land, he shall not render the *luzzi*-services (of that). If the land is vacated, or the men of the village give him (other land), he shall perform the *luzzi*-services.

§48 A *ḫipparaš*-man renders the *luzzi*-services. Let no one transact business with a *ḫipparaš*-man. Let no one buy his child, his land, (or) his vineyard(s). Whoever transacts business with a *ḫipparaš*-man shall forfeit his purchase price, and the *ḫipparaš*-man shall take back whatever he sold.

§XL (= late version of §48) (Even) if a *ḫipparaš*-man renders the *luzzi*-services, let no one transact business with a *ḫipparaš*-man. Let no one buy his child, his land (or) his vineyard(s). Whoever transacts business with a *ḫipparaš*-man shall forfeit his purchase price, and the *ḫipparaš*-man [shall take] back whatever he sold.

§49 [If] a *ḫipparaš*-man steals, there will be no compensation. But [if] (there is) a body which represents him, only that body shall give compensation. If they (i.e., the *ḫipparaš*-men) [were] to have to give (compensation for) theft, they would all have been dishonest, or would have become thieves. This one would have seized that one, and that one this one. [They] would have overturned the king's authority(?).

§XLI (= late version of §49) [If] a *ḫipparaš*-man steals, they will impose upon him no [compensation, or else a body which represents him] will [make compensation.] If [the *ḫipparaš*-men had been required ...] [*Continuation broken away.*]

§50 The ... [man] who ...-s in Nerik, Arinna or Ziplanta, and he who is a priest in any town — their houses are exempt, and their associates render the *luzzi*-services. In Arinna when the eleventh month arrives, [the house of him] at whose gate an *eyan* (tree or pole) is erected is likewise (exempt).

§51 Formerly the house of a man who became a weaver in Arinna was exempt, also his associates and relatives were exempt. Now only his own house is exempt, but his associates and relatives shall render the *luzzi*-

[37] I.e., the principal heir shall inherit the *luzzi*-obligation.

[38] Lit. "shall take bread from his table and give it to him."

services. In Zippalantiya it is just the same.

§52 A slave of a Stone House, a slave of a prince (or) a person entitled to wear a reed-shaped emblem(?) — any of such people who hold land among TUKUL-men, shall render the *luzzi*-services.

§53 If a man having a TUKUL-obligation and his associate live together, if they have a falling out, they shall divide their household. If there are on their land 10 persons (lit. heads), the man having a TUKUL-obligation shall receive 7 and his associate 3. They shall divide the cattle and sheep on their land in the same ratio. If anyone holds a royal grant by tablet, if they divide old land, the man having a TUKUL-obligation shall take 2 parts, and his associate shall take one part.

§54 Formerly, the *MANDA* troops, the troops of Sala, Tamalki, Hatra, Zalpa, Tashiniya and Hemuwa, the bowmen, the carpenters, the chariot warriors and their *karuḫaleš*-men did not render the *luzzi*-services, nor did they perform *šaḫḫan*-services.

§55 When (a delegation of) Hittites, men owing *šaḫḫan*-services, came, they did reverence to the father of the king, and said: "No one pays us a wage. They say to us: 'You are men required to perform your jobs as a *šaḫḫan*-service!'" The father of the king [stepped] into the assembly and declared under his seal: "You must continue to perform *šaḫḫan*-services just like your colleagues."[39]

§56 None of the coppersmiths is exempt from participating in ice procurement,[40] construction of fortresses and royal roads, or from harvesting vineyards. The gardeners render the *luzzi*-services in all the same kinds of work.

§57 If anyone steals a bull — if it is a weanling calf, it is not a "bull"; if it is a yearling calf, it is not a "bull"; if it is a 2-year-old bovine, that is a "bull." Formerly they gave 30 cattle. But now he shall give 15 cattle: 5 two-year-olds, 5 yearlings and 5 weanlings. He shall look to his house for it.

§58 If anyone steals a stallion — if it is a weanling, it is not a "stallion"; if it is a yearling, it is not a "stallion"; if it is a two-year-old, that is a "stallion." They used to give 30 horses. But now he shall give 15 horses: 5 two-year-olds, 5 yearlings and 5 weanlings. He shall look to his house for it.

[r] Exod 20:17; Deut 5:21

[s] Exod 20:17; Deut 5:21

§59 If anyone steals a ram, they used to give 30 sheep. Now he shall give [15] sheep: he shall give 5 ewes, 5 wethers and 5 lambs. And he shall look to his house for it.

§60 If anyone finds a bull and castrates it, (when) its owner claims it, (the finder) shall give 7 cattle: 2 two-year-olds, 3 yearlings, and 2 weanlings. He shall look to his house for it.

§61 If anyone finds a stallion and castrates it, (when) its owner claims it, (the finder) shall give 7 horses: 2 two-year-olds, 3 yearlings, and 2 weanlings. He shall look to his house for it.

§62 If anyone finds a ram and castrates it, (when) its owner claims it, (the finder) shall give 7 sheep: 2 ewes, 3 wethers, and 2 (sexually) immature sheep. He shall look to his house for it.

§63 If anyone steals a plow ox,[r] formerly they gave 15 cattle, but now he shall give 10 cattle: 3 two-year-olds, 3 yearlings, and 4 weanlings. He shall look to his house for it.

§64 If anyone steals a draft horse, its disposition is the same.[41]

§65 If anyone steals a trained he-goat or a trained deer or a trained mountain goat,[42] their disposition is the same as of the theft of a plow ox.[43]

§66 If a plow ox, a draft horse, a cow, or a mare[44] strays into another corral, if a trained he-goat, a ewe, or a wether strays into (another) pen, and its owner finds it, he shall take it back according to the law in full. He shall not have (the pen's owner) arrested as a thief.

§67 If anyone steals a cow, they used to give 12 oxen. Now he shall give 6 oxen:[45] he shall give 2 two-year-old oxen, 2 yearling oxen, and 2 weanlings. He shall look to his house for it.

§68 If anyone steals a mare, its disposition is the same (i.e., 2 two-year-olds, 2 yearlings and 2 weanlings).

§69 If anyone steals either a ewe or a wether, they used to give 12 sheep, but now he shall give 6 sheep: he shall give 2 ewes, 2 wethers and 2 (sexually) immature sheep. He shall look to his house for it.

§70 If anyone steals an ox, a horse, a mule, or an ass,[s] (when) its owner claims it, [he shall take] it according to the law in full. In addi-

[39] Presumably only a delegation of the men subject to the *ILKU*-obligation appeared before the king.

[40] Post-OH manuscripts omit "ice procurement."

[41] Lit., "is this very (same)."

[42] I.e., decoys used by hunters.

[43] A later copy incorrectly substitutes "its compensation is the same as that for a he-goat."

[44] NH text: "jenny."

[45] A later copy adds: "Now he shall give 6 oxen."

tion (the thief) shall give to him twice/ double. He shall look to his house for it.

§71 If anyone finds a (stray) ox, a horse, (or) a mule,[t] he shall drive it to the king's gate. If he finds it in the country, they shall present it to the elders. (The finder) shall harness it (i.e., use it while it is in his custody). When its owner finds it, he shall take it according to the law in full, but he shall not have him (sc. the finder) arrested as a thief. But if (the finder) does not present it to the elders, he shall be considered a thief.[u]

§72 If an ox is found dead on someone's property, the property-owner shall give 2 oxen. He shall look to his house for it.

§73 If anyone ...s a living ox, that is the same as (a case) of theft.

§74 If anyone breaks the horn or leg of an ox, he shall take that (ox) for himself and give an ox in good condition to the owner of the (injured) ox. If the owner of the ox says: "I will take my own ox," he shall take his ox, and (the offender) shall pay 2 shekels of silver.

§75 If anyone hitches up an ox, a horse, a mule or an ass, and it dies, [or] a wolf devours [it], or it gets lost, he shall give it according to the law in full. But if he says: "It died by the hand of a god," he shall take an oath (to that effect).

§76 If anyone impresses an ox, a horse, a mule or an ass, and it dies at his place, he shall bring it and shall pay its rent also.

§77a If anyone strikes a pregnant cow, so that it miscarries, he shall pay 2 shekels of silver. If anyone strikes a pregnant horse, so that it miscarries, he shall pay 3[46] shekels of silver.

§77b If anyone blinds the eye of an ox or an ass, he shall pay 6 shekels of silver. He shall look to his house for it.

§78 If anyone rents an ox and then puts on it a leather ... or a leather ..., and its owner finds it, he shall give 50 liters[47] of barley.

§79 If oxen enter (another man's) field,[v] and the field's owner finds (them), he may hitch them up for one day until the stars come out. Then he shall drive them back to their owner.

§80 If any (shepherd) throws a sheep to a wolf, its owner shall take the meat, but he (the shepherd) shall take the sheepskin.

§81 If anyone steals a fattened pig, they used to pay 40 shekels of silver. But now he shall pay 12 shekels of silver. He shall look to his house for it.

§82 If anyone steals a pig of the courtyard, he shall pay 6 shekels of silver. He shall look to his house for it.

§83 If anyone steals a pregnant sow, he shall pay 6 shekels of silver, and they shall count the piglets: for each 2 piglets he shall give 50 liters of barley. He shall look to his house for it.

§84 If anyone strikes a pregnant sow a lethal blow, its (i.e., the case's) settlement disposition is exactly the same.

§85 If anyone cuts out a piglet and steals it, he shall give 100 liters of barley.

§86 If a pig enters a grain-heap, a field or a garden, and the owner of the grain-heap, field (or) garden strikes it a lethal blow, he shall give it back to its owner. If he doesn't give (it back), he shall be considered a thief.

§87 If anyone strikes the dog of a herdsman a lethal blow, he shall pay 20 shekels of silver. He shall look to his house for it.

§88 If anyone strikes the dog of a dog trainer (or: hunter?) a lethal blow, he shall pay 12 shekels of silver. He shall look to his house for it.

§89 If anyone strikes a dog of the enclosure(?) a lethal blow, he shall pay one shekel of silver.

§90 If a dog devours lard, and the owner of the lard finds (the dog), he shall kill it and retrieve the lard from its stomach. There will be no compensation (for the dog).

§91 [If] anyone [steals bees] in a swarm, [formerly] they paid [... shekels of silver], but now he shall pay 5 shekels of silver. He shall look to his house for it.

§92 [If] anyone steals [2] or 3 bee hives, formerly (the offender) would have been exposed to bee-sting. But now he shall pay 6 shekels of silver. If anyone steals a bee-hive, if there are no bees in the hive, he shall pay 3 shekels of silver.

§93 If they seize a free man at the outset, before he enters the house, he shall pay 12 shekels of silver. If they seize a slave at the outset, before he enters the house, he shall pay 6 shekels of silver.

§94 If a free man burglarizes a house,[w] he shall pay only according to the law in full. Formerly they paid 40 shekels of silver as (fine) for the theft, but now [he shall pay] 12 shekels of silver. If he steals much, they will impose much upon him. If he steals little, they shall impose little upon him. He shall look to his house for it.

§95 If a slave burglarizes a house, he shall pay only according to the law in full. He shall

t Exod 23:4; Deut 22:1; 1 Sam 9-10
u Exod 22:3
v Exod 22:5
w Exod 22:2-3

[46] A NH manuscript reads: 2.
[47] Hittite: 1 *PARISU*.

pay six shekels of silver for the theft. He[48] shall disfigure/mutilate the nose and ears of the slave and they will give him back to his owner. If he steals much, they will impose much upon him; if he steals little, they will impose little upon him. [If] his owner says: "I will make compensation for him," then he shall make it. But [if] he refuses, he shall lose that slave.

§96 If a free man breaks into a grain storage pit, and finds grain in the storage pit, he shall fill the storage pit with grain and pay 12 shekels of silver. He shall look to his house for it.

§97 If a slave breaks into a grain storage pit, and finds grain in the storage pit, he shall fill the storage pit with grain and pay 6 shekels of silver. He shall look to his house for it.

§98 If a free man sets fire to a house, he shall rebuild [the house]. And whatever perished in the house — whether it is persons, [cattle or sheep], it is not ...

§99 If a slave sets fire to a house, his owner shall make compensation for him, and they shall disfigure the slave's nose and ears and return him to his owner. But if (the owner) will not make compensation, he shall forfeit that slave.

§100 If anyone sets fire to a shed, he shall feed his (sc. the owner's) cattle and bring them through to the following spring. He shall give back the shed. If there was no straw in it, he shall (simply) rebuild the shed.

§101 If anyone steals a vine, a vine branch, a ..., or an onion/garlic, formerly [they paid] one shekel of silver for one vine and one shekel of silver for a vine branch, one shekel of silver [for one *karpina*, one] shekel of silver for one clove of garlic. And they shall strike a spear on his [...] [Formerly] they proceeded so. But now if he is a free man, he shall pay 6 shekels [of silver]. But if he is a slave, he shall pay 3 shekels of silver.

§102 [If] anyone steals wood from a [...] pond, [if] he steals [one talent (= 30.78 kg) of wood], he shall pay 3 shekels of silver; if he steals 2 talents (= 61.56 kg) of wood, [he shall pay] 6 shekels of silver; if he steals [3] talents (= 92.34 kg) of wood, it becomes a case for the king's court.

§103 [If] anyone steals plants, if it is 0.25 square meters [of planting], he shall re-plant it and [give] one shekel of silver. [If it is 0.5] square meters of planting, he shall re-plant it and pay 2 shekels of silver.

§104 [If] anyone cuts down a pear(?) tree or plum(?) tree, he shall pay [... shekels] of silver. He shall look to his house for it.

x Exod 22:5

y Exod 22:4

§105 [If] anyone sets [fire] to a field, and (the fire) catches a fruit-bearing vineyard, if a vine, an apple tree, a pear(?) tree or a plum tree burns,[x] he shall pay 6 shekels of silver for each tree. He shall re-plant [the planting]. And he shall look to his house for it. If it is a slave, he shall pay 3 shekels of silver (for each tree).

§106 If anyone carries embers into his field, catches(??) a fruit-bearing (one), and ignites the field,[y] he who sets it (i.e., the fire [neuter]) shall himself take the burnt-over field. He shall give a good field to the owner of the (burnt-over) field, and he will reap it.

§107 If a person lets (his) sheep into a productive vineyard, and ruins it, if it is fruit bearing, he shall pay 10 shekels of silver for each 3,600 square meters.[49] [ ][50] But if it is bare, he shall pay 3 shekels of silver.

§108 If anyone steals vine branch(es) from a fenced-in vineyard, if (he steals) 100 vines/(fruit) trees, he shall pay 6 shekels of silver. He shall look to his house for it. But if (the vineyard) is not fenced in, and he steals vine branch(es), he shall pay 3 shekels of silver.

§109 If anyone cuts off fruit trees from their irrigation ditch, if (there are) 100 trees, he shall pay 6 shekels of silver.

§110 If anyone steals clay from a pit, [however much] he steals, he shall give the same amount in addition.

§111 [If] anyone forms clay for [an image] (for magical purposes), it is sorcery (and) a case for the king's court.

§112 [If] they give [to an *arnuwala*-man] the land of a man having a TUKUL-obligation who has disappeared, [for 3 years] they perform no [*šaḫḫan*-services], but in the fourth year he begins to perform *šaḫḫan*-services and joins the men having TUKUL-obligations.

§113 [If] anyone cuts down a vine, he shall take the cut-down [vine] for himself and give to the owner of the vine (the use of) a good vine. (The original owner of the cut-down vine) shall gather fruit from (the new vine) [until] his own vine recovers. ...

[§114 and 118 too broken for translation. §§115-117 lost in a lacuna]

§119 If anyone [steals] a duck (lit. pond bird) trained (as a decoy) [or] a mountain goat trained (as a decoy), [formerly] they paid [40] shekels of silver, but now [he shall pay]

[48] Another manuscript reads: "They."

[49] Hittite: 1 IKU, which equals 30 *gipeššar*.

[50] Two late manuscripts add: "He shall look to his house for it."

12 shekels [of silver]. He shall look [to his house for it].

§120 If anyone steals ...-ed birds [...], if there are 10 birds, he shall pay one shekel [of silver].

§121 If some free man steals a plow, and its owner finds it, (the owner) shall put [(the offender's) neck] upon the ..., and [he shall be put to death] by the oxen. So they proceeded formerly. But now he shall pay 6 shekels of silver. He shall look to his house for it. If it is a slave, [he shall pay] 3 shekels of silver.

§122 If anyone steals a wagon with all its accessories, initially they paid one shekel of silver, [but now] he shall pay [... shekels of silver]. He shall look [to his] house [for it].

§123 If [anyone steals a ..., ... Now he shall pay] 3 shekels of silver. He shall look to his house for it.

§124 If anyone steals a ... tree, he shall pay 3 shekels of silver. He shall look to his house for it. If anyone loads a wagon, [leaves] it in his field, and someone steals (it), he shall pay 3 shekels of silver. He shall look to his house for it.

§125 If anyone steals a wooden water trough, he shall pay [...] + one shekel of silver. If anyone steals a leather ... or a leather ..., he shall pay one shekel of silver.

§126 If anyone steals a wooden ... in the gate of the palace, he shall pay 6 shekels of silver. If anyone steals a bronze spear in the gate of the palace, he shall be put to death. If anyone steals a copper pin, he shall give 25 liters of barley. If anyone steals the threads (or strands of wool) of one bolt of cloth, he shall give one bolt of woolen cloth.

§127 If anyone steals a door in a quarrel, he shall replace everything that may get lost in the house, and he shall pay 40 shekels of silver. He shall look to his house for it.

§128 If anyone steals bricks, however many he steals, he shall give the same number a second time over. If [anyone] steals stones from a foundation, for 2 (such) stones he shall give 10 stones. If anyone steals a stela or a ... stone, he shall pay 2 shekels of silver.

§129 If anyone steals a leather ..., a leather ..., a [...], or a bronze bell(?) <of> a horse or a mule, formerly they paid 40 shekels of silver, but now [he shall pay] 12 shekels of silver. He shall look to his house for it.

§130 If anyone steals [...s] of an ox or a horse, [he shall pay ... shekels of silver.] He shall look to his house for it.

§131 If [anyone steals] a leather harness(?), he shall pay 6 shekels of silver. [He shall look to his house for it.]

§132 If a free man [steals ..., he shall pay] 6 shekels of silver. [He shall look to his house for it.] If he is a slave, [he shall pay 3 shekels of silver.]

§133 If a free man [steals ...,] he shall pay [...] shekels [of silver. He shall look to his house for it. If he is a slave, he shall pay ... shekels of silver.]

§142 [If] anyone drives [..., ... anyone steals] its wheel(s), he shall give 25 liters of barley [for each] wheel. [If he is a slave, he shall give ... of barley] for each wheel.

§143 If a free man [steals] copper shears(?) [or] a copper nail file(?), he shall pay 6 shekels of silver. [He shall look to] his house [for it]. If it is a slave, he shall pay 3 shekels of silver.

§144 If a barber gives copper [...s] to his associate, and (the latter) ruins them, he shall give [them] according to the law in full. If anyone cuts fine cloth [on/with] a *ḫanzan*, he shall pay 10 shekels of silver. If anyone cuts [...], he shall pay 5 shekels of silver.

§145 If anyone builds an ox barn, (his employer) shall pay him 6 shekels of silver. [If] he leaves out [...], he shall forfeit his wage.

§146a If anyone offers a house, a village, a garden or a pasture for sale, and another goes and pre-empts(?) him, and offers (lit. makes) a purchase price instead of (lit. upon) the (first) purchase price, as a fine for his offence he shall pay 40 shekels of silver, and buy (the items) [from the person] at the original prices.

§146b[51] [If] anyone offers a [...] for sale, and another pre-[empts(?)], for his offence he shall pay 10 shekels of silver. He shall buy at the original prices.

§147 [If] anyone offers an unskilled person for sale, and another person pre-empts(?), as the fine for his offence he shall pay 5 shekels of silver.

§148 [If] anyone [offers] an ox, a horse, a mule or an ass [for sale], and another person pre-empts(?), as the fine for his offence he shall pay ... shekels of silver.

§149 If anyone sells a trained person, and (afterwards, before delivery) says: "He has died," but his (new) owner tracks him down, he shall take him for himself, and in addition (the seller) shall give 2 persons (lit. heads) to him. He shall look to his house for it.

§150 If a man hires himself out for wages, (his employer) [shall pay ... shekels of silver] for [one month. If a woman] hires herself out for wages, (her employer) [shall pay ... shekels]

[51] §146b is omitted in the post-OH manuscripts.

for one month.

§151 If anyone rents a plow ox, [he shall pay] one shekel [of silver] for one month. [If] anyone rents a [..., he shall pay] a half shekel of silver for one month.

§152 If anyone rents a horse, a mule or an ass, he shall pay one shekel of silver [for one month].

§157[52] If a bronze axe[z] weighs 1.54 kg,[53] its rent shall be one shekel of silver for one month. If a copper axe weighs 0.77 kg, its rent shall be ½ shekel of silver for one month. If a bronze *tapulli*-tool weighs 0.5 kg, its rent shall be ½ shekel of silver for one month.

§158a If a (free) man hires himself out for wages, to bind sheaves, load them on wagons, deposit them in barns, and clear the threshing floors, his wages for 3 months shall be 1,500 liters of barley (= 3.75 shekels of silver).

§158b If a woman hires herself out for wages in the harvest season, her wages shall be 600 liters of barley (=1 shekel of silver) for 3 months' work.[54]

§159 If anyone hitches up a team of oxen for one day, its rent shall be 25 liters of barley.

§160a If a smith makes a copper box weighing 1½ minas, his wages shall be 5,000 liters of barley (=12.5 shekels of silver).

§160b If he makes a bronze axe weighing 2 minas, his wages shall be 50 liters of wheat (=0.33 shekel of silver).

§161 If he makes a copper axe weighing one mina, his wages shall be 50 liters of barley (=0.125 shekels of silver).

§162a If anyone diverts an irrigation ditch, he shall pay one shekel of silver. If anyone stealthily taps (water from) an irrigation ditch, he/it is ...ed. If he takes (water at a point) below (the other's branch), it is his (to use).

§162b [If] anyone takes [...], whosoever [...] he prepares, [...]. [If] anyone [...s] sheep from a pasture, [... will be] the compensation, and he shall give its hide and meat.

§163 If anyone's animals go loco (lit. are made divine),[55] and he performs a purification ritual upon them, and drives them back home, and he puts the mud(?) (used in the ritual) on the mud pile(?), but doesn't tell his colleague, so that the colleague doesn't know, and (the colleague) drives his own animals there, and they die, there will be compensation.

§164 If anyone goes (to someone's house) to impress (something), starts a quarrel, and breaks either the sacrificial bread or the libation vessel,

§165 he shall give one sheep, 10 loaves of bread, and one jug of ... beer, and reconsecrate his house. Until [a year's] time has passed he shall keep away from his house.

§166 If anyone sows (his own) seed on top of (another man's) seed,[aa] his neck shall be placed (lit. come to rest) upon a plow. They shall hitch up 2 teams of oxen: they shall turn the faces of one team one way and the other team the other. Both the offender and the oxen will be put to death, and the party who first sowed the field shall reap[56] it for himself. This is the way they used to proceed.

§167 But now they shall substitute one sheep for the man and 2 sheep for the oxen. He shall give 30 loaves of bread and 3 jugs of ... beer, and re-consecrate (the land?). And he who sowed the field first shall reap it.

§168 If anyone violates the boundary of a field[bb] and takes[57] one furrow off (the neighbor's field), the owner of the field shall cut 0.25 square meters of field (from the other's field), the owner of the violated field shall cut off a strip of his neighbor's land 0.25 meters deep along their common boundary and take it for himself. He who violated the boundary shall give one sheep (= 1 shekel), 10 loaves (= ca. 0.1 shekel), and one jug of ... beer and re-consecrate the field.

§169 If anyone buys a field and violates the boundary,[cc] he shall take a thick loaf and break it to the Sungod [and] say: "My scales have been flowing into the ground." And he shall speak thus: "Sungod, Stormgod. There is no quarrel."

§170 If a free man kills a snake, and speaks another's name, he shall pay 40 shekels of silver. If it is a slave, he alone shall be put to death.

§171 If a mother removes her son's garment, she is disinheriting her son. If her son comes back into (her house, i.e., is reinstated), (s)he takes her door and removes it, (s)he takes her ... and removes it, she (thus) takes them (i.e., the sons) back; she makes her son her

z 2 Kgs 6:5
aa Deut 22:9
bb Deut 19:14; 27:17
cc Deut 19:14; 27:17

[52] The OH manuscript q shows that there was no gap in which four additional laws (§§153-156 in Hrozny's numbering) might fit. We preserve the traditional numbering of §§157-200 for convenience of reference.

[53] So the OH manuscript. The NH manuscripts describe lighter axes, for the same rent, yielding a higher rate of rent per weight.

[54] A NH manuscript has: "He (the employer) shall give 600 liters of barley for two months' (work)."

[55] Others (e.g., Friedrich 1959:75) have translated this verb "are smitten by a god." The translation "are branded" (Goetze 1969:195) is impossible.

[56] A later manuscript reads "take."

[57] A later manuscript reads "drives."

son again.

§172 If anyone preserves a free man's life in a year of famine, (the saved man) shall give a substitute for himself. If it is a slave, he shall pay 10 shekels of silver.

§173a If anyone rejects a judgment of the king, his house will become a heap of ruins. If anyone rejects a judgment of a magistrate, they shall cut off his head.[dd]

§173b If a slave rebels against[58] his owner, he shall go into a clay jar.

§174 If (when) men are hitting each other, one of them dies, (the other) shall give one slave (lit. head).

§175 If either a shepherd or a steward[59] takes a free woman in marriage, she will become a slave for[60] either two or four years. They shall ... her children, but no one shall seize (their) belts.

§176a If anyone keeps a bull outside a corral,[61] [ee] it shall be a case for the king's court. They shall sell (the bull). (A bull is an animal which) is capable of breeding in (its) third year. A plow ox, a ram, (and) a he-goat (are animals which) are capable of breeding in (their) third year.

§176b If anyone buys a trained artisan: either a potter, a smith, a carpenter, a leather-worker, a fuller, a weaver, or a maker of leggings, he shall pay 10 shekels of silver.

§177 If anyone buys a man trained as an augur(?), he shall pay 25 shekels of silver. If anyone buys an unskilled man or woman, he shall pay 20 shekels of silver.

§178 The price of a plow ox is 12 shekels of silver. The price of a bull is 10 shekels of silver. The price of a fullgrown cow is 7 shekels of silver. The price of a yearling plow ox or cow is 5 shekels of silver. The price of a weaned calf is 4 shekels of silver. If the cow is pregnant with a calf, the price is 8 shekels of silver. The price of one calf is 2 (variant: 3) shekels of silver. The price of one stallion, one mare, one male donkey, and one female donkey are the same.

§179 If it is a sheep, its price is one shekel of silver. The price of 3 goats is 2 shekels of silver. The price of 2 lambs is one shekel of silver. The price of 2 goat kids is ½ shekel of silver.

§180 If it is a draft horse, its price is 20 (variant: 10) shekels of silver. The price of a mule is 40 shekels of silver. The price of a pastured horse is 14 (variant: 15) shekels of silver.[62] The price of a yearling colt is 10 shekels of silver. The price of a yearling filly is 15 shekels of silver.

§181 The price of a weaned colt (or) a weaned filly is 4 shekels of silver. The price of 4 minas of copper is one shekel of silver, of one bottle of fine oil is 2 shekels of silver, of one bottle of lard is one shekel of silver, of one bottle of butter/ghee is one shekel of silver, of one bottle of honey is one shekel of silver, of 2 cheeses is one shekel [of silver], of 3 rennets is one shekel of silver.

§182 The price of a ... garment is 12 shekels of silver. The price of a fine garment is 30 shekels of silver. The price of a blue wool garment is 20 shekels of silver. The price of an *ADUPLI* garment is 10 shekels of silver. The price of a tattered(?) garment is 3 shekels of silver. The price of a ... garment is 4 shekels of silver. The price of a sackcloth garment is one shekel of silver. The price of a sheer/thin tunic is 3 shekels of silver. The price of an (ordinary) tunic is [... shekels of silver]. The price [of one] (bolt of) cloth weighing 7 minas is [... shekels of silver]. The price of one large (bolt of) linen is 5 shekels of silver.

§183 The price of 150 liters of wheat is one shekel of silver. The price of 200 liters [of barley is ½ shekel of silver.] The price of 50 liters of wine is ½ shekel of silver, of 50 liters of [... is ... shekels of silver. The price] of 3,600 square meters of irrigated(?) field is 3 [shekels of silver. The price] of 3,600 square meters of ... field is 2 shekels of silver. [The price] of a (field) adjoining(?) it is one shekel of silver.

§184 This is the tariff, as it was ...ed in the city.

§185 The price of 3,600 square meters of vineyard is 40 shekels of silver. The price of the hide of a full-grown ox is one shekel of silver. The price of 5 hides of weanling calves is one shekel of silver, of 10 oxhides is 40 shekels of silver, of a shaggy sheepskin is one shekel of silver, of 10 skins of young sheep is one shekel of silver, of 4 goatskins one shekel of silver, 15 sheared(?) goatskins is one shekel of silver, of 20 lambskins is one shekel of silver, of 20 kidskins is one shekel of silver. Whoever buys the meat of 2 fullgrown cattle shall give one sheep.

§186 Whoever buys the meat of 2 yearling cattle

dd Deut 16:18

ee Exod 21:28-36

[58] Lit., *ara<w>ezzi* "exempts/frees himself from."

[59] "Steward" translates the Sumerogram AGRIG (Akk. *abarakku*). On this function in Hittite texts see Singer 1984.

[60] Or, less likely: "after." See §35.

[61] Lit., "dispenses with a bull's corral." See the goring ox cases in Exod 21:28-36.

[62] For what follows, another manuscript substitutes: "The price of a yearling filly is 15 shekels of silver. The price of a gelding(?) (or) a mare is [...] shekels of silver. The price of 4 minas of copper is one shekel [of silver]."

shall give one sheep. Whoever buys the meat of 5 weanlings shall give one sheep. (Whoever buys) the meat of 10 calves shall give one sheep. (Whoever buys) the meat of 10 sheep shall give one sheep. (Whoever buys) the meat of 20 lambs shall give one sheep. [If] anyone buys the meat of [20] goats, he shall give one sheep.

§187 If a man has sexual relations[63] with a cow,[64] [ff] it is an unpermitted sexual pairing: he will be put to death. They shall conduct him to the king's court (lit. gate). Whether the king orders him killed or spares his life, he shall not appear (personally) before the king (lest he defile the royal person).

§188 If a man has sexual relations with a sheep, it is an unpermitted sexual pairing: he will be put to death. They will conduct him [to the] king's [gate].[gg] The king may have him executed, or may spare his life. But he shall not appear before the king.

§189 If a man has sexual relations with his own mother,[hh] it is an unpermitted sexual pairing. If a man has sexual relations with (his own) daughter,[ii] it is an unpermitted sexual pairing. If a man has sexual relations with (his own) son,[65] [jj] it is an unpermitted sexual pairing.

§190 If they appear(?) with the dead — man, woman — it is not an offence. If a man has sexual relations with his step-mother,[kk] it is not an offence. But if his father is still living, it is an unpermitted sexual pairing.

§191 If a free man sleeps with free sisters who have the same mother and their mother[ll] — one in one country and the other in another, it is not an offence. But if it happens in the same location, and he knows (the relationship, the women are related), it is an unpermitted sexual pairing.[66]

§192 If a man's wife dies, [he may take her] sister [as his wife.][mm] It is not an offence.[67]

§193 If a man has a wife, and the man dies, his brother shall take his widow as wife. (If the brother dies,) his father shall take her. When afterwards his father dies, his (i.e., the father's) brother shall take the woman whom he had.[68] [nn]

§194 If a free man sleeps with slave women who have the same mother and their mother, it is not an offence. If brothers sleep with a free (woman), it is not an offence. If father and son sleep with the same female slave or prostitute,[oo] it is not an offence.

§195a If a man sleeps with his brother's wife, while his brother is alive, it is an unpermitted sexual pairing.

§195b If a (free) man has a free woman (in marriage) and approaches her daughter (sexually),[pp] it is an unpermitted sexual pairing.

§195c If he has the daughter (in marriage) and approaches her mother or her sister (sexually), it is an unpermitted sexual pairing.

§196 If anyone's male and female slaves enter into unpermitted sexual pairings, they (sc. the authorities) shall move them elsewhere: they shall settle one in one city and one in another. A sheep shall be offered in place of one and a(nother) sheep in place of the other.

§197 If a man seizes a woman in the mountain(s) (and rapes her), it is the man's offence, but if he seizes her in (her) house, it is the woman's offence: the woman shall die.[qq] If the (woman's) husband (lit. the man) finds them (in the act), he may kill them without committing a crime.

§198 If he brings them to the palace gate (i.e., the royal court) and says: "My wife shall not die," he can spare his wife's life, (but) he must also spare the lover[69] and "clothe his head." If he says, "Both of them shall die," they shall "roll the wheel."[70] The king may have them killed or he may spare them.

§199 If anyone has sexual relations with a pig (or) a dog,[71] [rr] he shall die. He shall bring him to the palace gate (i.e., the royal court). The king may have them (i.e., the human and the animal) killed or he may spare them, but he (the human) shall not approach the king. If an ox leaps on a man (in sexual excitement), the ox shall die; the man shall not die. They shall substitute one sheep in the place of the man and put it to death. If a pig leaps on a man (in sexual excitement), it is not an offence.

§200a If a man has sexual relations (lit. "sins") with

ff Exod 22:18; Lev 20:15-16
gg Deut 22:15; 2 Sam 19:8; Amos 5:10, 12, 15
hh Lev 18:7-8; 20:11
ii Gen 19:36; Lev 18
jj Lev 20:13
kk Lev 18:8; 20:11; 2 Sam 16:21; 20:3
ll Lev 18:17
mm Gen 29:30; Ezek 23:4
nn Gen 38; Deut 25:5-10; Ruth
oo Amos 2:7
pp Lev 18:17
qq Deut 22:25-26
rr Exod 22:18; Lev 18:23

[63] Lit., "sins." So also in §§188-190, 199-200.
[64] See Hoffner 1973; Haase 1976.
[65] Since the blood relationship is specified here, this is probably not a blanket prohibition of homosexual sex such as in Lev 20:13. See Hoffner 1973.
[66] One NH manuscript mistakenly adds: "It is not an offence."
[67] Another version reads: "If a woman's husband dies, his partner shall take his wife (in marriage). It is [not] an offence." See Hoffner 1997b:151f.
[68] A NH manuscript adds: "There is no offence."
[69] Cf. MAL A §15 (*COS* 2.132, below, p. 355).
[70] A symbolic gesture of uncertain significance.
[71] See Hoffner 1973.

either a horse or a mule,[72] it is not an offence, but he shall not approach the king, nor shall he become a priest.[73] If anyone sleeps with an *arnuwalaš*-woman, and also sleeps with her mother, it is not an offence.

§200b If anyone gives (his) son for training either (as) a carpenter or a smith, a weaver or a leather worker or a fuller, he shall pay 6 shekels of silver as (the fee) for the training. If the teacher makes him an expert, (the student) shall give (to his teacher) one person.

Telipinu Edict §49

And a case of murder (lit. blood) is as follows. Whoever commits murder, whatever the heir himself of the murdered man says (will be done). If he says: "Let him die," he shall die; but if he says: "Let him make compensation," he shall make compensation. But to the king let (him) not (come) at all.[ss]

[ss] Deut 19:11-13

Telipinu Edict §50

(Regarding cases) of sorcery in Ḫattuša: keep cleaning up (i.e., investigating and punishing) (all) instances (thereof). Whoever in the royal family knows sorcery (i. e., practices it), seize him and deliver him to the king's gate. But it will go badly for that man (C adds: and for his household) who does not deliver him.

[72] Perhaps this ancient sexual taboo applied to animals domesticated at that very early period in human history. Equids, domesticated only later, were never included.

[73] That is, he has committed no punishable crime, but he has become so defiled by the incident that he may not enter the king's presence or ever become a priest.

REFERENCES

Text: Laws §§1-100 are Series One (*CTH* 271), while laws §§101-200 are Series Two (*CTH* 272). Manuscripts of Series One are: A = KBo 6.2 + 19.1 + 22.62 + 22.61 + 19.1a; B = KBo 6.3 + 22.63; C = KBo 6.5; D + E = KBo 6.6 + 6.7; F = KBo 6.8 (F) (+) KUB 13.11 (F?) + KUB 29.15 (F‹) (+) KBo 19.3 (F›) (+) KBo 19.4 (Ffi); G = KBo 6.9; H (+) I = KUB 13.12 (H) (+) KUB 13.13 (I); I = See H; J = KUB 26.56; K = KUB 29.13; L = KUB 29.14 (L) (+) KBo 12.49 (L?); M = KUB 29.16 + KBo 19.2; N + V = KUB 29.17 (N) + KBo 14.64 (V); O (+) Q = KUB 29.18 (+) KUB 29.20; P = KUB 29.19; R = KBo 6.21; S = KBo 6.22; T = KBo 9.70; U = KUB 40.32; W = KBo 14.65 (+) Bo 88/5; X = KBo 12.48; Y = KBo 19.7; Z = KBo 9.69; AA = KBo 19.5; BB = KBo 22.65. Manuscripts A and M are in OH script; the rest are in NH script. Manuscripts for Series Two are: a = KBo 6.12; b = KUB 29.21 (+) 29.22 (+) 29.23; c = KBo 6.10 + 6.20; d = KBo 6.11; e = KBo 6.13 (+) KUB 13.30; f = KBo 6.14 + 6.18 (+) 6.19; g = KBo 19.6; h = KBo 19.9; i = KBo 6.17; j = KBo 6.16; k = KUB 29.24; l = Bo 92/113; m = Bo 8202; n = KUB 13.15 + KBo 19.7; o = KUB 29.26 (+) 29.27; p = KBo 6.26; q = KBo 14.66 + KUB 48.78; r = 11/p; s = HFAC 5; t = KBo 14.67; u = KUB 29.31; v = KBo 6.15; w = 684/c; x = KBo 9.71 + KUB 29.33 + KUB 13.14 + KUB 13.16; y = KUB 29.34 (+) 29.37; e? = KUB 13.30; z = KBo 22.66; aa = KUB 29.25 + KUB 29.28 + KUB 29.29 + 29.30 + 29.32 + 29.35 + 29.36 + 29.38 + KBo 25.5 + 25.85; bb = KBo 19.8; cc = "Bo 2111"; dd = HFAC 4; ee = VAS 127. Only manuscript aa in Series Two is in the OH script. The standard editions are Friedrich 1959; Imparati 1964; and Hoffner 1997b. Fairly recent translations are: Goetze 1969; Haase 1984; von Schuler 1982; and Hoffner 1997a. General surveys of Hittite law may be found in Güterbock 1954; Hoffner 1963 and 1995.

C. HIEROGLYPHIC INSCRIPTIONS

1. "IDEAL PRICES" (2.20)

KARKAMIŠ A2 (+3) (2.20A)[1]

J. D. Hawkins

The text comes from the first of a pair of inscribed stone door jambs excavated *in situ* at the entrance to the cella of the temple of the Storm-God in the lower city at Karkamiš.[2] Katuwa was the last of a four-generation line of rulers of the city dating approximately to the 10th century BCE,[3] and he and his father Suhi (II) left a number of such building inscriptions and much sculpture in the form of relief orthostats decorating building facades.

A recurring theme in such inscriptions is the favor of the gods and the prosperity of the author's reign, one element of which is a statement of ideal prices to emphasize the cheapness of living.[4] Such statements are found already in inscriptions of Mesopotamian rulers in the early 2nd millennium BCE, and reappear in those of Assurbanipal of Assyria and Nabonidus of Babylon probably as archaisms. Recognition of similar statements in the Hieroglyphic Luwian inscriptions of the early 1st millennium BCE was something of a surprise.

In the Mesopotamian versions of these statements, prices of commodities, above all barley but also oil, wine, wool, etc., are expressed in terms of so-much measure of commodity for one shekel of silver.[5] The idealized literary character of these statements is clear when they are compared with the more realistic tariffs of prices appended to law codes of Mesopotamia.[6] The Hittite Laws too contain such tariffs, but their prices may be expressed not in silver shekels but in sheep,[7] which reflects a standard equivalence 1 sheep = 1 shekel of silver, and probably shows the more primitive, less monetarized Hittite economy.

Katuwa's statement introduced here is repeated by him in another inscription and different context, in a more elaborate form (KARKAMIŠ A 11a)[8]. Other examples are found as far away as the Anatolian plateau, in particular on a partly preserved stele from Aksaray, the work of a certain Kiyakiya, probably to be identified with Kiakki of Sinuḫtu deported by Sargon II in 718 BCE.[9] This is the most detailed such statement known from the Hieroglyphic inscriptions, covering as it does three commodities, instead of simply barley, as at Karkamiš, and it was indeed the appearance of this inscription in 1978 that permitted the identification of these statements, when this new one was compared with the other examples. Thus the logogram for "barley" could be recognized, as well as the hieroglyphic Luwian word for "wine" (*matu*, cf. Greek *methú*, Sanskrit *madhu*, English *mead*). It is also noteworthy that Karkamiš uses the Assyrian measure the *homer* (or donkey(-load)), while the more distant Anatolia uses an unknown measure the *tiwatali*, apparently from the context about ⅓ of the *homer*.

§1 I am Katuwa the ruler, the Karkamišean Country Lord, the Country Lord Suhi's son.

§2 When Tarhunza[10] gave me my paternal succession,

§3 this Karkamišean Tarhunza had exalted the person neither for my father,

§4 nor for my grandfather had he exalted (the person),

§5 but for me Katuwa, the Karkamišean Country Lord he exalted the person,[11]

§6 and he looked on me with a smiling(?) face,

§7 and it in my *good-times* brought forth the Grain-God and the Wine-God[12] in the country.

§8 In my *good-times* for a sheep ten homers (of barley) stood,

§9 and I myself *thereupon* constructed these temples of Tarhunza for him with goodness.

(The text concludes with curses designed to protect the foundation and Katuwa's name attached to it)

[1] Hawkins 2000 no. II. 13 (+14).

[2] Woolley 1952:169f., pls. 34a-37a.

[3] Hawkins 2000:76-78.

[4] Hawkins 1986.

[5] Hawkins 1986:93f.

[6] Esp. the Laws of Eshnunna (*COS* 2.130). See Hawkins 1986:94f.

[7] See the Hittite Laws, *COS* 2.19 §§178-186.

[8] Hawkins 2000 no. II. 9.

[9] Ibid. no. X. 16.

[10] The Storm-God. See below Azatiwata, *COS* 2.21, n. 10.

[11] "Exalting the person." A common topos in these inscriptions. Cf. MARAŞ 4, §15, *COS* 2.22A, where I have translated "person" as "image." See also, KULULU 4, §4, *COS* 2.22B, where it is translated "soul" (§9 there).

[12] For the Grain God and the Wine God as symbols of prosperity, cp. *COS* 2.21, §§53, 55.

KARKAMIŠ A11a (2.20B)

In this parallel, closely similar passage, Katuwa records:

§7 My lord Tarhunza, Karhuha and Kubaba[13] loved me because of my justice,
§8 (not properly understood)
§9 and the Grain-God and the Wine-God for me [they brought forth],
§10 and in my *good-times* for a sheep the cost (?) (as) [so many] homers of barley stood,
§11 but I myself then constructed the temple with luxury for Karkamišean Tarhunza.

[13] The regular triad of gods invoked at Karkamiš. Besides Tarhunza, the Storm-God, the god Karhuha is a manifestation of the god known elsewhere in the Hittite world as Runza, the Stag-God, protector of wild animals, Resheph to the Semitic world: see *COS* 2.21, n. 19. Kubaba, the "Queen of Karkamiš," was the patron goddess of the city, and later passed through Anatolia, through veneration by the Phrygians, to become the Kubēbē/Kubēlē (Cybele) of the Greeks.

AKSARAY (2.20C)

This more recently discovered inscription has a more detailed statement, which provided the key to the understanding of comparable passages.

[Beginning of text lost]
§1 ... Tarhunza prospered the ...,
§2 and m[uch] came down from the sky,
§3 and much came up from the earth,
§4 and in those years for one sheep 30 *measures* of barley stood,
§5 20 *measures* of oil(?) [...]ed,
§6 [x] *measures* of wine stood.
§7 Because of my justice, I was dear to Tarhunza and all the gods there.
§8 And great kings and kings all *admired* this city.
(text continues)

REFERENCES

Texts: Hawkins 2000 no. II.13 (+ 14), II.9, X.16; (*COS* 2.20A only): Woolley 1952:169f., pls. 34a-37a. Studies: Hawkins 1986.

2. ROYAL INSCRIPTIONS

AZATIWATA (2.21)

J. D. Hawkins

The Karatepe inscriptions are famous as one of the ancient world's longest bilingual texts. The hilltop fortress of Karatepe was defended by a circuit of walls with two monumental gateways, each decorated with sculptured orthostats and a bilingual version of the same inscription in Phoenician and Hieroglyphic Luwian. The lower North Gate is better preserved with more of its sculpture and inscriptions *in situ* or just fallen from their plinths; the upper South Gate's stones were largely scattered and the text incomplete.

The site was discovered in 1946 by H. T. Bossert and Halet Çambel, and the main excavations exposing the gateways were rapidly completed, but further research and restoration has continued under Halet Çambel up to the present.[1] Bossert's publication of the bilingual text in a preliminary form was incomplete at the time of his death in 1960, and a final publication by Halet Çambel has appeared recently.[2]

The inscription is the work of a certain Azatiwata who was apparently a subordinate ruler subject to the royal house of Adana, referred to as the "house of Muksa" (see below, n. 16). He names as his patron the king of Adana, Awariku (see below, n. 11), and seems from his somewhat veiled language to have acted as guardian to Awariku's succession and a powerful regent of the kingdom.

[1] Çambel 1993.
[2] Çambel 1999.

The date of the buildings, sculptures and inscriptions, which are not necessarily all contemporary, has been much debated.[3] The sculptures show features datable to both the 9th and 8th centuries BCE,[4] while a late date is favored both for the Phoenician[5] and Hieroglyphic[6] scripts, and historically a date at the beginning of the 7th century BCE (the reign of Sennacherib in Assyria) looks suitable.[7] The possible identification of Awariku is relevant here.

The text is both the longest Phoenician and Hieroglyphic inscription; so it is equally important for both languages, quite apart from its bilingual aspect. In general, of course, the Phoenician throws light on the Hieroglyphic, but in some instances the reverse is true. The discovery and publication of the bilingual marks a most important stage in the decipherment of Hieroglyphic Luwian, which was reasonably advanced before its appearance, but has now been set on a sound footing by the translation of the parallel Phoenician (below, 2.31).[8]

§1 I am Azatiwata,[9] the Sun-blessed man, Tarhunza's[10] servant,
§2 whom Awariku[11] the Adanawean king promoted.[12]
§3 Tarhunza made me mother and father[a] to Adanawa;[13]
§4 and I caused Adanawa to prosper,
§5 and I *extended* the Adanawa *plain* on the one hand towards the west and on the other hand towards the east,
§6 and in my days there were to Adanawa all good things, *plenty* and *luxury*,
§7 and I fill the Paharean[14] granaries,
§8 and I made horse upon horse,
§9 and I made army upon army,
§10 and I made shield upon shield, all by Tarhunza and the gods.
§11 So I *broke* up the *proud*,
§12 and the evils which were in the land
§13 I [remov]ed out of the land.
§14 And I blessed my lord's house well,[15]
§15 and I did all good things for my lord's family,
§16 and I made it sit upon its father's throne.
§17 [not preserved in Hier. text; Phoen.: "and I established peace with every king."]
§18 and every king made me father [b] to himself because of my *justice* and my *wisdom* and my goodness.
§19 And I built strong fortresses [...] on the frontiers,
§20 where there were bad men, robbers,
§21 who had not served under Muksa's house,[16]
§22 and I, Azatiwata, put them under my feet.[c]
§23 So I built fortresses in those places,
§24 so that Adanawa might dwell peacefully.
§25 And I smote strong fortresses towards the west,
§26 which former kings had not smitten,
§27 who were before me.
§28 (So) I, Azatiwata, smote them,
§29 and I brought them down,
§30 and I settled them down towards the east, on my frontiers,
§31 and so I settled Adanaweans down ... there.
§32 In my days I *extended* the Adanawean frontiers on the one hand towards the west and on the other hand towards the east,
§33 and even in those places which were formerly feared,
§34 where a man fears to go the road,
§35 so in my days even women walk with spindles.[17]
§36 In my days there was *plenty* and *luxury* and

a Deut 32:6; 32:18
b Gen 45:8; Ps 109:14; Isa 22:21
c Josh 10:24; Pss 8:7; 110:2; 1 Kgs 5:3; 2 Sam 22:39 (= Ps 18:39); 1 Sam 25:24; Esther 8:3

[3] Summarized by Çambel 2000:9-11; Hawkins 1999:44f.

[4] Winter 1979; Deshayes 1981.

[5] Peckham 1968:116-119; Röllig 1999:73-81.

[6] Hawkins 2000:44 and n. 88, 67f., 460 f.

[7] Hawkins 1979; Garelli 1981; Desideri and Jasink 1990:133-146.

[8] Words in italic in the translation are dependent on the Phoen. for their interpretation.

[9] This name, also spelled *Azatiwara*, is a normal Luwian compound of *aza-*, "love," and *Tiwat*, the Sun-God. The consonantal outline is given most accurately by the Phoen. ʾ*ztwd* (note that intervocalic *d* > *r* is a regular Luwian development), while the vocalization is given by the Hieroglyphic: these combine to indicate *Azatiwada* (> *Azatiwara*).

[10] Tarhunza is the usual name of the Hittite-Luwian Storm-God, equated in the bilingual with the Phoen. Baʿal.

[11] Awariku has the same name as Urikki, king of Que (Plain Cilicia), named in the inscriptions of Tiglath-pileser III and Sargon II of Assyria (2nd half of the 8th century BCE). He could well be the same person, which would fix the date of the inscriptions, but he could also be a homonymous predecessor of Urikki. See below, *COS* 2.117A, note 4.

[12] This clause appears to define the position of Azatiwata as a subordinate ruler subject to the kings of Plain Cilicia.

[13] Adanawa clearly designates the city of Adana, capital of Plain Cilicia (the "Adanawa plain") and seat of the dynasty. The usual Phoen. equivalent is *dnnym*, probably to be vocalized *danunîm*, "the Danuna people," apparently a Semitism for the inhabitants of Adana. Phoen. also has ʿ*mq* ʾ*dn* for "plain of Adana."

[14] A city, = Phoen. *p*ʿ*r*, identified as classical *Pagri*, perhaps an earlier name of Mopsouhestia (Misis): see Bossert 1951:290-294.

[15] This and the following two rather cryptic phrases seem to show that Azatiwata acted as regent and guardian to Awariku's succession when the latter died or disappeared. The whole inscription, however, emphasizes how Azatiwata, though not king in Adana, exercised great power over the kingdom.

[16] Muksa (Phoen. *Mpš*) was at once identified as representing at least some aspects of *Mopsos* (*Moxos*) of Greek legend: see Hawkins 1995 with bibliography. It was remarkable to find him in the indigenous record regarded as the founder of the royal house of Adana.

[17] Recognized as a regular literary topos of peace and security. Cf. also Hoffner 1966.

good living,
§37 and peacefully dwelt Adanawa and the Adanawa *plain*.
§38 I built this fortress,
§39 and to it I put the name Azatiwataya.[18]
§40 So Tarhunza and Runza[19] were after me for to build this fortress.
§§41-46 [Missing in Hier. South Gate inscription. Fragmentary in North Gate inscription, preserved in Phoen.]
§47 and therein (i.e. in Azatiwataya) I caused Tarhunza to dwell,
§48 and every river-land [20] will begin to honor him: by (?) the year an ox, and at the cutting (?) a sheep and at the vintage a sheep.[21]
§49 Let him bless Azatiwata with health and life,[d]
§50 and let him be made highly preeminent over all kings!
§51 And may Tarhunza the highly blessed and this fortress's gods give to him, to Azatiwata, long days and many years and good abundance,[22]
§52 and let them give him all victory over all kings!
§53 And so let this fortress become (one) of the Grain-God and the Wine-God,
§54 and so the nations that dwell in (it).
§55 let them become (those) of sheep, oxen, the Grain-God, and the Wine-God!

d Mal 2:5; Prov 3:2

e Pss 72:5, 17; 89:37-38

§56 Much let them beget for us,
§57 and much let them multiply,
§58 and much let them be in service to Azatiwata and to Muksa's house, by Tarhunza and the gods!
§59 If anyone from (among) kings,
§60 or (if) he (is) a prince,
§61 and to him (there is) a princely name,
§62 proclaims this:
§63 "I shall delete Azatiwata's name from the gates here,
§64 and I shall incise my name";[23]
§65 or (if) he is covetous towards this fortress,
§66 and blocks up (?) these gates,
§67 which Azatiwata made,
§68 and proclaims thus:
§69 "I shall make the gates my own,
§70 and I shall incise my name for myself";
§71 or (if) from *covetousness* he shall block them up (?),
§72 or from badness or from evil he shall block up (?) these gates,
§73 may celestial Tarhunza, the celestial Sun, Ea and all the gods delete that kingdom, and that king and that man!
§74 Hereafter may Azatiwata's name continue to stand for all ages,
§75 as the moon's and the sun's name stands! [e]

[18] While Azatiwata clearly named his city after himself, the name so strikingly resembles the pre-classical name of the Pamphylian city Aspendos as recorded on its coins, Εστϝεδιιυς, as to raise the question whether Azatiwata's building programme might have extended as far west as Pamphylia.

[19] Runza (or Runtiya) is the usual Luwian name of the Stag-God, a tutelary deity often represented as supporter of the Storm-God, whose sphere of activity was the countryside and wild animals. The bilingual equates him with *Ršp ṣprm*, "Reseph of the Goats" (or "Birds").

[20] "River-land" is the usual Hittite expression for an inhabited, cultivated river valley. The problematic Phoen., *mskt* must be explained by reference to this: Morpurgo Davies and Hawkins 1987:270-272; Röllig 1999:60; Amadasi Guzzo, forthcoming.

[21] For the seasonal festivals at which a sheep is offered, Phoen. has "ploughing" and "reaping." It is not at all clear that the Hieroglyphic text provides exact equivalents. The second seems certain to be "vintage," and while the first could be "ploughing," "cutting" looks more likely.

[22] Hieroglyphic "abundance" is well established, Hawkins 2000:65, and Phoen. *ršʾt* should be interpreted by reference to it, which seems to rule out the translation "old age" (but cf. Röllig 1999:60).

[23] The offense referred to, misappropriation of the monument, is often banned in ancient inscriptions, which seems to imply that it was common.

REFERENCES

Text, Translations and Studies: Hawkins 2000; Bossert 1951; Çambel 1993; 1999; Deshayes 1981; Desideri and Jasink 1990; Garelli 1981; Hawkins 1979; 1995; Hawkins and Orthmann 1980; Peckham 1968; Röllig 1999; Winter 1979.

3. FUNERARY INSCRIPTIONS (2.22)

MARAŞ 4 (2.22A)

J. D. Hawkins

The inscription in Hieroglyphic Luwian is on a fragment of a colossal statue[1] recognizably of a type known from complete but uninscribed examples, notably the figure from Zinçirli, 3 m. high, of a typical neo-Hittite ruler, bearded, with hair in pot-hook curls, wearing a long fringed garment and belt with frontal tassel, sword on hip, holding a long staff of office.[2] This figure stands on a base of a pair of lions held centrally by a small hero figure,

[1] Hawkins 2000 no. IV.2.

[2] For an illustration, see e.g. Akurgal 1962 pls. 126-127.

and represents the ruler, deified after death, to receive funerary offerings, a practice referred to in inscriptions.[3] Though from Zinçirli, it clearly comes from a Karkamiš workshop, and fragments of a closely similar statue and base were found at the latter site.[4]

The Maraş fragment was clearly another such statue but the only inscribed example, the text giving the ruler's self-presentation of his deeds. This belongs in a tradition descending from the Hittite Empire: the last known Hittite king Suppiluliuma II records on a tablet that he made a statue of his late father Tudhaliya IV, inscribed it with his deeds and set it up in a rock sanctuary to receive offerings (see text *COS* 1.75, ii.4-16).

The author of MARAŞ 4, Halparuntiya II of Gurgum, is identified as a contemporary of the Assyrian king Shalmaneser III, to whom he paid tribute in 853 BCE.[5] In the next century, the Arameans borrowed this practice of the commemorative inscribed statue when Bar-Rakib king of Samʾal set up and inscribed in Aramaic a statue for his father Panammu II, who had fallen fighting for the Assyrians at the siege of Damascus in 733-732 BCE.[6]

§1 I am Halparuntiya the ruler, Gurgumean King,[7] the ruler Muwatali's son.[8]
§2 In the year in which I smote the city Hirika,[9]
§3 in that year I set up Tarhunza of the Domain.[10]
§4 I captured the city Iluwasi,[11]
§5 and I ...ed away Mount(?) Atursaliyanza,[12]
§6 and I trampled(?) the land Hirika,
§7 and for us I did not spare(?) the two countries.
§8 To my father and grandfather there was authority,
§9 but neither (my) father nor (my) grandfather "allowed it to themselves (?),"[13]
§10 But I, Halparuntiya "allowed it to myself (?),"[14] Muwatali's son, Muwizi's great-grandson.
§11 I exalted (my) father, grandfather, great-grandfather and forefather(?).
§12 [When] I captured the city Iluwasi,
§13 (of) the men I cut off the feet,[15]
§14 but the *children* I made eunuchs to us,
§15 and thereby I exalted my image for myself.
§16 But I came forth,
§17 and myself on my throne [I seated ...[16]]
(text breaks off)

[3] See Hawkins 2000:89, no. II. 6, §§28-34.
[4] Woolley 1952 pls. B53*a-b*, 54*a*, p. 192, but note that the figures are deified rulers, not gods as such.
[5] Grayson *RIMA* 3:23, ii.84. See below Kurkh Monolith, *COS* 2.113A.
[6] See the Panamuwa inscription (*KAI* #215), *COS* 2.37 below.
[7] Gurgum is the name of a small country with the capital city Marqas in Assyrian terminology, and Marqas has become modern Maraş (Marʿaş), city and province. The Hieroglyphic inscriptions use only Gurgum for city and country.
[8] Muwatali is named by Shalmaneser III in the year 858 BCE. See Grayson *RIMA* 3:16, i.40. See below Kurkh Monolith, *COS* 2.113A.
[9] Place names unknown though an identification of Hirika with Hilakku (Assyrian Rough Cilicia) has been proposed. See Neumann 1979.
[10] Special manifestation of the Storm-God Tarhunza.
[11] See note 9.
[12] See note 9..
[13] Literal translation not obviously meaningful but presumably idiomatic.
[14] See previous note.
[15] This barbaric act against captives is actually depicted on the Bronze Gates of Shalmaneser III, Halparuntiya's contemporary.
[16] The text breaks off with our hero reporting his accession.

REFERENCES

Text, Translation and Studies: Hawkins 2000 no. IV.2. Photo: Akurgal 1962 pls. 126-127.

KULULU 4 (2.22B)

J. D. Hawkins

This Hieroglyphic Luwian inscription was placed on a round-topped stele, running round all four sides, and broken off at the fourth line, but ending with an appended inscription across the top.[1] It is unique in beginning, "I *was* Ruwa ...," where all other such have "I am ...." It is clearly an example of the "speaking dead" addressing an audience from the tombstone, which is emphasized by the final appended notice that the dead man's nephew set it up for him. The inscription is also unusual in expressing an individual's concept of his soul, although this can be paralleled from cuneiform Hittite texts.[2] Though somewhat difficult to understand, the text apparently states that the speaker's soul

[1] Hawkins 2000 no. X.10.
[2] ibid., 446, §4.

has been put in (at birth) by the gods and is taken back by them (at death). In the Bronze Age the idea that the King (and Queen) at death "become a god" and join the divine company finds expression in the texts,[3] but it is not until the early Iron Age, with the appearance of inscribed tombstones for private individuals, that this notion is extended to non-royal folk.[4]

Ruwa is probably the same Ruwa who inscribed another stele from the same site Kululu, recording his construction of houses for his overlord Tuwati.[5] That inscription concludes: "When I shall depart into the presence of the gods ..., these houses will be here." This suggests that Ruwa even in his lifetime was preoccupied with the idea of personal immortality and "afterlife."

§1 I was Ruwa the Ruler, the Sun-blessed (man).
§2 Also my posterity (?) (is) Sun-blessed.
§3 The gods loved me ...,
§4 and they put into me a beloved soul.[6]
§5 Under my lords[7] (and) ... with my soul I ...ed,
§6 and I was dear to my lords,
§7 and they made me governor,
§8 and I was house-lord in the lords' house.
§9 For me the gods received the beloved soul put in (as) a ...[8].
§10 I blessed my lords well,[9]
§11 and I was every man's father,
§12 and for every (man) I honored the good,
§13 and for me my ... [...],
§14 and for my eunuchs ... [...]
(text breaks off)

Across the top of the stele is written:
§15 This stele Huli set up, Ruwa's brother's son,
§16 And he ....

[3] "To become a god" is a regular euphemism describing a king's death. Note also the Royal Death Ritual introduced by the words: "When in Hattuša a great sin occurs and either the king or the queen becomes a god ..." (Otten 1958:184)
[4] Hawkins 1980b; 1989.
[5] Hawkins 2000 no. X.9.
[6] The word here translated "soul" following the context as understood seems to mean literally "form, figure, image." The concept appears similar to that known from the classical world, the soul as an image or replica of the living person.
[7] It is not exactly clear who are meant by the speaker's "lords," probably his earthly superiors during his lifetime rather than the gods.
[8] The clause presumably describes the speaker's death.
[9] This and the following clauses seem to characterize the speaker's virtuous life.

REFERENCES

Text, Translation and Studies: Hawkins 2000 no. X.10; 1980b; 1989.

HITTITE BIBLIOGRAPHY

AKURGAL, E.
1962 *The Art of the Hittites*. London: Thames and Hudson.
ALP, S.
1950-51 "Die soziale Klasse der NAM.RA-Leute und ihre hethitische Bezeichnung." *JKF* 1:113-135.
1954 "The -N(N)- Formations in the Hittite Language." *Belleten* 18/72:456-458.
1979 "Das hethitisches Wort für 'Palast'." Pp. 17-25 in *Studies Meriggi*.
AMADASI GUZZO, M. G.
forthcoming "MSKT at Karatepe." *Or*.
BEAL, R.
1986 "The History of Kizzuwatna and the Date of the Šunaššura Treaty." *Or* 55:424-445.
1988 "The GIŠTUKUL-institution in Second Millennium Ḫatti." *AoF* 15:269-305.
1992 *The Organisation of the Hittite Military*. THeth 20. Heidelberg: Carl Winter-Universitätsverlag.
1993 "Kurunta of Tarhuntassa and the Imperial Hittite Mausoleum." *AnSt* 43:29-39.
BECKMAN, G. M.
1982 "The Hittite Assembly." *JAOS* 102:435-42.
1989-90 "Review of Otten 1988." *WO* 20-21:289-294.
1992 "Hittite Administration in Syria in the Light of the Texts from Ḫattuša, Ugarit, and Emar." BiMes 25. Malibu: Undena.
1996 *Hittite Diplomatic Texts*. WAW 7. Atlanta: Scholars Press.
1997 "New joins to Hittite Treaties." *ZA* 87:96-100.
BÖRKER-KLÄHN, J.
1993 "Zum Kolophon der Bronzetafel aus Boğazköy." *AoF* 20:235-237.
1994 "Der hethitische Areopag: Yerkapı, die Bronzetafel und der 'Staatsstreich'." *AoF* 21:131-160.
BOSSERT, H. T.
1951 "Die Phönizisch-Hethitischen Bilinguen von Karatepe." 1-2 Nachtrag. *JKF* 1/3:290-294.
BRYCE, T.
1982 *The Major Historical Texts of Early Hittite History*. Queensland, Australia: University of Queensland.
1988 "Tette and the Rebellions in Nuhassi." *AnSt* 38:21-28.
1989 "Ahhiyawans and Mycenaeans — An Anatolian Viewpoint." *Oxford Journal of Archaeology* 8:297-310.
1998 *The Kingdom of the Hittites*. Oxford: Clarendon Press.
ÇAMBEL, H.
1993 "Das Freilichtmuseum von Karatepe-Aslantaş." *Ist. Mit.* 43:495-509.
1999 *CHLI 2*.
CANCIK, H.
1976 *Grundzüge der hethitischen und alttestamentlichen Geschichtsschreibung*. Wiesbaden: O. Harrassowitz.
CARRATELLI, G. P.
1994 "La clausola del 'Testamento' di Hattusili I." *La parola della passato* 276:401-408.
COHEN, Y.
1997 Taboos and Prohibitions in Hittite Society: A Study of the Hittite Expression *natta āra* ("not right"). M.A. Thesis. Tel Aviv University.
CORNIL, P. AND R. LEBRUN.
1975-76 "Fragments hittites relatifs à l'Égypte." *OLP* 7-8:83-108.
DEL MONTE, G.
1985a "Un Nuovo Frammento degli 'Annali Completi' di Muršili II." *Athenaeum* NS 63:164-166.
1985b "Nuovi frammenti di trattati hittiti." *OA* 24:263-269.
1986 *Il trattato fra Muršili II di Ḫattuša e Niqmepa di Ugarit*. Oriens Antiqui Collecto 18. Roma: Istituto per l'Oriente C. A. Nallino.
1993 *L'annalistica ittita*. Testi del Vicino Oriente antico 4. Brescia: Paideia.
DEL MONTE, G. and J. TISCHLER.
1978 *Die Orts- und Gewässernamen der hethitischen Texte*. RGTC 6. TAVO B 7/6. Wiesbaden: Dr. Ludwig Reichert Verlag.
DESHAYES, J.
1981 "Remarques sur les monuments de Karatepe. I. - Problemès archéologiques." *RA* 75:32-46.
DESIDERI, P., and A. M. JASINK.
1990 *Cilicia. Dall'età di Kizzuwatua alla conquista macedone*. Universita degli Studi di Torino, Fondo di studi Parini-Chirio 1. Firenze: Casa Editrice Le Lettere.
DINÇOL, A. M.
1998 "The Rock Monument of the Great King Kurunta and Its Hieroglyphic Inscription." Pp. 159-166 in *Acts of the IIIrd International Congress of Hittitology. Çorum, September 16-22, 1996*. Ed. by S. Alp and A. Süel. Ankara: Grafik, Teknik Hazırlık Uyum Ajans.
EDEL, E.
1976 *Ägyptische Ärzte und ägyptische Medizin am hethitischen Königshof*. Rheinisch-Westfälische Akademie der Wissenschaften, Vorträge G 205. Opladen: Westdeutscher Verlag.
FORRER, E.
1926 *Die Boghazköi-Texte in Umschrift. Zweiter Band. Geschichtliche Texte*. WVDOG 42/2. Leipzig: J.C. Hinrichs'sche Buchhandlung.
FREYDANK, H.
1959 "Eine hethitische Fassung des Vertrages zwischen dem Hethiterkönig Šuppiluliuma und Aziru von Amurru." *MIO* 7:356-381.

FRIEDRICH, J.
1925 *Aus dem hethitischen Schriftum 1. Heft: Historische Texte, Staatsverträge, Königliche Erlasse, Briefe, Gesetze, wirtschaftliche Texte.* Der Alte Orient 24,3. Leipzig: Hinrichs.
1926 *Staatsverträge des Hatti-Reiches in hethitischer Sprache. 1. Teil.* MVAG 31.1. Leipzig: J. Hinrichs'sche Buchhandlung.
1952 *HW* 1.
1959 *Die hethitischen Gesetze.* Documenta et Monumenta Orientis Antiqui 7. Leiden: E. J. Brill.
GARELLI, P.
1981 "Remarques sur les monuments de Karatepe. III. - Les données assyriennes." *RA* 75:54-60.
GIORGIERI, M.
1991 "Magia e intrighi alla corte de Labarna-Hattusili." *IstLombRend* 124:247-277.
GOETZE, A.
1930 "Die Pestgebete des Muršiliš." *KlF* 1:161-251.
1933 *Die Annalen des Muršiliš.* MVAG 38. Leipzig: J. C. Hinrichs'sche Buchhandlung.
1955 *ANET*, 199-206, 529-530.
1969 "The Hittite Laws." Pp. 188-197 in *ANET.*
GORDON, C. H.
1965 *UT.*
GORDON, E. I.
1967 "The Meaning of the Ideogram ^{d}KASKAL.KUR = 'Underground Water-course' and its Significance for Bronze Age Historical Geography." *JCS* 21:70-88.
GRÉLOIS, J.-P.
1988 "Les Annales décennales de Mursili II (CTH 61, 1)." *Hethitica* 9:17-145.
GÜTERBOCK, H. G.
1954 "Authority and Law in the Hittite Kingdom." *JAOS* Suppl. 17:16-24.
1956 "The Deeds of Suppiluliuma as Told by his Son, Mursili II." *JCS* 10:41-68, 75-85, 90-98, 107-130.
1983a "The Hittites and the Aegean World." *AJA* 87:133-143.
1983b "Noch einmal die Formel *parnaššea šuwaizzi.*" *Or* 52:73-80.
1984 "Hittites and Akheaeans: A New Look." *PAPS* 128:114-122.
1989 "Hittite *kursa* 'Hunting Bag.'" Pp. 113-19 in *Studies Kantor.*
GÜTERBOCK, H. G., and E. HAMP.
1956 "Hittite *šuwaya-*." *RHA* XIV/58:22-25.
HAASE, R.
1956 "Über die Formel *parnaššeja šuwaizzi* in den hethitischen Gesetzestexten." *WO* 2:290-293.
1962 "Über neue Vorschläge zur Erklärung der hethitischen Formel *parnaššeja šuwaizzi.*" *BiOr* 19:117-122.
1976 "Über Tierdelikte in den sogenannten hethitischen Gesetzen." *Zeitschrift der Savigny-Stiftung, Römische Abteilung* 93:253-60.
1984 *Texte zum hethitischen Recht. Eine Auswahl.* Wiesbaden: Reichert.
HAWKINS, J. D.
1979 "Who was Azatiwatas?" *AnSt* 29:153-157.
1980a "Karkamiš." *RlA* 5:426-46.
1980b "Late Hittite Funerary Monuments." Pp. 213-225 in *RAI* 26.
1986 "Royal Statements of Ideal Prices: Assyrian, Babylonian, and Hittite." Pp. 93-102 in *Studies Mellink.*
1989 "More Late Hittite Funerary Monuments." Pp. 189-197 in *Studies Özgüç.*
1995 "Muksas." *RlA* 8/5-6:413.
2000 *CHLI 1.*
HAWKINS, J. D., and W. ORTHMANN.
1980 "Karatepe, A. Inschriften, Geschichte, B. Archäologische." *RlA* 5:409-414.
HEINHOLD-KRAHMER, S.
1977 *Arzawa: Untersuchungen zu seiner Geschichte nach den hethitischen Quellen.* THeth 8. Heidelberg: Carl Winter-Universitätsverlag.
1991-92 "Zur Bronzetafel aus Boğazköy und ihrem historischen Inhalt." *AfO* 38-39:138-158.
HOFFMAN, I.
1984 *Der Erlaß Telipinus.* THeth 11. Heidelberg: Winter.
HOFFNER, H. A., Jr.
1963 "The Laws of the Hittites." Brandeis University Ph. D. Dissertation.
1966 "Symbols for Masculinity and Femininity: Their Use in Ancient Near Eastern Sympathetic Magic Rituals." *JBL* 85:326-334.
1973 "Incest, Sodomy and Bestiality in the Ancient Near East." Pp. 81-90 in *Studies Gordon.*
1976 "Review of H. Otten and Chr. Rüster, *Keilschrifttexte aus Boğazköi* 22." *BiOr* 33:335-337.
1980 "Histories and Historians of the Ancient Near East: The Hittites." *Orientalia* 49:283-332.
1983 "A Prayer of Muršili II About His Stepmother." *JAOS* 103:187-92.
1992 "The Last Days of Khattusha." Pp. 46-52 in *The Crisis Years: The 12th Century B.C. From Beyond the Danube to the Tigris.* Ed. by W. A. Ward and M. S. Joukowsky. Dubuque, Iowa: Kendall/Hunt Publishing Company.
1995 "Legal and Social Institutions of Hittite Anatolia." Pp. 555-570 in *CANE.*
1997a "The Hittite Laws." Pp. 211-247 in *Law Collections from Mesopotamia and Asia Minor. Second Edition.* Ed. by M. T. Roth. WAW 6. Atlanta: Scholars Press.
1997b *The Laws of the Hittites. A Critical Edition.* Documenta et Monumenta Orientis Antiqui, 23. Leiden: E. J. Brill.
HOUWINK TEN CATE, Ph.
1966 "Mursilis' Northwest Campaigns — Additional Fragments of his Comprehensive Annals." *JNES* 25:162-191.
1967 "Mursilis' Northwestern Campaigns — a Commentary." *Anatolica* 1:44-61.
1979 "Mursilis' Northwestern Campaigns — Additional Fragments of His Comprehensive Annals Concerning the Nerik Region." Pp. 157-167 in *Studies Laroche.*

1979a "The Mashuiluwas Affair: A Join (KBo XIX 46) and a Duplicate (KBo IX 77) to Mursilis's Comprehensive Annals (12th year of his reign)." Pp. 267-290 in *Studies Meriggi*.
1992 "The Bronze Tablet of Tudhaliyas IV and its Geographical and Historical Relations." *ZA* 82:233-270.

HUEHNERGARD, J.
1993 "Meskene A. Philologisch." *RlA* 8:83.

IMPARATI, F
1964 *Le leggi ittite*. Incunabula Graeca 7. Roma: Edizioni dell'Ateneo.
1991 "Autorita centrale e istitutioni collegiali nel regno ittita." Pp. 161-181 in *Esercizio del potere e prassi della consultazione*. Ed. by A. Ciani and G. Diurni. Rome: Libreria Editrice Lateranense.
1992a "Le relazioni politiche fra Hatti e Tarhuntassa all'epoca di Hattusili III e Tuthaliya." Pp. 23-68 in *Quattro Studi Ittiti*. Ed. by F. Imparati. Eothen 4. Firenze: Edizione Librarie Italiane Estere (ELITE).
1992b "A propos des témoins du traité avec Kurunta de Tarhuntassa." Pp. 305-322 in *Studies Alp*.
1992c "Significato politico della successione dei testimoni nel trattato di Tuthaliya IV con Kurunta." *Istituto per gli studi micenei ed egeo-anatolici, Seminari* 59-86.

KAMMENHUBER, A.
1969 "Zur Textüberlieferung der Annalen des Hethiterkönigs Muršilis II." *Athenaeum* NS 47:168-172.
1970 "Keilschrifttexte aus Boğazköy (KBo XVI)." *Or* 39:548-567.

KLENGEL, H.
1964 "Neue Fragmente zur akkadischen Fassung des Aziru-Vertrages." *OLZ* 59:437-445.
1969 *Geschichte Syriens im 2. Jahrtausend v.u.Z.* VIO 70. 3 vol. Berlin: Akademie Verlag.
1977 "Zwei neue Fragmente zum akkadischen Aziru-Vertrag." *AoF* 5:259-261.
1992 *Syria 3000 to 300 B.C.* Berlin: Akademie Verlag.
1993 "Hugo Wincklers Tagebücher." *IM* 43:511-516.
1999 *Geschichte des Hethitischen Reiches*. HdO 1/34. Leiden: E. J. Brill.

KLINGER, J.
1992 "Fremde und Außenseiter in Ḫatti." Pp. 187-212 in *Außenseiter und Randgruppen*. Ed. by V. Haas. Xenia 32. Konstanz: Universitätsverlag Konstanz.

KLOCK-FONTANILLE, I.
1996 "Le testament politique de Ḫattušili Ier ou les conditions d'exercise de la royauté dans l'ancien royaume hittite." *Anatolia Antiqua* 4:33-66.

KÜHNE, C., AND H. OTTEN.
1971 *Der Šaušgamuwa-Vertrag*. StBoT 16. Wiesbaden: Otto Harrassowitz.

KÜMMEL, H. M.
1980 "Kizzuwatna." *RlA* 5:627-631.
1985 "Hethitische historisch-chronologische Texte." in *TUAT* 1/5:455-495.

LAROCHE, R.
1948 "Un point d'histoire, Ulmi-Tessub." *RHA* 8:40-48.
1968 "Textes de Ras Shamra en langue Hittite." *Ugaritica* 5:769-784.

LEBRUN, R.
1992 "Les traités hittites." Pp. 15-59 in *Traités et serments dans le proche-orient ancien*. Ed. by J. Briend, R. Lebrun and É. Puech. Paris: Impressions Dumas.

MARAZZI, M.
1984 "Überlegungen zur Bedeutung von *pankuš* in der hethitisch-akkadischen Bilinguis Ḫattušilis I." *WO* 15:96-102.
1986 *Beiträge zu den akkadischen Texten aus Boğazköy in althethitischer Zeit*. Rome: Dipartimento di studi glottoantropologici, Università "La Sapienza."
1992 "Das 'geheimnisvolle' Land Ahhijawa." Pp. 365-378 in *Studies Alp*.

MARGUERON, J-C.
1993 "Meskene B Archäologisch." *RlA* 8:84-93.

DE MARTINO, S.
1989 "Hattušili I e Haštayar: un problema aperto." *OA* 28:1-24.
1998 "Le accuse di Muršili II alla regina Tawananne secondu il testo KUB XIV 4" Pp. 19-48 in *Studi e Testi 1*. Ed. by S. de Martino and F. Imparati. Eothen 9. Firenze: Logisma.

MELCHERT, H. C.
1990 "Review of Otten 1988." *Kratylos* 35:204-206.
1991 "Death and the Hittite King." Pp. 182-187 in *Perspectives on Indo-European Language, Culture and Religion*. McLean, VA: Institute for the Study of Man.
1994 *Anatolian Historical Phonology*. Leiden Studies in Indo-European 3. Amsterdam/Atlanta: Rodopi.

MORA, C.
1998 "Kurunta, Prince." Pp. 85-91 in *Studi e Testi 1*. Ed. by S. de Martino and F. Imparati. Eothen 9. Firenze: Logisma.

MORAN, W. L.
1992 *The Amarna Letters*. Baltimore: Johns Hopkins.

MORPURGO DAVIES, A., and J. D. HAWKINS.
1987 "The Late Hieroglphic Luwian Corpus: Some New Lexical Recognitions." *Bibliothéque des Cahiers de l'Institut de Linguistique de Louvain* 37: *Hethitica* 8:267-295.

NEUMANN, G.
1979 "Zum Namen Kilikien." Pp. 2:429-437 in *Studies Meriggi*.

OTTEN, H.
1955 "Neue Fragmente zu den Annalen des Muršili." *MIO* 3:153-179.
1958 *Hethitische Totenrituale*. Deutsche Akademie der Wissenschaften zu Berlin. Institut für Orientforschung. Veröffentlichung 37. Berlin: Akademie Verlag.

1969 *Sprachliche Stellung und Datierung des Madduwatta-Textes*. StBoT 11. Wiesbaden: Otto Harrassowitz.
1988 *Die Bronzetafel aus Boğazköy: Ein Staatsvertrag Tuthalijas IV*. StBoT. Beiheft 1. Wiesbaden: Otto Harrassowitz.
1989 *Die 1986 in Bogazköy gefundene Bronzetafel. Zwei Vorträge (1. Ein hethitischer Staatsvertrag des 13. Jh. v. Chr.; 2. Zu den rechtlichen und religiösen Grundlagen des hethitischen Königtums)*. Innsbrucker Beiträge zur Sprachwissenschaft, Vorträge und Kleinere Schriften, 42. Innsbruck: Universität Innsbruck.

PECCHIOLI DADDI, F.
1992 "Note di storia politica antico-ittita." *SEL* 9:11-19.

PECKHAM, J. D.
1968 *The Development of the Late Phoenician Scripts*. HSS 20. Cambridge, MA: Harvard University Press.

RANOSZEK, R.
1950 "A propos de KUB XXIII 1." *ArOr* 18/4:236-242.

RÖLLIG, W.
1999 "Appendix I. The Phoenician Inscriptions." Pp. 50-81 in H. ÇAMBEL, *CHLI* 2.

VON SCHULER, E.
1965 *Die Kaškäer. Ein Beitrag zur Ethnographie des alten Kleinasien*. UAVA 3. Berlin: Walter de Gruyter.
1982 "Die hethitischen Gesetze." in *TUAT* 1/1:96-123.

SINGER, I.
1984 "The AGRIG in Hittite Texts." *AnSt* 34:97-127.
1990 "Aziru's Apostasy and the Historical Setting of the General's Letter." Pp. 113-183 in Sh. Izre'el and I. Singer. *The General's Letter from Ugarit*. Tel Aviv: Tel Aviv University.
1991a "A Concise History of Amurru." Pp. 134-195 in S. Izre'el, *Amurru Akkadian: A Linguistic Study*. Vol. 2. HSS 41. Atlanta: Scholars Press.
1991b "The 'Land of Amurru' and the 'Lands of Amurru' in the Šaušgamuwa Treaty." *Iraq* 53:69-74.
1992 "Hittite Cultural Influence in the Kingdom of Amurru." Pp. 231-234 in *RAI* 38.
1996 "Great Kings of Tarhuntassa." *SMEA* 38:63-71.

SOMMER, F., and A. FALKENSTEIN.
1932 *Die Aḫḫijava-Urkunden*. ABAW. Philosophisch-historische Abteilung n.F. 6. München: Verlag der Bayerischen Akademie der Wissenschaften.
1938 *Die hethitisch-akkadische Bilingue des Ḫattušili I. (Labarna II.)*. ABAW: Philosophisch-historische Abteilung n. F. 16. Munich: Verlag der Bayerischen Akademie der Wissenschaften.

SOUČEK, V.
1961 "Bemerkungen zur Schlussformel der hethitischen Gesetze (*parnaššea šuwaizzi*)." *ArOr* 29:1-29.

STARKE, F.
1981 "Die keilschrift-luwischen Wörter für Insel und Lampe." *KZ* 95:141-155.
1985 *Die keilschrift-luwischen Texte in Umschrift*. StBoT 30. Wiesbaden: Otto Harrassowitz.
1990 *Untersuchung zur Stammbildung des keilschrift-luwischen Nomens*. StBoT 31. Wiesbaden: Otto Harrassowitz.

STEFANINI, R.
1992 "On the Tenth Paragraph of the Bronze Tablet (ii 91 - iii 1)." *AGI* 67:133-152.

STEINER, G.
1989 "'Schiffe von Aḫḫiyawa' oder 'Kriegsschiffe' von Amurru im Šaušgamuwa-Vertrag?" *UF* 21:393-411.
1996 "Muršili I.: Sohn oder Enkel Labarna-Ḫattušilis I.?" *UF* 28:561-618.

SÜRENHAGEN, D.
1992 "Untersuchungen zur Bronzetafel und weiteren Verträgen mit der Sekundogenitur in Tarḫuntašša." *OLZ* 87:341-371.

TISCHLER, J.
1988 "Labarna." Pp. 347-358 in *Studies Otten*.

VAN DEN HOUT, Th. P. J.
1984 "Kurunta und die Datierung einiger hethitischen Texte." *RA* 78:89-92.
1995 *Der Ulmitešub-Vertrag. Eine prosopographische Untersuchung*. StBoT 38. Wiesbaden: Otto Harrassowitz.

WATKINS, C.
1997 "Luvo-Hittite *lapan(a)-*." Pp. ### in *Studies Puhvel*.

WEIDNER, E.
1923 *Politische Dokumente aus Kleinasien: Die Staatsverträge in akkadischer Sprache aus dem Archiv von Boghazköi*. Boghazköi-Studien 8 and 9. Leipzig: Hinrichs.

WEINFELD, M.
1983 "Divine Intervention in War in Ancient Israel and in the Ancient Near East." Pp. 121-147 in *HHI*.

WINTER, I. J.
1979 "On the Problems of Karatepe: the Reliefs and their Contexts." *AnSt* 29:115-151.

WOOLLEY, C. L.
1952 *Carchemish. The Excavations in the Inner Town*. Carchemish, Report on the Excavations at Jerablus, on Behalf of the British Museum, Part III. London: The Trustees of the British Museum.

YOUNGER, K. L., Jr.
1990 *Ancient Conquest Accounts: A Study of Ancient Near Eastern and Biblical History Writing*. JSOTSup 98. Sheffield: Sheffield Academic Press.

ZACCAGNINI, C.
1988 "A Note on Hittite International Relations at the Time of Tudhaliya IV." Pp. 295-299 in *Studies Caratelli*.

WEST SEMITIC MONUMENTAL INSCRIPTIONS

A. BUILDING AND DEDICATORY INSCRIPTIONS

1. MOABITE INSCRIPTIONS

THE INSCRIPTION OF KING MESHA (2.23)

K. A. D. Smelik

The inscription, which was carved on a black basalt stone, measuring 1.15 m. high and 60-68 cm. across, was discovered by the Alsatian missionary Klein at Dhiban in 1868. Due to the great interest in the stone shown by various Europeans in Palestine, the local population decided to demolish it and use the pieces as amulets in their granaries. The Frenchman Clermont-Ganneau, however, who had already had squeezes made of the stela, managed to get possession of two-thirds of the original stone. The fragments were sent to France and put together in the Louvre museum. Some of the gaps were filled on the basis of the squeezes. The end of the inscription is completely lost. The text, written in Moabite (or Israelite Hebrew?), dates around 835 BCE and belongs to the genre of building inscriptions. The Arabic numerals refer to the lines of the original text.

Introduction and Identification (1-3a)
I am Mesha,[a] the son of Kemosh[-yatti][1], the king of Moab, the Dibonite.[2]
My father was king over Moab for thirty years,
and I was king after my father.

Occasion for the Erecting of the Stela (3b-4)
And I made this high-place[3] for Kemosh[4] [b] in Karchoh,[5]
[...]
because he has delivered me from all kings(?),
and because he has made me look down on all my enemies.

Introduction to the Part on Military Achievements (5-7a)
Omri[c] was the king of Israel,
and he oppressed Moab for many days,
for Kemosh was angry with his land.[6]
And his son[7] succeeded him,
and he said — he too —
"I will oppress Moab!"
In my days did he say [so],
but I looked down on him and on his house,
and Israel has gone to ruin, yes, it has gone to ruin for ever![8]

The Return of the Land of Medeba (7b-9)
And Omri had taken possession of the whole la[n]d of Medeba,
and he lived there (in) his days and half the days of his son, forty years,
but Kemosh [resto]red it[9] in my days.
And I built Baal Meon,
and I made in it a water reservoir,
and I built Kiriathaim.

The Conquest of Ataroth (10-13)
And the men of Gad lived in the land of Ataroth from ancient times,[10]
and the king of Israel built Ataroth for himself,
and I fought against the city,
and I captured it,
and I killed all the people [from] the city as a sacrifice(?)[11] for Kemosh and for Moab, and I brought back the fire-hearth of his Uncle(?)[12] from there,

a 2 Kgs 1:1; 3:4

b Num21:29; Judg 11:24; 1Kgs11:7,33; 2 Kgs 23:13; Jer 48:7 (*qere*), 13, 46

c 1Kgs16:16-28

[1] The complete name of Mesha's father is not preserved in the Mesha inscription, but supplemented on the base of a reconstruction of another Moabite inscription found at Kerak in 1958 and published by Reed and Winnett 1963:1-9.

[2] Dibon (now Diban) was the capital of Moab at that time.

[3] *bmt*: a kind of sanctuary typical for Canaan. It also occurs frequently in the Hebrew Bible.

[4] National god of Moab.

[5] Possibly the name for a new quarter of the capital Dibon. The vocalization of the name is uncertain. Other possibilities: Kericho, Korcha, Kircho.

[6] According to the same principle, in Judg 3:12 the oppression of Israel by a Moabite king is explained as the result of YHWH's wrath with his people.

[7] According to the Hebrew Bible, this was Ahab (ruled 868-854 BCE). This is, however, not in accordance with the date given in line 8. For this reason, it is more probable that Omri's grandson Jehoram (ruled 851-840 BCE) is meant.

[8] Possible reference to the decline of Israel during the reign of Jehu (839-822 BCE); cf. 2 Kgs 10:32-33.

[9] Lit., "returned it." Other possibility: "lives there."

[10] This remark by Mesha shows that he was not acquainted with the tradition that Gad was one of the Israelite tribes who participated in the Exodus.

[11] Meaning uncertain. Part of ritual warfare was the massacre of the population of a conquered town in honour of the national god (also in ancient Israel).

[12] Some cultic device. Possibly, "Uncle" was a divine name or title.

and I hauled it before the face of Kemosh[13] in Kerioth,
and I made the men of Sharon live there, as well as the men of Maharith[14].

The Destruction of Nebo (14-18a)
And Kemosh said to me:
"Go, take Nebo from Israel!" [d]
And I went in the night,
and I fought against it from the break of dawn until noon,
and I took it,
and I killed [its] whole population,
seven thousand male citizens(?) and aliens(?),
and female citizens(?) and aliens(?),[15] and servant girls;
for I had put it to the ban [e] for Ashtar Kemosh.[16]
And from there, I took th[e ves]sels of YHWH,[17]
and I hauled them before the face of Kemosh.

The Conquest of Jahaz (18b-21a)
And the king of Israel had built Jahaz,
and he stayed there during his campaigns against me,[18]
and Kemosh drove him away before my face,
and I took two hundred men of Moab, all its division(?),[19]
and I led it up to Jahaz.
And I have taken it in order to add it to Dibon.

Mesha's Building Activities at Karchoh (21b-25)
I have built Karchoh,
the wall of the woods and the wall of the citadel,
and I have built its gates,
and I have built its towers,
and I have built the house of the king,
and I have made the double reser[voir for the spr]ing(?)[20] in the innermost part of the city.

d 1Sam 15:3

e Num 21:2-3; Josh 10:28-40; Judg 1:17; 21:11; 1 Sam 15:3; 1 Kgs 20:42

f Num 32:38; 1 Chr 5:8

g Isa 15:5; Jer 48:3, 5, 34

Now, there was no cistern in the innermost part of the city, in Karchoh,
and I said to all the people:
"Make, each one of you, a cistern in his house."
And I cut out the moat(?) for Karchoh by means of prisoners from Israel.[21]

Other Building Activities (26-27)
I have built Aroer,
and I made the military road in the Arnon.
I have built Beth Bamoth,
for it was destroyed.
I have built Bezer,
for [it lay in] ruins.

First Conclusion (28-29)
[And the me]n[22] of Dibon stood in battle-order,[23]
for all Dibon, they were in subjection.
And I am the kin[g over the] hundreds in the towns which I have added to the land.

Other Building Activities (30-31a)
And I have built [the House of Mede]ba[24]
and the House of Diblathaim[f]
and the House of Baal Meon,
and I brought there [...] flocks of the land.

Battle at Horonaim (31b-34)
And Horonaim,[g] there lived [...]
And Kemosh said to me:
"Go down, fight against Horonaim!"
I went down [...]
[and] Kemosh [resto]red it in my days.
and [...] from there [...]
[...]
[...]

Second Conclusion (34-)
And I ...

[13] The Kemosh sanctuary at Kerioth is meant.

[14] Mesha only combined the massacre of the original inhabitants with the resettlement of the conquered territory by his own population when he wanted to add the city to Moab (Ataroth and Jahaz; not Nebo).

[15] Meaning uncertain; for this translation, see Gibson, *SSI* 1:80-81.

[16] Ashtar is the male counterpart of Ashtarte/Ishtar; here combined with the national Moabite god Kemosh. For the significance of the ban (*ḥrm*), see Stern 1991.

[17] The earliest occurrence of the name of Israel's god in an inscription. Cf. also below, 2.47.

[18] In 2 Kgs 3, Jehoram attacks Moab from the South; in the Mesha inscription from the North (Jahaz). For a historical reconstruction see Smelik 1992:90-92.

[19] For the translation here, see Gibson, *SSI* 1:81.

[20] For the translation here, see Yadin 1969:18 n. 18.

[21] For the translation of this sentence, see Gibson, *SSI* 1:82.

[22] For the restoration of the text here, see Smelik 1992:71.

[23] For the translation here, see Lipiński 1971:339.

[24] For the restoration of the text here, see Miller 1974:14.

REFERENCES

Text: *KAI* 2:168-179; *SSI* 1:71-83; Translations: *ANET* 320-321; *DOTT* 195-199; *RTAT* 253-257 (E.T. 237-240); *TUAT* 247-248; Studies: Dearman 1989; Miller 1974; Smelik 1990; 1991:29-50; 1992; Stern 1991:19-56.

2. AMMONITE INSCRIPTIONS

THE AMMAN CITADEL INSCRIPTION (2.24)

Walter E. Aufrecht

The inscription is on an irregularly shaped rectangle of white limestone discovered on the Citadel of Amman, Jordan, in 1961. The face of the stone is chipped, causing several letters to flake off. The beginning and ending of each line are lost. The inscription is in the Archaeological Museum, Amman, Jordan (No. J 9000).[1] It has been dated paleographically to the (mid)-9th century BCE.[2]

Introduction: Command by the deity (line 1)
[The words of Mi]lkom:[3] [a] build for yourself entrances roundabout [

Curses and blessings (lines 2-8)
[ ] that all who surround you shall surely die [
[ ] I shall surely destroy. All who enter [
[ ] and amid (its) co[lum]ns (the) just will reside [
[ ] (the) innermost door[4] [b] [I shall surely] extinguish [
[ ] you shall gaze in awe in the midst of the porch
[[5]
[ ] and *š*[ ]*h̊* and *n*[ ]
[ ] ... peace to you and pe[ace

a 1 Kgs 11:5, 33; 2 Kgs 23:13
b Jer 36:23

[1] For the most recent discussions, see: *CAI* 154-163 (no. 59); Shea 1991:62-66; and Hübner 1992:17-21.

[2] Cross 1969:17.

[3] The inscription has been interpreted by most commentators as a building inscription of either a temple or of the Citadel itself. Most interpreters agree in reconstructing the phrase as if the god Milkom is speaking. Milkom may have been the national deity of Ammon. The name appears in the Bible and in several inscriptions, *CAI* nos. 1, 55, 57, 61, 127, 129, 147, 136. See the discussions by Puech 1977, Tigay 1987, and Aufrecht 1999a.

[4] Hicks 1983:53-55 takes *dlt* here (and in Jer 36:23) to mean "writing board."

[5] An alternative reading of this line is, "You shall be feared among the gods," *CAI* 162-163.

REFERENCES

Text: *CAI* 154-163 (no. 59). Studies: Aufrecht 1999a; Cross 1969; Fulco 1978; Hicks 1982; Hübner 1992; Puech 1977; Shea 1991; Tigay 1987.

THE TELL SĪRĀN INSCRIPTION (2.25)

Walter E. Aufrecht

The inscription is found on a 10 cm. long bronze-colored metal bottle made of copper, lead and tin. The bottle was found at Tel Sīrān, Jordan, in 1972. The end of the bottle was sealed by a pin through the neck. It contained dried barley, wheat, a few weeds and chunks of lead and copper. There are ninety-two letters in the eight-line inscription, all of which can be read clearly. The inscription is in the Archaeological Museum, Amman, Jordan (No. J 12943).[1] It has been dated paleographically to ca. 600 BCE.[2]

May the produce[3] of ᶜAmminadab[4] king of the Ammonites,[5] [a]
the son of Hissalᵓil[6] king of the Ammonites,
the son of ᶜAmminadab king of the Ammonites —
the vineyard and the garden(s)[b] and the hollow[7] and cistern[8] —

a 2 Sam 10:1; Jer 40:14
b Amos 4:9, 9:14

[1] For the most recent discussions, see: *CAI* 203-211 (no. 78) and Hübner 1992:27-31.

[2] Cross 1973a:14.

[3] Among the major studies of this inscription, two trajectories of translation and interpretation have developed: those who view the text as a building or commemorative inscription, and those who view it as a poem. The differences among the interpretations rest on the translation of the first word, *mᶜbd*, and those in lines four and five. Those who view the text as a building inscription translate *mᶜbd* as "works of." Others extend the meaning of this word to mean "poem." Coote 1980:93, made the sensible suggestion that this word refers to the contents of the bottle, translating "product of," *CAI* 207.

[4] This king (ca. 600 BCE) has the same name as his grandfather (line 3). The grandfather is likely the person mentioned on Asshurbanipal's Cylinder C (ca. 667 BCE), who is said to have paid tribute to the Assyrian king, *ANET* 294. The name is also found on Ammonite seals, *CAI* 40-43 (no. 17) and 96-99 (no. 40). For a new list of the Ammonite kings, see Cross (in press).

[5] The Ammonites, *bn ᶜmn*, lit. "sons of Ammon," were the Northwest Semitic speaking people who occupied part of Transjordan in the Iron Age. For the most recent discussions, see: Hübner 1992; Aufrecht 1999b; Aufrecht and Herr (in press); and Cross (in press).

[6] This king, otherwise unknown, may be dated to ca. 625 BCE, Cross (in press).

[7] Those who view the text as a building inscription interpret this word, *hᵓtḥr*, as a noun from the root *ḥrr*, meaning "hole," "tunnel," "hollow," or the like. Those who view the inscription as a poem take the word to be a verb from the root *ᵓḥr*, meaning "to be delayed," or from the root *ḥrh*, "to be hot," *CAI* 209.

[8] If a noun, the root of this word is *šwḥ* meaning, "pit," "tunnel," or "cistern." The word also appears in line 9 of the Moabite stela, *COS* 2.23; *KAI* 2.168. Those who view the inscription as a poem take the word to be a verb from the root *šḥt*, "to go to ruin," *CAI* 210-211.

cause rejoicing and gladness for many days (to come) and in years[9] *c*	*c* Deut 32:7, Ps 90:15	far off.

[9] The formulaic pair *ymt*, "days," and *šnt*, "years," also occurs in Ug.; Virolleaud 1957:39. Cf. below, p. 146, n. 9; p. 150, n. 32; p. 154, n. 13; p. 154 n. *f*.

REFERENCES

Text: *CAI* 203-211 (no. 78); Studies: Aufrecht 1999b; Aufrecht and Herr (in press); Coote 1980:93; Cross 1973a; in press; Hübner 1992; Virolleaud 1957.

THE AMMAN THEATRE INSCRIPTION (2.26)

Walter E. Aufrecht

This two-line inscription is on a fragmentary, triangular, black basalt stone measuring 26 x 17 cm at its widest. The surface of the stone is rough and pitted. A word divider in the form of a short stroke is found between the first and second words. The inscription is in the Archaeological Museum, Amman, Jordan (No. J 11686).[1] It has been dated paleographically to the late 6th century BCE.[2]

[ ] Baᶜal[3] I shall build [ ]
[ ] son of ᶜAmm[on][4]

[1] For the most recent discussions, see: *CAI* 151-153 (no. 58) and Hübner 1992:21-23.
[2] Cross 1975:11.
[3] This word means "lord" or "master," and is probably part of a proper name, an epithet designating the male deity of fertility, whose proper name was Hadad among the Amorites, Adad among the Mesopotamians, and Haddu among the Canaanites; Maier 1992:11.
[4] Most interpreters reconstruct "ᶜAmmon" or "ᶜAmminadab." It is also possible to understand it as "Ammonite(s)" or to read the first two letters as ᶜ*š*; *CAI* 153.

REFERENCES

Text: *CAI* 151-153 (no. 58); Studies: Ahlström 1984; Cross 1975; Fulco 1979; Hübner 1992; Maier 1992.

---

3. DEIR ᶜALLA

THE DEIR ᶜALLA PLASTER INSCRIPTIONS (2.27)
(The Book of Balaam, son of Beor)

Baruch A. Levine

The Deir ᶜAlla plaster inscriptions were discovered by H. Franken in 1967, and later published by J.Hoftijzer and G. van der Kooij 1976. They immediately awakened scholarly attention because the name of Balaam, son of Beor, the non-Israelite seer and diviner whose exploits and poetic orations are preserved in Numbers, chapters 22-24, appears several times in these inscriptions. What is more, the inscriptions speak of phenomena similar to those associated with the biblical Balaam; of divine visitations and visions, of signs and admonitions, of destruction and death, all in a language not very different from Biblical Hebrew. The Deir ᶜAlla inscriptions also refer to a divine council of inimical gods, and to El and his circle of friendly gods, and tell of intense magical activity, all of which lends to the Balaam texts a mythological character. The religio-ethnic identity of the author of these inscriptions remains uncertain, as does the identity of those for whom they were written (see below).

The first edition by Hoftijzer and van der Kooij provided color photographs, as well as copies and transcriptions. Unidentified fragments were also published. The texts were presented in two "Combinations," respectively, Combination I and Combination II. There is a full commentary, with introductory sections on the script and writing materials, including a discussion of the archaeological background by Franken, the excavator of Deir ᶜAlla. Caquot and Lemaire 1977 realigned the fragments of Combination I and in so doing added significantly to their comprehensibility. The proceedings of an international conference on the Deir ᶜAlla inscriptions, held in Leiden in 1989, present a re-evaluation of the inscriptions by most of those who had been engaged in their research, with updated information gathered from the ongoing excavations at the site (Hoftijzer and van der Kooij 1991).

What are being called "inscriptions" are actually texts pieced together from fragments of plaster that had fallen to the floor from the inner walls of a building. That structure was part of a manufacturing and distribution center located on the mound, where some religious activity may have taken place. The inscriptions, written in ink on plaster with a nib, were displayed on the walls. They belong to stratum IX at the site, which has been dated to the ninth and eighth centuries BCE, with the inscriptions, themselves, dated on the basis of laboratory tests to ca. 800 BCE (Ibrahim and van der Kooij 1991). Tel Deir ^{c}Alla is located about eight kilometers east of the Jordan, not far from the northern bank of the Zerqa river (the biblical Jabbok), which flows into the Jordan. The plaster inscriptions are on display in the Archaeological Museum in Amman, Jordan.

The interpretation of the inscriptions has been complicated from the outset by their fragmentary state and poor legibility, and by questions bearing on their language and cultural provenance. Serious disagreements remain as to correct readings, a situation which has produced more than a few alternative renderings of the texts. Puech 1987 and others have been successful in placing some initially unidentified fragments in the gaps of Combination I. In the first publication, the language of these inscriptions was simply identified as Aramaic, but subsequent analysis has altered scholarly opinion, favoring a local, or regional language bearing affinities to both the Aramaic and Canaanite groups, with opinion still divided on this question.

What has become clear is that the inscriptions are a product of the place where they were discovered: in the Valley of Succoth of biblical times, in the land of Gilead. They date from the period prior to the invasions of Tiglat-Pileser III (734-732 BCE), which resulted in mass deportations from the area. Given what is known of the immediate region in the early to mid-eighth century BCE, it is likely that Israelites constituted the principal element in the Gileadite population. It has been argued that, indeed, the inscriptions speak for Gileadite Israelites who worshipped El, a regional deity.

Although Balaam's name is not attested in what we have of Combination II, it is reasonable to conclude that the initial title "The Book of Balaam" named a collection of visions that encompassed both of the combinations thus far assembled, and additional sections that are preserved only in fragments. Since the inscriptions display a poetic character, they will be arranged in verse form, which adds to their clarity. Combination I can be read consecutively, despite its gaps, whereas Combination II, pending further attempts at its reconstruction, is less continuous, and will be presented as excerpts.

The contents of Combination I may be summarized as follows: Balaam is visited at night by gods sent to communicate to him a message from El, the high god. It is a message of doom, and Balaam is so distressed that he weeps and fasts for two days. Convening his intimates, Balaam discloses to them what has been revealed to him in the vision. A council ($mw^{c}d$ = Hebrew *mô*^{c}*ēd*) of inimical gods, opposing El, has commanded the goddess Shagar - and-Ishtar, a Venus figure of light and fertility, to sew up the heavens producing darkness, and never to speak again. Celestial darkness will cause frenzy on earth, with birds of prey shrieking. Balaam interprets the vision to refer to an impending disaster in the land. Grazing land will be lost to wild beasts, and the flocks will be scattered.

At this point, it becomes less clear what is happening. As interpreted here, the text relates that Balaam undertook the rescue of the goddess from the edict of the council of inimical gods, in accordance with the will of El who had forewarned him. Shagar-and-Ishtar is brought to various magical practitioners and oracles, as Balaam issues admonitions to her adversaries and dispatches powerful agents against them. The adversaries of Shagar-and-Ishtar suffer distress for all to see. Although the text becomes progressively more fragmentary, it is apparent that what had been threatened did not happen; the goddess did not sew up the heavens, and the land was not devastated. The adversaries heard incantations pronounced against them. Domesticated animals drove off the wild beasts.

Combination II begins by relating that after engaging in lovemaking, El constructed a netherworld, described as a "house" where no traveler enters, where no bridegroom goes. The text continues with descriptions of the netherworld reminiscent of Isaiah, chapter 14, the biblical oracle of Sheol. The word Sheol (*šʾl*) may actually occur in the text. We read that the corpse moans in the nether world. The unusual word used to designate a corpse, *nqr*, is known from Isa 14:19 in its Hebrew form, *nēṣer*. Alongside the depiction of the half-existence of kings in Sheol, of worm rot and shrouds, where human feelings and quests are lacking, we read of an unnamed, wise counselor being denied his craft; deprived of his ability to pronounce oracles and execrations. It is suggestive to associate such a fate with Balaam, the protagonist of Combination I, although Balaam's name is not attested in Combination II as we have it. In the following, uncertain translations are italicized.

COMBINATION I:

Title (line 1)
The misfortunes[1] of the Book of Balaam, son of Beor.[2] [a]
A divine seer[b] was he.[3]

The Theophany (lines 1-4)
The gods came to him at night,
And he beheld a vision[c] in accordance with El's utterance.[4]
They said to Balaam, son of Beor:
"So will it be done, with naught surviving,[5]
No one has seen [the likes of] what you have heard!"

Balaam Reports his Vision to his Intimates (lines 4-7)
Balaam arose on the morrow;
He summoned *the heads of the assembly* unto him,
And for two days he fasted, and wept bitterly.[d]
Then his intimates entered into his presence,[6]
And they said to Balaam, son of Beor:
"Why do you fast,
And why do you weep?"
Then he said to them:
"Be seated, and I will relate to you[7] what the Shaddai-gods[e] have planned,[8]
And go, see the acts of the gods!"[9] [f]

Balaam Describes the Celestial Vision and Its Aftermath in the Land (lines 7-13)
"The gods have banded together;
The Shaddai-gods have established a council.[10] [g]
And they have said to [the goddess] Shagar:[11]

a Num 22-24, esp. 24:3, 15; Num 31:8, 16, Deut 23:5; Josh 13:2; 24:9; Mic 6:5; Neh 13:2 *b* 2 Sam 24:11; 2 Kgs 17:13; Isa 30:10; Amos 7:12; Mic 3:7 *c* Num 22:8-13, 19-20; Gen 15:1; Num 24:4, 16; Ezek 13:7 *d* 1 Sam 1:10; Isa 30:9, Jer 22:10, Lam 1:2 *e* Gen 49:25, Num 24:4, 16; Isa 13:6; Ezek 1:24; 10:5; Joel 1:15; Pss 68:15; 91:1; Job (31 times), esp. 5:17; 6:14; 22:17; 40:2; *f* Num 23:23 *g* Isa 14:13; Ps 82:1

---

[1] Read *yissûrê* "the misfortunes of," namely, the misfortunes envisioned in "The Book of Balaam." The BH verb *yissēr* may mean "to afflict, punish " (Lev 26:28, 1 Kgs 12:11, Ps 39:12). In post-BH, sing. *yissôr*, plural *yissûrîn* mean "suffering(s), punishment(s)" (Levy 1964 2:250).

[2] The WS term *spr* (= Heb. *sēper*) refers to all types of written records, including collections of prophetic visions (Jer 36:11; Nah 1:1; Dan 12:4). The title *spr Blʿm br-Bʿr*: "The Book of Balaam, son of Beor" encompasses Combinations I and II, and probably subsequent sections that have been lost. The patronymic *br-bʿr* (= Heb. *ben Beʿor*) is written as one word, using the normal Aram. *br* (= *bar, bir*) for "son."

[3] The syntax is emphatic: *ʾš ḥzh ʾlhn hʾ* (= *ʾîš ḥôzēh ʾelāhîn hûʾ*) "a divine seer was he." Cf. *ʾîš hāʾelōhîm hûʾ* "The man of God was he" (1 Kgs 13:26). Others have parsed the words differently, reading *ʾaša ḥôzēh ʾelāhîn hûʾ* "who was a divine seer," expressing the relative *ʾš* (= *ʾaša*), with prosthetic *aleph*, which is current in Phoen.-Punic.

[4] Appropriately the *ḥzh* "seer" beholds a vision (*mḥzh* = *maḥazeh*), a term associated with Balaam in the biblical poems, where it is said of him: *ʾašer maḥazeh Šaddâi yeḥezeh* "who beholds the vision of Shaddai" (Num 24:3, 16). The term *mśʾ* (= *maśśāʾ*) "utterance" means, lit., what one says when he "raises" his voice, an action conveyed in the idiom *nāśāʾ qôl* "to raise one's voice." In biblical literature, Heb. *maśśāʾ* often defines prophetic utterances. See *c* above. It is the message of the god El (Heb. *ʾĒl*) which was revealed to Balaam, and which the gods who visited him at night had related to him. The gods came "to him" (*ʾlwh*), written with *aleph* instead of *ayin*. This shift reflects the interplay of the prepositional forms *ʿal* and *ʾel* in certain phases of Heb. and Aram., and recalls the Aram. form *ʿalôhî* "to him."

[5] The elliptical clause *kh ypʿl* (= *kôh yipʿal*) is to be taken as stative-passive: "So will it be done." The verb *pʿl* "to do" resonates in this inscription. (See note 9 below). The phrase *blʾ ʾḥrʾh* (= *belāʾ ʾaḥrāʾāh*) is best taken adverbially: "without anything coming after, surviving into the future." The form *ʾḥrʾh* (= *ʾaḥrāʾāh*) resembles that of Heb. *hālʾāh* "further on, beyond" (Num 17:11; 32:19).

[6] The term *ʿm* (= *ʿam*), in *ʿmh* (= *ʿammôh*) "his intimates," is usually taken to mean "people, nation," but it essentially connotes "clan, family." See Levine: 1989:142, s.v. Lev 21:4; Good 1983.

[7] The text reads *ʾḥwkm* (= *ʾaḥawwākûm*) "I will relate to you." The verb *ḥwy* "to show, tell," is common to the WS languages. Cf. Job 15:17: *ʾaḥawwekā, šemaʿ lî* "I will tell you; hear me!"

[8] The previously unattested plural, *šdyn*, is best vocalized *šaddāyîn* "Shaddai-gods" on the model of the Aram. gentilic plural *Yehûdāyîn* "those of Judah; Judeans" (*Qere*) in Dan 3:12. In fact, the frequent Heb. singular, *Šaddâi*, is also gentilic, and is best translated "the one of the mountain," referring to divine beings who inhabit mountains, or associated with them in myth. As such, *Šaddâi* would be cognate with Akk. *šaddāʾu* "mountain dweller." Cf. *CAD* Š 1:43, s.v. *šaddûʾa*; *HAL* 1319-1321, s.v. *Šaddâi* (see *e* above). Heb. *Šaddâi* is closely associated in biblical literature with *ʾĒl*, the presiding deity in the Deir ʿAlla inscriptions. The Deir ʿAlla *šaddāyîn* are deities allied with the other group of *ʾlhn* (= *ʾelāhîn*) "gods" who were opposing the chief god, El. The hypostasis of Shaddai in biblical literature is realized in personal names such as *ʿAmmîšaddâi* "Shaddai is my kin" (Num 1:6), and *Ṣurîšaddâi* "Shaddai is my rock" (Num 1:12).

[9] Gods are given to action, a thought conveyed by the verb *pʿl* "to do." Deir ʿAlla *pʿlt ʾlhn* (= *peʿullôt ʾelāhîn*) "the acts of the gods," recalls biblical *mah pāʿal ʾEl* "What El is about to do" (Num 23:24).

[10] For the biblical attestations of the Heb. term *môʿēd*, Deir ʿAlla *mwʿd*, see *g* above. On the high ridges of Mount Zaphon, referred to as *har môʿēd* "the mountain of the divine council," El and his council assembled (Isa 14:13). The notion that gods made common cause and "banded together" (*ʾtyḥdw*) in divine assemblies to deal with problems on earth and in heaven is pervasive in ancient Near Eastern literature; cf. Polley 1980; Mullen 1992. It is interesting to read here that the Shaddai-gods "established, set up" (Piel *nṣbw* = *niṣṣebû*) a divine council, whereas Ps 82:1 employs the Niphal, stative stem of the same verb: *ʾelōhîm niṣṣāb baʿadat ʾEl* "God stands up in the assembly of El."

[11] The text is restored to read *lš[gr]*, the first part of the goddess' name. Her full name is given near the end of COMBINATION I as *Šgr wʿštr* "Shagar and Ishtar" (see below, Note 17 [name partially restored], and Note 26 [complete name]). As first noted by Hoftijzer, this composite divine name evokes the biblical expression: *šegar ʾalāpêkā weʿašterôt ṣôʾnekā* "the issue of your herds and the fertility of your flocks" (Deut 7:13; 18:51; 28:4). In that expression, the plural of *ʿAštoret*, namely, *ʿaštārôt*, loses its status in divine nomenclature and comes to mean "feritility," the major attribute of the goddess in question. In contrast, the component *šgr* is hypostasized here. Note the Punic personal name, *ʿbdšgr* "servant / worshipper of Shagar," which demonstrates the same hypostasis; Benz 1972:163. It may be pure coincidence, but in the inscriptions from Emar, a Late Bronze Age town on the Euphrates, divine *Ša-ag-ga-ar* is listed as the recipient of offerings alongside the goddess *Nin-kur*, suggesting that this name may be that of a goddess. In any event, the context at Emar is suggestive for comparison with the inscriptions from Deir ʿAlla. The principal text (no. 378) is a list of gods and goddesses to whom offerings were brought. It begins by referring to Dagan as "Lord of cattle" (EN *bu-[qa-ri]*), and there is further reference to "Ashtar of the stars" (*ᵈAs-tar* MUL) and to "Ishtar, lady of the water sources" (*ᵈInanna* GAŠAN e-ni); Arnaud 1986:372, no. 378, lines 1, *12, 39, 44. It is surprising to find in a WS inscription the masculine form of the name of the goddess, namely, *ʿštr*, which is normal for East Semitic (cf. Akk. *Ištar*), instead of the feminine form, Heb. *ʿAštôret*, Phoen.-Punic *ʿštrt*,

'Sew up, close up[12] the heavens with dense cloud,
That darkness exist there, not brilliance[13]; [h]
Obscurity and not clarity;
So that you instill dread in dense darkness.
And — never utter a sound again!'"

"It shall be that the swift and crane will shriek insult to the eagle,
And a nest of vultures shall cry out in response.
The stork, the young of the falcon and the owl,
The chicks of the heron, sparrow and cluster of eagles;
Pigeons and birds, [and fowl in the s]ky."[14 i]

"And a rod [shall flay the cat]tle;[15]
Where there are ewes, a staff shall be brought.[j]
Hares — eat together!
Free[ly *feed*,] oh beasts [of the field]!
And [*freely*] drink, asses and hyenas!"[16]

Balaam Acts to Save the Goddess and the Land (lines 13-14)

Heed the admonition,[k] adversaries of Sha[gar-and-Ishtar]![17]
[skilled diviner.[18]
To skilled diviners shall one take you, and to an oracle;
[*To*] a perfumer of myrrh and a priestess.[19]
[*Who*] *covers his body* [*with oil*],
And rubs himself with olive oil.
To one bearing an offering in a horn;[20]
One augurer after another, and yet another.
As one augurer broke away *from his colleagues*.[21]
The strikers[22] departed [ ]

The Admonitions are Heeded; The Malevolent Gods are Punished, the Goddess Rescued, and the Land Saved (lines 14-18)

They heard incantations from afar.[23]
[ ]
Then disease was unleashed,[24]
And all beheld acts of distress.[25]
Shagar-and-Ishtar did not[26] [ ]
The piglet [drove out] the leopard;
And [the] drove out the young of [the].[27]
[ ] double offerings.
And he beheld [ ]

h Isa 4:5; 50:10; 59:9; 60:19; 62:1, 3; Ezek 1:4, 13, 27-28; 10:4; Joel 2:10; Amos 5:20; Hab 3:11; 2 Sam 22:13 ‖ Ps 18:13; Job 22:11-14

i Ezek 31:13; 32:4

j Jer 25:34-36; 51:23; Ezek 34:5-10; Amos 1:2; Zech 11:3; 13:7

k Jer 17:23; 32:33; 35:13; Prov 1:8; 4:1; 8:33

Ug. ʿ*ṯtrt*. And yet reference must be to a goddess, because the verbs of address are consistently feminine. The counterpart male aspect, expressed in Moabite and South-Arabic as ʿ*štr*, Ug. ʿ*ṯtr*, cannot be intended here. As will be clarified in due course, the Deir ʿAlla goddess Shagar-and-Ishtar expresses the synthesis of Ishtar and Venus. See Note 13 below.

[12] It is appropriate to speak of sewing up the heavens, since they are depicted as a tent flap (Ps 104:2). The verb *skr* "to close up, dam" is employed in Gen 8:2 to describe the shutting of the wells of the deep after the Flood.

[13] The text reads *ḥšk w*ʾ*l ngh* "darkness and not brilliance," a contrast well attested in biblical literature, where Heb. *nôgah* is most often associated with the light of heavenly bodies. See ***h*** above. In post-biblical Jewish literature, *nôgah* is the name given to Venus (Levy 1964 3:334). The synthesis of Ishtar-Venus in Mesopotamian culture is best known from the so-called *Venus Tablets of Ammiṣaduqa* newly edited by Reiner-Pingree (1975; 1981).

[14] The long list of birds, mostly birds of prey, is unusual. All may be identified, and many are included in the category of forbidden fowl in Lev 11 and Deut 14. Deir ʿAlla *ṣdh* "owl" is known from the Aram. treaties from Sefire (*KAI* 22, line 33; see below, 2.82). The restoration: [ʿ*p bš]myn* "[fowl in the s]ky" is by Puech 1987.

[15] Puech 1987 restores: *w[yḥšl.b]qr* "shall flay the cattle," based on the occurrence of the verb *ḥšl* "to peel off, hull" (Akk. *ḫašālu*) in an unidentified fragment, which reads: *bqr.lḥšl.wy*ʾ*kl* "Let him skin cattle and eat."

[16] Phonetically, Deir ʿAlla *qb*ʿ "hyena" is realized in post-biblical Heb. as *ṣābû*ʿ*a* (Levy 1964 4:166).

[17] The text reads *šm*ʿ*w mwsr* (= Heb. *šime*ʿ*û mûsār*) "heed the admonition." This is biblical diction. See ***k*** above. The name of the goddess is partially restored.

[18] The text is restored: *ḥ]km* "skilled diviner" from ensuing *lḥkmm* "to skilled diviners." Cf. Isa 3:3 *ḥakam ḥarāšîm* "one skilled in incantations" which is parallel with *nebôn laḥaš* "one expert in spells." In Gen 41:8, *ḥakāmîm* is listed alongside *mekaššepîm* "socrcerers" and in Exod 7:11 with *ḥarṭûmîm* "magicians."

[19] The feminine noun ʿ*nyh*, lit. "responder, answerer" is compared by Hoftijzer (1976:212, notes 79-82) with Akk. *āpiltu*, a known role at Mari. *CAD* A 1:170: "female answerers." Cf. in biblical usage *ma*ʿ*aneh* ʾ*elôhîm* "a divine response" (1 Kgs 18:24; Prov 16:1). In fact, all of the practitioners listed are women: *khnh* "priestess," *rqḥt mr* "perfumer of myrrh," and ʿ*nyh*.

[20] The text reads: *lnš*ʾ ʾ*zr.qrn* "to one bearing an offering [in] a horn," taking ʾ*zr* as a cognate of Ug. *uzr* "offering." The precise sense remains uncertain.

[21] The term *ḥšb* (Heb. *ḥôšêb*) is understood as one who "calculates," hence: "augurer." The text reads *ḥšb, ḥšb, wḥšb*, which may be taken as distributive: "augurers of all sorts." Puech 1987 restores ʾ*tntq* "he broke away" on the basis of an unidentified fragment.

[22] Puech 1987 restores *ḥbṣn* from an unidentified fragment and explains it on the basis of Aramaic-Syriac *ḥbṣ*, a variant of *ḥbṭ* "to strike, mill, crush," (Levy 1964 2:7). Hoftijzer cites Syriac *ḥebṣā*ʾ "crowd." Cf. Brockelmann 1966:211. These are the ones sent to afflict the adversaries of the goddess.

[23] The text reads *wšm*ʿ*w ḥršn mn rḥq* "They heard incantations from afar." Cf. Note 18 above, *hakām ḥarāšîm*. See Levy 1964 2:119, for post-biblical and Aram. forms, *ḥārāš* and *ḥaršā*ʾ "incantations." Cf. Brockelmann 1966:259 and Sokoloff 1990:216.

[24] Puech 1987 restores on the basis of a fragment: *[w]ypth lḥly*, lit. "He opened to disease."

[25] All beheld the distress inflicted on the adversaries of the goddess. Deir ʿAlla *qqn* (pl.) reflects a phonetic variant of Heb. forms such as *ṣûqāh* "distress, oppression" (Isa 8:22), and masc. *ṣôq* (Dan 9:25).

[26] This is the only place where the full name of the goddess, *Šgr-w-*ʿ*štr* is preserved. The name is followed by what appears to be a prefixed negative *l-* "not." The sense would be that the goddess "did not" sew up the heavens or, to put it another way, that she did not bring devastation on the land.

[27] Order and calm were restored. Domestic animals drove out wild beasts. The form *hqrqt* "she drove out" is the Haphel 3rd fem. perf. sing. of *qrq*, a phonetic variant of ʿ*rq* "to run away, abscond" (Job 30:17). *HAL* 841.

COMBINATION II:

EXCERPT A: *El builds a necropolis* (lines 6-7)
El satisfied himself with [lovemaking];[l]
And then El fashioned an eternal house;[1] [m]
[A house],
A house where no traveler [n] enters,[2]
Nor does a bridegroom enter there.

EXCERPT B: *A Half-existence in Sheol* (line 8)
Worm rot from a grave.
From the reckless affairs of men,
And from the lustful desires *of people*[3]

EXCERPT C: *The Rejection of a Seer* (line 9)
If it is for counsel, one will not counsel with you!
Or for advising him, one will not take advice![4]

EXCERPTS D-E: *More on Conditions in Sheol* (lines 10-11)
From the bed they cover themselves with a wrap.[o]
If you hate him, he will be mortally afflicted.[5]
If you [ ]
- - - - -
[Worm rot] is under your head.[p]
You shall lie on your eternal bedding,
To pass away [6] to [ ]

EXCERPTS F-G: *Kings and Other Corpses in Sheol* (lines 12-15)
[ ] in their heart.
The corpse moans in his heart[7] [q]
He moans [ ]
- - - - -
[ ] a daughter.
There, kings behold [ ].[r]
There is no mercy when Death seizes a suckling.[8]
And a suckling [ ];
And a suckling [ ];
A suckling [ ];
There [ ] shall be.
The heart of the corpse is desolate[9]
As he approaches [Sheol].
[ ].
To the edge of She[ol],[10] [s]
And the shadow of the hedge [ ].

EXCERPTS H-I: *An Oracle: The Quests of Kings and Seers Come to Naught* (lines 5-17)
"The quest of a king is moth rot,[11]
And the quest of [ ];
[ ] seers.

l Prov 7:18
m Qoh 12:5
n 2 Sam 12:4
o Isa 14:19
p Isa 14:11; Job 7:5; 17:4; 21:26; 25:6
q Isa 14:19
r Isa 14:9, 18
s Gen 37:35; Deut 32:22; Isa 14:9-15; 1 Sam 2:6; Isa 38:10, 18; Ezek 32:21, 37; Hos 13:14; Pss 18:6; 30:4; Prov 9:18; 17:13; 30:16; Qoh 9:10

[1] The text reads *byt* ᶜ*lmn* (= *bêt* ᶜ*ôlāmîn*), with the abstract pl. connoting "eternity." Further on, in EXCERPT D-E, we find the same concept of the grave as an eternal resting place, expressed by the plural *mškby* ᶜ*lmyka* (= *miškābê* ᶜ*ôlamâikā*) "your eternal bedding." As noted by Hoftijzer, Qoh 12:5 attests the sing. term: "For the human being is going to his eternal house" (*bêt* ᶜ*ôlāmô*). The Deir ᶜAlla inscriptions antedate the biblical Qoheleth. Cf. Hallo 1993:187f.; Williams 1977:500 [eternal house = grave]. In post biblical Jewish literature, *bêt (hā)*ᶜ*ôlāmîm* (also: *bêt* ᶜ*alemîn*), and related sing. forms, may refer either to the Temple of Jerusalem (after 1 Kgs 8:13), or to a burial ground. Levy 1964 1:224-228, esp. 227, s.v. *bet* ᶜ*ālam*. Cf. Sokoloff 1990:95. The sing. form occurs in an Aram. deed of grant from Nahal Ḥever on the Dead Sea, dated July 13, 120 CE. In it a father states to his wife, among other provisions, that he beqeathes his property to her "from the day I go to my eternal house (*lbyt* ᶜ*lmy* = *lebêt* ᶜ*ālamî*) and forever." Yadin, Greenfield and Yardeni 1996:384, line 21, *passim*. Cf. also below, p. 156., n. 3.

[2] *hlk* "traveler" is matched in 2 Sam 12:4 by the *hapax legomenon* in BH *hēlek* "traveler."

[3] The parallelism *pḥzy//šqy* "reckless affairs// lustful desires" recalls Ps 147:10: *šôqê hā*ᵓ*îš* "the lustful desires of man," related to Heb. *tešûqāh* "desire" (Gen 3:16; 4:7; Cant 7:11). Gen 49:4 has *paḥaz kammayîm* "as unstable as water," and cf. participial *pôḥēz* "shiftless" in Judg 9:4; Zeph 3:4, as well as abstract *paḥazût* in Job 23:32.

[4] The one being addressed is told that his counsel will no longer be sought. We have the parallelism of ᶜ*ṣh* (= Heb. ᶜ*ēṣāh*) "advice" and *mlk* (= *mulk*) "counsel." A similar thought is expressed further on, in EXCERPTS H-I. In post-biblical Heb. and Jewish Aram. the Nìphᶜal construction *nimlāk b-* and Ithpeᵓel, *yitmelek* mean "to take counsel with," as does the Deir ᶜAlla Ithpeᵓel *lytmlk b-* "He will not take counsel with." Levy 1964 3:128-130 s.v. *mālak, melak*. *DNWSI* 634 s.v. *mlk* 2. Sokoloff 1990:310, s.v. *mlk* #2.

[5] The translation is conjectural, at best, and not fully comprehensible, even though the text is clearly legible as *hn tšn*ᵓ*n y*ᵓ*nš*.

[6] *lḥlq* "to pass away, disappear" is to be related to Akk. *ḫalāqu*, and Ug. *ḫlq*, realized in BH as *ḥlq* III "to pass away, die," as distinct from *ḥlq* "to be smooth; to divide"; Levine 1995:139-149.

[7] The term *nqr* "corpse" is crucial to the interpretation of COMBINATION II. It is understood as a cognate of BH *nēṣer* "carrion, corpse" in Isa 14:19: "You have been cast from your grave like loathsome carrion (*kenēṣer nit*ᶜ*āb* "like a trampled corpse"). The *qoph* of the Deir ᶜAlla language realizes proto-Semitic *ḍod*, which is often realized in Heb. as a *ṣade*. Post-biblical Heb. attests a related noun *nēṣel*, or *nāṣāl* "putrid flesh" of a corpse (Mishnah, *Nāzîr* 7:2, ᵓ*Ahîlôt* 2:1), and the proto-Semitic *ḍod* is preserved in the Arabic verb *naḍala* "to extract, remove" Ibn-Manzur 1956 2:663, s.v. *naḍala*. Others have related Deir ᶜAlla *nqr* to the better attested Heb. noun *nēṣer* "offshoot, scion" (Isa 11:1; 60:21), interpreting the Deir ᶜAlla text to refer to a dead child.

[8] The line is difficult to interpret with certainty. It reads: *lyš bmyqḥ mwt* ᶜ*l rḥm*, lit. "There is not, when Death seizes a suckling, mercy." The noun ᶜ*l* (= Heb. ᶜ*ûl*) "suckling" occurs repeatedly in broken lines, suggesting that the vision of Sheol focuses on infant mortality. Death, or perhaps the god Mot, personified, snatches away infants mercilessly. Cf. ᶜ*ûl yāmîm* "infant," in contrast to *zāqēn* "graybeard" in Isa 65:20. Most relevant is Isa 49:15: "Can a woman forget her suckling child (ᶜ*ûlāh*), withholding compassion (*meraḥēm*) from the fruit of her womb?" Others prefer to translate ᶜ*l rḥm* as "suckling of the womb," reflecting Heb. *reḥem* "womb."

[9] The text reads *lbb nqr šhh*. I take Deir ᶜAlla *šhh* to be a variant of Heb. *š*ᵓ*h*, as in Isa 6:11: "Until such a time that towns lie desolate (ᵓ*im šā*ᵓ*û* ᶜ*ārîm*) without inhabitants."

[10] Restoring *l[š*ᵓ*l]* "to Sheol" on the basis of what follows: *lqṣh š[*ᵓ*l]* "to the edge of Sheol." The corpse groans as it approaches Sheol, which is surrounded by a hedge or wall (*mgdr*).

[11] *ssh* (= *sāsāh*) "moth rot" is taken to be a cognate of BH *sās* "rot"? parallel with ᶜ*āš* "moth" in Isa 51:8.

Your quest is distant from you.
To know how to deliver an oracle to his people.
You have been condemned for your speech,

t Num 22:11, 17; 23:8, 11, 25-27; Job 5:3

And [banned] from pronouncing words of execration." *t*

REFERENCES

Text: Hoftijzer and van der Kooij 1976; 1991; Studies: Arnaud 1986; Benz 1972; Brockelmann 1966; Caquot and Lemaire 1971; Good 1983; Hackett 1984; Hallo 1993; Ibn Manzur 1956; Ibrahim and van der Kooij 1991; Levine 1989; 1995; Levy 1964; Mullen 1992; Polley 1980; Puech 1987; Reiner and Pingree 1975; 1981; Sokoloff 1990; Williams 1977; Yadin, Greenfield and Yardeni 1996.

4. HEBREW INSCRIPTIONS

THE SILOAM TUNNEL INSCRIPTION (2.28)

K. Lawson Younger, Jr.

The inscription was discovered in 1880 on the wall of a Jerusalem tunnel that leads from the Gihon Spring to the pool of Siloam. The inscription occupies the lower half of a prepared panel that is approximately 0.50 m in height and 0.66 m in width. The tunnel winds through the Mizzi Ahmar dolomite rock for a length of approximately 533 m (corresponding roughly to the inscription's 1,200 cubits).[1] It is essentially an enlargement of natural karstic dissolution channels,[2] and was executed as part of a comprehensive design by Hezekiah's town planners (2 Kgs 20:20; 2 Chr 32:3-4, 30; Isa 22:11; Ben Sira 48:17). Both the execution of the tunnel and the inscription demonstrate careful adeptness. Cut by two groups of workmen progressing towards each other,[3] the tunnel's floor required accurate calculation since it runs smoothly at a 0.06% average slope with the height differential between the spring and exit being a very moderate gradient ($\approx$ 0.32 m).[4]

This commemorative inscription is not an "official"/"royal" inscription, but an "unofficial"/"common person" type text.[5] In this sense it is unique among ancient Near Eastern building/display inscriptions. It is not concerned with the recounting of the complete history of the excavation of the tunnel.[6] Instead, it is very much preoccupied with a specific moment on a specific day — the culmination of a great and exciting engineering project.[7]

In spite of a recent attempt to date the inscription on paleographic and archaeological grounds to the Hasmonean period,[8] the vast majority of scholars see the inscription dating to ca. 700 BCE (i.e. a product of Hezekiah's reign).[9]

[The day of][10] the breach.[a]
——————— [11]
This is the record of how the tunnel was breached.
While [the excavators were wielding[12]] their pick-axes,

a Isa 51:1

each man towards his co-worker,
and while there were yet three cubits for the brea[ch,]
a voice [was hea]rd
each man calling to his co-worker;

[1] Contrast the straight-line (i.e., rectilinear) distance from the spring to the pool which is only 320 m.

[2] Gill 1991; 1994; 1996.

[3] The reason for having two crews digging simultaneously was to halve the cutting time — an essential since an Assyrian attack was imminient. See the discussion of Abells and Arbit 1995:6.

[4] Gill 1991:1469; Shiloh 1993:711.

[5] Parker 1997:38-39. Cf. above pp. xxiiif.

[6] Sasson 1982:113.

[7] Shea 1988:431-435.

[8] Rogerson and Davies 1996:138-149.

[9] Hackett, Cross, McCarter, Yardeni, Lemaire, Eshel, and Hurvitz 1997:41-50, 68-69; Hendel 1996:233-237. Also note that geology may provide a clue to when the tunnel was dug through the dating of a stalactite. See Gill 1996:22.

[10] See Younger 1994:551 and nn. 29-30 for a discussion of the different suggested restorations.

[11] The inscription contains deliberate spaces that function as idea dividers. See Sasson 1982:113.

[12] For the possible restorations, see Younger 1994:544.

because there was a cavity[13] in the rock (extending) from the south to [the north].

So on the day of the breach,
the excavators struck,
each man to meet his co-worker,
pick-axe against pick-[a]xe.

Then the water flowed from the spring[14][b] to the pool,
a distance of one thousand and two hundred cubits.
One hundred cubits was the height of the rock above the heads of the excavat[ors.][15]

b 2 Chr 32:30

[13] The meaning of *zdh* has been the crux for this inscription. For a survey of the different proposals, see Younger 1994:549-550 and Parker 1997:52, n. 4. The geological conclusions of Gill 1996 seem to demand a geological type meaning for *zdh*: something like "cavity" or "fissure." See Lancaster and Long 1999:15-26; Younger 1994.

[14] For *mwṣ*ʾ, cf. 2 Chr 32:30.

[15] One hundred cubits (150 feet) was the maximum thickness of the rock at only one point, namely at the northern loop of the tunnel nearest the Gihon spring. It was not the average height.

REFERENCES

Text: *HAE* 1:178-189; *AHI* 68 (4.116); *SSI* 1:21-23; *KAI* 1:34; 2:186-188. Translations: *ANET* 321; *DOTT* 209-211; *TUAT* 2/4:555-556; *WAI* 64-71; Studies: Abells and Arbit 1995; Gill 1991; 1994; 1996; Hackett, Cross, McCarter, Yardeni, Lemaire, Eshel, and Hurvitz 1997; Hendel 1996; Lancaster and Long 1999; Pardee 1996; Parker 1997:36-42, 152-154; Rogerson and Davies 1996; Sasson 1982:111-117; Shea 1988; Shiloh 1993; Younger 1994.

5. PHOENICIAN INSCRIPTIONS

THE INSCRIPTION OF KING YAḤIMILK (2.29)

Stanislav Segert

The inscription on the limestone block (35 x 70 x 45 cm) was found in the ruins of the Crusader Castle in Byblos (Ğebail) in 1929 and published in the same year. Its seven lines are written over a text in "Byblos hieroglyphic" that is no longer clearly visible. Yaḥimilk's building inscription can be dated to about 950 BCE. It is now kept in the National Museum in Beirut.

Building inscription (lines 1-3a)
Building [1][a] which Yaḥimilk,[2] the king of Byblos/Gubal[3][b] built.[c]
He rebuilt[4][d] all ruins of these buildings.

The king deserves to be rewarded by gods (lines 3b-7)
May Baal/Master[5] of Heavens[6][e]
and Baala[t]/Mistress[7][f] of Byblos/Gubal
and the assembly[g] of holy gods[8] of Byblos/Gubal
prolong [h] the days[9] of Yaḥimilk
and his years over Byblos/Gubal,
for [he][10] (is) the righteous[11][i] king
and just king
at the face/before the holy[12] (gods) of Byblos/Gubal.

a 1 Kgs 9:1 *b* Ezek 27:9 *c* 1 Kgs 6:1-2 *d* Micah 3:12; Isa 58:12 *e* Gen 24:7; Jonah 1:9 *f* 1 Kgs 17:17 *g* Ps 89:7 *h* Exod 20:12; Deut 5:16; 6:2; 11:9; 25:15; 32:47; Ps 61:7; Prov 3:2 *i* Ps 140:14; Deut 9:5

[1] The word *bt* can mean various kinds of buildings, including "temple" or "palace."

[2] The reconstruction is based on Assyrian syllabic cuneiform *ia-ḫi-mil-ki*. The name can be interpreted as "may (the divine) King keep alive."

[3] In the syllabic cuneiform texts from the 14th century BCE, the name is given as *gublu* (with the case ending *-u*). In the Hebrew Bible the form *gᵉbāl* is attested, with reduction of the first vowel. The Phoenician form can be reconstructed as /gubal/. The Greek form *Bublos* goes back to the second millennium BCE, when in archaic Greek **gu-* changed into */bu-/*. This city was important economic and cultural center in antiquity.

[4] Lit., "he revived." Cf. 1 Chr 11:8.

[5] Baal (*bʿl*) "master (of the house)," "Lord," "Chief" was originally an epithet of this god, named primarily /had(a)d/. He was compared to Greek Zeus.

[6] Phoenician *bʿlšmm* is rendered in the cuneiform writing as *ba-al-ša-me-me*, in Greek as *baalsamēn*.

[7] The usual form is *bʿlt*. At the end of line 3 the final letter is omitted. This goddess is mentioned already in the 16th century BCE. She was later compared to Greek Aphrodite.

[8] Assembly of gods is often mentioned in Canaanite religious texts, including those from Ugarit.

[9] The word pair "days" — "years" is attested also in the HB; cf. Dahood 1972:203-205, and above p. 140, n. 9.

[10] The supposed equivalent [*h*ʾ] at the very end of the inscription is missing.

[11] The word pair indicating "righteousness" and "uprightness" appears in ancient Canaanite poetry, e.g. *KTU* 1.14:I:12-13. Cf. 1 Kgs 3:6.

[12] As "holy" (*qdš*), gods are characterized only in ancient Canaanite tradition.

REFERENCES

Text: *KAI* #4; 2:6-7; *SSI* 3:17-19. Translations: *ANET*, 653. Driver 1954 pl. 48, 1.7. Studies: Avishur 1976:7f., 12f.

THE KULAMUWA INSCRIPTION (2.30)

K. Lawson Younger, Jr.

The inscription, which is carved on a large orthostat, was discovered during the German excavations at Zinjirli (= Samʾal) in 1902. The orthostat's relief pictures Kulamuwa pointing with his right hand to divine symbols that fill part of the space at the top of the monument. The text, written in North Phoenician with Aramaic influences, dates around 830-820 BCE and belongs to the "memorial" genre (Miller 1974:9-18).

It is a highly rhetorical work utilizing symmetrical design. It divides into two roughly equal sections (lines 1-8; 9-16) by a line drawn across the monument and a double introduction (line 1 and line 9). There are two major units in each section that create a chiasm: A "The past contrasted with the present" (lines 2-5a), B "External or foreign affairs" (lines 5b-8) :: B′ "Internal or domestic affairs" (10-13), A′ "Curse: the future" (14-16).

Introduction: Identification (line 1)
I am Kulamuwa,[1] the son of Ḥayya.[2]

The Past Contrasted With the Present (lines 2-5a)
Gabbar[3] ruled over Yʾdy,[4]
but he achieved nothing.
BNH[5] also (ruled over Yʾdy),
but he achieved nothing.
And then my father Ḥayya,
but he achieved nothing.
And then my brother Šaʾil,[6]
but he achieved nothing.
But I am Kulamuwa, son of *TML*[7] —
what I achieved
(my) predecessors had not achieved.

External Affairs (lines 5b-8)
The house of my father was in the midst of mighty kings.[a]
And each one stretched forth his hand[8] to fight.[9] [b]
But I was in the hand of the kings like a fire consuming[c] the beard and like a fire consuming the hand.[10]
Now the king of the Danunians was more powerful than I (or: too powerful for me),[11]
But I engaged[12] [d] against him the king of Assyria.
A young woman was given for a sheep and a young man for a garment.[13]

a Ps 136:18

b Exod 22:7, 10; 24:11; Deut 25:11; Judg 5:26; 1 Sam 22:12; 26:9; 2 Sam 15:5; 1 Kgs 13:4; Job 28:9

c Exod 24:17; Deut 4:24; 9:3

d Deut 23:5; 2 Sam 10:6; 1 Kgs 15:18; 2 Kgs 7:6; 16:7; Isa 7:20; Neh 13:2

[1] The name *Klmw* is undoubtedly Anatolian. Starke investigates the Luwian components *kula* and *muwa*, and defines the name as "die Wehrhaftigkeit des Heeres besitzend" ("possessing the fighting ability of the army"). See Starke 1990:236, n. 806.

[2] This individual is mentioned in Shalmaneser III's inscriptions (see *COS* 2.113A, note 10; see also *RIMA* 3:16 [lines i.42, 53]; 3:23 [ii.83]).

[3] Also mentioned by Shalmaneser III. See *COS* 2.113A, p. 263 and *RIMA* 3:23 (ii.83).

[4] *Yʾdy* is the ancient non-Semitic name of Zinjirli. It was also known as *Samʾal* (cf. below 2.38 = Bar-Rakib 2-3; 2.35 = Zakkur 7; and Assyrian texts from Tiglath-Pileser III to Assurbanipal). The vocalization of *Yʾdy* is still uncertain.

[5] See Tropper 1993:32 and esp. plate 6; Lipiński 1974:45-61, esp. p. 49. While *bnh* appears to be the reading of line 3, the reading in line 16 appears to be *bmh*.

[6] The name is attested in Hebrew: Šāʾūl. See Swiggers 1983:137.

[7] For the reading *TML*, see Tropper 1993:33 and Young 1993. Some scholars have suggested that this is the name of Kulamuwa's mother. See Gibson *SSI* 3:36; Swiggers 1981:2, n. 6; 1983:138; and Young 1993:96-98.

[8] Avishur 1976:10; Tropper 1993:35.

[9] There are two ways in which the term *lḥm* has been understood: 1) "to eat, devour, consume" (see Müller 1985:638; Gibson *SSI* 3:34; Fales 1979:10); and 2) "to make war, fight" (see Tropper 1993:35; Swiggers 1983:139; Krahmalkov 1974:39-43). Cf. 1 Sam 22:12.

[10] There are two possible interpretations of *ʾš*: 1) *ʾš* is the relative pronoun attached to *km*. Thus the translation would be something like "And I was in the hand of the kings as if I had eaten my beard and as if I had eaten my hand" (see Röllig, *KAI* 2:31; Fales 1979:12; Müller 1985:638); and 2) *ʾš* is the word "fire" (cf. *ʾš ʾklt* to the biblical phrase "a consuming fire"). Here the term is used as a symbol of the humiliation of an enemy in the burning of the beard and hand. The context seems to demand that a description of earlier difficulties be followed at this point in the text by triumph. We would expect Kulamuwa to harm the very kings who stretched out the hand to destroy his dynasty (see Sperling 1988:331; Tropper 1993:36-37).

[11] Cf. the Amarna formula *da-an-nu* LÚ.SA.GAZ.MEŠ *eli-nu* :: "the Hapiru are too powerful for us" or "the Hapiru are more powerful than us" EA 299:18-19; 305:21-22; 307:8-10. See Liverani 1991:180, n. 13; and Parker 1997:222, n. 1.

[12] The "hiring" of armies was not unusual in the ancient Near East. See Lipiński 1974:50; Sperling 1988:332. Dion 1997:107 and note 118; and Parker 1997:80-81. For other explanations, see: Landsberger 1948:51; and Garbini 1977a:116-118.

[13] This is the most difficult sentence of the inscription. The problem is in identifying the subject of the verb *ytn*. There are at least five possibilities: 1) The Danunian king who had bad economic conditions after the Assyrian intervention (Gibson *SSI* 3:37; Müller 1985:639); 2) the Assyrian king whom Kulamuwa boasts of hiring cheaply (Rosenthal 1955:654; Fales 1979:19); 3) a parenthetical statement describing the heavy tribute Kulamuwa had to pay the king of Assyria (Röllig, *KAI* 2:33); 4) a parenthetical statement describing the depressed economic conditions

Introduction: Identification (line 9)
I am Kulamuwa, son of Ḥayya.
I sat upon the throne of my father.

Internal Affairs (lines 10-13)
Before the former kings, the *Muškabīm*[14] were living like dogs.[15 e]

But I was to some a father;
and to some I was a mother;
and to some I was a brother.

Now whoever had never possessed a sheep,[16]
I made lord of a flock.
And whoever had never possessed an ox,
I made owner of a herd and owner of silver and lord of gold.
And whoever from his childhood had never seen linen,
now in my days wore byssos.

And I took the *Muškabīm* by the hand,
and they showed (me) affection[17] like the affection of a fatherless child toward (its) mother.

Curse: The Future (lines 14-16)
Now whoever of my sons
who will sit (reign) in my place
and damages this inscription,
may the *Muškabīm* not honor the *Ba*ᶜ*rīrīm*,[18]
and may the *Ba*ᶜ*rīrīm* not honor the *Muškabīm*.

And whoever strikes out this inscription,
may Baᶜal Ṣemed,[19] (the god) of Gabbar, strike his head;
and may Baᶜal Ḥammon,[20 f] (the god) of Bamah,[21]
and Rakib-El,[22] the lord of the house (i.e., dynasty), strike his head.

e Ps 59:16

f Ezek 6:4,6; 2 Chr 14:4; 37:4

within Y᾿dy prior to the Assyrian intervention (O'Connor 1977:226); and 5) a climatic statement concerning the dramatic fall of prices from the Assyrian king's intervention. The inverted word order and the parallel of 2 Kgs 7:1-16 strengthen this interpretation. See Tropper 1993:38; and Liverani 1991:177-184.

[14] Meaning is still uncertain. Perhaps, the poor, indigenous population of Sam᾿al. See the discussion of Swiggers 1983:142-143; Dion 1997:253-254; 285-286.

[15] Tropper 1993:39-41, plate 8. For other interpretations, Landsberger 1948:52; *SSI* 3:37; Müller 1985:639; O'Connor 1977:22. Concerning Ps 59:16 see Tropper 1994:87-95.

[16] Lit., "see the face." See Landsberger 1948:52 and O'Connor 1977:22.

[17] See Dion 1974:88-89; Zevit 1990:342-343; and Tropper 1993:43-44.

[18] Meaning uncertain. This is no doubt a social group at Sam᾿al and is often seen by commentators as referring to the dominant, nomadic, immigrant Aramaic minority in the land (as opposed to the *mškbm* above). The term may have more ethnic than social connotations; Dion 1997:253-254; 285-286.

[19] See Tropper 1993:45.

[20] For this deity see Xella 1991:229-234.

[21] See note 5 above.

[22] Rakib-El occurs also in Kulamuwa's scepter inscription (*KAI* 25:4-6; see Lemaire 1990:323-327) and in later inscriptions from Zenjirli: Hadad (below, 2.36 = *KAI* 214:2, 3, 11, 18), Panamuwa (below, 2.37 = *KAI* 215:22), and Bar-Rakib (below, 2.38 = *KAI* 216:5; 217:7-8). For recent discussions of this deity see van der Toorn 1995:1296-1297; Teixidor 1987:371; Schmidt 1994:135, n. 135.

REFERENCES

Text: Tropper 1993:27-46; *KAI* 1:4-5; 2:30-34, 338; *SSI* 3:30-39; Translations and Studies: Avishur 1976; Dion 1974; 1995; 1997; Fales 1979; Garbini 1977a; Ishida 1985; Krahmalkov 1974; Landsberger 1948; Lemaire 1990; Lipiński 1974:45-61; Liverani 1991; Müller 1985; O'Connor 1977; Parker 1997:76-83; Rosenthal *ANET* 654; Sperling 1988; Swiggers 1981; 1983; Tropper 1993:27-46; 1994; Xella 1991; Zevit 1990.

THE AZATIWADA INSCRIPTION (2.31)

K. Lawson Younger, Jr.

In 1946, a Phoenician-Hieroglyphic Luwian bilingual inscription was discovered on portal orthostats at the Iron Age fortification of Karatepe on the west bank of the Çeyhan River in the ancient region of Cilicia, the modern province of Adana, Turkey. It is the longest extant Phoenician inscription and is preserved at three locations on the site: the Lower (North) Gate, the Upper (South) Gate, and on the skirt of a colossal divine statue which stood just inside the Upper Gate. The Lower Gate was carved on four orthostats in three columns and continues onto the base of a fifth orthostat and onto a stone lion. The text appears to date from the very end of the 8th century, or more likely from the beginning of the 7th century BCE.[1] Azatiwada was an agent of Awariku, the king of the Danunians (= Que[a]) and the text narrates his various accomplishments on behalf of the Danunians and his sovereign. For the Hieroglyphic Luwian (HL) inscription see *COS* 2.21 above.

[1] For the most recent discussion, see Hawkins 1995:1304.

Introduction: Epithets (i.1-2)
I am Azatiwada,
the blessed of Ba^cal,[2] servant of Ba^cal,
whom Awariku,[3] king of the Danunians, empowered.

Body: Azatiwada's Mighty Deeds (i.3-iii.2)
General establishment of Azatiwada's reign (i.3-13)
Ba^cal made me a father and a mother[4] [b] to the Danunians.
I caused the Danunians to live.[5] [c]
I enlarged the land of the plain of Adana from East[6] to West.[7]
Now there was in my days all good for the Danunians and abundance and luxury.

And I filled the granaries[8] of the city of Pahar.[9]
And I acquired[10] [d] horse upon horse, and shield upon shield, and army upon army,
by the grace of Ba^cal and the gods.[11]
And I smashed the rebels;[12]
And I crushed[13] all evil which was in the land.
And I established the house of my lord in goodness;
and I did good to the root [e] of my lord.
And I caused him to reign [f] upon the throne of his father.

And I made peace with every king.
And indeed every king made me as a father,[14] [g]
on account of my righteousness, my wisdom and the goodness of my heart.

[a] 1 Kgs 10:28; 2 Chr 1:16
[b] Deut 32:6; 32:18
[c] Gen 50:18-20
[d] 1 Kgs 10:26; Isa 30:1; Jer 4:20; Ps 61:7; Job 16:14; Prov 21:6
[e] Isa 11:1, 10
[f] 1 Kgs 2:24
[g] Gen 45:8; Ps 109:14; Isa 22:21
[h] Josh 10:24; Pss 8:7; 110:2; 1 Kgs 5:3; 2 Sam 22:39 (= Ps 18:39); 1 Sam 25:24; Esther 8:3

Building of fortifications and their impact (i.13-ii.9)
I built strong fortifications[15] in all the far regions of the borders,
in places where there had been evil men,
gang leaders,[16]
of whom not one man had ever been a vassal
to the house of Mopsos;[17]
But I, Azatiwada, placed them under my feet.[18] [h]
And I built fortifications in those places
so that they,[19] the Danunians, might dwell in the ease of their hearts.
And I humbled strong lands in the West,
which no king who was before me ever humbled.
But I, Azatiwada, have humbled[20] them.

I brought them down.
I settled them in the far regions of my borders in the East.
And I settled the Danunians there.

And they were in my days on all the borders of the Plain of Adana from the East to the West,
even[21] in places which formerly were feared,
where a man feared to walk the road.
But in my days, (especially) mine, a woman can walk alone with her spindles,[22]
by the grace of Ba^cal and the gods.
Now there was in all my days abundance and luxury and good living and ease of heart for the Danunians and for all the Plain of Adana.

---

[2] The meaning of *hbrk b^cl* is difficult. Some scholars suggest that *hbrk b^cl* should be translated "chief official (*habarakku*) of Ba^cl," arguing that *hbrk* is a loanword from Akk. *abarakku* (e.g. Lipiński 1974:45-46). Others understands *hbrk b^cl* as a construct "the (one) blessed (by)/of Ba^cal" (e.g. Greenfield 1972:179). The HL seems to support a religious honorific. See now Röllig 1999:58 and Younger 1998:33-35. A further complication for *hbrk* being a loanword from Akk. *abarakku* is the fact that the title *abarakku* in the Neo-Assyrian period had been replaced by *masennu* (*mašennu* in Neo-Babylonian). See Millard 1994:7, n. 14.

[3] Awariku is known from the inscriptions of Tiglath-Pileser III (*COS* 2.117A, note 4) and Sargon II. He is also mentioned in the Cebel Ires Daği inscription (*COS* 3).

[4] Cf. the Hittite inscription of Anitta where the phrase "father and mother" are used as a metonymy for "compassion."

[5] For the phrase *yḥw ʾnk ʾyt dnnym* "I caused the Danunians to live," see Amadasi Guzzo 1984:109-118. Cf. the usage in Egyptian, as well as in the Amarna Letters (EA 94. 65, 69; 136. 43; 147. 9; 169. 7).

[6] Lit. "the rising of the sun."

[7] Lit. "its setting."

[8] The term *^cqrt* is defined by Luwian *ka-ru-na-zi* "granaries, storehouses." Lipiński has attempted to link *^cqrt* with Akk. *ekurru/ekurrāt* (1974:47). See Röllig 1999:58.

[9] Pahar (Pahri in Assyrian sources) is probably to be located at Misis (classical Mopsuestia). See also Röllig 1999:58.

[10] Lit. "made." For the meaning of acquire, see Greenfield 1966:103-105 and *DNWSI* 926.

[11] On the term *ʾlm* see Younger 1998:28-31. See also Röllig 1999:59.

[12] Gevirtz understood *wšbrt mlṣm* to mean "and the assembly of the (divine) intermediaries" (1990:145-158). But the Luwian text clearly has a verbal clause in the place where *wšbrt mlṣm* occurs. Thus, it should be read as a verbal clause: "and I smashed the rebels." See Röllig 1999:59.

[13] See Younger 1998:15, note 26, and also *DNWSI* 1233-1234.

[14] The meaning is uncertain. See Bron 1979:60-62.

[15] See *DNWSI* 381; Bron 1979:64; and Röllig 1999:59.

[16] See Müller 1985:642.

[17] Ibid. See also Vanschoonwinkel 1990:185-211.

[18] Greenfield points out that the nuance of the figure is "to subjugate," or even closer to the idea "to conquer" (1971:253-268). Cp. Tukulti-Ninurta I's treatment of the captured Babylonian king Kaštiliaš: "I trod with my feet upon his lordly neck as though it were a footstool. Bound I brought him as a captive into the presence of Aššur, my lord" (*RIMA* 1:245).

[19] For the *nm* suffix as prospective, see Pardee 1987:140.

[20] Cf. the use of *^cnh* in the Mesha inscription with reference to Omri's oppression of Moab. See *COS* 2.23.

[21] The HL seems to support understanding the Phoen. conjunction in the sense of "even." Cf. also Gibson *SSI* 3:59.

[22] See Younger 1998:32-33.

Building the city and cultic innovations (ii.9–iii.2)
And I built this city.
And I gave it the name[23] [i] Azatiwadaya,[24]
since Ba^cal[25] and Resheph of the stags[26] commissioned me to build.
So I built it,
by the grace of Baᶜal and by the grace of Resheph of the stags,
in abundance and in luxury and good living and in ease of heart,
that it might be a guard (outpost) for the Plain of Adana and for the house of Mopsos.
since in my days there was for the land of the Plain of Adana abundance and luxury.[j]
And there was never any night for the Danunians in my days.[27]

And I built this city.
And I gave it the name Azatiwadaya.
I settled in it Baᶜal KRNTRYŠ.
Now all the river-land[28] shall offer a sacrifice to him:
a yearly sacrifice:[29] an ox;
and at the time of plowing: a sheep;
and at the time of reaping/harvesting: a sheep.

Closing: blessings and curses (iii.2–iv.3)
Blessings (iii.2-11)
Now may Baᶜal KRNTRYŠ bless[30] [k] Azatiwada[31]
with life and health,[l]
and mighty strength over every king;

may Baᶜal KRNTRYŠ and all the gods of the city give Azatiwada
length of days[m] and multitude of years and good prosperity,[32]
and mighty strength over every king.

And may this city be a possessor of grain and wine;[n]
and may this people who dwell in it be possessors of herds and possessors of flocks and possessors of grain and wine.

And may they immeasurably bear children;
and may they immeasurably become mighty;
and may they immeasurably serve Azatiwada and the house of Mopsos,
by the grace of Baᶜal and the gods.

Curses (iii.12–iv.1)
Now if a king among kings or a prince among princes,
if a man, who is a man of renown,[33] [o]
who shall erase the name of Azatiwada from this gate,
and shall place (his) name (on it) —

if indeed he shall covet this city,
and shall tear away this gate, which Azatiwada has made,
or shall make for himself a different gate,
and place (his) name on it —
if from covetousness he shall tear (it) away —
if from hate or from evil he shall tear away this gate —

then shall Baᶜal Shamem and El, creator of the earth,[34] [p] and Shemesh, the eternal, and the whole group of the children of the gods erase that kingdom, and that king, and that man who is a man of renown.[o]

Climactic invocation (IV.2-3)
Only may the name of Azatiwada be forever like the name of the sun and the moon![35] [q]

i Judg 8:31; Neh 9:7
j Ps 103:5
k Ps 29:11
l Mal 2:5; Prov 3:2
m Deut30:20; Ps 21:5; Prov 3:2
n Prov 3:10
o Gen 6:4
p Gen 14:19
q Pss 72:5, 17; 89:37-38

---

[23] For the idiom "to place a name," see Bron 1979:87.
[24] Based on the HL "Azatiwataya." See Röllig 1999:59-60. For a similar episode, cf. Ninurta-kudurrī-uṣur (*COS* 2.115B, lines iii.1′-22a′).
[25] Baᶜal = Tarhunzas.
[26] Phoen. *ṣprm* has been defined either as "he-goats" or "birds." Bron 1979:88, 185 and Müller 1985:643 favor the latter; Hawkins 1995:1300, Weippert 1969:200-210, the former. Garbini 1992:93-94 has proposed: "Rešeph of the talon." Amadasi Guzzo and Archi argue on the basis of the equivalence of ᵈKAL and *ršp ṣprm* that the graphical representation in the HL of a deer makes "stag" a superior definition to "bird" (1980:101).
[27] *DNWSI* 577-578, s.v. ll_2. For *mtm* see Röllig 1999:60.
[28] The Phoen. reads "Now all the river-land shall offer a sacrifice to him." The HL: "And every river-land will begin to honor him." For a full discussion see Younger 1998:36-40 and also Röllig 1995:206-208; 1999:60.
[29] See Younger 1998:19.
[30] Cf. Yeḥawmilk (*KAI* #10.8-10). See *COS* 2.32 below.
[31] For the blessings' structure, see Barré 1982:177-194 and Younger 1998:47.
[32] Various meanings for the Phoen. *ršʾt* have been proposed: (1) "authority," "rule" (Greenfield 1991a:145); (2) "old age" (Bron 1975:545-546; 1979:105-106; Barré 1981:1-3; Röllig 1999:60); (3) "property" (Müller 1985:644, n. 6a). and (4) "abundance, prosperity" (Morpurgo Davies and Hawkins 1987:272-275). see Younger 1998:40-41.
[33] Röllig (1999:60) suggests that the phrase *ʾdm ʾš ʾdm šm* may be understood as "a man who is (just) called a man" i.e. an ordinary human being without title of any sort (cf. *DNWSI* 1157 sub 3).
[34] *KAI* 1:25 (no. 129. 1): *lʾl qn ʾrṣ*.
[35] See Greenfield 1971:266-268; Röllig 1999:61.

REFERENCES

Text: Text: Phoen.: Röllig 1999:50-57; Bron 1979:8-25; *KAI* #26, 1:5; *SSI* 3:41-64; HL: Hawkins 2000; Meriggi 1967:69-103; Marazzi 1990:365-367. Studies: Amadasi Guzzo and Archi 1980; Amadasi Guzzo 1984; Barré 1981; 1982; Bron 1975:545-546; 1979; Garbini 1992; Gevirtz 1990; Greenfield 1971; 1972; 1991a; Greenstein 1995:2428-2432; Hawkins 1995; Lipiński 1974; Morpurgo Davies and Hawkins 1987; Müller 1985; Pardee 1987; Weippert 1969; Younger 1998.

THE INSCRIPTION OF KING YEḤAWMILK (2.32)

Stanislav Segert

The limestone stele measuring 113 x 56 x 24 cm was found in 1869 by a local planter of trees in the ruins of the ancient sanctuary of the Mistress of Byblos/Gubal. The missing lower right part was discovered much later at the excavation conducted by Maurice Dunand and published by him in 1939. On the upper part of the stele the goddess Baalat/Mistress of Byblos is depicted, sitting on a small throne, clothed in Egyptian style with winged sun on her head, holding a long sceptre in one hand and blessing with the other hand king Yeḥawmilk, who is offering her a large cup. The Persian style of clothing of the bearded king corresponds to the date of the inscription, 5th or 4th century BCE. Some parts of the inscription are damaged. The stele with the inscription is kept in the Louvre Museum in Paris.

Introduction of the king (lines 1-2a)
I am Yeḥawmilk,[1] king of Byblos/Gubal,[2]
son of Yeḥarbaal,[3]
son of son[a] / grandson of Urimilk,[4] king of Byblos/Gubal,
whom the Lady, Baalat/Mistress[5] of Byblos/Gubal made[b] king upon Byblos/Gubal.

King gratefully offered art works to the goddess of Byblos/Gubal (lines 2b-8a)
And I called [c] my Lady, Baalat/Mistress of Byblos/Gubal, [and] she heard my voice.[d]
And I made for my Lady, Baalat/Mistress of Byblos/Gubal
this altar of bronze,[6] [e] which is in this [court-yard],[f]
and this opening/engraving[7] [g] of gold,
which(is) opposite to this opening/engraving of mine,[8]
and this winged (disk)[9] of gold,
which (is) in the midst of the stone,
which (is) above this opening/engraving of gold,
and this portico and its columns.[10] [h]

a Prov 13:22
b 2 Chr 1:9
c Pss 120:1; 3:5
d 2 Sam 22:7; Jonah 2:3
e Gen 35:37; 1 Chr 21:22, 26; Exod 38:30; 2 Kgs 16:14; 2 Chr 4:1
f Exod 27:9; Jer 36:10
g 1 Kgs 6:31-35; Num 3:25-26; Ezek 8:7, 16; 41:20; 2 Chr 2:6(7), 13(14); Zech 3:9
h 1 Kgs 7:6, 18, 21
i 1 Kgs 7:16-20, 22
j 1 Kgs 6:15
k Ps 90:17
l Gen 28:3; Ps 67:7
m Pss 1:3(2); 143:11
n 1 Kgs 3:14
o Jer 37:2

and the capitals [11] [i] which (are) upon them,
and its roof.[j]
I, Yeḥawmilk, king of Byblos/Gubal, made (it) for my Lady, Baalat/Mistress of Byblos/Gubal,
as I called by lady, Baalat/Mistress of Byblos/Gubal,
and she heard my voice,
and made agreeableness[12] [k] to me.

Request of blessing for the king (lines 8b-11a)
May the Mistress of Byblos/Gubal bless[l] Yeḥawmilk, king of Byblos/Gubal,
may she keep him alive,[m]
and may she prolong his days and his years[13] [n] upon Byblos/Gubal,
for he (is) a righteous[14] king.
And may [the Lady], Mistress of Byblos/Gubal give [him] favor in the eyes of gods,
and in the eyes of the people of this land,[o]
and favor of the people of this land.[15]

The king's work has to be protected (lines 11b-18)
[Whoever you (are)],[16] every king and/or every

[1] The name *yḥwmlk* is formed with the factitive verbal pattern, "may the (divine) King keep alive." A similar name is attested in the Hebrew Bible (2 Chr 29:14); it is written in the text as *yḥwʾl*, but in the Masoretic note *w* is replaced by *y* and read *yᵉḥîʾēl*, "may he live, O God!" (or: "may El live"). Cf. Benz 1972:308.

[2] Cf. Yaḥimilk, *COS* 2.29, note 3 above.

[3] The name *yḥrbᶜl* can be interpreted differently, the most probable meaning is "may Baal liberate"; cf. Hebrew *ḥōr* "noble" (< "free"), Arabic *ḥ-r-r* II "to liberate."

[4] The name *ʾrmlk* can be reconstructed with the help of Assyrian cuneiform ú-ru-mil-ki as ʾūrumilk. The meaning is "King (is) my light," cf. Heb. *ʾûrîʾel* and *ʾōr/ʾûr* "light." Cf. Benz 1972:274.

[5] Cf. Yaḥimilk, *COS* 2.29, note 7 above.

[6] Stone altars from Megiddo and from Khorsabad (?) are presented in *ANEP* numbers 575 and 580. A bronze altar is mentioned in Exod 38:30.

[7] The object of gold is called *ptḥ*. This word can mean "opening," "entrance," "gateway" (Gibson), "door." The other possible interpretation points to Heb. *pittū(a)ḥ* "carved ornament," "engraving"; cf. Exod 28:11 and 36, both also concerning gold.

[8] Perhaps the king had his own entrance — cf. 2 Kgs 16:18 — or his image — cf. note 7 above.

[9] The noun *ᶜpt* is related to Heb. *ᶜwp* "to fly"; here it means "wing"; the winged sun disk is carved on the top of the stele.

[10] The word for "column" *ᶜmd* points to a portico or colonnade (*ᶜrpt*); cf. Bondi 1988:255-257.

[11] The damaged word is restored with help of Heb. *ktrt*; cf. 2 Kgs 25:17.

[12] This unusual word is used as an equivalent to *nᶜm* (cf. Heb. *nᶜm* Ps 90:17), as it indicates "pleasantness," "delight," and also suggests agreement, leading to peace.

[13] Cf. Yaḥimilk, *COS* 2.29, note 9 above.

[14] Cf. Yaḥimilk, *COS* 2.29, note 11 above.

[15] On this line words from the lines 10b-11a are exactly rendered, but it is possible that the scribe repeated the preceding formula, as he wanted to include the word for "favor" (*ḥn*).

[16] The words [*qnmy ʾt*] are restored according to the incription of Eshmunazar, king of Sidon, line 4; cf. Gibson, *SSI* 3:94, 97, 106-107; and Rosenthal, *ANET* 502. In *KAI* 10, line 11 (and in *GPP* 268) the gap is filled by [*wḥn lᶜn*] "and favor in the eyes," connecting it with the following *kl mmlkt* "(of) all kingdoms/kings."

(ordinary) man,[17]
who will do additional work on this altar
[and/or] this opening/engraving of gold
and/or on this portico,
my name, (that of mine), Yeḥawmilk, king of Byblos/Gubal,
[you must put with] yours on that work.
And if you will not put my name with yours,

p Micah 1:6
q Jer 49:10
r Jer 36:31; 22:28

and/or if you remove this work,
[and/or shif]t this [...][18] with its base upon/from[19] this place,
and (thus) uncover its foundation[p]/deposit[q](?),[20]
may the Lady, Mistress/Baalat of Byblos/Gubal putrefy[21] [him], that man and his seed,[r]
at the face of all gods[22] of By[blos]/Gu[bal].

[17] The word ᵓdm indicates an ordinary man in contrast to *mmlkt* "royalty," "king."

[18] The lower part of the inscription is badly damaged. Perhaps some word indicating "pillar" was in the gap.

[19] The preposition ᶜ*lt* means usually "upon," but after a verb of removing it can also indicate this movement, "from."

[20] Uncover the hidden foundation means to destroy the building which is above; cf. Micah 1:6. Uncovering precious things is mentioned in Isa 45:3, uncovering persons who are hiding in Jer 49:10. In this inscription most probably a foundation deposit is meant (cf. *KAI* 15), such as that found in 1926.

[21] The translation of *tsrḥ[w]* is based on post-biblical Hebrew; cf. "rotten name" *šm šrḥ* (to be read instead of *-h*) in Wis 42:11. The root *srḥ* in Syriac indicates mostly cutting in pieces. Either of these interpretation means "to destroy."

[22] Cf. Yaḥimilk, *COS* 2.29, note 12 above.

REFERENCES

Text: *CIS* I:#1; *KAI* #10; 2:11-15. *SSI* 3:93-99; Translations and studies: *ANET* 656. *ANEP* #477 (305). Moscati 1988:305.

6. OLD ARAMAIC INSCRIPTIONS

THE MELQART STELA (2.33)

Wayne T. Pitard

This short dedicatory inscription (four lines, with one letter on a fifth) is carved on the lower part of a basalt stela found in the late 1930's. It had been incorporated into a Roman period wall in the village of Bureij, near Aleppo, Syria. The text is surmounted by a relief of the god Melqart, who strides forcefully to the left carrying a fenestrated axe over one shoulder and an Egyptian ᶜ*ankh* in his right hand. Although the inscription is in Aramaic, the relief is Phoenician in style. The most significant controversy about the text centers on the identity of the donor, Bir-Hadad, the king of Aram. Earlier readings of the damaged name of Bir-Hadad's father on line 2 led scholars to identify Bir-Hadad with one of the kings of Aram-Damascus who had that name (cf. 1 Kgs 15:18; 2 Kgs 8:7-15; 13:24-25, where Ben-Hadad is the Hebrew rendering of the name). More recent studies of the line, however, have cast doubt on a relationship of this Bir-Hadad to Damascus. Many scholars now argue that he was the ruler of an area in northern Syria, perhaps Arpad. The script suggests that the stela dates to the second half of the ninth or early eighth century.

The stela[a] which Bir-Hadad[1] the son of Attar-

a Gen 28:18; 31:13; 35:14; Isa 19:19 b Gen 15:2, 8; Isa 7:7; Ezek 2:4; passim

hamek,[2] [ ] king of Aram[3], set up for his lord[b]

[1] This name means, "Son of (the god) Hadad." It is attested as a royal name in ninth and eighth century Aram Damascus. Names of the type Bir-DN are well attested in Aram. onomastics (Pitard 1988:18, n. 12).

[2] The left half of line 2, which includes the name of Bir-Hadad's father, is the poorest preserved part of the inscription. Numerous proposals for reading the name have been published over the years, including: Tab-Rimmon (Albright 1942; cf. 1 Kgs 15:18); Ezer the Damascene (Cross 1972); Ezer-Shamash (Lipinski 1975a); Hezion (Lemaire 1984a). Recent studies (Pitard 1988, Fitzmyer and Kaufman 1992, and Puech 1992) have supported a reading of Attar-hmk (ᶜ*trhmk*) or a closely related, ᶜ*trsmk*. Reading the fourth letter as an *s*, instead of an *h*, produces the name of Attar-sumki, a well-known king of the important north Syrian state of Arpad during the late ninth century. It is, then, tempting to identify the donor of this stela as Attar-sumki's son and successor. However, the surviving traces of the letter on the stone are more likely those of an *h* (Pitard 1988:6, 12). The verbal element, *hmk*, is ambiguous, but likely means "to subdue." Thus the name may mean, "(The god) Attar has subdued (his enemies)."

There is also controversy about what, if anything, follows the name Attar-hmk on the last third of line 2. Proposals for reading this section have been overwhelmingly divergent. This points to the fact that there is so little evidence for letters on that stone that it is best to conclude that either the traces of further words on the line have been entirely effaced, or that the latter part of the line was simply left blank by the scribe (Pitard 1988:7). See most recently Puech (1992:319), who lists earlier proposals and suggests reading "son of Attar-sumki, son of Hadrame."

[3] The term Aram was used to designate a number of states in Syria-Palestine and Mesopotamia during the first millennium. The Hebrew Bible often uses it to designate the state of Aram-Damascus, but also calls Aram-Zobah simply Aram. The Sefire inscription uses the term to designate the kingdom of Arpad. The Assyrians designated part of northern Syria as Aram during the tenth and ninth centuries, but by the mid-eighth

Melqart[4], to whom he made a vow[c] and who heard his voice.[d]

c Gen 31:13; Num 21:2-3; Judg 11:30-31; 2 Sam 15:7-8 *d* Deut 33:7; Josh 10:14; Ps 6:9; 27:7; 28:2, 6; 64:2

century they used the term to designate an area along the bank of the Tigris River. Thus its usage here is not a helpful indicator of the location of Bir-Hadad's kingdom.

[4] Melqart was the patron deity of the Phoen. city of Tyre, and he is not attested in any other Aram. inscription. His appearance on this stela in a decidedly Phoen. artistic style suggests that there was a substantial relationship between Bir-Hadad's kingdom and the Phoen. coast.

REFERENCES

Text: *KAI* #201, 2:203-204; *SSI* 2:1-4; Translations and Studies: *ANET* 655; Albright 1942; Bordreuil and Teixidor 1983; Cross 1972; Dunand 1939; Fitzmyer and Kaufman 1992; Lemaire 1984a; Lipinski 1975a; Pitard 1988; Puech 1992.

HADAD-YITHᶜI (2.34)

Alan Millard

In February 1979 a farmer uncovered a life-size basalt statue of a man at the edge of Tell Fekheriye on a branch of the Habur river, opposite Tell Halaf. The standing figure is carved in Assyrian style, without any emblems of rank. On the major part of his skirt are 38 ruled lines of Assyrian cuneiform script, set vertically (as on the Law-stele of Hammurabi), i.e. at right angles to the normal, while the back of the skirt carries 23 lines of Aramaic script engraved horizontally, with dots separating the words. There is now wide agreement that a date in the third quarter of the ninth century BCE is the most likely, taking together historical, stylistic, palaeographic and prosopographic features, as proposed by the original editors (Abou-Assaf, Bordreuil, Millard 1982), although a later date has been proposed on grounds of sculptural style by Spycket (1985) and an earlier one on the basis of the Aramaic script by Naveh (1987) and Cross (1995). This is the oldest lengthy Aramaic text published, bringing unexpected information on the early history of the Aramaic language; see Kaufman (1982), Muraoka (1984). It is also the only extensive bilingual Assyrian-Aramaic text and has stimulated many studies which cannot be cited here. The composition appears to be in two parts, the first (A) copied from a previous monument, the second (B) prepared for this statue. In A the Assyrian text is clearly primary, containing many stock phrases from the Assyrian scribal repertoire, of which the Aramaic is a fairly close translation, whereas B shows greater freedom, displaying linguistic equivalents rather than exact translation; see Fales (1983). Many terms in the Aramaic find parallels and echoes in biblical Hebrew, most extensively noted by Sasson (1985).

A *Identification*

The image of Hadad-yithᶜi[1] which he has set up [a] before Hadad[2] of Sikan,[3]
regulator of the waters of heaven and earth,
who rains down adundance,[b]
who gives pasture and watering-places to all lands,
who gives rest and vessels of food to all the gods, his brothers,
regulator of all rivers, who enriches[4] all lands,
the merciful god[c] to whom it is good to pray,
who dwells[d] in Sikan.

a Deut27:15; Judg 18:31; 2 Kgs 21:7 *b* 1 Kgs 3:13; Ps 65:9, 10 *c* Exod 34:6; Deut 4:31; Pss 86:15; 103:8 *d* 1 Sam 4:4; 2 Sam 6:2 = 1 Chr 13:6; 2 Kgs 19:15; Pss 2:4; 9:12; 99:1

[1] Hadad-yithᶜi's name means "Hadad is my salvation," incorporating the base *yšᶜ* seen in such biblical names as Joshua, Isaiah and Elisha. In this name as in certain other words in this text, the sibilant is written with *s* in place of the expected *š*, apparently a local peculiarity. The divine name Hadad is written *hd* here (but *hdd* where it stands alone), so may have been pronounced Had or Hadda.

[2] Hadad, the storm god, widely worshipped by the Aramaean tribes and attested in other cuneiform texts from Guzan (Sader 1987:11-13). The historical identification of this ruler depends upon that of his father; see note 7 below.

[3] Sikani, known from Assyrian texts, was evidently the ancient name for Tell Fekheriyeh, apparently also Wassukkanni of the second-millennium BCE Mitannian kingdom.

[4] "enriches" is a participial form from the base *ᶜdn*, denoting "pleasure, luxury" in BH, now seen with the same connotation in Old Aram. This cognate strengthens the case for deriving the name of the Garden of Eden from the same base, rather than from a Sum. word supposedly borrowed into Heb. (see Millard 1984). The epithets of Hadad here express his particular role, widely attested in cuneiform texts, one which biblical writers attribute to the God of Israel, e.g. Ps 65:9, 10; Isa 41:17-19.

Dedication

To the great god, his lord, Hadad-yithᶜi,
king[5] of Guzan,[6] [e] son of Sâs-nūrī,[7]
king of Guzan, set up and gave (the statue) to him,
so that his soul may live, and his days be long,
and to increase his years,[f]
and so that his house may flourish, and his descendants may flourish, and his people may flourish,
and to remove illness from him,[g] and for making his prayer heard, and for accepting the words of his mouth.[h]

Blessing and curses

Now whoever afterwards, when it is in disrepair,[8] re-erects it, may he put my name on it,
but whoever erases my name from it and puts his name, may Hadad,
the hero,[j] be his adversary.[9]

B *Rededication*

The statue[10] of Hadad-yithᶜi, king of Guzan and of Sikan and of Azran,[11]
for exalting and continuing his throne,[12]
and for the length of his life
and so that his word might be pleasing to gods and to people,
this image he made better than before.
In the presence of Hadad who dwells in Sikan, the lord of Habur,[13] [k] he has set up his statue.

Curses

Whoever removes my name from the furnishings of the house of Hadad,[l] my lord,
may my lord Hadad not accept[m] his food and water[n] from his hand,
may my lady Sûl[14] not accept food and water from his hand.
When he sows, may he not reap,[15] [o]
and when he sows a thousand (measures) of barley,[16] may he take (only) a fraction[p] from it.[q]
Should one hundred ewes suckle a lamb, may it not be satisfied.
Should one hundred cows suckle a calf, may it not be satisfied.
Should one hundred women suckle a child, may it not be satisfied.[r]
Should one hundred women bake bread in an oven, may they not fill it.[s]
May his men glean barley from a refuse pit to eat.
May plague, the rod of Nergal,[17] not be cut off from his land.

e 2 Kgs 17:6; 18:11 = Isa 37:12; 1 Chr 5:26
f Prov 3:2
g Exod 23:25; Deut 7:15
h Prov 4:10; Ps 19:14
j Deut 10:17; Ps 24:8; Isa 9:6; 10:21; Jer 32:18
k 2 Kgs 17:6; 18:11; 1 Chr 5:26
l Ezra 5:14
m Exod 29:25; Num 5:25; Judg 13:23
n Gen 18:4, 5; Deut 23:4
o Mic 6:15
p Dan 5:22, 28
q Deut 28:38; Isa 5:10; Hag 1:6
r Isa 66:11
s Lev 26:26

[5] "king" (*mlk*) stands in the Aram. text where the Assyrian has "governor" (*šākin māti*). The best explanation takes each text as directed at a different audience, the former to the local people, whose ruler erected the statue, the latter to representatives of the Assyrian emperor whose vassal the local ruler was. The appellation of the same man as "king" in one text and "governor" in another illustrates an ancient attitude to such titles which may be reflected in the application of "king" to Belshazzar in Dan 5; 7:1; 8:1, denoting his actual, although not his titulary role, after his father, Nabonidus, the actual king, departed to Arabia.

[6] Guzan, modern Tall Halaf; for its history see Sader 1987:5-45.

[7] Sâs-nūrī, "Shamash is my light," the name of Hadad-yithᶜi's father, is written Shamash-nūrî in Akk., the Aram. presenting the abbreviated, spoken form of the divine name Shamash, with Assyrian sibilant shift, reflected later in the Babylonian form Sheshbazzar, Ezra 1:8, 11; 5:14, 16 (see Berger 1971). This ruler of Guzan has been identified with Shamash-nuri, the eponym for 866 BCE, thus giving a date for the statue of his son within the next quarter of a century; see Abou-Assaf, Bordreuil and Millard (1982:103-05).

[8] The Aram. verb *ybl* is understood as "to wither, fail" on the basis of biblical Hebrew *nbl*, with Pardee and Biggs (1984:254); other proposals relate it to *nbl* from *bly* "to wither, be old" or from *npl* "to fall down" (Kaufman 1982:166; Greenfield and Shaffer 1983:113; Fales 1983:246).

[9] "Adversary" is a term used for a prosecutor in a lawsuit; cf. Isa 50:8; Assyrian legal contracts often call on Hadad to act in this way should the contract be broken.

[10] The monument is termed *dmwtᵓ* "image" at two points and *ṣlm* "statue" at two others, both words clearly referring to the same stone figure. While remembering that Aram. and Heb. are not identical, this parallel use suggests no significant differences of meaning should be sought between the two cognate Heb. words used in a similar way in Gen 1:26, 27; 5:3.

[11] Azran, Assyrian *zarani*, is otherwise unknown.

[12] The meaning of the Aram. expression here is uncertain; the text reads *lᵓrmwrdt krsᵓh* parallel to Akk. *tiriṣ kussišu*, which should mean something like "to continue his throne," but as yet has found no generally accepted interpretation.

[13] Habur is the river on which Guzan was situated.

[14] Sûl is the wife of Hadad, known as Shala in Babylonian; the unique Aram. writing here (*swl*) suggests her name was pronounced Sawl, Sôl, or Sûl. The use of *w* to mark *ô* ,or *û*, or possibly the diphthong *aw*, as well as *y* for *î* is one of the novelties of the text (see Muraoka 1984:83-87).

[15] This and the following "futility" curses follow the pattern "maximum effort — minimum return" (Fales 1982a) and have clear echoes in Aram. (Treaty of Sefire *COS* 2.82 below) and biblical texts, leading to the supposition that they have a WS origin; see Fales (1982a), Greenfield and Shaffer (1983:110), Pardee and Biggs (1984). But this may be contested (Millard 1993a:521-522).

[16] The word "barley" is written *šᶜryn* which some have linked with a unique biblical Heb. word written in the same way in Gen 26:12, thought to be a measure, but it is more reasonable to interpret it as "barley" here (written *šᶜrn* a few lines later), the actual measure being omitted as in Ruth 3:15; see Greenfield and Shaffer (1983:115), Sasson (1985:100 n. 13), Millard (1993a:523).

[17] Nergal, the Mesopotamian god of plague.

REFERENCES

Text: Abou Assaf, Bordreuil and Millard 1982; Translations and studies: *TUAT* 634-637; Berger 1971; Cross 1995; Fales 1982a; 1983; Greenfield and Shaffer 1983; 1985; Gropp and Lewis 1985; Kaufman 1982; Millard 1984; 1993a; Millard and Bordreuil 1982; Muraoka 1984; Naveh 1987; Pardee and Biggs 1984; Sader 1987; Sasson 1985; Spycket 1985.

THE INSCRIPTION OF ZAKKUR, KING OF HAMATH (2.35)

Alan Millard

H. Pognon bought parts of a basalt stele in north Syria which he published in 1907-8; they are now in the Louvre (AO 8185). Now 1.03 m. high, 62 cm. wide, the squared block was originally taller, the upper part carved with a figure in relief of which only the feet resting upon a dais or stool survive. Below the sculpture an inscription was engraved in Aramaic, starting on the front (A), continuing on the left (B) and right sides (C). This "memorial" text is damaged and incomplete. Circumstantial evidence points to a date shortly after 800 BCE.

Title (A line 1)
The monument which Zakkur,[1] [a] king of Hamath[2] [b] and Lu^{c}ash,[3] set up[c] for El-wer[4] [in Apish.[5]]

Record of divine rescue (A lines 1-17)
I am Zakkur, king of Hamath and Lu^{c}ash. I was a man of ^{c}Anah[6] and Ba^{c}lshamayn[d] [raised] me and stood beside me, and Ba^{c}lshamayn made me king over Hazrach.[e] Then Bar-Hadad,[f] son of Hazael,[g] king of Aram,[7] united against me s[even]teen kings[h]: Bar-Hadad and his army, Bar-Gush[8] and his army, the king of Que and his army, the king of ^{c}Amuq and his army, the king of Gurgum and his army, the king of Sam$^{\supset}$al and his army, the king of Meliz and his army [ ] seven[teen],[9] they and their armies. All these kings laid siege[i] to Hazrach. They raised a wall higher than the wall of Hazrach, they dug a ditch deeper than [its] ditch. Now I raised my hands[k] to Ba^{c}lshamayn and Ba^{c}lshamayn answered me.[l] Ba^{c}lshamayn [spoke] to me through seers and diviners.[10] [m] Ba^{c}lshamayn said to me, "Do not be afraid! Since I have made [you king, I will stand] beside you.[n] I will save you from[p] all [these kings who] have besieged you." [Ba^{c}lshamayn] also said to [me, "] all these kings who have [besieged you] and this wall [ ]."

Building inscription (B lines 1-15)
[ ] Hazrach [ ] for chariot [and] horseman[q] [ ] its king within it(?). I [built] Hazrach and added [to it] all [ ] defenses. [ ] and I put x x[ ] x x[ ] forts on every side. [I] built shrines in a[ll] my [land ?]. I built [ ]x Apish and [ ] the house [ ] and I set up this monument before [El-wer] and w[rote on] it my achi[evements].[r]

Curses (B lines 16-28, C 1,2)
[In future who]ever removes from this monument wha[t Zakkur king of Hamath [and Lu'ash] has [accomplished] and who[ever re]moves this monument from [befo]re El-wer and takes it away fr[om] its [place], or whoever throws it in [ ] x [ ] x [May Ba^{c}lshamayn and El[-wer[11]] and Shamash and Shahar [ ] and the gods of heav[en and the god]s of earth and Ba ^{c}lX[ ] x and x [ ] x x [ ] (C) [ ] the name of Zakkur and the name of [ ].

a Num 13:4; 1 Chr 4:26; 24:27; 25:2; 25:10; Neh 3:2; 10: 13; 12:35; 13:12; Ezra 8:14 *b* 2 Kgs 14:25, 28; Jer 49:23; Amos 6:2; Zech 9:2 *c* Gen 28:18, 22 *d* Zech 9:1 *e* 2 Kgs 13:3, 24 *f* 2 Kgs 13:3, 24 *g* 2 Kgs 8:7-15, 28, 29; 10:32; 13:22-25 *i* 1 Kgs 10:28 *h* 1 Kgs 20:1 *j* Mic 4:14 (5:1) *k* Ps 28:2 *l* Jon 2:3; cf. 2 Kgs 13:4, 5 *m* 1 Sam 9:6-9; 2 Sam 5:17-25; 1 Kgs 22:1-28 *n* Ps 91:15; Isa 41:9,10; 43:1; 44:2; 54:4,5; Jer 30:10 *p* Jer 1:8; 30:10, 11 *q* Exod 14:17 etc.; 1 Kgs 9:19; 2 Kgs 18:24 *r* 2 Sam 18:18

[1] The king's name, long read Zakir, is established by the Assyrian transcription ^{m}*za-ku-ri*, referring to the same ruler, on a stele defining the boundary between the states of Hamath and Arpad, found near Antakya. See Donbaz 1990:6-7, line 4. See *COS* 2.114A, note 5.

[2] A dynasty with Luwian (neo-Hittite) names ruled Hamath during the ninth century BCE; see Hawkins 1982, Sader 1987:185-230. Its frontier marked the northernmost limit of Israelite power (1 Kgs 8:65; 2 Kgs 14:25). For Aram. graffiti and seals found there, see Otzen 1990. The name is engraved in Aram. letters on an ivory label found at Nimrud, perhaps taken there as booty by Assyrian forces; see Millard 1962:42-43.

[3] Lu^{c}ash, earlier Nuhashshe, lay south-west of Aleppo. The name is engraved in Aram. letters on the back of a carved ivory found at Nimrud; cf. note 2 above.

[4] El-wer was a weather god known in east and north Syria; see Millard 1990:51. He is invoked in the Antakya stele mentioned in note 1 above.

[5] The name is restored on the basis of its later occurrence in the text and the likely provenance of the stele.

[6] For this rendering see Millard 1990 and note the writing of ^{c}Anah as ^{d}*ana*^{na} in an Assyrian legal document: Kwasman and Parpola 1991:198, 4.

[7] Aram at this time denoted the kingdom of Damascus.

[8] Gush, Agush, founded the Aramean dynasty Bit-Agush, based at Arpad (Tell Rifa'at) and faced Ashurnasirpal of Assyria about 877 BCE (Annals iii 77; Grayson 1976:143; 1991:218).

[9] While seven names are given, if seventeen is correct earlier, it can be accepted here; not all kings need have been named.

[10] The first word is cognate with Hebr. *ḥôzēh*, the second related to Hebr. PN ^{c}Oded (2 Chr 15:1, 8; 28:9) and known in Ug. Consulting diviners or oracles in crises was common throughout the Near East: see Greenfield 1971; Weippert 1981.

[11] For pairs of divine names see the Sefire Stelae 2.82 below.

REFERENCES

Text: *KAI* #202; *SSI* 2:6-17; Translations: *ANET* 501-502; *TUAT* 626-628; Studies: Donbaz 1990; Grayson 1976; 1991; Greenfield 1972; Hawkins 1982; Kwasman and Parpola 1991; Millard 1962; 1990; Otzen 1990; Sader 1987; Weippert 1981; Zobel 1971.

THE HADAD INSCRIPTION (2.36)

K. Lawson Younger, Jr.

Discovered in the village of Gerçin 7 km northeast of Zenjirli, dating to the mid-eighth century BCE, this large statue of the god Hadad contains a thirty-four line inscription on its lower portion. The statue originally stood about 4 m high, though the top portion is not preserved. It was erected by Panamuwa I, king of Yᵓdy (also known as Samᵓal) (see Dion 1997:99-105). The inscription, which is difficult due to poor preservation in a number of places, is written in Samalian Aramaic, the dialect of this north Syrian city-state (see Tropper 1993:287-296).

Introduction (line 1)
I am Panamuwa, son of Qarli,[1] king of Yᵓdy,
who have erected[2] this statue for Hadad in my eternal abode (i.e. "burial chamber").[3]

Panamuwa's divine authority and prosperous rule (lines 2-13a)
The gods Hadad and El and Rašap and Rakib-El and Šamaš supported me.
And Hadad and El and Rakib-El and Šamaš and Rašap[4] [a] gave the scepter of dominion[5] into my hands.

Rašap supported me.
So whatever I grasped with my hand,
[ ] (served?)
and whatever I asked from the gods,
they granted to me.
And the devastation(?) they restored.[6]
[ ]
[ ] a land of barley ...
[ ]
[... a l]and of wheat and a land of garlic [b] and a land of [ ] ...
Then [...]
And [...]
They cultivated the land and the vineyard.
They dwelt there [...].

And I, Panamuwa, reigned also on the throne of my father.
And Hadad gave into my hands a scepter of dominion.[7]
And I also cut of]f war and slander[8] from the house of my father.
And in my days also Yᵓdy ate and drank.[c]

And in my days it was commanded throughout al[l my lan]d to reconstruct ṬYRT[9] and to reconstruct ZRRY[10] and to build the villages[11] of the dominion.
And each one took his friend(?)[12]
And Hadad [and] El and Rakib-El and Šamaš and ᵓArqû-Rašap[13] gave abundance.[d]
And greatness was granted me.
And a sure covenant [e] was concluded with me.

And in the days when I gained dominion, a gift-offering(?)[14] was given to the gods;
[15]and they took the land from my hand.
and whatever I asked from the gods of the land, they gave to me.
And the gods of the land delighted[16] [in me, the son] of Qarli.

Hadad's commission (lines 13b-14)
Then Hadad gave the land for my [[17]];

a Deut32:24; Hab 3:5
b Deut 8:8
c 1 Kgs 4:20
d Ps 72:3-16
e Neh 10:1

[1] Vocalization is uncertain, though possibly *Qarli (based on a hieroglyphic Luwian form). See Lipiński 1994:204, n. 5.
[2] For the syntax of this clause see Segert, *AaG* 434; and Tropper 1993:255.
[3] Tawil (1974:42-43) and Gibson (*SSI* 2:65) translate *bᶜlmy* "from my youth." But see Tropper 1993:61, and *COS* 2.27 above p. 144, n. 1.
[4] Cf. this line 2b-3a: *wnt*n. bydy. hdd. ... ḥṭr. ḥlbbh.* and lines 8b-9a: *wntn. hdd. bydy*[.] [9]*ḥṭr ḥl*[*bbh*] below.
[5] Proposed meanings for *ḥlbbh* include: 1) "reign, rule" Dion 1974:88; Tropper 1993:62; 2) "succession" Fales 1982b:76-77; Greenfield 1987:69; Lipiński 1994:204; and 3) "blessing, prosperity" Sader 1987:163.
[6] See Tropper 1993:63-64. Tawil's translation "And they kept (me) alive for years" (1974:50) is very unlikely. See *DNWSI* 1177, s.v. *šnm*.
[7] See note 5 above.
[8] Lit., "sword and tongue."
[9] According to Tropper the epigraphically possible readings are: *ṭyrt* "the enclosures" and *ᶜyrt* "the cities" (1993:68-70).
[10] Uncertain meaning.
[11] See Dion 1997:254, n. 55.
[12] Or perhaps better in the context: "each one acquired his herd." See the discussion in Tropper 1993:70.
[13] For a discussion of this deity, see Lipiński 1983:15-21; 1994:210-211.
[14] The reading is uncertain. Tropper (1993:72) favors *mtn* "gift"; Lipiński (1994:204) favors *mt* "land."
[15-15] Alternatively: "and they indeed took from my hand. And whatever I asked from the gods, indeed they gave to me. And the gods truly delighted [in me, the son] of Qarli. Then Hadad indeed gave for my [ ]; he singled me out to build and during my dominion Hadad [ ] indeed gave me to build. So I have truly built."
The difference lies in the meaning of the difficult word *mt*. Three proposals have been made: 1) "always," linking *mt* with Mari Akk. **matay-ma* (Faber 1987); 2) "surely, indeed, truly," understanding an apheresis of the aleph, *ᵓ*mt* > *mt* (Tropper 1992); and 3) "land," a loan word from Akk. *mātu* (Lipiński 1976:232; 1977:100-101; 1994:204). There are difficulties with each proposal (see *DNWSI* 706-707 s.v. mt_1 and mt_6). None of them fits all the contexts where *mt* occurs in the Hadad and Panamuwa inscriptions. One cannot rule out the possibility that *mt* means "land," since it is now well-attested in OA inscriptions, though this meaning clearly does not fit the context of Panamuwa (*KAI* 215.4) or Hadad (*KAI* 214.28). But conversely, one cannot completely rule out apheresis of the aleph, though the evidence is hardly overwhelming in favor of it.
[16] *DNWSI* 1083 s.v. rqy_1 and Tropper 1993:74.
[17] Possibly read: *l*[*yr*]*ty* "for my [inherit]ance." See *DNWSI* 472 s.v. yrt_2; Lipiński 1994:204.

he singled me out to build,
and during my dominion Hadad [ ] gave me the land to build.
So I have built the land.[15]
And I have erected this statue of Hadad,
and the place of Panamuwa, son of Qarli, king of Y⁾dy, with the statue — a burial chamber.

Blessings (Lines 15b-18)
Whoever of my sons seizes the scepter,
and sits upon my throne,
and maintains power,[f]
and sacrifices to this Hadad,
[... an o]ath?
and sacrifices this [ ]
[ ] sacrifices to Hadad

Or, on the other hand, [ ]
then he says:
"May [the de]ad spirit[18] of Panamuwa [eat] with you (i.e. Hadad),
and may the dead spirit of Panamuwa dri[nk] with you."
May he remember eternally the dead spirit of Panamuwa with [Had]ad.[g]

[May he gi]ve this his sacri[fice to Hadad].
May he (i.e. Hadad) look favorably upon it;
May it be a tribute for Hadad and for El and for Rakib-El and Šamaš [and Rašap].

Reintroduction (lines 19-20a)[19]
I am Panamuwa [...] a hou[se for the go]ds of this city.
And [I built] it.
And I caused the gods to dwell in it.
And during my reign, I allotted [the gods] a resting place.
[And] they gave to me a seed of the bosom.[20]

Curses (Lines 20b-34)
[whoev]er of my sons seizes the scepter,
and sits on my throne,
and reigns over Y⁾[dy],
and maintains his power;
and sacri[fices to this Hadad],
[and does not remem]ber the name of Panamuwa,
(who) does (not) say:

f Isa 9:6; Prov 20:28

g Jer 16:5-9; Amos 6:4-7

h 1 Kgs 2; 16:11; 2 Kgs 10:6; 11:1; etc.

"May the dead spirit[21] of Pana[muwa] eat with Hadad,
and may the dead spirit of Panamuwa drink with H[adad];
[ ] his sacrifice
And may he (Hadad) not look favorably upon it,
and whatever he asks,
may Hadad not grant him;
And as for Hadad — may his wrath be poured out on him;[22]
[And] may he not give to him to eat because of (his) rage;
and may he withhold sleep from him in the night;
and may terror be given to him
And may he not [ ]
[ ] my kinsmen [or re]latives.

Whoever of my house seizes the scepter in Y⁾dy
and sits on my throne
and reig[ns in my place],
[May he not] stretch his hand with the sword against [ ] of my [hou]se[h] [either out of] anger or out of violence;
may he not do murder, either out of wrath or out of [ ];
And may no one be [put to death], either by his bow or by his word [or by his command].
But may [his kins]man plot the destruction[23] of one of his kinsmen or one of his relatives or one of his kinswomen.
[Or if any member of my house] should plot destruction;
may he (the king) assemble his male relatives,
and may he stand him in the middle.[24]

Indeed, he ("the accused") will pronounce his oath:
"Your brother has caused (my) destruction!"
If [he (i.e. "the accused") denies it, and] he lifts up his hands to the god of his father (i.e. Rakib-El),
and says on his oath:
"Behold, I have put these words in the mouth of a stranger!"
saying:
"May my eyes be fixed or troubled,
or [I have put] my commands in the mouth of the enemies' men!"

[18] For *nbš/npš* in this context, see Niehr 1994:63-65. *Nbš* appears to signify both "the dead spirit" of Panamuwa and, on the basis of the sense of a funerary monument, the cult image of the deceased king. Thus in the form of this cult image the dead spirit of Panamuwa could receive sacrifice (cf. the archaeological materials from Tel Halaf). Lines 15-18 indicate that when an offering was made before the statue of Hadad, both the god and the spirit of the deceased royal ancestor could receive the sacrifice. With the remembrance of the name "Panamuwa," blessing is invoked upon the descendant monarch. Cp. this ritual to the Mesop. *kispu* and the WS *marzeaḥ* (Greenfield 1973; 1987; Hallo 1992; 1996:209; Porten 1968:179-186). While nuances of royal ancestor worship are apparent, there are some distinctions (Niehr 1994:60-63; and Schmidt 1994:132-135).

[19] Cf. the double introduction in the Kulamuwa inscription above (2.30).

[20] The meaning of the phrase *zr*ᶜ *ḥb*⁾ is uncertain. See *DNWSI* 343 s.v. *ḥb*$_1$.

[21] See note 18 above. Lines 20-24 indicate that when an offering was placed before the statue of Hadad without a remembrance and offering to the spirit of the deceased royal ancestor (i.e. Panamuwa), Hadad would reject the offering and would bring a curse upon the offerer.

[22] See Tropper 1993:83.

[23] See *DNWSI* 1123 s.v. *šḥt*$_2$. There is a note of similarity at this point between the Hadad Inscription and the Hittite "Proclamation of Telipinu" with the interest in the shedding of royal blood and procedures given to deal with such. See *COS* 1.76.

[24] See Tropper 1993:89-90.

And if it is a male,
then may his male relatives be assembled,[25]
and may they pound him with stones; [i]
and if it is [a female],
then may her kinswomen be assembled,
and may they pound her with stones.[i]
But if indeed ruin (has struck) him himself,[26]
then your eyes should be weary of him,

i Lev 20:2; Deut 13:6-10; 17:5; 21:18-21; 22:13-21; Josh 7:25; 1 Kgs 12:18; 2 Chr 10:18; 24:21

either by his bow or by his power or by his words or by his instigation.[27]
you, then [ ] his right,
And [ ]
or you slay him in violence or in anger,
or you issue a decree against him,
or you incite a stranger to slay him,
may (the gods(?)) ... (slay?) ...

[25] For these clauses, see Huehnergard 1987:268-269.
[26] A very difficult sentence. See Tropper 1993:95.
[27] Or possibly "maneuvers." Quack points out a parallel in Sinuhe B 103-105 which states: "with my power, with my bow, with my maneuvers and with my capable plans."

REFERENCES

Text: *KAI* #214; Dion 1974:26-35; *SSI* 2:60-76; Tropper 1993:54-97. Studies: Faber 1987; Fales 1982b; Fitzmyer and Kaufman 1992:15-16; Greenfield 1973; 1987; Hallo 1992; Huehnergard 1983; 1987; Kaufman 1974; Klengel 1992; Lehmann 1994; Lipiński 1983; 1994:203-211; Niehr 1994; Quack 1993; Sader 1987:153-184; Schmidt 1994:132-135; Tawil 1973; 1974; Tropper 1993:54-97.

THE PANAMUWA INSCRIPTION (2.37)

K. Lawson Younger, Jr.

The inscription, engraved on the lower half of a statue, is written in Samalian Aramaic (see *COS* 2.36). It was discovered in the German excavations at Zinjirli. Bar-Rakib, the son of Panamuwa II, probably raised this monument early in his reign to memorialize his father because of his sudden and unexpected death during Tiglath-Pileser III's campaign against Damascus (733-732 BCE). The text also served Bar-Rakib's interests in that his legitimate right to rule is firmly established. Thus a date of 733-727 BCE is very probable for the inscription. The form of the Panamuwa inscription is that of the dedication genre although it has been modified and adapted for a human dedication. The statue was originally intended to be placed in front of the tomb of Panamuwa to serve as a memorial.[1] Elements of the memorial genre are also evident. Thus, these two genres have been incorporated in the composition.

Introduction (line 1)
This statue Bar-Rakib has set up for his father,
for Panamuwa, the son of Barṣūr, the king of Yᵓdy,
[in ...] the year [of his death(?)].

Body (lines 2-19a)
The Crisis (lines 2-6a)
My father, Panamuwa —
because of the loyalty of his father, the gods of Yᵓdy delivered him (i.e. Panamuwa) from the destruction[2]
which[3] was in the house of his father.
And the god Hadad stood with him.

a Judg 9:5; 2 Kgs 10:1-11

[ ] his throne against [ ].
And(?) he destroyed(?) [ ] in the house of his father.
And he killed his father Barṣūr;
and he killed seventy brothers of his father.[4] [a]
But my father mounted a chariot[5] ...
and [ ] lord [ ]
And(?) he pierced [ ] Panamuwa(?)
And (with) the rest of it[6] he indeed[7] filled the prisons.
And he made ruined cities more numerous than inhabited cities.
And it gave (?) [Panamuwa], son of Q[ar]li, (and

[1] In some way the statue was connected to the cult of the royal ancestors. See Niehr 1994:67-68 and also Greenfield 1973. Cf. Absalom's actions in 2 Sam. 18:18.
[2] See *DNWSI* 1123 s.v. *šḥt*$_2$. Cp. the opening to the Idrimi Inscription (*COS* 1.148). See Younger 1986:96.
[3] For the reading *ᵓzh*, see Tropper 1993:104 and plate 13. Others have read *ᵓlh* with the meaning of either "curse" or "conspiracy." But the second sign in Tropper's photograph clearly reads *z* and not *l*.
[4] Cf. the story of Abimelech's murder of his seventy brothers (Judg 9:5) and the execution of the seventy sons of Ahab (2 Kgs 10:1-11). See Fensham 1977.
[5] Cp. Idrimi's departure from Emar (see *COS* 1.148). This clause suggests the motif of the departure of the hero with only his essential equipment or personnel, after which he passes through alien territory and eventually assumes the throne. See Parker 1997:162, n. 34.
[6] i.e. "the house of his father."
[7] See *COS* 2.36 note 15-15 above for a discussion of the term *mt*. It seems doubtful for syntactic reasons that *mt* means "land" in this context (as proposed by Lipiński 1994:204). See Tropper 1992:448-453.

he spoke?) ...
"And if[8] you cause bloodshed[9] in my house,
and you also kill one of my sons,
then I also will make bloodshed in the land of Y°dy." [b]
Then [[10]] Panamuwa, son of Qa[r]li[11] ...

My father Panam<uwa>, son of Barṣūr(?), [he?] destroyed(?) in the la[nd][12]
[ ] ewe and cow and wheat and barley.
And a *parīs*[13] stood at a shekel; [c]
and a STRB-(measure) [of onions(?)/wine(?)[14]] at a shekel;
and two-thirds of a mina[15] of oil at a shekel.

The Restoration (lines 6b-11a)
Then my father, Pana[muwa, son of Ba]rṣūr, brought a gift[16] [d] to the king of Assyria.[17] [e]
And he made him king over the house of his father.
And he killed the stone of destruction[f] from the house of his father.

And ... (away) from the treasuries of houses of the land of Y°dy from ....
[ ]
And he opened[18] the prisons;
and he released the captives of Y°dy.

So my father arose,
and released the women in [ ].
[ ] the house of the women who had died,

b 2 Chr 21:12
c 2 Kgs 6:24-7:2
d Isa 18:7; Pss 68:30; 76:12
e 1 Kgs 15:17-22; 2 Kgs 16:5-9; 2 Kgs 6:24-7:20; 2 Sam 10:6; Deut 23:5b-6
f Isa 8:14
g 1 Kgs 10:27
h 1 Sam 8:11; 2 Sam 15:1; 1 Kgs 1:5

and he buried(?)[19] them(?) in ...
[and he seized(?)] the house (i.e., the palace) of his father.
And he made it better than before.
And it abounded with wheat and barley and ewe and cow in his days.
And then [the land[20]] ate [and drank ...]
The price was cheap.[21] [g]

And in the days of my father Panamuwa, he truly[22] appointed lords of villages and lords of chariots.
And my father Panamuwa was esteemed in the midst of mighty kings [from the east to the west].
[ ] my father surely possessed silver;
and surely he possessed gold.[23]
On account of of his wisdom and because of his loyalty, he then seized onto the skirt (robe)[24] of his lord, the mighty king of Assyria.

Panamuwa's Vassalship (lines 11b-19a)
[ ] of Assyria.
Then he lived
and Y°dy also lived.
And his lord, the king of Assyria, positioned him over powerful kings [as the head(?)].[25]
[ ]
[And he ran] at the wheel of his lord,[26] [h] Tiglath-Pileser, king of Assyria, (in) campaigns from the east to the west [and from the north to the south, over] the four quarters of the earth.

[8] Tropper reads *whnw* "and if" (1993:267).

[9] Lit., "set a sword."

[10] Dion restores *ḥl[y š]°l* "Panamuwa asked (vengeance for) those who had been killed" (1974:37).

[11] Some scholars restore: °*[b°b]* "my great-grandfather." See *KAI* 2:226; Dion 1974:37; *SSI* 2:78. For Qarli, see *COS* 2.36, note 1.

[12] Parker translates "(they) fled from the land" (1997:84 and n. 37).

[13] A small dry measurement ≈ a *se°ah* or perhaps less (≈ 7 quarters, 7.3 liters). For *parīs*, see Kaufman 1974:80.

[14] Tropper (1993:111) reads: *šmw* "onions." Greenfield states: "To judge from the Hieroglyphic Luwian material assembled by Hawkins (Hawkins 1986) a word for wine is needed here, since the *kaf* is doubtful, perhaps one should restore *ḥmr*" (Greenfield 1991:122, n. 7).

[15] Tropper argues for a reading of *snb* (without the ° at the beginning of the word) (1993:111). The term *snb* occurs on a lion-weight from Nineveh with the meaning of ⅔ of a mina. The comparative material makes the reading of *mšḥ* "oil" sure.

[16] Panamuwa must have brought tribute to Tiglath-Pileser III to gain his help. Tropper suggests reading *šy* "gift" (1993:112).

[17] Parker (1997:89-104) adeptly compares the story of Panamuwa II to the biblical accounts of Asa (1 Kgs 15:17-22), Ahaz (2 Kgs 16:5-9), the siege of Samaria (2 Kgs 6:24-7:20), as well as 2 Sam 10:6; Deut 23:5b-6.

[18] So Tropper 1993:114. Or alternatively "destroyed" through an Akk. root *pasāsu* "to destroy" (Lipiński 1977:102).

[19] Tropper 1993:115. Formerly read: *qnw°l*.

[20] Reading uncertain (Tropper 1993:115). Dion restores °*rq y°dy* (1974:37). Cp. Hadad 9: *wbymy gm °bl wšt° y°dy*.

[21] Concerning the motif of "ideal prices" in Panamuwa's day as compared to the previous depressionary conditions in Y°dy, see Hawkins 1986:93-102; Younger 1986:96-98; and Greenfield 1991:122.

[22] See *COS* 2.36, note 15-15. Lipiński (1994:205) translates: "he provided the land with chiefs of villages and chiefs of carting" or "he made the land proprietors of villages and proprietors of carting."

[23] There are two options for the understanding of *lw*: 1) it is an asseverative particle so that the translation is: "my father surely possessed silver; and surely he possessed gold." See Dion 1978:298-300; Tropper 1993:118; and 2) it is a concessive particle so that the translation is: "my father, though he were a possessor of silver, though a possessor of gold." See Gibson, *SSI* 2:81; Huehnergard 1983:571. The context seems, in my opinion, to argue for the former.

[24] The idiom "to grasp the hem (of a garment)" has been identified in Akk. (*sisikta(m) ṣabātu(m)*), Old Aram. (°*ḥz bknp*), BH (*hḥzyq bknp*: 1 Sam 15:27), and Ug. (°*ḫd bs°n*). It is derived from a gesture in which a suppliant beseeches, or indicates his submission to, his superior by grasping the hem of the superior's garment. Used alone, the locution serves to denote "supplication, importuning, submission to a superior." It establishes a closer relationship between suppliant and superior, especially between vassal and suzerain. See Greenstein 1982; Younger 1986:98, n. 31; and *COS* 2.137, note 4.

[25] A reading of *bmšn* "as vice-regent" has been suggested by Lipiński 1977:103. Tropper argues that the reading is epigraphically impossible (1993:120).

[26] Vassal kings were often obligated to participate with the Assyrian king in his campaigns (see Dion 1997:262; Na°aman 1991). Cf. Bar-Rakib 1:8-7. Cp. 1 Sam 8:11; 2 Sam 15:1; 1 Kgs 1:5.

And the population[27] of the east he brought to the west;
and the population of the west he brought to the east.
And [my] father [profited more than all other mighty kings][28]
And [to] his territory his lord Tiglath-Pileser, king of Assyria, [added] cities from the territory of Gurgum[29] and ...[30]
[And] my [fa]ther Panamuwa, son of Ba[rṣūr ...]
[[31]]
And my father, Panamuwa, died while following[32] his lord Tiglath-Pileser, king of Assyria, in the campaigns.
Even [his lord, Tiglath-Pileser, king of Assyria, wept for him;][33]
and his relative kings wept for him;
and all of the camp of his lord, the king of Assyria, wept for him.
And his lord, the king of Assyria, took [ ]
["may] his dead spirit [eat and drink."][34]
And he set up for him a memorial in the way.
And he brought my father from Damascus to Assyria.

i 2 Sam 18:18
j Judg 9:9, 13

In my days [...]
[And] his whole house we[pt] for him.

Conclusion (lines 19b-23)
And I am Bar-Rakib, son of Panamuwa.
Because of the loyalty of my father and because of my loyalty, my lord [Tiglath-Pileser, king of Assyria,] has caused me to reign [on the throne] of my father, Panamuwa, son of Barsur.

And I have set up this statue [to my father], to Panamuwa, son of Barṣūr.
And ?

And [[35]]
And [ ] the king [ ][36]
And [[37]] before the tomb of my father, Panammu[wa].

And this memorial is it.[i]
Thus, may Hadad and El and Rakib-El, the lord of the house, and Šamaš, and all the gods of Yʾdy [have favor on me the son of Panamuwa].[38]
[And may Rakib-El show favor][39] to me before gods and before men.[j]

[27] Lit., "the daughters."
[28] Tropper's suggested restoration based on Bar-Rakib 7-8.
[29] Gurgum's border was changed earlier by the Assyrians. See the Pazarcık Inscription, *COS* 2.114B and *RIMA* 3:201-205. See Dalley 1995:421.
[30] Tropper suggests [*wmn. q*]*wh* "[from the territory of Q]ue(?)" (1993:123).
[31] Concerning the possible meanings of a verb *mrg*, see the discussion of Tropper 1993:123-124.
[32] *lgry* is a metathesis of *rgl* (Friedrich 1951:162).
[33] For this restoration see Gibson *SSI* 2:80; and Dion 1974:206.
[34] Two possible restorations: 1) [*tʾkl. wtšt*][18]*y. nbšh.* "[may] his soul [eat and drink]" (Gibson *SSI* 2:80-81); or 2) [*whʾkl. whšq*][18]*y. nbšh.* "[and he caused/permitted] his soul [to eat and drink]" (Tropper 1993:125).
[35] Tropper suggests: "a lamb in the roasting position(?)" (1993:129-130).
[36] Tropper suggests: *wʿl. ybl. ʾmn. ys*m*k*. mlk*[*. ydyh*]. "And [upon a certain/reliable ram(?)] the king [should support(?) [his hands](?)" (1993:130).
[37] Tropper suggests restoring: "he should send out a ram (?)" (1993:130).
[38] Restored on the basis of Hadad 13. See Tropper 1993:130.
[39] Restored on the basis of Bar-Rakib 2:7-9. See Tropper 1993:131.

REFERENCES

Text: Tropper 1993:98-139; *KAI* #215; *SSI* 2:76-86. Translations and studies: *TUAT* 1/6:628-630; Dalley 1995; Dion 1974; 1978; Faber 1987; Fensham 1977; Fitzmyer and Kaufman 1992:16-17; Friedrich 1951; Friedrich and Röllig 1970; Greenfield 1991b; Greenstein 1982; Hawkins 1986; Huehnergard 1983; Lipiński 1977; Tropper 1992; 1993:98-139; Younger 1986:91-100.

THE BAR-RAKIB INSCRIPTION (2.38)

K. Lawson Younger, Jr.

Composed not long after the Panamuwa inscription (i.e. 733-727 BCE), the Bar-Rakib inscription was written in an Old Aramaic dialect which as been identified as "Mesopotamian Aramaic."[1] Its form is that of the memorial genre, though the emphasis is on Bar-Rakib's vassal loyalty to Tiglath-Pileser III of Assyria.[2] The inscription was discovered in excavations conducted at Zenjirli (cf. *COS* 2.36, 2.37, and especially 2.37).

[1] Greenfield 1978:95. There are eight inscriptions attributable to Bar-Rakib.
[2] The absence of a curse is "rather surprising." See Miller 1974:10, n. 6.

Introduction (lines 1-4a)
I am Bar-Rakib, son of Panamuwa, king of Samᵓal,
the servant of Tiglath-Pileser (III), lord of the four quarters of the earth.

The Accession (lines 4b-7a)
On account of the loyalty of my father and on account of my loyalty,
my lord, Rakib-El,[3] and my lord, Tiglath-Pileser, caused me to reign upon the throne of my father.

The Ascension of the Dynasty (lines 7b-15)
And the house of my father profited,[4] [a] more than all others.
And I ran at the wheel of my lord,[5] [b] the king of Assyria,
in the midst of powerful kings, lords of silver and lords of gold.

And I took control of the house of my father.
And I made it better than the house of any powerful king.
And my brother kings were desirous[6] for all that is the good of my house.

The Construction of the Palace (lines 16-20)
But there was not a good house[7] for my fathers, the kings of Samᵓal.
They had the house of Kulamuwa;
and it was a winter house for them;
and it was a summer house (too).

But I built this house![8] [c]

a Ps 105:44; Isa 53:11; Qoh 2:10; 4:4; 5:17
b 1 Sam 8:11; 2 Sam 15:1; 1 Kgs 1:5
c 2 Sam 7; 1 Kgs 4-8

[3] Lit., "The chariot driver of El." On this deity see Kulamuwa (*COS* 2.30, n. 22).
[4] For the possible meanings for the verb ᶜ*ml* see *DNWSI* 870-871 s.v. ᶜ*ml*₁. Parker translates "accomplished" (1997:160, n. 8).
[5] Cf. Panamuwa 13 (*COS* 2.37).
[6] The best understanding of the verb *htnᵓbw* is as an *Etpaᵓal* of *nᵓb*. See Kaufman 1974:153 and Younger 1986:101, n. 38.
[7] Probably a sandhi-writing, see Degen 1969:43.
[8] Cf. the same word play in the Davidic narrative: *byt* "temple," "palace," and "dynasty." (2 Sam 7; 1 Kgs 4-8).

REFERENCES

Text: Tropper 1993:132-139; *KAI* #216; *SSI* 2.87-92. Translations and studies: *TUAT* 1/6:630-631; Sader 1987:169-170; Younger 1986:100-103.

THE TELL DAN STELE (2.39)

Alan Millard

Three fragments of a basalt stele were found at Tell Dan in 1993 and 1994, re-used as building stones in structures dated on archaeological grounds to the eighth century BCE. The pieces fit together, with gaps. Across the smooth face run parts of thirteen lines of clearly incised Aramaic letters, with word-dividers, of a style best placed late in the ninth century BCE. An unknown number of lines is missing at the beginning and end, nor is the length of the lines known, allowing for a variety of reconstructions. The monument was apparently a "memorial" inscription, like those of Mesha, Kulamuwa and Zakkur of the same period.

[sa]id x [ ] and cu[t]
[ ] x my father[1] went u[p against him when] he fought at x[ ]
Then my father lay down[a] and went to his
[fathers]. There came up the king of I[s]rael[2]
beforetime in the land of my father, [but]
Hadad [ma]de [me] king[3] [b] [ ]
x[4] Hadad went before me[5] [c] [and] I went from x
[ ]
of my king(s)[6] I killed kin[gs?] who harnessed[7] [d] x

a 1 Kgs 2:10 etc.
b 1 Sam 15:11; 1 Kgs 3:7; 2 Chr 1:11
c Exod 13:21, 22; 32:1; Num 10:33; 14:14; Isa 52:12
d Gen 46:29; Exod 14:6; 2 Kgs 9:21

[1] The author is not identified. Hazael of Damascus (*COS* 2.40) is the most attractive candidate, but the reference to his 'father' in terms of a predecessor contradicts Assyrian and biblical statements that he was a usurper (2 Kgs 8:7-15; see *COS* 2.113G, note 3; 2.113C-F); without more of the text, speculation is pointless.
[2] This restoration assumes only one letter (*s*) is lost at the end of the line.
[3] Cp. Zakkur's claim that Baᶜlshamayn made him king (*COS* 2.35).
[4] The meaning of the first word in this line, as it stands, the pronoun "I," is unclear; it may be the end of a verb from the previous line.
[5] Gods were widely perceived as marching ahead of their loyal worshippers to give success; see Ashurnasirpal II's "annals" ii.25-26,27, 50, iii.52. See Grayson 1976:128, 130, 140 and 76 n. 305; 1991:203, 205, 216, with 134 n. to line 48 and the depictions of the god Ashur above the king in battle scenes on sculptures from his palace; Budge 1914: pls. XIVa, XVIIa, XXIIIa.
[6] Translation uncertain; the first editors rendered "my kingdom" (Biran and Naveh 1995:15-16), but "my kings" i.e. vassals, is also possible, cf. 1 Kgs 20:1.
[7] Translation uncertain.

[ch]ariots and thousands of horsemen[8] [e]
[ ]*rm*[9] son of [ ]
king of Israel and kill[ed]yahu son of [I
overthr]ew[10] the house of David.[11] [f] I set/imposed
[tribute ?]

x their land to [ ]
other and to [was/became kin]g over Is[rael]
siege against [ ]

e Exod 14:17 etc.; 1 Kgs 9:19; 2 Kgs 18:24
f 2 Sam 3:1, 6; 7:26; 2 Kgs 17:21; Isa 7:12, 13; 22:22; Jer 21:12; Zech 12:7ff

[8] "Thousands" could also be "two thousand."

[9] A restoration "[Jeho]ram son of [Ahab] king of Israel and killed [Ahaz]iah son of [Jehoram kin]g of Beth-David" is attractive historically (Kitchen 1997:32-34), although 2 Kgs 9:14-28 names Jehu as the killer and the expression "king of the House of PN" has grammatical problems. Possibly Hadad was the subject here, for the first person ending of the verb is not preserved. The number of missing letters is impossible to calculate with certainty, for, even if only one is to be restored at the end of the third line (n. 2), there is no proof that the stele was symmetrical, or that the lines were of equal length.

[10] The restoration suggested is [*wʾhp*]*k*, "and I overthrew." Cf. Sefire IC 19, 21 (*COS* 2.82) and 2 Sam 10:3.

[11] Beth-David, House or Dynasty of David: this understanding of the six letters *bytdwd* has been challenged because the words are not separated as are all others in this text. In the light of Aram. use, that is not compelling; see Rendsburg 1995. The numerous names for dynasties or states "House of" or "Son of PN" hark back to eponymous ancestors who, in some cases at least, are attested, e.g. Omri; Gush of Arpad; Sader 1987:99-136, 271-273. Linguistic arguments in favor of a place name have some force (Knauf, de Pury, and Römer 1994), although the divine name Dod supposed, is otherwise unknown, see Barstad 1995:493-98, but attempts to avoid any possible reference to an historical David (Cryer 1995; Thompson 1995) stem rather from a form of scepticism at odds with all known ancient practices.

REFERENCES

Text: Biran and Naveh 1993; 1995. Translations and studies: Barstad 1995; Budge 1914; Cryer 1995; Grayson 1976; 1991; Kitchen 1997; Knauf, de Pury, and Römer 1994; Lemaire 1994; 1998; Rendsburg 1995; Sader 1987; Thompson 1995.

THE HAZAEL BOOTY INSCRIPTIONS (2.40)

Alan Millard

Four brief dedicatory inscriptions refer to "our lord Hazael" who is to be identified as the usurper who took the throne of Damascus from Ben-Hadad (Assyrian Hadad-idri; cf. *COS* 2.125A) and ruled ca. 842-800 BCE; see Pitard 1987:145-160; Sader 1987:231-260.

A. A trapezoidal bronze plaque cast with figures in relief, a horse's nose-piece, was unearthed at the Hera temple in Samos in 1984; see Kyreleis 1988. One line of Aramaic letters is incised in the field. This discovery established the correct reading of a line of Aramaic letters incised upon a bronze horse's cheek piece found long before in the area of the temple of Apollo Daphnephoros in Eretria, Euboea (see Charbonnet 1986), showing that the inscriptions are duplicates; see Amadasi Guzzo 1987:17-20; Röllig 1988; Bron and Lemaire 1989; Ephʿal and Naveh 1989.

That which Hadad gave[1] [a] to our lord[b] Hazael from ʿAmq in the year when our lord crossed the river.[2] [c]

a Deut20:14; 1 Sam 30:23 *b* Dan 4:16, 21 *c* Gen 31:21; Exod 23:31; Num 22:5; 2 Sam 8:3 etc.

[1] The god Hadad made Hazael victorious and so gave him these objects among the booty. They were then selected and inscribed as votive offerings in accordance with the common practice of giving the deity part of the spoils of war (Gen 14:20; Num 31:25-54; 1 Chr 18:11). It is unlikely that they were originally presented to the Greek temples where they were found; they were probably looted from somewhere in Syria, perhaps the temple of Hadad in Damascus and passed through several hands to Greece.

[2] "The river" is understood to be the Euphrates, as in biblical and cuneiform texts, but in conjunction with ʿAmq, the plain of the Orontes, here could denote that river, see Millard 1993b:175*-176*.

B1. A fragmentary ivory plaque found in two pieces (which do not join) at Arslan Tash, ancient Hadatu, is thought to be from the edge of a bed.

[ ] x the people (or "Amma") for our lord Hazael in the year [ ] x [ ][1]

[1] Reconstruction as "the bed which the people (or 'Amma') offered to ... in the year of annexing Hawran" (Puech 1981; followed by Bron and Lemaire 1989:37) seems too imaginative (see Ephʿal and Naveh 1989:197 n. 24).

B2. Another ivory strip, from Nimrud[1] in Assyria, bears the end of a text:

Our [lor]d Hazael

[1] See Millard in Mallowan 1966:598.

REFERENCES

Text: *KAI* No. 232 (B1 only); *SSI* 2, No. 2 (B1 only); Bron and Lemaire 1989; Ephᶜal and Naveh 1989; Kyreleis 1988; Röllig 1998. Studies: Amadasi Guzzo 1987; Charbonnet 1986; Lemaire 1991b; Mallowan 1966; Millard 1993b; Pitard 1987; Sader 1987.

7. ARAMAIC DEDICATORY INSCRIPTIONS

THE ASWAN DEDICATORY INSCRIPTION (2.41)

Bezalel Porten

Usually known as the Aswan sandstone stela, this six-line building dedication inscription (Cairo J. 36448) was published by de Vogüé in 1903 (*TAD* D17.1). It is 44.2 cm wide (frontally), 27.5 cm high and 12.5 cm thick (in depth) and is engraved in cursive script whose proximate forerunners are attested in a clay tablet of 571/570 BCE (Louvre AO 21063; *SSI* 2:116-117; cf. the letters *aleph, beth, he, waw, zayin, yod, kaph*). Unlike other dedicatory inscriptions, both Phoenician and Aramaic, this one is dated (Sivan = Meḥir, 7 Artaxerxes). Since palaeographically the reign of Artaxerxes I is indicated, the resultant date would be June 6-13, 458 BCE.[1] So far unique in Achaemenid Egypt, the inscription formula may be compared to a Cilician inscription at Yale ("This statue Nanasht erected before ..." [*KAI* #258; *SSI* 2:153-154]). In both the Cilician and Elephantine inscriptions, the object described is indicated by a Persian loanword — *ptkr*, **patikara-* "statue" and *brzmdnᵓ*, **brazmādāna-* "shrine" respectively — and both follow a traditional Aramaic formulary: "Cultic object + demonstrative - verb - subject - indirect object" (*KAI* #215). The cultic site was dedicated by the Troop Commander of Syene, whose name is damaged, to a deity whose name is likewise damaged.

This[2] *shrine*[3] PN[4] the Troop Commander[5] [a] of Syene made[6] in the month of Sivan,[b] that is Meḥir, year seven of Artaxerxes[7] [c] the king[8] [for] DN[9] the god. Peace[10] [...] ...

a Gen 21:22, 32; 26:26; Judg 4:2; 1 Sam 14:50; 2 Sam 10:16; 2 Kgs 4:13; 5:1 *b* Esth 8:9 *c* Ezra 4:7-8, 11, 23; 6:14; Ezra 7 passim; 8:1; Neh 2:1; 5:14; 13:6

[1] Lemaire 1992:295-303 argued for a date in the reign of Artaxerxes II. But already in Artaxerxes II fifth year, Elephantine was controlled by Amyrtaeus (400 BCE [*TAD* B4.6:1]), who gave way a year later to Nepherites (*TAD* A3.9:3-4). Synchronous Babylonian-Egyptian double dating was standard in Egypt between 473 and 402 BCE; Porten 1990:16, 31.

[2] For use of the demonstrative at the beginning of dedicatory inscriptions see *KAI* #215, #258.

[3] An Old Persian loanword **brazmādāna-* (Bogoliubov 1966).

[4] The surviving letter traces (∘∘*dn*[...] or ∘∘*rn*[...]) do not allow for the restoration of *wydrng* Vidranga, as desired by Bogoliubov 1966 and Lemaire 1992:292.

[5] Aram. *rb ḥyl* = BH *śr ṣbᵓ*. Both officials were second in command, the Aram. to the *frataraka-*, "governor," and the biblical to the king. We have the names of four people in the fifth century BCE who bore this title: Rauk (*TAD* B5.1:3 [495]; D7.24:15), Naphaina (*TAD* A5.2:7 [post 434/433]), his son Vidranga (*TAD* A4.3:3; B2.9:4-5, 2.10:2, 4, 3.9:2-3 [420-416]), and Vidranga's son Naphaina (*TAD* 4.7:7 ‖ 4.8:6 [410]). A Vidranga appears in broken context in a fragmentary letter of 399 BCE (*TAD* A3.9:7). They functioned not only in a military capacity but in a judicial one as well, independently or alongside the governor (*TAD* B2.9:4-5).

[6] The verb ᶜ*bd* was regularly, if not exclusively, used to describe the fashioning of a ritual object; see *TAD* D20.1:2 = *COS* 2.60 here and cf. *DNWSI* 810-813.

[7] ᵓ*rtḥšsš* was the standard spelling of the royal name in Eg. Aram. texts, though once it is abbreviated to ᵓ*rtḥš* (TAD B3.3:1). In the Bible it was rendered ᵓ*rtḥšst*ᵓ (Ezra 7 passim) or ᵓ*rtḥššt*ᵓ (Ezra 4:7-8, 11, 23; 6:14 [separate source]).

[8] Palaeography and the historical situation point to Artaxerxes I. In his year 7 Babylonian Sivan and Eg. Meḥir converged for only a week, June 6-13.

[9] The preserved text reads [l∘]∘*wpd/rnḥty*. Unfortunately, what is perserved does not allow intelligible restoration. The attempt to restore Osirnakht (Lemaire 1992:293) cannot be sustained.

[10] The last legible word is another Old Persian loanword, *drwt*, *druvatāt-*, "peace, welfare" and must have introduced the concluding blessing to be bestowed upon the official who built the shrine and set the inscription.

REFERENCES

Text, translations and studies: *AC* #22; Bogoliubov 1966; *DAE* #75; Fitzmyer and Kaufman 1992:B3f3; Lemaire 1992; *TAD* D17.1.

8. PHILISTINE INSCRIPTIONS

THE EKRON INSCRIPTION OF AKHAYUS (2.42)

K. Lawson Younger, Jr.

Written in a lapidary style script developed by the Philistines at Ekron, the text is a royal dedicatory inscription for the temple of the goddess *Ptgyh* made by Akhayus,[1] the son of Padi, the ruler of Ekron. The royal names ("Padi" and "Akhayus") are names known from Assyrian sources: for Padi, the inscriptions of Sennacherib (*COS* 2.119B) and another inscription from Ekron (see n. 3 below); for Akhayus (vocalized in the Assyrian texts as Ikausu), the inscriptions of Esarhaddon and Aššurbanipal. On the basis of these names, the inscription dates to ca. 680-665 BCE.

The name Akhayus has been generally associated with the name of biblical ᵓākîš Achish, the Philistine king(s) of Gath in the times of Saul and Solomon (1 Sam 21:11-16; 1 Sam 27:1-29:9; 1 Kgs 2:39-40).

Dedication (lines 1-3)
The temple (house)[2] [a] that Akhayus, son of Padi,[3] son of Ysd, son of Ada, son of Yaᶜir, ruler[4b] of Ekron,[5c] built for PTGYH,[6] his lady.

Invocation (lines 4-5)
May she bless him,[7d] and prote[ct] him, and prolong his days,[d] and may she bless his [l]and.

a Isa 29:1
b Judg 3:3; Judg 9:6, 22; 16:5 etc; 1 Sam 5; 6; 7; 21:10; 27:2; 29:1, 6-7
c Josh 13:3, etc.
d - d Num 6:24-26

[1] For a vocalization as Akhayus, i.e. 'Αχαιος, meaning "Greek," see Gitin, Dothan, and Naveh 1997a:11; Naveh 1998:35-37. The name Achish appears in an Eg. list of names from Caphtor (Crete) from the 16th century BCE (Sasson 1997:632).

[2] Rainey (1998:242) points out that *bt bn* ᵓ*kyš* is a noun in construct with a clause acting as the *nomen rectum*. Cf. Isa 29:1.

[3] Padi is best known from the annals of Sennacherib (below, *COS* 2.119B) and now also from another inscription from Ekron that reads: *lb*ᶜ*l wlpdy* "for Baᶜal and for Padi." See Gitin and Cogan 1999. For Baᶜal at Ekron, cf. Baᶜal-Zebub in 2 Kgs 1:2-3. See Sasson 1997:634.

[4] The use of the phrase *šr* ᶜ*qrn* (instead of *mlk* ᶜ*qrn*) may be because: 1) it expresses the vassal's loyalty to the Assyrian king, 2) the term *šr* means king in the Philistine-Canaanite dialect, or 3) the phase is directed toward a particular audience. Cf. the Hadad-yithᶜi inscription (*COS* 2.34, n. 5): the Aram. has "king" (*mlk*), the Assyrian has "governor" (*šākin māti*) (cf. Isa 10:8). Note that the Philistine rulers are called *śar* (Judg 3:3; 16:5 etc; 1 Sam 5; 6; 7). Cf. also Judg 9:6 and 9:22. In 1 Sam 29, the title *sarnê pᵉlištîm* (29:1, 7, also *hassᵉrānîm* in v. 6) is used synonymously with *śārê pᵉlištîm* (29:3 [2x], 4). Akhayus (Achish) of Gath was called *melek* (e.g. 1 Sam 21:11; 27:2), perhaps because at that time he was the senior among the five Philistine rulers (Rainey 1998:243).

[5] For the spelling and vocalization of the name ᶜ*qrn*, see Rainey 1998:243. In Akk. it is spelled ^{uru}*Am-qar-ru-na* and ^{uru}*Am-qar-ru-u-na* = *Amqarūna* = *ᶜ*Amqarôna* < *ᶜ*Aqqarôna*). See Parpola 1970:16; and Hurvitz 1968:18-24.

[6] Much speculation has arisen over this Ekronite goddess. Gitin, Dothan and Naveh (1998:12) suggest an equation with Asherah (this deity's name appears on a votive jar inscription from Tel Miqne / Ekron). Schäfer-Lichtenberger (1998:64-76) vocalizes the goddess's name as Pythogajah and argues that she was Ekron's principal deity, positing possible connections between this Philistine goddess and the sanctuary at Delphi known as Pytho, which was the shrine of Gaia before the cult of Apollo became popular there. The principal goddess of the Mycenean period was a personification of mother earth which may be a further indication that the Philistines were of Mycenean origin.

Since the *gimel* in the word appears somewhat defectively written, some scholars have suggested different readings. Demsky (1997:1-5; 1998:53-58) reads *ptnyh* and equates with the Greek term πότνια — a title used in the addressing of females meaning "lady," "mistress," "queen." It is used to describe Athena and Artemis. Demsky equates its use in the inscription with Asherah. But there is a redundancy created by Demsky's proposal: *lptnyh* . ᵓ*dth* "for his lady/mistress, his lady." The term ᵓ*dt* is an epithet and thus *ptnyh* would seem to be a divine name. Görg (1998), however, suggests the reading *ptryh*, and equates this with a Canaanite goddess known from Ugarit. However, the ending in Ug. is *y* not *yh* (Sasson 1997:633). Moreover, the text seems to read *gimel*, not *nun* or *resh*.

[7] Cf. the Azatiwada inscription (*COS* 2.31) and the Kuntillet ᶜAjrud inscriptions (*COS* 2.47).

REFERENCES

Text: Text: Gitin, Dothan, and Naveh 1997a; 1997b. Studies: Demsky 1997; 1998a; 1998b; Gitin 1993; Naveh 1998; Rainey 1998; Schäfer-Lichtenberger 1998; Sasson 1997.

---

9. NABATAEAN INSCRIPTIONS

A NABATAEAN COMMEMORATIVE INSCRIPTION FROM ᶜAVDAT (2.43)

J. F. Healey

This is a rare example of a non-funerary Nabataean building inscription. Found ca. 2 km south of ᶜAvdat on what was probably a libation altar, it mentions a religious celebration (*mrzḥ*) connected with Dushara and is dated, though the reading of the date is uncertain.[1]

Event being recorded (lines 1-2a)
This is the dam (which was built) by ... and ... sons of ... (and his associates) the sons of Saruta.

Dedication and date (lines 2b-4)
This was at the *marzeaḥ*-festival[2] [a] of Dushara, the god of Gaia,[3] in the year 7(?) ... of King Rabbel, King of the Nabataeans, who brings life and deliverance to his people.[4]

a Jer 16:5; Amos 6:7

[1] The text is published and annotated by Negev 1963.

[2] The *marzeaḥ* (Heb. form) is a widespread phenomenon stretching from Ebla in the third millennium BCE to Marseilles in the first millennium CE and also alluded to in later Jewish sources. It refers to a communal celebration by members of a fraternity involving eating and drinking under the supervision of a symposiarch. Strabo refers to such celebrations by the Nabataeans. See *COS* 2.36, note 18.

[3] Gaia is the ancient form of the geographical name al-Jī, the name of the village to the east of Petra. This may have been the original (even pre-Nabataean) home of Dushara, the main Nabataean god.

[4] The date is far from certain, but the 7th year of Rabbel II (70-106 CE) was 76/77 CE. (This follows Meshorer 1975; Negev 1963 has the 18th year). The titulature "he who has brought life and deliverance to his people" is an Aramaic version of the Greek title *σωτήρ*.

REFERENCES

Meshorer 1975; Negev 1963.

THE DEDICATION OF A STATUE TO THE DIVINIZED NABATAEAN KING (2.44)

J. F. Healey

While belonging to a common genre of inscription commemorating an individual in the presence of a god,[1] this particular example is noteworthy for the possibility that the god in question is the divinized Nabataean king, Obodas. It also contains a probably poetic section, the meaning of which is uncertain, but which appears to be in Arabic. It thus contains the earliest Arabic known to us, from the 1st century CE.[2]

Commemoration (lines 1-2a)
May he who recites (this inscription) before the god Obodas be remembered for good and may whoever ... be remembered.[3]

Pious Act Commemorated (line 2b)
Garmalahi son of Taymalahi [set up] a statue before the god Obodas.[4]

Reason for Dedication (lines 4-5)
And he (Obodas) works without reward or favor, and he, when death tried to claim us, did not let it claim (us), for when a wound (of ours) festered, he did not let us perish.[5]

Autograph (line 6)
Garmalahi wrote (this) with his (own) hand.

[1] On the formula see Healey 1996.

[2] First published and translated by J. Naveh and S. Shaked in Negev 1986, this inscription has become the focus of intense scholarly interest, especially centered upon the Arabic section: Noja 1989; Bellamy 1990; Snir 1993; Ambros 1994; Kropp 1994.

[3] The formula "Remembered be PN before DN" is extremely common in inscriptions of this period (Nabataean, Palmyrene, Hatran, Jewish, Syriac, Greek). The basic idea behind it is clearly that anyone seeing the inscription should mention the name of the person who wrote the inscription. This would keep his or her memory alive before the god and bring blessing on the reciter of the name.

[4] Obodas was regarded as divine from the early first century CE onwards, though it is not clear which Obodas is meant, I (ca. 96-85 BCE) or III (30-9 BCE). This may have been a nationalistic move towards an ancestral cult. Theophoric personal names such as ᶜAbdᶜobodat ("servant of [the god] Obodas") reflect the same idea. Obodas was buried at ᶜAvdat (see Stephanus of Byzantium: Negev 1986:59-60). Despite the report of Stephanus, some have doubted that the god Obodas is a divinized king (Dijkstra 1995:319-321).

[5] The different commentators vary considerably in their translations of the Arabic. We provisionally follow Bellamy 1990.

REFERENCES

Ambros 1994; Bellamy 1990; Healey 1996; Kropp 1994; Negev 1986; Noja 1989; Snir 1993.

A NABATAEAN INSCRIPTION CONTAINING RELIGIOUS LAWS FROM THE ATARGATIS TEMPLE AT PETRA (2.45)

J. F. Healey

This inscription gives us a most tantalizing glimpse of Nabataean religious law in the 1st century CE. It is the religious aspect which is particularly unusual, since on secular law we are surprisingly well informed.[1] The inscription is preserved on a marble plaque which was originally attached to the temple wall along with (many?) others which proclaimed the religious law of this particular temple. The habit of placing religious laws in full view in temples is known from Jerusalem and from Hatra in the same period. In Jerusalem, the fragments of the law prohibiting non-Jews from going beyond the Court of the Gentiles have survived (see also literary reference in Josephus). In Hatra the laws on temple walls include strict rules about theft and an apparent rule that shoes were to be removed before entry.

In this case the law seems to be directed at priests, though there is so much difficulty in the text that our translation, based on that of the publishers of the inscription, must be regarded as tentative.[2]

Law on Taxation of Offerings (lines 1-3)
Whatever he receives[3] of silver or gold or offerings or provisions of any kind, or of silver (coinage) or bronze (coinage)[4] ...
and the other half (will be allotted) to the priests[5] [a] after the carrying out of a proclamation of delinquency[6] before this (time). Then there shall be allotted ...

a Lev 7:28-36; 10:12-15, etc.; Deut 18:1-8; 1 Sam 2:12-17; Neh 10:32-33

... concerning it, whoever does other than all of what is written above shall as a consequence repay that which was found out ...

Date (line 4)
On the fourth day of ʾAb, the 37th year of Ḥaretat, King of the Nabataeans, lover of his people.[7] And ...

[1] See Healey 1993.

[2] See Hammond, Johnson, and Jones 1986.

[3] Apparently this refers to the income of a priest or some other temple official (receiving offerings). Subsequent reference to priests receiving half may refer to some collective body.

[4] There is a distinction between precious metals and coinage.

[5] On temple taxes note Neh 10:32-33 and Josephus, *Antiquities*, III.191; Mishnah Shekalim 2:3, 4; 4:7-8; Yoma 6:1, etc.

[6] *ʾkryz ʿwn*: like the public proclamation of bankruptcy which protects the rights of creditors.

[7] The king, whose "nationalistic" title is normally added, is Aretas IV (9 BCE–40 CE) and the date is therefore 28/29 CE.

REFERENCES

Hammond, Johnson, and Jones 1986; Healey 1993b.

A NABATAEAN SHRINE INSCRIPTION FROM EGYPT (2.46)

J. F. Healey

This well-preserved inscription on a white limestone block is particularly important historically because of the detailed chronological synchronism it gives. It comes from the site of Tell esh-Shuqafiya in the eastern delta of lower Egypt and is dated to 34 BCE.[1] The Nabataeans were active in Egypt and have left many inscriptions there.

Dedication (lines 1-4a)
This is the shrine[2] which Wahballahi son of ʿAbdʾalgaʾ son of ʾAwsalahi made for the god Dushara who is in Daphne[3] — as it is called in Egyptian.[4]

Date (lines 4b-6)
The year 18 of Queen Cleopatra,[5] which is the year 26 of Maliku,[6] King of the Nabataeans, i.e. the year 2 of ʾAṭlah,[7] in the month of Nisan.

[1] The primary publication is Jones, Johnson, Hammond, and Fiema 1988.

[2] The Nabataean word (*rbʿtʾ*) indicates a *square* temple or shrine.

[3] Probably Tell ed-Defenna.

[4] Possibly "Daphne of the Egyptians."

[5] 34 BCE. For corrected dating see Fiema and Jones 1990.

[6] Or Maniku.

[7] Perhaps a local priest.

REFERENCES

Fiema and Jones 1990; Jones, Johnson, Hammond, and Fiema 1988.

B. VOTIVE INSCRIPTIONS

1. HEBREW INSCRIPTIONS

KUNTILLET ᶜAJRUD (2.47)

KUNTILLET ᶜAJRUD: INSCRIBED PITHOS 1 (2.47A)

P. Kyle McCarter

A number of Hebrew inscriptions, primarily religious in content, were found in excavations conducted during the 1970's by Ze'ev Meshel for the Tel Aviv Institute of Archaeology at the site of Kuntillet ᶜAjrud, a major crossroads in the northeastern Sinai. The inscriptions were found in the ruins of the better preserved of the two buildings found at the site, which have been dated archaeologically to the end of the ninth and the beginning of the eighth century BCE. Among the most important artifacts were two large pithoi bearing a number of inscriptions and other graffiti. The first pithos is decorated with various drawings, including a pair of ibexes feeding on a stylized tree of life, a cow suckling a calf, a partially preserved lion, and, of special interest, a pair of human-bovine figures in the traditional pose of man and wife, king and queen or god and consort. This last illustration appears immediately below and partially overlapping the blessing translated below. Though it has been vigorously argued that the two figures are representations of the Egyptian god Bes (Beck 1982:27-31; Hadley 1987:189-196; Keel and Uehlinger 218-223), the unmistakable bull's head, hooved feet and tail of the larger figure argue decisively in favor of interpreting him as the "Yahweh of Samaria" invoked in the adjacent inscription (cf. "the young bull of Samaria" in Hos 8:6), while the female breasts of the smaller figure, who stands slightly behind Yahweh and interlocks her arm with his (cf. Weippert 1988: 673), is evidently "his asherah."

Utterance of ᵓAshyaw the king[1] [a]: "Say to Yehallel and to Yawᶜasah and to [...]: 'I bless you by Yahweh[b] of Samaria[2] and his asherah[3][c]!'"	*a* 2 Kgs 13:9-19, 25; 14:8-17; 2 Chr 25:17-25 *b* 2 Sam 6:18; 1 Chr 16:2; Ps 129:8 *c* Exod 34:13; Deut 7:5; 12:3; 1 Kgs 14:15, 23; 16:33; 2 Kgs 13:16; 17:10; 18:14; 21:3; 23:14; cf. 1 Kgs 15:1; 18:19; 2 Kgs 21:7; 23:4, 7; Jer 17:2; 1 Chr 15:16

[1] Reading *ᵓšyw hmlk*. Though the *mem* of the title cannot be seen in published visible-light photographs, it is clear in infrared images. The king in question is Joash of Israel, the years of whose reign (ca. 802-787 BCE) correspond precisely with the paleographic dating of the Kuntillet ᶜAjrud inscriptions. The correspondence between *ᵓšyw*, "ᵓAshyaw," and biblical *ywᵓš*, "Joash" (originally Yawᵓash) is not problematic, the theophoric and verbal elements being transposed as in a number of other royal names known from the Bible (cf. Ahaziah [2 Kgs 8:24, etc.] and Jehoahaz [2 Chr 21:17, etc.], Jehoiachin [2 Kgs 24:6, etc.] and Jeconiah [Jer 24:1, etc.]), etc. Cf. *COS* 2.50, n. 3.

[2] The god of Israel as he was worshiped in Samaria. A distinctive feature of the Kuntillet ᶜAjrud inscriptions is that Yahweh is routinely identified by one of his local manifestations, the Yahweh of Samaria and the Yahweh of Teman (McCarter 1987:139-143). Though the genitive construction *yhwh šmrn* violates BH grammar, it is not surprising in inscriptional Hebrew in view of comparative evidence in related languages.

[3] In the Bible the word *ᵓăšērâ* is sometimes used in reference to a goddess, "Asherah," but more often it designates a wooden cult object — possibly an upright wooden pole, a carved image of a goddess, or even a sacred tree. Its use is usually condemned by the biblical writers, at least in part because of its association with a goddess. In light of this association, the formula employed at Kuntillet ᶜAjrud, "Yahweh of Samaria [or 'Teman'] and his asherah," suggests the pairing of the god of Israel with a consort. Various proposals have been made to explain the connection between the wooden cult object and the divine consort. Most probably, the abstract conceptualization of Yahweh's divine presence, as marked in the cult by the wooden object, was given concrete form — that is, hypostatized — and personified as female, then venerated as Yahweh's consort (McCarter 1987:143-49).

REFERENCES

Text: *AHI* 8.017; *HAE* 1:59-61; Translations and studies: Gilula 1978/79; Beck 1982; Emerton 1982; Lemaire 1984b; Weinfeld 1984; Hadley 1987a; McCarter 1987; Meshel 1979; 1987; Olyan 1988:25-34; Weippert 1988; Keel and Uehlinger 1998:225-226.

KUNTILLET ᶜAJRUD: INSCRIBED PITHOS 2 (2.47B)

P. Kyle McCarter

The second pithos from Kuntillet 'Ajrud, like the first, is decorated with a number of drawings, including a cow, an archer with his bow drawn, and a group of five human figures, standing with their hands extended as if in worship or supplication. The pithos also bears four separate inscriptions. First is a complete Hebrew abecedary, with the letters *pe* and ᶜ*ayin* reversed from their traditional order, as also found in the early twelfth-century BCE ostracon from ᶜIzbet Ṣarṭah and occasionally in the Bible (Prov 2:16-17; 3:46-51; 4:16-17; 31:25-26 [LXX]; cf. Ps 34:16-17); cf. *COS* 1.107. Second, adjoining the drawing of the supplicating figures, is a list of names: Shakanyaw, ʾAmoṣ, Shamaryaw, ʾEliyaw, ᶜUzziyaw and Miṣray. The third and fourth inscriptions are translated here.

A Fragmentary Blessing (lines 1-3)
[...] to Yahweh of the Teman[1] [a] and his asherah.[b] And may he grant (?) everything[2] that he asks from the compassionate god[3] [c] [...], and may he grant according to his needs[4] [d] all that he asks![5]

A Message of Blessing (lines 1-10)
Utterance of 'Amaryaw, "Say to[6] my lord: 'Is it well with you?[e] I bless you by Yahweh[f] of Teman[7] and his asherah. May he bless you and keep you,[g] and may he be with my lord!'"[h]

a Jer 49:7, 20; Ezek 25:13; Amos 1:12; Obad 9; Hab 3:3 *b* Exod 34:13; Deut 7:5; 12:3; 1 Kgs 14:15, 23; 16:33; 2 Kgs 13:6; 17:10; 18:4; 21:3; 23:14; cf. 1 Kgs 15:13; 18:19; 2 Kgs 21:7; 23:4, 7; Jer 17:2; 2 Chr 15:16 *c* Exod 34:6; Jon 4:2; Ps 86:15; Neh 9:31; cf. Joel 2:13; Pss 103:8; 111:4; 145:8; Neh 9:17; 2 Chr 30:9 *d* Exod 36:7; Jer 49:9; Obad 5; Prov 25:16 *e* Gen 29:6; 43:27; 2 Sam 18:32; 20:9; 1 Kgs 2:13; 2 Kgs 4:26 *f* 2 Sam 6:18; 1 Chr 16:2; Ps 129:8 *g* Num 6:24 *h* Gen 28:15

[1] The particular manifestation of the god of Israel invoked in this blessing is *yhwh htmn*, "Yahweh of the Teman," i.e., "Yahweh of the Southland," probably the local form of Yahweh worshiped in the vicinity of Kuntillet ᶜAjrud. "The Teman" or "Southland" is the biblical Teman, spelled *tmn* (*têmān*) here in the Israelite (northern) dialect of Hebrew, though the name also appears at Kuntillet ᶜAjrud in the Judahite (southern) form *tymn* (*taymān*). The initial article is an indication that Teman is understood as a region, "the Teman" or "the Southland."

[2] Reading *wyšʾl* [.] *kl*. Only the last two letters are certain.

[3] The apparent reading is *mʾš* . *ḥnn*, but the *šin* is uncertain, and the reading *mʾl* . *ḥnn* is suggested by the second Khirbet Beit Lei cave inscription (*COS* 2.53) as well as biblical *ʾēl raḥûm wᵉḥānûn*, "the gracious and compassionate god" (Exod 34:5, etc.)

[4] Reading *wntnldyhw* (apparently without the expected word divider) and interpreting the final sequence as the preposition followed by *dayyēhû*, lit., "according to his sufficiency." Weinfeld (1984:125-126) reads *wntn lh yhw klbbh*, "let Yahweh given him according to his wish," but the defective spelling of the divine name (*yhw*), though it appears (by scribal error?) on a stone bowl from Kuntillet ᶜAjrud, would be isolated in the pithoi and plaster texts, where the full spelling (*yhwh*) is consistently found, as elsewhere in the Iron Age epigraphic corpus.

[5] Reading *klbph*, lit., "everything that is in his mouth."

[6] A peculiarity of this inscription in comparison not only to biblical practice but to the rest of the epigraphic corpus is the attachment of the preposition *-l* (!) to the preceding word, as in *ʾmrl* . *ʾdny*, "Say to my lord," instead of the expected form *l-*, attached to the following word.

[7] In this case *yhwh tmn*, "Yahweh of Teman," occurs without the article (see n. 1 above).

REFERENCES

Text: *AHI* 8.018-22; *HAE* 1: 59-61. Translations and studies: Chase 1982; Keel and Uehlinger 1998:227; McCarter 1987; Meshel 1979; 1987:E (2.2); Weinfeld 1984.

KUNTILLET ᶜAJRUD: THE TWO-LINE INSCRIPTION (2.47C)

P. Kyle McCarter

Portions of at least three ink-on-plaster texts in very fragmentary condition were found where they had fallen on the floor of the so-called bench room, near the entryway of the main building at Kuntillet ᶜAjrud. One of these is illegible except for a single word that admits of no obvious interpretation. The second, translated here, consists of two incomplete lines of text in four fragments. There is insufficient continuous text to determine the exact relationship among the four parts of the inscription, and the fragment presented here is the only one well enough preserved for translation. A peculiarity of the plaster inscriptions is that they are written in Phoenician script, but features of phonology and morphology show that the language is Hebrew.

A blessing (lines 1-2)
[... May] he prolong (their) days,[1] [a] and be satisfied [...] Yahweh of the Teman[2] [b] has dealt favorably [with[c] ...]

a 1 Kgs 3:14; Deut 4:26, 40; 5:33; 11:9; 17:20; 22:7; 30:18; 32:47; Josh 24:31; Judg 2:7; Isa 53:10; Ps 72:5 (!); Prov 28:16; Job 29:18; Eccl 8:13 *b* Jer 49:7, 20; Ezek 25:13; Amos 1:12; Obad 9; Hab 3:3 *c* Exod 1:20; Num 10:32; Deut 8:16; 28:63; 30:5; Josh 24:20; Judg 17:13; 1 Sam 25:31; Jer 32:40-41; Zech 8:15; Ps 125:4

[1] Reading *yʾrk ymm* in preference to *ybrk ymm*, "May he *bless* their days ..." (Meshel, Renz *HAE*). Though the first letter is poorly preserved, the traces fit *ʾalep* better than *bet*, and the Hebrew phrase is more idiomatic and better suited to the context.

[2] For *yhwh htymn*, see Inscribed Pithos 2 (*COS* 2.47B, note 1). Note that the Judahite (southern) dialect (*hattaymān*) is used in the Two-Line Inscription.

REFERENCES

Text, translation and studies: *AHI* 8.015; *HAE* 1: 58; Meshel 1979; 1987:D (2).

KUNTILLET ᶜAJRUD: PLASTER WALL INSCRIPTION (2.47D)

P. Kyle McCarter

This inscription fell from the doorjamb of the entryway to the western storage room in the main building at Kuntillet ᶜAjrud. Preserved on the plaster are portions of five lines of a much longer text, which was poetic in character and similar in striking ways to certain theophanic passages found in archaic biblical poetry. Though the script is Phoenician, the language is probably Hebrew (cf. notes 3 and 5).

A Theophany of the Day of Battle (lines 1-5)
[...] When ᵓEl[1] shone forth[a] in [...] And mountains melted,[b] and peaks[2] grew weak[3] [...] Baᶜl[4] on the day of battle[5] [c] [...] on the day of batt[le ...]

a Deut 33:2; Hos 6:3; Isa 60:1 *b* Isa 34:3, Mic 1:4; Ps 97:5 *c* Hos 10:14; Amos 1:14; Prov 21:31

[1] Or "God." Despite the Phoen. script, the language and poetic style of this poem are distinctively Heb., like the other inscriptions at Kuntillet ᶜAjrud. In all probability, then, ᵓEl should be understood here as the god of Israel rather than a non-Israelite deity.

[2] To the enigmatic *pbnm*, compare *pabn-*, the common Hurrian word for "mountain." Though this (loan)word is not attested elsewhere in the Northwest Semitic lexica, the alternative, to read *gbnm* and compare Ps 68:16, fails on epigraphic grounds: The first letter is a perfect *pe* but unparalleled as *gimel*.

[3] Both *wymsn*, "and ... melted," and *wyrkn*, "and ... grew weak," end in the so-called paragogic *nun*, a well-known feature of Heb. but thus far lacking in Phoen. except in late forms influenced by Aram. (Friedrich and Röllig, *PPG* §135 and n. 2).

[4] In view of the distinctively Israelite literary character of this fragmentary poem, it seems probable that Baᶜl ("Lord") should be understood as an epithet of the god of Israel here rather than the name of a Canaanite or Phoen. god. Cp. the old debate over the meaning of *-baᶜl* in personal names in the Samaria ostraca of the early eighth century.

[5] The reading of this word seems to be *mlḥm*, with a word-divider following the final *mem*, indicating a pronunciation *milḥamā*. The lack of a final *mater* is consistent with Phoen. orthography, while the final *-ā* rather that *-at* shows that the language of the text is Heb. rather than Phoen.

REFERENCES

Text: *AHI* 8.023; *HAE* 1: 59; Meshel 1979; 1987:D (3). Translations and studies: Weinfeld 1984.

THE JERUSALEM POMEGRANATE (2.48)

K. Lawson Younger, Jr.

This inscription is carved on a thumb-sized ivory in the shape of a pomegranate (height 4.3 cm, diameter 2.1 cm). It has been dated on paleographic grounds to the end of eighth century BCE. Since the text circles on the pomegranate, there is some uncertainty concerning the starting and ending points. The text appears to mention a sanctuary of Yahweh which may possibly be associated with the temple in Jerusalem built by Solomon. Lemaire (1981; 1984c) has suggested that this ivory pomegranate may be part of a priestly scepter.[1]

lby[t yhw]h qdš khnm	Belonging to the tem[ple of Yahw]eh,[2][a] holy[b] to the priests.[3][c]

a Exod 23:19; 34:26; Deut 23:19; Josh 6:24; 1 Sam 1:7, 24; 3:15; 2 Sam 12:20; 1 Kgs 3:1; 6:37; 7:12, 40, 45, 48, 51 (‖ 2 Chr 5:1); 1 Kgs 8:11, 63, 64; 9:1 (‖ 2 Chr 7:11); 1 Kgs 9:10, 15; 10:5, 12 (‖ 2 Chr 9:4, 11); 1 Kgs 12:27; 14:26, 28 (‖ 2 Chr 12:9, 11); 1 Kgs 15:15, 18 (‖ 2 Chr 16:2); 2 Kgs 11:3 + (8x); 12:5 + (12x); 14:14; 15:35 (‖ 2 Chr 27:3); 2 Kgs 16:8, 14, 18; 18:15; 19:1, 14 (‖ Isa 37:1, 14); 2 Kgs 20:5, 8; 21:4, 5 (2 Chr 33:4, 5); 2 Kgs 22:3, 5, 8, 9 (‖ 2 Chr 34:15, 17); 2 Kgs 23:2 + (6x); 24:13 (‖ 2 Chr 36:10); 2 Kgs 25:9, 13, 16 (‖ Jer 52:13, 17, 20); Isa 2:2 (‖ Mic 4:1); Isa 38:20, 22; 66:20; Jer 7:2; 17:26; 19:14; 20:1, 2; 26:2, 7, 9, 10; 27:16, 18, 21; 28:1, 3, 5, 6; 29:26; 33:11 35:2, 4; 36:5, 6, 8, 10; 38:14; 41:5; 51:51; 52:13; Ezek 8:16; 10:19; 11:1; 12:10; 44:4, 5; Hos 8:1; 9:4; Joel 1:9, 14; 3:18; Hag 1:2, 14; Zech 7:3; 8:9; 11:13; 14:20, 21; Pss 23:6; 27:4; 92:14; 116:19; 118:26; 122:1, 9; 134:1; 135:2; Lam 2:7; Dan 1:2; Ezra 1:3, 7; 2:68; 3:8, 11; 7:27; 8:29; Neh 10:36; 1 Chr 6:16, 17; 9:23; 22:11, 14; 23:4, 24, 28, 32; 24:19; 25:6; 26:12, 22, 27; 28:12, 13, 20; 29:8; 2 Chr 3:1; 4:16; 7, 2, 11; 8:16; 20:5, 28; 23:5, 6, 18, 19; 24:4, 7, 8, 14, 18, 21; 26:19; 28:21, 24; 29:3 + (10x); 30:1, 15; 31:10, 11, 16; 33:15; 34:14; 35:2; 36:7, 14, 18
b Exod 28:36; 39:30; Zech 14:20 *c* Lev 21:7b-8; 22:9; 27:21; Ezek 22:26; 44:13

[1] Two inscribed Phoen. vessels in the form of pomegranates have been published (Heltzer 1996). Both are votive inscriptions reading, *lᶜštrt* "To ᶜAštarte" or "Belonging to ᶜAštarte." Heltzer feels that these add "strong confirmation that the publication of N. Avigad treats a really genuine object with a genuine dedicatory inscription" (1996:282).

[2] Kempinski (1990) suggested that the text should be restored and translated: *lby[t ᵓšr]h qdš khnm* "Belonging to the tem[ple of Asher]ah, holy to the priests." But there are difficulties with this restoration, see Hess 1996; Millard 1991. For *lbyt yhwh*, see the Temple of Yahweh ostracon (*COS* 2.50) below. The phrase *byt yhwh* also occurs in Arad ostracon 18.9 (Renz *HAE* 1:382-384). See esp. the comments of Pardee 1978:318.

[3] Avigad (1994) proposed to read the inscription with a different starting point: *qdš khnm lbyt [yhw]h* "Sacred donation for the priests of (in) the house of Yahweh." But see Renz *HAE* 1:193 and 2:27.

REFERENCES

Text, translations and studies: *AHI* 99.001.1; *HAE* 1:192-193; Avigad 1989; 1990; 1994; Kempinski 1990; Lemaire 1981; 1984.

JERUSALEM OSTRACON (2.49)
(The "Creator of the Earth" Ostracon)

P. Kyle McCarter

The ostracon, a fragment of the shoulder of a storage jar bearing three incomplete lines of Hebrew script written in ink, was found in 1971 during N. Avigad's excavations in the Jewish Quarter of Jerusalem. The poorly-preserved inscription is of special interest because of its third line, which may read "Creator of the Earth," a well-known epithet of the biblical and West Semitic god ᵓEl, though the orthography is problematic and the interpretation uncertain. The ostracon is datable on paleographical grounds to the end of the eighth century BCE (cf. Renz *HAE* 1:198).

List of Names
[...]yahu. ᵓAbbir[y]ahu[1]
[...]n. Mikayahu[2] son of [. . .]nh[. . .]
[...] Creator (?) of the Earth.[a]

a Gen 14:19; cf. Isa 40:28; 45:18

[1]The meaning of this name is "Yahweh is a Bull" (ᵓ*abbîr*, as in Isa 34:7 and Jer 46:15; cf. Ugaritic *ibr*, "buffalo," and probably Egyptian *ibr*, "stallion") or "Yahweh is Strong."

[2] That is, *mîkāyāhû* ("Who [among the gods] is like Yahweh?"), "Micaiah."

[3] The reading of this line (*qn* ᵓ*rṣ*) has been compared, esp. by Miller (1980), to the common epithet that characterizes the god ᵓEl as "the creator of the earth," which is attested in Northwest Semitic sources from Late Bronze Age Canaanite (reflected in Hittite *Ilkuniršа*) to Neo-Punic ᵓ*l qn* ᵓ*rṣ* in the second century CE. Its occurrence here in a Hebrew source is reminiscent of biblical ᵓ*ēl* ᶜ*elyôn qōnê šāmayim wā*ᵓ*āreṣ*, "ᵓEl, creator of heaven and earth," in Gen 14:19. This led Avigad to reconstruct the divine name ᵓ*l*, "ᵓEl," in the break at the beginning of the line, a restoration described by Miller as "almost inescapable." Admittedly, however, the spelling *qn* for *qōnē*, "creator," without the expected final *-h*, as expected in Hebrew orthography of this period, is anomalous (Miller, Lipiński, Renz *HAE*), and this led some scholars to propose alternative interpretations, such as [*z*]*qn* ᵓ*rṣ*, "elders of the land" (Lipiński; see Renz *HAE* 1: 198 n. c for other possibilities). Nevertheless, noting its frequent occurrence in Phoen. texts, the orthography of which did not employ final *-h* (Karatepe ᵓ*l qn* ᵓ*rṣ*; *KAI* 2:42-43), Miller (1980:45) suggests that it may be "a cultic or religious cliché in frozen form," and this suggestion is reinforced by the possibility that, as a common epithet, the epithet "creator-of-the-earth" might have come to be viewed as, in effect, a single word, *qn*ᵓ*rṣ*, as suggested already by Hittite *Kunirsha*.

REFERENCES

Text: *AHI* 4.201; *HAE* 1:197-98. Translations and studies: Avigad 1972; Lipiński 1990; Miller 1980; Smelik 1987:73 §156.

THE TEMPLE OF THE LORD OSTRACON (2.50)
(Moussaïeff No. 1)

K. Lawson Younger, Jr.

This is one of two ostraca in the Moussaïeff collection (for the other, see the Widow's Plea Ostracon, *COS* 3). It is a five-line inscription that records a royal contribution of silver by a king ᵓAshyahu to the temple of Yahweh to be made through the agency of a royal functionary named Zakaryahu. The ostracon is 10.9 cm x 8.6 cm, and is written in Hebrew script that dates[1] on the basis of palaeography to the time of Josiah (640-609 BCE) (Bordreuil, Israel, and Pardee 1996; 1998).

As[2] ᵓAshyahu[3] the king (has) commanded you to give in the hand of Zakaryahu[4] silver of Tarshish[5] [a] for the house of Yahweh[6] [b]: three shekels.[7]

a 1 Kgs 10:22; 22:49; Isa 60:9; Jer 10:9 Ezek 27:12; Jonah 1:3; Ps 72:10 *b* 2 Kgs 12:5ff; 22:3 etc.

[1] Interestingly, Ephᶜal and Naveh (1998) suggest that the ostracon (as well as its sister ostracon "the Widow's Plea") may not be genuine, but a modern forgery because of the great similarity of words and phrases with BH and known epigraphic materials. The very same facts are used by Becking to argue for genuineness (1998:5)! It should be remembered that the ink used on the inscriptions has been tested and appears to date from the time period (Bordreuil, Israel, and Pardee 1996:74-76).

[2] *k*ᵓ*šr* at the very beginning of a text is unknown in extrabiblical texts. Lang (1998) argues that *k*ᵓ*šr* can stand at the beginning of a Hebrew sentence and that the word should be construed as "Thus," or the like, having a kataphoric function (see also Becking 1998:6). However, the examples that Lang cites do not syntactically support his contention. Most of the examples are instances of the occurrence of the *k*ᵓ*šr* ... *kn* ... sentence type where the first (dependent) clause, *k*ᵓ*šr* ..., states: "as such and such has been commanded or spoken," and the second (independent) clause, *kn* ..., states: "so this such and such has been done or will be done (using ᶜ*śh*)." See Num 8:22b; 36:10; Josh 11:15; 14:5; 1 Kgs 2:38. 1 Kgs 2:38 is esp. helpful since it records a monarchic edict in the *k*ᶜ*šr* clause, and the subject's commitment to do this in the *kn* clause. Therefore the ostracon may simply employ this *k*ᵓ*šr* ... *kn* ... formula elliptically. The *k*ᶜ*šr* clause records "as ᵓAshyahu, the king, (has) commanded you ... and elliptically, the *kn* clause is understood, "so you will do"; or "so it will be done".

[3] The name ᵓAshyahu is attested among extrabiblical personal names (Zadok 1988; Renz *HAE* 2:61), though none of these persons are monarchs. Thus the name is problematic because no king of Israel or Judah is known by this name in the biblical materials. Nevertheless, there

are two biblical possibilities. First, this could be an inverted form of the name of Joash, king of Judah, 835-796 BCE (2 Kgs 11:21–12:21) (or much less likely Joash, king of Israel, 803-787 BCE, 2 Kgs 13:10-13). Second, this could be an inverted form of the name of Josiah, king of Judah, 640-609 BCE (2 Kgs 22:1, etc.). That royal names could be inverted is seen in the case of Jehoiachin (*Yehôyākin*, 2 Kgs 24:6 etc.), who was also called Coniah (*Konyāhû*, e.g. Jer 22:24) among a number of other variations of his name. Another example is Ahaziah (*ʾḥzyhw*) (of Judah) (2 Kgs 8:25) who is called Jehoahaz (*yhwʾḥz*) in 2 Chr 2:21:17. Finally, Becking (1998:6-9) discusses three other possibilities that are much less likely than either of the two Judahite kings (i.e. Joash or Josiah). Cf. the discussion in *COS* 2.47A, note 1 above.

[4] There are two possibilities for biblical identification: 2 Chr 24:20 mentions a Zechariah who, though full of the spirit of God, nevertheless was murdered by his uncle Joash; and 2 Chr 35:8 mentions a Zechariah who was a Levite "over the house of God" during the reign of king Josiah (Bordreuil, Israel, and Pardee 1996:53; Lang 1998:22).

[5] Silver from Tarshish had proverbial high quality (Jer 10:9). The location of Tarshish is uncertain. The Phoen. Nora inscription seems to refer to a Tarshish on Sardinia. More probably, Tarshish was located in Spain. See Baker 1992; Lipiński 1992.

[6] A reference to "the house of Yahweh" is known from one of the Arad ostraca (Renz *HAE* 1:384) as well as possibly from the Jerusalem Pomegranate (see Renz *HAE* 1:192-193; and *COS* 2.48 above). Whether ʾAshyahu is Joash or Josiah, it is most likely that this is a reference to the Solomonic temple in Jerusalem.

[7] Bordreuil, Israel and Pardee (1998:5) understand this to be a reference (however oblique) to the Judahite royal shekel and not to the *šeqel haqqōdeš* "sanctuary shekel" (cf. Exodus 30:13).

REFERENCES

Text: Bordreuil, Israel, and Pardee 1996; 1998. Translations and studies: Becking 1998; Ephʿal and Naveh 1998; Lang 1998.

---

2. ARAMAIC INSCRIPTIONS

TELL EL-MASKHUṬA LIBATION BOWLS (2.51)

Bezalel Porten

In 1954 the Brooklyn Museum acquired three inscribed libation bowls, and then a fourth in 1957. They were said to have been found at Tel el-Maskhuṭa, ca. 12 miles west of Ismailia, and were published by Isaac Rabinowitz in 1956 and 1959 (*TAD* D15.1-4). Three are to be dated to the first half of the fifth century (*TAD* D15.1-3 = *COS* 2.51A-C) and the fourth to the second half (*TAD* D15.4 = *COS* 2.51D). They were all dedicated to the North-Arabian goddess Hanilat, known to Herodotus as Alilat (iii.8), and three of the four bowls (*TAD* D15.2-4 = *COS* 2.51B-D) recorded the names of the donor. These indicate the same kind of onomastic assimilation found among the Arameans in Egypt (see Egyptian mortuary texts below (*COS* 2.60-65) and evidenced in the contemporary Teima stela (Ṣalamshezib son of Peṭosiri [*CIS* 2.113:9, 11, 21 = *KAI* #228]). Only the king of Kedar bore a fully Arabian name — Kainu son of Geshem (D15.4 = *COS* 2.51D), the latter identical with Biblical Geshem/Gashmu the Arabian, opponent of Nehemiah. The other donors had mixed Egyptian and Arabian names (Ṣeḥo son of Abdamru *COS* 2.51C) or only Egyptian names (Ḥarbek son of Pa(u)siri *COS* 2.51B). The Arabs who aided Cambyses in his conquest of Egypt may have been Kedarites, who would have then or shortly thereafter been stationed in Wadi Tumeilat, where they built a shrine to their deity Hanilat at Tel el-Maskhuṭa.[1] Their king Geshem was a threat to Nehemiah and some say was the Jašm son of Šahr renowned in Arabian Dedan. The prophet Isaiah had already associated the Dedanites with Kedar (Isa 21:13-17).

SILVER BOWL (Brooklyn Museum 54.50.36) (2.51A)
(First Half of Fifth Century BCE)

To Hanilat[2]

---

[1] For recent discussion on the identification of this site see Currid 1997:128-130.

[2] Elliptical for "Bowl which PN offered to Hanilat the goddess;" see inscriptions below. Rabinowitz 1956:2 thought this abridged form was "used when a donor preferred to remain anonymous." For discussion of the goddess Allat see *NSI* p. 222 and references in Rabinowitz (1956) 3. The name means "goddess" and this form of her name ("the [*hn*] goddess") occurs only here. Rabinowitz 1956:4, 8 argues for her identification with Atarsamain and Greek Athena.

REFERENCES

Text: Rabinowitz 1956; *TAD* D15.1. Studies: Dumbrell 1971; Fitzmyer and Kaufman 1992:B.3.f.12.

SILVER BOWL (Brooklyn Museum 57.121) (2.51B)
(First Half of Fifth Century BCE)

(That which)[3] Ḥarbek[4] son of Pa(u)siri[5] offered[6] [a]	*a* Ezra 7:17	to Hanilat the goddess[7]

[3] The scribe omitted the initial *zy*, "that which" found in the two inscriptions below.

[4] The name is Egyptian — *Ḥr-byk*, "Horus (the) Falcon" — as is that of the father. Ḥarbek must have been at least a third generation settler in Egypt.

[5] Pasiri = *pa-Wsir*, "He of Osiris."

[6] The stem *qrb* was used in Official Aramaic (*KAI* 2.229), Nabataean (*NSI* 100:1), and Palmyrene (*NSI* 133:1) with the sense of presenting an object to deity. See below on *COS* 2.60 (Serapeum offering table).

[7] It was proper in monuments, and not *de rigeur* in graffiti, to add masculine *ʾlhʾ*, "the god" or feminine *ʾlhtʾ*, "the goddess" to the divine name (cf. *COS* 2.41; *TAD* D20.3:2, *COS* 2.62 and 2.64; *KAI* 2.229). Strikingly, only one of the four bowls here has the addition of the title.

REFERENCES

Text: Rabinowitz 1959; *TAD* D15.1. Studies: Dumbrell 1971; Fitzmyer and Kaufman 1992:B.3.f.12; Honeyman 1960.

SILVER BOWL (Brooklyn Museum 54.50.32) (2.51C)
(First Half of Fifth Century BCE)

That which[8] Ṣeḥo son of Abdamru[9] offered[b] to	*b* Ezra 7:17	Hanilat

[8] Elliptical for "Bowl which (*zy*) Ṣeḥo ...;" see *KAI* 2.1, 4-7, 25, 201-202, 229 and discussion on Serapeum offering table below *COS* 2.60. The voiced dental in all the inscriptions discussed in this collection was expressed by *zayin*, thus *zy* not *dy* and *znh* not *dnh*; cf. *COS* 2.41.

[9] The praenomen is an Egyptian name (Ṣeḥo = *ḏd-ḥ*[*r*], "The Face Spoke") well known in Aramaic texts (see glossaries in *TAD* B and C) and the patronym occurs in Nabataean documents (Cantineau 1932:126). The name *ʿmrw* is found in Palmyrene (Stark 1971:45) and the root *ʿmr* is very popular in North Arabian names (Harding 1971:10-411). Is this root related to Biblical *ʿmry*, Omri (1 Kgs. 16:16)?

REFERENCES

Text: Rabinowitz 1956; *TAD* D15.3. Studies: Cantineau 1932; *DAE* No. 79; Dumbrell 1971; Fitzmyer and Kaufman 1992:B.3.f.12; Harding 1971; Stark 1971.

SILVER BOWL (Brooklyn Museum 54.50.34) (2.51D)
(Second Half of Fifth Century BCE)

That which Kainu[10] [c] son of Geshem[11] [d] king[12] of Kedar[13] [e] offered[f] to Hanilat	*c* Gen 4:1; 5:9 *d* Neh 2:19; 6:1-2, 6 *e* Gen 25:13 ‖ 1 Chr 1:29; Isa 21:16-17; 42:11; 60:7; Jer 2:10; 49:28; Ps 120:5; Cant 1:5 *f* Ezra 7:17

[10] The name is found in Nabataean inscriptions (Cantineau 1932:142) and the root *qyn* in North Arabian inscriptions (Harding 1971:492-493) and in Hebrew.

[11] Known as Geshem the Arabian, Geshem, or Gashmu, he was associated with Sanballat (Sin-uballiṭ) the Horonite and Tobiah the Ammonite servant (of the king?) in opposition to Nehemiah, governor of Judah (Neh. 2:19; 6:1-2, 6). His memory survived for a couple centuries so that the land of Goshen, where Jacob's family settled, was designated by the translator of the Septuagint as the land of Gesem of Arabia (LXX Gen. 45:10, 46:34). Some would identify Geshem with Jašm son of Šahr who appears in a Lihyanite inscription from Dedan dated to the fifth century BCE (Winnett 1937:50-51), but others are sceptical (Ephʿal 1982:210-214). The name is common in Nabataean (cf. *NSI* p. 255; see Contineau 1932:80 [where also *gšmw*]); Safaitic, Thamudic, Qatabanian, and Lihyanite inscriptions (as *jšm* [Harding 1971:162]).

[12] In his memoirs, Nehemiah withheld any title from his three opponents, although we know that Sanballat was "governor" (*pḥh*) of Samaria (*TAD* A4.7:29). Nor does Jašm (Geshem) bear a title in the Lihyanite inscription. During the time of Sennacherib, Ḥazail was styled "king of the Arabs" and his son Iauta is referred to by Ashurbanipal as "King of Kedar." For detailed discussion of the Kedarites see Ephʿal 1982.

[13] Filiated with Ishmael, Kedar was associated with Dedan, Edom, Nebaioth, and Arabia; possessed tents, flocks, and camels with their chiefs (*nśyʾym*) trading in lambs, rams, and goats. For geographical location see the references in Rabinowitz 1956:3.

REFERENCES

AC No. 44; Contineau 1932:142; *DAE* No. 78; Dumbrell 1971; Ephʿal 1982; Fitzmyer and Kaufman 1992:B.3.f.12; Harding 1971:492-493; *NSI*; Rabinowitz 1956; *TAD* D15.4; *SSI* 2:25; Winnett 1937:50-51.

C. MORTUARY INSCRIPTIONS

1. HEBREW INSCRIPTIONS

KHIRBET EL-QOM (2.52)

P. Kyle McCarter

This late eighth-century BCE epitaph appears on a slab of limestone recovered in 1967 after having been looted from a cave-tomb at the site of Khirbet el-Qom, about eight miles west of Hebron in the Judaean hills. The slab was originally part of a pillar adjoining one of the burial chambers in the tomb. The interpretation of the inscription, which is rather crudely written and not deeply incised, is hampered by the fact that much of the text has been retraced, with the result that many letters appear twice, sometimes superimposed on each other, so that it is often difficult for the epigraphist to decide which letters to read and which to ignore. The text surmounts a deeply incised representation of an inverted human hand, which, though it resembles the common Islamic talisman known as "the hand of Fatima," seems to have been in place before the Iron Age inscription was carved around it.

ᵓUriyahu, the rich[1]: (This is) his inscription. Blessed was Uriyahu to Yahweh,[a] and from his enemies,[2] [b] by his asherah,[3] [c] he saved him.[d]

(Written by?) ᵓOniyahu.[4]

a 1 Sam 15:13; 23:21; 2 Sam 2:5; Ps 115:15; Ruth 2:19, 20; 3:10 *b* 2 Sam 22:4 *c* Exod 34:13; Deut 7:5; 12:3; 1 Kgs 14:15, 23; 16:33; 2 Kgs 13:16; 17:10; 18:14; 21:3; 23:14; cf. 1 Kgs 15:1; 18:19; 2 Kgs 21:7; 23:4, 7; Jer 17:2; 1 Chr 15:16 *d* Ps 44:8

[1] Reading *hᶜšr*. This seems a strange way to identify the deceased, and in fact the *ᶜayin* is uncertain.

[2] When the overwriting described above is taken into account, the reading *wmṣryh* seems secure and is now accepted by most scholars (the objection of Olyan [1988:24 and n. 6] to the spelling of the suffix must be taken seriously, but despite the contraction in the sixth-century Lachish form, *ᵓnšw*, "his men," it is reasonable to suppose that the suffixed plural ending **-ayhū* remained uncontracted in the eighth century). Naveh (1979: 28-29) read *nṣry*, "my guardian," yielding a translation that has the merit of conforming to the Kuntillet ᶜAjrud blessing formula (see *COS* 2.47A-C): "Blessed be Uriahu by YHWH my guardian and by his Asherah."

[3] This phrase, *lᵓšrth*, was partially clarified by the discovery of the Kuntillet ᶜAjrud blessing formula ("Blessed be PN by Yahweh ... and his asherah!"), providing the clue that most interpreters of the Khirbet el-Qom text have followed (contrast Mittmann 1981). Thus Lemaire, arguing that the scribe wrote *lᵓšrth* out of sequence in Uriah's inscription, reconstructs *brk ᵓryhw lyhwh wlᵓšrth mmṣryh hwšᶜ lh*, "Blessed be Uriyahu by Yahweh and by his asherah; from his enemies he saved him!" In this way, Lemaire succeeds in producing a smooth and idiomatic reading that is consistent with the evidence of Kuntillet ᶜAjrud. The rearrangement is too arbitrary to inspire confidence, however (but cf. Miller 1981:315-20), and other solutions, interpreting *lᵓštrh* as a vocative particle with a personal name (Angerstorfer 1982, "O Ashirta"; Zevit 1984, "O Asherata," with "double feminization") and/or appealing to the canons of poetic syntax (O'Connor 1987) have been proposed. As translated above, the text is understood to give credit to Yahweh's asherah — that is, his divine presence as available in the cult (see *COS* 2.47A, note 3) — for Uriyahu's salvation from his enemies during his lifetime.

[4] The phrase *lᵓnyhw*, written just below the main inscription and to the viewer's left of the inverted hand, might be a indicator of the identity of the man who carved Uriyahu's inscription. Alternatively, it might be the laconic epitaph of another resident of the same burial chamber. Further down on the stone, on the same (left) side of the hand, appear two further lines, the meaning of which is enigmatic: *lᵓšrth wlᵓšrth*, "To his asherah, and to his asherah."

REFERENCES

Text: *AHI* 25.003; *HAE* 1: 199-211. Translations and studies: Angerstorfer 1982; Barag 1970; Dever 1969-70; Hadley 1987b; Jaroš 1982; Lemaire 1977; Margalit 1989; Miller 1981; Mittmann 1981; Naveh 1979; O'Connor 1987; Olyan 1988:23-25; Shea 1990; Tigay 1986:29-30; Zevit 1984.

THE KHIRBET BEIT LEI CAVE INSCRIPTIONS (2.53)

P. Kyle McCarter

These two inscriptions, along with several shorter texts and a number of graffiti, were discovered during road construction in a burial cave at the site of Khirbet Beit Lei, about five miles east of Lachish in the Judaean Shephelah. Though found in a burial cave, the texts are not conventional tomb inscriptions, and no grave-goods were found with them. They offer praise to the god of Israel and invoke his help and succor, suggesting that they were incised in the rock walls by refugees seeking shelter in the cave. This also explains the discrepancy between the archaeological date of the burial cave, which is of a standard eighth- or seventh-century type (Lemaire), and the palaeographical date of the script, which, though difficult to date because of its crude character, seems to belong to the beginning of the sixth century BCE (Cross; contrast Naveh, Lemaire and Mittmann: late eighth century; Gibson *SSI*: late sixth century).

Inscription A
Yahweh is the god of the whole earth.[a] The highlands of Judah[b] belong to the god of Jerusalem.[1] [c]

Inscription B
Intervene,[2] O[3] compassionate god![4] [d] Absolve, O[3] Yahweh!

a Isa 54:5; cf. Josh 3:11, 13; Mic 4:13; Zech 4:14; 6:5; Ps 97:5
b 2 Chr 21:11 *c* 2 Chr 32:19; cf. Ezra 7:19 *d* Jon 4:2; Exod 34:6; Ps 86:15; Neh 9:31; cf. Joel 2:13; Pss 103:8; 111:4; 145:8; Neh 9:17; 2 Chr 30:9

[1] The reading *hry yhdh lʾlhy yršlm* is essentially that of Lemaire (followed by Renz *HAE* 246), who, however, reads *yhwdh* despite the improbability of the internal vowel letter (*waw*) in a pre-exilic inscription. A substantially different interpretation of the entire text is offered by Cross (1970:299-302, followed in part by Miller 1981:320-332) and Weippert (1964:161-164).

[2] That is, *pqd* (Lemaire, Miller), but the reading is difficult. Cross reads *nqh*, "Absolve," as later in the line, and Naveh's original reading (corresponding to *pqd yh*, "Intervene, O ...") was *hmwryh*, "(Mount) Moriah ..."

[3] Interpreting *yh* with Cross as the vocative particle known also from Aram. and Arab. (*yā*) as well as Ug. (*y*). The alternative is to render *yh*, as "Yah," the shortened form of "Yahweh," which is well known from the Bible but always in specialized circumstances and often in textually troubled contexts. To the end of Inscription B, compare especially "Yah, Yahweh" in Isa 12:2 and 26:4, both of which are textually uncertain (Renz *HAE* 248. n. 3).

[4] That is, *ʾl ḥnn*, as also in Kuntillet ʿAjrud Pithos 2 (*COS* 2.47B, note 3).

REFERENCES

Text: *AHI* 15.005-008; *HAE* 1: 245-49; *SSI* 1: 57-58. Translations and studies: Cross 1970; Lemaire 1976; Miller 1981; Mittmann 1989; Naveh 1963; Weippert 1964.

THE ROYAL STEWARD INSCRIPTION (2.54)

P. Kyle McCarter

This damaged grave inscription was found beneath a modern building in a burial chamber hewn from the rock of the eastern slope of the Kidron Valley in the village of Silwan in southeastern Jerusalem. The tomb is widely believed to have been that of the Hezekiah's royal steward Shebna, who was condemned by the prophet Isaiah for, among other things, presuming to have a tomb cut for himself in the rock (Isa 22:15-25). Though he may have lost the office of royal steward at this time, he seems to have remained in Hezekiah's administration as a royal secretary, and in this capacity he was among the party sent by Hezekiah to negotiate with the Assyrians during Sennacherib's siege of Jerusalem in 701 BCE (2 Kgs 18:13-19:7 = Isa 36:1-37:7).

Identification of the Deceased (line 1)
This is [the tomb[1] of Sheban]iah,[2] [a] who is over the house.[3] [b]

Curse against Desecration of the Grave (lines 1-3)
There is no silver or gold here — only [his bones] and the bones of his maidservant[4] (who is) with him. Cursed be the man who opens this (tomb)!

a 2 Kgs 18:18, 26, 37; 19:2 Isa 22:15; 36:3, 11, 22; 37:2
b 1 Kgs 4:6; 16:9; 18:3; 2 Kgs 10:5; 15:5; 18:18; Isa 22:15; 36:3

[1] The fem. pronoun that begins the inscription (*zʾt*, "this") requires the reconstruction in the lacuna of a feminine noun, probably *qbrt*, "the tomb of, the grave of."

[2] Only the end of the name of the deceased (*-yhw*) is preserved after the lacuna. The reconstruction is based on the script of the epitaph, which requires a paleographic date at the end of the eighth or beginning of the seventh century, that is, to the reign of Hezekiah. We know of two individuals, Shebna (Isa 22:15) and Eliakim (Isa 36:3; 37:2) who held the position of "the one who is over the house" in Hezekiah's administration. Of these two names, only that of Shebna in its longer form *šbnyhw*, "Shebanyahu" or "Shebaniah" (cf. 1 Chr 15:24) fits here.

[3] The title *ʾšr ʿl hbyt*, "the one who is over the house," is well known from Heb. seals and the Bible, where it is held by high-ranking individuals (1 Kgs 4:6; 16:9; 18:3; etc.), who seem in particular to have had responsibility for the management of the king's household. For this reason, the position is often described as that of "royal steward," or "palace steward"; cf. *COS* 2.70D and T.

[4] While it is true that biblical law makes special provision for the protection of a woman who was part of a man's household but not his legal wife (Gibson *SSI* 1:25), it is still surprising to learn that Shebaniah was buried with a servant.

REFERENCES

Text: *AHI* 4.401; *HAE* 1:261–265; KAI 2:#191B; *SSI* 1:23–24. Translations and studies: Avigad 1953; Clermont-Ganneau 1871; Good 1979; Katzenstein 1960.

---

2. PHOENICIAN INSCRIPTIONS

THE SARCOPHAGUS INSCRIPTION OF ᵓAHIROM, KING OF BYBLOS (2.55)

P. Kyle McCarter

The limestone sarcophagus of King ᵓAhirom (*fl.* 1000 BCE) was found in 1923 during the French excavations at Byblos. ᵓAhirom's epitaph, commissioned by his son and successor, ᵓIttobaᶜl, is carved around the edge of the lid and the upper rim of the coffin. The inscription surmounts an elaborate relief, in which the king is depicted enthroned on a cherub throne and receiving offerings from a procession of dignitaries; women in mourning are depicted on the two ends of the coffin. The ᵓAhirom epitaph is the earliest known Phoenician inscription of substantial length.

Identification of the sarcophagus (line 1)
The sarcophagus[a] that ᵓIttobaᶜl,[1] son of ᵓAhirom,[2] the king of Byblos, made for ᵓAhirom, his father, when he placed him in eternity.[3] [b]

Curses against desecration of the sarcophagus (line 2)
And if a king among kings or a governor[c] among governors or the commander[4] of an army should rise up against[d] Byblos and uncover this sarcophagus, may the scepter[e] of his rule be uprooted,[f] may the throne of his kingship be overturned,[g] and may peace depart from Byblos! And as for him, may his inscription be effaced with the double edge[5] of a chisel (?)[6]!

a Gen 50:26 *b* Eccl 12:5 *c* Isa 22:15 *d* 1 Sam 11:1; 1 Kgs 14:25; 20:1; 2 Kgs 6:24; 16:9; 17:5; 18:9, 13; 24:10; Isa 7:1; 36:1; 2 Chr 12:2, 9; 16:1 *e* Isa 11:1 *f* Isa 14:5; Jer 48:17 *g* Ps 89:45

[1] ᵓIttobaᶜl was also the name of the mid-ninth century king of Tyre whose daughter, Jezebel, was the queen of King Ahab of Israel; though his name is vocalized ᵓ*etbaᶜal*, "Ethbaal," in MT, the correct Phoen. pronunciation is preserved in Josephus as *Ithōbalos* (*Apion* 1.156). A second ᵓIttobaᶜl of Tyre (*Tubaᵓlu* in Assyrian inscriptions) ruled at the end of the eighth century. See *COS* 2.117B, note 5; *ANET* 287, 288.

[2] In shortened form, Hirom, the name appears as that of at least two kings of Tyre: the first, the biblical Hiram, was a contemporary of David and Solomon, and the second (*Ḫirummu* in Assyrian records) ruled in the eighth century (*ANET* 283).

[3] No precise parallel to the expression "placed him in eternity" exists, though its meaning seems clear. A number of scholars (Albright 1947:155 n. 19; Galling 1950; Rosenthal, *ANET* 661), assuming a scribal error, would emend the text to read "as his abode in eternity" (*kš<b>th bᶜlm*). The proposal of Tawil (1970-71; accepted by Gibson, *SSI* 3:15), that *bᶜlm* is an abbreviation for *bt ᶜlm*, "(in) the house of eternity," is unlikely in an early Phoen. text.

[4] This meaning of Phoen. *tmᵓ*, which seems to occur in Punic as *tmyᵓ* (Tomback 1978:341), is probable from the context.

[5] The meaning of the final phrase is uncertain. To *lpp*, "with the double edge (of)," compare the use of *pîpîyyôt* in Ps 149:6.

[6] The conjecture that Phoenician *šbl* is some kind of tool, such as a chisel (Donner 1953-54:157 n. 16), is based entirely on context, and several other suggestions, none persuasive, have been made.

REFERENCES

Text: *KAI* 2:2-4, 338; *SSI* 3:12-16. Translations and studies: *ANET* 661; Albright 1947; Donner 1953-54; Dussaud 1924; Galling 1950; Greenfield 1971:254-257; Tawil 1970-71; Tomback 1978.

THE SARCOPHAGUS INSCRIPTION OF TABNIT, KING OF SIDON (2.56)

P. Kyle McCarter

Tabnit's sarcophagus was found in 1887 during the excavation of a shaft tomb in Sidon. It was manufactured in Egypt of black basalt, and it bears a hieroglyphic inscription that shows it was originally intended for an Egyptian general by the name of Pen-Ptah (Assman 1963). It was evidently brought to Phoenicia as plunder and appropriated as a coffin for Tabnit, who ruled Sidon in the second quarter of the fifth century BCE (see n. 1). The eight-line Phoenician inscription, primarily a warning to discourage grave robbers, is engraved beneath the hieroglyphic text at the base of the sarcophagus, which is now in the Museum of Antiquities in Istanbul.

Identification of the deceased (lines 1-3)
I, Tabnit,[1] priest of ʿAshtart,[2] king of the Sidonians, son of ʾEshmunʿazor,[3] priest of ʿAshtart, king of the Sidonians, am lying in this coffin.[a]

Warning against desecration of the sarcophagus (lines 3-8)
Whoever you are, any man who comes upon this coffin, do not, do not[3] open my cover and disturb me,[b] for no silver is gathered with me (and) no gold is gathered with me or any kind of riches.[4] I alone am lying in this coffin. Do not, do not open my cover and disturb me, for such a thing would be an abomination[c] to ʿAshtart! And if you do open my cover and disturb me, may you have[5] no offspring among the living[d] under the sun[e] or a resting place with the Repaʾim.[6] [f]

a Gen 50:26
b 1 Sam 28:15
c Deut 7:25; 12:31; 17:1; 18:12; 22:5; 23:19; 27:15
d Eccl 4:15; 6:8; 7:2; 9:9
e Eccl 4:15; 6:12; 9:9
f Isa 14:9; 26:14, 19; Ps 88:11; Job 26:5; Prov 2:18; 9:18; 21:16

[1] For historical and archaeological reasons the Sidonian dynasty founded by Tabnit's father, ʾEshmunʿazor I, must be dated to the fifth century BCE (Peckham 1968:78-87). Tabnit's reign, which was probably in the second quarter of the fifth century, was not a long one, as suggested by the testimony of the ʾEshmunʿazor inscription (*COS* 2.57), which indicates that Tabnit's son and heir, ʾEshmunʿazor II, was born after his father's death and that Tabnit's queen, ʾUmmiʿAshtart, ruled as regent with her minor son during his own short reign.

[2] ʿAshtart was the principal goddess of Sidon, whose king, at least in Tabnit's case, held the sacerdotal office of her chief priest.

[3] Note the emphatic repetition *ʾl ʾl*, "Do not, do not ...!" here and in line 5 below.

[4] To *mšr*, "riches," cp. Akk. *mašrû*, "wealth, riches" (Lipiński 1974).

[5] The text seems defective here, and most scholars reconstruct *y<k>n l<k>*, following the text of line 8 of the ʾEshmunʿazor inscription (*COS* 2.57).

[6] Deified royal ancestors — a group that appears frequently in the Ug. literature and occasionally in the HB, where the term also comes to refer to certain primordial inhabitants of Syria-Palestine and, in the Deuteronomistic literature, esp. Transjordan. For literature, see Hallo 1992:382-386.

REFERENCES

Text: *KAI* 2:17-19; *SSI* 3:101-105. Translations and studies: *ANET* 662; Assman 1963; Greenfield 1971:258-259; Hallo 1992:382-386; 1993:188-191; Lipiński 1974.

THE SARCOPHAGUS INSCRIPTION OF ʾESHMUNʿAZOR, KING OF SIDON (2.57)

P. Kyle McCarter

This black basalt sarcophagus, manufactured in Egypt and imported to Phoenicia, was found in 1855 in a shallow, rock-cut tomb in the Sidonian necropolis. After a false start on the head of the coffin itself, the stonecutter engraved the full inscription on the lid. ʾEshmunʿazor became king at the death of his father, Tabnit, in the mid-fifth century BCE. He was an infant at the time of his accession and lived to reign only fourteen years as a vassal ruler of the Persian Empire. The text recounts his achievements and those of his mother, who evidently served as regent during his reign (see further n. 9, and *COS* 2.56, note 1).

Introduction and date formula (lines 1-2)
In the month of Bul,[1] [a] in the fourteenth year — 14 — of the reign of King ʾEshmunʿazor,[2] king of the Sidonians, son of Tabnit,[3] king of the Sidonians, King ʾEshmunʿazor, king of the Sidonians, said:

The king's self-lamentation (lines 2-4)
I was snatched away[b] (when it was) not my time,[c] a man of a limited number[4] of days,[d] an invalid,[5] an orphan, the son of a widow[6]; and (now) I am lying in this coffin, in this grave in a place that I built.

Curses against desecration of the sarcophagus (lines 4-13)
Whoever you are, any ruler or any (ordinary) man, do not open this resting-place and look for anything in it, for nothing has been placed in it, and do not carry away the coffin of my resting-place and move me from this resting-place to another resting-place! Even if men tell you (something different), do not

a 1 Kgs 6:38
b Isa 38: 9-12; Ps 102:24-25; Job 10:20-22
c Job 22:16; Eccl 7:17
d Job 10:20; 14:1

[1] The month of Bul was the eighth month in the old Canaanite calendar used by the Phoenicians and, originally, the Israelites (cf. *bûl* in 1 Kgs 6:38); it corresponded to the later Jewish month of Marcheshvan.

[2] ʾEshmunʿazor II (ca. 465-451 BCE) was the son of Tabnit (ca. 470-465 BCE) and the grandson of ʾEshmunʿazor I (ca. 479-470 BCE). The dates for the kings of the ʾEshmunʿazor dynasty are those calculated by Peckham 1968:78-87.

[3] For Tabnit's epitaph, see *COS* 2.56.

[4] Several scholars have compared the obscure term *msk* to Syriac *sāk*, "end, limit, sum," which may be used in reference to the limit or summing-up of one's lifespan and commonly occurs in expressions stressing brevity.

[5] The term *ʾzrm* remains unexplained. It is also used of a type of *mulk* or child sacrifice (Tomback 1974:9), but the relationship of this technical term to the present context in far from clear. The conjectural translation "invalid" is based on the observations of G. R. Driver (cf. Gibson *SSI* 3:110).

[6] The meaning is presumably that Tabnit had died before ʾEshmunʿazor was born.

listen to their lies! For any ruler or (ordinary) man who opens the cover of this resting-place or carries off the coffin of my resting-place and moves from this resting place, let him have no resting-place with the Rephaʾim,[7] [e] let him not be buried in a grave, and let him have no son or offspring to take his place! And may the holy gods deliver him up to a mighty ruler who shall hold sway over him to bring an end to him — any ruler or (ordinary) man who opens the cover of this resting-place or carries off this coffin, or the offspring of that ruler or those (ordinary) men! Let him have no root below or fruit above[f] or form[8] among the living[g] under the sun![h] For I deserve pity: I was snatched away (when it was) not my time, a man of a limited number of days; an invalid, an orphan, the son of a widow was I.

e Isa 14:9; 26:14, 19; Ps 88:11; Job 26:5; Prov 2:18; 9:18; 21:16

f Amos 2:9; Job 18:16; cf. Isa 37:31

g Eccl 4:15; 6:8; 7:2; 9:9

h Eccl 4:15; 6:12; 9:9

The achievements of ʾEshmunʿazor (lines 13-20)
For I, ʾEshmunʿazor, king of the Sidonians, son of King Tabnit, king of the Sidonians, grandson of King ʾEshmunʿazor, kings of the Sidonians, and my mother, ʾUmmiʿashtart,[9] the priestess of ʿAshtart, our lady,[10] the queen, the daughter of King ʾEshmunʿazor, king of the Sidonians — we are the ones who[11] built the houses of the gods: [the house of ʿAshtar]t in Sidon-Land-of-the-Sea[12] and enthroned[13] ʿAshtart in the Majestic-Heavens [14]; and we are the ones who built the house of ʾEshmun, the holy prince,[15] at the spring of YDLL[16] on the hill, and enthroned him in the Majestic-Heavens; and we are the ones who built houses for the gods of Sidon in Sidon-Land-of-the-Sea, a house for Baʿl of Sidon[17] and a house of ʿAshtart-Name-of-Baʿl.[18] Moreover, the Lord of Kings[19] gave us Dor and Joppa, the majestic corn lands that are in the Plain of Sharon, in accordance with the mighty deeds that I performed, and we added them to the limits of the land so that they would belong to the Sidonians forever.

Final warning against desecration (lines 20-22)
Whoever you are, any ruler or any (ordinary) man, do not open my cover, and do not take off my cover and move me from this resting-place, and do not carry away the coffin of my resting-place, lest these holy gods deliver them up and they — that ruler or those (ordinary) men — be brought to an end forever!

---

[7] See the Tabnit inscription (*COS* 2.56, note 6).

[8] The sense of *tʾr* is "form, visible presence" (cf. Gibson *SSI* 3:111 n. 12).

[9] ʾUmmiʿashtart is a common Phoen. name (Benz 1972:62) meaning "My (divine) mother is (the goddess) ʿAshtart." Her role as regent during her son's reign is made clear by the language of the inscription: "... *we* are the ones who built the houses of the gods ..., and *we* are the ones who built the house of ʾEshmun ..., and *we* are the ones who built houses for the gods of Sidon .... Moreover, the Lord of Kings gave *us* Dor and Joppa ...."

[10] Probably a title of the goddess rather than another designation of the queen-mother.

[11] Assuming, with most scholars, that *ʾm* is a scribal error for *ʾš*.

[12] "Sidon Land-of-the-Sea" (*ṣdm ʾrṣ ym*) was evidently the same district of the city called "Sidon-of-the-Sea" (*ṣdn ym*) in one of the two building inscriptions of ʾEshmunʿazor's successor, Bodʿashtart (*KAI* 2: 24).

[13] Assuming, with most scholars, that *wyšrn* is a scribal error for *wyšbn*, the verb used immediately below in an identical context.

[14] Here and below, "the Mighty-Heavens," refers to a shrine or precinct within a temple — in this case the seaside temple built (or rebuilt) for ʿAshtart and below the hilltop temple of ʾEshmun.

[15] The same epithet is used of ʾEshmun in the two building inscriptions of ʾEshmunʿazor's successor, BodʿAshtart (*KAI* 2:23-25).

[16] "The spring of YDLL" is evidently the same as "the spring of YDL" mentioned in the Baʿlshillem inscription found in the temple of ʾEshmun at Bostan esh-Sheikh (Dunand 1965) north of Sidon, where the two inscriptions of Bodʿashtart, ʾEshmunʿazor's successor, were also found; the temple was located on a hill on the west bank of the river known today as the Nahr el-Awali, and "the spring of YDL(L)" must have been the ancient name of the source of this watercourse.

[17] The "Baʿl" (*bʿl*) or "Lord" of Sidon must have been the local genius of the city, a divine embodiment of Sidon itself. He is not known from other sources, however, and his relationship to ʾEshmun, who is usually understood to be the principal god of Sidon, is unclear.

[18] As her epithet "Name-of-Baʿl" indicates, this ʿAshtart was the consort of the city god, Baʿl of Sidon, and a personification of his cultically available presence (*šm*, "name").

[19] The title *ʾdn mlkm*, "Lord of Kings," or its equivalent was used from Assyrian to Hellenistic times, most often referring to the reigning emperor. In this case it denotes the Persian emperor (Peckham 1968: 80-86), probably Xerxes (486-465 BCE) or Artaxerxes I (465-425 BCE). The vassal-gift of Dor and Joppa with the Plain of Sharon was a generous one, including the port-city of Joppa as well as the whole of the former Assyrian province of Duru or Dor, including its rich farm lands and its own port.

REFERENCES

Text: *KAI* 2:19-23; *SSI* 3:105-114; Translations and studies: *ANET* 662; Benz 1972; Dunand 1965; Galling 1963; Garbini 1977b; Ginsberg 1963; Greenfield 1971:259-265; Peckham 1968; Tomback 1978.

THE FUNERARY INSCRIPTION FROM PYRGI (2.58)

P. Kyle McCarter

The Phoenician inscription is engraved on a sheet of gold leaf found in excavations at the site of ancient Pyrgi (Santa Severa), the principal port of the wealthy Etrurian city of Caere (modern Cerveteri, ca. 30 miles north of Rome on the Tyrrhenian coast), in the ruins of a temple dated archaeologically to ca. 500 BCE. The sheet was found together with two similar plaques bearing Etruscan inscriptions, one of which seems to correspond in content to the Phoenician text, though, unfortunately for our knowledge of the still incompletely understood Etruscan language, the two inscriptions do not constitute a true bilingual. The text records the dedication of a shrine to the Phoenician goddess ᶜAshtart, who was identified at Pyrgi with the Etruscan Uni, to whom the larger sanctuary was sacred. As shown by Knoppers (1992), the nature of the shrine was probably funerary, erected to commemorate the burial of a prominent individual, who was deified at death and is thus referred to in the inscription as "the god."

Dedication and construction of the shrine (lines 1-9)
To the Lady ᶜAshtart[1]: This holy place[2] which Thebariye Velinas, king over Kaysriye,[3] made and dedicated in the month of the Sacrifice of the Sun[4] as a gift (and) as a temple.[5] I built it because ʿAshtart requested it from me[a] in the third year of my reign in the month of Kirar[6] on the day of the burial of the god.[7]

A wish for the longevity of "the god" (lines 9-11)
And may the years during which[8] the god is in his house[9] be like these[10] stars![b]

a 2 Sam 7:4-6; 1 Kgs 8:17-21

b Isa 14:13 (?)

[1] In the Etruscan texts the divine name corresponding to ᶜAshtart is Unialastres, whose name has been explained as a combination of the names of the Etruscan goddess Uni (the Roman Juno) and the Phoen. goddess ᶜAshtart (Pallottino in Colonna, et al. 1964:84-85).

[2] The "holy place" was probably a shrine located within the precincts of the larger temple of Uni at Pyrgi (Garbini and Levi della Vida 1965:37). See also note 5 below.

[3] The vocalizations of the name of the Etruscan king and the Etruscan name of the city of Caere are based on the Etruscan texts. Thebariye is probably the equivalent of Latin Tiberius.

[4] Or "the month of the Sacrifices [pl.] of the Sun" (cf. Knoppers 1992:110-111). This month is also known from Phoen. inscriptions from Cyprus, though its position in the year is unknown. Knoppers (1992:111-112), noting the chthonic nature of the sun god in both Mesopotamian and Northwest Semitic religions, argues that the dedication of the shrine in this month is in keeping with the funerary character of the inscription.

[5] Reading *bmtn ᵓbbt*, with the *ᵓalep* understood as prosthetic (cf. Garbini and Levi della Vida 1965:41; Gibson *SSI* 3:156). The "temple" or "house" (*bt*) referred to here and in line 10 ("his house") was probably not the larger temple of Uni itself but rather the funerary shrine of the deified deceased ("the god").

[6] This month name appears several times in Phoen. and Punic texts, but, as in the case of the month of the Sacrifice of the Sun, the time of year to which it belonged is unknown. The same month-name (*Kiraru*) seems to have been known in northern Syria (Alalakh) already in the OB Period (*CAD* K 401).

[7] As convincingly argued by Knoppers (1992:114-117) the "god" (*ᵓlm*), which is frequently sing. in Phoen. (Tomback 1978:16-18), was probably a prominent citizen of Thebariye Velinas's kingdom whose burial and deification the shrine commemorates.

[8] Construing *lmᵓš* as *lm-* (the long form of the prep. *l-*) and the relative particle *ᵓš* (Février 1965:11, 14-15).

[9] The "god ... in his house" refers to the deceased deified and residing in his funerary shrine.

[10] The expression "like these stars" (*km hkkm ᵓl*) evidently expresses the pious hope that the years of the "god" residing in his "house" should be as numerous as the stars in the night sky, but the referent of *ᵓl*, "these," is admittedly rather vague, and this has provoked a number of other interpretations. The most ingenious is that of Dahood (1965), who took the phrase to mean "like the stars of ᵓEl," comparing *kôkᵉbê-ᵓēl*, "the stars of 'El," in Isa 14:13 and explaining the *-m* of *hkkm* as enclitic.

REFERENCES

Text, translations and studies: *KAI* 2:330-332; *SSI* 3:151-159; Colonna et al. 1964; Dahood 1965; Delcor 1968; Dupont-Sommer 1964; Ferron 1965; Février 1965; Fischer and Rix 1968; Fitzmyer 1966; Friedrich 1969; Garbini 1968; Garbini and Levi della Vida 1965; Heurgon 1966; Knoppers 1992.

3. ARAMAIC INSCRIPTIONS

THE TOMB INSCRIPTION OF SIᵓGABBAR, PRIEST OF SAHAR (2.59)

P. Kyle McCarter

Two funerary reliefs depicting deceased priests and inscribed with their epitaphs were found in 1891 at Nerab, southeast of Aleppo. The two inscriptions, which date to the early seventh century BCE, are written in the dialect known as Empire Aramaic, recognizable from a number of features of grammar and lexicon that show the influence of the dominant Assyrian language and culture of the period. The names of both priests honor the Assyrian god Sin, and it has been suggested that the sanctuary at Nerab was a satellite of the great temple of Sin at Harran (Gibson *SSI*

2:94). The epitaph translated here is written above a representation of the priest Siᵓgabbar, who is depicted in a seated position offering a libation at an altar, behind which is an attendant holding a fan.

Identification of the Deceased (lines 1-2)
Siᵓgabbar,[1] priest of Sahar[2] in Nerab. This is his picture.

The Piety of the Deceased (lines 2-6)
Because of my righteousness in his presence,[3] he gave me a good name and prolonged my days.[a] On the day I died, my mouth was not deprived of words, and with my eyes I beheld children of the fourth generation.[b] They wept for me and were greatly distraught.[4] But they did not place any silver or bronze with me; they placed me (here) with (only) my clothes, so that in the future my remains[5] would not be carried off.[6]

Warning against Desecration of the Sarcophagus (lines 6-10)
Whoever you are, who do (me) wrong[7] and carry me off, may Sahar, Nikkal[8] and Nusk[9] make his death ignominious, and may his posterity perish![c]

a 1 Kgs 3:14; cf. Deut 4:26, 40; 5:33; 11:9; 17:20; 22:7; 30:18; 32:47; Josh 24:31; Judg 2:7; Isa 53:10; Ps 72:5 (!); Prov 28:16; Job 29:18; Eccl 8:13
b Ps 128:6; Job 42:16 *c* Ps 37:38; 109:13

[1] The element *Siᵓ* is the West Semitic (Aram.) form of the name of the Mesopotamian god Sin (Kaufman 1970:271); thus Siᵓgabbar's name means "Sin is a warrior." [See also the Akk. attestation for the name, Parpola 1985. KLY].

[2] Sahar (*šhr* = *śhr*) was the Aramean moon-god (cf. Syriac *sahrā*, "moon").

[3] The assertion of "my righteousness in his presence" indicates, in the first place, simply that Siᵓgabbar's behavior met with Sahar's approval; but since Siᵓgabbar was a priest, the expression *qdmwh*, "before him, in his presence," refers more specifically to his performance of his sacerdotal duties in the service of the god.

[4] That is, *hwm ᵓthmw*. Evidently *hwm* (*hawm*) is a noun in cognate accusative construction rather than an infinitive absolute, for which we might have expected *hm* or *mhm* (cf. Gibson *SSI* 2:98 n. 6, but contrast Segert *AaG* 532).

[5] On this word (*ᵓrṣty*) see Kaufman (1974:50), who explains it in light of Akk. *eṣittu*, "bone, skeleton."

[6] The verb *lthns*, derived by some interpreters from a root *hns* (cf. Syriac *ᵓns*, "press, compel," which in the ᵓEthpeᵓel mean "be compelled, distressed," and Jewish Palestinian Aram. *ᵓns*. "oppress, overwhelm") is better explained as Hapᶜel of *nws* with the meaning "carry off" (*KAI* 2:210, 275, 276).

[7] Elsewhere in Aram., including Sefire III 20 (*COS* 2.82), and Hebrew the verb *ᶜšq* is transitive, meaning "oppress, do wrong (to), slander." Here the object is not expressed, but it may be implied or reverted from following verb.

[8] Nikkal is the Aram.-Phoen. version of the Sum.-Akk. Ningal, the consort of Sin.

[9] In Mesopotamian mythology Nuska or Nusku was esp. associated with the sacrificial flame, so that he is often described in modern literature as a "fire god." One of his most important roles was the expulsion of demons.

REFERENCES

Text, translations and studies: *KAI* 2:276; *SSI* 2:97-98; Kaufman 1970.

ARAMAIC MORTUARY TEXTS FROM EGYPT

Bezalel Porten

Achaemenid Egypt has yielded a half-dozen mortuary texts, one offering table and five stelae with Aramaic inscriptions. Their period of discovery spans two and one-quarter centuries (1704-1920's CE). Three certainly, and the others most likely, were found in the Memphis-Saqqarah area, and today each is housed in a different museum — Louvre in Paris (*COS* 2.60 [discovered 1851]), Musées Royaux d'Arts et d'Histoire in Brussels (*COS* 2.61 [1907]), municipal museum in Carpentras (*COS* 2.64 [1704]), and the Vatican in Rome (*COS* 2.65 [1860]). The one in the Staatliche Museen in Berlin was destroyed in World War II (*COS* 2.62 [pre-1877]) and the last one remains in an unknown storage site in Egypt (*COS* 2.63 [1920]). The Egyptian funerary scenes and the onomasticon indicate a ready adoption by Aramaean settlers of local practices, at the same time maintaining their native language, the *lingua franca* of the empire. Four stelae open with a blessing of the deceased (*COS* 2.61-64), three of them by the Egyptian god Osiris (*COS* 2.61-62, 2.64; cf. 2.65), who was slaughtered by his brother Seth and revived by his son Horus. The inscriptions came at the bottom of two or three registers of familiar Egyptian funerary scenes. The fifth stela inscription is merely a label identifying the deceased and it appears between two registers (*COS* 2.65). Two of the inscriptions are for a male (*COS* 2.63, 2.65), two for a female (*COS* 2.61, 2.64) and one for a couple (*COS* 2.62). This latter stela was prepared by a surviving son, adds a hieroglyphic inscription, and is dated to 4 Xerxes (482 BCE). The most famous of the stelae, that in Carpentras, is a quatrain of three four-beat bicola, internal rhyme in lines 2-3, and a concluding three-beat bicolon (*COS* 2.64). Twice the deceased, female and male, is designated by an Egyptian loanword meaning "(the) excellent (one)" (*COS* 2.64-65), while the Carpentras stela employs two more loanwords, one an epithet of deity, "Lord of Two Truths" (*nb mᵓᶜty*) and another of the defunct, "praiseworthy" (*ḥsyw*). Most of the names, both praenomen and patronym, are likewise Egyptian: *Bokrinf* father of

Tuma (*COS* 2.61), *Ḥor* father of Abah (*COS* 2.62), *Peṭees*[*e*] son of *Yhʾ*[...] (*COS* 2.63), *Tabi* daughter of *Taḥapi* (*COS* 2.64), and *Ankhoḥapi* son of *Takhabes* (*COS* 2.65). This is in stark contrast to the Jewish settlers in Egypt who preserved their Hebrew names. The names on the offering table were both Aramaean — Abitab son of Banit (*COS* 2.60). Though discovered in the Memphis Serapeum (thus dedicated to Osiris-Ḥapi = Serapis) in a Thirtieth Dynasty context (380-343 BCE), palaeographic considerations argue for an early fifth century date.[1] We may conjecture that along with numerous other tables, ours was moved from its original site to make way for the late pylon, in whose proximity they were then deposited. A new reading following recent collation presents a text which can best be understood as a calque on Egyptian grammar. In similar fashion, the Carpentras text (*COS* 2.64) may be seen as an abstract of Chapter 125 in the Book of the Dead (*COS* 2.12).[2]

[1] See Introduction to D20.1-6 in *TAD* D. Complete bibliography to these texts can be found there and in Fitzmyer and Kaufman 1992.

[2] These conclusions were worked out in conjunction with the Egyptologist John Gee and most of the Egyptological references are due to him. A joint article entitled "Aramaic Funerary Practices in Egypt" is scheduled to appear in the P.-E. Dion *Festschrift*.

OFFERING TABLE FROM THE MEMPHIS SERAPEUM (2.60)
(Early Fifth Century BCE)

Bezalel Porten

Written somewhat carelessly without clear word separation, this four-line text (Louvre A0 4824) is susceptible to different interpretations (see notes). The smoothest translation is achieved if we view it as a calque on Egyptian grammar. We surmise that the memorial offering-table was originally deposited in a public place outside the sanctuary proper. Offerings, whether periodic or occasional, would subsequently have been made to the deity, and the deceased would have taken his share therefrom. Bible and Apocrypha know of the practice of feeding the dead directly (Deut 26:14; Tob 4:17).

Offering-table[1] as an offering[2] of Banit[3] [a] to[4] Osiris-Ḥapi (Serapis)[5] (which) Abitab[6] [b] son of	*a* 2 Kgs 17:30 *b* 1 Chr 8:11	Banit made[7] for him[8] (so that)[9] he may be[10] before Osi>ḥ<ris-Ḥapi.[11]

[1] While the formula in this dedicatory inscription is familiar from Phoen. (cf. *KAI* 2.1, 4-7, 25) and Aram. (*KAI* 2.201-202, 215, 229, 239, 242-243, 258; *TAD* D17.1), the formulation here is syntactically elliptical. The first word always refers to the object dedicated, hence *ḥtpy* = Eg. *ḥtp.t* means here "offering table" (*Glossar* 338; cf. *DAE*, Lipiński 1978:111) and not "offering" (so *NSI*, *KAI*). The text regularly proceeded either with the relative ("which"), followed by verb-subject-indirect object (*KAI* 2.1, 4-7, 25, 201-202, 229), or with the demonstrative ("this"), likewise followed by verb-subject-indirect object (*KAI* 2.215, 258; *TAD* D17.1:1 = *COS* 2.41). In the first pattern the word order occasionally changed to subject-verb-indirect object (*KAI* 2.242-243). In our text the word order is verb (*ʿbd*)-subject (Abitab)-indirect object (*lh*). There is neither a relative nor a demonstrative pronoun. Conceivably, one may take the opening expression as a title and render: "Offering-table for the offering of Banit to Osiris-Ḥapi. Abitab son of Banit made it for him." The awkwardness is eliminated if we assume the grammar imitates an Eg. pattern wherein the relative marker *nty* (= Aram. *zy*) is omitted in the past tense, replaced by a special relative form of the verb, *r-sḏm.f*; see Johnson 1976:182.

[2] Official Aram. knows the use of the stem *qrb* both in the sense of approaching a person (*TAD* C1.1:50, 54, 57, 193-194) and presenting an offering to deity (*KAI* 2.229 [Teima]; *COS* 2.51B-D; cf. *TAD* A4.7:25, 28 ‖ 4.8:25, 27; Ezra 7:17). This is the only occurrence of the nominal form. Those who prefer the former sense point to the appearance of the defunct before Osiris for judgment (Book of the Dead, Chap. 125). But the terminology there is not "approach deity" but simply *iw r*, "come to (the hall)" (Lexa 1910:5) or *spr r*, "arrive at (the hall)" (Naville 1886:I, Pl. cxxxiii, line 1). Ordinarily in the Aram. inscriptions, the object would be dedicated (to a deity) for "the life" or "honor" of the deceased (references in *DNWSI* 812-813).

[3] A Mesopotamian female deity, appearing here in a rare but not unparalleled occurrence as a personal name; cf. Eg. *Ḥr*, "Horus" (*COS* 2.61). Banit was embraced by the Aramaeans and had a temple at Syene (*TAD* A2.2:1, 12, 2.3:7, 2.4:1). She appeared there and at Elephantine, at the same time as our text, in such personal masculine names as Banitsar (*TAD* A2.2:5, 2.6:8), Banitsarel (*TAD* 2.3:2), Baniteresh (*TAD* B2.1:19), and the dominant Makkibanit (*TAD* A2.1:8, etc.). In a Neo-Assyrian text from Nineveh involving Egyptians, a name that may be read Banitu appears as witness; Postgate 1976:No. 13:34 and n. on p. 103. In the Neo-Babylonian onomasticon, on the other hand, Banitu was found almost exclusively in female names; Tallqvist 1905:21-22. See further Cogan 1995.

[4] The preposition "to" appears in four votive bowl inscriptions (*COS* 2.51) but it alternates with "before" in blessings ("before:" *COS* 2.62; *TAD* D22:10-11, 16, 24, 26, 47, 49-52; "to:" *TAD* D22.13, 17-18, 29-32, 40-44).

[5] Upon death the Apis bull (*ḥpy*) became known as Osiris-Apis, Greek Serapis, and was buried in the Serapeum. Popular in Ptolemaic times, the term *Wsir Ḥpy* is found already in Serapeum stelae 22-23 dating to year 2 of Pimay (772 BCE); Malinine, Posener, and Vercoutter 1968:I, 21-23; II, Pl. viii. *Ḥpy* was a popular element in the personal names in these funerary texts — Taḥapi (*COS* 2.64) and Ankhoḥapi (*COS* 2.65). This fact suggested to Lévy 1927:285-286 that the respective stelae and the persons they commemorated stem from Memphis.

[6] A good West Semitic name ("[My] divine father is goodness"), occurring also in a graffito at the Seti Temple at Abydos: Abitab son of Shumtab (*TAD* D22:9).

[7] For the verb *ʿbd* in this context see *COS* 2.41.

[8] This word had been read *khy* and rendered "thus(?)" with no satisfactory etymology. Careful examination of the offering table reveals that the first letter is a *lamed* whose horizontal bar is mistakenly curved to the left rather than to the right. Read *lh*, "to him" (i.e. to Banit) and attach the *yod* to the following word (*yᶜbd*) (so Ada Yardeni). While word separation is not always clear in this text, there is noticeable space between *lh* and *yᶜbd*. It was not uncommon for a child to fashion the funerary object for the parent (cf. *COS* 2.62; *KAI* 2.1, 215; cf. *KAI* 2.239, 248 [husband]; references in *DNWSI* 812-813 passim).

[9] Aram. would normally employ the particle *kzy* to introduce a purpose (final) clause; Muraoka and Porten 1998:§52f. Its absence here is consonant with Eg. syntax which omits such a particle in the subjunctive *sḏm=f* in purpose clauses; see the hieroglyphic text in *COS* 2.62 below (*di.f qrst nfrt*, "so that he might give a good burial") and discussion in Johnson 1976:279-280, esp. E492B-D. Alternately, we may view the verb *yᶜbd* as jussive ("Let him be") and the construction as "two asyndetic clauses loosely hanging together" (T. Muraoka, written communication). This rendition, however, appears somewhat awkward.

[10] Aram. *ᶜbd* may be a calque of Eg. *iri* which besides its regular meaning of "do, make" may also mean "be, become." See the expression *ir=t wᶜ m-bꜣḥ pꜣ nb nṯr.w*, "may you be one before the lord of the gods" in parallel to *rpy=k m-bꜣḥ pꜣ nb nṯr.w*, "may you be rejuvenated before the lord of the gods"; P. Louvre E 10607, lines 7-8 in Smith 1993:23, Pl. 7; see also *Glossar* 36-37. Proper ritual, including offerings, would enable Banit to be an attendant in the presence of Serapis (cf. 2.64). This would be the sense of the Aram. verb if we took it conjecturally to mean "act." The verb also has the meaning of offering up a sacrifice, but with an object complement (*TAD* A4.7:21-22 ‖ A4.8:21), here to be understood as "make (offerings)." The clause would then express the determination of the son to attend to the funerary rites of his father. Reading *yᶜbr* and translating "Let it pass before Osiris-Ḥapi" does not seem to be an improvement. The simplest explanation is to assume an Eg. prototype, as argued above.

[11] The careless scribe, perhaps unskilled, anticipated the *ḥeth* of the second word in the line (*ḥpy*) already at the beginning of the line.

REFERENCES

CIS 2.123; *DAE* No. 84; Donner 1969; Fitzmyer and Kaufman 1992 B.3.e.8; *HNE* I, 128, 448, II, Pl. 28.2; Johnson 1976; *KAI* No. 268; Lévy 1927; Lexa 1910; Lipiński 1978; *NSI* No. 72; Malinine, Posener, and Vercoutter 1968; Muraoka and Porten 1998; Naville 1886; Postgate 1976; *TAD* D20.1; Smith 1993; Tallqvist 1905.

FUNERARY STELA (Brussels E. 4716) (2.61)
(Early Fifth Century BCE)

Bezalel Porten

Blessed[1] [a] be Tuma[2] daughter of Bokrinf[3] by[1] [a] Osiris.[4]	*a* Gen 14:19; Judg 17:2; 1 Sam 15:13; Ps 115:15; Ruth 3:10

[1] In the formula *brk* + *l/qdm*-DN, the deity has been considered not the agent but the indirect object of the preposition, thus "I bless you to/before DN, i.e. I pray to/before DN that he bless you"; Muraoka 1979:92-94; Muraoka and Porten 1998:§ 54d. Lipiński 1975:96-98 rendered it here "Be recommended to Osiris." For general discussion of this formula as commendation to deity cf. Scharbart 1975 2:279-308. The word *brk* occurs in four of the five stelae (*COS* 2.61-2.64), once with the preposition *qdm* (*COS* 2.62; see there *sub voce*). In the passive voice the dual formula occurs essentially in graffiti ("before" *TAD* D22:10-11, 16, 24, 26, 47, 49-52; "to:" D22.13, 17-18, 29-32, 40-44); in the active voice it appears in epistolary salutations (see references in *EPE* B1, n. 6). The passive formula also occurs in inscriptions from Hatra (*KAI* 2.244, 246 [*dkyr wbryk* PN *qdm* DN]) and in a Heb. tomb inscription (Dever 1971).

[2] The name is found frequently in Palmyra (Stark 1971:56; Lipiński 1975b:98) and a third century BCE Aram. ostracon mentions a "Tam wife of Malchiah son of Azgad" (*TAD* D7.57:4-5).

[3] Bokrinf = *bꜣk-rn.f*, "Servant of his Name," known through Greek transcription as Bocchoris, this name was borne by a well-known king of the Twenty-fourth Dynasty. See Lipiński 1975b:99-101.

[4] The name is here spelled *wsry*; in the other texts it is written with an initial *aleph*. The graffiti know three different spellings — *ꜣwsry* (*TAD* D22.10, 24), *ꜣsry* (*TAD* D22.13, 16), and *wsry* (*TAD* D22.11, 18).

REFERENCES

Lipiński 1975b; Muraoka 1979; Muraoka and Porten 1998; *RÉS* 1788; Scharbart 1975; Stark 1971; *TAD* D20.2

FUNERARY STELA FROM SAQQARAH (BERLIN GIPSFORMEREI 939 FORMERLY ÄM 7707 [destroyed WW II]) (2.62)

(482 BCE)

Bezalel Porten

Aramaic text

Blessed be Abah son of Ḥor[1] and Aḥatabu daughter of Adiyah,[2] all (told),[3] of Khastemeḥi the city[4] before Osiris the god.[5] Absali son of Abah,[6] his mother (being) Aḥatabu,[7] thus said[8] in year 4, month of Meḥir, (of) Xerxes[9] [a] the king[10] ...

a Esth 1:1, etc.; Dan 9:1; Ezra 4:6

[1] The son bore a hypocoristic Aram. name (cf. Abah father of Itu, an Aramaean scribe at Syene [*TAD* B2.2:16]) and the father an Eg. one (*Ḥr*, "Horus"), popular at Elephantine (*TAD* B3.10:10 ‖ 11:6, C3.4:16, 3.9:19, 3.10:3, 4.6:3, 4.8:7, etc.). The intermingling of Aram. and Eg. names was well-attested in the filiations of the Makkibanit letters sent to Syene and Luxor, probably from Memphis (*TAD* A2.1-7); cf. Nabushezib son of Peṭekhnum (*TAD* A2.1:15) and Makkibanit son of Psami (*TAD* A2.2:18).

[2] Here there are apparently two Aram. names. The praenomen has been explained as abbreviation of the Ersatzname *ʾḥt ʾbwh*, "Sister of her father" (*NSI*, *KAI*, *SSI*); Tallqvist 1905:3 compares Neo-Babylonian *Áḫ-at-bu-ú*. In the hieroglyphic text it is written *ʾḫtʾbw*. The patronym is identical with Heb. Adaiah, well attested in fifth century BCE Judah (Ezra 10:29, 39; Neh. 11:12 [*AC*]) but the stem is found in Moabite *ʿdʾl* (Zadok 1988:300), Nabataean *ʿdyw* (*CIS* 2.195:1 [*KAI*]; Cantineau 1932:127), Safaitic and Thamudic *ʿdy* (Harding 1971:410-411), Arabic ʿAdī, ʿAdiyāʾ [Jewish] (*EnIslam* 1:195-196 [reference from F. Rosenthal]). The name Adaios in the Greek inscriptions (adduced by Lipiński 1978a:105-106) may reflect ʾAdi and not ʿAdi (Wuthnow 1930:12; F. Rosenthal orally); likewise with similar spellings such as Addaios, Adeios, Adeou. Our name is not to be found in the well documented onomasticon of Elephantine. Given the pattern of name-giving among the Jews there it is questionable whether among the five names represented here this alone is Jewish; see Porten 1968:133-150. Positive determination would mean that the Jew Adaiah had assimilated to the pagan Aramaean-Egyptian society; Lévy 1927:287.

[3] Such enumeration of personal names was common in Aram. contracts (*TAD* B2.9:2-3, 2.11:2; 3.12:3, 11) and letters (*TAD* A6.3:5, 6.7:5).

[4] The word now read by A. Yardeni as *qrytʾ*, "the city" was formerly misread as *qrbtʾ* and erroneous derivations were proposed for the preceding *ḫstmḥ*. The newly retrieved formula is familiar from the Elephantine contracts with the addition of an ethnicon, "PN son of PN, Jew/Aramaean of Elephantine/Syene"; see discussion with references in *EPE* 153, n. 4. The site has been identified independently by K.-Th. Zauzich (orally) and J. Yoyotte 1995 with Khastemeḥi, adjacent to or identical with Marea at Egypt's western border where Herodotus (ii.30) cited the location of an outpost, just as at Elephantine.

[5] Several Aram. graffiti on the walls of the Osiris temple at Abydos likewise contained the formula "Blessed be PN (son of PN) before Osiris" (*TAD* D22.10-11, 13, 16-18, 24). Here he is identified as "the god" and in the accompanying hieroglyphic inscription as "the great god" (*nṯr ʿʾ*).

[6] Father and son both bear theophorous names compounded with *ʾb*, "father." In the Jewish onomasticon at Elephantine this element survived only in the female names Abihi (*TAD* A3.7:2; B6.3:10; C3.15:93, 103), Abiosher (*TAD* C3.15:107), and in the apparently related Abioresh, of unknown gender, though possibly feminine (*TAD* D9.14:3). It appeared more frequently in the Egyptian Aramaean onomasticon — the above-cited Abah from Syene and the Abitabs from Memphis and Abydos, Abihu father of Rochel ("Merchant" in Aram. [*TAD* B4.4:20]), feminine Abut(a)i on an Aswan sarcophagus (*TAD* D18:16), and the frequently attested Abieti in the Ptolemaic period (*TAD* D7.57:1-2; 8.9:13, 8.10:1; 9.15:1). The element *sly* appears in the abbreviated biblical names, mostly exilic, Salli/Sallu (Neh 11:7; 12:7, 20) and in female Sallua (*TAD* B6.4:7) and Salluah (*TAD* B4.6:10, 5.1:1, 6.4:3; C3.15:105) among the Elephantine Jews. Our name would mean "(Divine) Father Rejected (Sinners)" (cf. Ps 119:118; Lam 1:15; conversation with F. Rosenthal). For dubious derivation from Arabic *salaʾa*, taken to mean "replace, substitute" cf. *DAE*, p. 462; Zadok 1988:110, 112, n. 34.

[7] The addition of a mother in a filiation was common in Demotic documents but in Aram. contracts appears to be limited to a situation where the father may have had more than one wife (*TAD* B2.9:3, 2.10:3).

[8] "PN thus (*kn*) said" was a common formula in Imperial Aram. documents of all sorts — letters (*TAD* A4.7:4; 6.2:2, 6.3:6; etc.), court record (*TAD* B8.7:3), and the Bisitun inscription (*TAD* C2.1:8, etc.). Heb. had a different word order — "Thus (*kh*) said PN" (e.g. Gen 32:4).

[9] This Persian royal name was spelled in Aram. and Heb. in a variety of ways — *ḫšyrš* (*TAD* B4.4:1 [483 BCE]), *ḫšyʾrš* (here [482 BCE] and *TAD* D1.33b:1 [473 BCE]; B2.1:1 [471 BCE]), and *ʾḥšwrwš* (Esth *passim*; Dan 9:1; Ezra 4:5).

[10] The word order of this date formula (year, month, king) follows the Eg. pattern (see e.g. *EPE* C28-31, 33-35) rather than the Aram. one, which was month, year, king, on both monument (*TAD* D17.1 = *COS* 2.41) and in contracts (*TAD* B2-6). In 4 Xerxes = 482 BCE, the month of Meḥir = May 21-June 19. By 13 Xerxes = 473 BCE it became *de rigeur* to employ a synchronous Babylonian and Eg. month (*TAD* C3.8). See Porten 1990:16, 28.

Hieroglyphic text

1 *ḥtp-di-nswt Wsir ḫnty-imntyw nṯr ʿʾ nb ʾbḏw*
di.f qrst
nfrt n
2 *ẖrt-nṯr rn nfr ḥr-tp*
3 *tʾ n imʾḫy ḫr nṯr ʿʾ*
4 *nb pt ʾḫtʾ*
5 *bw*

(Transcription and translation by Miriam Lichtheim)

[1]A royal offering (to) Osiris Khentamenthes (= Lord of the Westerners), great god, lord of Abydos, that he may give a good burial in [2]the necropolis and a good name on [3]earth to the one honored before the great god, [4]lord of sky, Akhata[5]bu.

REFERENCES

AC No. 21; Cantineau 1932; *CIS* 2.122; *DAE* #85; Donner 1969; *EnIslam* 1960; *EPE*; Fitzmyer and Kaufman 1992:B.3.e.22; Harding 1971; *HNE* 1:448, 2:Pl. 28.1; *KAI* #267; Lévy 1927; *NSI* #71; Lipiński 1978; Porten 1968; 1990; *TAD* D20.3; Tallqvist 1905; *SSI* 2:119-120; Wuthnow 1930; Yoyotte 1995; Zadok 1988.

FUNERARY STELA (SAQQARAH; LOCATION UNKNOWN) (2.63)
(First Half of Fifth Century BCE)

Bezalel Porten

Blessed be Peṭees[e] son of *Yh*ʾ[[1]... by/before DN]

---

[1] The praenomen is Eg. (*p*ʾ*-dy-*ʾ*s.t*, "The [One] whom Isis Gave") but the fragmentary patronym is unrecoverable.

REFERENCES

Aimé-Giron 1939; Fitzmyer and Kaufman 1992:B.3.e.28; *TAD* D20.4.

FUNERARY STELA (CARPENTRAS) (2.64)
(First Half of Fifth Century BCE)

Bezalel Porten

This inscription may be entitled "The Immortalization of Taba." Its composer was well-versed in Egyptian funerary vocabulary. In a grammatically correct, well-fashioned quatrain he has deftly woven original Aramaic formulae — "Blessed be Tabi" (1a), "Before Osiris blessed be" (3a), "serve" (4a) — into translations of Egyptian terminology and formulary. Bicolon (1b) employs a traditional term for the deceased (*t*ʾ *mnḫt*) and associates it with Osiris. Bicolon (2) paraphrases two of the most attested clauses in the tomb autobiographies that contain negative confessions.[1] Bicola (3) and (4) are the earliest attestation of four benedictions recorded in Roman funerary papyri, with (3a) preferring traditional Aramaic terminology to Egyptian.[2] The a-b-c-d order of the clauses in the Egyptian text is completely altered (a-c-d-b) to create an Aramaic poetic balance:

a. *qdm* ʾ*wsry brykh hwy*	Before Osiris blessed be
a. ʿ*nḫ p*ʾ*y=f by r nḥe*	May his soul live forever
c. *hwy plḥh nm*ʿ*ty*	Do serve the Lord of the Two Truths
b. *mtw p*ʾ*y=f by šms Wsir*	and may his soul serve Osiris
d. *wbyn ḥsyh* [*l*ʿ*lm hwy*]	and among the praiseworthy [*forever be*].
c. *mtw=f ḫpr ńnw n*ʾ *ḥse.w Wsir*	and may he be among the praiseworthy of Osiris
b. *mn qdm* ʾ*wsry myn qḥy*	from before Osiris water take.
d. *mtw=f ṯ mw ḥr t*ʾ *ḥtp.t m-s*ʾ *Wsir*	and may he take water on the offering-table after Osiris

The final product in Aramaic is a precis of the process the deceased experiences through the final judgment and beyond, as elaborated in Book of the Dead, chapter 125 (*COS* 2.12).

(1a) Blessed be Tabi daughter of Taḥapi,[3] (2a) Anything evil[5] [a] she did not do	a Deut 17:1; 23:10; 2 Kgs 4:41 b Dan 3:8; 6:25	(1b) the excellent (one)[4] of Osiris the god. (2b) and the slander of a man[6] she did not say[7] [b] at all.[8]

---

[1] Thirty-four percent of the these autobiographies contain the "no evil" clause while twenty-seven percent contain the "no slander" clause; Gee 1998:173-178 (evil), 190-194 (calumny).

[2] Spiegelberg 1901:9-11; Lévy 1927:288-294, and esp. 293-294 for why the Eg. expression "live forever" would be unsuitable for an Aramaean.

[3] Both praenomen and matronym are Eg. — Tabi = *ta-b*ʾ, "She of the Ba," Taḥapi = *ta-Ḥp*, "She of Apis." Taba (also = *ta-b*ʾ) occurs frequently in the papyri (*TAD* B2.11:4-5, 12; 8.10:6; C3.17a:3, 3.19:8). Filiating a deceased (fe)male to mother rather than father was common in late Eg. funerary texts. The standard late period Book of the Dead was owned by Efonkh son of the woman Tsemminis (Lepsius 1842); see below *COS* 2.65.

[4] *tmnḥ*ʾ = *t*ʾ *mnḫ*, a term with special reference to the deceased, applied to a male in the Vatican stela (*COS* 2.65); the first of three Eg. loan words in this inscription. Though usually used as an adjective, it does occur as an epithet on a late gravestone — *mnḫ.t ḫr Ptḥ Skr Wsir*, "excellent (one) before Ptaḥ-Sokar-Osiris" (P. Cairo 31153:1 in Spiegelberg 1904 1:62; Lipiński 1978a:112, n. 148).

[5] The indef. pron. *mnd*ʿ*m* may function as a noun modified by an adj.; see Muraoka and Porten 1998:§ 44a. The comparable Heb. expression (*dbr r*ʿ) occurs in the Deuteronomist in a cultic sense. The Aram. expression and a similar Heb. one (*m*ʾ*wmh r*ʿ) also bear the meaning of physical harm (*TAD* A6.7:8; Jer. 39:12). The cognate Eg. statement would be *n ir=i isf.t*, "I have not done iniquity" (Book of the Dead chapter 125 A1).

[6] It is strange that Donner and Röllig *KAI* should call the word ʾ*yš* "a Canaanism!" It occurs in every type of document in the papyri.

[7] The expression *krṣn* ʾ*mr* is a var. of the idiomatic Akk. loan *qrṣn* ʾ*kl* (Dan 3:8, 6:25) < *karṣī akālu*; Kaufman 1974:63; *DNWSI* 537. Slander was condemned in Torah (Lev 19:16), Prophets (Jer 6:28), and Writings (Ps 34:4) and the sage Aḥiqar advised extreme caution in speech (*TAD* C1.1:80-83, 93, 141). The deceased was pure in deed and word.

[8] This word (*tmh*) is a crux. Metrically it overweighs the line. It is usually taken to mean "there" on earth as distinct from the world of the

(3a) Before Osiris blessed be;[9]	(3b) from before Osiris water take.[10]
(4a) Do serve[11] the Lord of the Two Truths[12]	(4b) and among the praiseworthy[13] [*forever be*].[14]

dead (*KAI*, *SSI*, *DAE*, *DNWSI* 1219-1220), but no Eg. parallel in funerary context supports this interpretation. The suggestion of Shea 1981 to restore metrical balance by reading it as the beginning of line 3 ("There before Osiris" in parallel to "from before Osiris") fails to explain why the scribe of this poem put it at the end of line 2. Lipiński 1978:112 took it as adjective "perfect," an interpretation rejected by *NSI*, who preferred the suggestion of Lagarde, citing Syriac *mtwm* (from *tmm*), "ever." Torrey 1926:247 proposed *tummā*, "completeness," as adverbial accusative "(not) at all." The Eg. autobiographies did not have a standard categorical denial of slander but only specific limited denials (e.g. "I never slandered anyone to the captain of the land;" Statue of *Ḏd-Ḏḥwty-iw=f-ᶜnḫ* [reign of Osorkon II] = Cairo JE 36697, line 20 in Janssen-Winkeln 1985 1:49; 2:456). As translated above, the Aram. would have affirmed an absolute denial in parallel to the absolute denial in the first half of the line.

[9] With inverted word order, verb first, this blessing appears regularly among the graffiti on the walls of the Temple at Abydos — "Blessed be PN before Osiris" (*TAD* D22.10-11, 13, 16, 24). The sequence "blessed-serve" is found in juxtaposition in reverse order in an Aram. statue inscription from Hatra where the king is designated *plḥ ᵓlhᵓ bryk ᵓlhᵓ*, "servant of the god, blessed of the god" (*KAI* 2.243).

[10] Imperative *qḥy* is no more a Canaanism (contra *KAI*) than is *ᵓyš* (cf. *TAD* D1.14:2); see Muraoka and Porten 1998:§12b, 33d. As the Eg. parallel indicates, the libation offering is made to Osiris and then the deceased takes the water "after" him to quench her thirst (so John Gee; cf. also Donner 1969, *KAI*). The Aram. text is fashioned to duplicate the preposition — *qdm* and then *mn qdm*; Lévy 1927:289.

[11] The verb *plḥ* takes the direct object (*TAD* B3.6:11); here it appears in a periphrastic imperative, indicating a "sense of urgency and insistence;" Muraoka and Porten 1998:§ 55g. Others translate "Be a servant/worshipper" (*NSI*, *KAI*, *SSI*).

[12] An Eg. loan word — *nb mᵓᶜ.ty* (*DAE*, 342, note s.), a known epithet of Osiris (Book of the Dead chap. 136 b S = Allen 1974:111). It is apparently applied to him in the Declaration of Innocence in the Book of the Dead, chap. 125 a § S 1 because that text concerns entering the *wsḫ.t mᵓᶜty*, "Hall of the Two Truths"; see *COS* 2.12. It appears both in the editions of the Eighteenth and Nineteenth Dynasties (Maystre 1937:13 = Allen 1974:97) through the Twenty-fifth and Twenty-sixth Dynasties (Verhoeven 1993 1:228, 15,13; 2:79*); see also Couroyer 1970:19-20. A different explanation of the Eg. loanword has yielded the translation "Do attend on the righteous ones" (*nmᶜty* < *nᵓ mᵓᶜ.ty*), this in parallel with the second hemistich, as restored, "and be among the beatified ones [of Osiris];" Lipiński 1977:112-115.

[13] Aram. *ḥsyh* < Eg. *ḥsy*, an epithet applied to the deceased (*Glossar*, 329-330). A Neo-Assyrian contract from Nineveh (Postgate 1976:No. 13) attaches the word *ḫasaya* to the Eg. patronym Aḥertais father of Nabu-riḫtu-uṣur. Usually taken as a gentilic it is now understood as our Eg. word; Lipiński 1978:114. But an epithet "deceased" is not attached to a patronym in either Akk. or Eg. documents (W. W. Hallo, J. Gee orally).

[14] Among the restorations proposed are *hwy šlymh*, "be complete" (*NSI*), *ḥyy lᶜlm*, "live forever" (Couroyer 1970:20-21; *SSI* 2:122), *zy ᵓwsry*, "of Osiris" (Lipiński 1978:112-115). In light of the Eg. parallel, it is tempting to restore *lᶜlm hwy*, "forever be," opening and closing the bicolon with the same verb and creating an internal rhyme (cf. Lévy 1927:290) but the blank space in the damaged text does not allow for such a full restoration.

REFERENCES

AC #49; Allen 1974; *CIS* 2.141; Couroyer 1970; *DAE* #86; *DNWSI*; Donner 1969; Fitzmyer and Kaufman 1992:B.3.f.18; Gee 1998; *Glossar*; *HNE* 1:91-92, 448, 2:pl. 28.3; Janssen-Winkeln 1985; *KAI* #269; Kaufman 1974; Lepsius 1842; Lipiński 1977; 1978a; Maystre 1937; Muraoka and Porten 1998; *NSI* #75; Postgate 1976; Shea 1981; Spiegelberg 1901, 1904; *TAD* D20.5; Torrey 1926; Verhoeven 1993; *SSI* 2:120-122.

FUNERARY STELA (VATICAN MUSEUM 1° SALA 22787) (2.65)

Bezalel Porten

Ankhoḥapi son of Takhabes,[1] excellent (one)[2] of Osiris the god.

[1] Both names are Eg., as in the Carpentras stela (2.64 above), here as there, the parent being female rather than male. Ankhoḥapi = *ᶜnḫ-Ḥp*, "May Apis live;" Takhabes = *ta-ḫᵓb.s*, "She of the Stars."

[2] The same Eg. loanword (*mnhᵓ* < *mnḫ*) as in the preceding inscription. Absent in this inscription is the traditional opening blessing.

REFERENCES

CIS 2.142; Donner 1969; Fitzmyer and Kaufman 1992:B.3.f.28; *HNE* 1:448, 2:Pl. 28.4; *KAI* #272.

TOMBSTONE INSCRIPTION (GRECO-ROMAN MUSEUM 18361) (2.66)
(ca. End Third Century BCE)[1]

Bezalel Porten

Among the tombstones uncovered at the necropolis in el-Ibrahimiya, Alexandria, in 1906 by E. Breccia were three of limestone with Aramaic inscriptions. They were published in 1907 by Clermont-Ganneau (*TAD* D21.4-6) and have

[1] The dating follows Lidzbarski (*ESE*). Most would date it to the early Ptolemaic period. Complete bibliography in Horbury and Noy 1992:#3.

been much discussed. The one reproduced here bears a name reminiscent of that of one of the last Davidides — Akkub son of Elioenai (1 Chr 3:24).[2] The praenomen, of course, is the hypocoristicon of Akabiah, the name here, and it is tempting, given the known practice of papponymy, to see in our deceased a descendant of the biblical figure. Breccia suggested that the buried were mercenaries. The inscription is spread across three lines and is painted in large red characters.

Akabiah[3] son of Elioenai[4] [a]	[a] 1 Chr 3:24; 4:36

[2] The sequence of Simeonite names Elioenai and Jaakobah (1 Chr 4:36) is most coincidental.

[3] The root of this name (ᶜ*qb*) is the same as that in Jacob and occurs in a variety of hypocoristica, borne primarily by Aramaeans, both at Elephantine/Syene (Akab [*TAD* C4.3:16; D1.1:12], Akbah [*TAD* A2.4:6] Akban [*TAD* B4.2:12] Akkub [*TAD* D11.2:1], Nabuakab [*TAD* A6.2:23, 28, etc.], and Ṣaharakab [*TAD* B3.9:10]) and in the Ptolemaic period at Edfu (Akban [D7.56:3]). It is well attested elsewhere, as well; for references see Abbadi 1983:44-46, 85. In post-exilic Judah the name Akkub is borne by gatekeepers (Ezra 2:42 ‖ Neh 7:45; 11:19; 12:25; 1 Chr 9:17), Levites (Neh 8:7), Nethinim (Ezra 2:45), and a Davidic descendant (1 Chr 3:24). This is the first occurrence of the name with the theophorous element *-yh*.

[4] This nominal sentence name with three elements (ᵓ*l-yw-*ᶜ*yny*, "To YHW are My-Eyes [Lifted Up]") is unique in the Israelite onomasticon; Zadok 1988:57. Borne in pre-exilic times by a Simeonite and Benjaminite (1 Chr 4:36; 7:8), it was popular in exilic times (Ezra 10:22, 27; Neh 12:41; 1 Chr 3:23-24).

REFERENCES

Abbadi 1983; Breccia 1907; Clermont-Ganneau 1907; *ESE* 49; Fitzmyer and Kaufman 1992:B.3.f.39.3; Horbury and Noy 1992; *TAD* D21.4; Zadok 1988.

4. NABATAEAN INSCRIPTIONS

THE NABATAEAN TOMB INSCRIPTION OF KAMKAM AT MADĀᵓIN ṢĀLIḤ (2.67)

J. F. Healey

The inscription, dated 1 BCE/CE, is the finest of 38 carved on Nabataean tomb facades (this one is tomb no. B 19) at the site of Madāᵓin Ṣāliḥ (ancient Ḥegra) in northern Saudi Arabia. The tombs were first described and the texts copied by C. Doughty in 1883. Subsequent work, especially by J. Euting and Frs A. Jaussen and R. Savignac (Jaussen and Savignac 1909), established the importance of this southern outpost of the Nabataean kingdom in the 1st century CE. The tomb inscriptions, many of which are precisely dated, are particularly informative on religion, social structure and legal matters. It is clear that the surviving texts were also preserved on papyrus in the legal archives of the city or one of its temples.[1]

Ownership (lines 1-2a)
This is the tomb which Kamkam daughter of Waᵓilat daughter of Ḥaramu and Kulaybat, her daughter, made for themselves and their descendants.[2]

Date[3] (lines 2b-3a)
In the month of Ṭebet, the ninth year of Ḥaretat, King of the Nabataeans, lover of his people.[4]

Curse (lines 3b-7a)
And may Dushara[5] and his throne and Allat of ᶜAmnad[6] and Manotu[7] and her Qaysha curse anyone who sells this tomb or who buys it or gives it in pledge or makes a gift of it or removes from it body or limb or who buries in it anyone other than Kamkam and her daughter and their descendants.[8]

[1] The fullest discussion of the inscription is to be found in Healey 1993:154-162.

[2] It is noteworthy that there are several Nabataean tombs owned by and designed for the use of women.

[3] December/January 1 BCE/CE.

[4] Aretas IV (9 BCE - 40 CE) is usually given the nationalistic title "lover of his people."

[5] Dushara ("the master of the Shara mountains") was the main Nabataean god. Astral in character, he is elsewhere called "the one who separates day from night" and "lord of the world." Dushara's "throne" (*mwtb*) was the object of separate veneration: see Healey 1993:156-158.

[6] The divine name Allat is borrowed from Arabic. The apparent geographical name ᶜ*mnd* cannot be identified.

[7] Manotu is known from early Islamic evidence as Manāt.

[8] The terminology is legalistic and it is reflected in such Nabataean legal papyri as have survived, notably those from the Babatha archive. See *COS* 3.

Fine[9] (lines 7b-10)
And whoever does not act according to what is written above shall be liable to Dushara and Hubalu[10] and to Manotu in the sum of 5 *shamads*[11] and to the exorcist-priest[12] for a fine of a thousand Haretite *sela*ᶜs,[13] except that whoever produces in his hand a document from the hand of Kamkam or Kulaybat, her daughter, regarding this tomb, this document will be valid.

The Mason[14] (lines 11-12)
Wahballahi son of ᶜAbdᶜobodat made it.

[9] The inclusion of fines in these texts is most unusual in the Semitic sphere (there is one Palmyrene example), but it is a characteristic feature of Lycian tomb inscriptions.

[10] Hubal: one of the pre-Islamic deities of Mecca.

[11] The *šmd* has no obvious cognate. It is most likely that it is some kind of monetary unit, probably a large unit.

[12] Nabataean ᵓ*pkl*ᵓ. It occurs quite frequently and is also found in Palmyrene and Hatran Aramaic and in Sabaic, Minaean and Lihyanite. Cf. already Akk. *apkallu*, Sum. AB-GAL, Kaufman 1974:34.

[13] The Nabataean *sela*ᶜ is the normal unit of silver coin (here specified as according to the standard established by the king Ḥaretat). It corresponds to the silver tetradrachm.

[14] It is common for masons to be named, and since genealogical information is given it is clear that a small number of mason families was at work at Madāᵓin Ṣāliḥ.

REFERENCES

Healey 1993; Jaussen and Savignac 1909.

THE NABATAEAN TOMB INSCRIPTION OF ḤALAFU AT MADĀᵓIN ṢĀLIḤ (2.68)

J. F. Healey

For general comments see the Kamkam inscription above. The Ḥalafu inscription is dated 31/32 CE and located on the facade of tomb no. E 18.[1]

Ownership (lines 1-7a)
This is the tomb which Ḥalafu son of Qosnatan[2] made for himself and for Suᶜaydu, his son, and his brothers, whatever male children may be born to this Ḥalafu,[3] and for their sons and their descendants by hereditary title for ever. And his children may be buried in this tomb: this Suᶜaydu and Manuᶜat and Ṣanaku and Ribamat and Umayyat and Salimat, daughters of this Ḥalafu. And none at all of Suᶜaydu and his brothers, males, and their sons and their descendants has the right to sell this tomb or write a deed of gift or anything else for anyone at all, except if one of them writes for his wife or for his daughters or for a father-in-law[4] or for a son-in-law a document for burial only.

Fine (lines 7b-9a)
And anyone who does other than this will be liable for a fine to Dushara the god of our lord[5] [a] in the sum of five hundred Haretite *sela*ᶜs and to our lord for the same amount, according to the copy of this deposited in the temple of Qaysha.[6]

[a] Gen 31:5; 32:10; 43:23, etc.

Date (lines 9b-10a)
In the month of Nisan, the fortieth year of Ḥaretat, King of the Nabataeans, lover of his people.[7]

Masons (line 10b)
Ruma and ᶜAbdᶜobodat, the masons.

[1] Fullest and most recent discussion: Healey 1993:226-231.

[2] This theorphoric name appears to be formed on the Edomite divine name Qos. There is a view that the Nabataeans were not newcomers into the Jordan area but descendants of the Edomites.

[3] The limitation to males is unique in the context of these inscriptions.

[4] The term for father-in-law, *nšyb*, is an Arabic loan, though it has been Aramaicized.

[5] The "god of our lord" is the "god of our lord the king" — the deity Dushara in the guise of (royal) family god. There is a certain analogy here with Albrecht Alt's "god of the fathers."

[6] "The copy" (*nsḥt*) is best paralleled in Akk. legal terminology (*nisḫu*, originally "extract," coming to mean in Neo-Babylonian "official record"). Here we have explicit evidence that there was a corresponding document lodged in a temple. We can assume that this other copy was on papyrus like the Nabataean legal documents from Naḥal Ḥever.

[7] The year is 31/32 CE. On the titulature see the Kamkam inscription above.

REFERENCES

Healey 1993; Jaussen and Savignac 1909.

A NABATAEAN FUNERARY INSCRIPTION FROM MADEBA (2.69)

J. F. Healey

There are two copies of this monumental funerary inscription, one in the Vatican, the other in the Louvre (AO 4454). They are identical except for a minor variation in line-division. In both exemplars words are separated by spaces; *scriptio continua* is the norm in Nabataean.[1]

Ownership (lines 1-7a)
This is the tomb and two funeral monuments above it which ᶜAbdᶜobodat the governor made for ᵓItaybel the governor,[2] his father, and for ᵓItaybel, the camp commandant who is in Luḥitu and ᶜAbarta, son of this ᶜAbdᶜobodat the governor; in the territory of their rule which they exercised twice for thirty-six years during the time of Ḥaretat, King of the Nabataeans, lover of his people.

Date (lines 7b-8)
And the above work was executed in his forty-sixth year.[3]

[1] For the main edition of the text see *CIS* 2 #196 (Vatican text). For discussion see Starcky 1980 and Healey 1993:247-248.

[2] Nabataean *ᵓsrtgᵓ* (< Greek στατηγός). Nabataean *strategoi* are mentioned in Josephus, *Ant.* XVIII.112.

[3] The date is 37/38 CE.

REFERENCES

CIS 2 #196; Healey 1993; Starcky 1980.

D. SEAL AND STAMP INSCRIPTIONS

1. SEALS AND SEAL IMPRESSIONS*

Jeffrey H. Tigay[1] *and Alan R. Millard*

Seals were used for stamping the names of their owners on clay bullae to seal letters and documents (1 Kgs 21:8; Isa 8:16; 29:11; Jer 32:9-14; Job 38:14; Esth 8:8; cf. Gen 38:18, 25; 41:42; Jer 22:24; Song 8:6; Esth 3:10), on pottery vessels to indicate ownership or some other type of relationship, and for other purposes. Hundreds of seals and seal impressions, containing inscriptions in Hebrew, Phoenician, Ammonite, Moabite, Edomite, Philistine, and Aramaic script are known, mostly from the eighth through sixth centuries BCE. The inscriptions, spread over one to four lines, usually contain the name of the seal's owner, often that of the owner's father and occasionally his grandfather, and sometimes the owner's title or some other phrase. They are a valuable source of information about history, religion, culture, government, and economy because of the onomastic information they contain, the fact that some of the owners are government or religious officials, that a few are individuals known from the Bible, and because of the objects to which they are affixed and the iconography on some of them. Seals that were found in controlled archaeological excavations are the most reliable sources of information; some of these come from occupation debris, as at Lachish (Diringer 1941), some from tombs (e.g. Barkay 1986:34), which are the most likely provenience for the majority. Bullae, often with imprints of papyrus on the back, were recovered in excavations at Lachish (Aharoni 1968:164-168) and Jerusalem (Shiloh 1986). Seals and bullae acquired on the antiquities market, notably the hoard of bullae published by Avigad (1986), are less reliable because their provenience is unknown, their date uncertain, and some may be modern forgeries.[2]

The seals may bear a design of imaginary, human or animal figures, floral or geometric motifs, with the inscription engraved above or below or in the field, sometimes clearly as an addition, usually in a space deliberately created. In this respect, Hebrew seals differ little from other West Semitic seals (see Bordreuil 1992; Sass and Uehlinger 1993). However, the majority of Hebrew seals carry only the owner's name and patronym or title, normally written in two lines divided by a ruling or simple design and enclosed in a border. The seals are usually under one inch in diameter, so the lettering is tiny, sometimes finely engraved, sometimes roughly cut and occasionally with errors.

HEBREW (2.70)

2.70A. Two bullae of Berechyahu son of Neriyahu the scribe, made by the same seal (Hebrew; provenience unknown).[3] These identical inscriptions are written in the Hebrew script of the seventh century BCE. This Berechyahu is probably Jeremiah's secretary "Baruch son of Neriyahu the scribe" (Jer 36:32). Baruch is the hypocoristicon, or nickname, for Berechyahu. The shorter form of Baruch's patronym, Neriyah, that appears in some biblical passages (such as Jer 36:4), reflects the form of the theophoric element that was common in the Second Temple period when earlier biblical manuscripts were recopied. Although the names Berechyahu and Neriyahu were common, the identification of this Berechyahu as Jeremiah's scribe is quite likely, for it is rare to find two individuals in the Bible and/or in Hebrew inscriptions who have both the same first name and patronym, especially among the relatively limited segment of the population that is likely to have owned seals (another case is the seal of Baruch's brother Serayahu son of Neriyahu [Avigad and Sass 1997 #390; Avigad 1978b:86-87; 1978a:56]; see also [C], below). The title "scribe" virtually clinches the identification.

(Belonging) to Berechyahu
son of Neriyahu[4]
the scribe

---

* [Millard furnished items 2.70 I-V and portions of the introduction, Tigay the rest. Ed.]

[1] Tigay notes: "I owe several helpful observations to Nili S. Fox."

[2] See Sass 1993:245-46; Naveh 1997:12; and the broader discussion of the problem of unprovenienced material by Fox 1997 chapter II, section C, 1.

[3] Avigad and Sass 1997 #417; Davies 1991 100.509; Avigad 1978a:52-56; 1978b:86-87; Deutsch and Heltzer 1994:37-38.

[4] The name Berechyahu means "YHWH has blessed (the family with this child)," while Neriyahu means "YHWH is my lamp." Like the vast majority of Israelite theophoric personal names of the Biblical period, both of these names contain the theophoric element *-yahu*, a short form

2.70B. The bulla of Jerahmeel, the king's son (Hebrew; provenience unknown).[5] This inscription is also in seventh-century script. This bulla, reportedly found in the same group as that of Berechyahu ben Neriyahu ([A], above), probably belonged to "Jerahmeel the king's son" who was sent by King Jehoiakim to arrest Baruch and Jeremiah (Jer 36:26). [For an actual seal with the same inscription, but of a different size see now Heltzer 1999.]

(Belonging) to Jerahmeel[6]
The king's son[7]

2.70C. The seal impression of Hananyahu son of Azaryahu (Hebrew; provenience unknown).[8] The inscription is written in the Hebrew script of the seventh century BCE. In view of the considerations discussed in (A) above, the owner of this seal may have been Hananyah son of Azur, denounced by Jeremiah as a false prophet (Jer 28; Azur is a hypocoristicon of Azaryahu).

(Belonging) to Hananyahu
son of Azaryahu[9]

2.70D. The bulla of Gedalyahu, over(seer of) the (royal) house (Hebrew).[10] This bulla, found on the surface at Lachish, is inscribed in the Hebrew script of the seventh century BCE. Some scholars believe that the owner of this seal was Gedaliah son of Ahikam son of Shaphan, whom the Babylonians placed in charge of the Jews remaining in Judah after the destruction of Jerusalem; he was assassinated shortly afterwards (2 Kgs 25:22-25; Jer 40:5-41:2). Gedaliah was from a family that held several high offices at the court of Judah, and since the Babylonians appointed him, it is plausible that he had already held a high office such as overseer of the palace. The back of the bulla contains imprints of the papyrus document to which it was affixed. Perhaps the document was a letter sent by Gedaliah from the palace to the defenders of Lachish before it fell to the Babylonians.

(Belonging) to Gedalyahu[11]
"Over(seer of) the (royal) house" (i.e. the palace steward)[12]

2.70E. The seal of Zecharyaw, Priest of Dor (Hebrew; provenience unknown).[13] The other side of the seal bears the inscription "(Belonging) to Zadok son of Micha͗," possibly the name of Zecharyaw's father. Both inscriptions are written in Hebrew script of the eighth century BCE.

[(Belonging) to Ze]charyaw[14]
Priest of Dor[15]

2.70F. The seal of Uzza son of Baalhanan (Hebrew; provenience unknown).[16] The script on the seal has been classified as Hebrew of the eighth century BCE.[17]

---

of YHWH (Yahweh). This form is usually anglicized as *-iah* at the end of a name, *Jeho-* at the beginning. The fact that this element is used so extensively, while no other deity's name is used in more than one or two percent of Israelite names, probably indicates, when combined with other evidence, that the vast majority of Israelites, particularly in the eighth-sixth centuries BCE, was exclusively Yahwistic. See Tigay 1986; Pike 1990.

[5] Avigad and Sass 1997 #415; Davies 1991 100.508; Avigad 1978a:52-56.

[6] The name Jerahmeel (Heb. Yeraḥmeʾel) means "May God have mercy."

[7] Several individuals mentioned in the Bible and on West Semitic seals are designated as "the king's son" (see 1 Kgs 22:26 = 2 Chr 18:25; 2 Kgs 15:5; Jer 36:26; 38:6; 2 Chr 28:7; for other seal inscriptions containing the title see Barkay 1993:109-114; cf. 2.70G, below). It is debated whether the phrase means simply "offspring of the king" (either of the current king or his predecessor) or is the title of some office not necessarily connected with royal descent; the former view is more likely. See the discussion by Brin 1969:433-465; Yeivin 1954:160; de Vaux 1961:119-120 Rainey 1969; 1975; Fox 1997 chap. III, section A, 1 and below , n. 38.

[8] Avigad and Sass 1997 #165; Davies 1991 100.024; Moscati 1951 67 #24.

[9] The name Hananyahu means "YHWH has been gracious," while Azaryahu means "YHWH has helped."

[10] Avigad and Sass 1997 #405; Davies 1991 100.149; Tufnell et al. 1953:347-348.

[11] The name Gedalyahu means "YHWH was (i.e., has shown himself) great."

[12] The title *ʾasher ʿal habayit* ([ʾ]*šr ʿl hby*[*t*]), known from the Bible and from inscriptions, cannot be defined precisely. It refers literally to the major domo of the royal palace, which was probably the original role of those who bore this title (see below, 2.70T). Eventually individuals bearing this title took on major state responsibilities and we find them active in political and diplomatic affairs as well (see particularly 2 Kgs 15:5; 18:17-18; 19:2-7; see also Gen 43:16, 19; 44:1, 4; 1 Kgs 4:6; 16:9; 18:3; 2 Kgs 10:5; 15:5; 18:18, 37; 19:2; Isa 22:15; 36:3; 37:2). See also Avigad 1953:137-152; 1979b:119-126 no. 1; de Vaux 1961:125, 129-131; Katzenstein 1960; Yeivin 1971; Layton 1990; Fox 1997 chap. III, section B, 1; for a possible Ug. parallel, see Good 1979. See *COS* 2.54 and 2.70T.

[13] Avigad and Sass 1997 #29; Davies 1991 100.323; Avigad 1975.

[14] The name Zecharyaw is the equivalent of Zecharyahu (Zachariah) and means "YHWH remembered," perhaps meaning that the Lord remembered Zecharyaw's parents and gave them this child. The form of the theophoric element, *-yaw* (anglicized as *-io* [*Jo-a* + the beginning of a name]) instead of *-yahu*, is more commonly found in inscriptions of north-Israelite provenience.

[15] Dor was a Canaanite harbor town on the coastal plain between Caesaria and Haifa. Its king was defeated by Joshua (Josh 12:23), but it was apparently only controlled by Israel from the time of David and Solomon (1 Kgs 4:11) until it was captured by Assyria in the latter part of the eighth century. The seal implies that there was a sanctuary, perhaps of YHWH, in the city in the eighth century.

[16] Avigad and Sass 1997 #297; Davies 1991 100.036; Diringer 1934:195 #36.

[17] Avigad 1987:197.

(Belonging) to Uzza,[18] so-
n of Baalhanan[19]

2.70G. The seal of Maadanah the king's daughter (Hebrew; provenience unknown).[20] The inscription, written in the Hebrew script of the seventh century BCE, is one of about a dozen known seal inscriptions of Israelite women. Most are on seals, but at least one is in a seal impression stamped on a jar handle, showing that it was used functionally and not merely as jewelry. This raises the possibility that Israelite women enjoyed at least some of the rights enjoyed by men who owned seals, such as holding office and perhaps signing contracts and other documents (Avigad 1987:205-206; 1988:8). But, as in the case of "the king's son," it is not clear whether "the king's daughter" means simply "princess" or implies that Maadanah held public office.

(Belonging) to Maadanah[21]
the king's daughter

2.70H. The seal of Pelayahu son of Mattityahu, Overseer of the Corvée (Hebrew; provenience unknown).[22] The inscriptions, on the front and back of the seal, are written in Hebrew script of the seventh century BCE. Pelayahu probably used side A of his seal for private purposes and side B for official ones.

Side A:
(Belonging) to Pelayah-
u[23] (son of)[24] Mattityahu[25]

Side B:
(Belonging) to Pelayahu
Over(seer of)
the Corvée[26]

2.70I. The seal of Nehemyahu son of Micayahu.[27] Both of these names are attested in the Bible (Neh 1:1 etc.; Judg 17:1 etc.).

(Belonging) to Nehemyahu son of Micayahu

2.70J. The seal of Yehoezer son of Yigdalyahu.[28] The patronymic recurs in Jer 35:4. For the owner's name cf. Yoezer in 1 Chr 12:7.

(Belonging) to Yehoezer son of Yigdalyahu

---

[18] The name Uzza, a hypocoristicon meaning "(the deity so-and-so) is strong," is known from the Bible and other Northwest Semitic inscriptions.

[19] The name Baalhanan, "Baal has been gracious," is also known from the Bible (a king of Edom, Gen 36:38-39; an official of David, 1 Chr 27:28); it is virtually synonymous with the Phoen./Carthaginian name Hannibal. The element *baal* is known in some names appearing in the Bible, the Samaria ostraca, and one or two other Heb. inscriptions; see, for example, Jerubbaal, Eshbaal, Meri(b)-baal, and Beeliada (Judg 6:32; 1 Chr 8:33, 34; 9:39, 40; 14:7); the Samaria ostraca clearly contain the names *ᵓbbᶜl* (SO #2:4), *bᶜlᵓ* (SO #1:7); *bᶜlzmr* (SO #12:2-3), *bᶜlᶜzkr* (SO #37:3), and *mrbᶜl* (SO #2:7); for other possibly baalistic names in the Bible and inscriptions, see Tigay 1986:7-8, 65-66. It means "lord," and scholars debate its significance in Hebrew names. In Canaanite names and texts it refers to the Canaanite storm-god Hadad (see below, n. 49). Some think it has the same meaning in the Hebrew names. If that is the case, these names reflect the worship of Baal by some Israelites or foreigners living in Israel, but they do not show widespread worship of him because they constitute a minuscule percentage of all Israelite theophoric names (Tigay 1986; Pike 1990). Others believe that it does not refer to the Canaanite deity but functions as an epithet of YHWH, synonymous with *ᵓadon*, "Lord." The Hebrew names *Yehobaᶜal* (Avigad 1988:8) and *ba-li-ya-a-ma* (in the Murashu archives of the fifth century BCE Babylonia; see Coogan 1976:15, 69), both meaning "YHWH is Lord," indicate that *baᶜal* was sometimes used as an epithet of YHWH (cf. also *Beᶜalyah*, borne by a contemporary of David in 1 Chr 12:6; the masoretic vocalization of *beᶜal-* indicates a perfect-tense verb, and the name must mean "YH(WH) rules"). Hos 2:18 (possibly from the approximate time and place of the Samaria ostraca) states this almost explicitly: "On that day ... you will call 'My Husband' (*ᵓiši*), and no more will you call Me 'My baᶜal.'"

[20] Avigad and Sass 1997 #30; Davies 1991 100.781; its authenticity has been doubted, Naveh 1997:12; Avigad 1978c.

[21] The previously unknown name Maadanah, derived from the same root as "Eden," means something like "luxury," "lubricity" (Greenfield 1984). See above *COS* 2.34, note 4.

[22] Avigad and Sass 1997 #20; Davies 1991 100.782; Avigad 1980.

[23] The name Pelayahu, "YHWH is wondrous" or "YHWH has acted wondrously," appears in its short form Pelaiah in Neh 8:7; 10:11.

[24] On side A the word *ben*, "son of," is omitted before the patronym, a common practice in Heb. seal inscriptions.

[25] The name Mattityahu (rendered as Mattathias in Greek and Matthew in English) means "Gift of YHWH." It appears in 1 Chr 15:18, 21; 25:3, 21, and in the short form Mattithiah in 1 Chr 9:31; 16:5; Ezra 10:43; Neh 8:4.

[26] The title "Over(seer of) the Corvée" is known from the Bible, where it is borne by Adoram/Adoniram son of Abda, Overseer of the Corvée in the days of David, Solomon, and Rehoboam (2 Sam 20:24; 1 Kgs 4:6; 5:28). Opposition to the corvée was the principal reason why northern Israel seceded from Judah, and Adoram/Adoniram was stoned to death by north Israelites at the time of the secession (1 Kgs 12:1-18). The continuation of the corvée into late seventh century Judah seems implied by Jeremiah's critique of Jehoiakim for forcing fellow Israelites to build his palace with no pay (Jer 22:13), but this seal is the only explicit evidence of the practice in that period.

[27] Avigad and Sass 1997 #265; Davies 1991 100.030.

[28] Avigad and Sass 1997 #1073; Davies 1991 100.421.

2.70K. The seal of Zephanyah (son of) Mattanyah.[29] Here the divine name is reduced to *yh* (usually anglicized as *-iah*), its least common abbreviation in pre-exilic documents, becoming usual later.

belonging to Zephanyah (son of) Mattanyah

2.70L. The seal of Yehoᶜadan daughter of Uriyahu.[30] That women could own seals in their own right — although only a few out of the total — is noted above, see 2.70G.

(Belonging) to Yehoᵓadan daughter of Uriyahu

2.70M. The seal of Abigail wife of Asayahu.[31] Another seal belonging to a woman.

(Belonging) to Abigail wife of Asayahu

2.70N. The seal of Hanan son of Hilqiyahu, the priest.[32] As a Hilqiah was High Priest in the time of Josiah (2 Kgs 22:4 etc.), this seal could have belonged to his son.

(Belonging) to Hanan son of Hilqiyahu, the priest

2.70O. The bulla of X son of Zakkur.[33] The bulla is incomplete, so the owner's name is unknown.

(Belonging) to [X] son of Zakkur, the physician[34]

2.70P. The bullae of Elyaqim squire of Yawkin.[35] When first found, imprints of this seal on jars were thought to belong to a servant of Jehoiachin, king of Judah, taken to Babylon by Nebuchadrezzar in 597 BCE (2 Kgs 24). But excavations at Lachish demonstrated that this type of jar belonged to the level destroyed by Sennacherib in 701 BCE, implying that the master lived earlier. The word 'squire' (*naᶜar*) applies to anyone who is not an independent citizen, yet not a slave, from a child (1 Sam 1:22) to a responsible man (2 Sam 9:9) as here.

(Belonging) to Elyaqim squire[36] of Yawkin

2.70Q. Seals of "servants" (ministers) of unnamed kings. At least eleven seals or impressions have been found with this title, denoting a certain position or rank, rather than simply 'slave' of the king.[37] Other seals belonged to sons of unnamed kings.[38]

(Belonging) to Obadyahu, "servant" (i.e. minister) of the king[39]

2.70R. Seals of "servants" (ministers) of named kings. The names of the masters can all be identified with eighth century kings of Israel and Judah; no other personal names occur after *ᶜbd*. For the last, note the existence of Eliakim, son of Hilkiah, in Hezekiah's court (2 Kgs 18:18 etc.), perhaps this seal owner's brother.[40]

(Belonging) to Shema, servant of Jeroboam
(Belonging) to Abiyaw servant of Uzziyaw
(Belonging) to Shebanyahu servant of Uzziyaw
(Belonging) to Ushna servant of Ahaz
(Belonging) to Yehozarah son of Hilqiyahu servant of Hizqiyahu

2.70S. The seal of Miqneyahu servant of Yahweh.[41] The unique title (*ᶜbd yhwh*) may indicate a high official in the temple, Cross 1983:62-63, argued for a singer, cf. Ps 135:1 etc.

(Belonging) to Miqneyahu servant of Yahweh

2.70T. The bulla of Adoniyahu, palace steward (*ᵓšr ᶜl hbyt*).[42] The title, literally 'who is over the house' is explained as 'in charge of the palace' by comparing 2 Kgs 15:5 with 2 Chr 26:21. Cf. note 12 above.

(Belonging) to Adoniyahu, "over(seer of) the (royal) house" (i.e. palace steward)[43]

---

[29] Avigad and Sass 1997 #340; Davies 1991 100.716.
[30] Avigad and Sass 1997 #38; Davies 1991 100.855.
[31] Avigad and Sass 1997 #31; Davies 1991 100.062.
[32] Avigad and Sass 1997 #28; Davies 1991 100.734.
[33] Avigad and Sass 1997 #420; Davies 1991 100.804.
[34] Gen 50:2; 2 Chr 16:12.
[35] Avigad and Sass 1997 #663; Davies 1991 100.108, 277, 486. See Ussishkin 1976.
[36] Gen 22:3; Exod 24:5; Judg 9:54; Jer 1:6.
[37] Avigad and Sass 1997 #9; Davies 1991 100.070.
[38] See Davies 1991 100.072, 110, 209, 252, 506, 507, 508, 719, 760, 784, and one daughter, 781; Avigad and Sass 1997:467; and #30.
[39] 1 Kgs 18:3 etc.
[40] Avigad and Sass 1997 ##2, 4, 3, 5, 407; Davies 1991 100.068, 065, 067, 141, 321.
[41] Avigad and Sass 1997 #27; Davies 1991 100.272.
[42] Avigad and Sass 1997 #404; Davies 1991 100.501, 502. See also *COS* 2.54.
[43] 2 Kgs 18:18; 19:2; Isa 22:15.

2.70U. Two bullae of the governor of the city (*śr hᶜyr*).[44] This title appears beneath figures cut in imitation of Assyrian style.

Governor of the city[45]

2.70V. The bulla of Eltolad.[46] This bulla indicates a fiscal process otherwise unrecorded. If the year is a regnal year, then it can only be that of Josiah of Judah, in the south of whose realm the town of Eltolad (Josh 15:30; 19:4) or Tolad (1 Chr 4:29) lay, i.e. 613 BCE.

In year 26, Eltolad, belonging to the king

AMMONITE (2.71)

Many seals inscribed with the first letters of the alphabet — from four to eight — are regarded as Ammonite; they are probably practice pieces; see Avigad and Sass 1997:366-371; Hestrin and Dayagi-Mendels 1979 ## 127, 129.

The seal impression of Milkom-or, minister of Baalyasha (Ammonite).[47] This seal was discovered in excavations at Tell el-ᶜUmeiri in Jordan.

(Belonging) to Milkom-or[48]
"servan-
t" (minister) of Baalyasha[49]

MOABITE (2.72)

The seal of Kemosham son of Kemoshel the scribe (Moabite; provenience unknown).[50] This seal is in the Moabite script of the eighth-seventh centuries BCE.[51]

(Belonging) to Kemosham[52]
(son of) Kemoshel[53]
the scribe

EDOMITE (2.73)

The bulla of Qawsgabar, king of Edom (Edomite).[54] This is one of the few known Edomite seal inscriptions (see Herr 1978:161-169). It was found at Umm el-Biyara in Jordan, near Petra.

(Belonging) to Qawsg[abar][55]
King of E[dom]

---

[44] Avigad and Sass 1997 #402; Bordreuil 1992:192; Davies 1991 100.402, 510.

[45] Judg 9:30; 1 Kgs 22:26; 2 Kgs 23:8; 2 Chr 34:8.

[46] See Avigad and Sass 1997 #421; Bordreuil 1992:193.

[47] Avigad and Sass 1997 #860; Herr 1985.

[48] The name Milkom-or means "Milkom is light." According to the Bible, Milkom was the national god of the Ammonites (1 Kgs 11:5, 33; 2 Kgs 23:13). His name is mentioned in one or two Ammonite inscriptions (Jackson 1983:10, 13, 74) but, oddly, rarely in Ammonite personal names. There are Milkomit (if the name is complete) in an Ammonite inscription from Tell el-Mazar, Jordan (Yassine and Teixidor 1986:48-49), and the seal inscription of one Tamak-ᵓel, where the patronym reads either "(son of) Bodmilkom (*bdmlkm*)" or, less likely, "son of Milkom (*br mlkm*)" (CIS 2:94); see Avigad 1965:225 n. 12; 1985:5 n. 25; cf. Cross 1973:128 n. 6. Most often, *ᵓel*, "god," serves as the theophoric element, which may suggest that El was the chief god of the Ammonites and that Milkom was his title, meaning something like "the King."

[49] The name Baalyasha (the name could also be read as Baalisha, comparable to Hebrew Elisha) means "the Lord (*baal*) has saved (*yashaᶜ*)" or "the Lord is salvation (*yeshaᶜ*)," referring either to the Canaanite storm god or some other deity. Since the title "minister" (*ᶜbd*, lit. "servant") commonly refers to the minister of a king in seal inscriptions, it is likely that Baalyasha/Baalisha was a king. Some think him identical with Baalis, king of the Ammonites ca. 586 BCE according to Jer 40:14 (the script is also compatible with the early sixth century). This seems possible, since the theophoric element *baal* is rare in Ammonite names and Baalis is the only other definite example. In this view Baalis, a name admittedly hard to explain, is an error for Baalyasha or Baalisha (the final *ᶜayin* may be reflected in the Septuagint of Jer 40:14, which renders Baalis as *Bel(e)isa*; see Herr 1985:172). However the Ug. names *bᶜls* and Baalasi indicate that Baalis is probably a name in its own right (Aḥituv 1992:241; see Gröndahl 1967:102, 115, 116).

[50] Avigad and Sass 1997 #1010; Hestrin and Dayagi-Mendels 1979 #2.

[51] Avigad 1970:289; Herr 1978:156-157.

[52] Kemosham means "Kemosh is a kinsman." Kemosh was the Moabite national deity, known from the Bible and Moabite inscriptions. See Num 21:29; Judg 11:24; 1 Kgs 11:7, 33; 2 Kgs 23:13; Jer 48:7, 13, 46. And also *COS* 2.23; Reed and Winnet 1963; Avigad and Sass 1997:373, 380-382.

[53] The name means "Kemosh is god."

[54] Avigad and Sass 1997 #1048; Bennett 1966:399-401.

[55] The name is restored on the basis of inscriptions of the Assyrian kings Esarhaddon (680-669 BCE) and Ashurbanipal (668-627 BCE) that mention Qawsgabri King of Edom (*ANET* 291, 294), almost certainly the same individual. The name means something like "Qaws is mighty" or "Qaws has prevailed" (on *gabri* see Noth 1928:190). Qaws was the Edomite deity, known from the postexilic name Barqos (Ezra 2:53 = Neh 7:55) and extrabiblical sources; see Vriezen 1965; Herr 1978:162, 164-165; Naveh 1975 ##1, 10, 20-21, 32-33, 43.

PHOENICIAN (2.74)

The seal of Yahzibaal (probably Phoenician; provenience unknown).[56] The script fits the ninth-eighth century.

(Belonging to) Yahzibaal[57]

PHILISTINE (2.75)

The seal of Abd-Ilib son of Shabeath, minister of Mittit son of Zidqa (Philistine; provenience unknown).[58] Mittit and his father Zidqa must be Mitinti II and Zidqa, the kings of Ashkelon mentioned in Assyrian inscriptions. Zidqa and his family were exiled to Assyria when Sennacherib conquered Ashkelon in 701 BCE, and Mitinti II paid tribute to Esarhaddon in 677 and to Ashurbanipal in 667.[59]

(Belonging) to Abd-Ilib[60]
son of Shabeath[61]
"servant" (i.e. minister) of Mittit[62] son of
Zidqa[63]

EARLY ARAMAIC (2.76)

The seal of Hadadezer (Aramaic).[64] This seal, found at Saqqarah, Egypt, is inscribed in the Old Aramaic script and orthography of ca. the eighth century BCE.

(Belonging) to Hadadezer[65]

ROYAL JUDAEAN SEAL IMPRESSIONS (2.77)

Over 1700 royal seal impressions, stamped on jar handles from at least 65 sites, are known.[66] With few exceptions, each impression contains the word *lamelekh* (*lmlk*), "(Belonging, or pertaining) to the king," on the top line, a four-winged scarab or a two-winged symbol (possibly the sun-disc) in the middle, and on the bottom line one of four place names: Hebron and Ziph in Judah, Sochoh in the Shephelah, and an otherwise unknown place whose name is spelled *mmšt*.[67] Such impressions have been found at most of the excavated sites in Judah, particularly Lachish, Jerusalem, and Ramat Raḥel, as well as at Tell en-Naṣbeh, Gibeon, Gezer, Beth Shemesh, Timnah, and elsewhere, including border sites in northern Israel and Philistia (apart from Arad, they have been found only rarely in the Negev). These impressions, mostly found in public buildings, are from the reign of Hezekiah at the end of the eighth century BCE.[68] Almost all of the "*lamelekh*" jars were probably manufactured and stamped at a single central location: neutron activation analysis of typical jars showed that all were made of the same clay, from the Shephelah, possibly

---

[56] Avigad and Sass 1997 #1143; Hestrin and Dayagi-Mendels 1979 #118; Avigad 1968:49.

[57] The name Yahzibaal, "May Baal see," meaning "May Baal look favorably upon" the bearer of the name, is similar to the Biblical names Yahziel and Yahzeyah, "May God/YH(WH) see" (Ezra 8:5; 10:15; 1 Chr 12:4; 16:6; 23:19; 24:23; 2 Chr 20:14). The theophoric element *baᶜal*, "Lord, Master," referring particularly to the storm-god, is very common in Phoenician and other Canaanite names. See Benz 1972:288-290; Gröndahl 1967:114-117.

[58] Avigad and Sass 1997 #1066; Aḥituv 1992:212. Main discussion by Bergman 1936:224-226; Naveh 1985:9, 18.

[59] *ANET* 287a, 291bc, 294b.

[60] The name Abd-Ilib is comparable to Biblical Abdiel, Obadiah, etc., and must mean "Servant of the deity Ilib (*ᵓlᵓb*)." The word *ᵓilᵓb* is known from Ug. and Akk. texts, where it means "god of the father," apparently something like an ancestral spirit. See UT Aqht i.27, 45; ii.16 (*COS* 1.103 and n. 6); *UT* 17:14; 44:3, 5; 72:1; 2004:5; Nougayrol et al. 1968:44 (no. 18 line 1), 45-46; Roberts 1972:secs. 27-28; Lambert 1981; cf. Old Akk. Ilaba, mentioned in UET 1, 275 ii.28 (cited in *CAD* G 25c); Albright 1968:141-142.

[61] Shabeath seems to be a variant of the name Sheba, known from the Bible and inscriptions (2 Sam 20:1, etc.; 1 Chr 5:13; SO #2:6; Aharoni 1975 #38:4; Avigad and Sass 1997 #356; cf. Shibᶜah[?] in Cowley *AP* #82:2; Bathsheba in 2 Sam 11:3, etc.; Yehosheba in 2 Kgs 11:2 = Yehoshabeath in 2 Chr 22:11; and Elisheba in Exod 6:23 etc., rendered Elisabeth [= Elishabeath] in the Septuagint). The underlying root *š-b-ᶜ* resembles the Heb. root(s) meaning "seven" and "swear," but the meaning of the names containing this element is uncertain.

[62] Mittit, "gift" (cf. Heb. *mattat*, 1 Kgs 13:7; Prov 25:14) is a hypocoristicon of a name meaning "gift of the deity so-and-so," comparable to Heb. Mattityahu (above, 2.70H). Cf. Hebrew Mattattah (Ezra 10:33) and Mattan (2 Kgs 11:8, etc.). The vocalization Mittit is not certain; it is based on the forms found in Assyrian inscriptions. See Benz 1972:356.

[63] Zidqa (Ṣidqa) is a hypocoristicon of a name meaning "The deity so-and-so is my vindicator," comparable to Heb. Zedekiah (*Ṣidqiyah[u]*), "YHWH is my vindicator" (2 Kgs 24:17, etc.; cf. Jer 23:6; Ps 4:2).

[64] Avigad and Sass 1997 #785; CIS 2:124; Galling 1941 no. 103; Herr 1978 Aram. #1.

[65] Hadadezer, "Hadad is (my) help," is a typical Aram. name. Essentially same name appears on an Aram. seal in the form *hdᶜdr* (CIS 2:77; Herr 1978 Aram. #73). Hadad, the storm god, was head of the Aramean pantheon. See Greenfield 1994:54-61. The same name was held by Hadadezer son of Rehob, King of Aram Zobah, defeated by David (2 Sam 8:3, 5; 10:16 [= 1 Chr 18:3, 5; 19:16], and by the king of Damascus in the days of Ahab (873-852 BCE) and Shalmaneser III (858-824 BCE). The name of the latter Hadadezer is represented in cuneiform as Adad-idri. See *COS* 2.113A, note 23.

[66] Vaughan 1996:219, 231-251; Fox 1997 chap. IV, section A, 2.

[67] Samples in Hestrin et al. 1973:95-99; Aḥituv 1992:139-140.

[68] Ussishkin 1976, 1977, 1979.

in the same workshop;[69] all the impressions were made from about twenty seals;[70] and some jars may have been stamped with a second seal carrying certain personal names, identical impressions of which appear on jars from several sites.[71]

The exact significance of the iconography and inscriptions on these impressions is uncertain. The winged figures may be royal symbols, perhaps symbolizing Judean independence and indicating the type or grade of the contents of the jars to which they were affixed. *lamelekh* probably means that the jars and their contents belong to the king. There are various theories about the significance of the place names. They may have been agricultural regions in which the royal estates were located (the additional seal impressions with personal names, stamped on some of the jars, may have belonged to government officials who had been given grants of crown land in those regions). Other possibilities are that they were district centers where products of royal estates, such as wine and oil, were gathered for marketing; that they refer to storage cities where food was kept in royal warehouses or where taxes in kind were collected; or that they were military garrisons or administrative centers to which, or from which, supplies were sent for royal bureaucrats and the Judean army, especially while Hezekiah was preparing to rebel against Assyria. The latter use may be reflected in the fact that most of these jars were found in destruction levels caused by the retaliatory Assyrian invasion of 701 BCE.[72]

PERSIAN PERIOD (2.78)

2.78A. Seals and seal impressions of the Persian province of Yehud (Aramaic)[73]

The one-word inscription *Yehud*, the name of the Persian province of Judah (Ezra 5:8), is inscribed on a seal and stamped on several hundred jar handles from various Persian-period sites in Judah and on several bullae from an unknown site (there are also coins similarly inscribed). The bullae gave official sanction to the documents to which they were affixed, and the stamped jar handles indicated that the contents of the jar belonged to the government, perhaps as taxes in kind.

2.78B. The bulla of Elnathan the Governor (Aramaic; provenience unknown).[74] For the seal of Elnathan's "maidservant," see below, 2.78C.

(Belonging) to Elnathan[75]
the Governor[76]

2.78C. The seal of Shelomit, "maidservant" of Elnathan the Governor (Hebrew in Aramaic script; provenience unknown).[77]

(Belonging) to Shelomit,[78]
Maidservant[79] of El<na>-
than the Gove[rnor]

---

[69] Mommsen, Perlman, and Yellin 1984.

[70] Mazar 1990:455.

[71] Avigad 1979a:37.

[72] See Avigad 1979a:37; Mazar 1990:455-458; Rainey 1982; Naᵓaman 1979; 1986; Fox 1997 chap. IV, section A, 2.

[73] Avigad 1976:3-4, 21-23. In these inscriptions, *Yehud* is spelled both fully (*yhwd*) and defectively (*yhd*).

[74] Davies 1991 106.017; Avigad 1976:5-7.

[75] The name Elnathan ("God has given [this child to his parents])" is known from the Bible; in the Persian period it was borne by two or three of Ezra's associates (Ezra 8:16).

[76] Aram. *pḥwᵓ*, apparently a variant of *pḥtᵓ*, equivalent to Heb. *hpḥh*; see Avigad 1976:6; cf. Avigad and Sass 1997:33 n. 45 (contrast the view of Greenfield and Naveh cited there). This was the title of provincial governors in the western part of the Persian empire, including Sheshbazzar, Zerubbabel, and Nehemiah who were governors of Judah (Hag 1:1; Ezra 5:14; Neh 5:14; 12:26), Sanballat, Governor of Samaria (below, COS 2.78D), and Bagohi, Governor of *Yehud*, mentioned in an Aram. papyrus from Elephantine (Cowley *AP* 30:1; *ANET* 492). See also the seals of an unnamed governor of *Yehud* and two other named governors (Avigad 1976:22-23).

[77] Davies 1991 106.018; Avigad 1976:11-13.

[78] The name Shelomit is related to *šalom*, "peace," "wellbeing," and *šalem*, "well," "unimpaired," and expresses a wish that its bearer will enjoy these blessings. It is known from the Bible and elsewhere as a name of both men and women (Lev 24:11; 1 Chr 23:18; etc.), including the daughter of Zerubbabel, Governor of Judah toward the end of the sixth century BCE (1 Chr 3:19); the owner of this seal could be the same Shelomit (Meyers and Meyers 1987:12-13).

[79] The significance of the description of Shelomit as "maidservant" is uncertain. Seals of two Ammonite "maidservants" are also known (Hestrin and Dayagi-Mendels 1979 ##28, 29). These women were hardly menials, since they would then have had no need to own seals. At the very least, they must have been secondary wives of prominent men, like the maidservant of the overseer of the palace, whose burial alongside the overseer is noted in the latter's tomb inscription from Siloam village (Avigad 1953; Hestrin et al. 1973 #24; *COS* 2.54). Conceivably, "maid-servant" is the feminine equivalent of ᶜ*ebed*, the "minister" of a king, and is used in some of these cases for female ministers of high officials. In any case, Shelomit did hold an important office in the Governor's administration. This is shown by the official character of the collection in which it was found: the collection included an official Yehud provincial seal and several Yehud bullae (2.78A), a bulla of the governor (2.78B), bullae containing the name of the province and other officials, and ten bullae of a scribe, as well as forty-four bullae of six other individuals; the only personal seal in the collection was that of Shelomit, suggesting that she was in charge of the collection and used both the provincial seal and

2.78D. The bulla of the son of Sanballat, Governor of Samaria (Hebrew).[80] This bulla was attached to an Aramaic deed of sale for a vineyard, written on papyrus, found at Wadi Daliyeh, north of Jericho. It probably dates from the reign of Artaxerxes III (358-338 BCE).

(Belonging) to [...]iah son of [San-]
ballat,[81] Governor of Samar[ia]

---

her own for official purposes. It is unclear whether her title "maidservant" refers to her official position or simply to her marital status, and whether she owed her position to that status (Avigad 1976:11-13, 30-32; see also Avigad and Sass 1997:33 n. 45).

[80] Davies 1991 100.408; Hestrin et al. 1973 #148; Aḥituv 1992:207-208; Cross 1971:47 and figs. 34-35; Naveh, 1982:115.

[81] Sanballat, spelled *snʾblṭ* in extrabiblical documents (Cross 1971:47 n. 4; Cowley *AP* 30:29), is a Babylonian name, originally *Sin-uballiṭ*, meaning "Sin (the moon god) gave life." "Sanballat" is the vocalization found in the Bible. The biblical Sanballat was the governor of Samaria who was Nehemiah's contemporary and opponent (Neh 2:10, 19; 3:33; 4:1; 6:1-14); he is also mentioned in the Elephantine papyri (Cowley *AP* 30:29). The document accompanying this bulla bears a date that is too late for this to be the Biblical Sanballat; he is probably his descendant (see Cross 1966:201-206). The Babylonian name does not necessarily imply that either Sanballat was a foreigner. Such names were common among Jews in the Persian period, and both of these men gave their sons Yahwistic names: those of Nehemiah's contemporary were named Delaiah and Shelemiah (Cowley *AP* 30:29), and the son of Sanballat named on this seal also had a Yahwistic name. For further discussion see Cross 1966; Williamson 1992.

REFERENCES

Texts and Translations: Avigad and Sass 1997; Davies 1991; Aḥituv 1992; Avigad 1979b; 1986; Barkay 1986; 1993; Bordreuil 1992; Cross 1971; 1973; 1983; Deutsch and Heltzer 1994; Herr 1978; 1985; Hestrin, R. et al. 1973; Hestrin and Dayagi-Mendels 1979; Sass 1993; Sass and Uehlinger 1993; Shiloh 1986; Ussishkin 1976; 1977; Yassine and Teixidor 1986.

THE SEAL OF ᶜAŚAYĀHŪ (2.79)

Michael Heltzer

The Hebrew seal is dated paleographically to the second half of the 7th century BCE.[1]

(Belonging) to ᶜAśayāhū
"servant" (minister) of the king

It is most probable that this ᶜAśayāhū of the seal is identical with "Aśayā, servant of the king," mentioned in 2 Kings 22:12, 14 and 2 Chronicles 34:20. He appears as one of the team, sent by king Josiah (*Yošiyāhū*) in the year 622 to the temple in connection with the finding of the book, which is by most scholars identified with Deuteronomy. Among the other persons of the team involved in this event was a Ḥilqiyāhu, the High Priest. There is a seal that reads: (1)*lḥnn b*(2)*n ḥlqyhw* (3)*hkhn* "Belonging to Ḥanan son of Ḥilqiyāhu, the priest.[2] There is also a seal impression dated ca. 600 BCE which reads: (1)*ᶜzryhw* (2)*bn ḥlqyhw* "ᶜAzaryāhū, son of Ḥilqiyāhū."[3] Moreover there are additional persons who are mentioned in the 2 Kings 22 and 2 Chronicles 34 whose seals or whose fathers' seals are known.[4]

---

[1] Deutsch and Heltzer 1994:49-51.

[2] Elayi 1987:54-56; 1992:680-685; above, *COS* 2.70N.

[3] Shiloh 1986: No. 27.

[4] Schneider 1991:26-33.

REFERENCES

Deutsch and Heltzer 1994; Elayi 1987; 1992; Shiloh 1986; Schneider 1991.

2. STAMPS

STAMPS (2.80)

Michael Heltzer

There are more than one hundred stamps on identical handles, and as proved by the examinations of D. Ussishkin in Lachish, they appear on one or two of the four handles where the others had the *lmlk* stamps (*COS* 2.77). These stamps belonged to more than 30 persons, who were the officials responsible for the standard measures of the jars.[1] The following are a few examples.

Yhwḥyl Šḥr	Yehoḥayil (son of) Šaḥar
lNḥm Hṣlyhw	(Belonging) to Naḥum (son of) Hiṣṣilyāhū
Šbnyhw ᶜzryhw	Šebanyāhū (son of) ᶜAzaryāhū

No seal which was used for stamping the handles before firing the jar was ever found.[2]

[1] See Garfinkel 1985:105-118.

[2] There is now known a stamped seal impression on a jar-handle clearly showing that the seal was cut from timber.

REFERENCES

Ussishkin 1977; Garfinkel 1985.

E. WEIGHT INSCRIPTIONS

HEBREW WEIGHT INSCRIPTIONS (2.81)

Alan Millard

Four hundred or more inscribed stone weights have been found, mostly in the area of Judah and made in the eighth and seventh centuries BCE. They are flat-based dome-shaped stones, with values engraved on the top. (Two weights have their values marked in ink which suggests the numerous uninscribed stones of the same type may have had their values noted in the same way.) The majority bear a sign like a loop, believed to denote the shekel, followed by a numeral in a system derived from Egyptian hieratic. A series of smaller weights bear single words and yet smaller ones numerical signs alone.

Shekel weights occur with the values 1, 2, 4, 8, 12, 16, 24, 40, the shekel being about 11.33 grams.

Fractions of the shekel named are *nṣp*, 5/6, *pym*, 2/3 and *bq*ᶜ, 1/2, their values being determined metrologically.

Discovery of the *pym* weights elucidated an obscure phrase in 1 Sam 13:21, which can now be rendered "the charge was two thirds of a shekel for ploughshares and mattocks ..."

The *bq*ᶜ occurs once in the Bible as the value of the nose-ring given to Rebekah by Eliezer, Gen 24:22.

The very small weights, marked 2, 3, 4, 5, 6, 7, 8, 10, are believed to be multiples of the *gerâ*, 1/20th of a shekel, see Exod 30:13; Lev 27:25, although a system of 24 *gerâ*s to the shekel fits the metrology better. The slightly heavier "shekel of the sanctuary" may be the special standard the texts specify.

Variation in weight between stones of the same value is rarely more than 5%, except in the very small ones. The cheating often condemned lay in using two sets of weights, heavy for buying and light for selling; see Deut 25:13; Prov 20:10, 23; Mic 6:11.

REFERENCES

Kletter 1991; 1998.

F. "FUNCTIONAL" INSCRIPTIONS

1. TREATIES

THE INSCRIPTIONS OF BAR-GAʾYAH AND MATIʿEL FROM SEFIRE (2.82)

Joseph A. Fitzmyer, S.J.

These inscriptions of Sefire (once called Sujin) were discovered by S. Ronzevalle in 1930 in a village southeast of Aleppo. Two of them became the property of the Damascus Museum in 1948. The third stele was acquired by the Beirut Museum in 1956. The three steles are related not only by their provenience, but also by their contents, script, and language. They are inscribed in Old Aramaic and date from the mid-eighth century, sometime prior to 740 BCE, the year in which Tiglath-pileser III conquered Arpad and made it part of the Assyrian empire.

STELE I

What remains of this inscription is engraved on three sides of a basalt stone, 51.5 inches high, which was cut subsequently to its engraving so that it lacks several letters at the end of the lines of face A and at the beginning of the lines of face B. The text that was engraved on face D is completed lost today. Also missing are several lines in the middle of the faces that are otherwise preserved.

Face A

The title, introducing the contracting parties (lines 1-6a)
The treaty[a] of Bar-gaʾyah,[1] king of KTK,[2] with Matiʿel,[3] the son of ʿAttarsamak,[4] the king [of Arpad; and the trea]ty of the sons of Bar-gaʾyah with the sons of Matiʿel; and the treaty of the grandsons of Bar-gaʾ[yah and] his [offspring] with the offspring of Matiʿel, the son of ʿAttarsamak, the king of Arpad; and the treaty of KTK with [the treaty of] Arpad; and the treaty of the lords of KTK with the treaty of the lords of Arpad; and the treaty of Ḥa[bur]u[5] with all Aram, and with Miṣr[6] and with his sons who will come after [him], and [with the kings of] all Upper-Aram and Lower-Aram and with all who enter the royal palace.

The gods who are witnesses to this treaty (lines 6b-14a)
And the st[ele with t]his [inscription] they have set up (as) this treaty. Now (it is) this treaty which Bar-gaʾ[yah] has concluded[7] [b] [in the presence of Assur] and Mullesh[8] in the presence of Marduk and Zarpanit, in the presence of Nabu and T[ashmet, in the presence of Ir and Nus]k, in the presence of Nergal and Laṣ, in the presence of Shamash and Nur, in the presence of S[in and Nikkal, in the pre]sence of Nikkar and Kadiʾah, in the presence of all the gods of Raḥbah and Adam(?)[9] [... in the presence of Hadad of A]leppo, in the presence of Sibitti, in the presence of El and ʿElyan,[10] [c] in the presence of Hea[ven and Earth,[d] in the presence of (the) A]byss and (the) Springs, and in the presence of Day and Night — all the god[s of KTK and the gods of Ar]pad (are) witnesses (to it).[e] Open your eyes,[f] (O gods!), to gaze upon the treaty of Bar-gaʾyah [with Matiʿel, the king of Arpad].

Curses against Matiʿel, if he violates the treaty (lines 14b-35a)
Now if Matiʿel, the son of ʿAttarsamak, the kin[g

a Isa 33:8 (read ʿdym; cf. 1QIsa[a] 27:8)
b Gen 15:18; Jer 34:18
c Gen 14:18-19
d Deut 4:26; 30:19; 31:28
e Gen 31:50
f 2 Kgs 19:16; Isa 37:17

[1] The name, meaning "son of majesty," may be a title, possibly for Šamši-ilu, the *turtanu* of northern Syria; see: Lemaire and Durand 1984:3-58.
[2] The place is still not identified with certainty. For recent discussion of it, see: Lemaire and Durand (ibid.); Fitzmyer 1995:167-174.
[3] Called Mati'ilu in related Akk. treaties.
[4] Called *Ataršumki* in related Akk. treaties.
[5] Instead of the name *Ḥbwrw*, one could rather read *ḥ[br*, "federation, union." So Dupont-Sommer, who supplied [ʾ*rrṭ*]*w*, "of Urartu," a restoration that has created many historical problems and is unlikely.
[6] Dupont-Sommer (1960:18) originally translated this last phrase, "et avec <le roi de> Muṣru," understanding *mṣr* as the name of a land. On the problems that this creates, see Garelli 1957:1469-1470; 1971. Others have interpreted *mṣr* as the name of a person. So Lipiński 1975a:25.
[7] Lit., "has cut" (as in I A 40). Cf. Heb. *kārat berît* (Gen 15:18; Jer 34:18).
[8] ʾ*šr*, pronounced in Assyrian fashion "Assur," is restored with certainty as the consort of *mlš*, which represents the Neo-Assyrian form *Mullissu* (< Mulliltu) or Ninlil. See Barré 1985.
[9] Interpreted as in I A 35.
[10] Here treated apparently as two gods; cf. Gen 14:18-19.

of Arpad], should prove unfaithful [to Bar-gaᵓyah, the king of KTK, and i]f the offspring of Matiᶜel should prove unfaithful [to the offpsring of Bar-gaᵓyah ... [... and if the Benê-]Gush[11] should be unfaithful ...] [ ]from YM[...] [... and should seven rams cover] a ewe, may she not conceive; and should seven nurses] anoint [their breasts and] nurse a young boy, may he not have his fill; and should seven mares suckle a colt, may it not be sa[ted; and should seven] cows give suck to a calf, may it not have its fill; and should seven ewes suckle a lamb, [may it not be sa]ted; and should seven hens(?) go looking for food, may they not kill(?) (anything)![12] [g] And if Mati[ᶜel] should be unfaithful <to Bar-gaᵓyah> [and to] his son and to his offspring, may his kingdom become like a kingdom of sand, a kingdom of sand, as long as Assur rules! (And) [may Ha]dad [pour (over it) every sort of evil (which exists) on earth and in heaven and every sort of trouble; and may he shower upon Arpad [ha]il-[stones]![h] For seven years may the locust devour (Arpad), and for seven years may the worm eat, and for seven [years may] TWY come up upon the face of its land![i] May the grass not come forth so that no green may be seen; and may its vegetation not be [seen]! Nor may the sound of the lyre[j] be heard in Arpad; but among its people (let there rather be) the din of affliction and the noi[se of cry]ing and lamentation![k] May the gods send every sort of devourer against Arpad and against its people! [May the mou]th of a snake [eat], the mouth of a scorpion, the mouth of a bear(?), the mouth of a panther. And may a moth and a louse and a [... become] to it a serpent's throat![13] May its vegetation be destroyed unto desolation! And may Arpad become a mound to [house the desert animal],[14] [l] the gazelle and the fox and the hare and the wild-cat and the owl and the [ ] and the magpie! May [this] ci[ty] not be mentioned (any more), [nor] MDRᵓ nor MRBH nor MZH nor MNLH nor Sharun nor Tuᵓim nor Bethel nor BYNN nor [... nor Ar]neh nor Ḥazaz nor Adam![15]

Curses with accompanying rites (lines 35b-42)
Just as this wax is burned by fire, so may Arpad be burned and [her gr]eat [daughter-cities]! May Hadad sow in them salt[m] and weeds(?), and may it not be mentioned (again)! This GNBᵓ and [ ] (are) Matiᶜel; it is his person. Just as this wax is burned by fire, so may Mati[ᶜel be burned by fi]re![n] Just as (this) bow and these arrows are broken, so may Inurta and Hadad break [the bow of Matiᶜel],[o] and the bow of his nobles! And just as the man of wax is blinded, so may Mati[ᶜel] be blinded![p] [Just as] this calf is cut in two, so may Matiᶜel be cut in two, and may his nobles be cut in two![q] [And just as] a [har]lot is stripped naked],[r] so may the wives of Matiᶜel be stripped naked, and the wives of his offspring, and the wives of [his] no[bles! And just as this wax woman is taken] and one strikes her on the face, so may the [wives of Matiᶜel] be taken [and]

Face B

The sacred character of the treaty (lines 1-15?)
[The treaty of Bar-gaᵓyah, king of KTK, with Matiᶜel, son of ᶜAttarsamak, the king of Ar]pad; and the treaty of the son of Bar-gaᵓyah with the sons of Matiᶜel; and the treaty of the [grandsons of Bar-]gaᵓyah with the offspring of Matiᶜel and with the offspring of any king who [will come up and rule] in his place, and with the Benê-Gush and with Bêt-ṢLL and with [all] Ar[am;[16] and the trea]ty of KTK with the treaty of Arpad; and the treaty of the lords of KTK with the trea[ty of the lords of Ar]pad and with its people. The treaty of the gods of KTK with the treaty of the g[ods of Arpad]. This is the treaty of gods, which gods have concluded. Blessed(?) forever be the reign of [Bar-gaᵓyah], a great king,[s] and from this happy treaty [ ] and heaven. [All the gods] shall guard [this] treaty.[t] Let not one of the words of thi[s] inscription be silent, [but let them be heard from] ᶜArqu(?) to Yaᵓd[i and] BZ, from Lebanon to Yabrud, from Damascu]s to ᶜAru(?) and M..W, [and fr]om the Valley to KTK [... in Bê]t-Gush and its people with their sanctuary(?), this treaty [...]YTH HŠK.HWᵓ. . in Muṣr and MRBH [...] DŠ. . . . .TM to Matiᶜel, son [of ᶜAttarsamak ...]

[A few letters are legible on lines 14-15; lines 16-20 are missing.]

The stipulations of the treaty (lines 21-45)
[...] to your house. And (if) Matiᶜel will not obey [and (if) his sons will not obey, and (if) his people will not o]bey, and (if) all the kings who will rule in Arpad [will not obey] the .[ ] [ ]. .LMNYN, you will have been unfaithful to all the gods of the treaty whi[ch is in this inscription.[u] But if you obey and car]ry out this treaty and say, "[I] am an ally," [I shall not be able to raise a hand] against you;[v] nor will my son be able to raise a hand against

g Lev 26:26
h Exod 10:4-5; Ps 105:32, 34
i Deut 28:38-42
j Ezek 26:13
k Zeph 1:10
l Isa 13:21
m Judg 9:45; Deut 29:22
n Ps 68:3
o Hos 1:5
p Jer 39:7
q Jer 34:18; Gen 15:10
r Jer 13:26-27
s 2 Kgs 18:28
t Pss 25:10; 119:2
u 2 Kgs 23:21
v Gen 37:22; Exod 22:7, 10

[11] Restored according to I B 3.

[12] The reading and meaning of this line is highly contested. Dupont-Sommer read it: *wšbᶜ bkth yhkn bšṭ lḥm wᵓl yhrgn*, which I have translated above. In light of Fakhariyah 22 (*COS* 2.34), Kaufman (1982:72) would rather read: *wšbᶜ bnth yᵓpn b..ṭ lḥm wᵓl ymlᵓn*, "and may his seven daughters bake bread in an oven(?) but not fill (it)." Cf. Lev 26:26. Cf. Fitzmyer 1995, ad loc.

[13] The division of the letters into words is disputed; see Fitzmyer 1995, ad loc.

[14] The restoration follows Isa 13:21.

[15] Most of these ancient places are not yet identified, especially those written in capital letters.

[16] Restored as in I A 5.

[your] son, or my offspring against [your] offspr[ing. And if] one of (the) kings [should speak a word] against me or one of my enemies (should so speak) and you say to any king, "What are you [going to do?" and he should raise a hand against] my son and kill him and raise his hand to take some of my land or some of my possessions, you will have been unfaith[ful to the trea]ty which is in this inscription. If one of (the) kings comes and surrounds <me>, [your] ar[my] must come [to me with every arch[er] and every sort [of weapon], and you must surround those who surround me and you must draw for me [...] and I shall pile corpse upon corpse in Ar[pad] ... some king LᵓWYN WMWT [...] and if on a day when (the) gods [...] the rebels, you (sg.) do not come with your army and (if) [you (pl.) do not] come with your (pl.) armies to strengthen my ho[u]se and [if your] off[spring does not] come to strengthen [my] offspring, [you will have been unfaithful to] the gods of the treaty which is in this inscription. And (when) [...] YᶜPN with me, I shall be able [to drink] water [of the well of ...]L; whoever lives around that well shall not be able to destroy (it) or raise a hand against the water of [the] wel[l]. [And the king] who will enter and take LBKH or Ḥ......, who will take ... BᶜH. [... to] destroy ᵓNGDᵓ . . MLHM . . M . . KD in the town of ᵓYMᵓM. And if (you do) not (do) so, you will have been unfaith[ful] [to the treaty] <which is in> this <inscription>. And if . . Q. LY . . . LᵓK.L . . . LHMY . Y.NŠᵓ, you shall send ..ᵓ. [...]M, and if you do not give (me) my provisions, [or] deduct provisions from me, and do not deliver (them), you will have been unfaithful to this treaty. [. . . You can[not] deduct provisions ᵓNḤ KᵓYM YQM LK, and you yourself will seek and will go [... to] your [cit]y and to your house YN. . ZRᵓ. . for myself [and for eve]ry person of my household and for Ṭ [...] in it your son(?); and the kings of Ar[pad] will not cu[t any]thing off from them because it is a living pact. [...] H.... ṬLL Hᵓ WSḤ Hᵓ WBL Hᵓ NTRḤM for yourself ᵓM. [...]. ... Kᶜ. . with you; so you will cut the ᵓPLᵓ. And if ... [...] NQ ... he will strengthen the QLBT of my house against ... L.Ḥ.ᵓY ᵓQL. ... [...]. . [against] my son or against one of my courtiers; and (if) one of them flees and com[es ...]

Face C

Conclusion (lines 1-9)
Thus have we spoken [and thus have we writ]ten. What I, [Matiᶜ]el, have written (is to serve) as a reminder for my son [and] my [grand]son who will come a[fter] me. May they make good relations [beneath] the sun[w] [for (the sake of) my] ro[yal hou]se that no ev[il may be done against] the house of Mat[iᶜel and his son and] his [grand]son for[ever]

w Qoh 1:3, 9, 14

Blessings (lines ?-16)
... may (the) gods keep [all evils] away from his day and from his house.

Curses (lines 17-24)
Whoever will not observe the words of the inscription which is on this stele or will say, "I shall efface some of its words," or "I shall upset the good treaty-relations and turn (them) [to] evil," on any day on which he will d[o] so, may the gods overturn th[at m]an and his house and all that (is) in it! May they make its lower part its upper part! May his sci[on] inherit no name!

STELE II

When stele II was obtained by the Damascus Museum, it consisted of about a dozen fragments. When assembled, they yielded the middle part of three sides of an inscribed monument similar to stele I. Stele II is clearly related to stele I, mentioning the same kings, Bar-gaᵓyah and Matiᶜel, and having very similar curses and stipulations, but it is not simply another copy of the same text. Hence the relation of the two steles is debated.

Face A

Curses (lines 1-14)
... [and should seven mares suckle a colt, may it not be sated; should seven cows give suck to a calf, may it n]ot have its fill; should seven [ewes suckle a lamb, may it not be sated; and should seven goats suck]le a kid, may it not be sa[ted; and should seven hens(?) go looking for food, may they not kill(?) (anything).[17] And if (Matiᶜel) should be un]faithful to Bar-gaᵓyah and to [his son and to his offspring, may his kingdom become like a kingdom of sand; and may his name be for]gotten, and may [his grav]e be ... [and for se]ven years thorns, ŠB[...] [... and for se]ven years may there be [...] [...] among all the nobles of ... [...] and his land. And a cry [... and may] the mouth of a lion [eat] and the mouth of [a ...] and the mouth of a panther [...]

[Lines 10-14 are practically illegible.]

Face B

Stipulations (lines 1-20)
... the treaty and the amity whi[ch] the gods have

[17] See n. 12 above.

made in [Arpad and among its people; and (if) Mati^{c}el will not obey], and (if) his sons will not obey, (if) his nobles will not obey, and (if) his people will not obey, and (if) [all the kings of Arpad] will not o[bey ...] YM who are watchful(?). But if you obey, (may) tranquility [... And] if you say in your soul and think in your mind,[a] ["I am an ally, and I shall obey Bar-ga$^{\supset}$yah] and his sons and his offspring," then I shall not be able to raise a ha[nd against you, nor my son against your son, nor my offspring against your offspring], either to rout them, or to destroy their name.[b] And [if one of my sons says, "I shall sit upon the throne] of my father, for he is babbling(?) and growing old," or (if) my son seeks [my head to kill me and you say in your soul, "Let him kill whomever he would kill," (then) you will have been unfaithful to all the gods [of the treaty which is in this inscription ...] [...]NK and Bêt-Gush and Bêt-ṢLL and [...] [...] and corpse ... upon corpse [...] [...] and on a day of wrath for all [...] [...] will come to my son and [my] grandsons [...] sons of [my] sons [...] from the hand of my enemies and [...], you will have been unfaithful [to this treaty ...] RB$^{\supset}$B..KMY ... ŠMR WBŠQ. [...] and let no one oppress him. If he oppresses (him) in QR[...] LHW.H ... if you should seek and not ... [...] you [will have been unfaithful to] all the [gods of the trea]ty which is in [this] inscription [...] [.]LY^{c} [...] he will surpass you until [.]HN [...] who will be stronger than you [...]

a Zech 7:10; 8:17

b Deut 7:24; 12:3

c Gen 28:19

Face C

Safekeeping of the inscribed treaty (lines 1-17)

... [and whoever will] give orders to efface [th]ese inscriptions from the bethels,[c] where they are [wr]itten, and [will] say, "I shall destroy the inscript[ion]s, and with impunity(?) shall I destroy KTK and its king," should that (man) be frightened from effacing the inscriptions from the bethels and say to someone who does not understand, "I shall engage (you) indeed(?)," and (then) order (him), "Efface these inscriptions from the bethels," may [he] and his son die in oppressive torment. [...] and all the gods of the [trea]ty which is in [this] inscription will [...] Mati^{c}el and his son and his grandson and his offspring and all the kings of Arpad and all his nobles and their people from their homes and from their days.

SEFIRE III

The nine fragments of this stele, when pieced together, yielded an extended text of 29 lines. In this case, the text was engraved only on one side of a broad slab, roughly 102 cm. x 72 cm. Though stele III is related to the other two steles, Bar-ga$^{\supset}$yah's name has been restored in III 25, and that may be questionable. But it does mention "the kings of Arpad" (lines 1, 3, 16, 27), which does relate it to the other two. Neither the beginning nor the end of this text is preserved; it contains only stipulations imposed on the kings of Arpad.

Concerning the surrender of plotters (lines 1-4a)

[... And whoever will come to you] or to your son or to your offspring or to one of the kings of Arpad and will s[pea]k [ag]ainst me or against my son or against my grandson or against my offspring, indeed(?), any man who rants(?)[18] [a] and utters evil words[b] against me, [you] must [not] accept such words from him. You must hand them (i.e., the men) over into my hands, and your son must hand (them) over to my son, and your offspring must hand (them) over to my offspring, and the offspring of [any of the ki]ngs of Arpad must hand (them) over to me. Whatever is good in my sight, I will do to them.[c] And if (you do) not (do) so, you shall have been unfaithful to all the gods of the treaty which is in [this] inscription.

Concerning the surrender of fugitives (lines 4b-7a)

Now if a fugitive flees from me, one of my officials, or one of my brothers, or one of my courtiers, or one of the people who are under my control, and they go to Aleppo,[19] you must not gi[ve th]em food or say to them, "Stay quietly in your place"; and you must not incite them against me. You must placate(?) them and return them to me. And if they [do] not [dwell] in your land, placate(?) (them) there, until I come and placate(?) them. But if you incite them against me and give them food and say to them, "Stay where [yo]u are[d] and do not (re)turn to his region," you shall have been unfaithful to this treaty.

Concerning freedom of passage (lines 7b-9a)

Now (as for) all the kings of my vicinity[20] [e] or any one who is a friend of mine, when I send my ambassador to him for peace or for any of my business or (when) he sends his ambassador[f] to me, the road shall be open to me. You must not (try to) dominate me in this (respect) or assert your authority over me concerning [it]. [And] if (you do) not (do) so, you shall be unfaithful to this treaty.

a Lam 4:20; Prov 1:23; Isa 11:15

b Qoh 8:3

c 2Sam 19:38; Josh 9:25; 2 Kgs 10:5

d Exod 16:29

e Gen 34:10; 42:34

f 1 Kgs 20:2

[18] Lit., "who causes the breath of his nostrils to boil"; cf. Lam 4:20; Prov 1:23; Isa 11:15.

[19] For Aleppo and its temple as a place of asylum, see Greenfield 1991a.

[20] The noun *sḥrty* may mean "trading area"; cf. the use of the verb *sḥr* in Gen 34:10; 42:34.

Concerning vengeance to be taken in the case of assassination (lines 9b-14a)
Now if any one of my brothers or any one of my father's household or any one of my sons or any one of my officers or any one of my [of]ficials or any one of the people under my control or any one of my enemies seeks my head to kill me[g] and to kill my son and my offspring — if they kill m[e], you must come and avenge my blood[h] from the hand of my enemies. Your son must come (and) avenge the blood of my son from his enemies; and your grandson must come (and) avenge the blo[od of] my grandson. Your offspring must come (and) avenge the blood of my offspring. If it is a city, you must strike it with a sword. If it is one of my brothers or one of my slaves or [one] of my officials or one of the people who are under my control, you must strike him and his offspring, his nobles(?), and his friends with a sword.[i] And if (you do) not (do) so, you shall have been unfaithful to all the gods of the [tr]eaty which is in this inscription.

Concerning plots against the suzerain (lines 14b-17a)
If the idea should come to your mind[j] and you should express with your lips[k] (the intention) to kill me; and if the idea should come to the mind of your grandson and he should express with his lips (the intention) to kill my grandson; or if the idea should come to the mind of your offspring and he should express with his lips (the intention) to kill my offspring; and if the idea should come to the [mi]nd of the kings of Arpad, in whatever way anyone[21] [l] shall die, you shall have been false to all the gods of the treaty which is in this inscription.

Concerning duty in a strife for succession to the throne (lines 17b-19a)
If [my] son, who sits upon my throne, quarrels <with> one of his brothers, and he would remove him, you shall not interfere[m] with them,[22] saying to him, "Kill your brother or imprison him and do no[t] let him go free." But if you really make peace between them, he will not kill and will not imprison (him). But if you do not make peace between them, you shall have been unfaithful to this treaty.

Concerning the reciprocal return of fugitives (lines 19b-20)
And as for [k]ings [of my vicin]ity, if a fugitive of mine flees to one of them, and a fugitive of theirs flees and comes to me, if he has restored mine, I will return [his; and] you yourself shall [no]t (try to) hinder me. And if (you do) not (do) so, you shall have been unfaithful to this treaty.

Concerning plots against the suzerain's household (lines 21-23a)
You shall not interfere in my house or (with) my grandsons or (with) the sons of my bro[thers or (with) the sons of my off]spring or (with) the sons of my people, saying to them, "Kill your lord, and be his successor! For he is not better than you."[n] Someone will avenge [my blood. If you do com]mit treachery against me or against my sons or against [my] offspring, you shall have been unfaith]ful to all the gods of the treaty which is in th[is] inscription.

*Concerning the territory of Tal*ᵓ*ayim* (lines 23b-27a)
[Talᵓay]im,[23] its villages, its lords, and its territory (once belonged) to my father and to [his house from] of old. When (the) gods struck [my father's] house, [it came to belong] to another.[o] Now, however, (the) gods have brought about the return[p] of my [father's ho]use, [and] my father's [house has grown great], and Talᵓayim[24] has returned to [Bar-gaᵓy]ah and to his son and to his grandson and to his offspring forever. [If my son quarrels and (if)] my [grand]son quarrels and (if) my offspring quarrels [with your offspring a]bout Talᵓayim and its villages and its lords, whoever will raise [... the ki]ngs of Arpad [...]LNH, you shall have been unfaithful to this treaty.

Concerning gifts (?) (lines 27b-29)
And if [ ] and they bribe in any way a king who will [... all th]at is beautiful and all that is go[od] [...]

g Jer 26:21; Ps 37:32
h 2 Kgs 9:7
i Deut 13:16; Josh 11:11; 1 Sam 22:19
j Isa 65:17; Jer 3:16
k Ps 16:4c
l Dan 7:13; 1QapGen 21:13; 11QtgJob 26:3
m Prov 6:19b
n 1 Kgs 19:4
o Deut 24:2
p Jer 33:7; Ps 126:1

[21] Lit., "a son of man." This is the earliest occurrence of this phrase in Aram., where it is used in a generic sense. Cf. Dan 7:13; 1QapGen 21:13; 11QtgJob 26:3.
[22] Lit., "you shall not send your tongue between them."
[23] The name is restored according to Sf III 25-26.
[24] Identified as *Talḫayim*, known from Akk. texts; see Noth 1961:156.

REFERENCES

Text: *KAI* 2:238-274, 342; *SSI* 2:18-5; *ANEP* 659-661; Translations and Studies: *TUAT* 1:178-189; Barré 1985; Dupont-Sommer and Starcky 1956; 1960; Fitzmyer 1995; Garelli 1957; 1971; Greenfield 1991a; Kaufman 1982; Lemaire and Durand 1984; Lipiński 1975a:27-76; McCarthy 1978; Noth 1961; Ronzevalle 1930-1931; van Rooy 1989.

G. MISCELLANEOUS INSCRIPTIONS

THE KETEF HINNOM AMULETS (2.83)

P. Kyle McCarter

These two tiny silver scrolls were found in 1980 by Gabriel Barkay during the excavation of a burial cave in Jerusalem near the Church of St. Andrew on a rocky hillside overlook the Valley of Hinnom — hence, Ketef Hinnom or "the Shoulder of Hinnom." When unrolled, the scrolls proved to be amulets containing several lines of Hebrew script, the preserved portions of which include blessings almost identical to the so-called priestly or Aaronid Benediction of Num 6:24-26. In design, the burial chamber is typical of the early sixth century BCE, and since the majority of the artifacts belong to that period, Barkay assigned a similar date to the two scrolls. The tomb continued in use until the first century BCE, however, and Renz (*HAE* 447-452) argues on paleographic and orthographic grounds that the inscriptions should be dated to the second or first century BCE — that they are written, in other words, in the archaizing Paleo-Hebrew script. Nevertheless, Yardeni (1991:179-180), the principal decipherer of the scrolls, has mounted a forceful argument on the same grounds for an early sixth-century date.

Amulet 1: concluding benediction (lines 14-19) [...] May Yahweh bless you[1] [and] keep you. May Yahweh cause his face to shine [on you[a] ...].	*a* Num 6:24-25a *b* Num 6:24-25a, 26b; cf. Ps 67:2	*Amulet 2: benediction* (lines 5-12) [...] May Yahweh bless you and keep you. May Yahweh cause his face[2] to shine [on] you[3] and give you peace[b] [...].

[1] The spelling in both amulets is *ybrk* in comparison to *ybrkk* in Num 6:24; this feature is attested elsewhere in epigraphic Heb. as early as the beginning of the ninth century (Kuntillet ᶜAjrud). See *COS* 2.47.

[2] The spelling of the third-person suffix after the formally plural noun "face" as *-yw* is a late orthographic feature, reminiscent of the MT but contrasting with inscriptional forms of the seventh-sixth centuries BCE, such as Yabneh Yam *ᵓlw*, "to him," and Lachish *ᵓnšw*, "his men." This supports Renz's argument for a Hellenistic date for the amulets. The same would be true of the *plene* spelling of *šlwm*, "peace," in the next line, though in that case the *waw* in question is doubtful (not read by Yardeni).

[3] The text of the second amulet includes no equivalent of Num 6:25b-26a, "... and be gracious to you. May Yahweh lift up his face to you ...." There seems to have been room at the end of the first amulet for *wyḥnk*, "... and be gracious to you," but the text is not extant.

REFERENCES

Text, translations and studies: *AHI* 4.301-302; *HAE* 1:447-56; Barkay 1986; 1989; 1992; Haran 1989; Rösel 1986; Yardeni 1991.

THE EL KHADR ARROWHEADS (2.84)

Gordon Hamilton

These five arrowheads, inscribed with Old Canaanite alphabetic letters, were found near Bethlehem and published between 1954 and 1980.[1] Their weight and size, between 9.5 and 10.5 cm, fall within normal parameters for arrowheads used for practical purposes.[2] Dating to ca 1100-1050 BCE,[3] these inscriptions provide witness both to literacy and goddess religion in Palestine during the late second millennium.

1 (The) Arrowhead of ᶜAbd-Labīᵓt[4] 2 (The) Arrowhead of ᶜAbd-Labīt[4] 3 (The) Arrowhead of ᶜAbd-Labīᵓt[4]	*a* Judg 3:31; 5:6	4 (The) Arrowhead of ᶜAbd-LᵓT[5] 5 ᶜAbd-Labīᵓt[4] Bin-ᶜAnat[6] [a]

[1] For the most recent discussions, see Mitchell 1985:137-148; Sass 1988:76-78; Cross 1993:542.

[2] See Mitchell 1985:140-142 and, for previous proposals, Cross 1979:103, n. 28.

[3] Since all five were purchased in the marketplace, their dating depends on combining the typological analysis of their scripts and the form of the arrowheads themselves. See Cross and Milik 1956:15-23 and Mitchell 1985:142-145; cf. Sass 1988:76.

[4] The name ᶜAbd-Labīᵓt on Arrowheads 1, 3 and the first name of 5 means "(The) Servant/Slave/Worshipper of (the) Lioness," a reference to a goddess, possibly ᶜAnat (Cross 1967:13*-14* and 1980:7). The spelling of the same name on Arrowhead 2, *ᶜbdlbt*, either shows an accidental omission of the *ᵓaleph* (so Cross 1980:5) or loss of that letter at the end of a syllable (Milik and Cross 1954:8).

[5] Cross (1980:5) interpreted the name on Arrowhead 4, ᶜbd-*LᵓT*, as exhibiting another error, the omission of a *bêt*. It is also possible to view the 2nd element, *lᵓt*, as a genuine name given **liᵓatum* in Amorite (Gelb 1980:312, 323) and *lēᵓâ*, Leah, in BH; the meaning might then be "(The) Arrowhead of (the) Servant/Slave/Worshipper of (the) Prevailing One," another reference to a goddess (cf. Lioness in 1, 2, 3 and ᶜAnat in 5).

[6] Bin-ᶜAnat either could be the name of the father of ᶜAbd-Labīᵓt or indicate that the latter was a member of an archers' guild (Cross 1980:7). For occurrences of the term on another arrowhead and elsewhere cf. Hallo and Tadmor 1977:4f. See also Beem 1991:158-162.

REFERENCES

Text: Milik and Cross 1954; Cross and Milik 1956. Studies: Cross 1967; 1979; 1980; Mitchell 1985; Sass 1988; Deutsch and Heltzer 1994:11-21.

THE GEZER CALENDAR (2.85)

P. Kyle McCarter

This limestone plaque, found at Gezer in 1908, is inscribed with a brief text associating the months of the year with various agricultural activities — hence its familiar designation as a "calendar." The limestone from which the small, hand-sized tablet is made is soft, and both surfaces show evidence of erasing and reuse. This suggests that it may have been a practice tablet and that its apparently formulaic inscription may have been a standard text used in scribal training. The text probably dates to the tenth century BCE, and its archaic language, which exhibits features not found in later inscriptional Hebrew, is probably most safely described as a South Canaanite dialect rather than specifically Hebrew.

A list of agricultural activities (lines 1-7)
His double-month[1] is ingathering.[2] [a] His double-month is sowing.[3] [b] His double-month is late-planting.[4] [c] His month[5] is chopping flax.[6] [d] His month is barley harvest.[e] His month is harvest and measuring (?).[7] His double-month is pruning.[f] His month is summerfruit.[g]

A personal name (margin)
Abiya.[8]

a Exod 23:16; 34:22; Isa 32:10 *b* Gen 8:22; Lev 26:5 *c* Amos 7:1 *d* Exod 9:31 *e* 2 Sam 21:9; Ruth 1:22; 2:23 *f* Lev 25:3-5; Cant 2:12 (?) *g* 2 Sam 16:1-2; Isa 16:9; Jer 40:10-12; 48:32; Amos 8:1-2; Mic 7:1

[1] Interpreting the difficult *yrḥw* with Albright (1943:22) as *yarḥēw*, a dual noun with masculine singular suffix vocalized according to the pronunciation of the South Canaanite dialect of Gezer in the tenth century.

[2] Probably the harvest of grapes and olives.

[3] That is, the planting of grain.

[4] Cf. Targumic Aram. *laqqîš*, which refers to late rain and other late-season activities.

[5] Instead of *yrḥw*, "his two months," we now have *yrḥ* (*yarḥō*), "his month," for four of the remaining five activities. The combination of four double-months and four single months yields a total of twelve.

[6] To *ᶜṣd pšt*, cf. BH *maᶜăṣād*, "axe," and [*pēšet*], *pištâ*, "flax."

[7] The reading *wkl* is problematic. The interpretation "measuring" is based on the root *kûl*, "contain, hold," and (presumably) by extension "measure." A form of the word seems also to occur in an agricultural context in line 5 of the Meṣad Hashavyahu (Yabneh Yam) inscription (*COS* 3).

[8] These three letters, *ʾby*, are written sideways at the edge of the tablet. They evidently represent a personal name, possibly that of the scribe. If the name is complete, it corresponds to a common hypocoristic pattern, shortened with final *-y*.

REFERENCES

Text: *EHO* 46–47; *KAI* 2:181-82; *SSI* 1:1-4; *AHI* 10.001. Translations and studies: *ANET* 320; Albright 1943; Diringer 1934:1-20, 337-338; Février 1948; Garbini 1954-56; Honeyman 1953; Lidzbarski 1909; Rahtjen 1961; Segal 1962; Talmon 1963; 1986; Wirgin 1960.

AN AMULET FROM ARSLAN TASH (2.86)

P. Kyle McCarter

Two small limestone plaques, bearing a series of inscriptions and drawings and perforated at the top for wall-mounting, were purchased in 1933 at Arslan Tash, Syria (ancient Ḫadattu). The first plaque, which was published in 1939, is translated here. The main text is written on the front and back of the plaque in the spaces not occupied by illustrations; it consists of six lines on the obverse, eight on the reverse, and three more on the edges. Depicted on the obverse is a winged sphinx inscribed with two lines of text and, beneath the sphinx, a wolf devouring a child and inscribed with yet another line of text. On the reverse is portrayed a warrior-god wielding an axe, on or alongside which are eight other short lines of text. While the language of the text is Phoenician or a local Canaanite dialect, the script is Aramaic, paleographically datable to the seventh century BCE. Somewhat surprisingly, the orthography sides with the language (Phoenician) rather than the script.

Main text: obverse (lines 1-6)
Incantations[a] against the Flyers,[1] the goddesses, (against) Sasm[2] son of Padrishishaʾ, the god, and against the Strangler of the Lamb.[3] The house I enter, you shall not enter![b]

Main text: reverse (lines 7-14)
The court I tread, you shall not tread! Ashur[4] has made[c] an eternal covenant[d] with us. He has made (a covenant) with us, along with all the sons of ʾEl[e] and the leaders of the council of all the Holy Ones,[f] with a covenant of the Heavens and Eternal Earth, with an oath of Baʿl,

Bottom edge (line 15)
Lord of Earth, with

Left edge (line 16)
an oath of Hawran,[5] whose mouth is true,

Right edge (line 17)
and his seven consorts, and the eight wives of Baʿl Qudsh.[6]

On the winged sphinx (lines 19-20)
Against the Flyers: From the dark chamber pass away! At once! At once, O night demons!

On the man-eating wolf (line 21)
In the house, against the Crushers (?)[7]: Go!

On the warrior-god (lines 22-29)
As for Sasm, let (the house) not be opened to him,[g] and let him not come down to the doorposts! Let the sun arise against Sasm! Pass away,[h] and forever fly away!

a Isa 3:20 *b* Exod 12:21-32 *c* Gen 15:18; Exod 34:10, 27; Deut 5:2, 3; 28:69; 29:13, 24; Josh 24:25; 1 Kgs 5:26; 2 Kgs 11:17; etc. *d* Gen 9:16; 17:7, 13, 19; Exod 31:16; Lev 24:8; Num 18:19; 25:13; 2 Sam 23:5; etc. *e* Gen 6:2, 4; Ps 29:1; 89:7; Job 1:6; 2:1; 38:7 *f* Zech 14:5; Ps 89:6, 8; Job 5:1; 15:15; Dan 8:13 *g* Ezek 46:12 *h* Isa 2:18

[1] Reading *l*ʿ<*p*>*t*ʾ. The *p* is missing, but the parallelism of ʿ*pt*ʾ, "Flyers," and *llyn*, "night demons," in the text on the sphinx strongly favors the reconstruction (Cross and Saley 1970:44 n. 5). Since the wolf must be the "Strangler of the Lamb" (see n. 3), the winged sphinx must either be one of the Flyers or, less likely, Sasm.
[2] For the little that is known about this god, who seems to be Hurrian in origin, see *KAI* 2:44. He is probably the warrior-god depicted on the reverse.
[3] As pointed out by du Mesnil du Buisson 1939, this demon finds a parallel in an Arabian she-wolf demon called Qarinat, who also has the epithet "Strangler of the Lamb" and who carried off children at night. She must be the wolf depicted on the obverse.
[4] Ashur, the god of Assyria, seems to have assumed the role of senior deity in northern Syria at this time when Ḫadattu was an imperial Assyrian administrative center (Zevit 1977:115). The alternative is to reconstruct ʾ*šr*<*t*>, "ʾAsherah," with Albright (1939:8 n. 16), or read a dialectal form (ʾ*aširō*) with Cross and Saley (1970:45 n. 17).
[5] Hawron or Horon, a Syro-Canaanite deity known from Ug. to Greco-Roman times, had a chthonic aspect, though his full character is not known.
[6] Evidently Baʿl Qudsh, "the Lord of Holiness," was an epithet of Hawron.
[7] Reading *lpḥṣt* with Cross and Saley (1970:46).

REFERENCES

Text: *KAI* 2: *SSI* 3:78-88. Translations and studies: *ANET* 658; Albright 1939; Caquot 1973; Cross and Saley 1970; Du Mesnil du Buisson 1939; Dupont-Sommer 1939; Gaster 1942; Lipiński 1978a:247-49; Röllig 1974; Torczyner 1947; van den Branden 1961; Zevit 1977.

THE TEL DAN BOWL (2.87)

P. Kyle McCarter

This short Aramaic inscription is incised on the base of bowl found among a collection of ninth- and eighth-century pottery from Tel Dan. It consists of six Aramaic letters, five of which are fully or partly extant, written alongside a five-pointed star.

(Belonging) to the butchers.[1] [a]

a 1 Sam 8:13; 9:23, 24; cf. Gen 37:36; 2 Kgs 25:8; Dan 2:14

[1] That is, *lṭb*[*ḥ*]*y*ʾ. The noun can mean "butchers" or "cooks," but titles like Hebrew *śr hṭbḥym* (Gen 37:36) and *rb ṭbḥym* (2 Kgs 25:8), both lit. "chief of the butchers" and Aram. *rb ṭbḥy*ʾ *dy mlk*ʾ (Dan 2:14), lit. "chief of the butchers of the king," came to designate high-ranking officers, and it is possible that the Tel Dan bowl belonged to such an individual.

REFERENCES

SSI 2:5-6; Avigad 1968b.

INSCRIBED NIMRUD IVORIES (2.88)

P. Kyle McCarter

A number of inscribed fragments of ivory inlay were found during the 1961 season of the British excavations of the stronghold of Fort Shalmaneser at Nimrud, the ancient Assyrian capital of Calah, on the east bank of the Tigris. The ivories, which bear both Aramaic and Hebrew inscriptions, are believed to have been brought to Calah as booty by the Assyrian army returning from campaigns in the West. The ivory plaque translated here is inscribed with well-written Hebrew characters dating paleographically to the middle of the eighth century BCE, and it is reasonable to surmise that it was part of the plunder taken from Samaria when the city fell to Shalmaneser V in 722 BCE. The first editor (Millard 1962) understood the preserved lines as an imprecation included in a votive or commemorative plaque to threaten with divine retribution anyone in the future who should damage the inscription.

[...] may Ya[hweh] shatter[1] [a] [... who come af]ter me, from great king[2] [to ... if they should co]me and efface[3] th[is ivory[b] ...]

a Pss 68:22; 110:5-6 *b* 1 Kgs 10:18; 22:39; Amos 3:15; 6:4; 2 Chr 9:17

[1] Millard's readings in the *editio princeps*, though highly tentative in view of the very fragmentary character of the text, have not been substantially improved upon and are generally followed here. The first sequence that admits of any possible interpretation is [...]*ypt*[.]*y*[*hwh* ...]. Millard identifies the verb as *ptt*, "break into pieces, shatter," which occurs in BH only as the infinitive in Lev 2:6, but which has reflexes in Syriac and Arabic.

[2] Millard may be correct in understanding *mmlk gdl*, "from great king," as the first part of such phrases found frequently in curses as "from great king to common man"; cf., for example, "Whoever you are, any ruler or any (ordinary) man" in the ᵓEshmunᶜazor epitaph (*COS* 2.57). As Millard also points out, if the ivory text read *mhmlk hgdl*, "from *the* great king," we would suspect a reference to the Assyrian emperor (*šarru rabû*) in this period (cf. 2 Kgs 18:19).

[3] That is, *wmḥw*, presumably a plural from *māḥâ*, "wipe, wipe out, obliterate, efface."

REFERENCES

Millard 1962; *SSI* 1:19-24; *AHI* 34.001-003; Lemaire 1976b.

WEST SEMITIC BIBLIOGRAPHY

ABBADI, S.
1983 *Die Personennamen der Inschriften aus Hatra*. Hildesheim/New York: Olms.
ABELLS, Z. and A. ARBIT.
1995 "Some New Thoughts on Jerusalem's Ancient Water Systems." *PEQ* 127:2-7.
ABOU ASSAF, A., BORDREUIL, P., and A. R. MILLARD.
1982 *La Statue de Tell Fekherye et son inscription bilingue assyro-araméenne*. Paris: Editions Recherche sur les civilisations.
AHARONI, Y.
1968 "Trial Excavation in the 'Solar Shrine' at Lachish, Preliminary Report." *IEJ* 18:157-169.
1975 *Ketovot Arad*. Jerusalem: Bialik Institute and Israel Exploration Society.
AḤITUV, S.
1992 *Handbook of Ancient Hebrew Inscriptions*. Encyclopaedia Biblica Library 7. Jerusalem: Mosad Bialik (in Hebrew).
AHLSTRÖM, G.
1984 "The Tell Siran Bottle Inscription." *PEQ* 116:12-15.
AIMÉ-GIRON, N.
1939 "Adversaria Semitica." *BIFAO* 38:40-43.
ALBRIGHT, W. F.
1939 "An Aramean Magical Text in Hebrew from the Seventh Century B.C." *BASOR* 76:5-11.
1942 "A Votive Stele Erected by Ben-Hadad I of Damascus to the God Melcarth." *BASOR* 87:23-29.
1943 "The Gezer Calendar." *BASOR* 92:16–26.
1947 "The Phoenician Inscriptions of the Tenth Century B.C. from Byblus." *JAOS* 67:153-60.
1968 *Yahweh and the Gods of Canaan*. Garden City, NY: Doubleday.
ALLEN, T. G.
1974 *The Book of the Dead*. Chicago: University of Chicago Press.
AMADASI GUZZO, M. G., and A. ARCHI.
1980 "La bilingue fenicio-ittita geroglifica di Karatepe." *VO* 3:85-101.
AMADASI GUZZO, M. G.
1984 "Le roi qui fait vivre son peuple dans les inscriptions phéniciennes." *WO* 15:109-118.
1987 "Iscrizioni semitiche di nord-ovest in contesti greci e italici (X-VII sec.a.C.)." *Dialoghi di Archeologia* 3rd series 5:13-27.
AMBROS, A. A.
1994 "Zur Inschrift von ᶜEn ᶜAvdat — eine Mahnung zur Vorsicht." *Journal of Arabic Linguistics* 27:90-92.
ANDERSEN, F. I.
1966 "Moabite Syntax." *Or* 35:81-120.
ANGERSTORFER, A.
1982 "Asherah als 'Consort of Jahweh' oder Ashirtah?" *BN* 17:7-16.
ARNAUD, D.
1986 *Emar*.
ASSMAN, J.C.
1963 "Zur Baugeschichte der Königsgruft von Sidon." *AA* 78:690-716.
AUFFRET, P.
1980 "Essai sur la structure littéraire de la stèle de Mésha." *UF* 12:109-124.
AUFRECHT, W. E.
1999a "The Religion of the Ammonites." Pp. 152-162 in *Ancient Ammon*. Ed. by B. MacDonald and R. W. Younker. Leiden: E. J. Brill.
1999b "Ammonite Texts and Language." Pp. 163-188 in *Ancient Ammon*. Ed. by B. MacDonald and R. W. Younker. Leiden: E. J. Brill.
AUFRECHT, W. E., L. G. and HERR.
In Press "The Civilizations of the Ammonites." *JAOS*.
AVIGAD, N.
1953 "The Epitaph of a Royal Steward from Siloam Village." *IEJ* 3:137-152.
1965 "Seals of Exiles." *IEJ* 15:222-232.
1968a "Notes on some Inscribed Syro-Phoenician Seals." *BASOR* 189:44-49.
1968b "An Inscribed Bowl from Dan." *PEQ* 100:42-44.
1970 "Ammonite and Moabite Seals." Pp. 284-295 in *Studies Glueck*.
1972 "Excavations in the Jewish Quarter of the Old City of Jerusalem, 1971 (Third Preliminary Report)." *IEJ* 22:193-200 and pl. 42B.
1975 "The Priest of Dor." *IEJ* 25:101-105.
1976 *Bullae and Seals from a Post-Exilic Judean Archive*. Qedem 4. Jerusalem: Institute of Archaeology, The Hebrew University of Jerusalem.
1978a "Baruch the Scribe and Jerahmeel the King's Son." *IEJ* 28:52-56.
1978b "The Seal of 'Seraiah (son) of Neriah.'" *EI* 14:86-87 (in Hebrew).
1978c "The King's Daughter and the Lyre." *IEJ* 28:146-151.
1979a "Hebrew Epigraphic Sources." Pp. 20-43 in *The World History of the Jewish People*. Ed. by A. Malamat, and I. Ephᶜal. First Series: Ancient Times. Vol. 4, Pt. 1: Political History. Jerusalem: Massada.
1979b "A Group of Hebrew Seals from the Hecht Collection." Pp. 119-126 in *Festschrift Rëuben R. Hecht*. Jerusalem: Koren.
1980 "The Chief of the Corvée." *IEJ* 30:170-173.
1985 "Some Decorated West Semitic Seals." *IEJ* 35:1-7.
1986 *Hebrew Bullae from the Time of Jeremiah*. Jerusalem: Israel Exploration Society (in Hebrew).
1987 "The Contribution of Hebrew Seals to an Understanding of Israelite Religion and Society." Pp. 195-208 in *Studies Cross*.
1988 "Hebrew Seals and Sealings and Their Significance for Biblical Research." Pp. 8-16 in *Congress Volume: Jerusalem, 1986*. SVT 40. Ed. by J. A. Emerton. Leiden: E. J. Brill.

1989 "The Inscribed Pomegranate from the 'House of the Lord.'" *Israel Museum Journal* 9:7-16.
1990 "The Inscribed Pomegranate from the 'House of the Lord.'" *BAR* 53:157-166.
1994 "The Inscribed Pomegranate from the 'House of the Lord.'" Pp. 128-137 in *Ancient Jerusalem Revealed*. Ed. by H. Geva. Jerusalem: Israel Exploration Society.

AVIGAD, N., and B. SASS.
1997 *Corpus of West Semitic Stamp Seals*. Revised and completed by B. Sass. Jerusalem: Israel Academy of Sciences and Humanities, Israel Exploration Society, and Institute of Archaeology, Hebrew University of Jerusalem.

AVISHUR, Y.
1976 "Studies of Stylistic Features Common to the Phoenician Inscriptions and the Bible." *UF* 8:1-22.

BAKER, D. W.
1992 "Tarshish." *ABD* 6:331.

BARAG, D.
1970 "Note on an Inscription from Khirbet el-Qom." *IEJ* 20:216-218.

BARKAY, G.
1986 *Ketef Hinnom. A Treasure Facing Jerusalem's Walls*. Jerusalem: Israel Museum, Catalogue 274.
1989 "The Priestly Benediction on the Ketef Hinnom Plaques." *Cathedra* 52:37-76 (in Hebrew).
1992 "The Priestly Benediction on Silver Plaques from Ketef Hinnom in Jerusalem." *TA* 19:139-194.
1993 "A Bulla of Ishmael, the King's Son." *BASOR* 290-291:109-114.

BARRÉ, M. L.
1981 "A Note on *rš*ᵓ*t* in the Karatepe Inscription." *JANES* 13:1-3.
1982 "An Analysis of the Royal Blessing in the Karatepe Inscription." *Maarav* 3/2:177-194.
1985 "The First Pair of Deities in the Sefîre I God-List." *JNES* 44:205-210.

BARSTAD, H. M.
1995 "Dod" Cols. 493-498 in *DDD*. Pp. 259-262 in 2nd Revised Edition, 1999.

BECK, P.
1982 "The Drawings from Ḥorvat Teiman (Kuntillet ᶜAjrud)." *TA* 9:3-68.

BECKING, B.
1998 "Does a Recently Published Paleo-Hebrew Inscription Refer to the Solomonic Temple?" *BN* 92:5-11.

BEEM, B.
1991 "The Minor Judges: A Literary Reading of Some Very Short Stories." Pp. 147-172 in *SIC* 4.

BELLAMY, J. A.
1990 "Arabic Verses from the First/Second Century: the Inscription of ᶜEn ᶜAvdat." *JSS* 35:73-79.

BENNETT, C.
1966 "Fouilles d'Umm el-Biyara." *RB* 73:399-401.

BENZ, F. L.
1972 *Personal Names in the Phoenician and Punic Inscriptions*. Studia Pohl 8. Rome: Pontifical Biblical Institute.

BERGER, P.-R.
1971 "Zu den Namen *ššbṣr* und *sin*ᵓ*sr*." *ZAW* 95:111-112.

BERGMAN, A.
1936 "Two Hebrew Seals of the ᶜ*Ebed* Class." *JBL* 55:221-226.

BIRAN, A., and J. NAVEH.
1993 "An Aramaic Stele Fragment from Tel Dan." *IEJ* 43:81-98.
1995 "The Tel Dan Inscription: A New Fragment." *IEJ* 45:1-18.

BLAU, J.
1980 "Short Philological Notes on the Inscription of Mešaᶜ." *Maarav* 2: 143-157.

BOGOLIUBOV, M. N.
1966 "An Aramaic Inscription from Aswan." *Palestinskiy Sbornik* 15:41-46 (in Russian).

BONDI, S. F.
1988 "City Planning and Architecture," Pp. 248-283 in *Moscati*.

BORDREUIL, P.
1992 "Sceaux inscrits des pays du Levant." *Dictionnaire de la Bible, Supplement* 12:86-212. Paris: Letouzey et Ané.

BORDREUIL, P., and J. TEIXIDOR.
1983 "Nouvel examen de l'inscription de Bar-Hadad." *AO* 1:271-276.

BORDREUIL, P., F. ISRAEL, and D. PARDEE.
1996 "Deux ostraca paléo-hébreux de la collection Sh. Moussaïeff." *Semitica* 46:49-76 and plates 7-8.
1998 "King's Command and Widow's Plea. Two New Hebrew Ostraca of the Biblical Period." *NEA* 61:2-13

BRECCIA, E.
1907 "La Necropoli de l'Ibrahimieh." *Bulletin de la Socièté Archéologique d'Alexandrie* 9:35-42.

BRIN, G.
1969 "The Title *ben (ha)melekh* and its Parallels." *AION* 29:433-465.

BROCKELMANN, K.
1966 *Lexicon Syriacum*. Hildesheim: Georg Olms.

BRON, F.
1975 "Phénicien *rš*ᵓ*t* = vieillesse." *AION* 35:545-546.
1979 *Recherches sur les inscriptions phéniciennes de Karatepe*. École pratique des Hautes études 2: Hautes études orientales 11. Genève/Paris: Librairie Droz.

BRON, F., and A. LEMAIRE.
1989 "Les inscriptions araméennes de Hazaël." *RA* 83:35-44.

BUDGE, E. A. W.
1914 *Assyrian Sculptures in the British Museum. Reign of Ashur-nasir-pal, B.C. 885-860*. London: The British Museum.

CANTINEAU, J.
1932 *Le Nabatéen*. Paris: Ernest Leroux.
CAQUOT, A.
1973 "Observations sur la première tablette magique d'Arslan Tash." *JANES* 5:45-51.
CAQUOT, A., and A. LEMAIRE.
1977 "Les Textes Araméens de Deir ᶜAlla." *Syria* 54:189-208.
CHARBONNET, A.
1986 "Le dieu au lions d'Erétrie." *AION. Archeologia e Storia antica* 8:123-154.
CHASE, D. A.
1982 "A Note on an Inscription from Kuntillet 'Ajrud." *BASOR* 246:63-67.
CIASCA, A.
1988 "Phoenicia." Pp. 140-151 in *Moscati*.
CLERMONT-GANNEAU, C.
1871 "Notes on Certain New Discoveries at Jerusalem. 1. Hebrew Inscription in Phoenician Characters." *PEFQS* 3:103.
1907 "L'antique nécropole juive d'Alexandrie." *CRAIBL* 234-243.
COGAN, M.
1995 "Sukkoth-Benoth." Cols. 1553-1556 in *DDD*.
COLONNA, G., M. PALLOTTINO, L. VLAD BORELLI, L. GARBINI, and G. GARBINI.
1964 "Scavi nel santuario etrusco di Pyrgi: Relazione preliminare della settima campagna, 1964, e scoperta de tra limine d'oro inscrite in etrusco e in punico." *Archaeologia classica* 16:49-117 and pls. 25-39.
COOGAN, M. D.
1976 *West Semitic Personal Names in the Murašu Documents*. HSM 7. Missoula, MT: Scholars Press.
COOTE, R. B.
1980 "The Tell Siran Bottle Inscription." *BASOR* 240:93.
COUROYER, B.
1970 "A propos de la stèle de Carpentras." *Semitica* 20:17-21.
CROSS, F. M.
1966 "Aspects of Samaritan and Jewish History in Late Persian and Hellenistic Times." *HTR* 59:201-206.
1967 "The Origin and Early Evolution of the Alphabet." *EI* 8:8*-24*.
1969 "Epigraphic Notes on the Ammān Citadel Inscription." *BASOR* 193:13-19.
1970 "The Cave Inscriptions from Khirbet Beit Lei." Pp. 299-306 in *Studies Glueck*.
1971 "Papyri of the Fourth Century B.C. from Dâliyeh." Pp. 45-69 in *New Directions in Biblical Archaeology*. Ed. by D. N. Freedman and J. C. Greenfield. Garden City, NY: Doubleday.
1972 "The Stele Dedicated to Melcarth by Ben-Hadad." *BASOR* 205:36-42.
1973a "Notes on the Ammonite Inscription from Tell Sīrān." *BASOR* 212:12-15.
1973b "Heshbon Ostracon II." *AUSS* 11:126-131.
1975 "Ammonite Ostraca From Heshbon, Heshbon Ostraca IV-VIII." *AUSS* 13:1-22, pls. 1-2.
1976 "Heshbon Ostracon XI." *AUSS* 14:145-48, pl. 15:A.
1979 "Early Alphabetic Scripts." Pp. 97-123 in *Symposia*.
1980 "Newly Found Inscriptions in Old Canaanite and Early Phoenician Scripts." *BASOR* 238:1-20.
1983 "The Seal of Miqnêyaw, Servant of Yahweh." Pp. 55-63 in *Ancient Seals and the Bible*. Ed. L. Gorelick and E. Williams-Forte. Malibu: Undena Publications.
1986 "An Unpublished Ammonite Ostracon from Ḥesbān." Pp. 475-89 in *Studies Horn*.
1993 "Newly Discovered Arrowheads of the 11th Century B.C.E." Pp. 533-542 in *BAT 1990*.
1995 "Palaeography and the Date of the Tell Fahariyeh Bilingual Inscription." Pp. 393-409 in *Studies Greenfield*.
In press "Ammonite Ostraca from Tell Hesbân." *Leaves From an Epigraphist's Notebook*.
CROSS, F. M., and J. T. MILIK.
1956 "A Typological Study of the El-Khadr Javelin- and Arrow-Heads." *ADAJ* 3:15-23.
CROSS, F. M., and R. J. Saley.
1970 "Phoenician Incantations on a Plaque of the Seventh Century B.C. from Arslan Tash in Upper Syria." *BASOR* 197:42-49.
CRYER, F. H.
1995 "A 'Betdawd' Miscellany. Dwd, Dwdᵓ or Dwdh?" *SJOT* 9:52-58.
CURRID, J. D.
1997 *Ancient Egypt and the Old Testament*. Grand Rapids: Baker.
DAHOOD, M.
1965 "Punic *hkkbm ᵓl* and Isa. 14:13." *Or* 34:170-172.
1972 "Ugaritic-Hebrew Parallel Pairs." Pp. 71-382 in *Ras Shamra Parallels I*. Ed. by L. R. Fisher. AnOr 49. Rome: Pontificium Institutum Biblicum.
DALLEY, S.
1995 "Ancient Mesopotamian Military Organization." *CANE* 1:413-422.
DAVIES, G. I.
1991 *AHI*.
DEARMAN, J. A. (editor).
1989 *Studies in the Mesha Inscription and Moab*. Atlanta: Scholars Press.
DEGEN, R.
1969 *Altaramäische Grammatik der Inschriften des 10.-8. Jh. v. Chr.* AKM 38/3. Wiesbaden: Harrassowitz.
DELCOR, M.
1968 "Une inscription bilingue étrusco-punique récemment découverte à Pyrgi, son importance réligieuse." *Le Muséon* 81:241-254.

DEMSKY, A.
1997 "The Name of the Goddess of Ekron: A New Reading." *JANES* 25:1-5.
1998a "A Royal Inscription from Ekron." *IEJ* 47:1-16.
1998b "Discovering a Goddess: A new Look at the Ekron Inscription Identifies a Mysterious Deity." *BAR* 24/5:53-58.
DEUTSCH, R., and M. HELTZER.
1994 *Forty New Ancient West Semitic Inscriptions*. Tel Aviv-Jaffa: Archaeological Center Publication.
DEVER, W. G.
1969-70 "Iron Age Epigraphic Material from the Area of Khirbet el-Kom." *HUCA* 40/41:159-169.
1971 "Inscription from Khirbet el-Kom." *Qadmoniot* 4:90-92 (in Hebrew).
DIJKSTRA, K. J.
1995 *Life and Loyalty*. Leiden: E. J. Brill.
DIRINGER, D.
1934 *Le iscrizioni antico-ebraiche palestinesi*. Florence: Felice le Monnier.
1941 "On Ancient Hebrew Inscriptions Discovered at Tell ed-Duweir (Lachish), I, II." *PEQ* 73:38-56, 89-106.
DION, P.-E.
1974 *La langue de Ya'udi: description et classement de l'ancien parler de Zenčirli dans le cadre des langues sémitiques du nord-ouest*. Waterloo: La Corporation pour la Publication des Études Académiques en Religion au Canada.
1978 "The Language Spoken in Ancient Samᵓal." *JNES* 37:115-118.
1995 "Aramaeans." In *CANE* 4:1281-1285.
1997 *Les Araméens à l'âge du fer: histoire politique et structures sociales*. Études bibliques, nouvelle série 34. Paris: J. Gabalda.
DONBAZ, V.
1990 "Two Neo-Assyrian Stelae in the Antakya and Kahramanmaraş Museums." *ARRIM* 8:5-24.
DONNER, H.
1953-54 "Zur Formgeschichte der Aḥīrām-Inschrift." *Wissenschaftliche Zeitschrift (Karl-Marx-Universität, Leipzig). Gesellschafts- und sprachwissenschaftliche Reihe* 2/3:283-287.
1969 "Elemente ägyptischen Totenglaubens bei den Aramäern Ägyptens." Pp. 35-44 in *Religions en Égypte hellénistique et romaine*. Ed. by P. Derchain. Paris: Presses Universitaires de France.
DORNEMANN, R. H.
1983 *The Archeology of the Transjordan in the Bronze and Iron Ages*. Milwaukee: Milwaukee Public Museum.
DRIVER, G. R.
1954 *Semitic Writing: From Pictograph to Alphabet*. The Schweich Lectures of the British Academy 1944. London: British Academy.
DUMBRELL, W. J.
1971 "The Tell el-Maskhuṭa Bowls and the 'Kingdom' of Qedar in the Persian Period." *BASOR* 203:33-44.
1960 *Encyclopaedia of Islam*. 2nd Edition. Leiden: E. J. Brill.
DU MESNIL DU BUISSON, C.
1939 "Une tablette magique de la région du Moyen Euphrate." Pp. 1:421-434 in *Studies Dussaud*.
DUNAND, M.
1939 "Stèle araméenne dédiée à Melqart." *BMB* 3:65-76.
1965 "Nouvelles inscriptions phéniciennes du temple d'Echmoun à Bostan ech-Cheikh près Sidon." *BMB* 18:105-109.
DUPONT-SOMMER, A.
1939 "L'Inscription de l'amulette d'Arslan Tash." *RHR* 120:133-159.
1964 "L'Inscription punique récemment découverte à Pyrgi." *JA* 252:282-302.
DUPONT-SOMMER, A., and J. STARCKY.
1956 "Une inscription araméenne inédite de Sfiré." *BMB* 13:23-41 (+ pls. i-vi).
1960 "Les inscriptions araméennes de Sfiré (stèles I et II)." *MPAIBL* 15:1-155 (+ pls. i-xxix).
DUSSAUD, R.
1924 "Les inscriptions phéniciennes du tombeau d'Aḥiram, roi de Byblos." *Syria* 5:135-57.
ELAYI, J.
1987 "Name of Deuteronomy's Author Found on a Seal Ring." *BAR* 13:54-56.
1992 "New Light on the Identification of Priest Ḥanan, son of Ḥilqiyahu (2 Kgs. 22)." *BiOr* 49:680-685.
EMERTON, J. A.
1982 "New Light on Israelite Religion: The Implications of the Inscriptions from Kuntillet ᶜAjrud." *ZAW* 94:2-20.
EPHᶜAL, I.
1982 *The Ancient Arabs. Nomads on the Borders of the Fertile Crescent 9th-5th Centuries B.C.* Jerusalem: Magnes Press.
EPHᶜAL, I., and J. NAVEH.
1989 "Hazael's Booty Inscriptions." *IEJ* 39:192-200.
1998 "Remarks on the Recently Published Moussaieff Ostraca." *IEJ* 48:269-273.
FABER, A.
1987 "On the Etymology and Use of Yaudi *mt*." *ZDMG* 137:278-284.
FALES, F. M.
1979 "Kilamuwa and the Foreign Kings: Propaganda vs. Power." *WO* 10:6-22.
1982a "Massimo Sforzo, Minima Resa: Maledizioni divine da Tell Fekheriye all'Antico Testamento." *Annali della facolta' di lingue e letterature straniere di ca' Foscari* 21:1-12.
1982b "Note di Semitico nordoccidentale." *VO* 5:75-83.
1983 "Le double bilinguisme de la statue de Tell Fekherye." *Syria* 60:233-250.
FENSHAM, F. C.
1977 "The Numeral Seventy in the Old Testament and the Family of Jerubbaal, Ahab, Panammuwa and Athirat." *PEQ* 109:113-115.
FERRON, J.
1965 "Quelques remarques à propos de l'inscription phénicienne de Pyrgi." *OA* 4:181-198.

FÉVRIER, J.G.
1948 Rémarques sur le calendrier de Gèzer. *Semitica* 1:33–41.
1965 "L'Inscription punique de Pyrgi." *CRAIBL* 11-13.
FIEMA, Z. T., and R. N. JONES.
1990 "The Nabataean King-List Revised: further observations on the second Nabataean Inscription from Tell Esh-Shuqafiya, Egypt." *ADAJ* 34:239-248.
FISCHER, W., and H. RIX.
1968 "Die phönizische-etruskischen Texte der Goldplättchen von Pyrgi." *Göttingischer Gelehrte Anzeigen* 220:64-94.
FITZMYER, J. A.
1966 "The Phoenician Inscription from Pyrgi." *JAOS* 86:287-297.
1995 *The Aramaic Inscriptions of Sefire*. Biblica et Orientalia 19a. Rev. ed. Rome: Biblical Institute.
FITZMYER, J. A., and S. A. KAUFMAN.
1992 *An Aramaic Bibliography, Part I: Old, Official and Biblical Aramaic*. Baltimore: Johns Hopkins University Press.
FOX, N. S.
1997 "Royal Functionaries and State-Administration in Israel and Judah During the First Temple Period." Ph.D Dissertation University of Pennsylvania.
FRIEDRICH, J.
1951 *Phönizisch-Punische Grammatik*. AnOr 32. Rome: Pontifical Biblical Institute.
1969 "Nochmals die phönizische Inschrift von Pyrgi." Pp. 205-209 in *Studies Altheim*. vol 1.
FRIEDRICH, J. and W. RÖLLIG.
1970 *PPG*.
FUENTES ESTAÑOL, M.-J.
1980 *Vocabulario Fenicio*. Biblioteca Fenicia 1. Barcelona: Biblioteca Fenicia.
FULCO, W. J.
1978 "The ᶜAmmān Citadel Inscription: a New Collation." *BASOR* 230:39-43.
1979 "The Amman Theatre Inscription." *JNES* 38:37-38.
GALLING, K.
1941 "Beschriftete Bildsiegel." *ZDPV* 64:121-202.
1950 "Die Achiram-Inschrift im Lichte der Karatepe-Texte." *WO* 1/5:421-425.
1963 "Eshmunazar und der Herr der Könige." *ZDPV* 79:140-151.
GARBINI, G.
1954-56 "Note sul 'calendario' di Gezer." *AION* 6:12–30.
1968 "Riconsiderando l'iscrizione di Pyrgi." *AION* 18:229-246.
1977a "L'iscrizione fenicia di Kilamuwa e il verbo *škr* in Semitico nordoccidentale." *BeO* 19:(=111-112):113-118.
1977b "L'iscrizione di Eshmun'azar." *AION* 37:408-412.
1992 "RŠP ṢPRM." *RSF* 20:93-94.
GARBINI, G., and G. LEVI DELLA VIDA.
1965 "Considerazioni sull'iscrizione punica di Pyrgi." *OA* 4:35-52.
GARELLI, P.
1957 "*Muṣur* (mât Muṣri)." *Dictionnaire de la Bible, Supplément* 5:1468-1474.
1971 "Nouveau coup d'oeil sur Muṣur." Pp. 37-48 in *Studies Dupont-Sommer*.
GARFINKEL, Y.
1985 "A Hierarchic Pattern in the Private Seal Impressions on the *lmlk* Jar-Handles." *EI* 18:105-118 (Hebrew).
GASTER, T. H.
1942 "A Canaanite Magical Text." *Or* 11:41-79.
GEE, J.
1998 Requirements of Ritual Purity in Ancient Egypt. Ph.D. Dissertation Yale University.
GELB, I.
1980 *Computer-Aided Analysis of Amorite*. AS 21. Chicago: The Oriental Institute of the University of Chicago.
GEVIRTZ, S.
1990 "Phoenician *wšbrt mlṣm* and Job 33:23." *Maarav* 5-6:145-158.
GILL, D.
1991 "Subterranean Waterworks of Biblical Jerusalem: Adaptation of a Karst System." *Science* 254:1467-1471.
1994 "How They Met." *BAR* 20/4:20-33.
1996 "The Geology of the City of David and its Ancient Subterranean Waterworks." Pp. 1-28 in *Excavations at the City of David 1978-1985 Directed by Yigal Shiloh*. Volume 4: *Various Reports*. Ed. by D. T. Ariel and A. de Groot. Qedem 35. Jerusalem: The Hebrew University.
GILULA, M.
1978/79 "To Yahweh Shomron and to his Asherah." *Shnaton* 3:129-137 (in Hebrew).
GINSBERG, H. L.
1963 "Roots Below and Fruit Above." Pp. 72-76 in *Studies Driver*.
GITIN, S.
1993 "Seventh Century B.C.E. Cultic Elements at Ekron." Pp. 248-258 in *BAT 1990*.
GITIN, S., and M. COGAN.
1999 "A New Type of Dedicatory Inscription from Ekron." *IEJ* 49:193-202.
GITIN, S., T. DOTHAN, and J. NAVEH.
1997a "A Royal Dedicatory Inscription from Ekron." *IEJ* 47:1-16.
1997b "A Royal Dedication Inscription from Tel Miqneh / Ekron." *Qadmoniot* 30:38-43 (in Hebrew).

GOOD, R. M.
1979 "The Israelite Royal Steward in the Light of Ugaritic ᶜl bt." *RB* 36:580-582.
1983 *The Sheep of his Pasture: a Study of the Hebrew Noun ᶜamm and its Semitic Cognates*. Chico CA: Scholars Press.
GÖRG, M.
1998 "Die Göttin der Ekron-Inschrift." *BN* 93:9-10.
GRAYSON, A. K.
1976 *ARI* 2. Wiesbaden: Harrassowitz.
1991 *RIMA* 2.
GREENFIELD, J. C.
1966 "Three Notes on the Sefire Inscription." *JSS* 11:98-105.
1971 "Scripture and Inscription: The Literary and Rhetorical Element in Some Early Phoenician Inscriptions." Pp. 253-268 in *Studies Albright*.
1972 "The Zakir Inscription and the Danklied." Pp. 174-191 in *Proceedings of the Fifth World Congress of Jewish Studies*. Vol 1. Jerusalem: World Union of Jewish Studies.
1973 "Un rite religieux Araméen et ses parallèles." *RB* 80:46-52.
1978 "The Dialects of Early Aramaic." *JNES* 37:93-99.
1984 "A Touch of Eden." Pp. 219-224 in *Orientalia J. Duchesne-Guillemin Emerito Oblata*. Leiden: Brill.
1987 "Aspects of Aramaic Religion." Pp. 67-78 in *Studies Cross*.
1991a "Some Glosses on the Sfire Inscriptions." *Maarav* 7:141-147.
1991b "Doves' Dung and the Price of Food: The Topoi of II Kings 6:24-7:2." Pp. 121-126 in *Studies Soggin*.
1991c "Asylum at Aleppo: A Note on Sfire III, 4-7." Pp. 272-278 in *Studies Tadmor*.
1994 "The Aramean God Hadad." *EI* 24:54-61.
GREENFIELD, J. C., and A. SHAFFER.
1983 "Notes on the Akkadian-Aramaic Bilingual Statue from Tell Fekherye." *Iraq* 49:109-116.
1985 "Notes on the Curse Formulae of the Tell Fekherye Inscription." *RB* 92:47-59.
GREENSTEIN, E. L.
1982 "'To Grasp the Hem' in Ugaritic Literature." *VT* 32:217-218.
1995 "Autobiographies in Ancient Western Asia." *CANE* 4:2421-2432.
GRÖNDAHL, F.
1967 *Die Personennamen der Texte aus Ugarit*. Studia Pohl 1. Rome: Pontifical Biblical Institute.
GROPP, D. M., and T. J. LEWIS.
1985 "Some Problems in the Aramaic Text of the Hadd-Yithᶜi Bilingual." *BASOR* 259:45-61.
HACKETT, J. A.
1984 *The Balaam Text from Deir ᶜAllā*. HSM 31. Chico: Scholars Press.
HACKETT, J. A., F. M. CROSS, P. K. MCCARTER, JR., A. YARDENI, A. LEMAIRE, E. ESHEL and A. HURVITZ.
1997 "Defusing Pseudo-Scholarship: The Siloam Inscription Ain't Hasmonean." *BAR* 23/2:41-50, 68-69.
HADLEY, J. M.
1987a "Some Drawings and Inscriptions of Two Pithoi from Kuntillet ᶜAjrud." *VT* 37:180-214.
1987b "The Khirbet el-Qom Inscription." *VT* 37:50-62.
HALLO, W. W.
1992 "Royal Ancestor Worship in the Biblical World." Pp. 381-401 in *Studies Talmon*.
1993 "Disturbing the Dead." *Studies Sarna* 183-192.
1996 *Origins*.
HALLO, W. W., and H. TADMOR.
1977 "A Lawsuit from Hazor." *IEJ* 27:1-11 and pl. i.
HAMMOND, P. C., D. J. JOHNSON, and R. N. JONES.
1986 "A Religio-Legal Nabataean Inscription from the Atargatis/Al-ᶜUzza Temple at Petra." *BASOR* 263:77-80.
HARAN, M.
1989 "The Priestly Blessing on Silver Plaques: The Significance of the Discovery at Ketef Hinnom." *Cathedra* 52:77-89 (in Hebrew).
HARDING, G. L.
1971 *An Index and Concordance of Pre-Islamic Arabian Names and Inscriptions*. Near and Middle East Series 8. Toronto: University of Toronto Press.
HAWKINS, J. D.
1982 "The Neo-Hittite States in Syria and Anatolia" in *CAH*² 3/1:372-441.
1986 "Royal Statements of Ideal Prices: Assyrian, Babylonian, and Hittite." Pp. 93-106 in *Studies Mellink*.
1995 "Karkemish and Karatepe: Neo-Hittite City-States in North Syria." *CANE* 2:1295-1307.
2000 *CHLI* 1.
HEALEY, J.
1993a *The Nabataean Tomb Inscriptions of Madāᵓin Ṣāliḥ*. JSSSup 1. Oxford: Oxford University Press.
1993b "Sources for the Study of Nabataean Law." *New Arabian Studies* 1:203-214.
1996 "'May He Be Remembered for Good': An Aramaic Formula." Pp. 177-186 in *Studies McNamara*.
HELTZER, M.
1996 "Two Inscribed Phoenician Vessels in the Form of Pomegranates." *AO* 14:281-282.
1999 "Two Ancient West Semitic Seals." *SEL* 16:45-47.
HENDEL, R.
1996 "The Date of the Siloam Inscription: A Rejoinder to Rogerson and Davies." *BA* 59/4:233-237.
HERR, L. G.
1978 *The Scripts of Ancient Northwest Semitic Seals*. HSM 18. Missoula, MT: Scholars Press.
1985 "The Servant of Baalis." *BA* 48:169-172.
1992 "Epigraphic Finds from Tell El-'Umeiri During the 1989 Season." *AUSS* 30:187-200.

HESS, R. S.
1996 "Asherah or Asherata?" *Or* 65:209-219.
HESTRIN, R.
1983 "Hebrew Seals of Officials." Pp. 50-54 in *Ancient Seals and the Bible*. Ed. by L. Gorelick and E. Williams-Forte. Monographic Journals of the Near East. Occasional papers on the Near East, v. 2/1. Malibu, CA: Undena.
HESTRIN, R. et al.
1973 *Ketovot Mesapperot* (*Inscriptions Reveal*). Israel Museum Catalogue no. 100. 2nd ed. Jerusalem: Israel Museum.
HESTRIN, R., and M. DAYAGI-MENDELS.
1979 *Inscribed Seals. First Temple Period*. Jerusalem: Israel Museum.
HEURGON, J.
1966 "The Inscriptions of Pyrgi." *JRS* 56:6-15.
HICKS, L.
1982 "*Delet* and *Mᵉgillāh*: A Fresh Approach to Jeremiah xxxvi." *VT* 33:46-66.
HILLERS, D. R., and E. CUSSINI.
1995 *Palmyrene Aramaic Texts*. Baltimore and London: Johns Hopkins.
HOFTIJZER, J., and G. VAN DER KOOIJ.
1976 *Aramaic Texts from Deir ᶜAlla*. Leiden: E. J. Brill.
1991 *The Balaam Text from Deir ᶜAlla Re-evaluated. Proceedings of the International Symposium held at Leiden, August 21-24, 1989*. Leiden and New York: E. J. Brill.
HONEYMAN, A. M.
1953 "The Syntax of the Gezer Calendar." *JRAS* 53–58.
1960 "Two Votaries of Han-ᵓIlat." *JNES* 19:40-41.
HORBURY, W., and D. NOY.
1992 *Jewish Inscriptions of Graeco-Roman Egypt*. No. 3. Cambridge/New York: Cambridge University Press.
HORN, S. H.
1986 "Why the Moabite Stone was Blown into Pieces: 9th-Century B.C. Inscription Adds New Dimension to Biblical Account of Mesha's Rebellion." *BAR* 12/3:50-61.
HÜBNER, U.
1988 "Die ersten moabitischen Ostraca." *ZDPV* 104:68-73.
1992 *Die Ammoniter: Untersuchungen zur Geschichte, Kultur und Religion eines transjordanischen Volkes in 1. Jahrtausend v. Chr.* Wiesbaden: Otto Harrassowitz.
HUEHNERGARD, J.
1983 "Asseverative **la* and Hypothetical **lu/law* in Semitic." *JAOS* 103:569-593.
1987 "The Feminine Plural Jussive in Old Aramaic." *ZDMG* 137:266-277.
HURVITZ, A.
1968 "*Ακκαρων = Amqar(r)una = ᶜqrwn*." *Lěšonénu* 23:18-24 (in Hebrew).
IBN MANZUR, M.
1956 *Lisān al-ᶜarab*. Beirut: al-Qahirah, J.M.A.
IBRAHIM, M. M.
1975 "Third Season of Excavations at Sahab, 1975 (Preliminary Report)." *ADAJ* 20:69-82, pls. 25-29.
IBRAHIM, M. M., and G. VAN DER KOOIJ.
1991 "The Archaeology of Deir ᶜAlla, Phase IX." Pp. 16-29 in Hoftijzer and van der Kooij 1991.
ISHIDA, T.
1985 "'Solomon Who is Greater Than David.' Solomon's Succession in 1 Kings I-II in the Light of the Inscription of Kilamuwa, King of YᵓDY-ŚAMᵓAL." Pp. 145-153 in *Congress Volume. Salamanca 1983*. Ed. J. A. Emerton. Leiden: E. J. Brill.
JACKSON, K. P.
1983 *The Ammonite Language of the Iron Age*. HSM 27. Chico, CA: Scholars Press.
JANSSEN-WINKELN, K.
1985 *Ägyptische Biographien der 22. und 23. Dynastie*. Wiesbaden: Harrassowitz.
JAROŠ, K.
1982 "Zur Inschrift Nr. 3 von Ḫirbet el Qom." *BN* 19:31-40.
JAUSSEN, A., and R. SAVIGNAC.
1909 *Mission archéologique en arabie*. I. Paris: Leroux & Geuthner.
JOHNSON, J. H.
1976 *The Demotic Verbal System*. Chicago: Oriental Institute of the University of Chicago.
JONES, R. N., D. J. JOHNSON, P. C. HAMMOND, and Z. T. FIEMA.
1988 "A Second Nabataean Inscription from Tell Esh-Shuqfiya, Egypt." *BASOR* 269:47-57.
KATZENSTEIN, H. J.
1960 "The Royal Steward (*Asher ᶜal ha-Bayith*)." *IEJ* 10:149-154.
KAUFMAN, S. A.
1970 "Siᵓgabbar, Priest of Sahr in Nerab." *JAOS* 90:270-271.
1974 *The Akkadian Influences on Aramaic*. AS 19. Chicago and London: The University of Chicago.
1982 "Reflections on the Assyrian-Aramaic Bilingual from Tell-Fakhariyeh." *Maarav* 3:137-175.
KEEL, O., and C. UEHLINGER.
1998 *Gods, Goddesses, and Images of God in Ancient Israel*. Minneapolis: Fortress.
KEMPINSKI, A.
1990 "Is It Really a Pomegranate from the 'House of the Lord'? — On: N. Avigad, «An Inscribed Pomegranate from the 'House of the Lord.'»" *Qadmoniot* 23:126 (Hebrew).
KITCHEN, K. A.
1997 "A Possible Mention of David in the Late Tenth Century BCE and Deity *Dod as dead as the Dodo?" *JSOT* 76:29-44.

KLENGEL, H.
1992 *Syria: 3000 to 300 BC. A Handbook of Political History*. Berlin: Akademie Verlag.
KLETTER, R.
1991 "The Inscribed Weights of the Kingdom of Judah." *Tel Aviv* 18:121-163.
1998 *Economic Keystones: The Weight System of the Kingdom of Judah*. JSOTSup 276. Sheffield: Sheffield Academic Press.
KNAUF, E. A., A. DE PURY, and Th. RÖMER.
1994 "*BaytDawid ou *BaytDod?" *BN* 72:60-69.
KNOPPERS, G. N.
1992 "'The God in His Temple': The Phoenician Text from Pyrgi as a Funerary Inscription." *JNES* 52:105-120.
KRAHMALKOV, C.
1974 "The Object Pronouns of the Third Person of Phoenician and Punic." *RSF* 2:39-43.
KROPP, M.
1994 "A Puzzle of Old Arabic Tenses and Syntax: the Inscription of ᶜEn ᶜAvdat" *Proceedings of the Seminar for Arabian Studies* 24:165-174.
KWASMAN, T., and S. PARPOLA.
1991 *Legal Transactions of the Royal Court of Nineveh, Part I, Tiglath-pileser III through Esarhaddon*. SAA 6. Helsinki: University Press.
KYRELEIS, H.
1988 "Ein altorientalischer Pferdeschmuck aus dem Heraion von Samos." *MDAIA* 103:37-61.
LAMBERT, W. G.
1981 "Old Akkadian Ilaba = Ugaritic Ilib." *UF* 13:299-301.
LANCASTER, S. P., and G. A. LONG.
1999 "Where They Met: Separations in the Rock Mass Near the Siloam Tunnel's Meeting Point." *BASOR* 315:15-26.
LANDSBERGER, B.
1948 *Sam'al. Studien zur Entdeckung der Ruinenstätte Karatepe. 1. Liefg*. Veröffentlichungen der Türkischen Historischen Gesellschaft 7, num. 16. Ankara.
LANG, B.
1998 "The Decalogue in the Light of a Newly Published Palaeo-Hebrew Inscription (Hebrew Ostracon Mousaïeff no. 1)." *JSOT* 77:21-25.
LAYTON, S. C.
1990 "The Steward in Ancient Israel: A Study of Hebrew *(ʾašer) ᶜal habbayit* in Its Near Eastern Setting." *JBL* 109:633-649.
LEHMANN, G.
1994 "Zu den Zerstörungen in Zincirli während des frühen 7. Jahrhunderts v. Chr." *MDOG* 126:105-122.
LEMAIRE, A.
1976a "Prières en temps de crise: les inscriptions de Khirbet Beit Lei." *RB* 83:552-568.
1976b "Notes sur quelques inscriptions sur ivoire provenant de Nimrud." *Semitica* 26:66-70.
1977 "Les inscriptions de Khirbet el-Qôm et l'Ashérah de Yhwh." *RB* 84:595-608.
1981 "Une inscription paléo-hébraïque sur grenade en ivoire." *RB* 88:236-239.
1984a "Le stèle araméene de Bar-Hadad." *Or* 53:337-349.
1984b "Date et origine des inscriptions hébraïques et phéniciennes de Kuntillet ᶜAjrud." *SEL* 1:131-143.
1984c "Probable Head of Priestly Scepter from Solomon's Temple Surfaces in Jerusalem." *BAR* 10/1:24-29.
1987 "Notes d'épigraphie nord-ouest sémitique." *Syria* 64:205-216.
1990 "SMR dans la petite inscription de Kilamuwa (Zencirli)." *Syria* 67:323-327.
1991a "La stèle de Mésha et l'histoire de l'ancien Israël." Pp. 143-169 in *Studies Soggin*.
1991b "Hazaël de Damas, roi d'Aram." Pp. 91-108 in *Studies Garelli*.
1992 "La stèle araméenne d'Assouan (RES 438, 1806): nouvel examen." Pp. 289-303 in *Studies Milik*.
1994 "Epigraphie palestinienne: nouveaux documents. I. Fragment de stèle araméenne de Tell Dan (IXe s. av. J.-C.)." *Henoch* 16:87-93.
LEMAIRE, A., and J.-M. DURAND.
1984 *Les inscriptions araméennes de Sfiré et l'Assyrie de Shamshi-ilu*. Geneva/Paris: Librairie Droz.
LEPSIUS, R.
1842 *Das Todtenbuch der Ägypter nach dem hieroglypischen Papyrus in Turin*. Leipzig: G. Wigand.
LEVINE, B. A.
1989 *Leviticus, JPS Torah Commentary*. Philadelphia: Jewish Publication Society.
1995 "The Semantics of Loss: Two Exercises in Biblical Hebrew Lexicography." Pp. 137-148 in *Studies Greenfield*.
LÉVY, I.
1927 "Les inscriptions araméennes de Memphis et l'Epigraphie funéraire de l'Égypte Gréco-Romaine." *JA* 210:281-310.
LEVY, J.
1964 *Wörterbuch über die Talmudim und Midraschim*. Darmstadt: Wissenschaftliche Buchgesellschaft. 4 volumes.
LEXA, F.
1910 *Das demotische Totenbuch der Pariser Nationalbibliothek*. Leipzig: J. C. Hinrichs.
LIDZBARSKI, M.
1909 "An Old Hebrew Calendar-Inscription from Gezer." *Palestine Exploration Fund Quarterly Statement* 41:26–29.
LIPIŃSKI, E.
1971 "Etymological and Exegetical Notes on the Mešaᶜ Inscription." *Or* 40:325-340.
1974 "From Karatepe to Pyrgi. Middle Phoenician Miscellanea." *RSF* 2:45-61.
1975a *Studies in Aramaic Inscriptions and Onomastics*. OLA 1. Leuven: Leuven University.
1975b "La stèle égypto-araméenne de Tummaʾ fille de Bokkorinif." *CdE* 50:93-104.
1976 "Review of P.-E. Dion 1974." *BiOr* 33:231-234.
1977 "North-West Semitic Inscriptions. A Review of Gibson, *Textbook of Syrian Semitic Inscriptions*." *OLP* 8:81-117.
1978a "North-west Semitic Inscriptions." *OLP* 8:81-107.

1978b "North Semitic Texts from the First Millennium B.C." Pp. 247-249 in *Near Eastern Religious Texts Relating to the Old Testament*. Ed. by W. Beyerlin. OTL. Philadelphia: Westminster.
1983 "The God ᵓArqû-Rashap in the Samalian Hadad Inscription." Pp. 15-21 in *Arameans, Aramaic and the Aramaic Literary Tradition*. Ed. by M. Sokoloff. Ramat-Gan: Bar-Ilan University.
1990 "*hnq*." *TWAT* 7/1-2:63-71.
1992 "Tarshish." P. 440 in *DDCP*.
1994 *Studies in Aramaic Inscriptions and Onomastics II*. OLA 57. Louvain: Peeters.

LIVER, J.
1967 "The Wars of Mesha, King of Moab." *PEQ* 99:14-31.

LIVERANI, M.
1991 "Kilamuwa 7-8 e II Re 7." Pp. 117-184 in *Studies Soggin*.

MAIER, W. A. III
1992 "Hadad." in *ABD* 1:11.

MALININE, M., G. POSENER, and J. VERCOUTTER.
1968 *Catalogue des stèles du Sérapeum de Memphis*. Paris: Éditions des Musées Nationaux.

MALLOWAN, M. E. L.
1966 *Nimrud and Its Remains*. London: John Murray.

MARAZZI, M.
1990 *Il Geroglifico anatolico: problemi di analisi e prospettive di ricerca*. Biblioteca di ricerche linguistiche e filologiche 24. Rome: Dipartimento di studi glottoantropologici università 'la Sapienza'.

MARGALIT, B.
1986 "Why King Mesha of Moab Sacrificed His Oldest Son." *BAR* 12/6:62-63, 76.
1989 "Some Observations on the Inscription and Drawing from Khirbet el-Qôm." *VT* 39:371-378.

MAYSTRE, C.
1937 *Les déclarations d'innocence livre des morts, chapitre 125*. Cairo: Institut Français d'Archéologie Orientale.

MAZAR, A.
1990 *Archaeology of the Land of the Bible* New York: Doubleday.

MAZAR, B.
1975 "ᶜEn Gev." *EAEHL* 2:381-385.

MAZAR, B., A. BIRAN, M. DOTHAN, and I. DUNAYEVSKY.
1964 "ᶜEin Gev. Excavations in 1961." *IEJ* 14:1-49.

MCCARTER, P. K., Jr.
1987 "Aspects of the Religion of the Israelite Monarchy: Biblical and Epigraphic Data." Pp. 137-155 in *Studies Cross*.

MCCARTHY, D. J.
1978 *Treaty and Covenant: A Study in Form in the Ancient Oriental Documents and in the Old Testament*. Rev. ed. Rome: Biblical Institute.

MERIGGI, P.
1967 *Manuale di eteo geroglifico 2/1: Testi neo-etei più o meno completi*. Incunabila Graeca 14. Rome. Edizioni dell' Ateneo.

MESHEL, Z.
1979 "Did Yahweh Have a Consort? The New Religious Inscriptions from the Sinai." *BAR* 5/2:24-35.
1987 *A Religious Centre from the Time of the Judaean Monarchy on the Border of Sinai*. Inscriptions: E (1). Israel Museum Catalogue 175. Jerusalem: Israel Museum.

MESHORER, Y.
1975 *Nabataean Coins*. Qedem 3. Jerusalem: Institute of Archaeology.

MEYERS, C. L., and E. M. MEYERS.
1987 *Haggai, Zechariah 1-8*. AB 25B. Garden City, NY: Doubleday.

MILIK, J. T., and F. M. CROSS.
1954 "Inscribed Javelin-Heads from the Period of the Judges: A Recent Discovery in Palestine." *BASOR* 134:5-15.

MILLARD, A. R.
1962 "Alphabetic Inscriptions on Ivories from Nimrud." *Iraq* 24:41-51.
1984 "The Etymology of Eden." *VT* 34:103-106.
1990 "The Homeland of Zakkur." *Semitica* 39:47-52.
1991 "Variable Spellings in Hebrew and Other Ancient Texts." *JTS* 42:106-115.
1993a "The Tell Fekheriyeh Inscriptions." Pp. 518-524 in *BAT 1990*.
1993b "Eden, Bit Adini and Beth Eden." *EI* 24:173*-177*.
1994 *The Eponyms of the Assyrian Empire 910-612 BC*. SAAS 2. Helinski: The Neo-Assyrian Text Corpus Project.

MILLARD, A. R., and P. BORDREUIL.
1982 "A Statue from Syria with Assyrian and Aramaic Inscriptions." *BA* 45:135-141.

MILLER, J. M.
1974 "The Moabite Stone as a Memorial Stela." *PEQ* 106:9-18.

MILLER, P. D., Jr.
1980 "El, Creator of the Earth." *BASOR* 239:43-46.
1981 "Psalms and Inscriptions." Pp. 311-332 in *Congress Volume, Vienna, 1980*. Ed. by J. A. Emerton. VTSup 32. Leiden: Brill.

MITCHELL, T.
1985 "Another Palestinian Inscribed Arrowhead." Pp. 136-153 in *Studies Tufnell*.

MITTMANN, S.
1981 "Die Grabinschrift des Sängers Uriahu." *ZDPV* 97:139-152.
1989 "A Confessional Inscription from the Year 701 BC Praising the Reign of Yahweh." *Acta Academica* 21/3:17-23.

MOMMSEN, H., I. PERLMAN, and J. YELLIN.
1984 "The Provenience of the *lmlk* Jars." *IEJ* 34:89-113.

MORPURGO DAVIES, A., and J. D. HAWKINS.
1987 "The Late Hieroglyphic Luwian Corpus: Some New Lexical Recognitions." *Bibliothéque des Cahiers de l'Institut de Linguistique de Louvain* 37: Hethitica VIII:267-295.
MOSCATI, S.
1951 *L'epigrafia Ebraica Antica. 1935-1950*. BibOr 15. Rome: Pontifical Biblical Institute.
1988 "Stelae." Pp. 304-327 in *Moscati*.
MULLEN, E. T.
1992 "Divine Assembly." *ABD* 2:214-217.
MÜLLER, H.-P.
1985 *TUAT* 1:638-640; 640-645.
MURAOKA, T.
1979 "Hebrew Philological Notes." *AJBI* 5:88-104.
1984 "The Tell-Fekherye Bilingual Inscription and Early Aramaic." *Abr-Nahrain* 22:79-117.
MURAOKA, T., and B. PORTEN.
1998 *A Grammar of Egyptian Aramaic*. Leiden: E. J. Brill.
NA᾿AMAN, N.
1979 "Sennacherib's Campaign to Judah and the Date of the LMLK Stamps." *VT* 29:61-86.
1986 "Hezekiah's Fortified Cities and the *LMLK* Stamp." *BASOR* 261:5-21.
1991 "Forced Participation in Alliances in the Course of the Assyrian Campaigns to the West." Pp. 80-98 in *Studies Tadmor*.
NAVEH, J.
1963 "Old Hebrew Inscriptions in a Burial Cave." *IEJ* 13:74-92.
1975 "Aramaic Ostraca." Pp. 165-204 in Aharoni 1975.
1979 "Graffiti and Dedications." *BASOR* 235:27-30.
1980 "Review of Herr 1978." *BASOR* 239:75-76.
1982 *Early History of the Alphabet*. Jerusalem: Magnes, and Leiden: Brill.
1985 "Writing and Scripts in Seventh-Century Philistia: The New Evidence from Tell Jemmeh." *IEJ* 35:9-18.
1987 "Proto-Canaanite, Archaic Greek and the Script of the Aramaic Text on the Tell Fakhariyah Statue." Pp. 101-113 in *Studies Cross*.
1997 "Preface." Pp. 11-13 in Avigad and Sass 1997.
1998 "Achish-Ikausu in the Light of the Ekron Dedication." *BASOR* 310:35-37.
NAVILLE, E.
1886 *Das aegyptische Todtenbuch der XVIII. bis XX. Dynastie aus verschiedenen Urkunden zusammengestellt und herausgegeben*. 2 vols. Berlin: A. Asher & Co.
NEGEV, A.
1963 "Nabataean Inscriptions from ᶜAvdat (Oboda)." *IEJ* 13:113-124.
1971 "A Nabatean Epitaph from Trans-Jordan." *IEJ* 21:50-52.
1986 "Obodas the God." *IEJ* 36:56-60.
NIEHR, H.
1994 "Zum Totenkult der Könige von Sam᾿al im 9. und 8. Jh. v. Chr." *SEL* 11:58-73.
NOJA, S.
1989 "Über die älteste arabische Inschrift, die vor kurzem entdeckt wurde." Pp. 187-194 in *Studies Macuch*.
NOTH, M.
1928 *Die Israelitischen Personennamen im Rahmen der gemeinsemitischen Namengebung*. BWANT. 3rd series, no. 10; Stuttgart: Kohlhammer.
1961 "Der historische Hintergrund der Inschriften von Sefîre." *ZDPV* 77:118-172.
NOUGAYROL, J., et al.
1968 *Ugaritica* 5.
O'CONNOR, M.
1977 "The Rhetoric of the Kilamuwa Inscription." *BASOR* 226:13-29.
1987 "The Poetic Inscription from Khirbet el-Qom." *VT* 37:224-330.
OLYAN, S. M.
1988 *Asherah and the Cult of Yahweh in Israel*. SBLMS 34; Atlanta: Scholars Press.
OTZEN, B.
1990 "The Aramaic Inscriptions." Pp. 267-318 in *Hama II.2. Les objets de la période dite Syro-Hittite (Age du fer)*. Ed. by P. J. Rijs, and M.-L. Buhl. København: Nationalmuseet.
PARDEE, D.
1978 "Letters from Tel Arad." *UF* 10:289-336.
1987 "Review of Gibson, *SSI* 3." *JNES* 46:137-142.
1996 "Siloam Tunnel Inscription." *OEANE* 5:41-42.
PARDEE, D., and R. D. BIGGS.
1984 "Review of Abou Assaf, Bordreuil and Millard 1982." *JNES* 43:253-257.
PARKER, S.
1997 *Stories in Scripture and Inscriptions. Comparative Studies on Narratives in Northwest Semitic Inscriptions and the Hebrew Bible*. New York-Oxford: Oxford University Press.
PARPOLA, S.
1970 *Neo-Assyrian Toponyms*. AOAT 6. Kevelaer: Butzon & Bercker.
1985 "Si'Gabbar of Nerab Resurrected." *OLP* 16:273-275.
PECKHAM, J. B.
1968 *The Development of the Late Phoenician Scripts*. Cambridge, MA: Harvard.

PIKE, D. M.
1990 *Israelite Theophoric Personal Names in the Bible and their Implications for Religious History*. Ph.D. dissertation University of Pennsylvania, 1990. (Photocopy, Ann Arbor, MI: UMI, 1993).
PITARD, W. T.
1987 *Ancient Damascus*. Winona Lake, IN: Eisenbrauns.
1988 "The Identity of the Bir-Hadad of the Melqart Stela." *BASOR* 272:3-21.
POLLEY, M. E.
1980 "Hebrew Prophecy Within the Council of Yahweh, Examined in its Ancient Near Eastern Setting." *SIC* 1:141-156.
PORTEN, B.
1968 *Archives from Elephantine*. Berkeley: University of California Press.
1990 "The Calendar of Aramaic Texts from Achaemenid and Ptolemaic Egypt." Pp. 13-32 in *Irano-Judaica* II. Ed. by S. Shaked and A Netzer. Jerusalem: Ben-Zvi Institut.
POSTGATE, J. N.
1976 *Fifty Neo-Assyrian Legal Documents*. Warminster: Aris and Phillips.
PUECH, E.
1977 "Milkom, le dieu ammonite, en Amos I 15." *VT* 27:117-125.
1987 "Les Admonitions de Balaam (premierè partie)." Pp. 13-30 in *Studies Grelot*.
1992 "La stèle de Bar-Hadad à Melqart et les rois d'Arpad." *RB* 99:311-334.
QUACK, J. F.
1993 "Eine ägyptische Paralle zu KAI 214:32f?" *ZDPV* 109:37-38.
RABINOWITZ, I.
1956 "Aramaic Inscriptions of the Fifth Century B.C.E. from a North-Arab Shrine in Egypt." *JNES* 15:1-9.
1959 "Another Aramaic Record of the North-Arabian Goddess Han-ᵓilat." *JNES* 18:154-155.
RAHTJEN, B. D.
1961 A Note concerning the Form of the Gezer Tablet. *PEQ* 93:70–72.
RAINEY, A. F.
1969 "'Ben Hamelekh' be-Ugarit ve-ᵓeṣel ha-Ḥittim." *Leshonenu* 33:304-308 (in Hebrew).
1975 "The Prince and the Pauper." *UF* 7:427-432.
1982 "Wine from the King's Vineyards." *EI* 16:177-181 (Hebrew).
1998 "Syntax, Hermeneutics and History." *IEJ* 48:239-251.
REED, W. L., and F. V. WINNETT.
1963 "A Fragment of an Early Moabite Inscription from Kerak." *BASOR* 172:1-9.
REINER, E., and D. PINGREE.
1975 *The Venus Tablets of Amiṣaduqa, Babylonian Planetary Omens 1*. BiMes 2. Malibu CA: Undena.
1981 *Babylonian Planetary Omens 2, Enuma Anu Enlil (EAE)*. Tablets 50-51. Malibu CA: Undena.
RENDSBURG, G. A.
1995 "On the Writing *bt-dwd* in the Aramaic Inscription from Tel Dan." *IEJ* 45:22-25.
ROBERTS, J. J. M.
1972 *The Earliest Semitic Pantheon*. Baltimore: Johns Hopkins University Press.
RÖLLIG, W.
1974 "Die Amulette von Arslan Taş." *NESE* 2:17-28.
1988 "Die aramäische Inschrift für Haza'el und ihr Duplikat." *MDAIA* 103:62-75.
1995 "Phoenician and the Phoenicians in the Context of the Ancient Near East." Pp. 203-214 in *I Fenici: ieri - oggi - domani. ricerche, scoperte, progetti, Roma, 3-5 marzo 1994*. Rome: Gruppo editoriale internazionale.
1999 "Appendix 1: The Phoenician Inscriptions." Pp. 50-81 in *CHLI 2*.
ROGERSON, J. R., and P. R. DAVIES.
1996 "Was the Siloam Tunnel Built by Hezekiah?" *BA* 59/3:138-149.
RONZEVALLE, S.
1930-1931 "Fragments d'inscriptions araméennes des environs d'Alep." *MUSJ* 15:237-260.
VAN ROOY, H. F.
1989 "The Structure of the Aramaic Treaties of Sefire." *Journal of Semitics* 1:133-139.
RÖSEL, H. N.
1986 "Zur Formulierung der aaronitischen Segens auf den Amuletten von Ketef Hinnom." *BN* 35:30-36.
ROSENTHAL, F.
1955 "Kilamuwa." In *ANET* 654.
SADER, H.
1987 *Les états araméens de Syrie depuis leur fondation jusqu'à leur transformation en provinces assyriennes*. Beiruter Texte und Studien 36. Beirut and Wiesbaden: F. Steiner Verlag.
SANDERS, T. K.
1997 "An Ammonite Ostracon from Tall al-'Umayri." Pp. 331-36 in *Madaba Plains Project 3*. Ed. by L. G. Herr, et al. Berrien Springs, MI: Andrews University Institute of Archaeology.
SASS, B.
1988 *The Genesis of the Alphabet and Its Development in the Second Millennium* BC. AAT 13. Wiesbaden: Harrassowitz.
1993 "The Pre-Exilic Hebrew Seals." Pp. 194-256 in Sass and Uehlinger 1993.
SASS, B., and C. UEHLINGER.
1993 *Studies in the Iconography of Northwest Semitic Inscribed Seals*. OBO 125. Fribourg: University Press, and Göttingen: Vandenhoeck & Ruprecht.

SASSON, V.
1982 "The Siloam Tunnel Inscription." *PEQ* 114:111-117.
1985 "The Aramaic Text of the Tell Fakhriyah Assyrian-Aramaic Bilingual Inscription." *ZAW* 97:86-103.
1997 "The Inscription of Achish, Governor of Ekron, and Philistine Dialect, Cult and Culture." *UF* 29:627-639.
SCHÄFER-LICHTENBERGER, C.
1998 "PTGJH — Göttin und Herrin von Ekron." *BN* 91:64-76.
SCHARBART, J.
1975 "*brk*." *TDOT* 2:279-308.
SCHMIDT, B.
1994 *Israel's Beneficent Dead. Ancestor Cult and Necromancy in Ancient Israelite Religion and Tradition.* FAT 11. Tübingen: J. C. B. Mohr.
SCHNEIDER, Ts.
1991 "Six Biblical Signatures. Seals and Seal Impressions of Six Personages Recovered." *BAR* 17/4:26-33.
SEGAL, J.B.
1962 "*yrḥ* in the Gezer Calendar." *JSS* 7:212–221.
SHEA, W. H.
1977 "Ostracon II from Heshbon." *AUSS* 15:117-25.
1981 "The Carpentras Stela: A Funerary Poem." *JAOS* 101:215-217.
1988 "Commemorating the Final Breakthrough of the Siloam Tunnel." Pp. 431-442 in *Studies Ehrman*.
1990 "The Khirbet el-Qom Tomb Inscription Again." *VT* 40:110-116.
1991 "The Architectural Layout of the Amman Citadel Inscription Temple." *PEQ* 123:62-66.
SHILOH, Y.
1986 "A Group of Hebrew Bullae from the City of David." *IEJ* 36:16-38.
1993 "Jerusalem: Period of the Monarchy. The Water Supply Systems." *NEAEHL* 2:709-712.
SMELIK, K. A. D.
1987 *Historische Dokumente aus dem alten Israel.* Kleine Vandenhoeck-Reihe 1528. Göttingen: Vandenhoeck & Ruprecht.
1990 "The Literary Structure of King Mesha's Inscription." *JSOT* 46:21-30.
1991 *WAI.*
1992 *Converting the Past: Studies in Ancient Israelite and Moabite Historiography.* OTS 28. Leiden: Brill.
SMITH, M.
1993 *The Liturgy of Opening the Mouth for Breathing.* Oxford: Griffith Institute, Ashmolean Museum.
SNIR, R.
1993 "The Inscription of ᶜEn ᶜAbdat: an early evolutionary stage of ancient Arabic poetry." *Abr-Naharain* 31:110-125.
SOKOLOFF, M.
1990 *A Dictionary of Jewish Babylonian Aramaic.* Ramat Gan: Bar Ilam University Press.
SPERLING, S. D.
1988 "*KAI* 24 Re-Examined." *UF* 20:323-337.
SPIEGELBERG, W.
1901 *Aegyptische und griechische Eigennamen aus Mummienetiketten der römischen Kaiserzeit.* Leipzig: J. C. Hinrichs.
1904 *Die demotischen Denkmäler.* Cairo: Institut Français d'Archéologie Orientale.
SPYCKET, A.
1985 "La statue bilingue de Tell Fekheriye." *RA* 79:67-68.
STARCKY, J.
1980 "Inscription nabatéenne de Madaba." Pp. 76-77 in *Inoubliable Petra: Le royaume nabatéen aux confins du désert.* Ed. by D. Homès-Fredericq. Bruxelles: Musées Royaux d'Art et d'Histoire.
STARK, J. K.
1971 *Personal Names in Palmyrene Inscriptions.* Oxford: Oxford University Press.
STARKE, F.
1990 *Untersuchung zur Stammbildung des keilschrift-luwischen Nomens.* StBoT 31. Wiesbaden: O. Harrassowitz.
STERN, P. D.
1991 *The Biblical Ḥerem.* BJS 211. Atlanta: Scholars Press.
SWIGGERS, P.
1981 "Notes on the Phoenician Inscription of Kilamuwa." *RSO* 55:1-4.
1983 "Commentaire philogique sur l'inscription phénicienne du roi Kilamuwa." *RSF* 11:133-147.
TALLQVIST, K. L.
1905 *Neubabylonisches Namenbuch.* Helsingfors.
TALMON, S.
1963 "The Gezer Calendar and the Seasonal Cycle of Ancient Canaan." *JAOS* 83:177–187.
1986 *King, Cult and Calendar in Ancient Israel.* Leiden and Jerusalem: Brill.
TAWIL, H.
1970-71 "A Note on the Aḥiram Inscription." *JANES* 3:33-36.
1973 "The End of the Hadad Inscription in the Light of Akkadian." *JNES* 32:477-482.
1974 "Some Literary Elements in the Opening Sections of the Hadad, Zākir, and Nērab II Inscriptions in Light of East and West Semitic Royal Inscriptions." *Or* 43:40-65.
TEIXIDOR, J.
1987 "Aramean Religion." Pp. 1:367-372 in *Encyclopedia of Religion.* Ed. by M. Eliade. New York: MacMillan.
THOMPSON, T. L.
1995 "'House of David': An Eponymic Referent to Yahweh as Godfather." *SJOT* 9:59-74.

TIGAY, J. H.
1986 *You Shall Have No Other Gods. Israelite Religion in the Light of Hebrew Inscriptions*. HSS 31. Atlanta: Scholars Press.
1987 "Israelite Religion: The Onomastic and Epigraphic Evidence." Pp. 157-194 in *Studies Cross*.
TOMBACK, R. S.
1978 *A Comparative Semitic Lexicon of the Phoenician and Punic Languages*. SBLDS 32. Missoula, Montana: Scholars Press.
TORCZYNER, H.
1947 "A Hebrew Incantation against Night-Demons from Biblical Times." *JNES* 6:18-29.
TORREY, C. C.
1926 "A Specimen of Old Aramaic Verse." *JAOS* 46:241-247.
TROPPER, J.
1992 "Samᵓalisch *mt* 'wahrlich' und das Phänomen der Aphärese im Semitischen." *Or* 61:448-453.
1993 *Die Inschriften von Zincirli. Neue Edition und vergleichende Grammatik des phönischen, samᵓalischen und aramäischen Textkorpus*. ALASP 6. Münster: Ugarit Verlag.
1994 "»Sie knurrten wie Hunde« Psalm 59,16, Kilamuwa:10 und die Semantik der Wurzel *lwn*." *ZAW* 106:87-95.
TUBB, J. N.
1988 "Tell es-Sa'idiyeh: Preliminary Report on the First Three Seasons of Renewed Excavations." *Levant* 20:23-88.
TUFNELL, O. et al.
1953 *Lachish III*. London: Oxford University Press.
USSISHKIN, D.
1976 "Royal Judean Storage Jars and Private Seal Impressions." *BASOR* 223:1-13.
1977 "The Destruction of Lachish by Sennacherib and the Dating of the Royal Judean Storage Jars." *Tel Aviv* 4:28-60.
1979 "Answers at Lachish." *BAR* 5/6:16-39.
VAN DEN BRANDEN, A.
1961 "La tavolette magica di Arslan Tash." *BeO* 3:41-47.
VAN DER TOORN, K.
1995 "Rakib-El." Pp. 1296-1297 in *DDD*.
VANSCHOONWINKEL, J.
1990 "Mopsos: Légendes et réalité." *Hethitica* 10:185-211.
VAUGHAN, A. G.
1996 "The Chronicler's Account of Hezekiah: The Relationship of Historical Data to a Theological Interpretation of 2 Chronicles 29-32. PhD. dissertation Princeton Theological Seminary.
1999 *Theology, History, and Archaeology in the Chronicler's Account of Hezekiah*. Archaeology and Biblical Studies 4. Atlanta: Scholars Press.
DE VAUX, R.
1961 *Ancient Israel*. New York: McGraw Hill.
VERHOEVEN, U.
1993 *Das saitische Totenbuch der Iahtesncht*. Bonn: R. Habelt.
VIROLLEAUD, Ch.
1957 *Le Palais royal d'Ugarit. Vol. 2. Textes en cunéiformes alphabétiques des Archives Est, Ouest et Centrales*. Ed. by Ch. Virolleaud. Paris: n.p.
VRIEZEN, Th. C.
1965 "The Edomite Deity Qaus." *OTS* 14:330-353.
WALLIS, G.
1965 "Die vierzig Jahre der achten Zeile der Mesa-Inschrift." *ZDPV* 81:180-186.
WEINFELD, M.
1984 "Kuntillet ᶜAjrud Inscriptions and Their Significance." *SEL* 1:121-130.
WEIPPERT, H.
1988 *Palästina in vorhellenistischer Zeit*. Handbuch der Archäologie, Vorderasien 2/1. Munich: C. H. Beck.
WEIPPERT, M.
1964 "Archäologischer Jahrsbericht." *ZDPV* 80:150-195.
1969 "Elemente phönikischer und kilikischer Religion in den Inschriften vom Karatepe." *XVII. Deutscher Orientalistentag. Vorträge, 1. ZDMGSup* 1/1:191-217.
1981 "Assyrische Prophetien der Zeit Asarhaddons und Assurbanipals." Pp. 71-117 in *ARINH*.
WILLIAMS, R. J.
1977 "Ägypten und Israel." *TRE* 1:492-505.
WILLIAMSON, H. G. M.
1992 "Sanballat." *ABD* 5:973-975.
WINNETT, F. V.
1937 *A Study of the Lihyanite and Thamudic Inscriptions*. Toronto: University of Toronto.
WIRGIN, W.
1960 "The Calendar Text from Gezer." *EI* 6:*9–*12.
WUTHNOW, H.
1930 *Die semitischen Menschennamen in griechischen Inschriften und Papyri des vorderen Orients*. Leipzig: Dietrich.
XELLA, P.
1991 *Baal Hammon. Recherches sur l'identité et l'histoire d'un dieu phénico-punique*. Collezione di Studi Fenici 32. Rome: Consiglio nazionale delle ricerche.
YADIN, Y.
1969 "Excavations at Hazor, 1968-1969: Preliminary Communiqué." *IEJ* 19:1-19.
YADIN, Y., J. C. GREENFIELD, and Y. YARDENI.
1996 "A deed of Grant in Aramaic Found in Nahal Ḥever: Papyrus Yadin 7." *EI* 25:383-403 (Joseph Aviram Volume) (Hebrew).

YARDENI, A.
1991 "Remarks on the Priestly Blessing on Two Ancient Amulets from Jerusalem." *VT* 41:176-185.
YASSINE, Kh., and J. TEIXIDOR.
1986 "Ammonite and Aramaic Inscriptions from Tell El-Mazar in Jordan." *BASOR* 264:48-49.
YEIVIN, S.
1954 "*ben-hamelekh*." Col. 160 in *Enṣiqlopedya Miqra'it* (*Encyclopaedia Biblica*). Ed. by E. L. Sukenik, et al. Jerusalem: Mosad Bialik.
1971 "*peqidut*." Cols. 547-548 in *Enṣiqlopedya Miqra'it* (*Encyclopaedia Biblica*). Ed. by E. L. Sukenik, et al. Jerusalem: Mosad Bialik.
YOUNG, I.
1993 "Klmw br Tml." *Syria* 70:95-98.
YOUNGER, K. L., Jr.
1986 "Panammuwa and Bar-Rakib: Two Structural Analyses." *JANES* 18:91-103.
1994 "The Siloam Tunnel Inscription — An Integrated Reading." *UF* 26:543-556.
1998 "The Phoenician Inscription of Azatiwada. An Integrated Reading," *JSS* 43:11-47.
YOYOTTE, J.
1995 "Berlin 7707. Un détail." *Transeuphratène* 9:91.
ZADOK, R.
1988 *The Pre-Hellenistic Israelite Anthroponymy and Prosopography*. Leuven: Peeters.
ZEVIT, Z.
1977 "A Phoenician Inscription and Biblical Covenant Theology." *IEJ* 27:110-118.
1984 "The Khirbet el-Qôm Inscription Mentioning a Goddess." *BASOR* 255:39-47.
1990 "Phoenician *nbš/npš* and its Hebrew Semantic Equivalents." *Maarav* 5/6:337-344.
ZOBEL, H.-J.
1971 "Das Gebet um Abwendung der Not und seine Erhörung in den Klageliedern des Alten Testaments und in der Inschrift des Königs Zakir von Hamath." *VT* 2:91-99.

AKKADIAN MONUMENTAL INSCRIPTIONS

A. BUILDING AND DISPLAY INSCRIPTIONS
(Akkadian and Sumerian)

1. OLD AKKADIAN INSCRIPTIONS

INSCRIPTION OF SARGON: FOUNDATION OF THE AKKADIAN EMPIRE (2.89)

Burkhart Kienast

This inscription, originally encarved on the socle of a statue, is preserved only on two clay tablets containing a collection of several inscriptions of Sargon (2334-2279 BCE), Rīmuš (2278-2270 BCE) and Maništūsu (2269-2255 BCE). The text deals with the defeat of Lugalzagesi of Uruk and his allies, a victory which eventually led to the foundation of the Akkadian Empire.

Titles of the king (lines 1-11)
Sargon, king of Akkade,
solicitor of Ištar,
king of the Universe,
anointed priest of An,
king of the Land,
governor of Enlil.

Victory over Lugalzagesi of Uruk (lines 12-34)
He won in battle with Uruk.
Fifty city-rulers he ...[1]
with the mace of Abā[2]
and he conquered the city.
and tore down its walls.
And he captured
Lugalzagesi, king of Uruk, in battle
(and) led him in a neck-stock
to the Gate (of the temple) of Enlil.

Victory over the city of Ur (lines 36-46)
Sargon, king of Akkade,
won in battle with Ur
and he conquered the city
and tore down its walls.

Victory over the state of Lagaš (lines 47-61)
He conquered É-nin-MAR.KI
and tore down its walls.
He conquered its territory
as well as Lagaš (down) to the sea;
he washed his weapons in the sea.

Victory over Umma (lines 62-70)
He won in battle with Umma
and he conquered the city
and tore down its walls.

Description of the empire (lines 71-108)
Sargon, king of the Land:
Enlil did not give him a rival,
(but) he gave him indeed
the Upper Sea and the Lower (Sea)
From the Lower Sea up to the Upper Sea
citizens of Akkade (now)
hold governorships.
Even Mari and Elam
stand (at service) before Sargon, king of the Land.
Sargon, king of the Land,
restored (?) Kiš
(and) let them both ... the city.[3]

Curse formula (lines 109-131)
As for one who removes this inscription,
may Enlil and Šamaš pull out his roots
and pick up his seed.
Whoever takes away this statue,
may Enlil take away his son;
may he break his weapon:
He shall not last before Enlil.

Colophon
Inscription on the socle (of a statue);
it is written in front of Lugalzagesi.

[1] The syntax requires at this place a predicate left out by the copyist.

[2] Abā is the clan god of the Sargonic kings. The name (^{d}A-ba$_4$) is read Ìl-a-ba$_4$ by others on ground of a late entry in a god list; see in detail Kienast 1990:203.

[3] Lines 103-108 are difficult. Frayne translates: "Sargon ... altered the two sites of Kiš. He made the two (parts of Kiš) occupy (one) city" following Edzard 1980:610f. This refers to the unification of Kiš and Ḫursagkalama in one city, which seems to be out of date. Our translation is based on the Sum. version of a bilingual parallel.

REFERENCES

Text: Gelb and Kienast 1990:170-174; Frayne 1993:13-15.

INSCRIPTION OF NARĀM-SÎN: DEIFICATION OF THE KING (2.90)

Burkhart Kienast

This inscription is preserved on the socle of a statue made of copper, representing a crouching male figure of a *laḫmu*-Monster with the upper part of the body missing. The statue was found 1975 near Bāṣetkī, a small village on the way from Mossul to Zākhō, during road construction. The text deals with the background of the deification of Narām-sîn and the erection of his chapel at Akkade. Henceforth rulers of Babylonia often wrote their name with the divine determinative to underline the claim of rulership over all of Babylonia, a custom that ended with the foundation of the Ḫammurabi Empire.

The king's title (lines 1-4)
Narām-Sîn, the Mighty,
king of Akkade:[a]

Summary of the great revolt (lines 5-19)
When the Four Quarters (of the world)
all together revolted against him,
he won nine batles in only one year
through the love Ištar showed to him
and he captured the kings
who had risen against him.

Request for deification (lines 20-56)
Because he strengthened
the base of his city
in these hard times,
(the citizen of) his city
requested him
from Ištar in E'anna,
from Enlil in Nippur,
from Dagān in Tuttul,[b]
from Ninḫursag in Keš,
from Enki/E'a in Eridu,
from Sîn in Ur,
from Šamaš in Sippar
(and) from Nergal in Kutha[c]
(to become) the god of their city
and they built a temple for him
in the midst of Akkade.

Curse formula (lines 57-74)
As for one who removes
this inscription,
may Šamaš
and Ištar
and Nergal,
the solicitor of the king,
and all those gods (mentioned)
pull out his roots
and pick up his seed.

a Gen 10:9-10
b 1 Sam 5:2-7, etc.
c 2 Kgs 17:30

REFERENCES

Text: Gelb and Kienast 1990:81-83; Frayne 1993:113-114. Studies: Hallo 1999b.

INSCRIPTION OF NARĀM-SÎN: CAMPAIGN AGAINST ARMĀNUM AND EBLA (2.91)

Burkhart Kienast

This inscription was originally encarved on the socle of a statue also showing the relief of a city on top of a mountain; it is preserved in three Old Babylonian copies on clay tablets from Ur. Exemplar A contains lines 1-118 and the captions describing the city, exemplar B has the lines 119-185 and two short captions while exemplar C seems to contain the complete text of A and B; the beginning of C is lost and therefore only a few lines (100-106) are parallel with A. The text deals with a campaign of Narām-Sîn to northern Syria and with the conquest of Armānum and Ebla.

Summary of the campaign (lines 1-60)
Concerning the fact[1]
from old from the creation of men
no one among the kings
had overthrown
Armānum and Ebla:
With the help of the weapon of Nergal
Narām-Sîn,[2] the Mighty,

[1] The beginning of the inscription is not given in the copy, probably because the original was in a fragmentary condition when copied. We expect the king's titles and a report on the cities conquered and the enemies captured or killed.

[2] The name of the king is written here and elsewhere in exemplar A with the divine determinative (^{d}*Na-ra-am-*^{d}EN.ZU), in exemplars B and C without it (*Na-ra-am-*^{d}EN.ZU). Therefore, Frayne argues that B and C represent an inscription different from A. But the reconstruction of C shows there is exactly the space needed for A lost and both exemplars, A and C overlap just in the unusual "*Declaration of Narāmsîn*" (see note 4). Given the fact that we deal here with an OB copy of unknown history the problem is still open for discussion.

opened the only path (there)
and he (Nergal) gave him
Armānum and Ebla.
He also granted him
the Amanus, the Cedar Forest,
and the Upper Sea.
Indeed,
with help of the weapon of Dagān,
who has made his kingship great,
Narām-Sîn, the Mighty,
conquered
Armānum and Ebla.
And from the bank of the Euphrates
until Ulisum
he subjugated the people
whom Dagān granted him recently
and they now carry
the basket (in service) of Abā, his god.
Finally, he won control
over the Amanus, the Cedar Forest.

Dedication formula (lines 61-81)
When Dagān
had rendered judgement
for Narām-Sîn, the Mighty,
and given Rīš-Adad, king of Armānum,[3]
in his hand,
so that he (Narām-Sîn) himself
could take him (Rīšadad) prisoner
in the midst of his 'entrance,'[3]
he (Narām-Sîn) fashioned his statue from diorite
and dedicated it to Sîn.

Declaration of Narām-Sîn (lines 82-118)[4]
Thus (said) Narām-Sîn, the Mighty,
king of the Four Quarters (of the world):
'Dagān gave me Armānum and Ebla
and I captured Rīš-Adad, king of Armānum.
And at that time I fashioned
a likeness of myself
and dedicated it to Sîn.
No one shall remove my name!
May my statue stand in front of Sîn.
What(ever) his god allots to someone
may he perform;
(but) the task I had to perform
was exceeding.[5]

Curse formula (lines 119-185)[6]
Whoever removes the name
of Narām-Sîn, the Mighty,
king of the Four Quarters (of the world),
and puts his name on the statue
of Narām-Sîn, the Mighty,
saying "(it is) my statue",
or shows (the statue) to another man
saying "remove his name
and put my name in,"
may Sîn, the owner of this statue,
and Ištar Annunītum,
An,
Enlil,
Abā,
Sîn,
Šamaš,
Nergal,
Ūm,
Ninkarak
(and) the great gods
all together
curse him with an evil curse;
he shall not hold the scepter for Enlil
nor the kingship for Ištar;
he shall not last before his god;
Ninḫursag and Nintu
shall not grant him
a son or heir;
Adad and Nisaba
shall not make his furrow prosper;
Enki/E'a shall fill
his (irrigation) ditch with mud
and not increase his understanding.
... ...[7]

Captions according to exemplar A:
Description af Armānum
(a) From the strong wall to the great wall:
130 cubits (is) the height of the mountain,
44 cubits (is) the height of the wall.
(b) From the outer wall to the strong wall:
180 cubits (is) the height of the mountain,
30 cubits (is) the height of the wall.
(c) In total: 404 cubits height
from the ground to the top of the wall.

---

[3] The name of the king of Armānum is rendered *Ri*-DA-[d]IM in line 67 and *Ri*-ID-[d]IM in line 93. The affair of Armānum has been compared with the Babylonian historical tradition, as e.g. given in the Chronicle of Early Kings (cf. Grayson 1975:154): "Narām-Sîn, the son (sic!) of Sargon marched against Apišal. He made a breach (in the city wall) (*pilšu ip-luš-ma*) and captured Rīšadad (*Ri-iš*[1]-[d]IM), king of Apišal, and the vizier of Apišal with his (own) hand." Here the name of the city of Apišal is obviously a play on the phrase *pilšu ipluš-ma*, and the "breach (in the city wall)" is a reference to the "entrance" (*nārabtum*) of our inscription. Since *Rīd-Adad* is not attested otherwise in the onomasticon, the emendation into *Rīš-Adad* is justified.

[4] The passage called "*Declaration of Narām-Sîn*" has a parallel only once in an inscription of Erridupizir (see Gelb and Kienast 1990:303-307, lines 58-80; Frayne 1993:221-223, lines ii 13-10'). It would be a very peculiar coincidence if in exemplars A and C of our text two different inscriptions with a "*Declaration of Narām-Sîn*" were represented, especially in view of the facts given in note 2.

[5] Lines 110-118 are difficult and especially the two last lines are without translation in Frayne and open to discussion.

[6] We expect in accordance with the parallel from an inscription of Erridupizir (see note 4) after the "*Declaration of Narām-Sîn*" some curse formulas; these are, in our view, given in exemplars B and C or otherwise lost as the beginning of the inscription of exemplar A.

[7] No translation is possible.

(d) He destroyed (?) the city Armānum.
Colophon 1
What (is written) on the side (of the statue) (facing) the chapel of the New Court.
(e) From the river to the outer wall:
196 cubits (is) the height of the mountain,
20 cubits (is) the height of the wall.
(f) From the outer wall to the strong wall:
156 cubits (is) the height of the mountain,
30 cubits (is) the height of the wall.
Colophon 2
What (is written) on the side (of the statue) (facing) the large statue of Sînerībam.

Captions according to exemplar B:
(a) [Above:] ..., Imlik.[8]
(b) Below:
The general of Sumer and Akkad, PN[8]

[8] Since we are dealing with a fragmentary inscription no arguments can be drawn from these two captions as to the relationship between exemplars A and B+C.

REFERENCES

Text: Foster 1982:27-36; Gelb and Kienast 1990:253-264; Frayne 1993:132-135.

---

2. EARLY OLD BABYLONIAN INSCRIPTIONS

ISIN DYNASTY

Hegemony over the land of Sumer and Akkad eventually passed from Akkad(e) to Ur (*COS* 2.138-141) and from Ur to Isin with the collapse of the Ur III state ca. 2004 BCE. Isin, the new center of power, was located at modern Ishan Baḥriyat. The site has been excavated since 1973 by an expedition of the Deutsche Forschungsgemeinschaft under the direction of B. Hrouda. The names of fifteen kings of the Isin I dcynasty are known; they reigned from 2017-1794 BCE.

ISHBI-ERRA (2.92)

Douglas Frayne

Ishbi-Erra, the first king of the Isin Dynasty, reigned ca. 2017-1985 BCE. A Sumerian royal inscription known from a contemporary tablet copy from Nippur records the fabrication by the king of a lyre for the god Enlil of Nippur.

(1-3) For the god Enlil, lord of the foreign lands, his lord,
(4-6) Ishbi-Err[a], mighty king, lord of <his> land
(7-9) fashioned a great lyre[a] for him, which ... the heart.
(10) He dedicated it [for his own] life.
(12-15) The name of the lyre is "Ishbi-Erra trusts in the god Enlil."

a Pss 33:2; 43:4; 49:4; 57:8; 71:22; 81:2; 92:3; 98:5; 108:2; 137:2; 147:7; 149:3

REFERENCES

Text: Kärki 1980:2; Frayne 1990:6-7.

SHU-ILISHU (2.93)

Douglas Frayne

The name of what is probably the third year of Shu-ilishu (the second king of the Isin I dynasty, who reigned ca. 1984-1875 BCE) commemorates the construction of a standard for the moon god Nanna, tutelary deity of Ur. The deed is recorded in a Sumerian school tablet copy excavated by Sir Leonard Woolley at Ur.

Standards, with divine or animal images on their tops, were often used in ancient Mesopotamia to muster and lead troops in battle (cf. for example, the depiction of troops with standards standing behind Naram-Sin in the famous

"Victory Stele" in the Louvre; see *ANEP* fig. 309). They are directly comparable to the standards of the Israelite tribes mentioned in Num 2:10.

(i.1-7) For the god Nanna, trusted one of heaven and earth, true princely son of the god Enlil, the lord who, as far as heaven and earth, uniquely surpasses the gods,
(i.8-14) Shu-ilishu god of his land, mighty king, king of Ur, beloved of the gods An, Enlil, and Nanna,
(i.15-22) a great divine standard,[a] a tree fit for a (rich) harvest, evoking wonder, colored with gold, silver, and shining lapis lazuli, ..., a sil[ver] image ...

Lacuna

(ii.1-7) he fashioned for him (the god Nanna) [when] he (Shu-ilishu) establish[ed] in their abodes [in U]r(?) the people] scattered as far away as A[nshan].
(ii.8-9) He dedicated it for his own life.

(A curse formula follows).

[a] Exod 17:15, 16; Num 2:10; Isa 5:26; 13:2; 18:3; Jer 4:21; 50:2; 51:27; Ps 74:4; Cant 2:4; 6:4, 10

REFERENCES

Kärki 1980:2-3; Frayne 1990:16-18.

ISHME-DAGAN (2.94)

Douglas Frayne

A Sumerian inscription found on various stamped or inscribed bricks from Nippur indicates that they originally came from a socle built by Ishme-Dagan (third king of the Isin I dynasty, who reigned c. 1953-1935 BCE) for the ceremonial mace of the god Ninurta, the god Enlil's second in command at Nippur. Isin-Larsa period account texts from Nippur record offerings made for this mace, an apparently impressive monument (Sigrist 1984:150). For a depiction of a possibly similar ceremonial mace erected to the god Ningirsu (a local variant of Ninurta at Girsu) by Gudea, see Börker-Klähn 1982:Plate volume fig. 89a.

Archaeological excavations in Mesopotamia have turned up numerous examples of stone and metal mace-heads (see Solyman 1968). They are comparable to the "war club" (KJV "maul") mentioned in the Bible.

(1-7) When the god Enlil had Ishme-Dagan, king of the land of Sumer and Akkad, take the god Ninurta, his might champion as bailiff,
(8-9) (Ishme-Dagan) fashioned for him (Ninurta) the *šita*-weapon, the mace[a] with fifty heads
(10-12) (and) set up his beloved weapon on a baked brick platform for him.

[a] Prov 25:18

REFERENCES

Kärki 1980:8-9; Frayne 1990:35-36.

LIPIT-ESHTAR (2.95)

Douglas Frayne

Numerous clay cones found or excavated at Isin record the construction by Lipit-Eshtar (the fourth king of the Isin I dynasty, who reigned ca. 1934-1924 BCE) of a storehouse (*ganīnum*) for the gods Enlil and Ninlil.

This text provides us with the earliest Akkadian translation of the Sumerian royal title lugal KI-EN-GI KI-URI, Akkadian *šar māt šumerim u akkadim*, "king of the land of Sumer and Akkad."

(1-19) I, Lipit-Eshtar, humble shepherd of Nippur, true farmer of Ur, unceasing (provider) for Eridu, *en*-priest suitable for Uruk, king of Isin, king of the land of Sumer and Akkad,[a] favorite of the goddess Eshtar,
(20-23) a storehouse of the ... offerings of the gods Enlil and Ninlil,
(24-26) in Isin, my royal city, at the palace gate,
(27-29) I, Lipit-Eshtar, son of the god Enlil,
(30-35) when I established justice in the land of Sumer and Akkad,
(36) built (it).

[a] Gen 10:10

REFERENCES

Kärki 1980:19-20; Frayne 1990:49-51.

UR-NINURTA (2.96)

Douglas Frayne

A tablet from Nippur contains the copy of one (or more) Sumerian royal inscriptions of Ur-Ninurta (the fifth king of the Isin I dynasty, who reigned ca. 1923-1896 BCE). The excerpted section deals with the fashioning of a statue depicting the king holding a votive goat kid at his breast; the statue was set up in the courtyard of the goddess Ninlil (Enlil's spouse) in Nippur. In Mesopotamia, as in Israel, kids were commonly used for sacrifical purposes.

(vi.6′-12′) I fashioned (for the goddess Ninlil[?]) a [copper] statue, whose form was endowed with my face, clasping a votive kid, standing to make supplications for me, an ornament of the main courtyard of the Gagishshua (temple).
(vi.13′-14′) I dedicated it to her for my own life.

(A curse formula follows).

a Num 15:11

REFERENCES

Kärki 1980:24-26; Frayne 1990:66-68.

UR-DUKUGA (2.97)

Douglas Frayne

A Sumerian cone inscription of Ur-dukuga, the thirteenth king of the Isin I dynasty (who reigned ca. 1830-1828 BCE), records the construction of a temple of the god Dagan in the royal city of Isin.

Dagan was an important Mesopotamian and West Semitic deity with major cult centres at ancient Tuttul (modern Tell Bi^{c}a near the junction of the Euphrates and Balih rivers) and Terqa (modern Tell ^{c}Asherah on the Euphrates about 13 km upstream from Mari). The etymology of the DN is unknown. While a connection with Hebrew *dāg* "fish" is highly unlikely, a connection of the Semitic root *dgn* when translated as "grain" is possible (*ABD* 2:2).

(1-3) For the god Dagan,[a] great lord of the foreign lands, the god who created him,
(4-20) Ur-dukuga, shepherd who brings everything (needed) for Nippur, superb farmer of the gods An and Enlil, provider of Ekur, who provides abundance for Eshumesha (and) Egalmah, who returned to the gods the regular offerings which had been expropriated from the sanctuaries, mighty king, king of Isin, king of the land of Sumer and Akkad, spouse steadfastly looked upon by the goddess Inanna,
(21-24) built for him the Edurkigara ("House — the well founded residence") in Isin, his shining beloved residence.

a Judg 16:23; 1 Sam 5:2-7; 1 Chr 10:10; 1 Macc 10:84; 11:4

REFERENCES

Kärki 1980:34-35; Frayne 1990:94-95.

LARSA DYNASTY

The city of Larsa (modern Sinkara) struggled with Isin for hegemony over the land of Sumer and Akkad in early Old Babylonian times. The site has been dug by a series of French expeditions in 1933-34 and 1967 (directed by A. Parrot), 1969-70 (directed by J.-Cl. Margueron) and since 1970 (directed by J.-L. Huot).

The names of fourteen kings of the Larsa dynasty are known; they reigned from ca. 2025-1763 BCE.

GUNGUNUM (2.98)

Douglas Frayne

Gungunum, the fifth member of the Larsa dynasty and its first effective king, reigned from ca. 1931-1906 BCE. A Sumerian cone inscription from Ur deals with the construction there of a storehouse for the sun god by En-ana-tuma, *en*-priestess of the moon god Nanna. Though installed by her father Ishme-Dagan of Isin (above, 2.94), she was allowed to keep her priestly office even after Larsa captured Ur from Isin. The sun god, Sumerian Utu, Akkadian Shamash, was the tutelary deity of the dynastic capital of Larsa.

(1-7) For the god Utu, offspring of the god Nanna, ... son of the Ekishnugal, whom the goddess Ningal bore, her lord,
(8-11) for the life of Gungunum, mighty man, king of Ur,
(12-17) En-ana-tuma, *zirru*-priestess, *en*-priestess of the god Nanna in Ur, daughter of Ishme-Dagan, king of the land of Sumer and Akkad,
(18-20) built his Ehili ("Charming House"), built his shining storehouse for him.
(21-22) She dedicated it to him for her own life.

REFERENCES

Kärki 1980:41; Frayne 1990:115-117.

NUR-ADAD (2.99A)

Douglas Frayne

A Sumerian inscription from Ur belonging to Nur-Adad, eighth king of the Larsa dynasty (who reigned ca. 1865-1850 BCE) deals with the king's construction of a KIR_4-MAḪ "great (bread) oven" and a DU_8-MAḪ (possibly "great *cauldron*") for the moon god Nanna. Copies of the text are inscribed on three copper cylinders and several clay cones that were found in a room northwest of the ziqqurrat at Ur; it is to probably to be identified as a temple kitchen. The Sumerian word KIR_4 "(bread) oven" was apparently borrowed into Akkadian as *kīru(m)* "kiln (for lime and bitumen)" and, in all likelihood is to be connected with Akkadian *kūru(m)*, "crucible, kiln, brazier" and Hebrew *kwr* "pot or furnace for smelting metals," (see reference ***a***).

(1-6) For the god Nanna, crown of heaven and earth, whose face is adorned with charming rays, the god Enlil's first-born son, his lord,
(7-25) Nur-Adad, mighty man, provider of Ur, king of Larsa, who makes first fruit offerings reach the Ekishnugal, who looks after the shrine Ebabbar, whom the youth, god Utu has truly chosen in his heart, one given the scepter by the god Nanna, subduer of the foreign lands for the god Utu, called by a good name by the god Ishkur,
(26-36) when he had made Ur content, had removed evil (and the cause for any) complaint from it, had regathered its scattered people (and) had given to the god Nanna, his lord, his (proper) boundary,
(37-41) at that time, a great (bread) oven[a] for the meals of the god Suen, which (also) provides bread for all the gods
(42-46) (and) a great *cauldron* cared for in the (dining) hall, roaring loudly at the morning and evening meals,
(47-48) he made for him (the god Nanna) and for his own life.
(49-50) He restored the traditional cleansing rites.
(51-56) May a long life-span (and) a reign of abundance come forth from the Ekishnugal for Nur-Adad, shepherd of righteousness.

a Deut 4:20; 1 Kgs 8:51; Isa 48:10; Jer 11:4; Ezek 22:18, 20, 22 Prov 17:3; 27:21

REFERENCES

Kärki 1980:51-52; Frayne 1990:140-142.

NUR-ADAD (2.99B)

A Sumerian clay cone records Nur-Adad's construction of Enki's *abzu* temple at Eridu.

(1-3) [For] the god En[ki], lord of Eridu, [his] lord,
(4-8) Nur-[Adad], mighty man, provider of Ur, king of Larsa, subduer of the foreign land for the god Utu,
(9-16) when he had restored Ur and Larsa, had resettled their scattered people in their residence,

their captive people ... the foundation tru[ly ...], Eridu [...],
(17-19) at that time (he did not let) any one who might do evil (against) the god Enki [enter] it.
(20-21) Divine lord Nudimmud was pleased at this.
(22-24) Beside his ancient temple (Nur-Adad) built anew for him (Enki) his Abzu (temple), the Emekukuga ("House which purifies the *me*'s").
(25-28) Into it he brought his throne, standard, (and) ancient treasures.

REFERENCES

Frayne 1990:146.

SIN-IDDINAM (2.100)

Douglas Frayne

A Sumerian inscription known from an Old Babylonian period tablet copy deals with the construction by Sin-iddinam (the ninth king of the Larsa dynasty, who reigned ca. 1849-1843 BCE) of a throne for the storm god Ishkur/Adad.

The inscription's account of two butting bull (figures) standing on either side of the base of the throne (lines 75-78) can be compared with the passage in 1 Kings 10:14 describing two lion (figures) standing by the armrests of king Solomon's throne. The biblical account, in turn, can be compared with the relief found on the stone sarcophagus of Ahiram, king of Byblos (*ANEP*[2] #458; cf. above, 2.55) and the scene carved on an ivory plaque from Megiddo (*ANEP*[2] #332); both show lion figures standing below the armrests of the ruler's throne (cf. *IDB* 4:637). In these two cases the lions have wings spreading backward in an apparent attitude of flight. They are, then, comparable to the Biblical winged *cherubim* which stood as sentinels and supports by God's throne (*IDB* 1:131). Hebrew *cherubim*, in turn, are likely connected with the Akkadian word *kurību(m)* "representative of a protective genius with specific non-human features" (cf. *IDB* 1:131); *kurību(m)* genii stood guard with other demons at doorways in Babylonian and Assyrian temples.

(1-8) For the god Ishkur, lord, an[gry] storm, [...] great storm of heav[en and earth], who trusts in his supremacy, foremost one, advocate, son of An, whose head is clothed in magnificence, lord, raging leader, great storm, in whose ... has no rival, who masses the clouds, at his rushing in the storm wind he causes the earth to tremble.
(9-17) In broad heaven he is a mighty wind which roars, whose [rum]ble is abundance. At his roar the land and the great mountains are afraid. Great champion, who holds the sceptre in the hand (and) is clothed in authority. At his thundering (over) the sea (and) covering the land with ra<diance>), great (hail)stones rain ... (which are) difficult to see through,
(18-24) In their ... they set up for him ... like a
(19-21) [...] like a reed.
(22-23) On their own accord, at his presence they lift ... to him. He spies the numerous people.
(25-33) Lord of abundance, who makes splendor plentiful, who gives sustenance to the land, merciful prince whose compassion is good, shade of Larsa, helper of Sin-iddinam in the field of battle, who stands in combat with the troops at his side, great lord, canal inspector of the gods An and Enlil,whose destiny cannot be rivalled, for his lord,
(34-40) Sin-iddinam, mighty man, humble prince who reverences the god Enlil, he is the "yea" of the Ekur, youth called by a good name by the god Nanna, provider of Ur, king of Larsa, king of the land of Sumer and Akkad,
(41-53) given broad wisdom and surpassing intelligence by the god Nudimmud, granted a good reign, a long life-span, and abundance without end by the god Ishkur, his personal deity, who puts in order the rites of Eridu, who perfects the offerings of the gods, wise one, who [r]estored the ancient *me*'s, one whom his numerous people tru]ly [ch]ose —
(54-67) a lofty [thron]e, [...] with surpassing form, placed for his [personal deity], [grand]ly made with [...] refined silver, [...] of the green heaven, [...] befitting his greatness, suitable for *sitting on* — amidst jubilation, he finished the work there.
(68-82) At that time, the god Ishkur, his (personal) deity, grandly sat down there on his throne of glory. Then, for the future (Sin-iddinam) made its form surpassing. He sought out a place for its rites and supreme *me*'s. He set below, on the right and left, two great wild bulls at the throne butt[ing] at the enemies of the king, a ... beast ... the A[nunna gods] set u[p] abundance [from] the horizon ... beside him. He [fashioned] its (cult) statue and [set it] on its (the throne's) lap.
(85-88) He ... there [...]

REFERENCES

Michalowski 1988:265-275; Frayne 1990:177-179.

WARAD-SIN (2.101A)

Douglas Frayne

A Sumerian cone inscription of Warad-Sin (the thirteenth king of the Larsa dynasty who reigned from 1834-23 BCE) records the construction of the chief storehouse in Ur. This building was apparently not a storeroom for grain, but rather a repository for precious objects donated to the city temples.

(1-4) For the god Nanna, lord who beams forth brightly in shining heaven, first-born son of the god Enlil, his lord,
(5-13) I, Kudur-mabuk, father of the Amorite land, son of Simti-shilhak, the one who is attentive to the god Enlil, who finds favor with the goddess Ninlil, who reverences the Ebabbar, provider of the Ekur, constant (attendant) for the Ekishnugal, the one who makes Nippur content,
(14-15) when the god Nanna agreed to my entreaty
(6-18) (and) delivered into my hands the enemies who had thrown down the top of the Ebabbar temple,
(19-21) he (the god Nanna) returned Mashkan-shapir and Kar-Shamash to Larsa.
(22-24) "Nanna, my lord, it is you who has done it, (as for) myself, what am I?"
(25-27) In respect of this, to the god Nanna, my lord, as I prayed fervently,
(28-38) I built the Ganunmah, the house of silver and gold, the god Suen's storehouse with heavy treasure — it had been built in the past (and) had become dilapidated — for my own life and for the life of Warad-Sin, my son, king of Larsa.
(39) I restored it.
(40-42) May the god Nanna, my lord, rejoice at my deed
(43-47) (and) grant to me a destiny of life, a good reign, (and) a throne with a secure foundation.
(48-49) May I be the shepherd, beloved of the god Nanna.
(50) May my days be long.

REFERENCES

Kärki 1980:97-98; Frayne 1990:214-216.

WARAD-SIN (2.101B)

Kudur-mabuk's construction of the throne of the god Nanna of Ur for his son Warad-Sin is known from two Sumerian school tablet copies found in Sir Leonard Woolley's excavations at Ur. The deed was commemorated in the name of the sixth year of Warad-Sin.

The two protective genie (Sumerian LAMMA) described in lines 68-75 of this text as protecting the god Nanna's throne may be compared with the Hebrew *cherubim* who guarded Yahweh's throne (*IDB* 1:131). Although the probable animal nature of these lamma's is not specified in this text, their decription as genii "stretched out towards the statue of me praying, as if (making) new *šuila* prayers and entreaties" suggests a connection with the Akkadian *kurībū* noted above (2.100), since the latter word is derived from a root (*krb*) meaning "to bless." What they stretched out is not specified; comparative evidence suggests it might have been wings. The four breed bulls mentioned in lines 78-79 can be compared with the two small bull heads depicted on the arm-rests of the throne of the Aramean ruler Bar-Rakib in the relief from Zinjirli (ancient Samᵓal) (*ANEP*² fig. 460; for the Bar-Rakib inscription see *COS* 2.38); in all four bull heads would have been placed at the corners of the king's throne.

(1-6) For the god Nanna, great lord, light which fills shining heaven, who holds the princely crown aloft, reliable god, who alternates days and nights, who establishes the months, who completes the year.
(7-9) In the Ekur he humbly receives the true decisions from the father who engendered him (Enlil) —
(10) son beloved of the goddess Ninlil,
(11-13) (for) the god Ashimbabbar, who listens to prayers and entreaties, his lord,
(14-35) (I), Kudur-mabuk, father of the Amorite land, son of Shimti-shilhak, the one who repaid a favor for the Ebabbar temple (and) adorned it for the god Utu, his lord, who gathered the scattered people (and) put in order their disorganized troops, who made his land peaceful, who smote the head of its foes, snare of his land, who smashed all the enemies, who made the youth, god Utu, supreme judge of heaven and earth, reside contentedly (in) his princely residence, in Larsa, the place of regular offerings.
(36-38) I, Kudur-mabuk, humble shepherd, who stands in supplication for the shrine Ebabbar,
(39-46) when the gods An, Enlil, Enki, and Ninmah had given to me, on account of my order by the

supreme decree of the gods Nanna and Utu, the true scepter suitable to lead the people (and) a reign with eternal *me*'s, whose *me*'s cannot be altered,
(47) on account of this, as I made an ardent prayer ...
(48-58) ..., shining star(s) radiance ... a ... awe-inspiring,
(59-60) that throne [was inlaid] with red gold,
(61-67) [...] the days which I live ... a work ... [...] a statue of the god Nanna [whose] fo[rm] was fashioned correctly ..., [...], ... grandly I ...
(68-71) A pair of protective genii ... [giving] good omens [...], being there daily ... [...] I set up on either side of it.
(72-75) I fixed them there here at the perimeter of that throne (area with their ...) stretched out towards the statue of me praying, as if (making) new *šuila* prayers and entreaties.[a]
(76-77) I sought out will-chosen *me*'s for the calf of heaven,[b] that was in its entirety a masterpiece.
(78-79) I fixed there four breed bulls.
(80-82) Its great seat was of *kiškanûm* wood. Its crosspieces, (depicting) a lion seizing a kid, were inlaid with refined silver.
(83-88) I dedicated it to him for my life and for the life of Warad-[Sin], my son, offspring of ... eternal name, son of ..., provider of Ur, who reverences] the E[babbar, king] of Larsa.

a Exod 25:18-20; 37:7-9; 1 Kgs 6:23-28; 8:6-7 Isa 37:16

b 1 Kgs 10:19

REFERENCES

Kärki 1980:122-126; Frayne 1990:219-222.

RIM-SIN (2.102A)

Douglas Frayne

A Sumerian cone inscription of Rim-Sin (the fourteenth king of the Larsa dynasty, who reigned ca. 1822-1763 BCE) records the construction of a temple of the god Dumuzi in Ur.

Dumuzi was in origin a Sumerian shepherd god who, with the goddess Inanna, served as tutelary deity of the ancient city of Badtibira (var.: Patibira), modern Tell al-Madaʾin. For the most recent discussion of the cult of Dumuzi see Kutscher 1990:29-44.

Dumuzi was the parade example of the tragic lover in Sumerian mythology; the Sumerian myth "Death of Dumuzi" describes how the hapless god was pursued and finally killed by five evil demons.

In astral terms, Dumuzi was equated by the ancients with the constellation they called the "Hired Man"; it corresponded in the main to the modern constellation of Aries ("The Ram") (Foxvog 1989). The heliacal setting of the constellation Aries during the fourth month of the Babylonian year (month Dumuzi) was apparently the annual occasion for wailing rites for the disappearing god. A Mari text (Dossin 1975:27-28; Kutscher 1990:42) dated to the month Abum (which alternates with Dumuzi) refers to cleansing rituals for (the statues of) Ishtar and Dumuzi, and another Mari text dated to the same month (but two years later) (Birot 1960 ARM(T) 175; Kutscher 1990:40) records a disbursement of grain for "wailing women" (MUNUS.MEŠ *ba-ki-tim*). The wailing that accompanied the Dumuzi cult was evidently a female prerogative.

Dumuzi was adopted as a fertility god under the name Tammuz by the inhabitants of Syro-Palestine. A passage in Ezekiel condemns the women of Jerusalem for their apostasy in wailing for "the Tammuz." In Syria Tammuz was often designated by his title Adonis (Greek Adonis from Semitic *adōn* "lord").

(1-6) For the god Dumuzi,[a] lord of offerings, beloved husband of the goddess Inanna, shepherd of the broad steppe, fit to to care for (all the creatures), his lord,
(7-11) Rim-Sin, prince who reverences Nippur, provider of Ur, king of Larsa, king of the land of Sumer and Akkad,
(12-19) built for the future the Eigarasu ("House filled with butterfat"), his beloved residence suitable for his habitation, for his own life and for the life of Kudur-mabuk, the father who engendered him.
(20-24) On account of this may the god Dumuzi, his lord, rejoice in him and multiply cattle and sheep for him in the pens and folds.

a Ezek 8:14

REFERENCES

Kärki 1980:153; Frayne 1990:275-276.

RIM-SIN (2.102B)

A different Sumerian cone inscription of Rim-Sin commemorates the construction of a temple of Nergal in Ur.

Nergal was a deity venerated by Assyrian deportees (especially those from Cuthah) who were re-located in Samaria following the downfall of Israel in 722 BCE.

(1-6) For the god Nergal,[a] supreme lord, who possesses great might, the one with a perfect fearsome splendor and aura, foremost one, who destroys all the evil foreign lands (and) piles up the rebellious land in heaps, his god,
(7-11) Rim-Sin, prince who reverences Nippur, provider of Ur, king of Larsa, king of the land of Sumer and Akkad,
(12-19) built for the future Eerimhashhash ("House which smashes the enemy"), his residence of valor suitable for habitation, for his own life and for the life of Kudur-mabuk, the father who engendered him.
(20-28) On account of this may the god Nergal, his divine creator, look at him with shining eyes, and dwell at his right side in the field of battle. May he conquer the foreign land that rebels against him.

a 2 Kgs 17:30

REFERENCES

Kärki 1980:157-158; Frayne 1990:277-278.

RIM-SIN (2.102C)

A Sumerian cone inscription from Ur records Rim-Sin's construction of the temple of Ninsiᵓana, here taken to be a male deity, who (as noted, see *COS* 2.139A) was likely a manifestation of the planet Venus as "Morning Star."

(1-16) For the god Ninsiᵓana, god whose station shines from clear heaven, whose light shines forth, lofty one, who fills the great hall, whose utterance is favorable, aristocrat, whose fiat (carries) weight in the assembly, who goes at the fore of the great gods, foremost hero, who perfectly executes the artful *me*'s, who truly puts instruction and counsel in heaven, judge, supreme adviser, who distinguishes (between) truth and falsehood, god with patient mercy, who provides a protective genius of well-being, a ... guardian spirit, and a very great life-span for the one who is in awe of him, for my lord,
(17-26) I, Rim-Sin, mighty man, whose offerings are the greatest for the shrine Nippur, who perfectly executes the *me*'s and rites of Eridu, reliable provider of Ur, who reverences Ebabbar, king of Larsa, Uruk, (and) Isin, king of the land of Sumer and Akkad,
(27-29) when the god Ninsiᵓana delivered all my enemies into my hands,
(30-40) on account of this, for the god Ninsiᵓana my lord, as I established a colleagueship (with him), I built in a pure place the Eeshbarzida ("House of reliable decisions"), suitable for his divinity, his residence which pleases him. I wrote my name there, on the lintel (and) door jamb of the temple, for the future.

REFERENCES

Kärki 1980:160-161; Frayne 1990:297-298.

RIM-SIN (2.102D)

A rock-crystal jar, probably once used to hold unguent, was dedicated in Sumerian to the god Mardu/Amurrum for the life of Rim-Sin by the king's chief physician.

The evidence of the vessel's inscription suggests that this purchased piece originally came from Larsa. It apparently belonged to a hoard from the Amurrum temple in Larsa that consisted of at least four pieces (see Braun-Holzinger 1984 nos. 192-194): (a) this vessel, (b) a "bronze" statue of a kneeling figure with an inscription dedicating the piece to the god Amurrum for the life of Hammu-rapi (see *COS* 2.107C below); (c) a "bronze" figure of a recumbent ram with an inscription dedicating the piece to the god Amurrum for the life of a king of Larsa whose name is unfortunately corroded away, and (d) a "bronze" statuette depicting three rampant goats standing on a pair of divine figures, likely Amurrum and Ashratum (their divine status is indicated by their horned crowns). All were apparently obtained through illicit excavations around the time of A. Parrot's excavations at Larsa in 1933-34. For color photos of objects (b) and (d), see Strommenger 1964:pl. xxx.

The cult of the god Amurrum, eponymous deity of the Amorites, was elevated to high status during the reigns of Warad-Sin and Rim-Sin of Larsa. This may be accounted for by the fact that the family dynasty at Larsa at this time was apparently of Amorite origin; Kudur-mabuk, father of Warad-Sin and Rim-Sin, styles himself in his royal inscriptions as "father of the Amorite land" and "father of Emutbala," the latter an Amorite tribal designation. Further evidence of the veneration of the god Amurrum at Larsa during the reign of Rim-Sin is provided by a hymn dedicated to the god Amurrum and his wife Ashratum; it ends with a prayer for the life of Rim-Sin (Gurney 1989:text no. 1; von Soden 1989).

At Ugarit a divine name cognate with Amurrum is the element Amrr in the compound Qdš-w-Amrr. While in Mesopotamia the divine pair Amurrum and Ashratum (the latter is cognate with Ugaritic Aṯirat) are linked as husband and wife, in Ugarit Amrr is demoted to a subservient role as helpmate of Aṯirat.

(1-2) To the god Mardu/Amurrum, his lord,
(3-5) for the life of Rim-Sin, king of Larsa,
(6-12) Shep-Sin, son of Ipqusha, the chief physician, the servant who reverences him, dedicated to him (this) vessel of rock-crystal, whose lip is inlaid with gold (and) whose base is inlaid with silver.

REFERENCES

Frayne 1990:305-306.

ESHNUNNA

Year names of Ibbi-Sin, the last king of the Ur III dynasty, cease on tablets from Eshnunna (modern Tell Asmar) during the third year of the king. Shortly thereafter Eshnunna became independent and remained so until it was defeated by Hammu-rapi of Babylon. Most of the extant Eshnunna inscriptions stem from excavations carried out by the Oriental Institute of the University of Chicago at Tell Asmar under the direction of H. Frankfort during the years 1930-35.

IPIQ-ADAD II (2.103)

Douglas Frayne

One of the most energetic of the rulers of Eshnunna was king Ipiq-Adad II; during his lengthy reign he greatly expanded the terrritory controlled by Eshnunna, a fact proclaimed by his adoption of the title "king who enlarges Eshnunna." A brick inscription from ancient Nerebtum (modern Ishchali) commemorates his donation of the city to the goddess Eshtar-Kititum.

(1) To the goddess Eshtar-Kititum,
(2-9) Ipiq-Adad (II), mighty king, king who enlarges Eshnunna, shepherd of the black-headed (people), beloved of the god Tishpak, son of Ibal-pi-El (I)
(10) donated Nerebtum to her.

REFERENCES

Greengus 1979:1; Frayne 1990:545-546.

URUK

About the time of Sin-iddinam of Larsa a small independent kingdom was established on the Lower Euphrates with its capital at the city of Uruk. The names of eight of its rulers are known. The kingdom came to an end ca. 1800 BCE with its capture by king Rim-Sin of Larsa.

SIN-KASHID (2.104)

Douglas Frayne

German excavations at Uruk have unearthed a large palace built by Sin-kashid, the probable founder of the Old Babylonian period Uruk dynasty. Innumerable bricks and clay tablets found in the walls of the palace (and scattered over the surface of the mound) commemorate its construction in Sumerian. Of interest is Sin-kashid's title "king of Amnanum," an Amorite tribal name.

(1-7) Sin-kashid, mighty man, king of Uruk, king of the Amnanum, built his royal palace.

REFERENCES

Kärki 1980:176-177; Frayne 1990:441-444.

ANAM (2.105)

Douglas Frayne

A Sumerian inscription found on small stone tablets from Uruk commemorates king Anam's construction of the wall of Uruk, a structure said to have been built in ancient times by divine Gilgamesh.

(1-4) Anam, chief of the army of Uruk, son of Ilan-shemea,
(5-8) who restored the wall of Uruk, the ancient work of divine Gilgamesh,
(9-12) constructed in baked brick (the moat) "Water roars as it goes around."

REFERENCES

Kärki 1980:190; Frayne 1990:474-475.

SIMURRUM — IDDI(N)-SIN (2.106)

Douglas Frayne

The city of Simurrum (for a possible location see Frayne 1997b), long the target of military campaigns waged by the Ur III kings Shulgi and Amar-Suena, gained its independence after the fall of the Ur III dynasty. In Early Old Babylonian times it served as the capital of a kingdom that likely stretched along the Zagros foothill road that ran from the area of the Diyala River to Arrapha (modern Kirkuk). Inscriptions naming two of its rulers, Iddi(n)-Sin and Zabazuna, are known. One of these, a rock inscription found near the village of Bardi-Sanjian in the Bitwatah district, deals with the setting up of a table for the goddess Eshtar.

(1-3) Iddi(n)-Sin, mighty king, king of Simurrum,
(4-5) Zabazuna (is) his son —
(6-11) Kullunum rebelled and waged war against Zabazuna.
(12-21) The gods Adad, Eshtar, and Nishba heard the word of Zabazuna (and) he (Zabazuna) destroyed the city (of Kullunum) and consecrated it to those gods.
(22-25) He set up a table of the goddess Eshtar, his lady.
(26-33) He who removes my work, or erases my inscription of because of its curse incites another (to do so),
(34-53) that man — may the gods Anum, Enlil, Ninhursag, Ea, Sin, Adad, lord of weapons, Shamash, lord of judgements, Eshtar, lady of battle, Ninsiᵓana, my god (and) the god Nishba, my lord, inflict on him an evil curse.
(54-57) May they destroy his seed and rip out his foundation.
(58-66) May they not grant him heir or offspring. May life be his taboo. As (when) there is *no* harvest, may it be difficult for his people.

REFERENCES

Al-Fouadi 1978; Frayne 1990:708-709.

3. LATE OLD BABYLONIAN INSCRIPTIONS

BABYLON

About the time of king Sumu-El of Larsa, an Amorite chief named Sumu-abum installed himself as ruler of Babylon, then an inconsequential town on the Arahtum canal north of Dilbat. Subsequently, kings of an Amorite dynasty were to rule in Babylon for a period of almost 300 years. Under the reigns of kings Sin-muballiṭ and Hammu-rapi there was a great expansion in the Babylonian realms; it culminated with Hammu-rapi's defeat of kings Rim-Sin of Larsa and Silli-Sin of Eshnunna. In so doing Hammu-rapi was able establish the hegemony of Babylon over the entire land of Sumer and Akkad, a feat unparalleled since the days of the Ur III state.

HAMMU-RAPI (2.107A)

Douglas Frayne

Hammu-rapi, the sixth king of the Babylon I dynasty reigned ca. 1792-1750 BCE. The name of his 23rd year commemorates the laying of the foundation of the wall of Sippar, that of year 25 the construction of the wall itself. These deeds were commemorated in a long cone inscription known in both Sumerian and Akkadian versions.

Ancient Sippar, cult center of the sun god Utu/Shamash was located at modern Abu Hatab. Excavations were carried out at the site for the British Museum by H. Rassam (1879-82), for the Imperial Ottoman Museum by V. Scheil (1894), for the Notgemeinschaft der Deutschen Wissenschaft by J. Jordan (1927), and for the College of Arts, Baghdad University by W. al-Jadir (since 1978).

The name Sepharvaim of 2 Kgs 17:24 was connected by early scholars with Mespotamian Sippar. The equation is almost certainly false; a more likely hypothesis connects Sepharvaim with the GN Sibraim of Ezek 47:16, a city situated between Hamath and Damascus (*IDB* 4:273). Unfortunately, the old reading Sippar has stuck and is now conventional; the correct form of the name would be Sippir.

A long held Mesopotamian tradition considered Sippar to be "the eternal city" (Akkadian *āl ṣâti*) normally spared from attack and exempted from corvée obligations.

(1-12) When the god Shamash, great lord of heaven and earth, king of the gods, with his shining face, joyfully looked at me, Hammu-rapi, the prince, his favorite, granted to me everlasting kingship (and) a reign of long days,

(13-27) made firm for me the foundation of the land which he had given me to rule, spoke to me by his pure word which cannot be changed to settle the people of Sippar and Babylon in peaceful abodes, (and) laid a great commission on me to build the wall of Sippar (and) to raise its head,

(28-35) at that time, I, Hammu-rapi, mighty king, king of Babylon, reverent one, who heeds the god Shamash, beloved of the goddess Aia, who contents the god Marduk, his lord,

(36-45) by the supreme might which the god Shamash gave to me, with the levy of the army of my land, I raised the top of the foundation of the wall of Sippar with earth (until it was) like a great mountain. I built (that) high wall.

(46-50) That which from the past no king among the kings had built, for the god Samas, my lord, I grandly built.

(51-55) The name of that wall is "By the decree of the god Shamash, may Hammu-rapi have no rival."

(56-61) In my gracious reign which the god Shamash called, I cancelled corvée duty for the god Shamash for the men of Sippar, the ancient city of the god Shamash.

(62-69) I dug its canal (and) provided perpetual water for its land. I heaped up plenty and abundance. I established joy for the people of Sippar.

(70-81) They pray (Sumerian: they prayed) for my life. I did what was pleasing to the god Shamash, my lord, and the goddess Aia, my lady. I put my good name in the mouths of the people (in order) that they proclaim it daily like (that of) a god and that it not be forgotten forever.

REFERENCES

Kärki 1983:6-10; Frayne 1990:333-336.

HAMMU-RAPI (2.107B)

The name of year 33 of Hammu-rapi commemorates the digging of the canal named "Hammu-rapi is the abundance of the people." This deed is commemorated in a stone foundation tablet which also describes the construction of "Fort-Sin-muballit" (Sin-muballit was Hammu-rapi's father). The foundation tablet likely came from this fortress.

(1-9) I, Hammu-rapi, mighty king, king of Babylon, king who makes the four quarters be at peace, who achives the victory of the god Marduk, shepherd who satisfies him,
(10-16) when the gods Anum and Enlil gave to me the land of Sumer and Akkad to rule, (and) entrusted their nose-rope into my hands,
(17-20) I dug the canal Hammu-rapi-nuhush-nishi ("Hammu-rapi is the abundance of the people"), which brings abundant water to the land of Sumer and Akkad.
(21-37) I turned both its banks into cultivated areas. I kept heaping up piles of grain. I provided perpetual water for the land of Sumer and Akkad (and) gathered the scattered peoples of the land of Sumer and Akkad (and) provided for them pastures and watering places.[a] In abundance and plenty I shepherded them. I settled them in peaceful abodes.
(38-49) At that time, I, Hammu-rapi, mighty king, favorite of the great gods, by the mighty strength which the god Marduk gave to me, raised high a tall fortress with great (heaps of) earth, whose tops were like a mountain. I built (it) at the intake of the Hammu-rapi-nuhush-nishi canal.
(50-57) I named that fortress Dur-Sin-muballit-abim-walidiia ("Fort Sin-muballit, father who engendered me"). (Thus) I made the name of Sinmuballit, the father who engendered me, preeminent (throughout) the (four) quarters.

[a] Ps 23:2

REFERENCES

Sollberger and Kupper 1971:216-217; Kärki 1983:13-15; Frayne 1990:340-342.

HAMMU-RAPI (2.107C)

A copper figurine in the Louvre bears a Sumerian dedicatory inscription to the god Mardu/Amurrum for the life of Hammu-rapi.

As noted (see *COS* 2.102D above), this figurine likely came from the hoard unearthed in illicit excavations in the area of the Amurrum temple in Larsa.

(1-2) For the god Mardu/Amurrum, his god,
(3-5) for the life of Hammu-rapi, king of Babylon,
(6-11) Lu-Nanna [...], son of Sin-leʾi, fashioned for him, for his life, a suppliant statue of copper, [its] face [plat]ed with gold.
(12-13) He dedicated it to him as his servant.

REFERENCES

Sollberger and Kupper 1971:219; Frayne 1990:360.

HAMMU-RAPI (2.107D)

A limestone slab from Sippar was dedicated in Sumerian to the goddess Ashratum, wife of the god Mardu/Amurrum, for the life of Hammu-rapi.

Ashratum's name is cognate with Ugaritic ʾAṯirat. Ashratum's epithet "daughter-in-law of An" follows from the fact that her husband Amurrum was conceived by the ancient Mesopotamians to be the offspring of the sky-god An. Similarly her connection with the mountain echoes Amurrum's epithet "lord of the mountain" (*bēl šadî*).

(1-10) For [the goddess Ash]ratum, daughter-in-law of the god An, the one suitable for ladyship, lady of voluptuousness and joy, tenderly cared for in the mountain, lady with patient mercy, who prays reverently for her spouse, his lady,
(11-13) for the li[fe] of Hammu-r[api], king of the Amo[rites],
(14-20) Itur-ashd[um], chief of the [Si]lakku canal (district), son of Shuba-il[an], the servant who re[verences her, set up] as a wonder a protective

genius befitting her d[ivi]nity, [in her] beloved residence.

REFERENCES

Sollberger and Kupper 1971:219; Frayne 1990:359-360.

SAMSU-ILUNA (2.108)

Douglas Frayne

A royal inscription of Hammu-rapi's son Samsu-iluna (the seventh king of the Babylon I dynasty who reigned ca. 1749-1712 BCE) known in both Sumerian and Akkadian versions on clay cylinders excavated at Tutub (modern Hafaji) records the construction of "Fort Samsu-iluna" on the banks of the Turul (Diyala) river. The deed was also commemorated in the name of year 24 of Samsu-iluna.

(1-6) Samsu-iluna, mighty king, king of Babylon, king of Kish, king who makes the four quarters be at peace,
(7-19) king who at the order of the gods An and Enlil slew all those who engaged in hostility against him, shepherd to whom the goddess Inanna gave her favorable omen and help, who bound the hands of all those who were disloyal, who made all evil ones disappear in the land,
(20-24) who caused bright daylight to come forth for the numerous people, foremost first-born son of Hammu-rapi, the lord who extended the land,
(25-41) king who subjugated the land of Idamaraz from the border of Gutium to the border of Elam with his mighty weapon, who conquered the numerous people of the land of Idamaraz, who demolished all the various fortresses of the land of Warum who had resisted him, who achieved his victory and made his strength apparent.
(42-49) After two months had passed, having set free and given life to the people of the land of Idamaraz whom he had taken captive, (and) the troops of Eshnunna, as many prisoners as he had taken,
(50-56) he (re)built the various fortresses of the land of Warum which he had destroyed (and) regathered and resettled its scattered people.
(57-65) At that time, Samsu-iluna, mighty man, in order that the people who dwelled along the banks of the Turul and Taban rivers might reside in peaceful abodes, that they might have no one who terrified them, (and) in order that all the land might sing the praise of his mighty valor,
(66-76) in the course of two months, on the bank of the Turul river, he built Fort Samsu-iluna. He dug its (surrounding) moat, piled up its earth there, formed its bricks, (and) built its wall. He raised its head like a mountain.
(77-89) On account of this the gods An, Enlil, Marduk, Enki, and goddess Inanna determined as his destiny (and) gave to him a mighty weapon that has no rival, (and) a life that like (that of) the gods Nanna and Utu is eternal.
(90-94) The name of that wall is "The god Enlil has made the land of those who had become hostile to him bow down to Samsu-iluna."

REFERENCES

Sollberger and Kupper 1971:226-227; Kärki 1983:39-43; Frayne 1990:388-391.

AMMI-DITANA (2.109)

Douglas Frayne

Ammi-ditana, Hammu-rapi's grandson and ninth king of the Babylon I dynasty, reigned ca. 1683-1647 BCE. A Sumerian inscription known from an original cone fragment and a much later Neo-Babylonian tablet copy commemorates his construction of the wall of Babylon.

(i.1-12) I, Ammi-di[tan]a, mighty king, king of Babylon, king of Kish, king of the land of Sumer and Ak[kad], king of all the Amorite land, I, descendant of Sumu-la-Il, [s]on of the great champion Abi-eshuh, favor[ite] of the god Enlil, belo[ved of the goddess ...]

Lacuna

(ii.1-4) In Babylon, the city of my kingship, he proc[laimed] his lofty decree [in] heaven and earth.
(ii.5-10) At that time, by the wisdom that the god En[ki verily granted] to me,

Lacuna

(ii.1′-3′) I made (Babylon) dwell in an abode of joy.
(ii.4′-8′) The name of that wall is "May Asarluhi turn into clay in the underworld the one who makes a breach in the clay (of the wall)."

(Colophon): (Property) of Bel-ushallim, son of D[a-bi]bi, the exorcist.

REFERENCES

Kärki 1983:45; Frayne 1990:411-412.

EKALLATUM — SHAMSHI-ADDU (2.110)

Douglas Frayne

Arguably the most energetic rulers of Old Babylonian times was the king Shamshi-Addu. The origins of this remarkable figure are obscure; while we know the name of his father (Ila-kabkabu) and his brother (Aminum), the original seat of his dynasty is still uncertain (it may have been ancient Ekallatum, probably modern Tell Haikal 17 km north of Aššur). Because of the campaigns directed by king Naram-Sin of Eshnunna against Ekallatum and Aššur eighteen years after Shamshi-Addu's accession to the throne, Shamshi-Addu fled southwards, finding refuge in Babylon. Shortly after the death of Naram-Sin of Eshnunna he returned to Ekallatum and three years later conquered Aššur. The king continued his conquests, founding a new capital city at Shubat-Enlil (modern Tell Leilan) in the Upper Habur region. His campaigns in the west culminated with the taking of the city of Mari and the installation of his son Iasmah-Addu as city ruler there.

In a long inscription found on stone foundation tablets from Aššur Shamshi-Addu records the construction of the Aššur temple equating it with the temple of the god Enlil.

(1-17) Shamshi-Addu king of the universe, builder of the temple of the god Aššur, pacifier of the land between the Tigris and Euphrates, by the command of the god Aššur who loves him, whom Anu and Enlil called by name for greatness among the kings who went before:
(18-58) The temple of the god Enlil which Erishum (I), the son of Ilu-shumma, had built and which had become dilapidated, and I abandoned it. I constructed the temple of the god Enlil, my lord, the fearful dais, the large chapel, the seat of the god Enlil, my lord, which were methodically made by the skilled work of the building trade within my city Aššur. I roofed the temple with cedar (beams). I erected in the rooms cedar doors with silver and gold *stars*. (Under) the walls of the temple (I placed) silver, gold, lapis lazuli, (and) carnelian; cedar resin, best oil, honey, and ghee I mixed in the mortar. I methodically made the temple of the god Enlil, my lord, and called it Eamkurkurra, "The Temple — Wild Bull of the Lands," the temple of the god Enlil, my lord, within my city, Aššur.
(59-72) When I built the temple of the god Enlil, my lord, the prices in my city Aššur, (were): two kor of barley could be purchased for one shekel of silver; fifteen minas of wool for one shekel of silver; and two seahs of oil for one shekel of silver, according to the prices of my city Aššur.
(73-87) At that time I received the tribute of the kings of Tukrish and of the king of the Upper Land, within my city, Aššur. I set up my great name and my monumental inscription in the land of Lebanon of the shore of the Great Sea.[a]
(88-98) When the temple becomes dilapidated: may whoever among the kings, my sons, renovates the temple anoint my clay inscriptions with oil, make a sacrifice, and return them to their places.
(99-135) Who(ever) does not anoint my clay inscriptions and my monumental inscriptions with oil, does not make a sacrifice, does not return them to their places, (but) instead alters my monumental inscriptions, removes my name and writes his (own) name (or) buries (the monumental inscriptions) in the earth (or) throws (them) into the water: may the gods Shamash, Enlil, Adad and Sharru-matim pluck the offspring of that king; may he and his army not prevail in the face of a king who opposes him; may the god Nergal take away by force his treasure and the treasure of his land; may the goddess Eshtar, mistress of battle, break his weapon, and the weapons of his army; may the god Sin, "god of my head," be an evil demon to him forever.

[a] Jos 9:1

REFERENCES

Meissner 1926:12-27; Grayson 1972:19-21; Grayson 1987:47-51.

MARI

The ancient city of Mari (modern Tell Hariri) was a major player on the Mesopotamian stage from Early Dynastic to Old Babylonian times. The site has been excavated by a long series of French expeditions led by A. Parrot (1933-38, 1951-74) and J.-Cl. Margueron (since 1979).

After a long period of rule by "viceroys" (*šakkanakkū*) in the Sargonic, Ur III and early Old Babylonian periods, the Amorite leader Iahdun-Lim was installed as "king" (LUGAL) in Mari. In a lengthy inscription found on foundation tablets from the Shamash temple in Mari he records his defeat of a coalition of Amorite tribes on the Upper Euphrates and his trip to the Mediterranean Sea.

IAHDUN-LIM (2.111)

Douglas Frayne

(1-16) To the god Shamash, king of heaven and earth, judge of gods and mankind, whose concern is justice, to whom truth has been given as a gift, shepherd of the black-headed (people), resplendent god, judge of those endowed with life, who is favorably inclined to supplications, who heeds prayers, who accepts entreaties, who gives a long-lasting life of joy to him who reveres him, who is the lord of Mari:
(17-27) Iahdun-Lim, son of Iaggid-Lim, king of Mari and the land of Hana, opener of canals, builder of walls, erector of steles proclaiming (his) name, provider of abundance and plenty for his people, who makes whatever (is needed) appear in his land, mighty king, magnificent youth,
(28-33) when the god Shamash agreed to his supplications and listened to his words, the god Shamash quickly came and went at the side of Iahdun-Lim.
(34-40) From distant days when the god El built Mari, no king resident in Mari reached the sea, reached the mountains of cedar and boxwood, the great mountains, and cut down their trees,
(41-50) But Iahdun-Lim, son of Iaggid-Lim, powerful king, wild bull of kings, by means of his strength and overpowering might went to the shore of the sea, and made a great offering (befitting) his kingship to the Sea. His troops bathed themselves in the Sea.
(51-66) (Next) he entered into the cedar and boxwood mountains, the great mountains, and cut down these trees — box, cedar, cypress, and *elammakum*. He made a commemorative monument, established his fame, and proclaimed his might. He made that land on the shore of the Sea submit, made it subject to his decree, and made it follow him. Having imposed a permanent tribute on them, they now bring their tribute to him.
(67-91) In that same year, — Laʾum, king of Samanum and the land of the Ubrabium, Bahlukullim, king of Tuttul and the land of the Amnanum, Aialum king of Abattum and the land of the Rabbum — these kings rebelled against him. The troops of Sumu-Epuh of the land of Iamhad came as auxiliary troops (to rescue him) and in the city of Samanum the tribes gathered together against him, but by means of (his) mighty weapon he defeated these three kings of ... He vanquished their troops and their auxiliaries and inflicted a defeat on them. He heaped up their dead bodies. He tore down their walls and made them into mounds of rubble.
(92-98) The city of Haman, of the tribe of Haneans, which all the leaders of Hana had built, he destroyed and made into mounds of rubble. Now, he defeated their king, Kasuri-Hala. Having taken away their population he controlled the banks of the Euphrates.
(99-107) For his own life he built the temple of the god Shamash, his lord, a temple whose construction was perfect with finished workmanship, befitting his divinity. He installed him in his majestic dwelling. He named that temple Egirzalanki ("House—rejoicing of heaven and earth").
(108-117) May the god Shamash, who lives in that temple, grant to Iahdun-Lim, the builder of his temple, the king beloved of his heart, a mighty weapon which overwhelms the enemies (and) a long reign of happiness and years of joyous abundance, forever.
(118-131) (As for) the one who destroys that temple, who ... it to evil and no good, who does not strengthen its foundation, does not set up what has fallen down, and cuts its regular offerings off from it, who effaces my name or has it effaced and writes his own name previously not there, or has it written there, or because of (these) curses incites another to do so,
(132-136) that man, whether he be king, viceroy, mayor, or common man,
(137-157) may the god Enlil, judge of the gods make his kingship smaller than that of any other king. May the god Sin, the elder brother among the gods, his brothers, inflict on him a great curse. May the god Nergal, the lord of the weapon, smash his weapon in order that he not confront warriors. May the god Ea, king of destiny, assign him an evil destiny (and) may the goddess bride Aia, the great lady, put in a bad word about him before the god Shamash forever. May the god Bunene, the great vizier of the god Shamash, cut his throat;

may he take away his progeny and may his offspring and descendants not walk before the god Shamash.

REFERENCES

Text: Dossin 1955:1-28; Sollberger and Kupper 1971:245-249; Frayne 1990:604-608. Studies: Malamat 1989:41-43, 107-121.

ZIMRI-LIM (2.112)

Douglas Frayne

After a period of rule over Mari by Shamshi-Addu of Ekallatum and his son Iasmah-Addu, Zimri-Lim, son of Iahdun-Lim, was able to reassert control of the "Lim" dynasty over Mari. He reigned in Mari for a period of about 15 years until his defeat at the hands of Hammu-rapi of Babylon.

An inscription known from four clay tablet copies records Zimri-Lim's building of an ice-house for the god Dagan in Terqa.

(1-4) Zimri-Lim, son of Iahdun-Lim, king of Mari, [Tuttul], and the land [of Hana],
(5-8) builder of an i[ce]-house, (something) which formerly n[o] k[ing had built] on the bank of the Euphrat[es],
(9) had ice of ... brought over and
(11-14) [had] an ic[e]-house [built] on the bank of the Euphrat[es], in Terq[a, the *city*] beloved of the god [Dagan].

REFERENCES

Sollberger and Kupper 1971:249; Frayne 1990:625.

4. NEO-ASSYRIAN INSCRIPTIONS

SHALMANESER III (2.113)

KURKH MONOLITH (2.113A)

K. Lawson Younger, Jr.

Inscribed on a large stone stela discovered at Kurkh, this version of the annals of Shalmaneser III is identified by Schramm as Recension A (*EAK* 2:70-72, 87-90). Since the text ends abruptly with the last narrated event being the battle of Qarqar (853 BCE), the inscription seems to date from 853-852 BCE. The monument was apparently carved in great haste resulting in numerous scribal errors (Tadmor 1961a:143-144). This is quite unfortunate since the stela contains the most detailed extant account of the battle of Qarqar in which Ahab, king of Israel, participated in an alliance with other kings of the west in opposition to Shalmaneser III.

(i.29b-36a)

In the month of Iyyar, the thirteenth day, I departed from Nineveh. I crossed the Tigris River (and) I traversed Mount Hasamu and Mount Diḫnunu. I approached the city of Laʾlaʾtu, which belonged to Aḫuni,[1] (the man) of Bīt-Adini.[2] [a] The fear of the splendor of Aššur, my lord, overwhelmed them. In order to save their lives they went up(stream). I razed, destroyed and burned the city. I departed from the city of Laʾlaʾtu. I approached the city of Tīl-Barsip,[3] the fortified city of Aḫuni, (the man) of Bīt-Adini. Aḫuni, (the man) of Bīt-Adini trusted in the massed might of his troops, and he became hostile against me in order to make war and battle. With the support of Aššur and the great gods, my lords, I fought with him. I decisively defeated him. I confined him to his city.

a Amos 1:5

[1] While Aḫuni paid tribute and gave up hostages to Aššurnaṣirpal II, he rebelled against Assyrian rule under Shalmaneser III. See *PNA* 1:84-85.

[2] For Bīt Adini, see Dion 1997:86-96; Millard 1993; Sader 1987:47-98. For Shalmaneser's campaign against Bīt Adini, see Ikeda 1999:271-273. For the equation with Bet-Eden (Amos 1:5), see Hallo 1960:38f.

[3] For Til Barsip (Tell Aḫmar), see Dornemann 1997b; Bunnens 1995. The hieroglyphic Luwian inscriptions indicate that the Luwian name of the city was Masuwari (see Hawkins 1996-97:110-111).

I departed from the city of Tīl-Barsip.[4] I approached the city of Burmarʾina, which belonged to Aḫuni, (the man) of Bīt-A[dini]. Besieging the city, I captured it. I felled with the sword 300 of their fighting men. I made a pile of heads in front of his city. In the course of my advance, I received the tribute of Ḫapini, the Tīl-Abnīan, Gaʾuni, the Sarugaean,[5] Giri-Adad, the Immerinaean: silver, gold, oxen, sheep, (and) wine.

(i.36b-39)
I departed from the city of Burmarʾina. I crossed the Euphrates in rafts (made of inflated) goatskins.[6] I received the tribute of Qatazilu, the Kummuḫite:[7] silver, gold, oxen, sheep, (and) wine. I approached the city of Paqaruḫbuni,[8] one of the cities belonging to Aḫuni, (the man) of Bīt-Adini, which is on the opposite bank of the Euphrates. I decisively defeated his land. I laid waste his cities. I filled the wide plain with the corpses (lit. "defeat") of his warriors. I felled with the sword 1,300 of their battle troops.

(i.40-41a)
I departed from the city of Paqaruḫbuni. I approached the cities of Mutalli, the Gurgumite.[9] I received the tribute of Mutalli, the Gurgumite: silver, gold, oxen, sheep, wine, (and) his daughter with her rich dowry.

(i.41b-51a)
I departed from the city of Gurgum. I approached the city of Lutibu, the fortified city of Ḫayāni,[10] the Samʾalite. Ḫayāni, the Samʾalite, Sapalulme, the Patinaean,[11] Aḫuni, (the man) of Bīt-Adini, (and) Sangara, the Carchemishite, put their trust in each other. They prepared for war. They marched against me to do battle. With the exalted power of the divine standard which goes before me (and) with the fierce weapons which Aššur, my lord, gave, I fought with them. I decisively defeated them. I felled with the sword their fighting men. Like Adad, I rained down upon them a devastating flood. I piled them in ditches (and) filled the extensive plain with the corpses of their warriors. Like wool, I dyed the mountain with their blood. I took away from them (lit. "him," i.e. Ḫayāni) numerous chariots (and) teams of horses. I made a pile of heads in front of his city. I razed, destroyed (and) burned his cities.

At that time, I praised the majesty of the great gods; I proclaimed the valor of Aššur and Šamaš. I made a large royal statue of myself (and) I wrote on it my heroic deeds (and) my victorious achievements. I erected (it) before the source of the Saluara River, at the foot of Mt. Amanus.

(i.51b-ii.10a)
I departed from Mt. Amanus. I crossed the Orontes River. I approached the city of Aliṣir (or Alimuš), the fortified city of Sapalulme, the Patinaean. Sapalulme, the Patinaean — in order to save his life — received into his military forces Aḫuni, (the man) of Bīt-Adini, Sangara, the Carchemishite, Ḫayāni, the Samʾalite, Katê, the Quean, Piḫirim, the Ḫilukaean,[12] Bur-Anate, the Yasbuqaean, Adānu, the Yaḫanaean. By the command of Aššur, my lord, I scattered their combined forces. Besieging the city, I captured it. I carried off valuable booty — numerous chariots (and) teams of horses. I felled with the sword 700 of their fighting men. In the midst of the battle, I captured Bur-Anate, the Iasbuqaean. I ca[ptured] the great cities of the Patinaean. I overwhe[lmed] like ruin mounds of the flood [the cities on the shore of the] upper [sea] of the land Amurru, also called the western sea. I received the tribute of the kings on the seashore. I marched justly (and) victoriously throughout the extensive region of the seashore. I made a statue of my lordship, establishing my reputation (lit. "name") for eternity. I erected (it) by the sea. I climbed Mt. Amanus (and) cut down beams of cedar (and) juniper. I marched to Mt. Atalur,[13] where the image of Anum-ḫirbe stands. (And) I erected my image with his image.

(ii.30b-35a)
In the eponymy of Aššur-bēlū-kaʾʾin,[14] in the month of Iyyar, the thirteenth day, I departed from Nineveh. I crossed the Tigris (and) I traversed Mounts Hasamu and Diḫnunu. I <approached> the city of Tīl-Barsip, the fortified city of Aḫuni, (the man) of Bīt-Adini. I captured (it). Aḫuni, (the man) of Bīt-Adini, in the face of the splendor of my fierce weapons and my ferocious battle array, crossed the Euphrates, which was [in flood], in order to save his life. He crossed over to strange lands. By the command of Aššur, the great lord, my <lord>, I seized the cities of Tīl-Barsip,

[4] For the reading of Tīl-Barsip in this line (i.33), see Yamada 1995 and Grayson *RIMA* 3:15 (note i.33).
[5] See Dion 1997:46, n. 106.
[6] See *CAD* D 202, s.v. *dušû*.
[7] The name Kummuḫ was applied to both the land and its capital city, which should be identified with the enormous site, *höyük* and lower town, of Samsat (Hawkins 1995b:92-93).
[8] Paqaruḫbuni (Paqaraḫubuni in Aššur Clay Tablet, *RIMA* 3:38, iii.17) was located in the modern province of Gaziantep (Hawkins 1995b:94).
[9] The land of Gurgum was located in the Maraş plain (Hawkins 1995b:93-94).
[10] Ḫayya of the Kulamuwa Inscription. See *COS* 2.30, n. 2. Samʾal, also known as Bīt-Gabbari, is modern Zinjirli.
[11] Patina is equated with Umq/Unqi, the modern Amuq, the plain of Antioch (Hawkins 1995b:94-95).
[12] The land of Ḫilakku was Plain and Rough Cilicia.
[13] Or Mt. Lallar. For a discussion of the mountain's name, see Grayson, *RIMA* 3:17, n. ii.10.
[14] I.e., 856 BCE. See Millard 1994:27. For this individual, see *PNA* 1:172.

Alligu, [Nappigu], (and) Rugulitu as my royal cities. I settled Assyrians in their midst. I founded inside palaces as my royal residences. I renamed Tīl-Barsip as Kār-Shalmaneser, Nappigu as Līta-Aššur, Alligu as Aṣbat-lā-kunu, (and) Rugulitu as Qibīt-[Aššur].

(ii.35b-40a)[15]

At that time, the city of (Ana)-Aššur-utēr-aṣbat, which the people of the land of Ḫatti call Pitru[b] (and) which is on the River Sagu[ra by the opposite bank] of the Euphrates, and the city of Mutkīnu, which is on the bank of the Euphrates, which Tiglath-pileser (I), my ancestor, a prince who preceded me, had established — at the time of Aššur-rabi (II), king of Assyria, the king of Aram[16] had taken (these two cities) away by force — I restored these cities. I settled Assyrians in their midst. While I was residing in the city of Kār-Shalmaneser, I received the tribute of the kings of the seashore and kings on the banks of the Euphrates: silver, gold, tin, bronze, bronze (and) iron vessels, oxen, sheep, garments with multi-colored trim, and linen garments.

(ii.78b-81a)

In the eponymy of Dayān-Aššur,[17] in the month of Iyyar, the fourteenth day, I departed from Nineveh. I crossed the Tigris. I approached the cities of Giammu on the River Baliḫ. They were afraid of my lordly fearfulness (and) the splendor of my fierce weapons; and with their own weapons they killed Giammu, their master. I entered the cities of Saḫlala and Tīl-ša-turaḫi. I took my gods into his palaces; (and) celebrated the *tašīltu*-festival in his palaces. I opened his treasury (and) saw his stored-away wealth. I carried off his possessions (and) property. I brought (them) to my city, Aššur.

(ii.81b-86a)

I departed from the city of Saḫlala. I approached the city of Kār-Shalmaneser. I crossed the Euphrates in its flood, for a second time[17a] in rafts (made of inflated) goatskins. In the city of Ana-Aššur-utēr-aṣbat, which is by the opposite bank of the Euphrates on the River Sagura (and) which the people of the land of Ḫatti call the city of Pitru, in (this city) I received the tribute of the kings on the opposite bank of the Euphrates — Sangara, the Carchemishite, Kundašpu, the Kummuḫite, Arame, (the man) of Bīt-Agūsi, Lalla, the Melidite, Ḫayāni, (the man) of Bīt-Gabbari, Qalparuda, the Patinaean, (and) Qalparuda, the Gurgumite: silver, gold, tin, bronze, (and) bronze bowls.

(ii.86b-102)

I departed from the Euphrates. I approached the city of Aleppo (Ḫalman). They were afraid to fight. They seized my feet. I received their tribute of silver (and) gold. I made sacrifices before Hadad[18] of Aleppo (Ḫalman).

I departed from the city of Aleppo (Ḫalman). I approached the cities of Irḫulēni,[19] the Hamathite.[20] [c] I captured Adennu, Pargâ, (and) Arganâ, his royal cities.[21] I carried off captives, his valuables, (and) his palace possessions. I set fire to his palaces.

I departed from the city of Arganâ. I approached the city of Qarqar.[22] I razed, destroyed and burned the city of Qarqar, his royal city. 1,200 chariots, 1,200 cavalry, (and) 20,000 troops of Hadad-ezer (*Adad-idri*)[23] of Damascus;[24] 700 chariots, 700 cavalry, (and) 10,000 troops of Irḫulēni, the Hamathite; 2,000 chariots,[25] (and) 10,000 troops of Ahab,[d] the Israelite (*Sirʾalāia*); 500 troops of Byblos;[26] 1,000 troops of Egypt;[27] 10 chariots (and) 10,000 troops of the land of Irqanatu (Irqata);[28] 200 troops of Matinu-baʾal of the city of Arvad;[29] [e] 200 troops of the land of Usanatu (Usnu);[30] 30 chariots (and) [ ],000 troops of Adon-baᶜal of the land of

b Num 22:5; Deut 23:5

c 2 Sam 8:9-10; 2 Kgs 14:28; 1 Chr 18:9-10

d 1 Kgs 17, etc.

e Gen 10:18; Ezek 27:8, 11; 1 Chr 1:16

[15] Cf. Aššur-dan II (*RIMA* 2:133-135; lines 23-32, 60-67); and Adad-nirari II (*RIMA* 2:150-151, 49b-60). Also possibly the Assyrian Chronicle, Fragment 4 (Grayson *ABC* 189); but see Pitard 1996:299.

[16] MAN KUR *a-ru-mu*. The king's identity is enigmatic. Malamat (1973:142) suggests Hadad-ezer (2 Sam 8:3; 10:16). But see Ikeda 1999:275.

[17] 853 BCE. See Millard 1994:27, 93. For the individual, see *PNA* 1:368.

[17a] Yamada (1998:92-94) argues that the phrase *ša šanûtēšu* means "another time, again," not "for a second time."

[18] Adad the stormgod, the city god of Aleppo. Cf. also the Sefire Inscription A (line 10), *COS* 2.82.

[19] For Irḫulēni, see Hawkins 1976-80a:162.

[20] For Hamath, see Hawkins 1972-75a:67-70; Dion 1997:137-170.

[21] These Hamathite campaigns with the captures of the cites Pargâ, Adâ (=Adennu), Qarqar, and Aštamaku (captured in the 848 campaign) are represented in the reliefs of Shalmaneser's bronze gates. See the discussion of Marcus 1987.

[22] See Dornemann 1997a.

[23] There is disagreement whether Hadad-ezer (Adad-idri) should be equated with the Ben-Hadad (II) of 1 Kgs 20-22. Favoring this identification, see Hallo 1960:39-40; Wiseman 1972-75. Against this identificaiton, see Pitard 1987:114-125; 1992a; and Kuan 1995:36-38; *PNA* 1:46.

[24] For the name KUR ANŠE-*šú* (*Imērišu* / *Ša-imērišu*), see Pitard 1987:14-17.

[25] There is debate over the accuracy of the numbers in this passage and especially the number of chariots attributed to Ahab. Some scholars argue that this is an accurate number (e.g. Elat 1975:29; Briquel-Chatonnet 1992:80-81; Kuan 1995:34-36). Others argue that this is a scribal error (e.g. Naʾaman 1976:97-102; Mitchell *CAH*[3] 3/1:479). De Odorico (1995:103-107) discusses the problem and concludes that the scribe decided on what had to be the approximate size of the Syro-Palestinian army (≈ 70,000) and tenfolded some numbers until he got this value.

[26] Tadmor argues for the emendation: *Gu-<bal>-a-a* "Byblos" (1961:144-145).

[27] *Mu-uṣ-ra-a-a* = "Egyptian." See Tadmor 1961:144-145; Borger *TUAT* 1/4:361, n. 92a; and Redford 1992:339. However, Lemaire (1993:152) and Dion (1997:164-165) read *Ṣumur*.

[28] Tell ᶜArqā northeast of Tripoli, Lebanon (Borger *TUAT* 1:361, n. 92b). See also Thalmann 1991. Cf. Gen 10:17.

[29] See Badre 1997; Bonatz 1993; Dion 1997:113-136.

[30] See Dion 1997:185, n. 66.

Šianu (Siyannu);[31] 1,000 camels of Gindibuʾ of Arabia;[32] [ ] hundred troops of Baʾasa, (the man) of Bīt-Ruḫubi, the Ammonite[33] — these 12 kings[34] he took as his allies.

They marched against me [to do] war and battle. With the supreme forces which Aššur, my lord, had given me (and) with the mighty weapons which the divine standard, which goes before me, had granted me, I fought with them. I decisively defeated[35] them from the city of Qarqar to the city of Gilzau.[36] I felled with the sword 14,000 troops,[37] their fighting men. Like Adad, I rained down upon them a devastating flood. I spread out their corpses (and) I filled the plain. <I felled> with the sword their extensive troops. I made their blood flow in the *wadis*(?)[38] [[39]]. The field was too small for laying flat their bodies (lit. "their lives"); the broad countryside had been consumed in burying them. I blocked the Orontes River with their corpses as with a causeway.[40] In the midst of this battle I took away from them chariots, cavalry, (and) teams of horses.

[31] See Bounni and al-Maqdissi 1992.

[32] Ephʿal 1982:75-76.

[33] The debate concerning the last allied participant has centered primarily on the word KUR *A-ma-na-a-a*. Commonly scholars (Luckenbill *ARAB* 1:§611; Oppenheim *ANET* 279; Naʾaman 1976:98, n. 20; Millard 1992:35) have understood this to refer to Ammon, the small Transjordanian state (Gen 19:38, etc.). Some scholars (Cogan 1984:255-259; Dion 1997:176, 186; *PNA* 1:275) have understood the word to refer to Amanah, the Anti-Lebanon mountain range (cf. 2 Kgs 5:12Q, Song 4:8). Moreover, beside the similarity of place name, Forrer (1928:134, 328) equated the patronym with Rehob, father of Hadad-ezer of Sobah, named in 2 Sam 8:3, suggesting Rehob was the dynastic name of the kings of Sobah. For a fuller discussion, see Rendsburg 1991.

[34] Possibly an erroneous addition since only eleven kings are listed (see Grayson *RIMA* 3:23, note ii.90-95); or possibly the twelfth king was erroneously omitted (Tadmor 1961:144-145); or as Reinhold suggests "das angegriffene Karkar" was the twelfth state (1989:125); or "Baʾasa, (the man) of Bīt-Ruḫubi, the Ammonite" is really a reference to two entities: Beth-Rehob and Ammon (Kuan 1995:32-34; Ikeda 1999:278); or possi-bly a rounding of the number to an even dozen, a conventional number with symbolic significance (De Odorico 1995:133-136). The last option seems preferable. Interestingly, one text of Shalmaneser III, carved along with a second inscription into a rock face at the Tigris' source, gives the number of the allied enemies as "15 cities of the seashore" (*RIMA* 3:94-95, line 21).

[35] While Shalmaneser may have captured the city of Qarqar, most scholars believe that his claim to victory over the coalition in the ensuing battle was in reality an Assyrian defeat, since he returned in 849 (his 10th year), 848 (his 11th year) and 845 (his 14th year) to fight against this same coalition with little greater success (see Hawkins 1972-75a:67). The two rock face inscriptions at the source of the Tigris refer to the "4th time" in which Shalmaneser faced this coalition (see *RIMA* 3:94-95, 95-96). There may have been some limited successes in these campaigns. E.g., in 848 he was apparently able to capture Aštammaku (see below *COS* 2.113B, ii.68-iii.15). For the resistance to Shalmaneser, see Dion 1995c.

[36] URU *gíl-za-ú*. However, Fort Shalmaneser Stone Throne Base (*RIMA* 3:107 line 32) and Fort Shalmaneser Door Sill (*RIMA* 3:107 line 27) read: URU *di-il-zi-a-ú*.

[37] In later versions of the annals, the number of enemies killed is 20,500, 25,000 and 29,000. See the discussions of De Odorico (1995:107) and Mayer (1995:46-47).

[38] Grayson *RIMA* 3:24.

[39] "The end of the line is incomprehensible" (Grayson *RIMA* 3:24, n. ii.99).

[40] Grayson (*RIMA* 3:24) and Borger (*TUAT* 1:362) translate *titurri* "bridge." See also *AHw* 1363 s.v. *titurum, titurru* "bridge." However, in this context with this verb (*kesēru* "to dam, stop up, clog, etc.") *CAD*'s "causeway" seems better. See *CAD* K 313.

REFERENCES

Text: 3 R pla. 7-8; *RIMA* 3:11-24; Brinkman 1978. Translations and studies: *DOTT* 47-49; *ARAB* 1:§§594-611; *ANET* 277-278; *TUAT* 1:360-362; Tadmor 1961a; Schramm *EAK* 2:70-72, 87-90; Kuan 1995:27-47; Dion 1997:184-190.

ANNALS: AŠŠUR CLAY TABLETS (2.113B)

K. Lawson Younger, Jr.

Written on clay tablets from Aššur dating to 842 BCE, this edition of the annals is identified as Recension C.[1] It narrates the military campaigns of Shalmaneser III in chronological order from the accession year to the sixteenth year by using regnal year formula: "in my Xth regnal year (*palû*)." It includes narration of Shalmaneser's campaigns against the coalition of kings that fought him in years 853, 849, 848 and 845 BCE. The text concludes with a summary of Shalmaneser's mighty achievements: a geographically arranged résumé of his conquests, a description of the appointment of governors, the increase of agricultural production, and the growth of the Assyrian army.[2]

(ii.19b-33)
In my sixth regnal year, I departed from Nineveh. I approached the cities on the banks of the Baliḫ (Paliḫ) River. They became afraid in the face of my mighty weapons (and) they killed Giammu, their city ruler. I entered the city of Tīl-turaḫi. I

[1] Schramm *EAK* 2:73-75. A unique feature of this text is the use of dividing lines on the tablet to separate the regnal years.

[2] Many of these are motifs first encountered in the annals of Tiglath-pileser I (see Grayson *RIMA* 2:7-8).

claimed the city as my own.

I departed from the Baliḫ (Paliḫ) River. I crossed the Euphrates in its flood. I received the tribute of the kings of the land of Ḫatti.

I departed from the land of Ḫatti. I approached the city of Aleppo (Ḫalman). I made sacrifices before Hadad of Aleppo (Ḫalman).

I departed from Aleppo (Ḫalman). I approached the city of Qarqar. Hadad-ezer (Adad-idri), the Damascene, (and) Irḫulēni, the Hamathite, together with twelve kings of the shore of the sea, trusted in their combined forces; (and) they marched against me to do war and battle. I fought with them. I felled with the sword 25,000 troops,[3] their fighting men. I took away from them their chariots, their cavalry (and) their military equipment. In order to save their lives they ran away. I boarded ships (and) I went out upon the sea.

(ii.55-67)
In my tenth regnal year, I crossed the Euphrates for the eighth time. I razed, destroyed, (and) burned the cities of Sangara, the Carchemishite.

I departed from the cities of the Carchemishite. I approached the cities of Arame. I captured the city Arnê, his royal city. I razed, destroyed (and) burned (it) together with 100 cities in its environs. I slaughtered their people. I plundered them.

At that time, Hadad-ezer (Adad-idri), the Damascene, (and) Irḫulēni, the Hamathite, together with twelve kings on the shore of the sea, trusted in their combined forces; and they marched against me to do war and battle. I fought with them. I decisively defeated them. I took away from them (their) chariots, their cavalry, (and) their military equipment. In order to save their lives they ran away.

(ii.68-iii.15)
In my eleventh regnal year, I departed from Nineveh. I crossed the Euphrates in its flood for the ninth time. I captured 97 cities of Sangara. I captured, razed, destroyed (and) burned 100 cities of Arame. I took to the slopes of Mt. Amanus.

I crossed Mt. Yaraqu (and) I descended to the cities of the people of Hamath. I captured the city of Aštammaku[4] together with 89 cities. I slaughtered their people. I plundered them.

At that time, Hadad-ezer (Adad-idri), the Damascene, (and) Irḫulēni, the Hamathite, together with twelve kings on the shore of the sea, trusted in their combined forces; and they marched against me to do war and battle. I fought with them. I decisively defeated them. I felled with the sword 10,000 troops, their fighting men. I took away from them (their) chariots, their cavalry, (and) their military equipment. On my return, I captured Aparāzu, the fortified city of Arame.

At that time, I received the tribute of Qalparunda: silver, gold, tin, horses, donkeys, oxen, sheep, blue-dyed wool, (and) linen garments. I climbed Mt. Amanus; (and) I cut beams of cedar.

(iii.24-33)
In my fourteenth regnal year, I mustered (the troops of my) extensive land in countless numbers. With 120,000 troops[5] I crossed the Euphrates in its flood.

At that time, Hadad-ezer (Adad-idri), the Damascene, (and) Irḫulēni, the Hamathite, together with twelve kings on the shore of the sea, above and below, mustered their troops in countless numbers. They marched against me. I fought with them. I decisively defeated them. I destroyed their chariots (and) their cavalry. I took away their military equipment. In order to save their lives they ran away.

(iv.26-36)
Conqueror from the upper and lower seas of the land of Nairi and the great sea of the west as far as Amanus mountain range, I ruled over the land of Hatti in its entirety. I (lit. "he") conquered from the source of the Tigris to the source of the Euphrates. I devastated like a flood from the land of Enzi to the land of Suḫni (Suʾunu), from the land of Suḫni to the land of Melid, from the land of Melid to the land of Daiēnu, from the land of Daiēnu to the city of Arṣaškun, from the city of Arṣaškun to the land of Gilzānu,[6] (and) from the land of Gilzānu to the city of Ḫubuškia.[7]

(iv.37-39)
In the lands and mountains over which I ruled, I appointed governors everywhere and imposed upon them tax, tribute, (and) corvée.[8]

(iv.40-44)
The gods Ninurta and Nergal, who love my priesthood, gave to me the wild beasts and commanded me to hunt. I killed from my ... chariot 373 wild bulls (and) 399 lions with my valorous assault. I

[3] See *COS* 2.113A note 37.

[4] For the identification of Aštammaku with Stūma between Idlib and Rīḫa, see Sader 1987:225.

[5] For a discussion of the size of the Assyrian army (120,000), see De Odorico 1995:107-112.

[6] Gilzānu may have been located on the western shores of Lake Urmia (Liverani 1992a:23); and/or perhaps on the plain of Ushnu (Ushnaviyeh) and Solduz with its most important center at Hasanlu (Reade 1979:175; 1995:35-36). Until the end of the 9th century, Gilzānu furnished the Assyrians with their best horses.

[7] For Ḫubuškia, see Lanfranchi 1995 and Medvedskaya 1995.

[8] Lit. "basket carriers."

drove 29 elephants into ambush.

(iv.45-48)
I hitched up plows in the districts of my land. I piled up more grain and straw than ever before. I hitched up teams of horses to 2,002 chariots (and equipped) 5,542 cavalry for the horses of my land.

(iv. 49-51)
The month of Tashrit, the twenty-second day, eponymy of Taklāk-ana-šarri, governor of the city of Nēmed-Ištar.[9]

[9] 842 BCE. See Millard 1994:28, 56.

REFERENCES

Text: *RIMA* 3:32-41; Michel 1947-52:7-20, 63-71, 454-475, pls. 1-3, 5-6, 22-24; Cameron 1950. Translations and studies: *ARAB* 1:§§627-639; *ANET* 278-279; Schramm *EAK* 2:73-75, 87-90.

ANNALS: CALAḪ BULLS (2.113C)

K. Lawson Younger, Jr.

This is a reconstructed recension (Recension D according to Schramm *EAK* 2:76-77) based on inscriptions on two monumental bulls found at Calaḫ and supplemented by two small fragments of inscribed stones. The edition apparently dates to 841 BCE[1] and is the first edition of Shalmaneser's annals that documents Shalmaneser's campaign in his eighteenth regnal year against Hazael of Damascus, and which also mentions the tribute paid to Shalmaneser by Jehu of Israel.

(12′b-19′)
In my sixth regnal year, I departed from Nineveh. I approached the cities on the banks of the Baliḫ (Paliḫ) River. They became afraid in the face of my mighty weapons (and) they killed Giammu, their city ruler. I entered the city of Tīl-turaḫi. I claimed the city as my own.

I departed from the Baliḫ (Paliḫ) River. I crossed the Euphrates in its flood. I received the tribute of the kings of the land of Ḫatti.

I departed from the land of Ḫatti. I approached the city of Aleppo (Ḫalman). I made sacrifices before Hadad of Aleppo (Ḫalman).

I departed from Aleppo (Ḫalman). I approached the city of Qarqar. Hadad-ezer (Adad-idri), the Damascene, (and) Irḫulēni, the Hamathite, together with twelve kings of the shore of the sea, trusted in their combined forces; and they marched against me to do war and battle. I fought with them. I felled with the sword 25,000 troops, their fighting men. I took away from them their chariots, their cavalry (and) their military equipment. In order to save their lives they ran away. I boarded ships (and) I went out upon the sea.

(29′-34′)
In my tenth regnal year, I crossed the Euphrates for the eighth time. I razed, destroyed, (and) burned the cities of Sangara, the Carchemishite.

I departed from the cities of the Carchemishite. I approached the cities of Arame. I captured the city Arnê, his royal city. I razed, destroyed (and) burned (it) together with 100 cities in its environs. I slaughtered their people. I plundered them.

At that time, Hadad-ezer (Adad-idri), the Damascene, (and) Irḫulēni, the Hamathite, together with twelve kings on the shore of the sea, trusted in their combined forces; and they marched against me to do war and battle. I fought with them. I decisively defeated them. I took away from them their chariots, their cavalry, (and) their military equipment. In order to save their lives they ran away.

(35′-41′)
In my eleventh regnal year, I departed from Nineveh. I crossed the Euphrates in its flood for the ninth time. I captured 97 cities of Sangara. I captured, razed, destroyed (and) burned 100 cities of Arame. I took to the slopes of Mt. Amanus.

I crossed Mt. Yaraqu (and) I went down to the cities of the Hamathites. I captured the city of Aštammaku together with 99 cities. I slaughtered their people. I plundered them. At that time, Hadad-ezer (Adad-idri), the Damascene, (and) Irḫulēni, the Hamathite, together with twelve kings on the shore of the sea, trusted in their combined forces; and they marched against me to do war and battle. I fought with them. I decisively defeated them. I felled with the sword 10,000 troops, their fighting men. I took away from them their chariots, their cavalry, (and) their military equipment. On my return, I captured Aparāzu, the fortified city of Arame.

[1] The date depends somewhat on whether one understands there to be a lacuna at the end of the text or not (see Grayson *RIMA* 3:42).

At that time, I received the tribute of Qalparunda, the Patinaean: silver, gold, tin, horses, oxen, sheep, (and) linen garments. I climbed Mt. Amanus; (and) I cut beams of cedar.

(44′b-47′a)
In my fourteenth regnal year, I mustered (the troops of my) extensive land in countless numbers. With 120,000 of my troops[2] I crossed the Euphrates in its flood.

At that time, Hadad-ezer (Adad-idri), the Damascene, (and) Irḫulēni, the Hamathite, together with twelve kings on the shore of the sea, above and below, mustered their troops in countless numbers. They marched against me. I fought with them. I decisively defeated them. I destroyed their chariots (and) their cavalry. I took away their military equipment. In order to save their lives they ran away.

(1″-27″)
In my eighteenth regal year, I crossed the Euphrates for the sixteenth time. Hazael [a] of Damascus trusted in the massed might of his troops; and he mustered his troops in great numbers. He made Mt. Saniru/Senir,[b] a mountain peak, which (lies) opposite Mount Lebanon, his fortress. I fought with him. I decisively defeated him. I felled with the sword 16,000 of his troops, his fighting men. I took away from him 1,121 of his chariots, 470 of his cavalry, together with his camp. In order to save his life he ran away. I pursued after him. I confined him in Damascus, his royal city. I cut down his orchards.[3] [c] I marched to the mountains of Ḫaurāni. I razed, destroyed and burned cities without number. I carried away their booty without number. I marched to the mountains of Baʾli-rasi[4] at the side of the sea. I erected a statue of my royalty there.

At that time, I received the tribute of the Tyrians and the Sidonians, and of Jehu (*Ia-ú-a*),[d] (man of) Bīt-Humrî (Omri).[5]
(lacuna?)

a 2 Kgs 8:7-15; 10:32-34
b Deut 3:9
c Deut 20:19
d 2 Kgs 9:1-10:36

[2] See *COS* 2.113B, note 5.
[3] For the destruction of orchards, see Cole 1995. For a similar context, see Tiglath-pileser III, *COS* 2.117A, note 32, and *COS* 2.2A, note 61.
[4] The identification of Baʾli-rasi is debated. Three locations have been proposed: (1) in the neighborhood of Tyre (Borger *TUAT* 1:366, n. 21a); (2) in the vicinity of the Nahr el-Kelb (Wiseman *DOTT* 49; Honigmann *RlA* 1:395); and (3) Mt. Carmel (Astour 1971:384-385; Green 1979:36). See the discussion in Dion 1997:196-197. "The ravaging of Beth-arbel by Shalman on the day of battle" (Hos 10:14) is understood by some scholars as a reference to an attack on the Israelite town by an Assyrian king, perhaps Shalmaneser III in connection with this campaign in 841 BCE (Astour 1971; Timm 1989:319-320).
[5] Clearly a reference to Jehu (Ungnad 1906; Halpern 1987:81-85). Naʾaman (1997a:19-20) argues that the transcription should be *Iu-ú-a mār Ḫumri* (see also Zadok 1997:20). Schneider (1995; 1996) has suggested that the phrase *mār* ^{m}*ḫu-um-ri-i* means "son (descendent) of Omri" and that Jehu was a descendent of the Omride dynasty, perhaps by a different branch than the ruling descendants of Ahab. But see the criticisms of Naʾaman (1998a:236-238) and Dion (1997:231, n. 36). The Assyrians often denoted countries by the name of the founder of the ruling dynasty at the time of their first acquaintance with it (e.g. "Bīt Baḫiani, Bīt Agusi, Bīt Ḫumri"), regardless of which dynasty was currently in power.

REFERENCES

Text: *RIMA* 3:42-48; Michel 1947-52:265-268. Translations and studies: *ARAB* 1:§§640-663, 671-672; *ANET* 279-280; *TUAT* 1:363-366; *EAK* 2:76-77, 87-88.

ANNALS: MARBLE SLAB (2.113D)

K. Lawson Younger, Jr.

Engraved on a large marble tablet (80 x 60 cm) found in the wall of the city of Aššur, this version of the annals can be identified as Recension E (Schramm *EAK* 2:77-78). The narration covers through Shalmaneser's twentieth year and therefore dates to 839 BCE.

(ii.13-25)
In my sixth regnal year, I approached the cities on the banks of the Baliḫ River. They killed Giammu, their city ruler. I entered the city of Tīl-turaḫi.

I crossed the Euphrates in its flood. I received the tribute of the kings of the land of Ḫatti.

Hadad-ezer (Adad-idri), the Damascene, (and) Irḫulēni, the Hamathite, together with twelve kings of the shore of the sea, trusted in their combined forces; and they marched against me to do war and battle. I fought with them. I decisively defeated them. I took away from them their chariots, their cavalry (and) their military equipment. I felled with the sword 25,000 troops, their fighting men.

(ii.51-iii.5)
In my eleventh regnal year, I crossed the Euphrates for the ninth time. I conquered 97 cities of Sangara. I took (the way) along the slopes of Mt. Amanus. I crossed Mt. Yaraqu. I went down to the cities of the Hamathites. I captured the city of Abšimaku (Aštammaku?) together with 89 cities.

At that time, Hadad-ezer (Adad-idri), the Damascene, (and) Irḫulēni, the Hamathite, together with twelve kings on the shore of the sea, trusted in their combined forces; and I fought with them. I decisively defeated them. I felled with the sword 10,000 troops, their fighting men.

(iii.14-25)
In my fourteenth regnal year, I mustered (the troops of my) extensive land in countless numbers. With 120,000 of my troops I crossed the Euphrates in its flood.

At that time, Hadad-ezer (Adad-idri), the Damascene, (and) Irḫulēni, the Hamathite, together with twelve kings on the shore of the sea, above and below, mustered their troops in countless numbers. They marched against me. I fought with them. I decisively defeated them. I took away their chariots, their cavalry (and) their military equipment. In order to save their lives they ran away.

(iii.45b-iv.15a)
In my eighteenth regnal year, I crossed the Euphrates for the sixteenth time. Hazael [a] of Damascus trusted in the massed might of his troops; and he mustered his army in great number. He made Mt. Saniru/Senir [b] a mountain peak, which (lies) opposite Mount Lebanon, his fortress. I felled with the sword 16,020 troops, his fighting men. I took away from him 1,121 of his chariots, 470 of his cavalry, together with his camp. In order to save his life he ran away. I pursued after him. I confined him in Damascus, his royal city. I cut down his orchards. I burned his shocks. I marched to the mountains of Ḫaurānu. I razed, destroyed and burned cities without number. I carried away their booty. I marched to the mountains of Baᵓli-raᵓsi at the side of the sea and opposite Tyre. I erected a statue of my royalty there. I received the tribute of Baᵓal-manzēr,[1] the Tyrian, and of Jehu (*Ia-a-ú*),[2] [c] (the man) of Bīt-Ḫumrî (Omri).

On my return, I went up on Mt. Lebanon. I set up a stela of my royalty with the stela of Tiglath-pileser (I), the great king who went before me.

[a] 2 Kgs 8:7-15; 10:32-34
[b] Deut 3:9
[c] 2 Kgs 9:1-10:36

[1] See *PNA* 1:242; Lipiński 1970 (note Josephus, *Against Apion* i.124).
[2] See *COS* 2.113C, note 5.

REFERENCES

Text: *RIMA* 3:50-56; Michel 1954-59:27-45; Safar 1951. Translations and studies: Schramm *EAK* 2:77-78; *TUAT* 1:366-367; Cogan and Tadmor 1988:334.

KURBAᵓIL STATUE (2.113E)

K. Lawson Younger, Jr.

Engraved on a statue of Shalmaneser (measuring 103 cm in height), the text belongs to Recension E of his annals. Since the last regnal year narrated is the twentieth, the statue must date to 839-838 BCE. While it belongs to the same recension as the Marble Slab (*COS* 2.113D), the narrative concerning Shalmaneser's eighteenth year campaign against Hazael more closely follows that of the Calaḫ Bulls (*COS* 2:113C). The statue was dedicated to the god Adad of Kurbaᵓil, but was discovered in excavations of Calaḫ. While it may have been brought to Calaḫ for repair (Oates 1962:16), it seems more likely that there was a shrine to Adad of Kurbaᵓil at Calaḫ since this deity was an important god in the Neo-Assyrian period.[1] Here only the eighteenth regnal year (841 BCE) is translated.[2]

(lines 21-30a)
In my eighteenth regnal year, I crossed the Euphrates for the sixteenth time. Hazael [a] of Damascus trusted in the massed might of his troops; and he mustered his army in great numbers. He made Mount Saniru/Senir,[b] a mountain peak, which (lies) opposite Mount Lebanon, his fortress. I fought with him. I decisively defeated him. I felled with the sword 16,000 of his men-of-arms. I took away from him 1,121 of his chariots, 470 of his cavalry, together with his camp. In order to save his life he ran away. I pursued after him. I confined him in Damascus, his royal city. I cut down his orchards. I marched to the mountains of Ḫaurāni. I razed, destroyed and burned cities without number. I carried away their booty without number. I marched to the mountains of Baᵓli-raᵓsi at the side of the sea. I erected a statue of my royalty there.

At that time, I received the tribute of the Tyrians, the Sidonians, and Jehu [c] (*Ia-ú-a*), (the man) of Bīt-Ḫumrî (Omri).

[a] 2 Kgs 8:7-15; 10:32-34
[b] Deut 3:9
[c] 2 Kgs 9:1-10:36

[1] Besides in the city of Kurbaᵓil, the deity, Adad of Kurbaᵓil, also had a major shrine in Assur. See Postgate 1983:367-368.
[2] Grayson notes: "The whole narrative begins with a broad geographical sweep of Shalmaneser's conquests, except for Babylonia, ending with a more explicit narrative of recent campaigns to the west and concluding with the first invasion of Que. This initial campaign against Que was apparently a great success (see *CAH* 3/1 p. 263) and it is not surprising that a statue would have been sculpted to commemorate it" (*RIMA* 3:59).

REFERENCES

Text: *RIMA* 3:58-61; Kinnier Wilson 1962:90-115. Translations and Studies: Schramm *EAK* 2:78-79; Oates 1962:16-17.

BLACK OBELISK (2.113F)

K. Lawson Younger, Jr.

Sculpted from black alabaster, the famous "Black Obelisk," is 2.02 meters in height and contains the longest account of Shalmaneser's reign, stretching down to the king's thirty-first regnal year.[1] It was discovered by Layard at Calaḫ in 1846. The text is identified as Recension F and dates to 828-827 BCE. The Obelisk is formed in the shape of a ziggurat, having four sides with five panels on each side containing reliefs of the tribute being brought to the king (*ANEP* 120-121). This form may reflect the special appeal which these temple towers appear to have had for the Assyrians (Porada 1983:16).[2] While each panel has an epigraph, the main text is found above and below the five panels on all four sides.

On the front side, the second panel or register contains the famous relief of Jehu of Israel (or his envoy) paying his tribute to Shalmaneser (see epigraph 2 below). The first or top register holds a scene of the ruler of Gilzānu, a land near Lake Urmia, paying his tribute (see epigraph 1 below). By juxtaposing the portrayals of the tribute from these two countries — the first being in the easternmost area of the empire and the second being in the southwesternmost area — the obelisk creates a pictorial merism stressing the gigantic extent of Shalmaneser's Assyrian empire (Green 1979; Porada 1983; Lieberman 1985).

(54b-66)[3]
In my sixth regnal year, I approached the cities on the banks of the Baliḫ River. They killed Giammu, their city ruler. I entered the city of Tīl-turaḫi. I crossed the Euphrates in its flood. I received the tribute of [all] the kings of the land of Ḫatti. At that time, Hadad-ezer (Adad-idri), the Damascene, (and) Irḫulēni, the Hamathite, together with the kings of the land of Ḫatti and on the shore of the sea, trusted in their combined forces; and they marched against me to do war and battle. By the command of Aššur, the great lord, my lord, I fought with them. I decisively defeated them. I took away from them their chariots, their cavalry (and) their military equipment. I felled with the sword 20,500 troops, their fighting men.

(87-89a)
In my eleventh regnal year, I crossed the Euphrates for the ninth time. I captured cities without number. I went down to the cities of the Hamathites. I captured 89 cities. Hadad-ezer (Adad-idri), the Damascene, (and) twelve kings of the land of Ḫatti stood together with their combined forces. I decisively defeated them.

a 2 Kgs 8:7-15; 10:32-34

(91b-92a)
In my fourteenth regnal year, I mustered (my) land. I crossed the Euphrates. Twelve kings marched against me. I fought <with them.> I decisively defeated them.

(97b-99a)[4]
In my eighteenth regnal year, I crossed the Euphrates for the sixteenth time. Hazael [a] of Damascus attacked to do battle. I took away from him 1,121 of his chariots, 470 of his cavalry together with his camp.

(102b-104a)
In my twenty-first regnal year, I crossed the Euphrates for the twenty-first time. I marched to the cities of Hazael of Damascus. I captured 4 of his fortified settlements. I received the tribute of the Tyrians, the Sidonians, and the Byblians.

Epigraph 1 (*RIMA* #87)
I received the tribute of Sūa,[5] the Gilzānean:[6] silver, gold, tin, bronze vessels, the staffs of the king's hand, horses, (and) two-humped camels.

[1] Since the Black Obelisk relates that the aged Shalmaneser dispatched Dayan-Aššur for the military expedition against the lands of Muṣaṣir and Gilzānu in 828 BCE (while he himself stayed in Calah), the obelisk, in a way, is effectively a memorial to Dayan-Aššur as well as to Shalmaneser III. See Reade 1981:159.

[2] The Assyrians may have thought that inherent in the shape of the ziggurat was the protective function of the deity of the ziggurat. Thus this protective function of the deity may explain the use of the miniature ziggurats at the tops of the obelisks on which were portrayed the king's important actions in the Middle Assyrian examples and the tribute of subjected peoples in the extant Neo-Assyrian obelisks (Porada 1983:17). See also Reade 1980:20-21.

[3] Cf. with the Kurkh Monolith's description of this campaign above (*COS* 2.113A, ii.86b-102).

[4] Cf. with the Calaḫ Bulls above (*COS* 2.113C, 1″-27″).

[5] ᵐ*šu-ú-a*. In the Kurkh Monolith, this name is also spelled ᵐ*a-su-ú* (*RIMA* 3:15, i.28) and ᵐ*a-sa-a-ú* (RIMA 3:21, ii.61).

[6] For the location of Gilzānu, see *COS* 2.113B, note 6.

Epigraph 2 (RIMA #88)
I received the tribute of Jehu (*Ia-ú-a*) (the man) of Bīt-Ḫumrî: silver, gold, a golden bowl, a golden goblet,[7] golden cups, golden buckets, tin, a staff of the king's hand,[8] (and) javelins(?).[9]

Epigraph 3 (RIMA #89)
I received the tribute of Egypt:[10] two-humped camels, a water buffalo (lit. "river ox"), a *rhinoceros*, an antelope, female elephants, female monkeys, (and) apes.

[7] See *CAD* Z 166 s.v. *ẓuqutu*; Landsberger and Gurney 1957-58:442.

[8] Elat notes that another monarch, Sūa, king of Gilzānu, is pictured on the Obelisk giving Shalmaneser *ḫuṭāre* "staffs." He argues for a distinction between *ḫuṭāru* and *ḫaṭṭu*. The latter he sees as a symbol of royal authority, i.e. a scepter. The former was a symbol of protection or ownership of property. Thus Jehu and Sūa, in handing over the *ḫuṭāru* to Shalmaneser III, "wished to symbolize that their kingdoms had been handed over to the protection of the king of Assyria" (1975:33-34). See *CAD* Ḫ 265 s.v. *ḫuṭāru* A.

[9] The transliteration and meaning is uncertain. Michel suggests that it is a kind of weapon, based on the reading GIŠ *bu-dil-ḫa-ti* (Michel 1954-59:141). Luckenbill translates "javelins" (*ARAB* 1:§590) (so also Cogan and Tadmor 1988:335). Oppenheim transliterates as GIŠ *pu-ru₄-ḫa-ti*, but does not translate (*ANET*, 281, n. 2). Wiseman translates "*puruḫati*-fruits" (*DOTT* 48-49). Apparently following von Soden (*AHw* 844, s.v. *pašḫu* II), Grayson (*RIMA* 3:149) transliterates: GIŠ *pu-aš-ḫa-ti* and translates "spears."

[10] The date of this tribute is uncertain. While Egypt participated in a minor way in the battle of Qarqar (853 BCE), it is doubtful that the tribute is connected to this conflict.

REFERENCES

Text: *RIMA* 3:62-71, 149-150; Michel 1954-59:137-157, 221-233. Translations and Studies: *ARAB* 1:§§553-593; *DOTT* 48-50; *ANET* 278-281; *TUAT* 1:362-363; *ANEP*² figs. 351-355; Schramm *EAK* 2:79-81, 87-90; Porada 1983; Lieberman 1985; Cogan and Tadmor 1988:335; Marcus 1987.

AŠŠUR BASALT STATUE (2.113G)

K. Lawson Younger, Jr.

This is a Summary or Display inscription which is incised on the front, left hip and back of a broken basalt statue of Shalmaneser. It was discovered in the 1903 German excavations at the entrance to a Parthian building where it had been moved from its original location at the Tabira Gate. The statue had been broken into two large and many small pieces and the head was missing. The text appears to date to 833 BCE based on the its inscriptional content.

The two portions translated here narrate Shalmaneser's campaign against the western "12" king coalition in 853 BCE and his campaign against Hazael of Damascus in 841 BCE.

(i.14-24)[1]
I decisively defeated Hadad-ezer (Adad-idri), the Damascene together with 12 kings, his allies. I laid low 29,000 of his men-of-arms like sheep. I threw the rest of their troops into the Orontes River. In order to save their lives, they ran away.

(i.25-ii.6)[2]
Hadad-ezer (Adad-idri) passed away. Hazael,[a] son of a nobody,[3] took the throne. He mustered his numerous troops; (and) he moved against me to do war and battle. I fought with him. I decisively defeated him. I took away from him his walled camp. In order to save his life he ran away. I pursued (him) as far as Damascus, his royal city. I cut down his orchards.

(Remainder of column too fragmentary for translation)

[a] 2 Kgs 8:7-15; 10:32-34

[1] Cf. the account of this campaign in the Kurkh Monolith (*COS* 2.113A, ii.86b-102).

[2] Cf. the narration of this campaign with its counterparts translated above: *COS* 2.113C (1″-27″); 2.113D (iii.45b-iv.15a); and 2.113E (21-30a).

[3] A clear declaration of Hazael's illegitimate regnal status. For discussion, see Pitard 1987:132-138. For the form of the name in the Šeh Ḥamad texts, see Fales 1993.

REFERENCES

Text: *RIMA* 3:117-119; Michel 1947-52:57-63; Messerschmidt 1911: no. 30. Translations and Studies: *ARAB* 1:§§679-683; *ANET* 280; Schramm *EAK* 2:82-83, 87-90; Pitard 1987:132-138; Cogan and Tadmor 1988:334.

BLACK STONE CYLINDER (2.113H)

K. Lawson Younger, Jr.

This short inscription is engraved on a small, black and white marble cylinder (1.5 x 4.1 cm) discovered on the northeast side of the small ziqqurrat in Aššur (i.e., the Anu-Adad temple). The cylinder was brought to Aššur by Shalmaneser as booty from Hazael of Damascus;[1] and was perhaps used as a foundation deposit for the city wall.

(lines 1-8)
Booty from the temple of the god Šēru[2] of the city of Malaḫa,[3] a royal city of Hazael [a] of Damascus, which Shalmaneser, son of Aššur-naṣir-pal, king of Assyria, brought back inside the wall of the Inner city (Aššur).

a 2 Kgs 8:7-15; 10:32-34

[1] For a contrast, see Hazael's Booty Inscriptions (*COS* 2.40).
[2] The deity mentioned here cannot be identified with certainty.
[3] The location of Malaḫa is uncertain.

REFERENCES

RIMA 3:151; Galter 1987:1, 13, 19; Michel 1947-52:269-270. Translations and Studies: *ANET* 281; Schramm *EAK* 2:92; *TUAT* 1:367.

THE DIE (*PŪRU*) OF YAḪALI (2.113I)

K. Lawson Younger, Jr.

In ancient Assyria, the system of dating was by eponym (see *COS* 1.136). Each year was named after the *līmu*, "eponym," who was a high officer of state. Inscribed clay cubes were used as dice for casting lots to determine the eponyms. This die (27 x 27 x 28 mm) belonged to Yaḫali, an official of Shalmaneser III. He held the office of eponym twice during Shalmaneser's reign (833 and 824 BCE).

The use of lots for many legal and commercial purposes is well attested throughout ancient Mesopotamian history. Presumably the inscribed lots were thrown, either by their owners or by an impartial third party, and priority was established by the location in which they fell. In the case of Yaḫali, perhaps the lot which fell closest to the statues of the gods Aššur and Adad took first place. On the other hand, it is possible that the lots were placed in a container and whichever "fell" out first was the lot taken.[1]

The term in this inscription translated "die" (i.e. *pūru*) provides the name for the festival of Purim in the book of Esther (cf. Esth 3:7) (Hallo 1983). Lots were used in a number of instances in the Hebrew Bible.[2] [a]

(Panel i)
Aššur, the great lord! Adad, the great lord! (This is) the die of Yaḫali, the Chief Steward (*masennu*)[3]

(Panel ii)
of Shalmaneser, king of Assyria; governor[4] of the city of Kibšuni, the land of Qumēni,

(Panel iii)
the land of Meḫrāni, the land of Uqi, (and) the land of Erimmi;[5] chief of customs. In his eponymy (assigned to him by) his die (*pūru*),

(Panel iv)
may the harvest of Assyria prosper and thrive. Before Aššur (and) Adad, may he throw his die.[6]

a Lev 16:7-10, 21-22; Josh 7:14; 14:2; 18:6; 1 Sam 14:42; 1 Chr 6:39-50, 54-80; Prov 16:33; Neh 10:34; Esth 3:7

[1] Hallo 1983:20. The typical verb used in all these contexts, in Sum. as well as in both dialects of Akk., is one of the many terms for "to fall" or "to throw."
[2] The Urim and Thummim may have also been a type of lot. See Exod 28:30; Deut 33:8; and Ezra 2:63.
[3] See Parpola, 1995:379-401. See also *CAD* M 1:363-364 s.v. *mašennu*. Importantly, Whiting notes: "The reading (amel)*masennu* for (LÚ)IGI.DUB is preferred over (amel)*abarakku* for the Neo-Assyrian period. There is no doubt, both from syllabic writings and Aramaic correspondences, that *masennu* was the correct reading in the seventh century. Since a syllabic writing of *masennu* appears already in the Nuzi texts and, apart from literary sources, there are no syllabic writings of *abarakku* after the Old Babylonian period (see *CAD* s.v. *abarakku* and *mašennu*), it is extrapolated that *masennu* was correct for the ninth and eighth centuries and probably for the Middle Assyrian period as well" (see Millard 1994:7, n. 14).
[4] Postgate (1995a:6-7) discusses this governorate of the *masennu*. He states: "There is clear evidence that this territory is in the mountains north and east of the Al-Kosh plain, in the region of Atrush."
[5] Both Millard and Hallo translate: "the Cedar Mountain." But Grayson comments: "The reading proposed by some scholars for our passage of KUR (= *šadê*) *e-ri-ni*[*m*?)] is unlikely; 'cedar mountain' would hardly be the name of a province." See also Postgate 1995a:6.
[6] Grayson reads: *li*-⌜*da*⌝-*a* from *nadû* "to throw, cast." Millard reads: *li-l*[*i*]-*a* from *elû* "come up," and translates: "may his lot come up (or

fall out)." Hallo: "may his lot (*pūru*) fall." Interestingly, the Black Obelisk reads: *ina* 31 BALA.MEŠ-*ia šá-nu-te-šú pu-ú-*⌜*ru*⌝ (175) *ina* IGI *aš-šur* dIŠKUR *ak-ru-ru* "In my thirty-first regnal year, I threw the die for a second time before Aššur and Adad" (*RIMA* 3:70, 174b-175a).

REFERENCES

RIMA 3:179; Hallo 1983; Millard 1994:8; Postgate 1995a:6-7.

ADAD-NIRARI III (2.114)

ANTAKYA STELA (2.114A)

K. Lawson Younger, Jr.

This inscription is carefully incised on a stone stela which was discovered by a farmer digging a well near the Orontes river about 1.5 km outside the city of Antakya (undoubtedly in the ancient territory of Unqi, see Hawkins 1995b:96). While the stela is damaged on the left side, from top to bottom, and on the top and top right corner, it records clearly the establishment of a boundary between Zakkur of Hamath and Ataršumki of Arpad, in which there was a cession to Arpad, presumably at the expense of Hamath, of an unknown city Nahlasi and a stretch of the Orontes river.[1] Notably, it is the king Adad-nirari and his commander-in-chief (*turtānu*), Šamši-ilu, who are recorded as jointly[2] establishing the boundary. The historical background seems to fit with the events of 796 BCE, the year of Adad-nirari's final western campaign. For the possibility that he is alluded to as a "savior" of Israel in 2 Kgs 13:5, see Hallo 1960:42 and n. 44.

(lines 1-3)
Adad-nirari,[3] great king, mighty king, king of the universe, king of Assyria, son of Šamši-Adad, mighty king, king of the universe, king of Assyria, son of Shalmaneser, king of the four quarters.

(lines 4-8a)
The boundary[3] which Adad-nirari, king of Assyria, (and) Šamšī-ilu, the commander-in-chief (*turtānu*), established between Zakkur,[5] the Hamathite, [and] Ataršumki,[6] son of Adrame: the city of Naḫlasi together with all its fields, its orchards [and] its settlements is Ataršumki's property. They divided the Orontes River between them. *This is*[7] the border.

(lines 8b-11a)
Adad-nirari, king of Assyria (and) Šamši-ilu, the commander-in-chief (*turtānu*), have released it (from obligations) free and clear to Ataršumki, son of Adrame, to his sons, and his subsequent grandsons. He has established his city (and) its territories [...] to the border of his land.

(lines 11b-19)
By the name of Aššur, Adad and Ber, the Assyrian Enlil,[8] the Assyrian [Ninli]l,[9] and the name Sîn, who dwells in Harran, the great gods [of] Assyria: whoever afterwards speaks ill of the terms of this stela, and takes away by force this border from the possession of Ataršumki, his sons, or his grandsons, ⌜and⌝ destroys the written name (and) writes another name: may [Aššur], Adad, and Ber, Sîn who dwells in Harran, the great gods of Assyria [whose] names are recorded [on] this stela, not listen to his prayers.

[1] It is very difficult to identify the scene of this action with the find-spot of the stela in the middle of Unqi (as does Weippert 1992:58-59). It is easier to suppose that the stela was somehow conveyed down the Orontes from an original emplacement in the neighborhood of Jisr eš Šuġur, where the location of an Arpad-Hamath frontier seems much more probable (Hawkins 1995b:96).

[2] The stela has a broken relief at the top which portrays two figures (Adad-nirari and Šamši-ilu) with a perpendicular object standing between them.

[3] For Adad-nirari III, see *PNA* 1:31-34.

[4] The word *taḫūmu* is used in these inscriptions with the meaning "border, territory" (*AHw* 1303) and with the meaning "boundary stone" (Donbaz 1990:5-7).

[5] For Zakkur, see *COS* 2.35.

[6] See Sefire treaty *COS* 2.82 (*KAI* 222 A lines 1,3,14), and a seal (Bordreuil 1986) (Dion 1997:374). The name is spelled c*trsmk* :: cAttarsumk(i?) "(the deity) cAttar is my support" (Lipiński 1975:61-62; *PNA* 1:236).

[7] NAM A is a problem. Grayson notes (following Donbaz): "One could read NAM as *ana* (an attested value of NAM), giving *ana-a* = *annâ*. Or should one regard this as metathesis for *a-nam* = *annâm*?" (*RIMA* 3:203, n. 8).

[8] See Donbaz 1990:7.

[9] The Assyrian name of Ninlil is Mullissu.

REFERENCES

Text: *RIMA* 3:203; Donbaz 1990. Translations and studies: Weippert 1992.

PAZARCIK / MARAŞ STELA (2.114B)

K. Lawson Younger, Jr.

This stela was discovered during the construction of the Pazarcık dam in the village of Kızkapanlı near Maraş, Turkey. The inscription found on the obverse of the stela belongs to Adad-nirari III (on the reverse is an inscription of Shalmaneser IV, see below *COS* 2.116). The text records the establishment of the boundary (*taḫūmu*) between Kummuh and Gurgum by Adad-nirari III (and surprisingly, his mother Sammuramat, also called Semiramis, see *COS* 2.114H below). This followed a battle at the city of Paqiraḫubuna against an Arpad-led alliance of nine kings (including Arpad). This event may be dated to 805 BCE[1] and Kummuh clearly appears here as an Assyrian client. Since Pazarcık lies on the Maraş-Malatya road,[2] it appears that the stela was found more or less *in situ*.

Not only is the text unusual for the mention of Adad-nirari's mother Sammuramat (Semiramis), but also for the fact that she is said to have crossed the Euphrates with Adad-nirari to attack Ataršumki of Arpad and his allies.

(lines 1-7a)
Boundary stone of Adad-nirari, king of Assyria,
son of Šamši-Adad, king of Assyria,
(and) Sammuramat (Semiramis),
the palace-woman[3] of Šamši-Adad, king of Assyria,
mother of Adad-nirari, mighty king, king of Assyria,
daughter-in-law of Shalmaneser, king of the four quarters.

(lines 7b-15a)
When Ušpilulume,[4] king of the Kummuḫites, caused Adad-nirari, king of Assyria, (and) Sammuramat (Semiramis),[5] the palace woman, to cross the Euphrates, I fought a pitched battle with them — with Ataršumki,[6] the son of Adrame, the Arpadite,[7] [a] together with eight kings who were with him at the city of Paqiraḫubuna.[8] I took away from them their camp. In order to save their lives they ran away.

[a] 2 Kgs 18:34

(lines 15b-18)
In this year, they erected this boundary stone between Ušpilulume, king of the Kummuḫites, and Qalparuda, son of Palalam, the king of the Gurgumites.

(lines 19-23)
Whoever takes (it) away from the possession of Ušpilulume, his sons, (or) his grandsons, may Aššur, Marduk, Adad, Sîn, and Šamaš not stand (with him) in his lawsuit. Interdict[9] of Aššur, my god, (and) Sîn,[10] who dwells in Ḫarran.

[1] The Eponym Chroncile records a campaign against Arpad for this year. See Millard 1994:33, 57; and Weippert 1992:55-60.
[2] See Astour 1979:82.
[3] See Parpola 1988:73-76.
[4] Hieroglyphic Luwian inscriptions from the region mention a king named Suppiluliuma who is probably the same king as Ušpilulume in this inscription. See the discussion of Hawkins 1995b:93.
[5] See Pettinato 1988; Weinfeld 1991. For other references see Hallo *Origins* 253-255.
[6] See previous inscription (Antakya) *COS* 2.114A, note 6.
[7] Arpad is modern Tell Rifāt, 30 km northwest of Aleppo. The capital of Bīt-Agusi only from the time of Adad-nirari III.
[8] See *COS* 2.113A (Shalmaneser III), note 8.
[9] See *CAD* I/J 57 s.v. *ikkibu*.
[10] See Stol 1995:1480-1481; Green 1992.

REFERENCES

Text: *RIMA* 3:204-205; Timm 1993; Donbaz 1990.

ORTHOSTAT SLAB OF UNKNOWN PROVENANCE (2.114C)

K. Lawson Younger, Jr.

This text is inscribed on a very fragmentary stone slab of unknown provenance. It seems to describe a western campaign of Adad-nirari III that may have included the defeat of Ataršumki of Arpad.

... [...]
They drew the yoke of [my lordship. The kings of the extensive land of Ḫatti] who, in the time of Šamši-[Adad, my father, had become strong and caused] the lords of the river[1] Or[ontes?] / Eu[phrates? to rebel ...] he heard [of my approach]

[1] The reading ÍD.A.[...] can be restored as either ÍD.A.[RAD] "the Euphrates" or ÍD *a*-[*ramtu*]. The text of the Antakya stela associates Ataršumki with the Orontes and may argue in favor of that restoration (see Grayson RIMA 3:206, n. 4′; Scheil 1917:159). However, Millard notes that the

and Ataršumki[2] ...] trusted [in his own strength, attacked to wage war and battle. I decisively defeated him. I took away his camp. [...] the treasure of [his pal]ace [I carried off.] [... Ataršumki], the son of Aramê,[3] [...] I received without number [...]

(lacuna)

river is the Euphrates in the Tell Sheik Hammad stela (*COS* 2.114D) which rules out the Orontes (Millard and Tadmor 1973:61).

[2] The restoration is "quite conjectural, but seems to fit the traces" (Millard and Tadmor 1973:61).

[3] The father of Ataršumki is Adrame in the Antakya Stela (*COS* 2.114A) and the Pazarcık Stela (*COS* 2.114B). Arame, (the man) of Bīt-Agūsi, was a tributary to Shalmaneser III. See Kurkh Monolith (*COS* 2.113A, ii.83).

REFERENCES

Text: *RIMA* 3:205-206; Millard and Tadmor 1973:60-61; Scheil 1917. Studies: Schramm *EAK* 2:118.

TELL SHEIK HAMMAD STELA (2.114D)

K. Lawson Younger, Jr.

This fragmentary text (81 x 48 cm) is inscribed on a broken black basalt stela found in 1879[1] at Tell Sheik Hammad (ancient Dūr-Katlimmu).[2] The fragment also preserves a partial relief of the king's portrait and divine symbols.

(lines 1-2)
[Adad-nirari, the great king,] the mighty [king], king of the universe, king of Assyria, son of Šamši-Adad, [king of the universe, king of Assyria, son of] Shalmaneser, king of the four quarters.

(lines 3-10)
[At the command of Aššur], I mustered my [chariotry, troops] (and) camp. [I ordered (them) to march] to the land of Ḫatti. I crossed the Euphrates in its flood. I descended [to the city of Paqarḫu]-buna.[3] Ataršumki[4] [the Arphadite and the kings] of the land of Ḫatti who had rebelled and [trusted in their own strength,] the fearful splendor of Aššur, my lord, [overwhelmed them]. [...] [In a sin]gle year, I con[quered] the land of Ḫatti [in its entirety ...].

[1] For a description of its discovery and description, see Millard and Tadmor 1973:57.

[2] See Kühne 1994; 1995:69-87, esp. 72. Assyrian attention to the steppe during the reign of Adad-nirari III is attested by inscriptions of this king from Tell Sheik Hammad / Dūr-Katlimmu, from Para (the western edge of the Sinǧar), from Tell al Rimah (see *COS* 2.114F) and from Sabaʾa (*COS* 2.114E). See Weippert 1992:43.

[3] See *COS* 2.113A (Shalmaneser III), note 8.

[4] See the Antakya inscription, *COS* 2.114A, note 6.

REFERENCES

Text: BM 131124; *RIMA* 3:206-207; Millard and Tadmor 1973. Translations and Studies: Schramm EAK 2:118; Tadmor 1973:141; *TUAT* 1:369.

SABAʾA STELA (2.114E)

K. Lawson Younger, Jr.

This inscription is engraved on a badly worn stone stela from Sabaʾa, south of Jebel Sinjar. The stela is 192 cm in height and contains a relief of the king along with divine symbols on its top and text below. Interestingly, about two-thirds of the text (lines 1-22) are a royal dedicatory inscription; then Nergal-ēreš, a governor under Adad-nirari III, is introduced with his titles (lines 23-25). Finally, the last lines (26-33) are concluding curses given by Nergal-ēreš. The text dates to 797 BCE or perhaps later, since it was in that year that Ḫindānu was added to Nergal-ēreš's domain by royal decree.[1]

(lines 1-5)
[To] Adad, canal-inspector of heaven and earth, son of Anu, the perfectly splendid hero who is mighty in strength, foremost of the Igigi-gods, warrior of the Anunnakki-gods, who is clothed with luminosity, who rides the great storms (and) is clothed with fierce splendor, who causes the evil one to fall, who carries the holy whip, who causes the light-

[1] For this decree, see *RIMA* 3:213-216, obv. 4-5.

ning bolt, the great lord, his lord.

(lines 6-11a)
[Adad-nir]ārī, great king, mighty king, king of the universe, king of Assyria, unrivalled king, wonderful shepherd, exalted vice-regent, who likes to pray (and) to offer sacrifices, whose shepherdship the great gods have made pleasing to the people of Assyria like a healing drug, and whose land (the gods) have widened;

son of Šamši-Adad, mighty king, [king of the universe], king of Assyria; son of Shalmaneser, commander of all rulers, scatterer of (the inhabitants of) enemy lands.

(lines 11b-20)
In the fifth year, <after> I had ascended nobly the royal throne, I mustered the land. I ordered the extensive troops of the land of Assyria to march to the land of Ḫatti. I crossed the Euphrates in its flood. The kings of the extensive [land of Ḫatti] who, in the time of Šamši-Adad, my father, had become strong and had withheld(?) their [tribute], by the command of Aššur, Marduk, Adad, Ištar, the gods who support me, (my) fearful splendor overwhelmed them and they submitted to me (lit. "they seized my feet"). Tribute (and) tax [...] they brought to Assyria (and) I received.

I ordered [my troops to march to the land of Damascus[2]]. I [confined] Mariʾ[3] [a] in the city of Damascus. [He brought to me] 100 talents of gold (and) 1,000 talents of silver as tribute. [...]

a 2 Kgs 13:24-25

b Judg 6:5; 7:12; Joel 1:4

(lines 21-22a)
At that time, I made a stela of my lordship. I inscribed on it my heroic victories (and) achievements. I erected it in Zabanni.

(lines 22b-25)
[The inscribed stone(?)] of Nergal-ēreš,[4] governor of the cities of Nemed-Ištar, Apku, Mari, the lands of Raṣappa,[5] Qatnu, the city of Dūr-katlimmu, Kār-Aššurnaṣirpal, Sirqu, the land of Laqê, the land of Ḫindānu, the city of Anat, the land of Suḫu (and) the city of (Ana)-Aššur-utēr-aṣbat.

(lines 26-33)
A later prince who takes this stela from its place; whoever covers (it) with dirt or puts (it) in a Taboo House, or erases the name of the king, my lord, and my name, and writes his own name;

may Aššur, the father of the gods, curse him and destroy his seed (and) his name from the land.

May Marduk [...] overthrow his rule. May he give him up to be bound by the hands (and) over the eyes.

May Šamaš, judge of heaven and earth, cause there to be darkness in his land so that no one can see the other.

May Adad, canal-inspector of heaven (and) earth, tear out (his) name; (and) may he attack like an onslaught of locusts[b] so that his land falls.

[2] Tadmor (1973:145) restores: *ana* KUR *šá*-ANŠE-*šú* DU.

[3] While there have been different proposals for the identity of Mariʾ of Damascus, most scholars identify him with Ben-Hadad III, the son of Hazael, mentioned in the Zakkur inscription (see *COS* 2.35). For further discussion see Pitard 1987:166-167.

[4] For Nergal-ēreš (803-775 BCE), see Galter 1990; Grayson 1993:27-28; Liverani 1992b:38-39; Fales 1992:106-107.

[5] The geographic pattern is counter-clockwise (Liverani 1992b:38). Cf. the counter-clockwise border descriptions for Judah (Josh 15:1-12) and Benjamin (18:12-20). For the province of Raṣappa, see Liverani 1992b and Fales 1992.

REFERENCES

Text: *RIMA* 3:207-209; Tadmor 1973:144-148; Unger 1916:8-12. Translations and studies: *ARAB* 1:§§734-737; *DOTT* 51-52; *ANET* 282; *TUAT* 1:369; Tadmor 1969; Schramm *EAK* 2:111-113.

TELL AL RIMAH STELA (2.114F)

K. Lawson Younger, Jr.

The stela was discovered at Tell al Rimah, near Jebel Sinjar, where it stood in "position inside the cella of a Late Assyrian shrine, set beside the podium, a placing that is unparalleled among the find spots of other royal stelae" (Page 1968:139). The monument is 130 cm in height and 69 cm in width. Like the Sabaʾa stela it has a relief of the king with divine symbols on the top and the text below. It also contains, like the Sabaʾa stela, an inscription of Adad-nirari III with a text of Nergal-ēreš, although this portion has been deliberately erased. It is uncertain when Nergal-ēreš fell from power and when the erasure would have taken place. Finally, like the Sabaʾa stela, it must date to 797 BCE or perhaps later, since it was in that year that Ḫindānu was added to Nergal-ēreš's domain by royal decree.[1]

To Adad, the greatest lord, powerful noble of the gods, first-born son of Anu, unique, awesome, lofty, the canal-inspector of heaven and earth, who rains abundance, who dwells in Zamaḫu, the great

[1] For this decree, see *RIMA* 3:213-216, obv. 4-5.

lord, his lord.

Adad-nirari, mighty king, king of the universe, king of Assyria; son of Samši-Adad, the king of the universe, king of Assyria; son of Shalmaneser, the king of the four quarters.

I mustered (my) chariots, troops and camps; I ordered (them) to march to the land of Ḫatti. In a single year,[2] I subdued the entire lands of Amurru (and) Ḫatti. I imposed upon them tax and tribute forever.

I (text: "he") received 2,000 talents of silver, 1,000 talents of copper, 2,000 talents of iron, 3,000 linen garments with multi-colored trim — the tribute of Mariʾ[3] [a] of the land of Damascus. I (text: "he") received the tribute of Joash (*Iuʾasu*)[4] [b] the Samarian, of the Tyrian (ruler), and of the Sidonian (ruler).

I marched to the great sea in the West. I erected a statue of my lordship in the city of Arvad which is in the midst of the sea. I climbed Mt. Lebanon; (and) I cut down timbers: 100 mature cedars, material needed for my palace and temples.

a 2Kgs 13:24-25

b 2Kgs 13:10-25

I (text: "he") received tributes from all the kings of the land of Nairi.

At that time, I ordered Nergal-ēreš, the governor of the lands of Raṣappa, Laqê, Ḫindānu, the city of Anat, the land of Suḫu, and the city of (Ana)-Aššur-(utēr)-aṣbat, my courtier: the city of Dūr-Ištar with its 12 villages, the city of Kār-Sîn with its 10 villages, the city of Dūr-katlimmu with its 33 villages, the city of Dūr-Aššur with its 20 villages, the city of Dūr-Nergal-ēreš with its 33 villages, the city of Dūr-Marduk with its 40 villages, the city of Kār-Adad-niriri with its 126 villages, in (the area of) Mt. Sangar, 28 villages in (the area of) Mt. Azalli?, the city of Dūr-Adad-niriri with its 15 villages in the land of Laqê, the city of Adad with its 14 villages in the land of Qatnu, — altogether 331 small towns, which Nergal-ēreš undertook to rebuild by the order of his lord.

Whoever shall blot out a single name from among these names, may the great gods fiercely destroy him.

[2] A literary convention in which several campaigns to Syria have been telescoped into one. See Younger 1990:122; Tadmor 1973:62, 143. Page 1968:141; 1969:483-484. For the campaigns, see Millard 1973; Weippert 1992.

[3] See *COS* 2.114E, note 3.

[4] ᵐ*Iu-ʾa-su* is to be identified with Joash. See Cogan and Tadmor 1988:147-152.

REFERENCES

Text: *RIMA* 3:209-212; Page 1968. Translations and Studies: Page 1969; Donner 1970; Millard 1973; Schramm *EAK* 2:113-115; Tadmor 1973; *TUAT* 1:368; Cogan and Tadmor 1988:335.

CALAH ORTHOSTAT SLAB (2.114G)

K. Lawson Younger, Jr.

Discovered in 1854 at Calah, the text was inscribed on a broken stone slab which was left on the mound of Nimrud. It is known only through its publication based on the paper squeezes[1] made by Norris on the site. Only the latter half of the inscription is translated here.

(lines 11-14)
I subdued from the bank of the Euphrates, the land of Ḫatti, the land of Amurru in its entirety, the land of Tyre, the land of Sidon, the land of Israel (Ḫumrî),[2] the land of Edom,[3] the land of Philistia,[4] as far as the great sea in the west. I imposed tax (and) tribute upon them.

(lines 15-21)
I marched to the land of Damascus. I confined Mariʾ,[5] the king of Damascus in the city of Damascus, his royal city. The fearful splendor of Aššur, my ("his") lord, overwhelmed him; and he submitted to me.[6] He became my vassal. 2,300 talents of silver, 20 talents of gold, 3,000 talents of bronze, 5,000 talents of iron, linen garments with multi-colored trim, an ivory bed, a couch with inlaid ivory, his property (and) his possessions without number — I received inside his palace in Damascus, his royal city.

[1] These paper squeezes were subsequently destroyed. See Galter, Reade and Levine 1986:27.

[2] KUR *ḫu-um-ri-i*. Cf. the attribution of Joash's tribute in Tell al Rimah Stela (2.114F, note 4): Joash, the Samarian.

[3] On Edom, see Millard 1992:35-39.

[4] KUR *pa-la-as-tú*.

[5] See *COS* 2.114E, note 3.

[6] Lit. "he seized my feet."

(lines 22-24)
The kings of the land of Chaldea became my vassals. I imposed on them tax and tribute in perpetuity. At Babylon, Borsippa, (and) Cuthah they delivered up the remnant offerings of the gods Bēl, Nabû, (and) Nergal. [I made] pure sacrifices.
(Lacuna)

REFERENCES

Text: *RIMA* 3:212-213; Tadmor 1973:148-150. Translations and studies: *ARAB* 1 §§738-741; *DOTT* 51; *ANET* 281-282; Schramm *EAK* 2:115-116; Millard 1973; *TUAT* 1:367-368.

STELA OF SAMMURAMAT (SEMIRAMIS) (2.114H)

K. Lawson Younger, Jr.

This engraved stela was discovered in the row of stelae unearthed by the German excavations in the southern part of the city wall built by Shalmaneser III at Aššur (Andrae 1913). Sammuramat (classical references know her as Semiramis) was the wife of Šamši-Adad V and mother of Adad-nirari III. It is a most unusual aspect of the reign of Adad-nirari that the queen mother attained such a high profile with her name appearing in royal inscriptions (see *COS* 2.114B above) and in her own inscribed stela translated here.

While Andrae theorized that the stelae formed a type of calendar for reckoning the years, it is more likely that the place was a depository for discarded monuments removed from the temple from time to time and placed respectfully in the position in which they were found. The stones would have stood in a shrine as substitutes for the persons named, possibly commemorating them after their lifetimes, as well as during them, as did stelae of similar shape in the west (Millard 1994:12).[1]

(lines 1-7)
Stela of Sammuramat (Semiramis), the palace-woman[2] of Šamši-Adad, king of the universe, king of Assyria, mother of Adad-nirari, king of the universe, king of Assyria, daughter-in-law of Shalmaneser, king of the four quarters.

[1] See further Miglus 1984 and Canby 1976. Canby suggests possible links with the biblical *maṣṣēbôt*. Gen 28:18, 22; 31:13; 35:14; Exod 23:24; 34:13; Deut 7:5; 12:3; 1 Kgs 14:23; 2 Kgs 3:2; 10:27; 18:4; 23:14; Hos 3:4; 10:1; etc.
[2] See Parpola 1988.

REFERENCES

Text: *RIMA* 3:226; Andrae 1913: no. 5. Translations and studies: *ARAB* 1:§§730-731; Schramm *EAK* 2:111; Canby 1976; Miglus 1984; Weinfeld 1991; Millard 1994:11-12.

OFFICIALS' INSCRIPTIONS (2.115)

The recent discoveries of cuneiform tablets from the Middle Euphrates, combined with older known documents, have enabled a more comprehensive picture to emerge of the situation in the Assyrian state during the eighth century BCE. During this period, Assyrian influence had so declined that the cohesive political entity represented in the rulers Aššur-nasir-pal II and Shalmaneser III had become geographically fragmented with various districts being ruled by a select few powerful men who might or might not pay lip service to the Assyrian king. In fact, while most of these individuals were high officials or governors in the "Assyrian" kingdom, this is clearly just a sham, because they otherwise behave like independent rulers (in some cases even alluding to their roles as "kings").[1] Brinkman has designated this a "period of local autonomy" in Assyrian regions as well as in Babylonia.[2] (For Nergal-ēreš, see above, *COS* 2.114E).

[1] For more discussion, see Dion 1995a; 1995b; Grayson 1993; 1994; 1995.
[2] Brinkman 1968:218-219.

ŠAMŠI-ILU — STONE LIONS INSCRIPTION (2.115A)

K. Lawson Younger, Jr.

This inscription was incised on two colossal, dark gray basalt lions that were discovered at Tell Ahmar (Tīl-Barsip/Kār Shalmaneser)[1] originally in 1908. A study of one of the lions in 1988 revealed that it was 258 cm in height; with a length of 250 cm; and a width of 120 cm (Roobaert 1990:127). While the text is in the form of a royal dedicatory inscription, its author is not an Assyrian monarch, as would be expected, but a commander-in-chief (the *turtānu*) named Šamši-ilu.[2] Thus it highlights his victorious campaign against the Urartian king Argištu (I) and erection of the two lions with their fierce names. There is no mention of the Assyrian king.

(lines 1-8a)

Aššur, great lord, king of the gods, [who] determines destinies;

Anu, mighty, foremost, progenitor of the great gods;

Enlil, father of the gods, lord of the lands, who makes kingship great;

Ea, the wise, king of the *apsû*, who grants wisdom;

Marduk, sage of the gods, lord of omens, commander of all;

Nabû, scribe of Esagil, possessor of the tablet of destinies[3] of [the gods], who resolves conflicts;

Sîn, luminary [of heaven and earth], lord of the lunar disk, who brightens the firmament;

Ištar, lady of wa[r and] battle, overturner of the fierce;

Gula, the great chief woman physician, wife of the hero of the gods, the son of mighty Enlil.

(lines 8b-11a)

[Šamši]-ilu, the commander-in-chief (*turtānu*),[a] the great herald,[4] [the administrator of] temples, chief of the extensive army, governor of the land of Ḫatti (and) of the land of the Guti, and all the land of Namri, conqueror of the mountains in the West, who lays waste [...], who overthrows the lands of Mušku and Urartu, who plunders its people, who devastates the lands of Utû, Rubû, Ḫatallu,[5] (and) Labdudu, who brings about their annihilation.

(lines 11b-13a)

When (at that time) Argištu,[6] the Urartian, the number of whose forces is massive like a heavy fog and who had not had relations with[7] any previous king, he (Argištu) rebelled and assembled the people together at the land of the Guti. He put his battle array in good order. All his troops marched toward the battleground in the mountains.

a 2 Kgs 18:17; Isa 20:1

(lines 13b-18)

By the command of the father, Aššur, the great lord, and the lofty mother of Ešarra, foremost among the gods, the goddess Ninlil; Šamši-ilu, the commander-in-chief (*turtānu*), the great herald, [the administrator of] temples, chief of the extensive army, concentrated the soldiers within these mountains. With the loud noise of the drums[8] (and) prepared weapons that dreadfully roar, he blew like the *imḫullu* wind.[9] He had his high-mettled horses that were harnessed to his chariot fly against him (Argištu) like the *Anzu*-bird;[10] and he decisively defeated him. He (Argištu) deserted; and his army (and) his assembly scattered. He was frightened by the battle, Like a thief I took (his) arrows away from him. I personally captured his camp, his royal treasure, (and) his [...].

(lines 19-24)

At that time, I erected two outstanding lions in the gate of the city of Kār-Shalmaneser, the city of my lordship, on the right and on the left; and I named them. The name of the first is: "The lion who [...], fierce *ūmu*-demon, unrivalled attack, who overwhelms the insubmissive, who obtains what his heart desires." The name of the second, which stands before the gate, is: "Who gores through resistance, who levels the enemy country, who casts out evildoers, (and) who brings in good people.

[1] For Tell Aḫmar, see Bunnens 1990; 1995. See *COS* 2.113A (Shalmaneser III), note 3.

[2] See Grayson 1993:27; 1994:74-80. Malamat (1953:25-26) argues that Šamši-ilu is referred to in Amos 1:5; Millard (1993:173*-177*) argues for a different understanding. For his golden cup inscription, see Fadhil 1990:482. For his votive inscription, see Reade 1987; Watanabe 1994:248.

[3] For the "Tablet of Destinies," see Paul 1973.

[4] For this office, see Sassmannshausen 1995.

[5] KUR *ḫa-⌜da(?)⌝-lu*. For the reading, see Grayson's remarks, *RIMA* 3:232, 11a. Liverani (1992b:37) reads this as a reference to the Ḫatallu tribe (or better, confederation of tribes). For the Ḫatallu, see *COS* 2.115B, note 7.

[6] For Argištu I, see *PNA* 1:129-130. For Urartu, see Zimansky 1995.

[7] Lit. "stretched out his hand to."

[8] Following Grayson *RIMA* 3:3:233.

[9] *imḫullu* wind refers to a specific type of destructive wind with supernatural qualities. See *CAD* I/J 116.

[10] The *Anzu*-bird was a monstrous bird, subject of various mythological stories.

REFERENCES

Text: *RIMA* 3:231-233; Thureau-Dangin 1930:11-21. Studies: Schramm *EAK* 2:120-121; Kuan 1995:108-112; Grayson 1993.

NINURTA-KUDURRĪ-UṢUR — SUḪU ANNALS #2 (2.115B)

K. Lawson Younger, Jr.

Discovered by Iraqi archaeologists in salvage work in the Ḥadītha Dam area, this four-column clay tablet was found at Sūr Jarᶜā and contains a lengthy account of Ninurta-kudurrī-uṣur. It was apparently composed in the seventh year of his "governorship" (see lines iv.38b′-40′).[1] Written in the Babylonian dialect with both Assyrian and Aramaic influences, the text describes Ninurta-kudurrī-uṣur's mighty achievements, especially his defeat of the Ḫatallu tribal confederation headed by the wily leader Šamaᵓgamni. It also records Ninurta-kudurrī-uṣur's victory over the city of Raᵓil and the capture of a caravan from Temā and Šabaᵓ.

(lines i.1-7a)

I, Ninurta-kudurrī-uṣur, governor of the land of Suḫu and the land of Mari, son of Šamaš-rēša-uṣur,[2] ditto[3] (governor of the land of Suḫu and the land of Mari), son of Iqīša-Marduk, ditto (governor of the land of Suḫu and the land of Mari), descendant of Adad-nādin-zēri, ditto (governor of the land of Suḫu and the land of Mari), the one of everlasting seed, distant descendant of Tunamissaḫ, son of Ḫammu-rāpi,[4] king of Babylon: the chosen, upon whom Šamaš and Marduk, Adad and Apla-Adad[5] [a] joyfully (and) radiantly glanced with their powerful shining faces; to whom they gave complete power and kingship[6] over the land of Suḫu; and for my allotted destiny they bestowed justice.

(lines i.7b-16a)

Barely three months had passed in the initial year of my governorship, when I sat on the throne of my father, when 2000 men of the Ḫatallu tribe[7] — from the Sarugu (clan) to the Luḫuāya[8] (clan) — with their archers and their military commanders[9] gathered together; and they imparted a command to each other.[10] Šamaᵓgamni, the herald (*nāgiru*)[11] of the Sarugu, who is thoroughly confused by falsehood, was their chieftain. They came up for a raid against the land of Laqê. And while in the steppe they thought to themselves, thus: "the governor of Suḫu is hostile to us. How will we go past to make a raid on the land of Laqê?"

(lines i.16b-27a)

Šamaᵓgamni, the herald (*nāgiru*) of the Sarugu and Iâᵓe, the son of Balammu,[12] [b] the Amatite,[13] their military commanders, said the following to them:

"Among the governors of the land of Suḫu, his ancestors, none dared to go to war against 1,000 Arameans. Now he must go to war against 2000 Arameans! If he does attack us, we will go to war against him and gain possession of the land of Suḫu. But if he does not attack, we will bring down the booty; and (more) troops will join us; and we will go and attack the houses[14] of the land of Suḫu; we will seize his cities of the steppe; and we will cut down their fruit trees."[15] [c]

(lines i.27b-30a)

They trusted in their strength and they advanced against the land of Laqê. They seized 100 villages of the land of Laqê; they plundered booty without number; and they turned the land of Laqê into ruin mounds.

(lines i.30b-32)

Adad-daᵓᵓānu, the governor of the land of Laqê, came to me with 4 chariots and 200 troops. He kissed the ground before me; and he entreated me

a Job 2:11; 8:1; 18:1; 25:1; 42:9

b Num 20-24

c Deut 20:19-20

[1] While Ninurta-kudurrī-uṣur never specifically calls himself "king," he does state in this inscription that the gods Šamaš, Marduk, Adad and Apla-Adad gave him "kingship over the land of Suḫu" (see note 6 below).

[2] Concerning this individual, see Mayer-Opificius 1995.

[3] The cuneiform repeating sign is used.

[4] See *COS* 2.107A-D.

[5] Apla-Adad (lit., "son of Adad") was a deity that was, in particular, worshipped in the Middle Euphrates region. The deity's name is known from personal names and from texts as well as on a cylinder seal discovered at Beer-Sheba (see *COS* 2.125A below). See Rainey 1973; Lipiński 1975. The strong link between Apla-Adad (Apladad) and the land of Suḫu may help the explication of the second friend of Job "Bildad the Shuhite" (Job 2:11; 8:1; 18:1; 25:1; 42:9). The name, Bildad, may be equated with the name, Apla-Adad (Apladad), and Shuhite may be equated with Suḫu. See Dion 1995a:72.

[6] LUGAL-*ú-tu šá* KUR *Su-ḫi*. This is a clear claim of kingship by Ninurta-kudurrī-uṣur. Cf. Hadad-yithᶜi, *COS* 2.34, note 5.

[7] The Ḫatallu tribe was a confederation of tribes composed of those mentioned here (i.e., the Sarugu and the Luḫuāya) and the Amatu (i.17 below). The confederation's homeland was located northeast of Suḫu in the Wadi Tharthar area. See Liverani 1992b and *COS* 2.115A, n. 5.

[8] *lu-ḫu-ú-a-a*: Frame *RIMB* 2:295.

[9] LÚ.SAG KALxBAD.MEŠ-*šú-nu*, "their head(s) of camps." See Dion 1995b:9 "heads of tents." Cf. the much later phrase *rwš hmḥnyh* "the head of the camp" in *DJD* ii 42[2].

[10] I.e., came to an agreement.

[11] For this title, see Sassmannshausen 1995; Parpola 1995.

[12] The name is spelled here: ᵐ*Ba-la-am-mu* (i.17); in *RIMB* 2:301, it is spelled: ᵐ*Ba-li-am-mu* (i.8). Dion (1995a:68-69) connects the paternal name to the biblical form Balaam, and the Amatu with Hamath. Cf. also the Deir ᶜAlla Inscription (*COS* 2.27).

[13] The Amatu clan.

[14] The word "houses" (É.MEŠ) probably refers to households, families, clans, etc. rather than to physical structures.

[15] For the cutting down of orchards, see Shalmaneser text *COS* 2.113C, note 3.

(for help). I accepted his entreaty.

(lines i.33-35)

Furthermore, Sîn-šallimanni,[16] the provincial governor of the land of Ruṣapu/Raṣappu, came against them (the Arameans) together with the entire strength of the land of Ruṣapu/Raṣappu. But (when) he saw them, he became afraid [...]

(lines i.36-?)

(But) I am Ni[nurta-kudurrī-uṣur ...]

(lacuna)

(lines ii.1-29a)

I brought upon them an inundation. From inside my chariot, I washed them away like [barley re]eds.[17] Like locusts the arrows whizzed over my camp. (But) no one in my camp fell dead! Although they wounded 38 soldiers in my camp, not one among them fell dead in the steppe.[18] I fell upon them (the Arameans) like a blazing fire, and I put to the sword 1,616 of their troops.[19] Furthermore, I removed the hands and lower lips of 80 of their troops; and I let them go free to (spread the news of my) glory. From the well of Makiri (and) the well of Gallabu and up to the well Suribu, at (these) three wells, I decisively defeated them. I annihilated them. I scattered their substantial auxiliary troops; and I broke up their troop contingents. I captured those who attempted to escape. I caused their blood to flow like waters of a river. The road with their corpses was visible[20] to the eagles and vultures.[21] [d] I filled the mountains and wadis with their skulls like mountain stones. Birds made nests in their skulls. 304 of their troops had quickly fled before me. (Since) my horses and my troops had become thirsty for water due to the fighting, I did not pursue them. 40 of (these) troops perished due to thirst for water. 254 of their troops got away. I killed 1,846 of their troops. This is a single defeat that Ninurta-kudurrī-uṣur, governor of the land of Suḫu and the land of Mari, inflicted upon the Ḫatallu (tribesmen). Šamaᵓgamni, the herald (*nāgiru*) of the Sarugu (clan), their leader, the dishonest servant whom the land of Suḫu, the land of Assyria and my fathers rejected,[22] I captured him. When I killed him, my heart calmed down. Having stripped off his skin like the skin of a sheep, I set (it) in front of the gate of Āl-gabbāri-bānî. I inflicted such a defeat as none of <my ancestors> had ever inflicted. My ancestors had defeated the enemy ten times, but they did not achieve as much as I.[23] In inflicting a single defeat, I surpassed my ancestors.

d Gen 15:11; 1 Sam 17:44

(lines ii.29b-35)

Anyone in the future who comes forward and says: "How [did] Ninurta-kudurrī-uṣur, governor of the land of Suḫu and the land of Mari, [inflict] this defeat?" (should be told that) I did [not] inflict (this) [by my own power, (but rather) I inflicted this][24] defeat by the power of Šamaš and Marduk, A[dad and Apla-Adad, the great gods]. [Anyone in the future] who comes forward and [should ask] the elders of [his] la[nd ...]

(lacuna)

(lines iii.1′-22a′)[25]

[...] I saw [... at] the well of Bukrê, but [...] had not been built(?). Above the well of Buk[rê ...] I discovered. It was depressions(?), a reed marsh. I opened it up and its water was abundant. Three routes which [...] which go to the land of Laqê, the city of Ḫindānu[26] and the land of Suḫu, which in the days of the governors of the land, my ancestors, who had left no mounted troops there <...> Anyone in the future who comes forward and says: "How is it that a stranger who passes by may drink from this water?" (should be told) that he may drink from the well which we formed(?).[27] Before my time, no city had been built there. I conceived the idea to build this city. While the priestly workforce[28] was making the bricks for it, before the city

[16] Sîn-šallimanni was governor of Raṣappu and held the office of eponym in 747 BCE (Millard 1994:43, 59). His march against the Arameans and his subsequent flight without battle, "no doubt, displeased his master the Assyrian king who removed him from office and possibly had him executed" (Grayson 1993:23).

[17] Restoration is based on *RIMB* 2:302 (ii.4-5) and *RIMB* 2:308 (i.15′).

[18] Lit., "no one among them (i.e. the 38), his corpse fell in the steppe."

[19] For an attempt to reconcile the various figures cited in these texts for the numbers of enemy who were killed and who got away alive, see Cavigneaux and Ismail 1990:352-353.

[20] Lines 14b-15a read: *ḫar-⌈ra⌉-nu ina* LÚ.ÚŠ.MEŠ-*šú-nu a-ru-ú u zi-bu in-na-aṭ-ṭal*. Cavigneaux and Ismail (1990:355) see possibly an Aramaic influence. They translate: "über ihre Leichen schwebten Adler und Geier hinunter :: over their corpses eagles and vultures hover." See also Frame *RIMB* 2:296. However, the verb could be a N Durative 3cs of *naṭālu* "to appear, become visible." The verb is singular; hence it seems that *ḫarrānu* is the subject. See *CAD* N 2:128 for this very form. However, RIMB 2:310 (i.19′-20′) reads: [*ḫar-ra*]-⌈*a*⌉-*ni i-na* LÚ.ÚŠ.MEŠ-*šú-nu* TI_8.MUŠEN (20) [*u zību in-na-a*]*ṭ-ṭal*.

[21] For birds of prey, cf. Gen 15:11; 1 Sam 17:44.

[22] Frame suggests reading for ii.25: *ú-šá-an-si*(*)-<*ku(?)*>-*šu*. See *RIMB* 2:293, n. i.41.

[23] For the motif of achieving what the ancestors could not, see Kulamuwa (*COS* 2.30, lines 2-5a).

[24] Following the suggested restorations of Frame *RIMB* 2:297.

[25] For this section cp. the inscription of Azatiwada (*COS* 2.31).

[26] The land of Ḫindānu was located between Laqê and Suḫu. The location of the city of Ḫindānu is uncertain (perhaps in the area of Abu Kemal, Dion 1995a:55-57; 1995b:6). See also Postgate 1972-75:415.

[27] See Cavigneaux and Ismail 1990:356; Frame *RIMB* 2:298, n. iii.11′.

[28] Following Frame (*RIMB* 2:298, n. iii.13′), the term *kinaltu/kiništu* is translated "the workforce," even though it is normally used in connec-

had been built (i.e. finished), a twenty-man band[29] [e] of Arameans came there, but one officer of the mounted troops whom I had stationed there on guard captured them! I built a city there and named it Dūr-Ninurta-kudurrī-uṣur.[30] I settled people in it (and) stationed mounted troops in it. For the sake of the security of the land of Suḫu, it (the city) is the open eyes of the land of Suḫu. No one in the future who comes forward should become negligent of this city (or) expel the inhabitants whom I settled in this city. For the sake of the security of the land of Suḫu, they should (continually) guard against the enemy. Just as I (did), he should not become negligent of this city.

e 2 Kgs 5:2; 6:15-23; 13:20; Hos 6:9

(lines iii. 22b′-32′)
I, Ninurta-kudurrī-uṣur, governor of the land of Suḫu and the land of Mari, discovered a tract of land (capable of being) cultivated on the top of a cliff and I conceived the idea of building a city there. When I had laid a stone foundation, I reinforced (it). I built a city upon (it), and named it Kār-Apla-Adad.[31] I [settled] 50 ..., citizens of the land of Suḫu, who had approached (me), Ninurta-kudurrī-uṣur, governor of the land of Suḫu and the land of Mari, about settling in (this) city, saying: "Settle us in your city!" I planted orchards near it. I built a temple to Apla-Adad and [...]. I settled inside (it) [...] of Apla-Adad, who had (previously) dwelt in the city of Anat. I established one *sūtu*[32] of bread and fine beer [...] as regular offerings for him. I presen[ted] (them) to the temple entrants[33] and the mayor. I built a palace for the governor there. I repaired the embankment(?) from the Euphrates; and I made it high; (and) I built a [...] upon it.
(lacuna)

(lines iv.1′-9a′)
I, Ninurta-ku[durrī-uṣur, governor of the land of Suḫu and the land of Mari: the *Akītu*-temple of the gods Adad] and Mešar (Mīšarum) — the great gods who dwell in the city of Udada — had become old and had been abandoned. None am[ong] my ancestors had paid attention (to it) and had rebuilt (it). I completely rebuilt this *Akītu*-temple; and I dedicated (it) to Adad and Mešar (Mīšarum),[f] the great gods, my lords, in order to ensure my good health (and) the well-being of my offspring, to prolong my days, to make my reign firm, (and) to defeat the land of the enemy.

f Pss 45:7; 67:5; etc.

(lines iv.9b′-15a′)
The palace of Enamḫe-zēra-ibni, governor of the land of Suḫu, (which is located in) the district of the city of Raʾil, which is in the middle of the Euphrates (river), had become old and I abandoned it. I built another palace above it: 64 cubits is its length (and) 12½ cubits is its width. I made it 20 cubits longer (and) 4 cubits wider than the palace of Enamḫe-zēra-ibni. I built (even) another palace above it. I made it 45 cubits long (and) 9 cubits wide.

(lines iv.15b′-26a′)
The people of Raʾil (and) their rebels, they had rebelled against my father, but my father had defeated them. At the beginning of my governorship, when I had sat on the throne of my father, the people of Raʾil rebelled against me; but I defeated them. In this regard, I did not pay (much) attention to it and did not make a relief (commemorating) it. No one in the future who comes forward should become negligent of the people of Raʾil! Regarding the city of Āl-gabbāri-bānî, the city which Šamaš-rēša-uṣur, governor of the land of Suḫu and the land of Mari, had built, I built an enclosure[34] around it. I made the city longer and wider, and I strengthened (it). The wall of the enclosure which I built is 13 cubits thick. I dug a moat around the city; and I surrounded the city on all sides with water.

(lines iv.26b′-38′)[35]
I, Ninurta-kudurrī-uṣur, governor of the land of Suḫu and the land of Mari: regarding the Temanites and Sabaeans,[36] [g] whose country is far away, from whom no messenger had ever come to me, and (who) had never travelled to meet me, their merchant caravan[37] came near to the water of the wells of Martu (Amurru?) and Ḫalatu, but it passed by and entered into the city of Ḫindānu. While in the city of Kār-Apla-Adad, I heard a report about them at noon; and I (immediately) harnessed (the horses of) my chariot. I crossed the river during the night and reached the city of Azlāyanu before noon of the next day. I waited in the city of Azlā-

g Ezek 27:17, 22f.

tion with temple personnel. See *CAD* K 386 s.v. *kiništu* "a class of priests of lowly status concerned with the preparation of food offerings."

[29] The word *gudūdu* is cognate to Heb./Aram. g^e*dûd* (See Cavigneaux and Ismail 1990:356, n. iii.14). The activities of these Aramean bands in this text parallels chronologically those of the Aramean and Moabite g^e*dûdîm* "bands" mentioned in the Elisha cycle (2 Kgs 5:2; 6:15-23; 13:20); and Hos 6:9; 7:1. Earlier cf. 1 Kgs 11:23-25; later 2 Kgs 24:2.

[30] For a similar episode, cf. the Azatiwada inscription (*COS* 2.31, ii.9–iii.2).

[31] Lit. "Quay of Apla-Adad."

[32] Approximately 10 liters.

[33] I.e., those privileged to enter the temple.

[34] The word written *a-di-ri* is a hapax and following the suggestion of Cavigneaux and Ismail (1990:357) and Frame (*RIMB* 2:299) it is translated here as "enclosure." It may be connected to the Heb. root *ʾzr*.

[35] For this passage and a discussion of Taimāʾ, see Liverani 1992c; Livingstone 1995:137-140; Kitchen 1997:134-135.

[36] Sabaʾ, South Arabia, biblical Sheba. See Kitchen 1997:127-128.

[37] Postgate (1995b:404) remarks: "*alaktu* has the sense of 'a (single) trip' especially with the concrete nuance of a merchant caravan."

yanu for three days and on the third day they approached. I captured 100 of them alive. I captured their 200 camels, together with their loads — blue-purple wool, ... wool, iron, <*pappar*>*dilû*-stones,[38] every kind of merchandise. I plundered their abundant booty and brought it back into the land of Suḫu.

In the 7th year of Ninurta-kudurrī-uṣur, governor of the land of Suḫu and the land of Mari, this report was made. Collated.

[38] Agates and onyxes were often used for their magical powers (Sax 1992). The *pappardilû* stone was one of these (Dalley 1999:77; Tallon 1995; Galter 1987:15). Agates for seals and beads were items traded by the South Arabians. Note the seal from ᶜAna with a South Arabian inscription made of agate (Collon 1987: #379).

REFERENCES

Text, translations and studies: Frame *RIMB* 2:294-300; Cavigneaux and Ismail 1990:343-357; Dion 1995a; 1995b; Grayson 1993; 1994; 1995.

NINURTA-KUDURRĪ-UṢUR — SUḪU ANNALS (#18) (2.115C)

K. Lawson Younger, Jr.

Inscribed on a stone stela discovered on the island of ᶜĀnā, this text describes a revolt of the city of Anat (before the days of Ninurta-kudurrī-uṣur) and the subsequent disaster when "the Assyrian" took action against the city. It records Ninurta-kudurrī-uṣur's restoration of the city, emphasizing his goodness and kindness.

(lines i.1-5)

I, Ninurta-kudurrī-uṣur, governor of the land of Suḫu and the land of Mari, son of Šamaš-rēša-uṣur, ditto[1] (governor of the land of Suḫu and the land of Mari), descendant of Adad-nādin-zēri, ditto (governor of the land of Suḫu and the land of Mari), the one of everlasting seed of Tunamissaḫ, son of Ḫammu-rāpi, king of Babylon.

(lines i.6-22a)

Tabnēa, the governor of the land of Suḫu, went up to Assyria with his tribute for an audience, but he ("the Assyrian") killed him in Assyria. Then the inhabitants of the city of Anat rebelled against the land of Suḫu. They joi[ned] hands with the Assyrian[2] and brought the Assyrian up to the city of Anat. (However) the Assyrian [to]ok the city of Anat neither by force nor by battle; (instead) the men — the citizens of the city themselves — (simply) gave (it) [to] the Assyrian. Afterwards, the Assyrian exiled them and scattered them over (all) the lands. He turned the houses on (both) the landside and the hillside of the city of Anat into heaps of ruins. Then the Assyrian settled his own men in the city of Anat.

(lines 22b-ii.19a)

From (the time of) Tabnēa, Iqīša-Marduk, and Nasḫir-Adad — three governors (in all) — for fifty years, the city of Anat was (under the control) of the Assyrian, (and also) for three years, in the days of Šamaš-rēša-uṣur, ditto (governor of the land of Suḫu and the land of Mari), my father, bef[ore] ... [... I sat on] the throne of [my] father. When the gods Adad and Apla-[Adad] set [...], the city of A[nat] returned (its allegiance) [to my father]. After four(?) [years], during which the city of Anat pros[pered(?)], [my father di]ed.[3] I [sat on] the throne of my father, I (re-)established the regular offerings, offe[rings, (...)] and religious festivals of the god Adad [...] according to the wording (of the commands) of Ḫam[mu]-rāp[i, king of Babylon, and] the father who begot me. [...] In addition, I settled people in the city of Anat on (both) the landside and on the hi[ll]side. I settled the city of Anat as (it had been) before, on (both) the landside and the hillside. I returned the gods of (both) the landside [and the hillside of] the city of Anat who had gone [t]o the city of Ribaniš[4] on account of the Assyrian [...] and I settled them in their dwelling(s), (just) as (they had been) before.

(lines ii.19b-25)

I built an *Akītu*-temple in the city of Anat: 1[00] cubits is its length (and) 16 cubits is its width. I built a ... palace beside (it): 47 cubits is its length (and) 8 cubits is its width. A palace of gladness [...]

(lines iii.1-7)

(No translation possible)

(lines iii.8-18)

[Anyone in the future who] comes forward [... I made] this foundation [10 cubits] deep. [I qua]rried large mountain-stones, laid the foundation, [and]

[1] The cuneiform repeating sign is used.

[2] It is unclear who "the Assyrian" is. While it may refer to an Assyrian governor, it more probably refers to the Assyrian king (cf. Cavigneaux and Ismail 1990:386). Apparently, Tabnēa would have taken his tribute to Assyria for an audience with the Assyrian monarch.

[3] Lit. "[went] to his fate."

[4] On the identification of this city, see the comments of Frame (*RIMB* 2:279).

made (it) firm. [I s]et my own name [with] his own [na]me. Anyone in the future [who] comes forward should revere the gods Adad and Apla-[Adad] and not become negligent of those who are favorable and those who are hostile to the city of Anat. Like me, may he (then) enjoy happiness!

REFERENCES

Text and translations: Cavigneaux and Ismail 1990:383-388, 437-439; *RIMB* 2:315-317.

NINURTA-KUDURRĪ-UṢUR — SUḪU ANNALS (#17) (2.115D)

K. Lawson Younger, Jr.

This inscription is engraved on a stone stela found on the island of ᶜĀnā. It also contains a relief of Ninurta-kudurrī-uṣur venerating the goddess Anat. In the text, Ninurta-kudurrī-uṣur describes his restoration of the statue and cult of the goddess after the desecration of the Assyrian following a revolt of the city of Anat against the land of Suḫu, narrated in *COS* 2.115C above. The same events are presented through political and religious filters.

(lines 1-9a)

For the goddess Anat, the perfect lady, most exalted of goddesses, strongest of goddesses, greatest of the Igīgu gods, excellent lady, whose godhead is splendid, splendid lady, whose valor is not equalled by (any of the other) goddesses, one who grasps the hand of the powerless, grants life, and gives instruction(s) to the king who reverences her, (one who) presents to the people of her settlements prosperity and abundance, who dwells in Ešuziana[1] — holy cella, the excellent shrine — the great lady, his lady.

(lines 9b-14)

I, Ninurta-kudurrī-uṣur, governor of the land of Suḫu and the land of Mari, son of Šamaš-rēša-uṣur, governor of the land of Suḫu and the land of Mari, descendant of Adad-nādin-zēri, governor of the land of Suḫu and the land of Mari, distant descendant of Tunamissaḫ, son of Ḫammu-rāpi, king of Babylon.

(lines 15-23a)

The people of Anat who live in the city of Anat rebelled against the land of Suḫu. They joined hands with the Assyrian and brought the Assyrian up to the city of Anat. (However), he defiled the city of Anat and its gods. He defiled the fine garment of the goddess Anat, the *ṣāriru*-gold, the precious stones, and all the (other) things befitting her godhead. Then he placed her (statue) by itself in a hidden place.

(lines 23b-32)

I, Ninurta-kudurrī-uṣur, governor of the land of Suḫu and the land of Mari, the servant who reverences her great godhead, brought Anat out from (that) hidden place and [returned] (her) fine garment, the [*ṣār*]*iru*-gold, and ... the precious stones. [I] made her godhead complete (again). Then I caused her to reside in [...]. I (re-)established the regular [offerings ... and] her [...] according to the wording (of the commands) of Ḫammu-rāpi, king of Babylon, a king who preceded me.

(lines 33-34)

(No translation possible)

(lacuna)

[1] Lit., "House, True hand of Heaven."

REFERENCES

Text and translations: Cavigneaux and Ismail 1990:380-383, 435-436; *RIMB* 2:317-318.

SHALMANESER IV — PAZARICIK / MARAŞ STELA (2.116)

K. Lawson Younger, Jr.

This inscription is incised on the back of the stone stela that contains an inscription of Adad-nirari III (see its description in *COS* 2.114B above). Like that earlier inscription, Shalmaneser IV's text confirms the boundary of Ušpilulume, king of Kummuḫ. It also contains the mention of another individual in a significant role in addition to the king of Assyria; in this case, Šamši-ilu, the commander-in-chief (*turtānu*) (see his inscription, *COS* 2.115A); Adad-nirari's text mentions his mother Sammuramat. Finally, the inscription makes reference to a campaign by Šamši-ilu against a Ḫadiyāni (*ḫa-di-a-ni*) of Damascus which resulted in tribute being given to the Assyrian monarch by the Damascene. This inscription dates to 773/772 BCE, the date of this particular campaign against Damascus.

(lines 1-3)
Shalmaneser, mighty king, king of Assyria, son of Adad-nirārī (III), mighty king, king of the universe, king of Assyria, son of Šamši-Adad (V), king of the four quarters.

(lines 4-10)
When Šamši-ilu, the commander-in-chief (*turtānu*), marched to the land of Damascus, the tribute of Ḫadiyāni,[1] [a] the Damascene — silver, gold, copper, his royal bed, his royal couch, his daughter with her extensive dowry, the property of his palace without number — I received from him.

(lines 11-13a)
On my return, I gave this boundary stone to Ušpilulume, king of the Kummuḫites.

(lines 13b-20)
Whoever takes (it) away from the possession of Ušpilulume, his sons, and grandsons, may Aššur, Marduk, Adad, Sîn, (and) Šamaš not stand (with him) at his lawsuit; may they not listen to his prayers; may they quickly smash his country like a brick; (and) may he no longer give advice to the king.[2]

Interdict of Aššur, my god, (and) Sîn, who dwells in Ḫarran.

a For a king having this name, though not the individual mentioned here, see 1 Kgs 15:18

[1] For ᵐ*ḫa-di-a-ni*, see Dion 1997:182, n. 47, 208-209; Timm 1993:75-77. Cp. the name ᵐ*ra-ḫi-[a]-ni* "Rezin" (see *COS* 2.117A, n. 2).

[2] These last two sentences (lines 18 and 19) pose great difficulties in both the correct reading of the cuneiform and the proper translation. For recent full discussions, see Zaccagnini 1993 and Ponchia 1991:8-12. Donbaz (1990:10), Timm (1993:58-59) and Grayson (*RIMA* 3:240) transliterate: (18) KUR-*su ki-i* SIG_4 *lu-šá-*⌈*bi(?)-ru(?)*⌉ *ur-ru-uḫ* (19) *mim-ma ina* UGU MAN *la i-ma-lik*, and translate: "may they quickly smash his country like a brick; (and) may he no longer give advice to the king." Ponchia 1991:8-11 follows Donbaz's transliteration and translation of line 18, but reads line 19 as: *mám-ma ina* UGU-*šú*?! *la i-ma-lik* "nessuno gli darà consiglio(?)." She proposes alternative interpretations of the line as "nessuno (gli) darà consigli (come) ad un re (*ina* UGU MAN)" or "mai più darà consigli al re." Zaccagnini (1993:55) argues for a different transliteration and translation of both lines: "May his country become quickly as small as a brick, in no way may he exercise kingship over the (legitimate) king."

REFERENCES

Text, translations and studies: *RIMA* 3:239-240; Zaccagnini 1993; Timm 1993; Ponchia 1991:8-12; Donbaz 1990.

TIGLATH-PILESER III (2.117)

THE CALAḪ ANNALS (2.117A)

K. Lawson Younger, Jr.

In the final years of Tiglath-pileser's reign,[1] the royal scribes composed what became the final "full" edition of his Annals, made up of seventeen *palû*'s (or regnal years). This edition was inscribed between two registers of reliefs on stone slabs already in place decorating the walls of Tiglath-pileser's palace at Calah (Nimrud). However, the palace was never completed, and the slabs were later dismantled by Esarhaddon. During early excavations, some of these slabs were recovered in Tiglath-pileser's palace while others were discovered in Esarhaddon's South-West Palace.

But many slabs were lost or destroyed in antiquity, or while being excavated. In fact, major portions of the originals have survived only in squeezes or hand copies made by the early discoverers: A. H. Layard, H. Rawlinson and G. Smith. The fragmentary state of the extant texts, along with difficulties in the squeezes and hand copies, makes it difficult to understand the Annals' contents and to arrange the material chronologically. Nevertheless, it is clear that the Annals of Tiglath-pileser can be divided into parallel series that differ in the number of lines per column: the seven-line series, the twelve-line series, and the sixteen-line series, originating from different halls. Finally, through much hard work and persistence of study, H. Tadmor has recently published the Calah recension of the Annals following the chronological order of the preserved twenty-eight annal units (1994:27-89).

(Ann. 21:1′-10′; Tadmor 54-55)
Bīt-[Agusi ...] in the midst of [...] of Ma[tiᵓil ...] I placed there. From Rezin[2] [a] [...] x talents of gold, 300 talents of silver, 200 talents of [...] 20 talents of ladanum,[3] 300 ... 30 [...] Kuštašpi, the Kummuḫite, [...], the Tyrian, Urikki,[4] [the Quean], [...] Pisiris, the Carchemishite, Tarḫulara, [the Gurgumite], [...] iron, elephant hides, elephant tusks (ivory), red-purple wool, [...]

a 2 Kgs 15:37; 16:5-9; Isa 7:1-8; 8:6

[1] The biblical texts concerning Tiglath-pileser are: 2 Kgs 15-16; Isa 7; 8:1-10, 23; 10:9; 17:1-3; Amos 6:2; 1 Chr 5:6, 26; 2 Chr 28:16-21.

[2] Concerning the name ᵐ*ra-ḫi-[a]-ni*, i.e., Rezin, see Pitard 1987:181; 1992b; Naᵓaman 1995c.

[3] ŠIM.*la-du-nu* "the aromatic plant." See *CAD* L 36 s.v. *ladinnu*.

[4] See the Karatepe bilingual: Hieroglyphic Luwian: *COS* 2.21, n. 11; Phoen.: *COS* 2.31. See also the Cebel Ires Daği inscription (*COS* 3).

(Ann. 25:1′-12′; Tadmor 56-59)
elephant hides, elephant tusks (ivory), red-purple wool, multi-colored garments, linen garments — numerous clothes of their lands. [...] weapons, spindle(s)[5] [...] I received within the city of Arpad. [Tutammu, king of the land of Unqi][6] broke [the loyalty oath sworn by the great gods] (and) forfeited his life.[7] My enemy [...] [he did not con]sult me. In my fury [...] of Tutammu, together with [his] nobles [...] I captured Kinalia,[8] [b] his royal city. His people, together with their possessions, [...] mules I counted in the midst of my army like sheep. [...] I set up my throne inside Tutammu's palace. [...] 300 talents of silver, by the heavy standard, 100 talents of [...] war equip[ment], multi-colored garments, linen garments, all kinds of spices,[9] the furnishings of his palace, [...] I reorganized (the administration of) Kinalia (as an Assyrian provincial capital). I [subdued] Unqi to its full extent. [...] I placed my eunuchs as governors over them.

b Isa 10:9; Amos 6:2

(Ann. 19*:1-12; Tadmor 58-63)
[...] Azriyau[10] [...] I seized and [...] tribute like that [of the Assyrians ...] the city of [...] his helper(s). The city of El[...] the cities of [Usnu], Siannu, [...[11]] Kašpuna, which are on the seashore, together with the towns [...] [up to Mount Saue], which nudges[12] the Lebanon, Mount Baᵓali-ṣapūna,[13] up to Anti-Lebanon,[14] the boxwood mountain, all the Mount Saue,[15] the province of Kar-Adad,[16] the city of Hatarikka,[17] the province of Nuqudina, [Mount Hasu], together with the towns of its environs, the city of Ara [...], both of them, the towns of their environs, all of Mount Sarbua, the city of Ašḫani, (and) the city of Yatabi, all of Mount Yaraqu, ... the city of Ellitarbi, the city of Zitanu, up to the city of Atinni ..., the city of Bumame[18] — 19 districts of Hamath together with the towns of their environs, which are on the western seashore, which in sin and criminal outrage were seized for Azriyau, I annexed to Assyria. I placed two of my eunuchs[19] over them as governors. [...] 83,000 (people) [...] in/from those cities in the province of Tuš[ḫan] I settled. I settled 1,223 people in the province of Ulluba.[20]

c 2Kgs 15:14-22, esp. 19

(Ann. 13*:10-Ann. 14*:5; Tadmor 69-71)
I received the tribute of Kuštašpi, the Kummuḫite, Rezin, the Damascene, Menahem,[21] [c] the Samarian, Hiram, the Tyrian, Sibittibiᵓil,[22] the Byblian, Urikki, the Quean, Pisiris, the Carchemishite, Eniil, the Hamathite, Panammuwa,[23] the Samᵓalite, Tarḫulara, the Gurgumite, Sulumal, the Melidite,

[5] GIŠ.*pilaqqu* "spindles." Cf. Esarhaddon's Succession Treaty, SAA 2:56 (lines 616-617): *ki-i* GIŠ.*pi-laq-qi lu-šá-aṣ-bi-ru-ku-nu ki-i* MÍ *ina* IGI LÚ.KÚR-*ku-nu le-pa-šu-ku-nu* "May (the gods) spin you around like a spindle, may they make you like a woman before your enemy."

[6] For the restoration, see Tadmor 1994:56, n. 2′.

[7] The Akk. ⌜*i*⌝-*miš nap-ša-ti-šú* appears cognate to the Heb. *mwᵓs npšw* (Prov 15:32). See Tadmor 1994:56.

[8] Kinalia/Kinalua (Tell Tayinat) was the capital of Unqi. Unqi was conquered and annexed in 738 BCE according to the evidence of the Eponym Chronicle. It is to be equated with biblical Kullani (Naᵓaman 1974:82-83; Tadmor 1994:58; Hawkins 1995b:95). Cf. Isa 10:9; Amos 6:2.

[9] ŠIM.ḪI.A DÙ.A-*ma* (*riqqē kalâma*) "all kinds of spices."

[10] The identification of this individual is uncertain. Three proposals have been made. Two of these proposals were based on a supposed join to *ITP* Ann 19* (= ICC 65), namely K 6205 — a fragmentary tablet that contains an account of a war against the land of *Yaudi* and a certain individual called [... *i*]*a-a-u* KUR *Ia-u-da-a-a*. Thus some scholars have proposed that Azriyau was the king of Yᵓdy/Samᵓal, the southeastern Anatolian state (e.g. Winckler 1893). This view, however, is the least likely since Yᵓdy/Samᵓal was always rendered KUR/URU *Samᵓal(la)* in Assyrian records, whereas *Yaudu/i* exclusively refers to Judah. Others suggested that Azriyau was Azariah, the powerful king of Judah (Tadmor 1961b; see also Roberts 1985). The third proposal was put forth by Naᵓaman (1974). He argued convincingly that K 6205 should be joined to another fragment and that both of these derive from the reign of Sennacherib (see the Azekah inscription, *COS* 2.119D below). This meant that the Azriyau of Tiglath-pileser's annals no longer was attributed to a particular country. Thus Naᵓaman (1995b:276-277) argued that this Azriyau was an otherwise unattested king of Hatarikka (biblical Hadrach), a Syrian state neighboring Hamath, and postulated an alternative reconstruction of the events of 739 and especially 738, the year in which Tiglath-pileser annexed Unqi, Hatarikka and the "19 districts of Hamath" (Ann 19*.9-10). See also Weippert 1976-80; Hawkins 1976-80b:273). Until new evidence is discovered, any interpretation of the Azriyau episode must remain conjectural. For further discussion, see Tadmor 1994:273-276; and *PNA* 1:240.

[11] Borger (*TUAT* 1:370) reads "Simya," which was a city south of Arvad.

[12] *it*]-*tak-ki-pu-ni*. Tadmor (1994:61) notes that in a geographic context *nakāpu* is unattested in Akk. and compares Heb. "*pgᶜ b*... in similar delimitations of boundaries (e.g. Josh 16:7; 19:22, 26; etc.)."

[13] Baᶜal-Ṣapūna. Jebel el-Aqra in northern Syria. See Röllig *RlA* 4:241-242.

[14] Lit. Mt. Ammanana. See Cogan 1984:255-259.

[15] For a discussion of the reading, see Tadmor 1994:60.

[16] Kar-Adad. Perhaps Aleppo, the center of storm-god worship. Cf. Hawkins 1972-75:53.

[17] Hatarikka is the Hazrik of the Zakkur inscription (*COS* 2.35). Cf. Heb. Hadrach (*ḥdrk*) of Zech 9:1.

[18] Perhaps this should be emended to URU *Bu-ta-me*. See Weippert 1973:42, n. 61.

[19] See Grayson 1995.

[20] The province was organized immediately after the campaign to Ulluba in 739 BCE.

[21] On the date of Menahem's tribute see Tadmor 1994:274-276. According to 2 Kgs 15:19, Menahem gave Pul of Assyria 1,000 talents of silver. That the names Tiglath-pileser (*Tukulti-apil-Ešarra*) and Pul (*Pūlu*) were used to designate a single ruler is no longer seriously called in question (Brinkman 1968:61). The name Pul is often understood as Tiglath-pileser's Babylonian throne name (Oded 1997:109). On the other hand, Brinkman (1968:61-62, n. 317; 240-241, n. 1544) and Tadmor (1994:280, n. 5) understand it either as Tiglath-pileser's original name or as a quasi-hypocoristic for the second element of the name Tiglath-pileser — *apil*. In either case, *pūlu*, *pīlu*, i.e. "limestone block," could also have served in folk etymology as a nickname for the ruthless empire-builder. See further Loretz and Mayer 1990:228-229.

[22] Spelled here (Ann. 13*:11): ᵐ*Si-bi-it-bi-ᵓi-li*. Spelled in Iran Stela (iii.A.7): ᵐ*Si-bít-ba-il*.

[23] See the Panammuwa inscription, *COS* 2.37.

Dadīlu,[24] the Kaskean, Uassurme, the Tabalian,[25] Ušḫitti, the (A)Tunean,[26] Urballâ,[27] the Tuḫanean, Tuḫamme, the Ištundian, Uirime, the Hubišnean, Zabibe, queen of the land of Arabia: gold, silver, tin, iron, elephant hides, elephant tusks (ivory), multi-colored garments, linen garments, blue-purple wool, and red-purple wool, ebony,[28] boxwood, all kinds of precious things from the royal treasure, live sheep whose wool is dyed red-purple, flying birds of the sky whose wings are dyed blue-purple, horses, mules, cattle and sheep, camels, she-camels together with their young.

(Ann. 23*:1′-18′; Tadmor 78-81)
[... of] Rezin[29] [the Damascene ...]. [I captured] heavy [booty] [...] his advisor [...] [(With) the blood of his] war[riors] I dyed a reddish hue the river of [...], raging [torrent]; [...], his courtiers, charioteers and [...], their weapons I smashed; and [...] their horses I [...]. I captured his warriors, archers, shield- and lance-bearers; and I dispersed their battle array. That one (i.e. Rezin), in order to save his life, fled alone; and he entered the gate of his city [like] a mongoose. I impaled alive his chief ministers; and I made his country behold (them). I set up my camp around the city for 45 days;[30] and I confined him like a bird in a cage.[31] His gardens, [...] orchards[32] without number I cut down; I did not leave a single one.

... the town of ...]ḫadara, the home of the dynasty of Rezin the Damascene, [the pl]ace where he was born, I surrounded (and) captured. 800 people with their possessions, their cattle (and) their sheep I took as spoil. I took as spoil 750 captives from the city of Kuruṣṣa (and) the city of Sama, 550 captives from the city of Metuna. I destroyed 591 cities of 16 districts of Damascus like mounds of ruins after the Deluge.

Annals 18 compared with Annals 24 (Tadmor 80-84)[33]

(Ann. 18:3′-13′)	d Josh 19:14	(Ann. 24:3′-16′)
[... of 16] districts of Bīt-[Ḫumria] (Is[rael)] I [leveled to the grou]nd ...		of 16 di[stricts of Bīt-Ḫumria (Israel)]
		[...]
[... captives from the city of ...]bara,	e 2 Kgs 21:19	[...] capti[ves from ...]
625 captives from the city of [...]		[...]
[...]		226 [captives from ...]
[... x captives from the city of] Ḫinatuna,[d]	f 2 Kgs 23:36	captives [from ...]
650 captives from the city of Ku[...]		[...]
[...]	g Josh 11:1, 5	400 [(+ x) captives from ...]
[... x captives from the city of Ya]tbite[e]		[...]
656 captives from the city of Sa... [...]		656 captives from the city of Sa... (altogether)]
[...]		13,520 [people ...]
[...]		with their posessions [I carried off to Assyria]
[...] the cities of Aruma[f] and Marum[g] [...]		[... the cities of Aruma and Marum]
[...]		[situated in] rugged mountains [I conquered (?) ...]

[24] Dadīlu or Tadīlu. Apparently a Luwian PN, see *PNA* 1:364.

[25] Uassurme of Tabal (Bīt-Burutaš) is known from Hieroglyphic Luwian as Wasussarma and ruled a minimum 738-730 BCE. See Hawkins and Postgate 1988:38. For a possible connection with Ben-Tabʾal (Isa 7:6), see Hallo 1960:49.

[26] Or Atunaean (Iran Stela, *COS* 2.117B). See Hawkins and Postgate 1988:35, 37-38.

[27] Urballa of Tuḫana is attested in a recently discovered Hieroglyphic Luwian-Phoenician bilingual found in 1986 in Ivriz, near Ereğli, Turkey. The inscription was commissioned by Muwaḫarna, the son of Warpalawa, king of Tuwana (Tuḫana, classical Tyana). Warpalawa may be identified with Urballu of Tuhana (ca. 738-710 BCE). See Dinçol 1994:117-128 and Röllig 1992:98.

[28] GIŠ *ušû* is probably "ebony." For a discussion of the *ušû* tree, see Stol 1979:34-49; *AHw* 1442.

[29] For the reading, see Tadmor 1994:78.

[30] The capture of Damascus and the execution of Rezin are only recorded in 2 Kgs 16:9.

[31] GIM *iṣ-ṣur qu-up-pi e-sir-šú*. This motif recurs in Sennacherib's description of his siege of Jerusalem during his campaign against Hezekiah in 701 BCE (*COS* 2.119B, note 9). Tadmor remarks: "The true sense of these passages is that of a total blockade, and the hyperbole is employed as a face-saving device to cover for a failure to take the enemy's capital and punish the rebellious king. In the case of Rezin, this was accomplished in the following year (732); in the case of Hezekiah, Sennacherib was forced to make do with heavy tribute delivered to Nineveh after his retreat" (1994:79, n. to 11′).

[32] For this motif in the earlier inscriptions of Shalmaneser III (also concerning a siege of Damascus), see Calah Annals *COS* 2.113C, note 3.

[33] See Naʾaman 1993:105; 1995b:271-275; Younger 1998:210-214.

REFERENCES

Text: Smith 1875; Rost 1892; Tadmor 1994:58-63; 69-71; 78-81; 80-84. Translations: *ARAB* 1:§§770-771, 772-774; 776-779; *DOTT* 54-55; *ANET* 282-283; *TUAT* 1:370-373; Naʾaman 1986a:125; 1995b:271-275.

THE IRAN STELA (2.117B)

K. Lawson Younger, Jr.

This inscription is incised on a stela from somewhere in western Iran, perhaps Luristan (Levine 1972:11). The exact provenance is unknown. It is the only known stela of Tiglath-pileser III. After his second campaign in the area in his 9th *palû* (regnal year) (i.e. 737 BCE), he set it up on the border of one of the states that he had defeated during that campaign.[1]

(lines iii.A.1-23)

The kings of the land of Ḫatti, (and of) Aram of the western seashore, the land of Qedar[2] [a] (and) the land of Arabia:[3] Kuštašpi, the Kummuḫite, Rezin,[4] the Damascene, Menahem,[b] the Samarian, Tuba᾿il,[5] the Tyrian, Sibitba᾿il,[6] the Byblian, Urik(ki),[7] the Quean, Sulumal, the Melidite, Uassurme, the Tabalian,[8] Ušḫiti, the Atunean, Urballâ, the Tuḫanean, Tuḫamme, the Ištundian, Uirime, the Ḫubišnean, Dadi-ilu, the Kaskean,[8] Pisiris, the Carchemishite, Panammuwa,[9] the [Sa]m᾿alite, Tarḫularu, the [Gur]gumite, Zabibe, the queen of the land of Arabia — I imposed on them tribute of silver, gold, tin, iron, elephant hides, elephant tusks (ivory), blue-purple (and) red-purple garments, multi-colored garments, linen garments, camels, (and) she-camels.

a Gen 25:13; Isa 21:16-17; 42:11; Jer 2:10; 49:28; Ezek 27:21; Ps 120:4[5]; 1 Chr 1:29

b 2 Kgs 15:19

(lines iii.A.24-30)

And as for Iranzu, the Mannaean,[10] Daltâ,[11] the Ellipian, the city rulers of the land of Namri, the land of Singibutu (and) all the eastern mountains — I imposed on them (as tribute) horses, mules, Bactrian camels, cattle (and) sheep (so that) I might receive[12] (it) regularly on an annual basis in the land of Assyria.

(lines iii.A.31-36)

I caused a stela to be made in the vicinity of the mountain, (and) I depicted on it (the symbols of) the great gods, my lords, (and) I engraved upon it my own royal image; and the mighty deeds of Aššur, my lord, and achievements of [my] hands, which were done throughout all the lands, I wr[ote] on it. [At] the border, which is at ... [...].

[1] See lines iii.A.31-36 and iii.B.1′-10′. See Levine 1972:15; Tadmor 1994:92. For different views on the stela's dating see Cogan 1973:97-98; Na᾿aman 1986b:81-82; Kuan 1995:150-152.

[2] KUR *Qid-ri*. This is the earliest mention of the Qedarites. See Ephᶜal 1982:83; Kitchen 1994:49-51, 117-119, 167-169, 237.

[3] Weippert treats KUR *a-ri-bi* as an appositive of KUR *qid-ri*. While this is possible, it is more likely that they are two separate entities parallel in ways to Ḫatti and Aram in the previous line.

[4] Here spelled: ᵐ*Ra-qi-a-nu*. In other texts the name is spelled: ᵐ*Ra-ḫi-a-nu* (e.g. *COS* 2.117A, note 1 above).

[5] ᵐ*Tu-ba-il* is most likely the Phoen. name ᾿*tb*ᶜ*l*, "Ethbaᶜal/Ittobaᶜl. See Zadok 1978:70-71 for the transcription of *ba-ìl* for *b*ᶜ*l*. See also Pitard 1987:185; Kuan 1995:153.

[6] See *COS* 2.117A note 22 above.

[7] See *COS* 2.117A note 4 above.

[8-8] For these kings, see *COS* 2.117A notes 24-26; Hawkins and Postgate 1988. For Dadīlu, see *COS* 2.117A, note 24.

[9] See the Panamuwa inscription, *COS* 2.37.

[10] See Postgate 1987-90. Ir᾿anzi seems to have remained pro-Assyrian until his death in ca 717 BCE.

[11] For Daltâ, the king of Ellipi, who plays a role in Tiglath-pileser III's and Sargon II's reigns, see *PNA* 1:375.

[12] *šat-ti-šam-ma am-da-na-ḫa-ra*. This verbal form is a GTN durative 1cs + vent. Both the *-tan-* infix and the durative tense stress the expected regularity of the tribute on a yearly basis.

REFERENCES

Text: Levine 1972; Tadmor 1994:90-110 (106-109). Translations and Studies: *TUAT* 1:378; Weippert 1973:29-32.

SUMMARY INSCRIPTION 4 (2.117C)

K. Lawson Younger, Jr.

Incised on fragmentary pieces of an apparent pavement slab, this summary inscription was discovered in excavations at Nimrud and left *in situ*. It is preserved in squeezes that are no longer extant. Thought originally to be part of the Tiglath-pileser's Annals (note Luckenbill *ARAB* 1:§§ 815-819 and Oppenheim *ANET* 283), Wiseman (1956:118) recognized correctly the text's affinity to Summary Inscriptions 1 and 9.

(lines 1′-8′a)

[...] which [...] the city of Hatarikka up to Mount Sau[e], [... the city of] Byblos, [...] the city of Ṣimirra, the city of Arqa, the city Zimar[ra], [... the city of] Usnu, [the city of Siannu, the city of Ma]᾿araba, the city of Ri᾿sisu[ri] [...] the cities [...] of the Upper [Sea] I ruled. I placed six [of my] eunuchs[1] [over] them [as governors].

[... the city of Kaš]puna,[2] which is on the shore of the Upper (text: Lower) Sea [... the city of ...]nite,[3] the city of Gil[ead?,[4] and] [the city of] Abel-...,[5] which are the border of Bit Ḫumri[a][6] — I annexed to Assyria the en[tire] wide land of [Bit-Ḫazaʾi]li.[7] [I plac]ed [x eunuchs over them] as governors.

(lines 8′b-15′a)[8]

Ḫanunu of Gaza, [who] fle[d before] my weapons, (and) escaped [to] Egypt — [I conquered] Gaza [... his royal city], [I seized] his property (and) his gods. [I made a (statue) bearing the image of the gods my lo]rds and my (own) royal image [out of gold]. I set (it) up in the palace [of Gaza]; (and) I counted it among the gods of their land; I established [their ...].

As for [him (i.e. Hanunu), the fear of my majesty] overwhelmed him and like a bird he flew (back) [from Egypt]. [...[9]] I returned him to his position and [I turned his city(?) into an Assyrian] em[porium (*kāru*)]. I received [gold], silver, multi-colored garments, linen garments, large [horses], [...].

(lines 15′b-19′a)

I carried off [to] Assyria the land of Bīt-Ḫumria (Israel),[10] [a] [... its] "auxiliary [army,"] [...] all of its people, [...] [I/they killed][11] Pekah,[b] their king, and I installed Hoshea [c] [as king] over them. I received from them 10 talents of gold, x talents of silver, [with] their [possessions] and [I car]ried them [to Assyria].

(lines 19′b-36′)[12]

As for Samsi, the queen of the land of Arabia, at Mount Saqurri I sle[w 9,400] of her warriors. I seized 1,000 people, 30,000 camels, 20,000 cattle [...] 5,000 (leather pouches) of all kinds of spices[13] [...] seats of her gods, [arms (and) staffs of her goddesses,] and her property. And she, in order to save her life, [... to] a desert, an arid place, like an onager [made off]. [The rest of her possessions] (and) her [ten]ts, her people's watchmen,[14] within her camp [I set on fire].

[Samsi], who took fright at my mighty [weapo]ns, she brought [to Assyria] to my [presence] camels, she-camels, [together with their young]. I installed an official administrator (*qēpu*)[15] over her; and [... 10,000 soldiers ...].

The people of Massaʾ,[16] [d] Temā, Sabaʾ,[e] [Ḫayappâ],[f] Badanu, Ḫatte, Idibaʾilu, [..., who dwell] on the border of the countries of the setting sun (western lands) [of whom no one (of my ancestors) knew and whose place is far] away, the fame of my lordship [(and of) my heroic deeds they heard, and they made supplication to] my lordship. [They brought before me]: gold, silver, [camels, she-camels, all kinds of spices], their tribute, as one; [and they kissed] my feet. I appointed [Idibiʾilu[17] as the prebend of the "Gatekeeper"[18]] facing Egypt [... of] Aššur I placed therein. [...] I made and [...] the yoke of Aššur, my lord, [I placed over them ... in all the lands through which] I have marched.

a 2 Kgs 15:29; 1 Chr 5:26

b 2 Kgs 15:25-31; 16:5; Isa 7:1-8:6

c 2 Kgs 15:30; 17:1-6

d Gen 25:13-15; Prov 30:1; 31:1; 1 Chr 1:29-30

e Job 1:15; 6:19

f Gen 25:4; 1 Chr 1:33

---

[1] Concerning eunuchs, see Grayson 1995; Deller 1999.

[2] Concerning the erroneous reading Rašpuna, see Wiseman 1951:21-24; and Tadmor 1985b.

[3] "One might restore here *[adi libbi* ^{uru}*Qa]*-⌜*ni*⌝-*te*: Biblical Kenath (Num 32:42, 1 Chr 2:23) modern Qanawat in the Hauran. However, other restorations are not excluded" (Tadmor 1994:139, n. 6′). Naʾaman (1995:105-106) suggests the restoration: [Min]nite. Cf. Judg 11:33.

[4] For the reading "the city of Gil[ead?]," see Tadmor 1994:139, 186. Cf. Hos 6:8. Naʾaman suggests that this is a reference to Mizpeh-Gilead (Judg 10:17; 11:29) (1995c:105-106). See also *COS* 117F, note 5.

[5] ^{uru}*A-bi-il*-x_1-x_2 has been identified with Abel-beth-Maʾacah of 2 Kgs 15:29. In fact, Rost read ^{uru}*A-bi-il-ak-k*[*a*] (1892:78) and ^{uru}*A-bi-il*-⌜*ak*⌝-⌜*ka*⌝ (pl. xxv). Tadmor, however, states: "This reading cannot be sustained any longer ... One might read ^{uru}*A-bi-il*-⌜*šiṭ*⌝-⌜*ṭi*⌝. Perhaps it is ʾ*bl hšṭym* of Num 33:48-49" (Tadmor 1994:139, note to 6′). Tadmor also adds: "If *A-bi-il*-x_1-x_2 is read *A-bi-il*-⌜*šiṭ*⌝-⌜*ṭi*⌝ and identified with Abel-shittim, 'located in the plains of Moab by the Jordan at Jericho' (Num 33:48-49), this would indicate that Aram on the eve of its fall controlled a much larger territory east of Jordan than I had suggested in *IEJ* 12 (1962) 114-122" (1994:281, n. 10). Naʾaman (1995c:105-106) argues for an identification with Abel-shittim. Recently, Oded suggested Abila (1997:110).

[6] On the spelling Bīt-Ḫumria instead of Bīt-Ḫumrî, see Zadok 1978:306.

[7] I.e. Aram Damascus.

[8] The prominence given to Gaza is probably due to economic factors, esp. in connection with the spice trade. See Ehrlich 1991, esp. 54.

[9] Tadmor (1994:140, n. 13′) suggests that this lacuna probably included a statement about Ḫanunu's submission and plea for forgiveness. On Hanunu's return and restoration to power in Gaza, see Ehrlich 1996:94-98.

[10] Concerning Tiglath-pileser III's deportations of the northern kingdom, see Younger 1998:201-214; Naʾaman 1993.

[11] The restoration of the verb describing Pekah's fate is uncertain. Possible restorations include: [*i*]-*du*-[*ku-ma*] "they killed" or [*a*]-*du*-[*uk-ma*] "I killed" (Tadmor 1994:141, n. 17′). Rost's restoration *is-ki-pu-ma* is doubtful. According to 2 Kgs 15:30, Hoshea assassinated Pekah.

[12] For this episode, see Ephʿal 1982:33-36, 83-86; Tadmor 1994:225-230.

[13] See Ephʿal 1982:128, n. 447; cf. *COS* 2.117A, note 9.

[14] *ḫurādāt nišēša ... ašrup*. Tadmor (1994:143, n. 24′) argues that in this context the phrase seems unlikely to refer to the burning of watchmen (*ḫurādu*). Thus he understands the phrase metaphorically and renders "safeguard(?)," referring to Samsi's encampment. However, if adolescent boys and girls could be burned (e.g. by Aššur-nasir-pal II), why not watchmen? The term *ḫurādu* seems to refer to a type of soldier (*CAD* H 244). See also Borger *TUAT* 1:374.

[15] This title was generally given to Assyrian officials of various ranks who supervised the policy and administration in provinces and vassal states. See *CAD* Q 264-268 s.v. *qīpu*.

[16] For these tribes, see Ephʿal 1982:215-218.

[17] See Ephʿal 1982:43.

[18] See *CAD* A 2:522 s.v. *atûtu*.

REFERENCES

Text: Smith 1875:284-285; Rost 1892:78-83; Tadmor 1994:136-143. Translations and studies: *ARAB* 1:§§ 815-819; *ANET* 283; *DOTT* 55; Spieckerman 1982:324-327; *TUAT* 1:373-374; Irvine 1990:62-69; Kuan 1995:62-69.

SUMMARY INSCRIPTION 7 (2.117D)

K. Lawson Younger, Jr.

This inscription is written on about half of a large tablet (23.4 x 17.5+ cm) which though it bears the label K 3751, was most probably discovered at Nimrud. The most detailed of Tiglath-pileser's summary inscriptions, it was likely composed in or shortly after his 17th *palû* (regnal year) (i.e., 729 BCE) (Tadmor 1994:154, 238-259). It preserves the only complete building account of Tiglath-pileser from Calah.

(lines R. 1′-6′)[1]
[...] I set on fire. [Samsi who took fright at my mighty weapons]; [she brought to As]syria to my presence [camels, she-camels, together with their young]. I instal[led an official administrator (*qēpu*)[2] ov]er her; and [... 10,000 soldiers ...].

[The people of Mas]saʾ, Temā, Sabaʾ, Ḫayappâ, Badanu, [Ḫatte, Idibaʾilu, ... who dwell on the border of the countries of the setting sun (western lands)] of whom no one (of my ancestors) knew and whose place is far away, the fame of my lordship [(and of) my heroic deeds they heard, and they made supplication to my lordship]. [They brought] be[fore me [gold, silver], camels, she-camels, all kinds of spices, their tribute, as one; [and they kissed my feet]. I appointed [Idi]biʾilu[3] as the prebend of the gatekeeper[4] facing Egypt. In all the (foreign) lands which [...]

(lines R. 7′-13′)[5]
[I received the tribute] of Kuštašpi, the Kummuḫite, Urik(ki), the Quean, Sibittibiʾil, the [Byblian, Hiram, the Tyrian, Pisiris, the Carchemishite, Eni]-il, the Hamathite, Panammuwa,[6] the Samʾalite, Tarḫulara, the Gurgumite, Sulu[mal, the Melidite, Dadīlu, the Kaskaean, U]assurme, the Tabalite, Ušḫitti, the Tunaean,[7] Urballâ,[8] the Tuḫanaean, Tuḫam[me, the Ištundaean, Urimmi, the Hubišnaean, Ma]tanbiʾil, the Arvadite, Sanipu, Ammonite, Salamanu, Moabite, [...] [Mi]tinti,[9] the Ashkelonite, Jehoahaz,[10][a] the Judahite, Qaušmalaka, the Edomite, Muṣ[..., the ...] (and) Hanunu, the Gazaean: gold, silver, tin, multi-colored garments, linen garments, red-purple wool, [all kinds of] costly articles, produce of the sea (and) dry land, the commodities of their lands, royal treasures, horses (and) mules broken to the yo[ke ...].

[a] 2 Kgs 16:5-8

(lines R. 14′-15′)
Uassurme, the Tabalite, acted as if he was the equal of Assyria and did not appear before me. [I sent to Tabal] my eunuch, the Chief-[Eunuch (*rāb ša-rēši*), ...]. I placed on his throne [Ḫu]lli, the son of a nobody. [I received as his tribute] 10 talents of gold, 1,000 talents of silver, 2,000 horses, [... mules].

(line R. 16′)
I sent my eunuch, the Chief-Eunuch (*rāb ša-rēši*)[11] to Tyre. [I received] from Metenna, the Tyrian, [his tribute]: 150 talents of gold[12] (and) [2,000 talents of silver].

[1] See Ephᶜal 1982:34-36.
[2] See *COS* 2.117C, note 15.
[3] See Ephᶜal 1982:93.
[4] See Summary Inscription 4 (*COS* 2.117C, note 18).
[5] Noticeably missing from this list are references to Damascus, Samaria, Tyre and Arabia, nations that had paid tribute on earlier occasions. There are also new nations that are listed as tributaries (including Judah). Thus the list includes vassal kings who submitted in 738 BCE as well as those who submitted in 734 BCE. Concerning the composition of the list, see Weippert 1973:53; Ephᶜal 1982:29, n. 76; Tadmor 1994:258; but note Irvine 1990:43; Kuan 1995:162-163.
[6] See the Panamuwa inscription, *COS* 2.37.
[7] Or Atunaean. See Iran Stela, *COS* 2.117B.
[8] See *COS* 2.117A, note 27.
[9] For a recent discussion of this Mitinti and the fragmentary annalistic passages concerning him, see Naʾaman 1998c.
[10] ᵐ*Ia-ú-ḫa-zi* KUR *Ia-ú-da-a+a*. This is the full name of Ahaz, king of Judah who sent to Assyria to ask for aid against Rezin of Damascus and Pekah of Israel (2 Kgs 16:5-8). See Wiseman 1976-80; Hallo 1999a:36 and nn. 3-5.
[11] LÚ.GAL.SAG is the *rāb ša-rēši*, not the *rab šaqê* (contra Luckenbill *ARAB* 2:§§ 802-803; Oppenheim *ANET* 282; Wiseman *DOTT* 56). See Tadmor 1983; Grayson 1995.
[12] Concerning the amount of gold paid in tribute, see Tadmor's remarks (1994:171, n. 16′).

REFERENCES

Text: Smith 1875:256-285; Rost 1892:54-77; Tadmor 1994:154-175. Translations and studies: *ARAB* 1:§§787-804; *ANET* 282; *DOTT* 55-56; Spieckermann 1982:324-327; *TUAT* 1:374-375; Na⁾aman 1986b:72-73; Irvine 1990:40-41; Kuan 1995:161-164.

SUMMARY INSCRIPTION 8 (2.117E)

K. Lawson Younger, Jr.

This inscription (ND 400, now BM 131982) is found on a well-baked tablet fragment (8.6 x 10.8 cm) discovered at Nimrud in 1950. While it may be possible that the inscription is part of the same tablet as Summary Inscription 7 (K 3751), this is far from certain (it may be an additional copy).

(lines 1′-9′)
[...] [...] his [...] on dry land [...] [...] I made (them) pour out [their lives]. That city[1] to[gether with ...] [...] in the midst of the sea I devastated them and anni[hilated them]. [...] and he was afraid. He put on sackcloth[2] [...] [...] of ivory, ebony, inlaid with precious stones and gold, together with [...] [...] ivory, fine oil, all kinds of spices, horses[3] of E[gypt] [...] from Kašpuna, which is on the shore of the [Upper] Sea, [as far as ...] under the control of my eunuch, the governor of Ṣi[mirra, I placed].

(lines 10′-13′)[4]
[...] I filled [the plain] with the bodies of their warriors [like gras]s, [together with] their belongings, their cattle, their sheep, their asses [...] [...] within his palace [...] [...] I accepted their plea to [forgive] their rebellion (lit. "sin") and s[pared] their land.

(lines 14′-19′)
[...] [Ḫan]unu, the Gazaean [a] feared my powerful weapons and [escaped to Egypt]. [I conquered Gaza ...]. [x talents] of gold, 800 talents of silver, people together with their possessions, his wife, [his] sons, [his daughters ...] [I seized his property (and) his gods]. [I made] an image of the great gods, my lords, <and> an image of my lordship out of gold.[5] [I set (it) up in the palace of Gaza; (and) I counted it among the gods of their land]; I established the[ir ...].

As for him (i.e. Hanunu), like a bird [he flew (back)] from Egypt. [... I returned him to his position and] I turned [his city(?)] into an Assyrian [emporium]. [I set up] my royal stela in the city of the brook of Egypt,[6] a river[-bed ...] I removed [... from ... x talents of gold, x + 100 talents] of silver and [I brought] (it) to Assyria.

(lines 20′-23′)
[...] had not submitted [to the kings], my predecessors and who had not sent (them) any message, [heard about] the conquest of the land of [...] [... the fear of the splendor of Aššur, my lord, overwhelmed him] and fear seized him. [He sent me] his ambassadors[7] to do obeisance [...] [...] Siruatti, the Me⁾unite,[8] [b] whose [territory is] "below" Egypt,[9] [...] exalted [...], my own extensive conquest he he[ard, and fear overwhelmed him ...]. [...]

(lines 24′-27′)
[As for Samsi, the queen of the land of Arabia], I defeated 9,400 (of her people) at Mount Saqurri [...] [...] [I seized] her [gods], arms (and) staffs of her goddess, [and her property]. [And she, in order to save her life, ... to a desert, an arid place], made off [like an on]ager. The res[t of her posses-

a Amos 1:6-8

b 1 Chr 4:41; 2 Chr 20:1; 26:7

[1] Two proposals for the identification of this island city have been made: 1) Arvad (Alt 1953:152-153; Oded 1974:46; Irvine 1990:47-48; Tadmor 1994:282); and 2) Tyre (Eph^cal 1982:30; Na⁾aman 1995b:268-271). It is more likely that Tyre is the entity in view, though this cannot be absolutely certain due to the fragmentary state of the tablet. See also Kuan 1995:166.

[2] TÚG.*sa-gu*. While both *CAD* and *AHw* distinguish between *sagu*, a type of clothing ("penitential garb" *CAD* S 289) and *saqqu* "sack," Tadmor suggests that it is likely that the distinction is phonological/dialectical rather than lexical, *sagu* being the Assyrian form. Hence not only was sackcloth worn among West Semitics as a sign of mourning and penitence, but also in Assyria. Cf. Jonah 3:6-9.

[3] Egypt was known for its special breed of "large horses."

[4] The identification of the enemy of Tiglath-pileser in these lines is uncertain. Scholars have suggested the following: Tyre (Tadmor 1994:282); Israel (Alt 1953:151-157; Na⁾aman 1986b:72-73; 1995:268-271); or either Damascus, a Phoenician city-state, or Israel (Eph^cal 1982:30).

[5] According to Tadmor (1994:177) there was only one object (not two) that was set up in Gaza — a golden statue of the king with with symbols of the deities engraved on it. Concerning the Assyrian imperial cult, see Cogan 1974:48-52 and 1993.

[6] Concerning the reading, see Tadmor 1994:178. While Na⁾aman identifies the Naḥal Miṣraim with Wadi Besor (1979; 1980a), it is still preferable to identify it with Wadi el-Arish (see Rainey 1982).

[7] *ṣīrāni*. This term becomes an Akk. loanword in Heb. *ṣîr* (cf. Isa 18:2; Jer 49:14; Prov 13:17). See Machinist 1983:730, n. 65.

[8] This is an extra-biblical attestion of the Menuites. See the discussion of Eph^cal 1982:68-71, 219-220. For Siruatti, the Me⁾unite, see Na⁾aman 1997b.

[9] Probably refers to northern Sinai.

sions (and) her tents, her people's watchmen], [within her camp] I set on fire. Samsi took fright at my mighty weapons, [she brought to Assyria to my presence camels], she-camels, together with [their young], [...]

REFERENCES

Text: Wiseman 1951; Tadmor 1994:154-157, 176-179. Translations and studies: Spieckermann 1982:324-327; *TUAT* 1:375-376; Na'aman 1986b:72-73; 1995b; Irvine 1990:44-56; Kuan 1995:164-167.

SUMMARY INSCRIPTION 9-10 (2.117F)

K. Lawson Younger, Jr.

The text is written on a large, very fragmentary clay tablet[1] (18.4 cm wide) which was recovered in excavations at Nimrud in 1955. The reverse of the tablet preserves narrations of Tiglath-pileser's Levantine campaigns, arranged geographically and set off by rulings across the surface of the tablet.

Summary Inscription 10 (K 2649),[2] following Tadmor's designation (1994:180), is a tiny fragment (2.5 x 5.6 cm) which may be a part of the same tablet as Summary Inscription 9.[3] Tadmor uses K 2649 to restore some missing parts of Summary 9. As in his edition, these restorations are italicized in the translation.

(lines R. 1-31)

[The city of Hata]rikka, as far as Mount Sa[ue], the city of *Kašpuna on the shore of the Upper* (text: *Lower*) *Sea*, [(and) the city of Ṣimirra and the city of Arqa] I annexed to Assyria. [I placed over them] *two eunuchs as governors*.

The wide [land of Bīt]-Ḫaza'ili (Aram-Damascus) in its entirety,[4] from Mount [Leb]*anon as far as the city of Gilea*[d,[5] Abel ...[6] [on the bor]der of Bīt-Ḫurmia (Israel) *I annexed* to Assyria. [I placed] *my eunuch* [over them as governor].

[Hi]ram, the Tyrian, who plotted(?)[7] together with Rezin [...]. I captured [the city of] Maḫalab,[8] his fortified city, together with (other) large cities. Their plunder [...]. He came before me and kissed my feet. [I received] 20 talents of [gold ...] multi-colored [garments], linen garments, eunuchs, male singers and fem[ale] singers ... [... horses] of Egypt [...].

[I captured the land of Bīt-Ḫumria (Israel)] to its fu[ll extent ...] [I carried off to Assyria] ... [together with] their possessions. [... [I placed Hoshea][a] as king over them. [...] before me to the city of Sarrabani[9] [...]

a 2 Kgs 15:30

[... from ...] x + 100 talents of silver I carried off and [brought to Assyria].

[Hanunu, the Gazaean, feared my powerful weapons and] escaped [to Egypt]. [I conquered] Gaza, [his royal city]. I made [a statue bearing the image of the great gods, my lords, and my (own) royal image out of gold]. [I set it up] in the palace of Ga[za]. [I counted it among the gods of their land ... As for him (i.e. Hanunu), like] a bird [he flew (back)] from Egypt. [... I returned him to his position and I turned] his [city] into an Assyrian emporium (*kāru*).

[As for Samsi, the queen of the land of Arabia], I felled with the sword [... at Mount Saqurri]. And all of [her] ca[mp ...] [... all kinds of spices] without number, [her] gods [I seized]. [And she, in order to save her life, ... to a desert], an arid place, [made off] like an onager. [The rest of her possessions (and) her tents, her people's watchmen], within her camp [I set on fire]. [Samsi took fright at my mighty weapons; camels], she-camels together with [their you]ng, [she brought to Assyria to

[1] These ND-fragments (ND 4301 + ND 4305 + ND 5422) were published by Wiseman 1956 and 1964.

[2] K 2649 was published by Leeper 1918:35.

[3] Borger (*TUAT* 1:376-378) gives a translation based on a composite text drawn from the fragments.

[4] Probably a reference to all of Rezin's territories (including any Israelite holdings), not simply Aram-Damascus proper.

[5] URU *Ga-al-'a-*⌈*a*⌉(?)-[*di*]. Cf. Hos 6:8. For the reading see Tadmor 1994:186, n. 3. See Summary Inscription 4, *COS* 2.117C, note 4.

[6] See Summary Inscription 4, *COS* 2.117C, note 5.

[7] ND 4301 reads: ŠA.KU.NA. Tadmor emends to *iš*(sic)-*ku-na*, and from K 2649 adds: ⌈*pi*⌉-⌈*i*⌉(!)-⌈*šú*⌉.

[8] The conquest of Maḫalab and the submission of Hiram are only mentioned here.

[9] This sentence appears to mention Hoshea's (or more likely, his messengers') appearance before Tiglath-pileser with tribute at Sarrabani in southern Babylonia (see Parpola *NAT* 306).

my presence]. I installed over her [an official administrator (*qēpu*)] and 10,000 soldiers [...]

[... who] had not submitted to the kings, my predecessors, and [had never sent his message] [...] heard about [the conquest of the land of Ḫat]ti. The fear of the splendor of Aššur, my lord, [overwhelmed him] [and fear seized him. He sent his ambassadors[10]] to my presence, to Calah, [to do obeisance].

[... From Metenna the Tyr]ian 50 talents of gold, 2,000 talents of silver [I received as his trib]ute.

[Uassurme, the Tabalite, acted as if he was the equal of Assyria and] did not appear before me. [I sent to Tabal] my eunuch, [the Chief-Eunuch (*rāb ša-rēši*)]. [I placed on his] thr[one Ḫull]i, the son of a nobody. [I received as his tri]bute [10 talents of gold, 1,000 talents of silver, 2,000 horses, ...].

[...] nobody [among] the kings, my ancestors, [...]; [I received] his tribute.

[10] See Summary Inscription 8, *COS* 2.117E, note 7.

REFERENCES

Text: Wiseman 1956; 1964; Tadmor 1994:180-191, esp. 186-191. Translations and studies: Weippert 1973:37; Ephᶜal 1982:33-36; Spieckermann 1982:324-327; *TUAT* 377-378; Irvine 1990:56-62; Kuan 1995:182-186.

SUMMARY INSCRIPTION 13 (2.117G)

K. Lawson Younger, Jr.

This inscription is engraved on a poorly preserved colossal bas-relief from Nimrud that depicts a large figure with a mace. The inscription is incised across the large figure. While a number of scholars have treated the text as a part of Tiglath-pileser's Annals,[1] others have noted its non-chronological elements as evidence of its summary type. In Tadmor's recent treatment, he suggests that the inscription is a summary inscription of a special category (1994:198-199).

(lines 1′-2′)[2]
[...] [...] to Calah before me [...]

(lines 3′-16′)[3]
[As for Samsi, the queen of the land of] Arabia, at Mount Sa[qurri ...] [...] her [ent]ire camp [...] [... And she, who] took fright [at my (mighty) weapons], [...] brought to Assy]ria [to my presence]. [I ins]talled [an official administrator (*qēpu*) over her]; and [10,000] sold[iers[4] ...] I made [...] bow down to my [feet]. The people of [Massaᵓ, Temā, Sab]aᵓ, Ḫaya[ppâ], [Badanu, Ḫat]te, I[dibaᵓilu], [..., who dwell on the bor]der of the countries of the setting sun (western lands) [whose place is far away, the fa]me of my lordship (and [of) my heroic] de[eds they heard], [They brought before] me: gold, silver, camels, [she-camels], all kinds of spices, their tribute, as [one]; [and they kis]sed my feet. Their gifts [...] I appointed Idibiᵓilu[5] as [the prebend of the "Gatekeeper"[6]] facing [Egyp]t.

(lines 17′-18′)
[The land of Bīt-Ḫumria (Israel)], all [of whose] cities I leveled [to the ground] in my former campaigns, [...] I plundered its livestock, and I spared only (isolated) Samaria. [I/They overthrew Pek]ah, their king.[7]

[1] E.g. Rost 1872:211-228; Luckenbill *ARAB* 1:§§778-779; Oppenheim *ANET* 283; Borger *TUAT* 372.
[2] An apparent reference to the arrival of tribute from a foreign king (Tadmor suggests the king of Egypt(?), 1994:198) while Tiglath-pileser is staying in Calah. This may be linked to the statement in the Eponym Chronicle for the year 730 BCE that the king stayed "in the land" (Millard 1994:45, 59).
[3] This is the shortest version concerned with the defeat of Samsi.
[4] For the reading with a discussion of past misunderstandings of the text, see Tadmor 1944:200-201.
[5] See Summary Inscription 4, *COS* 2.117C, note 17.
[6] See Summary Inscription 4, *COS* 2.117C, note 18.
[7] See Summary Inscription 4, *COS* 2.117C, note 11.

REFERENCES

Text: Layard 1851:66; Smith 1875:285-286; Rost 1892:36-38; Tadmor 1994:198-203. Translations: *ARAB* 1:§§778-779; *ANET* 283; *TUAT* 372.

SARGON II (2.118)

THE ANNALS (2.118A)

K. Lawson Younger, Jr.

In very early excavations (1843-44), P. E. Botta uncovered fourteen large rooms of the palace of Sargon II[1] at ancient Dūr-Šarrukīn (modern Khorsabad). The doorways and walls of these rooms were adorned with slabs having sculptured reliefs along with inscriptions. Further excavations were undertaken at the site by T. V. Place in 1852-54. In connection with the early excavations, E. N. Flandin made excellent drawings of the slabs. These together with Botta's copies were published in 1849-50.[2] Based on the drawings and especially on plaster squeezes that were also made during the early excavations, H. Winckler (1889) and A. G. Lie (1929) attempted to restore the Annals of Sargon from Khorsabad.[3] Through further discoveries of texts of Sargon II as well as additional work, a very useful edition of Sargon's Annals has recently been published (Fuchs 1994).

(lines 10-18)[4]

[...] [the Samar]ians,[5] [who had agreed with a hostile king] [...] [...] [... who c]ause my victory. [I fought with them and decisively defeated them]. [...] [...] carried off as spoil. 50 chariots for my royal force [I ...] [the rest of them I settled in the midst of Assyria.[a]] [... I re]settled and I made it greater than before. People of lands conquer[ed ...] [...] tax I imposed upon them as on Assyrians. [I opened the sealed] har[bor of Egypt]. [The Assyrians and the Egyptians] I mingled [t]ogether and made them trade with each other.

(lines 23b-25)

In my second regnal year, Ilu-biᵓdi,[6] [the Hamathite],[7] [...] the wide [land ...] at Qarqar[8] he gathered. The oath [...] [... Arpad, Ṣimirra] Damascus, and Sa]mari[a he caused to rebel against me] [...]

(lines 53-57)

[...] and Reᵓe, his [commander-in-chief (*turtānu*)], came to his assistance, and he marched against me to do war and battle. In the name of Aššur, my lord, I inflicted a defeat on them. Reᵓe fled alone like a shepherd[9] whose flock is robbed, and he disappeared.

[Ḫa]nunu I seized with the hand; and I brought him as a prisoner to my city Aššur. I razed, destroyed, and burned Raphia. I carried off 9,033 inhabitants together with their great property.

a 2 Kgs 17:6, 23; 18:11

b Gen 10:2

(lines 72-78)

In my fifth regnal year, Pisiri, the Carchemishite,[10] sinned against the treaty of the great gods, and he sent a message to Mita (Midas),[11] the king of Muski.[12] [b] I lifted up my hands to Aššur, my lord; and I brought forth him together with his family as prisoners. I plundered gold, silver, along with the property of his palace, and the sinful inhabitants of Carchemish, who (had supported) him, along with their possessions. I brought them to Assyria. I gathered 50 chariots, 200 cavalry, and 3000 infantrymen from them and I added (them) to my royal contingent. I settled inhabitants of the land of Assyria in the city of Carchemish; and I imposed on them the yoke of Aššur, my lord. The people of Papa and Lallakna — dogs who were brought up in my palace, had spoken ...ly to Kakmê — I deported them from their place and [settled them] in Damascus, in the land of Amurru [...]

(lines 120b-123a)

The Tamudi, Ibadidi, Marsima[ni] and Hayappâ, who live in distant Arabia, in the desert, who knew[13] neither overseer nor commander, who never brought tribute to any king — with the help of Aššur, my lord, I defeated them. I deported the rest of them. I settled them in Samaria/Samerina.

[1] The biblical texts that may be related to Sargon II are: 2 Kgs 17:1-24; 18:1-12; Isa 10:27-32; 14:4b-21; 20:1.

[2] For further discussion of these wall reliefs, see Albenda 1986.

[3] For some of the problems and difficulties with these editions, see Tadmor 1958.

[4] The restoration of this section is very dependent on the Nimrud Prisms (esp. Prism D).

[5] Becking (1992:39-45) has recently argued that since the Annals are fragmentary at this particular point, they may, in fact, not refer to the conquest of Samaria. However, see Fuchs 1994:82. For the issues surrounding the fall of Samaria, see Younger 1999.

[6] In Sargon's inscriptions, the name of the king of Hamath is spelled *Ilu-biᵓdi* and *Yau-biᵓdi*. Some scholars interpret the *Yau-* as a Yahwistic theophoric element (Malamat 1963:7; Cogan and Tadmor 1988:166; with variation, Dalley 1990:27, 31; Zevit 1991:363-366). Other scholars are doubtful of a Yahwistic theophoric element in the name (Lipiński 1971:371-373). See also Hawkins 1976-80c; Dion 1997:169, n. 142.

[7] For Hamath, see Hawkins 1972-75a:67-70; Dion 1997:137-170.

[8] Same site as Shalmaneser III's battle in 853 BCE (see *COS* 2.113A, note 22).

[9] Akk. *rēᵓû* which is used as a wordplay on the name of the Egyptian commander Reᵓe. For older attempts to links his name with "So, king of Egypt" (2 Kgs 17:4), see Borger 1960; Kitchen 1986:374-375; Cogan and Tadmor 1988:196.

[10] For Carchemish, see Hawkins 1997; 1976-80c.

[11] I.e., Midas of Phrygia.

[12] Muski or Muški is identified with Meshech (Gen 10:2).

[13] The Arab tribes are the subject and not the object of *idūma* (see Cogan and Tadmor 1988:337; and Becking 1992:103).

(lines 249-262)[14]
Azuri,[15] the king of Ashdod,[16] [plo]tted to with[hold his tribute], and he sent (messages) to the neighboring kings [hostile to Assyria]. Because he committed crimes again[st the people of his country], I abo[lished] his ru[le] (and) plac[ed] Aḫimiti, his favorite brother, as king [over them]. The Hittites,[17] who (always) speak treachery, [hated] his rule. [Ya]dna,[18] who had no claim to the throne, who was like them, and had [no respect for rulership], they elevated over them. [In the anger of my heart], with my own chariot and with my cavalry — who never leave my [side in (hostile or) friendly territory] — I [quickly] marched to Ashdod, [his royal city]. I besieged (and) conquered Ashdod, Gi[mtu][19] and [Ashdod-Yam].[20] I counted as boo[ty] the gods who dw[elt] in them, him[self], [together with the people of his land, gold, silver, (and) the property of his palace]. I reorganized those cities. I settled there the people of the lands, the conquest of my hands. I placed my eunuchs as governors over them; and I counted them with the people of Assyria; and they bore my yoke.

[14] Tadmor (1958:79) states: "The assumption that an Assyrian Commander-in-Chief (*turtanu*) fought against Ashdod in 712 BC agrees with the date in Isa. 20:21ff. 'The year that Tartan came into Ashdod ... and took it.'" He also argues: "There are, however, some indications that Sargon had intervened in the affairs of Ashdod prior to the expedition of 712: e.g., the replacement of Aziru with Aḫimetu. However, the narrative of the campaign against Ashdod in the Annals (11th yr. = 711) was shifted by the scribes from the 9th yr. = 712 in the prism in order to extend the brief narrative of events of 712" (1958:92-94).

[15] For this monarch, see *PNA* 1:240.

[16] For Ashdod, see Dothan 1993. Fragments of an Assyrian victory stela were found in excavations at Ashdod. See Tadmor 1971; Kapera 1976; Cogan and Tadmor 1988: pl. 11b.

[17] Used figuratively of the Westerners, namely, here, the Ashdodites.

[18] Elsewhere Yamani. Yadna may be a scribal error (Borger *TUAT* 1:380, n. 254a; Edzard 1976-80). For the campaign against Ashdod, see Kapera 1972-73; 1987; Mattingly 1981; Reade 1976; Redford 1992; Spalinger 1973; 1978; Tadmor 1958. Cf. Tang-i Var (*COS* 2.118J) below.

[19] Generally identified with Gath.

[20] This site (located on the coast) was evidently built by Yamani to serve as a rear base for the main city in times of danger. See Kaplan 1993.

REFERENCES

Text: Fuchs 1994:82-188, 313-342; Lie 1929:2-13, 20-23, 38-41; Winckler 1889:4-7, 12-13, 16-17, 24-25, 40-43. Translations and studies: *ARAB* 2:§4; *ANET* 284; *TUAT* 1:378-379; Tadmor 1958:34; Becking 1992:39-45.

THE BOROWSKI STELA (2.118B)

K. Lawson Younger, Jr.

This text is inscribed on a broken stone stela,[1] belonging to a type of stela which was set up locally to commemorate events in the district. Thus it was probably incised after the successful completion of the campaign in Syria and Palestine in 720 BCE. This document reveals what had not been known before its publication, namely that thousands of Assyrians were "guilty" of rebellion according to Sargon. Those mentioned in the stela, however, he pardoned and deported to Hamath.

I gathered from them 200 chariots, 600 cavalry, shield and lance (bearers); and I added them to my royal contigent. I pardoned 6,300 guilty Assyrians;[2] and showed mercy on them; and I settled them in Hamath. I imposed on them tribute, gifts, and corvée work, as my royal fathers[3] had imposed on Irḫulēni[4] of Hamath. Future rulers should heed the kindly deeds of the god Aššur, and they should teach later generations to reverence him. The people of of the land Ḫatti and of the land of Arime, who live in Bīt-Agusi and Unqi, to their whole extent ...

[1] It is only 58 cm in height and 35.6 cm in width.

[2] Most likely these were part of the Assyrian army units who had offended Sargon by supporting a more legitimate successor to Shalmaneser V (Lambert 1981:125).

[3] Sargon's rise to power came on the heels of the death of Shalmaneser V, whose death recent research has shown was the result of natural causes (see Younger 1999:468, n. 28). Some scholars conclude that since Shalmaneser V died a natural death, Sargon II was not a usurper (Becking 1992:22, n. 6; Naʾaman 1990:218, n. 37; Vera Chamaza 1992:21-33). But just because Shalmaneser V may have died a natural death does not mean that Sargon was the legitimate heir to throne. The ensuing internal difficulties indicated in the sources demonstrate a significant struggle for the throne in Assyria at this time. The cumulative evidence seems to point to an illegitimate power seizure by Sargon. See Tadmor 1981:26-29; Dalley 1985:33.

[4] A king of Hamath in the days of Shalmaneser III. See *COS* 2.113A, ii.86b-102.

REFERENCES

Text and translation: Lambert 1981.

THE AŠŠUR "CHARTER" (2.118C)

K. Lawson Younger, Jr.

The text (K. 1349) is inscribed on a fragmentary tablet 6.9 cm x 12.0 cm and describes the restoration of privileges[1] to the city of Aššur. The fragment offers a brief but clear representation of the internal political situation of Assyria during Sargon II's ascent to the throne. It appears that the text was written only a few years[2] after Sargon came to power since he states in line 16 "in my second regnal year." In the section of the document relating Sargon's activities of 720 BCE (lines 16-28), Samaria's involvement in the coalition against Sargon is clearly linked to the leadership of Ilu-biʾdi (Yau-biʾdi) of Hamath (see Younger 1999:471-473).

(lines 16-17a)

In my second regnal year,[3] when I had sat on the royal throne and had been crow[ned] with the crown of lordship, I smashed the forces of Ḫumbanigaš, king of Elam; I decisively defeated him.[4]

(lines 17b-28)

Il[ubiʾdi[5] of] Hamath, not the rightful holder of the throne, not fit(?) for the palace, who in the shepherdship of his people, did [not attend to their] fate, [but] with regard to the god Aššur, his land (and) his people he sought evil, not good, and he treated contemptuously. He gathered Arpad and Samerina, and he turned (them) to his side [...] h[e] kill[ed] [a]nd he did not leave anyone alive [...] I raised [my hand to Aššur]; and in order to conquer H[a]math [...] [... of the extensive the land of Amurru]. I prayed[6]; and Aššur, the [great] god ... heard [my prayer] and received my supplication [...] I caused [my forces] to take [the way to the land of Amu]rru.[7] Ha[math [...] earlier times, who had learned fame [...] I subdued [the inhabitants of the land of Amu]rru. [...] I brought [them t]o my [c]ity, the city of Aššur, a[nd ...]

[1] What made up this "privileged status" (*kidinnu* or *kidinnūtu*) was apparently exemption from both *ilku* and *tupšikku* (Vera Chamaza 1992:26-27).

[2] Tadmor concludes that the Aššur Charter is "superior to all other Annalistic sources of Sargon as to historical reliability and exactness of dating" (1958:32).

[3] See Sargon's Annals above, COS 2.118A, lines 23-25.

[4] The reference is to the Battle of Der; see *COS* 2.118I, n. 2.

[5] See Sargon's Annals, *COS* 2.118A, note 6.

[6] Here understanding *maḫāru* meaning "to pray (to a deity)." See *CAD* M 1:61.

[7] I.e., Syria-Palestine.

REFERENCES

Text: Saggs 1975; Winckler 1893-94:pl. 1; 1897 1:403-405. Translations and studies: *ARAB* 2:§§133-135; *TUAT* 1:387; Tadmor 1958:31-32; Becking 1992:34-36; Vera Chamaza 1992.

NIMRUD PRISMS D & E (2.118D)

K. Lawson Younger, Jr.

A number of fragmentary clay prisms were discovered in excavations at Nimrud in 1952-53. These fragments form two prisms: D, comprised of ND 2601 + 3401 + 3417, and E, comprised of ND 3400 + 3402 + 3408 + 3409.[1] These two prisms are duplicate and fortunately allow restoration of a more continuous text. Most of the column translated here comes from prism D.

(iv.25-41)

[The inhabitants of Sa]merina, who agreed[2] [and plotted][3] with a king [hostile to][4] me, not to do service and not to bring tribute [to Aššur] and who did battle, I fought against them with the power of the great gods, my lords. I counted as spoil 27,280 people, together with their chariots, and gods,[a] in which they trusted. I formed a unit with 200 of [their] chariots for my royal force. I settled the rest of them in the midst of Assyria. I repopulated

[a] 2 Kgs 17:7-8

[1] There were additional fragments discovered as well. But only the two prisms are relevant here.

[2] Dalley (1985:36) suggests reading *kamālu* instead of *gamālu*. However, *kamālu* is doubtful since it is not found in such contexts in the royal inscriptions. It is most often used with deities as the subject (*CAD* K 109). Thus *gamālu* seems more probable.

[3] The most probable restoration seems to be either [*ikpudu*] — used twice by Sargon in his Letter to the God and used by Assurbanipal in the phrase: *ša itti RN ikpudu lemuttu* "who plots evil against Assurbanipal" (*CAD* K 173), or *ibbalkitu* — seems less likely though it is used in Sargon's inscriptions (*CAD* N 1:13-14).

[4] For the restorations of lines 25-28, see Younger 1999:469-471.

Samerina more than before.[5] I brought into it people from countries conquered by my hands. I appointed my eunuch as governor over them. And I counted them as Assyrians.

(lines 42-49)
I caused the awe-inspiring splendor of Aššur, my lord, to overwhelm the people of the land of Egypt and the Arabians; and at the mention of my name their hearts palpitated, (and) their arms collapsed. I opened the sealed [borders(?)][6] of Egypt, and I mingled together the people of Assyria and Egypt. I made them trade [with each other].

[5] Dalley (1985:36) reads this as a hendiadys, *uttir ... ušešib* "I made the population greater." Tadmor (1958:34) reads "the city of Samaria I resettled and made it greater than before," reading *ú-še-me* (from *ewû, emû*) instead of *ú-še-šib* (from *ašābu*).

[6] Borger (*TUAT* 1:382) proposes [*ki-s*]*ur-re*; Tadmor (1958) suggests [*ka*]*r-ri*.

REFERENCES

Text: Gadd 1954:179-180, pls. xlv, xlvi; Tadmor 1958:34; Spieckermann 1982:349-350. Translations and studies: Cogan and Tadmor 1988:200, 336; *TUAT* 1:382; Dalley 1985:36; Na^ʾaman 1990:209-210; Becking 1992:28-31.

THE GREAT "SUMMARY" INSCRIPTION (2.118E)

K. Lawson Younger, Jr.

Discovered at Khorsabad (see introduction to Sargon's Annals above, *COS* 2.118A), this summary inscription stood on the wall slabs of rooms 4, 7, 8 and 10 in Sargon's palace.

(lines 23-27)
From my accession year to my fifteenth regnal year, I decisively defeated Humbanigaš, the Elamite, in the district of Der.

I besieged and conquered Samarina. I took as booty 27,290[1] people who lived there. I gathered 50 chariots from them. I taught the rest (of the deportees) their skills.[2] I set my eunuch over them, and I imposed upon them the (same) tribute as the previous king (i.e. Shalmaneser V).

Hanunu, the king of Gaza, along with Reʾe, the commander-in-chief (*turtānu*) of Egypt, marched against me to do war and battle at Raphia. I inflicted a decisive defeat on them. Reʾe became afraid at the noise of my weapons, and he fled, and his place was not found. I captured with my own hand Hanunu, the king of Gaza. I received the tribute of Pharaoh,[3] the king of Egypt, Samsi,[4] the queen of Arabia, Ithamar, the Sabean[5]: gold, herbs of the mountain, horses and camels.

(lines 33-36a)
Yau-biʾdi, the Hamathite, a *ḫupšu*-man,[6] with no claim to the throne, an evil Hittite, was plotting in his heart to become king of Hamath. He caused Arpad, Ṣimirra, Damascus and Samaria to rebel against me, had unified them (lit. made them one mouth) and prepared for battle. I mustered the masses of Aššur's troops and at Qarqar, his favorite city, I besieged and captured him, together with his warriors. I burned Qarqar. Him I flayed. I killed the rebels in the midst of those cities. I established harmony. I gathered 200 chariots, 600 cavalry from among the people of Hamath, and I added (them) to my royal contingent.

(lines 90-112a)
Azuri, the king of Ashdod, plotted in his heart to withhold tribute, and he sent (messages) to the neighboring kings, hostile to Assyria. Because he committed crimes against the people of his coun[try], I abolished his rule. I placed Aḫimiti, his favorite [brother],[7] as king over them. The Hittites, who (always) speak treachery, hated his rule.

Yamani,[8] who had no claim to the throne, who was like them, and had no respect for rulership, they elevated over them. In the ebullience of my heart, I did not gather the masses of my troops, nor did I organize my camp. With my warriors — who never leave my side in (hostile or) friend[ly terri]tory — I marched to Ashdod. Now when this Yamani heard from afar the approach of my cam-

[1] Nimrud Prism has 27,280 deportees, *COS* 2.118D. For the Battle of Der, see *COS* 2.118C, n. 4.
[2] For the interpretation of this sentence, see Younger 1999:469.
[3] For *Pirʾu šār Muṣuri* (ca. 713 BCE), see Naʾaman 1974:32 and n. 29. For Reʾe, see *COS* 118A, n. 9.
[4] See Tiglath-pileser III *COS* 2.117C, note 12.
[5] Kitchen 1994; 1997. Cf. the name of Aaron's youngest son, Exod 6:23, etc.
[6] Following Borger *TUAT* 1:383, n. 33b. Cf. Heb. *ḥopšî* denoting a lower class; Ug. *ḫpṯ*, *ḫbṯ*; see Heltzer 1981:54, n. 56.
[7] *AHw* 1310 "bevorzugter Bruder."
[8] For Yamani and this campaign of Sargon, see *COS* 2.118A, note 18 above.

paign, he fled to the border area of Egypt which is on the border with Meluḫḫa,[9] and his place was not found. I besieged (and) conquered Ashdod, Gimtu (Gath) and Ashdod-Yam. I counted as booty his gods, his wife, his sons, his daughters, the property, the possessions (and) treasures of his palace, together with the inhabitants of his land. I reorganized those cities. I settled there the peoples of the lands, the conquest of my hands, from [the area] of the east. [I placed my eunuchs as governors over them]. I counted them with the people of Assyria and they bore my yoke.

The king of Meluḫ[ḫa][9]—who in ... land of U[r]izzu, an inaccessible place, a way [... who]se ancestors [from the] distant [past] until now had nev[er se]nt their messengers to the kings, my ancestors, in order to inquire about their well-being — heard from af[ar] of the might of the gods [Aššur, Nabû], (and) Marduk. The [fear]ful splendor of my majesty overwhelmed him and panic overcame him. He put him (Yamani) in handcuffs and manacles, [fe]tters of iron, and they brou[ght] (him) the long journey to Assyria (and) into my presence.

[9] In the Neo-Assyrian texts, Meluḫḫa refers to Nubia. Heimpel 1987 and 1993-97 overlooks these references. For this king see COS 2.118J, lines 19-21.

REFERENCES

Text: Fuchs 1994:189-248, esp. 197, 343-355; Winckler, Sargon, 100-103; 114-117. Translations and studies: *ARAB* 2:§§55, 62; *ANET* 284-285; *TUAT* 1:383-384; Dalley 1985:34-35; Timm 1989-90:73; Becking 1992:25-26.

THE SMALL "SUMMARY" INSCRIPTION (2.118F)

K. Lawson Younger, Jr.

The text was discovered in room 14 of Sargon's Khorsabad palace.

(lines 11b-18a)

Yamani,[1] the Ashdodite, became afraid of my weapons, and he abandoned his wives, his sons, (and) his daughters, and he fled to the border area of Egypt which is on the border with Meluḫḫa,[2] and lived like a thief (there). I placed my eunuchs as governors over all of his extensive land and his flourishing[3] people. I extended the territory of Aššur, king of the gods.

[...] The fearful splendor of Aššur, my lord, [ov]erwhelmed [the king of the land of M]eluḫḫa[2] and they put iron fetters on his (Yamani's) hands and feet. He (the king of Meluḫḫa) had him (Yamani) brought to Assyria into my presence. [... I plundered Šinuḫtu, Samerina[4] and the entire land of Bīt-Ḫumria (Israel). The Ionians, who live in the midst of the western sea, I caught like fish. I deported the land of Kasku, the land of Tabal (and) the land of Ḫilakku. I drove away Mita (Midas), king of Muski. I decisively defeated Egypt at Raphia, and I counted Hanunu, the king of Gaza, as booty.

I subdued the seven kings of the land of Ia,[5] a district of the land of Iadnana,[6] whose homes lie a seven days' journey in the middle of the western sea.

[1] See *COS* 2.118A, note 18 above.

[2] See *COS* 2.118E, note 9.

[3] See *AHw* 1156 s.v. *šamḫu* and Fuchs 1994:308, n. 308.

[4] Becking comments: "it is a remarkable fact that 'Samerina and the whole land of Omri' are mentioned in one line with URU *Ši-nu-uḫ-tú* in Cilicia which Sargon conquered during a campaign in his fourth *palû* = 718 BCE" (1992:27-28). For Šinuḫtu, see *COS* 2.118I, n. 5.

[5] For the subjugation of these Cypriote kings, see Naʾaman 1998b.

[6] Lipiński (1991) argues that the term Iadnana, the most common name for Cyprus in the Assyrian royal inscriptions, may be interpreted as "the island of the Danunians."

REFERENCES

Text: Fuchs 1994:75-81, esp. 76, 307-312; Weissbach 1918:175-185; Winckler 1889:82-83; Translations: *ARAB* 2:§79-80; *ANET* 285; *TUAT* 1:385; Becking 1992:27-28.

PAVEMENT INSCRIPTION 4 (2.118G)

K. Lawson Younger, Jr.

The text was inscribed on a pavement slab for the gates at Dūr-Šarrukīn (Khorsabad).

(lines 31-41)
(Sargon II) ... who conquered Samaria and the entire land of Bīt-Ḫumria (Israel);[1] who plundered Ashdod (and) Šinuḫtu,[2] who caught the Ionians[3] like fish in the middle of the sea; who deported the Kasku, all of Tabal, and Ḫilakku; who drove away Mita (Midas), the king of Muski; who decisively defeated Egypt at Raphia, and counted Hanunu, king of Gaza, as spoil.

[1] Var.: *ka-a-šid* [uru]*Sa-mir-i-na gi-*[*mi*]*-ir* É *Ḫum-ri-a*.
[2] See Nimrud Inscription (*COS* 2.118I, note 5).
[3] KUR *Ia-am-na-a-a*. Perhaps these are Ionian pirates on the Cilician coast. See Röllig 1976-80b.

REFERENCES

Text: Fuchs 1994:259-271, esp. 261, 359-362; Borger *BAL*², 59-63, 131-132, 322-326; Winckler 1889 1:146-157, 2:pls. 38-40. Translations: *ARAB* 2:§§99-100; *ANET* 284; *TUAT* 1:386; Becking 1992:27.

THE CYLINDER INSCRIPTION (2.118H)

K. Lawson Younger, Jr.

Discovered at Khorsabad, the text is inscribed on four barrel cylinders (two in the Louvre at Paris and two in the British Museum in London). The inscription commemorates the founding of Sargon's new capital at Dūr-Šarrukīn.

(lines 19-20)[1]
(Sargon) who subjugated the extensive land of Bīt-Ḫumria (Israel), who inflicted a decisive defeat on Egypt at Raphia, and who brought Hanunu, king of Gaza, to Aššur as a prisoner, who conquered the Tamudi, the Ibadidi, the Marsimani and the Hayappâ, of whom the remainder I removed and settled in the land of Bīt-Ḫumria (Israel).

[1] Interestingly, events of 720 BCE (subjugation of Israel, the defeat of Hanunu of Gaza, Egyptians at Raphia) are joined with events of 717 BCE (the conquest of the Arab tribes and their deportations to Samaria).

REFERENCES

Text: Fuchs 1994:34 (lines 19-20); Lyon 1883 4:19-20. Translations: *ARAB* 2:§§116-118; *TUAT* 1:386.

THE NIMRUD INSCRIPTION (2.118I)

K. Lawson Younger, Jr.

Inscribed on two slabs from Calah (Nimrud), this text is a summary inscription recording Sargon's restoration of Aššur-naṣir-pal II's palace. One slab is in Assyrian characters, the other in Babylonian. While the inscription is not dated, it appears to date to late 717 or early 716 BCE (Naᵓaman 1994:19-20).

(line 7-12)
Pious prince, who met with Ḫumbanigaš,[1] king of Elam, in the district of Der[2] and defeated him; the subduer of Judah [a] which lies far away;[3] deporter of the land of Hamath, whose hands captured Yaubiᵓdi, their king; repulser the land of Kakmê,

[a] Isa 10:27-32

[1] The battle against Ḫumbanigaš at Der, the subjugation of Hamath, and the subduing Judah took place in 720 BCE. See *COS* 2.118C, n. 4.
[2] Concerning the site of Der, see de Meyer 1997. Concerning the battle, see Brinkman 1984:40-50, esp. p. 48. Sargon's texts claim that he was the winner of the battle of Der. See Annals (lines 21-22); Nimrud inscription (line 7); Tang-i Var Inscription (line 16). The other sources declare the Elamites as winners (see the Babylonian Chronicle I i.33-37); or the Elamites/Babylonians (Marduk-apla-iddina Nimrud stela, lines 17-18; Gadd 1953:123). See Hallo 1960:53.
[3] For possible connections of this phrase to a campaign of Sargon II against Judah in the 720 BCE context, see Sweeney 1994; Younger 1996;

the wicked enemy; who set in order the disordered land of the Manneans; who gladdened the heart of his land; who extended the border of Assyria.

Diligent ruler, snare of the unsubmissive, whose hand captured Pisiri, king of Ḫatti, and set his official over Carchemish,[4] his city; deporter of the city of Šinuḫtu,[5] who brought Kiakki,[6] king of Tabal, to Aššur, his city, and placed his yoke on the land of Muski; conqueror the land of the Manneans, the land of Karallu and the land of Pattiru; avenger of his land; who defeated the distant Medes as far as the rising sun.

Na᾿aman 1994; Hallo 1999a:36f. Cf. the interesting parallel in the Nimrud Prism: *mu-šak-niš* KUR *Ma-da-a-a ru-qu-ú-ti* "the subduer of the distant Medes" (Gadd 1954:200; Tadmor 1958:38-39). For the Isaianic passage, see Christensen 1976.

[4] The conquest of Carchemish dates to 717 BCE.

[5] Šinuḫtu is to be located at Aksaray (Hawkins 1995b:99). For the episode recording this deportation, see Annals lines 68b-71.

[6] In 718 BCE, Sargon removed Kiakki of Šinuḫtu for disloyalty and intrigue with Mita of Muski (Midas of Phrygia). He gave Šinuḫtu to Kurti of Atuna, a successor of Tiglath-pileser III's contemporary Ušḫitti (see the Iran Stela of Tiglath-pileser, *COS* 2.117B). A stela from Aksaray names a ruler Kiyakiya, who seems likely to be the same as Kiakki of Šinuḫtu. See Hawkins 1995b:99; Hawkins and Postgate 1988:37.

REFERENCES

Text: Winckler 1889 1:168-173. Translations: *ARAB* 2:§§136-138; *ANET* 287; *TUAT* 1:387; Na᾿aman 1994:17-18.

THE TANG-I VAR INSCRIPTION (2.118J)

K. Lawson Younger, Jr.

Discovered in Iranian Kurdistan in 1968, this cuneiform inscription is found on a Neo-Assyrian relief that is carved into a niche in a rock face on the flanks of the Kūh-i Zīnāneh in the Tang-i Var mountain pass. The niche is approximately 170 cm in height and 150 cm in width and some 40 m above ground level. The relief depicts an Assyrian king in a standard pose, standing and facing right with his right hand raised and his left hand holding an object (perhaps a scepter). Apparently, the relief and inscription were engraved in this niche to commemorate the Assyrian campaign of 706 BCE carried out against the land of Karalla[1] by Sargon's officials and very likely carved in that year (Frame 1999:51). This is the only Assyrian rock relief known to have been made in the time of Sargon II. Unfortunately, the inscription is badly worn. Nevertheless, through photographs taken in the early 1970s,[2] G. Frame has recently published a very informative preliminary edition (Frame 1999).

(lines 11-12)

Sargon, great king, mighty king, king of the world, king of Assyria, governor of Babylon, king of the land of [Sumer and Ak]kad, favorite of the great gods, perfect hero, [...] man, pious [prince], marvellous man, [...] shepherd, [...].

(lines 13-15)[3]

Aššur, Nabû(?), (and) Marduk, the gods [my] helpers, granted [me] a kingship [without] equal and [have ex]tolled my good [fa]me reach to the utmost. I un[dertoo]k[4] the [res]tor[at]ion of Sippar, Ni[ppur], (and) Babylon (and) I recom[pen]sed the citizens of [*kidinnu*-status],[5] as man[y as] there were, for all the wrongful damage (suffered by) [them]. I re[in]stated the exemption from taxation of Bal[til][6] which had been interrupted. Regarding the city of Ḫarran [...] gate of [the peo]ple [...] I set up a *kidinnu*-symbol[7] (indicating their privileged status).

(lines 16-18)[8]

I smashed the army of Ḫumbanigaš, the Elamite. I destroyed the land of K[aral]la,[9] the land of Šurda, the city of Ki[šes]im, the city of Ḫarḫar, [the land] of the Medes, (and) the land of Elli[pi ...]. I laid waste to the land of Urartu, plundered the city of [Muṣaṣi]r (and) the land of the Manneans; I mauled the land[s of Andia (and) Zikirtu, (and)] allowed [... a]ll their settlements to live [...]. I conquered

[1] The passage (lines 37-44) that narrates this campaign in the inscription is badly preserved and only partially legible.

[2] François Vallat took these photographs while dangling from a rope! (see Frame's description, 1999:34).

[3] See Display Inscription from Room 14 (lines 2-3 and 5).

[4] *ša PN, PN, PN zāninūssun eteppuša* (*e-tep-pu-šá*). *CAD* E 225 s.v. *epēšu* + *zāninūtu* "to act as provider and caretaker." Cf. *ša Sippar Nippur Bābili u Barsip zāninūssun e-tep-pu-šá* "I undertook the restoration of Sippar, Nippur, Babylon and Borsippa." Winckler 1889 no. 56:3, and passim in Sargon.

[5] I.e. "privileged status."

[6] I.e. Aššur.

[7] *CAD* K 343 s.v. *kidinnu*.

[8] See Display Inscription from Room 14 lines 7-10 and note such texts as Pavement Inscription no. 4 lines 14-27.

[9] See Röllig 1976-80a; and esp. Frame 1999:48-52.

the rulers of the land of Hamath, the city of Carche[mish, the city of Kummu]ḫi, (and) the land of Kammanu; I set governors over their lands [...].

(lines 19-21)
I plundered the city of Ashdod. Yamani, its king, feared [my weapons] and [...]. He fled to the region of the land of Meluḫḫa and lived like a thief[10] (there). Šapatakuʾ[11] (Shebitku[12]),[a] king of the land of Meluḫḫa, heard about the mig[ht] of Aššur, Nabû, (and) Marduk which I had [demonstrated] over all lands [...]. He put (Yamani) in manacles and handcuffs [...] he had him brought before my presence like a captive.

(line 22)
[I depopulated] all the lands of Tabālu, Kasku (and) Ḫilakku; I [took away] settlements belonging to Mita (Midas), king of the land of [Mu]sku, and reduced his land.

a Gen 10:7; Isa 18:1-3; 20; 30:1-7

b 2Kgs 20:12; Isa 39:1

(line 23)
At the city of Raphia (Rapiḫu) [I defeated] the vanguard of the army [of Egypt]; and I counted as bo[ot]y the king of the city of Gaza who had not submitted to my [yo]ke.

(line 24)
I subdued seven kings of the land of Iāʾ, a region of the l[and of] Iadnāna (Cyprus)[13] — whose home is situated at a distance[14] of [...] [in the mid]dle of the Western Sea.

(line 25-26a)
Moreover, my hands defeated Marduk-apla-iddina (Merodach-baladan),[b] king of the land of Chaldea, who dwelled on the shore of the sea (and) who ex[erc]ised kingship over Babylon against the wi[ll of the gods]. Moreover, all the land of Bīt-Yakin [...]

[10] I.e. "in hiding."

[11] From the photographs published by Frame, I read the signs of the name: ⌈m⌉ ⌈*šá*⌉-*pa*-⌈*ta*⌉-*ku*-⌈*u*ʾ⌉.

[12] The Tang-i Var inscription indicates, by naming Shebitku as the king who extradited Yamani from Egypt, that Shebitku was already ruler by 706, at least four years earlier than has generally been thought. See the discussion of Frame 1999:52-54 and Redford 1999. Cf. COS 2.118A, note 18. For the possible biblical allusions, see Astour 1965.

[13] See Lipiński 1991:64. He argues that the word Iaʾ renders the Phoen. ʾ*y* "island," and *Iadnāna* should probably be interpreted in the sense of "Island of the Danunians."

[14] For this line, see Frame 1999:45.

REFERENCES

Text: Frame 1999; Sarfarāz 1968-69. Translation: Frame 1999. Studies: Frame 1999; Redford 1999.

SENNACHERIB (2.119)

SENNACHERIB'S FIRST CAMPAIGN: AGAINST MERODACH-BALADAN (2.119A)

Mordechai Cogan

The date of this earliest of Sennacherib's campaigns is disputed; it was directed against Merodach-baladan, who had seized the opportunity of Sargon's death (705 BCE) to proclaim himself king of Babylon, in opposition to the upstart rebel Marduk-zakir-shumi. Levine (1982) favors a date from winter 704 through early 702, while Brinkman (1984) opts for 703-702, considerably shortening the time span of the abundant military activities detailed in the inscription. Unlike his predecessors, Sennacherib did not reign as king of Babylon upon routing Merodach-baladan; rather he appointed the pro-Assyrian Bel-ibni to the throne.

The Babylonian mission sent by Merodach-baladan to Jerusalem [a] is frequently associated with the period of rebellion prior to the campaign described, suggesting that Babylonians and Judeans coordinated their insurgencies against Assyria (Brinkman 1964:31-33; Hallo 1999a:37). Another option dates the Jerusalem visit to the reign of Sargon, ca. 713 BCE, during Merodach-baladan's earlier rule in Babylon (Cogan and Tadmor 1988:260-263).

The text bears no colophon date, but certainly predates the "Bellino cylinder" inscription that relates both the first and second campaigns and is dated to mid-702 BCE.

(lines 5-15) At the beginning of my reign, when I had majestically ascended the throne and ruled the people of Assyria with obedience and peace, Merodach-baladan, king of Karduniash (i.e., Babylonia), an evil rebel, of treacherous mind, doer of evil, for whom truth is sinful, turned to Shutur-Nahhunte, the Elamite, for help, sent him gold and silver and precious stones, requesting his help. He (i.e., the

a 2Kgs 20:12-19; Isa 39:1-8; 2Chr 32:31

Elamite) sent him General[1] [b] Imbappa, with his troops, Tannanu, the "third man," [c] 10 commanders, together with Nergal-nasir, the Sutean, fearless in battle, 80,000 bowmen, [chariots, wagons, mules and h]orses, to his aid in Sumer and Akkad. He, [Merodach-baladan, Larsa], Ur, Eridu, Kullab, Kissik, Nimid-Laguda, Bit-Yakin, Bit-Amukkani, Bit-Salli, Bit-Dakkuri, all the Chaldeans, as many as there were, who (dwell) by the banks [of the Tigris, the Tuᵓumuna, the Riḫilu, the Ubudu], the Yadaqqu, the Kipre, the Maliḫu, [who (dwell) by the banks of the Euphrates, the Gurumu, the Ubulu, the Damu]nu, the Gambulu, the Ḫindau, the Ruᵓua, the Buqudu, [who (dwell) by the banks of the Uqnu, the Ḫamranu, the Ḫagru], the Nabatu, the Liᵓtau — unsubmissive Arameans who do not know field crops,[2] Nippur [...], Borsippa, Kutha, all of Babylonia, he gathered together as one and prepared for battle.

(lines 16-19) They reported these evil deeds to me, Sennacherib, who is pious in heart. I raged like a lion and gave the order to march into Babylonia against him. He, the image of an evil demon, heard of the march of my campaign. Horses and bowmen of the Elamites, Arameans, and Chaldeans, together with Nabu-nasir and the 10 commanders of Elam who do not know field crops — a force without number with them — he strengthened their ranks and brought them into Kutha. He set watch at the outposts against the advance of my campaign. I readied my chariot teams, (and) on the twentieth day of Shebat,[d] I set out from Assur at the head of my army, like a mighty wild ox. I did not wait for my forces, nor did I hold back for the rear guard.

(lines 20-30) I ordered the Rabshakeh[e] and my governors to Kish ahead of me: "Take the road against Merodach-baladan (and) keep him under strong watch." He (i.e., Merodach-baladan) saw my governors and sallied forth with all his troops through the gate of Zamama and did battle with my officers in the plain of Kish. The enemy's onslaught was great against my officers and they could not withstand it. They sent messengers for help to me (while I was) in the plain of Kutha. In my wrath, I made a fierce assault upon Kutha; I slaughtered their warriors round about its wall like sheep and took the city. I took out and counted as spoil the horses and bowmen of the Elamites, the Arameans, and the Chaldeans, the commanders of the king of Elam, Nabu-nasir, as well as the rebel inhabitants of the city. I raged like a lion; I stormed like the flood. I set my face, together with my merciless warriors, against Merodach-baladan. And he, doer of evil, saw the advance of my campaign from afar. Fear fell upon him and he abandoned all of his forces and fled to Guzummani. Tannanu, together with the armies of the Elamites, the Chaldeans and the Arameans, who stood at his side and had come to his aid — I defeated them and shattered his forces. Adinu, son of the wife[3] of Merodach-baladan, together with Bazqanu, brother of Iatie, queen of the Arabs, together with their armies, with my own hands I took alive as captives. I myself seized the chariots, wagons, horses, mules, asses, dromedaries (and) Bactrian camels which had been abandoned during the battle. In the joy of my heart and with shining countenance, I hurried to Babylon and entered the palace of Merodach-baladan to oversee the property and goods (stored) there.

(lines 31-38) I opened his treasuries. Gold, silver, vessels of gold and silver, precious stones, beds, armchairs, a processional carriage — a royal appurtenance — inlaid with gold and silver, property and goods of all kinds, without number, an enormous treasure, his wife, the women of his palace, his housekeepers, male and female musicians, eunuchs, courtiers, attendants, palace slaves who keep his royalty in good spirits, all the craftsmen as many as there were, I brought (them) out and counted as spoil.

I hurried after him. I sent my warriors to Guzummani into the swamps and the marshes. They searched for him for five days, but his (hiding) place was not found. The rest of the horses of his troops, which had no place to rest and had fled from him (as swiftly) as deer, and had not gone with him, I gathered together from the steppe and the hills.

(lines 39-50) In the course of my campaign, ... (the names of 26 towns are listed),[4] in all 33 fortified towns, walled towns of Bit-Dakkuri, with 250 villages within their borders; ... (the names of 8 towns are listed), in all 8 fortified towns, walled towns of Bit-Saᵓalli, with 120 villages within their borders; ... (the names of 39 towns are listed), in all 39 fortified towns, walled towns of Bit-Amukkani, with 350 villages within their borders; ... (the names of 8 towns), in 8 fortified towns, walled towns of Bit-Yakin, with 100 villages within their borders; a total of 88 fortified towns, walled towns of Chaldea (i.e., Babylonia), with 820 villages within their borders, I besieged, I conquered, I plundered.

b 2 Kgs 18:17; Isa 20:1

c 1 Kgs 9:22; 2 Kgs 7:2; 9:25; 15:25, etc.

d Zech 1:7

e 2 Kgs 18:17, etc.

[1] Lit. "the tartan."

[2] An expression referring to the nomadic life style of the Arameans. In a similar manner, the Amorite tribes who entered Mesopotamia in the late 3rd millennium BCE were styled "who know no grain" and "who dig up mushrooms at the foot of the mountain." See Klein 1996. For Nergal-nasir, the Sutean, see Heltzer 1981:96.

[3] Perhaps to be read "sister" (Brinkman 1964:25, n. 140).

[4] An error of transcription may account for the missing seven names; cf. Ephᶜal 1982:40, n. 106.

(lines 51-62) I provisioned my troops with barley and the dates of their groves, (and) their produce from outlying regions. I destroyed, devastated and burned (their towns) and turned them into forgotten tells. I took out the Aramean and Chaldean elite forces who were in Uruk, Nippur, Kish and Hursagkalamma, together with their rebel inhabitants and counted (them) as spoil. I provisioned my troops with barley and dates of their groves, from the field which they had worked, (and) the produce from outlying regions, for their sustenance.

I installed Bel-ibni, son of a building inspector, a native-born Babylonian, who was raised in my palace like a young puppy.

On my return, I captured the Tu᾿muna, Riḫilu, Yadaqqu, Ubudu, Kipr[e, Maliḫu, Gurumu, U]bulu, Damunu, Gambulum, Ḫindaru, Ru᾿ua, Baqudu, Ḫamranu, Ḫagranu, Nabatu, Li᾿ta[u, all of them unsubmissive Arameans], and despoiled them.

In the course of my campaign, I received the heavy tribute of Nabu-bel-shumati, the administrator of Hararati: gold, silver, large *musukkanu*-timber, asses, dromedaries, cattle and sheep. I slew the warriors of Ḫirimmu, a dangerous enemy, who had not submitted to any of the kings, my predecessors. Not a soul escaped. I reorganized that district: one ox, 10 lambs, 10 homers of wine, 20 homers of the best quality dates, I imposed as dues for (the temples of) the gods of Assyria, my lords. I returned to Assyria with the great spoil of 208,000 men, 7,200 horses and mules, 11,073 asses, 5,230 camels, 800,100 ewes, excluding the men, asses, camels, and sheep, the shares which my troops had carried off and appropriated for themselves; and the enemy warriors, strong power, who had not submitted to my yoke, I cut down with the sword and hung on stakes.

REFERENCES

Text: BM 113203; Smith 1921; Luckenbill 1924:48-55; Frahm 1997:42-45; Studies: Brinkman 1964:6-53; 1984:54-59; Eph^cal 1982; Frahm 1997:42-45; Klein 1996; Levine 1982:29-40; Smith 1921.

SENNACHERIB'S SIEGE OF JERUSALEM (2.119B)

Mordechai Cogan

This is probably the most discussed Neo-Assyrian inscription, due to its providing a complimentary report, from the Assyrian point of view, of the military operations in Judah, in particular the investment of Jerusalem, portrayed so extensively in the Bible (2 Kgs 18:13-19:37; Isa 36-37; 2 Chr 32:1-22). The cuneiform text summarizes the campaign of Sennacherib in 701 BCE, undertaken to quell the revolt of vassal states in the West which had broken out upon the death of Sargon four years earlier. Because of the literary nature of compositions in which events are grouped topically rather than chronologically, i.e., they are grouped under the rubrics of "the submissive" or "the defeated" (Tadmor 1985a), a strict itinerary of the campaign cannot be re-created. Sennacherib's scribes portray Hezekiah as being roundly defeated, submitting to his overlord and sending a substantial tribute payment to Nineveh at the conclusion of the campaign. The contradictory conclusion in the biblical record, which describes the miraculous defeat of the Assyrian army (2 Kgs 19:35), has given rise to a number of alternative reconstructions (Gonçalves 1986), no one of which has gained general scholarly assent.

There is no record of a further western campaign during Sennacherib's reign, and the oft-times posited second encounter between Hezekiah and Sennacherib some fifteen years later is untenable, considering the development of events in the West during the first quarter of the seventh century.

The earliest copy of the cuneiform text (= the Rassam cylinder) bears the date Iyar 700 BCE, a half year or so after the end of hostilities.

In my third campaign, I marched against Hatti.[1] The awesome splendor of my lordship overwhelmed Lulli, king of Sidon, and he fled overseas far-off.[2] The terrifying nature of the weapon of (the god) Ashur my lord overwhelmed his strong cities, Greater Sidon, Lower Sidon, Bit-zitti, Sariptu, Mahaliba, Ushu, Akzib, Akko, walled cities (provided) with food and water for his garrisons, and they bowed in submission at my feet. I installed Tuba᾿lu on the royal throne[3] over them and im-

[1] I.e., "Upper Syria."

[2] Added in prism dated 697: "and disappeared forever" (i.e., died).

[3] Var.: "his royal throne,"

posed upon him tribute and dues for my lordship (payable) annually without interruption.

The kings of Amurru,[4] all of them — Minuḫimmu of Samsimuruna,[5] Tubaʾlu of Sidon, Abdiliʾti of Arvad, Urumilki of Byblos, Mitinti of Ashdod, Puduilu of Beth-Ammon, Chemosh-nadbi of Moab, Ayarammu of Edom — brought me sumptuous presents as their abundant audience-gift, fourfold, and kissed my feet.

As for Ṣidqa, king of Ashkelon, who had not submitted to my yoke — his family gods, he himself, his wife, his sons, his daughters, his brothers, and (all the rest of) his descendants, I deported and brought him to Assyria. I set Sharruludari, son of Rukubti, their former king, over the people of Ashkelon and imposed upon him payment of tribute (and) presents to my lordship; he (now) bears my yoke. In the course of my campaign, I surrounded and conquered Beth-Dagon, Joppa, Bene-berak, Azor, cities belonging to Ṣidqa, who did not submit quickly, and I carried off their spoil.

The officials, the nobles, and the people of Ekron who had thrown Padi,[6] their king, (who was) under oath and obligation to Assyria, into iron fetters and handed him over in a hostile manner to Hezekiah, the Judean, took fright because of the offense they had committed. The kings of Egypt, (and) the bowmen, chariot corps and cavalry of the kings of Ethiopia assembled a countless force and came to their (i.e. the Ekronites') aid. In the plain of Eltekeh, they drew up their ranks against me and sharpened their weapons. Trusting in the god Ashur, my lord, I fought with them and inflicted a defeat upon them. The Egyptian charioteers and princes, together with the charioteers of the Ethiopians, I personally took alive in the midst of the battle. I besieged and conquered Eltekeh and Timnah and carried off their spoil. I advanced to Ekron and slew its officials and nobles who had stirred up rebellion and hung their bodies on watchtowers all about the city. The citizens who committed sinful acts I counted as spoil, and I ordered the release of the rest of them, who had not sinned. I freed Padi, their king, from Jerusalem and set him on the throne as king over them and imposed tribute for my lordship over him.

a 2 Kgs 18:13-19:37; Isa 36-37; 2 Chr 32:1-22

b 2 Kgs 18:14

As for Hezekiah, the Judean,[7] [a] I besieged forty-six of his fortified walled cities and surrounding smaller towns, which were without number. Using packed-down ramps and applying battering rams, infantry attacks by mines, breeches, and siege machines,[8] I conquered (them). I took out 200,150 people, young and old, male and female, horses, mules, donkeys, camels, cattle, and sheep, without number, and counted them as spoil. He himself, I locked up within Jerusalem, his royal city, like a bird in a cage.[9] I surrounded him with earthworks, and made it unthinkable[10] for him to exit by the city gate. His cities which I had despoiled I cut off from his land and gave them to Mitinti, king of Ashdod, Padi, king of Ekron and Ṣilli-bel, king of Gaza,[11] and thus diminished his land. I imposed dues and gifts for my lordship upon him, in addition to the former tribute, their yearly payment.

He, Hezekiah, was overwhelmed by the awesome splendor of my lordship, and he sent me after my departure to Nineveh, my royal city, his elite troops (and) his best soldiers, which he had brought in as reinforcements to strengthen Jerusalem, with 30 talents of gold, 800 talents of silver,[b] choice antimony, large blocks of carnelian, beds (inlaid) with ivory, armchairs (inlaid) with ivory, elephant hides, ivory, ebony-wood, boxwood,[12] multicolored garments, garments of linen, wool (dyed) red-purple and blue-purple, vessels of copper, iron, bronze and tin, chariots, siege shields, lances, armor, daggers for the belt, bows and arrows, countless trappings and implements of war, together with his daughters, his palace women, his male and female singers.[12] He (also) dispatched his messenger to deliver the tribute and to do obeisance.

[4] I.e., the West.
[5] To be distinguished from Menachem of Israel; see Weippert 1993-97.
[6] For this royal name at Ekron, see above, *COS* 2.42.
[7] Added in "Chicago" Prism dated 691: "who had not submitted to my yoke."
[8] Perhaps "storm ladders."
[9] For this cliché, see *COS* 2.117A, n. 31.
[10] Lit.: "taboo."
[11] Var. in Bull Inscription (Frahm, No. 4): "I gave it (i.e. his land) to the kings of Ashdod, Ashkelon, Ekron and Gaza."
[12-12] Omitted in "Chicago" Prism; replaced there by: "abundant treasure of all kind."

REFERENCES

Text: Frahm 1997:53-55, lines 32-58; Luckenbill 1924:29-34, col. ii:37-iii:49; p. 60, lines 56-58. Translations: *ARAB* 2.239-240, 284; *ANET* 287-288; *DOTT* 66-67; Borger in K. Galling, *TGI*[2] 67-69; *TUAT* 1/4 388-390. Studies: Tadmor 1985a; Hallo 1999a (with previous literature).

SENNACHERIB — LACHISH RELIEF INSCRIPTION (2.119C)

Mordechai Cogan

A four-line epigraph, inscribed in a rectangular block to the left of the seated figure of the king reviewing captives filing out of Lachish. The detailed relief,[1] which depicts the assault and capture of the Judean city, enjoyed a most prominent position in a suite of rooms in the palace of Sennacherib at Nineveh, so that "a visitor [to the palace] might justifiably conclude that the surrender of Lachish was the high point of the western campaign" (Russell 1991:252). Though commemorated in outstanding fashion in this wall relief, the battle of Lachish did not come in for specific mention in the "official" annal account of the campaign of 701 BCE (cf. *COS* 2.119B); the choice of Lachish as the representative of the battles in Judah may have been influenced by the presence of the king on the scene.

Sennacherib, king of the universe, king of Assyria, seated upon a sedan chair,

a 2 Kgs 19:8; 2 Chr 32:9

the spoils of Lachish[a] passed before him.

[1] For photograph of reliefs and their reconstructions in the archaeological context, see Ussishkin 1982; for artistic and architectural analysis, see Russell 1991:202-209; 252-257. Cf. also Yadin 1963:428-439; Hallo 1960:59 and figs. 2-3.

REFERENCES

Luckenbill 1924:156, i.37; *ANET*, 288; *TUAT* 1:391.

SENNACHERIB: THE "AZEKAH" INSCRIPTION (2.119D)

Mordechai Cogan

The remains of twenty-one lines of a tablet, one fragment of which (K 6205) was formerly ascribed to Tiglath-pileser III (*ANET* 282b), the other (82-3-23, 131) to Sargon. The reference to the Judean city of Azekah, as well as the name of Hezekiah (partially restored) definitively set the location of the battles in Judah, but there is still some question as to their date. Naʾaman (1974), who joined the two fragments, opined that the description fits the western campaign of Sennacherib in 701 BCE; others (e.g., Frahm 1997) argue for a date during Sargon's reign (712 or even earlier 720). In either case, the elevated, poetic style of the surviving lines resembles that of Sargon's "Letter to the god Ashur," written at the end of the campaign to Urartu, reporting in magnificent detail the king's triumph.

1-2 (scattered signs)
3 [Ashur, my lord, support]ed me and to the land of Ju[dah I marched. In] the course of my campaign, the tribute of the ki[ngs of ... I received].
4 [by the mig]ht (?) of Ashur, my lord, the district [of Hezek]iah of Judah, like [ ]
5 [ ] the city of Azekah,[a] his stronghold, which is between my [ ] and the land of Judah [ ]
6 [ ] located on a mountain peak, like countless pointed ir[on] daggers, reaching to high heaven
7 [ ] were strong and rivaled the highest mountains; at its sight, as if from the sky [ ]
8 [by packed-down ra]mps, and applying mighty (?) battering rams, infantry attacks by mi-n[es]
9 [the approach of my cav]alry they saw, and heard the sound of Ashur's mighty troops and they were afraid [ ]
10 [I besieged (?)] I conquered, I carried off its spoil. I tore down, I destroyed [ ]
11 [the city X] a royal [city] of the Philistines,[b] which He[zek]iah had taken and fortified for himself [ ]
12 [ ] (scattered signs) [ ] like a tree [ ]
13 [ ] surrounded by great t[o]wers, most difficult [ ]
14 [ ] a palace, like a mountain, was barred in from of them, high [ ]
15 [ ] it was dark, and the sun never shone on it, its waters were located in dar[kn]ess, its outflow [ ]
16 [ ] its mo[uth (?)] was cut with axes and a moat was dug around it [ ]
17 [soldiers] skilled in battle, he stationed in it, he girded his weapons, in order to [ ]
18 [ ] I had the people of Amurru,[1] all of them, carry earth [ ]
19 [against them. For a third time, [ ] great, like a pot [I smashed]

a Jer 34:7

b Mic 1:10-16

[1] I.e., the West.

20 [cattle and sh]eep, from its midst I t[ook out, and as] spo[il I counted.]

21 (illegible signs)

REFERENCES

Na᾿aman 1974:25-39; Galil 1992:113-119; Frahm 1997:229-232; Hallo 1999a:40.

SENNACHERIB: THE CAPTURE AND DESTRUCTION OF BABYLON (2.119E)

Mordechai Cogan

The Bavian Rock Inscription of Sennacherib was chiseled on the walls of the gorge of the Gomel River, whose waters were fed into the Jerwan aqueduct, a major link in the king's project to irrigate the plains surrounding Nineveh. The historical section of the inscription concentrates on the "second campaign" against Babylon that varies from the prism text (where it is numbered the "eighth" and last campaign of the king) in tone; its dispassionate description reflects a sense that Sennacherib's "Babylonian problem" was behind him (Brinkman 1973; Weissert 1997) . The date of the events in Babylonia, as determined by the prism inscriptions, is 689 BCE.

The standard introduction praising the gods and king is followed, in an unusual editorial displacement, by a description of the building project commemorated in this inscription. Detailed are the canals and water courses constructed to bring water to the thirsty fields of Nineveh, their dedication and the rewarding of the builders. The king's military undertakings follow.

(lines 34-43) In the same year as the flowing of that canal which I dug, I arrayed the forces in the plain of Halule against Ummanmenanu king of Elam and the king of Babylon, with the many kings of the mountains and sea who (had come) to their aid. By the word of the god Ashur, the great lord, my lord, I advanced into their midst like a fierce arrow and defeated their armies. I scattered their concentrations (and) I shattered their troops. I took alive in that battle the princes of the king of Elam, together with Nabu-shum-ishkun, son of Merodach-baladan king of Babylon.[a] (As for) the king of Elam and the king of Babylon, the fear of my mighty battle overcame them and they defecated in their chariots and they fled back to their lands in order to save their lives. And they did not return, (thinking): Perhaps Sennacherib king of Assyria will become angry and will set out for Elam once again. Fear and terror were poured out over all of Elam and they left their land to save their lives. Like an eagle, they settled on steep mountains; like a pursued bird, their hearts were beating and they did not come down as long as they lived (lit. "until the day of their fate" [i.e., their death]), (nor) did they make war.

(lines 43-54) In my second campaign, I marched quickly against Babylon which I was set upon conquering. Like the onset of a storm I swept, (and) like a fog I enveloped it. I laid siege to that city; with mines and siege machines, I personally took it — the spoil of his mighty men, small and great. I left no one. I filled the city squares with their corpses. Shuzubu,[1] king of Babylon, together with his family and his [ ], I brought alive to my land. I handed out the wealth of that city — silver, gold, precious stones, property and goods — to my people and they made it their own. My men took the (images of the) gods who dwell there and smashed them. They took their property and their wealth. Adad and Shala, the gods of Ekallate, which Marduk-nadin-ahhe, king of Babylon had taken and carried off to Babylon during the reign of Tiglath-pileser (I), king of Assyria, I brought out of Babylon and returned them to their place in Ekallate.

I destroyed and tore down and burned with fire the city (and) its houses, from its foundations to its parapets. I tore out the inner and outer walls, temples, the ziggurat[2] of brick and earth, as many as there were, and threw them into the Arahtu river. I dug canals through the city and flooded its place with water, destroying the structure of its foundation. I made its devastation greater than that of "the Flood."[b] So that in future days, the site of that city, its temples and its gods, would not be identifiable, I completely destroyed it with water and annihilated it like inundated territory.

a 2 Kgs 20:12; Isa 39:1

b Gen 6:17–8:22; Ps 29:10

[1] I.e., Mushezib-Marduk of Bit-Dakkuri; he had seized the throne towards the end of 693 BCE.

[2] I.e., "temple-tower."

REFERENCES

Luckenbill 1924:78-85; Levine 1982:48-51; Brinkman 1984:63-65, 67-68; Frahm 1996:151-154; Weissert 1997.

ESARHADDON (2.120)

William W. Hallo

Sennacherib's destruction of Babylon (see *COS* 2.119E) was condemned by the city's later Chaldaean rulers. Nabopolassar, the founder of the Chaldaean Dynasty, declared war on the Assyrians and saw their destruction as just retribution (Gerardi 1986); Nabonidus, the last king of the Dynasty, also considered Sennacherib's assassination as evidence of divine retribution (*ANET* 309; Beaulieu 1989:105, 115). In much the same spirit, Sennacherib's assassination was juxtaposed with his (failed) siege of Jerusalem in 701 BCE by the biblical author (2 Kgs 19:36f. = Isa 37:37f.) as if to say *post hoc ergo propter hoc* (Hallo 1999a). Under these circumstances, it was understandable that his son and successor, Esarhaddon (681-669 BCE), marshalled all the physical and spiritual resources of the Assyrian empire to reverse the effects of his father's depredations (Porter 1993). He rebuilt Babylon and, in his inscriptions from and about the city, he went out of his way to express his solicitude for it, and for Marduk, its patron deity. Recension B of his major Babylon inscription includes the following passage ("episode 10" in Borger's edition):

Until the days were elapsed that the heart of the great lord Marduk should be appeased and he would find peace with the country against which he had raged, 70 years were to elapse, but he wrote [11] years (instead) and took pity and said: Amen!

This is explained more fully in Recensions A and D as follows:

He (Marduk) had written 70 years as the quantity of its (the city's) exile (lit.: lying fallow) but merciful Marduk — soon his heart was appeased and he turned the upper into the lower (figure) so that he decreed its resettlement for 11 years.

The meaning is that the numeral 70, written in cuneiform as 60 + 10, was turned into 11 by the simple device of writing 10 + 60, or rather 10 + 1 (60 and 1 are alike written with a single vertical wedge), i.e. turning the left (= upper in the older direction of cuneiform writing) into the right (= lower) wedge (Shaffer 1981). For other examples of "metathesis of numerals" see Beaulieu 1995. An exile of 70 years is also predicted by Jeremiah (25:12, 29:10), and alluded to in 2 Chr 36:22 = Ezra 1:1, though in fact it proved to be closer to 50 years (Tadmor 1999).

REFERENCES

Borger 1956:15.

---

5. NEO-BABYLONIAN INSCRIPTIONS

Paul-Alain Beaulieu

After the fall of the Assyrian Empire at the end of the 7th century BCE, power shifted back to Babylon, whose rulers inherited most of the territories formerly ruled by the kings of Assyria. During this relatively short but brilliant period (626-539 BCE) the kings of the Neo-Babylonian dynasty embellished their capital with numerous architectural wonders. They also extensively rebuilt the temples of Babylonia,[1] which had been left in a state of disrepair for centuries because of economic stagnation, civil disorders, and repeated foreign interference. Almost all the inscriptions of the Neo-Babylonian empire are building inscriptions which contain little historical information. In fact two of the inscriptions translated here (*COS* 2.121, 123A) are among the few such texts which allude to historical events. On the other hand, these inscriptions are of great importance for understanding the culture and religious ideology of that period. They are written in the Standard Babylonian idiom of Akkadian, but display a number of peculiarities derived from their imitation of much older styles of royal inscriptions, in particular the inscriptions of the First Dynasty of Babylon (ca. 1894-1595 BCE). Many of them are written in an archaizing script which imitates the lapidary script of the Old Babylonian period. For many inscriptions two editions are known, one in archaizing, the other in Neo-Babylonian script. In spite of these antiquarian tendencies, Neo-Babylonian building inscriptions display several important innovations, notably the concluding prayer to the deity to whom the inscription is dedicated.[2]

[1] The essential information on each temple is collected in George 1993. For Babylon itself, see *COS* 2.120.

[2] Similar prayers occasionally occur in the inscriptions of the Sargonid kings of Assyria, but they became a regular feature of building inscriptions only during Neo-Babylonian empire.

NABOPOLASSAR (2.121)

NABOPOLASSAR'S RESTORATION OF IMGUR-ENLIL, THE INNER DEFENSIVE WALL OF BABYLON (2.121)

Paul-Alain Beaulieu

Nabopolassar (626-605 BCE) was the founder of the Neo-Babylonian dynasty. He revolted against the Assyrians, ousted them from Akkad (i.e. Babylonia), and eventually helped the Medes to destroy the Assyrian empire. The following inscription discovered during the Iraqi restoration work on the site of Babylon and first published in 1985 commemorates Nabopolassar's rebuilding of the inner defensive wall of Babylon, the wall Imgur-Enlil "the god Enlil has been favorable."[1] The king also states his humble origins and his defeat of the Assyrians.[2] This composition is remarkable for its elaborate poetic praise of the wall Imgur-Enlil, for the royal oath recorded in the third section, and finally for its concluding part where the traditional curse against eventual violators has been transformed into a wisdom address to future generations, a theme borrowed from Akkadian pseudo-historical and sapiential literature. It is written in archaizing script.

Royal Titulary (i.1-6)
Nabopolassar, the king of justice, the shepherd called by Marduk, the creature of Ninmenna[3] - the supreme lady, the queen of queens - the one to whom Nabû and Tashmêtu[4] strech their hand, the prince beloved by Ninshiku.[5]

Royal Autobiography (i.7-ii.5)
When I was young, although I was the son of a nobody, I constantly sought the sanctuaries of Nabû and Marduk my lords. My mind was preoccupied with the establishment of their prescriptions and the complete performance of their rituals. My attention was directed at justice and equity. Shazu,[6] the lord who fathoms the hearts of the gods of heaven and the netherworld,[7] who constantly observes the conduct[8] of mankind, perceived my inner thoughts and elevated me, me the servant who was anonymous among the people, to a high status in the country in which I was born. He called me to the lordship over the country and the people. He caused a benevolent protective spirit to walk at my side. He let (me) succeed in everything I undertook. He caused Nergal, the strongest among the gods, to march at my side; he slew my foes, felled my enemies. The Assyrian, who had ruled Akkad because of divine anger and had, with his heavy yoke, oppressed the inhabitants of the country, I, the weak one, the powerless one, who constantly seeks the lord of lords, with the mighty strength of Nabû and Marduk my lords I removed them[9] from Akkad and caused (the Babylonians) to throw off their yoke.

Rebuilding of Imgur-Enlil (ii.6-41)
At that time Nabopolassar, king of Babylon, the one who pleases Nabû and Marduk, I, (for) Imgur-Enlil - the great fortification wall of Babylon, the original boundary-post which has been made manifest since olden days, the solid border as ancient as time immemorial, the lofty mountain peak[10] which rivals heavens, the mighty shield which locks the entrance to the hostile lands, the wide enclosure of the Igigi, the spacious courtyard of the Anunnaki, the staircase to heaven, the ladder to the netherworld, the station of Lugalirra and Meslamtae, the outdoor shrine[11] of Ishtar the great lady, the place of the throwing stick[12] of Dagan the hero, the camp enclosure of warrior Ninurta, the temple of the divine protection of Anu and Enlil, the shrine artfully designed by Ea the lord of Eridu, the fortification ground of the great gods, whose foundations the Igigi and the Anunnaki had (originally) established in the jubilation of their hearts, (whose work) they had artfully carried out (and which) they had raised to its top, (which) because of old

[1] For a history of the walls of Babylon, Imgur-Enlil and Nemetti-Enlil, see George 1992:343-351.

[2] The chronology of Nabopolassar's war against the Assyrians in Babylonia is discussed in Beaulieu 1997:367-394.

[3] Lit., "the lady of the tiara," a mother goddess at home in southern Babylonia, mostly Ur and Uruk. This might point to Nabopolassar's southern origin.

[4] The consort of the god Nabû.

[5] A name of the god Ea/Enki, the god of wisdom, magic, and of the Apsu (the subterranean waters). Ea/Enki was at home in Eridu, located in the southernmost area of Iraq. This might also indicate Nabopolassar's southern origin.

[6] A name of the god Marduk which means "he who knows the heart."

[7] This is an explanation of the name Shazu, which also occurs in the Babylonian Epic of Creation, Tablet VII, line 35.

[8] The word is *takkaltu*, perhaps to be emended to *tallaktu* "way, conduct." See al-Rawi 1985:6-7, note to col. i.16.

[9] Namely, the Assyrians, referred to in the singular in the preceding verses.

[10] For a different interpretation see al-Rawi 1985:7, note to col. ii.11. I follow *CAD* G s.v. *ginû* B.

[11] The word *ibratu* refers to outdoor shrines, probably niches located on the street or in private courtyards. Topographical descriptions of Babylon mention 180 such shrines of Ishtar in the capital (George 1992:68-69, line 86).

[12] Since the word *tilpanu*, translated here as "throwing stick," can also denote the bow in late royal inscriptions (*AHw* s.v.), it is possible that this passage refers to the battlements on the wall from which the soldiers threw spears and javelins at the besieging enemy.

age had weakened and caved in, whose walls had been taken away[13] because of rain and heavy downpours (and) whose foundations had heaped up and accumulated into a mound of ruins — I levied the troops of Enlil, Shamash and Marduk, had (them) wield the hoe, imposed (on them) the corvée basket. From the bank of the Araḫtu canal, (on) the upper side near the gate of Ishtar, down to the (other) bank of the Araḫtu canal, (on) the lower side near the gate of Urash, I removed its accumulated debris, surveyed and examined its old foundations, and laid its brickwork in the original location. On the edge of the netherworld I established its base. I surrounded the east bank with a mighty mountainous belt.[14]

Burying the Foundation Deposit (iii.1-21)
Nabopolassar, the humble one, the submissive one, the worshiper of Nabû and Marduk, the shepherd who pleases Papnunanki,[15] the one who inspects the old foundations of Babylon, the one who discovers (inscribed) brick(s) from the past,[16] the one who carries out the work on the original, eternal foundations, the one who wields the hoe of the Igigi, the one who carries the corvée basket of the Anunnaki, the builder of Imgur-Enlil for Marduk my lord, I, in order that no future king whosoever remove my well chosen words (and) in order that no words are made to supersede my speech, I swore the oath of Marduk, my lord, and of Shamash, my god: "(Woe on me) if my utterances are not true, but false!"[17] At that time I found the royal statue of one of my predecessors who had rebuilt that wall and, in a secure place, in the great foundations, together with my own statue, I placed (it) for eternity.

Wisdom Address to Future Generations (iii.22-36)
Any king, at any time, whether a son or a grandson who will succeed me, (and) whose name Marduk will call to rulership of the country, do not be concerned[18] with feats of might and power. Seek the sanctuaries of Nabû and Marduk and let them slay your enemies. The lord Marduk examines utterances and scrutinizes the heart. He who is loyal to Bēl,[19] his foundations will endure. He who is loyal to the son of Bēl[20] will last for eternity. When that wall becomes dilapidated and you relieve its disrepair, in the same manner as I found the inscription of a king who preceded me and did not alter its location, find my own inscription and place it with your inscription. By the command of Marduk the great lord, whose command is not revoked, may your fame be established forever.

[13] The verb *ut-ta-as-sú-ú* must be a Dt stem of *nesû*, previously unattested for this root.

[14] Al-Rawi emended this passage from *e-bi-iḫ dan-num* to *e-pé-šum*! *dan-num*, but this seems unnecessary. Different interpretations of *e-bi-iḫ* have since been offered: George 1991 ("cincture, belt") and Farber 1991 ("mount Ebiḫ, mountain"). I follow Vanstiphout 1991, who posits a deliberate ambiguity. This ambiguity is already expressed in the Sum. composition Inanna and Ebiḫ. It should be noted that the interpretation of *ebiḫ* as a proper noun (mount Ebiḫ) solely because it lacks an ending is not mandatory in consideration of the occurrence of several endingless nouns in the same text (e.g. col. i.17: *ib-rat šá* ᵈINNIN *šar-rat ra-bi-tim*).

[15] A name of Zarpanītu, the wife of Marduk, who was also known under the designation Bēltiya "my lady."

[16] The phrase *muttû libitti ša waḫrâtim* means lit. "who discovers the brick(s) of the future," but in this context *(w)aḫrâtu* must mean "past." Akk. expressions of remote time usually apply to both past and future, but this is the first occurrence of *(w)aḫrâtu* referring to the past. Al-Rawi emends to *ma*!*-aḫ-ra-tim*, but this does not seem necessary.

[17] This oath formula recalls very similar oaths found in the inscriptions of Rīmush and Manishtūshu, the two sons and successors of Sargon of Akkad, nearly two millennia earlier. Is it possible that Nabopolassar is here emulating an inscription of one of these rulers found during the restoration of Imgur-Enlil, and that it is the same ruler of whom he claims to have discovered a statue? Building activities in Babylon are mentioned as early as the reign of Shar-kali-sharri, who claims to have built the temples of Anunītu and Ilaba in KÁ.DINGIR.KI.

[18] The shift from third to second person, and vice versa (*COS* 2.123A, n. 21), is customary in this type of address.

[19] Bēl, literally "lord," is a name of Marduk.

[20] The son of Bēl is presumably Nabû, the son and vizier of Marduk and patron god of Borsippa.

REFERENCES

Text: Al-Rawi 1985; Farber 1991; George 1991a; 1991b; Vanstiphout 1991; Beaulieu 1997.

NEBUCHADNEZZAR II (2.122)

NEBUCHADNEZZAR II'S RESTORATION OF THE EBABBAR TEMPLE IN LARSA (2.122A)

Paul-Alain Beaulieu

This inscription is recorded on several clay cylinders and baked bricks found at Larsa, all written in Neo-Babylonian script. It commemorates the rebuilding of Ebabbar, the temple of the sun god Shamash at Larsa, by Nebuchadnezzar II (605-562 BCE), the son and successor of Nabopolassar and the real architect of Neo-Babylonian hegemony.

Nabonidus restored Ebabbar again in his 10th regnal year (546-45 BCE). He claims that Nebuchadnezzar did not find the original foundation deposit before rebuilding the temple, this being apparently the reason why it quickly fell into disrepair. Nebuchadnezzar's inscription is indeed ominously silent concerning the finding of a foundation deposit, but insists that the god Marduk directly ordered him to restore the temple. The Sippar cylinder of Nabonidus, translated below (*COS* 2.123A), makes the same observation for the other temple of Shamash, the Ebabbar of Sippar. The inscription follows the standard Neo-Babylonian pattern, with the royal titulary in first position (royal name — epithets — *anāku* "I"), then the description of the building work with its surrounding circumstances (clauses *īnu* "when" and *ina ūmīšu* "at that time"), and the concluding prayer.

Royal titulary (i.1-6)
Nebuchadnezzar, king of Babylon, the humble one, the submissive one, the pious one, the worshiper of the lord of lords, the caretaker of Esagil and Ezida, the legitimate heir of Nabopolassar, king of Babylon, I,

Rebuilding of Ebabbar (i.7-ii.11)
when Marduk, the great lord, the wisest among the gods, the proud one, gave me the shepherdship of the country and the people, at that time Ebabbar, the temple of Shamash in Larsa, which since distant days had turned into a mound of ruins, in whose midst sand had accumulated and (whose) ground plan could no longer be identified, during my reign the great lord Marduk became reconciled to that temple. He aroused the four winds and removed the sand inside it so that the ground plan could be discovered. He specifically ordered me, Nebuchadnezzar, king of Babylon, the servant who worships him, to restore that temple. I surveyed and inspected its old foundations, spread consecrated soil above its old foundations and set up its brickwork. Ebabbar, the legitimate temple (and) residence of Shamash, my lord, for Shamash, who dwells in Ebabbar in the midst of Larsa, the great lord, my lord, did I rebuild.

Concluding prayer to Shamash (ii.12-26)
O Shamash, great lord, when you enter Ebabbar, your lordly seat, in joy and gladness, look joyfully upon the work of my gracious hands, and may a life of distant days, the stability of the throne, the long duration of my reign (and) [the defeat of my enemies][1] be set (for me) on your lips. May the thresholds, the locks, the bolts (and) the doors of Ebabbar, without ceasing, speak of me favorably in your presence.

[1] The passage between brackets appears only in the Yale exemplar published as YOS 9:140.

REFERENCES

Text: I R, plate 51, no.2 (copy); Stephens 1937:35-36; Langdon 1912:96-97; Berger 1973:249-251. Translations: Seux 1976:510; Foster 1993 2:746.

NEBUCHADNEZZAR II'S RESTORATION OF E-URIMIN-ANKIA, THE ZIGGURAT OF BORSIPPA (2.122B)

Paul-Alain Beaulieu

This inscription is recorded on clay cylinders found in the ruins of the ziggurat of Borsippa. Duplicates are known in both Neo-Babylonian and archaizing scripts. Like the preceding, this inscription follows the standard Neo-Babylonian pattern, but the *īnu* clause has been expanded to include a review of the previous building works of Nebuchadnezzar dedicated to the gods Marduk and Nabû, the patron deities of the Neo-Babylonian dynasty.

Royal titulary (i.1-9)
Nebuchadnezzar, king of Babylon, the loyal shepherd, the one permanently selected by Marduk, the exalted ruler, the one beloved by Nabû, the wise expert who is attentive to the ways of the gods, the tireless governor, the caretaker of Esagil and Ezida, the foremost heir of Nabopolassar, king of Babylon, I,

Previous work on the shrines of Marduk and Nabû (i.10-26)
when Marduk, my great lord, duly created me and ordered me to take care of him, Nabû, the administrator of the totality of heaven and the netherworld, put in my hands the just scepter. (In) Esagil, the temple of heaven and the netherworld, the residence of the Enlil[1] of the gods, Marduk, (and) E-

[1] Enlil was the head of the pantheon before Marduk usurped that position at the end of the second millennium BCE, after which the title "Enlil of the gods" was commonly applied to the latter to celebrate his role as king of the gods.

umusha, his lordly cella, I applied shining gold (glaze) instead of plaster. Ezida[2] I built anew and with silver, gold, choice gems, copper, *musukkannu*-wood (and) cedar-wood, I completed its work. E-temen-anki, the ziggurat of Babylon, I rebuilt (and) completed and with glazed bricks of pure blue color I raised it to its summit.

Rebuilding of E-urimin-ankia (i.27-ii.15)
At that time E-urimin-ankia, the ziggurat of Borsippa, which a former king had built and elevated to forty-two cubits but had not raised to its summit, (which) since remote days had fallen into ruins and whose drainage openings had not been kept in order, whose brickwork rain and downpours had taken away, whose covering of glazed bricks had become dismantled and the brickwork of whose cella had accumulated into a mound of debris, Marduk, my great lord, prompted me to rebuild it. I did not change its location and did not alter its foundations. In a propitious month, on an auspicious day, I (began to) repair the destroyed brickwork of its cella and its destroyed glazed bricks covering (and to) set back up its ruined portions, and I placed my own inscription in its repaired parts. (Then) I began to rebuild it and to raise it to its summit. [I built it anew as in olden times, I raised it to its summit as in days of yore].[3]

Concluding prayer to Nabû (ii.16-31)
O Nabû, legitimate heir, exalted vizier, pre-eminent one, beloved by Marduk, look joyfully (and) favorably upon my deeds and grant me as a gift a long life, satiety with extreme old age, stability of throne, long duration of reign, defeat of adversaries, (and) conquest of the land of the enemies. On your reliable writing board which establishes the border of heaven and the netherworld, decree the lengthening of my days, inscribe for me extreme old age.[4] [a] Cause my deeds to find acceptance before Marduk, the king of heaven and the netherworld, the father your begetter. Speak favorably on my behalf, (and) let (these words) be set on your lips: "Nebuchadnezzar is indeed the king (who is) a caretaker!"[5]

a Exod 32:32-33; Isa 4:3

[2] The temple of the god Nabû in the city of Borsippa.
[3] The passage between brackets, though apparently essential to complete this section, appears in only one of the duplicates. It is possible that this expanded version was written after the actual rebuilding of the temple, while the others may have been composed before and served primarily as foundation deposits, which were of course put in the foundations before the rebuilding began.
[4] Nabû is hailed here as the god of the scribal art, who holds the "tablets of destinies" on which are inscribed the fates of all individuals. Cf. Paul 1973.
[5] Seux (1976:512, n. 1) argues for translating this as a precative: "May Nebuchadnezzar be a king (who is) a caretaker." Foster (1993 2:744) prefers an asseverative meaning "Nebuchadnezzar is surely a provident king," and this indeed fits the context better.

REFERENCES

Text: I R, plate 51, no.1 (copy); Berger 1973:270-272; Translations: Langdon 1912:98-101; Seux 1976:511-512; Foster 1993 2:744.

NABONIDUS 2.123

THE SIPPAR CYLINDER OF NABONIDUS (2.123A)

Paul-Alain Beaulieu

This long and complex inscription occurs in several exemplars and fragmentary duplicates, all clay cylinders inscribed in Neo-Babylonian script and found in the remains of the Ebabbar temple in Sippar. One exemplar was found in Babylon, in the so-called "palace museum," along with many older inscriptions removed from their original contexts; it is now preserved in Berlin. The inscription commemorates the rebuilding of three temples by Nabonidus (556-539 BCE), the last king of Babylon, and it dates after Nabonidus' return from northern Arabia in his thirteenth regnal year. The first section, devoted to the rebuilding of Ehulhul, is remarkable for its direct historical allusions to the war between the Persians and the Medes. This war resulted in the victory of Cyrus, who was very probably Nabonidus' ally before he turned against him and conquered the Neo-Babylonian empire in the fall of 539 BCE. The second section is devoted to the Ebabbar temple of Sippar, which was restored in the third year of Nabonidus. It is a new, shorter edition of the building inscription originally composed for that occasion. Finally the third section is devoted to the rebuilding of Eulmash, the temple of the goddess Anunītu, a form of Ishtar, in Sippar-Anunītu. The entire inscription was probably composed on the occasion of the rebuilding of Eulmash.

Royal titulary (i.1-7)
I, Nabonidus, the great king, the strong king, the king of the universe, the king of Babylon, the king of the four corners, the caretaker of Esagil and Ezida, for whom Sîn and Ningal in his mother's womb decreed a royal fate as his destiny,[a] the son

a Jer 1:4-5

of Nabû-balāssu-iqbi, the wise prince, the worshiper of the great gods,[1] I,[2]

Rebuilding of Ehulhul in Harran (i.8-ii.25)

Ehulhul, the temple of Sîn in Harran, where since days of yore Sîn, the great lord, had established his favorite residence - (then) his heart became angry against that city and temple and he aroused the Mede, destroyed that temple and turned it into ruins[3] — in my legitimate reign Bēl (and) the great lord, for the love of my kingship, became reconciled with that city and temple and showed compassion.[4] In the beginning of my everlasting reign they sent me a dream. Marduk, the great lord, and Sîn, the luminary of heaven and the netherworld, stood together.[5] Marduk spoke with me: "Nabonidus, king of Babylon, carry bricks on your riding horse, rebuild Ehulhul and cause Sîn, the great lord, to establish his residence in its midst." Reverently I spoke to the Enlil of the gods, Marduk: "That temple which you ordered (me) to build, the Mede surrounds it and his might is excessive."[6] But Marduk spoke with me: "The Mede whom you mentioned, he, his country and the kings who march at his side will be no more." At the beginning of the third year they aroused him, Cyrus, the king of Anshan, his second in rank.[7] [b] He scattered the vast Median hordes with his small army. He captured Astyages, the king of the Medes, and took him to his country as captive. (Such was) the word of the great lord Marduk and of Sîn, the luminary of heaven and the netherworld, whose command is not revoked. I feared their august command, I became troubled, I was worried and my face showed signs of anxiety. I was not neglectful, nor remiss, nor careless. For rebuilding Ehulhul, the temple of Sîn, my lord, who marches at my side, which is in Harran, which Assurbanipal, king of Assyria, son of Esarhaddon, king of Assyria, a prince who preceded me, had rebuilt, I mustered my numerous troops, from the country of Gaza on the border of Egypt, (near) the Upper Sea[8] on the other side of the Euphrates, to the Lower Sea,[9] the kings, princes, governors and my numerous troops which Sîn, Shamash and Ishtar my lords had entrusted to me, (and) in a propitious month, on an auspicious day, which Shamash and Adad revealed to me by means of divination, by the wisdom of Ea and Asalluhi, with the craft of the exorcist, according to the art of Kulla, the lord of foundations and brickwork, upon (beads of) silver (and) gold, choice gems, logs of resinous woods, aromatic herbs (and cuts of) cedar (wood), in joy and gladness, on the foundation deposit of Assurbanipal, king of Assyria, who had found the foundation deposit of Shalmaneser,[10] the son of Assurnasirpal, I cleared its foundations and laid its brickwork. I mixed its mortar with beer, wine, oil and honey and anointed its excavation ramps with it. More than the kings my fathers (had done), I strengthened its building and perfected its work. That temple from its foundations to its parapet I built anew and completed its work. Beams of lofty cedar

b Isa 42:1; 45:1

[1] These two epithets refer to the father of Nabonidus, Nabû-balāssu-iqbi, who does not appear in ancient sources outside his son's inscriptions.

[2] The prologue with the royal titulary adheres to the pattern *anāku* — royal titulary — *anāku*, also found in some inscriptions of Assurbanipal. The restoration of Ehulhul is also recorded in the inscriptions of that king, and not surprisingly many coincidences of wording between them and the present inscription can be detected. Nabonidus in fact mentions that he discovered the old foundation deposits of Assurbanipal during the excavations of Ehulhul.

[3] The Medes, who allied themselves with Nabopolassar, the founder of the Neo-Babylonian dynasty, to overthrow the Assyrian empire in the last quarter of the 7th century, are presented here as the agents of divine wrath. Another inscription of Nabonidus informs us that in 610 BCE they sacked the city of Harran, which had become the last stronghold of Assyrian resistance after the fall of Nineveh two years earlier.

[4] Here the British Museum exemplar has ^{d}EN EN GAL-*ú* "Bēl, the great lord," which is the common name of Marduk, while the Berlin exemplar has ^{d}EN.ZU EN GAL-*ú* "Sîn, the great lord." This variant was very probably intentional, providing one more example of Nabonidus trying to assimilate Marduk to Sîn. In addition, the verbs *is-li-mu* and *ir-šu-ú ta-a-a-ri* in that same sentence are plural: "they became reconciled and showed mercy." Therefore the sequence ^{d}EN/^{d}EN.ZU EN GAL-*ú* must be interpreted as "Bēl/Sîn (and) the great lord," the "great lord" being Sîn in one exemplar, and Marduk in the other. In the following passage Sîn and Marduk indeed act as one deity.

[5] This passage probably refers to an astronomical conjunction of the moon (the god Sîn) and the planet Jupiter, identified in Babylonia with the god Marduk. An actual astronomical observation need not be involved, however, since conjunctions of celestial bodies seen in dreams possessed equal significance. Cf. Oppenheim 1956:202f.

[6] The region of Harran was evidently still under Median control at the time of Nabonidus' accession to the throne.

[7] The interpretation of Cyrus' epithet is uncertain. The Akkadian reads ÌR-*su ṣa-aḫ-ri* (*arassu ṣaḫri*), lit. "his young servant." *CAD* (Ṣ 182, s.v. *ṣihru*) proposes the following translation: "Cyrus, king of Anshan, his (Astyage's) subject, the second (of his name)." Seux (1969:228-229) follows *CAD* and translates the passage as follows: "ils (= Marduk et Sîn) dressèrent contre lui Cyrus II, roi d'Anzan, son vassal, et avec son armée réduite il mit en pièces l'immense (armée des) Mèdes." However, the evidence that *ṣaḫri* means "the second" is tenuous, and the more common meaning "servant, subordinate," seems more appropriate. The old theory that Cyrus is presented here as the servant of Marduk (and Sîn), providing a possible parallel to Isaiah 42:1, seems difficult to uphold, mainly because the two gods act together and are grammatically the subjects of plural verbs, while the possessive pronoun suffixed to *ardu* "servant" (*arassu*) is singular. This, however, should not be viewed as impossible considering the other ambiguities deliberately embedded in this narrative. Another difficulty arises on the biblical side, since it is by no means assured that God's "servant" in Isaiah 42:1 is Cyrus. The expression refers, more likely, to Israel as God's servant. However, Cyrus is directly mentioned in Isaiah 45:1 as the instrument of God's will, in the same manner as he is the agent of the gods Marduk and Sîn in the Sippar cylinder.

[8] This is the Mesopotamian designation for the Mediterranean Sea.

[9] This is the designation for the Persian Gulf.

[10] Shalmaneser III, son of Assurnasirpal II, reigned as king of Assyria from 858 to 824 BCE. For his inscriptions, see *COS* 2.113A-H.

trees, a product of Lebanon,[c] I set up above it.[11] Doors of cedar wood, whose scent is pleasing, I affixed at its gates. With gold and silver (glaze) I coated its walls and made it shine like the sun. I set up in its chapel a 'wild bull' of shining silver alloy, fiercely attacking my foes. At the Gate of Sunrise I set up two 'long-haired heroes'[12] coated with silver,[13] destroyers of my enemies,[14] one to the left, one to the right. I led Sîn, Ningal, Nusku and Sadarnunna my lords in procession from Babylon my royal city and, in joy and gladness, I caused them to dwell in its midst, a dwelling of enjoyment. I performed in their presence a pure sacrifice of glorification, presented my gifts and filled Ehulhul with the finest products, and I made the city of Harran, in its totality, as brilliant as moonlight.

c Judg 9:15; Isa 2:13; 14:8; Pss 29:5; 104:16

Prayer to Sîn (ii.26-43a)

O Sîn, king of the gods of heaven and the netherworld, without whom no city or country can be founded, (nor) be restored, when you enter Ehulhul, the dwelling of your plenitude, may good recommendations for that city and that temple be set on your lips. May the gods who dwell in heaven and the netherworld constantly praise the temple of Sîn, the father their creator. As for me, Nabonidus, king of Babylon, who completed that temple, may Sîn, the king of the gods of heaven and the netherworld, joyfully cast his favorable look upon me and every month, in rising and setting,[15] make my ominous signs favorable. May he lengthen my days, extend my years, make my reign firm, conquer my enemies, annihilate those hostile to me, destroy my foes. May Ningal, the mother of the great gods, speak favorably before Sîn, her beloved, on my behalf. May Shamash and Ishtar, his shining offspring,[16] recommend me favorably to Sîn, the father their creator. May Nusku, the august vizier, hear my prayer and intercede (for me).

Burying the foundation deposit (ii.43b-46)

The inscription written in the name of Assurbanipal, king of Assyria, I found and did not alter. I anointed (it) with oil, performed a sacrifice, placed it with my own inscription and returned it to its (original) place.

Rebuilding of Ebabbar in Sippar (ii.47-iii.7)

For Shamash, the judge of heaven and the netherworld, (concerning) Ebabbar, his temple which is in Sippar, which Nebuchadnezzar, a former king, had rebuilt and whose old foundation deposit he had looked for but not found - (yet) he rebuilt that temple and after forty-five years the walls of that temple had sagged[17] — I became troubled, I became fearful, I was worried and my face showed signs of anxiety. While I led Shamash out of its midst (and) caused (him) to dwell in another sanctuary, I removed (the debris) of that temple, looked for its old foundation deposit, dug to a depth of eighteen cubits into the ground and (then) Shamash, the great lord, revealed to me (the original foundations of) Ebabbar, the temple (which is) his favorite dwelling, (by disclosing) the foundation deposit of Narām-Sîn, son of Sargon, which no king among my predecessors had found in three thousand and two hundred years.[18] In the month Tashrītu, in a propitious month, on an auspicious day, which Shamash and Adad revealed to me by means of divination, upon (beads of) silver (and) gold, choice gems, logs of resinous woods, aromatic herbs (and cuts of) cedar (wood), in joy and gladness, on the foundation deposit of Narām-Sîn, son of Sargon, not a finger's breadth too wide or too narrow, I laid its brickwork. Five thousand massive (beams of) cedar wood I set up for its roofing. Lofty doors of cedar wood, thresholds and pivots I affixed at its gates. Ebabbar, together with E-kun-ankuga its ziggurat, I built anew and completed its work. I led Shamash, my lord, in procession and, in joy and gladness, I caused him to dwell in the midst of his favorite dwelling.

Burying the foundation deposit (iii.8-10)

The inscription in the name of Narām-Sîn,[19] son of Sargon, I found and did not alter. I anointed (it) with oil, made offerings, placed (it) with my own inscription and returned it to its (original) place.

[11] That is to say, for the roofing.

[12] On the identification of this mythological being as a "long-haired hero" see Green *RlA* 8:248-249; also Black and Green 1992:115.

[13] The meaning of the word *ešmarû* is uncertain. It refers either to a type of silver or to a silver alloy. See *CAD* E, s.v.

[14] It is uncertain whether the phrases "fiercely attacking my foes" and "destroyers of my enemies" are just epithets or describe the posture in which these mythological beings were depicted. They could also be names given to the statues.

[15] A similar statement concerning Sîn of Harran occurs in the Neo-Assyrian letter SAA 10:13. It is uncertain whether the daily rising and setting of the moon is meant. The expression *ina nipḫi u rībi* could refer in this case to the beginning and end of the month, which were of particular ominous significance in Mesopotamia.

[16] Lit. "the offspring of his luminous womb."

[17] Nabonidus is stressing the fact that failure to find the original foundation deposit before laying the new foundations of the temple led to its premature fall into disrepair.

[18] Narām-Sîn reigned, according to the commonly accepted chronology, between ca. 2254 and 2218 BCE. The figure given by Nabonidus is therefore erroneous by some fifteen hundred years. He was the grandson (not son) of Sargon of Akkad. Cf. above, *COS* 2.90-91.

[19] In ii.57 the name Nāram-Sîn: "the one beloved by Sîn," is written ^{I}*na-ra-am-*^{d}30; in ii.64: ^{I}*na-ra-am-*^{d}EN.ZU; and here, in ii.8: ^{I}*na-ra-am-*DINGIR. The appellation DINGIR, Akk. *ilu* "god" for the moon-god is occasionally attested in Mesopotamian religious texts, but it became especially popular with Nabonidus, who made it a component of his theological reform.

Prayer to Shamash (iii.11-21)
O Shamash, great lord of heaven and the netherworld, light of the gods your fathers, offspring of Sîn and Ningal, when you enter Ebabbar your beloved temple, when you take up residence in your eternal dais, look joyfully upon me, Nabonidus, king of Babylon, the prince your caretaker, the one who pleases you (and) built your august chapel, (and) upon my good deeds, and every day at sunrise and sunset, in the heavens and on the earth, make my omens favorable, accept my supplications and receive my prayers. (With) the scepter and the legitimate staff which you placed in my hands may I rule forever.

Rebuilding of Eulmash in Sippar-Anunītu (iii.22-38a)
For Anunītu — the lady of warfare, who carries the bow and the quiver, who fulfills the command of Enlil her father, who annihilates the enemy, who destroys the evil one, who precedes the gods, who, at sunrise and sunset, causes my (ominous) signs to be favorable — I excavated, surveyed and inspected the old foundations of Eulmash, her temple which is in Sippar-Anunītu, which for eight hundred years, since the time of Shagarakti-Shuriash,[20] king of Babylon, son of Kudur-Enlil, no king had rebuilt, and on the foundation deposit of Shagarakti-Shuriash, son of Kudur-Enlil, I cleared its foundations and laid its brickwork. I built that temple anew and completed its work. Anunītu, the lady of warfare, who fulfills the command of Enlil her father, who annihilates the enemy, who destroys the evil one, who precedes the gods, I caused her to establish her residence. The regular offerings and the (other) offerings I increased over what they were and I established for her.

Prayer to Anunītu (iii.38b-42)
As for you, O Anunītu, great lady, when you joyfully enter that temple, look joyfully upon my good deeds and every month, at sunrise and sunset, petition Sîn, the father your begetter, for favors on my behalf.

Burying the foundation deposit and address to future generations (iii.43-51)
Whoever you are whom Sîn and Shamash will call to kingship and in whose reign that temple will fall into disrepair and who will build it anew, may he[21] find the inscription written in my name and not alter (it). May he anoint (it) with oil, perform a sacrifice, place it with the inscription written in his own name and return it to its (original) place. May Shamash and Anunītu hear his supplication, receive his utterance, march at his side, annihilate his enemy (and) daily speak good recommendations on his behalf to Sîn, the father their creator.

[20] Shagarakti-Shuriash, son of Kudur-Enlil, belonged to the Kassite dynasty. He reigned between ca. 1245 and 1233 BCE. The time distance given by Nabonidus is erroneous by one century.

[21] The change of person is here from second to third, while in the inscription of Nabopolassar translated above (*COS* 2.121, n. 18) the change was from third to second.

REFERENCES

Text BM exemplar: V R, plate 64 (master copy); Berlin Museum exemplar: VS 1, no. 53 (copy); Langdon 1912:218-229; Berger 1973:371-375. Translations: Seux 1976:518; Beaulieu 1989:34, 107-108, 210-211, 214; Foster 1993 2:755.

NABONIDUS' REBUILDING OF E-LUGAL-GALGA-SISA, THE ZIGGURAT OF UR (2.123B)

Paul-Alain Beaulieu

This inscription, recorded on several clay cylinders found at Ur in the remains of the ziggurat, is probably the last building inscription of Nabonidus. It attests to the intensity of the king's personal devotion to the moon god Sîn, and to his attempt to impose him as supreme deity of the Neo-Babylonian empire. Sîn is praised as "king/lord of the gods of heaven and the netherworld," a position normally reserved for Marduk, and as "'gods' of the gods," an innovative title which reveals the king's fervor and theological boldness. Sîn is also consistently referred to as 'gods,' a plural formation which recalls the designation *elohîm* for the god of Israel. The inscription refers to the original builders of the ziggurat, Ur-Nammu and his son Shulgi, the first two rulers of the third dynasty of Ur (reigned ca. 2112-2095 and ca. 2094-2047 BCE; cf. *COS* 2.138-139). Nabonidus indirectly quotes their foundation deposits which he allegedly discovered during the excavation of the ziggurat. Although the inscriptions and year names of Ur-Nammu refer to his building works in Ur, no surviving inscription of his or of his son Shulgi specifically refers to the building of E-lugal-galga-sisa. The prayer to Sîn which concludes the inscription mentions Belshazzar (Bēl-šar-uṣur), Nabonidus' son and heir to the throne, who appears in many business and administrative transactions from his reign. All known copies of this inscription are written in Neo-Babylonian script.

Royal titulary (i.1-4)
Nabonidus, king of Babylon, caretaker of Esagil and Ezida, worshiper of the great gods, I,

Rebuilding of the ziggurat (i.5-ii.2)
E-lugal-galga-sisa, the ziggurat of Egishnugal,[1] which is in Ur, which Ur-Nammu, one of the kings who preceded me, had built but not completed (and) whose work his son Shulgi had completed, (for) in the inscriptions of Ur-Nammu and Shulgi his son I read that Ur-Nammu had built that ziggurat but not completed it (and that) Shulgi his son had completed its work, now that ziggurat had become old and on the ancient foundations which Ur-Nammu and Shulgi his son had built, that ziggurat, as in former times, with bitumen and baked bricks I repaired its damaged parts and for Sîn, the lord of the gods of heaven and the netherworld, the king of the gods, the 'gods' of the gods, who dwells in the great heavens, the lord of Egishnugal, which is in Ur, my lord, I built anew.

Prayer to Sîn (ii.3-31)
O Sîn, my lord 'gods',[2] king of the gods of heaven and the netherworld, 'gods' of the gods, who dwells in the great heavens, when you joyfully enter that temple, may good recommendations for Esagil, Ezida, Egishnugal, the temples of your great godhead,[3] be set on your lips, and instill reverence for your great godhead (in) the hearts of its[4] people so that they do not sin against your great godhead. May their foundations be as firm as heaven. As for me, Nabonidus, king of Babylon, save me from sinning against your great godhead and grant me as a present a life of long days, and as for Belshazzar,[5] [a] the eldest son my offspring, instill reverence for your great godhead (in) his heart and may he not commit any cultic mistake, may he be sated with a life of plenitude.

[a] Dan 5

[1] The temple complex of the moon god in Ur.
[2] ii.3 reads as follows: [d]30 *be-lí* DINGIR.MEŠ. Although this has so far always been translated as "O Sîn, lord of the gods," the text clearly says "O Sîn, my lord 'gods'." The compound "lord of the gods" should be written *be-el* DINGIR.MEŠ or EN DINGIR.MEŠ, as is the case earlier in the inscription. The plural designation DINGIR.MEŠ, Akk. *ilū*, *ilī* or *ilāni*, is occasionally attested for the moon god Sîn in Mesopotamian texts. Nabonidus favored it for its obvious monotheizing connotations. It should be noted that in the duplicate discovered at Ur during the 1960-61 season the same line reads [d]30 EN DINGIR.MEŠ (ii.5), providing one more case of Nabonidus deliberately creating ambiguities to illustrate a theological point, since the logogram EN can be read *bēlī* "my lord" as well as *bēl* "lord of (the gods)" in the construct state. The ambiguity is also increased by the fact that in the somewhat artificial idiom of Neo-Babylonian building inscriptions the spelling *be-lí* could also be understood as a frozen form borrowed from OB building inscriptions, but without its original grammatical function.
[3] By attributing Esagil and Ezida, the temples of Marduk and Nabû, to the god Sîn, Nabonidus is proposing a syncretism between the three deities and an outright usurpation of Marduk's prerogatives by the moon god.
[4] UN.MEŠ-*šú*, where the pronoun refers either to the temple(s) mentioned before, or to Nabonidus, or to the "godhead" of Sîn (with *šú* for *šá*). Another possibility is to understand ŠÚ as a logogram for *kiššatu*, in which case UN.MEŠ ŠÚ would mean "the people of the universe."
[5] Belshazzar appears in Dan 5 as the son of Nebuchadnezzar, though he was in reality the son of Nabonidus.

REFERENCES

Text: I R, plate 68, no.1 (master copy); Langdon 1912:250-253; As-Siwani 1964; Berger 1973:355-359; Translations: Seux 1976:521; Beaulieu 1989:35-37, 61-62; Foster 1993 2:756.

6. ACHAEMENID INSCRIPTIONS

CYRUS

CYRUS CYLINDER (2.124)

Mordechai Cogan

The Cyrus cylinder (BM 90920 + BIN II, n. 32), discovered at Babylon in 1879, has been of continuing interest for the light it sheds on Persian imperial policy towards subject peoples as reflected in its description of the restoration of the cult of Marduk in Babylon. The biblical report of the permission granted by Cyrus to rebuild the temple of YHWH in Jerusalem (Ezra 1:1-6; 6:1-5; 2 Chr 36:22-23) is considered another example of this practice (cf. Kuhrt 1983). In the cuneiform text, Cyrus reviews the history of his rise to kingship in Babylon at the summons of Marduk, who, in response to evil deeds of Nabonidus, acted to save his city. Cyrus renewed the fortunes of the enslaved Babylonians and restored the neglected cult centers of the land. The dedicatory nature of the inscription, which follows traditional Mesopotamian patterns of composition, was only recently clarified with the joining of a fragment to the end of the text which describes the restoration of the fortifications of Babylon (Berger 1975). The Cyrus cylinder is evidence for the continuity of the Babylonian scribal tradition under the Persians, whose rule was welcomed and supported by the native elite.

(lines 3-8) An incompetent person was installed to exercise lordship over his country. [...] he imposed upon them.[1] An imitation of Esagila[2] he ma[de ?], for Ur and the rest of the sacred centers, improper rituals [ ] daily he recited. Irreverently, he put an end to the regular offerings; he [ ], he established in the sacred centers. By his own plan, he did away with[3] the worship of Marduk, the king of the gods; he continually did evil against his (Marduk's) city. Daily, [without interruption ...], he [imposed] the corvée upon its inhabitants unrelentingly, ruining them all.

(lines 9-19) Upon (hearing) their cries, the lord of the gods became furiously angry [and he left] their borders; and the gods who lived among them forsook their dwellings, angry that he had brought (them) into Babylon. Marduk [ ] turned (?) towards all the habitations that were abandoned and all the people of Sumer and Akkad who had become corpses; [he was recon]ciled and had mercy (upon them). He surveyed and looked throughout all the lands, searching for a righteous king whom he would support. He called out his name:[a] Cyrus, king of Anshan;[4] he pronounced his name to be king over all (the world). He (Marduk) made the land of Gutium and all the Umman-manda[5] bow in submission at his feet. And he (Cyrus) shepherded with justice and righteousness all the black-headed people, over whom he (Marduk) had given him victory. Marduk, the great lord, guardian (?) of his people, looked with gladness upon his good deeds and upright heart. He ordered him to march to his city Babylon. He set him on the road to Babylon and like a companion and friend, he went at his side. His vast army, whose number, like the water of the river, cannot be known, marched at his side fully armed. He made him enter his city Babylon without fighting or battle;[6] he saved Babylon from hardship. He delivered Nabonidus, the king who did not revere him, into his hands. All the people of Babylon, all the land of Sumer and Akkad, princes and governors, bowed to him and kissed his feet. They rejoiced at his kingship and their faces shone. Ruler by whose aid the dead were revived and who had all been redeemed from hardship and difficulty,[7] they greeted him with gladness and praised his name.

a Isa 44:28; 45:1-4

(lines 20-22a) I am Cyrus, king of the world, great king, mighty king, king of Babylon, king of Sumer and Akkad, king of the four quarters, son of Cambyses, great king, king of Anshan, grandson of Cyrus, great king, king of Anshan, descendant of Teispes, great king, king of Anshan, (of an) eternal line of kingship, whose rule Bel (i.e., Marduk) and Nabu love, whose kingship they desire for their hearts' pleasure.

(lines 22b-28) When I entered Babylon in a peaceful manner, I took up my lordly reign in the royal palace amidst rejoicing and happiness. Marduk, the great lord, caused the magnanimous people of Babylon [to ...] me, (and) I daily attended to his worship. My vast army moved about Babylon in peace; I did not permit anyone to frighten (the people of) [Sumer] and Akkad. I sought the welfare of the city of Babylon and all its sacred centers. As for the citizens of Babylon, upon whom he imposed corvée which was not the god's will and not befitting them, I relieved their weariness and freed them from their service (?). Marduk, the great lord, rejoiced over my [good] deeds. He sent gracious blessings upon me, Cyrus, the king who worships him, and upon Cambyses, the son who is [my] offspring, [and upo]n all my army, and in peace, before him,[8] we move [about].

(lines 28-36) By his exalted [word],[8] all the kings who sit upon thrones throughout the world, from the Upper Sea to the Lower Sea,[9] who live in the dis[tricts far-off], the kings of the West,[10] who dwell in tents, all of them brought their heavy tribute before me and in Babylon they kissed my feet. From [Ninev]eh (?), Ashur and Susa, Agade, Eshnunna, Zamban, Meturnu, Der, as far as the region of Gutium, I returned the (images of) the gods to the sacred centers [on the other side of] the Tigris whose sanctuaries had been abandoned for a long time, and I let them dwell in eternal abodes. I gathered all their inhabitants and returned (to them) their dwellings. In addition, at the command of Marduk, the great lord, I settled in their habitations, in pleasing abodes, the gods of Sumer and Akkad, whom Nabonidus, to the anger of the lord of the gods, had brought into Babylon. May all the gods whom I settled in their sacred centers ask

[1] The subject is Nabonidus, the last king of Babylon (555-539 BCE).

[2] The cultic misdeeds of Nabonidus, his neglect of the temple of Marduk in Babylon in favor of the temple of Sîn in Harran, are the subject of a satirical composition by the king's opponents (*ANET* 312-315).

[3] Tentative translation; with Borger: *[ig]mur karšussu.*

[4] Site in southern Iran, mentioned in titulary of Elamite kings in 2nd millennium BCE, and used by Cyrus to point to his legitimate dynastic line.

[5] The reference is to the Medes, using terms from Sum. times for barbarian highlanders who often raided the riverine valleys of Mesopotamia.

[6] The Babylonian Chronicle No. 7 (*COS* 1.137) confirms the peaceful entry into Babylon.

[7] Berger (1970; 1973:196f., 213) understands this as a reference to the (statues of) deities saved from death and destruction.

[8-8] Or: "we lavishly prais[ed his] exalted [divinity]."

[9] I.e., from the Mediterranean Sea to the Persian Gulf.

[10] Lit. "Amurru."

daily of Bel and Nabu that my days be long and may they intercede for my welfare. May they say to Marduk, my lord: "As for Cyrus, the king who reveres you, and Cambyses, his son, [ ] a reign." I settled all the lands in peaceful abodes.

(lines 37-44) [ ] I increased the offerings [to x] geese, two ducks and ten turtledoves above the former (offerings) of geese, du[cks, and turtledoves [ ]. I sought to strengthen the [construction(?)] of Dur-Imgur-Enlil, the great wall of Babylo[n]. [ ] The bricks at the bank of the ditch, which a former king had built, [but had not comple]ted its construction [ ] , on the outside, which no former king had made, a levy of workmen of Babylonians, [with bitumen] and bricks, I built anew. [ ] overlaid in copper. The thresholds and the pivo[ts] their [doors]. [An inscription with] the name of Ashurbanipal, a king who had proceeded me [I sa]w.[11] [(two lines missing) ... for e]ternity.

[11] An inscription bearing the name of the Assyrian king was discovered during the reconstruction work on the wall. For a text of Ashurbanipal commemorating his work on Imgur-Enlil, see VAB 7, 234-239.

REFERENCES

Text: Berger 1975; Kuhrt 1983. Translations: *ANET*, 315-316; *DOTT*, 92-94; Borger in Galling, *TGI*^{2}, 82-84.

B. VOTIVE SEAL INSCRIPTIONS

VOTIVE SEAL INSCRIPTIONS (2.125)

William W. Hallo

Votive objects were designed to carry inscriptions praying for the long life of the donor (who could be the king) and/or designated beneficiaries, normally members of his family (or the king). They could be pure works of art such as statues, steles, or beads, or they could be artistic replicas of objects used in the daily life of the donor, such as bowls or axes, ships for a merchant or weapons for a soldier. Seals can be recognized as votives when they were inscribed in a positive sense so that their text was to be read off from the seal itself, not from its impression on a clay tablet or vessel. For a particularly significant example, see Lee 1993.

1. Rimut-ilani (2.125A)

This seal was found in controlled excavations at Beer-Sheba in the Negev (Israel). There is no indication as to how it got there, but the seal owner's father is either identical with or at least a namesake of Hadad-idri, king of Damascus in the ninth century,[1] and the script of the inscription would be compatible with that time. Note, however, that the direction of the script (from top to bottom, not from left to right), might suggest either an earlier date or deliberate archaizing.[2]

> To the divine Apil-Adad,[3] the great lord, his lord, Rimut-ilani, son of (H)adad-idri, made and donated (this cylinder seal).

2. Nabu-apla-iddina (2.125B)

This four-sided bead is described as a seal in its inscription. It provides a parallel of sorts to the seal from Beer-sheba, since it mentions the same unusual divine name. The donor is a namesake of a king of Babylon who ruled in the first half of the ninth century, but had a different patronymic.

> A seal of lapis lazuli — Nabu-apla-iddina, son of Shamash-eresh, for the well-being of his life, the length of his days (and) the furthering of his cause, to the divine Gabra the spouse of the divine Apil-Adad his lord he donated.

3. Marduk-zakir-shumi (2.125C)

At 19 cm high, this is one of the largest seals known, a worthy votive offfering from a king of Babylon (second half of the ninth century BCE) to the city's principal deity.

> For the divine Marduk, the great lord, heroic, lofty, exalted, lord of all, lord of lords, high judge, rendering decisions for the inhabited world, lord of foreign lands, lord of Babylon, dwelling in the temple Esagil, his lord — Marduk-zakir-shumi, king of the world, the prince who worships him — for the well-being of his life, the safety of his offspring, the length of his days, the stability of his reign, the overthrowing of his enemies, and the ever going peacefully before him — (this) seal of shining lapis lazuli which is artfully set in ruddy gold as the ornament of his (Marduk's) neck he caused it to be made and donated it.

---

[1] See *COS* 2.40.

[2] For dating the change, see Hallo 1982:114-115.

[3] For this deity, see above, *COS* 2.115B, note 5 (Apla-Adad).

REFERENCES

Texts: Rainey 1973; Frame 1995:104f. Studies: Watanabe 1994.

C. WEIGHT INSCRIPTIONS

WEIGHT INSCRIPTIONS (2.126)

Marvin A. Powell

Most weights from ancient Mesopotamia bear no mark at all, partly because the vast majority are small with little room for inscription; however, many weights that could have been marked for unit of mass have no markings either. Weights with masses of one-half mina (ca. 250 grams) and higher are usually marked for mass, and more elaborate inscriptions are largely limited to these larger weights. Dating is often problematic, because a large proportion of weights in western collections derive from the antiquities market or from uncertain archaeological context, and this problem is complicated by the fact that some weights were reused, carried off as booty, and/or preserved as heirlooms. The brevity of most weight inscriptions and the tendency to use logographic-ideographic script occasionally makes identification of language a matter of an educated guess.

This selection is organized in (approximate) chronological order, oldest first. Published mass and "implied mina norms" are given to assist the reader in interpretation, but it must be borne in mind that these are approximations whose precision depends upon the accuracy of the modern weighing, the state of conservation of the object, and the accuracy of the ancient standard. There are large numbers of still unpublished and unstudied weights in Iraq and in Turkey and quite a few in Syria.

126A. Elongated barrel, from Tell Sweyhat, Syria; probably Naram-Sin or later.

1 mina.[1]

126B. Duck, excavated at Susa, probably Akkad period.

(1) mina.[2]

126C. Ellipsoid, excavated at Susa, probably Akkad period.

1 little mina.[3]

126D. Duck, provenance unknown, Old Akkadian.

10 minas,[4] in cloth/wool(?),[5] true, of *Uṣi-ina-pušqim*.[6]

126E. Fragment, probably from a duck weight, of unknown provenance, with Old Babylonian script similar to the Laws of Hammurabi.[7]

Stone(weight), 1 talent, palace of Sin-iribam.[8]

---

[1] 472.2+ grams; dated by palaeography and associated pottery paralleling Mallowan's "Late Sargonid" from Brak and Jidle Level 5; Holland 1975:75-76. This weight seems to be normed on a standard distinct from the Babylonian and is perhaps related to the later "mina of Carchemish"; see Powell 1990:516.

[2] 538 grams; Powell 1971:255.

[3] 2.90 grams; Powell 1971:271. A "little mina" is one-third of a shekel. The shekel contained three "little minas" or 180 barleycorns. The number on this weight is written with a horizontal wedge resembling those which normally precede talents but not minas and shekels. Thus, the "1" may symbolize "60 (barleycorns)." The implied mina norm is 522 grams, but the margin of error is much higher for small weights; the intended norm could easily lie anywhere within 500 to 540 grams.

[4] 5371+ grams; Powell 1971:205, 251; Borger *HKL* 1:506 (correct reading of PN and identification as Old Akkadian). The stone has suffered slight damage, implying a mina norm a bit above 537 grams.

[5] Unclear; probable reading: ŠÀ TÚG.

[6] Unidentified person.

[7] Clay 1915:28, no. 30.

[8] Tenth king of Larsa, 1842-1841 BCE.

126F. Elongated barrel, provenance unknown, probably late Old Babylonian.

Stone(weight), 2/3 shekel,[9] true, of Šamaš.[10]

126G. Elongated barrel, provenance unknown (brought to the French excavations at Susa, where it was hastily copied and weighed), late Kassite or early Neo-Babylonian.

3 minas,[11] true, of Kilamdi-Marduk, temple-head of Kiš.[12]

126H. Duck, excavated at Babylon, probably early first millennium.

1 talent,[13] true, of Mušallim-Marduk,[14] "son" of the temple-head of Kiš,[15] whoever takes it away, let Šamaš take him away![16]

126I. Duck, excavated at Susa, late Kassite or early Neo-Babylonian.

2 1/2 minas,[17] true, of Naṣiri, son of Kidin-Gula, descendant of Arad-Ea.

126J. Duck, found at Nippur, Second Dynasty of Isin.

Stone(weight), 10 minas,[18] Napsamenni,[19] head seer,[20] chief priest[21] of Enlil, servant of Marduk-šapik-zeri,[22] king of Babylon.

126K. Duck, found by A. H. Layard at Nimrud (perhaps carried there as booty), Second Dynasty of Isin.

30 minas,[23] true, Nabu-šumu-libur,[24] king of the world.[25]

---

[9] Powell 1971:207, 268. Mass published as 5.3 grams; reweighed by R. B. Y. Scott: 5.344 grams; reweighed by M. A. Powell: 5.3545 grams. It has lost a small chip; the implied mina norm is in the 500 gram range.

[10] A one-third shekel weight of Shamash in Brussels was published by Speleers 1925:22 no. 215 (text, description, mass, which is given as "3" grams). AbB 13 (1994) no. 112 gives a good idea of how such temple standards functioned in the business world beyond the temple: one party has sent a second party silver on behalf of a third party and instructs the second party to pay the third party back using the "stone(weight) of Shamash."

[11] 1425 grams, implied mina: 475 grams; Powell 1971:207, 253.

[12] Also represented by an ellipsoid in the British Museum weighing 79.35 grams published by Thureau-Dangin 1927:71 with the inscription "[one-sixth?] mina, true, Kilamdi-Marduk(!), the temple-head of Kish"; cf. Powell 1971:207, 261. The British Museum stone is pierced, which is not normal for ellipsoids and may reflect subsequent use as an amulet.

[13] 29680 grams plus a small percentage due to surface loss; the implied mina is about 495 grams. Powell 1971:206, 249.

[14] This Mušallim-Marduk seems otherwise unattested. He can hardly have been the Amukanu chief who submitted to Shalmaneser III (discussed by Brinkman 1968:198); see Powell 1993-97.

[15] "Son" means "descendant"; for a parallel to the expression, see Brinkman 1968:230 n. 1454.

[16] *šá* TÙM (= *itabbalu*) [d]UTU *lit-bal-šu'*; for parallels, see Hunger 1968:177-178 + nos. 240-241, 256 (Shamash).

[17] 4915.3+ grams; Powell 1971:206, 251. The original mass was close to 5000 grams, implying a mina norm around 2000 grams. This belongs to a small group of weights whose masses represent "quadruple" norms. The metrological motives for these norms remain unclear; however, these "2 1/2 minas" correspond to 10 normal Babylonian minas and to 60 Persian/Elamite *karša*. Thus, one of these "quadruple minas" would contain 24 *karša*, suggesting an underlying duodecimal system that has been adjusted to mesh with Babylonian norms. See below (number 13) for a possible example of Babylonian norms adjusted to mesh with western standards.

[18] Mass not published; Biggs 1969:16 no. 56; Brinkman 1968:335.

[19] Also attested according to Biggs 1969:16 on a Nippur text dated to the 2nd year of the preceding king, Marduk-nadin-aḫḫi, where he is called "seer, chief priest."

[20] UGULA AZU = *akil barî.*

[21] NU-ÈŠ = *nešakku.*

[22] Seventh king of the Second Dynasty of Isin, 1081-1069 BCE (Brinkman).

[23] 14589.551+ grams; Powell 1971:206, 250. The stone has lost around 200 grams, which would make the mina standard around 493 grams.

[24] Eleventh and last king, 1033-1026 BCE (Brinkman), of the Second Dynasty of Isin.

[25] LUGAL *šár* = *šar kiššati*; what precisely is to be understood under this term in each era and context is far from clear, as is illustrated by use of this title for a Babylonian king who ruled but eight years and whose reign marked the end of a dynasty during what appears to have been an era of increasing chaos.

126L. Elongated barrel, provenance unknown, perhaps early 8th century.

20 shekels,[26] true, palace of Nabu-šumu-lišir,[27] descendant of Dakkuru, the Isinite(?), overseer of the temple(?) of Marduk.[28]

126M. Duck, found east of the ziqqurrat at Assur, Tiglath-Pileser III (745-727 BCE).

3 (minas),[29] palace of Tukulti-apil-ešarra, king of the world, king of the land of [Aššur].

126N. Bronze lion, from Northwest palace at Nimrud, Shalmaneser V (727-722 BCE).

Palace of Šulman-ašarid, king of Aššur, 5 minas of the king.[30]

126O. Truncated pyramid with rounded top, provenance uncertain, Nebuchadrezzar II (605-562 BCE).

[2] minas[31] true, property of Marduk king of gods, copy of a weight which Nabu-kudurri-uṣur king of Babylon, son of Nabu-apla-uṣur king of Babylon, made true[32] as a copy of a weight of Šulgi, a former king.

---

[26] Written 1/3 (i.e., of a mina) GÍN; 164.3 grams. Powell 1971:206, 259; Brinkman 1968:215 and n. 1338 (collation on squeeze), 363-364.

[27] Nabu-šumu-lišir cannot be dated precisely.

[28] Translation of the difficult last line, LÚ.PA.TE.PA.SI(??) ᵈAMAR.UTU," is based on a provisional reading LÚ.PA.ŠE! UGULA É ᵈAMAR.UTU. For LÚ.PA.ŠE, see Borger 1970:5-8.

[29] 2775+ grams[1]; Nassouhi 1927:14-15 no. VI (text), 17 (photo). Marked with three strokes. This duck weight on the "double standard" originally weighed around 3 kilograms. For discussion of the "double standard," see Powell 1990:515-516. Powell 1992:906 has suggested that the motivation for this "double mina" was to approximate 100 western shekels. Thirty such "double minas" would be 3000 western shekels and would approximate both the Babylonian and western talent. This still seems a likely solution.

[30] Also inscribed in Aramaic: "five minas of the land, five minas of the king" plus 5 strokes. Published mass: 5042.805+ grams; Powell 1971:251; Mallowan 1966:109. This is again the "double" standard, for which see above (number 13, Tiglath-Pileser III).

[31] 978.309 grams; Powell 1971:254.

[32] *ú-kin-ni*. This use of *kânu* can hardly mean "to place" (so *CAD* K 163a) but must rather belong under the broad category of "establishing as true," already attested in Ur III inscriptions (see, e.g., *COS* 2.149, 5, Shulgi below).

REFERENCES

Text: 126A: Holland 1975. 126B: MDP 12:6. 126C: MDP 12:11. 126D: Stephens 1937:#63. 126E: Frayne 1990:188. 126F: BIN 2:20. 126G: Pézard *RA* 9 (1912) 107-109; *ZDMG* 70 (1916) 52. 126H: *MDOG* 38 (1908) 16. 126I: MDP 12:8. 126J: Biggs 1969:16 and 42 #56. 126K: Brinkman 1968:147, n. 887. 126L: Brinkman 1968:215, n. 1338. 126M: Tadmor 1994:214. 126N: Mallowan 1966:109 and nn. 9-10. 126O: MDP 12:29.

D. “FUNCTIONAL” INSCRIPTIONS

1. TREATIES

ABBAEL'S GIFT OF ALALAKH (*AT* 1) (2.127)

Richard S. Hess

This Old Babylonian text from Alalakh Level VII records the background behind the gift of the city of Alalakh as a reward for military efforts. Gifts of lands and towns are also reported in Joshua 13 where, as in *AT* 1, they serve as a recollection of past events. See also Joshua 20 and 21 and the towns of asylum and of the Levites, both of which are presented as gifts of towns from the tribes to these groups. A similar gift of towns appears in *AT* 456. Both in the Bible and at Alalakh these gifts either are closely attached to or actually form part of treaty documents or divine covenants (see Josh 8:30-35; 24:1-28).

Historical Background (lines 1-10)[1] [a]
When his brothers rebelled against Abbael their lord, then Abbael, aided by Hebat, Addu and the spear [of Ishtar] went to Irride.[2] [b] He [conquered?] Irride and captured his [ene]my.

At that time Abbael, according to his gracious heart, gave Alalakh in exchange for Irride, which his father gave.[3] [c]

At the same time, Yarimlim,[4] so[n of Hammu]rapi and servant of Abbael brought up [...] Ishtar.

Stipulations (lines 11-13a)
...Ab]bael (which) ... Yarimlim ... he shall give him city for city.

Curses (lines 13b-20)
whoever changes the word[5] [d] that Abbael has made for Yarimlim and does evil to his descendants,
may Addu dash him in pieces with the weapon in his hand,
may Hebat Ishtar break his spear,
may Ishtar give him up to the hand of his conquerors,[6] [e]
may Ishtar impress femaleness into his maleness.

a Gen 4; Judg 9; 2 Sam 13-14; 1 Kgs 1-2
b 1 Sam 21:1-9
c 1 Kgs 9:11-13, 16; 2 Chr 8:2
d Deut 5:32; 17:20; 28:19; Josh 1:7; 23:6; 2 Chr 34:2; Prov 4:27; Isa 30:21
e Lev 26:36-39

[1] The rebellion of brothers is a common theme (e.g., Gen 4) and one that is known in the Bible among royalty (Judg 9; 2 Sam 13-14; 1 Kgs 1-2).

[2] Cf. the special dedication of the spear of Goliath in a sanctuary, 1 Sam 21:1-9.

[3] For gifts and payments of towns, see 1 Kgs 9:11-13, 16; 2 Chr 8:2.

[4] Na᾿aman (1980b) inserts ALAM-*šu a-na* É here and translates that Yarimlim "brought up [his statue to the temple] of Ishtar." This translation is based upon a reconstruction.

[5] The expression "changes the word" (*a-wa-at ... ú-na-ak-ka-ru*) recalls similar expressions of betrayal to covenants often expressed as warnings to turn neither to the right nor to the left, e.g. Deut 5:32; 17:20; 28:19; Josh 1:7; 23:6; 2 Chr 34:2; Prov 4:27; Isa 30:21.

[6] That an enemy is given control over the treaty breaker forms part of biblical curses, e.g., Lev 26:36-39.

REFERENCES

Text and Translation: *AT* 25 and pl. i. Studies: Na᾿aman 1980b.

THE AGREEMENT BETWEEN IR-ADDU AND NIQMEPA (*AT* 2) (2.128)

Richard S. Hess

This is a treaty text from the Middle Babylonian period of Alalakh (Level IV). The stipulations are largely concerned with citizens of Niqmepa's lands who, for various reasons, find themselves in the land of Ir-Addu. The clauses provide for extradition of these people back to the lands of Niqmepa. Fugitives were a common cause for concern as witnessed in the second millennium law codes: Ur-Nammu §17; Lipit-Ishtar 12-13; Eshnunna 50; Hammurabi 16-20 (*COS* 2.153; 2.154; 2.130; 2.131, respectively). See Roth 1995/1997.

I. *Introduction* (lines 1-4)

1 The seal of Ir-Addu the king of Tunip

2 The text of the divine oath of Niqmepa king of Mukiš

3 and of Ir-Addu king of Tunip. In this manner Niqmepa and Ir-Addu

4 [...] have now made an agreement[1] between them:

II. *Stipulations* (lines 5-76)

5 [If ...] whether merchants or Sutean troops[2]

6 [...] you ... all your enemies

7 [...] you shall not go to war. If it is barley, emmer, or oils,

8 [...]

9 [...] [... you] shall give.

---

10 [If ... th]ere is

11 [... you] protest

12 [... of] copper

13 [...] you shall search for them

14 [... if] they should say

15 [... fr]om Mukiš, we [are citizens]

16 you shall kill those troops.

---

17 If anyone from my country approaches your land to live there,

18 If you hear of it, you must report it.

19 If he lives in your country, you must seize him and give him up.

---

20 If there are captives from my country whom they sell in your country

21 you must seize them along with the one who sold them, and give them to me.

---

22 If a fugitive slave, whether male or female, flees from my country to yours,

23 you must seize him and return him. If anyone else seizes him

24 and gives him to you, you [shall keep him] in your prison.

25 When his owner arrives, you shall hand him over.

26 If the slave is not there, you shall provide an escort so that in the city where he is

27 the owner can seize the fugitive. (In the city) where the fugitive is not residing, the mayor[3] [a] and five of his witnesses

28 shall declare the following oath: "If my slave stays with you, you must notify me (= the owner)."

29 If they do not agree to the oath, then you must return his slave to him.

30 If they do swear and afterwards they produce his slave,

[a] Deut 21:1-9

31 then they are thieves. Their hands shall be cut off.

32 6,000 copper shekels will be paid to the palace for the slave.

---

33 If a man, woman, ox, donkey, or horse in anyone's house [is found and the owner]

34 identifies it, but he (= the person in whose house it is found) says, "I got it by purchase,"

35 if he produces the merchant, then he is clear. But if he does

36 not produce the merchant who can identify that he took it...

37 he will declare with an oath. If...

38 But if he does not agree to the oath, then...

---

39 If you hold a man in custody, and you... with another man

40 he will go (free?). If (they break?) his fetters,

41 they shave off his slave mark...

42 and someone captures him, then he is a thief. If he declares...

43 then he will state with an oath, "If..."

44 If he does not agree to an oath, then he is a thief and (shall be treated) like a thief.

45 If the criminal, whether man, woman or child, goes from his house (and)

46 he (= the owner) seizes him, he is a thief and so his owner shall swear it:

47 "Surely I did not seize him on a journey of his own doing."

---

48 If a thief from your land steals from my land...

49 he breaks into a house or town and they seize him, (they shall put him) into a prison.

50 Whenever his owner comes, the owner of the house will take the following oath:

51 "You took it from the burgled house."

52 He shall produce his witnesses. They shall set his guilt on his head

53 and destroy(?) him. Then he will be a slave.

54 If they do not swear against him (as witnesses), then he shall go free.

---

55 [If people of my land] enter your land to preserve themselves from starvation,

56 you must protect them and you must feed them like (citizens of) your land.

57 Whenever they want to come to my land,

58 you must gather and return them t[o my land.]

59 You shall not detain a single family in your land.

---

60 If a man of my land [enters] your land to

---

[1] The expression, "an agreement between them," translates, *[i-n]a bi-ri-šu-nu*. Is this related to the Heb. "covenant" (*bᵉrîth*)?

[2] Cf. Heltzer 1981:80.

[3] The use of the local officials of the town to swear judicial oaths clearing the town of guilt also occurs for the laws of the unknown murderer

preserve himself from starvation,
61 and he says, "Surely there is..."
62 he is a criminal [...]
63 They shall bring him [...]
64 you [...]
65-67 [ ]
68 then the cri[minal

69 If there is a city, or if ... [ ]
70 They live with the guards of my city ... [ ]
71 a city ... [ ] you will seize them
72 If their city ... [ ] you will seize them.

73 As for the king of the Hurrian lord's army, if there is en[mity with the army of the Hurrian, my lord], then I
74 will not break the oath of my lord, the king of the Hurrian army,
75 (unless) he shall indeed release (me from) the words from the oath.

b Deut28:49-68

76 Seal of Niqmepa, the king of Alalakh.

III. *Curses* (lines 77-79)
(left side)
77 Whoever transgresses these matters, Addu the l[ord of divin]ation, Shapash the lord of judgment,
78 Sin, and the great gods will destroy him. [Let] his name and seed[4] [*b*] [per]ish from the lands.
79 Let them make him forsake his throne and his scepter ...

(Seal)
1. The great king Abban
2. son of Sharran
3. servant of Addu
4. favored of Addu
5. possession[5]
6. of Ḫebat.

in Deut 21:1-9, although the exact number of elders is not specified in the Bible.

[4] Cf. the covenant curses involving loss of land and seed in Deut 28:49-68.

[5] The term translated here as "possession" is *sikiltu*. It is cognate to that used by Israel's God to describe a special relationship with Israel in Exod 19:5 (*s*[e]*gullâ*). As a divine epithet of a special relationship with a person, this term is almost exclusive to Alalakh. In two additional occurences (not epithets) it is used in Middle Babylonian (*CAD* S 245; Hess 1994a:204).

REFERENCES

Text: Photo: Smith 1939 pl. xviii, 3 and 5. Copy: *AT* pls. i-iii. Transliteration: *AT* 26-28; Dietrich and Loretz 1997:214-222. Translations: *AT* 28-30; Speiser 1954:23; Tsevat 1958:111-112; Reiner 1969:531-532; Dietrich and Mayer 1996:177-179; Dietrich and Loretz 1997:215-223.

AGREEMENT BETWEEN PILLIA AND IDRIMI (*AT* 3) (2.129)

Richard S. Hess

Like *AT* 2, this text stipulates only the extradition of fugitives.

I. *Introduction* (lines 1-5)
1 A tablet of agreement (was made)
2 when Pillia
3 swore a divine oath,
4 and made this agreement
5 [be]tween them.

II. *Stipulations regarding fugitives* (lines 6-43)
6 Fugitives who are among them
7 they shall always return.
8 Pillia's fugitive
9 whom Idrimi seizes

a Lev 27:2-8

10 to Pillia
11 he shall return.
12 Idrimi's fugitive
13 whom Pillia seizes
14 to Idrimi
15 he shall return. Whoever
16 seizes a fugitive
17 shall return him to his owner.
18 If he is a man,[1] [*a*] 500 (shekels) of copper
19 (the owner) will give as his reward.[2]
20 If she is a woman,[1] [*a*]
21 he will give 1,000 (shekels) of copper

[1] The value of a female fugitive here is twice that of a male. This contrasts with the biblical values of men and women set for the votive offerings in Lev 27:2-8. See Wenham 1978.

[2] The meaning of "equivalent price" for *mištannu*, was suggested by Wiseman who derived it from Akk. *šina* "two." A different meaning, "reward, pay," was suggested on the basis of an Indo-Iranian etymology proposed by Mayrhofer 1965. This has been followed by the Akk. dictionaries *CAD* and *AHw*. The question of the derivation raises issues for the translation of *mišneh* in biblical texts such as Deut 15:18. See Tsevat 1994. Tsevat provides bibliography of the earlier discussion and summarizes the issues while advocating "duplicate, equivalent" for the evaluation of the slave's service in comparison to that of a hired laborer.

22 as his reward.
23 If a fugitive
24 of Pillia
25 enters the land of Idrimi,
26 and no one there seizes him
27 but his owner seizes him,
28 then no reward
29 shall be given. If
30 a fugitive of Idrimi
31 enters the land of Pillia,
32 and no one there
33 seizes him but his owner
34 seizes him, then no reward
35 shall be given.
36 In whatever city
37 they declare a fugitive (to be),
38 the mayor and 5 notables
39 shall swear an oath.[3]
40 From whatever day Baratarna
41 swears the oath with Idrimi
42 from that day
43 it is decreed that a fugitive is to be returned.

III. *Curse* (lines 44-47)
44 Whoever transgresses the words of
45 this tablet,
46 may Adad, Shapash, Išḫara, and all the gods
47 destroy him.

[3] See comment for *AT* 2 (*COS* 2.128, note 2). For a Talmudic parallel see Tsevat 1958:126.

REFERENCES

Text: Copy: *AT* pl. iv. Transliteration: *AT* 31-32. Translation: *AT* 31; Reiner 1969:532.

2. LAWS

THE LAWS OF ESHNUNNA (2.130)

Martha Roth

After the fall of the Ur III Dynasty, the north Mesopotamian city of Eshnunna, east of Babylon, fell under the sway of the Amorite settlers in the region. Under King Naram-Sin of Eshnunna, Eshnunna became one of the great military powers at the end of the nineteenth and the beginning of the eighteenth centuries BCE, alternately warring and allying with the other great powers of the time, Assur (or the Kingdom of Upper Mesopotamia), Mari, Elam, and Babylon. A successor to Naram-Sin, King Dadusha, *may* be referred to in the fragmentary superscription of the text here, although little else is known about this king. The kingdom of Eshnunna came to an end under his successor Ibal-pi-el II, when King Hammurabi captured the city during his thirty-first regnal year, 1766 BCE.

The composition is known from three school exercise texts; there is no literary prologue or epilogue preserved. This is the earliest extant of the Akkadian-language collections of laws. There are great similarities in content with the other known law collections, especially with the Laws of Hammurabi, and despite the lack of a framing structure, this composition stands within the scribal-legal tradition of the Laws of Ur-Namma, Lipit-Ishtar, and Hammurabi (*COS* 2.153, 154, 131).[1]

Superscription
Appointment to the throne (lines i.1-7)
[...] day 21 [...] of the gods Enlil and Ninazu, [when Dadusha ascended to] the kingship of the city of Eshnunna [and entered] into the house of his father, [when] he conquered with mighty weapons within one year the cities Ṣupur-Shamash [and ... on] the far bank of the Tigris River [...].

The Laws

§1 300 SILA of barley (can be purchased) for 1 shekel of silver. 3 SILA of fine oil — for 1 shekel of silver. 12 SILA of oil — for 1 shekel of silver. 15 SILA of lard — for 1 shekel of silver. 40 SILA of bitumen — for 1 shekel of silver. 360 shekels of wool — for 1 shekel of silver. 600 SILA of salt — for 1 shekel of silver. 300 SILA of potash — for 1 shekel of silver. 180 shekels of copper — for 1 shekel of silver. 120 shekels of wrought copper — for 1 shekel of silver.

§2 1 sila of oil, extract(?) — 30 SILA is its grain equivalent. 1 sila of lard, extract(?) — 25 SILA is its grain equivalent. 1 sila of bitumen, extract(?) — 8 SILA is its grain equivalent.

§3 A wagon together with its oxen and its driver — 100 SILA of grain is its hire; if (paid in) silver, ⅓ shekel (i.e., 60 barley corns) is its

[1] The most recent edition is in Roth 1995/1997, on which this translation is based, and to which the reader is referred for details of sources and earlier editions.

hire; he shall drive it for the entire day.

§4 The hire of a boat is, per 300-sila capacity, 2 SILA; furthermore, [x] SILA is the hire of the boatman; he shall drive it for the entire day.

§5 If the boatman is negligent and causes the boat to sink, he shall restore as much as he caused to sink.

§6 If a man, under fraudulent circumstances, should seize a boat which does not belong to him, he shall weigh and deliver 10 shekels of silver.

§7 20 SILA of grain is the hire of a harvester; if (paid in) silver, 12 barleycorns is his hire.

§8 10 SILA of grain is the hire of a winnower.

§9 Should a man give 1 shekel of silver to a hireling for harvesting — if he (the hireling) does not keep himself available to work and does not harvest for him, he shall weigh and deliver 10 shekels of silver.

§9A 15 SILA is the hire of a sickle, and the broken blade(?) shall revert to its owner.

§10 10 SILA of grain is the hire of a donkey, and 10 SILA of grain is the hire of its driver; he shall drive it for the entire day.

§11 The hire of a hireling is 1 shekel of silver, 60 SILA of grain is his provender; he shall serve for one month.

§12 A man who is seized in the field of a commoner among the sheaves at midday shall weigh and deliver 10 shekels of silver; he who is seized at night among the sheaves shall die, he will not live.[a]

§13 A man who is seized in the house of a commoner, within the house, at midday, shall weigh and deliver 10 shekels of silver; he who is seized at night within the house shall die, he will not live.

§14 The hire of a fuller, per one garment valued at 5 shekels of silver — 1 shekel is his hire; (per one garment) valued at 10 shekels of silver — 2 shekels is his hire.

§15 A merchant or a tapster will not accept silver, grain, wool, oil, or anything else from a male or female slave.

§16 The son of a man who has not yet received his inheritance share or a slave will not be advanced credit.

§17 Should a member of the *awīlu*-class bring the bridewealth to the house of his father-in-law — if either (the groom or bride then) should go to his or her fate, the silver shall revert to its original owner (i.e., the widower or his heir).

§18 If he marries her and she enters his house and then either the groom or the bride goes to his or her fate, he will not take out all that he had brought, but only its excess shall he take.[2]

§18A Per 1 shekel (of silver) interest accrues at the rate of 36 barleycorns (= 20%); per 300 SILA (of grain) interest accrues at the rate of 100 SILA (= 33⅓%).

§19 A man who lends against its corresponding commodity(?) shall collect at the threshing floor.

§20 If a man loans ... grain ... and then converts the grain into silver, at the harvest he shall take the grain and the interest on it at (the established rate of 33⅓%, i.e.,) 100 SILA per 300 SILA.

§21 If a man gives silver for/to his/its ..., he shall take the silver and the interest on it at (the established rate of 20%, i.e.,) 36 barleycorns per 1 shekel.

§22 If a man has no claim against another man but he nonetheless takes the man's slave woman as a distress, the owner of the slave woman shall swear an oath by the god: "You have no claim against me"; he (the distrainer) shall weigh and deliver silver as much as is the value(?) of the slave woman.[b]

§23 If a man has no claim against another man but he nonetheless takes the man's slave woman as a distress, detains the distress in his house, and causes her death, he shall replace her with two slave women for the owner of the slave woman.

§24 If he has no claim against him[3] but he nonetheless takes the wife of a commoner or the child of a commoner as a distress, detains the distress in his house, and causes her or his death, it is a capital offense — the distrainer who distrained shall die.

§25 If a man comes to claim (his bride) at the house of his father-in-law, but his father-in-law wrongs(?) him and then gives his daughter to [another], the father of the daughter shall return two-fold the bridewealth which he received.[c]

§26 If a man brings the bridewealth for the daughter of a man, but another, without the consent of her father and mother, abducts her and then deflowers her, it is indeed a capital offense — he shall die.[d]

§27 If a man marries the daughter of another man without the consent of her father and mother, and moreover does not conclude the nuptial feast and the contract for(?) her father and mother, should she reside in his house for even one full year, she is not a wife.

a Exod 22:1-2; Isa 38:1

b Deut 24:6

c Judg 15:1-2

d Deut22:23-27

[2] Subjects in the final clause are uncertain, and the resolutions outlined are not clear. For discussion of possibilities, see Yaron 1988:179-190.

[3] I.e., the "commoner" mentioned later in the provision.

§28 If he concludes the contract and the nuptial feast for(?) her father and mother and he marries her, she is indeed a wife; the day she is seized in the lap of another man, she shall die, she will not live.[4] [e]

§29 If a man should be captured or abducted during a raiding expedition or while on patrol(?), even should he reside in a foreign land for a long time, should someone else marry his wife and even should she bear a child, whenever he returns he shall take back his wife.

§30 If a man repudiates his city and his master and then flees, and someone else then marries his wife, whenever he returns he will have no claim to his wife.

§31 If a man should deflower the slave woman of another man, he shall weigh and deliver 20 shekels of silver, but the slave woman remains the property of her master.

§32 If a man gives his child for suckling and for rearing but does not give the food, oil, and clothing rations (to the caregiver) for 3 years, he shall weigh and deliver 10 shekels of silver for the cost of the rearing of his child, and he shall take away his child.

§33 If a slave woman acts to defraud and gives her child to a woman of the *awīlu*-class, when he grows up — should his master locate him, he shall seize him and take him away.

§34 If a slave woman of the palace should give her son or her daughter to a commoner for rearing, the palace shall remove the son or daughter whom she gave.

§35 However, an adoptor who takes in adoption the child of a slave woman of the palace shall restore (another slave of) equal value for the palace.

§36 If a man gives his goods to a *naptaru* for safekeeping, and he (the *naptaru)* then allows the goods which he gave to him for safekeeping to become lost — without evidence that the house has been broken into, the doorjamb scraped, the window forced — he shall replace his goods for him.[f]

§37 If the man's house[5] has been burglarized, and the owner of the house incurs a loss along with the goods which the depositor gave to him, the owner of the house shall swear an oath to satisfy him at the gate of (the temple of) the god Tishpak: "My goods have been lost along with your goods; I have not committed a fraud or misdeed"; thus shall he swear an oath to satisfy him and he will have no claim against him.

§38 If, in a partnership, one intends to sell his share and his partner wishes to buy, he shall match any outside offer.[6]

§39 If a man becomes impoverished and then sells his house, whenever the buyer offers it for sale, the owner of the house shall have the right to redeem it.[g]

§40 If a man buys a slave, a slave woman, an ox, or any other purchase, but cannot establish the identity of the seller, it is he who is a thief.[h]

§41 If a foreigner, a *naptaru,* or a *mudû* wishes to sell his beer, the tapster shall sell the beer for him at the current rate.

§42 If a man bites the nose of another man and thus cuts it off, he shall weigh and deliver 60 shekels of silver; an eye — 60 shekels; a tooth — 30 shekels; an ear — 30 shekels; a slap to the cheek[7] he shall weigh and deliver 10 shekels of silver.[i]

§43 If a man should cut off the finger of another man, he shall weigh and deliver 20 shekels of silver.[i]

§44 If a man knocks down another man in the street(?) and thereby breaks his hand, he shall weigh and deliver 30 shekels of silver.

§45 If he should break his foot, he shall weigh and deliver 30 shekels of silver.

§46[8] If a man strikes another man and thus breaks his collarbone, he shall weigh and deliver 20 shekels of silver.

§47 If a man should inflict(?) any other injuries(?) on another man in the course of a fray, he shall weigh and deliver 10 shekels of silver.

§47A If a man, in the course of a brawl, should cause the death of another member of the *awīlu*-class, he shall weigh and deliver 40 shekels of silver.

§48 And for a case involving a penalty of silver in amounts ranging from 20 shekels to 60 shekels, the judges shall determine the case against him; however, a capital case is only for the king.

§49 If a man should be seized with a stolen slave or a stolen slave woman, a slave shall lead a slave, a slave woman shall lead a slave woman.[j]

§50 If a military governor, a governor of the canal system, or any person in a position of

e Lev 20:10; Deut 22:22; Isa 38:1

f Exod 22:7-8

g Lev 25:29-30

h Exod 22:1-2

i Exod 21:24; Lev 24:20, Deut 19:21

j Exod 22:3, 6

[4] Yaron (1988:284-85) maintains his earlier position that it is the lover and not the woman who is the subject of *imât ul iballuṭ* "s/he shall die, s/he shall not live," and that her punishment is left to her husband; but see Roth 1988. For the idiom and its parallels see Hallo 1999:41 and nn. 65-67.

[5] I.e., the house of the depositary, the *naptāru* "resident alien" of §36.

[6] For other interpretations, see Yaron 1988:227-235.

[7] "Slap to the cheek" is a reference to a physical or social assault to a person's honor; see Roth 1995:27-36; and *COS* 2.131 §§202-205.

[8] On §§46, 47, 47A, see Roth 1990.

authority seizes a fugitive slave, fugitive slave woman, stray ox, or stray donkey belonging either to the palace or to a commoner, and does not lead it to Eshnunna but detains it in his house and allows more than one month to elapse, the palace shall bring a charge of theft against him.

§51 A slave or slave woman belonging to (a resident of) Eshnunna who bears fetters, shackles, or a slave hairlock will not exit through the main city-gate of Eshnunna without his owner.

§52 A slave or slave woman who has entered the main city-gate of Eshnunna in the safekeeping of a foreign envoy shall be made to bear fetters, shackles, or a slave hairlock and thereby is kept safe for his owner.

§53 If an ox gores another ox and thus causes its death, the two ox-owners shall divide the value of the living ox and the carcass of the dead ox.[k]

§54 If an ox is a gorer and the ward authorities so notify its owner, but he fails to keep his ox in check and it gores a man and thus causes his death, the owner of the ox shall weigh and deliver 40 shekels of silver.

§55 If it gores a slave and thus causes his death, he shall weigh and deliver 15 shekels of silver.

k Exod 21:28-36

§56 If a dog is vicious and the ward authorities so notify its owner, but he fails to control his dog and it bites a man and thus causes his death, the owner of the dog shall weigh and deliver 40 shekels of silver.

§57 If it bites a slave and thus causes his death, he shall weigh and deliver 15 shekels of silver.

§58 If a wall is buckling and the ward authorities so notify the owner of the wall, but he does not reinforce his wall and the wall collapses and thus causes the death of a member of the *awīlu*-class — it is a capital case, it is decided by a royal edict.

§59 If a man sired children but divorces his wif e and then marries another, he shall be expelled from the house and any possessions there may be and he shall depart after the one who ..., [...] the house ...[9]

§60[10] [If] a guard is negligent in guarding [a house], and a burglar [breaks into the house], they shall kill the guard of the house that was broken into [...], and he shall be buried [at] the breach without a grave.

[9] The interpretation of the provision is disputed, revolving around the identity (or identifies) of the subjects in the subclauses of the apodosis; see the summaries of the discussion in Yaron 1988:214ff. and in Westbrook 1988: 72ff.

[10] The provision is damaged, and the restorations and interpretation are uncertain; here, I follow the treatment put forward by Landsberger 1968:102.

REFERENCES

Text: Goetze 1948a; Yaron 1969/1988; Roth 1995/1997:57-70. Translations and Studies: *ANET* 161-163; *TUAT* 32-38; Goetze 1956; Eichler 1987; Finkelstein, 1970; Landsberger 1968; al-Rawi 1982; Roth 1988; 1990; 1995; 1995/1997:57-70; Saporetti 1984:41-48; Yaron 1969/1988; Westbrook 1988; 1994.

THE LAWS OF HAMMURABI (2.131)

Martha Roth

By the beginning of the second millennium, Amorite and other nomadic population groups integrated into Mesopotamian urban political and social life. The Amorite Sumu-abum (ca. 1894-1881 BCE) settled in Babylon, in the wasp-waist center of Mesopotamia, at the time that the rival cities of Isin and Larsa were struggling for dominance in the south. He and his successors for one hundred years stayed focused largely on their immediate geographical area, engaging in local political and military consolidation, fortification and temple building projects, canal maintenance, and some military actions. By the time the sixth ruler of this dynasty, Hammurabi (ca. 1792-1750 BCE), came to the throne, he found himself circumscribed by the rising powers of Larsa to the south, the Kingdom of Upper Mesopotamia to the north, Mari to the west, and Eshnunna and Elam to the east. In his first years, Hammurabi, like his predecessors, remained involved in building projects in Babylon itself, but then turned outward and began military forays into other territories; by his thirty-second regnal year, he had decisively defeated all the rivals mentioned. As "King of Sumer and Akkad," Hammurabi now had the luxury of turning his attention again to domestic programs, largely neglected during the years of military efforts. It is at this point that the law collection inscribed on the monumental stelae was compiled and publicized in multiple copies placed in major cities of his realm, fulfilling Hammurabi's repeated claims of a just and righteous rule. In all this, Hammurabi and his law collection stand firmly in the stream of tradition of his royal predecessors in other dynasties and other cities of Mesopotamia, beginning at least with Ur-Namma and Lipit-Ishtar, although the product of Hammurabi's efforts is by far the longest, most polished, and most comprehensive.

Hammurabi's son and successor Samsu-iluna also enjoyed a long reign (ca. 1749-1712 BCE), but the empire Hammurabi consolidated began to splinter soon after his death. By the beginning of the sixteenth century, the much reduced city of Babylon fell to invading Hatti forces. Hammurabi himself, however, achieved and retained enormous personal appeal as a charismatic leader both during his lifetime and after. The enduring power of Hammurabi's name and deeds is dramatically demonstrated by the seven and a half foot tall stela with the most complete edition of the Laws, which was taken from Sippar as booty to Susa by conquering Elamites five hundred years later.

In addition to the famous monument, some fifty manuscripts are known to record all or part of the laws, prologue, and epilogue of the composition. The manuscripts range from those contemporary with the time of Hammurabi through to the middle of the first millennium, and come from a variety of sites. The scribes in schools studied and copied the Laws, and engaged in exercises resulting in commentaries to and extracts of the composition, and even one Sumerian-Akkadian bilingual.[1]

Prologue (lines i 1-v 25)

Elevation of Marduk to head of the pantheon (lines i 1-26)

When the august god Anu, king of the Anunnaku deities, and the god Enlil, lord of heaven and earth, who determines the destinies of the land, allotted supreme power over all peoples to the god Marduk, the firstborn son of the god Ea, exalted him among the Igigu deities, named the city of Babylon with its august name and made it supreme within the regions of the world, and established for him within it eternal kingship whose foundations are as fixed as heaven and earth,

Appointment of Hammurabi to the throne (lines i.27-49)

at that time, the gods Anu and Enlil, for the enhancement of the well-being of the people, named me by my name: Hammurabi, the pious prince, who venerates the gods, to make justice prevail in the land, to abolish the wicked and the evil, to prevent the strong from oppressing the weak, to rise like the sun-god Shamash over all humankind, to illuminate the land.

Attributes and benefactions of Hammurabi to the temples and cities in his realm (lines i.50-v.13)

I am Hammurabi, the shepherd, selected by the god Enlil, he who heaps high abundance and plenty, who perfects every possible thing for the city Nippur, (the city known as) band-of-heaven-and-earth, the pious provider of the Ekur temple;

the capable king, the restorer of the city Eridu, the purifier of the rites of the Eabzu temple;

the onslaught of the four regions of the world, who magnifies the reputation of the city Babylon, who gladdens the heart of his divine lord Marduk, whose days are devoted to the Esagil temple;

seed of royalty, he whom the god Sin created, enricher of the city of Ur, humble and talented, who provides abundance for the Egishnugal temple;

discerning king, obedient to the god Shamash, the mighty one, who establishes the foundations of the city of Sippar, who drapes the sacred building of the goddess Aja with greenery, who made famous the temple of Ebabbar which is akin to the abode of heaven;

the warrior, who shows mercy to the city of Larsa, who renews the Ebabbar temple for the god Shamash his ally;

the lord who revitalizes the city of Uruk, who provides abundant waters for its people, who raises high the summit of the Eanna temple, who heaps up bountiful produce for the gods Anu and Ishtar;

the protecting canopy of the land, who gathers together the scattered peoples of the city of Isin, who supplies abundance for the temple of Egalmaḫ;

dragon among kings, beloved brother of the god Zababa, founder of the settlement of Kish, who surrounds the Emeteursag temple with splendor, who arranges the great rites for the goddess Ishtar, who takes charge of the temple of Ḫursagkalamma;

the enemy-ensnaring throw-net, whose companion, the god Erra, has allowed him to obtain his heart's desire, who enlarges the city of Kutû, who augments everything for the Emeslam temple;

the fierce wild bull who gores the enemy, beloved of the god Tutu, the one who makes the city of Borsippa exult, the pious one who does not fail in his duties to the Ezida temple, <the dwelling of> the god of kings;

the one who is steeped in wisdom, who enlarges the cultivated area of the city of Dilbat, who heaps up the storage bins for the mighty god Urash;

the lord, worthy recipient of the scepter and crown bestowed upon him by the wise goddess Mama, who devised the plans of the city of Kesh, who provides the pure food offerings for the goddess Nintu;

the judicious one, the noble one, who allots pasturage and watering place for the cities of Lagash and

[1] The most recent edition is in Roth 1995/1997, on which this translation is based, and to which the reader is referred for details of sources and earlier editions.

Girsu, who provides plentiful food-offerings for the Eninnu temple;

who seizes the enemies, beloved of (the goddess Ishtar) the able one, who perfects the oracles of the city of Zabala, who gladdens the heart of the goddess Ishtar;

the pure prince, whose prayers the god Adad acknowledges, appeaser of the heart of the god Adad, the hero in the city of Karkara, who installs the proper appointments throughout the Eudgalgal temple;

the king who gives life to the city of Adab, who organizes the Emaḫ temple;

lord of kings, peerless warrior, who granted life to the city of Mashkan-shapir, who gives waters of abundance to the Emeslam temple;

wise one, the organizer, he who has mastered all wisdom, who shelters the people of the city of Malgium in the face of annihilation, who founds their settlements in abundance, who decreed eternal pure food offerings for the gods Enki and Damkina who magnify his kingship;

leader of kings, who subdues the settlements along the Euphrates River by the oracular command of the god Dagan, his creator, who showed mercy to the people of the cities of Mari and Tuttul;

the pious prince, who brightens the countenance of the god Tishpak, who provides pure feasts for the goddess Ninazu, who sustains his people in crisis, who secures their foundations in peace in the midst of the city of Babylon;

shepherd of the people, whose deeds are pleasing to the goddess Ishtar, who establishes Ishtar in the Eulmash temple in the midst of Akkad-the-City;

who proclaims truth, who guides the population properly, who restores its benevolent protective spirit to the city of Assur;

who quells the rebellious, the king who proclaimed the rites for the goddess Ishtar in the city of Nineveh in the Emesmes temple;

the pious one, who prays ceaselessly for the great gods, scion of Sumu-la-el, mighty heir of Sîn-muballiṭ, eternal seed of royalty, mighty king, solar disk of the city of Babylon, who spreads light over the lands of Sumer and Akkad, king who makes the four regions obedient, favored of the goddess Ishtar, am I.

Establishment of justice in the land (lines v.14-25)
When the god Marduk commanded me to provide just ways for the people of the land (in order to attain) appropriate behavior, I established truth and justice as the declaration of the land, I enhanced the well-being of the people.

a Exod 20:16; 23:1-3; Deut 5:20; 19:16-21

b Exod 21:37; 22:1-2

c Exod 20:15; Lev 19:11, 13; Deut 5:19

At that time:

The Laws

§1 If a man accuses another man and charges him with homicide but cannot bring proof against him, his accuser shall be killed.[a]

§2 If a man charges another man with practicing witchcraft but cannot bring proof against him, he who is charged with witchcraft shall go to the divine River Ordeal, he shall indeed submit to the divine River Ordeal; if the divine River Ordeal should overwhelm him, his accuser shall take full legal possession of his estate; if the divine River Ordeal should clear that man and should he survive, he who made the charge of witchcraft against him shall be killed; he who submitted to the divine River Ordeal shall take full legal possession of his accuser's estate.

§3 If a man comes forward to give false testimony in a case but cannot bring evidence for his accusation, if that case involves a capital offense, that man shall be killed.

§4 If he comes forward to give (false) testimony for (a case whose penalty is) grain or silver, he shall be assessed the penalty for that case.

§5 If a judge renders a judgment, gives a verdict, or deposits a sealed opinion, after which he reverses his judgment, they shall charge and convict that judge of having reversed the judgment which he rendered and he shall give twelvefold the claim of that judgment; moreover, they shall unseat him from his judgeship in the assembly, and he shall never again sit in judgment with the judges.

§6 If a man steals valuables belonging to the god or to the palace, that man shall be killed, and also he who received the stolen goods from him shall be killed.[b]

§7 If a man should purchase silver, gold, a slave, a slave woman, an ox, a sheep, a donkey, or anything else whatsoever, from a son of a man or from a slave of a man without witnesses or a contract — or if he accepts the goods for safekeeping — that man is a thief, he shall be killed.

§8 If a man steals an ox, a sheep, a donkey, a pig, or a boat — if it belongs either to the god or to the palace, he shall give thirtyfold; if it belongs to a commoner, he shall replace it tenfold; if the thief does not have anything to give, he shall be killed.[c]

§9 If a man who claims to have lost property then discovers his lost property in another man's possession, but the man in whose possession the lost property was discovered declares, "A seller sold it to me, I purchased it in the presence of witnesses," and the owner of the lost property declares, "I can bring witnesses who can identify my lost property," (and then if) the buyer produces the seller who sold it to him and the witnesses in whose presence he purchased it, and also the owner of the lost property produces the witnesses who can identify his lost property — the judges shall examine their cases, and the witnesses in whose presence the purchase was made and the witnesses who can identify the lost property shall state the facts known to them before the god, then it is the seller who is the thief, he shall be killed; the owner of the lost property shall take his lost property, and the buyer shall take from the seller's estate the amount of silver that he weighed and delivered.[d]

§10 If the buyer could not produce the seller who sold (the lost property) to him or the witnesses before whom he made the purchase, but the owner of the lost property could produce witnesses who can identify his lost property, then it is the buyer who is the thief, he shall be killed; the owner of the lost property shall take his lost property.

§11 If the owner of the lost property could not produce witnesses who can identify his lost property, he is a liar, he has indeed spread malicious charges, he shall be killed.

§12 If the seller should go to his fate, the buyer shall take fivefold the claim for that case from the estate of the seller.

§13 If that man's witnesses are not available, the judges shall grant him an extension until the sixth month, but if he does not bring his witnesses by the sixth month, it is that man who is a liar, he shall be assessed the penalty for that case.

§14 If a man should kidnap the young child of another man, he shall be killed.[e]

§15 If a man should enable a palace slave, a palace slave woman, a commoner's slave, or a commoner's slave woman to leave through the main city-gate, he shall be killed.

§16 If a man should harbor a fugitive slave or slave woman of either the palace or of a commoner in his house and not bring him out at the herald's public proclamation, that householder shall be killed.

§17 If a man seizes a fugitive slave or slave woman in the open country and leads him back to his owner, the slave owner shall give him 2 shekels of silver.

§18 If that slave should refuse to identify his owner, he shall lead him off to the palace, his circumstances shall be investigated, and they shall return him to his owner.

§19 If he should detain that slave in his own house and afterward the slave is discovered in his possession, that man shall be killed.

§20 If the slave should escape the custody of the one who seized him, that man shall swear an oath by the god to the owner of the slave, and he shall be released.

§21 If a man breaks into a house, they shall kill him and hang him in front of that very breach.[f]

§22 If a man commits a robbery and is then seized, that man shall be killed.[g]

§23 If the robber should not be seized, the man who has been robbed shall establish the extent of his lost property before the god; and the city and the governor in whose territory and district the robbery was committed shall replace his lost property to him.

§24 If a life (is lost during the robbery), the city and the governor shall weigh and deliver to his kinsmen 60 shekels of silver.[h]

§25 If a fire breaks out in a man's house, and a man who came to help put it out covets the household furnishings belonging to the householder, and takes household furnishings belonging to the householder, that man shall be cast into that very fire.

§26 If either a soldier or a fisherman who is ordered to go on a royal campaign does not go, or hires and sends a hireling as his substitute, that soldier or fisherman shall be killed; the one who informs against him shall take full legal possession of his estate.

§27 If there is either a soldier or a fisherman who is taken captive while serving in a royal fortress, and they give his field and his orchard to another to succeed to his holdings, and he then performs his service obligation — if he (the soldier or fisherman) should return and get back to his city, they shall return to him his field and orchard and he himself shall perform his service obligation.

§28 If there is either a soldier or a fisherman who is taken captive while serving in a royal fortress, and his son is able to perform the service obligation, the field and orchard shall be given to him and he shall perform his father's service obligation.

§29 If his son is too young and is unable to perform his father's service obligation, one third of the field and orchard shall be given to his mother, and his mother shall raise him.

§30 If either a soldier or a fisherman abandons his field, orchard, or house because of the service obligation and then absents himself, another person takes possession of his field, orchard, or house to succeed to his holdings and performs the service obligation for three years — if he then returns and claims his field, orchard, or house, it will not be given

d Exod 21:37; 22:3
e Exod 21:16; Deut 24:7
f Exod 22:2-3
g Lev 5:21-26; 19:11, 13
h Deut 21:1-11

to him; he who has taken possession of it and has performed his service obligation shall be the one to continue to perform the obligation.

§31 If he should absent himself for only one year and then return, his field, orchard, and house shall be given to him, and he himself shall perform his service obligation.

§32 If there is either a soldier or a fisherman who is taken captive while on a royal campaign, a merchant redeems him and helps him to get back to his city — if there are sufficient means in his own estate for the redeeming, he himself shall redeem himself; if there are not sufficient means in his estate to redeem him, he shall be redeemed by his city's temple; if there are not sufficient means in his city's temple to redeem him, the palace shall redeem him; but his field, orchard, or house will not be given for his redemption.

§33 If either a captain or a sergeant should recruit(?) deserters or accepts and leads off a hireling as a substitute on a royal campaign, that captain or sergeant shall be killed.

§34 If either a captain or a sergeant should take a soldier's household furnishings, oppress a soldier, hire out a soldier, deliver a soldier into the power of an influential person in a law case, or take a gift that the king gave to a soldier, that captain or sergeant shall be killed.

§35 If a man should purchase from a soldier either the cattle or the sheep and goats which the king gave to the soldier, he shall forfeit his silver.

§36 (Furthermore), the field, orchard, or house of a soldier, fisherman, or a state tenant will not be sold.

§37 If a man should purchase a field, orchard, or house of a soldier, fisherman, or a state tenant, his deed shall be invalidated and he shall forfeit his silver; the field, orchard, or house shall revert to its owner.

§38 (Furthermore), a soldier, fisherman, or a state tenant will not assign in writing to his wife or daughter any part of a field, orchard, or house attached to his service obligation, nor will he give it to meet any outstanding obligation.

§39 He shall assign in writing to his wife or daughter or give to meet an outstanding obligation only a field, orchard, or house which he himself acquires by purchase.

§40 (However), a *nadītu,* a merchant, or any holder of a field with a special service obligation may sell her or his field, orchard, or house; the buyer shall perform the service obligation on the field, orchard, or house which he purchases.

§41 If a man accepts a field, orchard, or house of a soldier, fisherman, or state tenant in an exchange and gives him a compensatory payment (for the difference in value), the soldier, fisherman, or state tenant shall reclaim his field, orchard, or house and shall also keep full legal possession of the compensatory payment which was given to him.

§42 If a man rents a field in tenancy but does not plant any grain, they shall charge and convict him of not performing the required work in the field, and he shall give to the owner of the field grain in accordance with his neighbor's yield.

§43 If he does not cultivate the field at all but leaves it fallow, he shall give to the owner of the field grain in accordance with his neighbor's yield, and he shall plow and harrow the field which he left fallow and return it to the owner of the field.

§44 If a man rents a previously uncultivated field for a three-year term with the intention of opening it for cultivation but he is negligent and does not open the field, in the fourth year he shall plow, hoe, and harrow the field and return it to the owner of the field; and in addition he shall measure and deliver 3,000 SILA of grain per 18 *iku* (of field).

§45 If a man leases his field to a cultivator and receives the rent for his field, and afterwards the storm-god Adad devastates the field or a flood sweeps away the crops, the loss is the cultivator's alone.

§46 If he (the owner) should not receive the rent for his field (before the catastrophe destroys the field) or he leases out the field on terms of a half share or a third share (of the yield), the cultivator and the owner of the field shall divide whatever grain there is remaining in the agreed proportions.

§47 If the cultivator should declare his intention to cultivate the field (in the next year) because in the previous year he did not recover his expenses, the owner of the field will not object; his same cultivator shall cultivate his field and he shall take (his share of) the grain at the harvest in accordance with his contract.

§48 If a man has a debt lodged against him, and the storm-god Adad devastates his field or a flood sweeps away the crops, or there is no grain grown in the field due to insufficient water — in that year he will not repay grain to his creditor; he shall suspend performance of his contract and he will not give interest payments for that year.

§49 If a man borrows silver from a merchant and gives the merchant a field prepared for planting with either grain or sesame[2] (as a pledge for the loan) and declares to him, "You cultivate the field and collect and take away as much grain or sesame as will be grown" — if the cultivator should produce either grain or sesame in the field, at the harvest it is only the owner of the field who shall take the grain or sesame that is grown in the field, and he shall give to the merchant the grain equivalent to his silver which he borrowed from the merchant and the interest on it and also the expenses of the cultivation.

§50 If he gives (to the merchant as a pledge for the loan) a field already plowed and sown with either <grain> or sesame, (at the harvest) it is only the owner of the field who shall take the grain or sesame that is grown in the field and he shall repay the silver and the interest on it to the merchant.

§51 If he does not have silver to repay, he shall give to the merchant, in accordance with the royal edict, <either grain or> sesame according to their market value for his silver borrowed from the merchant and the interest on it.

§52 If the cultivator should not produce grain or sesame in the field, he will not alter his agreement.

§53 If a man neglects to reinforce the embankment of (the irrigation canal of) his field and does not reinforce its embankment, and then a breach opens in its embankment and allows the water to carry away the common irrigated area, the man in whose embankment the breach opened shall replace the grain whose loss he caused.

§54 If he cannot replace the grain, they shall sell him and his property, and the residents of the common irrigated area whose grain crops the water carried away shall divide (the proceeds).

§55 If a man opens his branch of the canal for irrigation and negligently allows the water to carry away his neighbor's field, he shall measure and deliver grain in accordance with his neighbor's yield.

§56 If a man opens (an irrigation gate and releases) waters and thereby he allows the water to carry away whatever work has been done in his neighbor's field, he shall measure and deliver 3,000 SILA of grain per 18 *iku* (of field).

§57 If a shepherd does not make an agreement with the owner of the field to graze sheep and goats, and without the permission of the owner of the field grazes sheep and goats on the field, the owner of the field shall harvest his field and the shepherd who grazed sheep and goats on the field without the permission of the owner of the field shall give in addition 6,000 SILA of grain per 18 *iku* (of field) to the owner of the field.

§58 If, after the sheep and goats come up from the common irrigated area when the pennants announcing the termination of pasturing are wound around the main city-gate, the shepherd releases the sheep and goats into a field and allows the sheep and goats to graze in the field — the shepherd shall guard the field in which he allowed them to graze and at the harvest he shall measure and deliver to the owner of the field 18,000 SILA of grain per 18 *iku* (of field).

§59 If a man cuts down a tree in another man's date orchard without the permission of the owner of the orchard, he shall weigh and deliver 30 shekels of silver.

§60 If a man gives a field to a gardener to plant as a date orchard and the gardener plants the orchard, he shall cultivate the orchard for four years; in the fifth year, the owner of the orchard and the gardener shall divide the yield in equal shares; the owner of the orchard shall select and take his share first.[i]

i Lev 19:23-25

§61 If the gardener does not complete the planting of (the date orchard in) the field, but leaves an uncultivated area, they shall include the uncultivated area in his share.

§62 If he does not plant as a date orchard the field which was given to him — if it is arable land, the gardener shall measure and deliver to the owner of the field the estimated yield of the field for the years it is left fallow in accordance with his neighbor's yield; furthermore he shall perform the required work on the field and return it to the owner of the field.

§63 If it is uncultivated land, he shall perform the required work on the field and return it to the owner of the field, and in addition he shall measure and deliver 3,000 SILA of grain per 18 *iku* (of field) per year.

§64 If a man gives his orchard to a gardener to pollinate (the date palms), as long as the gardener is in possession of the orchard, he shall give to the owner of the orchard two thirds of the yield of the orchard, and he himself shall take one third.

§65 If the gardener does not pollinate the (date palms in the) orchard and thus diminishes the yield, the gardener [shall measure and deliver] a yield for the orchard to <the owner of the orchard in accordance with> his neighbor's yield.

[2] Or "linseed"; see the discussion and literature cited in *CAD* Š 3:306f. s.v. *šamaššammu*.

gap §a If a man borrows silver from a merchant and his merchant presses him for payment but he has nothing to give in repayment, and therefore he gives his orchard after pollination to the merchant and declares to him, "Take away as many dates as will be grown in the orchard as payment for your silver" — the merchant will not agree; the owner of the orchard himself shall take the dates that are grown in the orchard, he shall satisfy the merchant with silver and the interest on it in accordance with the terms of his contract, and only the owner of the orchard shall take the dates that are grown in the orchard in excess (of the debt).

gap §b If a man intends to build a house and his neighbor [...]

gap §c [If ...] he will not give to him [...] for a price; if he intends to give grain, silver, or any other commodity for a house encumbered by a service obligation and belonging to the estate of his neighbor which he wishes to buy, he shall forfeit whatever he gave; it shall return to its owner. If that house is not encumbered by a service obligation, he may buy it; he may give grain, silver, or any other commodity for that house.

gap §d If a man should work his neighbor's uncultivated plot without his neighbor's permission, in the house [...] his neighbor [...]

gap §e [If ... a man] declares [to the owner of a rundown house], "Reinforce your scalable wall; they could scale over the wall to here from your house," or to the owner of an uncultivated plot, "Work your uncultivated plot; they could break into my house from your uncultivated plot," and he secures witnesses — if a thief [breaks in] by scaling the wall, the owner [of the rundown house shall replace anything which is lost by] the scaling; if [a thief breaks in by access through the uncultivated plot], the owner [of the uncultivated plot] shall replace anything [which was lost ...]; if [...]

gap §f [if ...] house [...]

gap §g If [a man rents a house ... and] the tenant gives the full amount of the silver for his annual rent to the owner of the house, but the owner of the house then orders the tenant to leave before the expiration of the full term of his lease, the owner of the house, because he evicted the tenant before the expiration of the full term of his lease, shall forfeit the silver that the tenant gave him.

gap §h [If] a tenant intends to purchase [the house of a commoner, ...] the rent obligation which he shall perform, in order to purchase the house of a commoner, [...] which he shall place [...] he shall place it [...]; if he is abroad(?) [...] of the commoner; if he does not purchase (the house) [he shall forfeit the silver that] he took and [the house of the commoner shall revert to] its owner.[3]

gap §§i, j, k [...]

gap §l [If a man borrows silver ...] he shall weigh and deliver his silver and the interest on it at the harvest; if he has nothing to give, [he shall give to him] any of his property, any commodity or grain; if he has ... to give, [...]

gap §m If a merchant who for [...] ... for 5 shekels of silver [...] he did not write for him a sealed document [...] ... the son of a man ... that one ... they shall kill him.

gap §n If a man's slave [...] he shall weigh and deliver 20 shekels of silver, and that slave [...] complete ... he shall be killed.

gap §o [If] a man [...] another man [...] silver [...]

gap §§p, q [...]

gap §r [If...] to [...] wages [...] silver [...]; if that man who [...] does not [...] he shall forfeit the silver that he gave.

gap §s If either a male slave or [a female slave ..., they shall return him] to [his] master; if [...] he beats(?) him, they will not return him [to] his [master].

gap §t If a merchant gives grain or silver as an interest-bearing loan, he shall take 100 SILA of grain per GUR as interest (= 33⅓%); if he gives silver as an interest-bearing loan, he shall take 36 barleycorns per shekel of silver as interest (= 20%).

gap §u If a man who has an interest-bearing loan does not have silver with which to repay it, he (the merchant) shall take grain and silver in accordance with the royal edict and the interest on it at the annual rate of 60 SILA per 1 GUR (= 20%); if the merchant should attempt to increase and collect the interest on the (silver) loan [up to the grain interest rate of 100 SILA of grain] per 1 GUR (= 33⅓%), [or in any other way beyond] 36 barley corns [per shekel (= 20%) of silver], he shall forfeit whatever he had given.

gap §v If a merchant gives grain or silver at interest and he then takes [...] grain or silver as in-

[3] Taken by Donbaz and Sauren (1991:8-13) as a variant of the preceding provision presented here separately as gap §g.

terest according to the amount of his capital sum, [...] the grain and silver, his capital and interest [...], the tablet recording [his debt obligation shall be broken].

gap §w If a merchant [...] should take [...] interest and [...], then does not deduct the payments of either grain [or silver] as much as [he received, or] does not write a new tablet, or adds the interest payments to the capital sum, that merchant shall return twofold as much grain as he received.

gap §x If a merchant gives grain or silver as an interest-bearing loan and when he gives it as an interest-bearing loan he gives the silver according to the small weight or the grain according to the small *sūtu*-measure but when he receives payment he receives the silver according to the large weight or the grain according to the large *sūtu*-measure, [that merchant] shall forfeit [anything that he gave].[j]

j Lev 19:35-36; Deut 25:13-16; Hos 12:8; Amos 8:5; Prov 11:1; 20:10; 20:23

gap §y If [a merchant] gives [...] as an interest-bearing loan, [...] he shall forfeit anything that he gave.

gap §z If a man borrows grain or silver from a merchant and does not have grain or silver with which to repay but does have other goods, he shall give to his merchant in the presence of witnesses whatever he has at hand, in amounts according to the exchange value; the merchant will not object; he shall accept it.

gap §aa [If a man ...] like [...]

gap §bb [If...] he shall be killed.

gap §cc If a man gives silver to another man for investment in a partnership venture, before the god they shall equally divide the profit or loss.

§100 If a merchant gives silver to a trading agent for conducting business transactions and sends him off on a business trip, the trading agent [shall ...] while on the business trip; if he should realize [a profit] where he went, he shall calculate the total interest, per transaction and time elapsed, on as much silver as he took, and he shall satisfy his merchant.

§101 If he should realize no profit where he went, the trading agent shall give to the merchant twofold the silver he took.

§102 If a merchant should give silver to a trading agent for an investment venture, and he incurs a loss on his journeys, he shall return silver to the merchant in the amount of the capital sum.

§103 If enemy forces should make him abandon whatever goods he is transporting while on his business trip, the trading agent shall swear an oath by the god and shall be released.

§104 If a merchant gives a trading agent grain, wool, oil, or any other commodity for local transactions, the trading agent shall return to the merchant the silver for each transaction; the trading agent shall collect a sealed receipt for (each payment in) silver that he gives to the merchant.

§105 If the trading agent should be negligent and not take a sealed receipt for (each payment in) silver that he gives to the merchant, any silver that is not documented in a sealed receipt will not be included in the final accounting.

§106 If the trading agent takes silver from the merchant but then denies the claim of his merchant, that merchant shall bring charges and proof before the god and witnesses against the trading agent concerning the silver taken, and the trading agent shall give to the merchant threefold the amount of silver that he took.

§107 If a merchant entrusts silver to a trading agent and the trading agent then returns to his merchant everything that the merchant had given him but the merchant denies (having received) everything that the trading agent had given him, that trading agent shall bring charges and proof before the god and witnesses against the merchant, and because he denied the account of his trading agent, the merchant shall give to the trading agent sixfold the amount that he took.

§108 If a tapster should refuse to accept grain for the price of beer but accepts (only) silver measured by the large weight, thereby reducing the value of beer in relation to the value of grain, they shall charge and convict that tapster and they shall cast her into the water.

§109 If there should be a tapster in whose house criminals congregate, and she does not seize those criminals and lead them off to the palace authorities, that tapster shall be killed.

§110 If a *nadītu* or[4] an *ugbabtu* who does not reside within the cloister should open a tavern or enter a tavern for some beer, they shall burn that woman.[4a]

[4] Or: "If a *nadītu* who is an *ugbabtu* ..."

[4a] See Roth 1998.

§111 If a tapster gives one vat of beer as a loan(?), she shall take 50 SILA of grain at the harvest.

§112 If a man is engaged in a trading expedition and gives silver, gold, precious stones, or any other goods to another under consignment for transportation, and the latter man does not deliver that which was consigned to him where it was to be consigned but appropriates it, the owner of the consigned property shall charge and convict that man of whatever consignment he failed to deliver, and that man shall give to the owner of the consigned property fivefold the property that had been given to him.

§113 If a man has a claim of grain or silver against another man and takes grain from the granary or from the threshing floor without obtaining permission from the owner of the grain, they shall charge and convict that man of taking grain from the granary or from the threshing floor without the permission of the owner of the grain, and he shall return as much grain as he took; moreover, he shall forfeit whatever he originally gave as the loan.

§114 If a man does not have a claim of grain or silver against another man but distrains a member of his household, he shall weigh and deliver 20 shekels of silver for each distrainee.

§115 If a man has a claim of grain or silver against another man, distrains a member of his household, and the distrainee dies a natural death while in the house of her or his[5] distrainer, that case has no basis for a claim.

§116 If the distrainee should die from the effects of a beating or other physical abuse while in the house of her or his distrainer, the owner of the distrainee shall charge and convict his merchant, and if (the distrainee is) the man's son,[6] they shall kill his (the distrainer's) son; if the man's slave, he shall weigh and deliver 20 shekels of silver; moreover, he shall forfeit whatever he originally gave as the loan.

§117 If an obligation is outstanding against a man and he sells or gives into debt service his wife, his son, or his daughter, they shall perform service in the house of their buyer or of the one who holds them in debt service for three years; their release shall be secured in the fourth year.[k]

§118 If he should give a male or female slave into debt service, the merchant may extend the term (beyond three years), he may sell him; there are no grounds for a claim.

§119 If an obligation is outstanding against a man and he therefore sells his slave woman who has borne him children, the owner of the slave woman shall weigh and deliver the silver which the merchant weighed and delivered (as the loan) and he shall thereby redeem his slave woman.

§120 If a man stores his grain in another man's house, and a loss occurs in the storage bin or the householder opens the granary and takes the grain or he completely denies receiving the grain that was stored in his house — the owner of the grain shall establish his grain before the god, and the householder shall give to the owner of the grain twofold the grain that he took (in storage).[l]

§121 If a man stores grain in another man's house, he shall give 5 SILA of grain per GUR (i.e., per 300 SILA) of grain as annual rent of the granary.

§122 If a man intends to give silver, gold, or anything else to another man for safekeeping, he shall exhibit before witnesses anything which he intends to give, he shall establish a contract, and (in this manner) he shall give goods for safekeeping.

§123 If he gives goods for safekeeping without witnesses or a contract, and they deny that he gave anything, that case has no basis for a claim.

§124 If a man gives silver, gold, or anything else before witnesses to another man for safekeeping and he denies it, they shall charge and convict that man, and he shall give twofold that which he denied.

§125 If a man gives his property for safekeeping and his property together with the householder's property is lost either by (theft achieved through) a breach or by scaling over a wall, the householder who was careless shall make restitution and shall restore to the owner of the property that which was given to him for safekeeping and which he allowed to be lost; the householder shall continue to search for his own lost property, and he shall take it from the one who stole it from him.

§126 If a man whose property is not lost should declare, "My property is lost," and accuse his city quarter, his city quarter shall establish against him before the god that no property of his is lost, and he shall give to his city quarter twofold whatever he claimed.

k Exod 21:2-11; Lev 25:48-50; Deut 15:12-18

l Exod 22:6-9

[5] The Akk. *nipûtu* is fem., hence the fem. pronoun, but the person or animal given in distress could be male or female.

[6] Or: "(if the distress is) a member of the *awīlu*-class."

§127 If a man causes a finger to be pointed in accusation against an *ugbabtu* or against a man's wife but cannot bring proof, they shall flog that man before the judges and they shall shave off half of his hair.

§128 If a man marries a wife but does not establish a contract for her, that woman is not a wife.

§129 If a man's wife should be seized lying with another male, they shall bind them and cast them into the water; if the wife's master allows his wife to live, then the king shall allow his subject (i.e., the other male) to live.[m]

m Deut 22:22

§130 If a man pins down another man's virgin wife who is still residing in her father's house, and they seize him lying with her, that man shall be killed; that woman shall be released.[n]

n Deut 22:23-27

§131 If her husband accuses his own wife (of adultery), although she has not been seized lying with another male, she shall swear (to her innocence by) an oath by the god, and return to her house.

§132 If a man's wife should have a finger pointed against her in accusation involving another male, although she has not been seized lying with another male, she shall submit to the divine River Ordeal for her husband.[o]

o Num 5:11-31

§133a If a man should be captured and there are sufficient provisions in his house, his wife [..., she will not] enter [another's house].

§133b If that woman does not keep herself chaste but enters another's house, they shall charge and convict that woman and cast her into the water.

§134 If a man should be captured and there are not sufficient provisions in his house, his wife may enter another's house; that woman will not be subject to any penalty.

§135 If a man should be captured and there are not sufficient provisions in his house, before his return his wife enters another's house and bears children, and afterwards her husband returns and gets back to his city, that woman shall return to her first husband; the children shall inherit from their father.

§136 If a man deserts his city and flees, and after his departure his wife enters another's house — if that man then should return and seize his wife, because he repudiated his city and fled, the wife of the deserter will not return to her husband.

§137 If a man should decide to divorce a *šugītu* who bore him children, or a *nadītu* who provided him with children, they shall return to that woman her dowry and they shall give her one half of (her husband's) field, orchard, and property, and she shall raise her children; after she has raised her children, they shall give her a share comparable in value to that of one heir from whatever properties are given to her sons, and a husband of her choice may marry her.

§138 If a man intends to divorce his first-ranking wife who did not bear him children, he shall give her silver as much as was her bridewealth and restore to her the dowry that she brought from her father's house, and he shall divorce her.

§139 If there is no bridewealth, he shall give her 60 shekels of silver as a divorce settlement.

§140 If he is a commoner, he shall give her 20 shekels of silver.

§141 If the wife of a man who is residing in the man's house should decide to leave, and she appropriates goods, squanders her household possessions, or disparages her husband, they shall charge and convict her; and if her husband should declare his intention to divorce her, then he shall divorce her; neither her travel expenses, nor her divorce settlement, nor anything else shall be given to her. If her husband should declare his intention to not divorce her, then her husband may marry another woman and that (first) woman shall reside in her husband's house as a slave woman.[p]

p Deut 22:13-19, 28-29

§142 If a woman repudiates her husband, and declares, "You will not have marital relations with me" — her circumstances shall be investigated by the authorities of her city quarter, and if she is circumspect and without fault, but her husband is wayward and disparages her greatly, that woman will not be subject to any penalty; she shall take her dowry and she shall depart for her father's house.

§143 If she is not circumspect but is wayward, squanders her household possessions, and disparages her husband, they shall cast that woman into the water.

§144 If a man marries a *nadītu,* and that *nadītu* gives a slave woman to her husband, and thus she provides children, but that man then decides to marry a *šugītu*, they will not permit that man to do so, he will not marry the *šugītu*.

§145 If a man marries a *nadītu,* and she does not provide him with children, and that man then decides to marry a *šugītu*, that man may marry the *šugītu* and bring her into his house; that *šugītu* should not aspire to equal status with the *nadītu*.

§146 If a man marries a *nadītu,* and she gives a slave woman to her husband, and she (the slave) then bears children, after which that slave woman aspires to equal status with her mistress — because she bore children, her mistress will not sell her; (but) she may place upon her the slave-hairlock and reckon her with the slave women.

§147 If she does not bear children, her mistress may sell her.

§148 If a man marries a woman, and later *la᾿bum*-disease[7] seizes her and he decides to marry another woman, he may marry; he will not divorce his wife whom *la᾿bum*-disease seized; she shall reside in quarters he constructs and he shall continue to support her as long as she lives.

§149 If that woman should not agree to reside in her husband's house, he shall restore to her her dowry that she brought from her father's house, and she shall depart.

§150 If a man awards to his wife a field, orchard, house, or movable property, and makes out a sealed document for her, after her husband's death her children will not bring a claim against her; the mother shall give her estate to whichever of her children she loves, but she will not give it to an outsider.

§151 If a woman who is residing in a man's house should have her husband agree by contract that no creditor of her husband shall seize her (for his debts) — if that man has a debt incurred before marrying that woman, his creditors will not seize his wife; and if that woman has a debt incurred before entering the man's house, her creditors will not seize her husband.

§152 If a debt should be incurred by them after that woman enters the man's house, both of them shall satisfy the merchant.

§153 If a man's wife has her husband killed on account of (her relationship with) another male, they shall impale that woman.

§154 If a man should carnally know his daughter, they shall banish that man from the city.[q]

§155 If a man selects a bride for his son and his son carnally knows her, after which he himself then lies with her and they seize him in the act, they shall bind that man and cast him into the water.

§156 If a man selects a bride for his son and his son does not yet carnally know her, and he himself then lies with her, he shall weigh and deliver to her 30 shekels of silver; moreover, he shall restore to her whatever she brought from her father's house, and a husband of her choice shall marry her.

q Lev 18:6-18:1; 20:10-21; Deut 27:20-23

r Lev 18:7; 20:11

s Gen 35:22; 49:3-4; 1 Chr 5:1

§157 If a man, after his father's death, should lie with his mother, they shall burn them both.[r]

§158 If a man, after his father's death, should be discovered in the lap of his (the father's) principal wife who had borne children, that man shall be disinherited from the paternal estate.[s]

§159 If a man who has the ceremonial marriage prestation brought to the house of his father-in-law, and who gives the bridewealth, should have his attention diverted to another woman and declare to his father-in-law, "I will not marry your daughter," the father of the daughter shall take full legal possession of whatever had been brought to him.

§160 If a man has the ceremonial marriage prestation brought to the house of his father-in-law and gives the bridewealth, and the father of the daughter then declares, "I will not give my daughter to you," he shall return twofold everything that had been brought to him.

§161 If a man has the ceremonial marriage prestation brought to the house of his father-in-law and gives the bridewealth, and then his comrade slanders him (with the result that) his father-in-law declares to the one entitled to the wife, "You will not marry my daughter," he shall return twofold everything that had been brought to him; moreover, his comrade will not marry his (intended) wife.

§162 If a man marries a wife, she bears him children, and that woman then goes to her fate, her father shall have no claim to her dowry; her dowry belongs only to her children.

§163 If a man marries a wife but she does not provide him with children, and that woman goes to her fate — if his father-in-law then returns to him the bridewealth that that man brought to his father-in-law's house, her husband will have no claim to that woman's dowry; her dowry belongs only to her father's house.

§164 If his father-in-law should not return to him the bridewealth, he shall deduct the value of her bridewealth from her dowry and restore (the balance of) her dowry to her father's house.

§165 If a man awards by sealed contract a field, orchard, or house to his favorite heir, when the brothers divide the estate after the father goes to his fate, he (the favorite son) shall take the gift which the father gave to him and apart from that gift they shall equally divide the property of the paternal estate.

[7] The disease or illness *la᾿bu* may refer to a contagious skin disease; see Stol 1993:143 with literature.

§166 If a man provides wives for his eligible sons but does not provide a wife for his youngest son, when the brothers divide the estate after the father goes to his fate, they shall establish the silver value of the bridewealth for their young unmarried brother from the property of the paternal estate, in addition to his inheritance share, and thereby enable him to obtain a wife.

§167 If a man marries a wife and she bears him children, and later that woman goes to her fate, and after her death he marries another woman and she bears children, after which the father then goes to his fate, the children will not divide the estate according to the mothers; they shall take the dowries of their respective mothers and then equally divide the property of the paternal estate.

§168 If a man should decide to disinherit his son and declares to the judges, "I will disinherit my son," the judges shall investigate his case and if the son is not guilty of a grave offense deserving the penalty of disinheritance, the father may not disinherit his son.[t]

§169 If he should be guilty of a grave offense deserving the penalty of disinheritance by his father, they shall pardon him for his first one; if he should commit a grave offense a second time, the father may disinherit his son.

§170 If a man's first-ranking wife bears him children and his slave woman bears him children, and the father during his lifetime then declares to (or: concerning) the children whom the slave woman bore to him, "My children," and he reckons them with the children of the first-ranking wife — after the father goes to his fate, the children of the first-ranking wife and the children of the slave woman shall equally divide the property of the paternal estate; the preferred heir is a son of the first-ranking wife, he shall select and take a share first.

§171 But if the father during his lifetime should not declare to (or: concerning) the children whom the slave woman bore to him, "My children," after the father goes to his fate, the children of the slave woman will not divide the property of the paternal estate with the children of the first-ranking wife. The release of the slave woman and of her children shall be secured; the children of the first-ranking wife will not make claims of slavery against the children of the slave woman. The first-ranking wife shall take her dowry and the marriage settlement which her husband awarded to her in writing, and she shall continue to reside in her husband's dwelling; as long as she is alive she shall enjoy the use of it, but she may not sell it; her own estate shall belong (as inheritance) only to her own children.

§172 If her husband does not make a marriage settlement in her favor, they shall restore to her in full her dowry, and she shall take a share of the property of her husband's estate comparable in value to that of one heir. If her children pressure her in order to coerce her to depart from the house, the judges shall investigate her case and shall impose a penalty on the children; that woman will not depart from her husband's house. If that woman should decide on her own to depart, she shall leave for her children the marriage settlement which her husband gave to her; she shall take the dowry brought from her father's house and a husband of her choice shall marry her.

§173 If that woman should bear children to her latter husband into whose house she entered, after that woman dies, her former and latter children shall equally divide her dowry.

§174 If she does not bear children to her latter husband, only the children of her first husband shall take her dowry.

§175 If a slave of the palace or a slave of a commoner marries a woman of the *awīlu*-class and she then bears children, the owner of the slave will have no claims of slavery against the children of the woman of the *awīlu*-class.

§176a And if either a slave of the palace or a slave of a commoner marries a woman of the *awīlu*-class, and when he marries her she enters the house of the slave of the palace or of the slave of the commoner together with the dowry brought from her father's house, and subsequent to the time that they move in together they establish a household and accumulate possessions, after which either the slave of the palace or the slave of the commoner should go to his fate — the woman of the *awīlu*-class shall take her dowry; furthermore, they shall divide into two parts everything that her husband and she accumulated subsequent to the time that they moved in together, and the slave's owner shall take half and the woman of the *awīlu*-class shall take half for her children.

§176b If the woman of the *awīlu*-class does not have a dowry, they shall divide into two parts everything that her husband and she accumulated subsequent to the time that they moved in together, and the slave's owner

[t] Deut 21:18-21

shall take half and the woman of the *awīlu*-class shall take half for her children.

§177 If a widow whose children are still young should decide to enter another's house, she will not enter without (the prior approval of) the judges. When she enters another's house, the judges shall investigate the estate of her former husband, and they shall entrust the estate of her former husband to her latter husband and to that woman, and they shall have them record a tablet (inventorying the estate). They shall safeguard the estate and they shall raise the young children; they will not sell the household goods. Any buyer who buys the household goods of the children of a widow shall forfeit his silver; the property shall revert to its owner.

§178 If there is an *ugbabtu*, a *nadītu*, or a *sekretu* whose father awards to her a dowry and records it in a tablet for her, but in the tablet that he records for her he does not grant her written authority to give her estate to whomever she pleases and does not give her full discretion — after the father goes to his fate, her brothers shall take her field and her orchard and they shall give to her food, oil, and clothing allowances in accordance with the value of her inheritance share, and they shall thereby satisfy her. If her brothers should not give to her food, oil, and clothing allowances in accordance with the value of her inheritance share and thus do not satisfy her, she shall give her field and her orchard to any agricultural tenant she pleases, and her agricultural tenant shall support her. As long as she lives, she shall enjoy the use of the field, orchard, and anything else which her father gave to her, but she will not sell it and she will not satisfy another person's obligations with it; her inheritance belongs only to her brothers.

§179 If there is an *ugbabtu*, a *nadītu*, or a *sekretu* whose father awards to her a dowry and records it for her in a sealed document, and in the tablet that he records for her he grants her written authority to give her estate to whomever she pleases and gives her full discretion — after the father goes to his fate, she shall give her estate to whomever she pleases; her brothers will not raise a claim against her.

§180 If a father does not award a dowry to his daughter who is a cloistered *nadītu* or a *sekretu*, after the father goes to his fate, she shall have a share of the property of the paternal estate comparable in value to that of one heir; as long as she lives she shall enjoy its use; her estate belongs only to her brothers.

§181 If a father dedicates (his daughter) to the deity as a *nadītu*, a *qadištu*, or a *kulmašītu* but does not award to her a dowry, after the father goes to his fate she shall take her one-third share[8] from the property of the paternal estate as her inheritance, and as long as she lives she shall enjoy its use; her estate belongs only to her brothers.

§182 If a father does not award a dowry to his daughter who is a *nadītu* dedicated to the god Marduk of the city of Babylon or does not record it for her in a sealed document, after the father goes to his fate, she shall take with her brothers her one-third share[9] from the property of the paternal estate as her inheritance, but she will not perform any service obligations; a *nadītu* dedicated to the god Marduk shall give her estate as she pleases.

§183 If a father awards a dowry to his daughter who is a *šugītu*, gives her to a husband, and records it for her in a sealed document, after the father goes to his fate, she will not have a share of the property of the paternal estate.

§184 If a man does not award a dowry to his daughter who is a *šugītu*, and does not give her to a husband, after the father goes to his fate, her brothers shall award to her a dowry proportionate to the value of the paternal estate, and they shall give her to a husband.

§185 If a man takes in adoption a young child at birth and then rears him, that rearling will not be reclaimed.

§186 If a man takes in adoption a young child, and when he takes him, he (the child?) is seeking his father and mother, that rearling shall return to his father's house.

§187 A child of (i.e., reared by) a courtier who is a palace attendant or a child of (i.e., reared by) a *sekretu* will not be reclaimed.

§188 If a craftsman takes a young child to rear and then teaches him his craft, he will not be reclaimed.

§189 If he should not teach him his craft, that rearling shall return to his father's house.

§190 If a man should not reckon the young child whom he took and raised in adoption as equal with his children, that rearling shall return to his father's house.

---

[8] That is, not the preferential (double) inheritance share of a primary heir, but the single share of any other heir; the terminology derives from the paradigmatic case of two heirs in which the estate is divided into three parts.

[9] See note at §181.

§191 If a man establishes his household (by reckoning as equal with any future children) the young child whom he took and raised in adoption, but afterwards he has children (of his own) and then decides to disinherit the rearling, that young child will not depart empty-handed; the father who raised him shall give him a one-third share[10] of his property as his inheritance and he shall depart; he will not give him any property from field, orchard, or house.

§192 If the child of (i.e., reared by) a courtier or the child of (i.e., reared by) a *sekretu* should say to the father who raised him or to the mother who raised him, "You are not my father," or "You are not my mother," they shall cut out his tongue.

§193 If the child of (i.e., reared by) a courtier or the child of (i.e., reared by) a *sekretu* identifies with his father's house and repudiates the father who raised him or the mother who raised him and departs for his father's house, they shall pluck out his eye.

§194 If a man gives his son to a wet nurse and that child then dies while in the care of the wet nurse, and the wet nurse then contracts for another child without the consent of his father and mother, they shall charge and convict her, and, because she contracted for another child without the consent of his father and mother, they shall cut off her breast.

§195 If a child should strike his father, they shall cut off his hand.[u]

§196 If an *awīlu* should blind the eye of another *awīlu*, they shall blind his eye.[v]

§197 If he should break the bone of another *awīlu*, they shall break his bone.

§198 If he should blind the eye of a commoner or break the bone of a commoner, he shall weigh and deliver 60 shekels of silver.

§199 If he should blind the eye of an *awīlu*'s slave or break the bone of an *awīlu*'s slave, he shall weigh and deliver one-half of his value (in silver).[w]

§200 If an *awīlu* should knock out the tooth of another *awīlu* of his own rank, they shall knock out his tooth.

§201 If he should knock out the tooth of a commoner, he shall weigh and deliver 20 shekels of silver.

§202 If an *awīlu* should strike the cheek of an *awīlu* who is of status higher than his own, he shall be flogged in the public assembly with 60 stripes of an ox whip.

§203 If a member of the *awīlu*-class should strike the cheek of another member of the *awīlu*-class who is his equal, he shall weigh and deliver 60 shekels of silver.

§204 If a commoner should strike the cheek of another commoner, he shall weigh and deliver 10 shekels of silver.

§205 If an *awīlu*'s slave should strike the cheek of a member of the *awīlu*-class, they shall cut off his ear.

§206 If an *awīlu* should strike another *awīlu* during a brawl and inflict upon him a wound, that *awīlu* shall swear, "I did not strike intentionally," and he shall satisfy the physician (i.e., pay his fees).[x]

§207 If he should die from his beating, he shall also swear ("I did not strike him intentionally"); if he (the victim) is a member of the *awīlu*-class, he shall weigh and deliver 30 shekels of silver.[y]

§208 If he (the victim) is a member of the commoner-class, he shall weigh and deliver 20 shekels of silver.

§209 If an *awīlu* strikes a woman of the *awīlu*-class and thereby causes her to miscarry her fetus, he shall weigh and deliver 10 shekels of silver for her fetus.[z]

§210 If that woman should die, they shall kill his daughter.

§211 If he should cause a woman of the commoner-class to miscarry her fetus by the beating, he shall weigh and deliver 5 shekels of silver.

§212 If that woman should die, he shall weigh and deliver 30 shekels of silver.

§213 If he strikes an *awīlu*'s slave woman and thereby causes her to miscarry her fetus, he shall weigh and deliver 2 shekels of silver.

§214 If that slave woman should die, he shall weigh and deliver 20 shekels of silver.

§215 If a physician performs major surgery with a bronze lancet upon an *awīlu* and thus heals the *awīlu*, or opens an *awīlu*'s temple with a bronze lancet and thus heals the *awīlu*'s eye, he shall take 10 shekels of silver (as his fee).

§216 If he (the patient) is a member of the commoner-class, he shall take 5 shekels of silver (as his fee).

§217 If he (the patient) is an *awīlu*'s slave, the slave's master shall give to the physician 2 shekels of silver.

§218 If a physician performs major surgery with a bronze lancet upon an *awīlu* and thus causes the *awīlu*'s death, or opens an *awīlu*'s temple with a bronze lancet and thus blinds the *awīlu*'s eye, they shall cut off his hand.

u Exod 21:15
v Exod 21:23-25; Lev 24:18-20; Deut 19:21
w Exod 21:20-21, 26-27
x Exod 21:18-20; Num 35:9-15
y Exod 21:12-14; Num 35:9-34; Deut 19:1-13
z Exod 21:22-25

[10] See note at §181.

§219 If a physician performs major surgery with a bronze lancet upon a slave of a commoner and thus causes the slave's death, he shall replace the slave with a slave of comparable value.

§220 If he opens his (the commoner's slave's) temple with a bronze lancet and thus blinds his eye, he shall weigh and deliver silver equal to half his value.

§221 If a physician should set an *awīlu*'s broken bone or heal an injured muscle, the patient shall give the physician 5 shekels of silver.

§222 If he (the patient) is a member of the commoner-class, he shall give 3 shekels of silver.

§223 If he (the patient) is an *awīlu*'s slave, the slave's master shall give the physician 2 shekels of silver.

§224 If a veterinarian performs major surgery upon an ox or a donkey and thus heals it, the owner of the ox or of the donkey shall give the physician as his fee one sixth (of a shekel, i.e., 30 barleycorns) of silver.

§225 If he performs major surgery upon an ox or a donkey and thus causes its death, he shall give one quarter(?)[11] of its value to the owner of the ox or donkey.

§226 If a barber shaves off the slave-hairlock of a slave not belonging to him without the consent of the slave's owner, they shall cut off that barber's hand.

§227 If a man misinforms a barber so that he then shaves off the slave-hairlock of a slave not belonging to him, they shall kill that man and hang him in his own doorway; the barber shall swear, "I did not knowingly shave it off," and he shall be released.

§228 If a builder constructs a house for a man to his satisfaction, he shall give him 2 shekels of silver for each SAR of house as his compensation.

§229 If a builder constructs a house for a man but does not make his work sound, and the house that he constructs collapses and causes the death of the householder, that builder shall be killed.

§230 If it should cause the death of a son of the householder, they shall kill a son of that builder.

§231 If it should cause the death of a slave of the householder, he shall give to the householder a slave of comparable value for the slave.

§232 If it should cause the loss of property, he shall replace anything that is lost; moreover, because he did not make sound the house which he constructed and it collapsed, he shall construct (anew) the house which collapsed at his own expense.

§233 If a builder constructs a house for a man but does not make it conform to specifications so that a wall then buckles, that builder shall make that wall sound using his own silver.

§234 If a boatman caulks a boat of 60-GUR capacity for a man, he shall give him 2 shekels of silver as his compensation.

§235 If a boatman caulks a boat for a man but does not satisfactorily complete his work and within that very year the boat founders or reveals a structural defect, the boatman shall dismantle that boat and make it sound at his own expense, and he shall give the sound boat to the owner of the boat.

§236 If a man gives his boat to a boatman for hire, and the boatman is negligent and causes the boat to sink or to become lost, the boatman shall replace the boat for the owner of the boat.

§237 If a man hires a boatman and a boat and loads it with grain, wool, oil, dates, or any other lading, and that boatman is negligent and thereby causes the boat to sink or its cargo to become lost, the boatman shall replace the boat which he sank and any of its cargo which he lost.

§238 If a boatman should cause a man's boat to sink and he raises it, he shall give silver equal to half of its value.

§239 If a man hires a boatman, he shall give him 1,800 SILA of grain per year.

§240 If a boat under the command of the master of an upstream-boat collides with a boat under the command of the master of a downstream-boat and thus sinks it, the owner of the sunken boat shall establish before the god the property that is lost from his boat, and the master of the upstream-boat who sinks the boat of the master of the downstream-boat shall replace to him his boat and his lost property.

§241 If a man should distrain an ox, he shall weigh and deliver 20 shekels of silver.

§242/243 If a man rents it for one year, he shall give to its owner 1200 SILA of grain as the hire of an ox for the rear (of the team), and 900 SILA of grain as the hire of an ox for the middle (of the team).

§244 If a man rents an ox or a donkey and a lion kills it in the open country, it is the owner's loss.[aa]

§245 If a man rents an ox and causes its death either by negligence or by physical abuse, he shall replace the ox with an ox of compara-

[aa] Exod 22:12-15

[11] Or IGI.5.GÁL "one fifth."

ble value for the owner of the ox.

§246 If a man rents an ox and breaks its leg or cuts its neck tendon, he shall replace the ox with an ox of comparable value for the owner of the ox.

§247 If a man rents an ox and blinds its eye, he shall give silver equal to half of its value to the owner of the ox.

§248 If a man rents an ox and breaks its horn, cuts off its tail, or injures its hoof tendon, he shall give silver equal to one quarter of its value.

§249 If a man rents an ox, and a god strikes it down dead, the man who rented the ox shall swear an oath by the god and he shall be released.[bb]

§250 If an ox gores to death a man while it is passing through the streets, that case has no basis for a claim.[cc]

§251 If a man's ox is a known gorer, and the authorities of his city quarter notify him that it is a known gorer, but he does not blunt(?) its horns or control his ox, and that ox gores to death a member of the *awīlu*-class, he (the owner) shall give 30 shekels of silver.

§252 If it is a man's slave (who is fatally gored), he shall give 20 shekels of silver.

§253 If a man hires another man to care for his field, that is, he entrusts to him the stored grain, hands over to him care of the cattle, and contracts with him for the cultivation of the field — if that man steals the seed or fodder and it is then discovered in his possession, they shall cut off his hand.

§254 If he takes the stored grain and thus weakens the cattle, he shall replace twofold the grain which he received.

§255 If he should hire out the man's cattle, or he steals seed and thus does not produce crops in the field, they shall charge and convict that man, and at the harvest he shall measure and deliver 18,000 SILA of grain for every 18 *iku* of land.

§256 If he is not able to satisfy his obligation, they shall have him dragged around[12] through that field by the cattle.

§257 If a man hires an agricultural laborer, he shall give him 2,400 SILA of grain per year.

§258 If a man hires an ox driver, he shall give him 1,800 SILA of grain per year.

§259 If a man steals a plow from the common irrigated area, he shall give 5 shekels of silver to the owner of the plow.

§260 If he should steal a clod-breaking plow or a harrow, he shall give 3 shekels of silver.

bb Exod 22:9-10

cc Exod 21:28-36

dd Exod 22:9-14

ee Deut 25:4

§261 If a man hires a herdsman to herd the cattle or the sheep and goats, he shall give him 2400 SILA of grain per year.

§262 If a man [gives] an ox or a sheep to a [herdsman ...]

§263 If he should cause the loss of the ox or sheep which were given to him, he shall replace the ox with an ox of comparable value or the sheep with a sheep of comparable value for its owner.

§264 If a shepherd, to whom cattle or sheep and goats were given for shepherding, is in receipt of his complete hire to his satisfation, then allows the number of cattle to decrease, or the number of sheep and goats to decrease, or the number of offspring to diminish, he shall give for the (loss of) offspring and byproducts in accordance with the terms of his contract.

§265 If a shepherd, to whom cattle or sheep and goats were given for shepherding, acts criminally and alters the brand and sells them, they shall charge and convict him and he shall replace for their owner cattle or sheep and goats tenfold that which he stole.

§266 If, in the enclosure, an epidemic[13] should break out or a lion make a kill, the shepherd shall clear himself before the god, and the owner of the enclosure shall accept responsibility for him for the loss sustained in the enclosure.[dd]

§267 If the shepherd is negligent and allows mange(?) to appear in the enclosure, the shepherd shall make restitution — in cattle or in sheep and goats — for the damage caused by the mange(?) which he allowed to appear in the enclosure, and give it to their owner.

§268 If a man rents an ox for threshing, 20 SILA of grain is its hire.[ee]

§269 If he rents a donkey for threshing, 10 SILA of grain is its hire.

§270 If he rents a goat for threshing, 1 sila of grain is its hire.

§271 If a man rents cattle, a wagon, and its driver, he shall give 180 SILA of grain per day.

§272 If a man rents only the wagon, he shall give 40 SILA of grain per day.

§273 If a man hires a hireling, he shall give 6 barleycorns of silver per day from the beginning of the year until (the end of) the fifth month, and 5 barleycorns of silver per day from the sixth month until the end of the year.

§274 If a man intends to hire a craftsman, he shall

[12] Akk. expresses this in the active voice ("they shall drag him around ...").

[13] Lit. "a plague (or touch) of the god."

give, per [day]: as the hire of a ..., 5 barleycorns of silver; as the hire of a woven-textile worker, 5 barleycorns of silver; as the hire of a linen-worker(?), [x barleycorns] of silver; as the hire of a stone-cutter, [x barleycorns] of silver; as the hire of a bow-maker, [x barleycorns of] silver; as the hire of a smith, [x barleycorns of] silver; as the hire of a carpenter, 4(?) barleycorns of silver; as the hire of a leatherworker, [x] barleycorns of silver; as the hire of a reed-worker, [x] barleycorns of silver; as the hire of a builder, [x barleycorns of] silver.

§275 If a man rents a [...-boat], 3 barleycorns of silver per day is its hire.

§276 If a man rents a boat for traveling upstream, he shall give 20 barleycorns of silver as its hire per day.

§277 If a man rents a boat of 60-GUR capacity, he shall give one sixth (of a shekel, i.e., 30 barleycorns) of silver per day as its hire.

§278[14] If a man purchases a slave or slave woman and within his one-month period epilepsy then befalls him, he shall return him to his seller and the buyer shall take back the silver that he weighed and delivered.

§279 If a man purchases a slave or slave woman and then claims arise, his seller shall satisfy the claims.

§280 If a man should purchase another man's slave or slave woman in a foreign country, and while he is travelling about within the (i.e., his own) country the owner of the slave or slave woman identifies his slave or slave woman — if they, the slave and slave woman, are natives of the country, their release shall be secured without any payment.

§281 If they are natives of another country, the buyer shall declare before the god the amount of silver that he weighed, and the owner of the slave or slave woman shall give to the merchant the amount of silver that he weighed, and thus he shall redeem his slave or slavewoman.

§282 If a slave should declare to his master, "You are not my master," he (the master) shall bring charge and proof against him that he is indeed his slave, and his master shall cut off his ear.

Epilogue

Summation (lines xlvii.1-8)

These are the just decisions which Hammurabi, the able king, has established and thereby has directed the land along the course of truth and the correct way of life.

Hammurabi fulfills the gods' charge (lines xlvii.9-58)

I am Hammurabi, noble king. I have not been careless or negligent toward humankind, granted to my care by the god Enlil, and with whose shepherding the god Marduk charged me. I have sought for them peaceful places, I removed serious difficulties, I spread light over them. With the mighty weapon which the gods Zababa and Ishtar bestowed upon me, with the wisdom which the god Ea allotted to me, with the ability which the god Marduk gave me, I annihilated enemies everywhere, I put an end to wars, I enhanced the well-being of the land, I made the people of all settlements lie in safe pastures, I did not tolerate anyone intimidating them. The great gods having chosen me, I am indeed the shepherd who brings peace, whose scepter is just. My benevolent shade is spread over my city, I held the people of the lands of Sumer and Akkad safely on my lap. They prospered under my protective spirit, I maintained them in peace, with my skillful wisdom I sheltered them.

Erection of the monument (lines xlvii.59-78)

In order that the mighty not wrong the weak, to provide just ways for the waif and the widow, I have inscribed my precious pronouncements upon my stela and set it up before the statue of me, the king of justice, in the city of Babylon, the city which the gods Anu and Enlil have elevated, within the Esagil, the temple whose foundations are fixed as are heaven and earth, in order to render the judgments of the land, to give the verdicts of the land, and to provide just ways for the wronged.

Blessings (lines xlvii.79-xlix.17)

I am the king preeminent among kings. My pronouncements are choice, my ability is unrivaled. By the command of the god Shamash, the great judge of heaven and earth, may my justice prevail in the land. By the order of the god Marduk, my lord, may my engraved image not be confronted by someone who would remove it. May my name always be remembered favorably in the Esagil temple which I love.

May any wronged man who has a case come before the statue of me, the king of justice, and may he have my inscribed stela read aloud to him, thus may he hear my precious pronouncements and may my stela reveal the case for him; may he examine his case, may he calm his (troubled) heart, (and may he praise me), saying:

"Hammurabi, the lord, who is like a father and begetter to his people, submitted himself to the command of the god Marduk, his lord, and achieved victory for the god Marduk everywhere. He gladdened the heart of the god Marduk, his

[14] See Stol 1993, esp. pp. 133-135.

lord, and he secured the eternal well-being of the people and provided just ways for the land."

May he say thus, and may he pray for me with his whole heart before the gods Marduk, my lord, and Zarpanitu, my lady. May the protective spirits, the gods who enter the Esagil temple, and the very brickwork of the Esagil temple, make my daily portents auspicious before the gods Marduk, my lord, and Zarpanitu, my lady.

May any king who will appear in the land in the future, at any time, observe the pronouncements of.justice that I inscribed upon my stela. May he not alter the judgments that I rendered and the verdicts that I gave, nor remove my engraved image. If that man has discernment, and is capable of providing just ways for his land, may he heed the pronouncements I have inscribed upon my stela, may that stela reveal for him the traditions, the proper conduct, the judgments of the land that I judged, the decisions of the land that I rendered, and may he, too, provide just ways for all humankind in his care. May he render their judgments, may he give their verdicts, may he eradicate the wicked and the evil from his land, may he enhance the well-being of his people.

I am Hammurabi, king of justice, to whom the god Shamash has granted (insight into) the truth. My pronouncements are choice, and my achievements are praiseworthy. If that man (a future ruler) heeds my pronouncements which I have inscribed upon my stela, and does not reject my judgments, change my pronouncements, or alter my engraved image, then may the god Shamash lengthen his reign just as (he has done) for me, the king of justice, and so may he shepherd his people with justice.

Curses (lines xlix.18–li.91)
(But) should that man not heed my pronouncements, which I have inscribed upon my stela, and should he slight my curses and not fear the curses of the gods, and thus overturn the judgments that I judged, change my pronouncements, alter my engraved image, erase my inscribed name and inscribe his own name (in its place) — or should he, because of fear of these curses, have someone else do so — that man, whether he is a king, a lord, or a governor, or any person at all,

may the great god Anu, father of the gods, who has proclaimed my reign, deprive him of the sheen of royalty, smash his scepter, and curse his destiny.

May the god Enlil, the lord, who determines destinies, whose utterance cannot be countermanded, who magnifies my kingship, incite against him even in his own residence disorder that cannot be quelled and a rebellion that will result in his obliteration; may he cast as his fate a reign of groaning, of few days, of years of famine, of darkness without illumination, and of sudden death; may he declare with his venerable speech the obliteration of his city, the dispersion of his people, the supplanting of his dynasty, and the blotting out of his name and his memory from the land.

May the goddess Ninlil, the great mother, whose utterance is honored in the Ekur temple, the mistress who makes my portents auspicious, denounce his case before the god Enlil at the place of litigation and verdict; may she induce the divine king Enlil to pronounce the destruction of his land, the obliteration of his people[15] and the spilling of his life force like water.

May the god Ea, the great prince, whose destinies take precedence, the sage among the gods, all-knowing, who lengthens the days of my life, deprive him of all understanding and wisdom, and may he lead him into confusion; may he dam up his rivers at the source; may he not allow any life-sustaining grain in his land.

May the god Shamash, the great judge of heaven and earth, who provides just ways for all living creatures, the lord, my trust, overturn his kingship; may he not render his judgments, may he confuse his path and undermine the morale of his army; when divination is performed for him, may he provide an inauspicious omen portending the uprooting of the foundations of his kingship and the obliteration of his land; may the malevolent word of the god Shamash swiftly overtake him, may he uproot him from among the living above and make his ghost thirst for water below in the netherworld.

May the god Sin, my creator, whose oracular decision prevails among the gods, deprive him of the crown and throne of kingship, and impose upon him an onerous punishment, a great penalty for him, which will not depart from his body; may he conclude every day, month, and year of his reign with groaning and mourning; may he unveil before him a contender for the kingship; may he decree for him a life that is no better than death.

May the god Adad, lord of abundance, the canal-inspector of heaven and earth, my helper, deprive him of the benefits of rain from heaven and flood from the springs, and may he obliterate his land through destitution and famine; may he roar fierce ly over his city, and may he turn his land into the abandoned hills left by the Flood.

[15] Var.: "his city."

May the god Zababa, the great warrior, the first-born son of the Ekur temple, who travels at my right side, smash his weapon upon the field of battle; may he turn day into night for him, and make his enemy triumph over him.

May the goddess Ishtar, mistress of battle and warfare, who bares my weapon, my benevolent protective spirit, who loves my reign, curse his kingship with her angry heart and great fury; may she turn his auspicious omens into calamities; may she smash his weapon on the field of war and battle, plunge him into confusion and rebellion, strike down his warriors, drench the earth with their blood, make a heap of the corpses of his soldiers upon the plain, and may she show his soldiers no mercy; as for him, may she deliver him into the hand of his enemies, and may she lead him bound captive to the land of his enemy.

May the god Nergal, the mighty one among the gods, the irresistible onslaught, who enables me to achieve my triumphs, burn his people with his great overpowering weapon like a raging fire in a reed thicket; may he have him beaten with his mighty weapon, and shatter his limbs like (those of) a clay figure.

May the goddess Nintu, august mistress of the lands, the mother, my creator, deprive him of an heir and give him no offspring; may she not allow a human child to be born among his people.

May the goddess Ninkarrak, daughter of the god Anu, who promotes my cause in the Ekur temple, cause a grievous malady to break out upon his limbs, an evil demonic disease, a serious carbuncle which cannot be soothed, which a physician cannot diagnose, which he cannot ease with bandages, which, like the bite of death, cannot be expunged; may he bewail his lost virility until his life comes to an end.

May the great gods of heaven and earth, all the Anunnaku deities together, the protective spirit of the temple, the very brickwork of the Ebabbar temple, curse that one, his seed, his land, his troops, his people, and his army with a terrible curse.

May the god Enlil, whose command cannot be countermanded, curse him with these curses, and may they swiftly overtake him.

REFERENCES

Text: Harper 1904; Driver and Miles 1952; 1955; Borger 1979; Donbaz and Sauren 1991; Roth 1995/1997:71-142. Translations and studies: *ANET* 163-180; Finet 1973; *TUAT* 1:39-79; Saporetti 1984:49-92; Roth 1995; 1995/1997:71-142; 1999.

THE MIDDLE ASSYRIAN LAWS (2.132)
(Tablet A)

Martha Roth

A number of cuneiform tablets preserving thematic collections of laws were excavated in the Assyrian capital of Assur. The tablets are datable to about the eleventh century BCE, but are copies of compositions that probably date to fourteenth-century originals, and the language is the Middle Assyrian dialect. The laws recorded are thus as much as five hundred years later than the well-known Sumerian and Akkadian law collections of Ur-Namma of Ur, Lipit-Ishtar of Isin, Dadusha(?) of Eshnunna, and Hammurabi of Babylon. During this interval, following the end of the Old Babylonian dynasty of Hammurabi, the political landscape of Mesopotamia had shifted, and by the time of King Tiglath-pileser I (ca. 1114-1076 BCE) the dominant forces — the Hittites in Anatolia, the Egyptians in the Mediterranean coastal areas, and the Kassites in southern Mesopotamia — all had fallen before the Assyrian military power.

Each Middle Assyrian Laws tablet records what we might call a "chapter" with an apparently well-defined theme. The best preserved tablet, known as Tablet A, is inscribed with eight columns, each with about one hundred lines, recording rules and regulations detailing circumstances involving mostly women and incidentally other dependents.

There is one known duplicate manuscript which dates to the Neo-Assyrian period, suggesting that the composition retained value at least in the scribal curriculum.[1]

The Laws

A §1 If a woman, either a man's wife or a man's daughter, should enter into a temple and steal something from the sanctuary in the temple and either it is discovered in her possession or they prove the charges against her and find her guilty, [they shall perform(?)] a divination(?), they shall inquire of the deity; they shall treat her as the deity instructs them.

A §2 If a woman, either a man's wife or a man's daughter, should speak something disgraceful or utter a blasphemy, that woman alone bears responsibility for her offense; they shall have no claim against her husband, her sons, or her daughters.

A §3 If a man is either ill or dead, and his wife should steal something from his house and give it either to a man, or to a woman, or to anyone else, they shall kill the man's wife as well as the receivers (of the stolen goods). And if a man's wife, whose husband is healthy, should steal from her husband's house and give it either to a man, or to a woman, or to anyone else, the man shall prove the charges against his wife and shall impose a punishment; the receiver who received (the stolen goods) from the man's wife shall hand over the stolen goods, and they shall impose a punishment on the receiver identical to that which the man imposed on his wife.[a]

A §4 If either a slave or a slave woman should receive something from a man's wife, they shall cut off the slave's or slave woman's nose and ears; they shall restore the stolen goods; the man shall cut off his own wife's ears. But if he releases his wife and does not cut off her ears, they shall not cut off (the nose and ears) of the slave or slave woman, and they shall not restore the stolen goods.

A §5 If a man's wife should steal something with a value greater than 300 shekels of lead from the house of another man, the owner of the stolen goods shall take an oath, saying, "I did not incite her, saying, 'Commit a theft in my house.'" If her husband is in agreement, he (her husband) shall hand over the stolen goods and he shall ransom her; he shall cut off her ears. If her husband does not agree to her ransom, the owner of the stolen goods shall take her and he shall cut off her nose.

A §6 If a man's wife should place goods for safekeeping outside of the family, the receiver of the goods shall bear liability for stolen property.

A §7 If a woman should lay a hand upon a man and they prove the charges against her, she shall pay 1,800 shekels of lead; they shall strike her 20 blows with rods.

A §8 If a woman should crush a man's testicle during a quarrel, they shall cut off one of her fingers. And even if the physician should bandage it, but the second testicle then becomes infected(?) along with it and becomes ...,[2] or if she should crush the second testicle during the quarrel — they shall gouge out both her [...]-s.[3] [b]

A §9 If a man lays a hand upon a woman, attacking her like a rutting bull(?), and they prove the charges against him and find him guilty, they shall cut off one of his fingers. If he should kiss her, they shall draw his lower lip across the blade(?) of an ax and cut it off.

A §10 [If either] a man or a woman enters [another man's] house and kills [either a man] or a woman, [they shall hand over] the manslayers [to the head of the household]; if he so chooses, he shall kill them, or if he chooses to come to an accommodation, he shall take [their property]; and if there is [nothing of value to give from the house] of the manslayers, either a son [or a daughter ...]

A §11 [If ...]

A §12 If a wife of a man should walk along the main thoroughfare and should a man seize her and say to her, "I want to have sex with you!" — she shall not consent but she shall protect herself; should he seize her by force and fornicate with her — whether they discover him upon the woman or witnesses later prove the charges against him that he fornicated with the woman — they shall kill the man; there is no punishment for the woman.[c]

A §13 If the wife of a man should go out of her own house, and go to another man where he resides, and should he fornicate with her knowing that she is the wife of a man, they shall kill the man and the wife.[d]

a Exod 21:37-22:3
b Deut 25:11-12
c Deut 22:22-27
d Lev 20:10; Deut 22:22

[1] The most recent edition is in Roth 1995/1997, on which this translation is based, and to which the reader is referred for details of sources and earlier editions.

[2] Restoration [*e*]-*ri-im-ma* "became inflamed(?), atrophied(?)," remains uncertain; see *CAD* E 295 s.v. *erimu* discussion section.

[3] Possible restorations include "eyes" and "breasts"; see Paul 1990:337-38 with notes.

A §14 If a man should fornicate with another man's wife either in an inn or in the main thoroughfare, knowing that she is the wife of a man, they shall treat the fornicator as the man declares he wishes his wife to be treated. If he should fornicate with her without knowing that she is the wife of a man, the fornicator is clear; the man shall prove the charges against his wife and he shall treat her as he wishes.

A §15 If a man should seize another man upon his wife and they prove the charges against him and find him guilty, they shall kill both of them; there is no liability for him (i.e., the husband). If he should seize him and bring him either before the king or the judges, and they prove the charges against him and find him guilty — if the woman's husband kills his wife, then he shall also kill the man; if he cuts off his wife's nose, he shall turn the man into a eunuch and they shall lacerate his entire face; but if [he wishes to release] his wife, he shall [release] the man.[e]

A §16 If a man [should fornicate] with the wife of a man [... by] her invitation, there is no punishment for the man; the man (i.e., husband) shall impose whatever punishment he chooses upon his wife. If he should fornicate with her by force and they prove the charges against him and find him guilty, his punishment shall be identical to that of the wife of the man.

A §17 If a man should say to another man, "Everyone has sex with your wife," but there are no witnesses, they shall draw up a binding agreement, they shall undergo the divine River Ordeal.[4] [f]

A §18 If a man says to his comrade, either in private or in a public quarrel, "Everyone has sex with your wife," and further, "I can prove the charges," but he is unable to prove the charges and does not prove the charges, they shall strike that man 40 blows with rods; he shall perform the king's service for one full month; they shall cut off his hair;[5] moreover, he shall pay 3,600 shekels of lead.

A §19 If a man furtively spreads rumors about his comrade, saying, "Everyone sodomizes him,"[6] or in a quarrel in public says to him, "Everyone sodomizes you," and further, "I can prove the charges against you," but he is unable to prove the charges and does not prove the charges, they shall strike that man 50 blows with rods; he shall perform the king's service for one full month; they shall cut off his hair;[5] moreover, he shall pay 3,600 shekels of lead.[g]

A §20 If a man sodomizes his comrade and they prove the charges against him and find him guilty, they shall sodomize him and they shall turn him into a eunuch.

A §21 If a man strikes a woman of the *awīlu*-class thereby causing her to abort her fetus, and they prove the charges against him and find him guilty — he shall pay 9,000 shekels of lead; they shall strike him 50 blows with rods; he shall perform the king's service for one full month.[h]

A §22 If an unrelated man — neither her father, nor her brother, nor her son — should arrange to have a man's wife travel with him, then he shall swear an oath to the effect that he did not know that she is the wife of a man and he shall pay 7,200 shekels of lead to the woman's husband. If [he knows that she is the wife of a man], he shall pay damages and he shall swear, saying, "I did not fornicate with her." But if the man's wife should declare, "He did fornicate with me," since the man has already paid damages to the man (i.e., husband), he shall undergo the divine River Ordeal; there is no binding agreement. If he should refuse to undergo the divine River Ordeal, they shall treat him as the woman's husband treats his wife.

A §23 If a man's wife should take another man's wife into her house and give her to a man for purposes of fornication, and the man knows that she is the wife of a man, they shall treat him as one who has fornicated with the wife of another man; and they treat the female procurer just as the woman's husband treats his fornicating wife. And if the woman's husband intends to do nothing to his fornicating wife, they shall do nothing to the fornicator or to the female procurer; they shall release them. But if the man's wife does not know (what was intended), and the woman who takes her into her house brings the man in to her by deceit(?), and he then fornicates with her — if, as soon as she leaves the house, she should declare that she has been the victim of fornication, they shall release the woman, she is clear; they shall kill the fornicator and the female procurer.

e Jer 13:26-27; Ezek 16:37-39; 23:24-45; Hos 4-5

f Num 5:11-31

g Gen 19:1-14; Lev 18:22; 20:13

h Exod 21:22-25

[4] Cf. Frymer-Kensky 1984.

[5] Or "beard."

[6] Lit. "has sex with."

But if the woman should not so declare, the man shall impose whatever punishment on his wife he wishes; they shall kill the fornicator and the female procurer.

A §24 If a man's wife should withdraw herself from her husband and enter into the house of an Assyrian, either in that city or in any of the nearby towns, to a house which he assigns to her, residing with the mistress of the household, staying overnight three or four nights, and the householder is not aware that it is the wife of a man who is residing in his house, and later that woman is seized, the householder whose wife withdrew herself from him shall [mutilate] his wife and [not] take her back. As for the man's wife with whom his wife resided, they shall cut off her ears; if he pleases, her husband shall give 12,600 shekels of lead as her value, and, if he pleases, he shall take back his wife. However, if the householder knows that it is a man's wife who is residing in his house with his wife, he shall give "triple."[7] And if he should deny (that he knew of her status), he shall declare, "I did not know," they shall undergo the divine River Ordeal. And if the man in whose house the wife of a man resided should refuse to undergo the divine River Ordeal, he shall give "triple"; if it is the man whose wife withdrew herself from him who should refuse to undergo the divine River Ordeal, he (in whose house she resided) is clear; he shall bear the expenses of the divine River Ordeal. However, if the man whose wife withdrew herself from him does not mutilate his wife, he shall take back his wife; no sanctions are imposed.

A §25 If a woman is residing in her own father's house and her husband is dead, her husband's brothers have not yet divided their inheritance, and she has no son — her husband's brothers who have not yet received their inheritance shares shall take whatever valuables her husband bestowed upon her that are not missing. As for the rest (of the property), they shall resort to a verdict by the gods, they shall provide proof, and they shall take the property; they shall not be seized for (the settlement of any dispute by) the divine River Ordeal or the oath.

A §26 If a woman is residing in her own father's house and her husband is dead, if there are sons of her husband, it is they who shall take whatever valuables her husband bestowed upon her; if there are no sons of her husband, she herself shall take the valuables.

i Gen 38; Deut 25:5-10; Ruth 4

A §27 If a woman is residing in her own father's house and her husband visits her regularly, he himself shall take back any marriage settlement which he, her husband, gave to her; he shall have no claim to anything belonging to her father's house.

A §28 If a widow should enter a man's house and she is carrying her dead husband's surviving son with her (in her womb), he grows up in the house of the man who married her but no tablet of his adoption is written, he will not take an inheritance share from the estate of the one who raised him, and he will not be responsible for its debts; he shall take an inheritance share from the estate of his begetter in accordance with his portion.

A §29 If a woman should enter her husband's house, her dowry and whatever she brings with her from her father's house, and also whatever her father-in-law gave her upon her entering, are clear for her sons; her father-in-law's sons shall have no valid claim. But if her husband intends to take control(?) of her, he shall give it to whichever of his sons he wishes.

A §30 If a father should bring the ceremonial marriage prestation and present <the bridal gift> to the house of his son's father-in-law, and the woman is not yet given to his son, and another son of his, whose wife is residing in her own father's house, is dead, he shall give the wife of his deceased son into the protection of the household of his second son to whose father-in-law's house he has presented (the ceremonial marriage prestation). If the master of the daughter who is receiving the bridal gift decides not to agree to give his daughter (in these altered circumstances), if the father who presented the bridal gift so pleases, he shall take his daughter-in-law (i.e., the wife of his deceased son) and give her in marriage to his (second) son. And if he so pleases, as much as he presented — lead, silver, gold, and anything not edible — he shall take back in the quantities originally given; he shall have no claim to anything edible.[i]

A §31 If a man presents the bridal gift to his father-in-law's house, and although his wife is dead there are other daughters of his father-in-law, if he so pleases, he[8] shall marry a daughter of his father-in-law in lieu of his deceased wife. Or, if he so pleases, he shall

[7] The amount and nature of the compensation indicated by *šalšāte*, "one-third" or "triple," of what commodity it consists, and to whom it is paid, all remain obscure.

[8] Text: "the father-in-law" (error).

take back the silver that he gave; they shall not give back to him grain, sheep, or anything edible; he shall receive only the silver.

A §32 If a woman is residing in her own father's house and her [...] is given, whether or not she has been taken into her father-in-law's house, she shall be responsible for her husband's debts, transgression, or punishment.

A §33 If a woman is residing in her own father's house, her husband is dead, and she has sons [...], or [if he so pleases], he shall give her into the protection of the household of her father-in-law. If her husband and her father-in-law are both dead, and she has no son, she is indeed a widow; she shall go wherever she pleases.

A §34 If a man should marry a widow without her formal binding agreement and she resides in his house for two years, she is a wife; she shall not leave.

A §35 If a widow should enter into a man's house, whatever she brings with her belongs to her (new) husband; and if a man should enter into a woman's (house), whatever he brings with him belongs to the woman.

A §36 If a woman is residing in her father's house, or her husband settles her in a house elsewhere, and her husband then travels abroad but does not leave her any oil, wool, clothing, or provisions,[9] or anything else, and sends her no provisions from abroad — that woman shall still remain (the exclusive object of rights) for her husband for five years, she shall not reside with another husband. If she has sons, they shall be hired out and provide for their own sustenance; the woman shall wait for her husband, she shall not reside with another husband. If she has no sons, she shall wait for her husband for five years; at the onset of(?) six years, she shall reside with the husband of her choice; her (first) husband, upon returning, shall have no valid claim to her; she is clear for her second husband. If he is delayed beyond the five years but is not detained of his own intention, whether because a ... seized him and he fled or because he was falsely arrested and therefore he was detained, upon returning he shall so prove, he shall give a woman comparable to his wife (to her second husband) and take his wife. And if the king should send him to another country and he is delayed beyond the five years, his wife shall wait for him (indefinitely); she shall not go to reside with another husband. And furthermore, if she should reside with another husband before the five years are completed and should she bear children (to the second husband), because she did not wait in accordance with the agreement, but was taken in marriage (by another), her (first) husband, upon returning, shall take her and also her offspring.

A §37 If a man intends to divorce his wife, if it is his wish, he shall give her something; if that is not his wish, he shall not give her anything, and she shall leave empty-handed.

A §38 If a woman is residing in her own father's house and her husband divorces her, he shall take the valuables which he himself bestowed upon her; he shall have no claim to the bridewealth which he brought (to her father's house), it is clear for the woman.

A §39 If a man should give one who is not his own daughter in marriage to a husband — if (this situation arose because) previously her father had been in debt and she had been made to reside as a pledge — and a prior creditor should come forward, he (i.e., the prior creditor) shall receive the value of the woman, in full, from the one who gives the woman in marriage; if he has nothing to give, he (i.e., the prior creditor) shall take the one who gives the woman in marriage. However, if she had been saved from a catastrophe, she is clear for the one who saved her. And if the one who marries the woman either causes a tablet to be ... for him or they have a claim in place against him, he shall [...] the value of the woman, and the one who gives (the woman) [...]

A §40 Wives of a man, or [widows], or [any Assyrian] women who go out into the main thoroughfare [shall not have] their heads [bare]. Daughters of a man [... with] either a ...-cloth or garments or [...] shall be veiled, [...] their heads [... (gap of ca. 6 lines) ...] When they go about [...] in the main thoroughfare during the daytime, they shall be veiled. A concubine who goes about in the main thoroughfare with her mistress is to be veiled. A married *qadiltu*-woman is to be veiled (when she goes about) in the main thoroughfare, but an unmarried one is to leave her head bare in the main thoroughfare, she shall not veil herself. A prostitute shall not be veiled, her head shall be bare. Whoever sees a veiled prostitute shall seize her, secure witnesses, and bring her to the palace entrance. They shall not take away her jewelry, but he who has seized her takes her clothing; they shall strike her 50 blows with rods; they shall pour hot pitch over her head. And if a man should see a veiled pro-

[9] Paul 1969 and 1990 compares Exod 21:10 as well as LE §32 (above, p. 334) and LH §178 (above, p. 347).

stitute and release her, and does not bring her to the palace entrance, they shall strike that man 50 blows with rods; the one who informs against him shall take his clothing; they shall pierce his ears, thread them on a cord, tie it at his back; he shall perform the king's service for one full month. Slave women shall not be veiled, and he who should see a veiled slave woman shall seize her and bring her to the palace entrance; they shall cut off her ears; he who seizes her shall take her clothing. If a man should see a veiled slave woman but release her and not seize her, and does not bring her to the palace entrance, and they then prove the charges against him and find him guilty, they shall strike him 50 blows with rods; they shall pierce his ears, thread them on a cord, tie it at his back; the one who informs against him shall take his garments; he shall perform the king's service for one full month.[j]

A §41 If a man intends to veil his concubine, he shall assemble five or six of his comrades, and he shall veil her in their presence, he shall declare, "She is my *aššutu*-wife"; she is his *aššutu*-wife. A concubine who is not veiled in the presence of people, whose husband did not declare, "She is my *aššutu*-wife," she is not an *aššutu*-wife, she is indeed a concubine. If a man is dead and there are no sons of his veiled wife, the sons of the concubines are indeed sons; they shall (each) take an inheritance share.

A §42 If a man pours oil on the head of a woman of the *a*ʾ*īlu*-class on the occasion of a holiday, or brings dishes on the occasion of a banquet, no return (of gifts) shall be made.

A §43 If a man either pours oil on her head or brings (dishes for) the banquet, (after which) the son to whom he assigned the wife either dies or flees, he shall give her in marriage to whichever of his remaining sons he wishes, from the oldest to the youngest of at least ten years of age. If the father is dead and the son to whom he assigned the wife is also dead, a son of the deceased son who is at least ten years old[k] shall marry her. If the sons of the (dead) son are less than ten years old, if the father of the daughter wishes, he shall give his daughter (to one of them), but if he wishes he shall make a full and equal return (of gifts given). If there is no son, he shall return as much as he received, precious stones or anything not edible, in its full amount; but he shall not return anything edible.

j Gen 24:65; Isa 38:14, 19; 47:1-4

k Gen 38:11

A §44 If there is an Assyrian man or an Assyrian woman who is residing in a man's house as a pledge for a debt, for as much as his value, and he is taken for the full value (i.e., his value as pledge does not exceed that of the debt), he (the pledge holder) shall whip (the pledge), pluck out (the pledge's) hair, (or) mutilate or pierce (the pledge's) ears.

A §45[10] If a woman is given in marriage and the enemy then takes her husband prisoner, and she has neither father-in-law nor son (to support her), she shall remain (the exclusive object of rights) for her husband for two years. During these two years, if she has no provisions, she shall come forward and so declare. If she is a resident of the community dependent upon the palace, her [father(?)] shall provide for her and she shall do work for him. If she is a wife of a *ḫupšu*-soldier, [...] shall provide for her [and she shall do work for him]. But [if she is a wife of a man(?) whose] field and [house are not sufficient to support her(?)], she shall come forward and declare before the judges, "[I have nothing] to eat"; the judges shall question the mayor and the noblemen of the city to determine the current market rate(?) of a field in that city; they shall assign and give the field and house for her, for her provisioning for two years; she shall be resident (in that house), and they shall write a tablet for her (permitting her to stay for the two years). She shall allow two full years to pass, and then she may go to reside with the husband of her own choice; they shall write a tablet for her as if for a widow. If later her lost husband should return to the country, he shall take back his wife who married outside the family; he shall have no claim to the sons she bore to her later husband, it is her later husband who shall take them. As for the field and house that she gave for full price outside the family for her provisioning, if it is not entered into the royal holdings(?), he shall give as much as was given, and he shall take it back. But if he should not return but dies in another country, the king shall give his field and house wherever he chooses to give.

A §46 If a woman whose husband is dead does not move out of her house upon the death of her husband, if her husband (while alive) does not deed her anything in writing, she shall reside in the house of (one of) her own sons, wherever she chooses; her husband's sons shall provide for her, they shall draw up an

[10] Problems in restoration and interpretation of A §45 are discussed by Postgate 1971:502-8 and Aynard and Durand 1980:9-13.

agreement to supply her with provisions and drink as for an in-law whom they love. If she is a second wife and has no sons of her own, she shall reside with one (of her husband's sons) and they shall provide for her in common. If she does have sons, and the sons of a prior wife do not agree to provide for her, she shall reside in the house of (one of) her own sons, wherever she chooses; her own sons shall provide for her, and she shall do service for them. And if there is one among her husband's sons who is willing to marry her, [it is he who shall provide for her; her own sons] shall not provide for her.

A §47 If either a man or a woman should be discovered practicing witchcraft, and should they prove the charges against them and find them guilty, they shall kill the practitioner of witchcraft. A man who heard from an eyewitness to the witchcraft that he witnessed the practice of the witchcraft, who said to him, "I myself saw it," that hearsay-witness shall go and inform the king. If the eyewitness should deny what he (i.e., the hearsay-witness) reports to the king, he (i.e., the hearsay-witness) shall declare before the divine Bull-the-Son-of-the-Sun-God, "He surely told me" — and thus he is clear. As for the eyewitness who spoke (of witnessing the deed to his comrade) and then denied (it to the king), the king shall interrogate him as he sees fit, in order to determine his intentions; an exorcist shall have the man make a declaration when they make a purification, and then he himself (i.e., the exorcist) shall say as follows, "No one shall release any of you from the oath you swore by (or: before) the king and his son; you are bound by oath to the stipulations of the agreement to which you swore by (or: before) the king and by his son."[l]

A §48 If a man <wants to give in marriage> his debtor's daughter who is residing in his house as a pledge, he shall ask permission of her father[11] and then he shall give her to a husband. If her father does not agree, he shall not give her. If her father is dead, he shall ask permission of one of her brothers and the latter shall consult with her (other) brothers. If one brother so desires he shall declare, "I will redeem my sister within one month"; if he should not redeem her within one month, the creditor, if he so pleases, shall clear her of encumbrances and shall give her to a husband. [...] according to [...1 he shall give her [...]

l Exod 22:17; Lev 20:27; Deut 18:10-14

m Exod21:22-25

n Exod22:16-17; Deut 22:28-29

A §49 [...] like a brother [...]. And if the prostitute is dead, because(?) her brothers so declare they shall divide shares [with(?)] the brothers of their mother(?).

A §50 [If a man] strikes [another man's wife thereby causing her to abort her fetus, ...] a man's wife [...] and they shall treat him as he treated her; he shall make full payment of a life for her fetus. And if that woman dies, they shall kill that man; he shall make full payment of a life for her fetus. And if there is no son of that woman's husband, and his wife whom he struck aborted her fetus, they shall kill the assailant for her fetus. If her fetus was a female, he shall make full payment of a life only.[m]

A §51 If a man strikes another man's wife who does not raise her child, causing her to abort her fetus, it is a punishable offense; he shall give 7,200 shekels of lead.

A §52 If a man strikes a prostitute causing her to abort her fetus, they shall assess him blow for blow, he shall make full payment of a life.

A §53 If a woman aborts her fetus by her own action and they then prove the charges against her and find her guilty, they shall impale her, they shall not bury her. If she dies as a result of aborting her fetus,[12] they shall impale her, they shall not bury her. If any persons should hide that woman because she aborted her fetus [...]

A §54 [If...] or slave women [...]

A §55 If a man forcibly seizes and rapes a maiden who is residing in her father's house, [...] who is not betrothed(?), whose [womb(?)] is not opened, who is not married, and against whose father's house there is no outstanding claim — whether within the city or in the countryside, or at night whether in the main thoroughfare, or in a granary, or during the city festival — the father of the maiden shall take the wife of the fornicator of the maiden and hand her over to be raped; he shall not return her to her husband, but he shall take (and keep?) her; the father shall give his daughter who is the victim of fornication into the protection of the household of her fornicator. If he (the fornicator) has no wife, the fornicator shall give "triple" the silver as the value of the maiden to her father; her fornicator shall marry her; he shall not reject(?) her. If the father does not desire it so, he shall receive "triple" silver for the maiden, and he shall give his daughter in marriage to whomever he chooses.[n]

[11] Text: "Her father will ask ..."

[12] Or "If the fetus dies as a result of the (attempted) abortion"(?).

A §56 If a maiden should willingly give herself to a man, the man shall so swear; they shall have no claim to his wife; the fornicator shall pay "triple" the silver as the value of the maiden; the father shall treat his daughter in whatever manner he chooses.

A §57 Whether it is a beating or [... for] a man's wife [... that is (specifically)] written on the tablet [...]

A §58 For all punishable offenses [...] cutting off [...] and... [...]

A §59 In addition to the punishments for [a man's wife] that are [written] on the tablet, a man may [whip] his wife, pluck out her hair, mutilate her ears, or strike her, with impunity.

Subscript

Month 2, day 2, eponymate of Sagiu.

REFERENCES

Texts: Driver and Miles 1935; Aynard and Durand 1980; Roth 1995/1997:153-194. Translations and studies: *ANET* 180-188; Cardascia 1969; *TUAT* 1:80-92; Saporetti 1984; Paul 1990; Roth 1995/1997:153-194.

THE NEO-BABYLONIAN LAWS (2.133)

Martha Roth

For almost a thousand years after the fall of the Old Babylonian dynasty of Hammurabi, the Assyrian empires held dominance throughout most of the Near East before the Neo-Babylonian dynasty (ca. 635-539 BCE), established following the defeat of the Assyrians by the combined Median and Babylonian forces, assumed the central military, political, and cultural position in the area. The first rulers of this dynasty, Nabopolassar (ca. 625-605 BCE) and Nebuchadnezzar II (ca. 604-562 BCE), consciously emulated the postures, rhetoric, and activities of the Hammurabi dynasty in order to establish their dynasty as legitimate linear successor to the great empires of the past.

One tablet dating to the Neo-Babylonian period preserves a copy of a damaged or incomplete original compilation of fifteen laws or cases. At the beginning of the last column of the obverse, in an area that could contain about ten lines, there is centered a short two-line notation that reads, "Its case (or judgment, etc.) is not complete and is not written (here)." This note is to be understood either as an indication that the original from which this tablet was copied was damaged (a situation usually marked by the expression *ḫīpi eššu* "new break," *ḫīpi labīru* "old break," etc.), or, perhaps more likely, that there was a case pending whose results would be summarized in this space at a later time.[1]

The Laws

§1 [...] in the presence of the owner of the field [...] in the presence of the owner of the field [...] the owner of the field [...] they wrote [...] year 2 [...] the king [...]

§2 [A man who ...] field [...] pastures [...] he pastures [...] the testimony which he will provide ... of the field [...], he shall give [grain] in accordance with the (yields of his) neighbor to the owner of the field; [... as much as] he pastured, he shall give grain in accordance with the (yields of his) neighbor.

§3 [A man who opens] his well to the irrigation outlet but does not reinforce it, and who thus causes a breach and thereby [floods] his neighbor's field, shall give [grain in accordance with the (yields of his)] neighbor [to the owner of the field].

§4 [...] an onager [...] he shall give.

§5 A man who seals a tablet as owner of (i.e., who buys) a field or a house in another's name, but does not make out a contract of proxy for the matter or does not take a copy of the tablet — it is the man in whose name the tablet and sale document are written who shall take the field or house.

§6 A man who sells a slave woman against whom a claim arises so that she is taken away — the seller shall give to the buyer the silver (of the purchase price) in its capital amount according to the sale document. Should she bear children (while in the possession of the buyer), he shall give half a shekel of silver each.

§7 A woman who performs a magic act or a ritual purification against(?) (i.e., in order to affect?) a man's field, or a boat, or a kiln, or anything whatsoever — (if it is a field, then concerning) the trees (or: wood) among which(?) she performs the ritual, she shall give to the owner of the field threefold its yield. If she performs the purification

[1] The most recent edition is in Roth 1995/1997, on which this translation is based, and to which the reader is referred for details of sources and earlier editions.

against(?) (i.e., in order to affect?) a boat, or a kiln, or anything else, she shall give threefold the losses caused to the property (text: field). Should she be seized [performing the purification] against(?) (i.e., in order to affect?) the door of a man's [house], she shall be killed.[2] [a]

§x Its case[3] is not complete and is not written (here).

§8 A man who gives his daughter in marriage to a member of the *amēlu*-class, and the father (of the groom) commits certain properties in his tablet and awards them to his son, and the father-in-law commits the dowry of his daughter, and they write the tablets in mutual agreement — they will not alter the commitments of their respective tablets. The father will not make any reduction to the properties as written in the tablet to his son's benefit which he showed to his in-law. Even should the father, whose wife fate carries away, then marry a second wife and should she then bear him sons, the sons of the second woman shall take one third[4] of the balance of his estate.

§9 A man who makes an oral promise of the dowry for his daughter, or writes it on a tablet for her, and whose estate later decreases — he shall give to his daughter a dowry in accordance with the remaining assets of his estate; the father-in-law (i.e., the bride's father) and the groom will not by mutual agreement alter the commitments.

§10 A man who gives a dowry to his daughter, and she has no son or daughter, and fate carries her away — her dowry shall revert to her paternal estate.

§11 [A wife who ...] fate [carries her away (...)] to a son [...] — she shall give her dowry to her husband or to whomever she wishes.

a Exod 22:17

§12 A wife whose husband takes her dowry, and who has no son or daughter, and whose husband fate carries away — a dowry equivalent to the dowry (which her husband had received) shall be given to her from her husband's estate. If her husband should award to her a marriage gift, she shall take her husband's marriage gift together with her dowry, and thus her claim is satisfied. If she has no dowry, a judge shall assess the value of her husband's estate, and shall give to her some property in accordance with the value of her husband's estate.

§13 A man marries a wife, and she bears him sons, and later on fate carries away that man, and that woman then decides to enter another man's house — she shall take (from her first husband's estate) the dowry that she brought from her father's house and anything that her husband awarded to her, and the husband she chooses shall marry her; as long as she lives, they shall have the joint use of the properties. If she should bear sons to her (second) husband, after her death the sons of the second and first (husbands) shall have equal shares in her dowry. [...]

§14 [...] her husband [...] she shall take [...] to her father [...]

§15 A man who marries a wife who bears him sons, and whose wife fate carries away, and who marries a second wife who bears him sons, and later on the father goes to his fate — the sons of the first woman shall take two-thirds of the paternal estate, and the sons of the second shall take one-third. Their sisters, who are still residing in the paternal home [...]

Subscript

[... king of] the city of Babylon.

[2] See Roth 1995/1997:149 note 7.

[3] The Akk. word *dīnu* is translatable as "case," "decision," or "judgment," and refers both to the entire proceedings of a suit or trial and to the decision rendered by the officiating judge. The antecedent of "its" in LNB §7 is not clear; the reference could be to a defective original exemplar from which this tablet was copied, or to a court case that has not yet been decided.

[4] I.e., not the preferential or double share; see note to LH §181.

REFERENCES

Text: Peiser 1889; Driver and Miles 1955:324-347; Petschow 1959; Szlechter 1971; 1972; 1973; Roth 1995/1997:143-149. Translations and studies: *ANET* 197-198; *TUAT* 1:92-95; Saporetti 1984:117-120; Roth 1995/1997:143-149.

3. EDICTS

THE EDICTS OF SAMSU-ILUNA AND HIS SUCCESSORS (2.134)

William W. Hallo

The dynasty of Hammurapi survived his death by over 150 years (1749-1595 BCE).[1] But such was the fame of his laws that his five successors did not openly dare to replace them. Instead they apparently contrived to modify them by issuing relatively briefer collections of laws in the form of edicts. The process began with Hammurapi's immediate successor, his son Samsu-iluna (1749-1712), continued with what may have been an edict of Ammi-ditana (1683-1647)[2] and concluded with Ammi-saduqa (1646-1626). The translation is based on the last edict, which is the best preserved, with significant variants from the earlier one(s) given in the footnotes.

Preamble

Document of the ... when [the king] (re)-estab[lished] equity for the land.[3]

§1 The arrears of the farmers,[4] shepherds, fellmongers[5] of the pasture lands, or (any other) tenants[6] of the palace[7] are remitted for the sake of strengthening them and treating them righteously;[8] the collection-agent may not dun the property[9] of the tenant.

§2 The "board of trade"[10] of Babylon, the boards of trade of the land, (and) the compensator who are assigned to the tax-collector in the end-of-the-year tablet — their arrears which [date] from the year (called) "By king Ammi-ditana the debts of the land which they had repeatedly incurred were remitted"[11] to the month Nisannu[12] of <the year> (called) "King Ammi-saduqa, whose princeship the divine Enlil had magnified, dawned truly like the Sungod over his nation (and) set its numerous people on the right path"[13] [a] are remitted because the king established equity for the land; the tax-collector may not dun their property.

§3 Whoever has given barley or silver to an Akkadian or an Amorite[14] either [as a loan at in]terest or as demand-loan [...] and has had a (legal) document drawn up (about it) — because the king has established equity for the land, his tablet will be voided; he may not collect barley or silver according to the wording of the tablet.

§4 But if from the second day of the last month of the year (called) "King Ammi-ditana destroyed the wall of Udinim which Dam(i)q-ilishu had built"[15] he has demanded and collected repayment of a loan outside of the season for collection, he must, because he has demanded and collected repayment outside of the season for collection, return that which he has collected and misappropriated.[16] [b] He who does not return it according to the royal edict will die.[17]

§5 Whoever has given barley or silver as a loan at interest or as a demand-loan to an Akkadian or an Amorite and in his sealed document which he had drawn up has committed fraud[18] by having it written up as a purchase

a Lev 25; Deut 15; etc.

b 2 Sam 12:4

[1] All dates given in this section are BCE and conform to the "middle chronology," according to which Hammurapi reigned from 1792-1750.

[2] So tentatively Kraus 1984:293. His suggestion is followed here, though it is not entirely excluded that his Edict "X" is simply another exemplar of Samsu-iluna's Edict. Lieberman 1989:251 and Jursa 1997:142 favor Abi-eshuch (1711-1684).

[3] The Edict of Samsu-iluna devotes the entire preamble to a date, by month, day and year, the last expressed in an unusually complete form (in Sum.) of the name of the eighth year of the king (1742).

[4] I.e. *iššakku*'s, at this time a class of privileged farmers or landed gentry; see *CAD* s.v.

[5] An administrative functionary concerned with the disposal of animal carcasses.

[6] I.e., <*našī*> *bilātim*, lit.: "tribute bearers." Cf. *COS* 2.131 §§36-38, 41 ("state tenant").

[7] Samsu-iluna is broken here but probably omits "of the palace" and has sing. forms for the four professions mentioned.

[8] Samsu-iluna has instead as motivating clause: "because the king has established equity."

[9] Lit.: "shout against the house."

[10] Lit.: "the wharf, quay."

[11] I.e. the 21st year of Ammi-saduqa's father and predecessor or 1663. Note that this and the next date formula are both cited in Sum., in their full official form.

[12] I.e. the first month.

[13] I.e. Ammi-saduqa's first (full) year on the throne, or 1646. The implication is that 17 years had elapsed between these two royal remissions of debts. For the "periodicity" of such acts and their comparison with biblical *yôbel* and *šemiṭṭa* cf. Hallo 1995:90f. and literature cited there (n. 59).

[14] The two principal ethnic elements in Babylonia at the time.

[15] I.e. 1647, the last year of the preceding reign and the year immediately preceding the presumed date of this edict. The Dam(i)q-ilishu in question is probably the third king of the Sealand Dynasty.

[16] *lequ*, "take," is here used in the sense of "take legitimately but in abuse of power"; cf. the next § and §113 of the Laws of Hammurapi as well as the Hebrew cognate *lqḥ* in 2 Sam 12:4 and in the Meṣad Ḥashavyahu ostracon for which see Dobbs-Allsopp 1994:50.

[17] This provision is quoted almost verbatim in a letter from the time of Samsu-iluna; see Hallo 1995:82.

[18] So with Finkelstein 1969:52 against Kraus 1979.

or as a bailment, and has thus misappropriated interest — they shall bring his (the debtor's) witnesses and con[vict him] (the creditor) of misappropriating interest.[19] Because he has falsified his sealed document, his sealed document will be voided.

§6 A creditor may not dun the property of an [Akkadian] or an Amorite to whom he extended credit. If he duns, he dies.

§7 If a man has given barley or silver as a loan and has had a document drawn up, then hangs on to the document and says: "I did *not* give it as a loan or as a demand-loan, I gave it for purchase, as an advance (for a commercial venture), or for some other purpose," the man who received barley or silver from the entrepreneur shall bring his witnesses to the effect that the lender has altered the wording of the document. Before the deity he shall declare (it) and because (the lender) has changed his document and moreover has altered the words, he shall give[20] six-fold. If he cannot meet his responsibility, he shall die.

§8 An Akkadian or an Amorite who has received barley, silver or movable property for purchase, for business travel, for partnership or advance — his document will not be invalidated. He must pay according to the wording of his contracts.

§9 (A lender) who has given barley, silver or movable property for purchase, for business travel, for partnership, (or) as an advance to an Akkadian or an Amorite and has had a sealed document drawn up (and) in the sealed document which he has had drawn up the entrepreneur has had it written that once its deadline has passed then the silver bears interest, or else has entered into additional contracts — he need not return it as per the wording of the contracts; the barley or silver which he has received ... he must return but the (additional) contracts are remitted to the Akkadian or Amorite.

§10 [As to the merchandise of the pal]ace — to the mercantile association[21] of Babylon, of Borsippa, of Isin, of Larsa, of Idamaras, of Malgium, of Mankisum, of Shitullum — [to the extent of] half the purse the purchase will be given to them in the palace, half they will supply; of the merchandise, it will be given to them in the palace exactly according to the price of the city.

§11 If an entrepreneur who retails the merchandise of the palace has drawn up a sealed document in (regard to) the arrears of a tenant (of the palace) up to (an amount) like the merchandise which he has received in (i.e. from) the palace, and moreover he has received the sealed document of the tenant, the merchandise according to the wording of his sealed document has not been given to him in the palace or else he has not received (it) from the tenant — because the king has remitted the arrears of the tenant(s), that entrepreneur shall clear himself (by oath) before the deity (to the effect that) "I have taken nothing from the tenant of that which is according to the sealed document," and once he has so cleared himself, he shall bring the sealed document of the tenant. They[22] shall confront each other, make the (necessary) deductions, and remit[23] to the entrepreneur out of the purchase which is according to the wording of their sealed document which the entrepreneur drew up for the palace as much as he drew up for the entrepreneur according to the sealed document of the tenant.

§12 A fellmonger of the land[24] who takes delivery [of cadavers] before the deity from the hands of a cattle-herder, a herder of sheep, (or) a herder of goats of the palace and who pays the palace one and a half sheqel together with the hide per naturally deceased cow, one-sixth sheqel + 5 grains together with the hide as well as one and two-thirds pounds + 5 sheqel wool per naturally dead ewe, (or) one-[...] silver together with the hide and two-thirds pounds goats hair per goat — because the king established equity for the land one will not collect their arrears. The [...] of the fellmongers of the land will not be supplied.

§13 The arrears of the porters which were given to a collector for collecting — it is remitted; it will not be collected.

§14 The arrears of Suhum in barley (subject to a share-cropping deduction of) one-third and the arrears in barley (subject to a share-cropping deduction of) one-half — because the king has established equity for the land, it is remitted; it will not be collected; the property of[25] Suhum will not be dunned.

[19] Cf. n. 16 above.
[20] Ammi-ditana in error or: its six.
[21] I.e. kar; cf. above note 10. The word is omitted here, but repeated with each subsequent geographical name.
[22] I.e. the creditor and debtor.
[23] I.e. forgive.
[24] I.e. of Babylonia.
[25] Ammi-ditana inserts: "the people of."

§15[26] A tax-collector who collects a tithe[27] on the yield of a field, sesame or a minor crop of a tenant, a dignitary, grandees, a subordinate, a soldier, a "fisher," or (the bearer) of any (other) duty of Babylon and its environs — because the king has established equity for the land, it (the tithe) is remitted; it shall not be collected, (but) the barley pertaining to the purchasing (of the palace) and the ancillary income (of the tenant) will be tithed according to the old tax-rate.

§16 An alewife of the environs who pays out silver for the barley of the brewer[28] to the palace — because the king has established equity for the land, the collection-agent shall not dun for their arrears.

§17 An alewife who has sold beer or barley on credit shall not collect for whatever she has sold on credit.

§18 An alewife or an entrepreneur who by means of an untrue seal [...] shall die.

§19 A soldier or "fisher" who rents a field for three years [for the purpose of opening the field to cultivat]ion shall not perform [his obligatory labor by the side of an ancillary source of income]. In this year, because the king has established equity for the country, the soldier or "fisher" shall pay either one-third or one-half (of the yield of the field)[29] depending on the share (normally due to an owner) of (i.e. in) his city.

§20 If a citizen[30] of Numhia, of Emutbal, of Idamaras, of Uruk, of Isin, of Kisurra, [or of Malgium] — an obligation requires him to give his [child], his wife, [or himself] for silver, to work off the debt or as a security deposit, because the king has established equity for the land, (the obligation) is remitted; his release is granted.

§21 If a slave-woman (or) slave — "born in the house" [c] of a citizen[31] of Numhia, of Emutbal, of Idamaras, of Uruk, of Isin, of Kisurra, of Malgium, or of the land — for a full price is sold for money, or else is made to work off a debt, or else is deposited as security: his release will not be granted.

§22[32] A "compensator" of the military governor of the land who forces barley, silver or wool on a soldier or a "fisher" for harvesting or for performing (other) labor shall die. The soldier or "fisher" may carry off whatever has been forced on him.

c Gen 17:12-13, 23, 27; Lev 22:11

[26] Omitted by Ammi-ditana. The "fisher" (*bāʾiru*) is "a military auxiliary" (*CAD* B 32); cf. *COS* 2.131 §§26-39 ("fisherman").
[27] For this meaning of *makāsu*, see Hallo 1998:209f.
[28] Ammi-ditana: barley and silver of the brewer.
[29] I.e. the share due to the owner, in this case presumably the palace.
[30] Lit. "son"; the word is repeated with each of the following geographical names.
[31] See note 30 above.
[32] Samsu-iluna and Ammi-ditana omit.

REFERENCES

Kraus 1958; 1965; 1979; 1984; Finkelstein 1961; 1969; Bar-Maoz 1980; Sweet 1986; Charpin 1987; Lieberman 1989; Hallo 1995; 1998.

4. BOUNDARY STONES

THE "SUN DISK" TABLET OF NABÛ-APLA-IDDINA (2.135)

Victor Hurowitz

This inscription, beautifully engraved on a black stone tablet measuring 7" x 11 5/8" x 2", was found at Abu-Habbah (= Sippar) in 1881 by H. Rassam and is now in the British Museum.[1] A relief occupying the top third of the obverse shows a large disk sitting on a table, suspended by ropes held by two deities.[1a] To the right of the disk and facing it, the sun-god Šamaš is seated on a throne under a canopy.[2] To the left of the disk, facing it and Šamaš, are a priest, a king, and a goddess. The text dates to 20 Nisannu in the thirty-first year of Nabû-apla-iddina (spring of ca 839 BCE; column 6 line 28),[3] king of Babylon, but was discovered in a clay box containing impressions of inscrip-

[1] There has been, to date, no comprehensive treatment covering all parts of this inscription. Naʾaman (1972:6-7) translates the entire text anew, save the curses, and offers several improvements. Jacobsen (1987:20-23) discusses in detail the first half of the inscription and the light it sheds on cult statues in Mesopotamian.
[1a] For a very late echo of the scene depicted, see Maimonides, *Guide to the Perplexed* Bk. 3, Ch. 29, as pointed out by Reiner 1996. Note also *ANEP* 653 for a sun disc on a table.
[2] For translations of the epigraphs identifying the characters in the relief see King 1912:120-121, notes.
[3] Nabû-apla-iddina's dates are not known exactly. See Brinkman 1968:182f., n. 1121.

tions of Nabonidus (555-539 BCE). The inscription has the content, language, literary structure and function of the so-called *kudurru*'s and like them is engraved on hard black stone with a relief. It differs only in shape and type of relief.[4] Like the *kudurru*'s it is a monument commemorating a royal grant of real-estate and income to a priest.[5] [a] The first half of the inscription (i.1–iv.34) describes how the image of Šamaš was lost and eventually restored, and the deed for which the priest is rewarded, namely, the "discovery" of a model of the lost image which enabled the king to fashion a new one. The rest of the document (iv.35–vi.31) stipulates the privileges granted. Some scholars have suggested that the reported discovery was a pious fraud, while others claim the entire document to be a pious fraud.[6] The text is a narrative which combines prose and poetic elements.

The disappearance of Šamaš's statue and cult (i.1-12)
Šamaš, the great lord,
resident of Ebabarra[7] which is inside Sippar,
whom, during the confusion and disturbances in (the land of) Akkadê,
the Suteans,[8] the wicked enemy,
had disturbed and obliterated (his)[9] form[10] —
his (cultic) ordinances were forgotten,
and his appearance and appurtenances disappeared,
and no-one saw (them) anymore;

Unsuccessful attempts to recover statue (i.13-23)
So Simbar-Šihu, king of Babylon,[11]
inquired about his appearance,
but he (Šamaš) did not turn to him his face.[12]
His image and his appurtenances he (the king) did not see,
so a disk of the blazing sun which is before Šamaš he suspended,[13]
and established his offerings;
and Ekur-šum-ušabši, the high priest[14] of Sippar, the diviner
he had take responsibility (for them).

Decline in cult (i.24-ii.17)
In the famine and starvation under king Kaššu-nādin-ahhe[15]
that offering was cut off,[16] [b]
and the (fragrant) sacrifice[17] ceased.[18] [c]

In (the days of) Eulmaš-šākin-šumi the king,[19]
Ekur-šum-ušabši, the high-priest of Sippar, the diviner,[20]
approached the king his lord
and: "the regular offering of Šamaš has ceased" he said;
so one SILA of food, and one SILA of drink,
the food allowance of the manager of Esagila,[21]
(to be taken) from the regular offering of Bel,[22] [d]
he (the king) established for Šamaš,
and (to) Ekur-šum-ušabši, high-priest of Sippar, the diviner, he granted (it).
A garden in the territory of Newtown[23] which is in Babylon,
he gave to Šamaš,
and (to) Ekur-šum-ušabši, the high priest of Sippar, the diviner,
he entrusted (it).[e]

a Exod 25-Lev 10
b Joel 1:9
c Dan 11:31; 12:11
d Isa 46:1; Jer 50:2; 51:44
e Num 35:1-8; Jos 21; Ezek 45:1-4

[4] Modern scholars sometimes refer to the inscription as a *kudurru*, but this may be a misnomer. In vi.43 the text refers to itself as a *narû*, a general term for "monument." For the function of such stones see Hurowitz 1997:1-4.
[5] Weinfeld (1970:185, nn. 5, 10) includes the *kudurru*'s, to which this text is essentially identical, among the ANE grants providing prototypes for biblical covenants of the unconditional type. In its combination of cult legend with stipulation of priestly allowances, King 1912:36 resembles the Priestly sections of Exod 25–Lev 10 which describe the fabrication of the Tabernacle and incorporate in it the laws of sacrifice.
[6] Brinkman 1968:189f., n. 1159; Powell 1991:30.
[7] Lit. "Bright House."
[8] See Heltzer 1981:90-93.
[9] Following Naʾaman 1972. The antecedent of the pronominal suffix *-šu*, "its" or "his," is ambiguous. Others take it to refer to the temple. This is doubtful since the text concerns the statue rather than the temple.
[10] *uṣurtu* is used in i.8; iii. 2, 19, 30 to designate an object with a form as well as a model of an object. Cf. BH *ṣûrā*, Ezek 43:11.
[11] 1026-1009 BCE. This king's name has been read also as Simbar-Šipak or Simmaš-šihu. See Brinkman 1968:150-155.
[12] I.e. the god did not pay attention to the king. For *pāni nadānum* see Cohen 1993:234; 25.
[13] For interpretation of the Akk. term *niphu* see Brinkman 1976. The disk set up is probably the one shown in the relief. Since Šamaš and the sun are one and the same, a sun-shaped disk was considered a proper representation of the god and could substitute temporarily for the missing anthropomorphic image. This form of the sun is visible to everyone, so it need not be divinely revealed to the king. Cf. Reiner 1996.
[14] The title *šangû*, translated here "high priest," designates the chief temple administrator.
[15] Brinkman 1968:156-157.
[16] To Akk. *satukku ipparis*, "the offering was cut off" cf. Heb. *hokrat minḥāh wānesek mibbêt YHWH*, "offerings and libations were cut off from the House of the Lord" (Joel 1:9, and cf. 13).
[17] The *surqinnu* offering is often described as fragrant (see *CAD* S s.v.). Cf. Heb. *rēyaḥ niḥōaḥ*.
[18] To Akk. *baṭil surqinnu* (i.28) and *ginê Šamaš baṭil* (ii.1-2), both meaning "the sacrifce ceased," cf. *hûsar hattāmîd* (Dan 11:31; 12:11), and esp. Mishnaic Heb. *bāṭal hattāmîd* (Ta'anit 4:6).
[19] Brinkman 1968:160-162.
[20] Šamaš was the patron deity of divination, so it is entirely appropriate that the high priest in his temple serve in this capacity.
[21] Marduk's temple in Babylon. Lit., "House with the raised head."
[22] Marduk, lit., "Lord."
[23] *Ālu eššu* was a quarter in the north-east of Babylon. See George 1992 passim, esp. 375-376.

Commission of Nabû-apla-iddina by Marduk and Šamaš (ii.18-iii.18)
Afterwards,
Nabû-apla-iddina[24]
king of Babylon,
called by Marduk,[f]
beloved of Anum and Ea,
pleaser of the heart of Ṣarpanitu,[25]
the heroic male, who is suited for kingship,
bearer of a fierce bow,
overthrower of the wicked enemy, the Sutean,
whose sin was very great,
who[26]
to avenge Akkadê,
(to) settle cult centers,
(to) found divine daises,
(to) form forms,
(to) perfectly perform (cultic) ordinances and laws,
(to) establish offerings,
(and to) make bread offerings lavish,
the great lord Marduk,
a just scepter,
(and) performing shepherdship of humanity,
had placed in his hand —
Šamaš, the great lord,
who, for many days,
had been angry with the land of Akkadê
and had wrathfully shown his neck,[27] [g]
in the term of Nabû-apla-iddina, king of Babylon,
became placated,
and turned towards (him) his face.[28]

Revelation of a model of the lost statue (iii.19-iv.11)
A form of his image, a baked piece of clay,
(showing) his appearance and appurtenances,
across the Euphrates,
on the west bank (of the city)[29] was seen,[h]
and Nabû-nādin-šumi, the high priest of Sippar, the diviner,
from the seed of Ekur-šum-ušabši, the high priest of Sippar, the diviner,
that form of the image,
to Nabû-apla-iddina, the king, his lord, revealed;[30]
and Nabû-apla-iddina, king of Babylon,
to whom making that image was commanded,
and who was so selected,
saw that image,
and his face smiled,
joyous was his inside.[31]

Manufacture and induction of the new statue (iv.12-34)
To fashioning that image[32]
he set his mind,
and by the skill of Ea,[33]
by the craft of Nin-ildu, Kusig-banda, Ninkurra, Ninzadim,
with red gold
and bright lapis-lazuli,
the image of Šamaš the great lord
he correctly tended to.[34]
By the purification rites of Ea and Asalluhi,[35]
in the presence of Šamaš,
in E-kar-zaginna[36]
which is on the bank of the Euphrates,
he washed its (the image's) mouth,[37]
and it (the image) sat in its abode.[38]
Sacrifices, as the heart's desire,
of huge oxen,
plump, lovely, and fat sheep,
he sacrificed;
and with honey, wine, and flour,
he made the locks overflow.[39] [i]

f Isa 42:6
g Jer 18:17
h Exod 25:9, 40; 27:8; Num 8:4; 2 Kgs 16:10; Ezek 43:11; 1 Chr 28:11-19
i Exod 30:26-29; 40:9-11; Lev 8:10

[24] The royal name is followed by a string of seven titles. See Brinkman 1968:182-192 for Nabû-apla-iddina's reign and 189 for translation of ii.18–iii.10.

[25] Marduk's spouse.

[26] The commission consists of eight infinitive phrases which are indirect objects of the main verb. The subject "the great lord Marduk" provides a break between the seventh and eighth, following a well known pattern by which a linguistic form is repeated seven times, building up to a climax in the eighth repetition.

[27] Akk. *itti Akkadê ikmelu išbusu kišassu* followed by *salīma iršīma usahhira pānīšu* is comparable to *ᶜōrep welōᵓ pānîm ᵓerᵓēm beyôm ᵓêdām* in Jer 18:17.

[28] See Cohen 1993:235.

[29] For *balri šalām Šamši*, see George 1992:377-378.

[30] For revelation of forms of temples and various cultic objects see Hurowitz 1992a:168-170; Lee 1993.

[31] Cf. Cohen 1993:231-232.

[32] For iv.12-28, see George 1992:302.

[33] Ea is god of wisdom, including artistic skill. The four gods listed after him are patron deities of several individual crafts and technologies. They appear together, with certain variations, in other texts dealing with the production of cult statues, e.g., Erra (*COS* 1.113) tablet i.155-160; Borger *Asarh.* 89:23.

[34] By using the word *kunnû*, "to tend to with care," the text avoids stating explicitly that the king made the statue, and solves thereby the theological problem of a human creating a god. See Jacobsen 1987:23-29 for the expression of this idea in the mouth-washing ceremony.

[35] Asalluhi is Marduk when functioning in the realm of magic. For the origin of Asalluhi and the history of his being subsumed under the figure of Marduk see Sommerfeld 1982 passim and esp. 13-18.

[36] This temple is regularly associated with the mouth-washing and mouth-opening rituals. See George 1992 passim, esp. 302-303.

[37] The mouth-washing ritual (*mīs pî*) was the ritual *par excellance* for purifying the newly fashioned divine statue and turning it into a living god. See Jacobsen 1987 and now Walker and Dick 1999.

[38] The new statue is installed in Ebabbara. See Hurowitz 1992:260-284.

[39] For use of oil in dedication ceremonies see Hurowitz 1992:278-279.

The grant to the priest (iv.35-vi.16)[40] [j]

At that time —
of Nabû-apla-iddinna,
king of Babylon,
his heart rejoiced,
and shining was his countenance.[41]
Towards Nabû-nādin-šumi, high priest of Sippar, the diviner
he lifted his face.[42]
With his bright face,
(and) his ruddy countenance,[43]
(and) his beautiful (generous) eyes,[44] [k]
happily he looked at him.[45]

1 And one *sila* of food, one *sila* of drink,
the old regular offering of Šamaš
along with the orchard
which Eulmaš-šākin-šumi the king
(to) Ekur-šum-ušabši,
the high-priest of Sippar, the diviner,
had granted (Nabû-apla-iddina reaffirmed);

2 FROM the food, drink, confection, beef, mutton, fish, and vegetables,[46]
which as an innovation Nabû-apla-iddina, king of Babylon, to Šamaš, Aja, and Bunene had established:
THE first half of the king's share
is (to be) the food allowance of the high priest;

3 FROM the sheep of the king's sacrifices of the entire year: (THE high priest will receive) the loins, the skin, the hind-quarters, the muscles, half the stomach, half the intestines, two knuckle-bones, and a vessel of meat-broth;[47]

4 FROM the sacrifices of cattle and sheep of the worshipper[48]:
(THE high priest's portion is to be) as above;[49] [l]

5 FROM the five prebends of the *ērib-bīti*[50] office:
(THE high priest is to receive) two portions of food, drink, confection, beef, mutton, fish, and vegetables;

6 (FROM the) butchers'[51] [m] prebend and (from) the internal organs:
(THE high priest is to receive a portion) equivalent to that of two *ērib-bīti* priests;

7 FROM the small and enlarged regular offerings from the customary dues of the city —
(from) the flour offering of the worshipper,
and (from) whatever is brought into Ebabarra:
THE first half of the king's share
is the food allowance of the high priest,
as well as two portions like those of two *ērib-bīti*-priests;

Beautiful garments of all sorts belonging to Šamaš, Aja and Bunene:[52] [n]
a linen[53] garment;
a *pulḫu* garment;
a *qarbītu* garment;
a *šerʾitu* garment;
a wrap;
a sash;
a red wool garment;
a purple wool garment; [o]
a large *qarbītu* garment;
and a *tēlītu*[54] [p] of the *kāribu*-priest;

For the seventh day of Nisannu, a *šerʾitu* garment;
for the tenth day of Ajjaru a *šerʾitu* garment;
for the third day of Ululu a *qarbītu* garment;
for the seventh day of Tašrītu a *qarbītu* garment;
for the fifteenth day of Arahsamna, a *šerʾitu* garment;
for the fifteenth day or Addaru, a *qarbītu* garment;

j Exod 29:27-28; Lev 6-7; Num 18:8-32; Deut 18:3-5; 1 Sam 2:13-17; Ezek 44:30
k Deut 15:9; 28:54, 56; Prov 23:6 etc.
l Lev 4:10, 20, 21, 31, 35
m 1 Sam 9:23
n Judg 8:27; Isa 30:22
o Jer 10:9
p 1 Sam 2:19

[40] This section is similar in function to the neo-Assyrian grants to priests such as Postgate 1969: no. 42-48, 51 and 52-53, and the Punic tariffs from Marseilles (*KAI* 69 = *COS* 1.98) and Carthage (*KAI* 74 = *ANET* 503).

[41] See Muffs 1969:130-131, 202; 1992:124-125, 134:24. Descriptions of happiness associated with giving are metaphors expressing volition.

[42] See Fishbane 1983:117.

[43] A physiologically correct description of a smiling, happy face. Not "healthy appearance" as *CAD* Z 120b s.v. *zīmu*.

[44] *damqat inīšu*, "beauty of his eyes" (iv.45) is usually taken to mean "bright eyed" and an expression of volition or kindness, but it probably has an added nuance of "generously." It is the equivalent of BH *ṭôb* ᶜ*ayin* ("One good of eye [*ṭôb* ᶜ*ayin*] will be blessed for he gives his food to the poor" Prov 22:9) and the common Rabbinic term ᶜ*ayin yāpāh* (eg. T. Betza 29b "a woman measures out flour on the holiday and puts it into her dough in order that she will remove the required sacrificial portion generously — *be*ᶜ*ayin yāpāh*.) The opposite term ᶜ*ayin rā*ᶜ*āh*, "bad eye," means "stingy" (see Deut 15:9; 28:54, 56; Prov 23:6 etc.).

[45] The text lists seven prebends granted the priest. Each of passages 2-7 stipulates first the source of the prebend, and then the quantity granted.

[46] Seven types of foodstuffs are mentioned.

[47] See McEwan 1983:194, n. 27.

[48] The word *kāribu*, translated here "worshipper" may designate a type of priest.

[49] King, not appreciative of the structure of the list, translated "in accordance with the following list." It is clear, however, that the reference is to what is mentioned previously and not further on. For internal reference in a list of sacrificial dues see Lev 4:10, 20, 21, 31 and 35 where the Heb. *kaʾăšer* parallels the Akk. *kīma annîm*.

[50] A type of priest. Lit., "one who enters the temple."

[51] *AHw* s.v. *ṭābiḫūtu*. See 1 Sam 9:23 and Deller 1985.

[52] Ten types of garments are listed. See Matsushima 1993; 1994; Waetzold 1980.

[53] *AHw* s.v. *pulḫu* reads *kitê! ṣubāt pulḫu* (of the deity).

[54] *AHw* 1345a translates "Ertrag(sabgabe)." Perhaps the text refers to divine clothing contributed by worshippers.

a total of six beautiful garments for the entire year,
a gift of the king, belonging to Šamaš, Aja and Bunene;

(All of the above) Nabû-apla-iddina
king of Babylon,
(to) Nabû-nādin-šumi,
high priest of Sippar, the diviner, his servant granted;[55]
and in order that it (the prebend) not be vindicated,
he sealed it,
and displayed it (this document) for ever.[q]

Witnesses (vi.17-31)
At the sealing of that document
Marduk-šum-ukīn son of Habban, the dirge singer;
Ittabši-ilu son of Ea-rimanni, the minister;
Marduk-šāpik-zēri son of Tuballaṭ-Ištar, the cup-bearer;
and Marduk-balassu-iqbi son of Arad-Ea,[56] the governor
were present.

At Babylon, Nisannu the twentieth,

q Lev 7:35-36

r Deut 7:24

s 1 Kgs 13:24; Jer 9:21

t 2 Kgs 9:10, 35-37; Jer 8:2; 14:16; 16:4, 6; 25:33; Ps 79:3

the thirty-first year of Nabû-apla-iddina king of Babylon.
Copy (of a document marked) "The royal seal for assigning prebends."[57]

Maledictions to protect the grant (vi.32-55)[58]
Whoever in the future
who in the palace authoritatively will stand,
and the grant of king Nabû-apla-iddina will vindicate,
and to someone else will grant it;
(or) will from the food make a diminution,
(or) to the governor will assign it,
or to himself will take it;
or by some evil action
that monument he will destroy —

that person,
by the word of Šamaš, Aja[59] and Bunene[60]
masters of the decisions of the great gods,
may his name perish,[r]
may his seed be gathered up;
in hunger and starvation
may his life come to an end;
may his corpse fall down[61] [s]
and someone to bury it may it not have![62] [t]

[55] This passages recapitulates in summary form iv.35-46 and completes the sentence. The two passages together constitute an inclusio enveloping the list of seven prebends. For similar structures in some *kudurru*'s see Hurowitz 1992b:40-41, n. 7.

[56] Arad-Ea is not the biological father of Marduk-balassu-iqbi, but the *pater familias* of a long line of high officials mentioned in numerous documents over a period of several hundred years.

[57] Kienast 1987:172-173.

[58] This section first lists potential violations of the grant and against the document itself, followed by the maledictions proper.

[59] Šamaš's spouse.

[60] Šamaš's vizier.

[61] To Akk. *limqut šalmassu*, "may his corpse fall" cf. *wenāpelāh niblat hā'ādām kedōmen* "the corpse of the man will fall like dung" (Jer 9:21). A more frequent expression combines *nebēlāh* with *hošlak* (1 Kgs 13:24), equivalent to Akk. *šalamtam nadû*, "to cast the corpse away."

[62] For not being buried see 2 Kgs 9:10, 35-37; Jer 8:2; 14:16; 16:4, 6; 25:33; Ps 79:3.

REFERENCES

Text: King 1912:#36. Picture: *ANEP* 529; Dick 1999:59. Studies: Brinkman 1968:182-192; 1976; Cohen 1993; Fishbane 1983; George 1992; Heltzer 1981; Hurowitz 1992a; 1992b; 1997; Jacobsen 1987; Kienast 1987; Lee 1993; McEwan 1983; Matsushima 1993; 1994; Muffs 1969; 1992; Na'aman 1972; Oppenheim 1949; Postgate 1969; Powell 1991; Reiner 1996; Sommerfeld 1982; Waetzold 1980; Weinfeld 1970.

5. ROYAL GRANTS

WILL OF AMMITAKU LEADER OF ALALAKH (2.136)
(*AT* 6*)

Richard S. Hess

This Middle Bronze Age (Level VII) text may be compared to the account of David's arrangement for the public proclamation of Solomon as king and his successor in 1 Kings 1. Both examples reflect the concern for royal succession which provides for the stability of the government.

1 Ammitaku
2 the governor of Alalakh,[1] [a]
3 during his lifetime,
4 in the presence of Yarimlim the king,
5 his lord,
6 he willed his house:
7 his city house, city areas, fields,
8 and whatever is his,
9 just as his father and his mother
10 had appointed him to be king
14 he has appointed
11 Hammurabi his son,
12-13 whom Nawarari bore to him, to be governor of the city.[1] [a]
15 Thus he said:
16 ... Hammurabi my son
17-18 [...]
19-20 There is no other heir.
21 Hammurabi is the lord of my city
22 and my house.
23 He is the servant of Yarimlim the king
24 my lord.

Witnesses:
25 Wirišilazuḫi a *šangu*-priest,
26 Nawari a canal worker,[2]
27 Zu[k]raši overseer of the army,
28 Warimuza a šatammu administrator,
29 Subaḫali a šangu priest,
30 Ammia a governor,
31 Arammara a judge,
32 Ikunbali a steward,
33 Ari-Teššub a scribe,
34 Bani-Dagan overseer of the citizens.

35 In the month of Ḫiyari, the seventeenth day,
36 the year when king Yarimlim
38 slew
37 the leader of Qa<t>na(?).

a 2 Sam 10:6, 8

[1] The use of the Akk. word for "man" *amīlu* in construct with the name of the town ruled may have parallels in the biblical text. See 2 Samuel 10:6, 8; Hess 1990.

[2] Read here *sēkiru*, "canal worker" for LÚ A.DU$_8$.IGI! (= A.IGI.DU$_8$?).

REFERENCES

Text: *AT* 33-34 and pl. v. Translation: *AT* 33.

LAND GRANT *AT* 456* (2.137)

Richard S. Hess

This Middle Bronze Age (Level VII) document from Alalakh begins with a record of eight towns that Abbael gave to Yarimlim. Yarimlim in turn gave to Abbael Uwiya (lines 1-9). Adrate (see also *AT* 79 where Adrate is exchanged between Yarimlim and Ammitaku) is given in exchange for some areas (lines 11-12). Six towns are then noted as in the possession of Yarimlim (lines 13-18).

As a land grant this is an important document for comparison with the land grant texts of Joshua 13-21. In both *AT* 456 and Joshua the past gifts or exchanges of towns and lands are reviewed (lines 1-18; see Joshua 13) as a background for the present gift or exchange of land (lines 19ff.; see Joshua 14-21). Also in both texts the transfer of towns is set in the context of a greater agreement, a treaty or a covenant (see Joshua 8:30-35; 24). See also Hess 1994b; 1996a; 1996b:59-60.

Review of past exchanges of towns (lines 1-18)
1 The city of Emar together with its pasture land(?),[1] [a]
2 Zar[ ]at,
3 [ ]na,
4 Naštarpi,
5 Zabunap,
6 Kazkuwa,
7 Ammakki,
8 Parrie,
9 in exchange for the town Uwiya.
10 The town Adrate
11 in exchange for the land which
12 is in[ ].
13 Amame,
14 Aušun,
15 Ḫalliwa,
16 Zikir,
17 Murar,
18 Irridi — Yarimlim [ruled them(?)].

Yarimlim's history of loyalty (lines 19-30)
19 Zitraddu, the governor of [Irridi],

a Josh 21; 24

[1] For references to towns with their surrounding pasture lands or districts, see Joshua 24 and the list of Levitical towns. There the term is used repeatedly with the towns mentioned (Hess 1996b:281).

20 revolted against Yarimlim and
21 [then he led (?)] robber bands(?)
22 and brought them to Irridi, his city.
23-24 He incited the whole land to rebel against Abbael [ ].
25 The mighty weapon [ ]
26 with silver, gold, lapis lazuli, crystal(?), and the great [wea]pon
27 of the weather god. (As for Abbael,) he seized Irridi and
28 captured the enemy bands(?).
29 To Aleppo
30 he returned in peace.

Abbael's gift of Alalakh (lines 31-39)

<He said:>

31 "Irridi is destroyed.
32 Will I give it to my brother?
33 In exchange for Irridi
34 [which] rebelled [against] him
35 [and which I captur]ed and d[estroyed,]
36 [Alal]akh
37 [I will give to Ya]rimlim.[2] [b]
38 The town of Murar, in addition to [his shar]e,
39 I will add to it." Abbael

Abbael's oath of the perpetuity of the gift (lines 40-42)[3] [c]

40 swore the oath to Yarimlim
41 and cut the neck of a lamb, <saying:>
42 "If I take back what I have given you <may I be cursed.>"

Acts of disloyalty that cause the gift to be forfeited (lines 43-76)

43 If ever in the future
44 Yarimlim sins against Abbael, or
45 [if] he gives away Abbael's secrets
46 to another king,
47 or if he lets go of the hem of Abbael's garment
48 and grasps the hem of another king's garment,[4] [d]
49 his towns and lands
50 he shall [forfeit]. If a descendant of
51 Yarimlim sins against Abbael,
52 (or a descendant of Abbael),
53 if he rel[ease]s the h[em] of Abbael's
54 garment, (or that of a descendant of Abbael),
55 and if he seizes the hem of another king's garment,
56 his towns and lands
57 he shall forfeit. If a descendant of
58 [Y]arimlim [tries to] sell his town
59 their older brother
60 shall bu[y it]
60-61 and give it to a descendant of Abbael.
62 He shall not give it to another person.
63 If a descendant of Yarimlim
64 [ ] not [ ] descendant of Abbael [ ]
65 If [ ] his tow[ns]
66 [ ] exists
67 town[s n]ot [ ]
68 Aḫi-Ṣad[uq] son [of]
69 Irpa[dda]
70 Niqma[ddu]nu[ ]
71 [ ]
72 N[a]
73 [ ]
74 Yari[ml]im
76 caused to swear
75 oaths.

b 1 Kgs 9:11-13, 16; 2 Chr 8:2

c Gen 15:18-21; Jer 34:18-20

d 1 Sam 15:27-28; 24:1-22; 1 Kgs 11:29-32

---

[2] For gifts of towns from one leader to another, see *AT* 1; *AT* 52; 1 Kgs 9:11-13, 16; 2 Chr 8:2.

[3] See Gen 15:18-21 where Abraham slaughters animals and separates the carcasses. This occurs before the presence of God and the subsequent covenantal blessing. Just as the giver of the town in *AT* 456 swears by his life, as symbolized by the sacrifice of the lives of the animals, so God swears by his divine life in Gen 15. See also Neo-Assyrian treaties with this oath as well as Mari texts, Sefire I and Jer 34:18-20. These are discussed in Hess 1994c and Malamat 1995.

[4] The act of grasping the hem here implies some sense of loyalty to the sovereign. See Saul's tearing of Samuel's hem (1 Sam 15:27-28) where the prophet represents God and the divine blessing of rulership which has been taken away from Saul. David's act of cutting the hem of Saul's garment (1 Sam 24:1-22) also symbolizes the sense in which David held Saul's life in his hands and could have "cut it off" as well. See also 1 Kgs 11:29-32 and the Panammuwa inscription (*COS* 2.37, note 24).

REFERENCES

Text: Wiseman 1958:125-128; Draffkorn 1959:95-96. Translations: Wiseman 1958:129; Draffkorn 1959:95-96.

AKKADIAN BIBLIOGRAPHY

ALBENDA, P.
1986 *The Palace of Sargon, King of Assyria: Monumental Wall Reliefs at Dur-Sharrukin, from the Original Drawings Made at the Time of their Discovery in 1843-1844 by Botta and Flandin.* Editions Recherche sur les Civilisations, Synthèse 22. Paris: Editions Recherche sur les Civilisations.

AL-FOUADI, A.-H.
1978 Inscriptions and Reliefs from Bitwātah." *Sumer* 34:122-29.

AL-RAWI, F. N. J.
1982 "Assault and Battery." *Sumer* 38:117-120.
1985 "Nabopolassar's Restoration Work on the Wall *Imgur-Enlil* at Babylon." *Iraq* 47:1-13, and pl. 1.

ALT, A.
1953 "Tiglathpilesers III. erster Feldzug nach Palästina." *Kleine Schriften zur Geschichte des Volkes Israel.* 2:150-162.

ANDRAE, W.
1913 *Die Stelenreihen in Assur.* WVDOG 10. Leipzig: Hinrichs.

AS-SIWANI, S. M. A.
1964 "A Prism from Ur." *Sumer* 20:69-77.

ASTOUR, M.
1965 "Sabtah and Sabteca: Egyptian Pharaoh Names in Genesis 10." *JBL* 84:422-425.
1971 "841 B.C.: The First Assyrian Invasion of Israel." *JAOS* 91:383-389.
1979 "The Arena of Tiglath-pileser III's Campaign against Sardurri II (743 B.C.)." *Assur* 2/3:69-91.

AYNARD, M.-J., and J.-M. DURAND.
1980 "Documents d'Epoque Médio-Assyrienne." *Assur* 3:1-54.

BADRE, L.
1997 "Arwad." *OEANE* 1:218-219.

BAR-MAOZ, Y.
1980 "The Edict of Ammiṣaduqa." Pp. 40-74 in *Studies Kutscher* (Hebrew; Engl. summary pp. lviii-lix).

BEAULIEU, P.-A.
1989 *The Reign of Nabonidus, King of Babylon (556-539 BC).* YNER 10. New Haven/London: Yale University Press.
1995 "An Excerpt from a Menology with Reverse Writing." *ActSum* 17:1-14.
1997 "The Fourth Year of Hostilities in the Land." *BaM* 28:367-394.

BECKING, B.
1992 *The Fall of Samaria: An Historical and Archaeological Study.* SHCANE 2. Leiden: E. J. Brill.

BERGER, P.-R.
1970 "Zum Kyros II.-Zylinder VAB 3." *UF* 2:337-338.
1973 *NBK.*
1975 "Der Kyros Zylinder mit Zusatzfragment BIN II Nr. 32 und die akkadischen Personennamen in Danielbuch." *ZA* 64:192-234.

BIGGS, R. D.
1969 "The Ninth Season (1964/65)." Pp. 9-16 in *Cuneiform Texts from Nippur, the Eighth and Ninth Seasons.* Ed. by G. Buccellati and R. D. Biggs. AS 17. Chicago: The University of Chicago Press.

BIROT, M.
1960 *ARM(T)* 9.

BLACK J., and A. GREEN.
1992 *Gods, Demons and Symbols of Ancient Mesopotamia.* London: British Museum.

BONATZ, D.
1993 "Some Considerations on the Material Culture of Coastal Syria in the Iron Age." *EVO* 16:123-157.

BORGER, R.
1956 *Asarh.*
1960 "Das Ende des ägyptischen Feldherrn Sib'e = *swʾ.*" *JNES* 19:49-53.
1970 "Vier Grenzsteinurkunden Merodachbaladans I. von Babylonien." *AfO* 23:1-16.
1979 *BAL*^{2}.

BÖRKER-KLÄHN, J.
1982 *Altvorderasiatische Bildstelen und vergleichbare Felsrelief.* Baghdader Forschungen 4. Mainz am Rhein: Verlag Phillip van Zabern.

BOTTA, P. E., and E. N. FLANDIN.
1849-50 *Monument de Ninive.* 5 Volumes. Paris: Imprimerie Nationale.

BOUNNI, A., and M. AL-MAQDISSI.
1992 "Tell Sianu. Un nouveau chantier syrien." Pp. 129-140 in *Studies Karageorghis.*

BRAUN-HOLZINGER, E.
1984 *Figürliche Bronzen aus Mesopotamien.* Prähistorische Bronzefunde 1/4. München: C. H. Beck.

BRINKMAN, J. A.
1964 "Merodach-baladan II." Pp. 6-53 in *Studies Oppenheim.*
1968 *PKB.*
1973 "Sennacherib's Babylonian Problem: an Interpretation." *JCS* 25:89-95.
1976 "A Note of the Šamaš Cult at Sippar in the Eleventh Century B.C." *RA* 70:183-184.
1978 "A Further Note on the Battle of Qarqar and Neo-Assyrian Chronology." *JCS* 30:173-175.
1984 *Prelude to Empire. Babylonian Society and Politics, 747-626 B.C.* Occasional Publications of the Babylonian Fund 7. Philadelphia: University Museum.

BRIQUEL-CHATONNET, F.
1992 *Les relations entre les cités de la côte phénicienne et les royaumes d'Israël et de Juda.* OLA 46. Louvain: Peeters.

BUNNENS, G.
1990 *Tell Aḫmar: 1988 Season*. Supplement of Abr-Nahrain 2. Louvain: Peeters.
1995 "Til Barsib under Assyrian Domination: A Brief Account of the Melbourne University Excavations at Tell Ahmar." Pp. 17-28 in *Assyria 1995*.

CAMERON, G.
1950 "The Annals of Shalmaneser III, King of Assyria." *Sumer* 6:6-26, pls. 1-3, 5-6, 22-24.

CANBY, J. V.
1976 "The *Stelenreihen* at Assur, Tell Halaf, and *Maṣṣēbôt*." *Iraq* 38:113-128.

CARDASCIA, G.
1969 *Les lois assyriennes*. Paris: Les Éditions du Cerf.

CAVIGNEAUX, A., and B. Kh. ISMAIL.
1990 "Die Statthalter von Suḫu und Mari im 8. Jh. V. Chr." *BaM* 21:321-456.

CHARPIN, D.
1987 "Les décrets royaux à l'époque Paléo-Babylonienne, à propos d'un ouvrage récent." *AfO* 34:36-41.

CHRISTENSEN, D. L.
1976 "The March of Conquest in Isaiah X 27c-34." *VT* 26:385-399.

COGAN, M.
1973 "Tyre and Tiglath-Pileser III: Chronological Notes." *JCS* 25:96-99.
1974 *Imperialism and Religion — Assyria, Judah and Israel in the Eighth and Seventh Centuries B.C.E.* SBLMS 19. Missoula, MT: Scholars Press.
1984 "From the Peak of Amanah." *IEJ* 34:255-259.
1993 "Judah Under Assyrian Hegemony: A Re-examination of Imperialism and Religion." *JBL* 112:403-414.

COGAN, M., and H. TADMOR.
1988 *II Kings. A New Translation with Introduction and Commentary*. AB 11. Garden City, NY: Doubleday & Company.

COHEN, C.
1993 "The Priestly Benediction (Num 6:24-26) in the Light of Akkadian Parallels." *Tel Aviv* 20:228-238.

COLE, S. W.
1995 "The Destruction of Orchards in Assyrian Warfare." Pp. 29-40 in *Assyria 1995*.

COLLON, D.
1987 *First Impressions: Cylinder Seals in the Ancient Near East*. London: British Museum.

COOPER, J. S.
1986 *SARI*.

DALLEY, S. (see also Page, S.)
1985 "Foreign Chariotry and Cavalry in the Armies of Tiglath-Pileser III and Sargon II." *Iraq* 47:31-48.
1990 "Yahweh in Hamath in the 8th Century B.C.: Cuneiform Material, and Historical Deductions." *VT* 40:21-32.
1999 "Sennacherib and Tarsus." *AnSt* 49:73-80.

DELLER, K.
1985 "Köche und Küche des Aššur-Tempels." *BaM* 16:347-376.
1999 "The Assyrian Eunuchs and Their Predecessors." Pp. 303-311 in *POANE*.

DICK, M. B.
1999 *Born in Heaven, Made on Earth: the Making of the Cult Image in the Ancient Near East*. Winona Lake, IN: Eisenbrauns.

DIETRICH, M., and O. LORETZ.
1997 "Der Vertrag von Ir-Addu von Tunip und Niqmepa von Mukiš." Pp. 211-242 in *Studies Astour*.

DIETRICH, M., and W. MAYER.
1996 "Hurritica Alalaḫiana (I)." *UF* 28:177-188.

DINÇOL, B.
1994 "New Archaeological and Epigraphical Finds from Ivriz: A Preliminary Report." *Tel Aviv* 21:117-128.

DION, P.-E.
1995a "Les Araméens du moyen-euphrate au VIIIe siècle à la lumière des inscriptions des maîtres de Suhu et Mari." Pp. 53-73 in *Congress Volume. Paris, 1992*. VTSup 61. Leiden: E. J. Brill.
1995b "The Syro-Mesopotamian Border in the VIIIth Century BC: The Aramaeans and the Establishment." *BSMS* 30:5-10.
1995c "Syro-Palestinian Resistance to Shalmaneser III in the Light of New Documents." *ZAW* 107-:482-489.
1997 *Les Araméens à l'âge du fer: histoire politique et structures sociales*. Études Bibliques, nouvelle série no 34. Paris: J. Gabalda.

DOBBS-ALLSOPP, F.
1994 "The Genre of the Meṣad Ḥashavyahu Ostracon." *BASOR* 295:49-55.

DONBAZ, V.
1990 "Two Neo-Assyrian Stelae in the Antakya and Kahramanmaraş Museums." *ARRIM* 8:5-24.

DONBAZ, V., and H. SAUREN.
1991 "Ni 2553+2565, a Missing Link of the Hammurabi Law-Code." *OLP* 22:5-28.

DONNER, H.
1970 "Adadnirari III. und die Vasallen des Westens." Pp. 49-59 in *Studies Galling*.

DORNEMANN, R. H.
1997a "Qarqur, Tell." *OEANE* 4:370-371.
1997b "Til Barsip." *OEANE* 5:209-210.

DOSSIN, G.
1955 "L'inscription de fondation de Iaḫdun-Lim, roi de Mari." *Syria* 32:1-28.
1975 "Tablettes de Mari." *RA* 69:23-30.

DOTHAN, M.
1971 *Ashdod II-III. The Second and Third Seasons of Excavations 1963, 1965. Soundings in 1967.* Volume 1: *Text.* Volume 2: *Figures and Plates.* ᶜAtiqot. English Series 9-10. Jerusalem: Department of Antiquities and Musuems.
1993 "Ashdod." *NEAEHL* 1:93-102.
DRAFFKORN, A.
1959 "Was King Abba-AN of Yamḫad a Vizier for the King of Ḫattuša?" JCS 13:94-97.
DRIVER, G. R., and J. MILES.
1935 *The Assyrian Laws.* Oxford: Clarendon. Reprint, Darmstadt: Scientia Verlag Aalen, 1975.
1952 *The Babylonian Laws: 1. Legal Commentary.* Oxford: Clarendon Press.
1955 *The Babylonian Laws: 2. Transliterated Text, Translation, Philological Notes, Glossary.* Oxford: Clarendon Press.
EDZARD, D. O.
1976-80 "Jamani." *RlA* 5:255.
1980 "Kiš. A. Philologisch." *RlA* 5:607-613.
1991 "Irikagina (Urukagina)." *AO* 9:77-79.
EHRLICH, C. S.
1991 "Coalition Politics in Eighth Century B.C.E. Palestine: The Philistines and the Syro-Ephraimite War." *ZDPV* 107:48-58.
1996 *The Philistines in Transition: A History from ca. 1000-730 BCE.* Leiden: E. J. Brill.
EICHLER, B.
1987 "Literary Structure in the Laws of Eshnunna." Pp. 71-84 in *Studies Reiner.*
ELAT, M.
1975 "The Campaigns of Shalmaneser III Against Aram and Israel." *IEJ* 25:25-35.
EPHᶜAL, I.
1982 *The Ancient Arabs.* Jerusalem: Magnes Press.
FADHIL, A.
1990 "Die Grabinschrift der Mullissu-mukannišat-Ninua aus Nimrud/Kalḫu und andere in ihrem Grab gefundene Schriftträger." *BaM* 21:482.
FALES, F. M.
1992 "Mari: An Additional Note on 'Raṣappu and Ḫatallu.'" *SAAB* 6:105-107.
1993 "West Semitic Names in the Šeh Ḫamad Texts." *SAAB* 7:146.
FARBER, W.
1991 "The city wall of Babylon — a belt-cord?" *NABU* 1991:45-46, No.72.
FINET, A.
1973 *Le Code de Hammurapi.* Paris: Les Éditions du Cerf.
FINKELSTEIN, J. J.
1961 "Ammiṣaduqa's Edict and the Babylonian 'Law Codes'." *JCS* 15:91-104.
1969 "The Edict of Ammiṣaduqa: a New Text." *RA* 63:45-64, 189-190.
1970 "On Some Recent Studies in Cuneiform Law." *JAOS* 90:131-143.
FISHBANE, M.
1983 "Form and Reformulation of the Biblical Priestly Blessing." *JAOS* 103:115-121.
FORRER, E.
1928 "Baᵓasa." *RlA* 1:328.
FOSTER, B. R.
1982 "The Siege of Armanum." *JANES* 14:27-36.
1993 *BM.*
FOXVOG, D.
1989 "Astral Dumuzi." Pp. 103-108 in *Studies Hallo.*
FRAHM, E.
1997 *Einleitung in die Sanherib-Inschriften.* AfO Beiheft 26. Vienna: Institut für Orientalistik der Universität.
FRAME, G.
1995 *RIMB* 2.
1999 "The Inscription of Sargon II at Tang-i Var." *Or* 68:31-57 and pls. i-xviii.
FRAYNE, D. R.
1990 *RIME* 4.
1993 *RIME* 2.
1997a *RIME* 3/2.
1997b "On the Location of Simurrum." Pp. 243-269 in *Studies Astour.*
FRYMER-KENSKY, T.
1984 "The Strange Case of the Suspected Sotah (Numbers V 11-31)." *VT* 34:11-26.
FUCHS, A.
1994 *Die Inschriften Sargons II. aus Khorsabad.* Göttingen: Cuvillier.
1998 *Die Annalen des Jahres 711 v. Chr.* SAAS 8. Helsinki: The Neo-Assyrian Text Corpus Project.
GADD, C. J.
1953 "The Inscribed Barrel Cylinder of Marduk-apla-iddina II." *Iraq* 15:123-134.
1954 "Inscribed Prisms of Sargon II from Nimrud." *Iraq* 16:173-201 and pls. xlv, xlvi.
GALIL, G.
1992 "Judah and Assyria in the Sargonid Period." *Zion* 57:111-133 (Hebrew).
GALTER, H. D.
1987 "On Beads and Curses." *ARRIM* 5:11-30.
1990 "Eine Inschrift des Gouverneurs Nergal-ereš in Yale." *Iraq* 52:47-48.

GALTER, H. D., J. E. READE, and L. D. LEVINE.
1986 "The Colossi of Sennacherib's Palace and their Inscriptions." *ARRIM* 4:27-32.
GELB, I. J., and B. KIENAST.
1990 *Die Altakkadischen Königsinschriften des Dritten Jahrtausends v. Ch.* FAOS 7. Stuttgart: F. Steiner.
GEORGE, A. R.
1991a "Seven words." *NABU* 1991:16, No. 19.
1991b "The city wall of Babylon — a belt cord." *NABU* 1991:70-71, No. 101.
1992 *Babylonian Topographical Texts.* OLA 40. Louvain: Peeters.
1993 *House Most High. The Temples of Ancient Mesopotamia.* Mesopotamian Civilizations 5. Winona Lake, IN: Eisenbrauns.
GERARDI, P.
1986 "Declaring War in Mesopotamia." *AfO* 33:30-38.
GOETZE, A.
1948 "The Laws of Eshnunna Discovered at Tell Harmal." *Sumer* 4:63-91.
1956 *The Laws of Eshnunna.* Annual of the American Schools of Oriental Research 31.
GONÇALVES, F. J.
1986 *L'expédition de Sennachérib en Palestine dans la littérature hébräique ancienne.* Paris: J. Gabalda.
GRAYSON, A. K.
1972 *ARI* 1.
1975 *ABC.*
1987 *RIMA* 1.
1993 "Assyrian Officials and Power in the Ninth and Eighth Centuries." *SAAB* 7:19-52.
1994 "Studies in Neo-Assyrian History II: The Eighth Century BC." Pp. 73-84 in *Studies Smith.*
1995 "Eunuchs in Power. Their Role in the Assyrian Bureaucracy." Pp. 85-98 in *Studies von Soden.*
1999 "The Struggle for Power in Assyria. Challenge to Absolute Monarchy in the Ninth and Eighth Centuries B.C." Pp. 253-270 in *POANE.*
GREEN, A.
1993-97 "Mischwesen B." in *RlA* 8:248-249.
GREEN, A. R.
1979 "Sua and Jehu: The Boundaries of Shalmaneser's Conquest." *PEQ* 111:35-39.
GREEN, T. M.
1992 *The City of the Moon God. Religious Traditions of Ḫarran.* Leiden: Brill.
GREENGUS, S.
1979 *Old Babylonian Tablets from Ishchali and Vicinity.* Uitgaven van het Nederlands Historisch-Archeologisch Instituut te Istanbul 44. Leiden: Nederlands Instituut voor het Nabije Oosten.
GURNEY, O.
1989 *Literary and Miscellaneous Texts in the Ashmolean Museum.* OECT 11. Clarendon Press: Oxford.
HALLO, W. W.
1960 "From Qarqar to Carchemish: Assyria and Israel in the Light of New Discoveries." *BA* 23:34-61.
1962 "The Royal Inscriptions of Ur: A Typology." *HUCA* 33:1-43.
1982 "Review of C. B. F. Walker, *Cuneiform Brick Inscriptions.*" *JCS* 34:112-117.
1983 "The First Purim." *BA* 49:19-29.
1995 "Slave Release in the Biblical World in Light of a New Text." Pp. 79-93 in *Studies Greenfield.*
1998 "Sharecropping in the Edict of Ammisaduqa." Pp. 205-216 in *Studies Frerichs.*
1999a "Jerusalem under Hezekiah: An Assyriological Perspective." Pp. 36-50 in *Jerusalem: Its Sanctity and Centrality to Judaism, Christianity, and Islam.* Ed. by L. I. Levine. New York: Continuum.
1999b "They Requested Him as God of Their City: a Classical Moment in the Mesopotamian Experience." Pp. 22-35 in *The Classical Moment: Views from Seven Literatures.* Ed. by S. Holst-Warhaft and D. R. McCann. Lanham, MD: Rowman & Littlefield.
HALPERN, B.
1987 "Yaua, Son of Omri, Yet Again." *BASOR* 265:81-85.
HANDY, L. K.
1997 *The Age of Solomon. Scholarship at the Turn of the Millennium.* SHCANE 11. Leiden: E. J. Brill.
HARPER, R. F.
1904 *The Code of Hammurabi, King of Babylon.* Chicago: University of Chicago Press.
HAWKINS, J. D.
1972-75a "Hamath." *RlA* 4:67-70.
1972-75b "Ḫalab." *RlA* 4:53.
1976-80a "Irhuleni." *RlA* 5:162.
1976-80b "Izrijau." *RlA* 5:273.
1976-80c "Karkemish." *RlA* 5:426-446.
1995a "Karkamish and Karatepe: Neo-Hittite City-States in North Syria." *CANE* 2:1295-1307.
1995b "The Political Geography of North Syria and South-East Anatolia." Pp. 87-101 in *NAG.*
1996-97 "A New Luwian Inscription of Hamiyatas, King of Masuwari." *Abr-Nahrain* 34:108-117.
1997 "Carchemish." *OEANE* 1:423-424.
HAWKINS, J. D., and J. N. POSTGATE.
1988 "Tribute from Tabal." *SAAB* 2:31-40.
HEIMPEL, W.
1987 "Das untere Meer." *ZA* 77:22-91.
1993-97 "Meluḫḫa." *RlA* 8:53-55.
HELTZER, M.
1981 *The Suteans.* Istituto Universitario Orientale. seminario di Studi Asiatici. Series Minor 13. Naples: Instituto universitario orientale.

HESS, R. S.
1990 "Splitting the Adam: The Usage of ᵓĀDĀM in Genesis i-v." Pp. 1-15 in *Studies in the Pentateuch*. VTSup 41. Ed. by J. A. Emerton. Leiden: E. J. Brill.
1994a "Alalakh Studies and the Bible: Obstacle or Contribution?" Pp. 199-215 in *Studies King*.
1994b "Late Bronze Age and Biblical Boundary Descriptions of the West Semitic World." Pp. 123-138 in *Ugarit and the Bible: Proceedings of the International Symposium on Ugarit and the Bible. Manchester, September 1992*. UBL 11. Ed. by G. Brooke, A. Curtis and J. Healey. Münster: Ugarit-Verlag.
1994c "The Slaughter of the Animals in Genesis 15:18-21 and Its Ancient Near Eastern Context." Pp. 55-65 in *He Swore an Oath: Biblical Themes from Genesis 12-50*. Ed. by R. S. Hess, P. E. Satterthwaite, and G. J. Wenham. Second edition. Carlisle: Paternoster; Grand Rapids: Baker. First edition, Cambridge: Tyndale House, 1993.
1996a "A Typology of West Semitic Place Name Lists with Special Reference to Joshua 13-21." *BA* 59:160-170.
1996b *Joshua. An Introduction and Commentary*. Tyndale Old Testament Commentaries. Leicester and Downers Grove: IVP.

HOLLAND, T. A.
1975 "An inscribed weight from Tell Sweyhat, Syria." *Iraq* 37:75-76.

HUNGER, H.
1968 *Babylonische und assyrische Kolophone*. AOAT 2. Neukirchen-Vluyn: Neukirchener Verlag.

HUROWITZ, V. (A.)
1992a *I Have Built You an Exalted House. Temple Building in the Bible in Light of Mesopotamian and Northwest Semitic Writings*. JSOTSup 115 = JSOT/ASOR Monograph Series 5. Sheffield: Sheffield Academic Press.
1992b "Some Literary Observations of the Šitti-Marduk Kudurru (BBSt. 6)." *ZA* 82:39-59.
1997 *Divine Service and its Rewards. Ideology and Poetics in the Hinke Kudurru*. Beer-Sheva 10. Beer-Sheva: Ben-Gurion University of the Negev Press.

IKEDA, Y.
1999 "Looking from Til Barsip on the Euphrates: Assyria and the West in Ninth and Eighth Centuries B.C." Pp. 271-302 in *POANE*.

IRVINE, S. A.
1990 *Isaiah, Ahaz, and the Syro-Ephraimite Crisis*. SBLDS 123. Atlanta: Scholars Press.
1994 "The Southern Border of Syria Reconstructed." *CBQ* 56:21-41.

JACOBSEN, T.
1987 "The Graven Image." Pp. 15-32 in *Studies Cross*.

JURSA, M.
1997 "'Als König Abi-ešuḫ gerechte Ordnung hergestellt hat': eine bemerkenswerte altbabylonische Prozessurkunde." *RA* 91:135-145.

KAPERA, Z. J.
1972-73 "Was YA-MA-NI a Cypriot?" *Folia Orientalia* 14:207-218.
1976 "The Ashdod Stele of Sargon II." *Folia Orientalia* 17:87-99.
1987 "The Oldest Account of Sargon II's Campaign against Ashdod." *Folia Orientalia* 24:29-39.

KAPLAN, J.
1993 "Ashdod-Yam." *NEAEHL* 1:102-103.

KÄRKI, I.
1980 *Die sumerischen und akkadischen Königsinschriften der altbabylonischen Zeit*. I. *Isin, Larsa, Uruk*. Studia Orientalia. Ed. by the Finnish Oriental Society 49. Helsinki.
1983 *Die sumerischen und akkadischen Königsinschriften der altbabylonischen Zeit*. II. Studia Orientalia. Ed. by the Finnish Oriental Society 55:1. Helsinki.

KIENAST, B.
1987 "NA_4 KIŠIB LUGAL *ša šiprēti*." Pp. 167-174 in *Studies Reiner*.
1990 "*Narāmsîn mut* ᵈINANNA." *Or* 59:196-203.

KING, L. W.
1912 *Babylonian Boundary-Stones*. 2 Vols. London: British Museum.

KINNIER WILSON, R.
1962 "The Kurbaᵓil Statue of Shalmaneser III." *Iraq* 24:90-115 and pls. xxx, xxxiii-xxxv.

KITCHEN, K. A.
1986 *Third Intermediate Period*. 2nd Edition. Warminster: Aris and Phillips.
1994 *Documentation for Ancient Arabia*. Part 1. Chronological Framework and Historical Sources. The World of Ancient Arabia Series. Liverpool: Liverpool University Press.
1997 "Sheba and Arabia." Pp. 126-153 in *The Age of Solomon. Scholarship at the Turn of the Millennium*. SHCANE 11. Ed. by L. K. Handy. Leiden: E. J. Brill.

KLEIN, J.
1996 "The Marriage of Martu: The Urbanization of 'Barbaric Nomads.'" *Michmanim* 9:83-96.

KRAUS, F. R.
1958 *Ein Edikt des Königs Ammi-ṣaduqa von Babylon*. SD 5.
1965 "Ein Edikt des Königs Samsu-iluna von Babylon." Pp. 225-231 in *Studies Landsberger*.
1979 "Akkadische Wörter und Ausdrucke, XIII: *tā(w)ītum/*uwwûm*." *RA* 73:135-141.
1984 *Königliche Verfügungen in altbabylonischer Zeit*. SD 11.

KUAN, J. K.
1995 *Neo-Assyrian Historical Inscriptions and Syria-Palestine*. Jian Dao Dissertation Series 1. Hong Kong: Alliance Bible Seminary.

KÜHNE, H.
1994 "The Urbanization of the Assyrian Provinces." Pp. 55-84 in *Nuove fundazioni nel Vicino Oriente Antico: Realtà e ideologia*. Ed. by S. Mazzoni.
1995 "The Assyrians on the Middle Euphrates and the Ḫabur." Pp. 69-85 in *NAG*.

KUHRT, A.
1983 "The Cyrus Cylinder and Achaemenid Imperial Policy." *JSOT* 25:83-97.

KUTSCHER, R.
1990 "The Cult of Dumuzi/Tammuz." Pp. 29-44 in *Studies Artzi*.
LAMBERT, W. G.
1981 "Portion of Inscribed Stela of Sargon II, King of Assyria." P. 125 in *Ladders to Heaven. Art Treasures from Lands of the Bible*. Ed. by O. W. Muscarella. Toronto: McCelland and Stewart.
LANDSBERGER, B.
1968 "Jungfräulichkeit." Pp. 65-403 in *Studies David*.
LANDSBERGER, B., and O. R. GURNEY.
1957-58 "Practical Vocabulary Assur." *AfO* 18:328ff.
LANFRANCHI, G. B.
1995 "Assyrian Geography and Neo-Assyrian Letters. The Location of Ḫubuškia Again." Pp. 127-137 in *NAG*.
LANGDON, S.
1912 VAB 4.
LAYARD, A. H.
1851 *Inscriptions in the Cuneiform Character from Assyrian Monuments*. London: Harrison & Son.
LEE, T. G.
1993 "The Jasper Cylinder Seal of Assurbanipal and Nabonidus' Making of Sin's Statue." *RA* 87:131-136.
LEEPER, A. W. A.
1918 *CT* 35.
LEMAIRE, A.
1993 "Joas de Samarie, Barhadad de Damas, Zakkur de Hamat: La Syrie-Palestine vers 800 av. J.-C." *EI* (*Avraham Malamat Volume*) 24:148*-157*.
LEVINE, L. D.
1972 *Two Neo-Assyrian Stelae from Iran*. Toronto: Royal Ontario Museum.
1982 "Sennacherib's Southern Front: 704-689 B.C." *JCS* 34:28-58.
LIE, A. G.
1929 *The Inscriptions of Sargon II, King of Assyria*. Part 1. *The Annals. Transliterated and Translated with Notes*. Paris: Librairie Orientaliste Paul Geuthner.
LIEBERMAN, S. J.
1985 "Giving Directions on the Black Obelisk of Shalmaneser III." *RA* 79:88.
1989 "Royal 'Reforms' of the Amurrite Dynasty." *BiOr* 46:241-259.
LIPIŃSKI, E.
1970 "Baʾli-Maʾzer II and the Chronology of Tyre." *RSO* 45:59-65.
1971 "An Israelite King of Hamath?" *VT* 21:371-373.
1975 "Apladad." *Or* 45:53-74.
1991 "The Cypriot Vassals of Esarhaddon." Pp. 58-64 in *Studies Tadmor*.
LIVERANI, M.
1992a *Studies on the Annals of Ashurnasirpal II*. 2: *Topographical Analysis*. Dipartmento di Scienze storiche, archeologiche e antropologiche dell'Antichità, Quaderni di Geografica Storica 4. Rome: Universitá di Roma "La Sapienza."
1992b "Raṣappu and Hatallu." *SAAB* 6:35-40.
1992c "Early Caravan Trade Between South-Arabia and Mesopotamia." *Yemen* 1:111-115.
LIVINGSTONE, A.
1995 "New Light on the Ancient Town of Taimāʾ." Pp. 133-143 in *Studia Aramaica*.
LORETZ, O., and W. MAYER.
1990 "Pūlu-Tiglatpileser III. und Menahem von Israel nach assyrischen Quellen und 2 Kön 15,19-20." *UF* 22:221-231.
LUCKENBILL, D. D.
1924 *Annals of Sennacherib*. OIP 2. Chicago: University of Chicago.
LYON, D. G.
1883 *Keilschrifttexte Sargon's König von Assyrien (722-705 v. Chr.)*. Leipzig: J. C. Hinrichs'sche Buchhandlung.
MCEWAN, G. J. P.
1983 "Distribution of Meat in Eanna." *Iraq* 45:187-198.
MACHINIST, P.
1983 "Assyria and its Image in First Isaiah." *JAOS* 103:719-737.
MALAMAT, A.
1953 "Amos 1:5 in the Light of the Til Barsip Inscriptions." *BASOR* 129:25-26.
1963 "Aspects of Foreign Policies of David and Solomon." *JNES* 22:1-17.
1973 "The Arameans." Pp. 134-155 in *POTT*.
1989 *Mari and the Early Israelite Experience*. Schweich Lectures 1984. Oxford: Oxford University Press.
1995 "A Note on the Ritual of Treaty Making in Mari and the Bible." *IEJ* 45:226-229.
MALLOWAN, M. E. L.
1966 *Nimrud and Its Remains*. 3 Vols. London. Collins.
MARCUS, M. I.
1987 "Geography as an Organizing Principle in the Imperial Art of Shalmaneser III." *Iraq* 49:77-90.
MATSUSHIMA, E.
1993 "Divine Statues in Ancient Mesopotamia: Their Fashioning and Clothing and Their Interaction with the Society." Pp. 207-217 in *Official Cult and Popular Religion in the Ancient Near East. Papers of the First Colloquium on the Ancient Near East — the City and its Life held at the Middle Eastern Culture Center in Japan (Mitaka, Tokyo) March 20-22, 1992*. Heidelberg: C. Winter.
1994 "On the Material Related to the Clothing Ceremony *lubuštu* in the Later Periods in Babylonia." *ActSum* 16:177-200.
MATTINGLY, G. L.
1981 "An Archaeological Analysis of Sargon's 712 Campaign against Ashdod." *NEASB* 17:47-64.

MAYER, W.
1995 *Politik und Kriegskunst der Assyrer*. ALASPM 9. Münster: Ugarit-Verlag
MAYER-OPIFICIUS, R.
1995 "Das Relief des Šamaš-rēš-uṣur aus Babylon." Pp. 333-348 in *Studies von Soden*.
MAYRHOFER, M.
1965 "Ein arisch-ḫurritischer Rechtausdruck in Alalakh?" *Or* 34:336-337.
MEDSVEDSKAYA, I.
1995 "The Localization of Hubuškia." Pp. 197-206 in *Assyria 1995*.
MEISSNER, B.
1926 "Die assyrischen Königsinschriften von Ititi bis auf Irêba-Adad." Pp. 2-37 in *IAK*.
DE MEYER, L.
1997 "Der, Tell ed-." *OEANE* 2:145-146.
MICHALOWSKI, P.
1988 "Sin-iddinam and Iškur." Pp. 265-275 in *Studies Sachs*.
MICHEL, E.
1947-52 "Die Assur-Texte Salmanassars III. (858-824)." *WO* 1:7-20, 63-71, 265-268 389-394, 454-475.
1954-59 "Die Assur-Texte Salmanassars III. (858-824)." *WO* 2:27-45; 137-165; 221-241.
MIGLUS, P. A.
1984 "Another Look at the 'Stelenreihen' in Assur." *ZA* 74:133-140.
MILLARD, A. R.
1973 "Adad-nirari III, Aram, and Arpad." PEQ 105:161-164.
1992 "Assyrian Involvement in Edom." Pp. 35-39 in *Early Edom and Moab: The Beginning of the Iron Age in Southern Jordan*. Ed. by P. Bienkowski. Sheffield: J. R. Collis.
1993 "Eden, Bit Adini and Beth Eden." *EI* (*Avraham Malamat Volume*) 24:173*-177*.
1994 *The Eponyms of the Assyrian Empire 910-612 BC*. SAAS 2. Helinski: The Neo-Assyrian Text Corpus Project.
MILLARD, A. R., and H. TADMOR.
1973 "Adad-Nirari III in Syria: Another Stele Fragment and the Dates of His Campaigns." *Iraq* 35:57-64.
MUFFS, Y.
1969 *Studies in the Aramaic Legal Papyri from Elephantine*. Leiden: E. J. Brill.
1992 *Love and Joy. Law, Language and Religion in Ancient Israel*. New York and Jerusalem: The Jewish Theological Seminary of America.
NA᾽AMAN, N.
1972 *Sources for the History of the Assyrian Empire. The First Millennium B.C.E.* (in Hebrew) 6-7. Tel Aviv: Students' Union Publishing House.
1974 "Sennacherib's 'Letter to God' on his Campaign to Judah." *BASOR* 214:25-39.
1976 "Two Notes on the Monolith Inscription of Shalmaneser III from Kurkh." *Tel Aviv* 3:89-106.
1978 "Looking for KTK." *WO* 9:220-239.
1979 "The Brook of Egypt and Assyrian Policy on the Border of Egypt." *Tel Aviv* 6:68-90.
1980a "The Shihor of Egypt and Shur that is Before Egypt." *Tel Aviv* 7:95-109.
1980b "The Ishtar Temple at Alalakh." *JNES* 39:209-214.
1986a *Borders and Districts in Biblical Historiography*. Jerusalem Biblical Studies 4. Jerusalem: Simor.
1986b "Historical and Chronological Notes on the Kingdoms of Israel and Judah in the Eighth Century B.C." *VT* 36:71-92.
1990 "The Historical Background to the Conquest of Samaria (720 BC)." *Biblica* 71:206-225.
1993 "Population Changes in Palestine Following the Assyrian Deportations." *Tel Aviv* 20:104-124.
1994 "The Historical Portion of Sargon II's Nimrud Inscription." *SAAB* 8:17-20.
1995a "Hazael of ᶜAmqi and Hadadezer of Beth-rehob." *UF* 27:381-394.
1995b "Tiglath-Pileser III's Campaigns Against Tyre and Israel (734-732 B.C.E.)." *Tel Aviv* 22:268-278.
1995c "Rezin of Damascus and the Land of Gilead." *ZDPV* 111:105-117.
1997a "Transcribing the Theophoric Element in North Israelite Names." *NABU* 1997:19-20, No. 19.
1997b "Siruatti the Me᾽unite in a Second Inscription of Tiglath-pileser III. *NABU* 1997:139, No. 4.
1998a "Jehu Son of Omri: Legitimizing a Loyal Vassal by his Overlord." *IEJ* 48:236-238.
1998b "Sargon II and the Rebellion of the Cypriote Kings against Shilṭa of Tyre." *Or* 67:239-247.
1998c "Two Notes on the History of Ashkelon and Ekron in the Late Eighth-Seventh Centuries BCE." *Tel Aviv* 25:219-227.
NA᾽AMAN, N., and R. ZADOK.
1988 "Sargon's Deportations to Israel and Philistia." *JCS* 40:36-46.
NASSOUHI, E.
1927 *Textes divers relatifs à l'histoire de l'Assyrie*. MAOG 3/1-2. Leipzig: E. Pfeiffer.
OATES, D.
1962 "The Excavations at Nimrud (Kalhu), 1961." *Iraq* 24:16-17, pl. viii.
ODED, B.
1974 "The Phoenician Cities and the Assyrian Empire in the Time of Tiglath-Pileser III." *ZDPV* 90:38-49.
1997 "The Inscriptions of Tiglath-Pileser III: Review Article." *IEJ* 47:104-110.
DE ODORICO, M.
1995 *The Use of Numbers and Quantifications in the Assyrian Royal Inscriptions*. SAAS 3. Helinski: The Neo-Assyrian Text Corpus Project.
OPPENHEIM, A. L.
1949 "The Golden Garments of the Gods." *JNES* 8:172-193.
1956 *The Interpretation of Dreams in the Ancient Near East*. TAPhS 46/3. Philadelphia: American Philosophical Society.

PAGE, S. (see also Dalley, S.)
1968 "A Stela of Adad-Nirari III and Nergal-Ereš from Tell Al Rimah." *Iraq* 30:139-153.
1969 "Joash and Samaria in a New Stela Excavated at Tell al Rimah, Iraq." *VT* 19:483-484.
PARPOLA, S.
1988 "The Neo-Assyrian Word for Queen." *SAAB* 2:73-76.
1990 "A Letter from Marduk-apla-uṣur of Anah to Rudamu/Urtamis, King of Hamath." Pp. 257-265 in *Hama II/2. Les objets de la période dite syro-hittite (âge du fer)*. Ed. by P. J. Riis and M.-L. Buhl. Copenhagen: National Museet.
1993 *Letters from Assyrian and Babylonian Scholars*. SAA 10. Helsinki: Helinski University Press.
1995 "The Assyrian Cabinet." Pp. 379-401 in *Studies von Soden*.
PAUL, S.
1969 "Exod 21:10: a Threefold Maintenance Clause." *JNES* 28:48-53.
1973 "Heavenly Tablets and the Book of Life." *JANES* 5:345-353.
1990 "Biblical Analogues to Middle Assyrian Law." Pp. 333-350 in *Religion and Law*. Ed. by E. B. Firmege et al. Winona Lake: Eisenbrauns.
PEISER, F.
1889 "Anhang." Pp. 923-928 in *Sitzungsberichte der Königlichen Preussischen Akademie der Wissenschaften zu Berlin*.
PETSCHOW, H.
1959 "Das neubabylonische Gesetzesfragment." *Zeitschrift der Savigny-Stiftung für Rechtsgeschichte* 76:36-96.
PETTINATO, G.
1988 *Semiramis. Herrin über Assur und Babylon, Biographie*. Zürich and München: Artemis.
PITARD, W. T.
1987 *Ancient Damascus*. Winona Lake, IN: Eisenbrauns.
1992a "Ben-Hadad." *ABD* 1:663-665.
1992b "Rezin." *ABD* 5:708-709.
1996 "An Historical Overview of Pastoral Nomadism in the Central Euphrates Valley." Pp. 293-308 in *Studies Young*.
PONCHIA, S.
1991 *L'Assira e gli stati transeufratici nella prima metà dell'VIII secolo a.C.* Padua: Sargon.
PORADA, E.
1983 "Remarks About Some Assyrian Reliefs." *AnSt* 33:13-18.
PORTER, B. N.
1993 *Images, Power, and Politics: Figurative Aspects of Esarhaddon's Babylonian Policy*. Philadelphia: American Philosophical Society.
POSTGATE, J. N.
1969 *Neo-Assyrian Royal Grants and Deeds*. Studia Pohl: Series Maior 1. Rome: Pontifical Biblical Institute.
1971 "Land Tenure in the Middle Assyrian Period: A Reconstruction." *BSOAS* 34:496-520.
1972-75 "Hindanu." *RlA* 4:415.
1983 "Kurbaʾil." *RlA* 6:367-368.
1987-90 "Mannäer." *RlA* 7:340-342.
1995a "Assyria: the Home Provinces." Pp. 1-17 in *NAG*.
1995b "Some Latter-Day Merchants of Aššur." Pp. 403-406 in *Studies von Soden*.
POWELL, M. A.
1971 *Sumerian Numeration and Metrology*. Ph.D. diss. University of Minnesota.
1990 "Masse und Gewichte." *RlA* 7:457-517.
1991 "Narām-Sîn, Son of Sargon: Ancient History, Famous Names, and a Famous Babylonian Forgery." *ZA* 81:20-30.
1992 "Weights and Measures." *ABD* 6:897-908.
1993-97 "Mušallim-Marduk." *RlA* 8:444.
RAINEY, A. F.
1973 "The Cuneiform Inscription on a Votive Cylinder from Beer-Sheba." Pp. 61-70 and pl. 26 in *Beer-Sheba I: Excavations at Tel Beer-Sheba 1969-1971 Seasons*. Ed. by Y. Aharoni. Publications of the Institute of Archaeology 2. Tel Aviv: Tel Aviv University Institute of Archaeology.
1982 "Toponymic Problems (cont.): The Brook of Egypt." *Tel Aviv* 9:131-132.
READE, J. E.
1976 "Sargon's Campaigns of 720, 716, and 715 B.C.: Evidence from the Sculptures." *JNES* 35:95-104.
1979 "Hasanlu, Gilzanu, and Related Considerations." *AMI* 12:175-181.
1980 "The Rassam Obelisk." *Iraq* 42:1-22.
1981 "Neo-Assyrian Monuments in their Historical Context." Pp. 143-168 in *ARINH*.
1987 "A Shamshi-ilu Dedication." *ARRIM* 5:53.
1995 "Iran in the Neo-Assyrian Period." Pp. 31-42 in *NAG*.
REDFORD, D. B.
1992 *Egypt, Canaan, and Israel in Ancient Times*. Princeton: Princeton University Press.
1999 "A Note on the Chronology of Dynasty 25 and the Inscription of Sargon II at Tang-i Var." *Or* 68:58-60.
REINER, E.
1969 "Akkadian Treaties from Syria and Assyria." *ANET* 531-541.
1996 "Suspendu entre ciel et terre." Pp. 311-313 in *Studies Spycket*.
REINHOLD, G. G. G.
1989 *Die Beziehungen Altisraels zu den aramäischen Staaten in der israelitisch-judäischen Königszeit*. Europäische Hochschulschriften XXIII/368. Frankfurt-Bern-New York-Paris: Peter Lang.
RENDSBURG, G.
1991 "Baasha of Ammon." *JANES* 20:57-61.
ROBERTS, J. M. M.
1985 "Amos 6.1-7." Pp. 155-166 in *Studies Anderson*.

RÖLLIG, W.
1976-80a "Karalla." *RlA* 5:405.
1976-80b "Ionier." *RlA* 5:150.
1992 "Asia Minor as a Bridge between East and West: The Role of the Phoenicians and Aramaeans in the Transfer of Culture." Pp. 93-102 in *Greece between East and West: 10th-8th Centuries B.C.*. Ed. by G. Kopeke and I. Tokumaru. Mainz: Verlag Philipp von Zabern.
ROOBAERT, A.
1990 "The City Gate Lions." Pp. 126-135 in Bunnens 1990.
ROST, P.
1892 *Die Keilschrifttexte Tiglat-Pilesers III.*, I: *Einleitung, Transcripton und Übersetzung. Wörterverzeichnis mit Commentar*; II: *Autographierte Texte*. Leipzig: Verlag von Eduard Pfeiffer.
ROTH, M. T.
1988 "'She will die by the iron dagger': Adultery and Marriage in the Neo-Babylonian Period." *JESHO* 31:186-206.
1990 "On LE ¶¶ 46-47A." *NABU* 1990:70-71, No. 92.
1995 "Mesopotamian Legal Traditions and the Laws of Hammurabi." *Chicago-Kent Law Review* 71/1:13-39.
1995/1997 *Law Collections from Mesopotamia and Asia Minor*. 2nd Edition. 1997. SBLWAW 6. Atlanta: Scholars Press.
1998 "The Priestess and the Tavern: LH §110." Pp. 445-464 in *Studies Borger*.
RUSSELL, J. M.
1991 *Sennacherib's Palace without Rival at Nineveh*. Chicago: University of Chicago.
SADER, H.
1987 *Les états araméens de Syrie depuis leur fondation jusqu'à leur transformation en provinces assyriennes*. Beiruter Texte und Studien 36. Beirut and Wiesbaden: F. Steiner Verlag.
SAFAR, F.
1951 "A Further Text of Shalmaneser III. From Assur." *Sumer* 7:3-21, pls. 1-3.
SAGGS, H. W. F.
1975 "Historical Texts and Fragments of Sargon II of Assyria. I. The 'Aššur Charter.'" *Iraq* 37:11-20 and pl. ix.
SAPORETTI, C.
1984 *Le leggi della Mesopotamia*. Studi e manuali di archeologia 2. Firenze: Casa Editrice le Lettere.
SARFARĀZ, A. A.
1968-69 "Sangnibištah-i mīhī-i Ūrāmāmānāt (A Cuneiform Inscription on Stone from Ūrāmāmānāt)." *Majallah-i Barrasīhā-i Tārīkhī* 3/V:13-20 and 14 pls.
SASSMANNSHAUSEN, L.
1995 "Funktion und Stellung der Herolde (*nigir/nāgiru*) im Alten Orient." *BaM* 26:85-194.
SAX, M.
1992 "The Composition of the Materials of First Millennium BC Cylinder Seals." Pp. 104-114 in *Archaeological Sciences 1989: Application of Scientific Techniques to Archaeology*. Oxbow Monographs Series 9. Oxford: Oxbow.
SCHEIL, V.
1917 "Notules, XXXV. Fragment d'une inscription de Salmanasar, fils d'Aššurnaṣirpal." *RA* 14:159-160.
SCHNEIDER, T. J.
1995 "Did King Jehu Kill his Own Family." *BAR* 21/1:26-33, 80.
1996 "Rethinking Jehu." *Biblica* 77:100-107.
SEUX, M.-J.
1969 "Cyrus serviteur de Marduk?" *RB* 76:228-229.
1976 *Hymnes et prières aux dieux de Babylonie et d'Assyrie*. LAPO 8. Paris: Les Éditions du Cerf.
SHAFFER, A.
1981 "'Up' and 'down', 'front' and 'back'; *Gilgamesh* XI, 78, and *Atrahasis* III 29-31." *RA* 75:188f.
SIGRIST, R. M.
1984 *Les* sattukku *dans l'Ésumeša durant la période d'Isin et Larsa*. BiMes 11. Malibu: Undena Publications.
SMITH, G.
1875 *Assyrian Discoveries*. London: S. Bagster & Sons.
SMITH, S.
1921 *The First Campaign of Sennacherib, King of Assyria, B.C. 705-681*. London: Luzac.
1939 "A Preliminary Account of the Tablets from Atchana." *Antiquaries' Journal* 19:39-48.
VON SODEN, W.
1989 "Zu dem altbabylonischen Hymnus an Anmartu und Ašratum mit Verheissungen an Rīm-Sîn." *NABU* 1989:78, No. 105.
SOLLBERGER, E., and R. KUPPER.
1971 *IRSA*.
SOLYMAN, T.
1968 *Die Entstehung und Entwicklung der Götterwaffen in alten Mespotamien und ihre Bedeutung*. Beirut: Henri Abdelnour.
SOMMERFELD, W.
1982 *Der Aufstieg Marduks. Die Stellung Marduks in der babylonischen Religion des zweiten Jahrtausends v. Chr.* AOAT 213; Neukirchen-Vluyn: verlag Butzon & Bercker Kevelaer.
SPALINGER, A.
1973 "The Year 712 B.C. and its Implications for Egyptian History." *JARCE* 10:95-101.
1978 "The Foreign Policy of Egypt Preceding the Assyrian Conquest." *CdÉ* 53:22-47.
SPEISER, E. A.
1954 "The Alalakh Tablets." *JAOS* 74:18-25.
SPELEERS, L.
1925 *Recueil des inscriptions de l'Asie Antérieure des Musées Royaux du Cinquantenaire á Bruxelles. Textes sumériens, babyloniens et assyriens*. Bruxelles.

SPIEKERMANN, H.
1982 *Juda unter Assur in der Sargonidenzeit*. FRLANT 129. Göttingen: Vanderhoeck & Ruprecht.
STEPHENS, F. J.
1937 *Votive and Historical Texts from Babylonian and Assyria*. YOS 9. New Haven and London: Yale University Press.
STOL, M.
1979 *On Trees, Mountains, and Millstones in the Ancient Near East*. Mededelingen en Verhandelingen van het Vooraziatisch-Egyptische Genootschap "Ex Oriente Lux" 21. Leiden: Ex Oriente Lux.
1993 *Epilepsy in Babylonia*. Cuneiform Monographs 2. Groningen: Styx.
1995 "Sîn." *DDD* 1480-1481.
STROMMENGER, E.
1964 *Five Thousand Years of the Art of Mesopotomia*. New York: Harry N. Abrams.
SWEENEY, M. A.
1994 "Sargon's Threat against Jerusalem in Isaiah 10,27-32." *Biblica* 75:457-470.
SWEET, R. F. G.
1986 "Some Observations on the Edict of Ammiṣaduqa Prompted by Text C." Pp. 579-600 in *Studies Horn*.
SZLECHTER, E.
1971 "Les Lois Néo-Babyloniennes." *RIDA* 18:43-107.
1972 "Les Lois Néo-Babyloniennes." *RIDA* 19:43-127.
1973 "Les Lois Néo-Babyloniennes." *RIDA* 20:43-50.
TADMOR, H.
1958 "The Campaigns of Sargon II of Aššur: A Chronological-Historical Study." *JCS* 12:22-40, 77-100.
1961a "Que and Muṣri." *IEJ* 11:143-150.
1961b "Azriyau of Yaudi." *ScrHier* 8:232-271.
1969 "A Note on the Sabaᵓa Stele of Adad-nirari III." *IEJ* 19:46-48.
1971 "Fragments of an Assyrian Stele of Sargon II." Pp. 1:192-197 and 2:pls xcvi and xcvii in *Dothan 1971*.
1973 "The Historical Inscriptions of Adad-Nirari III." *Iraq* 35:141-150.
1981 "History and Ideology in the Assyrian Royal Inscriptions." Pp. 13-34 in *ARINH*.
1983 "Rab-saris and Rab-shakeh in 2 Kings 18." Pp. 279-285 in *Studies Freedman*.
1985a "Sennacherib's Campaign to Judah: Historiographic and Historical Considerations." *Zion* 50:65-80 (Hebrew).
1985b "'Rashpuna' — A Case of Epigraphic Error." *EI* (*Nahman Avigad Volume*) 18:180-182.
1989 "On the Use of Aramaic in the Assyrian Empire: Three Notes on the Reliefs of Sargon." *EI* (*Yigael Yadin Volume*) 20:149-152 (Hebrew).
1994 *The Inscriptions of Tiglath-Pileser III King of Assyria*. Jerusalem: The Israel Academy of Sciences and Humanities.
1999 "'The Appointed Time Has Not Yet Arrived': the Historical background of Haggai 12." Pp. 401-408 in *Studies Levine*.
TALLON, F.
1995 *Les pierres précieuses de l'Orient ancien: des Sumériens aux Sassanides*. Les dossiers du Musée du Louvre 49. Exposition-dossier du départment des antiquités orientales. Paris: Réunion des musées nationaux.
THALMANN, J.-P.
1991 "L'âge du Bronze à Tell ᶜArqa (Liban): Bilan et perspectives (1981-1991)." *Berytus* 39:21-38.
THUREAU-DANGIN, F.
1927 "Poids en hématite conservés au Musée Britannique." *RA* 24:69-73.
1930 "L'inscription des lions de Til-Barsib." *RA* 27:11-21.
1933 "La stèle d'Asharné." *RA* 30:53-56, pl. 1.
TIMM, S.
1989 *Moab zwischen den Mächten. Studien zu historischen Denkmälern und Texten*. ÄAT 17. Wiesbaden: Harrassowitz.
1989-90 "Die Eroberung Samarias aus assyrisch-babylonischer Sicht." *WO* 20-21:62-82.
1993 "König Hesion II. von Damaskus." *WO* 24:55-84.
TSEVAT, M.
1958 "Alalakhiana." *HUCA* 29:109-134.
1994 "The Hebrew Slave according to Deuteronomy 15:12-18: His Lot and the Value of His Work, with Special Attention to the Meaning of משנה." *JBL* 113:587-595.
UNGER, E.
1916 *Reliefstele Adadniraris III. aus Saba'a und Semiramis*. Publicationen der Kaiserlich Osmanischen Museen 2. Konstantinopel: A. Ihsan.
UNGNAD, A.
1906 "Jaua, mâr Ḫumri." *OLZ* 9 cols:224-227.
USSISHKIN, D.
1982 *The Conquest of Lachish by Sennacherib*. Tel Aviv: Tel Aviv University.
VANSTIPHOUT, H. L. J.
1991 "A further note on Ebīḫ." *NABU* 1991:71f., No. 103.
VERA CHAMAZA, G. W.
1992 "Sargon II's Ascent to the Throne: The Political Situation." *SAAB* 6:21-33.
1994 "Der VIII. Feldzug Sargons II. Eine Untersuchung zu Politik und historischer Geographie des späten 8. Jhs. v. Chr. (Teil 1)." *AMI* 27:91-118.
WAETZOLD, H.
1980 "Kleidung. A. Philologisch." *RlA* 6:18-31.
WALKER, C., and M. B. DICK.
1999 "The Induction of the Cult Image in Ancient Mesopotamia: the Mesopotamian *mīs pî* Ritual." Pp. 55-121 in Dick 1999.
WATANABE, K.
1994 "Votivsiegel des Pān-Aššur-lāmur." *ActSum* 16:239-252.

WEINFELD, M.
1970 "The Covenant of Grant in the Old Testament and in the Ancient Near East." *JAOS* 90:184-203.
1991 "Semiramis: Her Name and Her Origin." Pp. 99-103 in *Studies Tadmor*.
WEIPPERT, M.
1973 "Menachem von Israel und seine Zeitgenossen in einer Steleninschrift des assyrische Königs Tiglathpileser III. aus dem Iran." *ZDPV* 89:29-53.
1976-80 "Israel und Juda." *RlA* 5:205.
1992 "Die Feldzüge Adadnararis III. nach Syrien: Voraussetzungen, Verlauf, Folgen." *ZDPV* 108:42-67.
1993-97 "Miniḫimmu." *RlA* 8:215-216.
WEISSBACH, F. H.
1918 "Zu den Inschriften der Säle im Palaste Sargon's II. von Assyrien." *ZDMG* 72:161-185.
WEISSERT, E.
1997 "Creating a Political Climate: Literary Allusions to *Enūma Eliš* in Sennacherib's Account of the Battle of Halule." Pp. 191-202 in *RAI* 39.
WENHAM, G.
1978 "Leviticus 27:2-8 and the Price of Slaves." *ZAW* 90:264-265.
WESTBROOK, R.
1988 *Old Babylonian Marriage Law*. AfO Beiheft 23. Horn: Berger & Söhne.
1994 "The Old Babylonian Term *napṭārum*." *JCS* 46:41-46.
WINCKLER, H.
1889 *Die Keilschrifttexte Sargons. Band I. Historisch-sachliche Einleitung, Umschrift und Übersetzung, Wörterverzeichnis*. Leipzig: E. Pfeiffer 1889.
1893 "Das syrische Land Jaudi und der angebliche Azarja von Juda." Pp. 1:1-23 in *Altorientalische Forschungen*. I. Leipzig: E. Pfeiffer, 1897.
1892 "Beiträge zur Quellenscheidung der Königbücher." *Alttestamentliche Untersuchungen*. Leipzig: E. Pfeiffer.
1893-94 *Sammlung von Keilschrifttexten*, II. *Texte verschiedenen Inhalts*. Leipzig: E. Pfeiffer.
1897 *Altorientalische Forschungen*. I. Leipzig: E. Pfeiffer.
1903 *Die Keilschrifttexte und das Alte Testament*. Ed. by E. Schrader. Berlin: Reuther & Reichard.
WISEMAN, D. J.
1951 "The Historical Inscriptions from Nimrud." *Iraq* 13:21-26.
1956 "A Fragmentary Inscription of Tiglath-Pileser III from Nimrud." *Iraq* 18:117-129.
1958 "Abban and Alalaḫ." *JCS* 12:124-129.
1958 *DOTT*.
1964 "Fragments of Historical Texts from Nimrud." *Iraq* 26:118.
1972-75 "Hadadezer." *RlA* 4:38.
1976-80 "Jehoahaz." *RlA* 5:274.
YADIN, Y.
1963 *The Art of Warfare in Biblical Lands*. 2 Vols. New York: McGraw-Hill.
YAMADA, Sh.
1995 "Tīl-bur-si-ip, the Correct Reading of the Problematic Place Name Ki-x-(x)-qa in Shalmaneser III's Kurkh Monolith (col. i.33)." *NABU* 1995:24-25, No. 30.
1998 "The Manipulative Counting of the Euphrates Crossings in the Later Inscriptions of Shalmaneser III." *JCS* 50:87-94.
YARON, R.
1969/1988 *The Laws of Eshnunna*. 2nd rev. ed. 1988. Jerusalem: Magnes Press, and Leiden: Brill.
YOUNGER, K. L., Jr.
1990 *Ancient Conquest Accounts: A Study of Ancient Near Eastern and Biblical History Writing*. JSOTSup 98. Sheffield: Sheffield Academic Press.
1996 "Sargon's Campaign Against Jerusalem — A Further Note." *Biblica* 77:108-110.
1998 "The Deportations of the Israelites." *JBL* 117:201-227.
1999 "The Fall of Samaria in the Light of Recent Research." *CBQ* 61:461-482.
ZACCAGNINI, C.
1993 "Notes on Pazarcik Stela." *SAAB* 7:53-72.
ZADOK, R.
1978 *On Western Semites in Babylonia During the Chaldean and Achaemenian Periods: An Onomastic Study*. Revised Edition. Jerusalem: Wanaarta.
1997 "Jehu." *NABU* 1997:20, No. 20.
ZEVIT, Z.
1991 "Yahweh Worship and Worshippers in 8th-Century Syria." *VT* 41:363-366.
ZIMANSKY, P. E.
1995 "The Kingdom of Urartu in Eastern Anatolia." Pp. 1135-1146 in *CANE*.

SUMERIAN MONUMENTAL INSCRIPTIONS

A. BUILDING AND DISPLAY INSCRIPTIONS

1. NEO-SUMERIAN INSCRIPTIONS

UR III DYNASTY

UR-NAMMU (2.138A)

Douglas Frayne

An eight-line brick inscription from the temenos wall at Ur records the construction by Ur-Nammu (the first king of Ur III dynasty, who reigned ca. 2112-2095 BCE) of the "wall of Ur." Ancient Ur, the dynastic capital, was located at modern Tell al-Muqayyar The site was excavated in 1850 by Loftus, 1855 by Taylor, 1918 by Thompson, 1919 by Hall, and from 1922-34 by a joint expedition of the British Museum and the University Museum of the University of Pennsylvania under the direction of Sir Leonard Woolley.

(1-2) For the god Nanna, his lord,
(3-4) Ur-Nammu, king of Ur,[a]

[a] Gen 11:28, 31; 15:7; Neh 9:7

(5-8) built his temple (and) built the wall of Ur.

REFERENCES

Kärki 1986:5; Steible 1991:102-104; Frayne 1997:25-26.

UR-NAMMU (2.138B)

Douglas Frayne

A ten-line inscription found on two door sockets records Ur-Nammu's construction of Enlil's Ekur temple in Nippur. Nippur (modern Nuffar) was the religious capital of the Sumerians; its city god Enlil was the effective head of the Sumerian pantheon. The city was excavated by a joint expedition of the University of Pennsylvania and the Babylonian Exploration Fund from 1889-1900, by a joint expedition of the Oriental Institute of the University of Chicago and the University Museum of the University of Pennsylvania from 1948-52, by a joint expedition of the Oriental Institute of the University of Chicago and the American Schools of Oriental Research until 1962, and by an expedition of the Oriental Institute alone until 1990.

(1-3) For the god Enlil, lord of the foreign lands, his lord,
(4-7) Ur-Nammu, mighty man, king of Ur, king of the lands of Sumer and Akkad,
(8-10) built for him the Ekur, his beloved temple.

REFERENCES

Kärki 1986:9; Steible 1991:110; Frayne 1997:75-76.

UR-NAMMU (2.138C)

Douglas Frayne

A ten-line inscription found on bronze canephores, stone foundation tablets, and a door socket records Ur-Nammu's construction of the goddess Inanna's Eanna temple in Uruk (modern Warkāʾ). Uruk was excavated by a team of archaeologists from the Deutsche Orient-Gesellschaft, Berlin from 1912-13 and 1925-1939, and by a team from the Deutsches Archäologisches Institut, Berlin, and the Deutsche Orient-Gesellschaft, Berlin, from 1954 on.

Inanna, one of the highest ranked Sumerian goddesses, was equated by the ancients with Akkadian Ishtar; the latter name is cognate with Canaanite Ashtarath and Hebrew Ashtaroth (*IDB* 1:255).

(1-3) For the goddess Inanna, lady of Eanna, his lady,
(4-7) Ur-Nammu, mighty man, king of Ur, king of the lands of Sumer and Akkad,
(8-10) built and restored her temple for her.

REFERENCES

Kärki 1986:7-8; Steible 1991:107-108; Frayne 1997:71-72.

UR-NAMMU (2.138D)

Douglas Frayne

A tablet copy of a royal inscription of Ur-Nammu deals with a campaign against the Elamite King Kutik-Inshushinak (Puzur-Inshushinak). The copy was found at Isin, excavated by the Deutsche Forschungsgemeinschaft under B. Hrouda since 1973. Elam was the ancient name for the land east of Sumer and Akkad, corresponding in part to modern-day Iran. Of interest in this text is the mention of the land of Akkad in connection with cities situated in the Diyala River region. This fact may give us as clue as the location of the as yet undiscovered capital city of Akkad.

Lacuna

(v′.1′-6′) [...] (I), Ur-Nammu, mighty man, king of Ur, king of the lands of Sumer and Akkad, dedicated (this object) for my (Text: his) life.
(v′.7′-10′) At that time the god Enlil gave ... to the Elamites.
(v′.11′-13′) In the territory of highland Elam,[a] they drew up against one another for battle.
(v′.14′-23′) Their(?) king, Kutik-Inshushinak — Awal, Kismar, Mashkan-sharrum, the [la]nd of Eshnunna, the [la]nd of Tutub, the [lan]d of Simudar, the [lan]d of Akkad, the peop[le ...]

Lacuna

I took as booty (and) brought to the god Enlil, my lord, in Nippur, (and) marked it for him. The remainder I presented as a gift to my troops.

[a] Gen 10:22; 14:1, 9; Isa 11:11; 21: 2; 22:6; Jer 25: 25; 49:34-39; Ezek 32: 24; Dan 8:2; 1 Chr 1:17

REFERENCES

Wilcke 1987:109-11; Frayne 1997:65-66.

SHULGI (2.139A)

Douglas Frayne

A steatite foundation tablet of unknown provenance — it probably came from Uruk — deals with the construction by Shulgi (the second king of the Ur III dynasty, who reigned ca. 2094-2047 BCE) of a temple to the goddess Ninsiʾana.

Ninsiʾana, a form of the goddess Inanna, appears in two aspects in Sumerian texts, one female (likely the planet Venus as the "Evening Star" as in this text), and one male (likely the planet Venus as the "Morning Star" as in the Rim-Sin inscription, *COS* 2.102C above). The female Ninsiʾana is equivalent to Inanna (see above, *COS* 2.138C).

(1-2) For the goddess Ninsiᵓana, his lady, (3-6) Shulgi, mighty man, king of Ur, king of the lands of Sumer and Akkad (7-8) built her temple for her.

REFERENCES

Steible 1991:210; Frayne 1997:117.

SHULGI (2.139B)

Douglas Frayne

An eight-line brick inscription records Shulgi's construction of Inanna's temple E-dur-anki in Nippur. The temple was excavated during 1955-58 and 1960-61 by a team of archaeologists from the Oriental Institute of the University of Chicago and the University Museum of the University of Pennsylvania.

(1-2) For the goddess Inanna, his lady, (3-6) Shulgi, mighty man, king of Ur, king of the lands of Sumer and Akkad, (7-8) built her E-dur-anki ("House, Bond of Heaven and Earth, i.e., Underworld") for her.

REFERENCES

Steible 1991:216-217; Frayne 1997:128-130.

SHULGI (2.139C)

Douglas Frayne

A Neo-Babylonian tablet copy of a Shulgi inscription records the king's construction of the E-meslam temple, shrine of the underworld god Nergal in Cuthah (modern Tell Ibrahim). Sargon II of Assyria, after his conquest of Samaria, repopulated the former capital city with inhabitants of Cuthah (*IDB* 1: 752).

(1-4) Šulgi, mighty man, king of Ur, king of the lands of Sumer and Akkad, (5-8) who built the E-meslam temple, temple of the god Meslamta-eᵓa in Cuthah.[a]

A colophon follows.

[a] 2 Kgs 17:24, 30

REFERENCES

Kärki 1986:30; Steible 1991:157-158; Frayne:1997:132-133.

SHULGI (2.139D)

Douglas Frayne

An eight-line Sumerian brick inscription from Susa (modern Shush in western Iran) records Shulgi's construction of the temple of the god Inshushinak, tutelary deity of Susa (for Susa, cf. Neh 1:1; Esth 1-4, 8-9, passim; Dan 8:2). The site of Susa has been excavated since 1897 by successive teams of French archaeologists.

(1-4) Shulgi, mighty man, king of Ur, king of the lands of Sumer and Akkad,		(5-7) built for the god Inshushinak his temple. (8) He restored it for him.

REFERENCES

Kärki 1986:31; Steible 1991:160-61; Frayne:1997:138-139.

AMAR-SUENA (2.140A)

Douglas Frayne

A nine-line inscription known from two foundation tablets and a bronze canephore[1] from Uruk records the construction by Amar-Suena (third king of the Ur III dynasty, who reigned ca. 2046-2038 BCE) of a temple for the goddess Inanna under her surname Ninsiʾana.

(1-3) For the goddess Inanna/Ninsiʾana, his lady, (4-7) Amar-Suena, mighty man, king of Ur, king		of the four quarters, (8-9) built her temple for her.

[1] I.e., a figurine showing the king carrying a basket on his head — presumably with the symbolic first load of earth or bricks; see Hallo 1962:11.

REFERENCES

Kärki 1986:77-78; Steible 1991:231; Frayne: 1997:259-260.

AMAR-SUENA (2.140B)

Douglas Frayne

A thirteen-line brick inscription from Eridu (modern Abu Shahrain) records Amar-Suena's construction of Enki's *abzu* temple. Sumerian *abzu* "sweet underground source" may conceivably be connected with the "abyss" of Gen 7:11, but the connection is far from certain. Abu Shahrain was excavated by Loftus in 1849, Taylor in 1855, Thompson in 1918, Hall in 1919, and by a team of Iraqi archaeologists under the direction of F. Safar from 1946-49.

(1-3) Amar-Suena, the one called by name by the god Enlil in Nippur, (5-9) supporter of the temple of the god Enlil,	*a* 1 Kgs 7:23-26; 2 Chr 4:2-5	mighty king, king of Ur, king of the four quarters, (10-11) for the god Enki, his beloved lord, (12-13) built his beloved Abzu[1] [a] for him.

[1] For a possible comparison with the "molten" or "bronze sea" of Solomon's temple, see *ABD* 5:1061f.

REFERENCES

Kärki 1986:75-76; Steible 1991:226-228; Frayne 1997:260-262.

IBBI-SIN (2.141A)

Douglas Frayne

A twenty-two line inscription known from clay cones, a stone foundation tablet and an Old Babylonian(?) tablet copy deals with the construction of the "great wall" (likely a temenos wall) of Ur by Ibbi-Sin (the fifth and last king of the Ur III Dynasty, who reigned ca. 2028-2004 BCE).

(1-5) Ibbi-Sin, god of his land, mighty king, king of Ur, king of the four quarters,
(6-7) on account of the great love of the god Suen,
(8-10) reached the decision to expand Ur.
(11-13) Therefore, in order to make the land secure and to make the highlands and lowlands bow down (before him),
(14-17) he surrounded his city with a great wall, whose *loop-holes* cannot be reached, and which was like a yellow (or green) mountain.
(18-19) He found places in its (the wall's) footings for foundation deposits.
(20-22) The name of that wall (is) "Ibbi-Sin is the noble canal-inspector."

REFERENCES

Kärki 1986:136-137; Steible 1991:279-281; Frayne: 1997: 368-369.

IBBI-SIN (2.141B)

Douglas Frayne

An inscription known from an Old Babylonian tablet copy deals with Ibbi-Sin's fashioning of a golden *šikkatu* vessel (Sumerian BUR-ŠAGAN, Akkadian *pūr šikkatu*) "a large container used for the storage of oil" from gold that had been taken as booty from Susa.

An idea of the kind of motifs that may have decorated this vessel may be gained by studying the iconographic elements adorning Early Dynastic period steatite vessels of Iranian manufacture (see Lamberg-Karlovsky 1988:46-37). "Bison" and snake motifs figure commonly on these vessels.

(1-5) For the god Nanna, whose radiance spreads over his people, the lord who alone is a luminous god, his lord,
(6-10) Ibbi-Sin, god of his land, mighty king, king of Ur, king of the four quarters,
(11-16) when he roared like a storm against Susa, Adamshah, (and) the land of Awan, made them submit in a single day, and took their lord(s) as bound captive(s),
(17-22) a golden *šikkatu* vessel, a masterpiece whose decorations — (depicting) *a kusarikku* ("bison"),[1] snakes, and radiant dark rain (clouds) — are of unceasing wonder,
(23-26) which (during) the "Exalted Festival," the *highpoint* of the year, (being) the lustration of the god Nanna, performs without end the "mouth-opening" ritual at the place of the (secret) treasure-chest —
(27) he fa[shioned] for him (the god Nanna)
(28-29) (and) dedicated for his (own) life.

[1] See Wiggerman and Green 1993-97:242 (3); 245 (3); 249f.

REFERENCES

Kärki 1986:146-147; Steible 1991:285-291; Frayne 1997: 370-371.

2. OLD BABYLONIAN INSCRIPTIONS

ISIN I DYNASTY

See above, *COS* 2.92-94, 96-97

LARSA DYNASTY

See above, *COS* 2.98-102

URUK DYNASTY

See above, *COS* 2.104-105

BABYLON I DYNASTY

See above, *COS* 2.107A, C, D, 108-109

B. VOTIVE INSCRIPTIONS

VOTIVE INSCRIPTIONS

William W. Hallo

Like the Biblical vow (*neder*),[a] the Mesopotamian votive offering was of two kinds: before the fact or after. In the former, it was made in the hope of a favor to be granted by the deity in the future, as expressed in the Latin motto *do ut das*, "I give that you might give." The most general and common "votive motive" in this case was "for (long) life" of the donor and/or designated beneficiaries in both Sumerian and Akkadian examples (for the latter see above, *COS* 2.125). In the latter case, a votive offering would represent the fulfillment of the vow to "pay" (cf. Hebrew *shallem*) for the sought-for beneficence once it had been granted. It is best illustrated by archival records of such donations (called *a-ru-a* in Sumerian) by the "seafaring merchants of Ur" and their wives under the Dynasty of Larsa (Oppenheim 1954). The first example chosen illustrates the former kind.

IBBI-SIN (2.142)

Old Babylonian copy on a clay tablet of a royal inscription of neo-Sumerian date originally carved on the sculpture of an exotic animal, perhaps a leopard.

For Nanna, the impetuous bullock of Heaven, the lord who is first-born son of Enlil, his master, Ibbi-Sin, the god of his nation, the mighty king, the king of Ur, the king of the four heavenly quarters — (of) a "dappled dog" of Meluhha (= India ?) that had been brought to him as tribute (or: as a diplomatic gift) from Marhashi (in Iran) he fashioned its image and made a votive offering of it to him (Nanna) for the sake of his (Ibbi-Sin's) (long) life. Of the "dappled dog" — "Let him catch (the enemy)!" is its name.

[a] Lev 27:2; Num 30:3; Deut 23:22 etc.

REFERENCES

Text: Frayne 1997:373f. Studies: Steinkeller 1982:253f.

LUGAL-MURUBE SON OF ZUZU (2.143)

Dogs were sacred to Nintinuga, the goddess of healing, perhaps because they were thought to aid recovery by licking wounds. Numerous skeletons of dogs have been found in Isin, her sacred city, where she was worshipped as Nin-Isina, "our lady of Isin," or as Gula, "the great (goddess)." The following literary text records the fashioning and dedication of the sculpture of a dog to the goddess as a votive offering. The donor, whose name may have to be read as Lugal-nisage, is well known as author of a literary letter, as a *neshakku*-priest of Enlil at Nippur, and as the son of the head of the great scribal academy at Nippur, variously known as Enlil-alsha or (here) as Zuzu, a nickname meaning approximately "Mr. Know-it-all" (Hallo 1977:57).

Lugal-murube, son of Zuzu the headmaster of (the scribal school of) Nippur, fashioned for Nintinuga Tuni-lusha ("her spell cures a man"), her messenger dog. On that account, a dog will always wag (his) tail for his mistress (and) nibble (at wounds?) for her. Queen of heaven and earth, food provider, steward[1] [a] of Enlil, sweet breast which satisfies all the lands and provides abundance, the one who examines the very heart of the paralysis-disease demon, who inspects its bones, who counts(?) the tendons of life and the tendons of death, and cures their joints, who knows the symptoms of those afflicted by stroke or depression, healing physician, exorcist who from the moment of entering sees into

[a] Gen 41:43

[1] Sum. AGRIG, Akk. *abarakku* can be compared to Heb. *abrek*.

the heart of men, my lady - that which I have fashioned I have named Tuni-lusha, I have named you Ubanshaga ("She who has cured"). When the sick man (?) draws breath (again) the paralysis-demon will be appeased. My name will be invoked together with your name. At your entrance one will seek your place. I have named (him) Tuni-lusha. May she (Nintinuga) see me as long as I live. When I die may she let me drink clear water in the netherworld.

REFERENCES

Text and studies: Ali 1966; Civil 1969.

C. SEAL INSCRIPTIONS

SEAL INSCRIPTIONS

William W. Hallo

Sumerian seal inscriptions are known by the thousands, both from recovered seals and from the impressions of lost seals preserved on tablets, envelopes, bullae, doorknobs and vessels. Out of this abundance, two will be chosen here for their inherent interest and their relevance to biblical history and archaeology respectively.

BABATI (2.144)

The queen-mother wielded great influence in Sumer as she did in Judah and Israel, where she was known as *gevira* and *shegal* respectively (de Vaux 1961:117-119). The latter term presumably derives from Akkadian *ša ekalli*, lit. "she of the palace," and this in turn from Sumerian É.GAL, "palace" (cf. Hebrew *hêkāl*). In the case of Abi-simti, Babati used his sister's influence to attain multiple posts for himself — military, civilian and clerical — within the Ur III empire.

Shu-Sin, mighty king,[1] king of Ur, king of the four heavenly quarters, presented (this seal) to Babati the archivist, the royal comptroller, the military governor of Awal, the temple-administrator of ..., the canal-inspector of the sweet waters, the temple-administrator of the twin goddesses Belat-Shuhnir and Belat-Terraban, the brother of Abi-simti his (Shu-Sin's) beloved mother, his servant.

[1] Frayne restores "mighty (man)," based perhaps on the seal inscription of Babati the scribe (*ENES* 637), but such usage under Shu-Sin "may be considered errors of ... commission on the part of the scribes or seal cutters" there and in the parallels cited in *EMRT* 70 n. 5 according to *EMRT* 93; they are unlikely to have been committed on the seal of the king's uncle!

REFERENCES

Text: Frayne 1997:340f. Studies: Whiting 1976; Walker 1983.

SERVANTS OF KINGS (2.145)

In Old Babylonian times, it became customary for royal officials to indicate their status and that of their sovereign implicitly — rather than explicitly — by resorting to a formula, A son of B servant of C, in which C was understood to be a ruler and A his appointee.[1] Much the same usage was followed in Judah and Israel, as shown by numerous archaeological finds there (above, *COS* 2.70R). In the following Old Babylonian examples, personal names are mostly Akkadian (or Amorite); realm is added in parentheses.

Ur-Shubula, son of Sha-...-a, servant of Ishbi-Irra (of Isin).

Warad-Shamash, son of Ziyatum, servant of Bur-Sin (of Isin).

Iku(n)-mishar, servant of Zabaia (of Larsa).

Sin-iddinam, son of Illatia, servant of Gungunum (of Larsa).

Dagania, servant of Sumu-abum (of Babylon).

Marduk-mushallim the scribe, son of Siatum, servant of Hammurapi (of Babylon).

Ili-iddinam, son of Manum, servant of Anam (of Uruk).

Akshak-shemi, son of Warassa, servant of Ipiq-Adad (of Eshnunna).

Ana-Sin-taklaku, son of Darish-libur, servant of Zimri-Lim (of Mari).

[1] It is not certain whether the formula was read in Sum. or Akk.

REFERENCES

Texts: Frayne 1990:7, 73, 112f., 119f., 324, 364, 552, 635. Studies: Weidner 1952; Nagel 1958; Kupper 1959; Hallo 1962:19f.

D. WEIGHT INSCRIPTIONS

WEIGHT INSCRIPTIONS

Marvin A. Powell

This selection is organized in (approximate) chronological order, oldest first (see the Akkadian Weight Inscriptions above, *COS* 2.126A-O for further introductory comments). Published mass and "implied mina norms" are given to assist the reader in interpretation, but it must be borne in mind that these are approximations whose precision depends upon the accuracy of the modern weighing, the state of conservation of the object, and the accuracy of the ancient standard.

2.146A. Rare, archaic shape (like a scrotum), pierced at top, perhaps from Girsu/Telloh, Presargonic.

Mina of wool rations,[1] Dudu,[2] temple-head.[3]

2.146B. Spindle-shaped, a form rare in Babylonia, probably from Girsu/Telloh, late Presargonic.

15 shekels,[4] (of) Ningirsu, Iri-KA-gina,[5] "king" of Girsu.[6]

2.147. Ellipsoid, from Lagash area, probably Akkad or Ur III period.

1 mina,[7] Dudu,[8] temple-head of URUxÚB}2*tenû*?.KI.[9]

2.148. Duck, probably from Girsu/Telloh, Ur III period.

2 talent stone(weight),[10] Ur-Ningirsu, ensi of Lagaš.

---

[1] 680.485 grams; Powell 1971:205, 255; Cooper 1986:68. The mass is about a third heavier than later mina-standards from around the time of Naram-Sin of Akkad onward. Distinct norms for wool or cloth are characteristic of the earlier era. A similar stone weight (A 252) in the Oriental Institute, Chicago, said to be from Adab, is inscribed "2 (minas) of wool rations" and weighs 1108.69 grams + about 30-50 grams in weight loss.

[2] Probably Dudu, the temple-head of Ningirsu mentioned in inscriptions of Entemena (Enmetena) and who in a dedicatory plaque refers to himself as the "temple-head superior" (SANGA MAḪ) of Ningirsu (Cooper 1986:66-68). He was perhaps the father of Enentarzi and is probably identical with the (deceased) "Dudu the temple-head" who receives offerings in DP 41 and RTC 59 (the place names in these texts are locatives rather than genitives).

[3] "Temple-head" renders SANGA, Akk. *šangû*. Often rendered "priest," the duties of this official seem to have been primarily administrative. He is one of the few officials besides kings who appear as the authority for weight standards.

[4] 119.30 grams; Powell 1971:207, 260; Cooper 1986:82. The mass, if correctly published, implies a mina of 477.2 grams, low by comparison with norms from the time of Naram-Sin and later, but very few inscribed weights datable to Presargonic times or earlier are known. Fifteen-shekel weights (a quarter of a mina) are extremely rare, this mass usually being weighed by ten and five shekel combinations.

[5] As Edzard (1991) has pointed out, the name of this individual, usually read Urukagina or Uru'inimgina (see *COS* 2.152, n. 1) was probably pronounced Irikagina or Iri'inimgina. In the first element, URU and IRI ("city") are probably only dialectical variants.

[6] The title "king (LUGAL) of Girsu" probably means that the inscription dates from after the seventh year of Irikagina. The translation "king" is makeshift. We know almost nothing about what this term implied in the Presargonic era.

[7] 497.5 grams; Powell 1971:206, 255 (place name incorrectly read there).

[8] Not the same as Dudu the temple-head in number 1 above; with Cooper 1986:68. Character of inscription, shape of stone, and mass all point to a date later than Presargonic.

[9] Reading of the toponym not entirely certain. URUxÚB*tenû* (damaged in this inscription) is the sign that actually occurs on Presargonic tablets, and careful copyists have reproduced this sign (e.g., in VS 14 170 5.3; *DP* 212 2.2-3).

[10] 60555 grams; Powell 1971:206, 249. The largest inscribed and intact weight yet discovered. Implied mina norm: 504.625 grams; this is very close to that of the five mina weight of Šu-Sin (number 6 below) and to the later standard of the Daric.

2.149. Four-sided pyramid with rounded top (a rare shape revived in the first millennium by Nebuchadrezzar II and Darius the Great), provenance unknown, Ur III period.

For Nanna his lord, Šulgi, mighty man, king of Ur, king of the four regions, has made true[12] 1/2 mina.[13]

2.150. Ellipsoid, from Girsu/Telloh, Ur III.

5 minas,[14] true, Šu-Su'en, mighty king, king of Ur, king of the four regions.

2.151. Duck, unknown provenance, Ur III.

(1/3 mina),[15] Ur-E-sua the stone shaper,[16] son of Ur-Ninzu, stone shaper[16] of the king.

---

[12] [M]U-NA-GI-I[N]; the Sum. verb written GI-IN, GI-NA, etc., used in a legal sense of establishing something as true and with weights, is probably an early loan from Akk. *kânu*. See above, *COS* 2.126O (Nebuchadrezzar). For Ur III parallels, see Hallo 1962:17, 34, 42.

[13] 248 grams; Powell 1971:206, 256-257. Implied mina: 496 grams.

[14] 2510.975 grams; Powell 1971:206, 252. Implied mina: 502.195 grams.

[15] 168.50 grams; Powell 1971:259. The first line of the four-line inscription, where one expects "1/3 mina true," is blank, perhaps because engraving of the mass would have made the weight below standard. [Or perhpas the inscription was copied from a seal. Note the peculiar writing of the sign DÍM.]

[16] "Stone shaper" is written with the word-sign ZADIM in the first case and, in the second case, is spelled ZA-DÍM. For another example, probably also Ur III, of a (ten shekel) weight marked only with the name of a stone shaper, see Powell 1971:260-261 (81.87).

REFERENCES

Texts: 2.146A: Sollberger 1956:44 (Ent. 78); 2.146B: Sollberger 1956:61 (Ukg. 58); 2.147: Sollberger 1956:44 (Ent. 77); 2.148: CT 33:50; 2.149: Frayne 1997:153f. #50; 2.150: Frayne 1997:332f. #22; 2.151: Scheil 1925:152.

E. "FUNCTIONAL" INSCRIPTIONS

1. SUMERIAN LAWS

REFORMS OF URU-INIMGINA (2.152)

William W. Hallo

The last ruler of the "First Dynasty of Lagash" (ca. 2570-2342 BCE) is known in the literature variously as Uru-inimgina or Uru-kagina (ca. 2351-2342 BCE).[1] He promulgated the first known systematic legal reforms which, though not yet cast in the casuistic (conditional) form of later precedent law, nevertheless stand at the head of the long tradition of "social justice in ancient Israel and in the ancient Near East" (Weinfeld 1995).

In the conclusion to one version of the Reforms, he summed up his ideal succinctly as a compact made with the patron deity of Lagash-Girsu not to allow widows and orphans to be handed over to the powerful men of the state (as distrainees for default). In more general terms ("that the powerful not oppress the weak" or the like), that sentiment was to be echoed later in the laws and hymns of Ur-Nammu and Shulgi of Ur, Ishme-Dagan and Lipit-Ishtar of Isin, and Hammurapi of Babylon, and much later still in the inscriptions of Sargon II and Assurbanipal of Assyria and Darius I of Achaemenid Persia.[2] It is also reflected in a petition addressed, most likely, to Samsu-iluna of Babylon.[3] In Israel, the weak classes were expanded to include not only widow and orphan but also "the stranger, for ye were strangers in the land of Egypt" (e.g. Exod 22:20f.).

The Reforms of Uru-inimgina are preserved in six inscriptions representing three different versions. Five of these inscriptions are found on clay nails, the sixth on an oval clay plaque.[4] Each version deals separately with abuses and reforms.[5] The following excerpt includes the prologue, some of the abuses, the corresponding reforms, and the conclusion, including a final building inscription.[6]

For the divine Nin-Girsu, the warrior of the divine Enlil, Uru-inimgina, the king of Lagash, built for him the Tirash-palace, built for him the Antasurra, built for him the temple of the divine Ba'u, built for him the Bursag, his house of daily offerings,[7] built for him his sheep-shearing shed of Uruku;[8] for the divine Nanshe he constructed the canal "Going-to-Nina," her beloved canal whose mouth (lit. "tail") carries for her to the heart of the sea;[9] he built for him (her?) the walls of Girsu.

From days of old, since the seed (first) came forth, at that time the ship-captain seized the ship, the herdsman seized the donkey, the herdsman seized the sheep, the fisherman seized the fisheries; the anointed priests measured out the deposited barley in Ambar;[10] the shepherds of the wool-bearing sheep deposited money (lit. "silver") instead of a white sheep; the surveyor, the chief lamentation-priest, the steward, the brewer (and) the overseers deposited money instead of an offering-lamb;[11] the oxen of the gods plowed the onion-patch of the ruler, the onion-patches and cucumber-patches of the ruler were located in the best fields of the gods; the *sanga*-priests hitched goring oxen [a] to the donkey-teams;[12] [b] the ruler's troops divided up the barley of the *sanga*-priests ...

(But) the standards from of old (still) existed. When the divine Nin-Girsu, the warrior of the

[a] Exod 21:28-32, 35f.

[b] Deut 22:10; Isa 1:3

[1] For proposed readings of the name, see Edzard 1991; Lambert 1992; Selz 1992; and above, *COS* 2.146B, n. 5.

[2] Full references in Hallo 1990:205f.

[3] Hallo *BP* 149f.

[4] The plaque was last edited by Donbaz and Hallo 1976.

[5] For their correlation see Diakonoff 1958.

[6] For a complete translation see Cooper 1986:70-74.

[7] For the BUR-SAG as storage-house or brewery see *COS* 1.162 n. 11. Cooper 1986:70 and n. 3 takes it as belonging to Ba'u, hence "her ... offerings."

[8] Lit., "the holy city," the sacred precinct of Lagash. For the "sheep-shearing shed" in month names and in archival texts, see Lambert 1957:140f.; Cohen 1993:61, 202.

[9] For this canal see in detail Carroué 1986.

[10] Lit. "the swamp" — a region of Girsu-Lagash (characterized by a forest).

[11] For this provision, see Lambert 1957.

[12] Or simply: the meandering oxen. For the two discrete meanings of DU_7-DU_7 see Heimpel 1968:300-307. On either reading the practice violates the biblical injunction against yoking ox and ass together (Deut 22:10). Cf. the Sum. proverb "The stubborn ox is made to follow (the leader), the balky donkey is forced onto the straight path." For this and other references to ox and ass in law and literature see Hallo 1990:213f.

divine Enlil, had bestowed upon Uru-inimgina the kingship of Lagash, having taken him by his hand out of the midst of 36,000 men,[13] he (re)established the norms of old: the commands which his king the divine Nin-Girsu had commanded him were seized upon.

The ship-captain he removed from the ship, he removed their herdsman from the donkeys and from the sheep, he removed the fisherman from the fisheries, he removed the granary supervisor from the deposited barley of the anointed priests, he removed their tax-collector from the money which had been deposited instead of a white sheep, instead of an offering-lamb; he removed the tax-collector from the corvée-duty which the *sanga*-priests had borne for the palace; he put the house of the ruler (and) the fields of the ruler in (the hands of) the divine Nin-Girsu his king; he put the house of the "woman's house" (and) the fields of the "woman's house" (into the hands of) the divine Ba'u his queen; he put the house of the crown-prince (and) the fields of the crown-prince into (the hands of) the divine Shul-shagana his king. From the border of the divine Nin-Girsu to the sea there was no tax-collector ...

A citizen of Lagash living in debt, (or) who had been condemned to its prison for impost, hunger, robbery, (or) murder — their freedom he established. Uru-inimgina made a compact with the divine Nin-Girsu that the powerful man would not oppress the orphan (or) widow.[c]

c Deut 14:29; etc.

In the course of that year, the "small canal which Girsu possesses"[14] he constructed for the divine Nin-Girsu, its name which it had from of old he placed on it, Uru-inimgina called its name "The divine Nin-Girsu is reliant by (virtue of) Nippur." The canal "Going-to-Nina" he brought there for her (Nanshe), the canal which is holy, whose interior is resplendent, may it (ever) bring flowing waters for the divine Nanshe!

[13] A cliché of the royal inscriptions of Lagash, based on the sexagesimal system of counting (60 x 60 x 10). Enmetena, an earlier ruler, was chosen out of 3600 (60 x 60) men, Gudea, a later ruler, claims to have been selected out of 216,000 (60 x 60 x 60).

[14] Name or epithet?

REFERENCES

Text: Sollberger 1956:48-55. Translations: M. Lambert 1956; Cooper 1986:70-74. Studies: M. Lambert 1956; 1957; Diakonoff 1958; Krispijn 1983; Carroué 1986; Steinkeller 1991.

THE LAWS OF UR-NAMMA (UR-NAMMU) (2.153)

Martha Roth

At the end of the third millennium BCE, the Sumerian city-states had been subject to the occupations of the Akkad Dynasty of Sargon the Great and then of the barbarian Gutian invaders from the east. These foreign invaders finally were expelled by King Utu-hegal of Uruk (biblical Erech). After Utu-hegal's death, his brother Ur-Namma, governor in Ur, assumed leadership throughout the region, conquered the city of Lagash (which had been the seat of Gudea's Second Dynasty of Lagash), assumed the royal epithet "King of Sumer and Akkad" (i.e., of all Lower Mesopotamia) and claimed divine parentage; Ur-Namma thus founded the Third Dynasty of Ur (or Ur III Dynasty). Ur-Namma's peacetime attention turned to temple and civic building campaigns, restoration and maintenance of the vital canal system, and royal patronage of the arts and literature. He died an untimely death in battle with the Gutians, and his widow Watartum, the mother of his son and successor Shulgi, commissioned a long and moving funeral lament.

It is now generally agreed that the royal sponsor of these laws is King Ur-Namma (r. 2112-2095 BCE), although some still maintain that it was his son Shulgi (2094-2047 BCE) who had the composition drafted. The difficulty in attribution involves the literary style of the prologue. While some Sumerian royal hymns refer to the king in a combination of second and third person voices and others exclusively express self-praise in the first person, the prologue combines a third-person introductory section laudatory of the named Ur-Namma with a series of first-person boasts of the (possibly unnamed) king's accomplishments. The details of these accomplishments neither contradict nor decisively confirm the known details of the reigns of either Ur-Namma or his son Shulgi.

Sumerian, which enjoyed a literary revival under the kings of the Ur III Dynasty, died out as a living language by the Old Babylonian period, the time during which our surviving copies of this composition were made. The composition is known to us now from three manuscripts from Nippur and Ur. Only a prologue of about 170 lines and thirty-seven laws are preserved. The paragraph numbering used here (and in Roth 1995a) accounts for some newly discovered fragments, and thus differs from earlier editions.[1]

Prologue

Appointment of Ur-Namma to the throne (lines 1-86)

... Ur-Namma, the mighty warrior, king of the city of Ur, king of the lands of Sumer and Akkad ... he established 21,600 SILA of barley, 30 sheep, 30 SILA of butter, per month, as regular offerings ... in the land. When the gods An and Enlil turned over the kingship of the city of Ur to the god Nanna,

at that time, for Ur-Namma, son born of the goddess Ninsun, for her beloved house-born slave, according to his (the god Nanna's) justice and truth ... gave to him ... I promoted Namhani to be the governor of the city of Lagash. By the might of the god Nanna, my lord, I returned Nanna's Magan-boat to the quay(?), and made it shine in the city of Ur.

Existing abuses and corruptions (lines 87-103)

At that time, the *nisku*-people had control of the fields, the sea captains had control of the foreign maritime trade those who appropriate(?) [the oxen] ... those who appropriate(?) [the sheep ...]

Establishment of justice in the land (lines 104-113)

[At that time, (I)], Ur-Namma, [mighty warrior, lord of the city of Ur, king of the lands of Sumer and] Akkad, [by the might] of the god Nanna, my lord, [by the true command of the god Utu(?)], I established [justice in the land].

Political and economic reforms (lines 114-170)

Trade reforms (lines 114-124)

[...] I returned. I established freedom for the Akkadians and foreigners(?) in the lands of Sumer and Akkad, for those conducting foreign maritime trade (free from) the sea-captains, for the herdsmen (free from) those who appropriate(?) oxen, sheep, and donkeys.

Liberation of oppressed populations (lines 125-134)

At that time, by the might of Nanna, my lord, I liberated Akshak, Marad, Girkal, Kazallu, and their settlements, and for Uṣarum, whatever (territories) were under the subjugation of Anshan.

Standardization of weights and measures (lines 135-149)

I made the copper BA.RI.GA-measure and standardized it at 60 SILA. I made the copper seah-measure, and standardized it at 10 SILA. I made the normal king's copper seah-measure, and standardized it at 5 SILA. I standardized (all) the stone weights (from?) the pure(?) 1-shekel (weight) to the 1-mina (weight). I made the bronze 1-sila measure and standardized it at 1 mina.

Transportation routes made secure (lines 150-161)

At that time, [I regulated] the riverboat traffic on the banks of the Tigris River, on the banks of the Euphrates River, on the banks of all rivers. [I secured safe roads for] the couriers(?); I [built] the (roadside) house. [I planted] the orchard, the king placed a gardener in charge of them.

Establishment of equitable justice (lines 162-170+)

I did not deliver the orphan to the rich. I did not deliver the widow to the mighty. I did not deliver the man with but one shekel to the man with one mina (i.e., 60 shekels). I did not deliver the man with but one sheep to the man with one ox.

I settled (in independent settlements?) my generals, my mothers, my brothers, and their families; I did not accept their instructions(?), I did not impose orders. I eliminated enmity, violence, and cries for justice. I established justice in the land.

At that time:

The Laws

§1 If a man commits a homicide, they shall kill that man.[a]

§2 If a man acts lawlessly(?), they shall kill him.

§3 If a man detains(?) (another), that man shall be imprisoned and he shall weigh and deliver 15 shekels of silver.

§4 If a male slave marries a female slave, his beloved, and that male slave (later) is given his freedom, she/he will not leave (or: be evicted from?) the house.

§5 If a male slave marries a native woman, she/he shall place one male child in the service of his master; the child who is placed in the service of his master, his paternal estate, ... the wall, the house, [...]; a child of a native woman will not be owned by the master, he will not be pressed into slavery.

§6 If a man violates the rights of another and deflowers the virgin wife of a young man, they shall kill that male.[b]

§7 If the wife of a young man, on her own initiative, approaches a man and initiates sexual relations with him, they shall kill that woman;[2] that male shall be released.

§8 If a man acts in violation of the rights of another and deflowers the virgin slave woman of a man, he shall weigh and deliver 5 shekels

[a] Exod 21:12-14; Num 35:9-34; Deut 19:11-12

[b] Deut 22:23-29

[1] The most recent edition is in Roth 1995/1997, on which this translation is based, and to which the reader is referred for details of sources and earlier editions.

[2] Var.: "the man (i.e., the husband) shall kill that woman."

of silver.

§9 If a man divorces his first-ranking wife, he shall weigh and deliver 60 shekels of silver.

§10 If he divorces a widow, he shall weigh and deliver 30 shekels of silver.

§11 If a man has sexual relations with the widow without a formal written contract, he will not weigh and deliver any silver (as a divorce settlement).

§12 If [...]

§13 If a man accuses another man of... and he has him brought to the divine River Ordeal but the divine River Ordeal clears him, the one who had him brought (i.e., the accuser) shall weigh and deliver 3 shekels of silver.

§14 If a man accuses the wife of a young man of promiscuity but the River Ordeal clears her, the man who accused her shall weigh and deliver 20 shekels of silver.[c]

§15 If a son-in-law [enters] the household of his father-in-law but subsequently the father-in-law [gives his wife to his (the son-in-law's) comrade], he (the father-in-law) shall [weigh and deliver to him (the jilted son-in-law)] two-fold (the value of) the prestations [which he (the son-in-law) brought (when he entered the house)].[d]

§16 If [...], he shall weigh and deliver to him 2 shekels of silver.

§17 If [a slave or(?)] a slave woman [...] ventures beyond the borders of (his or) her city and a man returns (him or) her, the slave's master shall weigh and deliver [x] shekels of silver to the man who returned (the slave).

§18 If [a man] cuts off the foot of [another man with ...], he shall weigh and deliver 10 shekels of silver.[e]

§19 If a man shatters the ...-bone of another man with a club, he shall weigh and deliver 60 shekels of silver.

§20 If a man cuts off the nose of another man with ..., he shall weigh and deliver 40 shekels of silver.

§21 If [a man] cuts off [the ... of another man] with [..., he shall] weigh and deliver [x shekels of silver].

§22 If [a man knocks out another man's] tooth with [...], he shall weigh and deliver 2 shekels of silver.

§23 If [...]

§24 [If ...], he shall bring [a slave woman]; if he has no slave woman, he shall instead weigh and deliver 10 shekels of silver; if he has no silver, he shall give him whatever of value he has.[3]

§25 If a slave woman curses someone acting with the authority of her mistress, they shall scour her mouth with one SILA of salt.[4]

§26 If a slave woman strikes someone acting with the authority of her mistress, [...].

§27 [If ...]

§28 If a man presents himself as a witness but is demonstrated to be a perjurer, he shall weigh and deliver 15 shekels of silver.[f]

§29 If a man presents himself as a witness but refuses to take the oath, he shall make compensation of whatever was the object of the case.

§30 If a man violates the rights of another and cultivates the field of another man, and he sues (to secure the right to harvest the crop, claiming that) he (the owner) neglected (the field) — that man shall forfeit his expenses.

§31 If a man floods(?) another man's field, he shall measure and deliver 900 SILA of grain per 100 SAR of field.

§32 If a man gives a field to another man to cultivate but he does not cultivate it and allows it to become wasteland, he shall measure out 720 SILA of grain per 100 SAR.

§33 If a man ... another man ...

§37 [...] he shall weigh and deliver to him.

c Deut 22:13-19

d Judg 14-15

e Exod 21:24; Lev 24:20; Deut 19:21

f Exod 20:16; Deut 5:20

[3] Text (in error): "he will not give him anything."

[4] Different interpretations of this provision are given by Finkelstein 1969:70; Römer 1982:22; Sauren 1990:41-42.

REFERENCES

Text: Kramer and Falkenstein 1954; Szlechter 1955; Finkelstein 1969; Yildiz 1981; Roth 1995/1997:13-22. Translations and studies: *ANET* 523-525; *TUAT* 1:17-23; Kramer 1983; Saporetti 1984:21-25; Roth 1995/1997:13-22.

THE LAWS OF LIPIT-ISHTAR (2.154)

Martha Roth

The last ruler of the Ur III Dynasty, Ibbi-Sin (the son or brother of King Shu-Sin), held the throne for twenty-four years in the face of the increasing pressures from the Elamite invaders from the east and the Amorite incursions from the west. With the collapse of Ur III hegemony, one of Ibbi-Sin's governors, Ishbi-Erra of Mari, founded his own dynasty at Isin (modern Ishan Bahriyat), south of Nippur, and ruled from 2017-1985 BCE. Isin became the cult center for the goddess Gula, patron deity of the healing arts, and the city continued to be identified with physicians and healing throughout Mesopotamian history.

The next two hundred years (called the Isin-Larsa Period) saw the political pendulum swing between the cities of Isin and Larsa, each of which claimed to be the heir to the Ur III legacy, until the unification of the region under the Old Babylonian king Hammurabi. The literary legacy, too, was maintained at the great scribal centers in Nippur, where hymns in praise of the dominant ruler were composed. The fall and destruction of the great city of Isin at the hands of her rival Larsa was commemorated in a mournful lament in the established Sumerian tradition.

Lipit-Ishtar, the fifth king of the First Dynasty of Isin, ruled from 1934-1924 BCE. Toward the end of his reign, his contemporary and rival at Larsa, King Gungunum, decisively captured the important city of Ur, gaining a significant moral and strategic advantage over Isin. Before this shift in influence, the Isin scribes had conscientiously followed the literary and cultural traditions of the Ur III rulers, and the Isin kings, like their Ur III predecessors, assumed the royal epithet "King of Sumer and Akkad." The traditions of royal self-praise and of commitment to the establishment and administration of justice in the land are evident too in the collection of Lipit-Ishtar's laws. More than fifteen manuscripts, almost all from Nippur, preserve parts of the Sumerian composition, and fragments of one or more stone stelae can be identified, suggesting monumental display and publication of the work. Almost all of the prologue and epilogue are preserved, and almost fifty law provisions, although many are still fragmentary and gaps remain.[1]

Prologue

Appointment of Lipit-Ishtar to the throne (lines i.1-37)

[When] great [god An, father of the gods], and the god Enlil, [king of the lands, the lord who determines] destinies, gave a favorable reign and the kingship of the lands of Sumer and Akkad to the goddess Ninisina, child of An, pious lady, for whose reign [...] rejoicing, for whose brilliant glance ..., in the city of Isin, her treasure house(?), established by the god An,

at that time, the gods An and Enlil called Lipit-Ishtar to the princeship of the land — Lipit-Ishtar, the wise shepherd, whose name has been pronounced by the god Nunamnir — in order to establish justice in the land, to eliminate cries for justice, to eradicate enmity and armed violence, to bring well-being to the lands of Sumer and Akkad.

Establishment of justice in the land (lines i.38-55)

At that time, I, Lipit-Ishtar, the pious shepherd of the city of Nippur, the faithful husbandman of the city of Ur, he who does not forsake the city of Eridu, the befitting lord of the city of Uruk, the king of the city of Isin, king of the lands of Sumer and Akkad, the heart's desire of the goddess Inanna, by the command of the god Enlil, I established justice in the lands of Sumer and Akkad.

Political and economic reforms (lines ii.1-40)

Liberation of oppressed populations (lines ii.1-15)

At that time, I liberated the sons and daughters of the city of Nippur, the sons and daughters of the city of Ur, the sons and daughters of the city of Isin, the sons and daughters of the lands of Sumer and Akkad, who were subjugated [by the yoke(?)], and I restored order.

Enforcement of familial and state obligations (lines ii.16-40)

With a ... decree(?) I made the father support his children, I made the child support his father. I made the father stand by his children, I made the child stand by his father.

I imposed service (equally) on the household of a living father and on the undivided household [of brothers]. I, Lipit-Ishtar, son of the god Enlil, obligated those in a household of a living father and in an undivided household of brothers to service for seventy (days per year), I obligated those in a household of dependent workers to service for ten days per month ... the wife of a man ... the son of a man ... [(more than two columns lost)]

[...] the troops (col. vi) ... the property of the paternal estate... (col. vii) ... the son of the governor, the son of the palace official, ...

[At that time:]

The Laws

§a If a man rents an ox for the rear of the team, he shall measure and deliver 2400 SILA of grain for two years as its hire; for an ox for the front or middle, he shall measure and deliver 1800 SILA of grain (for two years) as its hire.

§b If a man dies without male offspring, an unmarried daughter shall be his heir.[a]

§c If [a man dies] and his daughter [is married(?)], the property of the paternal estate [...], a younger sister, after [...] the house [...]

§d If [a ...] strikes the daughter of a man and causes her to lose her fetus, he shall weigh and deliver 30 shekels of silver.[b]

§e If she dies, that male shall be killed.

§f If a ... strikes the slave woman of a man and causes her to lose her fetus, he shall weigh and deliver 5 shekels of silver.

§g If [...]

§4 [If ... the] boat [is lost], he shall [replace] the boat.

a Num 27:1-11; 36:1-12

b Exod 21:22-25

[1] The most recent edition is in Roth 1995/1997, on which this translation is based, and to which the reader is referred for details of sources

§5 If a man rents a boat and an agreed route is established for him, but he violates its route and the captain(?) ... in that place — he has acted lawlessly; the man who rented the boat shall replace the boat and [he shall measure and deliver (in grain) its hire].

§6 [...] he shall give as his gift.

§7 If he leases his orchard to a gardener in an orchard-lease, the gardener shall plant [...] for the owner of the orchard and he shall have the use of the dates from one-tenth of the palm trees.

§7a If a man [...]

§8 If a man gives another man fallow land for the purpose of planting an orchard but he does not complete the planting of the orchard, they shall give the fallow land which he neglected to one who is willing to plant the orchard as his share.

§9 If a man enters the orchard of another man and is seized there for thievery, he shall weigh and deliver 10 shekels of silver.

§10 If a man cuts down a tree in another man's orchard, he shall weigh and deliver 20 shekels of silver.

§11 If a man — adjacent to whose house another man has neglected his fallow land — (if this) householder declares to the owner of the fallow land: "Your fallow land has been neglected; someone could break into my house. Fortify your property!" and it is confirmed that this formal warning was given, the owner of the fallow land shall restore to the owner of the house any of his property that is lost.

§12 If a man's female slave or male slave flees within the city, and it is confirmed that (the slave) dwelt in a man's house for one month, he (the one who harbored the fugitive slave) shall give slave for slave.

§13 If he has no slave, he shall weigh and deliver 15 shekels of silver.

§14 If a man's slave contests his slave status against his master, and it is proven that his master has been compensated for his slavery two-fold, that slave shall be freed.

§15 If a *miqtu*-person is a gift of the king, he will not be appropriated.

§16 If a *miqtu*-person goes into service to a man of his own free will, that man will not restrict(?) him, but he (the *miqtu*) shall go wherever he wishes.

§17 If a man, without grounds(?), accuses another man of a matter of which he has no knowledge, and that man cannot prove it, he shall bear the penalty of the matter for which he made the accusation.[c]

c Deut 19:16-21

§18 If the master or mistress of an estate defaults on the taxes due from the estate and an outsider assumes the taxes, he (the master) will not be evicted for three years; (but after three years of defaulting on the taxes) the man who has assumed the tax burden shall take possession of the estate and the master of the estate will not make any claims.

§19 If the master of the estate [...]

§20 If a man rescues a child from a well, he shall [take his] feet [and seal a tablet with the size of his feet (for identification)[2]].

§20a ... when ... fosterage.

§20b If a man does not raise the son whom he contracted to raise in an apprenticeship, and it is confirmed before the judges, he (the child) shall be returned to his birth mother.

§20c If a man [does not raise] the daughter whom he contracted to raise [...]

§21a [If ...] marries, the (marriage) gift which is given by(?) her/his paternal estate shall be taken for her/his heir. [...]

§21b[3] [If ...] is given to a wife, her/his brothers will not include for division (among their inheritance shares) the (marriage) gift which had been given by(?) her/his paternal estate, but [...]

§22 If, during a father's lifetime, his daughter becomes an *ugbabtu*, a *nadītu*, or a *qadištu*, they (her brothers) shall divide the estate considering her as an equal heir.

§23 If a daughter is not given in marriage while her father is alive, her brothers shall give her in marriage.

§23a If he takes a slave [...] he dies [...] an outsider [...] marries(?) [...]

§23b If a man [...]

§24 If the second wife whom he marries bears him a child, the dowry which she brought from her paternal home shall belong only to her children; the children of the first-ranking wife and the children of the second wife shall divide the property of their father equally.

§25 If a man marries a wife and she bears him a child and the child lives, and a slave woman also bears a child to her master, the father shall free the slave woman and her children; the children of the slave woman will not divide the estate with the children of the master.

§26 If his first-ranking wife dies and after his wife's death he marries the slave woman (who had borne him children), the child of

and earlier editions.

[2] The restoration is based on *ana ittišu* III iii 39ff.; see Leichty 1989.

[3] Possibly a continuation of the provision, rather than a new one.

his first-ranking wife shall be his (primary) heir; the child whom the slave woman bore to her master is considered equal to a native free-born son and they shall make good his (share of the) estate.

§27 If a man's wife does not bear him a child but a prostitute from the street does bear him a child, he shall provide grain, oil, and clothing rations for the prostitute, and the child whom the prostitute bore him shall be his heir; as long as his wife is alive, the prostitute will not reside in the house with his first-ranking wife.

§28 If a man's first-ranking wife loses her attractiveness or becomes a paralytic, she will not be evicted from the house; however, her husband may marry a healthy wife,[4] and the second wife shall support the first-ranking wife.[5]

§29 If a son-in-law enters the household of his father-in-law and performs the bridewealth presentation, but later they evict him and give his wife to his comrade, they shall restore to him two-fold the bridewealth which he brought, and his comrade will not marry his wife.

§30 If a young married man has sexual relations with a prostitute from the street, and the judges order him not to go back to the prostitute, (and if) afterwards he divorces his first-ranking wife and gives the silver of her divorce settlement to her, (still) he will not marry the prostitute.

§31 If a father, during his lifetime, gives his favored son a gift for which he writes a sealed document, after the father has died the heirs shall divide the (remaining) paternal estate; they will not contest the share which was allotted, they will not repudiate their father's word.

§32 If a father, during his lifetime, designates the bridewealth for his eldest son, and he (the son) marries while the father is still alive, after the father has died the heirs [shall ...] the estate [...] from the paternal estate [...] the bridewealth they shall [...] the bridewealth [...]

§32a [...]

§33 If a man claims that another man's virgin daughter has had sexual relations but it is proven that she has not had sexual relations, he shall weigh and deliver 10 shekels of silver.

§34 If a man rents an ox and cuts the hoof tendon, he shall weigh and deliver one-third of its value (in silver).

§35 If a man rents an ox and destroys its eye, he shall weigh and deliver one-half of its value (in silver).

§36 If a man rents an ox and breaks its horn, he shall weigh and deliver one-quarter of its value (in silver).

§37 If a man rents an ox and breaks its tail, he shall weigh and deliver one-quarter of its value (in silver).

§38 [If a man ...], he. shall weigh and deliver (in silver).

Epilogue

Accomplishment of fair judicial procedure (lines xxi.5-17)

In accordance with the true word of the god Utu, I made the lands of Sumer and Akkad hold fair judicial procedure. In accordance with the utterance of the god Enlil, I, Lipit-Ishtar, son of Enlil, eradicated enmity and violence. I made weeping, lamentation, shouts for justice, and suits taboo. I made right and truth shine forth, and I brought well-being to the lands of Sumer and Akkad. [...]

Erection of monument, blessings (lines xxi.36-48)

[...] all humankind. When I established justice in the lands of Sumer and Akkad, I erected this stela. He who will not do anything evil to it, who will not damage my work, who will <not> efface my inscription and write his own name on it — may he be granted life and breath of long days; may he raise his neck to heaven in the Ekur temple; may the god Enlil's brilliant countenance be turned upon him from above.

Curses (lines xxi.49–xxii.52)

(But) he who does anything evil to it, who damages my work, who enters the treasure room, who alters its pedestal, who effaces this inscription and writes his own name (in place of mine), or, because of this curse, induces an outsider to remove it — that man, whether he is a king, an *ēnu*-lord, or an ENSI-ruler [... may he be completely obliterated ...]

May [... the god ...], primary son of the god Enlil, not approach; may the seed not enter; ... the mighty one, the seed ... May he who escapes from the weapon, after he enters (the safety of) his house, may he not have [any heirs]. May [the gods ...], Ashnan, and Sumukan, lords of abundance, [withhold(?) the bounty of heaven and] earth. [...]

May [...] the god Enlil [...] revoke the gift of the lofty Ekur temple. May the god Utu, judge of heaven and earth, remove the august word. [...] its foundation bring into his house(?) ... May he make his cities into heaps of ruins. May the foundations of his land not be stable, may it have no king. May

[4] Var.: "a second wife."

[5] Var.: "he shall support the second wife and the first-ranking wife."

the god Ninurta, mighty warrior, the god | | Enlil, [...]

REFERENCES

Text: Szlechter 1957; 1958; Civil 1965; Roth 1995/1997:22-35. Translations and studies: *ANET* 159-161; *TUAT* 1:23-31; Saporetti 1984:27-34; Leichty 1989; Roth 1995/1997:22-35.

F. *TEMPLE HYMNS OF GUDEA*

THE CYLINDERS OF GUDEA (2.155)

Richard E. Averbeck

The composition known as the Cylinders of Gudea is inscribed on two large cylinders (i.e., hollow clay barrels), referred to as Cylinders A and B. The rims of the two cylinders are ca. 2.9 and 2.5 cm thick, respectively. Cylinder A is 61 cm long and 32 cm in diameter, and has 30 columns of writing parallel to the long axis. Cylinder B is 56.5 cm long and 33 cm in diameter, and has 24 columns of writing. Most columns have between 20-30 lines of writing (actually separate lined-off "cases" containing multiple lines), depending on how long the individual lines are in the particular column. Since Cylinder B is shorter it tends to have fewer lines per column than Cylinder A (Edzard 1997:69, 88).

The Cylinders were recovered in broken condition during the eleven campaigns of the French excavations at Tello (ancient Girsu, the administrative center of Gudea's Lagash) between 1877 and 1900 under the direction of Ernest de Sarzec (published in de Sarzec 1884-1912). The two Cylinders have been pieced back together and the *editio princeps* of the cuneiform text itself is a very fine hand copy by the renowned F. Thureau-Dangin (Thureau-Dangin 1925). As it stands now, the text is in relatively good condition except for the later part of Cylinder B and a few small broken sections in Cylinders A and B.

There are a number of leftover unplaced fragments, some of which scholars have attempted to use in restoring the broken sections of Cylinder B with limited success and a lack of consensus (Thureau-Dangin 1925:plates liii-liv; Baer 1971; Jacobsen 1987b:441-444; and now esp. Edzard 1997:88-89, 101-106, 232-233). Some scholars insist that there was a lost third Cylinder, which was the first part of a trilogy, and to which a number of the fragments belong. It may have consisted of hymns praising the temple, a recounting of events leading to the building of the temple, and perhaps Gudea's election as ruler of Lagash (Jacobsen 1987b:386). Others argue that, in light of the overall structural coherence and seeming completeness of the composition as we have it on Cylinders A and B, the original existence of a non-extant third Cylinder is unlikely (see the full discussion in Averbeck 1997:40-49).

The Cylinders were apparently written to celebrate or perhaps commemorate Gudea's building and dedication of a new Eninnu temple for the god Ningirsu, the patron deity of Lagash. The sequence of temple building projects recounted in Gudea Statue I (see Edzard 1997:52) suggests that he undertook this project early in his reign. Unfortunately, the dates of Gudea's reign in Lagash are not certain (cf. Steinkeller 1988 with Jacobsen 1987b:386 and Klein 1989b:289 n. 3). He ruled Lagash either just before Ur-Nammu established the Third Dynasty of Ur, or perhaps his reign overlapped with the early part of the Third Dynasty of Ur, which is dated to ca. 2112-2004 BCE (Ur-Nammu reigned ca. 2112-2095 BCE and Shulgi 2094-2047 BCE).

The Gudea Cylinders constitute one of the longest and most impressive, complex, and unique compositions in the Sumerian literary répertoire. Because this text is so unique, it has been difficult to assign it to a particular genre. In general, there is no evidence of it belonging to the scribal canon, since no other copies in any form have been found, and it is certainly not archival (i.e., economic or administrative). The Cylinders are not really "monumental" either, since they are not inscribed on a monument, unless the Cylinders themselves are viewed as monuments. The composition has affinities with the Sumerian Temple Hymn Collection (Sjöberg and Bergmann 1969:6), but as a royal temple building text it also has some features of royal inscriptions (Averbeck 1997:49-59).

The overall structural similarity between the Gudea Cylinders and other ANE building texts, including the various biblical accounts, has been the subject of much research in recent years (see esp. Hurowitz 1992:25-26, 32-67, 129-337). There are basically five stages: (1) the decision to build with an expression of divine sanction (Cyl. A i-xii and 1 Kgs 5:17-19 [Eng. 3-5]), (2) preparations for the building, including materials, workers, and laying foundations (Cyl. A xiii-xx and 1 Kgs 5:20-32 [Eng. 6-18]), (3) description of the construction process, the buildings, and their furnishings (Cyl. A xxi-xxx and 1 Kgs 6-7), (4) dedication prayers and festivities (Cyl. B i-xviii and 1 Kgs 8), and (5) divine promises and blessings for the king (Cyl. B xix-xxiv and 1 Kgs 9:1-9). See Hurowitz 1992:56, 109-110. Regarding comparisons with the tabernacle account (Exod 25-40) and Ezekiel's temple (Ezek 40-48), see Hurowitz 1985:21-26 and Sharon 1996:103-105, respectively.

With regard to the Gudea Cylinders as a Sumerian literary composition, it has been cogently argued that there is a subgenre of Sumerian royal hymns known as "building and dedication hymns," which includes the Gudea Cylinders and three other compositions (Klein 1989a). Based on this form critical investigation, once again a modified five-fold structural analysis has been proposed for the Gudea Cylinders: (1) commissioning of the building enterprise (Cyl. A i.1-xii.20; cf. 1 Kgs 5:16-19 [Eng. 2-5]), (2) preparations and building of the temple by Gudea (Cyl. A xii.21–xxix.12; cf. 1 Kgs 6-7), (3) praise of the Eninnu (Cyl. A xxix.13-xxx.12), (4) dedication of the Eninnu (Cyl. B i.1-xx.12; cf. 1 Kgs 8), and (5) blessing of the Eninnu and Gudea (Cyl. B xx.13–xxiv.8; cf. 1 Kgs 9:1-9). See Klein 1989a:28 and 1989b:294 n. 34, and the discussion in Averbeck 1997:59-62.

This general shape of the composition as a temple building text and, more specifically, a building and dedication hymn, however, does not settle the question of its internal literary structure. Of course, the most obvious structural break is between Cylinder A (construction of the Eninnu) and Cylinder B (dedication of the Eninnu). Both Cylinders begin with a prologue and end with an epilogue (Cyl. A i.1-11 and xxx.6-14, Cyl. B i.1-11 and xxiv.9-15), followed immediately by a colophon (Cyl. A xxx.15-16 and Cyl. B xxiv.16-17). Within the body of the text a relatively frozen formula occurs five times at major breaks between movements of the composition, resulting in a recognizable seven-fold structure. Another formula guides the reader through the very complicated third section of Cylinder A. Both formulas reflect the ritual nature of the composition as well as the building and dedication processes recounted in it. Moreover, both are used in other Sumerian compositions with similar effects (Averbeck 1997:62-76; and see esp. the notes on Cyl. A vii.9-10 and xiv.5-6 below).

This yields the following comprehensive literary structure for the main body of the Gudea Cylinders: (1) the initial dream and its interpretation (Cyl. A i.12–vii.8), (2) incubation of a second dream (Cyl. A vii.9–xii.19), (3) the construction of the new Eninnu (Cyl. A xii.20–xxv.19), (4) furnishing, decorating, supplying, and praising the temple complex (Cyl. A xxv.20–xxx.5), (5) preparations for the induction of Ningirsu and his consort, Baba, into the new Eninnu (Cyl. B i.12–ii.6), (6) induction of Ningirsu and Baba into the new Eninnu (Cyl. B ii.7–xiii.10), and (7) the housewarming celebration of the induction of Ningirsu and Baba into the new Eninnu (Cyl. B xiii.11–xxiv.8).

CYLINDER A:

Prologue (Cyl. A i.1-11)

On a day when destiny was being decreed in heaven and earth,[1]

Lagash lifted (its) head toward heaven in great stature,[2]

(and) Enlil looked at lord Ningirsu with favor.

In our city the long enduring thing(s)[3] did surely appear in splendor.

(i.5) Surely the heart did overflow,

surely the heart of Enlil did overflow,

[1] In myths and epics the decreeing of destiny was conceived of as having taken place in the primeval days (van Dijk 1964-65:16-34). It has been suggested that this event was regularly reenacted on a yearly holiday, most likely New Years Day, and that this is the very occasion on which Gudea experienced his first dream (Cyl. A i.15-21; Krispijn 1982:84-85). Moreover, it has even been proposed that Cyl. A i.1-9 actually refers back to the destiny decreed for Lagash in those primeval days, the most important element of that destiny being the regular flood of the Tigris that brought agricultural fertility and abundance to the Lagash region (Heimpel 1987b:316-317).

Within the Cylinders themselves, however, *nam—tar* "to decree destiny" sometimes seems to be used in a way that precludes a reference back to primeval times or even a one-time occasion during the year. E.g, although Cyl. A xix.10-11 is somewhat broken, it is clear enough that Enki "decreed destiny" in the process of molding the first brick. As far as we can tell from the text, this day was special because of that event, not because it was a New Year's day or anything of the kind. Cyl. A xxvi.3-5 refers to the eastern facade of the Eninnu as a place for "decreeing destiny." This was the direction of the sunrise and, corresponding to that, it was the place where Utu's standard was displayed. Cyl. B v.16 refers to the sunrise as the time of "destiny decreeing" (i.e., decision making), when the temple was determined to be acceptable and, therefore, was occupied by the divine couple.

Therefore, although it is possible that Cyl. A i.1 refers back to primeval days or to a regular annual day of decreeing destiny, it is just as possible that it simply refers to a particular day on which Enlil decreed a special destiny of blessed abundance for Lagash and Ningirsu. On that day, therefore, Ningirsu called for the building of a new Eninnu (Cyl. A i.10-11), and the wise and pious ruler, Gudea, was there ready to attend to his wishes (Cyl. A i.12-14). Cyl. B i.3 suggests that Enlil's decree in Cyl. A i.1-9 was actually a decree of good destiny for the temple. For a general introduction to "decreeing destiny" and related expressions in ancient Mesopotamia with comparisons and contrasts to related biblical concepts see Lambert 1972.

[2] The noun *me*, rendered "stature" in this line, is one of the most difficult and debated words in the Sum. lexicon. For a helpful recent summary of the discussion and secondary literature see Klein 1997:211-212 (cf. also Averbeck 1997:82 n. 98). The noun may derive from the verb *me* "to be," and on that basis its basic meaning would be "essence." It is commonly used as an abstract noun in reference to the basic elements of material culture, various cultural institutions (religious, social, and political), and the rules, principles, attributes, capacities, and functions that make the whole cultural system work properly. With regard to the latter, in one way or another, *me* virtually always relates to how things actually function or the nature of the effect that they have. In that sense, it is not just a matter of abstract essence. Aside from that, *me* sometimes refers to a symbol associated with a particular *me*, or a two-dimensional representation of that symbol engraved or painted on a sign, banner, or standard of some kind. See the notes on Cyl. B ii.8 and vi.23 below for more on the meaning and significance of *me* in the Gudea Cylinders.

In Cyl. A i.2 *me* seems to refer to the exalted position and importance (i.e., "stature"; the lit. espression is *me-gal-la* lit. "in great *me*") of Lagash on this occasion of determining destiny in heaven and earth (cf. line 1). Edzard, however, translates "Lagash proudly looked up, sure of itself," taking *me* to mean "self" (lit. "in great self," see Sum. variant *ME-te-na* / *ní-te-na*, where *ní* = Akk. *ramānu* "self"; cf. the references and explanations in Alster 1974 and Klein 1989b:292).

[3] The rendering "the long enduring thing(s)" is based on reading *nì-ul* (*UL* = *ul* = Akk. *ṣâtu* "distant time, distant past"; see Sjöberg 1974:116). Others read *nì-du*$_7$ (*UL* = *du*$_7$ = Akk. [*w*]*asmu* "perfect, fitting, proper, appropriate") and, therefore, translate "the appropriate thing(s)" (e.g., Jacobsen 1987b:388).

surely the heart did overflow,
surely the flood water did shine brightly, rising awesomely,
surely the heart of Enlil, being the Tigris river, did bring sweet water.[4] [a]
(i.10) Concerning the temple, its king (Ningirsu) proclaimed there and then:
"As for the Eninnu, I will make its stature appear in splendor in heaven and earth."

I. *Gudea's Initial Dream and its Interpretation* (Cyl. A i.12–vii.8)[5]

Gudea's attentive piety (Cyl. A i.12-14)

The ruler (Gudea), being a man of wide wisdom, had been paying close attention,
lauding (Ningirsu) with all great things,
properly arranging perfect ox and perfect he-goat (for sacrifice).[6] [b]

Gudea's first dream (Cyl. A i.15-21)

(i.15) The decreed brick lifted its head toward him,
stretched out its neck toward him to build the holy temple.
On that day in a night vision[7] (he saw) his king,[c]
Gudea saw the lord Ningirsu,
(and) he commanded him to build his temple.[8] [d]
(i.20) The Eninnu, its stature being the greatest,
he displayed to him.[9] [e]

a 2 Sam 7:1-2 (= 1 Chr 17:1); 1 Kgs 5:1-8 (= 2 Chr 1:14-2:10) *b* 1 Kgs 3:3-15; 5:9-14 (= 2 Chr 1:7-13); 1 Chr 28:6-10; *c* Gen 40:1-23; 41:1-36; Num 12:6; Dan 2:1-45; 4:4-27 *d* Exod 20:24; 25:1-9; 2 Sam 7:1-7, 12-18; 1 Chr 17:1-6, 11-12; 21:28-22:19; 28:2-3 *e* Exod 25:9, 40; 26:30; 27:8; Num 8:4; Josh 22:28; 2 Kgs 16:10; 1 Chr 28:11-19; Ezek 40-42; 43:10-12

[4] The building of temples was closely associated with fertility, abundance, and prosperity in the ANE. The Gudea Cylinders open with a statement of general economic prosperity as the background for the call to build the temple. Enlil determined a good destiny for Lagash (Cyl. A i.1-4) leading to or consisting of the overflow of Enlil's heart (Cyl. A i.5-8) in the form of the seasonal flood of the Tigris river that fertilized the agricultural land of the Lagash region (Cyl. A i.9). Later, in Gudea's second dream, Ningirsu promised that on the very day that the ruler engaged in the building of the temple for him he would make sure that abundance flowed for Lagash in support of the people and the project (Cyl. A xi.1–xii.9; see the note on Cyl. A xi.6 below). Finally, as a result of the successful completion of the temple, once again there is the overflow of the heart of the gods, which recalls the seasonal flood of the Tigris river that brought prosperity with it (Cyl. A xxv.20-21; cf. this with Cyl. A i.5-9 above). Regarding the importance of the Tigris river in ancient Lagash and its literary tradition see Heimpel 1987b.

The principle of economic prosperity is also expressed in the Ug. Baal Epic (*COS* 1.86) where the outcry of Baal for a temple of his own is heard by El (*CTA* 4 iv.40-57). The permission to build is directly associated with fertility in the land (*CTA* 4 iv.58–v.81). The Bible depicts the latter days of David and the whole reign of Solomon as a time of rest and prosperity. David was not allowed to build the temple (2 Sam 7), but the prosperity of Solomon is underlined leading directly to his construction of the Jerusalem temple (1 Kgs 5:1-8 [4:20-28], 5:18 [4], and 2 Chr 1:11-2:10). See Anderson 1987:91-126; Averbeck 1987:189-193; Hurowitz 1992:322-323; Meyers and Meyers 1987:65-66, Sharon 1996:99-102.

[5] For the overall literary structure of the Gudea Cylinders, see the introduction above and the note on Cyl. A vii.10 below.

[6] Claims of royal wisdom in association with temple building are common in the ANE (see Sweet 1990:99-101). The first mention of Gudea in both Cylinder A and B comes immediately after their respective introductory prologues. In both instances he is introduced as a wise and pious ruler who was paying special cultic attention to the gods (Cyl. A i.12-14 and B i.12-14). Solomon was likewise marked by the sex qualities of character at the beginning of his reign (1 Kgs 3:3-15), and this is reinforced in the immediate context of the temple building narrative (1 Kgs 5:9-14 [Eng. 4:29-34]; 2 Chr 2:11-12). Previously, David himself had exhorted his son to excel in piety for the building of the temple (1 Chr 28:6-10).

[7] Sum. *maš-gi*$_6$ "night vision," a phonetic writing for *máš-gi*$_6$ (Cyl. A i.17 and 27), is a close synonym used interchangeably with *ma-mu* "dream," which is, in turn, a phonetic writing of *ma-mú* (Cyl. A i.29, iii.25, iv.13, 14, v.12), all referring to the initial dream (cf. also *ma-mu* in Cyl. A xii.13, but referring to the second dream). Both are lexical equivalents for Akk. *šuttu* "dream" (*AHw* 1292b-1293). In response to the first dream, in which Ningirsu commissioned Gudea to build him a new temple (Cyl. A i.14-21), Gudea went to Nanshe, the "dream interpreter" of the gods, to receive her interpretation of the dream (Cyl. A i.24–ii.3; on dream interpretation see the note on ii.3 below).

Dreams, dream incubations, and dream interpretation are a major concern in the Gudea Cylinders as well as in other ANE temple building texts (Hurowitz 1992:51, 143-151). They were some of the primary means through which Gudea discerned Ningirsu's will for the building of his new Eninnu temple. It is not certain that Gudea's first dream was incubated, but to obtain the second and third dreams he clearly went through ritual procedures (e.g., offerings, extispicies, and prayers) and laid down to sleep specifically and intentionally to receive a dream revelation from Ningirsu (see the notes on Cyl. A viii.3 and xx.8 below).

Dreams were an important means of divine revelation in ancient Israel too, according to the Bible. The prophets were known for receiving oracles from God through dreams (Num 12:6). Jacob had a revelatory dream or two at Bethel (Gen 28:10-22; cf. also 35:9-15). Joseph interpreted dreams in Egypt (Gen 40-41), and Daniel in Babylon (Dan 2 and 4). Many more examples could be cited. See Averbeck 1987:506-579.

[8] The need for a divine call or at least divine permission to build a temple is well established in ANE literature. Sometimes the deity initiated the process as, e.g., in the Harran inscriptions of Nabonidus (*ANET* 562-563; Hurowitz 1992:144 n.1) and Exod 25:1-9. This also seems to be the case in Gudea Cyl. A, although P. Steinkeller (personal communication) is of the opinion that Cyl. i.1-21 follows a pattern something like this: Lagash requests permission to build a new Eninnu temple (lines 1-2, 4), the chief god, Enlil, who is in charge of the *me*'s, approves the increase of *me*'s for the Eninnu and proclaims it to Ningirsu (lines 3, 5-11), the attentive ruler, Gudea, overhears Enlil's address to Ningirsu, (lines 12-14), and the next night the pious ruler receives a dream in which he is commissioned to rebuild the temple (lines 15-21).

There are other instances in which a ruler initiated the process by asking permission from the deity, but was denied. According to the Curse of Agade, e.g., Naram-Sin requested permission to build a temple for Inanna in Agade, but it was denied to him through repeated divination. The destruction of Agade had been pre-ordained (Cooper 1983a:54-55, 239-240, and 244). This can be compared to the denial of David's temple building ambitions. Several complementary explanations for this are given in the Bible. First, the Lord had not requested a temple (2 Sam 7:5-7; 1 Chr 17:4-6). Second, the Lord was more interested in building a house for David than in David building a house for him (2 Sam 7:12-13 and esp. 1 Chr 17:10b-16). Third, David had defiled himself by shedding much blood in warfare (1 Chr 22:6-8; 28:2-3). Fourth, David had too many wars to fight to dedicate his time and resources to the project (1 Kgs 5:17[3]). See Ishida 1977:85-93; McCarter 1984:225-229; Ota 1974.

In other instances permission was granted. E.g., through divination Shamash and Adad granted the pious king Esarhaddon permission to rebuild a temple (Steele 1951:5 and Borger 1956:3 iii.33–iv.6). Similarly, on the divine level, after several attempts Baal was finally successful at gaining permission to have a temple built for himself (*CTA* 4). In ancient Israel it was common to build altars where a theophany had occurred (e.g., Gen 12:7; Judg 6:24-26). This was affirmed in the law (Exod 20:24) and, in fact, was the means by which David discerned the proper location of the first temple (1 Chr 21:28-22:5; cf. 2 Sam 24:16-25). See Ellis 1968:6-7; Ishida 1977:85-99; de Vaux 1961:277; Weinfeld 1972:247-250.

[9] Gudea gained his first glimpse of the new Eninnu in his initial dream (Cyl. A i.20-21). He was troubled by the dream because the precise

Gudea's anxiety over the dream (Cyl.A i.22–ii.3)
Gudea, his heart being stirred up,
tired himself over the command (saying):[10] [f]
"I must tell it to her! I must tell it to her!
(i.25) May she stand by me in regard to this command!
Me being the shepherd, she has entrusted me with the office of authority.[11] [g]
The thing which the night vision brought to me,
I do not know its meaning.
I must take my dream to my mother!
(ii.1) My dream interpreter who is clever in her practice,
Nanshe, my sister, the goddess of Sirara,
may she reveal its meaning to me!"[12] [h]

Gudea travels by boat to Nanshe's temple. Along the way he stops at the Bagara temple to pray to Ningirsu and Gatumdug. After arriving at Nanshe's town and entering her temple, he describes his dream to her in detail (Cyl.A ii.4–v.10).[13]

f Gen 41:8; Exod 33:18-23; Judg 13:21-22; Isa 6:5; Dan 2:1-4, 10-13; 4:5, 19
g 2 Sam 5:2 (= 1 Chr 11:2); 2 Sam 7:7 (= 1 Chr 17:6); Pss 23; 78:70-72; Jer 3:15; 23:1-4; Ezek 34:2, 8, 10, 23; Zech 11:4-17; Mic 5:3[4]
h Gen 40-41; Dan 2 and 4
i Dan 2:31-33

Nanshe's interpretation of Gudea's dream (Cyl. A v.11–vi.13)
To the ruler, his mother, Nanshe, gave an answer:
"O my shepherd, I myself will surely interpret your dream for you.
With regard to the man who was great like heaven (and) great like earth, [i]
as to his head, (being) a god, as to his arms (? wings?),
(v.15) (being) the Anzu bird, as to his lower parts, (being) a flood storm,
(and) on the right (and) on his left (two) lions lying down;
it was surely my brother Ningirsu.[14]
He commanded you to build the shrine of his Eninnu.
The sunlight that came forth from the horizon for you
(v.20) was your (personal) god, Ningishzida. He came forth for you from the horizon like sun-

details of the structure and how to actually proceed with the building project were not clear to him (Cyl. A i.22-23, 27-28, iv.20-21). Therefore, he decided to consult Nanshe, the dream interpreter of the gods, for an interpretation of the dream (Cyl. A i.22–iv.4; see Cyl. A ii.1-3 below and the note there).

In the Gudea Cylinders and other ANE temple building texts, the construction of a divinely pleasing sanctuary necessarily involved receiving and following a detailed and divinely revealed plan. The same is true in the Bible, but unlike Gudea, who needed to virtually pry the details of the plan out of the deity through cultic means, this information is readily forthcoming in ancient Israel (Exod 25:1-9; 1 Chr 28:11-19; Ezek 40-42). The revealed *tabnît* "plan" or "pattern" of the biblical tabernacle, the temple, and their furniture (see specifically Exod 25:9, 40; 26:30; 27:8; Josh 22:28; 1 Chr 28:11-12, 19; cf. Ezek 43:10-12) corresponds to both the *giš-ḫur* ("plan") of the temple and the visionary picture of the completed sanctuary in the Gudea Cylinders. See Hurowitz 1992:168-170; Jacobsen 1976b:80-81; Sarna 1986:200-203, and the notes on Cyl. A vi.5, xvii.17, and xix.20 below.

[10] Sum. *šà-ga-ni sud-rá-àm* (lit. "his heart being distant") in line 22 is rendered "his heart being stirred up" because of the parallel in Cyl. A ix.2 where Ningirsu's heart is said to be "highly disturbed" (Sum. *šà an-gim sud-rá-ni* lit. "his heart distant like heaven"; cf. Cyl. A vii.4-5). In the latter context, Ningirsu's heart is clearly disturbed like the sea with its rolling breakers, a roaring stream, a destructive flood, a wild storm, and fast flowing water that cannot be dammed up (Cyl. A viii.23–ix.1). Others translate in Cyl. A i.22, e.g, "his heart was not to fathom" (referring to Ningirsu's heart, Jacobsen 1987b:389), or "(although) having a far reaching mind" (referring to Gudea's heart of extensive knowledge and deep understanding, Edzard 1997:69).

Gudea was disturbed by the dream because he did not understand it and, therefore, did not know how to proceed from that point (see also the note on Cyl. A viii.22 below). Thus, he "wearied himself" over the command and determined to go to Nanshe for interpretive help and advice (Cyl. A i.24–ii.3; cf. v.11–vii.8). Both the Egyptian Pharoah of Joseph's day and Nebuchadnezzar had similar responses to their ominous dreams (Gen 41:8; Dan 2:1-4, 10-13). Theophanies, visions, and dreams were by nature awesome and dangerous (Exod 33:18-23), and often struck the fear of death in the hearts of those who experienced them (e.g., Exod 19:16 with 20:19; Judg 6:22-23; 13:21-22; Isa 6:5).

[11] As the ruler of his people, Gudea is often referred to, or refers to himself, as the "shepherd" (*sipa*; Cyl. A xvi.25, Cyl. B ii.5) or "faithful shepherd" (*sipa-zi*; Cyl. A vii.9, xi.5, xiv.5, xxiv.9, xxv.22, Cyl. B ii.7, viii.17; note esp. the regular use of this title in the structural formulas that shaped the composition as a whole). These are the earliest references to "faithful shepherd" as a royal motif (Hallo 1983:14-15). Gudea is the shepherd appointed and authorized by Nanshe (Cyl. A i.26, v.12, xiii.19), and "the shepherd called (i.e., chosen) in the heart of Ningirsu" (Stat. B ii.8-9; cf. also Stat. B iii.8-9 and Stat. D i.11-12, Edzard 1997:31-32, 41) to be his "obedient shepherd" (Cyl. B xiii.12).

"Shepherd" is well-known as a royal epithet in the ANE (Seux 1967:441-446). See, e.g., before Gudea in Lugalzagesi 1 iii.35-36 "the leading shepherd" (Cooper 1986:94-95), and after Gudea in the prologue to the Code of Hammurabi i.50-53 "Hammurabi, the shepherd, called by Enlil, am I" (*ANET* 164). The Lord called David to "shepherd my people Israel," which means that he was to "be a ruler over Israel" (2 Sam 5:2 = 1 Chr 11:2; cf. Ezek 34:23-24). We know that this was not simply a stock motif emptied of its original meaning because, according to Ps 78:70-72, David was called to shepherd Israel with the care, integrity, and skill that he had learned as a shepherd of sheep.

Israel experienced a plenitude of bad shepherds in its long history (Jer 23:1-4; Ezek 34:1-10), and it seemed that there were always more to come (Zech 11:4-17). However, the Lord also promised that he would eventually raise up a good Davidic shepherd (Ezek 34:23-24; cf. Mic 5:1-3[2-4]). The Lord sought out shepherds after his own heart to shepherd Israel (Jer 3:15-18; cf. 1 Sam 13:14) and, in fact, he himself was the ultimate shepherd of ancient Israel (Ps 23; Ezek 34:11-22). Similarly, Ningirsu could be referred to as the "shepherd" of ancient Lagash (Cyl. B vi.17-18). See Averbeck 1987:234-235 n. 237.

[12] Gudea's first dream was a "symbolic dream" that required interpretation if the ruler was to understand its full "meaning" or "intent" (Sum. *šà* lit. "heart" in ii.3; see the note on Cyl. A viii.22 below). Female dream interpreters are well known in ancient Mesopotamia, and in Cyl. A iv.12 the goddess Nanshe is referred to as "the dream interpreter of the gods." Nanshe did indeed interpret the dream (Cyl. A v.11–vi.13), but then advised Gudea to present a well-fashioned war chariot and present it to Ningirsu in order to incubate a second dream (Cyl. A vi.14–xix.6). On dream interpretation in particular, see Asher-Greve 1987 and the literature cited there (cf. Oppenheim 1956:221-225).

In the Bible both Joseph (Gen 40-41) and Daniel (Dan 2 and 4) became known as interpreters of dreams. Both of them attributed this ability to their God (Gen 40:8; 41:16; Dan 2:22-23, 27-30, 47). See Hurowitz 1992:148 n. 4.

[13] Virtually all the details of the dream are repeated *mutatis mutandis* in Nanshe's interpretation of the dream. See Cyl. A v.11–vi.13 below.

[14] Ningirsu of Lagash is virtually identifiable with Ninurta of Nippur (Cooper 1978:11; Heimpel 1996:22; and esp. Jacobsen 1976b:127-134),

light.
The young woman who was going forth in front (with) a place of sheaves made (? on her?),
who was holding a stylus of fine silver,
who had placed a star tablet on her knees
(and) was consulting it;
(v.25) she was most certainly my sister, Nisaba.
(vi.1) For the building of the temple according to its holy star(s)
she called out to you.
The second (man), being a warrior, bent (his) arm
(and) held a slate of lapis lazuli;
(vi.5) being Nindub, he was copying the plan of the temple.[15]
The holy carrying-basket standing before you, the holy brick-mold properly prepared,
(and) the decreed brick placed in the brick-mold;
it was most certainly the true brick of the Eninnu.
With regard to the beautiful poplar tree on which your eyes were fixed,
(vi.10) in which the *tigidlu* bird was passing the day in song;
(for zeal) to build the temple, sweet sleep will not enter your eyes.[16] [j]
With regard to the donkey stallion pawing the ground for you at the right side of your king,
it is you pawing the ground like a choice donkey (eager to get) at the Eninnu."

Nanshe's advice to Gudea (Cyl. A vi.14–vii.8)
"Let me advise (you)! May you take my advice!
(vi.15) When you have stepped ashore at Girsu, the chief temple of the Lagash region,
have torn loose the seal of your storehouse, have set out wood from it,
have fashioned a perfect chariot for your king,
have harnessed a donkey stallion to it,
have adorned that chariot with fine silver and lapis lazuli,
(vi.20) have made the arrows protrude from the quiver like (rays of) sunlight,
have carefully prepared the *ankara* weapon, the arm of warriorship,
have fashioned his beloved standard for him,
have inscribed your name on it;
(when) with his beloved lyre, the dragon of the land,
(vi.25) the famous harp, his instrument of counsel,
for the warrior who loves gifts,
(vii.1) your king, lord Ningirsu,
(when) you have brought them to the Eninnu for the shining Anzu bird;
(then) what you speak softly he will accept as being nobly spoken.
The heart of the lord, which is highly disturbed,
(vii.5) (the heart) of Ningirsu, the son of Enlil, will become calm for you.
He will reveal the plan of his temple to you.
The warrior, his stature being the greatest,
will laud it magnificently for you."[17]

j Ps 132:2-5

II. *Gudea's Second Dream* (Cyl. A vii.9–xii.19)

Narrative transition to Gudea's incubation of a second dream (vii.9-10)
The faithful shepherd Gudea
(vii.10) had come to know what was important, (so) he proceeded to do it.[18]

and both are sometimes visually or descriptively represented as the lion-headed or man-headed bird of prey known as the Anzu bird, something like the description given here in Cyl. A v.13-17 (cf. iv.14-19). The image retains features of Ningirsu as the god of rainstorm and fertility, but also and most especially the god of warfare, which is important in the Gudea Cylinders (see Porada 1992:69-72 and Jacobsen 1987b:394 n. 26; cf. the similar description of Inanna in Sargon's dream, Cooper 1983:77, 80, lines 19-24). At the end of her interpretation of the dream Nanshe advises Gudea to fashion a fine war chariot for Ningirsu in order to coax him to reveal more about his expectations regarding the temple to be built (Cyl. A vi.14–vii.8; cf. Cyl. B xiii.14–xiv.12 and the note on Cyl. A vii.10).

There are some striking similarities between the image in Gudea's dream and that of Nebuchadnezzar in Dan 2:31-33. The central figure of both was a giant (statue of a) man. Both figures are described beginning at the head and then moving to the chest or arm area, and finally the lower regions of the body (belly, legs, and feet). Moreover, in both dreams there is a sequence of actions surrounding the central figure.

Of course, the images are not the same, and Gudea's is not described as a "statue," but rather as a living figure of the god, Ningirsu, commanding Gudea to build his temple (Cyl. A v.17-18). The actions associated with the figure are also dissimilar (compare Cyl. A iv.22–v.10 and v.19–vi.13 with Dan 2:34-45). Although Ezekiel's theophany (Ezek 1) is textually distant from his temple restoration vision (Ezek 40-48), one could nevertheless also argue for some level of transformed correspondence between it and Gudea's description of Ningirsu (Sharon 1996:106-107).

[15] In her interpretation (Cyl. A v.21–vi.5), Nanshe explained that in the dream, among other things, the goddess Nisaba was consulting the tablet of the heavenly star(s) so that Gudea could construct the temple according to its holy star(s). Moreover, the god Nindub was copying the "plan" (*giš-ḫur*) of the temple onto a slate of lapis lazuli. Nanshe later advised Gudea to construct a fine war chariot for Ningirsu and present it to him (Cyl. A vi.14–vii.8), so that the god would look favorably upon the ruler and, therefore, reveal the *giš-ḫur* ("plan") of the temple (vii.6-8). Two subsequent dream incubations (Cyl. A viii.2–ix.5 and xx.6-8) and numerous other ritual preparations and procedures eventually led to the desired result. The details of the plan of the new temple (Cyl. A xix.20-21) and even a clear vision of the completed structure were granted to Gudea (xx.9-11). See the notes on Cyl. A i.21 above, and Cyl. A xvii.17 and xix.20 below.

[16] Regarding the "*tigidlu* bird" in line 10, see Civil 1987. The initial dream included a call for Gudea to work tirelessly, day and night, to accomplish the building of the new temple (Cyl. A vi.11), and this is what he did (Cyl. A xvii.5-9; xix.20-27; cf. also Stat. F ii.2-5 in Edzard 1997:47). Similar expressions of tireless compulsion for building the temple in Jerusalem are used of David (Ps 132:2-5), who, although he was not allowed to build the temple in his day, spared no expense or energy in making preparations for Solomon to do so (1 Chr 22:14-19; 28:2-29:5). See Hurowitz 1992:324-325. For the image of the donkey, see Tsevat 1962.

[17] See the note on Cyl. A vi.5 above.

[18] Cyl. A vii.9-10 is the first occurrence of the major structural formula that occurs five times and divides the composition into seven major sections (see the introduction above, and Averbeck 1997:66-71 for discussion and occurrences of the formula in other compositions as well). The sentence has two verbs. The first is *ḫamṭu* (*mu-zu*), referring to the previous section, and the second is *marû* (*ì-ga-túm-mu*), leading to what

Following Nanshe's advice (vi.14–vii.8) Gudea builds a chariot for Ningirsu and presents it to him as a gift in preparation for incubating a dream (vii.11–viii.1).

Gudea incubates the second dream (Cyl. A viii.2–ix.4)

Afterwards, he spent days at the temple, [k]
he spent nights.[19]
He quieted the assembly (of people), turned away conflict,
(viii.5) eliminated all disruptive speech from the area.
At the Shugalam, the awe-inspiring place, the place where judgment is rendered,
the place (from which) Ningirsu looks out over all the lands,
a fat sheep, a fat-tail sheep, (and) a fattened kid the ruler
laid down on the skin of an unmated female kid.[20]
(viii.10) Juniper, being the pure plant of the mountain, he stuffed into the fire;
cedar resin, being the fragrance of the god,
gave off its incense.
He rose up before his lord in the assembly (and) prayed to him;
he stepped up to him in the Ubshukkinna, put his hand to his nose (in humble salute):[21]
(viii.15) "O my king Ningirsu, the lord who returns

k Gen 46:1-4; 1 Kgs3:4-5 (= 2 Chr 1:6-7)

follows (the preformative *ì-ga-* implies sequence). A literal rendering would be, "The faithful shepherd Gudea had come to know what was great, he proceeded to carry out what was great." See Averbeck 1997:67 n. 73 for further discussion of the grammar (cf. Hurowitz 1992:52-53).

First, in the immediate context here Nanshe had just previously advised Gudea to fashion a war chariot and offer it as a gift to Ningirsu. This was intended to persuade the deity to be more forthcoming with revelations about the temple that Gudea had been commissioned to build for him (Cyl. A vi.14–vii.8). Gudea complied with her advice (vii.11-29) and then moved directly into dream incubation rituals and procedures (vii.30–ix.4). He thereby induced Ningirsu to appear a second time in a less enigmatic dream (ix.5–xii.11; cf. the first dream in i.12-21, Gudea's description of it to Nanshe in iv.14–v.11, and Nanshe's interpretation in v.12–vi.13).

The formula occurs a second time in Cyl. A xii.20, where it makes the transition from Gudea's confirmation of the second dream through extispicy (xii.12-19) to the ritual and pragmatic work of building the new Eninnu (xii.21–xxv.21). Another formula divides this large and complicated section into five (or six) segments (see the note on Cyl. A xiv.5-6). The third occurrence of the major formula is in Cyl. A xxv.22-23, where it makes the transition from the narrative remark announcing the completion of the temple (xxv.20-21) to the outfitting of the completed temple and its associated structures (xxv.24–xxx.5).

The fourth time the formula appears is in the early part of the second Cylinder (Cyl. B ii.7-8). In this instance, it marks the transition from Gudea's initial prayers and rituals in preparation for the consecration, dedication, and divine occupation of the new temple (i.12–ii.6), to the actual induction of Ningirsu and Baba, and their attending deities, into the new Eninnu (ii.9–xiii.10). Finally, the formula occurs in expanded form for the fifth time in Cyl. B xiii.11-13, where it signals the transition from the narrator's summary of divine support for the new Eninnu (xii.26–xiii.10), to the housewarming celebration of the induction of Ningirsu and Baba into their new home (xiii.14–xxiv.8).

[19] Cyl. A viii.2–ix.4 describes the procedures for incubating the second dream (cf. the notes on Cyl. A i.17 above and xx.8 below). After following Nanshe's instructions to fashion a new war chariot and present it to Ningursu (Cyl. A vii.11–viii.1; cf. the goddess's instructions in vi.14–vii.8), Gudea proceeded to incubate a second dream revelation. His goal was to gain further information about how to proceed with the building project commissioned to him in the first dream (see Cyl. A i.14-21 and the notes there).

Cyl. A viii.2-3 introduces the multiple-day incubation scene in the temple. The incubation procedures included complete silence and lack of conflict in the assembly (viii.4-5), various kinds of sacrifices and purification procedures (viii.6-12), and a prayer to Ningirsu requesting that he be more forthcoming regarding the temple (see the note on Cyl. A viii.19 below for the details). In a third dream, which was also incubated, Gudea saw a vision of the completed temple (Cyl. A xx.5-11; see the note on Cyl. A xx.8).

Dream incubation is known elsewhere in Sum. and other ANE literature. E.g., according to the Sum. Sargon Legend, it was through dream incubation that Sargon the Great foresaw that he would take over the kingdom from Zababa. According to the Gilgamesh epic, Gilgamesh incubated dreams as he and Enkidu approached their battle with Humbaba. The beginning of the Ug. Aqhat epic describes how Daniel spent six days and nights incubating a dream.

As with Gudea's first dream (see the note on Cyl. A i.17 above), in the Bible it is often difficult to determine whether or not a dream was incubated (Gnuse 1984:38). Solomon (1 Kgs 3:4-5; 2 Chr 1:6-7), and perhaps Jacob (Gen 46:1-4 [cf. 26:23-25]), incubated dreams by presenting offerings at altars or sanctuaries and lying down to sleep there. Some scholars propose that the close connection between temple building and dream incubation in the Gudea Cylinders is discernible also in the relationship between Solomon's incubated dream and the building of the Solomonic temple. Note the close proximity of the two in 2 Chr 1-2 (cf. esp. Kapelrud 1963 and Weinfeld 1972:250-254). This explanation of the text is, however, highly questionable (Rummel 1981:277-284; Kenik 1983:181-182 and n. 1; Brekelmans 1982). One interpretation of Ps 17:3 ("you have visited me at night") combined with v. 15b ("when I awake I will be satisfied with your likeness") is that it refers to the incubation of a dream during the night and the joy of the morning thereafter (Kraus 1988:247, 249). For other possible reflections of dream incubation in the Psalms see Kraus 1986:132 and 147, and for further discussion see Ackerman 1991:112-120; Averbeck 1987:506-579; Butler 1998:18-19, 73, 217-239; Gnuse 1984:11-55; McAlpine 1987:155-179; Miller 1985:230-231.

[20] This line is particularly difficult. Lit., one could read lines 8-9, "a fat sheep, a fat-tail sheep, a fattened kid; the ruler an unmated female kid made lie down in its skin." Edzard (1997:74) and Jacobsen (1987b:398) take it to mean that the ruler made the animals in line 8 lie down "on the skin" of the unmated female kid in line 8. The reference to the "skin" (Sum. *kuš*) of an animal in the context of dream incubation suggests, however, that this is somehow related to the well-documented sleeping of the incubant on the skin of a sacrificed animal in later incubation rituals. See Ackerman 1991:94-108 for a good summary of the sources from the wider Mediterranean world.

The *unmated* female kid would seem to reflect the concern for purity. Perhaps when the ruler would lie down to sleep and incubate a dream he would lie down on this skin (cf. Cyl. A ix.5-6). Previously, he would have identified the skin as a place of supplication by offering the other animals to Ningirsu on it. The plural days and nights mentioned in Cyl. A viii.2-3 suggest that he went through this procedure several times. In any case, the syntax of the passage is awkward. Perhaps we could take it to mean that the animals in line 8 would have previously been offered as sacrifices to Ningirsu, and it is the ruler who would lie down each night on the skin of an unmated female kid in line 9.

[21] The Ubshukkinna was a relatively public (see *un-gá* lit. "among the people" in line 13; *un* = Akk. *nišū* "mankind, people, inhabitants") meeting place (*ukkin* in Ubshukkina = Akk. *puḫru* "assembly") located somewhere in the courtyard of the temple (Jacobsen 1976b:86).

The Sum. verbal expression *kiri$_4$ šu gál* means lit. "to place hand to nose" and is used often in the context of obeisance and prayer. For a review of occurrences in Sum. literature, discussion, and references to iconographic evidence see Averbeck 1987:463-468 and the literature cited there.

to the Aḫush,[22]
the true lord, the semen ejaculated by the great mountain,
the glorious hero who has no challenger,
Ningirsu, I would build your temple for you
(but) I do not have my signal.[23]
(viii.20) O warrior, you have called for the long enduring thing(s),
(but) O son of Enlil, lord Ningirsu,
I do not know the heart of it from you.[24]
Your heart, rising like the sea,
crashing down like waves,
(viii.25) roaring like fast flowing water,
destroying cities like a flood,
striking at the rebel land(s) like a storm;
(ix.1) O my king, your heart is fast flowing water that cannot be stopped up,
O warrior, your heart is distant like heaven,
O son of Enlil, lord Ningirsu,
as for me, what do I know from you?"

Ningirsu speaks to Gudea in a dream (Cyl. A ix.5–xii.11)

(ix.5) For a second time to the one lying down, to the one lying down
he stepped up to the head, was touching (him) briefly(?) (saying):
"That which you will build for me, that which you will build for me,
O ruler, my temple which you will build for me,
O Gudea, in order to build my temple I will indeed give you its signal,[25]
(ix.10) the pure heavenly star(s) of my ritual procedure(s) I will indeed proclaim to you.
My temple, the Eninnu founded by An,

l Ezek 47:1-12; Hag 1:2-11; 2:15-19; Zech 9:9-13

its capacities are the greatest capacities, exceeding all capacities;
the temple whose king looks far into the distance,
as at the screeching of the Anzu bird
(ix.15) heaven trembles (at its screeching).
Its terrifying radiance reaches up to heaven.
The great fearfulness of my temple is cast over all the foreign lands.
At (the mention of) its name all the foreign lands assemble from the horizon,
Magan and Meluhha descend from their mountains.

Ningirsu continues with a description of his own divine position and powers as the occupant of the Eninnu (ix.20–x.14) and his other temples (x.15–x.29).

(xi.1) My temple, the foremost temple of all the lands,
the right arm of Lagash,
the Anzu bird screeching throughout heaven,
the Eninnu, my royal temple;
(xi.5) O faithful shepherd Gudea,
when you bring your faithful hand to bear for me [l]
I will cry out to heaven for rain.
From heaven let abundance come to you,
let the people receive abundance with you,
(xi.10) with the founding of my temple
let abundance come![26]
The great fields will lift up (their) hand(s) to you,
the canal will stretch out its neck to you,
(up to) the mounds, places to which water does not (normally) rise,
(xi.15) the water will rise for you.
Sumer will pour out abundant oil because of you,
will weigh out abundant wool because of you.
When you fill in my foundation,

[22] Edzard and others take Sum. *a-ḫuš* to refer to "fierce (*ḫuš*) water (*a*)," and therefore translate, "who turns back fierce waters." We know from elsewhere, however, that it could also refer to a temple shrine known as the Aḫush (Falkenstein 1966:167; Steible 1982:2.106 n. on line 3; pointed out to me by Å. Sjöberg and the late H. Behrens).

[23] In Cyl. A viii.18-19 Gudea proclaims to Ningirsu that he would go ahead and build the temple, but he was in need of a *giskim* "signal" (= Akk. *ittu*) before he could proceed. The term *giskim* occurs again at the beginning and end of the incubated dream for which the ruler was praying at this moment (see Cyl. A ix.7–xii.11). At the beginning of the dream Ningirsu announces that he will indeed grant Gudea his *giskim* (ix.9), and at the end he promises further *giskim* when needed (xii.10-11). The first "signal" was the dream itself. In it Ningirsu, who had already appeared with Anzu-bird features in the first dream (see the note on Cyl. A v.17 above), begins with a corresponding description of the temple as having the awe-inspiring characteristics of the Anzu bird (Cyl. A ix.14-15). The Anzu bird nature of the temple is mentioned again at the beginning of the second part of the dream (xi.3), in which Ningirsu called the ruler to actually begin the construction of the Eninnu and promised him proper support and supply in the process (xi.6–xii.9).

At the very end of the dream Ningirsu promises Gudea that he will know his "signal" in that day (referring forward to the time when he had begun the construction of the Eninnu) when "I (Ningirsu) have touched your arm with fire" (Cyl. A xii.10-11, see the note there). This refers forward to another time when he would receive a "signal" so that he could proceed further with the construction of the temple. It is most likely the third dream, which was also incubated, that Ningirsu is referring to here (see the note on Cyl. A xx.8 below).

[24] In addition to not having the proper *giskim* "signal" as a guide during the building process (see the note on Cyl. A viii.19 above), Gudea also did not know Ningirsu's exact "meaning" or "intent" (Sum. *šà* lit. "heart"; see the note on Cyl. A ii.3 above) with regard to the original dream "command" (lit. *inim* "word"; see the combination of these two terms in Cyl. A i.23–ii.3, iii.24-28, and finally xix.28–xx.1). Therefore, another part of the prayer request in the dream incubation procedure was that, in a play on words, Ningirsu would make known the "intent" (*šà*; Cyl. A viii.20-22) of his command, but this would require that the deity's storming "heart" (*šà*) would become calm (viii.23–ix.4; cf. the Nanshe's rationale in vii.4-8). This was accomplished in two stages. Gudea came to know the "intent" of Ningirsu through the first incubated dream (Cyl. A xii.18-19) and more became clear to him later, after the successful fashioning of the first brick (Cyl. A xix.28).

[25] See the note on Cyl. A viii.19 above.

[26] Gudea Cyl. A xi.6-8 and 18-25 are strikingly similar to Hag 2:18-19, where the day of the founding of the temple is the day when the Lord would begin to bless the people with abundance (cf. Hag 1:2-11; 2:15-17; and also Zech 9:9-13). Ezek 47:1-12 describes the waters flowing from under the threshold of the restored temple eastward to the Arabah and bringing fertility and abundance to the region through which it flows. See the note on Cyl. A i.9 above and Averbeck 1987:189-193; Hurowitz 1992:322-323; Meyers and Meyers 1987:65-66; Sharon 1996:99-102.

when you bring your faithful hand to bear for me at my temple,
(xi.20) (then) to the mountain range, the place where the north wind dwells,
I will direct my steps.
The man of abundant strength, the north wind — from the mountain range, the pure place,
I will have it blow straight to you.
When it has given fortitude of heart to the people,
(xi.25) one man will do the work of two men.[27]
At night moonlight will continually go forth for you,
at midday sunlight will continually go forth for you daily.
(xii.1) The day will build the temple for you,
the night will make it grow for you.
From below, *ḫalub*
and *biḫan*(?) wood I will have come to you.
(xii.5) From above, cedar, cypress, and *zabalum* wood I will have brought to you freely(?).
From the mountain of ebony trees
I will have ebony wood brought to you.
From the mountain of stone, the great stone of the mountain range
I will have cut into blocks for you.
(xii.10) In that day, when I have touched your arm with fire[28]
you will surely know my signal."
Gudea awoke, having been asleep.
He trembled, having had a dream.
To the command of Ningirsu
(xii.15) he bowed the head (in submission).
He reached into the white he-goat.
He performed an extispicy; his extispicy was favorable.
The heart of Ningirsu,
being (clear as) daylight, went forth for Gudea.

III. *The Construction of the New Eninnu* (Cyl. A xii.20–xxv.21)

Narrative transition to the initial stages of construction (xii.20)

He had come to know what was important, (so) he proceeded to do it.[29]

A. Initial Excavations, Social Calm, Purity, and Preparation of Brick Mold and Hoe (Cyl. A xii.21–xiv.6)[30]

Gudea initiates the building project (Cyl. A xii.21–xiii.15)

(xii.21-22) The ruler set forth instructions in his whole city as if to one man.
All Lagash land acted with a unified heart like sons of the same woman.
It took hold of tools, tore out shrubs,
(xii.25) (and) stacked the (torn up) foliage in piles(?).

Gudea eliminates social, legal, and economic strife and abuse, as well as physical and ritual impurity from the city (xii.26–xiii.15).[31]

Gudea prepares the brick-mold and hoe, and purifies the sacred area (Cyl. A xiii.16–xiv.6)

He made a he-goat lie down before the box of the brick-mold(?);
invoked (an extispicy for) the brick over the he-goat.
He looked with favor at the hoe;
the shepherd, whose name is called by Nanshe, established it in princely form.[32]
(xiii.20) The box of the brick-mold, which he designed;
the hoe, which he established in princely form;

[27] The translation here follows Edzard and Jacobsen, but it could also mean "one man will work with another" (Sum. *lú-aš lú-min-da kin mu-da-ak-ke₄* lit. "one man, with two men [or, a second man], he will do work").

[28] The expression "touched your arm with fire" has been interpreted in various ways. Landsberger suggested that the forthcoming *giskim* "signal" would literally include an accompanying sensation that Gudea's arm was burning (Landsberger 1964:72; cf. the note on Cyl. A viii.19 above). Jacobsen translates "the fire will touch your borders" (Sum. *á* can mean either "arm" or "border"), suggesting that it refers to the future purification of the foundation plot by fire. The actual construction of the building could begin once the fire reached the borders of the foundation plot (see Jacobsen 1987b:403 and n. 56 where he refers to Cyl. A xiii.25 *sic*; cf. Cyl. A xiii.12-13).

The translation here takes the expression to be a metaphorical way of referring to Gudea's sleepless energetic obsession to fulfill the commission to build the temple. This was described in Nanshe's interpretation of the first dream (Cyl. A vi.9-13) but not actually experienced by the ruler until Cyl. A xvii.5–xx.4 (note esp. xvii.7-9 and xix.21-27). It was only after this was fulfilled that Gudea came to understand the full intent (*šà* lit. "heart") of Ningirsu regarding the construction of the new Eninnu (Cyl. A xix.28–xx.1; cf. the notes on Cyl. A i). Thus, the final *giskim* "signals" consisted of the various oracles and divinations described in Cyl. A xx.2-11, including another incubated dream (see the note on Cyl. A xx.8 below).

[29] See the note on Cyl. A vii.10 above.

[30] For an explanation of the literary structure of Gudea Cyl. A xii.21–xxv.19 reflected in these headings see the note on Cyl. A xiv.6 below.

[31] The elimination of social, legal, and economic strife and abuse, as well as physical and ritual impurity from the city and sanctuary were major concerns. In Cyl. A xii.26–xiii.15 Gudea enforced this in order to set the stage for making the first brick (Cyl. A xiii.16-23 and xviii.3–xix.19; cf. also the purification of the city in xiii.24-25, and the more expanded parallel version of this in Stat. B iii.6–v.11, Edzard 1997:32). See the translation of Cyl. B xvii.18–xviii.11 (and the note on xviii.11) for similar concerns during the seven-day dedication festival.

[32] Cyl. A xiii.16-23 is difficult, but clearly recounts the initial preparations for the making the first brick, the actual fabrication of which is described in Cyl. A xviii.3–xix.19 (see the note on Cyl. A xix.19 below). These initial preparations involved, above all, divinatory approval of the "box (or perhaps 'shed') of the brick-mold" (xiii.16, 20, Sum. *pisan-ù-šub-ba*; compare Heimpel 1987a:206-207 with Jacobsen 1987b:404 and Edzard 1997:77) and the "hoe" (xiii.18, 21, reading *KA.AL* as *zú-al(a)* lit. "tooth of the hoe," normally written *al-zú*) or perhaps "clay pit" (taking *KA.AL* as a genitive *ka-al(a)* lit. "mouth of the hoe" = Akk. *kalakku* "excavation"; Heimpel 1987a:206-208).

With regard to the latter, in favor of reading *zú-al* "hoe" see the writing ^{giš}*zú-al* in *RA* 16 (1919):19 ii.25 in a delivery text (one cannot "deliver" a "clay pit") with the determinative for something made of wood, along with ^{giš}*al-zú-dili* "hoe with one tooth" (Hoe and Plow 174, cf. *COS* 1.580;

being the Anzu-bird of the standard of his king,
he caused (them) to shine brightly as protective emblems.[33]
He was purifying the city for him (Ningirsu), (its) heights and depths(?), (down) to the underground waters(?);[34]
(xiii.25) he was cleansing the heights(?) for him.
Juniper, being the pure plant of the mountain, he stuffed into the fire;
cedar resin, being the fragrance of the god, gave off its incense.
For him the day was for prayer offering(s);
he was passing the night in petition.
(xiv.1) The Anunna gods of all Lagash land;
to build the temple of Ningirsu
they stood with Gudea
in prayer and supplication.
(xiv.5-6) For the faithful shepherd, Gudea, it was cause for rejoicing.[35]

B. Gathering of Laborers, Provisions, and Raw Materials (Cyl. A xiv.7–xvii.4?)

At that time the ruler imposed a levy on his land.[36] [m]
On his whole country,
on the Guedinna of Ningirsu,
(xiv.10) he imposed a levy.

The following materials, their source, and their transport are of special interest:

Wood (Cyl. A xv.19–xvi.1)[37]
Into the cedar mountain, which no man can enter,[n]
(xv.20) for Gudea the lord Ningirsu
prepared the way.
He (Gudea) cut down its cedars with great axes.
For the *Sharur* weapon, the right arm of Lagash,
the flood weapon of his king,
(xv.25) he dressed (the logs).
Being like majestic snakes floating on water,
from the cedar mountain range, cedar rafts,
from the cypress mountain range,
cypress rafts,
(xv.30) from the *zabalum* mountain range,
zabalum rafts,
great big spruce trees, plane trees,
and *eranum* trees;
their great big rafts, which floated (downstream),
(xv.35) at the majestic quay of Kasurra

m Exod 35:10-19; 36:1-4; 1 Kgs 5:27-32[13-18]; 2 Chr 2:1-2

n 1 Kgs 5:20-24[6-10]; 2 Chr 2:3-16

references courtesy of Åke Sjöberg, personal communication). If *pisan* means "box" of the brick-mold, then we have two primary implements for the making of bricks, the hoe for mixing the clay and the brick-mold into which the clay was poured. The particular hoe and brick-mold were selected by extispicy. For another interpretation, see Hallo 1962:9.

[33] The rendering here takes Sum. *urì* "protective emblems" (line 23) to be a reference to the brick-mold and the hoe (lines 20-21), which take on the character and function of Ningirsu's Anzu bird standard in this context (line 22). Others take it to be the pole on which the regular Anzu-bird standard of Ningirsu was raised for display (Heimpel 1987a:209; cf. Jacobsen 1987b:404 "upright"), or the actual banner affixed to the pole (Edzard 1997:77). The reference to "designing" the brick-mold in line 20 suggests that perhaps the brick-mold had the design of the Anzu-bird on it. In the immediately following context, the brick-mold and hoe may have been paraded around as part of the purification procedures for the temple foundation area (xiii.24-27).

[34] The rendering here follows *PSD* B:199 (cf. the notes in Averbeck 1987:639 nn. 259 and 260). According to that interpretation, the line reads lit., "the height (Sum. u_5 = Akk. *šaqû* "high") the depth (Sum. *U* = $buru_3$ = "hole, cavity; depth") toward the underground water (Sum. *BAD* = *idim* = Akk. *nagbu* "underground water") the city was purifying for him." Others read the line differently: lit. "a mound (= same as above) toward eighteen *iku* (Sum. *U* = $buru_3$ = Akk. *buru* = "18 *iku*" of ground or surface area) six *iku* (Sum. *BAD* = $eše_3$ = "6 *iku*" of ground or surface area) the city was purifying for him." Thus, "a mound up to 24 *iku* the city was purifying for him" (Edzard 1997:77; cf. Jacobsen 1987b:404).

[35] Cyl. A xiv.5-6 is the first occurrence of a *minor* structural formula that occurs four (or five) times, dividing the third and most complicated section of Cylinder A (xii.21–xxv.21) into five (or six) segments (see the note on Cyl. A vii.10 for the *major* structural formula and overall structure of Gudea Cylinders A and B). See Averbeck 1997:71-74 for discussion of this minor formula and its uses in other compositions as well (cf. Hurowitz 1992:53-54). We are not sure whether it occurs four or five times because the text is broken at Cyl. A xvii.1-4, and the subject after the break is different from before it. The formula may have appeared again in the break (Averbeck 1997:72).

The grammar and translation of the formulaic sentence has been much debated (see Averbeck 1997:71-72 n. 88 for sources and discussion). It reads: *sipa-zi gù-dé-a ḫúl-la-gim im-ma-na-ni-íb-gar*, and may be rendered lit., "It (*-b-* verbal infix refers to the previous accomplishment) established (*gar*) (something) like (*-gim*) rejoicing (*ḫúl-la*) there (*-ni-*) for the faithful shepherd, Gudea (*sipa-zi gù-dé-a* plus the *-na-* verbal infix meaning 'for')." Others take *ḫúl-la-gim* plus the verb *gar* to mean "to make joy like a festival," and render the sentence something like this: "For the faithful shepherd, Gudea, it was like a festival day." In either case the point is that Gudea truly rejoiced over what had just been accomplished.

In the present context he had successfully made preparation and purification of the populace, sacred precinct, and brick-mold, and had attained the cooperation of the Anunna gods in the ongoing work of the project (Cyl. A xii.21–xiv.4). The next clear use of the formula is in Cyl. A xvii.28, after Gudea had gathered laborers and materials (xiv.7–xvii.4?; text broken at xvii.1-4, see remarks above), and surveyed and laid out the sacred area (xvii.5-27). The third occurrence is in Cyl. A xx.4, after the successful fabrication and presentation of the first brick (xvii.29–xx.3). Finally, the formula occurs a fourth time in Cyl. A xx.12, after the oracular confirmation of the architectural plan (xx.5-11). The final segment of this section of the document comes after the last instance of the formula, and provides an extended account of the actual construction of the new temple (xx.13–xxv.19). The whole section ends with the third occurrence of the major structural formula (xxv.22-23; see the note on Cyl. A vii.10 above).

[36] The term *zi-ga* "rising" in Cyl. A xiv.7, 10, 13, etc. combines with the verb *gar* "to set, establish" or *gál* "to (cause to) be" to attain the meaning "to impose a levy." According to Cyl. A xiv.7-28, Gudea levied laborers and the provisions to support them from the various regions of the land in order to build the temple. Likewise, Moses and Solomon levied laborers when they built the tabernacle and the temple, respectively (Exod 35:10-19; 36:1-4; 1 Kgs 5:27-32[13-18]; 2 Chr 2:1-2).

[37] Gudea had wood brought from various places all over the ANE for the building of the temple (Cyl. A xv.6–xvi.1; cf. Stat. B v.21-36 and v.45–vi.2). This included cedar wood from the cedar mountain range in northern Syria, along the upper Mediterranean coast (Cyl. A xv.19-25). The parallel passage in Stat. B v.28 refers to this specifically as the Amanus mountains (Edzard 1997:33). Solomon obtained cedar from the same

(xvi.1) [he (Gudea) moored for him (Ningirsu)].

[perhaps another lost line?]

Stone (Cyl. A xvi.3-6)[38]
[Into the stone mountain, which no man can enter,
for Gudea] the lord [Ningir]su
(xvi.5) [prepar]ed the way.
Its great big stones he brought in their blocks. [o]

The account of transporting stones and bitumen continues (xvi.7-12).

Precious metals and stones (Cyl. A xvi.13-32)
To the ruler who built the Eninnu,
great things came to his aid.
(xvi.15) From Kimash the copper mountain range
called itself for him.
He unloaded its copper from its raft(?).[39]
To the man who was about to build the temple of his king,
to the ruler, gold from its mountain
(xvi.20) was brought in its dust (form).[40] [p]

The account continues with the gathering of other precious metals and stones (xvi.21-32).

C. Surveying and Laying Out the Sacred Area (Cyl. A xvii.5-28)

Enki reveals the design of the temple complex to Gudea (Cyl. A xvii.5-17)
(xvii.5) He [prolonged] the da[ys for him];

o 1 Kgs 5:29-32[15-18]; 2 Chr 2:2, 17-18 (cf. 1 Chr 22:2-5; 28:14-18)

p Exod 35:5, 22; 1 Kgs 6:20-22, 30, 35; 2 Chr 3:4-10; 4:19-5:1 (cf. 1 Chr 22:14-16)

q Ps 132:2-5

r Ezek 40

he prolonged the nights for him(?).[41]
For the sake of building the temple of his king,
he did not sleep at night,
he did not bow the head in sleep at noon.[42] [q]
(xvii.10) Being the one at whom Nanshe looked with favor,
being the man of the heart of Enlil,
being the ruler ... (?) of Ningirsu,
Gudea, being born in a lofty sanctuary
by Gatumdug;
(xvii.15-16) Nisaba opened the house of wisdom for him,
Enki prepared the plan of the house for him.[43]

Gudea proceeds to survey and measure off the sacred area where the temple was to be built (xvii.18-28), concluding with lines 26-28:

(xvii.26) It being the right field(?), he laid the measuring cords (on it),[44] [r]
drove in stakes at its borders, and checked (the measurements) himself.
It was cause for rejoicing for him (Gudea).[45]

D. Fabricating, Presenting, and Placing the First Brick (Cyl. A xvii.29–xx.4)

Gudea makes the first brick (Cyl. A xvii.29–xix.15)
During the evening he went to the old temple in supplication.
(xviii.1) At the throne room of the Girnun, Gudea

geographical region through Hiram, king of Tyre (1 Kgs 5:20[6]; cf. 2 Sam 5:11-12 and 7:2), and both Gudea and Hiram floated them to their destinations in the form of rafts (see Cyl. A xv.26–xvi.1 and 1 Kgs 5:23[9]). See *ANET* 268-269 and Hurowitz 1992:205-207.

[38] The lineation of column xvi is uncertain at the beginning because the text is broken, but the main substance of it can be restored from Cyl. A xv.19-21.

Both Gudea (Cyl. A xvi.3-12; cf. Stat. B vi.59-63, Edzard 1997:35) and Solomon (1 Kgs 5:29-32[15-18]; 2 Chr 2:2, 17-18 [cf. 1 Chr 22:2-5; 28:14-18]) had large stones quarried and brought to them for laying the foundations of their respective temples. See *ANET* 268-269 and Hurowitz 1992:205-207.

[39] For this translation of this line see *PSD* A1:61. Others take it to refer to the actual mining of the copper (e.g., Edzard 1997:79 and Jacobsen 1987b:408).

[40] Gudea (Cyl. A xvi.13-32), Moses (Exod 35:5, 22), and Solomon (1 Kgs 6:20-22, 30, 35; 2 Chr 3:4-10; 4:19-5:1 [cf. 1 Chr 22:14-16]) all collected and used gold and other precious metals and stones in the construction of their sanctuaries. See *ANET* 268-269 and Hurowitz 1992:206.

[41] Line 5 is quite broken, but the first *ud* (= "day") and the *mu-* verbal prefix are relatively clear. The translation of line 6 offered here follows Falkenstein's view that we should read *DUGUD DUGUD* as gi_{25}-gi_{25} = gi_6-gi_6 "nights" (Falkenstein 1978:1.7-8). If this is correct, then "day" in line 5 suggests that these two lines should be treated as corresponding doublets. Others take *DUGUD DUGUD* as a reference to rain clouds (e.g., Edzard 1997:79 and Jacobsen 1987b:409). Falkenstein's analysis fits well with the following lines.

[42] For Gudea's single-minded devotion and untiring effort in building the temple reflected in Cyl. A xvii.5-9 see also Cyl. A vi.11 above and the note there. See also the discussion in Hurowitz 1992:324-325.

[43] Although some of the details are unclear to us and subject to various interpretations, Nisaba's appearance along with Enki has to do with Enki's preparing a proper "plan" (*giš-ḫur*; cf. Cyl. A v.21–vi.5). In this instance, *giš-ḫur* may refer to the plan of the temple complex as a whole. Cyl. A xvii.29 refers to Gudea going to the old Eninnu, and xviii.6-9 speaks of Gudea going out from the "holy city" (i.e., the temple complex) for a "second time." Gudea Statue B, on which is inscribed a shorter but parallel account of the building of the new Eninnu, has the ruler sitting with a tablet resting on his lap (see Johansen 1978:10 and plates 19-22). On the tablet there is a diagram of a walled-in area with six gate areas. Heimpel has argued convincingly that this diagram depicts the external walls of the Eninnu complex, and with this we agree. He also suggests on the basis of his interpretation of one inscription that the actual sanctuary of Ningirsu within the complex was called the "White Eagle (Anzu-bird) House" (Sum. *é* $anzu_2$-$babbar_2$, Heimpel 1996:19; regarding $anzu_2$ see the note on Cyl. A v.17 above). The latter point seems less certain, but it is true that a separate Tarsirsir sanctuary of Baba was also part of the complex (Heimpel 1996:22; see Cyl. A xxvi.9-11 and Gudea Stat. E ii.14-20, Edzard 1997:43).

Therefore, it seems that Cyl. A xvii.17 refers to the revelation of the *giš-ḫur* "plan" of the overall temple complex, and Cyl. A xix.20-27 describes the initial stages of Gudea's proper implementation of the plan in close association with the proper making of the first brick (Cyl. A xvii.3–xix.19). See also the notes on Cyl. A i.21 and vi.5 above (cf. vii.6-8).

[44] Some read Sum. GAN_2 = *iku* = Akk. *ikû* an area of land a little smaller than an acre (ca. 60 yards square), rather than Sum. GAN_2 = $gana_2$ = Akk. *eqlu* "field." *PSD* A2:9 translates, "he laid the measuring cords down on (every) cultivated field and put pegs at its borders," but this context is concerned with a particular field, the "right field." Ezekiel was shown a vision of a man measuring the dimensions of the temple walls and gates (Ezek 40).

[45] See the note on Cyl. A xiv.6 above.

was calming the heart
for him (Ningirsu).
Day dawned, he bathed,
(and) dressed himself suitably(?).
(xviii.5) The sun was shining brightly for him.
Gudea went out a second time from the holy city
(and) offered up a perfect bull and a perfect he-goat.
He went to the temple
(and) put his hand to his nose (in humble salute).
(xviii.10) The holy basket, the rightly decreed brick-mold,[46]

[line too broken to read]

... head lifted high he went along.
Lugalkurdub ('King Who Shakes the Mountains') went before him,
(xviii.15) Igalim ('Bison Door') followed behind him,
Ningishzida ('Lord of the Good Tree'), his (personal) god, was leading him by the hand.
In the box of the brick-mold he libated fine(?) water.
While *adab*, *šim*, and *ala* instruments resounded for the ruler,
he anointed the brick hoe,(?)[47]
(xviii.20) hoed in honey, butter, and ... oil;
sap and resin(?) from various kinds of trees
he worked into the paste.
He picked up the holy carrying basket (and) stepped up to the brick-mold.
Gudea put the clay into the brick-mold.
(xviii.25) He made the long enduring thing appear in splendor;
the brick of the temple he set forth in splendid appearance.
The lands sprinkled (it) with oil;
sprinkled (it) with (essence of) cedar.
(xix.1) His city and all Lagash land joyously
passed the day with him.

s Zech 4:7(?)

t 1 Sam 6:10-12

(Later) he shook the brick-mold (and) the brick fell into the sunlight (to dry).
At the hoe (used for mixing) of the clay in its mold(?)
(xix.5) he looked with gratification.
(With) *ḫašur* resin and sap
he anointed (the brick).
Over the brick which he had made in the brick-mold
Utu (the sun god) rejoiced.
(xix.10) In his mold, which rises like a lofty canal,
king En[ki decre]ed destiny.
... (?) he entered into the temple.
He lifted the brick out of the box of the brick-mold.
(Like) a holy crown lifted up to heaven,
(xix.15) he lifted the brick up and carried it around among his people.[48] [s]

Gudea energetically devotes himself to laying out the plan of the temple (Cyl. A xix.16-27)

Being (like) the holy team of Utu tossing the(ir) head(s);
being (like) that brick lifting its head toward heaven,
like the cow of Nanna (the moon god), ready to be hitched in its pen;
he placed the brick (and) walked about in the temple.
(xix.20) Gudea was laying out the plan of the temple.[49]
Being (like) Nisaba, who understands numbers,
like a young man building a house for the first time,
sweet sleep was not entering his eyes.
Like a cow that keeps its eye on its calf, [t]
(xix.25) he went to the temple in constant worry.
Like a man who puts (only) a little food in his mouth,
he did not tire from being constantly on the go.[50]

[46] For helpful translations as well as philological and interpretive remarks on Cyl. A xviii.10–xix.20 see Heimpel 1987a:206-211.

[47] For the translations "box" and "hoe" in lines 17-19 see the note on Cyl. A xiii.19 above.

[48] The first and foremost event in laying the foundation of the temple was making the first brick, the so-called "destined brick" (Sum. *sig₄-nam-tar-ra*; Cyl. A vi.7; cf. i.15, v.7, vi.7) or "true brick of the Eninnu" (Sum. *sig₄-zi-é-ninnu*; Cyl. A vi.8). There were two separate parts of the process (Heimpel 1987a:210): the previous preparations for making the first brick (Cyl. A xiii.16-23; see the note on Cyl. A xiii.19 and 23 above) and now the actual making of the first brick with great ritual pomp and circumstance (Cyl. A xviii.3–xix.19). Finally, he placed the first brick as the ritual initiation of the actual construction of the new temple.

Later we hear of Gatumdug, the mother goddess of Lagash, giving birth to the bricks used to build the Eninnu (Cyl. A xx.17-18). In other places *sig₄* "brick" refers to the new Eninnu as a whole "brickwork" (Cyl. A xxi.25, B i.3, xiii.7, xx.15, 16, 18) even "the destined brickwork" (Cyl. B xxi.18-19). The first "destined brick" was in a sense the prototype of the Eninnu as a whole and needed to be fabricated in a way that honored it, the future temple as a whole, and Ningirsu himself.

Although there is no clear biblical parallel, some biblical scholars have compared Gudea's first brick and the "first" or "former brick" (Akk. *libittu maḫrītu*) in the Mesopotamian *kalû*-ritual for rebuilding temples with the "head" or "former stone" (Heb. *hāʾeben hārʾōšāh*) referred to in Zech 4:7 (Halpern 1978:170-171). Others associate Zechariah's stone with the dedication of the temple (e.g., Hurowitz 1992:261 n.2), but in its context Zech 4:9 does indeed refer to laying the foundation of the second temple in Jerusalem.

[49] According to the original dream, the revelation of the plan of the temple was to be closely associated with the molding of the first brick (Cyl. A vi.3-8), and Gudea would then work feverishly to complete the construction of the temple (vi.9-13). This corresponds to the sequence here of molding the first brick (Cyl. A xvii.3–xix.19), and then feverishly working to to lay out the plan of the temple at the sacred site (xix.20-27). Cp. the notes on Cyl. i.21, vi.5, and xvii.17 above.

[50] See the note on Cyl. A vi.11 above.

Gudea gains full understanding of Ningirsu's intentions for the temple (Cyl. A xix.28–xx.4)
The heart of his king had come forth like daylight.
(xx.1) The command of Ningirsu was displayed for Gudea like a banner.
In his heart that summoned (him) to build the temple,
a man delivered a propitious oracle.
It was cause for rejoicing for him.[51]

E. Oracular Confirmation of the Architectural Plan (Cyl. A xx.5-12)

He performed an extispicy; his extispicy was favorable.
He cast barley on moving(?) water; its appearance was right.
Gudea lay down as an oracular dreamer;
a command went forth to him.[52]
The building of the temple of his king,
(xx.10) the separation of the Eninnu from heaven and earth,
was displayed there for him before his eyes.
It was cause for rejoicing for him.[53]

F. Construction of the Temple (Cyl. A xx.13–xxv.19)

The various gods now take up their specific tasks in the construction of the temple from the divine perspective (Cyl. A xx.13-23).

u Zech 4:8-10; Ezra 3:8-13

v 1 Kgs 8:31-53

w Exod 3:1; 15:17; Isa 2:2-3 (= Mic 4:1-2); Pss 2:6; 48:2-4[1-3]

Gudea participates directly in the actual construction of the temple (Cyl. A xx.24-27)
Gudea, the temple builder, [u]
(xx.25) put the carrying basket of the temple on (his) head like a holy crown.
He laid the foundation; made the footings for the walls(?).[54]
He gave a blessing, "the plumb-line aligns the bricks."[55] [v]

Gudea continues blessing the house for a total of seven times (xxi.1-12) and then sets the door frames (xxi.13-18).

Gudea and the gods build the temple high toward heaven like the mountains (Cyl. A xxi.19-23)
They were making the temple grow (high) like a mountain range;
(xxi.20) making it float in mid-heaven like a cloud;
making it raise its horns like an ox;
making it raise (its) head high in the mountains like the *gišgana* tree of the Abzu,
making the temple raised (its) head high in heaven and earth like a mountain range.[56] [w]

Further laudatory figurative descriptions of various features of the Eninnu follow (xxi.24–xxii.23), followed, in turn, by an account of the shaping and setting up of six stone stelae around the temple complex (xxii.24–xxiv.7). The account of the fourth stelae well-illustrates the pattern for all six:

---

[51] See the note on Cyl. A xiv.6 above.

[52] This particular dream incubation stands as the last in a series of three distinct divination procedures. They include extispicy (xx.5), reading a configuration of grain cast upon water (xx.6; cf. perhaps the casting of flour on water in the *mīs pî* ritual series, Jacobsen 1987a:23 and 25, and see Butler 1998:229 and the literature cited there), and incubation of a dream (xx.7-11; cf. the notes on Cyl. A i.17, 21, and esp. viii.3, 19 above). In this case, there is no new revelation given in the dream. That had already been received in the process of fashioning the first brick (Cyl. A xvii.29–xx.1 and the notes on xvii.17 and xix.20 above). The purpose of the multiple divination procedures here was to confirm that all was well and that it was now time to begin the full-scale construction of the temple (Cyl. A xx.13–xxv.21). Thus, in this second incubated dream the temple appeared complete in every detail perched high on the temple platform between heaven and earth (xx.9-11), a vision to which Gudea responded with great joy (xx.12; see the note on Cyl. A xiv.6 above).

[53] See the note on Cyl. A xiv.6 above.

[54] Laying the temple's foundation (Sum. *temen*) was, of course, an essential starting point filled with importance (see Ellis 1968). Cyl. A xx.15-26 has Enki, Nanshe, Gatumdug, Baba, *en* and *lagal* priests, the Anunna gods, and Gudea himself directly involved, and the following lines and columns recount various aspects of the process, all in poetic form. Biblically, the significance of the foundation of the temple appears in Ezra 3 and Zech 4.

The second half of line 26 is difficult. Thureau-Dangin (1907:110-111) and many others since him have taken *á-gar* as a writing of *é-gar* "wall" with vowel harmony, and translate "set the walls on the ground." There is, however, evidence that *á-gar* refers to some kind of "spade" (see the discussion and literature cited in Dunham 1980:399 n. 2 and Römer 1965:62 n. 151; cf. PSD A 2:60). If the latter is correct, then this clause refers to wielding a tool rather than setting walls.

[55] According to the rendering here, Cyl. A xx.27–xxi.12 records seven blessings that Gudea pronounced as he laid the foundation of the new Eninnu (see Jacobsen 1987b:413-414 nn. 98-102 for helpful explanations). There may be a remote parallel to the seven requests that Solomon made on behalf of the people of Israel at the dedication of the temple in Jerusalem (1 Kgs 8:31-53). The content and intention of Gudea's blessings, however, are not similar to Solomon's requests. See Hurowitz 1992:288 n. 1 and 296 n. 1, and the literature cited there.

Recently, Suter has revived the proposal by Lambert and Tournay that we should read *sá-mu-sum* (or *si*) "he laid a square," rather than *silim-mu-sum* "he gave a blessing" in Cyl. A xx.27, xxi.1, 3, 5, 7, 9, and 11. In that case, *sá* would be a shortened writing for *ki-sá* "platform" (cf. Dunham 1982:38-39). She interprets the statements that follow each instance of the expression as similes corresponding to the progressive building up of a seven step temple tower (ziggurat), atop which the Eninnu sanctuary was to be built (Suter 1997; cf. Suter 1995:100-102 and Lambert and Tournay 1948a:418 and 1951). If this is correct, then the biblical parallel outlined above would not hold true even in a general way.

[56] The new Eninnu is sometimes described as a "mountain" (Sum. *kur*, Cyl. A xxii.10, xxiv.11, Cyl. B i.5-6, 9, xxiv.9) or "mountain range" (Sum. *ḫur-sag*, Cyl. A xxi.19, 23, xxiv.15-16, xxx.10, Cyl. B i.4), which had its foundation embedded in the "deep" (Sum. *abzu*, Cyl. A xx.15, xxii.11, Cyl. B xiii.3) and its top rising high between earth and heaven (Cyl. A xx.10, xxi.16, 19-23, xxiv.8-17, Cyl. B i.1-2, 6-9, xxiv.9, 14). Observe that Cyl. B begins and ends with this motif (Cyl. B i.1-9 and xxiv.9-15). In point of fact, the temple was built on a tower of some sort, whether a ziggurat or not (see the note on Cyl. A xx.27 above). So it did stand out physically above the surrounding area.

The residence of deities on mountains is well-established as a common motif in the ANE. In the Ug. Baal Epic, e.g., the abode of the chief god "El" is represented as being situated on a mountain in some texts (see *COS* 1.244-245 nn. 16 and 29; cf. Smith 1994:25-30). Moses and later the whole nation of Israel met God at Sinai, "the mountain of God" (Exod 3:1, 12; 4:27; 18:5; 19:1-3; 24:13). In the Song of the Sea reference is made to the mountain of the Lord's inheritance, his dwelling place, his sanctuary (Exod 15:17). Mount Zion is said to be the Lord's "holy mountain" (Ps 2:6) in the "far north" (Ps 48:1-3[2-4]), and "the mountain of the house of the Lord" will be "the chief of the mountains" in the

(xxiii.25) The stone which he set up before the Shugalam:
"The king at whose name the mountain lands tremble,
the lord Ningirsu,
made Gudea firm upon his throne,"
he named that stone.[57] [x]

Further laudatory figurative descriptions of various features of the Eninnu follow (xxiv.8–xxv.19).

IV. *Furnishing, Decorating, Supplying, and Praising the Temple Complex* (Cyl. A xxv.20–xxx.5)

x 1 Sam 13:14; 16:1-13; 1 Kgs 2:15; 1 Chr 28:5

y Exod 25:10-28:43; 30:1-10; 36:8-38:31; 1 Kgs 6:14-38; 7:13-51

Narrative transition to furnishing, decorating, and supplying the temple complex (Cyl. A xxv.20-23)
(xxv.20) He had built (it)! After he had finished (it),
being that the heart of the gods was overflowing,[58]
the faithful shepherd Gudea had come to know what was important,
(so) he proceeded to do it.[59]

Laudatory account of Gudea decorating, furnishing, and supplying the temple complex (xxv.24–xxix.12), closing praise of the new Eninnu (xxix.13–xxx.5), epilogue praising Ningirsu and the Eninnu (xxx.6-14), and colophon (xxx.15-16). [y]

CYLINDER B:

Prologue (Cyl. B i.1-11)
The temple, mooring pole of the land,
which grows (high) between heaven and earth;
the Eninnu, the true brickwork, (for) which Enlil decreed a good destiny;
the beautiful mountain range, which stands out as a marvel,
(i.5) (and) which towers above the mountains;
the temple, being a big mountain, reached up to heaven;
being Utu, it filled heaven's midst;
the Eninnu, being the shining Anzu-bird,
spread its talons over the mountain.
(i.10) The people were set firm there, the land was standing (still) there (in awe),
(and) the Anunna gods just stood there in admiration.

V. *Gudea's preparations for the induction of Ningirsu and Baba into the new Eninnu* (Cyl. B i.12–ii.6)

Gudea's attentive piety (Cyl. B i.12-19)
The ruler, being wise and knowledgeable,
bowed low before the divine;
bowed to the ground submissively(?) in prayer and supplication.[60]
(i.15) The ruler spoke a supplication unto the god of his city.
He added more bread to the bread ration of the temple;
added more sheep to the evening meal of mutton.
Bowls, being (like) the abundance of heaven's wide expanse(?),
he set up in front of it (the temple).

Gudea prays to the Anunna gods (Cyl. B i.20–ii.6)
He stepped up to the Anunna gods
(and) made a petition: "O Anunna, O Anunna, pride of Lagash land;
(ii.1) guardian deities of all lands, whose command overflows (like) high water,
which will carry away any man who tries to stop it up;
(but) the faithful young man, the man at whom you look,
life is prolonged for him;
(ii.5) I, the shepherd, have built the temple, (and) would bring my king into his temple.
O Anunna gods, may you invoke a petition on my behalf!"

VI. *The induction of Ningirsu and Baba into the new Eninnu* (Cyl. B ii.7–xiii.10)

Narrative transition to the induction of Ningirsu and Baba into the new Eninnu (Cyl. B ii.7-8)
The faithful shepherd Gudea
had come to know what was important, (so) he proceeded to do it.[61]

last days (Isa 2:1-2 = Mic 4:1-2; Wildberger 1991:88-89). See the discussion in Averbeck 1987:147-154, 199-204; Clifford 1972:9-25 and Clifford 1984.

[57] The names of most of these stelae reflect well upon Gudea, but the fourth is especially significant because it specifically affirms his right to the throne: Cyl. A xxiii.25-29. This mention of Gudea's selection and confirmation by Ningirsu to be the ruler of Lagash corresponds to the common doctrine in the ANE that the legitimate king was divinely chosen and commissioned. This is an important factor in the establishment of both David (1 Sam 13:14; 16:1-13) and Solomon (1 Kgs 2:15; 1 Chr 28:5) on the throne of Israel (see de Vaux 1961:100-101.).

[58] See the note on Cyl. A i.9 above.

[59] Regarding the structural importance of Cyl. A xxv.22-23 see the note on Cyl. A vii.10 above. The rest of Cyl. A is taken up largely with poetic descriptions of various aspects of the new temple and its furniture, and the temple as a whole. Cf., e.g., Exod 25-38 and 1 Kgs 6-7, although the biblical descriptions are not poetic.

[60] See the note on Cyl. A i.14 above.

[61] The structural formula occurs first in Cyl. B after Gudea had enlisted the support of the Anunna gods in praying to Ningirsu that he and his consort, Baba, would occupy the newly constructed Eninnu (i.20–ii.6; note the formula in Cyl. B ii.7-8, and cf. the note on Cyl. A vii.10 above). Immediately after the formula, the text depicts Gudea going to the old temple (i.e., the old Eninnu, ii.11), where he prayed directly to Ningirsu and Baba that they would indeed take up residence in the new temple (ii.16–iii.1). Within the prayer, just before the petition, Gudea reported the completion of the temple in terms that echo, *mutatis mutandis*, the parallel lines in his first petitionary prayer to Ningirsu: "O warrior, you commanded me, (so) let me execute it well for you. O Ningirsu, let me build your temple for you" (Cyl. A ii.13-14; cp. Cyl. B ii.19b-21 below).
In this prayer, however, Gudea does not echo the next line in Cyl. A ii.15, where he continues "(and) let me perfect the *me* for you," referring

Gudea prays to Ningirsu and Baba (Cyl. B ii.9–iii.1)
His good *Udug*-spirit walked in front of him;
(ii.10) his good *Lamma*-spirit followed behind him.
To his king, at the long enduring temple, the old temple, his place of habitation,
to the lord Ningirsu
Gudea surely made great gifts.
He stepped up to the lord in the Eninnu
(ii.15) and made a petition:
"O my king, Ningirsu,
the lord who returns to the Aḫush,[62]
the lord whose speaking takes precedence,
the male child of Enlil; O warrior, you commanded me
(ii.20) (and) I performed faithfully for you.
O Ningirsu, I have built your temple for you,
(so) may you enter (it) in festive joy. [z]
O my Baba, I have set up your bed-chamber(?) for you,
(iii.1) (so) settle into it comfortably."[63]

z 1 Kgs 8:12-13 (= 2 Chr 6:2)

Ningirsu comes from Eridu to enter the temple (Cyl. A iii.2-12)
His plea having been heard,
the warrior, the lord Ningirsu,
accepted the prayer and supplication from Gudea.
(iii.5) The (old) year being gone, the (last) month being at an end,
the new year stepped forward in heaven.
The (first) month entered its house,
(and) three days passed in that month.[64]
Ningirsu having come from Eridu,[65]
(iii.10) brilliant moonlight was shining.
It illuminated the land, (and) the (new) Eninnu
rivaled the newborn Suen (the moon god).

With the help of the gods, Gudea puts the house into a final state of readiness for the divine couple (iii.13–iv.12), and makes the whole land rest peacefully the night before their arrival at dawn the following morning (iv.13-24).

to the *me* of the temple. For general remarks on the Sum. term *me*, see the note on Cyl. A i.2 above. Building the temple well, according to Ningirsu's standards, was one thing, and that had already been accomplished in Cyl. A. Perfecting the *me* of the temple was still another thing, and that was yet to be accomplished in the process of dedicating the temple. It included the proper installation of all the attending deities, each "with" his or her *me* (Cyl. B vi.11–xiii.10; see the note on Cyl. B vi.23 below and the involvement of Suen, the moon god in Cyl. B xiii.4-5), as well as the offering of Gudea's special gifts of a war chariot with all its associated weapons (Cyl. B xiii.13–xiv.12; note the direct connection to *me* in xiv 8) and utensils and furniture for eating and sleeping (Cyl. B xiv.13-24).

As a result of all this, "The temple lifted its head in great *me*" (Cyl. B xvi.3; cf. xx.21), and Ningursu and Baba actually took up residence in the new Eninnu (Cyl. B xvi.4–xvii.11). In close association with the divine occupation of the temple the narrator remarks that Gudea "had built the Eninnu, had perfected its *me*" (Cyl. B xvii.13-14). Here is the echo of Cyl. A ii.15 (see the remarks above). Thus, in the interval between the prayer in Cyl. B ii.16–iii.1 and the narrator's explanation in Cyl. B xvii.13-14 Gudea had accomplished what we might refer to as the proper "*me*-ing" or "activating" of the temple's functions. He had made it luxuriously inhabitable for the divine couple.

[62] See the note on Cyl. A viii.15 above.

[63] After enlisting the help of the Anunna gods (Cyl. B i.15–ii.6), Gudea went to the old Eninnu (ii.11) in order to announce the completion of the new Eninnu to Ningirsu and his consort Baba (written Ba-Ú, read Ba-ba$_6$) and invited them to take up residence in it (Cyl. B ii.16–iii.1). Solomon's proclamation at the dedication of the temple in 1 Kgs 8:13 (= 2 Chr 6:2) seems to correspond to this, but note 1 Kgs 8:27-30. Cf. Weinfeld 1972:35 and 195.

[64] There are four key time references in Cylinder B. First, Cyl. B iii.5-11 refers to Ningirsu's return from a trip to Eridu after three days had elapsed in the first month of the new year (see the note on Cyl. B iii.8-9 below). Second, Cyl. B iv.22–v.2 narrates Ningirsu's initial entrance into the new Eninnu at early dawn on the following (fourth) day, and his consort Baba with him (v.10). The third key time reference describes the coming of full daylight (Cyl. B v.19). As previously promised (Cyl. B i.20–ii.6), the Anunna gods assisted in the proceedings of the inaugural day (v.22), and the various attending deities paraded in review before Ningirsu as they took up their positions in the new temple (B vi.11–xii.25). This must have taken up a good portion of the day. The last major section of the composition opens with the ruler's presentation of special gifts to Ningirsu and Baba (see the note on Cyl. B xiii.14-17), after which the divine couple is described as reveling in all the features and provisions of their glorious new habitation (Cyl. B xvi.3–xvii.11).

Finally, the fourth important time reference is Cyl. B xvii.18-19, which refers to a seven-day temple dedication festival, during which time the whole region maintained purity and peace (xvii.20–xviii.11) while the gods celebrated at a fine banquet (xix.16-17). This seven-day banquet apparently began with the meal provided for the gods on the very day that Ningirsu and Baba arrived and entered into their new abode (cf. Cyl. B v.20–vi.2).

[65] After hearing Gudea's prayer in the old Eninnu (Cyl. B ii.11–iii.1), Ningirsu accepted Gudea's offerings (iii.2-4) and undertook a journey to Eridu (iii.9-11; cf. viii.13-16). We are not told precisely why he traveled to Eridu, but it is clear that Enki, the patron deity of Eridu, was one of the chief deities most closely associated with temple building in Sumer. From the Gudea Cylinders alone we can see that he was responsible for the design of the temple (Cyl. A xvii.17), the approval of the first brick (Cyl. A xix.10-11), and the embedding of the temple's foundation (Cyl. A xx.15; cf. Cyl. B xiii.3). Also, Eridu is the site of some of the oldest known temples in southern Babylonia, and the first temple hymn in the Sum. temple hymn collection is dedicated to Enki's Abzu in Eridu (Sjöberg and Bergmann 1969:17-18). For an overview and general remarks on journeys to Eridu see Green 1975:268-276.

These factors as well as the fact that he makes this journey right after Gudea's report that the temple was finished (cf. Cyl. B ii.19-22), suggest that Ningirsu may have traveled to Eridu to make a similar report to Enki, on the divine level. Moreover, Enki and Eridu are closely associated with purity and purification procedures, which are the major concern of the next two and a half columns (Cyl. B iii.11–v.24). Included in this is a reference to Asar, who is often associated with Enki and Eridu in purification contexts (see, e.g., Michalowski 1993:152-156 on text A line 14). Also, Nindub is called "the lofty purification priest of Eridu," and Enki issued oracles as the various deities went about their tasks of purification (Cyl. B iv.1-5; cf. v.22-24). Note also Gudea Stat. B iv.7-9, which says that "He (Gudea) built the temple of Ningirsu in a pure place like Eridu" (see Edzard 1997:32).

Thus, the immediate context before and after the reference to Ningirsu's journey to Eridu suggests that he went there to report to Enki and enlist his support in the necessary purification procedures. Finally, since the induction of the various attending deities with their *me*'s into the temple is such an important part of the following context (Cyl. B vi.11–xii.25), and since Enki was viewed as the deity in charge of the *me*'s (see, e.g., *COS* 1.522), therefore, Ningirsu might also have traveled to Eridu to obtain Enki's support in the proper "*me*-ing" of the temple (see also the notes

Ningirsu and Baba enter into the new temple (Cyl. B v.1-19)

The warrior, Ningirsu, was entering into the temple;
the king of the house came.[66]
Being (like) an eagle gazing at a wild bull;[67]
the warrior, his entering into his temple
(v.5) being (like) a storm roaring into battle,
Ningirsu was coming into his temple.
Being (like) the Abzu sanctuary at festival time,
the king surely paraded forth from his temple.
It was (like) the sun rising over Lagash land.
(v.10) Baba's going to her bed-chamber(?)
being (like) a faithful woman taking care of her house;
her entering by the side of her bed(?)
being (like) the Tigris at high water;
her sitting down beside her ... (?)
(v.15) being the lady, the daughter of holy An, a beautiful garden bearing fruit;
sun rising; destiny being decreed;
Baba entering into her bed-chamber;
Lagash land being in abundance,
day dawned, Utu lifted (his) head high over Lagash in the land.[68]

Offerings are presented and purification and divination procedures are performed (v.20-vi.10).

Installation of attending deities (Cyl. B vi.11-xii.25)

Each of the attending deities is installed into their temple office and its responsibilities according to the following pattern:

Igalim (Cyl. B vi.11-23)

To guide aright the hand of the one who does righteousness;
to put the wood (neck stock) on the neck of the one who does evil;
to keep the temple true; to keep the temple good;
to give instructions to his city, the sanctuary Girsu;
(vi.15) to set up the throne of decreeing destiny;
to put into the hand the scepter of prolonged day(s);
for Gudea, the shepherd of Ningirsu,
to lift (his) head toward heaven as (if wearing) a beautiful crown;
to appoint the leather-clad, the linen-clad, (and) the head-covered one(s)(?)
(vi.20) to (their) position(s) in the courtyard of the Eninnu;
the great door, the pole of Girnun, the chief constable of Girsu;
Igalim, his (Ningirsu's) beloved son,
was passing in review before the lord Ningirsu with his emblem (of office).[69]

After the installation of the minor attending deities, the major gods of the pantheon are characterized as supporters of the new temple (xii.26-xiii.10).

VII. *The housewarming celebration of the induction of Ningirsu and Baba into their new Eninnu* (Cyl. B xiii.11-xxiv.8)

Narrative transition to the celebration of the induction of Ningirsu and Baba into the new Eninnu (Cyl. B xiii.11-13)

The powerful steward of Nanshe,
the obedient shepherd of Ningirsu,
had come to know what was important, (so) he proceeded to do it.[70]

Gudea presents housewarming gifts to Ningirsu and Baba (Cyl. B xiii.14-xvi.2)

Upon the temple, the man who built the temple,
(xiii.15) Gudea, the ruler

on Cyl. A i.2 and B ii.7-8 above).

[66] See the note on Cyl. B iii.8 above.

[67] Jacobsen suggests that this pictures Ningirsu as a scavenger bird circling to pounce on the carcass of a dead bull in the wild (Jacobsen 1987b:429 n. 15).

[68] See the note on Cyl. B iii.8 above.

[69] Cyl. B vi.11-xvii.12 is surrounded by expressions that recall Cyl. A i.1-4. First, Cyl. B v.16 refers to the determination of destiny at the dawn of the new day (cf. Cyl. A i.1). Second, Cyl. B vi.8 refers to Ningirsu lifting his head high in the great *me*'s (= the "greatest stature"?; *me-gal-gal-la*, cf. the note on Cyl. A i.2 above). Third, Cyl. B xvii.12 refers to the fact that the ruler had succeeded in gloriously establishing "the enduring thing(s)" (*nì-ul*; or perhaps read *nì-du₇* "the appropriate thing[s]"; see the note on Cyl. A i.4 above) of the city (cf. Cyl. A i.4), and concludes that he had both built the Eninnu and now "perfected its *me*" (Cyl. B xvii.13-14; see the note on Cyl. B ii.8 above).

Thus, in the meantime, on this inaugural day Gudea had seen to the proper installation of all the *me*'s necessary for the effective functioning of the temple. Cyl. B vi.11-xii.25, in particular, recounts the various supporting deities "passing in review before" (or "going over to"; Sum. *dib*) Ningirsu "with his *me*" (*me-ni-da*) as they are incorporated into the temple as members of the staff (Cyl. B vi.23, vii.11, 23, viii.9, 22, ix.4-5, 14, x.2, 8, 15, xi.2, 26, xii.6, 17-18, 25). See Jacobsen 1976b:81-83 for a helpful description of the basic functions of each of these deities in the temple estate.

There have been several interpretations of the expression *me-ni-da—dib*. Edzard translates "he (Gudea) brings along (*dib*) with himself (*me-ni-da*) and introduces to the lord Ningirsu ...," taking *me* to simply mean "self" (see the note on Cyl. A i.2 above). Most, however, take *me* as the renowned Sum. term for the elements of their cultural system (see the note on Cyl. A i.2 above). Jacobsen understood the subject of the verb to be the deity in the context and rendered *me-ni-da* as "was going about his duties for the lord Ningirsu" (*dib* = Akk. *bâ'u* "to go along"; Jacobsen 1987b:431-436). Cooper took Gudea, not the deity, to be the subject of the verb, and translated the expression "He (Gudea) made him (the deity) ... pass in review with his *me*'s before lord Ningirsu" (*dib* = Akk. *etēqu* "to pass"; Cooper 1978:159 and n. 2). More recently, Klein has proposed rendering the expression "He (Gudea) lets such and such deity go over to (*dib* = Akk. *bâ'u*) Ningirsu with his symbol/emblem," or "he (Gudea) lets such and such deity pass before (*dib* = Akk. *etēqu*) Ningirsu with his symbol/emblem" (Klein 1997:217-218). In that case, *me* here actually refers to a two dimensional representation of the symbol associated with the *me*, which had been engraved or painted on a sign, banner, or standard of some kind.

[70] See the note on Cyl. A vii.10 above.

of Lagash,
was bestowing gifts.[71]

The gifts included a well-decorated war chariot with its associated weapons (xiii.18–xiv.12), and utensils and furniture for eating and sleeping (xiv.13-22).

After accepting the gifts, the divine couple settles into their fully supplied and fully functional residence (xiv.23–xvii.11).

Gudea prepares a temple dedication banquet for Ningirsu (Cyl. B xvii.12–xix.17)

He made the long enduring thing(s) of his city appear in splendor.
Gudea built the Eninnu;
he perfected its stature.[72]
(xvii.15) He made fat and cream enter into its dairy house.
He put bread into its house of holy ... (?).
He cancelled debts (and) cleared the hands (of criminals).[73]
When his king entered into the temple,
for seven days[74] [aa]
(xvii.20) the slave girl did become equal with her mistress;
the slave did walk beside the master;
(xviii.1) in his city the unclean one did sleep on its outside edge(?).
He removed speaking(?) from the evil tongue;
turned back anything evil from that(?) house.
To the laws of Nanshe and Ningirsu
(xviii.5) he paid close attention.
He did not deliver the orphan up to the rich man;
he did not deliver the widow up to the powerful man.
In the house that had no male heir,
he installed its daughter as the heir.[bb]
(xviii.10) A day of majestic justice arose for him;
he put his foot on the neck of (the) evil one(s) and complainer(s).[75] [cc]
Like Utu (the sun god), the city
went forth from the horizon.

aa 1 Kgs 8:2, 65; Ezek 45:21-25; 2 Chr 7:9; cf. Lev 23:34

bb Num 27:1-11

cc Ezek 42:13-14, 20; 43:6-12

On his head he wound(?) a turban(?).
(xviii.15) Before holy An
he made himself known.
He was entering with head held high like an ox.
In the sanctuary of the Eninnu
he offered up perfect ox and perfect he-goat.
(xviii.20) A tall bowl was standing (there)
(and) he was pouring wine from it.
The Ushumgalkalamma ('dragon-of-the-land') instrument was standing there with the *tigi* instrument,
(xix.1) (and) the *ala* instrument, being (like) a storm wind, was resounding for him.
Atop a ... (?), the ruler
did surely stand out.
His city marveled (at him).
(xix.5) Gudea ...

[lines 6-11 completely broken]

... [abun]dance [went forth] from ...;
the land was making spotted barley grow for him.
Along with the ruler, Lagash
(xix.15) increase in abundance.
Having entered into the new Eninnu, the warrior
prepared a fine banquet for the lord Ningirsu.

The gods take their seats at the divine banquet table (Cyl. B xix.18-?)

An he seated for him on the big side (of the table).
Next to An he seated Enlil.
(xix.20) Next to Enlil
he seated Ninmaḫ.[76]

Large sections of Cyl. B xx–xxiii are missing, but from what remains we know that it consists of blessings and good destinies determined for Ningirsu, Eninnu, and Gudea by the various gods in attendance at the divine banquet. The final blessing is pronounced for Gudea himself:

A blessing for Gudea (Cyl. B xxiii.18–xxiv.8)[77]

"Your (Gudea's personal) god, the lord Ningishzida, being descendant of An;

[71] The last major section of the Cylinders begins with Gudea offering special gifts to Ningirsu (Cyl. B xiii.14–xvi.2), and, although the text is broken, seems to end with Ningirsu pronouncing a special blessing of prosperity and longevity upon the ruler (Cyl. B xxiii.16–xxiv.8; see the note on Cyl. B xxiv.6 below). Compare the chariot in Cyl. B xiii.18–xiv.12 with the one described in Cyl. A vi.14–vii.8.

[72] See the note on Cyl. B ii.8 above.

[73] The parallel line in Gudea Stat. B vii.29 testifies that the last sign should be *luḫ* "to wash" not *gar* "to put, set." The scribe allowed his eye to slip up to the previous line and, therefore, wrote *gar* by mistake (Å. Sjöberg, personal communication).

[74] Gudea's seven day temple dedication festival mentioned in Cyl. B xvii.18-19 (cf. Stat. B vii.30, Edzard 1997:36) parallels Solomon's dedication of the temple during the seven day feast of booths in the seventh month (1 Kgs 8:2; cf. also Ezek 45:21-25). Actually, there were apparently two sets of seven day festivals on this occasion, one for the altar and the other for the temple as a whole (1 Kgs 8:65-66; 2 Chr 7:8-9). The numerous multiples of seven in association with building and dedicating temples in the ANE is impressive. Cp. the seven day period for consecrating the priests (Lev 8:33), and esp. the seven years that it took to build Solomon's temple (1 Kgs 6:38), and the seven days for building Baal's temple (*CTA* 4 vi.24-38). See the note on Cyl. B iii.8 above and Levenson 1988:78-79; Sarna 1986:145-148, Sharon 1996:107.

[75] Upon the occupation of the temple by Ningirsu and Baba, and during the seven-day temple dedication period and banquet of the gods, the ruler enforced social and ritual regulations similar to those established for the initial stages of the building of the Eninnu. Compare Cyl. B xvii.18–xviii.11 with Cyl. A xii.25–xiii.15. See also the note on Cyl. A xiii.15 above and the literature cited in Wildberger 1991:50-51. Ritual sanctity and purity is also emphasized in Ezekiel's temple building program (note esp. Ezek 42:3-14, 20; 43:6-12), although concerns for social justice and equity do not seem to be articulated there. For the overall problem of physical impurities in sacred space see Lev 12-16. See Greenberg 1984:191-194; Sharon 1996:102-103. For variations on the millennial topos in xviii.6-11, see Hallo 1990:205f. Cf. Exod 22:21-24; Deut 24:17-18; Isa 1:17; Jer 7:5-6.

[76] The text is broken after line 21 so the seating arrangements at the seven-day divine temple dedication banquet may have included other gods and goddesses besides An, Enlil, and Ninmaḫ. For an explanation of these lines and the Ug. parallels see Ferrara and Parker 1972:38-39.

[77] Here we break into a speech in progress, not knowing exactly where it starts because of the broken condition of the text.

your divine mother, Ninsumuna, being the mother
who gives birth to faithful offspring,
(xxiii.20) who loves offspring;
the one born by the faithful cow in woman-fashion
are you.
The faithful young man who goes forth from
Lagash land,
(xxiv.1) you are Ningirsu's.
From below to above let your name be famous.

dd 2 Sam 7:4-17 (= 1 Chr 17:3-15); 1 Kgs 8:14-21; 9:1-9 (= 2 Chr 7:11-22); Ps 78:68-70

O Gudea, what you say
no man disregards(?).
(xxiv.5) A ... (?) young man known by An are you.
O my(?) ruler,[78] the house determines (a good)
destiny for you(?).
O Gudea, son of Ningishzida,
let life be prolonged for you.[79] *dd*

Epilogue praising Ningirsu and the Eninnu (xiv.9-15) and colophon (xiv.16-17).

[78] The reading of xxiv.6 is important and, at the same time, problematic. Some scholars read [*en*]*si*$_2$-[*m*]*u* "my ruler" and others read [*en*]*si*$_2$-[*z*]*i* "faithful ruler." The former would assure us that Ningirsu was the one addressing Gudea in the blessing, although the latter reading would not exclude that possibility. The ending of the *mu* and *zi* signs is very similar. However, on the photographs of this portion of Cyl. B kindly sent to me by Béatrice André-Salvini (Conservatrice-en-chef of the Louvre Départment des Antiquités Orientales), the size, depth, and shape of the remnants of the sign compared with other *mu* and *zi* signs in close proximity to it suggest that it was originally a *mu* sign. If it is not Ningirsu, it is An, Enlil, Nanshe, Enki, or perhaps another deity in attendance at the divine banquet.

[79] The close association of temple building with the responsibilities and blessings of kingship is well established in the ANE (McCarter 1984:224-225). Although the latter part of the second cylinder is broken, the last pronouncement is reserved for special praise and promise to Gudea. Cyl. B xxiii.16–xxiv.8 clearly records a divine decree of prosperity and long life for Gudea for his care in building the temple.

Similarly, Solomon was promised special blessing after completing the construction of the temple, but in his case it depended upon continued fidelity to the Lord (1 Kgs 9:1-9). The blessedness of temple building is also reflected elsewhere in the Bible (2 Sam 7:4-17 = 1 Chr 17:3-15; 1 Kgs 8:14-21; and Ps 78:68:70).

REFERENCES

Text: Thureau-Dangin TCL 8 (1925). Transliterations, translations, and studies: *ANET* 268; Averbeck 1987:582-712 and 1997; Edzard 1997:68-106; Falkenstein 1953, 1966, 1978; Heimpel 1987 and 1996; Jacobsen 1987b:386-444; Klein 1989a and b; Kramer 1969:26-34; Lambert and Tournay 1948a, 1948b, 1950; Suter 1995:414-425 and 1997; Thureau-Dangin 1905:134-199 and 1907:88-141; Wilson 1996; Zólyomi 1998.

SUMERIAN BIBLIOGRAPHY

ACKERMAN, S.
1991 "The Deception of Isaac, Jacob's Dream at Bethel, and Incubation on an Animal Skin." Pp. 92-120 in *Priesthood and Cult in Ancient Israel*. Ed. by G. A. Anderson and S. M. Olyan. JSOTSup 125. Sheffield: Sheffield Academic Press.

ALI, F. A.
1966 "Dedication of a Dog to Nintinugga." *ArOr* 34:289-293.

ALSTER, B.
1974 "EN.METE.NA: 'His Own Lord.'" *JCS* 26:178-180.

ANDERSON, G. A.
1987 *Sacrifices and Offerings in Ancient Israel: Studies in their Social and Political Importance*. HSM 41. Atlanta: Scholars Press.

ASHER-GREVE, J.
1987 "The Oldest Female Oneiromancer." Pp. 27-32 in *RAI* 33.

AVERBECK, R. E.
1987 "A Preliminary Study of Ritual and Structure in the Cylinders of Gudea." 2 vols. Ph.D. dissertation, Dropsie College, Annenberg Research Institute. Ann Arbor, Michigan: University Microfilms International.
1997 "Ritual Formula, Textual Frame, and Thematic Echo in the Cylinders of Gudea." Pp. 37-93 in *Studies Astour*.

BAER, A.
1971 "Goudéa, Cylindre B, Colonnes XVIII a XXIV." *RA* 65:1-14.

BORGER, R.
1956 *Asarh*.

BREKELMANS, C. H. W.
1982 "Solomon at Gibeon." Pp. 53-59 in *Studies van der Ploeg*.

BUTLER, S. A. L.
1998 *Mesopotamian Conceptions of Dreams and Dream Rituals*. AOAT 258. Münster: Ugarit-Verlag.

CARROUÉ, F.
1986 "Le 'Cours-d'Eau-Allant-à-NINA^{ki}'." *ActSum* 8:13-57.

CIVIL, M.
1965 "New Sumerian Law Fragments." Pp. 1-12 in *Studies Landsberger*.
1969 "Le Chien de Nintinugga." *RA* 63:180.
1987 "The Tigidlu Bird and a Musical Instrument." *NABU* 1987:27, No. 48.

CLIFFORD, R. J.
1972 *The Cosmic Mountain in Canaan and the Old Testament*. HSM 4. Cambridge, Massachusetts: Harvard Univ. Press.
1984 "The Temple and the Holy Mountain." Pp. 107-124 in *The Temple in Antiquity*. Ed. by T. G. Madsen. Provo, Utah: Brigham Young University.

COHEN, M. E.
1993 *The Cultic Calendars of the Ancient Near East*. Bethesda, MD: CDL Press.

COOPER, J. S.
1978 *The Return of Ninurta to Nippur: an-gim dím-ma*. AnOr 52. Rome: Biblical Institute Press.
1983a *The Curse of Agade*. Baltimore: Johns Hopkins University Press.
1983b "The Sumerian Sargon Legend." *JAOS* 103:67-82.
1986 *SARI*.

DIAKONOFF, I. M.
1958 "Some Remarks on the 'Reforms' of Urukagina." *RA* 52:1-15.

VAN DIJK, J.
1964/65 "Le motif cosmique dans la pensée sumérienne." *ActOr* 28:1-59.

DONBAZ, V., and W. W. HALLO.
1976 "Monumental Texts from Pre-Sargonic Lagash." *OA* 15:1-9.

DUNHAM, S.
1980 "A Study of Ancient Mesopotamian Foundations." Ph.D. dissertation, Columbia University. Ann Arbor, Michigan: University Microfilms International.
1982 "Bricks for the Temples of Šara and Ninurra." *RA* 76:27-41.

EDZARD, D. O.
1991 "Irikagina (Urukagina)." *AO* 9:77-79.
1997 *RIME* 3/1.

ELLIS, R. S.
1968 *Foundation Deposits in Ancient Mesopotamia*. YNER 2. New Haven: Yale University Press.

FALKENSTEIN, A.
1953 "Tempelbau-Hymne Gudeas von Lagasch." Pp. 137-182 in *SAHG*.
1966 *Die Inschriften Gudeas von Lagaš*. AnOr 30. Rome: Pontificium Institutum Biblicum.
1978 *Grammatik der Sprache Gudeas von Lagaš*. AnOr 28-29. 2 vols. Second edition. Rome: Pontificium Institutum Biblicum.

FERRARA, A. J., and S. B. PARKER.
1972 "Seating Arrangements at Divine Banquets." *UF* 4:37-39.

FINKELSTEIN, J. J.
1969 "The Laws of Ur-Nammu." *JCS* 21:39-48.

FRAYNE, D. R.
1990 *RIME* 4.
1997 *RIME* 3/2.

GNUSE, R. K.
1983 *The Dream Theophany of Samuel*. Lanham, Maryland: University Press of America.
GREEN, M. W.
1975 "Eridu in Sumerian Literature." Ph.D. dissertation. Chicago: Univ. of Chicago.
GREENBERG, M.
1984 "The Design and Themes of Ezekiel's Program of Restoration." *Interpretation* 38:181-208.
HALLO, W. W.
1962 "The Royal Inscriptions of Ur: a Typology." *HUCA* 33:1-43.
1977 "Seals Lost and Found." BiMes 6:55-60.
1983 "Sumerian Historiography." Pp. 9-20 in *HHI*.
1990 "Proverbs Quoted in Epic." Pp. 203-217 in *Studies Moran*.
HALPERN, B.
1978 "The Ritual Background of Zechariah's Temple Song." *CBQ* 40:167-190.
HEIMPEL, W.
1968 *Tierbilder in der Sumerischen Literatur*. Studia Pohl 2. Rome: Pontificum Institutum Biblicum.
1987a "Gudea's Fated Brick." *JNES* 46:205-211.
1987b "The Natural History of the Tigris according to the Sumerian Literary Composition Lugal." *JNES* 46:309-317.
1996 "The Gates of the Eninnu." *JCS* 48:17-29.
HUROWITZ, V.
1985 "The Priestly Account of Building the Tabernacle." *JAOS* 105:21-30.
1992 *I have Built you an Exalted House: Temple Building in the Bible in Light of Mesopotamian and Northwest Semitic Writings*. JSOTSup 115. Sheffield: Sheffield Academic Press.
ISHIDA, T.
1977 *The Royal Dynasties in Ancient Israel*. BZAW 142. Berlin: Walter de Gruyter.
JACOBSEN, T.
1967 "Some Sumerian City-Names." *JCS* 21:100-103.
1976a "The Stele of the Vultures Col. I-X." Pp. 247-259 in *Studies Kramer*.
1976b *The Treasures of Darkness*. New Haven: Yale University Press.
1987a "The Graven Image." Pp. 15-32 in *Studies Cross*.
1987b *The Harps That Once ... Sumerian Poetry in Translation*. New Haven: Yale University Press.
JOHANSEN, F.
1978 *Statues of Gudea Ancient and Modern*. Mesopotamia: Copenhagen Studies in Assyriology 6. Copenhagen: Akademisk Forlag.
KAPELRUD, A. S.
1963 "Temple Building, a Task for Gods and Kings." *Or* 32:56-62.
KÄRKI, I.
1986 *Die Königsinschriften der dritten Dynastie von Ur*. Studia Orientalia. Ed. by the Finnish Oriental Society 58. Helsinki.
KENIK, H. A.
1983 *Design for Kingship: The Deuteronomistic Narrative Technique in 1 Kings 3:4-15*. SBLDS 69. Chico, California: Scholars Press.
KLEIN, J.
1989a "Building and Dedication Hymns in Sumerian Literature." *ActSum* 11:27-67.
1989b "From Gudea to Šulgi: Continuity and Change in Sumerian Literary Tradition." Pp. 289-301 in *Studies Sjöberg*.
1997 "The Sumerian *me* as a Concrete Object." *AoF* 24:211-218.
KRAMER, S. N.
1969 *The Sacred Marriage Rite*. Bloomington, Indiana: Indiana University Press.
1983 "The Ur-Nammu Law Code: Who Was Its Author?" *Or* 52:453-56.
KRAMER, S. N., and A. FALKENSTEIN.
1954 "Ur-Nammu Law Code." *Or* 23:40-51.
KRAUS, H.-J.
1986 *The Theology of the Psalms*. Minneapolis: Augsburg Publishing House.
1988 *Psalms 1-59: A Commentary*. Minneapolis: Augsburg Publishing House.
KRISPIJN, Th. J. H.
1982 "De Tempelbouw van Gudea van Lagash." Pp. 81-103 in *Oosters Genootschap in Nederland* 11. Leiden: Brill.
1983 "De hervormingen van Uruinimgina van Lagaš (24e eeuw v. Chr.)." Pp. 126-130 in *Schrijvend Verleden*. Ed. by K. R. Veenhof. Leiden: Ex Oriente Lux.
KUPPER, J.-R.
1959 "Sceaux-cylinders du temps de Zimri-Lim." *RA* 53:97-100.
LAMBERG-KARLOVSKY, C.
1988 "The 'International-Style' Carved Vessels". *Iranica Antiqua* 23:45-73.
LAMBERT, M.
1956 "Les 'Réformes' d'Urukagina." *RA* 50:169-184.
1957 "Documents pour le § 3 des 'Réformes' d'Uukagina." *RA* 51:139-144.
LAMBERT, M. and R. TOURNAY.
1948a "Le Cylindre A de Gudea." *RB* 55:403-437.
1948b "Le Cylindre B de Gudea." *RB* 55:520-543.
1950 "Corrections au Cylindre A de Gudea." *ArOr* 18/3:304-320.
1951 "Review of Parrot, Ziggurats et Tour de Babel." *RA* 45:33-40.
LAMBERT, W. G.
1972 "Destiny and Divine Intervention in Babylon and Israel." Pp. 65-72 in *The Witness of Tradition*. Ed. by M. A. Beek et al. Leiden: E. J. Brill.
1992 "The Reading Uru-KA-gi-na Again." *AO* 10:256-258.

LANDSBERGER, B.
1964 "Einige unerkannt gebliebene oder verkannte Nomina des Akkadischen (part 3)." *WO* 3:48-79.
LEICHTY, E.
1989 "Feet of Clay." Pp. 349-356 in *Studies Sjöberg*.
LEVENSON, J. D.
1988 *Creation and the Persistence of Evil: The Jewish Drama of Divine Omnipotence*. Princeton, New Jersey: Princeton University Press.
MCALPINE, T. H.
1987 *Sleep, Divine and Human in the Old Testament*. JSOTSup 38. Sheffield, England: Sheffield Academic Press.
MCCARTER, P. K., Jr.
1984 *2 Samuel*. AB 9. Garden City, New York: Doubleday and Company.
MEYERS, C. L., and E. M. MEYERS.
1987 *Haggai and Zechariah 1-8*. AB 25B. Garden City, New York: Doubleday and Company.
MICHALOWSKI, P.
1993 "The Torch and the Censer." Pp. 152-162 in *Studies Hallo*.
MILLER, P. D.
1985 "Eridu, Dunnu, and Babel: A Study in Comparative Mythology." *HAR* 9:227-251.
NAGEL, W.
1958 "Glyptische Probleme der Larsa-Zeit." *AfO* 18:319-322.
OPPENHEIM, A. L.
1954 "The Seafaring Merchants of Ur." *JAOS* 74:6-17.
1956 *The Interpretation of Dreams in the Ancient Near East*. Transactions of the American Philosophical Society, vol. 46 pt. 3. Philadelphia: The American Philosophical Society.
1966 "Mantic Dreams in the Ancient Near East." Pp. 341-350 in *The Dream and Human Societies*. Ed. by G. E. Von Grunebaum and R. Caillois. Berkeley: Univ. of California Press.
OTA, M.
1974 "A Note on 2 Sam 7." Pp. 403-407 in *Studies Myers*.
PORADA, E.
1992 "A Lapis Lazuli Disk with Relief Carving Inscribed for King Rimuš." Pp. 69-72 in *RAI* 38.
RÖMER, W. H. Ph.
1965 *Sumerische "Königshymnen" der Isin-Zeit*. DMOA 13. Leiden: E. J. Brill.
1982 "Aus den Gesetzen des Königs Urnammu von Ur." Pp. 17-23 in *TUAT* 1/1.
ROTH, M. T.
1995/1997 *Law Collections from Mesopotamia and Asia Minor*. 2nd Edition, 1997. SBLWAW 6. Atlanta: Scholars Press.
RUMMEL, S.
1981 "Narrative Structure in the Ugaritic Texts." Pp. 221-332 in *Ras Shamra Parallels*, vol. 3. Ed. by Stan Rummel. AnOr 51. Rome: Pontificium Institutum Biblicum.
SAPORETTI, C.
1984 *Le leggi della Mesopotamia*. Studi e manuali di archeologia 2. Firenze: Casa Editrice le Lettere.
SARNA, N. M.
1986 *Exploring Exodus: The Heritage of Biblical Israel*. New York: Schocken Books.
DE SARZEC, E.
1884-1912 *Decouvertes en Chaldée*. Paris: Ernest Leroux.
SAUREN, H.
1990 "Á-ÁŠ, ÁŠ, AŠ, 'Concubine.'" *RA* 84:41-43.
SCHEIL, V.
1925 "Passim." *RA* 22:141-162.
SELZ, G. J.
1992 "Zum Namen des Herrschers URU-INIM-GI-NA(-K): ein neuer Deutungsvorschlag." *NABU* 1992:34-36, No. 44.
SEUX, M. J.
1967 *Épithètes royales akkadiennes et sumériennes*. Paris: Letouzey et Ané.
SHARON, D. M.
1996 "A Biblical Parallel to a Sumerian Temple Hymn? Ezekiel 40-48 and Gudea." *JANES* 24:99-109.
SJÖBERG, Å. W.
1974 "Hymn to Numušda with a Prayer for king Sîniqīšam of Larsa and a Hymn to Ninurta." *OrSuec* 22:107-121.
SJÖBERG, Å. W., and E. BERGMANN.
1969 *The Collection of Sumerian Temple Hymns*. TCS 3. Locust Valley, New York: J. J. Augustin.
SMITH, M. S.
1994 *The Ugaritic Baal Cycle*. VTSup 55. Leiden: E. J. Brill.
SOLLBERGER, E.
1956 *Corpus des Inscriptions "Royales" Présargoniques de Lagaš*. Geneva: E. Droz.
STEELE, F. S.
1951 "The University Museum Esarhaddon Prism." *JAOS* 71:1-12.
STEIBLE, H.
1982 *Die altsumerischen Bau- und Weihinschriften*. FAOS 6. Ed. by B. Kienast. 2 vols. Wiesbaden: Franz Steiner.
1991 *Die neusumerischen Bau- und Weihinschriften. Teil 2. Kommentar zu den Gudea-Statuen; Inschriften der* III. *Dynastie von Ur; Inschriften der* IV. und "V." *Dynastie von Uruk; Varia*. FAOS 9/2. Stuttgart: Franz Steiner.
STEINKELLER, P.
1982 "The Question of Marḫaši: a Contribution to the Historical Geography of Iran in the Third Millennium B.C." *ZA* 72:237-265.
1988 "The Date of Gudea and his Dynasty." *JCS* 40:47-53.
1991 "The Reforms of UruKAgina and an Early Sumerian Term for 'Prison.'" *AO* 9:227-233.

SUTER, C. E.
1995 "Gudea's Temple Building: A Comparison of Written and Pictorial Accounts." Ph.D. dissertation, University of Pennsylvania. Ann Arbor, Michigan: University Microfilms International.
1997 "Gudeas vermeintliche Segnungen des Eninnu." *ZA* 87:1-10.
SWEET, R. F. G.
1990 "The Sage in Mesopotamian Palaces and Royal Courts." Pp. 99-107 in *The Sage in Israel and the Ancient Near East*. Ed. by J. G. Gammie and L. G. Perdue. Winona Lake: Eisenbrauns.
SZLECHTER, E.
1955 "Le Code d'Ur-Nammu." *RA* 49:169-76.
1957 "Le Code de Lipit-Ištar (I-II)." *RA* 51:57-82; 177-196.
1958 "Le Code de Lipit-Ištar (III)." *RA* 52:74-90.
THUREAU-DANGIN, F.
1905 *Les Inscriptions de Sumer et d'Akkad: Transcription et Traduction*. Paris: Ernest Leroux, 134-199.
1907 *Die Sumerischen und Akkadischen Königsinschriften*. Vorderasiatische Bibliothek I. Band Abteilung 1. Leipzig: J. C. Hinrichs'sche Buchhandlung, 88-141.
1925 *Les Cylinders de Goudéa*. TCL 8. Paris: Paul Geuthner.
TSEVAT, M.
1962 "A Reference to Gudea of Lagash in an Old Mari Text." *OA* 1:9-10.
DE VAUX, R.
1961 *Ancient Israel: Its Life and Institutions*. 2 vols. New York: McGraw-Hill Book Company.
WALKER, C. B. F.
1983 "Another Babati Inscription." *JCS* 35:91-96.
WEIDNER, E.
1952 "Könige von Ešnunna, Mari, Jamhad in altbabylonischen Siegelzylinder-Legenden." *Jahrbuch für Kleinasiatische Forschung* 2:127-143.
WEINFELD, M.
1972 *Deuteronomy and the Deuteronomic School*. London: Oxford University Press.
1995 *Social Justice in Ancient Israel and in the Ancient Near East*. Jerusalem: Magnes; Minneapolis: Fortress.
WHITING, R. M.
1976 "Tiš-atal of Nineveh and Babati, Uncle of Šu-Sin." *JCS* 28:173-182.
WIGGERMAN, F. A. M., and A. GREEN.
1993-97 "Mischwesen." *RlA* 8:222-264.
WILCKE, C.
1987 "Inschriften 1983-84 (7.-8. Kampagne)" in *Isin-Išān-Baḥrīyāt* III. *Die Ergebnisse der Ausgrabungen* 1983-84. ABAW. Neue Folge Heft 94. München. Verlag der Bayerischen Akademie der Wissenschaften.
WILDBERGER, H.
1991 *Isaiah 1-12: A Commentary*. Minneapolis: Fortress Press.
WILSON, E. J.
1996 *The Cylinders of Gudea: Transliteration, Translation and Index*. Alter Orient und Altes Testament, Bd. 244. Neukirchen-Vluyn: Neukirchener Verlag und Verlag Butzon & Bercker Kevelaer.
YILDIZ, F.
1981 "A Tablet of Codex Ur-Nammu from Sippar." *Or* 50:87-97.
ZÓLYOMI, G.
1998 *The Building of Ningirsu's Temple*. The Electronic Text Corpus of Sumerian Literature. London: Oxford University. http://www.etcsl.orient.ox.ac.uk/ section2/c217.html.